The Bowker Annual

The Bowker Annual

of Library & Book Trade Information

32nd Edition   1987

Compiled and edited by
Filomena Simora

Executive Editor   **Consulting Editor**
Margaret M. Spier   **Dorothy Pollet Gray**

Sponsored by
**The Council of National Library and
Information Associations, Inc.**

R. R. BOWKER COMPANY
NEW YORK & LONDON

Published by R. R. Bowker Company,
   a division of Reed Publishing (USA) Inc.
Copyright © 1987 by Reed Publishing (USA) Inc.
All rights reserved
International Standard Book Number 0-8352-2333-7
International Standard Serial Number 0068-0540
Library of Congress Catalog Card Number 55-12434
Printed and bound in the United States of America

Contents

Part 1
Reports from the Field

International Reports

National Associations

Part 2
Legislation, Funding, and Grants

Funding Programs and Grant-Making Agencies

Part 3
Library/Information Science
Education, Placement, and Salaries

Part 4
Research and Statistics

Library Research and Statistics

Book Trade Research and Statistics

Part 5
Reference Information

Part 6
Directory of Organizations

Preface

In its thirty-second edition, *The Bowker Annual* continues to rise to the challenge of meeting the expanding information needs of the library, book-trade, and information-industry communities.

This year's *Annual* is the first to focus on a theme: "Access to Information." How information is controlled and disseminated, who is able to access information, and the problems faced by special populations are critical issues for both information workers and society as a whole. Addressing the topic of the free flow of information are reports by Kenneth E. Dowlin, Pikes Peak Library District (on technology); Harold C. Relyea, Congressional Research Service (on government information); and Judith Krug, ALA Office of Intellectual Freedom (on censorship). Covering the area of special populations are articles by Bernard Vavrek, Center for the Study of Rural Librarianship; Frank Kurt Cylke, National Library Service for the Blind and Physically Handicapped; and Ann Knight Randall, ALA Committee on Minority Concerns. Yet another way of providing access to materials, preservation of fragile library materials, ensures that they will be available to library users both now and in the future. The Council on Library Resources report in Part 2 covers the work being done in this area by the Commission on Preservation and Access.

To keep you posted on important trends and developments, we have reports on copyright, networking, information standards, and our concise and informative news reports from *Library Journal, School Library Journal*, and *Publishers Weekly.* New to the association reports this year is the American Society for Information Science. And for all of you with wanderlust, we have Hannelore B. Rader's report on International Personnel Exchanges and Warren Horton's article on Library Services in Australia.

Statistics are the backbone of the *Annual* and once again we offer you the essential data you need: average book and periodical prices, library acquisition expenditures, book sales and output, and placement and salaries. We also provide the latest information on legislation and funding to help you obtain the financial support available to you.

The Library/Information Science Education, Placement, and Salaries section features an article by Michael Buckland celebrating the one-hundredth year of library education, and of special interest is the ALA Executive Summary on Accreditation.

Rounding out this year's volume are up-to-date bibliographies on publishing, librarianship, high technology, and a new bibliography of Z39 Standards; Notable Books and Bestsellers of 1986; the Directory of Organizations; and the 1987–1988 calendar of events.

Thanks are due to the many contributors who gave of their time and expertise to create this year's book. The special quality of *The Bowker Annual* is that it is a book written by peers for peers.

Consulting Editor Dorothy Pollet Gray provided invaluable assistance, most notably with the selection of a theme, the identification of contributors, and the preparation

of the headnotes introducing the special reports. Her knowledge and enthusiasm are much appreciated.

Nancy Bucenec, Production Editor, once again worked tirelessly to keep the book on track and compile the directory sections.

Special thanks are reserved for Manuscript Editor and Compiler Filomena Simora who each year takes the mass of diverse information that goes into *The Bowker Annual* and refines and structures it into one cohesive volume.

Margaret M. Spier
Executive Editor, *The Bowker Annual*

Part 1
Reports from the Field

News Reports

LJ News Report, 1986

Karl Nyren

Senior Editor, *Library Journal*

Libraries in 1986 could thank Congress for turning back raids by the administration on already appropriated library funds and for blocking attempts to attack 1987 funding. The Gramm-Rudman-Hollings bulldozer, however, which Congress lamentably let loose on the nation, hit hard and visibly, even cutting hours at the Library of Congress (LC). Congress relented in the case of LC and restored most of the lost funding. (The entire LC budget, after all, was less than the surplus the Pentagon had *not* been able to spend in 1985.) Congress also let federal revenue sharing slide to an end, although the program has supported a great many local social services, including libraries. Many are scrambling to find alternate funding.

The National Scene

Access to information continued under attack in Washington; the Office of Management and Budget (OMB) pushed through its controversial Circular A-130, which will cut information dissemination by federal agencies sharply. New obstacles to the use of the Freedom of Information Act (FOIA) were instituted in many agencies; the State Department had the worst record, with only 30 percent of FOIA requests answered. Official admission of a "disinformation" policy aimed at the U.S.S.R., but affecting U.S. citizens and even legislators, presented librarians and researchers with a whole new information problem.

Privatization, the turning over of government operations to private interests, continued to be pushed by the White House. The Government Printing Office was so busy putting out printing contracts that it had to open a third satellite office in San Diego. At year's end, OMB ordered the "full privatization" of NTIS, the National Technical Information Service. Privatization also flourished in another form: Private firms are developing major commercial ventures under the umbrella of publicly guaranteed bond funding, some involving library construction projects.

International Exchanges

In 1986, the average member of the American Library Association (ALA) placed international activity by the association very low on the association's want list, but the out-

Note: Adapted from *Library Journal*, January 1987.

side world continued to press in on librarians and many were involved internationally in a variety of trends and events that continued despite ALA members' lack of interest. For example, it was noted in 1986 that translations, worldwide, were up 67 percent in the last 25 years.

ALA led the way in one sense by agreeing to work with the United States Information Agency (USIA) in several international ventures that would involve librarians and people in publishing. The USIA was already suspect for its refusal to grant certain films "educational" status to ease their international distribution, apparently because it considered their content inimical to the interests of the United States. In federal court, the agency was adjudged to be censoring, and ordered to provide the educational status desired by the film producers.

At the same time, Baker & Taylor was cementing a deal with the Soviets for book sales. And ALA could point out that in 1986 it put the news service Interpress up on its ALANET system, thus providing libraries with a new access to news originating in the Third World. It also took the lead in helping Mexican libraries recover from earthquake damage by launching an aid fund.

The library school at the University of Maryland established an Institute for International Information Programs late in 1985, and Catholic University in 1986 established a new link with French libraries.

Around the Globe

China continued to be a focus of international library activity. The Project Emperor videotape, directed by Simmons Professor Ching-Chih Chen, was completed early in 1986. Gale Research funded a new award for Chinese–U.S. understanding. The University of Hawaii undertook to provide training to Chinese English-language specialist librarians.

Japan was the site of a high-level gathering of academic librarians who were laying foundations for greater cooperation and communication among university and research libraries. In the meantime, the University of Toronto Library Automation System (UTLAS) launched the export to Japan of cataloging in Japanese. Bechtel, which has the contract to distribute SEC data, expanded operations to export data to Japan as well as to Canada.

A group of U.S. libraries shipped some 20 tons of books to the Philippines. Rochester, New York, librarians found that the Vietnam War had left them with an extensive colony of Laotians, a new public for library services.

South Africa, already in Coventry with ALA, found libraries among the investors who were divesting themselves of holdings in firms doing business in South Africa. Chicago Public Library, Minneapolis Public Library, and Berkeley Public Library (California) were among them. Apartheid and South Africa cropped up as issues in cataloging when Forest Press, publisher of the Dewey Decimal Classification (DDC), drew the concerted ire of African librarians for uncritically accepting and publishing an update on DDC for Africa drawn up by SAILIS, the white South African library association.

Nicaragua, focus of a blazing political scandal in the last days of 1986, had been cropping up sporadically in the library news. A Dallas librarian went there on a Fulbright. A New York library union and a group of MIT librarians were raising money for Nicaraguan libraries and a library school.

In the troubled Middle East, the largest Muslim library in the world opened in

Mecca. While the White House was shipping weapons to the Iranians for their war on Iraq, a former chair of the Department of Library Science at the University of Teheran, John Harvey, was busy collecting information on what has happened to the librarians and libraries of Iran, once at the forefront of that nation's Westernization.

Ventures in Automation

Library automation vendors continued to pioneer international ventures: OCLC's LS/2000 was the first automated system in Central America; CLSI expanded its French market to Aix-en-Provence and its U.K. outreach to City University in London; Access Innovations set up operations in Amsterdam; Data Research Associates moved into Canada with an installation in Ontario; the ADONIS document delivery system of an international consortium of publishers was readying for a pilot test; and Carlyle was installing a network for Australia's CAVAL consortium in Victoria. [See the report "Library Services in Australia" in the International Reports section of Part 1 — *Ed.*]

It was, however, a two-way street, with UTLAS, Blackwell/North America, and Geac expanding their involvement with U.S. libraries. The German DOBIS/LIBIS (IBM) system is being installed at Emory University, and a new U.S. service office is being opened.

OCLC was increasing its international activities, exploring access to the riches, European and Asian, of the Bibliothèque Nationale. It is also active in Scandinavia, the low countries, Germany, Italy, the Vatican, Australia, Taiwan and China, and Japan.

The September OCLC Users Council heard President and CEO Rowland Brown sing the praises of international expansion, listing benefits to U.S. libraries, including copy cataloging of foreign materials, new access to international resource sharing, and improvement of international document delivery. Profits from international ventures would provide economic gain in the increased value of the database as well as maintaining a competitive position against other utilities operating internationally.

Brown also went into detail on the formidable difficulties of establishing operations in Europe. OCLC's European expansion will be cautious, involving, for the most part, microcomputer applications, CD-ROM, tape distribution, and dial access. Further export of the LS/2000 system will be held up while a "more readily transportable" system is developed.

Interchanges between OCLC and the Library of Congress at the Users Council meeting left the distinct impression that a turf issue is arising. Henriette Avram, according to the report of the meeting issued by OCLC, said that "LC sees itself as the interface between national agencies abroad and bibliographic organizations in the United States." In a section on discussion among the delegates, it was reported that "OCLC believes that it has reviewed its basic international strategy with LC. Henriette Avram disagreed."

Funding for Libraries

State-level Ups and Downs

Across the nation, oil states were pinching pennies while others were enjoying new prosperity, some of it from cheap oil; their libraries fared accordingly. A long-buried time bomb in California legislation was triggered by the drop in inflation, threatening local

library funding anew. The measure, passed at the same time as the infamous Proposition 13, limits increases in municipal spending to the current rate of inflation. A Florida book tax and a New Mexico "smokeless tobacco tax" were two failed oddball state-level attempts to improve library funding.

There were meteoric ups and downs in 1985 in state library funding, with the downs mostly in the energy-producing states: Alabama, Mississippi, New Mexico, Oklahoma, Wisconsin, and Wyoming. Mississippi lost some 20 percent of its state library staff. Wisconsin public library systems took a 10 percent cut. In many other states, funding was up: New York's $16 million jump led the way, followed by California, Georgia, Connecticut, and Massachusetts, where an influx of new money will build Boston Public Library resources, equalize services statewide, and push innovation.

Connecticut and Pennsylvania were outstanding for their proactive legislative programs, especially Pennsylvania's coalition of 72 legislators committed to libraries. New York is considering new, direct funding for individual public libraries, with $2 per capita being asked.

The November elections marked a watershed in state funding as libraries sought alternatives to lost federal revenue sharing money and faced new taxpayer revolts. The results appear to be almost uniformly encouraging.

Public Libraries: Bad News and Good News

The year 1986 was a bad one for many great urban public libraries. Baltimore's Enoch Pratt took a $200,000 cut and faced the loss of a dozen positions; a drop in the sales tax was blamed for salary and service cuts at Dallas Public; New Orleans Public was struggling along with donations from businesses and volunteer help; Minneapolis voters rejected dreams of growth, as did Kansas City, Missouri, in April, only to vote major new library funding in November.

Houston Public, like all other services of the city, was facing deep personnel cuts and possible consolidation with county library services. The Cleveland Public Library appeared to be coping without the $2.7 million it lost as the result of a new tax distribution formula in Ohio. Most of the money went to the Cuyahoga County Library, which is doing fine as a result. There was also a new round of talks about a merger of the Cleveland and Cuyahoga County library systems, but some insiders say there is little chance of that becoming a reality.

Denver Public was fighting a long decline by cutting more costs, but increasing services in a bid for better support. Saginaw Public was one Michigan library climbing back to health with a 30 percent budget increase. Newark Public, once a disaster area of library funding, was continuing its 1985 "banner year" with new increases in all areas of activity. Not all New Jersey libraries were so happy, however. The Orange Public Library, home base of Marvin Scilken, the U*N*A*B*A*S*H*E*D* L*I*B*R*A*R-*I*A*N, was reeling under the effect of a 12 percent cut below the 1985 budget.

The Atlanta/Fulton County Library continued the prosperous ways it has enjoyed since the merger of city and county authority: In 1986 it was hiring 76 new staffers, and branch buildings were going up all over the county. Jacksonville and Alachua County, Florida, are a similar success story. Following creation of a city–county library district, funding authorities allocated $1.7 million to buy new books for the branch libraries. Six Arizona county libraries won independent district taxing status in 1986, releasing them from perennial competition for funds with other county services.

Fort Worth was one Texas library in the black; it received $10 million for new library construction in 1985. Boston Public Library, after a long period of decline, welcomed its new director, Arthur Curley, by turning the corner financially and, with renewed state support, started to build resources, hire long-needed staff, and renovate deteriorating central library and branch buildings.

Massachusetts still has its Proposition 2½ tax cap, but the town of Rockland overturned it at the polls to win a $1 million addition. Maryland's Prince George's County Memorial Library made a paper tiger of that state's TRIM taxing cap by winning an 86 percent victory in a bond issue for new branch construction.

California public libraries began in 1986 to feel the effect of a sleeper tax cap: Proposition 4, passed some years ago and almost forgotten. It limits the annual tax increase a municipality can levy to the annual increase in inflation. With 1986's sudden drop in inflation, many communities are finding that they cannot make their customary annual increases in spending.

Networking

Document Delivery

The delivery of the document (book, article copy, etc.) to the reader is the be-all and end-all of library networking and library cooperation, although this is not always apparent. Concerns with turf and empire building put the spotlight on system structures, automation, and competition among agencies. Document delivery, therefore, is given pride of place in this report on networking and cooperation.

Library news pages in 1986 carried word of a significant name change. The BLLD (British Lending Library Division), which has been promoting document delivery worldwide, henceforth is to be known as the British Document Supply Centre, a somewhat more businesslike name.

UTLAS is going after a neglected document delivery market, the small library, in a new arrangement with University Microfilms International that makes the volume price discounts enjoyed by big customers available to the small ones. One study reported that document delivery from University Microfilms is faster than traditional interlibrary loan, but more expensive. Another competitor, Information on Demand, claimed that it could deliver NTIS documents faster and cheaper than NTIS itself.

Wisconsin libraries were noted as setting up a self-supporting, multitype library document delivery operation, charging a flat $4 per item delivered. European sources claimed that the satellite technology they are now developing will give them a commanding lead over American satellite document delivery.

SUNY/OCLC, which had been using Purolator for delivery among its member libraries, switched to United Parcel Service for a better business arrangement. Late in 1986, however, one SUNY network member reported pulling out and making its own arrangement with UPS at a better price.

Both the Washington State Library and the Fred Meyer Trust have been supporting experiments in the ambitious use of facsimile transmission, plus a courier service, to speed document delivery in the vast spaces of the American Pacific Northwest. At year's end, the reports of it were glowing, as they were from a similarly large-scale experiment concluded recently in Illinois.

The document delivery story in 1986 was one of growing competition among entre-

preneurs and library agencies and between technologies, with facsimile transmission staking out a growing share of the market. When the fourth-generation FAX machines come in, it will be even stronger.

Finally, the advent of disc technology throws a new uncertainty into the document delivery scene, offering the possibility of buying the database and doing one's own instant document delivery.

Public and Private Sectors

National and regional organizations from both the public and private sectors, as well as those involved in both camps, are the major mechanisms for networking. A decade ago they were mutually suspicious, but of late they have been drawing together, resembling each other more and more and having little difficulty in working together. There is competition, but it tends to pit for-profit against for-profit as much as not-for-profit against for-profit.

There were echoes in 1986 of the old hostility: One issue of the Information Industry Association's *Friday Memo* voiced a fear that the library networks are growing too powerful. On another occasion, library consultant Bonnie Juergens, in a discussion of standards, held that the nature of networks has to do with sharing—something basically in conflict with vendor competition.

But the vendors in 1986 acted like membership organizations: OCLC, which once wanted the image, if not the legal reality, of a private sector entrepreneur, made much of its claim to be a membership organization, operating for the good of and at the pleasure of its library members. CLSI pointed to the 20 million library card holders being served by its automation systems—a substantial user community indeed—and only the largest among several other turnkey system user populations.

Turnkey vendors like CLSI moved with unexpected alacrity to participate in the Linked Systems Project; SOLINET and UTLAS, a regional not-for-profit and an international for-profit firm, found no difficulty in handling each others' products, authority control, and record processing in this case. Ron Gardner, at one network meeting, noted that the networks are getting more like the vendors—as vendor products become more and more acceptable to them. SUNY/OCLC, a not-for-profit regional network, is marketing the Carlyle automation system, and NELINET, according to Director Laima Mockus, may also market the Carlyle system, now that "NELINET is getting more entrepreneurial" and feeling the need for something other than OCLC, which is "not affordable to many of our members."

The Network Utilities

Three major utilities—OCLC, WLN, and UTLAS—had a busy year and were much in the news. RLIN, on the other hand, was not making big headlines, although the search is on for a replacement for Richard McCoy, president of RLIN's parent, the Research Libraries Group, who reported substantial progress on the Linked Systems Project (proposing to link the databases of LC, RLIN, OCLC, and WLN). RLIN was handling an increasing amount of cataloging for its members, as well as responding to their needs in several other areas.

OCLC's member libraries, as well as the regional networks and brokers of its services and products, are looking with both anticipation and apprehension for the dawning

of the results of the Oxford Project: the enhancement and upgrading of the entire OCLC online system that promises new levels of access, easier manipulation of data, better training and support, and new user friendliness.

The issues keeping OCLC and some of the regional networks from signing a new contract are still there, but there is a new spirit of tolerance among the networks, marked by a moratorium on legal hostilities. Their formerly united front has been breached by ILLINET, which has signed a new contract with OCLC, but there have been no public recriminations. Toward year's end, even closer network/OCLC relations were promised by the creation of a new, high-level liaison position to provide a steady stream of communication among users, trustees, officers, and staff involved in OCLC and the regional networks.

Copyright of the OCLC database is still a cloudy area. Both the regionals and OCLC have tactfully said less and less about it, although some member libraries are playing it safe by copyrighting their own cataloging. A Wisconsin legal ruling recently held that bibliographic records created on OCLC are public records and cannot be copyrighted, but there appears to have been no immediate impact on network/utility relations. OCLC has said that it will contest the ruling.

OCLC pulled out of its commitment to provide an online acquisitions and serials system, and despite a flurry of anguish (notably among federal librarians) over "vendor abandonment," it is a *fait accompli* and already being forgotten. When an organization gets a certain critical mass, it gets away with many things for which a small one would draw instant retribution. In any case, the affected libraries are being offered a replacement in the INNOVACQ system of Innovative Interfaces.

OCLC today, which may be the closest thing we'll ever see to a national library/information network, noted its 11 millionth interloan transaction in 1986, and if it can survive what one observer called the transition from "totalitarian networking to a (possible) anarchy," it may well consolidate its national position even more. OCLC is also moving to diversify and expand its library market presence. About to come off the OCLC research and development drawing boards is a batch of new products and services including a compact disc cataloging package, an OCLC LINK "gateway" to databases, an upgraded LS/2000 circulation system, a CD-ROM retrieval system, and more.

It is worth noting that the dream of a national library network, in which libraries themselves would have a more active role vis à vis utilities and vendors, is not fully laid to rest. At ALA Midwinter 1986, a joint statement issued by the Library of Congress, the National Library of Medicine, and the Medical Library Association reasserts the need for network linkages, for standards and adherence to them, but bewails the decline in the cooperative spirit and the rise of entrepreneurship in networking, the attractions of inexpensive automation, and "the false lure of autonomy."

In 1986, UTLAS International noted its passing of the 29 million mark in the number of records in its database. Eight California libraries now use UTLAS for authority work, and five of them also turn to UTLAS for retrospective conversion. UTLAS is now able to interface with seven of the most active turnkey automation systems, to offer them database upgrade service. It has acquired the ALIS III (formerly Data Phase) library automation system, a technologically superior system that has lacked vendor support services, and is satisfying older customers as well as acquiring new ones. A frankly commercial, for-profit enterprise, UTLAS doesn't devote effort to being seen as a "membership" affair; it does come across as a vendor who gives customers what they want.

The Western Library Network, which has a lot of less affluent libraries in its service

area, is going vigorously into CD-ROM editions of its database, offering cheaper cataloging and no charges for telecommunications or inquiry. It dropped the price of adding
records to its database substantially in 1986, to encourage more use by small libraries,
and it also launched an online interlibrary loan system.

The Regional Networks

The primary income received by regional networks is still the fee they collect for broker-
ing OCLC service to their member libraries. They are aggressively seeking new sources
of income, including the vending of products that may compete with some sold by
OCLC.

Relations grew quite cool with OCLC over the copyright issue and differences
about what should be in their contracts, but OCLC seems to have felt no hardship from
the systems' refusal to negotiate contracts except together, and the loose alliance that
holds the systems together is fraying. Lately, a new spirit of compromise and cooperation has emerged.

Within their regions, they see larger member libraries building their system staffs
toward the day when they will no longer be dependent on the network. More and more
stand-alone systems are being created. Local networking is on the rise and the regionals
recognize this as a new area of opportunity, without fully knowing what to do about it.

They see continuing demand for their services in consulting, and for their mediation of access to non-OCLC databases like RLIN and WLN. One of the more vigorous
initiatives taken by a regional network has been SOLINET's LAMBDA project, providing an online service to many of its client libraries. Shortly before the end of 1986,
however, SOLINET announced that LAMBDA was being dropped.

Louella Wetherbee, AMIGOS executive director and the source of much of the preceding report on regional networks, in a dynamic presentation in 1985 in Albany, New
York, also predicted less member dependence on telecommunications as discs move in.
She sees more local expertise developing, and more decision making going on at lower
levels, as we "move from totalitarian networking to possible anarchy."

Entropy?

It seems appropriate to ask whether some of the things happening at the regional level
do not signal a growing entropy. There are signs of a depletion of the spirit of cooperation abroad. Two Mississippi cooperative systems have had to deal with secession; one
has had to be completely disbanded and reorganized. At a major California conference
on networking, the term "resource rape" was bandied about by libraries skeptical of
parasitic neighbors.

The two-year debate over "third-level reference" referral in the Golden State
achieved new levels of emotion. In 1985, the California State Library announced it
would end LSCA funding of two regional reference centers, BARC in San Francisco and
SCAN in Los Angeles. The state's systems and libraries are up in arms, and are asking
where the money will be spent if not on BARC/SCAN. In the clamor at the November
meetings of the state's LSCA advisory body and the CLA meetings, scorn was heaped
on consultant Barbara Robinson's study of the problem. Several library leaders in the
state seemed to agree with one state library staffer who said the issue was hardly worthy
of the two-year debate it caused. "The bottom line," he said, "is only one million bucks
and 4,000 questions."

Statewide interlibrary loan, at this writing, appeared to be at an end in Arizona, as

negotiations between the Phoenix Public Library and the state library agency for renewal of the interlibrary loan contract broke down in September. The major resource library of New York's Westchester Library System, White Plains, is threatening to leave the system rather than agree to loss of the subsidy it gets for resource sharing. After two decades of public library systems in Illinois, Indiana, and New York, and as those systems poise on the brink of evolution into multitype systems, studies of system effectiveness have raised the possibility of shakeups.

A longer view was taken by Betty Turock in a research study reported in *Library and Information Science Research*. She found a number of problem areas in multitype networking that call for substantial restructuring if the multitype model of cooperation is to prosper. Among them: bureaucratic fat, poor communications, lack of attention to patron and member library needs, and problems in the areas of governance, funding, and evaluation.

A report that countered pessimistic views of networking came from Bernard Sloan, director of the statewide LCS system based at the University of Illinois. He cites statistics from his big, active operation that identify the four smallest members as net lenders.

The still growing, very active area of state networking would seem to be the best case to present against entropy of the cooperative spirit. In 1986, networking progress was reported by New York, Iowa, South Carolina, Maine, New Hampshire, and Kansas, to name only a few. The state library agencies, seasoned in dealing with local public libraries and learning fast about academic, school, and special libraries in multitype settings, are for the most part stable underpinnings for the further development of the local and multitype networking that appears to be tomorrow's order of business.

Automation

Library automation continues to spread rapidly, even to very small libraries, now that microcomputer-based systems are both cheap and reliable. Pioneering efforts, aimed at moving the automation frontier ahead still further, are being funded at New York University and Vanderbilt University. Several new cooperative automation ventures serve three or more libraries, often of different types.

Concern over and interest in improving catalog and database searching capabilities are growing. One concern is that a strict approach to searching not destroy the organic, sometimes unpredictable, course of research and the serendipity that has always been a part of it. A similar concern has been expressed in the area of cataloging, where the growing extension of machine control over the cataloging process could supplant a healthy evolution in thought by a rigid adherence to rules and precedent.

A study of ARL researchers found that the computer resources available to them are still far too few, especially those existing outside their own university, and they tend also to underutilize library resources on campus, preferring not to personally consult library staff. A Peat Marwick study found that 50 percent of the top academic and public libraries have automated catalogs, interloan, acquisitions, and circulation and all are involved to some extent in automation. A prime concern of all is telecommunications.

Automation Changes Everything

Automation is steadily causing the elimination or reassignment of library staff. The most surprising instance in 1986 was in Portage, Wisconsin, where the volunteer staff,

once a busy group sorting circulation records, sending out reserves, etc., were all eliminated by automation.

A possibly inevitable clash between reality and the automation dream came about at Union College, Nebraska, where it was announced that every dorm room had a terminal hooked up to the library's online catalog. Not too many weeks later it was announced that Union College was deep in fiscal red ink.

The courtship between the academic library and the campus computer center continued in 1986 in tentative fashion. At SUNY Binghamton, the library hailed progress toward a desired joining of forces in the establishment of a "data center" in the library, with consequent reorganization of reference services. A more comfortable sharing arrangement, the extension of one library's system to serve a neighboring library, was developing into a familiar pattern. Wayne State's NOTIS system was announced as available to its neighbors. A DYNIX system was serving Lower Columbia College, and Longview Public Library in Washington. A Bergen County, New Jersey, consortium was sharing a collectively financed DRA ATLAS system with member libraries. The Las Vegas/Clark County Library extended its Geac system to serve the library at Nellis AFB.

Onward with Discs

Disc technology took large strides forward, and the development of the High Sierra standards, a landmark accomplishment of the disc industry, set the stage for standardization and rapid growth. Uncertainties about the library future of CD technology remain, particularly concern about the development of a hardware standard to allow libraries to employ more than one CD product without buying special devices for each.

A minor flood of publications and databases formerly available either in print or online began to appear in CD-ROM. Libraries were offered disc versions of *Books in Print*, University Microfilms *Dissertation Abstracts*, and the LISA database of library and information center information. The hegemony over chemical information enjoyed by Chemical Abstracts was challenged by ISI and Academic Press with their *Index Chemicus* and *Chemsmart*.

DEC offered portions of technological databases on disc, including Compendex and NTIS. The appearance of standard library reference works on disc aroused criticism, especially because only one person at a time can consult a reference work stored on CD-ROM, whereas a multivolume encyclopedia can be used by several at once.

In the case of one library, cost considerations led to its keeping both the print and the CD-ROM versions of one source, but its abstracts were dropped. CD-ROM is also being looked at as a tool for preservation, cataloging, and networking, competing with microfilm, online MARC services, and telecommunications-dependent networking.

Reference Robots?

Expert systems grew in visibility in 1986, with some librarians thinking of them as slavish to handle the "dogwork" at the reference desk, but others looked to this new development for exploration of new mental frontiers. Examples of the former could be found in the ANSWERMAN project of the National Agricultural Library, a system for the retrieval of information from reference books, as well as experiments reported at the University of Waterloo (Ontario, Canada) and the University of Washington. There were

proposals for the employment of expert systems to counter staff shortages and staff burnout from a heavy reference desk load. Projects at the University of Pittsburgh and Drexel were reported under way, and one at Stanford's Lane Library was reported to be working on medical decision making. The Pittsburgh project in particular suggested a view of library expert systems as far indeed from the notion of a robot at the reference desk.

The Cost of High Tech

The funding of automation includes both the initial capital expense and the subsequent maintenance costs. One proposal put forth would include both maintenance costs and software fees in the original package price—a course that would run afoul of the fact that, all too often, the funding that a library can raise is only enough for just the basic system and all too often for a system that is seriously under capacity. Another method proposed, and tried, by Missouri's Kansas City Public Library is lease purchase financing. Still another open to some urban libraries is LSCA for major urban resource library materials.

Micros for the Public

A variety of reports about micros in libraries turned up in 1986. The New York Public Library said that micros in its branches were being used by 3,000 patrons a month. The Microcomputer Center at the Toledo Public Library was one of several reporting an assortment of both micro hardware and software now available to the public, with the aim of encouraging computer literacy; no results have yet been reported.

One academic library found that the experience gained by the reference staff in teaching microcomputer use, all traced to familiarity with micros, has led to more use by both faculty and students, an enhanced image of librarians, and new operational efficiencies. Another library is reported trying out the microcomputer as a "town meeting"—a machine set up in the library allows people to engage in dialogue with fellow citizens on matters of social concern. Only two cheers for the micro came from staff of the Suffolk County Library System in New York. They find that the micros are good for public relations, showing the library to be an up-to-date place, but actually most of the usage is by children playing games.

The Reference Connection

The Association of Research Libraries issued *End User Searching Services*, reporting on a number of findings from the experience of member libraries. These included the perception that end user searching is now accepted and growing; that leading the way are the specialized subject departments and libraries; that most libraries are planning end user programs; and that still to be determined is whether end user searching or mediated searching yields the best results. Much interest is shown in new technology alternatives, including in-house mounted databases and CD-ROM databases. One major public library, Maryland's Prince George's County Memorial Library, reports that it is making online reference service available in its branches.

Vendor Systems

AutoGraphics announced its COMEBACK, a backup system for the union catalog using microforms and doing the job, it says, cheaper than a microcomputer, videodisc, or CD-ROM. Bibliofile, a strong contender for the lower end of the MARC cataloging market, now found in many small and medium-sized libraries, reported a new user service that would help users share cataloging and resources. Carlyle was moving strongly into the market with a system at Boston University and another in Australia; it was selected by SUNY/OCLC as a local library system for its member libraries. CLSI, Inc. gets credit for the biggest win of the year: a single circulation system to handle the branches of the New York Public and the branch and main libraries of the Brooklyn Public Library.

Data Phase, which sold its ALIS III system to UTLAS, was still in business, and its systems at Chicago Public, Memphis/Shelby County, and Garland (Texas) were reportedly healthy. One customer gave the credit to Data Phase's almost trouble-free software and its reliance on Data General (DG) computers, which puts most customers in easy distance of the excellent service provided by DG.

Data Research Associates (DRA) is negotiating for the installation of a circulation system at the Queens Borough Public Library in New York City. At year's end it was being sued by the Harrington Library Consortium in Amarillo, Texas, for theft of software developed by the library. DRA is in turn suing the library and charging it with theft of DRA software. It is meanwhile installing an UTLAS system at the University of Lowell in Massachusetts as well as one in North York, Ontario, and claims that its new processors give it the "fastest, best Boolean product" as well as new potential for cost saving.

DOBIS/LIBIS, the system developed in Germany and marketed in Europe, the Middle East, and Canada, but rarely in the United States despite its use of IBM hardware, is installing its first system (since the one a few years back in Douglas County, Oregon) at Emory University. DOBIS has also opened an office in Milford, Connecticut.

DYNIX was caught in a disagreement in Sioux City. The library staff and board had, with much effort, settled on DYNIX as the system best suited to their needs, only to face opposition from city hall, which decided that the library should use the same hardware as the city. Otherwise, DYNIX was extending its range from Washington State to Palo Alto; Portage, Michigan; and England.

Although Geac's parent company was in financial difficulties at year's end, and trading in its stock was halted for a period, it was ambitiously tackling a project in France that will involve thousands of terminals and robotic retrieval of materials. Geac was also installing systems at the University of Washington, an Australian network, and Wyoming. "Too much business, not enough people trained in installation," was one observer's comment.

INLEX was installing systems in Webster Groves (Illinois), Chesapeake Public (Maryland), and Jefferson-Madison Regional (Virginia). It also acquired Joe Matthews, one of the top names in library automation consulting, as vice president for operations.

INNOVACQ was working with OCLC to replace the utility's abandoned serials and acquisitions systems as well as developing interfaces with several more automated systems. It was also creating a system for three New York law libraries, making it possible for them to share online their serials holdings.

NOTIS briefly considered giant TBG, but backed off to the satisfaction of those

who see the nonprofit, cooperative style of NOTIS as something that would be lost if it were spun off by Northwestern. One pointed out that the kind of conflict over software that has DRA and the Harrington Consortium at odds couldn't happen with NOTIS, where users of the system are free to modify software and do so, sharing the results — free — with other NOTIS users. New installations include Notre Dame, University of Iowa, Library of Michigan, and Wichita State University.

OCLC's LS/2000 system was reported to be edging into the black at the end of 1986, but efforts to introduce it in Europe were to be discontinued. A Johns Hopkins installation late in the year was its eighty-third, and its installation at the University of Costa Rica made it the first online system in Central America.

The microcomputer-based system SC350 was offered by OCLC after it decided not to continue support of its online acquisitions/serials system. Milwaukee Public liked the new system, but found it lacked the capacity to handle its serials load. Consequently, it found local software talent capable of modifying the OCLC software and came up with a satisfactory custom-designed system.

Ocelot, the Canadian-based system, announced that it would work not only in both French and English but several more European languages, making it a competitor for polyglot honors with the DOBIS system, which has handled non-Roman alphabets as well as several European languages.

SIRSI reported a spurt of activity in 1986, with new installations at the Defense Nuclear Agency in Alexandria (Virginia), Fort Monroe Technical Library (Virginia), State of Georgia Public Library Services, and Old Colony Network (Massachusetts).

SYDNEY, the former Easy Data System, has been adapted to microcomputers and is now in some 60 libraries. It has also moved to DEC VAX hardware for larger libraries.

TECHLIB, a Battelle BASIS-based turnkey system by Information Dimensions, Inc., is reported to be approaching a full-text system with the capacity to store chapter headings from books.

ULISYS announced a new interface between two DEC VAX 11/780s at the San Diego Processing Corp. to an AutoGraphics UNIVAC 90/80 in Monterey Point, California, using IBM emulator software to transmit daily MARC records to catalogs at San Diego Public and San Diego County libraries.

UTLAS, now in the ranks of turnkey vendors with its UTLAS T/50 system, promptly found major clients in the University of Toronto and Stanford's Lane Medical Library.

VTLS, the Virginia Tech Library System, won contracts with the National Agricultural Library, the Newberry Library, 24 small West Virginia libraries, and the Federal Energy Regulatory Commission (replacing a CLSI system). It was also marketing LC cataloging on videodisc.

Library Buildings

Cost and Construction

Only 13 new academic library buildings are reported for fiscal 1986 in *LJ*'s December architectural issue. The big one is the University of Iowa Law Library, a $15 million project. The largest in new floor space, however, is Texas Woman's University, a $10 million job that has 135,000 square feet. Some of the other big projects: two $8 million main/system buildings in Irving and Richmond, Texas; a $6 million main library in Na-

perville, Illinois; and two $4 million projects: a main library in Atlantic City, New Jersey, and a Kansas City, Kansas, branch. Other notable ones are the Health Sciences Library at Tufts; the Albany Law School Library, New York; the University of Oklahoma in Norman; and Aguadilla Regional College in Puerto Rico.

Additions and renovations account for much more academic library space. The big ones are to be found at the University of Alaska, Fairbanks; Lehigh University; Wesleyan in Middletown, Connecticut; Florida Atlantic; Bucknell; Medical College of Wisconsin, Milwaukee; and Midwestern State in Wichita Falls, Texas.

Spending for public library construction in 1986 was matched in recent years only in 1982. Total funding of $150,313,337 produced fewer new buildings than in 1985: 69 against 99 in 1985. Federal funding fell sharply, from $17 million to $10 million, but state funding was up slightly from $5 million to almost $9 million. Local funding made the big difference, $110 million over 1985's $97 million and the highest figure yet since 1982's $112 million.

Creative and Cooperative

Unusual public library projects were found in the 1986 survey. The new Central Library in Irving, Texas, has its own video production complex. In Richmond, Texas, the new library has an outdoor amphitheater seating 250, with a plaza, fountain, and recessed stage. Weslaco, Texas, library patrons have a media center, theater with projection room, stage lighting and sound systems, and dressing rooms.

The North Park Library of Richmond, Virginia, has a building manufactured to library specs by Coastal Modular Corp.; it sits in a shopping center on land provided by Safeway, Inc. The new library in Glendale, Wisconsin, serves four separate municipalities; it is housed on the first floor of a new building shared with apartments and offices. The library in Apache Junction, Arizona, shares a project with a senior citizens center. East Hampton, Connecticut, shares with both preschool and senior centers. In Naperville, Illinois, children can read in seating designed like a trolley car, and strangers can find their way around town by consulting a 13' x 13' bronze city map inlaid in the sidewalk.

At the West Wyandotte Branch of the Kansas City Public Library (Kansas), patrons will find a "distributive multifunctional AV center with 22 individual audio and video receiving centers throughout the library." Best of all may be in Massachusetts, at the Milford Town Library's children's park, with a huge dog statue named Dewey, in honor of Melvil, who married a Milford woman.

Notable Projects

On June 12, the Frances Howard Goldwyn Hollywood Regional Library, a branch of the Los Angeles Public Library ravaged by arson, reopened bigger and better than ever. Orlando, Florida, opened its big, new main public library on April 6. The huge project to build the new British Library obtained financing for its £60 million second stage of the estimated £250 million total cost when it is finished in the next century. A half-dozen new mall kiosk libraries were noted, all highly successsful and admired by all except those who frown on libraries acting as "free bookstores." Notable were those in Kansas City (Missouri), Atlanta, and St. Paul.

Rebuilding the service infrastructure is a theme increasingly heard. The big new

public library building program now being financed by the Illinois State Library was sold to the voters on that basis. Other ambitious area building programs can be found today going full force in Atlanta-Fulton County, New Mexico, and New York. Seattle is refurbishing its Carnegie library branches, and the main library in Youngstown, Ohio, now securely in the National Register of Historic Buildings, will be preserved in its original glory. The Folger Shakespeare Library in Washington, D.C., reopened its renovated Great Hall, and the New York Public Library opened, with great fanfare, its remodeled and enhanced main library behind the lions on New York City's Fifth Avenue.

Work in Progress

In both academic and public library construction, the number and size of projects underway at the end of June 1986 show a healthy increase over 1985. At that point, 408 public library projects were in progress, as against 345 for 1985. The total cost of 1986 work in progress was $466 million, up from $377 million. College and university buildings under construction on June 30 numbered 64, up from 50. The apparently small number of academic projects, compared to the 408 public library projects, is deceiving, since the cost of college and university libraries in progress was $333 million, up from $231 million last year. The projects tend to be much larger, and small projects perhaps are not being reported. About 6 million square feet were added in new public library space, but a surprising 4 million in academic library space.

Capital Financing

Among major financing victories earlier in 1986 were Fort Worth's $10 million for a new library; a $1 million bond issue for an addition to the library in Boynton Beach, Florida; and a really enthusiastic prolibrary vote (74 percent) for a $2.5 million bond issue in Bloomfield Township, Michigan. A mall kiosk branch opened in St. Paul, with the help of $250,000 raised by a Friends group. A Pew grant of $1.5 million will be put toward the $12 million enlargement of Princeton's Firestone Library. A $3.9 million bond issue was voted in Middle Island, New York, for that community's first permanent library facility; and a $5 million bond issue for a building program passed in Wake County, North Carolina.

Unusual financing approaches were found in Tucson, which will get a new main public library as part of an intricate public/private financing package. The first example of a form of financing noted in 1985 by new legislation in California — special assessment bonds — gave Akron, Ohio, badly needed parking space, which will be paid for by commercial users of the new parking deck. Kansas City, Missouri, will get new library branches and a rebuilt main library paid for by a loan that it is empowered to pay back from its newly granted $3 million a year operating funds.

Two good bureaucrats in Washington, Nathan Cohen and Robert Klassen, are given much of the credit for a ruling that could save libraries a large amount of money. It had been understood that if a library put LSCA funds into a building and then sold or abandoned the building within 20 years, those LSCA dollars would have to be repaid. Last year, libraries in Virginia and Georgia won the right to transfer the equity involved to new projects.

Presidential Libraries

The Carter Library opened October 1, although its access road and some parts of the building are still to be completed. The Nixon Library is on the verge of construction as a result of generous donors and despite temporary loss of federal funding pending the outcome of controversy over title to some of his papers. The Reagan Library is moving ahead in planning, and it will be the last of the increasingly lavish memorials that presidents have been erecting to themselves. Reagan has signed legislation limiting the size of presidential libraries following, but not including, his pyramid. It requires that the sponsors raise 20 percent of the cost of both construction and upkeep.

Books on the Road

Bookmobile service was being phased out in some communities and is as healthy as ever in others. The Prince George's County Memorial Library, Maryland, had to reprint its widely used criteria for planning bookmobile service. Gerstenslager, one of the biggest bookmobile makers, bowed out of the market, but the Blue Bird School Bus Co. was supplying chassis units to Lee's Custom Coaches of Largo, Florida, for a line of big, new models. In Massachusetts an unusual bookmobile, devoted completely to large print, took to the roads. And believers in the future of the bookmobile in Louisiana are in the process of creating a new model bookmobile design for use in that state.

Asbestos Cleanups

A continuing drain on the scarce money available for library construction was noted in 1986. It is costing Long Beach, New York, $1.1 million to get rid of its asbestos. A Cuyahoga County Branch was closed for similar work. The Metropolitan Library System in Oklahoma County, forced to borrow money at high interest to pay its bills, blamed the unexpected cost of asbestos cleanup. The bill was $370,000 for Youngstown and Mahoning County, Ohio. The Santa Monica Public Library, California, had to close its doors for a whole year, as did the Maine State Library.

Energy Conservation

The fear of another OPEC reduction in oil supplies has moderated, but libraries are still making a point of saving on energy costs, both in new construction and in maintenance. Troy-Miami County has abandoned its pioneering total solar library, but the Mesa Public Library, Arizona, points out that its Dobson Ranch Branch will have natural lighting throughout. The Houston Public Library, in a city that is a casualty of the slump in oil use, has engaged Johnson Controls for an energy maintenance program that is expected to pay for itself in savings. San Diego University's Love Library expects to save $42,000 a year from a complete relamping.

The Endangered Library

Fire and flood, hurricanes, earthquakes, thievery, and even disorderliness continue to make physical security a full-time concern. In 1986 two spectacular arson fires ravaged the main building of the Los Angeles Public Library, just as it was reopening its Holly-

wood branch, an earlier arson disaster. Down the California coast a few hundred miles, San Diego County reopened its Fallbrook branch, which had also been destroyed by arson. St. Louis County, forewarned by the experience of less fortunate libraries, when installing a built-in book return, fireproofed it heavily as a matter of course.

Blind malice appears to motivate library arson, but one psychologist has suggested that the individuals involved are seeking some kind of notice from an institution that they perceive as the apex of community respectability. Theft, on the other hand, another burgeoning enemy of libraries, and its practical motivation, has become almost accepted, and so are measures to counter it. Yet there was something depressing about the Boise High School students' very practical gift to their school library: a 3M Tattle-Tape Model 1350 theft detector.

Among the covetous in 1986 was a staff member of the Paterson, New Jersey, Public Library, who enjoyed a steady supplementary income for a while from a fellow staffer, whom he turned on to cocaine and then into a customer for her daily supply. She found the money by writing fraudulent checks. The rare books librarian at Boston College, Ralph Coffman, allegedly took in about $160,000 from the sale of about 40 of the library's rare books. Earlier in his career, he claimed to have served on the ethics committee of the Society for the Management of Information Science, an organization that seems to have disappeared without a trace, if it ever existed.

Electricity and electronic radiation are more impersonal but still real hazards. Librarians in 1986 were warned about electrical hazards from fiche readers, and their lurking uneasiness about radiation from video screens was answered by news that a serious and large-scale study is being undertaken to find out if radiation from this source can indeed harm people. Incidents of microcomputers being destroyed by lightning aroused new interest in devices to protect both the hardware and the persons who might be using it during a storm.

The reliance of libraries on computers leaves them open to disaster rooted in human unreliability, as the San Jose Public Library learned when 267,000 circulation records vanished by mistake. It is notable that the library staff was very surprised that most people returned their books instead of taking the opportunity to steal them.

Water damage, unlike fire and theft, is a matter of Mother Nature or, at worst, human failings rather than malice. Water, abetted by wind, damaged 2,000 catalog cards at the Jackson County Campus of Mississippi Gulf Coast Junior College when Hurricane Elena winds took the roof off. The careless failure to shut off an air-conditioning valve at the Smithsonian Institution wrecked facilities and materials at the Museum Reference Center.

Whether caused by storm, high water, or burst plumbing, water damage is so common that it appears inevitable, and librarians have been busy in developing countermeasures. Susan George and Cheryl T. Naslund, writing in the April *C&RL News*, treated Dartmouth's extensive experiences with water damage as a "learning experience," and discussed preventive measures to be taken, including supplies to stockpile against the inevitable. Similarly, California librarians attended a July panel at San Jose State University on library preparedness for earthquakes. A slide/tape program on caring for water-damaged books was issued by the Illinois Cooperative Conservation Program; and a basic preservation information kit was issued by the Northeast Document Conservation Center for $8.

The unruliness of youth is a fact of life to the public librarian who has to deal with it by hiring proctors and sometimes even armed guards. But some academic librarians

face the same problem and must meet it by methods of crowd control that seem out of place in a college library. This was brought home forcefully by a paper delivered at the ACRL Conference in Baltimore by Sally S. Small and Maureen E. Strazdon. "Reduction of Noise in Two Campus Libraries of a Major University" (Penn State) discussed in matter-of-fact terms the management of disruptive behavior among the citizens of tomorrow, using measures like getting rid of all lounge seating and breaking up areas large enough for groups to assemble in, as well as picking up ID cards at the door and holding them in order to identify culprits apprehended by security personnel.

Preservation

Activity in preservation of library materials continued to accelerate in 1986. State-level planning and action were reported from New York (with the first statewide preservation plan), Illinois (a new five-year plan), New Jersey (a new preservation unit at the state library), and Oklahoma with its Higher Education Task Force. Surveys of collections, including many funded by ARL for member libraries, brought the expected dire results, like Northwestern's finding that nine of ten books need treatment, and the Smithsonian's discovery that 30.4 percent of its collection is brittle. Preservation education went international with a Vienna conference on the teaching of preservation. Awards of preservation fellowships were noted at Columbia, as well as a new course at Simmons.

Cooperation for preservation was a watchword among libraries, but also between library organizations and others concerned with preservation. Staff of regional conservation centers, including museum, art, history, and textile people joined librarians at a major conference in La Jolla, California. Bibliographic utilities RLG and OCLC have agreed to share preservation-related data, and agreement is being sought in the library community on the kind and amount of preservation data that should be made available on MARC records. A conservation cooperative in New York state, the Regional Conference of Historical Agencies, is making it possible for small libraries and museums to buy the expensive materials needed for in-house preservation work at bulk rates. The library preservation community may have already acquired its bibliographic cornerstone with the establishment at the University of Maryland of a major preservation-related collection that will be available on OCLC.

Photocopying for preservation was the subject of a December 9 conference at the National Archives. Two new copiers promised gains in both preservation and access: the British face-up photocopier and a very thin copier capable of being slid between pages of a book open only a few millimeters. Optical disc technology is being explored by the Library of Congress, but after a two-year study Smithsonian staff ruled it out for preservation at this time.

Among the materials snatched back from destruction in 1986 were 16.4 million pages of California newspapers, Holocaust materials at the National Archives and Records Service, political posters at the Hoover Institution, rare horticultural books at the Missouri Botanical Gardens, the European migrant press, Richard Morris Hunt drawings, and the original illustration of Rudolph the Red Nosed Reindeer.

Mass deacidification, the only hope now to save a substantial number of books approaching brittleness in our libraries, took a major setback with the failure of the Library of Congress and Northrup Services to achieve an upsizing to commercial scale of the diethyl zinc process. At year's end LC contracted with the chemical firm Texas Alkyls to try again to develop a workable process. (Texas Alkyls, incidentally, is the firm

that supplies LC with its diethyl zinc, and presumably would be the supplier of the chemical if the DEZ process is upsized satisfactorily.) On December 2, Congressman Vic Fazio proposed that the DEZ process be reviewed by an outside panel. He also pointed out that LC has been spending a great deal more on deacidification than his Subcommittee on the Legislative Branch has authorized, drawing from other authorized expenditures.

Meanwhile, the main alternative to DEZ, the Wei T'o system, put in another trouble-free year at the National Library of Canada archives, while its spray version continued to perform well at Princeton and at several commercial book restorers. State and regional preservation organizations were reported studying the Wei T'o process in 1986, including Ohio, Illinois, and Oklahoma state-level agencies. A national meeting of law librarians in Washington in July heard a mass deacidification briefing from leaders in the field. Research and development of deacidification is reported underway at both the Bibliothèque Nationale and the British Library, both of which are working on processes similar to the Wei T'o process.

Acid-free paper is becoming more common; one library observed that something like 40 percent of the books it was buying are on acid-free paper. Harvard has a new policy of not letting any materials under its control be printed except according to stringent conditions, including acid-free paper. During 1986 more heartening news was heard of a new paper pulping process that promises to make factory changeover to acid-free technology both cheaper and better than acid paper manufacture. A curious twist was reported from SUNY Stony Brook, where decaying microfilms of a Yeats collection are being printed (full size) on acid-free paper, much to the satisfaction of scholars working on the material.

Librarians

ALA and SLA Set Records

The American Library Association had a prosperous year with its new Executive Director Tom Galvin. Financial clouds were for the moment at least dispelled and years of financial chaos appeared to be clearing up. ALA's thriving publishing operations (income, $6.5 million) continued to grow as a source of income, and plans for a more extensive journal publishing operation were revealed. At the same time, the ALA divisions, formerly in the ascendant and threatening to place the central ALA organization in the shade, slipped financially.

Conference attendance in New York set new records, with more than 16,228 librarians and their combined purchasing power drawing 5,671 exhibitors. A new round in the traditional debates on priorities appeared to be launched in New York. Although "priorities" continue to be identified with the eternal verities of librarianship—intellectual freedom and access to all information for all persons—the members were shown by one survey to want their association first of all to use its influence to get more money for them and their libraries as a first "priority."

The Special Libraries Association, in its new headquarters in Washington, D.C., lived up to its intention to become more involved in national issues affecting libraries and information, speaking up vigorously on matters like privatization and the administration's reductions in the flow of government information. A survey reported in 1986 found SLA members younger than ever, with 55 percent aged 31–45. The largest group

(49 percent) is in corporate libraries, 83 percent have a master's in library/information science, and 76 percent have been on the job for five years or more. Their numbers are also growing steadily, topping 12,000 for the first time.

Getting Help: Consultants and Experts

The number and activities of consultants in library and information science appear to be still growing. A trend toward the formation of more or less formal groups or firms is also apparent. Among those increasingly active in 1986 was JNR Associates, which was writing a long-range plan for continuing education in Washington State and producing a widely noted document for planning by small libararies. RMG Consultants was developing a five-year automation plan for a group of southeastern New York library systems and advising Tulane on its $1 million automation project.

HBW Associates was instrumental in guiding the breakup of the Jackson Metropolitan Library System, Mississippi, and the formation of a new system based on its strongest members. HBW added something new to its list of services and specializations: an executive search service. Gossage Regan, to judge by the ads it has been running, is already well established in the library personnel search field.

Library schools, with their concentrations of specialists qualified in various fields, are natural places to look for research expertise. A team from Drexel went beyond this in 1986 to take on a $100,000 assignment to design a system to enable the National Park Service to do a better job of handling queries from the public.

Library Education

The topics of interest in education for librarianship in 1986, the centennial year for American graduate library education, were recruitment, upgrading professional skills in research libraries, enrollment, library school survival, curriculum changes, preservation training, growing shortages in some specializations, competencies, accreditation, and, surprisingly, book arts. Recruitment reappeared after several years as a prime concern. ALA Executive Director Tom Galvin called for a major effort to produce the librarians capable of moving librarianship from "a document delivery operation to information transfer." In California, a state-level recruitment operation, the California Library School Recruitment Project, was launched, conducted a massive survey of library personnel needs, and developed impressive recruiting materials. [See the special report "Library Education: A Centenary" by Michael Buckland in Part 3 — Ed.]

The need for new management in larger libraries is being addressed in several programs: the Council on Library Resources intern program, the University of Michigan's Research Library Residency Program, Louisiana State's new 24-hour post master's for certification in automation, Hawaii's new interdisciplinary doctorate, and Michigan's two new curricula for information managers and library associates. Libraries themselves are addressing the problem in in-house efforts. Two noted in 1986 were the mentor programs reported to be functioning successfully at the University of California, Berkeley, and the University of Texas at Austin.

Although the library school at the University of Michigan claimed a 40 percent increase last year in enrollment, many library schools are in dubious straits. Survival is being discussed at Emory and Peabody; the University of Chicago gave its library school a new lease on life; the defunct Case Western library school's library found a new

home at the University of Alabama. In the United Kingdom drastic reductions in the number of librarians produced annually were being discussed. In the effort to keep afloat in a changing world, library schools continued to change their names and their curricula to appeal to a broader potential clientele.

The new concern for preservation has not only stimulated the offering of courses for both administrators and craftspersons; it has apparently revived interest in rare book librarianship and the book arts. At Columbia's Rare Books School, 17 courses were offered, 12 of them for the first time. A new program in the book arts was launched at Occidental College, alma mater of bookman and library guru Lawrence Powell.

Sharing Accreditation

After a long study, the report of the ALA/USOE accreditation project led by UCLA's Robert Hayes was delivered to ALA, urging that ALA pursue the possibility of other organizations sharing responsibility and costs with ALA for the accreditation of information and library programs. Various associations responded to the challenge, but all seemed less than enthusiastic about the suggestion that they might have to provide some of the money for the program. The report was received by the ALA executive board, and referred back to ALA's Standing Committee on Library Education without much direction nor any budget to take the proposal to share accreditation further.

Librarian Requirements

Another idea that seemed worthwhile a year or two back was the determination of just what competencies are required in a librarian/library science worker by employers. King Research labored mightily to answer the question, but its answer was rejected out of hand by library educators. They faulted King's sampling methods and, despite the fact that several had offered proposals to do the study, were severely critical of the whole idea of competency-based education.

A somewhat different approach, and a more fruitful one for research libraries, was suggested in a January *College & Research Libraries* article by Ronald Powell and Sheila Creth. Their "Knowledge Bases and Library Education" reported on the rating by Association of Research Libraries members of 56 knowledge bases important for new librarians to have. Besides the traditional core knowledge of librarianship, ARL libraries want recruits with capabilities in automation, management, and personnel work. The application of the concept of knowledge bases would seem to offer a highly adaptable approach, enabling even the highly specialized library or library department to enunciate its personnel needs and requirements.

Fighting Discrimination

While the federal government was cutting back Equal Opportunity activities, the Library of Congress claimed success in countering discrimination with its Graduate Cooperative Education Program. In San Jose, progress was made toward equal pay for librarians, as people in a female-dominated occupation — without going so far as to admit publicly that the city was moving toward "comparable worth." On November 4, San Francisco voters solidly supported pay equity and voted for the money to effect it.

Cuyahoga County Public Library (Ohio) at year's end announced a renewed com-

mitment to affirmative action on ethnic discrimination, with scholarships and more active recruiting of blacks. In another area, sex discrimination, Cuyahoga was under fire. Linda Silver, who has been acting director of CCPL twice, while men were recruited for the post, filed charges of sex discrimination; at year's end the case was still being heard. The University of Wyoming Libraries has also been charged with an equal pay complaint, now under investigation.

Occupational Health Hazards

A British study that ranked librarianship lowest in stress among occupations ranging from clergy and nannies to construction workers and journalists drew indignation from more than one librarian, and discussions among personnel directors at ALA/New York included stress as a serious problem. Charles Bunge of the University of Wisconsin (Madison) library school faculty offered useful workshops on stress management at several conferences, including that of his faculty peers in ALISE. Practical suggestions for relieving stress caused by VDT work appeared in a paper delivered at the ACRL meeting in Baltimore: "Job Design for the Automated Technical Services Environment" by Kathleen M. Hayes.

Drugs were recognized as a problem by one Oklahoma public library board, which considered a harsh policy against employees involved in substance abuse either as a seller or a user, then changed its position and agreed to include in the policy new provisions for assistance to employees with a problem. The use by academic libraries of Employee Assistance Programs (EAPs) sponsored by their universities was noted as under study by two Texas Tech librarians.

Radiation hazards from VDT screens, a nagging fear especially to women of childbearing age, will apparently get its first substantial and controlled study by the National Institute for Safety and Health, in a study launched in fall 1986. Earlier in the year, concern intensified when a Swedish study warned that cancer had been induced in mice by VDT radiation.

Staff health programs have been reported by libraries only rarely, although there are frequent mentions in newsletters of individuals participating in jogging and exercise programs. Dallas Public librarians were reported a year or so back to be spending their lunch hours doing group Jane Fonda exercises. The single mention in 1986 was the report of a "wellness" program at the Baltimore County Public Library. An evaluation found that for most of the participants the program had lasting benefits in maintaining a more healthful way of life.

The Salary Situation

Some progress is being made toward correcting the imbalance in salaries of librarians as workers in a female-dominated occupation. Massachusetts librarians voted to set $20,000 as the current professional beginning salary, on the grounds that it should at least equal the salary paid beginning teachers. New York librarians voted similarly to peg library salaries at the level of new teachers with master's degrees.

The Special Libraries Association reported salaries of its members up $4,500 over 1982 levels. (SLA has appointed a task force, chaired by James Matarazzo of Simmons, to "determine the value of the information professional.") The Association of Research Libraries reported that the median salary of its librarians had increased by 5.3 percent to

$27,485 in 1985. Entry-level salaries rose 6.1 percent to $17,507. The Medical Library Association reported late in 1986 that the median salary of its members is $28,870 and most of them consider their paycheck either "good" or "very good."

Trouble for Boards

Two occurences in 1986 reminded one of the latent hostility that exists between independent library boards and municipal authorities. In Indiana, a move to put local elected officials in control of libraries was defeated. In Nebraska, proposals by the governor for changes in the state library commission would have removed the requirement that the director be a librarian and would have taken away the commission's appointive power and given it to the director of cultural affairs.

A new threat to citizen library boards has emerged with the escalation of insurance costs. In one case, a library board in Mississippi resigned en masse because the library could no longer afford liability insurance.

People of 1986

Richard Ackeroyd became Connecticut State Librarian . . . *Vivian Arterbery*, formerly director of libraries for Rand Corporation, is now executive director of NCLIS . . . *Hugh Atkinson*, University of Illinois librarian for the past ten years, died on October 24 . . . *Toni Carbo Bearman*, formerly executive director of NCLIS, is now dean of the School of Library and Information Science at Pittsburgh.

Daniel J. Boorstin, Librarian of Congress, will retire as of June 1987 . . . *Larry Brandwein*, Brooklyn Public's deputy director, is now director . . . *Margaret Chisholm,* dean of the University of Washington Library School, is ALA president for 1987–88.

Robert B. Croneberger, formerly State Librarian and Archivist, Tennessee State Library and Archives, is now director of Carnegie Library of Pittsburgh . . . *Richard De Gennaro*, director of libraries at University of Pennsylvania, will become director of New York Public Library on February 1, 1987.

Kenneth F. Duchac, director of the Brooklyn Public Library, will retire in early 1987 . . . *Elizabeth Futas*, formerly associate professor, Division of Library and Information Management, Emory University, is now professor and director of the Graduate School of Library and Information Studies, University of Rhode Island . . . *Gilbert Gude* resigned as director of LC's Congressional Research Service.

Ervin J. Gaines, director of Cleveland Public Library, died . . . *Matthew J. Higgins*, formerly Assistant State Librarian at the New Hampshire State Library, is now State Librarian and Director . . . *Monteria Hightower*, formerly director of downtown services, Seattle Public Library, is now associate commissioner for libraries and State Librarian of Missouri.

Norman Horrocks left his post as director of the School of Library Service at Dalhousie University to become vice president of editorial at Scarecrow Press . . . *E. J. Josey*, formerly chief of the Bureau of Specialist Library Service, New York State Education Department, is now professor at the School of Library and Information Science, University of Pittsburgh.

Richard W. McCoy retired as president of the Research Libraries Group . . . *Marilyn Gell Mason*, formerly director, Atlanta-Fulton Public Library, became director of the Cleveland Public Library . . . *Anne Mathews* of the University of Denver's Gradu-

ate School of Librarianship and Information Management has been named director of library programs at the Office of Educational Research and Improvement.

Major Owens, our "librarian in Congress," easily won reelection in Brooklyn . . . *Boyd W. Rayward*, formerly dean of the Graduate Library School at University of Chicago, is now head of the School of Librarianship, University of New South Wales, Australia . . . *Eleanor Jo Rodger*, formerly chief of network services at Enoch Pratt Free Library, is now executive director of the Public Library Association.

Frances Stuart Schwenger, formerly acting director, Metropolitan Toronto Reference Library, Ontario, Canada, became director at MTRL . . . *David H. Stam*, formerly Andrew W. Mellon director of the research libraries of NYPL, is now university librarian at Syracuse . . . *Roderick G. Swartz*, State Librarian of Washington since 1975, died.

Kenneth Y. Tomlinson, vice president and executive editor of *Reader's Digest*, is the new NCLIS chair . . . *Robert Penn Warren* is LC's first official U.S. poet laureate . . . *Dorman Winfrey* retired as Texas State Library director . . . *Sam G. Whitten*, educator at University of Texas Graduate School of Library and Information Science, died.

Ella Gaines Yates, formerly assistant director of administration for the Friendship Force in Atlanta, is now the Virginia State Librarian . . . *Nancy L. Zussy*, formerly Acting State Librarian at Washington State Library, became State Librarian.

SLJ News Report, 1986

Bertha M. Cheatham

Managing Editor/News and Features Editor, *School Library Journal*

Celebration and change were the positive hallmarks of the year 1986. In the realm of celebration, New York City held festivities for the restoration of the Statue of Liberty on July Fourth, just after the one hundredth and fifth annual conference of the American Library Association ended. ALA's most successful conference attracted over 16,000 participants. The American Association of School Librarians also found cause for celebration—its fourth national conference coincided with its thirty-fifth anniversary and drew a record 3,000 registrants to Minneapolis.

It was also a year of change—a record number of publishing companies were sold to domestic and foreign conglomerates, national professional associations acquired new leadership, and the Democrats gained control of the Senate. Libraries were caught short with abrupt abolition of federal revenue sharing. In some communities voters rejected library tax-support measures; library administrators had to seek new ways of coping with budget strictures. Some school boards found themselves deeply enmeshed in court battles over religious freedom issues. Shortages persisted in the supply of qualified professionals to fill vacant positions in public and school libraries that serve children.

Note: Adapted from *School Library Journal*, December 1986, where the article was entitled "The Year in Review."

Revenue Sharing Ends

In October 1986, 39,000 local governments (many of which were midway through their fiscal 1986–1987 budget) received their last revenue sharing check. For the past 14 years, revenue sharing had supported education and boosted public library budgets, although libraries had to compete with fire departments and other local public agencies for the extra dollars.

In its lifetime, revenue sharing supplied over $82.5 billion to local governments, including $3.9 billion in 1986. The real effect of this loss will be felt in 1987 by large urban school systems and public libraries. The cities will have to use local taxes to supplement now-defunct revenue sharing funds or find means of paring down municipal services.

Education: Ongoing Issues

Total education expenditures were expected to reach $278 billion by the end of 1986. The American public is becoming more aware of the costs of attaining excellence in education. This awareness grew from the widespread publicity over *A Nation at Risk* and other reports challenging the effectiveness of U.S. public schools.

Television joined in efforts to inform parents about progress made toward the excellence called for in the series of publications issued by the U.S. Department of Education. More publicity in the form of a special program titled *Whose School Is It?*, produced by the National Education Association and Ted Turner's WTBS, went into approximately 40 million homes at the beginning of American Education Week in November. "This is the first time that the NEA has utilized a major television network to convey a message on education of this magnitude to the American public," said NEA President Mary H. Futrell. Congress also supported education by passing spending and other education-related bills, despite haggling over deficit reduction measures required under the Gramm-Rudman-Hollings budget balancing law. Nevertheless, a $50 million dropout prevention act was defeated.

The allocation for the Chapter 2 State Block Grant under the Education Consolidation and Improvement Act for FY 1986–1987 is $529,337,000. A 1984–1985 U.S. Education Department study of the block grants shows that support for libraries dropped, with large allocations of Chapter 2 funds going to computer acquisitions. The funds are allocated at the discretion of local school districts. Ninety-nine percent of districts received Chapter 2 funds in the 1984–1985 school year; the median district allowance was $6,422.

Bennett Seeks Pals

Education Secretary William J. Bennett garnered more than his share of news headlines in 1986. "The outspoken, often-controversial Bennett has done more to bring educational issues to the forefront than any previous education secretary. He is willing to voice an opinion on anything — from values education, to parents' right to choice of schools, to how to handle drug education. But experts in these fields seldom agreed with all of his opinions.

With the late 1986 publication of *First Lessons: A Report on Elementary Education in America* directed to parents and other citizens, Bennett partially redeemed him-

self with school and public librarians serving children. Unlike the earlier *What Works: Research about Teaching and Learning,* this most recent in a series of reports on the status of U.S. education finally recognizes that school and public libraries are important to the educational process. Bennett said, "Youngsters need ready access to books" and called for a campaign to ensure that every child gets a public library card by the end of the 1987 school year. Appearing at the National Conference of the American Association of School Librarians in Minnesota, Bennett made an effort to clarify the intention of earlier reports that neglected to mention school libraries, an oversight brought to his attention by many readers of Lillian N. Gerhardt's editorial "Be a Bennett Pen Pal" published in the May 1986 issue of *School Library Journal.*

After pointing out areas for improvement in elementary school curricula, Bennett concluded that the schools are doing a good job. However, Bennett's critics took exception to specific recommendations. One was that business executives, army officers, successful publishers, and other business leaders might be encouraged to undergo an apprenticeship and take over the administrative function of elementary school principals. Bennett and Defense Secretary Caspar Weinberger signed an agreement to urge retired military personnel to join the ranks of our nation's teachers.

The teaching profession is making some strides forward in various areas. Teachers' pay is *slowly* rising and now averages about $26,650; five states now have starting salaries above $18,000 (California is highest at $20,222 per year). But teacher shortages will continue, especially among those qualified to teach math, advanced science, and foreign languages. Fewer college students are taking graduate education courses, teachers are retiring, the teaching force is graying, and the teacher turnover is escalating as the "brightest and best" leave for other fields. Kindergarten enrollments will continue to rise over the next few years as children of the post–World War II baby-boom generation enroll their own children in school.

"Educators under Siege"

"This year's censorship is a portrait of educators under siege," commented Anthony T. Podesta, president of People for the American Way. "In the middle of a drug epidemic . . . educators are being pressured by the censors to end drug education programs. In the face of a crisis of teen pregnancy, censors are pushing to eliminate sex education."

It is estimated that nearly 45 percent of public libraries and 30.9 percent of public schools in Georgia, Alabama, Tennessee, and Louisiana have been targets of censors since 1980, according to a report published by the American Civil Liberties Union. In the "Bible Belt," Christian fundamentalists are becoming more vociferous in their demands that schools abolish curricula that do not support their religious beliefs. This issue and the growing disenchantment of parents with the instructional methods in public schools have resulted in a transfer of children to nonpublic schools and a rise in the number of parents educating children at home.

Major court battles in 1986 involved creation science, a long-standing and troublesome issue. Conservative religious groups are also opposing books that they feel encourage vulgar language, undermine parental authority, promote the occult, and contain sexual content.

The *Edwards* vs. *Aguillard* suit now in the courts challenges the constitutionality of a Louisiana law, the so-called Balanced Treatment for Creation-Science Act. This requires that textbooks, library materials, and educational programs include balanced

coverage of "creation science" and evolution, both to be taught as theories rather than as scientific facts. It also states that each local school board must develop and provide a curriculum guide for public school teachers on how to present creation science, and that the governor designate a panel of seven creation scientists to assist local school boards in developing curricula that are acceptable to all parents. The case is now on the Supreme Court's docket.

In Mobile, Alabama, Christian fundamentalist parents filed suit to have 39 social studies and history textbooks plus 7 home economics textbooks removed from Mobile County schools. "One of the basic issues is 'What is secular humanism?' " said Judge W. Brevard Hand, "Is it a religion? Is it being taught?" He has not yet announced his decision in the *Smith* vs. *Board of Education* lawsuit brought by the Mobile parents.

Midway through the fall school term, a ruling from Greenville, Tennessee, stunned educators and intellectual freedom fighters. Citing the Freedom of Religion Amendment, Judge Thomas G. Hull decided in favor of seven fundamentalist parents against the Hawkins County school board. Judge Hull ruled that the schools must offer free public education without violating the First Amendment rights of students, who are no longer required to use the textbook that caused the controversy. At issue was *Riders on the Earth*, a 1983 sixth-grade reader published by Holt, Rinehart & Winston. The complainants identified 16 antireligious themes in the text, including evolution; pacifism; witchcraft; supernaturalism; male/female role reversals; and situational ethics. One alternative Hull suggested is an opt-out program. The students whose parents have denied them permission to use the texts could go to study halls or to the school library during classroom reading instruction and receive reading lessons from parents at home.

Hull's ruling creates a dilemma for textbook publishers who try to produce texts to please all of the different religious groups. They are already under tremendous pressure to meet high standards set by evaluation committees of state departments of education.

Meese Battles Pornography

After a year of hearings, and controversy about how they were conducted, Attorney General Edwin Meese's Commission on Pornography released its published report in July 1986, just after the annual conference of the American Library Association ended. Among the conclusions of the 1,960-page report was that some forms of pornography cause sexual violence. The report recommended that state and local prosecutors crack down on pornography and urged citizen vigilance in the form of "watch groups" that would file complaints. Some see this report as a trend toward new morality enforcement. After receiving a letter from the commission hinting that they might be cited for distributing pornography, many chain stores, such as 7-Eleven, stopped selling *Playboy, Penthouse*, and *Forum*.

When some critics said the report gave would-be censors a great deal of ammunition, Meese defended the commission and denied that the report fostered censorship. Even the panel of experts serving on his commission was not satisfied with the research and the findings. Two commissioners — Judith Becker of Columbia University and Ellen Levine, editor of *Woman's Day* — dissented. They did not agree with what others considered "degrading" material, nor did they concur with the conclusions reached by a commission they claimed lacked both sufficient time and money for original research. Despite its titillating contents, which caused an early rush to buy the report, the public and the national press soon appeared to lose interest. Meese, however, was determined

not to let up on his mission — he vowed to form a Justice Department task force to aid in his fight against porn.

Book Targeted in England

While U.S. school systems are trying to figure out how and when or whether to teach children about troublesome topics such as child abuse/abduction, AIDS, homosexuality, and divorce, a debate rages about how far to go in teaching sex education in England. The Inner London Education Authority is defending a book titled *Jenny Lives with Eric and Martin,* a Danish import about a five-year-old girl who lives with her homosexual father and his lover. The book is not in school libraries; it is only available from a book lending center run by the Authority.

According to a recent report, this book is one of 27 books used in schools that English groups have campaigned to have removed from classrooms in an effort to delete any lessons on sex outside of marriage. The controversy erupted in September, when Education Secretary Kenneth Baker asked the Authority to remove it from London's 1,084 schools. He described it as "homosexual propaganda" and said there was no place for it in any school, but he does not have the power to ban books.

Parents at one school burned copies of *Jenny* and sent children home for a day in protest. The government, which supports the teaching of sex education in school courses, has recommended that the book be banned. The Authority maintains it is up to each school to decide what should be taught, but conservative lawmakers are still pressing to have *Jenny* and the other 26 books banned.

Show Me! — In Trouble Again!

A fundamentalist minister, Reverend Eric Smith, heard *Show Me!* (St. Martin's, 1975) discussed on a Christian television show, and did not like what he heard. He checked the book out of the library and took it to the FBI and to the local police department to ask if its contents violated federal child pornography laws. Neither agency backed his claim, so he took his complaint to the Alameda County Library Advisory Commission. After deliberation, members voted 14-1 to keep the title in the library's circulating collection. Although it is shelved in the adult section under sex education, any patron can check it out.

Speak English Only?

Results of a test administered by the U.S. Census Bureau revealed that 13 percent of all U.S. adults are illiterate in English. Of these, about 37 percent speak a language other than English at home (14 percent are literate in their own language); 82 percent are immigrants; 21 percent entered the United States in the last six years.

California's Proposition 63, which voters approved in the November 1986 election, makes English the official language of the state. A similar measure has been introduced in Dade County (Florida) where Cubans and Haitians make up a large segment of the population. Observers predict that such laws will encourage prejudice against non-English-speaking residents in schools and in the job market; they are concerned that other states might follow California's lead. It should be noted that some cities are taking

an opposite route—residents of Atlanta and Osceola, Florida, have proudly declared their cities both multilingual and multicultural.

First Amendment Awareness

By a large majority, Maine voters defeated a referendum that would have made it a crime to sell or promote obscene material. The powerful Christian Civic League fought for the measure, but the campaign waged by Maine Citizens against Government Censorship was more powerful, leading to the defeat of the measure.

A positive approach to informing ninth- and tenth-grade students about the First Amendment was seen in Iowa, where the State Library received a $10,000 grant from the National Endowment for the Humanities to formulate and conduct a summer seminar dealing with religious freedom as guaranteed by the U.S. Constitution's First Amendment. Parents also read documents dealing with historic background of the First Amendment and potentially controversial materials found on library shelves.

Los Angeles Rebuilds

April 29, 1986 is a date that no staff member of the Central Library in Los Angeles will ever forget. A raging fire that started in the stacks whipped through the 60-year-old structure and destroyed 20 percent of the collection. Arson was suspected, and an artist's rendering of the suspected arsonist was published in the library press to no avail. On September 3 the arsonist struck again.

The damage was extensive, and the repairs costly. Over 395,000 books were lost; over 600,000 books with smoke damage were warehoused, then moved to a temporary library setup in the former Bullock's Department Store. The library expects to reopen in spring 1987. Library administrators report that 602,000 books were water damaged and are being treated in two freezer locations; 20,000 frozen books have been processed in the McDonnell Douglas vacuum chamber, dried, and warehoused; 200,000 books are in a Central Library off-site depository.

LC Cuts and Protests

In February 1986, Librarian of Congress Daniel J. Boorstin testified before an appropriations subcommittee of the U.S. House of Representatives and warned that the cuts suffered by LC as a result of the Gramm-Rudman-Hollings budget-ceiling legislation were "disastrous—for Congress, for the nation, and for the world of learning." LC's operating budget had been cut by $18.3 million. Boorstin immediately took action: cutting the reading room hours of the prestigious library, from 77.5 hours to 54.5 per week; threatening to reduce staff; clamping a freeze on hiring. Book buying was to drop 13.3 percent, or $626,000. Patron demonstrations, including a protest sit-in, ensued. These drew the attention of the news media, which publicized the library's plight. Eventually, legislators found $867,000 in supplemental funds, and Boorstin restored library hours and other services.

There was a public outcry when Boorstin eliminated the publication of a braille issue of *Playboy* after $103,000 was cut from LC's appropriation—the exact cost for producing *Playboy* in braille. ALA joined with other organizations in a suit that

charged the First Amendment rights of blind people were being violated. Judge Thomas F. Hogan upheld the complaint.

Sex Bias Charged

A sex bias complaint was filed by Linda Silver with the Equal Employment Opportunities Commission (EEOC) against the Cuyahoga County Public Library. Silver charged that the library passed over her for a promotion because she is a woman. Despite her more than 20 years of active service, during which she served twice as acting director and was responsible for the library's getting a bigger share of Ohio's intangible tax income, the board members failed to appoint her to the top post. Silver made the complaint in the hope that it might inspire and support other women in library service who are denied appointment to top administrative positions by library boards. EEOC failed to support her complaint. Silver has not announced whether she will take her charge to court.

Literacy Update

One in every five adults, 27 million Americans, is functionally illiterate; 45 million are only marginally literate. Over half of the adults currently on welfare are functionally illiterate. The national campaign to make the public aware of the illiteracy problem and the work to alleviate it continues on a wide scale.

To gain public support for books and reading, the Center for the Book of the Library of Congress is continuing its "Year of the Reader Program" for the tenth year. President Reagan signed the proposal into law in October 1986, and similar Centers for the Book in Florida, Illinois, Michigan, Oklahoma, Oregon, Minnesota, North Dakota, South Dakota, and Wisconsin are developing projects to spread the message to the public.

"Literacy: Your Child's Future" was the theme of the 1986 Harriet Dickson Reynolds in Celebration of the Child Program at the Houston Public Library this fall. Experts in literature for children and young adults discussed the necessity of reading aloud, how to select books for children, and other ways parents can be involved in a child's reading development.

Apartheid Protest

The proliferation of local and city ordinances restricting public agencies from doing business with vendors who have business interests in South Africa hit one book jobber in the pocketbook. Ordinances in San Francisco and Chicago require that Baker & Taylor submit a signed affidavit to the effect that its parent company W. R. Grace, which owns two small companies in South Africa, is not involved with any apartheid-enforcing agency. In early fall, Baker & Taylor had yet to respond to the libraries' requests for signed waivers.

Taking a direct approach, the board of the Minneapolis Public Library voted to adopt a resolution condemning apartheid, barring investment of trust funds in companies that do business with South Africa, and stating its intention to divest itself of holdings in such institutions or companies.

The American Library Association also took a major step on this issue — the divestiture of all South African companies from its endowment portfolio was completed in fall 1986.

Textbooks Evaluated

California's Department of Education continues its "get tough" policy requiring that textbooks meet rigid standards of accuracy and excellence. In 1985, textbook publishers got fair warning when the State Curriculum Development and Supplemental Materials Commission rejected more than 20 science textbooks. In 1986, the review commission held firm on its resolve not to purchase unreliable, poorly written textbooks. By a 10–1 vote, the commission rejected every math textbook submitted by 14 publishers for use in its public schools, kindergarten through eighth grade. The reason? None of the texts met new, stricter state requirements for teaching mathematics.

The publishers, who stand to lose much money, were given a year to revise more than 150 textbooks and teachers' manuals. For example, Laidlow is expected to spend another $2 million on revisions of mathematics textbooks that cost about $2 million to produce. This affects more than $25 million in California annual textbook purchases. The chief complaint, according to one of the 43 members of the commission, is that math textbooks continue to emphasize learning by memorization of rules rather than the understanding of mathematical concepts, and that workshops and supplemental materials continue to emphasize a "fill-in-the-blanks" strategy rather than approaches that can help students visualize concepts.

This get-tough policy was initiated in 1985 largely through the efforts of State Education Superintendent Bill Honig, who wants to upgrade the standards of textbook instruction with materials that are more accurate and more relevant to the curriculum.

Publishing Acquisitions

Takeovers and buyouts were reported almost weekly in the financial pages of the nation's press. In late December 1985, CBS sold Holt, Rinehart & Winston to the Holzbrinck Group of Stuttgart, West Germany. In 1986, Time Inc. entered the education market when it purchased Scott, Foresman for $520 million in cash. Toronto-based International Thomson Organization acquired South-Western Publishing, a leading high school and college business education publisher. Other sales in 1986 were the following:

- Greenwood Press bought Praeger.
- Nelson sold Dodd Mead to ten company officers.
- Harper & Row bought Winston Seabury.
- Globe Pequot bought Auburn Publishing.
- Gulf & Western bought Silver Burdett.
- Karl Navarre bought Atlantic Monthly.
- Penguin bought NAL and Dutton.
- Macmillan bought Hayden.
- Harcourt Brace Jovanovich bought CBS's textbook unit.
- Bertelsmann, which owns Bantam, acquired Doubleday.

Book sales continue to be stable. The Association of American Publishers reported 1985 sales totaled $9,878,500,000; $1.48 billion of which were textbook sales and $1.99 billion were trade book sales. Book prices are continuing to rise, and libraries are spending more to buy far fewer books than in previous years. This inflationary trend is expected to continue, and librarians are seeking ways to diminish the impact of higher book prices and lower discounts. Bookstores are continuing to reap profits on toy books.

But the spending tide may turn. "A modest improvement [in U.S. book sales] over the coming five years" is predicted by analyst John P. Dessauer, director of the Center for Book Research at the University of Scranton, Pennsylvania. Dessauer expects that schools will expend more monies over this period. "Schools have expended $1.2 billion in acquiring 257 million books for textbook and library use in 1981; by 1985 the figure had risen to $1.7 billion for 275 million books. In 1990 schools are anticipated to spend $3 billion for 344 million books."

One way to counteract rising book costs that deplete budgets is through cooperative purchasing. Schools and public libraries in the 12-county Norweld Cooperative in Ohio have been buying books, mainly paperbacks, from B. Dalton at 25 percent discount. They report that they have enjoyed excellent service, particularly with special orders.

School Library Statistics

An estimated 93 percent of 78, 455 schools have school library media centers. This statistic was taken from a preliminary report of a survey conducted by the U.S. Department of Education's Center for Statistics. Of the schools surveyed, 17 percent of the library's budget was spent on computer hardware; the total mean expenditure for materials acquisition was $7,577, and the average media center spent $6.24 per pupil for books.

Innovative Programs

Nuclear annihilation was the topic of a program at the West Hartford Public Library in Connecticut early in 1986. Adults and children over age ten heard a professor of pediatrics and psychiatry talk about the issues and how to allay the anxiety of children growing up in a "nuclear age."

A toy collection for disabled children was initiated in the Onondaga County (New York) Public Library, with the aid of the state office of Mental Retardation and Developmental Disabilities Planning Council. "Project Adapt" allows youngsters to use toys with their hands or feet, a voice activator, or a "puff and sip" straw.

State News Roundup

California

Ninety employees of the Berkeley Public Library (librarians, supervisors, library assistants, pages, aides, and technicians) received a 6 percent cost-of-living raise and each will receive two comparable worth salary adjustments within a year. Part-timers working fewer than 20 hours a week received paid leave for the first time as well as a 15 percent reclassification upgrade.

An ambitious statewide California Reading Initiative was launched in 1986. Its goal is to get children to read and to enjoy literature by introducing a host of selected general trade book titles in the classroom. This program provides an excellent opportunity for public and school librarians to share their book expertise with teachers, parents, and students, although the first booklist appeared to lack any fine tuning from librarians.

Illinois

Illinois celebrated School Library Day 1986 by holding tours, receptions, and programs. Governor James Thompson, a staunch library supporter, issued a proclamation recognizing the special day. Highland Park School District 108 won the prestigious School Library Media Program of the Year Award for 1986.

After 114 years of continuous service, the Chicago Public Library is confronting its most difficult challenge to date: the need for a new facility for its central library. It is now housed in a warehouse, with books in storage, a dwindling staff, and a new director, John B. Duff. Plans for another facility have met with opposition by critics in a continuing controversy over the site to be chosen for the library.

Maryland

It is estimated that 60.5 percent of women with children work outside the home, and that 7 million children are on their own after school; 5.5 million are in day-care centers. The Hyattsville branch of the Prince George's County Memorial Library System set up a Parent-Child Room to aid working parents. The room also has activities for latchkey children who stay at the library until a parent or older sibling returns home.

Massachusetts

The Massachusetts Library Association was one of several associations (see New York) that voted to endorse a recommendation for a minimum salary level. MLA recommended $20,000 for entry-level public librarians with MLS degrees. The minimum salary level for teachers in the state is $18,000. MLA set its sights higher to reflect more expensive education requirements.

Early in 1986, Boston Public Library was unable to fill about 70 vacancies and had to curtail weekend hours at some branches; many branches do not have a full-time children's librarian. Midyear, BPL realized a $1.63 million budget increase and expects to replenish its collections. It may also hire a children's librarian for every branch.

Ohio

Cleveland Public Library suffered a huge $2.7 million budget loss resulting from the transfer of funding from Cleveland Public to the Cuyahoga County Public Library. It was forced to cut back in staff (30 positions), eliminate a bookmobile, and spend less for books, magazines, and preservation of old materials. Marilyn Gell, formerly director of the Atlanta-Fulton Public Library, was appointed CPL director.

New York

New York Library Association's Council approved a recommendation in fall 1986 calling for a minimum salary for beginning librarians. The recommendation stated that, in each community, the salary should be equal to salaries of entry-level teachers who have master's degrees. At the current pay scale statewide, NYLA says this means a $24,800 annual salary for librarians.

New York made a significant stride forward in developing a regional database of all library holdings using state grants totaling $1.7 million and $405,000 in LSCA Title III funds. New York's goal is to have a database of 57 million records incorporating academic, research, public, and school libraries.

Pennsylvania

Pennsylvania has completed its CD-ROM laser library disc database listing the holdings of more than 100 school, academic, and public libraries.

Technology

Experts in electronic media remain cautious about teachers' use of media. David A. England, director of the National Teachers of English Commission on Media, states: "Until teachers are prepared to use media, and until they have actual models of media use, we're fighting a losing battle. Students are growing up immersed in media. With every generation, the need for media literacy increases. But there's no corresponding increase in teachers' use of media. If we're to make any progress with media in education, it has to begin with teacher education." Librarians are taking advantage of every workshop and in-service course possible and are becoming increasingly knowledgeable about this technology, often serving as advisers and resource staff in schools.

Some tech highlights of the year follow:

- Quality Education Data's 1986 census of U.S. school districts reveals that 42 percent of all public schools have at least 11 microcomputers; 86 percent are using VCRs for instruction. Only 5,167 or 6.3 percent of schools lack micros.
- Compact disc circulation in San Bernardino City Library tops the circulation of LP records. Supervising Librarian David Davis says they are "more cost effective since they are nearly impervious to damage."
- NICEM, the National Information Center for Educational Media, a listing available in print and online, is now sold on CD-ROM for about $800 a year.
- Milwaukee County Federated Library System reports that videotape circulation is up 77 percent, a dramatic increase over the 1985 circulation: 2,069 cassettes were circulated 86,517 times. The Milwaukee Public Library opened six new multimedia centers stocked with computers, compact discs, videotapes, and audiocassettes.
- New York Public Library estimates over 3,000 people a month use microcomputers installed in 24 branches; patrons use them for personal and business accounting, educational programs, BASIC programming, and games.

Organizations in Brief

The national library and education associations experienced some familiar difficulties in 1986: eroding membership; problems in fiscal management and budget deficits; lack of a leadership role in the field; staffing changes.

AECT

Lyn Gubser, executive director of the Association for Educational Communications and Technology (AECT) since 1983, resigned in July. Stanley Zenor, who replaced him, was given a new title — association manager. AECT is still trying to eradicate debts, boost a declining membership, and get a firm grip on determining future directions.

IASL

In June, over 150 registrants from all over the world convened at the International Association of School Librarianship in Halifax, Nova Scotia, to hear delegates discuss the theme "The School Library — Window on the World."

SSLI

The newly formed Society of School Librarians International (SSLI) was announced via a press release in February 1986. It was organized by former directors and by active members of American Association of School Librarians (AASL), assisted by Alice Fite, who served as executive director of AASL for 12 years. According to one organizer, Frances Dean, a past president of AASL, "[SSLI] was conceived . . . to meet the needs of school library professionals and their students . . . who live in a global society." SSLI's charter meeting in Philadelphia drew about 500 members and exhibitors.

CLA

Canadian Library Association announced that its executive director for over ten years, Paul Kitchen, resigned after a disagreement with its board of directors. CLA is attempting to overhaul its structure and decision-making procedures and implement ways of increasing membership.

NCLIS

Vivian J. Arterbery, former library director of the Rand Corporation in Santa Monica, California, was named executive director of the National Commission on Libraries and Information Science. She succeeded Toni Carbo Bearman, who, after serving as NCLIS executive director for five years, resigned to become dean of the University of Pittsburgh School of Library and Information Science.

ALA in Transition

At the American Library Association's annual conference, Executive Director Thomas J. Galvin delivered his first annual report. Galvin (who succeeded Robert Wedgeworth

in 1985) said his work was "never boring" and promised improved membership services. He insisted there was no crisis in ALA's financial status.

In late October, in a review of ALA's financial status, the executive board was informed that three ALA divisions were in serious financial straits: American Library Trustee Association (ALTA); Association of Specialized and Cooperative Library Agencies (ASCLA); and the Young Adult Services Division (YASD). Deputy Director Roger Parent explained that loss in divisional membership creates a financial drain since personal members' dues support salaries of headquarters staff and divisional programs. Each ALA division must maintain at least 3,000 members in order to be self-supporting, said Parent. All three of the above-mentioned divisions have memberships under 2,000. A special committee, chaired by past ALA President Beverly P. Lynch, will study options for financially strapped divisions. Lynch had a very productive presidential year in 1985–1986.

A Forecast of Needs

"Our diverse and complex society demands creative and innovative libraries," said ALA President Regina U. Minudri, the twenty-sixth woman to serve as president of the 110-year-old organization. "Bilingualism, multiculturalism, and integration make new demands on libraries. We may need new skills and new ways of identifying these needs of communicating, and a willingness to accept those who may be different."

Youth Divisions

AASL

At the beginning of the year, the American Association of School Librarians was faced with administrative problems and a $29,507 budget shortfall, but members were eager to get on with the business of running an effective, efficient, energized organization responsive to its membership. Following the departure of Executive Director Alice E. Fite, who resigned in 1985, Ann Carlson Weeks took over as executive director soon after the Midwinter Conference. Marilyn E. Miller, who filled in for 1985–1986 President Shirley Aaron before she officially became 1986–1987 president, continued Aaron's mission of studying AASL's structure and seeking the recommendations of an Organizational Evaluation Committee. Despite initial reservations of some directors when OEC recommendations were presented, AASL's board of directors voted to reduce the size of future boards and make a number of organizational changes, pending membership approval at ALA's 1987 annual conference in San Francisco.

Much of AASL's year was spent finalizing plans for its fourth national conference in Minnesota, which received high praise from those who attended it in September. Future plans call for new school library standards, under development by a four-person writing team, with September 1987 the proposed publication date. ALA will publish, advertise, and assist in the implementation of the long-awaited document.

ALSC

A stable financial status and a stable member enrollment holds the Association for Library Service to Children on a steady course. President Gail M. Sage said a top priority was to contend with the critical shortage of children's librarians. It was reported that

there are three open positions for every person enrolled in library schools. ALSC will produce a recruitment brochure in an attempt to attract others to the field.

In addition to developing recruitment strategies, Jane Botham, 1986–1987 ALSC president, says that the division is focusing on ways to break the cycle of illiteracy in families where parents are nonreaders. An ALA preconference program on reading to infants, planned for San Francisco, will deal with encouraging parents to read to very young children and with the use of book-related materials at home.

Susan Roman was appointed to fill the vacancy created when ALSC Executive Director Ann Weeks resigned.

YASD

Despite its growing financial difficulties, the Young Adult Services Division managed to have a productive year. It even launched an ambitious project to train YA librarians to design and implement humanities programs, thanks to a generous grant from the National Endowment for the Humanities. Executive Director Evelyn Shaevel is coordinating the four regional training workshops.

SLJ's Pick of the Year

When librarian Ann Scarpellino, of the Ramsey (New Jersey) Free Public Library, discovered a serious error in *First Love: A Young People's Guide to Sexual Information* by sexologist Dr. Ruth Westheimer, she called its publisher, Warner Books. In the guide, readers are erroneously advised that it is safe to have intercourse during the week before and the week of ovulation. Warner hastily pulled 115,000 copies from stores and offered to replace all copies sold during the three months it was on the bookstore shelves. The corrected edition bore a new red cover. Said Westheimer, "The book first came out in white, but I made a mistake. I blushed, now it's red."

PW News Report, 1986

John F. Baker

Editor in Chief, *Publishers Weekly*

The year 1986 was one of escalation in many areas of the publishing industry: Sales of a number of hardcover books assumed mass market proportions; extravagant advances continued for what looked like guaranteed bestsellers, with James Clavell's *Whirlwind* bringing a record $5 million; publishers themselves continued to amalgamate into ever-larger entities, with several combinations moving up behind 1985's Simon & Schuster/Prentice-Hall merger, still in the biggest-publisher slot. Prominent among them were two major international incursions, by the Bertelsmann group in the United States, which added Doubleday/Dell and the book clubs to Bantam; and by Penguin in

Note: Adapted from *Publishers Weekly*, January 9, 1987, where the article was entitled "1986: Looking Back."

London, which added New American Library and Dutton to their Viking Penguin flagship. Time Inc. bought Scott, Foresman, and Holt, Rinehart & Winston and W. B. Saunders went to Harcourt Brace Jovanovich (while Holt trade books went to Germany's Von Holtzbrinck). At the end of the year, a similar move created the biggest (in terms of sales) bookstore chain, when Barnes & Noble bought an insufficiently profitable B. Dalton chain from Dayton Hudson. And these were only the biggest such matings; literally dozens of smaller ones continued to change the face of U.S. publishing—while at the same time smaller, specialized publishers went on multiplying, reaching at last estimate a total well over 18,000.

The Ailing Trade Book Market

But was all this happening in a healthy overall market for trade books? Not really. The year began with heavier-than-usual returns, perked up a little in terms of sales in spring, nosedived in the summer and fall and, by the time the Christmas season approached, was struggling to stay slightly ahead of 1985—at a time when it was generally agreed that pricing had advanced far enough as a corrective for lagging sales. Adult hardcovers, helped by the mass bestsellers, moved upward a little, and children's books continued their steady advance; but in most categories sales were flat or down. It sometimes seemed, in fact, that more copies were being sold of far fewer books, and that the book business was moving closer to the boom-or-bust mentality of Broadway or the movies. And for the first time since the discounting craze first took hold at the beginning of the decade, there were signs of a retreat: the closing of the Pickwick chain and the slowing of Crown expansion, for example.

Against this background, there were signs of shrinkage within the trade business. Macmillan announced heavy future list-cutting among its family of lines, and Arbor House also said it would prune its list by nearly 50 percent within two years—likely harbingers of slenderizing to come.

Publishing Pressures: Old and New

New pressures were brought on publishers, and old ones were sometimes relieved: the virtual death of the Copyright Act's manufacturing clause, enabling publishers to look overseas for printing of works all or mostly text, was an example of the latter, and so was the responsiveness of the Reagan administration to efforts to end piracy of American books. Administration-threatened library and school funding cuts, mostly blocked by Congress, seemed never to arrive.

On the other hand, the present administration is no friend to publishers in the censorship area, and the spring report of the Meese Commission on Pornography gave no cause for rejoicing. As expected, it drew connections, in what was criticized as a highly unscientific manner, between pornography and crime, and while it specifically exempted print media from many of its strictures, it encouraged citizen action against stores carrying publications perceived as harmful.

Bookselling News

Large and long-established publishers also found an unwelcome new wrinkle in a lottery instituted by the American Booksellers Association to assign prime space at the annual

trade show and convention. Carried out in response to complaints from smaller and newer publishers about their locations, the lottery gave some decidedly unchoice spots to some big houses, with fallout still to come.

Another chapter in the long struggle of independent bookstores to secure from publishers discount terms comparable to those provided the chains was written in a November decision by a California judge. Acting on a suit by the Northern California Booksellers Association against Avon Books, pleading unfair discount practices, the judge found that Avon's study of the comparative cost of doing business with chains and independents did not justify its extra discounts to the former. If the ruling is upheld on appeal, it could mean considerable changes in bookseller-publisher relations.

AAP News

Within the Association of American Publishers, discontent focused on several issues, including the role in it of large and small publishers, finances and dues, Washington and New York activities, and its effectiveness in representing publishers' interests. This came to a head in an unusually outspoken annual meeting, but by then former executive director Townsend Hoopes had retired, to be swiftly replaced by Nicholas Veliotes, former U.S. Ambassador to Egypt.

International Developments

Happenings outside our borders impinged on publishers in two important ways. Considerable discontent was expressed with a Canadian government policy reinforcing the native publishing industry, which decreed that Canadian subsidiaries of foreign-based companies should be turned over to majority Canadian ownership; and the situation was exacerbated when the Canadian government, acting in response to U.S. protectionism in timber, imposed a 10 percent import tariff on U.S. trade books. This seemed equally unpopular with Canadian publishers and booksellers, but remained in place at year's end. And the turmoil in the United States over disinvestment in South Africa reached into the book world when a number of cities, including Chicago and San Francisco, informed Baker & Taylor that they would cease to purchase books from the company for their library systems until B & T's parent, W. R. Grace Co., disinvested from South Africa.

Personnel Losses

Two major publishing figures long identified with their publishing houses died during the year: Cass Canfield of Harper & Row, at 88, and Donald Klopfer, cofounder with Bennett Cerf of Random House, at 84. A most untimely death was that of Judy-Lynn Del Rey, founder of the line of science fiction and fantasy books that bears her name, who died at 43, after suffering a brain hemorrhage.

Networking and Resource Sharing in 1986: Facilitating Access to Information

JoAn S. Segal

Executive Director
Association of College and Research Libraries,
American Library Association

A few key books and articles published in 1986 affirm the role of networking in facilitating access to information. More than in previous years, the literature reflects a concern for the user, carried to its furthest by Michael Gorman, who asserted in spring 1986 that "libraries and cooperation cannot be separated" and put forth the concept of "The Library," meaning the fusion of all libraries through cooperation; "The Library," library service from the user's view. His forthright essay attacks "selfishness," based on narrow concepts of ownership, and decrys "the notion that certain materials 'belong' to certain libraries, and that people who use other libraries are not 'entitled' to use those materials." Gorman's vision is of a meganetwork: many cooperative endeavors to which all library users will have free and convenient access.[1]

But Gorman is not a voice crying in the wilderness; his opinions are repeated in others' work. Norm Stevens criticized the Network Advisory Committee's (NAC) *Common Vision* document,[2] asserting it did not recognize the extent to which networks are built from the bottom up.[3] The NAC itself embraced at year's end a concept of "The Nation's Library" as the aggregate of all available information resources, and included in its statement of a common vision of networking, "All users should have access on a timely basis to the information they require without being faced with costs beyond their own or society's means."[4]

As networking reaches a period of maturity, the trend seems to be people-oriented. If 1985 was characterized by a move from the term "networks" to "networking," 1986 is the year when networkers began to talk about "access" and "users," at least more than they have in the past few years.

But it would be dishonest to disregard the stresses on library cooperation. The decentralizing influences cited in this report in the 1986 *Bowker Annual* continue.[5] Not only has there been more local system development, but the notion that a library can get along without cooperating was strongly expressed in 1986. The White Plains (New York) Public Library, for instance, threatened to secede from the Westchester Library System over the loss of its resource sharing subsidy.[6] Cleveland Public and Cuyahoga County libraries argued over the sharing of tax monies, with Cuyahoga County calling for a merger of the two libraries.[7] Tom Ballard continued his campaign against resource sharing. His book was published in November by the American Library Association.[8]

In an extension of private sector attacks on nonprofits, the Information Industry Association (IIA) and the Association of American Publishers (AAP) announced they would set up a task force to address their "concern at the expansion of network activities into electronic services and network control over materials and technology buying decisions."[9] In California, the debate over multitype networking led to the charge·that large institutions might be subject to "resource rape" by smaller, "parasitic" ones.[10]

Key Writings

The 1986–1987 edition of Susan K. Martin's *Library Networks* is completely new, with excellent historical sections, touching on nonautomated networks as well as the usual

computerized ones, and shedding the light of her informed opinion on many of the events in network development.[11] Martin clarifies the distinction, not obvious in the late 1970s and early 1980s, between automation and networking. She accepts the need to continue use of large databases for interlibrary loan (ILL), document delivery, collection management, and access to machine-readable data files. In analyzing governance problems in networks, she thoughtfully considers the role of the large library directors, who were the original network prime movers, but who subsequently turned their attention to other spheres. Martin devotes a chapter to important players in the private sector, where much development is taking place. She pinpoints the year 1983 as a key one in which contracts seemed suddenly to take on importance, where they had previously been considered routine. A good chapter focuses on linking and local systems and on the spiral nature of local system development, with movement in the late 1960s from locally developed systems to networks, subsequent network growth, new local systems developed largely by vendors, and with network linkages still important. Martin points out that the changes in networks reflect the changes in libraries themselves.

Henriette Avram addressed the Florida State University Conference on Multitype Library Cooperation in Tallahassee in February; her paper later appeared in the *Journal of Academic Librarianship*.[12] She stressed four areas of important networking issues:

- Local systems, where the temptation of autonomy may subvert the desire to link with others
- Linking, with development of the LSP having gone beyond just a promise, but not far beyond
- Linking standards development, a sine qua non for network development
- Database ownership, a problem that has taken on increased importance, now that linking is more possible (here Avram clearly states the issue from several points of view through the use of specific cases)

Mel Jacob makes predictions about five areas with potential impact on networking in the future.[13] She foresees gloomy economic conditions, including shrinking resources leading to reallocation, a need to question who pays for what, and continued concern for telecommunications costs. In the technology sphere, she emphasizes standards; increased control, including international barriers; and more service-based research and development such as intelligent gateways. Social factors of note will include changes in demographics, a shift in values toward the perception of information as a commodity, and increased liability of all kinds. She foresees more lifelong learning, including much retraining, a need for computer literacy, and increased obsolescence of plant, equipment, and even staff. In the area of government and legislation, she predicts problems with access to government-funded information, a possible tax on information as hard industry wanes, and questions of control and ownership of information.

Betty Turock tests her model of multitype networks.[14] She identifies as problems that may be more than theoretical: bureaucratic structure, financial dependence on outside sources, communication with members rather than funders and legislators, and a traditional versus an organic structure. Charles Meadow presented some interesting systems theory implications for networks of all kinds in a paper to ASIS.[15] He points out that information networks, which share content and facilities for transmitting and processing that content, cause a change in the environment, which in turn creates a demand for change in network facilities. He asserts that the jump in speed of information ex-

change causes users to question what they are willing to do now rather than later. He sees roles and allegiances in networks changing as the environment is altered.

Developments in 1986

The Linked Systems Project

After four years of serious research and development, word of real accomplishment began to appear in 1986. In February, a news report in *Library Journal* described the first phase computer-to-computer telecommunications link "to speed authority data from LC to RLIN" and announced that 2,800 records were being sent each day.[16] Henriette Avram's technical and historical article, which appeared in March, is full of figures of models, linkages, database building and implementations. The article explains that authority records were the first ones transmitted because authority work is so expensive. Avram points out that, in the future, bibliographic data will also be shared, as will interlibrary loans. She notes international implications of the project and describes the standards development process as an "open" one.[17]

In spring 1986, Ray Denenberg's paper appeared, describing the Linked Systems Project/Standard Network Interconnection (LSP/SNI) test facility, where vendors can test their implementations for correct functioning of the Standard Network Interconnection protocols. He notes some of the limitations of the test facility, giving much needed detail.[18]

Reports of the ALA New York conference describe the Library and Information Technology Association (LITA) program where Avram, Richard Dougherty, and Hugh Atkinson discussed LSP implications for support of local and regional networking.[19]

Richard McCoy's article in the October *Library Journal* is a highly practical piece describing the results of four years of work in standards, protocols, and agreements.[20] Although not much progress is visible, the project is successfully transferring records and does allow intersystem searches in its present implementation. McCoy describes testing by commercial vendors, which will lead to linking of local systems. (Geac's tests of a BOBCAT/RLIN link are well in progress, for example.) He predicts that searching will be possible within two years; impressive scenarios for intersystem searches are described in sidebars. McCoy points out the advantage of adding directly to a foreign database rather than tape loading. Although charges for use of linking have yet to be seriously considered, they will be a factor in the cost of networking. The use of the OSI/ISO protocol family is praised because of its use in other parts of the economy and especially internationally.

Predicting a broad protocol for all searching based on OSI by 1990, McCoy suggests we will be able to "get more out of our databases." He also foresees further international extensions, linkable local systems, and the ability of a local user to move from the Public Access Catalog to the "home network," for example, OCLC or RLIN, from the library terminal. Policy issues and basic problems of cooperation and competition are yet to be overcome, but McCoy believes LSP will be a key element in the future of library services and cooperation.

Finally, the November 7 Association of Research Libraries newsletter contains a good LSP description.[21] The article points out that LSP is already having an impact on resource availability because the existence of an authority record speeds up cataloging. In fall 1986, National Authority Cooperative Project (NACO) participants began testing the record contribution procedure, transferring from RLIN to LC.

Standards

Work on standards continued in 1986. All the articles on LSP mention the OSI/ISO standard, most of them in a positive vein. The need for a standard command language was addressed by Hildreth,[22] who points out the numerous differences encountered by users of multiple systems. NISO Committee G is working on this standard.

Interlibrary Loan

Several interesting studies of the impact of automation on interlibrary loan were reported. Devenish-Cassell described the effect of three automated systems in New York State on a county library in Syracuse, New York.[23] Abbott and Kavanagh pointed out some unanticipated outcomes of using a hierarchical path for interlibrary loans, and described their resource sharing management system.[24]

Potter, in response to Ballard, cites statistics from the University of Illinois at Urbana–Champaign showing an increase in both borrowing and lending.[25] He concludes that there is an untapped demand for resource sharing. Finally, ARL's *SPEC/Flyer* for September announced increased interlibrary loan volume, the charging of fees of $10 to $15 on average, some cost sharing with other libraries through agreements, and an awareness of the potential for "elitism" caused by the imposition of ILL fees. An aside to this study was the note that many ARL libraries in RLIN also "subscribe" to OCLC for additional ILL holdings.

Also interesting is the regular "Library to Library" column in the *Wilson Library Bulletin*. Written by veteran ILL librarian Rod Henshaw, the column has treated, among other issues, international interlibrary loan.

Document Delivery

Telefacsimile, long flirted with by libraries, must be growing in popularity. Evaluation of a project in Illinois indicates high success for the group of libraries using it.[26] The Fred Meyer Trust fax directory shows tremendous growth since the last edition.[27]

Hickey and Calabrese reported the development of a prototype electronic document delivery system by OCLC.[28] The authors describe trends in information equipment and the particulars of the new system, which outputs copy on a high-speed laser printer after receipt of digital transmission.

Delivery of physical items is still carried out by many networks and systems. Reported in 1986 was the switch from Purolator to UPS by the SUNY/OCLC network, which carries out delivery services on contract in New England, eastern Pennsylvania, New Jersey, Delaware, and Maryland, as well as New York State.[29]

Medical Networking

Several important developments took place in health and medical information networks. As the National Library of Medicine passed its sesquicentennial, announcement was made of the availability of GRATEFUL MED, a front-end software system for searching MEDLINE and CATLINE, making these available to end users.[30] The library sponsored a symposium in March on developing Integrated Academic Information Management Systems (IAIMS), "comprehensive, integrated information networks of computer-based systems and services in academic institutions," and applying such sys-

tems to advancing health science education, research, patient care, and management.[31] In November, the Unified Medical Language System (UMLS) project was announced. The goal is to make terminology transparent to searchers.[32] Smith also reported on these items and updated information about the Regional Medical Networks.[33]

Two statewide projects were reported in 1986, one in Connecticut[34] and one in Washington.[35] Each involves libraries providing access to consumer health information. The Washington Consumer Health Information Network has as its goal the building of collections, preparation of a directory, and improved resource sharing. MEDLINK, the Massachusetts Medical Information Link, has enlarged its service area to include medical and health science libraries outside the state. Using ALANET, MEDLINK offers interlibrary loan, communication, ordering of documents from University Microfilms International (UMI) and other vendors, plus all other ALANET services.[36]

Preservation

A significant advance was made in cooperation for preservation when OCLC and RLIN agreed to exchange machine-readable tapes containing catalog records of preservation master microforms and major microform sets. In the first exchange, each gave about 40,000 records to the other. A librarian can now determine whether another library has already preserved a particular item and can have access to the cataloging of individual titles in major microform sets.[37]

ARL received a significant grant to create a Microform Masters File of preservation microforms for 27 libraries in five high-priority subject areas, with the help of the Library of Congress.[38]

Telecommunications

Although some major telecommunications projects were begun, no great breakthroughs took place in 1986. An excellent article describing the state of the art came from Lynch and Brownrigg,[39] who discuss the need for librarians to understand telecommunications, give them an excellent briefing on the topic, and describe the political and economic, as well as the technical problems. Announcement was made of a prototype wide-area packet radio network, based on the work of these two authors.[40]

Knowledge Industry Publications published a collection of telecommunications networking papers under Mel Jacob's editorship, which should be of great help to those involved with designing systems and networks, including the development and implementation of standards.[41]

Union Lists of Serials

A long-awaited step in union listing took place in 1986 with the announcement that the Minnesota Union List of Serials (MULS) would be loaded into the OCLC database in 1987.[42] AMIGOS has contracted to convert the paper files; MINITEX will maintain the list through OCLC. MULS, a highly valued tool in the region, will be much appreciated in its online incarnation.

Organizations, Agencies, Consortia, Networks, Systems, Utilities, Foundations, Vendors, and Associations Involved in Networking in 1986

During 1986, the artificial distinctions between the private and nonprofit sectors were even further blurred. As Utlas takes its place firmly in the for-profit sector and as commercial vendors increasingly produce and market products for groups of libraries, rather than single institutions, the list of what once may have been called "networks" has greatly expanded and includes a broad range of entities that may be called by any of the names in the heading of this section, as well as some others.

Bibliographic Utilities – OCLC

On August 26, OCLC celebrated the fifteenth anniversary of the first online contribution to the database.[43] Again, OCLC posted significant growth in its various output measures: more members (6,738), more terminals (7,413), more books cataloged (24.6 million), more ILL's (2.7 million), more catalog records (44 million), more LS/2000 users (a total of 146 at the end of FY 1986), and record revenues ($78.6 million, with $8.2 million going into corporate equity, for a total there of $45.8 million).[44]

A dominant theme for OCLC in 1986 was the "Oxford Project," one of those accidental names that sticks (although reports are that the colloquial in-house nickname is "The Noose"). More than a project, this three-year effort will cost $40 million and will result in a complete redesign of the OCLC system – the first real total system overhaul ever. The four goals of the project are to increase system power, flexibility, and availability; to support distributed processing, including access to distributed optical disc or other high-density memory as available; to enable OCLC to control its telecommunications environment to ensure cost-effective service; and to set the stage for electronic delivery of the contents of books and other library materials.[45] That is, OCLC intends to move beyond (but not away from) bibliographic control, toward general access to information.

The OCLC Users Council met three times during the year. Highlights included a forum (February) on networking and the national database, during which President Rowland Brown and RLIN's Richard McCoy took a highly cooperative stance and a generally optimistic view of the future, citing their "distinct, noncompetitive missions"; election of two Users Council members to the OCLC board of trustees: Doris Brown, DePaul University, and Francis Buckley, Detroit Public; election of new officers: Ralph Russell of SOLINET as president-elect, and Dilys Morris, Drew Racine, and Ron Leach, at-large; and appointment of an Ad Hoc Committee on Less-Than-Full-Service-Networks. The Users Council agreed that OCLC should take a leadership role in creating a national/international database, in database linking, and in access for OCLC members to other databases, and that OCLC should include in the database a variety of materials and formats and should seek alternatives to a centralized database.[46]

Contract issues remained unresolved, as bulletins were issued from time to time announcing that all would soon be well. ILLINET, demurring from any involvement with OCLC except in connection with online services, signed a contract with OCLC, as did individual libraries on the West Coast served by the OCLC service center PACNET, but no contracts were signed with the full-service networks desiring to provide a complete range of OCLC products and services to their members. In Wisconsin, the state

attorney general ruled that "computerized catalog records are public records," asserting that they are not protected by copyright, and advising Wisconsin libraries to review the opinion before entering into a new OCLC contract.[47] However, a new liaison post was established, as a coordinator was sought for the Regional OCLC Network Directors Advisory Committee (RONDAC).

Research at OCLC was impressive. The organization invests large amounts of its revenue in "mission-oriented" projects aimed at all aspects of library automation and networking, as well as development of new products and services. Its new research publication is full of impressive projects and of the credentials of outstanding staff members.[48] The Office of Research has a new director, Martin Dillon. The Office of Technical Planning is headed by Howard Turtle. All serve under Michael McGill, vice president, research and technical planning.

Some of the new products and services coming from OCLC during the year included *OCLC Micro*, a bimonthly journal covering use of M-300 work stations, not only for OCLC purposes, but for a variety of other functions; a prototype reference work station being tested at Vanderbilt University;[49] TAPECON, a new retrospective conversion service that upgrades a tape of abbreviated or non-OCLC MARC format records to OCLC MARC format;[50] and a gateway service, originally dubbed UNISON, but renamed OCLC-LINK, after an embarrassing trade-name conflict of minor proportions.[51]

Cooperative projects throughout the year included the establishment of the North Carolina Information Network in collaboration with SOLINET, Western Union's EASYLINK, and the North Carolina State Library;[52] the preservation information exchange with RLIN mentioned earlier; work on the Linked Systems Project; and a conference cosponsored with the Johnson Foundation bringing together eight university research teams to discuss information policies.[53]

In the international arena, OCLC concluded an agreement with the Deutsches Bibliotheksinstitut to explore ways they might reduce effort and unit cataloging costs by building databases to be shared internationally;[54] a contract for the use of MICROCON for retrospective conversion with the Université Libre de Bruxelles, Belgium;[55] and an accord with the French Direction des Bibliothèques, des Musées et de l'Information Scientifique et Technique (DBMIST), to see whether sharing records would be useful to both.[56]

Bibliographic Utilities—RLG/RLIN

The research libraries continued to cooperate on numerous projects of importance through RLG and RLIN. In the September 1986 issue of *RLG News*, RLG announced a strategic planning effort that involved the organization's central staff and board with a consulting firm in developing, first, an internal document on strategic choices, for discussion purposes, and finally a strategic plan.[57] The plan comes at a time when RLG has concluded seven years of expansion, has solved its major technical and financial problems, has a stable membership adequate to support it, and a balanced budget.

The RLG mission is "to facilitate access to information on behalf of scholarship and research in member institutions." The statement points out that cooperative action is taken, not to reduce costs, but to be more effective in doing what needs to be done. Some of the principles set forth in the plan define RLG as

- A member-owned cooperative
- Program-driven, with a database as support for the program

- Having primary contact with the library in the institution, but serving the entire campus
- Aiming at unmet needs, rather than duplicating others' work
- Using RLIN as its network and union database and for linking
- A service provider
- Engaging in cooperative programs

RLG programs are of three types. The Library-Based Programs include Library Technical Systems and Bibliographic Control; Shared Resources; Cooperative Collection Management and Development; and Preservation. Special Interest Programs are often short-range programs in specific areas, such as art and architecture, law, or archives, manuscripts, and special collections. The Research Information Program concentrates on the information needs of various disciplines and is currently focusing on integrated co-management of bibliographic, biographical, geographic, and statistical information.

RLIN Systems Projects include linking, maintenance and enhancements, technical infrastructure changes, improvements and additions to the database, technical support, and microcomputer or work station applications.

RLG announced (also in the September issue of the *News*) that it no longer assumes growth in the membership, now at 36 owner-members, as a factor in its planning, although it will continue to market to appropriate institutions. It plans to give more attention to its 11 associate and 31 special members.

In the economic sphere, RLG acknowledged the problem all networks must face as transactions — once the background of the charging system — migrate to local systems. RLIN has always relied more heavily than OCLC and its networks on fixed charges, such as annual membership fees. It will increase its dependence on these price agreements in the future, funding development, as well as operations, from such annual fees.

Issues of interest to RLG as indicated by topics of discussion at meetings are the crucial issues of networks at the end of 1986: the relationship of libraries and computer centers in research institutions; information as a commodity, particularly within the context of links between the private sector and the higher education establishment; the growing gap between the information rich and the information poor; and governance.

Announced during the year was a milestone in cataloging of materials in Asian alphabets (CJK), with the one-hundred-thousandth catalog record input.[58] CLASS continues to offer RLIN services to nonmembers, either on a cataloging or search-only basis.[59]

Richard McCoy stepped down as RLG president at the end of the year. After four years at the helm of the organization, McCoy leaves it in sound financial shape, after its major period of growth, and in a highly cooperative mood. McCoy pointed to personal plans as his reason for leaving and suggested this was a good time for transition in the organization.

Bibliographic Utilities — Utlas

Utlas is included here among the bibliographic utilities, rather than among commercial vendors, because the nature of its services more closely parallels that of the utilities, even though it now clearly belongs in the private sector. The ability to differentiate the private and public sector providers on the basis of the products and services they provide has essentially ceased to exist.

The entry of Utlas into the U.S. market, which has been gradually taking place since 1980, when the Rochester Institute of Technology became an Utlas user, became highly visible during 1986.[60] It officially calls itself Utlas International, rather than UTLAS, in order to clearly differentiate itself from its earlier affiliation with the University of Toronto. Two important events for Utlas were the impact of its merger with Carrollton Press, which took place in 1985, and its purchase of Tandem equipment, which permitted it to acquire the ALIS III system from DataPhase.[61]

Bibliographic Utilities — WLN

Several interesting changes in the Western Library Network (WLN) during 1986 indicated a strong desire to remain a major force in networking, especially in the Pacific Northwest. Early in the year, WLN announced that it had acquired a larger computer, an Amdahl 470 v/8, which would allow faster batch processing and lead to high-speed, high-density disc storage capacity.[62]

In summer 1986, WLN announced a change in pricing and policies, expanding its services to smaller libraries and encouraging the addition of holdings to its database. The price to add holdings is now only 15 cents.[63] Inquiries to the database, formerly priced at 11 cents, will now cost between 16.5 and 20 cents. In addition, all products and services will be available to all libraries, regardless of membership category.

A CD-ROM product was announced in fall 1986, which will accommodate the 8.5-million-item resource directory and will be updated quarterly. Dubbed "LaserCat," the project results from a large grant.[64]

Other Commercial Vendors

Large-scale networking and cooperative projects among commercial vendors and between vendors and nonprofit organizations were common in 1986. A few examples are given here to indicate the scope.

The Wyoming statewide circulation system, providing a state database and eventually offering access for a number of functions, passed its full-load test.[65] Ebsco announced interfaces with Geac, NOTIS, and CLASS.[66] Information Transform announced a software program that will allow users to create MARC records without learning MARC terminology, using a menu-driven system.[67] Faxon made it possible to link terminals in a local area network to its LINX system on a point-to-point basis, using a dedicated line.[68] Geac created LAN capability in its application for the Bibliothèque Nationale in Paris.[69] BiblioFile is supporting a group of school libraries in Maryland, using floppy discs to build their database.[70]

OCLC Networks

In May 1986, OCLC issued "Principles and Guidelines for Transfer of OCLC-Derived Machine-Readable Records." The document sets out the conditions under which member and nonmember libraries may use records from the OCLC database and the kind of agreements nonmember libraries would make in order to use such records. This document, addressing some of the key issues surrounding the negotiation of network/OCLC contracts, was the topic of considerable discussion among networks during the year.[71]

In February, David Brunell was elected chair of the network directors, with Mary Ann Mercante as chair-elect and Laima Mockus as treasurer.[72]

As reported earlier, OCLC signed contracts with ILLINET and with the independent libraries served by PACNET. OCLC began negotiations with several other networks, including AMIGOS, Michigan Library Consortium (MLC), SOLINET, and SUNY/OCLC.[73] In May, BCR defined unresolved contract issues as including the following:

1 Should OCLC be limited to one price increase per year, and of no more than 10 percent? Should OCLC be required to charge each network the same prices?

2 Should networks have the right of first refusal to handle all new OCLC products and services?

3 Should new contracts be binding for the brief period proposed by OCLC, or should they be in effect for a multiyear period?

4 What are the rights for the use and transfer of OCLC-derived records by networks, and by general members of OCLC?[74]

At a June 17 meeting in Dublin, networks discussed problems of marketing OCLC products. After debating a number of issues, they concluded that networks should be more involved in product development and that OCLC should provide some financial support for network demonstrations of new products.[75]

AMIGOS contracted with Blackwell/North America for authority control services for its members.[76] It also agreed to trade services with Utlas, with AMIGOS providing the collection analysis service and Utlas providing authority control.[77] The AMIGOS copyright claim was put on "hold" during contract negotiations, and AMIGOS and SOLINET agreed to a joint membership meeting in 1987 on managing resource sharing.[78]

BCR announced a new membership arrangement for groups of libraries in nonmember states and reduced the state member fee.[79] It began offering the BiblioFile CD-ROM system as a source of cataloging information for smaller libraries that are unable to afford OCLC services and as a retrospective conversion alternative for larger libraries. It held a preconference on reducing telecommunications costs at the Colorado/Mountain Plains Library Association Joint Conference, strengthened its microcomputer systems offerings, and showed increasing financial strength.[80]

The Michigan Library Consortium (MLC) added some Utlas services, as did the Missouri Library Network Corporation (MLNC).[81] The Carnegie Library of Pittsburgh returned to membership in the Pittsburgh Regional Library Consortium, from which it had defected three years before, when its director at the time was instrumental in the formation of AFLI, a "low-cost" network.

SOLINET continued strong in the Southeast, supporting network developments among its members, including involvement in development of the Triangle Research Libraries network, the North Carolina State Network, and Florida, Virginia, and Kentucky networking efforts. The network developed and published lists of trends and issues in networking in the Southeast that are, in fact, generalizable to networking throughout the United States. The ten issues are

• Ownership and use of bibliographic records
• Lack of inexpensive computerized collection analysis services

- "Wait and see" attitude to linking disparate systems
- Archaic guidelines on state and intrastate networking
- Relationships among state and interstate programs
- Economic factors, including tax structures
- Political uncertainties
- Nonlibrary information providers
- Lack of awareness by nonlibrarians of the value of networking
- Lack of understanding among administrators and coordinators in libraries and networks that they need to be both informed and conversant on networking problems and organizational issues

Sixteen trends included

- Proliferation of hardware and software options
- Increasing financial problems of vendors
- Rising communications costs
- Slow progress on linking of distributed databases
- Increase of nonhierarchical interlibrary loan patterns
- Stronger local multitype networks
- Liberalized intrastate interlibrary loan policies
- More laser disc use
- Increased facsimile transmission
- More common use of local area networks
- More statewide networks, with a need for coordination at the interstate level
- Reliance on LSCA funding for state and intrastate networks
- Information as a marketable commodity
- Need for increases in staffing to meet network obligations

Two regionally specific trends were identified: the increasingly two-party nature of politics in the South and the key role of southern legislators in U.S. Congress library committees.[82]

Phasing out its LAMBDA online service, SOLINET noted that increased telecommunications costs and development of local systems had lessened demand.[83]

The SUNY/OCLC network selected the Carlyle system for its members. With a major hardware installation at the network offices in Albany, the system will allow the libraries to "pay as they go" in creating local catalogs, without the necessity for making large up-front capital expenditures.[84]

CLASS

The Cooperative Library Authority for Systems and Services (CLASS) continued to offer a broad range of services in 1986 both in California and elsewhere. New contracts allowing CLASS to offer discounts on the prices of certain vendors' products were praised in the library press.[85] In a letter to the editor of *Library Journal*, Ron Miller, CLASS executive director, pointed out that the network makes access to RLIN available to more than 600 libraries through searching contracts.[86]

Network Advisory Committee

In 1986, the Network Advisory Committee (NAC) continued its work on a statement of a common vision, begun late in 1985. Although a preliminary version of the statement was criticized by Norman Stevens as giving "little recognition of the extent to which networks are built from the bottom up,"[87] the works contributing to the final statement and the discussion surrounding them are characterized by a great awareness of the distributed nature of networking, the decentralizing forces, and the needs of the user.

At year's end, the statement "Library Networking: Statement of a Common Vision" was being sent to the National Commission on Libraries and Information Science, to update NAC's earlier program document. The statement contains four concepts:

- "The Nation's Library"—the aggregate of all available information resources
- The importance of standards
- The importance of equity of access for all the nation's citizens
- The role of the NAC in highlighting the benefits of networking to the nation and its libraries

The concept of "a national network," interpreted as a centralized network at the national level, has been supplanted by that of "nationwide networking," which allows individuals, libraries, consortia, and systems and networks at various levels of aggregation to be linked for the purpose of getting access to information. Such linking is dependent on standards, and forms the foundation for a nation providing equal access to information for all.[88]

CRL

The Center for Research Libraries revised its governance and fee structure in spring 1986. Described as "a cooperative library of uncommonly held, infrequently used research materials that are cost-avoiding extensions of its members' own collections," the center provides "easy and dedicated access" to its materials. The new policy categorizes clients in three classes, offers greater access and lowest charges to the largest libraries, but allows for service to others as well.[89]

State Networks

Growing strength in networking at the state level was obvious during 1986. An increase in multitype networking provoked controversy in some places, but paved the way for state networks involving all types of libraries.

In California, the repercussions of the 1985 California Conference on Networking continued to be felt. The phasing out of the "third-level" reference centers, specifically the Bay Area and Southern California centers (BARC and SCAN), evoked concern.[90] The fear that large libraries would be subject to "resource rape" as smaller, "parasitic" libraries called upon their collections, was reported in 1986.[91] At the 1986 California Library Association conference, discussion over multitype networking was heated. State Librarian Gary Strong characterized the "central issue" as "whether or not we really want to work together." Speakers foresaw many changes for California library services.[92]

Colorado Regional Library Service Systems celebrated its tenth anniversary as multitype organizations, with the anniversary motto "Working Together Works."[93] Federal LSCA funding, for which the systems compete each year, has supported innovative system projects, but adequate funding remains a chimera.[94]

Iowa has moved its networking efforts to a microcomputer-based system. The I-LITE system, a set of round robin ILL arrangements, has been replaced by ICAN, the Iowa Computer Assisted Network. The microcomputers are expected to save $70,000 a year in operational costs of the interlibrary loan operation and to afford libraries the opportunity to develop other computer applications.

Minnesota has created a school library network using MITINET, Hank Epstein's Information Transform system. Some 59 school districts are involved, with more than 250,000 titles and 6 million holdings.[95]

ACCESS PENNSYLVANIA features statewide library cards, fees paid to "net lenders," and a CD-ROM catalog for high school and public libraries. The state has increased its funding of libraries by 15 percent.[96]

The South Carolina State Library entered the first phase of its statewide networking effort with 46 county libraries participating. Hardware and software are from Data Research Associates (DRA); the database will contain 650,000 records. The addition of dial access for academic libraries is expected in 1987.

Other Groups

Activities supported by the Fred Meyer Charitable Trust in the Pacific Northwest have furthered cooperative activities there. Murr, Williams, and Miller's *Information Highways* used an innovative model for presenting data about communication in that region.[97] Early in 1986, the Trust put three quarters of a million dollars into grants for pilot delivery projects aimed at demonstrating and evaluating the benefits of innovative methods (including fax, teletext, PCs, scanning cameras, and computer networks) of delivering information from many sources to people needing the information.[98] In September the Fred Meyer–funded Library and Information Resources for the Northwest (LIRN) announced that it had acquired new telefacsimile equipment and had produced an official directory of all telefax installations in libraries in the Northwest.[99]

Consortial activities cannot be covered completely in this article. Two interesting examples in the 1986 literature are the York Public Libraries Network and the Colorado Alliance of Research Libraries (CARL). Five municipal library systems in Ontario created a unified database, using IBM PCs, on a "shoestring budget." Using Geac software for database control, control of jointly owned hardware and software, and individually owned terminals, the network has proved cost-effective.[100]

In discussing the design of the CARL System at the Clinic on Library Applications of Data Processing, Shaw makes an interesting philosophical point. The user may only manipulate and use the online public access catalog by learning the rules of how to use that catalog, he says. But the understanding of those rules prevents the user from perceiving innovatively or conceiving of new ways to use the system. The CARL designers have kept this in mind as they designed a system where users would feel in control and where experimentation would be promoted. In addition, the system is expanding to include nonbibliographic files. The Colorado research libraries consortium's system has been adapted for use in the public library at Colorado Springs, where community resources and other factual information files have been loaded into the online catalog.[101]

(A photo of the CARL online catalog in use at the University of Colorado, Boulder, appears in *Information from the University of Colorado Libraries* 1(2), 2-3, Spring 1986.)

The addition of abstracting and indexing information to the CONSER database marks an enhancement for library networking and cooperation that will be greatly appreciated.[102]

People

Some important personnel changes that took place in the networking world in 1986 include the election of Doris Brown (De Paul University) and Francis Buckley (Detroit Public Library) to the OCLC board of trustees; appointment of Clarence R. Walters, former Connecticut State Librarian, to OCLC program director for state and public libraries; the move of Toni Carbo Bearman from NCLIS to the University of Pittsburgh Library School and subsequent appointment of Vivian J. Arterbery to the NCLIS executive directorship; and the untimely deaths of Rod Swartz, Washington State Librarian, who had played a key role in the development of the Western Library Network, and of Hugh Atkinson, leader in the development of the Illinois LCS and staunch, though not uncritical, advocate of OCLC.

Conclusion

The concept of library networking and cooperation as servants of access to information emerged from several sources during 1986. The possibility that the years of toil in the vineyards of automation might yield as fruit easier access to libraries and information by users is very exciting, but some resistance to resource sharing and cooperation still remains to be overcome.

Notes

1. Michael Gorman, "Laying Siege to the 'fortress library,' " *American Libraries* 17, no. 5 (May 1986): 325-328.

2. *Toward a Common Vision in Library Networking. Proceedings of the Library of Congress Network Advisory Committee Meeting, December 9-11, 1985* (Washington, D.C.: Library of Congress, 1986). Network Planning Paper no. 13.

3. Norman Stevens, "Our Profession," *Wilson Library Bulletin* 61, no. 4 (December 1986): 58-59.

4. Joseph Shubert and Carol Henderson, Memo on NAC meeting of December 10-12, 1986.

5. JoAn S. Segal, "Library Networking and Resource Sharing in 1985," in *The Bowker Annual of Library & Book Trade Information*, 31st ed. (New York: R. R. Bowker, 1986).

6. "White Plains Threatens to Leave Westchester (NY) Library System," *Library Hotline* XV, no. 41 (December 1, 1986): 2.

7. "Cleveland Public and Cuyahoga County Square Off," *Library Hotline* XV, no. 41 (December 1, 1986): 1.

8. Thomas Ballard, *The Failure of Resource Sharing* (Chicago: ALA, 1986).

9. "IIA and AAP on Networks," *Library Journal* 111, no. 7 (April 15, 1986): 25.

10. Paul Kittle and Kathleen Puffer, Editorial, *Online Magazine* 10, no. 4 (July 1986): 6-8.

11. Susan K. Martin, *Library Networks, 1986–1987: Libraries in Partnership* (White Plains, N.Y.: Knowledge Industry Publications, 1986).

12. Henriette D. Avram, "Current Issues in Networking," *Journal of Academic Librarianship* 12, no. 4 (September 1986): 205–209.

13. Mary Ellen Jacob, "The Moving Target: Future Trends in Networking," *Bulletin of the American Society for Information Science* 11, no. 6 (August–September 1985): 12–14.

14. Betty Turock, "Organization Factors in Multitype Library Networking: A National Test of the Model," *Library and Information Science Research* 8, no. 2 (April–June 1986): 117–154.

15. Charles T. Meadow, "Networks and Distributed Information Services," *Journal of the American Society of Information Science* 37, no. 6 (November 1986): 405–408.

16. "Authority Data Now Online in Linked Systems Project," *Library Journal* 111, no. 3 (February 1, 1986): 24.

17. Henriette D. Avram, "The Linked Systems Project: Its Implications for Resource Sharing," *Library Resources and Technical Services* 30, no. 1 (January–March 1986): 36–46.

18. Ray Denenberg, "The LSP/SNI Test Facility," *Library Hi Tech* 4, no. 1 (Spring 1986): 41–49.

19. "ALA Meets at Ground Zero, New York City. Conference Report," *Wilson Library Bulletin* 61, no. 1 (September 1986): 16 et passim.

20. Richard W. McCoy, "The Linked Systems Project," *Library Journal* 111, no. 1 (October 1, 1986): 33–39.

21. "Current Status of the Linked System Project," *Association of Research Libraries Newsletter* no. 132 (November 7, 1986): 3.

22. Charles E. Hildreth, "Communicating with Online Catalogs and Other Retrieval Systems: The Need for a Standard Command Language," *Library Hi Tech* 4, no. 1 (Spring 1986): 7–11.

23. Ann Devenish-Cassell, "Electronic Impacts on Library Resource Sharing: A Case Study," *Catholic Library World* 57, no. 5 (March/April 1986): 221–224.

24. Peter Abbott and Rosemary Kavanagh, "Electronic Resource Sharing Changes Interloan Patterns," *Library Journal* 111, no. 16 (October 1, 1986): 56–58.

25. William Gray Potter, "Creative Automation Boosts ILL Rates," *American Libraries* 17, no. 4 (April 1986): 244–246.

26. "Fax in Illinois: A Success Story," *Library Journal* 111, no. 17 (October 15, 1986): 23.

27. "New Fax Directory Sees Telefacsimile Spreading," *Library Journal* 111, no. 17 (October 15, 1986): 15.

28. Thomas B. Hickey and Andrew M. Calabrese, "Electronic Document Delivery: OCLC's Prototype System," *Library Hi Tech* 4, no. 1 (September 1986): 65–71.

29. "Purolator Dropped for UPS by SUNY/OCLC Service," *Library Journal* 111, no. 9 (May 15, 1986): 24.

30. "GRATEFUL MED: A New Way to Search MEDLINE," *National Library of Medicine News* 41, no. 2 (February 1986): 4–5.

31. "Second IAIMS Symposium Emphasizes Health Sciences Education," *National Library of Medicine News* 41, no. 4 (April 1986): 1–2.

32. "Unified Medical Language System," *National Library of Medicine News* 41, no. 11 (November 1986): 1–2, 10–11.

33. Kent A. Smith, "Medical Information Systems," *Bulletin of the American Society for Information Science* 12, no. 4 (April/May 1986): 17–18.

34. "Connecticut's HEALTHNET: Consumer Reference Service," *Library Journal* 111, no. 8 (May 1, 1986): 58.

35. "Washington Health Information Project Aims to Be Statewide Model," *Library Journal* 111, no. 8 (May 1, 1986): 58.

36. "MEDLINK Expands as ALANET's Medical Library Specialty Network," *Information Resources & Library Automation* 22, no. 6 (November 1986): 8.

37. "OCLC and RLG Share Microfilm Records," *Library Journal* 111, no. 9 (May 15, 1986): 20.

38. "Grant for Microform Masters File," *Association of Research Libraries Newsletter*, no. 130 (June 18, 1986): 1.

39. Clifford A. Lynch and Edwin W. Brownrigg, "The Telecommunications Landscape: 1986," *Library Journal* 111, no. 16 (October 1, 1986): 40–46.

40. "California Packet Radio Project," *Library Journal* 111, no. 17 (October 15, 1986): 22.

41. M. E. L. Jacob, ed., *Telecommunications Networks: Issues and Trends* (White Plains, N.Y.: Knowledge Industry Publications for ASIS, 1986).

42. "Minnesota Union List of Serials to Be Converted for Availability via OCLC," *OCLC Newsletter* no. 165 (November 1986): 5.

43. Phil Scheiber, "OCLC System Celebrates 15th Year," *OCLC Newsletter* no. 164 (August 1986): 10.

44. OCLC, *Annual Report* (Dublin, Ohio: OCLC, 1986).

45. "The New OCLC System, A Special Report," *OCLC Newsletter* no. 161 (February 1986): 1–16.

46. "User Group Recommendations on OCLC and National Network," *Library Journal* 111, no. 9 (May 15, 1986): 18.

47. "Wisconsin OCLC Records Are Ruled to Be Public Records," *Library Journal* 111, no. 16 (October 1, 1986): 22.

48. OCLC Offices of Research and Technical Planning, *Annual Review of OCLC Research January–June 1986* (Dublin, Ohio: OCLC, 1986).

49. "OCLC Tests CD-ROM Reference Package at Vanderbilt," *Advanced Technology/Libraries* 15, no. 12 (December 1986): 2, 4.

50. Ibid., p. 4.

51. "WILSONLINE to Be Available via OCLC Service," and "VU/TEXT to Be Available through OCLC," *Wilson Library Bulletin* 61, no. 10 (September 1986): 10–12.

52. "North Carolina Chooses Easylink for Statewide Information Network," *Advanced Technology/Libraries* 15, no. 12 (December 1986): 7.

53. OCLC, *Annual Report*.

54. "OCLC and Deutsches Bibliotheksinstitut," *Advanced Technology/Libraries* 15, no. 12 (December 1986): 4.

55. "Major European Retrospective Conversion Contract Announced," *OCLC Newsletter* no. 164 (August 1986): 9.

56. "French Administration and OCLC Sign Accord to Explore International Library Cooperation," *OCLC Newsletter* no. 162 (April 1986): 1–2.

57. "RLG Chooses Some Strategic Directions," *RLG News* no. 11 (September 1986): 2–3.

58. "RLG 100,000th Catalog Record Input in CJK," *American Libraries* 17, no. 5 (May 1986): 369.

59. Ron Miller, "RLIN Has CLASS" (letter), *Library Journal* 111, no. 16 (October 1, 1986): 14.

60. Ron Chepesiuk, "Special Report: Utlas Enters the U.S. Market," *Wilson Library Bulletin* 60, no. 8 (April 1986): 30–31.

61. "Utlas Tandem Hardware," *Bulletin of the American Society for Information Science* 12, no. 4 (April/May 1986): 22.

62. "WLN Acquires a Larger Computer," *Wilson Library Bulletin* 60, no. 6 (January 1986): 11.

63. "WLN Makes Changes in Pricing and Policies," *Wilson Library Bulletin* 61, no. 1 (September 1986): 10.

64. "WLN Adopts Laser Disc for Holdings Database," *Library Journal* 111, no. 14 (September 1, 1986): 131.

65. "Wyoming Geac System Passes Full-Load Test," *Library Journal* 111, no. 10 (June 1, 1986): 52.

66. "New EBSCO Interfaces: Geac, NOTIS, CLASS," *Library Journal* 111, no. 18 (November 1, 1986): 28.

67. "Information Transform Offers MITINET/MARC Software," *Library Hi Tech News*, no. 31 (October 1986): 15–16.

68. "Faxon Local Network Connection," *Library Hi Tech News*, no. 31 (October 1986): 2.

69. "Geac Extends Automation to Include LAN Capability," *Library Journal* 111, no. 9 (May 15, 1986: 24.

70. "Networking a CD-ROM-Based System: BiblioFile in Maryland," *Library Hotline* XV, no. 41 (December 1, 1986): 5.

71. "OCLC/Network Impasse Ending," *American Libraries* 17, no. 7 (July 8, 1986): 506.

72. "Brunell Named Network Director Chair," *Action for Libraries* XII, no. 2 (February 1986): 1.

73. *Ibid.*

74. "Unresolved contract issues," *Action for Libraries* XII, no. 5 (May 1986): 1–2.

75. "Networks Discuss Problems of Marketing OCLC Products," *Library Hotline* XV, no. 28 (September 1, 1986): 8.

76. "UTLAS and Blackwell/NA Increase Library Involvement," *Library Journal* 111, no. 10 (June 1, 1986): 30.

77. "AMIGOS & UTLAS Trade Services," *Library Journal* 111, no. 5 (March 15, 1986): 14.

78. "AMIGOS & SOLINET Set Joint Membership Meeting," *Library Journal* 111, no. 8 (May 1, 1986): 16.

79. "BCR Board Adopts Group Membership Category and Reduces State Fee," *Action for Libraries* XII, no. 4 (April 1986): 3.

80. "BCR Inaugurates BiblioFile CD-ROM System," *Action for Libraries* XII, no. 6 (June 1986): 2.

81. "UTLAS and Blackwell/NA Increase Library Involvement," *Library Journal* 111, no. 10 (June 1, 1986): 30.

82. "Networking Trends and Issues in the Southeast," *SOLINET Memorandum* (December 16, 1986).

83. "SOLINET Drops Online LAMBDA Service," *Library Hotline* XV, no. 39 (November 17, 1986): 5.

84. "Carlyle System Chosen for SUNY/OCLC Network," *Library Journal* 111 no. 8 (November 1, 1986): 26.

85. "CLASS Discounts Respond to New Price Awareness," *Library Journal* 111, no. 12 (July 1986): 21.

86. Miller, "RLIN Has CLASS."

87. Stevens, "Our Profession."

88. Shubert and Henderson, Memo on NAC meeting.

89. "Center for Research Libraries Sets New Governance and Fees," *Library Journal* 111, no. 8 (May 1, 1986): 17.

90. "Californians Debate Phase Out of BARC and SCAN," *Library Journal* 111, no. 1 (January 1986): 18.

91. Kittle and Puffer, Editorial.

92. "Californians Debate Networking Proposals," *American Libraries* 18, no. 1 (January 1987): 30.

93. Jean A. Major, "Colorado's Multitype Library Systems," *Colorado Libraries* 12, no. 3 (September 1986): 9.

94. S. Jane Ulrich, "System Program Showcase: Ten Years of Cooperation," *Colorado Libraries* 12, no. 3 (September 1986): 17–19.

95. "Schools Share CD-ROM Data," *American Libraries* 17, no. 10 (November 1986): 745.

96. "Access Pennsylvania," *American Libraries* 17, no. 5 (May 1986): 302–303.

97. L. E. Murr, J. B. Williams, and R. E. Miller, "Mapping Information Delivery Networks: The Objectives, the Methods, the Benefits, and the Model," *Library Hi Tech* 4, no. 1 (Spring 1986): 51–63.

98. "Fred Meyer Charitable Trust: Information Delivery Grants," *Library Journal* 111, no. 9 (May 15, 1986): 18.

99. "FAX in the Northwest," *Library Journal* 111, no. 14 (September 1, 1986): 138.

100. Jane Horrocks, "The York Public Libraries Network: A Unique Model for Co-operative Automation," *Canadian Library Journal* 43, no. 1 (February 1986): 31–34.

101. Ken Dowlin and Ward Shaw, "Aristotle Meets Plato in the Library Catalog," in "What Is User-Friendly, a Composite Report on the 23d Annual Clinic on Library Applications of Data Processing," *Library Hi Tech News* no. 31 (October 1986): 6.

102. "CONSER Serials Base Adds Abstracting, Indexing Info," *American Libraries* 17, no. 11 (December 1986): 820–821.

Information Standards in 1986

Sally H. McCallum

Network Development and MARC Standards Office
Library of Congress

Electronic manuscripts and CD-ROM (compact disc read-only memory) file structures headed the list of important standards for the information community that were circulated for comment or ballot by the National Information Standards Organization (NISO) Z39 in 1986. NISO is an affiliate of the American National Standards Institute (ANSI) that has responsibility for developing standards for libraries, information organizations such as indexing and abstracting services, publishers, and specialized library equipment manufacturers.

As an ANSI affiliate, NISO uses the consensus process for setting standards. Under this process, which follows ANSI rules, each draft standard is submitted to the NISO voting membership for comment and vote. Negative votes are resolved through a procedure that may result in change in the text of the standard and subsequent reballoting. The standard is also advertised by ANSI for review by interested persons outside NISO. When review and balloting are complete, the draft standard is submitted to ANSI for approval and publication. This carefully structured process contributes to the (frequently long) time it takes to complete a standard, but it also increases the acceptance and use of the standard by practitioners in the industry.

At the annual membership meeting of NISO in April 1986, presentations were heard on three topics important to the NISO constituency: CD-ROM database publishing standards, electronic publishing standards, and preservation standards. NISO was active in all three of these areas in 1986, in addition to carrying out work on other topics related to publishing and to description of and access to materials.

CD-ROM

A CD-ROM is an optical disc on which a very large amount of digitized information is stored. After a master disc is created, copies can be made for a relatively small extra cost. However, standardization is sorely needed for basic file structure on the CD-ROM so that manufacturers of hardware and software that access the discs can target a standard approach to the digitized information. Part of the standardization requirements for read-only compact discs falls under the purview of NISO. The first standard in this area was ready for ballot at the end of 1986.

The initial work on the standard for CD-ROM file structure was carried out by a small ad hoc group of representatives of hardware vendors, called the High Sierra Group. The NISO standards committee responsible for the proposed standard received the High Sierra document in late summer, and after several meetings ANSI Z39.60, draft *Volume and File Structure of CD-ROM for Information Interchange*, was ready for NISO ballot. This standard specifies the attributes and placement on the compact disc of information that describes the CD-ROM itself, relates it to other CD-ROMs (if needed), specifies the files, and gives requirements for input and output data streams to application programs. With new CD-ROM publications being announced in the publishing and database vendor communities each week (or so it seems), standardization of the CD-ROM technology will be very important to libraries and informatin centers.

Electronic Publishing

The second topic at the NISO annual meeting was presented by J. Sperling Martin, director of the American Association of Publishers (AAP) Electronic Manuscript Project, to develop a standard electronic manuscript preparation and markup syntax. AAP submitted the draft standard to NISO in summer 1986 and the resulting ANSI Z39.59, *American National Standard for Electronic Manuscript Preparation and Markup*, was balloted in the fall.

The electronic manuscript standard describes the general schema for tagging data elements in a manuscript and provides tags for many commonly occurring manuscript elements, including author name, title, chapter heads, and the like. If the standard's procedures are followed, a manuscript can be processed on any computer.

The proposed standard could be the keystone to hastening the publishing process, eliminating many steps where errors could be introduced, and opening the door to a number of new developments in publishing. Instead of a manuscript being keyed by the author, again (perhaps) by the editor, and finally by the typesetter, the author's version could be used directly for final preparation and markup. The manuscript becomes a structured file that gives publishers freedom to create many kinds of published products, either print or electronic.

The electronic manuscript standard is a specific application of the Standard Generalized Markup Language (SGML), an International Organization for Standardization (ISO) standard. The new NISO draft standard is related to SGML in the same way that the USMARC formats are related to ANSI Z39.2, *Bibliographic Information Interchange*.

Preservation Standards

The urgent need for standards in many areas of book preservation was the topic of the third presentation at the NISO annual meeting. NISO had taken a first step into this

area with the publication of ANSI Z39.48, *Permanence of Paper for Printed Library Materials*, in 1984. The symbol ∞, which indicates a desirable alkalinity of paper for printing, has become widely known in just two years. Publishers are increasingly meeting the specified paper quality standards, and the Library of Congress (LC) has requested information on the paper to be used by publishers for the galley pages they send LC to obtain prepublication cataloging data.

During 1986, NISO members voted to form a standards committee to work out the specifications for coated papers, to be added to ANSI Z39.48, which treats only uncoated papers. The determination of these requirements will be a complex task because of the variety of coatings available. The extension of the standard to cover coated papers is an important step for libraries and other information services that collect published items.

NISO also began its first project concerned with bindings for printed materials. A standards committee to develop a standard for hardcover edition bindings held its initial meetings in 1986. This standard will cover margins, materials such as thread, adhesives, spine linings, boards and covers, methods for leaf attachment, and other operations.

A final area of preservation in which NISO is working concerns the technical specifications for storage that contribute to the life of paper-based items, such as relative humidity, temperature, air quality, and lighting. A draft standard was completed and circulated for comment in 1986. Several who commented on the standard thought that more technical experimentation and evidence was needed to make the requirements more specific. NISO is seeking funding to support laboratory work to give a firmer base to the recommendations in the standard.

Bibliographic Description

NISO began or continued work in 1986 on five standards that facilitate bibliographic description of items by libraries and indexing services. All five standards concern specifications for the organization or labeling of items so that the data necessary for description of the item are clearly presented. Two such standards originally published in 1981 were up for review: ANSI Z39.15, *Title Leaves of a Book*, and ANSI Z39.32, *Information on Microfiche Headings*. The first specifies the content of book title pages; the second, the eye-legible headers that appear at the top of microfiche. Both standards were reaffirmed without change and thus remain in effect for another five years.

A similar but more inclusive standard for the title page, data page, and organization of technical reports that was first approved in 1974 was not reaffirmed when it was reviewed in 1984. In spring 1986, a new greatly enlarged draft of ANSI Z39.18, *Scientific Technical Reports: Organization, Preparation, and Production*, was circulated for comment. The new draft gives detailed guidelines for the title page, other front matter, body, and appendixes, as well as specifications for presentation of tables, graphs, equations and formulas, and terminology. Its final section treats report production — graphic design, typography, layout, and binding. ANSI Z39.18 was revised by the responsible standards committee and recirculated for ballot in the fall. This standard, if followed, could greatly assist libraries in controlling technical report material, which for various reasons often does not follow the standards used for published material.

Another packaging and labeling standard that was actively developed in 1986 is one for computer software. This standard, expected to be ready for comment in 1987, will cover labeling, citing, and advertising of computer software. Currently undergoing revi-

sion is a standard that facilitates the description of serial items, ANSI Z39.1, *Format and Arrangement of Serials.*

Access to Material

Standards for expressing holdings and for borrowing items have been under development in NISO for many years. In early 1986, ANSI Z39.44, *Serial Holdings Statement*, specifying the form of holdings statements at both the summary and detailed levels, replaced ANSI Z39.42, which specified serial holdings statements at only the summary level. In spring 1986, NISO members reviewed the first version of a standard for non-serial holdings statements.

Proposed standard ANSI Z39.57, draft *Holdings Statement for Non-Serial Items*, covers all monographic items, including multivolume monographs, excluded from the serial holdings standard. The new standard explicitly deals with all media that fit a non-serial publication pattern. Z39.57 was distributed for comment in spring 1986 and then revised by the standards committee and forwarded for NISO ballet in December 1986.

As libraries move into development of integrated systems, the two standards for serial and nonserial holdings are most timely. These systems include or are scheduled to include serial check-in and shelf-list holdings information as a logical extension of the online catalog and circulation. Small incompatibilities in the present drafts of Z39.44 and Z39.57 will need to be reconciled in order for the two standards to be used efficiently in integrated systems.

A major use of holdings data is to facilitate interlibrary loan. NISO distributed for comment in fall 1986 a draft standard, *Interlibrary Loan Data Elements*, that describes the data elements used in interlibrary loan transactions. This standard began as the standard for the printed interlibrary loan form that had been agreed upon within the American Library Association. As with other standards for printed forms, the orientation of the standard was changed early in its development to identification and description of data elements to be used for the transaction no matter the type of transmission used—mail, teletype, or telecommunications. The draft standard describes data elements needed to identify the item unambiguously, to reply to requests, and to identify the organizations involved in the transactions.

Other Standards Activity

Three additional NISO draft standards were forwarded for review and comment in 1986. The first, *Computerized Serials Orders, Claims, Cancellations, and Acknowledgements*, is a companion to the 1985 standard ANSI Z39.49, *Computerized Book Ordering*. The serial ordering standard specifies a variable length record format for the four types of communications specified in its title.

A significant, but somewhat controversial, draft standard for a common command language for use in automated systems was circulated for comment in 1986. The standards committee had the difficult task of establishing a logical, consistent set of commands and linking them with expected behavior on systems. Because no existing system will fit the new standard exactly, much controversy has ensued, as reviewers from established systems suggest changes to move the draft standard closer to their requirements.

The proposed standard could have a positive effect on systems development. If the

standard were widely followed, a library or information service user would be able to carry out basic searching on a new database or system with the common command tools learned in other search situations. The draft standard is referred to as ANSI Z39.58, draft *Common Command Language for Online Interactive Retrieval*.

A final standard that circulated for comment in 1986 is one for ANSI Z39.56, *Serial Issue and Article Identifiers*. When completed, this standard could facilitate both interlibrary loan and collection of photocopy fees by publishers.

NISO Management

The NISO Office continues to be housed at the National Bureau of Standards (Administration Building, Library E106, U.S. Department of Commerce, Gaithersburg, Maryland 20899). Theodore Brandhorst, director of the ERIC Processing and Reference Facility, currently serves as chairperson of the NISO board of directors. Patricia R. Harris is executive director, with responsibility for operations, the NISO office, and liaison with ANSI in New York City. The NISO board is composed of persons representing publishing, libraries, and information services. Current members include Mary Ellen Jacob (vice chairperson), Dana J. Pratt, Anita DeVivo, Ernest Muro, Joseph H. Howard, Paul Evans Peters, James E. Rush, and Richard Rowe.

The 60 current NISO voting members include publishers, abstracting and indexing services, library associations, information consultants, library networks, computer manufacturers, libraries, and other agencies that support information services. Five organizations joined NISO during the year: Data Research Associates, MINITEX, JERA, Inc., Apple Computers, Inc. and University Microfilms International.

The three membership categories maintained by NISO are full voting membership, information membership, and supporting membership. The support category was created in 1986 in response to requests from larger corporations only partially involved in activities under NISO's scope. These firms wanted to support and to be kept informed of NISO developments, but they did not want to vote on all NISO standards. (Full voting members are required to participate in order to keep their membership.)

To Obtain Standards

Copies of approved ANSI and ISO standards can be obtained from the American National Standards Institute, 1430 Broadway, New York, New York 10018. Copies of many of the draft standards are available from the NISO office.

Special Reports:
Access to Information

As we complete the shift from an industrial to a service-based economy, the value and importance of information in our lives becomes dramatically evident. In his keynote article, Kenneth E. Dowlin asserts that indeed the time has come when access to information must be acknowledged as a basic human right. A national access to information policy is needed to assist librarians with their special responsibility to protect the public's right to knowledge and information. The library profession should also lead in developing minimum standards of access to information and in promoting the compatability of information systems. Creating a community information and communications system is another important step librarians can take to ensure the basic right of public access.

Access to Information: A Human Right?

Kenneth E. Dowlin

Director, Pikes Peak Library District, Colorado Springs, CO 80901

As U.S. society moves toward the twenty-first century, there are indications that the economy of the United States has shifted from an industrial to a service base. This shift raises major societal questions. There is concern that the quality of life may well decline if the majority of workers are in service jobs. How many people can be employed in the fast food business, stores, government, or restaurants? A large body of literature promotes the information age as the salvation of American civilization with information as the new "industrial" product. But can information be treated as an "industrial" product? What will happen to those who, because of a lack of education, income, technology, or simply motivation, do not have adequate access to information? Access to certain kinds of information must be considered a basic human right in the information age:

1 Information relevant to issues to be decided by voters
2 Information pertaining to candidates for public office
3 Information essential for the individual to cope with his or her environment
4 Information about governments (federal, state, or local)
5 Information relevant to the consumption of the basic necessities (i.e., food, medicine, housing, transportation)
6 Information to improve health

7 Information to increase safety

8 Information to increase employment opportunity and enhance careers

Why do people need access to information?

- To learn lessons from history in the hope that mistakes will not be repeated
- To gain a sense of belonging from knowing the culture of their ancestors
- To cultivate pride in themselves and their community
- To select those who govern
- To be informed consumers
- To care for their bodies and minds
- To coexist with their fellow human beings through understanding
- To understand that today's actions in the environment will affect the future
- To sort through persuasive commercial messages
- To resist distorted information from ideologies that threaten the American way of life
- To preserve human rights where they exist and to encourage them where they do not exist

Barriers to Information Access

Although having access to information is in everyone's self-interest, many barriers limit this access—even in a country that attempts to follow the principles contained in its Constitution and Bill of Rights.

Legalistic Barriers

The governments of some countries try to impede the flow of information (1) from other countries, due to the notion that the national culture must be preserved at all costs and that foreign influence will dilute or contaminate the culture, and (2) within the country, believing that citizens have no right to read, hear, or see information that is not approved by the government. Certain kinds of information are censored even in governments that do not practice political censorship. The debate over providing sex education to children still rages in the United States in many localities.

The trend toward privatization in the United States, or placing more and more of the dissemination and indexing of government-created informational products in the hands of the private sector, has many people concerned that access will be denied to those who cannot pay. Also, certain types of industry attempt to use the law to provide unreasonable control over information they produce. One of the more controversial cases is the suit by the motion picture producers against Sony, contending that videocassette recorders in the home would reduce the potential revenue from Hollywood productions. Fortunately, the U.S. Supreme Court sided with the consumers.

Another factor is the time lag in laws that do not keep up with technology. Rapid change in technology makes it difficult for the U.S. Congress to maintain current policies relative to copyright and patents. Congress took decades to respond to the need to protect computer software ownership rights.

Competitive Forces

Another barrier to information access involves the competitive forces of corporate secrecy, media conglomeration, and the growth of transnational corporations. In a free market society the ownership of information is critical: Access to corporate information must be strictly controlled.

As technology has allowed mass message distribution throughout the country (perhaps the entire free world), the number of input channels to those distribution channels has decreased. Consolidation of publishing, the news media, and the entertainment media into less than 100 U.S. corporations—many with overlapping boards of directors—results in a sameness in all of the media and requires one to have a great deal of money to use the media to communicate information.

The growth of corporations whose operations are global in scale creates a new environment for the transfer of information from one country to another. (A number of countries, alarmed by transnational data flow, have passed legislation to restrict information transfer.) These corporations have disproportionate control of information by virtue of their communications technology and their size; some are larger than many nations and their headquarters are located in countries that have the most favorable business climate. Among them are the international companies located outside the United States that repurchase most of the insurance sold in the world.

Technological Barriers

Even in the age of information, technology can create key barriers to information access. A number of recent polls indicate that the majority of citizens receive their news from television, an almost totally ephemeral medium, but few people know how to access the news from last week, last month, or last year. Although Vanderbilt University archives the network news, there is almost no archiving of local television news and other local productions. Will the traces of an entire civilization be relegated to the ether of the atmosphere?

The lack of technical standards, knowledge, and hardware presents significant problems for information access. Although the electronics industry continues to show dramatic increases in product capability as prices continue to drop, different brands of equipment don't connect to each other. Unless you buy a television and a VCR from the same manufacturer, it is doubtful that the remote control from one will function with the other. A major barrier to the linking of library computer systems in the United States is the lack of interconnectability of the hardware.

Despite major marketing efforts by companies, many people still do not know how to use technology to increase their access to information. Unfortunately, marketing efforts are intended to stimulate sales, not use. Even the educational community, which has made major investments in computer hardware and software, seldom teaches students to use the computer as a tool for information access. Communications capability could be added to microcomputers at marginal cost, yet it is not included.

Many people do not have the equipment needed to access the existing information systems, either because they don't have the money to purchase the hardware, or they don't see a need for the hardware, or because they can't keep up with the endless changes in hardware arising from built-in product obsolescence. Virtually any technology that increases the breadth of distribution of information tends to decrease the access of the individual to the medium. Today, there are satellites that can broadcast throughout most

of North America. Yet those who have the ability to transmit the information to the satellite are few in number.

Perceptual Barriers

Many people are unaware that they need information in the first place. It is difficult to know what you don't know. Also, the censorship of information for religious or economic reasons, or simply to control other people, has a long history. Those who believe that the individual is best qualified to determine what he or she should read, see, or hear must constantly work to prevent others from building constraints on the free flow of information.

Economic Barriers

In a society where publicly subsidized information is valued — in theory — but where the user-pays philosophy is employed, we must recognize the constraints of economic barriers. Many people do not have the money to purchase the information they need. A person with money can purchase the services of an accountant, an attorney, a tutor, an architect. Those who do not have the money must rely on the collective conscience of the communities in which they live.

Strategies to Reduce Barriers

The impact of technology goes beyond simple hardware considerations. Electronic information technology increases the capacity for both control and access. It increases the likelihood of the sale of information and of the privatization of databases, tends to base access on the ability to pay, and, perhaps of most concern, allows for the massive concentration of power in transnational corporations. Those who control the technology decide on the amount of control versus access for the average person.

Although the United States has taken more steps to promote and preserve its citizens' right to information access than perhaps any other country, the public nevertheless perceives a lack of direction on the federal level. The library profession needs to assume leadership in developing minimum standards of access to information. As citizens, librarians must become involved in the political process to support efforts to create a national access to information policy. Until such time as a commonly accepted level of access is ensured in the United States, denial of access will continue to hamper economic and social progress.

Librarians also must provide leadership in the use of technology in the communities they serve. Computer systems can be implemented for housekeeping tasks, to build community resource files, and to create a community information and communications systems. Lack of ownership of hardware or lack of training should not be a barrier to information access in a community with an active library.

The library profession must take a strong stance concerning the ability of electronic information systems to interface with machines by different manufacturers or different media. Libraries should use the most effective tool available to them, the economic tool: They should refuse to purchase technological systems that do not interface.

According to Herbert Schiller, a professor at the University of California at San Diego, the field of librarianship contains a paradox: Although the skills and leadership

of librarians are critical to society in the information age, other, more powerful elements in the information game discount the importance of publicly funded libraries because of their traditionally passive role.* The library profession needs to make a shift of at least two dimensions in the basic tenets of the profession: that of changing from a passive role (i.e., bibliographic control) to an active role (i.e., the creation of databases and other information products), and that of moving beyond the print medium as the focus for library collections. Not only can electronic technology be used for such housekeeping tasks as circulation, acquisitions, and cataloguing but it also provides the tools to create the information needed by the community. The hardware for the online public access catalog can also be used to create databases of social services. Video will be perhaps the most effective information source for the future, replacing books.

In the information age the ability of librarians to strive for, defend, and increase access to information will not only have impact on the profession but on the communities librarians serve. A committed, trained, and caring profession is required to safeguard existing access to information and to ensure access in the years ahead. The technology used in libraries may change, but the role of publicly funded libraries and information centers to provide subsidized access to information will not.

*Herbert Schiller, "Information and the Crisis Economy," speech delivered at Mountain Plains Library Association/Colorado Library Association Joint Conference, October 1986.

Ready access to federal government information currently is threatened by three types of challenges: national security restrictions, fiscal constraints, and the impact of new technologies. In expanding the application of classifiable information, the Reagan administration has reversed the trend of the last 30 years. Moreover some existing means of acquiring government information are being weakened and both the volume and variety of government publications are being reduced. The privatization of the National Technical Information Service and the effects of OMB Circular A-130 also have important implications for access to federally produced information. Harold C. Relyea of the Congressional Research Service explores these current trends and their implications for our democractic system of government.

Access to Federal Government Information

Harold C. Relyea

Congressional Research Service
Library of Congress, Washington, DC 20540

Information is the currency of democracy. The truth of this statement was well appreciated 200 years ago, when James Madison, the principal author of the Bill of Rights, penned the following memorable and often quoted observation:

Note: The views expressed here are solely those of the author and are not attributable to any other source.

A popular Government without popular information, or the means of acquiring it, is but a Prologue to a Farce or a Tragedy; or perhaps both. Knowledge will forever govern ignorance: And a people who mean to be their own Governors must arm themselves with the power which knowledge gives.[1]

Today, the popular information of which Madison wrote becomes available to the populace on the initiative of either the government or parties outside the government using some "means of acquiring it." Certainly there are a variety of reasons why the federal government itself chooses voluntarily to provide information to the public. However, because such efforts can become self-serving, many of them have been characterized as "public relations," "flackery," "propaganda," or "disinformation."

Means of acquiring government information by the populace are of at least two kinds. The Freedom of Information Act (FOIA) and the Government in the Sunshine Act exemplify laws establishing procedures for accessing government records and policy-making meetings. In addition, there are surrogates of the public who facilitate the availability of government information. They include the press, the library community, and a variety of so-called public interest organizations, as well as elements of the information industry.

Few leaders in the federal government would take issue with Madison's comment on the importance of popular information for the functioning and preservation of popular government. A truly sovereign people must have government information for minimal reasons of protecting their individual rights as well as promoting the well-being of the larger community or society. However, some recent developments in federal information policy and practice do not appear to support this ideal. For example, national security controls on government information continue to increase; means of acquiring government information, such as the Freedom of Information Act, are being weakened; and both the volume and variety of government publications are being reduced. In addition, new economy concerns in government and growing use of new information technology by the departments and agencies suggest other difficulties regarding information access. These and other aspects of federal government information availability are considered here, beginning with the area of government-initiated information provision, moving next to the sphere of citizen-initiated information access, and then examining national security controls on government information.

Government-Initiated Information Provision

A major innovation in government-initiated information provision occurred in late February 1986, when the U.S. Senate temporarily authorized live gavel-to-gavel radio and television broadcast of its floor proceedings. Radio coverage began on March 12; television broadcasting initially started on a closed-circuit, in-house basis on May 1 and became available to the public on June 2. The Senate made the broadcasting arrangements permanent on July 29. Similar broadcasting of House floor proceedings has been operational since early 1979.

The retirement of chief justice Warren Burger prompted speculation that the Supreme Court might soon permit television coverage of oral arguments and the delivery of opinions. A steadfast opponent of Supreme Court broadcasting, Burger turned down various pleas from the press in March and April for radio and/or television coverage of arguments on the Gramm-Rudman-Hollings Balanced Budget Act. In a handwritten note to Mutual Broadcasting, he said: "When you get Cabinet meetings on the air, call

me!"[2] There has been concern that broadcasting might distort Court proceedings or result in filmed segments being used for commercial purposes. Later, however, Burger did allow television cameras into the Court building for live coverage of a press conference announcing his retirement, the elevation of William Rehnquist to chief justice, and the nomination of Antonin Scalia to the high bench. About the same time, Bill Moyers apparently filmed an interview with Burger in the courtroom for a CBS documentary on the Constitution.[3]

Elsewhere, the U.S. Court of Appeals for the Fifth Circuit determined that judicial rules prohibiting the televising, recording, or photographing of federal criminal trials do not violate the First Amendment.[4] During the year, there were other court rulings concerning the availability of or access to judicial branch information. For example, in late June, the Supreme Court decided that the public has a First Amendment right to attend most pretrial hearings in criminal cases.[5] In a September ruling, the U.S. Court of Appeals for the Third Circuit found there is a common law right of access to real estate settlement documents filed with a court.[6]

But, while congressional floor proceedings were becoming open to live broadcast coverage, another, more traditional avenue of congressional information was not faring so well. A March 14 "Dear Colleague" letter from the Joint Committee on Printing announced "sizable reductions in the numbers of printed copies of the *Congressional Record*, committee prints, hearings, and other types of Congressional publications." These changes resulted from a 4.3 percent funding cutback prompted by the Gramm-Rudman-Hollings Act. Consequently, as of June 2, members of the public are entitled to receive only one free copy of bills, reports, public laws, or other such materials usually distributed from the congressional document rooms.[7] Multiple copies and exhausted items may be purchased from the Superintendent of Documents. In addition, the numbers of copies of committee hearing volumes and committee prints usually delivered to committees is being cut by half, the remaining supply being reserved for the use of only members and staff of Congress. The provision of congressional documents to depository libraries apparently is unaffected by this new policy.

However, the continued government sale of some reports cannot be ensured. In late April, the Department of Commerce requested public comment on the prospect of all or part of the National Technical Information Service (NTIS) being operated by the private sector.[8] Some contend that such privatization would result in savings for the government; others view it as a way to curtail foreign-government acquisition of sensitive U.S. technical data; and there are also those who regard it as divestiture of an activity more properly performed by private business. The department's intentions regarding NTIS apparently will not be known until the president unveils the budget in early spring.

Public-Initiated Information Access

Some of the recent policy developments affecting public-initiated information access address abiding issues of the past few years. For example, both the Carter and Reagan administrations pursued amendments limiting the scope and effect of the FOIA. Legislation of this type, supported by the White House, was adopted by the Senate in 1984 but did not receive House endorsement. Subsequently, FOIA amendments affording greater protection of business information were perfected in the House and enacted by that chamber in September 1986.[9] The Senate, however, failed to take action on the measure before final adjournment. Nonetheless, amendments to the FOIA were realized

during the Ninety-ninth Congress. During the course of Senate consideration of omnibus antidrug legislation, a nongermane provision modifying the FOIA was attached to the bill,[10] and was still in the measure when it reached the president's desk for signature.[11] It affords greater protection of law enforcement records, liberalizes fee waiver arrangements, and obligates the Office of Management and Budget to issue agency guidelines concerning FOIA fees and fee waivers.

Of related interest is OMB Circular A-130. The object of considerable discussion and speculation,[12] it was formally issued in late December 1985.[13] In many places, the language of the directive is rather vague and general, and there has been little indication thus far as to how it will be implemented. However, the circular appears to have a potentially significant bearing on the FOIA to the extent that it serves as a means for determining the kinds of information the agencies may possess and the media of agency information collection, maintenance, and disssemination. Further, provisions of A-130 promoting cost effectiveness and maximum feasible reliance on the private sector in information operations may be used to justify privatization and fair market value fees for information deemed to be commercially valuable. Indeed, the circular may prove to be too generous in its grants of administrative discretion in information management, thus lending itself to political abuse. Consequently, its implementation merits close scrutiny.

Also, Gramm-Rudman-Hollings Act cutbacks and recent fiscal austerity within the agencies have begun to affect FOIA operations. In late April, a lawsuit for more expeditious processing of an FOIA request at the Department of Health and Human Services (HHS) was set aside by the district court for the District of Columbia "without prejudice, with the right to reopen after a reasonable time has expired." The court recognized that HHS staff losses slowed request processing, but was persuaded that the department, operating on a "first in, first out" basis, was making a good faith response effort.[14]

In other FOIA litigation, the U.S. Court of Appeals for the District of Columbia ruled in early January that the legality of Department of Justice guidelines used by agencies to determine fee waivers could be judicially challenged and, accordingly, remanded two consolidated instant cases to the district court.[15] In late April, the district court found that the Department of State's refusal to waive reproduction costs for a journalist was "illegal," but declined in that lawsuit to rule directly on the validity of the Justice guidelines regarding fee waivers.[16] Subsequently, in late July, the district court determined in one of the remanded cases that the Justice guidance was consistent with the FOIA and therefore valid. However, continued reliance on the fee waiver criteria outlined in the Justice guidance would require, said the court, that regulations based on the guidelines be published in the *Federal Register* and made subject to the notice and comment provisions of the Administrative Procedure Act.[17] Elsewhere, the U.S. Court of Appeals for the Third Circuit, sitting *en banc*, ruled that the press has no constitutional right of access to government documents because there is no historical tradition of such a right. However, four judges took issue with this position and signed a dissenting opinion arguing that the right of access to government documents was, indeed, implicit in the First Amendment.[18]

As a consequence of subcommittee hearings held in 1985, the House Committee on Government Operations issued a report on the electronic collection and dissemination of information by federal agencies. Among other considerations, it urged the agencies to "use modern technology to improve the range and quality of public access to agency records," to "make reasonable attempts to allow public users of agency information to share the benefits of automation," and to "retain the ability to provide promptly paper

copies of public records maintained electronically whenever those records are requested under the Freedom of Information Act."[19]

The issue being addressed concerned technological access. Not long before, a district court had ruled that "(1) a requester does not have absolute right to designate the format as well as the content of a requested agency record, and (2) although for instant plaintiff and under the current pricing system the computer tape offered the least expensive and most convenient means of access the agency offered a satisfactory alternative in the form of microfiche cards."[20] This ruling clearly suggests that a federal agency has unilateral discretion to determine the format or medium in which information sought pursuant to the FOIA will be released, and may do so without regard to efficiency or economy considerations. Thus, in satisfying a FOIA requester, an agency may determine that online computer access is appropriate or that certain computer reprogramming is necessary, both of which are costly undertakings. Similarly, it appears that as agencies increasingly resort to the electronic collection, maintenance, and dissemination of information, they may respond to FOIA requests without regard to whether or not a requester has recourse to the machinery necessary to read records in an electronic medium.

The committee report also took issue with the restricted access status of MEDLARS (Medical Literature Analysis and Retrieval), a computerized index of biomedical literature that is maintained and operated by the National Library of Medicine and sold by NLM to public users either in the form of online computer search services directly from the National Library or in the form of machine-readable copies of the database (computer tapes). The capital costs of the computer hardware and other expenses of generating the MEDLARS database are paid from appropriated funds. Revenues resulting from MEDLARS are turned over to the Treasury as miscellaneous receipts. Relying on a 1976 decision of the U.S. Court of Appeals for the Ninth Circuit, NLM maintains that MEDLARS computer tapes, which are copies of the database, are not agency records and therefore are not available for the nominal charges prescribed by the FOIA.[21] The committee report concluded that this court decision "is incorrect both as a matter of law and as a matter of policy."[22] It expressed concern "that the model of information control established by the NLM might be used elsewhere in government," that other "Federal Government electronic information systems might also become subject to similar restrictions," and "that, in establishing electronic information systems, Federal agencies might also acquire copyright-like controls over public information."[23] These potentialities, of course, have implications for the future operation of the FOIA and public access to government information.

Finally, in the last weeks of the Ninety-ninth Congress, qualified approval was given to the sixth set of regulations governing access to the materials of office of former President Richard M. Nixon. These regulations arise from the special protective custody afforded the Nixon records by the Presidential Recordings and Materials Preservation Act of 1974.[24] In August, a resolution was reported[25] and accepted in the Senate on implementing the new regulations, but rejecting a Department of Justice interpretative memorandum justifying executive privilege claims by Nixon.[26] An October report by the House Committee on Government Operations also gave approval to the access regulations, but renounced the Justice memorandum.[27]

National Security Concerns

Throughout U.S. history, the federal government has sought to protect information thought to be vital to the defense and survival of the country. From time to time, how-

ever, controversy has arisen over the nature, scope, and exercise of authority in this regard.[28] During the past several years, increased national security controls on information and communication in the United States have renewed this dispute. The Soviet invasion of Afghanistan and the end of détente prompted new national security limitations on traditional scientific communication.[29] Such restrictions seemed to become more prevalent and numerous with the arrival of the Reagan administration, affecting teaching, travel, foreign film and publication distribution, and news reporting.[30] Sometimes existing authority was more broadly interpreted and applied; sometimes new restrictions were generated. Sometimes government information was at issue; sometimes private data was the object of control. Moreover, whether or not any greater security for the nation has truly resulted is highly questionable.

Modern security classification policy, based on a presidential executive order, was inaugurated in 1940. During the past 30 years, three presidents issued directives successively narrowing the bases and discretion for assigning official secrecy to agency information and materials. The Reagan administration's order of April 1982 reversed this trend by expanding the categories of classifiable information, mandating that information falling within these categories be classified, making reclassification authority available, admonishing classifiers to err on the side of classification, and eliminating automatic declassification arrangements.[31]

When considering a prior security classification program in 1971, Justice Potter Stewart had warned ". . . when everything is classified, then nothing is classified, and the system becomes one to be disregarded by the cynical or the careless, and to be manipulated by those intent on self-protection or self-promotion."[32] The Reagan order did not improve the situation. Thus, it is no surprise that recent official evaluations of information security arrangements have concluded that too much material is classified.[33]

In March 1983, President Reagan signed National Security Decision Directive 84. It required, among other provisions, that all present and future executive branch employees with authorized access to Sensitive Compartmented Information, a kind of intelligence data, sign a nondisclosure agreement obligating them to lifetime prepublication review of their unofficial writing. However, as a consequence of congressional protest of this policy and a temporary statutory prohibition of the practice,[34] Reagan suspended the provision in early 1984. Nonetheless, the General Accounting Office recently reported that "the suspension has had little effect on prepublication review requirements" because the administration has been requiring federal personnel with access to SCI to sign Form 4193. In use since 1981, it obligates the signatory to lifetime prepublication review. In its survey, GAO found "the agencies did not know the number of former employees covered by these agreements." Thus, "the total number of agreements now in effect is unknown." The agencies did indicate, however, "that at least 240,776 individuals have signed the agreements."[35] GAO also discovered that 49,225 individuals with the FBI and Defense Intelligence Agency had signed employment agreements that require prepublication review.[36] And in 1985, 139 books, 5,053 articles, 3,484 speeches, and 14,144 other pieces of writing underwent government prepublication review.[37] GAO did not include the CIA or National Security Agency in its survey.

Finally, national security controls are beginning to have significant impact on some fundamental expectations about government information availability. In fall 1985, the Department of Defense refused to give a congressional committee access to a report on the DOD system of command and control for nuclear weapons because the study contained "sensitive" information and data supposedly derived from the department. The report had been prepared by the Office of Technology Assessment, a legislative branch agency, at the request of the committee.[38]

In early December 1985, the full U.S. Court of Appeals for the Fourth Circuit ruled on a criminal case determination in which the defendant sought disclosure of classified information as part of his defense. When the majority issued their opinion on the decision, portions of it were classified.[39] Although there was statutory accommodation of this practice,[40] two legal experts were prompted to warn: "Once loosed, the idea of secrecy in criminal proceedings may prove hard to cabin."[41]

In late September 1986, during the course of Senate consideration of an authorization bill for the federal intelligence community, Senator Jesse Helms offered amendments to the legislation. The details of the amendments were secret, but one provision reportedly enhanced the independence of the Defense Intelligence Agency. The director of Central Intelligence, William Casey, had opposed the proposals. As adopted by the Senate, they amended the classified annex to the committee report on the intelligence authorization measure. This annex supposedly contains dollar amounts and personnel ceilings for all the intelligence and intelligence-related programs authorized by the bill. It is made an integral part of the intelligence authorization act, however, by the statute itself. Thus, Helms's amendments, which seemingly give substantive policy direction to the intelligence community, arguably constitute secret statutory law.[42]

Conclusion

Apart from the long-standing impediments of government self-interest and bureaucratic inertia, government information availability is seriously threatened by at least three challenges: national security restrictions, fiscal constraints, and technology. Each of these begs thoughtful consideration. National security controls are necessary, but have become so pervasive and cumbersome of late that the integrity of the security system is in jeopardy. Similarly, economy in government is desirable, but can be used to stifle information access — for example, through reductions of staff for administering the FOIA — or thwart it, perhaps by privatization or otherwise neither collecting nor generating certain data. And while technology should be utilized to enhance government information availability, it can, of course, be used to create physical or economic barriers.

The opportunity to address these issues arises as the nation celebrates the bicentennial of the Constitution. Nowhere does that great document compel the American people to trust their government. Thus, those who lead the state should be willing to disclose information responsibly, not only to enhance public knowledge of its activities but also to cultivate a degree of trust or, at least, to dispel distrust. No quarter of the government can afford to frustrate the people for long in this regard without some consequential cost — the farce, tragedy, or both against which Madison so eloquently warned.

Notes

1. Letter to W. T. Barry, August 4, 1822, in Gaillard Hunt, ed., *The Writings of James Madison*, Vol. IX (New York and London: Putnam's, 1910), p. 103.

2. *Access Reports* 12, March 26, 1986, p. 12.

3. Ibid., July 2, 1986, p. 10.

4. *United States v. Edwards*, No. 85-3585 (CA 5th Cir. March 31, 1986).

5. *Press-Enterprise Company v. Superior Court of California for the County of Riverside*, No. 84-1560 (S. Ct. June 30, 1986).

6. *Bank of America National Trust and Savings Association* v. *Hotel Rittenhouse Associates*, No. 85-1753 (CA 3rd Cir. September 9, 1986).

7. See *Congressional Record* 132, May 21, 1986, p. S6347; ibid., May 22, 1986, p. H3161.

8. See *Federal Register* 51, April 28, 1986, pp. 15868–15870.

9. See *Congressional Record* 132, September 22, 1986, pp. H7876–H7880.

10. See ibid., September 27, 1986, pp. S14033, S14038–S14041, S14119; ibid., September 30, 1986, pp. S14295–S14300.

11. See PL 99-570, The Anti-Drug Abuse Act of 1986.

12. See, for example, Francis J. Buckley, Jr., "Federal Government Information Policies: A Library Perspective," in Filomena Simora, ed., *The Bowker Annual of Library and Book Trade Information*, 31st ed. (New York and London: R. R. Bowker, 1986), pp. 80–88; Eileen D. Cooke and Carol C. Henderson, "Legislation and Regulations Affecting Libraries in 1985," in Simora, ibid., p. 218; Kenneth B. Allen. "Legislation Affecting the Information Industry in 1985," in Simora, ibid., p. 233.

13. See *Federal Register* 50, December 24, 1985, pp. 52730–52751.

14. *Fox* v. *Department of Health and Human Services*, Civ. No. 86-0879 (DC DC April 25, 1986).

15. *Better Government Association* v. *Department of State*, No. 84-5723 (CA DC January 3, 1986); *National Wildlife Federation* v. *Department of Interior*, No. 84-5928 (CA DC January 3, 1986).

16. *Goldberg* v. *Department of State*, Civ. No. 85-1496 (DC DC April 29, 1986).

17. *Better Government Association* v. *Department of State*, Civ. No. 83-2998 (DC DC July 31, 1986).

18. *Capital Cities Media* v. *Chester and Pennsylvania Department of Environmental Resources*, No. 85-5132 (CA 3rd Cir. July 21, 1986).

19. See U.S., Congress, House, Committee on Government Operations, *Electronic Collection and Dissemination of Information by Federal Agencies: A Policy Overview*, H. Rept. 99-560, 99th Cong., 2d sess. (Washington, D.C.: GPO, 1986), p. 11.

20. *Dismukes* v. *Department of Interior*, 603 F. Supp. 760 (DC DC 1984).

21. See *SDC Development Corporation* v. *Mathews*, 542 F. 2d 1116 (CA 9th Cir. 1976).

22. H. Rept. 99-560, op. cit., p. 35.

23. Ibid., p. 36.

24. 88 Stat. 1695.

25. See U.S., Congress, Senate, Committee on Governmental Affairs, *National Archives and Records Administration Regulations Governing Preservation, Protection of, and Public Access to Nixon Administration Presidential Materials Meet Statutory Test and Should Be Implemented*, S. Rept. 99-402, 99th Cong., 2d sess. (Washington, D.C.: GPO, 1986).

26. See *Congressional Record* 132, August 15, 1986, p. S11784.

27. See U.S., Congress, House, Committee on Government Operations, *Access to the Nixon Presidential Materials Should Be Governed by NARA Regulations, Not OMB or DOJ Actions*, H. Rept. 99-961, 99th Cong., 2d sess. (Washington, D.C.: GPO, 1986).

28. See, generally, Harold C. Relyea, "The Presidency and the People's Right to Know," in Harold C. Relyea, ed., *The Presidency and Information Policy* (New York: Center for the Study of the Presidency, 1981), pp. 9–29.

29. See Harold C. Relyea, "Increased National Security Controls on Scientific Communication," *Government Information Quarterly* 1, no. 2 (1984): 177–207; Harold C. Relyea, ed., *Striking a Balance: National Security and Scientific Freedom—First Discussions*. (Washington, D.C.: American Association for the Advancement of Science, 1985).

30. See, generally, Eve Pell, *The Big Chill* (Boston: Beacon Press, 1984); U.S., Congress, House,

Committee on the Judiciary, *1984: Civil Liberties and the National Security State*. Hearings, 98th Cong., 1st and 2d sess. (Washington, D.C.: GPO, 1984).

31. See U.S., Congress, House, Committee on Government Operations, *Security Classification Policy and Executive Order 12356*, H. Rept. 97-731, 97th Cong., 2d sess. (Washington, D.C.: GPO, 1982); Richard C. Ehlke and Harold C. Relyea, "The Reagan Administration Order on Security Classification: A Critical Assessment," *Federal Bar News & Journal* 30 (February 1983): 91-97.

32. *New York Times Company v. United States*, 403 U.S. 713 at 729 (1971).

33. See U.S., Congress, House, Committee on the Judiciary, Subcommittee on Civil and Constitutional Rights [and] Committee on Post Office and Civil Service, Subcommittee on Civil Service, "Preliminary Joint Staff Study on the Protection of National Secrets" (Washington, D.C., October 25, 1985), pp. 3-4; U.S. Department of Defense, *Keeping the Nation's Secrets: A Report to the Secretary of Defense by the Commission to Review DOD Security Policies and Practices* (Washington, D.C., November 1985), pp. 18-19, 48-50; U.S., Congress, Senate, Select Committee on Intelligence, "Recommendations on Information Security" (Washington, D.C., December 1985), pp. 8-11; U.S., Congress, Senate, Committee on Governmental Affairs, Permanent Subcommittee on Investigations, *Federal Government's Security Clearance Programs*, S. Rept. 99-230, 99th Cong. 2d sess. (Washington, D.C.: GPO, 1986), p. 18; U.S., Congress, Senate, Select Committee on Intelligence, *Meeting the Espionage Challenge: A Review of United States Counterintelligence and Security Programs*, S. Rept. 99- , 99th Cong., 2d sess. (Washington, D.C.: GPO, 1986), pp. 111-114 (typescript).

34. 97 Stat. 1061.

35. U.S., General Accounting Office, *Information and Personnel Security: Data on Employees Affected by Federal Security Programs*, GAO/NSIAD-86-189FS (Washington, D.C. September 1986), pp. 2-3; see also Stephen Engelberg, "Security Rule Died but Lived On," *New York Times*, October 23, 1986, p. B10.

36. U.S., General Accounting Office, op. cit., p. 23.

37. Ibid., p. 24.

38. See Walter Andrews, "Nuclear Warning System Report Demanded by Panel," *Washington Times*, September 27, 1985, p. 2A; U.S., Congress, House, Committee on Government Operations, *Our Nation's Nuclear Warning System: Will It Work if We Need It?*, Hearing, 99th Cong., 1st sess. (Washington, D.C.: GPO, 1986), pp. 83-109, 125-128.

39. See *United States v. Smith*, 780 F. 2d 1102 at 1105-1106 (CA 4th Cir. 1985). Portions of the trial court opinion also were classified; see *United States v. Smith*, 592 F. Supp. 424 at 443 (DC ED Va 1984).

40. See 18 U.S.C. App. 9(b).

41. Harold Edgar and Benno C. Schmidt, Jr., "*Curtiss-Wright* Comes Home: Executive Power and National Security Secrecy," *Harvard Civil Rights-Civil Liberties Law Review* 21 (Summer 1986): 389.

42. See *Congressional Record* 132, September 24, 1986, pp. S13566-S13571; Stephen Engelberg, "Senate Endorses Helms Measure Directing C.I.A.," *New York Times*, September 26, 1986, pp. A1, A22.

As Judith Krug of the ALA Office of Intellectual Freedom points out in her report, the year 1986 witnessed formidable new pressures on freedom of access to information. Among them were the new restrictions on sensitive unclassified information — with implications for such material in private data banks — and the report of the attorney general's Commission on Pornography. The Churchill, Tennessee, textbook case exemplifies the increasing prevalence of religious views as the motivating force behind new censorship atttempts in school and public libraries. The library community responded to these challenges with pleas for tolerance of diversity and warnings about the implications for a procensorship climate.

An Environment of Censorship, 1986

Judith F. Krug

Director
Intellectual Freedom Office, American Library Association

In 1986, attacks on access to information were more intensive than at any time since Ronald Reagan was elected president of the United States. His administration, in fact, set the environment not only in which these attacks occurred, but in which these attacks could — and were urged — to occur. In an administration fraught with contradictions, there is nevertheless a continuing irony: Although the Reagan administration promotes a hard-line antiprotectionist policy in foreign trade, it goes out of its way to hinder the free flow of information.

As far back as September 1983, noted First Amendment attorney Floyd Abrams characterized the Reagan administration's information policy as

> unique in history — clear, coherent and, unlike that of some recent administrations, not a bit schizophrenic. More important, it seems at odds with the concept that widespread dissemination of information from diverse sources furthers the public interest. In fact, it appears to be hostile to the basic tenet of the First Amendment that a democracy requires an informed citizenry to argue and shape policy.

Abrams said further:

> . . . This is an administration that seems obsessed with the risks of information, fearful of its potential for leading the public to the "wrong" conclusions. . . . It is a view . . . that treats information as if it were a potentially disabling contagious disease that must be controlled, quarantined, and ultimately cured.[1]

ACLU Executive Director Ira Glasser agreed with these sentiments, adding that this administration "sees the free flow of information as a threat and seeks increasingly to

Note: The views expressed here are solely those of the author and are not attributable to any source. For related discussion on the Freedom of Information Act, see "Access to Federal Government Information" by Harold C. Relyea (earlier in this section of Part 1) and "Legislation Affecting the Information Industry in 1986" in Part 2 — *Ed.*

insulate governmental decisions from public debate."[2] Three years later, the administration apparently has no intention of altering its course regarding the withholding of information from the American public. In fact, 1986 saw several additional attempts to limit access to information.

Attempts to Limit Information Availability

In April, the Department of Commerce announced a "Study of Alternatives for Privatizing the National Technical Information Service [NTIS]." The mission of NTIS is to centralize the collection, announcement, and dissemination of U.S. government-sponsored research and development reports and translations of foreign technical literature. Many librarians across the country have expressed concern that if such activities were undertaken by private groups, ready access to technical information could be severely limited.

As the year was drawing to a close, the Department of Defense (DOD) undertook a two-pronged effort against commercial online databases. In November, using the mantle of national security, then National Security Adviser John Poindexter signed an order creating a new security designation for government information called "sensitive." The order instructs federal departments to review the "human, financial, industrial, agricultural, technological and law enforcement information" they generate to determine its sensitivity to national security. Information termed "sensitive" cannot be released publicly, although technically it is not classified information.

The second effort by the Department of Defense stems from the department's growing perception that the export of high technology data should be as strictly controlled as the export of high technology goods. The DOD seeks to limit access to unclassified material in private data banks, an effort that appears to be part of a systematic campaign, based on a two-year-old directive from President Reagan, to censor scientific papers, restrict telecommunications satellite operations, and ban the use of U.S. supercomputers by Soviet scientists.

In December, information industry executives of private data banks, such as Mead Data Central, said they had been informed that rules governing access to commercial data would be forthcoming. The recommendation is expected to require foreign nationals to have an export license to access commercial databases. In addition, database proprietors might be required to install software to monitor database use. Such requirements, of course, are instituted to make it difficult for the Soviet bloc to gather the information contained in the data banks.

Using yet another avenue to limit the availability of information, the administration recommended massive changes in the Freedom of Information Act (FOIA). Although the Ninety-ninth Congress set aside all major proposals to amend the FOIA, in the headlong rush of its closing days, Congress tacked a major amendment to the FOIA onto the omnibus drug control bill, the Anti-Drug Abuse Act of 1986. The amendment, presented by Senator Orrin Hatch (R–Utah), passed without hearings or press coverage. It exempts from release under the FOIA some records of law enforcement agencies, including certain files of the Freedom Bureau of Investigation pertaining to foreign intelligence, counterintelligence, and "international terrorism."

The amendment also included some changes in fee and waiver provisions, which constituted an effort to undo the Department of Justice's 1983 guidelines. Under the new provisions, fees are generally limited in the case of news media and writers, and

waivers are provided for "public interest" FOIA requests. At year's end, confusion about the meaning of these amendments was compounded by what at times seems "whimsical" enforcement of the FOIA.

Prepublication Review

In November, the General Accounting Office made public its latest report to Congress on *Information and Personnel Security: Data on Employees Affected by Federal Security Programs*. The report was in response to a November 1985 request from Representative Jack Brooks, chair of the House Committee on Government Operations, and Representative William A. Ford, chair of the House Committee on Post Office and Civil Service. The report made clear that prepublication review is alive and well – and being used extensively.

Prepublication review requires any government employee, current or past, with any level of security clearance, to obtain permission from the government before publishing material that might be classified. Prepublication review orders apply to everything federal employees write for the general reading public, including newspaper and magazine articles, books, lectures, and even fiction. In short, employees are urged to submit for review anything that might contain information garnered during federal government service.

Prepublication review began in 1981 with the issuance of Form 4193, a nondisclosure agreement with lifetime prepublication review requirements, that agency employees with access to "sensitive compartmented information" (SCI) were obliged to sign. It was used only in regard to SCI, that is, intelligence or intelligence-related material requiring special handling.

In March 1983, the president issued National Security Decision Directive (NSDD) 84, formalizing the prepublication review requirements. Although the president subsequently suspended this aspect of NSDD 84, the suspension had little effect, since employees are still required to sign the old version of Form 4193 before being granted access to SCI.

The Federal Bureau of Investigation requires all its employees to sign its own nondisclosure agreement, which contains a lifelong prepublication review provision. In many instances, federal employees working on non-SCI special access programs also are required to sign similar agreements. The total number of employees subject to prepublication review regulations on December 31, 1985 was 3,534,481.

Although attempts to limit the public's access to information by limiting its availability appear to be part of an overall plan, they have not garnered the public notoriety attached to the Attorney General's Commission on Pornography and the textbook trial in Churchill, Tennessee. Both not only reflected but also contributed to the censorship-prone environment.

Commission on Pornography

In many ways, the tone of 1986 was set by the Commission on Pornography. For the first half of the year, attention was focused on the closing of the hearings.

In a 30-page report entitled *Rushing to Censorship*, American Civil Liberties Union (ACLU) Legislative Counsel Barry W. Lynn charged that the procedures used by

the commission to gather and evaluate evidence had been "so intellectually indefensible that they tainted the integrity and credibility of any final recommendations." Many critics of the commission urged that the panel's methods be critically examined before the scheduled release of its report in June, and Lynn contended that if its methods were not examined in this manner, the report could "generate a steamroller effect in Congress, with adverse impact on First Amendment guarantees."

On July 9, 1986, the Commission on Pornography finally issued its report. A month later, on August 9, the ALA Intellectual Freedom Committee (IFC) met in Chicago to review the report and to identify the implications, if any, for libraries and librarians. The meeting resulted in the preparation and issuance of an "Advisory Statement on the Report of the Attorney General's Commission on Pornography," which was based on the testimony then-ALA President Beverly P. Lynch had presented to the commission on July 24, 1985.

In her testimony Lynch had pointed out the potential chilling effect that the commission's work could have on the free flow of information and ideas. She had urged that no new restrictions be recommended on access to materials of any kind and, indeed, that some of the existing restrictions be eliminated. Lynch had based her recommendations on the belief that citizens in a constitutional republic need a great deal of information and ideas on all possible topics of interest in order to govern themselves effectively.

In its review of the report, the IFC noted the commission's dismissal of ALA's concerns, and called the limitations proposed by the commission on what people may read, cavalier and specious. ALA's advisory continued:

The conduct of the Commission's hearings and its use of research findings and methodology supporting the Report were flawed. The Commission authorized no original scientific research and appears to have misrepresented some of the social science data considered in the preparation of the Report.

In the Commission's hearings there was a clear absence of significant debate as evidenced by capricious acceptance of some testimony, rejection of countervailing testimony, biased cross-examination of witnesses, and the admitted lack of thorough discussion of final recommendations, except those on child pornography.

The most pernicious aspect of the Report, in the opinion of the ALA Intellectual Freedom Committee, is its potential for heightening an already threatening procensorship climate in the United States.

The general tenor of the Report is that associated with a "call to arms." For example, in its suggestions for citizen and community action, the Commission states "citizens groups may wish to focus on materials which are not legally obscene and which are constitutionally protected from government regulation." This Report advises citizens that "to remain quiet" is to approve such materials; it fails to recognize that lack of protest may just as easily indicate tolerance for different points of view, as protected by the First Amendment.

In view of the frequent individual and group attacks on libraries for making available materials, with and without illustrations and in many formats, no comfort can be taken from the Commission's characterizations of libraries' concerns as a "phantom danger" nor can any assurance be found in the Commission's protection of "the printed word." Most libraries are publicly supported and are especially vulnerable to pressures from officials and governing bodies reacting to public feelings about "controversial" works.

The American Library Association has long advocated the need to rally community support in defense of intellectual freedom before censorship attacks occur. This Report, itself an attack and a provocation to further attacks, makes it urgent to bring together all of those forces and individuals in the community who support the First Amendment to the

Constitution, since much that the Commission advocates is not consistent with that Amendment or even with current obscenity laws.

In general, while the Commission encourages people "to object to the objectionable" and "to tolerate the tolerable," the inherent message of the First Amendment is tolerance for the objectionable. Since library collections can be expected to include materials which some persons will find objectionable, an understanding of the meaning and purpose of the First Amendment is crucial to the defense of those collections.

The advisory closed with recommendations for measures that librarians, libraries, and state library associations can undertake to prepare themselves for further attacks on library materials.

Contrary to expectations, no flood of attempts to remove materials from the nation's public and school libraries followed. But as early as July, incidents began to occur that confirmed the Intellectual Freedom Committee's concerns about the potential of the commission's report for "heightening an already threatening procensorship climate in the United States."

The July 1986 issue of the *Phyllis Schlafly Report* was devoted to heralding the conclusions of Attorney General Meese's commission. Schlafly included a section on "Pornography and Libraries," stating that "librarians want a unique right to evade anti-pornography laws," and reminding her readers that "public libraries are maintained with taxpayer's money and they should be subject to the ultimate supervision of the taxpaying public." Her final comment urged readers to "check your local public library and find out whether it is obeying the laws against child pornography."

By year's end, the number of incidents had begun to pick up, and reports to the ALA Office for Intellectual Freedom were increasing.

Tennessee Textbook Case

When all is said and done, however, perhaps the most telling action of 1986 was the Churchill, Tennessee, textbook case, *Bob Mozert et al.* v. *Hawkins County Public Schools et al.* On October 24, 1986, Judge Thomas G. Hull of the U.S. District Court for the Eastern District of Tennessee ruled that the Hawkins County Public Schools had violated the First Amendment rights to the "free exercise of religion" by failing to allow conservative Christian fundamentalist children to abstain from participation in the school's regular program of reading instruction. The plaintiffs, seven sets of parents, had objected to certain themes that they claimed are prevalent in the Holt, Rinehart & Winston series used to teach reading in grades K-8. Although the complaint was focused on the Holt, Rinehart & Winston series, testimony at trial demonstrated that the plaintiffs objected to a range of ideas and methods of teaching that are common to virtually all of the nonsectarian basal reading series on the market today and used throughout the nation's public schools.

The wide scope of the plaintiffs' objections can perhaps be conveyed by a few examples. Maintaining that it "is a violation of scriptural principles to eliminate roles, to do away with any stereotype roles of men and women," they objected to "favorable stories about the women's rights movement" or to any portrayal of a woman challenging her husband's authority. Objecting to their children being exposed to the beliefs and practices of religious groups who did not share their particular view of fundamentalist Christianity, unless the "error" of these other religious views is pointed out, the plain-

tiffs objected to a statement in a selection from *The Diary of Anne Frank*, in which Anne states, "I wish you had a religion, Peter. . . . Oh, I don't mean you have to be Orthodox . . . or believe in heaven or hell and purgatory and things. . . . I just mean some religion." This statement, they say, implies that one religion is as good as another.

The plaintiffs objected to their children being encouraged to use their imagination "beyond the limitation of scriptural authority," maintaining that it would violate their religious beliefs for a teacher to encourage children to imagine what it would be like to be disoriented, to describe "the world community of the future as they would like to see it," to pretend to have wings and fly over their community, or to ask them to "close your eyes and let the sounds that you hear set your thoughts and moods." The families objected to their children being encouraged to question and make moral judgments on their own. Thus, they maintained that it violates their religious convictions for a teacher to ask students whether lying or stealing is morally wrong or for a story to portray someone lying, unless the person who lies suffers bad consequences as a result.

As noted, the judge held for the plaintiffs. An appeal has been filed and at year's end was pending. The decision, however, was extremely narrow and related only to the children of the seven sets of parents who had filed suit and only in regard to the Holt, Rinehart & Winston reading series used to teach reading in grades K-8. In his decision, Judge Hull said that it could not be considered as precedent for other cases.

Nevertheless, the tone of the complaint and the requested resolution of the conflict herald an increasing intolerance that cannot but affect every citizen's access to information in every library in the country. The solution requested by the plaintiffs in the Tennessee case was the installation of a public education system based on fundamentalist Christian principles — yet another instance of groups using the constitutional guarantees to further their own personal value system at the expense of all others' values and principles.

Survey of Censorship

Similar clashes were evident in the reports of increasing numbers of censorship attempts at individual school and public libraries throughout the nation. In September, People for the American Way issued its fourth annual survey of censorship, *Attacks on the Freedom to Learn, 1985-1986*.[3] The study documented a 35 percent increase of "censorship incidents" in the nation's schools and libraries between 1985 and 1986, and a 117 percent increase over the group's first survey four years ago. Most importantly, the report documented a significant shift in the nature of the attacks. Where in the past critics tended to target "dirty books," the current trend is to target ideas with which the would-be censors disagree. More than in the past, the driving force is the censors' religious views.

According to the study, censorship is increasing in all parts of the country and in both rural and urban school districts. In the 1985-86 school year, 39 percent of the attacks on library books and curricula reported by the survey actually led to removal or restriction of the materials. Four years earlier, only 23 percent of all censorship efforts were successful.

Although the report emphasized that censorship efforts do not originate solely with the political and religious right, it noted that at least 43 percent of efforts reported were organized by such groups as Phyllis Schlafly's Eagle Forum, Beverly LaHaye's National Legal Foundation, and the relatively new National Association of Christian Educators.

The report pointed out that Citizens for Excellence in Education, a component group of the National Association of Christian Educators, has pledged to bring "public education back under the control of Christians" and to do so by taking "complete control of all local school boards."

Conclusion

The year 1986 was one of intense pressures on access to information. The probability that such pressures will continue to grow during the waning years of the Reagan presidency is substantial. Those who care about free access to information are faced with the challenge to increase the level of tolerance of the American public, for without tolerance, there is no diversity, and it is on diversity that pluralism depends.

Notes

1. Floyd Abrams. "The New Effort to Control Information," *New York Times Magazine*, September 25, 1983.
2. ACLU Public Policy Report, *Free Speech, 1984: The Rise of Government Controls on Information, Debate and Association* (New York: American Civil Liberties Union, July 1983).
3. *Attacks on the Freedom to Learn, 1985–1986* (Washington, D.C., People for the American Way, 1986).

Geographic barriers to information access traditionally have consigned rural residents to the category of "information have-nots." Today rural libraries — which comprise the majority of our public libraries — are undergoing both crisis and rebirth. A prevailing scarcity of financial, human, and information resources makes it very difficult for rural libraries to meet the diverse demands of an influx of new residents. However, rural librarianship is riding a wave of professional self-awareness and recognition while exploiting the potential of new information technologies. In the following article, Bernard Vavrek of the Center for the Study of Rural Librarianship explores the implications for access to information in rural America.

Rural Libraries: The Era of Consolidation

Bernard Vavrek

Coordinator, Center for the Study of Rural Librarianship,
College of Library Science
Clarion University of Pennsylvania, Clarion, PA 16214

In relation to information access, the United States supports at least two societies — the haves and the have-nots. Included in the latter category is the vast majority of rural communities throughout America — nonmetropolitan areas with such unfamiliar names as Atlanta, Michigan; Wayne, Maine; and Sligo, Pennsylvania.

The U.S. Bureau of the Census chooses to define nonmetropolitan areas by default: a population center of 2,500 or more individuals. The Center for the Study of Rural Librarianship also includes the scale 2,501–25,00 inhabitants as a model and normally tracks both groups. (More than 80 percent of the communities supporting public libraries in the United States are rural communities of 25,000 or fewer people, and more than 60 percent have 2,500 or fewer persons. Pennsylvania has the largest rural population in the country, with more than 3 million people.) Beyond these numerical determinations are such matters as geographic isolation and whether the library is an autonomous organization rather than a branch library of a system. Although other types of libraries flourish in rural America, public and school models tend to be the most common.

The Rush to the Countryside

For the first time in the history of the United States, more people are moving to rural areas than to metropolitan areas. Nonmetropolitan towns are clearly attracting a diversified audience. Among the factors that account for this reversal are interstate highway systems, increased population mobility, an expanding service economy, the availability and growth of institutions of higher education, and the movement of job opportunities to small towns. Unable to locate affordable housing in the central city or in the suburbs, young couples, particularly those with children, are being forced to seek living accommodations in nonmetropolitan areas. Americans are also looking for a "better way of life." The real and imagined values of small-town living – meaningful, interpersonal relationships, safe places, clean air and water, the backyard garden, and close proximity to recreational areas – are part of the appealing culture in which the new rural population hopes to participate.

For the residents of small towns that are being transformed from quaint villages to thriving municipalities, the change can be most unnerving – not only for the newcomers, who are confronted with decidedly inadequate educational facilities, but for the local residents as well, who were content with the status quo. The public library is probably the only library (and information provider) in its service area attempting to meet users' needs. It will be hard-pressed to provide for the information needs of new rural residents who may expect such library amenities of metropolitan living as online access to NewsNet or a subscription to *Byte* magazine to be available in their newly adopted community.

The Rural Library

With a typical collection size of 25,000 volumes, the library's task is decidedly ambitious. Depending on the definition of rural used, the annual expenditure can range from $22,000 to $69,000, with the higher amount representing the working capital for the typical rural library in a community ranging from 2,501–25,000 people. It must also be remembered that library services are being provided by an autonomous library (i.e., independent of a branch library system) located at least 50 miles from the next city of 25,000 people. (These average distances vary considerably depending on the state being visited, as my colleagues in Michigan, Texas, and California are quick to remind me.)

Library Personnel

Library staff usually consists of one to three full-time personnel, with a one-person operation not uncommon. (One will rarely find a staff person designated as reference librarian. Specialization is not a luxury of the typical nonmetropolitan library.) At present, only about 25 percent of the full-time staff members performing library managerial functions have completed the requirements for the master's of library science degree. Regardless of the form of educational pursuit, i.e., whether one is seeking an academic degree or participating in continuing education workshops, the rural environment presents its own unique obstacles. Assuming that a replacement is available to keep the facility open, the librarian must also consider the relative distance that must be navigated. While traveling by plane to a workshop is an option, it may first necessitate a two-hour drive to the closest metropolitan airport. The geographic dispersal of library schools is another factor that hinders the staff person's decision to participate in educational programs.

Library Cooperation

Another factor affecting the unification of rural libraries relates directly to the rural library's inability to exist by itself in an information society. Library cooperation in the form of networks, at whatever level, offers crucial opportunities for the geographically remote library to compete. Without networking, there is little hope that the typical small public library can offer much in the way of timely and accurate reference information. Indeed, there is a definite risk that the community information center could evolve into nothing more than a lending library for books, with the reemergence of the subscription library as a typical community model.

On the positive side, things "rural" are increasingly being used as a rallying point by both librarians and legislators. With the role of county government being augmented because of the new form of federalism in the United States, hopefully the rural librarian will have an additional ally on the county level. But the library's plight may appear only a modest need among so many other compelling concerns as unemployment, providing for the homeless, and so on.

Automation

The final element that contributes to the consolidation of nonmetropolitan libraries is automation. Aside from the continuing instances of libraries without telephones or suitable electrical wiring to adopt new communication facilities, there is renewed confidence that technology will enable the rural librarian to join the ranks of the "haves" while not requiring a move from the hometown. Numerous examples throughout the United States support the computer's contribution to rural library services.

There is also a potential danger in the new technology. Extreme care must be exercised that the automation of the small library does not bring with it a direct decline in the willingness of the librarian to deal with clients face to face. Interpersonal relationships continue to be the major way in which rural people share information. Irreparable harm already has been done to the institutional role of the library in society by librarians who have overenthusiastically adopted automation without clear reasons for their actions.

The Future Outlook

Whether American librarianship has been content to look the other way when the concerns of small-town librarianship have been enunciated is a matter for future historians to decide. In fairness, however, it should be mentioned that for a variety of reasons, rural librarians have not been card-carrying members of national library associations. Also, geographic isolation has had a tendency to keep the problems of rural librarians individualized. As a consequence, their needs have not been represented. This neglect, from whatever source, has had a pernicious effect on the morale of those working in rural libraries. Fortunately, circumstances are now changing.

In addition to the mediation of rural library consultants, the activities of state library agencies, and the efforts of state library associations, both the American Library Association and the American Society for Information Science have demonstrated their interests in smaller models of library service. Proliferating throughout the country as well have been numerous workshops and conferences whose themes have been directed toward nonmetropolitan libraries. Also of note is the generation of regional and statewide groups, usually as adjuncts of state library associations, that are organizing in the interest of dealing with the special problems related to librarianship in nonmetropolitan areas.

Timing, it seems, is a central factor in making progress. Small-town librarianship is presently riding a wave of development and growth commensurate with the current demographics of the United States. As small businesses support the U.S. economy, likewise it is the small community public library that is the nucleus of librarianship in the United States. The library community's responsibility to nurture this model of library service is enormous. What are the alternatives?

Information access is also problematic for ethnic and racial minority groups. These groups are affected by a combination of limitations including illiteracy, language barriers, economic distress, and cultural isolation. In addition, factors such as the charging of fees for services, the lack of minority programs and services in regular library budgets, and the limited recruitment, training, and development of minority library personnel all influence service to a group that comprises one-fifth of the population of the United States. Ann Knight Randall, chairperson of the ALA Committee on Minority Concerns, discusses the problems faced by this special population, focusing on the implementation plan for Equity at Issue *which seeks to identify problems and recommend actions to improve library service to minorities.*

Library Service to Minorities

Ann Knight Randall

Chair, ALA Committee on Minority Concerns

In 1985–1986, library service to minority groups was highlighted as an important information access issue by the American Library Association. The four major minority groups that were the subject of special focus are African Americans, Hispanic Ameri-

cans, Asian Americans, and Native Americans. According to the 1980 U.S. Census, 46,012,932 people, or one-fifth of the U.S. population, belong to the four major ethnic groups. (This is a conservative estimate.) By the first quarter of the twenty-first century, one in three U.S. residents is expected to be a member of a racial or ethnic minority group. In the urban or metropolitan centers, the numbers are expected to exceed 50 percent. These forecasts of population composition changes are not new. The need to develop strategies to meet the educational and information needs of new or emerging Americans has been apparent for some time.

Ethnic and racial minority groups represent a set of library users or nonusers who may have demonstrated problems associated with one or more of the following limitations: (1) illiteracy; (2) non-English language speaking; (3) economic distress; (4) cultural isolation; and (5) limited experience with publishing and preservation of written materials. A major issue of the information age is the degree to which access to information will be denied because of such economic factors as special fees for services, for example access to electronic databases in community agencies and academic institutions. Problems associated with the gap between privileged patrons served by wealthy institutions and those confined to locations where limited information resources are available have received much attention in the library and information science literature. Cultural isolation is a special problem for young people and older Americans who do not have easy access to adequate resources by and about their ethnic group. Each of these problems suggests the need for a variety of resources and strategies, involving library staffing, budget allocation for supportive services and programs, and the informed selection and maintenance of library collections.

The American Library Association has accepted the challenge to provide leadership in the improvement of information services to the nation's minorities. Through its various divisions, offices, and units, the association has been involved in developing programs and strategies. The problem, however, is complex, and it cuts across the boundaries of units that focus on specific functions or types of information environments. The coordinating mechanisms within the ALA must be strengthened and tightened to combat this problem. Current ALA activity builds on its earlier information access initiatives and those of other information agencies.

Background

The NCLIS Task Force on Cultural Minorities

In 1982, the National Commission on Libraries and Information Science issued a report that updated and expanded the 1979 report of the White House Conference on Library and Information Services.[1] In response to concerns that the special needs of minority groups were omitted from the WHCLIS report, NCLIS appointed the Task Force on Cultural Minorities chaired by E. J. Josey. The task force issued 42 recommendations, 34 of which were adopted by NCLIS. The recommendations addressed five major topical areas: library and information needs of cultural minorities (in general); library personnel; services and programs; materials and resources; and financing library programs for minorities. The eight recommendations that were not adopted by NCLIS suggested the need for a stronger role in working with professional library associations, with publishers and producers of library materials and technology, and with other government units to accomplish goals that were beyond the scope of NCLIS. Specifically, the rejected recommendations dealt with research on library personnel; publication of minor-

ity materials free of stereotyping; state financing for minority programs in libraries, and fees as barriers to service, especially in minority communities.

ALA President's Committee on Library Services to Minorities

In 1984, ALA President-Elect E. J. Josey appointed the special President's Committee on Library Services to Minorities, co-chaired by Elizabeth Martinez-Smith and Binnie Tate Wilkin (in 1984-1985) and Marva DeLoach and Albert Milo (in 1985-1986). The committee report, *Equity at Issue*, was revised and accepted by ALA Council and the Executive Board at the ALA annual meeting in New York in June 1986.[2]

Equity at Issue provides a historical and problem-oriented analysis of the status of library and information services to minorities in all types of libraries. It cites a study by Gerard Gill, *Meanness Media*, which documents the decline in library services to minorities. It also includes the results of another study by Lorene Brown, dean, Atlanta University, School of Library and Information Studies, documenting the decline in the education and recruitment of minorities to the library profession.

Equity at Issue offers 22 recommendations for action by ALA and its constituent and affiliated units and groups. Acknowledging that support to education and social services is being reduced throughout the nation, the report urges ALA to seek NCLIS support for priority recommendations:

> We strongly believe that there is an immediate need for the library profession, ALA in particular, and its concerned partners in higher education and the private sector to develop a concrete program of recruitment, training, development and upward mobility for cultural minority personnel. We further believe that the library and information needs of ethno-cultural minorities, the fastest growing segments of the nation's population, must be adequately met in order for them to share equally in governing our society and in the rewards of economy. Equal access to information is imperative for cultural minorities. . . . We further urge ALA to reaffirm its commitment to minorities by providing responsive leadership in eradicating inequity in the profession.[3]

ALA Committee on Minority Concerns

The responsibilities of the Committee on Minority Concerns, as outlined in the *ALA Handbook of Organization,* are:

> To provide a mechanism that represents the interests and concerns of ethnic minority librarians; to work closely with the ALA Office for Library Outreach Services; to serve as liaison with the ALA office advisory committees, division boards or division committees, or other membership units, the ALA affiliated ethnic minority associations and the nonaffiliated minority causes; to provide Council and Membership with reports and information needed for the establishment of policies and actions related to the interests and concerns of ethnic minority librarians; and to establish contact with nonlibrary organizations whose purposes and activities are designed to serve the needs of ethnic minority groups.[4]

In 1985-1986, the committee surveyed ALA staff liaison officers to determine the programs and activities that had been instituted in response to the 1977 ALA Resolution on Racism and Sexism Awareness. Their finding was that activity was concentrated within

a small number of ALA committees and units, and that the impact overall on the organization was relatively limited.

At the 1987 ALA midwinter meeting in Chicago, the Committee on Minority Concerns issued a preliminary report to the ALA Council in response to the *Equity at Issue* document.[5] The committee recommended that all ALA divisions and units be urged to cooperate on specific goals within their charge and within the major priorities of ALA as they relate to minorities. It further recommended that relationships with legislative groups, professional organizations in all levels of education, and other library associations, be strengthened or established toward the attainment of these goals. ALA Council approved a plan of action to be coordinated by the Committee on Minority Concerns, placing priority on specific *Equity at Issue* recommendations:

- To promote the removal of all barriers to library and information services, particularly fee charges and language barriers.
- To promote the publication, production, and purchase of print and nonprint materials that present positive role models of cultural minorities.
- To promote full funding for existing legislative programs in support of minority education and training, and to explore alternative funding sources for scholarships, fellowships, and assistantships to encourage minority recruitment into librarianship.
- To promote training opportunities for librarians, including minorities, in order to teach effective techniques for generating tripartite public funding to be used to upgrade library services to minorities.
- To promote the incorporation of minority programs and services into the regular library budgets in all types of libraries, rather than the tendency to support these activities solely from "soft monies" such as private grants or federal monies.
- To promote equity in funding adequate library services for minority populations, in terms of professional and nonprofessional personnel, materials, resources, facilities and equipment.
- To promote supplemental support for library resources on cultural minorities by urging local, state, and federal government, and the private sector, to provide funding such as block grants.
- To promote increased public awareness of library resources and services, as well as the importance of libraries in all segments of society, especially targeting minority communities.
- To promote the determination of output measures through the encouragement of community needs assessments, giving special emphasis to assessing the needs of cultural minorities.
- To promote staff development opportunities for minority librarians, especially leading toward increased promotions and upward mobility.

The Office of Library Outreach Services (OLOS)

The Office of Library Outreach Services (OLOS) has primary responsibilities within ALA headquarters for the coordination of association activities relating to minority

groups. Its three major objectives are: (1) To promote the provision of service to the urban and rural poor, of all ages, including minority group persons who may experience discrimination; (2) to encourage the development of user-oriented informational and educational library services to meet the needs of the urban and rural poor, ethnic minority groups, the underemployed, school dropouts, the semiliterate and illiterate and those isolated by cultural differences; and (3) to ensure that librarians and others have information, access to technical assistance, and continuing education opportunities to assist them in developing effective outreach programs. From 1973 to 1986 Jean Coleman was director of OLOS. Helen Wright of the ALA Publishing Office is serving as interim director in 1987. OLOS works closely with an advisory committee, chaired by Susan Luevano, Santa Ana College, in 1986–1987.

In 1985–1986, OLOS initiated a number of significant programs to fulfill its major objectives.

1 *ALA Internship Program.* To train minority librarians from the four focus ethnic groups. The successful candidates will spend a year working at ALA headquarters.

2 *Assembly of Library Literacy Programs.* To formalize the role of libraries in literacy education activities within ALA and to maintain a focal point for literacy activities that extend beyond the unit membership committees.

3 *Survey of Library Schools and Courses.* The OLOS 1980 survey is being updated by William Cunningham, University of Maryland, College of Library and Information Science. The purpose of the survey is to describe programs that include library outreach services, services to ethnic groups and literacy education.

4 *Clearinghouse Information on Outreach and Literacy Programs in Public Libraries.* OLOS will maintain a file of program profiles.

5 *Coalition for Literacy.* OLOS participation in the coordination of this effort is continuing. ALA has launched a three-year drive to help America's estimated 27 million adult illiterates. The coalition works with the Advertising Council, Inc., to raise public awareness of adult functional illiteracy and to stimulate interest in local community activities. A nationwide telephone referral service has been established. Additionally, technical assistance is provided to communities seeking to develop literacy programs or form local literacy coalitions.

6 *Dual Language Illiteracy Workshop.* The needs of language minorities will be addressed in a workshop in Chicago, during March 1988.

7 *Preconference on Library Literacy Programs and Computer Assisted Instruction (CAI).* To bring together speakers, hardware and software providers active in CAI activities that focus on literacy.

8 *Annual Conference Programs.* The 1986 program featured Mary Groda-Lewis who overcame dyslexia and illiteracy prior to becoming a physician, and whose story was dramatized in the film *Love Mary*. The 1987 program, "Mentorship: Third World Managers," will focus on ways in which professional development assistance can be provided to minority librarians.

OLOS also serves as liaison to other ALA units and affiliated groups addressing the information needs of minorities (see the list of library organizations and ALA units at the end of this article).

Diversity: The Challenge to America's Libraries

The special theme selected by ALA President Regina U. Minudri for 1986–1987 is "Diversity."[6] At the 1986 ALA Annual Conference in New York, President Minudri reflected on the implication for libraries of the Statue of Liberty's one-hundredth birthday celebration. In recent decades, "new Americans" have come from Third World nations, rather than from Europe, but the basic problems of illiteracy, poverty, unemployment or underemployment, and related social issues are familiar. Libraries have a role in assisting these new Americans to appreciate and share their culture, while at the same time incorporating the new skills necessary for meaningful participation in the American workforce. Minudri includes service to special groups such as the disabled, the aged, the working single parent, especially in female households, in her challenge to libraries. The role for libraries is to meet these information needs in creative ways while cooperating with other professionals in education and social agencies.

At the 1987 midwinter meeting, Minudri organized the President's Program "Showcase of Exemplary Library Programs," selected from information centers that have the "capacity to recognize, respond and react to changing clientele and changing needs." The programs were selected for excellence according to four categories as follows:

- *Library Service to American People of Color.* "Library Services to Cultural Minorities" Montgomery County Public Library, Rockville, Maryland, Agnes Griffen, Director, and Linda L. Tse, cultural minorities librarian.
- *Library Literacy Programs.* "Join the Team and Be a Winner—Read!" Yorktown Elementary Instructional Media Center, Yorktown, Indiana, Mary M. Wolcott, information specialist.
- *Library Services for the Disabled.* "Serving the Needs of the People" DuPage Library System, Geneva, Illinois, Sharon Hoffman, special services librarian.
- *Library Services for New Americans.* "Asian Shared Information and Access Project" South State Cooperative Library System, Huntington Park, California, Kate Seifert, director.

Other ALA Activities

The Office of Library Personnel Resources (OLPR) has among its many concerns the effective recruitment of minority librarians, and the implementation of library education programs. In 1985–1986, OLPR worked closely with OLOS to collect data on program activities addressing minority concerns within ALA units, and it conducted forums on minority recruitment at the ALA midwinter and annual conferences. Its list of Minority and Women's Organizations in Librarianship is updated annually. Margaret Myers is the OLPR director.

The legislative programs coordinated by the ALA Washington Office are also vital to minority interests. Recently, it demonstrated to members of Congress the importance of the Title II-B fellowship funds for attracting and supporting minority librarians in master's and doctoral programs.

The Committee on the Status of Women in Librarianship sponsors program and publication activities of interest to minorities. Its 1987 preconference focuses on "Librarians as Colleagues: Working Together across Racial Lines."

A Selected List of Library Organizations and ALA Units Related to Ethnic Minority Groups

American Indian Librarians

OLOS Library Service for American Indian People
Janice Beaudin, Chair
University of Wisconsin Library
600 N. Park St., Madison, WI 53706

American Indian Library Association
Rhonda Harris Taylor, President
Rte. 2, Box 410, Bullard, TX 75757

Asian/Pacific American Librarians

Asian/Pacific American Librarians Association
Asha Capoor, President
Baker and Taylor
652 Main St., Bridgewater, NJ 08804

Black Librarians

Black Caucus of the American Library Association
Marva De Loach, Chair
Milner Library
Illinois State University, Normal, IL 61761

Black Studies Librarianship Discussion Group
(Association of College and Research Libraries)
Willie Mae Dawkins, Co-Chair
Library and Learning Center
University of Wisconsin–Parkside
Kenosha, WI 53141;
    and
Steven S. Newsome, Co-Chair
Banneker-Douglas Museum
84 Franklin St., Annapolis, MD 21401

Chinese American Librarians

Chinese American Librarians Association
Marjorie H. Lee, President
Rutgers University Library

169 College Ave., New Brunswick, NJ 08903;
    and
Amy Seetoo Wilson, Executive Director
University Microfilms International
300 N. Zeeb Rd., Ann Arbor, MI 48106

Ethnic Minorities

Ethnic Materials Information Exchange Roundtable (EMIERT)
Edith Maureen Fisher, Chair
Central University Library C-075-R
University of California, San Diego
La Jolla, CA 92093

Minority Concerns Committee (ALA Council)
Ann K. Randall, Chair
City College of CUNY
5333 N. Academic Center, New York, NY 10031

Minority Women Oral History Task Force
(Committee on the Status of Women in Librarianship)
Mary Walters, Chair
1659 W. 81 St., Los Angeles, CA 90047

Hispanic Librarians

Library Services to the Spanish Speaking
(Reference and Adult Services Division)
Robert Caban, Chair
2897 Royal Path Ct., Decatur, GA 30030

Reforma; National Association to Promote Library Service to the Spanish Speaking
Elena Tscherny, President
Public Library, Washington, D.C.
9001 G St. N.W., Rm. 410, Washington, DC 20001

Summary

The ALA president's task force report *Equity at Issue* represents the key focus on minorities for libraries in 1985–1986. ALA has enthusiastically endorsed the report's recommendations. To achieve public awareness of the significance of libraries and their responsibilities for providing information services to all sectors of the population the recommendations must now be incorporated into ALA policy and transmitted to relevant ALA units for action.

Notes

1. National Commission on Libraries and Information Science, *Report of the Task Force on Library and Information Services to Cultural Minorities* (Washington, D.C., NCLIS, 1983).
2. American Library Association, Report of the President's Committee on Library Services to Minorities, *Equity at Issue: Library Services to the Nation's Four Major Minority Groups, 1985–1986* (Chicago, ALA, 1986), CD 30, 85–86.
3. *Equity at Issue*, p. 11.
4. American Library Association, *ALA Handbook of Organization, 1986–1987*, p. 19.
5. American Library Association, *Report of the Minority Concerns Committee to the ALA Council.* 1987 Midwinter Conference (Chicago, ALA, 1987), CD 19.
6. Minudri, Regina U. "Diversity: The Challenge to America's Libraries," Inaugural Address, ALA President, July 2, 1986.

Handicapped people require methods of access to information above and beyond those treated elsewhere in this section. One continuing problem has been identifying available materials; another is delivery in a usable format. In his article on access to information for visually and physically handicapped persons, Frank Kurt Cylke, Director of the National Library Service for the Blind and Physically Handicapped, considers current breakthroughs in delivery and access. Developments involve cooperation among many services, organizations, and individuals in both the public and private sectors. Computerized braille, synthesized speech output, and greatly simplified cassette players are among the technological enhancements helping to make access to information more of a reality for handicapped citizens.

Access to Information for Blind and Physically Handicapped Persons: Recent Developments

Frank Kurt Cylke

Director

National Library Service for the Blind and Physically Handicapped,
Library of Congress, Washington, DC 20542

The development of a knowledge base usually requires the use of many audio/visual/sensory sources to identify and access appropriate information. When one has full use of all natural senses, the process is difficult. When one does not, the process becomes extraordinarily complex.

A plethora of handicapping conditions requires information to be presented in alternative formats. (For the purposes of this report, handicaps are those conditions requiring audio and/or braille output to be useful.) If all information sources must be processed and transformed to audio or tactile form, output limits are immediately imposed on availability and access. Traditionally, sighted individuals have translated print and other visual information for handicapped individuals — either reading or brailling — on demand. But how does a handicapped person know what is available and, therefore, what to demand? Another problem has been delivery of materials in a usable format.

Many services, organizations, and individuals in both the public and private sectors work to provide handicapped people with access to information. These include traditional libraries, radio reading programs, and producers of "on-demand" materials for individuals. Public and school library services offered to the handicapped are similar to those for nonhandicapped individuals in many ways. Books, periodicals, and other materials are selected on merit, organized, and placed in a collection for use by the identified public. For handicapped individuals, materials are made available in audio or braille format. In academic libraries, however, where service is user specific, informational material is primarily provided on request. Selection of text and class-related readings does not generally present a problem, but there is a problem of identification in choosing research materials.

To help the handicapped meet professional and personal information needs, Recording for the Blind (RFB), a national nonprofit agency, lends tape-recorded educational texts to blind and print-handicapped students and professionals free of charge.

The NLS Program

Public library service is provided through a free national library program of braille and recorded materials for blind and physically handicapped persons that is administered by the National Library Service for the Blind and Physically Handicapped (NLS), Library of Congress. With the cooperation of authors and publishers who grant permission to use copyrighted works, NLS selects and produces full-length books and magazines in braille and on recorded disc and cassette. Reading materials are distributed to a cooperating network of 56 regional and more than 100 subregional (local) libraries where they are circulated to eligible borrowers. Reading materials and playback machines are sent to borrowers and returned to libraries by postage-free mail. Established by an act of Congress in 1931 to serve blind adults, the program was expanded in 1952 to include children, in 1962 to provide music materials, and in 1966 to include individuals with other physical impairments that prevent the reading of standard print.

Eligibility

Anyone who is unable to read or use standard printed materials as a result of temporary or permanent visual or physical limitations may receive service. A survey sponsored by NLS found that 2 million persons with some type of visual impairment may be eligible, and another million with physical conditions such as paralysis, missing arms or hands, lack of muscle coordination, or prolonged weakness could benefit from the use of reading materials in recorded form.

Circulation and Readership

For FY 1985, network libraries reported a total circulation of nearly 20 million books and magazines to 565,000 individuals and institutions in the United States and its territories and to American citizens living abroad. (See Table 1.) Recorded discs accounted for nearly 11 million items circulated, recorded cassettes 8,229,000 items, and braille 703,600 items. Many regional and subregional libraries also have collections of large-type books for circulation to handicapped readers.

Books and Magazines

Books are selected on the basis of their appeal to a wide range of interests. Bestsellers, biographies, fiction, and how-to books are in great demand. The national book collection currently contains more than 43,000 titles, with a total of approximately 11 million copies of braille and recorded books. Each year approximately 2,000 press-braille, disc, and cassette titles are mass-produced for distribution through network libraries. In addition, about 200 braille titles are produced by volunteers and circulated in limited quantities to readers. Through a union catalog available on michofiche and in computerized form, every network library has access to the entire NLS book collection and to the resources of several cooperating agencies. More than 70 magazines on disc and in braille are offered through the program.

Equipment and Accessories

Playback equipment is loaned free to readers for as long as recorded materials provided by NLS and its cooperating libraries are being borrowed. Talking-book machines are designed to play disc-recorded books and magazines at 8 rpm and 16 rpm; cassette-book machines are designed for cassettes recorded at $15/16$ ips and the standard speed of $17/8$ ips on two and four sides. Available accessories for playback equipment include headphones and pillowphones. Readers with very limited mobility may request a remote-control unit; hearing-impaired readers may be eligible for an auxiliary amplifier for use with headphones.

Table 1 / Circulation: National Library Service for the Blind and Physically Handicapped, Library of Congress Network

Medium/FY	Total Circulation*	Total Readership	Circulation per Readership
Disc			
1980	11,275,700	331,600	34.0
1985	10,697,500	296,940	36.0
Cassette			
1980	4,952,400	254,160	19.5
1985	8,229,100	349,370	23.6
Braille			
1980	660,600	19,410	34.0
1985	703,600	18,320	38.4
Total			
1980	16,888,700	605,170	27.9
1985	19,630,200	664,630	29.5

*Includes direct-circulation magazines and interlibrary loan.

Research and Development

The NLS research program is directed toward improving the quality of reading materials and related equipment, controlling program costs, and reducing the time required to deliver services to users. The latest advances in computer technology are being used to (1) improve the cost-effectiveness of braille production, (2) develop an automated book circulation system, and (3) provide a communications link among NLS, all participating libraries, book and magazine producers, and distribution centers.

Funding

The NLS program is funded annually by Congress. The FY 1986 appropriation is approximately $33,761,000. Regional and subregional libraries receive funding from state, local, and federal sources. The combined expenditure for the program is approximately $60 million.

Federal

The Library of Congress budget was cut by $18.3 million for FY 1986, which runs from October 1, 1985 to September 30, 1986. All LC divisions and services were affected, including congressional research, copyright, acquisitions, and books for blind and physically handicapped individuals. The NLS portion of the reduction came to more than $4 million, representing an effective 11.7 percent reduction from FY 1985 funding.

Such deep cuts meant reductions in every area of the budget. These affected direct-service items for patrons — such as production of books, magazines, publications, and machines — and program items such as travel for consultants and for people staffing exhibits, transportation of exhibit material, staff training, monies for outside consultants and for consumer representation on committees, and even monies to purchase print books for transcribing into braille or recording on disc and cassette.

Because approximately 90 percent of the annual NLS budget goes to provide materials for patrons, the largest amount of savings came from these accounts. The most significant materials reductions were in the number of titles selected for recorded books and in the number of copies to be produced, a corresponding reduction in the number of braille books and copies, and a limit on the amount to be used for production of cassette playback machines.

Private Sector

At the same time federal funds were being reduced, Recording for the Blind was making significant gains. In 1985, RFB received a $1.5 million multipurpose grant from the W. K. Kellogg Foundation, and the money was used in 1986 to modernize thoroughly procedures. Under the terms of the grant, those improvements include the following:

- Replacing, at a cost of $300,000, all aging cassette duplicating equipment with the newest generation of high-speed duplicating machines.
- Upgrading and expanding computer capacity almost threefold.
- Expanding capacity to record scientific and technical books by providing $600,000 to help defray the start-up and early operating costs of two studios devoted to recording scientific and technical material.

- Providing $400,000 for expanding and intensifying development efforts over the next five years to attract major gifts from corporations, foundations, and individuals to cover anticipated increases in RFB's annual operating budget, meet additional one-time capital needs, and create a modest permanent endowment.

To ensure rapid turnaround for borrowers, RFB brought its cataloging methods into line with those used by NLS. The standardized cataloging methods make it possible to find titles, authors, or subjects much more quickly and easily. This action also helped make possible inclusion of RFB titles in the NLS union catalog, which will list 60,000 RFB textbooks and upwards of 20,000 NLS leisure reading titles, so that borrowers everywhere will have easier access to recorded books.

Service

Reference Books

NLS made a commitment in 1986 to expand substantially the number of reference works available for blind and physically handicapped people. Because of their bulk (braille) and the difficulty of locating recorded entries, reference materials present particular access problems for the handicapped. In *Books in Our Future*, a 1985 report to Congress on "the changing role of the book," Daniel J. Boorstin, Librarian of Congress, lists this goal as one of the five positive steps for the Library of Congress.

The first press-braille edition of Bartlett's *Familiar Quotations* (15th edition) is now being produced. It will take at least one year to complete and will consist of about 106 volumes. The project is a cooperative venture of NLS and the National Federation of the Blind (NFB). With the permission of the publishers, Little, Brown and Company, NFB will make both hard- and softcover editions available at cost for personal purchase in the United States and abroad.

The first recorded dictionary for visually handicapped individuals was provided by NLS in 1983, using a voice-indexing technique for locating information. Other reference books recently selected for the NLS collections include *America in the Twentieth Century*, by Frank B. Freidel; *International Directory of Tactile Map Collections; An Outline History of the World*, by Herbert Davis; *The Reader's Companion to World Literature*, by Lillian Horstein; and *Webster's New Geographical Dictionary*.

Public Libraries

Local public libraries are becoming increasingly important to NLS network library efforts for closer contact with patrons. Using existing space and staff interested in appropriate collections, network libraries are establishing small browsing or demonstration centers in public libraries. Setup costs are generally low and visibility is high using this approach, and network libraries have a better chance of reaching those who could benefit from their services.

Public libraries are also sponsoring programs to help increase awareness of services and materials. Some libraries have extended the deposit-collection concept to include innovative equipment distribution points, aids and appliances displays, and reading areas with informational materials. The key to the success of these efforts is careful planning and close cooperation between the network library and the public library.

Senior Citizens

Older adults in nursing and convalescent homes, retirement homes, senior day centers, hospitals, and other residential settings are among the most underserved groups of blind and physically handicapped individuals. About 50 percent of the senior citizens in these settings are eligible for, but very few are using, the NLS program materials. Many are not aware of the services available, including popular magazines and books in recorded formats; long-term loan of playback equipment; and special accessories such as headphones, pillow-speakers, remote control units, and extension levers for use by severely physically handicapped readers. Often senior citizens are reluctant to admit that they need the service.

Two NLS studies have indicated the importance of reaching seniors. In 1977–1979 NLS conducted a survey of the potentially eligible nonuser population in the United States. The resulting study reported more than 3 million potentially eligible users. Of this total, 47 percent, or 1.4 million, were aged 65 or over. This number is continuing to grow. NLS also learned that 54 percent have a primary limitation that is visual, 62 percent have a combination of visual and physical limitations, 77 percent are retired, and 47 percent never heard of NLS.

In another study, NLS learned from a 1979–1981 user survey that about 50 percent of all patrons served by the NLS program at the time were 65 years of age and older. NLS also learned that of these older Americans who were receiving service 38 percent have a disability that began when they were over 65, 65 percent have a visual handicap, 75 percent are retired, and 74 percent have incomes of $10,000 or less.

To address these concerns and encourage more use of talking books by seniors, NLS has undertaken a national effort to increase and improve services. This comprehensive campaign aims to meet the needs of seniors through development of new, easy-to-use equipment, targeted reading lists in special formats, and expanded outreach efforts. Special handbooks are being prepared to help professionals working with seniors, including a program handbook and videocassette introduction for health care personnel and a notebook manual for network libraries. The goal is to make the act of reading more comfortable, enticing, and accessible for eligible older readers who have impairments.

Technology

Easy Machine

The Easy cassette machine (E-1), a player with only two controls, has recently been evaluated by network librarians serving blind and physically handicapped individuals and selected library patrons in the final testing phase scheduled before production. The E-1 machine was developed in response to a consumer need identified in the 1979 NLS user survey, which revealed that 40 percent of library patrons did not have a cassette machine. Many of them, particularly elderly people, found the standard model too complicated.

The E-1 machine has been designed to be as simple and automatic as possible. It has two main controls: a sliding switch that starts the machine, rewinds the cassette if necessary, and selects the volume; and a push button that rewinds the tape if the reader wants to review information. The cassette is ejected by sliding open a door and depressing the cassette. The machine also features automatic side change on a cassette. At the

end of each side of a tape, the machine automatically plays the next side; the cassette does not need to be turned over. Because of the automatic side change, the machine can play nonstop for up to six hours.

Computer Circulation System

READS, the NLS computer software system for automatic circulation of materials to patrons, has completed its developmental phases and is ready for installation in network libraries. The system can maintain patron and inventory records and handle circulation procedures for libraries serving up to 6,000 patrons. The READS program is available to network libraries from NLS. Libraries must provide the personal computers and other hardware necessary for operation.

A planning guide is available for use by libraries considering installing the system. The guide lists materials needed, outlines space considerations, and covers planning for installation and conversion. Photographs illustrate the different parts of the computer and materials for the system. It also contains case histories describing the different approaches of the three pilot libraries.

Speech Device Provides Access to READS

The Kentucky regional library has become the first NLS network site for a speech output system that makes READS accessible to blind staff members. The Speaqualizer was developed by the National Federation of the Blind and consists of a programmed expansion board that fits inside the computer, a connecting cable, and a combination keypad and speaker. The keyboard has 19 keys that permit the user to issue 36 different commands. The system allows the entire screen to be read. Single lines, words, or characters may be checked and spelled out phonetically if necessary. The unit is self-contained and does not have to borrow memory from the computer itself.

Computer Braille

With the introduction of braille transcription software for microcomputers, the Disk Output Service was born at the National Braille Association (NBA) in 1985. NBA volunteers provide handcopied braille on request of individuals. Computer programs enable braillists to produce masters more rapidly and with comparative ease. They also enable computer braille to be duplicated on floppy disk or cassette for direct use with computers or paperless braille devices.

Facilities

While architectural improvements and facility enhancements occur regularly in libraries serving blind and physically handicapped patrons, there are always outstanding examples that demonstrate the progress of access improvement.

Michigan

The Michigan regional library for the blind and physically handicapped will occupy a major portion of the ground floor in a new library building scheduled for completion in

1987. The new library, museum, and archives building will be part of the capitol complex of downtown Lansing. The new facility will feature a central Courtyard of the Counties and will have a landscaped entrance and tree-bordered parking lots.

Missouri

Wolfner Memorial Library, the regional library for the blind and physically handicapped in Missouri, is in spacious new quarters in the Truman State Office Building across the street from the state capitol in Jefferson City as of late June 1985. The new location, which consolidates the various divisions of the Missouri State Library in the heart of the state capital, should result in greater efficiency leading to improvements in service. Another major advantage is that Wolfner Library was able to switch from time sharing on the computer at the St. Louis Public Library to running its own Digital Equipment Corporation VAX 750, which is directly connected by telephone to the main computer at the Coordinating Board for Higher Education.

Texas

The Texas regional library for the blind and physically handicapped has initiated a state-of-the-art Research/Reading Center that could be duplicated in other libraries. The center is designed to meet the needs of the growing number of professionals who are disabled. (According to a May 1985 article in *USA Today*, more disabled people are entering the fields of politics, business, education, sports, advertising, and the media. The article further notes that even though 15 million disabled people of working age could work with training and resources — and most want to — 10 million are nevertheless unemployed.)

Along with Apollo Readers and tape and record players, the Research/Reading Center houses a Kurzweil Reading Machine, microcomputers, and a braille printer. With this equipment, disabled patrons can read print copy, have copy translated to and from braille and print, and edit. Using Braille-Edit discs, patrons can print out copies in either braille or standard print. In addition, because the Reseach/Reading Center is located adjacent to the Reference Unit in the regional library, all the amenities of a public library, including a browsing collection, study tables, and a story hour for children, are also available.

Centralizing Resources

Two projects may be cited as examples of efforts to expand existing services and awareness of such services.

Associated Services for the Blind

Three Philadelphia-based organizations have merged to create a new multiservice agency for blind persons. Associated Services for the Blind, Inc. (ASB), united the efforts of Volunteer Services for the Blind, Radio Information Center for the Blind, and the Nevil Institute for Rehabilitation and Service. W. Benjamin Holmes is the executive

director of the new agency, which is located in the Nevil Building, a ten-story structure at 919 Walnut St., Philadelphia, Pennsylvania 19107.

The three agencies involved in the merger have a history of dedicated, quality service to blind people, beginning in 1874 with the predecessor of the Nevil Institute. The new consolidated agency is better able to take a broad view in identifying unmet needs and planning for expanded services. The association allows individuals access to a wide range of services by contacting a single agency.

More than 300 volunteers and approximately 100 paid staff are involved in providing services through ASB. These services include production of special format publications, radioreading, social and rehabilitation services, Optacon and Versa-Braille training, evaluation of technical aids, and public education on blindness and prevention of blindness. Volunteers also provide in-person reader service and visitor and escort services.

ASB operates on an annual budget of approximately $2.6 million and its wide range of services reaches more than 6,000 persons annually. ASB is funded through grants and contracts with federal and state governments, United Way, private foundations, gifts, and fees based on the client's ability to pay. A board of directors and a consumer advisory panel guide the work of the agency.

The NLS Multistate Center for the North, which is administered by ASB, and the Philadelphia regional library are also housed in the Nevil Building. Sharing a location provides patrons with easier access to all services.

Radio Reading Services

The nation's 155 special radio stations for blind, physically handicapped, and elderly people opened an office in Washington, D.C., in 1986 to keep abreast of legislative and agency developments affecting radio services. The Association of Radio Reading Services is located at 1133 20th St. N.W., Washington, DC 20036, in offices donated by the American Association of Retired Persons.

The national office serves as a communication link among the radio stations, keeps them regularly informed of news, and writes and distributes sample public service announcements and tips on how to use them to member stations. Another of the new services is an idea exchange on such subjects as staffing, fund raising, programming, outreach, and technical aspects of broadcasting.

The director of the new national office is Bernard Posner, recently retired as executive director of the President's Committee on Employment of the Handicapped. All staff members are volunteers.

Outreach

Informing eligible readers about available services is an essential element in providing access to information. A recent public education campaign in Illinois illustrates the extensive effort involved. "Share Our Voices, Feel Our Words" is the slogan that is helping to increase the number of blind and physically handicapped patrons throughout Illinois. It is the motto of a well-orchestrated campaign by the Illinois regional library to double the number of new patrons in the state from an annual average of 3,000 to 6,000 as a prelude to a five-year plan that will double the entire patron load from 15,000 to 30,000. The Illinois library system, which works through the regional library in Chicago and 15

subregional libraries throughout the state, now serves 15,000 patrons out of an estimated potential of 200,000.

The campaign was launched when author Harry Mark Petrakis of Chicago was inducted into the Illinois Library Network Hall of Fame. At a special ceremony at the Chicago Public Library Cultural Center, Petrakis autographed special-format copies of his books and talked about the art of storytelling with readers.

Federal Agency and
Federal Library Reports

National Commission on Libraries
and Information Science

General Services Administration Bldg.
Seventh & D Sts. S.W., Suite 3122, Washington, DC 20024

Dorothy P. Gray

Research Associate

In November 1986 the U.S. National Commission on Libraries and Information Science (NCLIS) celebrated its fifteenth anniversary as an independent federal agency. Officially created by PL 91–345 in 1970, NCLIS held its first meeting in fall 1971. The anniversary was a time for reflecting on the many accomplishments of the first 15 years and for looking ahead to new directions and leadership.

In October 1986, the U.S. Senate confirmed Kenneth Y. Tomlinson as the fourth chairman of NCLIS. He was sworn in for a five-year term by Secretary of Education William Bennett on November 18. A former director of the Voice of America, Tomlinson is executive editor of *Reader's Digest*. Vivian J. Arterbery, library director at the Rand Corporation and a former president of the Special Libraries Association, became the commission's new executive director in November 1986.

Most of the commission's work during 1986 focused on four major program areas: (1) improvement of library and information services to meet changing needs, (2) access to information, (3) information technology and productivity, and (4) policy planning and advice.

Improvement of Library/Information Services

The commission continued to initiate partnerships to benefit the elderly, the fastest growing population group in the United States, as part of its continuing interest in improving library and information services to older Americans. At its April 1986 meeting, NCLIS announced the signing of an agreement with ACTION, the principal federal agency for administering volunteer service programs. NCLIS and ACTION agreed to work cooperatively at the national level and through their respective networks to promote the improvement and better use of library and information services to older Americans through voluntary activities.

Under the agreement, the two agencies will work together in a variety of ways to

enhance the use of public libraries as community-based institutions that provide essential services to the elderly. The agreement will support and strengthen the efforts of professional librarians who are trying to promote volunteer opportunities for the elderly as well as better use of library/information services by elderly persons.

NCLIS signed a similar agreement in 1985 with the Administration on Aging, Department of Health and Human Services, which has resulted in improved cooperation between libraries and agencies that serve the aging at the state and local levels.

Access to Information

NCLIS has always emphasized the importance of library and information services in the learning process and the development of essential skills needed to find and use information effectively. Recently, the commission launched a new Information Skills Program that aims to (1) define what is meant by information skills, (2) identify questions and problems related to the development of these skills, and (3) examine the possibility of a recognition program for those doing an outstanding job in teaching these skills. During 1985 and 1986, NCLIS convened several informal meetings of school library media program experts, resulting in a concept paper written at the commission's request by Jacqueline Mancall, Shirley Aaron, and Sue Walker. Entitled "Educating Students to Think: The Role of the School Library Media Program," the paper was published with accompanying comments in the Fall 1986 issue of *School Library Media Quarterly*. The commission is working with government and private sector representatives to examine the most effective methods of disseminating the ideas in the concept paper.

Last year's *Bowker Annual* (pp. 89–112) reprinted the commission's 1985 study, "The Role of Fees in Supporting Library and Information Services in Public and Academic Libraries." In response to the NCLIS report, the American Library Association Office for Research developed plans for a survey that will document sources of nontax sources of income for public libraries, with special emphasis on services for which public libraries charge fees, the categories of persons to whom fees are charged, the amount of revenue received from fees, and the uses made of that revenue. The H. W. Wilson Foundation has provided a grant to fund the survey.

Information Technology and Productivity

In 1986, NCLIS cosponsored and participated in two of a series of trilateral meetings on the Role of Information in the Economy. These conferences convened decision makers from industry, academia, and government from the United States, the United Kingdom, and Canada in order to (1) identify and measure the contributions of information to the economy, (2) share information among leaders in the three countries, and (3) disseminate summary reports of useful information. The private sector provided support for the meetings, including electronic conferencing and publishing.

The first meeting, held May 26–28 near Boston, was a forum for current information and expert views on the relationship between the growth of the information sector and national economies as a whole. Presentations from representatives of the three countries provided a foundation for discussion of national differences as well as universal trends in the growth of the information sector since the publication of Machlup's pioneering work, "The Production and Distribution of Knowledge in the United States" in 1962.

The British Library hosted the second trilateral meeting, held October 31–November 2 in England, which focused on The Role of the Public Sector in the Information Infrastructure. This conference examined the role of government and libraries in the creation and distribution of information. The final meeting in the series is scheduled for spring 1987 in Canada. A report summarizing the three meetings and reprinting key papers will be published by the Institute for Research on Public Policy in Canada. NCLIS is sharing results of the meetings through print and other media to help ensure that the findings reach decision makers in all sectors.

Policy Planning and Advice

Throughout the year, NCLIS has been working to involve the nation's libraries as focal points in the celebration of the bicentennial of the U.S. Constitution. The NCLIS Committee on the Bicentennial of the Constitution submitted to the chairman of the Commission on the Bicentennial of the U.S. Constitution a list of proposed projects, including a nationally televised, interactive panel discussion on the Constitution, a nationwide recognition program for exemplary school library programs and collections on the bicentennial, and a program of civic bicentennial celebrations and public forums to be held in local libraries.

The commission continued to work with Congress, the White House Conference on Library and Information Services Taskforce (WHCLIST), and the entire library/information community to plan for a second White House Conference on Library and Information Services in 1989. On April 8, Representative Major Owens (D-N.Y.) held a hearing before the House Subcommittee on Postsecondary Education that included testimony on the plans for the conference. (Legislation for the conference was introduced in 1985 and had attracted more than 200 cosponsors in both houses of Congress by the end of 1986.)

In August, NCLIS hosted a luncheon meeting with representatives from approximately 15 national library/information organizations in order to share information on progress and plans toward the 1989 conference. Many associations have already established White House Conference committees, and others have passed resolutions in support of the conference. Several federal agencies that have appointed White House Conference liaisons were represented at the meeting. A meeting with the Federal Library and Information Center Committee in November brought federal librarians up to date on progress toward the conference and enlisted their support in the planning process.

After the U.S. withdrawal from UNESCO, the State Department asked NCLIS—which formerly served as the secretariat for the U.S. National Committee for the UNESCO General Information Program—to continue to advise on matters relating to international library, information, and archives programs. When funding became available under PLs 99-83 and 99-190 to maintain and support continued U.S. participation in certain international activities previously supported by UNESCO, NCLIS was asked to work with the library/information community to identify priority programs in the international information, library, and archives area that meet the State Department's criteria.

In July 1986, NCLIS received a total of $115,000 from the State Department for transfer to six approved projects. The recipients, amounts, and purposes of the grants follow.

1 Support for the operation of the International Federation for Documentation (FID) Clearinghouse on Education and Training at Syracuse University for one year ($20,000)

2 Support for an International Federation of Library Associations and Institutions (IFLA) seminar on Latin American regional cooperation and library association leadership ($25,000)

3 Support for U.S. participation in the 1986 FID Conference and Congress, including seminar activity ($10,000)

4 Support for enhanced U.S. participation, via the National Information Standards Organization, in international information standards-setting bodies and for education and training in this area in the United States ($35,000)

5 Support for a U.S. training program for foreign conservationists under the auspices of the U.S. National Archives and Records Administration and the International Council on Archives ($20,000)

6 Travel support for a U.S. observer delegation to the 1986 UNESCO General Information Program Intergovernmental Council Meeting ($5,000)

The projects were completed or underway by the end of 1986, and progress reports will be received in 1987.

NCLIS will continue to work with the State Department to channel any available funding into appropriate international library/information programs.

National Technical Information Service

U.S. Department of Commerce, 5285 Port Royal Rd.,
Springfield, VA 22161

Ruth S. Smith

Director, Office of Customer Services

The National Technical Information Service (NTIS) is a self-supporting agency of the Department of Commerce. Its mission, as established by PL 81-776, is ". . . to search for, collect, classify, coordinate, integrate, record and catalog such information from whatever sources, foreign and domestic, that may be available . . . to make such information available to industry and business, to State and local Governments, to other agencies of the Federal Government, and to the general public. . . ." Under the provisions of Title 15, United States Code 1151-1157, NTIS is required to recover all costs through the sale of its large archive of information products and services.

NTIS has a number of cooperative arrangements with private industry and with government organizations, both foreign and domestic, to ensure continued growth and expansion of its collection. Each year NTIS adds some 70,000 titles to its collection, which includes technical reports; federally developed data files, software programs, and inventions; and foreign technology. Materials in the collection are made permanently available to the public to encourage U.S. innovation and productivity. (See 1983 edition of *The Bowker Annual*, pp. 93–94, for background information on NTIS and its predecessor organizations.)

Relations with the Private Sector

Privatization of NTIS and cooperation with private organizations are recent issues that reflect government policy as put forth in Office of Management and Budget (OMB) Circulars A-76 and A-130. The message is: Do not compete with the private sector; use the private sector to the maximum degree possible in achieving the agency's mission.

Privatization Study

In response to a request from OMB for a study and a plan on how to privatize NTIS, the secretary of commerce formed a Privatization Study Group, made up of representatives from various units of the Department of Commerce, reflecting legal, congressional, management, and other points of view.

A notice was published in the April 28, 1986, *Federal Register* requesting interested parties to submit comments about privatization issues of concern to them. Some 138 responses were received—primarily from the user community (information professionals and library associations in particular), from industry representatives, from government sources that use NTIS to distribute documents, and from members of Congress. A majority of respondents favored maintaining NTIS in its present form. One concern of respondents was that federal agencies and foreign sources are under no obligation to submit material to NTIS. (This is accomplished through interagency, intergovernmental, and other cooperative agreements.)

The study group gathered additional comments at an open workshop meeting held at the Department of Commerce on July 30, 1986. More than 100 people attended—50 percent were users (from all parts of the country), 20 percent represented government interests, and 30 percent were industry representatives. The final report was prepared in October 1986. OMB's final recommendation concerning this issue is expected to be implemented in FY 1988.

Partnership Arrangements

Partnership arrangements within government and with private organizations, both profit and nonprofit, will continue to be encouraged. Among the partnership arrangements NTIS presently has with U.S. government agencies and foreign sources are the following:

- NTIS has cooperative agreements with more than 85 foreign government sources for the acquisition of foreign technology reports for the NTIS collection.
- NTIS has interagency agreements with more than 400 agencies for the collection, dissemination, and archiving of information and provides these agencies with feedback for publication control.
- NTIS serves as the collection agency for fees paid to the National Library of Medicine (for MEDLARS online use and for interlibrary loan), to the National Agricultural Library (for interlibrary loan), and to the Defense Technical Information Center (for reports and other services provided by DTIC to the Defense community).
- The NTIS Bibliographic Database, which lists all titles added to the collection since mid-1964, is made available for online searching through lease agreements with services such as BRS Information Technologies, DIALOG Information

Services, Mead Data Central, System Development Corporation, and several overseas vendors.

- Published searches are computer searches of the literature covered in 20 databases of organizations participating in this program. These include American Petroleum Institute (API), Engineering Information, Inc. (EI), Information Services of the Physics and Engineering Communities (INSPEC), World Textile Abstracts (WTA), and others. The searches themselves are performed under contract to NTIS by NERAC, Inc.

- Three large public libraries signed three-year agreements with NTIS to particpate in a library ordering program. These libraries are now handling orders for NTIS documents as an extension of the services they offer to patrons. More libraries will be added to the program as interest is shown and mutual agreements can be arranged.

Products and Services

In 1986, the NTIS collection exceeded 1.7 million titles, all of which are permanently available for sale. During the year, NTIS supplied its customers with more than 4 million documents and microforms, generating more than $22 million in revenue.

Data Files and Software

More than 2,500 federally generated databases, data files, and computer programs are now in the NTIS inventory. During FY 1986, a total of 624 federally generated databases and computer programs were added to the NTIS sales inventory, a 280 percent increase over the FY 1985 effort. A major acquisition consisted of some 400 computer programs from the Department of Energy's National Energy Software Center. By acquiring the Federal Reserve Board's Call/Income tapes, NTIS has expanded the growing area of economic and statistical databases.

The number of data files and computer programs available for distribution on diskettes for microcomputers increased from 31 in FY 1985 to 73 in FY 1986. A major acquisition was the National Library of Medicine's "Grateful Med" microcomputer software. More than 3,000 copies of this bestselling software were sold in FY 1986. Other new floppy disks contain data from the Office of Management and Budget, Bureau of Mines, and the National Oceanic and Atmospheric Administration.

In 1986, the NTIS Center for the Utilization of Federal Technology (CUFT) developed the new Federal Applied Technology Database and made it available to the online search services for public access. This database provides electronic access to information about some of the best U.S. government technologies and resources.

Publications

Directories developed in 1986 and published by CUFT in paper form include the following:

- *The Directory of Federal and State Business Assistance, a Guide for New and Growing Companies* (PB86-100344) lists more than 180 federal and 400 state programs. Every contact listed offers assistance for day-to-day business needs of new and growing companies.

- *The Directory of Federal Laboratory and Technology Resources, a Guide to Services, Facilities, and Expertise* (PB86-100013) provides information on hundreds of federal agencies, laboratories, and engineering centers willing to share their expertise, equipment, facilities, and special services to aid research and engineering efforts.

Revised Subject Classification

NTIS revised the subject classification schemes used in its basic announcement products, including the NTIS Bibliographic Database. Previously two schemes were used: the 22 COSATI subject categories and the 39 more detailed NTIS subject categories. Beginning in January 1987, all COSATI categories were absorbed into the NTIS subject category scheme. The change was designed to achieve continuity among all the announcement products by using a single subject classification scheme better suited for the input NTIS receives and geared toward easy information retrieval for the average user.

Patent Licensing

NTIS handles the licensing of federally owned inventions. In FY 1986, more than 100 patent applications were received from NTIS-source federal agencies and publicized for licensing. A total of 51 new licenses were granted to companies in the private sector, 33 of which were small businesses. In FY 1985, 147 government employee/inventors shared in $69,000 of inventor awards and such awards are expected to grow to $300,000 based on FY 1986 revenues. NTIS filed 166 foreign patent cases on 16 U.S. inventions to continue protection of U.S. export sales, now at the $60 million level.

New Directions

Foreign Technology

Expansion of the NTIS collection of foreign technology will accelerate, to make U.S. industry more competitive in the world marketplace. Also, a translation program will be considered to make more accessible foreign reports now received by NTIS in languages other than English.

Electronic Dissemination

With the amount of government information assembled in electronic format steadily increasing, NTIS will attempt to meet the demand for information in this format. The role of NTIS in electronic dissemination will be enhanced, making available many more federal agency data files.

Partnerships

An increase in the number of partnership arrangements with the private sector will be encouraged, to make a rich variety of sources accessible for the benefit of government, the nation's research and development efforts, and U.S. business and industry. The aim is to do the best job possible in fulfilling the NTIS mission to collect, organize, announce, and make available to the public the unclassified results of government-sponsored research and development.

National Archives and Records Administration

Washington, DC 20408
202-523-3000

James Gregory Bradsher

Archivist, Office of Management and Administration

On April 1, 1985, the National Archives and Records Service, a constituent part of the General Services Administration, became an independent agency in the executive branch of the federal government and was renamed the National Archives and Records Administration. This change, which was a return to the status enjoyed by the National Archives from 1934 to 1949, had long been advocated by many users of the archives and by professional organizations associated with the archives.

Independence did not change the legal responsibility of the National Archives and Records Administration to identify, preserve, and make available to the federal government and to the people of the United States all forms of government records not restricted by law that have been determined to have sufficient historical, informational, or evidential value to warrant their continued preservation. All executive branch agencies of the U.S. government are obliged by law to cooperate with the archives and to transfer all historically valuable federal records more than 30 years old to the archives, if the records are not needed for continuing agency business. In 1978, presidential records, formerly considered the private property of the president who created them, were declared government property and subject to the archives' authority. The lower federal courts are included under the archives' jurisdiction. Although the Supreme Court and both houses of Congress are not, they elect to deposit their official noncurrent records in the National Archives, and they also set the specific access regulations for these records. The archives inspects agency records, establishes standards for records retention, and provides guidance and assistance to the agencies with respect to adequate and proper documentation of the policies and transactions of the government.

The National Archives, 1935–Present

When the United States established a National Archives in 1935, it was the last major nation to do so. The act of establishment also created the National Historical Publications Commission (renamed the National Historical Publications and Records Commission in 1975), a quasi-independent body headed by the Archivist of the United States and directed to promote the publication of original source material and to aid nonfederal records projects. The Federal Register was created as an office of the archives in 1935. This office provides official notice to the public through various publications of federal laws and administrative regulations, communicates the president's policies by the publication of his official documents and papers, and provides indexes and other finding aids to ensure ready access to all its publications. It also publishes annually *The United States Government Manual*, which provides comprehensive information on the agencies of the legislative, judicial, and executive branches, and includes information on quasi-official agencies, international organizations in which the United States participates, and boards, committees, and commissions. With the creation of the Franklin D. Roosevelt Library in 1939, the presidential libraries system was begun. (See the 1983

edition of *Bowker Annual of Library & Book Trade Information*, pp. 120–123, for a separate report on the presidential libraries.)

The Federal Property and Administrative Services Act of 1949 transferred the National Archives to the newly created General Services Administration and changed the name to the National Archives and Records Service, to reflect the agency's dual responsibilities for records and archives. These responsibilities were clarified and expanded in the Federal Records Act of 1950. It was in that year that the National Archives began establishing a series of records centers across the country to hold semiactive records, not needed for the daily business of the government but often required by law to be retained for a fixed period of time, in low-cost storage pending final disposition. During the late 1960s, when the storage capacity of the National Archives building was reached, a network of regional archives was created. These depositories, usually located in the same building as regional records centers, hold both microfilm and original records of particular significance to the geographic area where they are located. On April 1, 1985, the National Archives became an independent agency, the National Archives and Records Administration.

The National Archives System

The National Archives occupies a massive classic structure on a site bounded by Pennsylvania and Constitution Avenues and Seventh and Ninth Streets, Northwest, exactly halfway between the White House and the Capitol in Washington, D.C. Designed by John Russell Pope, the building contains 21 levels of stack areas for records, which are controlled for temperature and humidity and equipped with smoke detection devices, sprinkler systems, and, in a select area, a halon gas system to protect against fire. In addition to miles of stacks, the building contains research rooms, office space, laboratory space, a theater, exhibit areas, and the 75-foot-high rotunda in which the Declaration of Independence, the Constitution, and the Bill of Rights are on permanent display. As part of the nation's bicentennial celebration of the signing of the Constitution, two major exhibits are scheduled for the rotunda and circular gallery exhibit areas: "The American Experiment: Creating the Constitution" (October 1986–February 1989) and "The American Experiment: Living with the Constitution" (April 1987–September 1988).

Five other Washington and suburban locations hold various administrative offices; government cartographic and architectural records and the Richard Nixon presidential materials; and the National Audiovisual Center, which rents and sells to the public, on behalf of other federal agencies, their motion pictures, slides, and tapes.

The National Archives also operates 23 other locations around the country. Two major national centers are the Washington National Records Center in Suitland, Maryland, and the National Personnel Records Center in St. Louis. Other National Archives centers are located in or near Boston, New York City, Philadelphia, Atlanta, Chicago, Dayton, Kansas City, Fort Worth, Denver, San Francisco, Los Angeles, and Seattle. Located within each of the centers is an archives branch (except for Dayton, which has none, and Philadelphia, where the archives branch is in a separate downtown location), and a federal records center. The nine other National Archives buildings are presidential libraries or museums: the Herbert Hoover Library in West Branch (Iowa), the Franklin D. Roosevelt Library in Hyde Park (New York), the Harry S. Truman Library in Independence (Missouri), the Dwight D. Eisenhower Library in Abilene (Kansas), the John

F. Kennedy Library in Columbia Point (Massachusetts), the Lyndon B. Johnson Library in Austin (Texas), the Gerald R. Ford Library in Ann Arbor (Michigan), the Ford Museum in Grand Rapids (Michigan), and the Jimmy Carter Library in Atlanta (Georgia).

The Archivist of the United States, who is appointed by the president with the advice and consent of the Senate, is assisted by a deputy and seven assistant archivists, each having specific program or support function responsibilities. The major organizational elements are Management and Administration, the National Archives, Federal Register, Federal Records Centers, Presidential Libraries, Records Administration, and Public Programs. The executive director of the National Historical Publications and Records Commission is on the level of an assistant archivist. Special staffs reporting to the Archivist are Archival Research and Evaluation, Audits and Compliance, Congressional Relations, Pubic Affairs, and Legal Services.

The staff of the National Archives—approximately 2,000 full-time equivalents (FTEs)—is about equally divided between Washington and the rest of the country. For 1987, the agency's budget is $100.3 million, about 40 percent of which is spent on space, utilities, phones, postage, and the like; most of the remainder is expended on preservation activities and staff salaries.

An annual accounting of the activities and finances of the National Archives and Records Administration (including the National Historical Publications and Records Commission) can be found in the *Annual Report of the National Archives*, which is available from the Public Affairs Office.

Holdings of the Archives

The holdings of the National Archives are of two types: those in federal records centers awaiting to be destroyed or transferred to the National Archives and those that have been determined to have enduring value. Holdings of the first type, more than 14.6 million cubic feet of records, are in the physical custody of the National Archives, but remain under the legal control of the agency of origin. Most of these records are from the Department of Defense, the Department of the Treasury (Internal Revenue Service), the Department of Health and Human Services (Social Security Administration), and the Veterans Administration. Records of the second type, those of enduring value, are both records of the federal government and donated materials from private sources. The latter materials (except for donated film) are mostly in the presidential libraries; all presidential materials made or received before 1981 are considered private property.

The current estimate of the holdings in the archives is almost 1.5 million cubic feet of records, including 3 billion paper documents, 91 million feet of motion pictures, 5 million still photographs, 1.6 million maps, 151,000 video and sound recordings, 9.7 million aerial photographs, and 3,600 reels of computer tape. The records date from 1774 papers of the Continental Congress to the recent past. The presidential libraries estimate their holdings at 200.8 million pages of papers, 13.3 million feet of motion pictures, 3.4 million photographs, 29,192 hours of sound recordings, 14,007 hours of videotapes, 197,115 museum objects, and 180,218 pages of oral history interviews.

The National Archives building and the presidential libraries also have book collections designed to assist researchers working with archival sources. Of particular interest to librarians is the record set of the publications of the federal government, consisting of 1.8 million items the core of which was formerly the library of the Government Printing

Office's Public Documents Division. This is the most comprehensive set of federal publications in existence — dating from 1790 to 1979 — but it is not complete, especially for the years before 1895. The main collection, transferred from the GPO in 1972, is added to periodically.

Using the Archives

Researchers desiring to consult records in the main archives building are issued a research card, which must be shown when entering the Central Research Room. Those wishing to use only microfilm sign in at the Microfilm Reading Room. Consultants are available to assist researchers, and there are also guides, lists, inventories, indexes, and other finding aids, such as the *The Guide to the National Archives of the United States* (1974), which is currently being revised, and the *Catalog of National Archives Microfilm Publications*, which is updated annually. Copies of documents or microfilm can be obtained at modest prices, and printed facsimiles of many historical documents are available for purchase.

Microfilm of materials of interest primarily to genealogists is available for interlibrary loan through a commercial firm for a modest charge.

The National Archives building is open for research Monday through Friday from 8:45 A.M. to 10:00 P.M. and on Saturdays from 8:45 A.M. to 5:00 P.M.; it is closed Sunday and on every federal holiday. Researchers are also welcome in the archives branches outside Washington and at the presidential libraries, all of which issue their own lists of holdings and maintain their own research rooms. Hours of the archives branches and the presidential libraries vary; researchers should check to determine the exact times. Up-to-date information on accessions and openings of records in all parts of the National Archives and Records Administration can be obtained by consulting the lists published in the quarterly *Prologue: Journal of the National Archives*.

United States Information Agency Library and Book Programs

Library Programs Division/Book Programs Division
301 Fourth St. S.W., Washington, DC 20547

Richard Fitz

Chief, Library Programs Division

In the aftermath of World War II, the United States established a network of overseas libraries to provide information about American interests and policies to citizens of other countries and to improve understanding of American actions, attitudes, and values. Today, after four decades of profound and often tumultuous change in international affairs and within the United States itself, this network continues to operate in more than 120 countries under the stewardship of the United States Information Agency (USIA), known abroad as the United States Information Service (USIS).

Library Programs

Although the basic purposes of USIA library programs have remained constant, the services provided have changed to reflect new patron interests and needs, the development of indigenous library collections and services in host countries, new communications and information-processing technologies, advances in library science itself, and — of course — the vicissitudes of the USIA budget.

Organization

USIA now operates 146 special libraries in 88 countries and a headquarters library in Washington, D.C. Overseas, the USIS libraries are staffed by more than 480 foreign service national (FSN) employees and supported by 21 regional and country librarians, American foreign service specialists who assist in designing and administering USIS library programs that are uniquely adapted to local conditions. In addition, USIA supports library collections in 90 binational cultural centers and other foreign institutions, including major universities and research institutes.

USIS Library Programs Abroad

USIA library services and holdings vary significantly from country to country, depending on the objectives of the USIS post (the public affairs office of the American embassy) and the needs of the patrons served. As greater emphasis is placed on outreach and reference/research services for foreign opinion leaders, USIS librarians function increasingly as subject specialists with direct access to the wealth of information sources in the United States. In recent years, more than 40 USIS libraries in Europe, Latin America, Asia, and Africa have begun accessing online database services (principally DIALOG, NEXIS, and Legislate), using international value-added networks for this purpose, as well as dedicated lines provided by the Department of State.

At the same time, USIS libraries are giving increased attention in their circulating collections to long-term objectives, including improved understanding of American intellectual and cultural history, American economic and social institutions, and American political traditions. The reading interests of foreign university and secondary school students are of particular interest to USIS libraries in this regard.

With collections ranging in size from several hundred to more than 30,000 volumes, USIS libraries seek to provide a balanced cross section of outstanding American contributions in the social sciences and humanities, often in cities where such access is extremely limited or virtually nonexistent. More than 4 million patrons visited these libraries in 1986, and nearly 1.75 million items were circulated.

Washington Support

USIS posts overseas rely heavily on the 45 librarians and technicians of the USIA Library Programs Division in Washington, D.C. The division's bibliographics staff publishes a variety of selection tools to support overseas collection development and outreach services and to facilitate acquisition of new materials. A central acquisitions staff oversees the complex process of purchasing and delivering books, periodicals, and documents to libraries in every part of the world. The Library Programs Division pro-

vides professional cataloging for USIS library materials on request and is developing a worldwide union list of periodical holdings in USIS libraries. Washington-based services include rapid delivery of significant U.S. documents and think-tank reports and a weekly alert service to articles from current American periodicals. The division's interlibrary loan and document delivery services are routinely available to all USIS libraries, as needed.

Given their distance from the United States and the limited size of their library collections, USIS posts often turn for assistance to the reference staff of the Library Programs Division in Washington, D.C., especially with difficult or esoteric requests. The Reference Branch now handles about 150 overseas reference requests per month, transmitted by mail, telegram, telefacsimile, electronic mail, and telephone. As the source of last resort, the headquarters reference staff provides everything from simple address information to comprehensive packages of materials on major issues of public policy.

DIALOG, NEXIS, VuText, Legislate, Wilsonline, and other online database systems have become essential tools for coping with the high volume and tight deadlines of reference requests from USIS posts overseas and USIA program offices in Washington, D.C., including the Voice of America. Equally important, USIA posts and program offices can draw on a headquarters collection of 65,000 books, more than 800 journals, and several special collections, as well as the collections of other federal, state, and private sector libraries via interlibrary loan.

Public Diplomacy Query (PDQ) System/Overseas Automation

In addition to its more traditional services, the Library Programs Division indexes most program and foreign policy materials acquired by USIA for overseas distribution. The index is available online to USIS posts and Washington program offices on a USIA computer using Battelle Labs's BASIS information storage and retrieval software. The division plans to add full text of program materials and relevant policy statements from USIA and other U.S. government agencies beginning in 1987.

USIA is also testing microcomputer library software in USIS libraries overseas. A growing number of USIS libraries use WANG and IBM personal computers for online database searching, electronic mail, word processing, and spreadsheet applications. In 1987, microcomputer-based acquisitions systems will be evaluated and acquired for five test sites around the world.

Book Programs

Both the library and the book programs of USIA are designed to help foreign audiences get useful information about the United States in a timely and effective way. The USIA Book Programs Division supports the publication of American books abroad in English and in translation, as well as the export of American books that contribute to a better understanding of the United States. The division works closely with foreign publishers to encourage translations and reprints of important American titles abroad. It works with the American publishing industry in a variety of ways to expand the awareness and availability of American books overseas, including book fairs, circulating book exhibits, and donation of American books to foreign institutions.

Book Translations and Reprints

Translations and reprints of American titles have always been at the heart of USIA overseas book programs. The Book Programs Division works with foreign publishers to produce more than half a million copies annually of full-length U.S. trade books, textbooks, condensations, and serializations in English and in foreign languages. Titles are chosen to reflect a broad range of American thought in subjects of importance to long-term U.S. interests.

To support translations into major world languages, the Book Programs Division operates several regional book offices overseas, including Mexico City, Barcelona, Buenos Aires, and Cairo. French translations are the responsibility of an African Regional Services office in Paris. USIS posts cooperate with USIA book officers in Washington to handle translations and English reprints in other major countries, such as China, India, and Brazil.

Book Promotion

USIA conducts programs to promote the sale and distribution of American books overseas in close cooperation with the book-export efforts of the American publishing industry. Participation in foreign book fairs is given a high priority in this regard. In 1986, USIA sponsored and organized book exhibits at more than 20 book fairs, including the Frankfurt International Book Fair.

Circulating book exhibits provide further opportunities to acquaint foreign publishers, booksellers, and readers with American books. Up to a half dozen exhibits in multiple sets are produced each year for circulation worldwide. Each exhibit is organized around a theme, such as American literary prize winners, health and sports, English-language teaching, and children's literature. The exhibits travel to as many as 150 USIS posts overseas, where they are displayed at book fairs, professional meetings, scholarly seminars, cultural events, and academic institutions.

Donated Books

American publishers often donate books with small sales potential to nonprofit organizations. Many of these books have great value overseas, particularly in less developed and developing countries where commercial distribution of American books is difficult or impossible. USIA works with private sector organizations to get hundreds of thousands of these books into the hands of those who can benefit from them overseas.

Copyright

USIA has a special interest in encouraging respect for international copyright conventions by all nations. The Book Programs Division works closely on this issue with the U.S. Copyright Office, the Center for the Book at the Library of Congress, and the International Copyright Information Center (INCINC) in Washington, D.C. The division channels copyright questions about American books to INCINC or directly to the copyright holders.

Informational Assistance

American publishers should direct inquiries about export problems, rights, book exhibits, and participation in other USIA book activities to the Book Programs Division, Bureau of Educational and Cultural Affairs, USIA, Washington, DC 20547. Non-U.S. publishers should turn for assistance to the Cultural Affairs Office of the American embassy in their country, a nearby Regional Book Office, or directly to the Book Programs Division in Washington, D.C.

Federal Library and Information Center Committee

James P. Riley

Executive Director

Library of Congress, Adams Bldg., Rm. 1026B
Washington, DC 20540
202-287-6055

The Federal Library and Information Center Committee (FLICC) is an interagency committee serving federal library and information centers worldwide. Whereas the formal committee focuses on pilot projects and educational and policy issues, its operational unit, FEDLINK, administers information services contracts on behalf of member libraries and other federal participants. Additionally, the membership funds the operation of the FLICC/FEDLINK Microcomputer Demonstration Center.

The Federal Library and Information Center Committee marked its twenty-first year of operation in FY 1986 with sustained growth and plans for reshaping the committee to meet the challenges of the Information Age and the twenty-first century. During FY 1986, FEDLINK grew to become the largest library network in the nation in terms of both membership/participants (1,001) and dollars of service (approximately $40.5 million), retaining its status as the only library network operating nationwide. During 1986, FEDLINK also doubled, from 26 to 52, the services it makes available to the federal sector at discount prices.

As the successful fiscal year closed, FLICC had already begun planning to set long-term goals to better serve the federal information community in the face of the burgeoning information technology and growing budgetary constraints. A FLICC task force, chaired by FLICC Chairman Designate Ruth Ann Stewart, was formed to review the recommendations in the recently completed *The Federal Library and Information Center Committee: A Planning Study*. The task force is to come up with recommendations to help shape future FLICC policy regarding its role in the national information scene, as well as the size of its membership and the nature and extent of its services. Task force findings will be submitted to the FLICC membership in FY 1987 for review and further action.

The *Planning Study*, a 52-page report on FLICC's current status and future role, was prepared by Joseph Donohue, a contract consultant and a former professor at the College of Library and Information Science of the University of South Carolina. The seven-part study was compiled after an in-depth review of the FLICC office files for the

period 1965-1985—the first two decades of FLICC operation—and 55 interview meetings covering 83 respondents. Major concerns identified by the study are professional standards, A-76, Performance of Commercial Activities, economic factors, and physical threats to library and information facilities and services. The study identifies as future challenges the Information Society, Information Resource Management, privatism, and national service.

FLICC Subcommittee Activities

At bimonthly FLICC Executive Advisory Committee (EAC) meetings and quarterly membership meetings FLICC policies are formulated in broad, general terms. The various FLICC subcommittees and ad hoc groups implement these policies.

FEDLINK, first among equals of the various subcommittees, is headed by an Executive Advisory Council (EAC). The chairman of the FEDLINK EAC serves as liaison with the FLICC Executive Advisory Committee. Other subcommittees include Binding, Collection Development, Education, On-Line Serials Control, Personnel, and Program Development. Recently organized subcommittees will oversee the updating of the *Procurement of Library Materials in the Federal Government*, published by the Federal Library Committee (FLICC's original name) in 1968; and a FEDLINK Book Buying Program, a program for libraries to purchase monographs similar to the existing, very successful, program for the purchase of serial subscriptions.

The Education Subcommittee developed and helped implement a variety of general education programs in 1986. FLICC's third annual "Forum on Federal Information Policies" drew a crowd of 200 federal library and information center managers to the Mumford Room of the Library of Congress on February 12. The focus of the meeting was implementation of recent policies on electronic collection, storage, and dissemination of government information and the Office of Management and Budget's Circular A-130 on Management of Federal Information Resources. Congressman George Brown, Jr., of California gave the keynote address, followed by a variety of information experts, including Robert Gellman, counsel, Subcommittee on Government Information, Justice, and Agriculture. For the first time, proceedings were videotaped for later viewing by FLICC members around the nation and abroad. A summary of proceedings, *FLICC Forum on Federal Information Policies: Their Implementation and Implications for Information Access*, was prepared for fall publication by the Library of Congress.

The Program Development Subcommittee, established to consider ways of improving and facilitating communications relating to library technology and automation in the federal sector, moved forward with a number of projects during FY 1986. Among them were CD-ROM and Expert Systems developmental projects assigned to the Microcomputer Demonstration Center for implementation and an IDEA/LIST project (Investigation, Development, Early Application of Library and Information Systems Technology), a proposed inventory of projects for research, development, or early application of advanced information technologies carried on by, in, or with the support of the federal government.

Other Library Issues

OCLC Europe

An agreement was signed on behalf of FLICC and its FEDLINK members with OCLC Europe to provide OCLC services to federal libraries and information centers. The first services of OCLC Europe to be implemented will be cataloging and interlibrary loan at

the headquarters of the U.S. Army, Europe (USAREUR) in Heidelberg, West Germany. The 107 libraries that USAREUR services should benefit significantly from this agreement. Other federal libraries and information centers in Europe are expected to make use of the agreement.

CENDI Projects

On behalf of FLICC, the Library of Congress engaged consultant Madeline Henderson to conduct a study of a common data element dictionary for technical reports and guidelines for descriptive cataloging of such reports. In 1986, FLICC's executive director met with the director of the National Technical Information Service, representing the CENDI group (composed of the Departments of Commerce, Energy, Defense, and NASA), and Madeline Henderson to review the final report relating to the study. With FLICC's approval, Henderson has prepared an extensive discussion of the project for publication in *Government Publications Review*. As a result of the study, the NTIS file of standard corporate names and accompanying codes has become the authority file for the CENDI group, and the same decision was made for use of the NTIS file of Standard Technical Report Numbers. Such resource sharing agreements are expected to improve productivity and be cost beneficial to the CENDI group.

Personnel Study

In response to a request from librarians in the Washington, D.C., area, FLICC engaged consultant Raymond Crosby to examine the causes of inconsistencies in grade-level treatment of Librarians (GS-1410) and Technical Information Service (GS-1412) series. The study will survey several library/information centers. FLICC also contracted Crosby to review the Office of Personnel Management's "Tentative Standards for Executive, Managerial, and Supervisory Grade Evaluation Guide." On the basis of that review, FLICC submitted its comments on the guide to OPM on August 29, 1986.

Publications

A desktop publishing unit was added to the FLICC Office in FY 1986 in order to centralize and expedite issuances from the office to the federal library and information center community. FLICC is moving toward quarterly issuance of the *FLICC Newsletter* and bimonthly issuance of the *FEDLINK Technical Notes*.

Federal Library and Information Network (FEDLINK)

The FEDLINK program offers any federal agency, primarily through its library or information center, the opportunity to enhance the information resources available to meet the requirements of its personnel. Through FLICC/FEDLINK, federal agencies have cost-effective access to a number of automated services for online research databases, as well as online cataloging and interlibrary loan, and automated acquisitions and serials control. Other services include serials subscription services and CD-ROM products.

During FY 1986, FEDLINK participation grew to 1,001 agency libraries, information centers, and offices cooperating in the use of 52 contractual services that resulted in

2,164 interagency agreements for approximately $40.5 million of service. Of the 2,164 agreements, 1,615 were renewals and 549 were new. The large number of new agreements was the result of FEDLINK's expanded program of services, especially serials subscription services and the ITI Technical Logistics Reference Network. These figures represent increases of approximately 33 percent in the number of interagency agreements for all FEDLINK services.

Online Information Retrieval Services

The growth in the use of online retrieval services, as depicted by interagency agreements, was also 33 percent in FY 1986. Well over half of the interagency agreements in 1986 involved services from DIALOG, BRS, and LEXIS/NEXIS.

Online Library Services

Use of the online products and services contract with OCLC continued to expand in FY 1986. The number of federal libraries increased from 497 in FY 1985 to 567 in FY 1986. In addition to using the cataloging subsystem, federal libraries made increased use of the interlibrary loan subsystem, borrowing approximately 45,000 items in the second quarter of FY 1986. Also, SC350, OCLC's microcomputer-based serials control system, was purchased by 17 federal libraries, as interest in microcomputer technology continues to increase. The ordering of 171 M300 work stations and 179 microenhancers during FY 1986 confirms this trend.

The FEDLINK staff provided 85 OCLC training sessions in 1986. For FY 1987, FEDLINK has revised its course offerings and created a new descriptive catalog that includes not only the OCLC classes but also the courses from the Microcomputer Center and a list of forums, workshops, and seminars from the Federal Library and Information Center Committee.

Shared Retrieval Services

To support shared retrieval services, vendor contracts were continued or expanded with BRS Information Technologies, CompuServe, DIALOG Information Service, Information General Corporation, Mead Data Central, System Development Corporation, and the West Publishing Company.

Tape Processing

Three tape processing contracts with Blackwell North America, Informatics General Corporation, and Library Systems and Services, Inc., were awarded in FY 1986. Twenty agencies used the contracts for the processing of FLICC/FEDLINK OCLC and in-house tapes to produce various products and to be utilized as input for local online systems.

Retrospective Data Conversion

FY 1986 contracts were awarded to Biospherics, OCLC, and SOLINET for the purpose of converting existing catalog records into a machine-readable bibliographic file.

Optical Disc/CD-ROM Mastering

To enable members to create optical disc/CD-ROM masters, FEDLINK contracted with the Digital Equipment Corporation and Image Conversion Technologies.

A unique meeting of FEDLINK vendors was organized by the FEDLINK fiscal section on September 16 to introduce them to the new FY 1987 services package. The approximately 100 vendor representatives who attended obtained instructions and information on the fiscal procedures of FEDLINK and the Library of Congress.

Microcomputer Demonstration Center

The FLICC/FEDLINK Microcomputer Demonstration Center completed its third year of operation, providing specialized microcomputer troubleshooting, consultation, and technical support to a federal library and information center community that is learning to use over 400 modified OCLC/IBM microcomputers and at least as many equivalent IBM compatibles.

The Library of Congress

Washington, DC 20540
202-287-5000

Evelyn W. McCleaf

Information Office

Budget cuts under the Balanced Budget and Emergency Deficit Control Act of 1985 (PL 99-177), commonly referred to as the Gramm-Rudman-Hollings Act, were a dominant concern at the Library of Congress in 1986. Appropriations for FY 1986 were reduced by 4.3 percent as a result of the presidential sequestration order that went into effect in March, mandated by the Gramm-Rudman-Hollings Act. This was a cut of $9.8 million from the amount appropriated to the library in the Legislation Branch Appropriations Act for FY 1986, which was already $8.5 million less than the amount appropriated the previous year. These reductions affected all areas of the library: Reduced hours of service in the reading rooms, beginning in early March, were the occasion for articles in the press and objection and protest by some library users. The National Referral Center, originally established in the 1960s, was abolished. Budgetary constraints caused a reduction-in-force (RIF) and a paucity of vacancies. In February, the library notified 70 staff members that their jobs were being abolished due to the need to reduce operating costs. Eventually, because of the displacement rights of these employees, an additional 54 staff members were affected. The Personnel Operations Office processed only 331 appointments this year, as compared to 824 last year. Because of the budgetary situation, it was also necessary to suspend the library's Intern Program for outside applicants from library schools.

A highlight of 1986 was the appointment of Robert Penn Warren as the first Poet Laureate/Consultant in Poetry. Appointed to the library staff in 1986 was Ruth Ann Stewart as assistant librarian for National Programs.

During 1986 the library's Cataloging Distribution Service (CDS) reorganized, from

six sections into four: Customer Services, Computer Applications, Fiscal, and Distribution sections.

Cultural activities of particular note at the library included appearances by Garrison Keillor, William Golding, and Consultant in Poetry Gwendolyn Brooks. Among other cultural activities were exhibits such as *Riders on the Earth Together: Expressions of Faith in the Middle East and Asia*, some 130 objects demonstrating varied expressions of religious faith in Asia and the Middle East; *Books in the Grand Tradition*, 68 of the library's large-format books spanning the fifteenth to twentieth centuries; and *A Nation of Readers: An Exhibition Celebrating Reading in America*, a compilation of 41 prizewinning photographs.

Despite the trend of fewer acquisitions because of budgetary restraints, significant gifts were made during 1986. One was the donation by the National Broadcasting Company (NBC) of its entire collection of some 20,000 early television programs.

Staff, Budget, and Services

In FY 1986, the Library of Congress employed a staff of 4,802. It operated on a budget of $210,522,000 from Congress in direct appropriations (including $867,000 from the Urgent Supplemental Appropriations Bill, which restored some of the funds cut under Gramm-Rudman-Hollings), $10,614,000 in fees from its Cataloging Distribution Service and the Copyright Office, and $7,419,980 in obligations from gift and trust funds.

The library's collections totaled 84,694,819 items—including 14,045,520 books in the classified collections; 8,502,541 nonclassified books, pamphlets, technical reports, and other printed materials; 3,727,270 musical works; 1,149,065 recorded discs, tapes, and audio materials in other formats; 36,175,568 manuscripts; 3,862,328 maps; 6,653,286 microfiche, microfilms, and micro-opaques; and 10,637,251 motion pictures, photographs, posters, prints, drawings, videotapes, and other visual materials.

Library staff members welcomed some 2,309,303 users and visitors and answered 1,165,458 inquiries in person, 524,859 by telephone, and 147,165 by mail. The library conducted 2,752 tours for 63,408 visitors. The staff also completed 433,666 research assignments for Congress through the Congressional Research Service. The library aided scholars and researchers by circulating 3,176,956 volumes for use within the library, and made loans of 153,780 volumes outside the library.

Preservation

Budget reductions in 1986 seriously affected binding and rebinding, motion picture preservation, preservation microfilming, and phased conservation supplies. In addition, staff reductions affected the preparation of material for various preservation procedures.

Completion of a Mass Deacidification Facility, to be constructed at Ft. Detrick, Maryland, was delayed due to engineering problems experienced in the diethyl zinc (DEZ) deacidification test facility at Goddard Space Flight Center that led to two different incidents of fire, one in December and again in February. The library is proceeding with a contractor, Texas Alkyls, Inc., to undertake engineering studies and to redesign a pilot book deacidification facility. The pilot facility is to test and verify the design features of the chemical delivery system for a large-scale facility.

In April, the Preservation Office was represented at an international conference in Vienna, Austria, which considered the subject of the preservation of library materials, sponsored by the Conference of Directors of National Libraries in cooperation with the International Federation of Library Associations and Institutions (IFLA) and UNESCO.

National Library Service for the Blind and Physically Handicapped

For the first time jointly sponsored by the National Library Service for the Blind and Physically Handicapped and the National Library of Canada, the 1986 Conference of Librarians Serving the Blind and Physically Handicapped Individuals was held in Cincinnati, Ohio, in July, centered around the theme "Quality Effort – Quality Service."

Two national mini conferences were held. A national automation conference included updates on two new automation systems, NLSNET and READS, discussions of automation planning, user-group meetings, and a discussion of computer aids and appliances for blind and physically handicapped users. A national children's services conference focused on the needs of children who use the national program and ways to improve services to children nationally.

The Ad-Hoc Publications Advisory Group met in May to develop a series of recommendations for improvements in NLS/BPH program publications, which include *Talking Book Topics, Braille Book Review*, program catalogs, and bibliographies.

The American Foundation for the Blind, New York City, was engaged to peform a pilot test to determine the feasibility of reusing excess cassettes. The pilot test, if successful, could allow NLS/BPH to produce *Talking Book Topics* on recycled cassettes. The reuse of materials may result in significant savings for the NLS/BPH program.

In further efforts to reduce costs of managing and implementing the NLS/BPH program, other program reductions included dropping *Braille Magazine of the Quarter*, eliminating a young adult recorded periodical, the closing of the MultiState Center for the South, placing ceilings on all magazine subscriptions nationally, reducing the fiscal year cassette book production program by 100 titles, eliminating the hand-transcribed volunteer braille-book program, and reformatting and consolidating production of network bulletins to the national network of cooperating libraries.

A Committee on Technology for the Blind and Physically Handicapped was established to address such topics as consumer access to the BLND database, a reference circular on computer applications and related topics, a demonstration/communications center at NLS/BPH, narration of computer books, and other equipment-related topics.

During 1985 an amendment to the appropriations bill for the legislative branch for FY 1986 stipulated a $103,000 cut in funds earmarked for the production of books in braille. This had been the exact amount sought to continue the publication of *Playboy* in braille. Librarian of Congress Daniel J. Boorstin issued a statement saying, "I feel profound regret at the action of the House of Representatives to reduce the appropriations of the Library of Congress as its way of censoring material made available to the blind community through our Library of Congress service. . . . Censorship has no place in a free society." Subsequently the U.S. Court for the District of Columbia found that the discontinuance of publication of *Playboy* in braille had been a violation of the First Amendment. The court then ordered the resumption of the production and distribution of *Playboy* in braille.

American Folklife Center

In 1986, the American Folklife Center featured many activities in a year-long observance of its tenth anniversary. Among them were a colloquy on folklife and university education; a symposium that focused on education from other vantage points, entitled "Folklife and Public Education"; and many cultural activities, including music, dance, and crafts.

The Federal Cylinder Project began its final phase—dissemination of tape copies of wax-cylinder recordings and related documentation to the American Indian tribes among which they were recorded, including information on resources for archiving the tapes and programs for utilizing them.

As a follow-up to two of the center's field projects in New Jersey and Utah, final reports were prepared for the Pinelands Folklife Project and the Grouse Creek Survey. The center has entered into a collaborative agreement with the Florida Department of State on the Florida Maritime Heritage Survey Project. The center has also entered into a cooperative agreement with state and local agencies for a new field project in Lowell, Massachusetts, that will explore the living neighborhood and ethnic cultures of that well-known mill town.

The two-sided videdisc *The Ninety-Six: A Ranch in Northern Nevada* and its accompanying 84-page booklet was issued. They describe a cattle ranch in Paradise Valley, a small community near Winnemucca, Nevada.

Folklife Annual, 1985, the first in a series, has proven successful and drawn wide praise.

The center was reauthorized by Congress for the next three fiscal years, beginning October 1, 1987.

Collections

As already reported, the number of items in the library's collections increased to 84,694,819 items in the fiscal year. In an effort to effect economies, acquisition policies were refined and purchases of publications of secondary importance were minimized while allowing for the continued receipt of research materials of vital interest.

The office also revised blanket order specifications, giving dealers less latitude in making selections for the library, and placing more responsibility on the recommending officers in supplementing the dealers' selections.

A massive serials review project continued throughout the year. Efforts were made to deselect all but a few representative samples of foreign popular periodicals. Increased reliance was placed on receiving serials through exchange, gift, and copyright. At year's end, the number of current periodical subscriptions recommended for cancellation stood at approximately 2,000.

The Preservation Policy Committee submitted recommendations for the systematic deacidification of the massive retrospective classified collections. The committee suggested that those classes of greatest importance to the library's overall mission—and those containing a significant number of books that will need to be retained in original format—should be included in the earliest phases of the program.

The office worked closely with the National Preservation Program Office and the divisions of Research Services to arrange for the library's participaton in the ever-increasing number of interlibrary cooperative microfilming projects. These include

American imprints through 1920 from Class CS (U.S. local history) for the Research Libraries Group's Americana preservation project and Chinese monographs and serials of the early twentieth century.

The Geography and Map Division received the gift of the first fire insurance atlas of London, produced in the 1790s. The Rare Book and Special Collections Division received a rare book of verse by Paul Laurence Dunbar entitled *Majors and Minors*, printed in 1896, and a major addition to its Anarchism and Radical Pamphlet collections with the acquisition of the Paul Avrich Collection.

Cataloging and Networking

In November 1985, the Visual Materials Online System was implemented, a product of several years' efforts. Concurrent with the implementation of Visual Materials was the mounting of a MARC file of 74,000 audiovisual records that previously were not online in the library.

More than 1,600 manuscript collections were described for the 1985 volume of the *National Union Catalog for Manuscript Collections*. This was the year to begin planning for the automation of NUCMC. In an effort to prepare for the automation, the Manuscript Section began to prepare name authority records according to procedures in place for the other Processing Services cataloging units.

As the fiscal year ended, the MARC Editorial Division completed two major contracts. A special project, called the Series Flip, matched 6,886 series authority records with 57,341 bibliographic records to change the series information to correct *AACR 2* form. A second bibliographic project, called Bib Flip II, updated 38,487 bibliographic records to match *AACR 2* forms of name authority headings. A major new focus for the division is the development of online input and update to the PREMARC file.

The Name Authority Cooperative (NACO) concentrated its efforts to expand cooperative name authority and bibliographic projects into new areas. There are currently 41 libraries contributing records to the library. Five new institutions joined NACO in 1986: Ohio State University, University of Maryland, University of Pittsburgh, University of California/San Diego, and the Center for Research Libraries. By the end of the fiscal year, NACO libraries had contributed more than 208,000 name authority records to the Library of Congress file (more than 43,000 records were submitted in FY 1986). This was also the first year that NACO participants submitted series authority records – six member libraries volunteered to contribute records and received training. The University of Chicago expanded its contributions to include original cataloging of rare books.

Among other cooperative cataloging projects in 1986 was the project with the University of Illinois Slavic and East European Library, which agreed to contribute bibliographic records for monographs published from 1986 forward by seven Soviet publishers.

A new cooperative endeavor, the National Coordinated Cataloging Program (NCCP), is under development by Processing Services, members of the Research Library Advisory Committee to OCLC, Inc., and members of the Research Libraries Group. An initial pilot project will involve eight NACO libraries contributing full-level bibliographic records to the Library of Congress database; these records will subsequently be distributed through the Linked Systems Project and the MARC Distribution Services.

The Network Advisory Committee met in December to discuss "a common vision

for nationwide networking and a plan to realize it," and again in July to discuss implementation of the plan. The Network Development and MARC Standards Office prepared Update number 2 to *Authorities: A MARC Format*, and Update number 13 to *MARC Formats for Bibliographic Data*. USMARC documentation is being redesigned, and new versions of the existing publications are being produced using microcomputers. The office completed specifications for converting UKMARC records into USMARC records.

Other Educational and Cultural Activities

In addition to the *Folklife Annual* already mentioned, American folklife was also the subject of volume 2 of *The Federal Cylinder Project: A Guide to Field Cylinder Collections in Federal Agencies*, titled *Northeastern Indian Catalog, Southeastern Indian Catalog*. The African Section initiated an annual series, *U.S. Imprints on Sub-Saharan Africa: A Guide to Publications Cataloged at the Library of Congress*.

Once again a number of publications issued by the library had origins in lectures or conferences, including *The Invisible World: Libraries and the Myth of Cultural Exchange*, by Daniel J. Boorstin; *George Orwell Nineteen Eighty-Four: The Man and the Book*, papers and discussions from a conference in the spring; *Samuel Beckett: Nayman of Noland*, by Richard Ellmann; and *Poets and Anthologists: A Look at the Current Poet-Packaging Process*, originally presented by Poetry Consultant Reed Whittemore.

Another publication, long in preparation, is *Civil War Manuscripts*, a specialized guide to selected collections in the Manuscript Division. The final imprint of the National Referral Center was issued in June: *Information Resources in the Arts*. Other contributions to research in area studies were *Chinese Newspapers in the Library of Congress: A Bibliography* and volume 14 of *Antarctic Bibliography*. Finally, to bring some of the library's most important publications to the attention of the reading public, a catalog entitled *Library of Congress Selected Publications, 1986–1987* was issued, listing 44 books published by the library and offered for sale through the U.S. Superintendent of Documents.

The library produced a 21-minute videotaped "Tour of the Library of Congress" for sale ($25) to the public through its card and gift catalog and sales counters. The videotape was selected for distribution by the Book-of-the-Month Club in spring 1987.

For the second year, the CBS television network, assisted by the library's Information Office, produced "American Treasury," short-format programs about information and items in the collections of the Library of Congress, aired daily.

A volunteer program was established, staffed by retired library employees, to answer inquiries from visitors.

In addition to the exhibits already described, the library mounted in 1986 a number of special collection exhibits, including *A Celebration of the Fourth Centenary of La Galatea*, marking the four-hundredth anniversary of the publication of the first novel by Cervantes; *Surveyors of the Pacific: Charting the Pacific Basin, 1768–1842*, featuring surveys of 22 expeditions to the vast uncharted Pacific Basin; *The Spirit of the Place: Photographs by Paul Strand*, which captures the character of the working people of Mexico, New England, France, and Italy; *Latin American Port Cities*, some 40 maps of the Spanish Main (1650–1850) reflecting the development of major Atlantic ports in Latin America and the Caribbean; and *Coronelli Globes*, a permanent exhibit of a pair of 3½-foot-diameter globes constructed in the early 1690s, one a terrestrial and the other a celestial globe. *Porgy and Bess*, a Performing Arts Library exhibition, commemorates the fiftieth anniversary of the first performance of this famous American opera.

National Agricultural Library

U.S. Department of Agriculture, Beltsville, MD 20705
301-344-3778

Eugene M. Farkas

Chief, Education and Information Staff

The nation's agricultural information network, coordinated by the National Agricultural Library (NAL), was significantly strengthened in 1986 when NAL established new formal agreements and working arrangements with a broad spectrum of public and private sector institutions at the state, federal, and international levels. Adaptation of new technologies to help meet growing demand for library information and expanded coverage of agricultural materials were primary objectives of these agreements. Policy cooperation and communication between NAL and land-grant university and other agriculture-related libraries were facilitated through special briefing and discussion sessions held at the annual conference of the American Library Association (ALA), the Federal Interagency Field Librarians (FIFL) Workshop, and project meetings with representatives of concerned institutions.

Joint Projects with University Libraries

Text Digitizing, Storage, Retrieval

More than 50 land-grant and other agriculture-related university libraries agreed to support and participate in a cooperative pilot project to establish and evaluate a text digitizing image system for preserving and providing computer access to the content of agricultural library materials. If proven feasible, this process could provide access to masses of material that would otherwise be unavailable. NAL will prepare CD-ROM discs containing both digitized text and page images and make them available to cooperating libraries for use and evaluation. The University of Vermont was named project coordinator under a cooperative agreement.

Fifteen institutions, mostly land-grant university libraries, are participating in phase II of the full-text storage and retrieval laser disc project. Originally launched in 1984, the first phase of this project focused on evaluating the potential of videodisc used in conjunction with microcomputers to store and disseminate agriculturally related full-text databases. *The Pork Industry Handbook* — a major teaching and resource tool of the pork industry — and 200,000 records from AGRICOLA, NAL's master bibliographic database, were placed on the first videodisc. The second phase takes a closer look at the conversion and mastering process, using 12 different U.S. Department of Agriculture (USDA) and State Cooperative Extensive Service publications on a second disc.

Interactive Instruction

NAL began working with the University of Maryland to design, produce, and evaluate *AGRICOLearn*, an interactive course for instruction in the online searching of the AGRICOLA database. This course will contain many tracks for the user to follow and choices for the user to make. Text for the course will be on a computer floppy disc, with

motion videos, still pictures, graphics, or animation and sound available on a laser videodisc for access as needed. The system is intended primarily for one-on-one use, but also may assist an instructor. Land-grant institutions will be asked to test and evaluate the final product.

The University of Maryland also participated in a pilot project to explore the effectiveness of laser videodisc technology as a storage medium for photo collection. Under a cooperative agreement with NAL, the university mastered a videodisc containing 34,000 images from the 500,000 images in the Forest Service Photo Collection, the largest collection of its kind in the world, now part of the library's resources. The disc and the bibliographic file will be evaluated by regional offices of the Forest Service, USDA, and will be made available to other libraries and photo collections.

Cataloging/Indexing

With the goal of providing improved access to state agricultural publications, 34 land-grant university libraries participated in a joint project with NAL to acquire, catalog or index, and offer document delivery of experiment station and Extension Service materials. NAL entered bibliographic records into its AGRICOLA database and provided backup document delivery service. In another cooperative program, also intended to expand coverage of agricultural topics, libraries with strong agriculture-related collections—including the U.S. Department of the Interior, the University of Illinois, and Ohio State University—added records of their unique agricultural holdings to AGRICOLA.

Cooperation with Federal Agencies

Interaction and cooperation with other federal agencies regarding collection development, special collections, database building, and publications increased markedly during 1986.

Collection Development

NAL and the National Library of Medicine (NLM) reached an agreement concerning the collection and servicing of human nutrition materials after reviewing 26 subsumed areas of this field. The purpose of this project is to ensure broader coverage and prompt processing of relevant human nutrition information while minimizing costly duplication of effort. The two national libraries entered into a similar agreement in 1985, when they decided to share collection development responsibilities in various fields of veterinary medicine.

Significant special collections of materials on remote sensing, food irradiation, and animal welfare were transferred to NAL from the Johnson Space Center, Houston, Texas; the USDA's Eastern Regional Research Center, Wyndmoor, Pennsylvania, and its Beltsville, Maryland, Research Center, respectively. A comprehensive collection of materials on Agent Orange (used as a defoliant in Vietnam) was obtained from the Veterans Administration. Other major donations included materials on poultry from the American Poultry Historical Society and a special collection belonging to the late Charles Valentine Riley, pioneer scientist and entomologist, which was placed on permanent exhibit in NAL's new Special Collections Reading Room.

Forestry, Food Irradiation

Expanded coverage of forestry materials in the NAL/AGRICOLA database are to be provided under an interagency agreement with the Forest Service (FS). The FS will support additional cataloger/indexer positions at the library to do the primary work and will also station other FS personnel there to reduce overlap and consolidate processing of materials. In another cooperative project, the USDA's Food Safety and Inspection Service (FSIS) began working with NAL to develop a database on safety, nutrition, and other aspects of food irradiation based on materials received by the library from the Agriculture Research Service at Wyndmoor and other sources.

As the result of a continuing agreement with the Environmental Protection Agency (EPA), NAL has produced 13 commodity-oriented environmental bibliographies useful in the regulation of pesticides, as well as for research in the field of plant or commodity protection. Subject titles for the series include protection of corn, soybeans, pome fruits, stone fruits, wheat, rice, citrus, sorghum and millets, hays, conservation tillage, peanuts, and chemigation. The bibliographic compilations were funded by the EPA with technical assistance provided by that agency.

International Activities

Internationally, NAL focused its efforts on making agricultural literature from non-Western nations more fully available worldwide, on strengthening bibliographic database coverage, and on coordination in the use of controlled vocabularies.

International Database, Vocabulary

Online domestic access to the foreign literature cited in AGRIS, the international agricultural literature database of the United Nations (UN), was made possible by NAL, its U.S. sponsor, through arrangement with a major commercial database system. AGRIS, a cooperative, centralized system, in which more than 100 national and multinational centers take part, is produced by the UN's Food and Agriculture Organization (FAO). The library prepares a special monthly tape consisting solely of citations to U.S. imprints, extracted from its AGRICOLA database, for input into AGRIS. NAL also worked cooperatively with the Commonwealth Agriculture Bureaux (CAB) and provided leadership in synchronizing the AGRIS- and CAB-controlled vocabularies for use among the three libraries.

NAL Director Joe Howard and Technical Services Chief Sarah Thomas visited the People's Republic of China on a two-week study and lecture tour at the invitation of the Chinese Academy of Agriculture Sciences (CAAS). Plans were discussed for the indexing of important Chinese agricultural literature in AGRIS, as well as cooperation with NAL in areas of collection development, acquisition of materials, document delivery, staff exchange, and improved publications exchange partnerships.

NAL Library Services and Operations

NAL services and operations were extended and strengthened in 1986 in areas ranging from information centers to expert systems, from collection management to user fees. (See Table 1 for a summary of primary NAL activities for FYs 1986 and 1987.)

Table 1 / Summary of Primary NAL Activities, FYs 1986–1987

	Estimated Productivity	
Type of Activity	FY 1986 (Actual)	FY 1987 (Est.)
Serial issues added	201,136	185,000
Number of titles cataloged	18,934	19,000
Articles indexed	93,000	100,000
Volumes bound	941*	3,000
Document requests filled	235,971	244,000
Reference inquiries answered	23,946	27,000
Automated searches conducted	10,719	15,000
Current awareness (CALS) searches	181,980†	190,000
Current awareness (CALS) profiles by all database	2,141	2,300

*Reduced level due to lower fund availability.
†Reduced number reflecting a review of users and profiles.

New Information Centers

In 1986, NAL established four additional specialized information centers concentrating on subjects of current agricultural concern—alternative farming systems, animal welfare, fiber and textiles, and family—to provide selective, in-depth access to worldwide literature on a given topic and to offer other related information services. This brought to ten the number of such centers in operation, the others being in the fields of food and nutrition, biotechnology, food irradiation, aquaculture, horticulture, and critical agricultural materials.

In a related move, NAL began exploring the development of computer-based expert systems that will help users obtain answers to questions on agricultural topics. Since such systems mimic the advisory work done by human experts—in this case, reference librarians—the first such NAL system was produced by and for the librarians who operate NAL's Aquaculture Information Center. Other such systems will be tailored to the needs of librarians and users at the other specialized information centers at NAL.

Integrated Library System

An integrated library system (ILS) incorporating the latest computer technology will be installed at the National Agricultural Library during the next two years. The system will be used to manage the library's 1.9-million-volume collection, eliminating currently fragmented, multiple computer operations and resulting in significant savings in time and money. Patrons will have greater access to the collection, including more timely delivery of materials and direct electronic access to bibliographic records through an online catalog. Virginia Tech Library Systems, Inc., of Blacksburg, Virginia, will install the system under contract.

Scholar/Fellowship Programs

A scholar-in-residence program was established at NAL with the objective of attracting distinguished researchers in agriculture to make in-depth use of its preeminent collections. A prominent historian of U.S. agriculture and a specialist in aquaculture and marine science were appointed as the first participants in this program. The library also

signed a cooperative agreement with the University of Maryland's Department of History establishing a fellowship program in ornamental horticulture at the university. The program, funded through a gift donation to NAL, will focus on the historical development of marketing research and information services for the ornamental horticulture industry.

Following the 1985 conversion of the Washington, D.C., branch library into a reference center, the 250,000 volumes on agricultural economics/statistics formerly housed there were moved to the main library in Beltsville. To make space, the existing NAL collection was shifted and part of the ninth floor was converted to compact shelving. Turnaround time for processing NAL document delivery requests with call numbers was reduced to 24 hours, marking a significant improvement in services to patrons. The greater efficiency in lending operations was the result of reorganization and policy and procedural changes.

Software Demonstrations

A new software demonstration center was established at the library in recognition of the growing importance of computer technology in American agriculture. The center's program was designed to provide the increasing number of microcomputer users with the opportunity to evaluate agriculture-related software products on NAL microcomputers. At the same time, more than 120 microcomputer software programs acquired by NAL's Food and Nutrition Information Center were made available to professionals in the fields of food and human nutrition for review and evaluation in areas of diet analysis, food service management, and nutrition education.

Two open houses were held in spring and fall 1986 featuring exhibits and briefings on the specialized information centers, demonstrations of new technologies, and explanations of other user service. Some 500 people attended from the USDA and other federal agencies, trade associations and other private sector organizations, and area libraries.

User Fee Policy

Effective January 1, 1987, NAL announced a policy of charging for extended information and research services. Under this policy, most categories of users—with the exception of USDA personnel—will be billed for information support services in excess of a threshold level. The threshold level is defined as one hour of staff time or $25 in computer usage costs. The new fee program will allow a broader spectrum of users to utilize reference-research services than was previously possible. In the past, largely due to budgetary constraints, comprehensive in-depth reference assistance was reserved for USDA personnel and other selected audiences.

Other NAL Activities

NAL introduced its official logo, the first since the library was founded in 1862. The new logo is a bold and dramatic representation of NAL in the information age. It will serve as the library's trademark, signifying dynamic leadership in the collection and dissemination of agricultural information.

The sesquicentennial of Texas statehood was marked with a celebration and the

opening of an exhibition at the library in Beltsville. The exhibit, entitled "Settling the Land: Utilization of the Arid Lands of Texas," was sponsored by the Southwest Collection and the International Center for Arid and Semi-Arid Land Studies at Texas Tech University, Lubbock.

National Library of Medicine

8600 Rockville Pike, Bethesda, MD 20894
301-496-6308

Robert B. Mehnert

Public Information Officer

The National Library of Medicine (NLM) celebrated its sesquicentennial year in 1986. From a handful of books on a shelf in the office of the Army Surgeon General in 1836, the institution has grown into a biomedical communications complex unparalleled in the world. The celebratory events that took place during 1986 are briefly described at the end of this report.

Highlights of 1986

MEDLINE

There were a number of noteworthy events in 1986 involving MEDLARS and MEDLINE. In February, NLM introduced to the biomedical community a new software package that permits health professionals and other individuals to use their personal computers to easily search MEDLINE, its backfiles, and CATLINE. GRATEFUL MED, as it is called, resides on a floppy disc and eliminates the need for the user to know the library's medical subject headings and other technical aspects of online searching. By the end of 1986, about 3,000 copies of GRATEFUL MED had been sold by the National Technical Information Service. Because of the success of GRATEFUL MED and other user-friendly systems for searching MEDLINE, NLM no longer requires training before assigning an access code.

The increasing use of MEDLINE by individual health professionals is one important reason for the dramatic growth of the system in number of users in 1986. By the end of the year there were 6,000 members of NLM's network—4,200 institutions and 1,800 individuals. Usage also continues to climb: The number of online and offline searches rose almost 15 percent over 1985, to 3.4 million. (See Table 1 for other selected statistics.)

On October 27, 1986, the library celebrated the fifteenth anniversary of MEDLINE by providing free online access for the day. The event was well publicized in advance, and as a result, total usage for the day was 1,860 hours, exceeding by 600 hours the previous record. The experience was a useful "stress test" under real-life conditions.

MEDLARS

Two new members were added in 1986 to the MEDLARS international network. The first was Egypt's Academy of Scientific Research and Technology, in Cairo. The second

Table 1 / Selected Statistics*

Library Operation	Volume
Collection (book and nonbook)	3,709,000
Serial titles received	22,600
Articles indexed for MEDLINE	317,000
Titles cataloged	20,300
Circulation requests filled	365,000
For interlibrary loan	120,000
For on-site users	245,000
Computerized searches (all MEDLARS databases)	3,396,000
Online	3,011,000
Offline	385,000

*For the year ending September 30, 1986.

was the Chinese Academy of Medical Sciences in Beijing. These new centers bring to 16 the number of formal arrangements between NLM and its foreign partners for international MEDLARS access. Through the outreach of these 16 centers, MEDLARS bibliographic search services are provided to many more countries around the globe.

The library has signed a number of collaborative experimental agreements with private companies to make it possible for firms to develop and market optical disc products containing MEDLARS bibliographic data. Using CD-ROM (compact disc-read only memory) format, for example, a user could search NLM's databases much more conveniently in the home or office, without incurring online charges. The first such disc containing MEDLARS data became commercially available in 1986.

DOCLINE and TOXNET

Two online systems introduced in 1985 have proved welcome information resources for the biomedical community. DOCLINE, the automated document request and referral system, had 1,000 participating libraries by the end of 1986. Each day, some 1,000 interlibrary loan requests are entered into DOCLINE to be electronically routed to the nearest medical library that holds the needed item. The system requires no more than 30 seconds for a request to be input. The second new system, TOXNET, provides ready access to vital toxicological and chemical information for retrieval by emergency response teams, clinicians, poison control centers, and researchers.

The RML Network

New contracts have been signed with all seven regional medical libraries (RMLs) to continue their services through 1990. Among the important functions of the RML network are coordinating regional interlibrary loan activities (including DOCLINE), developing regional bibliographic locator tools, and regional cooperative resource development programs. In addition to the regional medical libraries, the network comprises 125 resource libraries, 4,000 health science libraries of all descriptions, and the NLM itself.

New Preservation Section

A Preservation Section was established within the Public Services Division in 1986. This section will oversee the implementation of a preservation plan prepared by the library's

staff and approved by the board of regents. Late in 1986, the library awarded a contract for almost $1 million to microfilm books and journals over the next year. The plan is for 35 million pages, or 45,000 volumes, to be filmed over four years. The board of regents was planning to hold a hearing in January 1987 on the subject of acid-free (permanent) paper and its use in medical publishing.

Unified Medical Language System

The library continues its efforts to develop a Unified Medical Language System (UMLS). Such a system has been proposed as a mechanism for intelligent linking and switching among the many disparate vocabularies and classifications currently employed in automated medical information systems. The UMLS, as proposed, would be in the form of an integrated series of automated tools that can be invoked to interpret questions, classify new medical information, and provide the intelligent links necessary to retrieve or process the whole range of information relevant to a particular inquiry. To begin development of the UMLS, contracts were awarded in 1986 to four universities, where leading medical informatics researchers will conduct background studies to obtain key information needed to design the system. NLM itself will be experimenting with automated methods for mapping and merging thesauri and with developing a group of exemplary search questions to be used in testing and evaluating research results. The library will also investigate approaches to linking MEDLINE records to related biotechnology databases.

Developments in Biotechnology

The subject of biotechnology information is one of increasing importance within the medical community. The sciences of molecular biology and molecular genetics (which is what is meant by "biotechnology") have spawned an immense amount of data about the human genes that control life processes. NLM is proposing an ambitious program to collect and control these data using modern information-handling techniques—the creation of a National Biotechnology Information Center is one possibility.

Long-Range Plan

A long-range plan to guide the library over the next 20 years was completed in 1986 and approved by the board of regents. Final editing is now taking place, and the plan will be published early in 1987. The plan commits the library to improve its collections and methods of access. It recommends new database systems that contain "facts" (as opposed to bibliographic records), and it foresees new interconnections and gateways among a host of biomedical knowledge bases. The plan also calls for enhancing the Regional Medical Library Network and for NLM to continue in its role as an innovator in medical informatics and health professions education.

National Learning Demonstration Center

The new National Learning Demonstration Center completed its first full year of operation. The center contains a wide variety of medical education software and computer and communications equipment and is used extensively to acquaint visitors with avail-

able educational technology. It also serves as a site for staff and visiting scientists to produce and test computer-based systems for health education. The center has proved very popular with visitors and staff, and work has begun to enlarge its facilities. The new center is a part of the Lister Hill National Center for Biomedical Communications, NLM's research and development component.

Lister Hill National Center

The Lister Hill National Center continues its development of a videodisc-based Electronic Document Storage and Retrieval System, the TIME project (a voice-recognition videodisc-based patient simulation program), and several projects involving artificial intelligence techniques. One of the most ambitious of these is AI/RHEUM (artificial intelligence in rheumatology). AI/RHEUM, intended for the nonspecialist practitioner, has both a diagnostic consultant component and a patient management component. The system "knows" 26 rheumatologic diseases and has been tested with more than 500 documented clinical cases with a resulting high degree of accuracy. In addition to its developmental work in medical education and practice, the Lister Hill Center has several projects to improve the library's systems for indexing, cataloging, and other information-handling activities.

Sesquicentennial Celebration

The library, celebrating its one-hundredth and fiftieth anniversary in 1986, took that opportunity to engage in a vigorous outreach program to acquaint the health professions and the general public with NLM. The library sponsored several one-day colloquia, held an open house, invited 120 science writers and journalists to an orientation of the library, sponsored a medical film festival, installed a special exhibit in the main catalog area, inaugurated a new Visitors Center, and held a barbecue/picnic for employees. This last event was sponsored by the new organization, the Friends of the National Library of Medicine. The Friends also sponsored two other events: an evening at Ford's Theatre in Washington, D.C. (where the library was located in the last century), and a formal banquet honoring both the library and American Nobel laureates in medicine, physiology, and chemistry.

Conclusion

Quoting from President Reagan's January 29, 1986 proclamation:

> American citizens, for whom the health of their loved ones is always of primary concern, can take great pride in their National Library of Medicine, which takes life-giving knowledge from research, organizes it, and transmits it to those who can best use it to fight disease and disability and to improve the quality of life for us all.

Educational Resources Information Center

Ted Brandhorst

ERIC Processing and Reference Facility,
4833 Rugby Ave., Suite 301, Bethesda, MD 20814
301-656-9723

In November 1985, the National Institute of Education (NIE), the parent agency of the Educational Resources Information Center (ERIC), changed its name to the Office of Educational Research and Improvement (OERI). The new organization remains a unit of the U.S. Department of Education.

The year 1986 marked the twentieth anniversary of the ERIC system. The first issue of *Resources in Education (RIE)* — then *Research in Education* — was published in November 1966. Since that time, ERIC has cataloged, indexed, and abstracted/annotated 606,402 bibliographic entities (265,600 documents and 340,802 journal articles), has produced more than 4,500 information analysis products synthesizing this vast literature, and has distributed more than 250 million microfiche around the world containing the full text of the documents processed. Access to the ERIC database is provided online by all of the major online vendors, and ERIC has remained for several years the fourth most searched database in the United States and the most searched database in the area of the social sciences/humanities. ERIC has a well-earned reputation as the U.S. national bibliographic database for the field of education. In 1986, *Resources in Education* announced 12,474 document accessions; *Current Index to Journals in Education (CIJE)* announced 17,776 journal article accessions.

New Products/Publications

Directory of ERIC Information Service Providers

The *Directory of ERIC Information Service Providers* was issued in June 1986. It is a comprehensive list of 891 organizations (780 in the United States, 111 in 22 other countries) that offer some level of ERIC service. Each entry states (among other things) whether the organization subscribes to the ERIC abstract journals and the ERIC microfiche, collects ERIC Clearinghouse information analysis products, does computer searches of the ERIC database, or provides users with access to the *Thesaurus of ERIC Descriptors*. Full address, contact point, and telephone information is provided. The *Directory* is free.

ERIC Thesaurus

The eleventh edition of the ERIC *Thesaurus*, published by Oryx Press in November 1986, contains 9,459 index terms (of which 5,296 are main entry descriptors and 4,163 are synonyms or other unused terms). New to this edition are 224 descriptors, 190 synonyms, and several hundred scope note and cross-reference modifications. It is available from Oryx Press for $65.

ERIC Digests

ERIC Digests are short (1-2-page) write-ups on topics of high interest to practitioner-level educators. They are designed specifically to provide the busy teacher, administra-

tor, counselor, or other practitioner with synthesized information of direct and immediate relevance, together with pointers to other sources for more details. Since 1985, the ERIC Clearinghouses have made the production of ERIC Digests a priority activity. An "ERIC Digests Online" (EDO) full-text file is already up on ED-Line via The Source and may be mounted elsewhere during 1987.

ERIC on Compact Laser Disc (CD-ROM)

In August 1986, OERI and SilverPlatter, working in partnership, shipped the first ERIC CD-ROM product. A disc containing both *RIE* and *CIJE* data from January 1983 to the present was sent to a group of charter subscribers. The disc is updated quarterly. The retrieval software is provided on an accompanying floppy disc. Subscribers only need an IBM-PC (or equivalent) with 512K of internal memory together with a CD-ROM data disc drive to operate the system. The backfile (1966–1982) is available on two discs for a one-time purchase price of $2,000.

In November 1986, DIALOG also announced an ERIC CD-ROM product. It offers a current disc, containing data from 1981, to be updated quarterly on subscription for $1,950. The backfile (1966–1980) and the current file are available together for a $3,450 recurring annual license fee. The DIALOG CD-ROM attempts to emulate the DIALOG 2 capabilities insofar as is possible and requires an IBM-PC with at least a 10-megabyte hard disc and a CD-ROM data disc drive.

The CD-ROM systems provide users with the advantages of a fixed-cost self-contained system not dependent on connect time, telecommunications charges, and output volume.

Changes to Existing Products

RIE Subscription Price

Following price reevaluation by the Government Printing Office (GPO), *Resources in Education* benefited from a subscription rate reduction. Effective February 1985, the price was lowered from $95 to $56 per year, for 12 monthly issues, making it one of the information bargains of the year.

ERIC Microfiche Price

Effective October 20, 1986, the ERIC Document Reproduction Service (EDRS) was granted a modest price increase for ERIC microfiche. For microfiche provided by subscription, the increase was $0.002 (two mils) per fiche (from $0.078 per fiche to $0.080 per fiche). For microfiche provided on-demand, the increase was $0.03 per title from $0.75 per title [up to five fiche] to $0.78 per title). Even so, with the price reductions of the past few years, the cost of a year's subscription to ERIC microfiche is down to approximately $1,300 per year (from a previous high of approximately $2,000 per year).

ERIC Microfiche Film Base

Several years ago, the ERIC microfiche were changed from a diazo film base to a vesicular film base because vesicular offered a considerable price advantage. Now that diazo film has become cost competitive, and because of the various other advantages offered

by diazo film (for example, it is more durable and rugged, more easily reproduced fiche-to-fiche), EDRS changed back to diazo distribution fiche effective March 1986.

ERIC Clearinghouse Changes

The ERIC Clearinghouse for Social Studies/Social Science Education (SO), which was located at the Social Science Education Consortium in Boulder, Colorado, moved to the Social Science Development Center at Indiana University in Bloomington, Indiana. The new Clearinghouse began operations in January 1986.

Future Directions

Education Statistics

ERIC has conceived two projects to make education statistics more accessible to its users. One project involves creating a directory file that will list existing bodies of statistical data pertaining to education. Each entry will fully describe and index a data file and will inform the user as to the file's availability and any publications that summarize its content. The files of the Center for Education Statistics, CES (formerly the National Center for Education Statistics, NCES), will be the first files cataloged and indexed. This project is underway. The other project involves the actual mounting of selected statistical files online and providing users with direct access to them for searching, answering questions, and data manipulation to arrive at new graphs, tables, totals, and configurations of the data. This project is in the planning stage.

InterEd: An International ERIC-like File

During 1986, meetings and discussions were held among representatives of the *Australian Education Index (AEI)*, the *British Education Index (BEI)*, the *Canadian Education Index (CEI)*, and ERIC. The objective was to explore possible coordination of activities and collaborative projects that would eliminate or reduce any duplication or overlap among the four groups, that would lead to convergence of practice and authority lists, and that might result in an integrated "family" of databases covering the total English-language literature of education. (The group of representatives is tentatively called InterEd; the non-U.S. files as a group are called ERIC International.) These exploratory discussions were undertaken without any specific funding, but all participants are optimistic that some concrete progress toward the goals will be made in 1987.

ERIC Redesign Study Panel

In 1986, OERI formed an 18-person ERIC Redesign Study Panel to examine ways in which ERIC could be strengthened and improved. Two meetings were held and several discussion papers were issued. Although no final report was prepared, the minutes of the meetings contained several suggestions for improvement. For example, in the subject coverage area, better coverage of the arts and humanities and of secondary education was recommended. Additional efforts were recommended to train members of the educational community in the use of ERIC. Practitioners and their needs should continue

to be a high priority for ERIC, both in terms of the kinds of materials acquired and in the kinds of products offered. No specific recommendations were made by the panel for the restructuring of the ERIC Clearinghouse network.

On December 8, 1986, OERI, pursuing the redesign effort, issued a document entitled "ERIC in its Third Decade," and public comment was solicited. This document is described as a "statement of principles," to be followed later by an "implementation" paper. OERI found ERIC's major shortcomings to be (1) lack of an institutional policy to guide the system, (2) failure to reach all potential ERIC users, (3) not stressing the practitioner strongly enough in acquisitions and dissemination efforts, (4) little systematic attention to marketing and dissemination efforts, and (5) inadequate integration with other information systems (including those within OERI).

Some of the new emphases planned by OERI for ERIC are (1) extending the user community, (2) stressing the dissemination and information marketing function, (3) linking ERIC with OERI's regional laboratories and research centers, (4) using National Diffusion Network (NDN) state facilitators as "ERIC agents," (5) forming "adjunct" ERIC Clearinghouses that will contribute to the ERIC system but on a voluntary no-government-funding basis, (6) offering toll-free telephone numbers in each ERIC Clearinghouse, (7) using the latest technology, (8) engaging in international cooperation with counterpart organizations abroad, (9) stressing cost sharing in contract solicitations, (10) giving a balanced treatment to the various kinds of educational literature, and (11) supporting the OERI priority on education statistics.

Regarding the structure of ERIC Clearinghouses, where major changes have been rumored, OERI's paper states: "Changes in American education dictate some new combinations of 'hybrid' configurations. We plan to organize the domains of future ERIC Clearinghouses around major functional categories of American education that are now and will be salient during the next decade."

Copyright, 1986

Christopher A. Meyer

Senior Attorney and Policy Planning Advisor, U.S. Copyright Office

The year 1986 was one in which many major copyright developments of interest to U.S. rightsowners and observers had a distinctly international flavor. The Supreme Court decided no copyright cases, and Congress passed no copyright legislation. The "inferior" courts, to use the constitution's somewhat archaic appellation, were as busy as usual, and some interesting cases were decided, but most of the really novel developments in 1986 occurred overseas, or at least with respect to international copyright matters.

Note: The opinions expressed herein are those of the author and do not represent the positions, if any, of the Copyright Office, the Library of Congress, or the U.S. government.

Legislative Developments

The second session of the Ninety-ninth Congress passed no copyright legislation but, at least in the international context, was nonetheless one of the most interesting and even important sessions in a number of years.

Because Congress took no steps to save it, a largely unlamented portion of the copyright law expired on July 1, 1986. For the first time in 95 years, the U.S. copyright law does not contain a "manufacturing clause." This small but real piece of protectionist trade legislation residing in the copyright law had been created in 1891 as part of the United States' grudging and parsimonious entry into the world of international copyright. At that time, the clause granted copyright to books of all authors, foreign and domestic, only on the condition that they were manufactured—printed and bound—in the United States. Over the years, the scope of the clause grew smaller and smaller so that the final version, a product of the major copyright revision in 1976, covered only the English-language literary works of American authors, and then only with respect to imports of more than 2,000 copies of a copyrighted title. Although this sounds less harsh, its impact fell most severely on precisely the books that make up the bulk of sales in the United States, that is, bestsellers written by U.S. nationals.

In the 1976 revision, Congress had tried to let the clause run out, by providing that it would expire on July 1, 1982. But, when that year arrived, complete with a substantial economic recession, Congress proved unwilling to appear insensitive to any employment issue, no matter how contrived. Despite several reputable estimates of the clause's minuscule effect on employment in the book manufacturing industry, Congress not only voted to extend the clause until 1986, but voted overwhelmingly to override the president's veto of the extension bill. Perhaps surprisingly, given the size of the trade deficits of the mid-1980s, the Congress in 1986 proved willing to let the clause go peacefully. Although bills were introduced to extend the clause, and to give the U.S. Trade Representative the power to negotiate it away, country-by-country, in return for trade concessions of other types, none ever reached the floor of either house. The relevant subcommittee chairmen, Senator Charles McC. Mathias (R-Md.) and Representative Robert W. Kastenmeier (D-Wisc.), together with a more coordinated and aggressive administration effort, played a substantial role in permitting the "sunset" provisions to take effect.

Rumors in Washington that the clause would reappear in trade legislation or elsewhere lasted until the Ninety-ninth Congress adjourned *sine die*. There remains, of course, the perpetual possibility that some future Congress will bring the clause back, but, for the moment at least, U.S. authors and publishers are free to negotiate with printers throughout the world for the manufacture of U.S. editions of their books.

One tangential effect of the clause's expiration is to move the U.S. copyright law closer to compatibility with the Berne Convention for the Protection of Literary and Artistic Works. This is the oldest of the multilateral copyright treaties, having first come into force in 1886. The United States has never adhered to it because its copyright law contains certain provisions that the treaty does not permit. With the passage of the present law, and the death of the manufacturing clause, U.S. copyright law is now closer to "Berne compatibility" than it has ever been. But it is not compatible enough to permit U.S. adherence to the treaty.

Among the most serious impediments to U.S. adherence are the provisions in U.S. law that: (1) condition copyright in published works upon the use of a copyright notice or the taking of precise curative steps after publishing a work without a notice; (2) require renewals of copyrights acquired before 1978 in order for those copyrights to last

longer than 28 years (the Berne minimum is 50 years after an author's death); and (3) create a "compulsory license" for music publicly performed on jukeboxes. In addition, the absence of copyright protection for works of architecture and "moral rights"— particularly the right of an author to prevent publication of his or her works without correct attributions of authorship and to prevent the mutilation or distortion of that work—also seems incompatible with Berne.

To rectify some of these incompatibilities, and ostensibly to permit the United States to adhere to the treaty, Senator Mathias, in recognition of Berne's centenary and in anticipation of his own retirement from the Senate, introduced a bill to amend the copyright law. It was introduced very late in the session in an election year, and no hearings were ever held. But the bill probably will prove to have been a precursor of much more robust Berne activity in the One-hundredth Congress, and possibly beyond. A concerted effort by the Reagan administration and at least some copyright industries is likely to lead, if not to Berne adherence, to a full-flowered debate on the pros and cons of the treaty in the next year or two.

International Developments

The year 1986 was one in which recent congressional and executive initiatives with respect to foreign copyright protection for the works of U.S. authors began to bear fruit. In the early 1980s Congress began conditioning certain foreign aid and tariff concessions for developing countries on their improved treatment of the whole gamut of U.S. intellectual property rights. For the first time, authorities in nations with which the United States had no copyright relations whatsoever became willing at least to talk to the United States about copyright matters. Particularly in East Asia, where rapid economic development is combined with near-total disrespect for foreign copyrights, U.S. copyright owners suffered substantial losses to unchecked piracy.

The first development in 1986 in that region was Taiwan's official proclamation that U.S. works were entitled to "national treatment" in Taiwanese courts. This meant that U.S. copyright owners could go into courts there on the same basis as residents of Taiwan, which served both to make access to courts cheaper and quicker and to increase the probability of success once inside the courthouse. Although the copyright situation in Taiwan remained a long way from perfect, great progress clearly had been made since the days, in the not too distant past, when Taiwan was the pirate capital of the copyright universe. The measure of the progress is the substantial increase in royalty and other revenues from Taiwan that U.S. publishers now earn.

In late 1985, the Reagan administration had announced that it had begun an investigation of copyright and patent protection for U.S. works in the Republic of Korea. The objective was to determine whether the absence of effective protection amounted to an unfair trade practice, thus setting the stage for possible retaliation on the trade front against Korea's substantial exports to the United States. During the course of the investigation, the Korean government undertook to revise the Korean copyright law so as to provide protection, in substantial accordance with international norms, for copyrighted works in all media, and to adhere to the Universal Copyright Convention in 1987, thus providing a basis for modern copyright relations between the United States and Korea.

Another major development was the progress made in Singapore toward complete revision of that important country's copyright law. By taking Australian law as a model, the Singapore government demonstrated its intention to adopt a modern copyright law.

After a series of public hearings at which U.S. and other foreign interests made their views known, the Parliament moved toward what appeared to be the inevitable enactment of a sound copyright law that would provide the basis for bilateral copyright relations between the United States and Singapore.

Two major international developments occurred within the United States in 1986. First, President Reagan sent the Berne Convention for the Protection of Literary and Artistic Works to the Senate for ratification. Congressional sentiment in 1986 was that the copyright law would have to be amended before placing the ratification issue before the Senate for a vote, but the act demonstrated the intention, at least, to adhere to Berne.

In a completely different forum, the United States succeeded in getting intellectual property placed on the agenda of the new Uruguay round of multilateral trade negotiations. These negotiations, which will shape the world's trading rules for the rest of this century under the General Agreement on Tariffs and Trade (GATT), may lead to the eventual adoption of a copyright "code" administered under the GATT, and will at all events guarantee that the U.S. view on the importance of respect for intellectual property as part of the world's trading system will be heard.

Judicial Developments

After two years of deciding important cases concerning fair use of copyrighted works, *Universal City Studios, Inc. v. Sony Corp. of America*, 464 U.S. 417 (1984), and *Harper & Row, Inc. v. Nation, Inc.*, 105 S.Ct. 2218 (1985), the Supreme Court conducted no copyright business in 1986. But other federal courts decided important cases about fair use, the scope of copyright protection for computer software, the meaning of copyright protection for choreography, and the ownership of copyright in television broadcasts of baseball games.

The computer cases decided in 1986 are among the most interesting in that genre since the first few cases, several years ago, made it clear that software, in all its manifestations, was copyrightable. Having determined that source code, object code, applications software, and operating systems were all protectable by copyright, courts have more recently begun to tackle the more conceptually difficult and ultimately even more important questions like "How strong is a software copyright?" "How much code must be taken to constitute an infringement?" and "What is fair use in a software context?"

Two cases decided in 1986 make it appear that software copyright may be far stronger than some of its earliest advocates appear to have intended, almost to the extent that patentlike protection for the theoretically uncopyrightable process or method of operation that underlies a program may have come, somehow, to be protected by copyright. The lesson to be drawn from *Whelan Assoc., Inc. v. Jaslow Dental Laboratory, Inc.*, 797 F.2d 1222 (3d Cir.), and *Broderbund v. Unison World, Inc.*, 648 F.Supp. 1127 (N.D.Cal.), appears to be that courts are willing to protect, via copyright, the "look and feel" of a program, when it operates a computer system. By borrowing language from cases concerning dramatic and conventional literary works, the courts appear to be comparing the internal structure of a program and the video monitor "screens" that its operation may generate to the details of a play or novel that have long been understood to be copyrightable.

One problem with applying such "look and feel" analyses to computer software cases is that software copyright was designed to protect the original writings of software

authors but not to protect the way in which a computer operates. Put another way, a software copyright owner was supposed to have copyright rights against those who would steal the language — the owner's writings — but not against those who would take the owner's "idea" and write their own — possibly better — software. An early analysis of the subject noted that anyone should always be free to study the operation of a computer system that was running copyrighted software and then, through his or her own work, seek to make other computer systems perform the same functions, as long as he or she did not take the expression of the copyrighted software.

Although courts continue to speak of the difference between uncopyrightable ideas and copyrightable expressions, it is not entirely clear that they identify the "idea-expression" dividing line in a manner that facilitates competition among legitimate entrepreneurs in the software industry. In *Whelan*, the court described the plaintiff-copyright owner's idea as "the efficient running of a dental laboratory." Although this is certainly an idea in the ordinary sense of the word, by calling it an "idea" in the copyright context means, for the court, that any work done by the plaintiff to make that idea operational gets treated as copyright expression, rather than as an unprotectable ideas. Thus the court looks at the defendant's program not as courts have traditionally looked at literary works, but at its file structures and outline. In short, this seems rather like protecting the "algorithm," or mathematical process, that most previous courts and commentators took to be uncopyrightable.

In the *Broderbund* case, the court held, as it had in *Whelan*, that "the over-all structure, sequencing, and organization of the program could be distinguished from the idea underlying the program, and that the former constituted expression of the latter." By following this route, courts may come close to granting very strong protection, in the name of copyright, to the way in which programs work, rather than to the language they contain.

The question whether a particular use of another's copyrighted work is "fair," was, as always, an important topic in copyright litigation in 1986. Familiar questions included whether a parody of a popular song constituted copyright infringement and whether a commercial use of someone else's copyrighted materials could be "fair." New ground was broken with respect to whether a victim of a parody could reproduce the parody for fund-raising purposes and the scope of fair use with respect to unpublished works received additional attention.

In *Fisher* v. *Dees*, 794 F.2d 432 (9th Cir.), a disc jockey requested the copyright owner's permission to prepare and record a parody of the popular song "When Sunny Gets Blue." After failing to receive such permission, the disc jockey proceeded to release a comedic record album containing such a parody. The court held that this use was fair. It noted that the refusal of permission was not relevant to the question of fair use since to hold otherwise would be to let copyright owners, rather than Congress and the courts, determine the law's meaning.

A second parody case, *Hustler Magazine, Inc.* v. *Moral Majority, Inc.*, 796 F.2d 1148 (9th cir.), involved the unique question whether it was a fair use for the Reverend Jerry Falwell's Moral Majority to reproduce a parody of an advertisement, when the copyright in the parody belonged to a "men's" magazine. Falwell reproduced the parody so as to raise funds from people on his mailing list, many of whom might be expected to object to a sexually explicit magazine's production of a parody in which Reverend Falwell appeared in an unflattering manner. Most parody cases involve the owner of copyright in a "serious" work arguing that a parody infringes his rights; in this case the owner of copyright in the parody sought relief against the Moral Majority's reproduc-

tion of the parody. The court held here that copying the parody was fair use, since the defendant's use was for both commercial and noncommercial purposes, and since there could be little or no harm to plaintiff's sales from defendant's copying and distributing the parody.

In *Maxtone-Graham* v. *Burtchaell*, 803 F.2d 1253 (2nd Cir.), a priest wrote a book about abortion from a "right-to-life" perspective, 4.3 percent of which was taken verbatim from a previous book of interviews with women who either had considered or had had an abortion. The "pro-choice" author of the first book sued, and the courts confirmed the priest's use was fair, because his purpose was to use the interviews for criticism and comment, because second uses of essentially factual works are more likely to be fair than second uses of works of fiction, because a relatively small part of the second book consisted of material from the first, and because the economic harm to the plaintiff was small. An amusing note with respect to this case is that Harper and Row, which had argued against fair use in the *Nation* case, here took advantage of the doctrine, since it was the paperback publisher of the priest's book.

In *Educational Testing Services, Inc.* v. *Katzman*, 793 F.2d (3rd Cir.), a "coaching" service provided its students with test materials to assist them in preparing for various copyrighted standardized apptitude and achievement tests. The copyright owner alleged that the service prepared its materials by having its employees take such standardized tests and memorize portions thereof. Because of the commercial nature of the coaching service, the unique nature of standardized tests, and the fact that the service's use of questions forced the copyright owner to remove the questions from its future tests, the court ruled that the service's use was not fair.

The scope of fair use in unpublished works is clearly smaller than with respect to those that have been published. How small, we do not yet know, but the Congress in 1976, in enacting the present law, and the Supreme Court in 1985, in the *Nation* case, suggest that it is rarely available. In *Salinger* v. *Random House, Inc.*, Copyright L. Reporter (CCH), ¶26,029 (S.D.N.Y.), the court held that the unpublished letters of J. D. Salinger, the reclusive novelist, were entitled to copyright protection but that their paraphrasing by his unauthorized biographer amounted to fair use. The basis for the decision was the scholarly purpose of the biography and the remote chance that this use would have any negative economic impact on the author. (The Court of Appeals reversed this decision early in 1987; that decision will be discussed in the next edition of the *Bowker Annual*.)

Questions concerning whether a particular work is sufficiently "original" to qualify for copyright protection offer as many permutations as the questions involving fair use. Two such cases decided by the U.S. Court of Appeals for the Eighth Circuit in 1986 make it clear that they are just as difficult, as well. In *Toro Co.* v. *R & R Products Co.*, 787 F.2d 1208, the court considered a case brought by a lawnmower manufacturer against the manufacturer of replacement parts for its lawnmowers. The copyright complaint was based in part on the plaintiff's system of numbering its parts, since the defendant used the same numbers to identify its compatible replacement parts. The court, in ruling against the plaintiffs' copyrights claim, said that the use of an arbitrary numbering system "falls short of even the low threshold of [copyrightable] originality," and that "The expression itself is nothing more than the public domain numbers."

This case might well not merit inclusion in this report, but for the same court's decision, some six months later, in *West Publishing Co.* v. *Mead Data Central, Inc.*, 799 F.2d 1219. There the case turned on whether a computer system operator could intersperse asterisks and numbers throughout computer files containing public domain judi-

cial decisions, where the asterisks and numbers served to identify the pagination employed by a publisher who produced printed books containing the same public domain decisions. Here the court found an infringement, over a strenuous dissent. The basis for the decision appears to be that the court believed that the care and labor expended by the book publisher in performing its typesetting and pagination functions gave it some sort of "sweat-of-the-brow" copyright. The dissent cited the *Toro* case and earlier cases as meaning that the routine process of pagination could never be copyrightable. All of this was done in the context of a motion for a preliminary injunction, which means that a full-dress trial may lie ahead. Some cynics have suggested that the plaintiff's status as one of the larger employers in the Minneapolis area was not lost on the Minneapolis courts who have heard the case thus far. If the current result remains in place after a trial, then the scope of copyright may prove to be greater than its most devoted advocates believed.

The final cases of note in 1986 dealt with works that might well not have received copyright protection under previous copyright laws. In *Horgan* v. *Macmillan, Inc.*, 789 F.2d 157 (2d Cir.), the court held that the choreographic copyright in a ballet would be infringed if the photographs proved, in the time-honored copyright phrase, to be "substantially similar" to the ballet. This reversed a decision of the trial court that because the motion of the ballet could not be reproduced from still photographs, that there could be no infringement. Although choreography has been protectable by copyright in the United States since 1978, this is the first case to consider just how such copyrights should be treated.

Finally, in *Baltimore Orioles, Inc.* v. *Major League Baseball Players' Association, Inc.*, 805 F.2d 663 (7th Cir.), the court ruled that the professional athletes who perform on television do so as employees of their teams, meaning that for copyright purposes the teams are authors of "works made for hire," which in turn means that the players have no copyright interest in the monies paid by broadcasters to major league baseball teams for the public performance rights in baseball games. Because the scope of copyright in live television broadcasts of sporting events has been at least somewhat unclear, the decision here adds precedential weight to the legislative opinion that copyright is available for works fixed simultaneously with their transmission to the public.

Even without any Supreme Court activity, the body of judicial decisions concerning copyright provide several interesting and important milestones in U.S. copyright law. If the computer software and pagination copyright trends continue, then the traditional scope of copyright may be expanded to an extent that most copyright experts might have found hard to imagine just a few years ago.

International Reports

International Personnel Exchanges for Librarians

Chairperson, IRC/IRRT Joint Committee on International Exchange of Librarians and
Information Professionals, American Library Association

Personnel exchanges between the United States and other countries have been of considerable interest to library and information professionals for many years. This interest has been especially growing since the United States hosted the 1985 IFLA Conference in Chicago. The withdrawal of the United States from the United Nation's Educational, Scientific, and Cultural Organization (UNESCO) on December 31, 1984, may have also stimulated interest in such exchanges on the part of foreign librarians.

The Decline in U.S. Organizational Support

The International Relations Committee (IRC), a standing committee of the ALA Council, has been in existence for more than 30 years. It is charged with promoting the exchange of librarians between the United States and other countries; encouraging and facilitating the use of library and bibliographic techniques and knowledge throughout the world; assisting in the exchange of professional information, ideas, and literature between the United States and other countries; and coordinating the activities of other units of ALA within this field.

The ALA International Relations Round Table (IRRT) was established in 1949 as a membership unit to further the development of librarians' interests and the resolution of problems in the field of international library relations. IRRT serves as a channel of communication and counsel between the IRC and ALA members and provides hospitality and information to visitors from abroad.

In 1981, budgetary constraints caused the elimination of the International Relations Officer position within ALA headquarters. International relations matters are now usually referred to the ALA Executive Office, but they have become generally more diffused within ALA units. The majority of the ALA divisions have created committees or task forces to deal with international relations matters. Sadly, however, the ALA membership has assigned the lowest priority to international relations.

Because of the elimination of the International Relations Officer position at ALA headquarters, both the IRRT and the IRC have had to deal with an increasing number of international relations issues. One particular need that has emerged is for a central clearinghouse, to assist librarians from the United States and foreign countries to exchange positions, work on special projects in other countries, exchange information, materials, and expertise, and so on.

In 1986, the chair of the IRC, Mohammed Aman, created a subcommittee of the IRC, the IRC/IRRT Joint Committee on International Exchange of Library and Information Professionals. This committee was charged with the preparation of guidelines for exchanges with librarians throughout the world; identifying sources of funding for particular areas of the world; compiling a list of agencies and groups that sponsor exchanges and/or act as clearinghouses; and preparing a list of librarians who have been involved in international exchanges. In addition to representatives from IRC and IRRT, committee memerbership includes representatives from the Association for Library and Information Science Education (ALISE), the Public Library Association (PLA), the Association of College and Research Libraries (ACRL), the American Association of Law Libraries (AALL), the U.S. Information Agency (USIA), the National Commission on Libraries and Information Science (NCLIS), the Music Library Association (MLA), the American Association of School Librarians (AASL), Seminars on the Acquisition of Latin American Library Materials (SALALM), the Standing Committee on Library Education (SCOLE), the ALA Resources and Technical Services Division (RTSD), as well as individuals who have been on international job exchanges or are planning to be involved in one.

A Survey of Opportunities

At this time few formal international job exchange programs exist for librarians in the United States. The majority of the exchanges are arranged on a person-to-person basis with approval from employers. A few librarians and library schools have foreign job exchange programs on a sporadic basis, notably Chicago Public Library, Milwaukee Public Library, Cleveland Heights-University Heights Public Library, Ohio University, Simmons College, Vanderbilt University, Washington State University, University of Wisconsin-Milwaukee, and Northern Illinois University. Others have expressed an interest in such staff exchanges and are beginning to plan for them.

A few more opportunities are available for librarians who want to obtain professional experience in a foreign country through study tours and special consulting programs. An example of the latter is the new Library/Book Fellows Program, a cooperative venture between ALA and USIA, administered by Robert P. Doyle at ALA. This program aims to place American library and book service professionals in foreign institutions for a period of several months to one year. Most countries provide proposals for projects for which U.S. professionals are to be recruited. Up to 8 fellows will be placed in foreign countries in 1987; the program will be expanded to include 20 fellows during 1988–1989. The project hopefully will revitalize international library and book exchanges while enriching U.S. librarians' professional overseas experience.

Job opportunities for librarians in foreign countries vary greatly. Some library schools include listings from foreign countries in their placement bulletins. Occasionally, job ads for positions in foreign countries do appear in library publications and the *Chronicle of Higher Education*. The journal of the International Federation of Library Associations and Institutions (IFLA), published four times a year, provides a listing of persons wishing to exchange positions outside their own country, as does *Leads* issued by IRRT and *Library Times International Guide to Library Placement Sources*, prepared by Margaret Myers from ALA's Office for Library Personnel Resources (OLPR). The OLPR publication also includes information on overseas job possibilities. Other sources for such information are listed here.

- ACRL/NEC AdHoc Committee on Librarian Exchanges: Jeremy Slinn, Library, Boston College, 140 Commonwealth Ave., Boston, MA 02167.
- Academy for Education Development: Abby Yodelson, 1255 23rd St. N.W., Washington, DC 20037. Sponsors visits of foreign librarians to the United States.
- ALA/ACRL: JoAn Segal, 50 E. Huron St., Chicago, IL 60611. Exchanges for academic librarian clearinghouse since 1981 (France, Australia, United Kingdom).
- ALA-PLA International Relations Committee: Harry Campbell, Box 624, Sta. K, Toronto, Ont., M4P 2H1, Canada. 416-485-8063. Public library study tours abroad.
- ALA/Office of Library Personnel Resources: Margaret Myers, 50 E. Huron St., Chicago, IL 60611. All types of international exchanges, very informal.
- American Association of Law Libraries, Special Committee on International Placement: Lauri Flynn, Paul L. Boley Law Library, 10015 S.W. Terwilliger Rd., Portland, OR 97219.
- Bureau of International Library Staff Exchange (LIBEX): Tony Hiller, College of Librarianship Wales, Aberystwyth, Dyfed SY23 3AS, Wales, Great Britain. Exchanges with Canada, the United States, and other countries.
- Center for French-American Studies: Raymond V. Vondran, Dean, School of Library and Information Science, Catholic University, Washington, DC 20064. 202-635-5085.
- Foreign Relations Bureau, German Library Institute: Elizabeth Simon, 1000 Berlin 19, Riehlstr. 13, West Germany. International library staff exchanges.
- Institute of International Education: Sandra Cervera, 809 United Nations Plaza, New York, NY 10017. 212-883-8241.
- International Library Exchange Center (ILEC): Harold Smith, Box 26, Park College, 8700 Riverpark Dr., Kansas City, MO 64152-3795. 816-741-2000. Information, personnel, and materials exchanges.
- U.S. Information Agency (Fulbright and other librarian exchanges), Institutional Partnership Research Program: Janet Gilligan, Library Programs, 301 Fourth St. S.W. Rm. 314, Washington, DC 20547. 202-485-2915.

A more complete but somewhat dated directory is Diane Stine's "A Librarian's Directory of Exchange Programs Study Tours, Funding Sources and Job Opportunities Outside of the U.S." (1982), available for $1.50 from ALA.

Funding Sources

The IRC/IRRT Joint Committee on International Exchange of Librarians and Information Professionals is in the process of developing a list of possible funding sources for international job exchanges. At this time the following four sources offer the best possibilities:

- IREX International Research & Exchanges Board, 126 Alexander St., Princeton, NJ 08540-7102. 609-683-9500. Offers special grants to individual scholars and institutions to foster collaboration and exchange. ALA is a participating association.

- Council for International Exchange of Scholars (CIES), 11 Dupont Circle N.W., Box U, Washington, DC 20036-1257. 202-939-5401. Takes part in the administration of the mutual educational exchange program under the Fulbright-Hayes Act as it applies to university lecturing and advance research.
- Council on Library Resources (CLR), 1785 Massachusetts Ave. N.W., Washington, DC 20036. 202-483-7974. Cooperative research grants are given for carefully developed proposals that exhibit an imaginative approach to solving problems or analyzing subjects of current interest in libraries.
- Institute of International Education, 809 United Nations Plaza, New York, NY 10017. 212-984-5326. Fulbright Collaborative Research Grants available for joint research abroad by teams of two or three U.S. graduate students or recent postgraduate researchers.

Guidelines for International Exchanges

Any library and information professional contemplating a job exchange with a professional in a foreign country is in need of a variety of information to plan and implement such a project. The IRC/IRRT Joint Committee on International Exchange of Librarians and Information Professionals has developed both a checklist and a comprehensive guide. The brief "Checklist for Preparing for an International Exchange" (Figure 1) is also being translated into several languages. The comprehensive "Your International Job Exchange: A Preparation Guide for Librarians," prepared by Linda Williamson and the IRC/IRRT Joint Committee, will be available from Robert P. Doyle at ALA in August 1987. It will provide potential job exchangers with information on necessary documents, a listing of housing and transportation possibilities, essential planning information, a list of specific responsibilities, and medical and tax tips.

Summary

With U.S. library and information services viewed by other countries as models, U.S. librarians and information professionals must not only continue to share their expertise with librarians in other countries but must also learn from their foreign colleagues to avoid becoming parochial. This is particularly important at a time when newly developed technologies are making faster and better communication feasible internationally, to provide not only scholars and researchers but all users with pertinent information. Learning from one another to use the latest technology to provide information and sharing with each other expertise in problem solving on an international basis will not only improve information handling worldwide but will improve international communication and understanding.

Figure 1. Checklist for Preparing for an International Exchange

Once you have found an exchange partner and administrative approval has been secured, you are faced with a number of questions that need to be resolved. This brief checklist, representing the collective wisdom of librarians who have planned and carried out international job exchanges, is a starting point.

Who will pay your salary?

It might be your host institution if you and your partner switch salaries as well as jobs.

It might be your home institution if you and your partner are granted paid leaves of absence to work abroad. (*Note:* This plan would probably make it easier for your host institution and your host country's government to allow you to enter a work situation there; it should also reduce complications for your home institution.)

It might be a sponsoring agency if you have received a grant to work abroad.

Will you need a special visa or work permit?

Inquire into this well ahead of your proposed departure date.

How will your exchange affect any benefits offered through your home institution?

You may need to make special arrangements for either continuing or discontinuing medical insurance, life insurance, retirement funds, etc., during your absence.

Will your income be enough to meet your expenses?

You will want to gather information about costs of living in your host country.

You should plan for extra expenses at the start of your visit, for travel while you are overseas, etc.

What kinds of bank accounts and credit cards will you need both at home and in your host country?

Who will handle your business affairs while you're away from home?

If possible, appoint an agent to take care of your banking, to pay regular bills, and to handle mail coming to your home.

Where will you live while abroad?

Perhaps your host institution will assist you in renting a home.

Perhaps you will exchange residences with your partner. If so, you will want to be sure your insurance coverage is adequate; you will want to come to agreement on who pays the various household bills (water, electricity, heating fuel, trash collection, etc.), on who is responsible for yard work, and on the care of pets, if any. Instruction booklets for appliances, and a list of service people to call in case of emergency would be useful for your exchange partner.

Will you exchange automobiles?

If so, be sure to check your insurance policy for coverage of your car with your exchange partner as driver, and your coverage as the driver of your exchange partner's car. You'll want to come to agreement on who is responsible for routine maintenance of the car, registration/licensing, parking stickers, paying damages in case of an accident, etc.

Will you need to get a driver's license in your host country?

You may be able to use your current driver's license.

You may want to obtain an International Driving Permit.

You might want to get a driver's license in your host country, especially as it may be a useful means of identification.

What medical insurance will you need while you are abroad?

Does your host country require any special vaccines or inoculations?

Look into these well ahead of time!

How will your exchange affect your tax situation, both at home and abroad?
    Check into this carefully, as it could affect your plans for the length of your exchange.

Note: This checklist was developed by the IRC/IRRT Joint Committee on International Exchange of Librarians and Information Professionals with special assistance from Linda Williamson.

Library Services in Australia: The National Perspective

Warren M. Horton

Director General, National Library of Australia,
Parkes Place, Canberra, ACT 2600, Australia

Australia has a population of 15 million people inhabiting a landmass the size of the continental United States. The distance across both continents is also the same, and Australia experiences much the same difficulties of transport and communication as the United States. But the harsh dry climate of much of the Australian interior has confined 70 percent of the Australian population to the "koala triangle" of the more fertile and wet southeast, and most of Australia's major public libraries were begun to serve the needs of an urban population.

    Although the median age of the population is 30 years — younger than that of many European countries — the number of aged in the population is increasing. European and Asian migration to Australia has been substantial: In 1947, only 10 percent of the population was born overseas, as opposed to 21 percent in 1981. The resulting mixture of cultures, languages, and age groups has placed specific strains on library services, especially services to non-English speakers. The commonwealth government is presently examining proposals for formulation and implementation of a national language policy that, it is hoped, will help to redress some of the present inequities of service.

Historical Perspective

The first libraries in Australia were subscription libraries established by early settlers for recreational reading. By 1870 state libraries in Sydney and Melbourne were established, together with the two oldest universities and their libraries, and public library services continued to develop along state lines. In the 1940s, most states passed acts providing for the establishment of a state library board and the provision of free library services supported by local government bodies from rate revenue with a state government subsidy. As a result few areas in Australia are without free public library service. Improve-

ments in library collections, services, and professional training followed the passage of these acts.

National Library of Australia

The National Library of Australia was an informal part of the Parliamentary Library until 1960, when it was officially established by an act of Parliament. The National Library collection includes library materials relating to Australia and its people. The library produces the national bibliography, provides central cataloging services, and maintains union catalogs, including national union catalogs for monographs and serials. Through its Australian MARC Record Service (AMRS), which uses Australian, U.S. Library of Congress, and British Library MARC data, the library provides cataloging records in machine-readable or card form.

The Australian Bibliographical Network

Established by the National Library in November 1981, the Australian Bibliographical Network (ABN) is a national online bibliographic system based on cooperative participation. It has participants in every state and territory and provides services to libraries of all types. Its membership reflects the involvement of state, university, college, public, and special libraries, as well as the National Library. Since its introduction, 108 libraries have joined ABN as full participants, and there are 320 dial-up customers and 35 review centers. The system uses the Western Library Network (USA) software.

The ABN system has the potential to support a wide range of library services. Its primary function is shared cataloging: to eliminate the duplication of original cataloging, a time-consuming and costly operation, by allowing the cataloging of any participant to be shared immediately with and copied by any other participant. ABN also provides inquiry, bibliographic verification, and library location services. Because the system has been designed to perform multiple functions, further subsystems can be added when available resources permit and demand is justified. Acquisitions and ILL subsystems are available, but as yet are not in operation. Provision has been made for the system to interface with other networks and computer systems.

As a cooperative venture in library resource sharing, ABN has two management committees that draw their members from the wider library community. The ABN Network Committee provides policy and administrative advice to the director-general; the other committee advises on cataloging standards and their implementation.

Other National Library Activities

The National Library acts as the Australian focus for a number of international programs and systems, including the United Nations Educational, Scientific and Cultural Organisation's General Information Program and its Asian Scientific and Technological Information Organization (ASTINFO), International Serials Data System (ISDS), and the International Information System on Research in Documentation (ISORID). As part of its multifaceted leadership role, the National Library provides staff and some financial support to the Australian Advisory Council on Bibliographical Services (AACOBS), a national advisory body on which are represented libraries, information

services, archives, and other institutions concerned with organized collections of information and bibliographical data. AACOBS plans for and recommends to appropriate authorities on the development and use of Australian bibliographical and library and information services and promotes and facilitates cooperation among libraries and other institutions to work toward the acceptance of national and international standards. AACOBS initiates and supports research. Membership is by subscription from all types of libraries. In conjunction with the Australian Department of Health, the National Library acts as the center for the Australian Medline Network. The Australasian Medical Index (AMI), a database of Australasian publications on human health and medicine that are not covered by the large international databases, was launched on the Australian Medline Network in 1985. Apart from Japan, Australia is the most heavily used center for life sciences information outside the United States.

The library accesses publicly available Australian and overseas databases made available through AUSINET and overseas vendors. It also acts as coordinator for library services for the disabled and provides bibliographical services, including the national union catalog for braille and audio materials. A works in progress file prevents unnecessary duplication by Australian producers.

State Libraries

Most state libraries had their origins in the nineteenth century. All state libraries are "public" libraries insofar as they are open to everyone. Each is an agency of the state, controlled by a board of trustees and financially supported by its state government. Library staff are state government employees.

The state library in each state and territory serves as the major research and reference collection for the people of the particular area. The board that administers each library is responsible for providing such support services as consultancy services to local public libraries. These services vary from state to state. In Western Australia, the library board is responsible for the acquisition of books for all local public libraries.

Each state library has a general collection based on a reference collection developed for the public of that state. In addition, each has a special collection of Australiana with a particular bias toward the home state. The Mitchell Library in the State Library of New South Wales has a world-class Australiana collection.

Public Libraries

A well-established network of 310 public library systems serves the people of Australia, with some 1,300 access points throughout the country, including mobile libraries in areas of new population growth. The libraries are supported by grants from both local government authorities and from the state governments, although there is no uniform pattern throughout the states. The state library boards usually provide consultancy and other special services, as well as administering the state financial grant.

University and College Libraries

Each of the 19 universities in Australia supports a library that caters to its teaching and research needs. These libraries are mainly funded by grants from the commonwealth

government. Their collections, especially those of the older university libraries, form a most important resource for the Australian interlibrary loan system. The 47 libraries at colleges of advanced education offering tertiary education equal to but different from that offered at universities provide for the needs of their students and staff.

School Libraries

In 1984, there were 9,998 school libraries in Australia, 7,544 of which were in government school systems and the rest in independent schools. The libraries in government schools are administered through the School Library Service in each state and territory. All school libraries do not have a qualified teacher-librarian in charge.

Special Libraries

The number of libraries serving companies in the Australian private sector is not known. Most commonwealth and state departments have a library, and some—such as the commonwealth Departments of Defense and Health—have a large network of libraries throughout the country. The Library Association of Australia's *Directory of Special Libraries* lists special libraries in the country.

Commonwealth Scientific, Industrial and Research Organisation

The Commonwealth Scientific, Industrial and Research Organisation (CSIRO) library system supports the work of the organization's divisions. The CSIRO Central Library coordinates a network of some 70 libraries, providing acquisitions, bibliographic reference, and document support for the entire system. Although CSIRO has substantial collections of monographs and serials in science and technology, it has no legally specified role to collect and provide scientific and technical publications for the nation.

National and Cooperative Developments

The Australian Libraries and Information Council, established in 1982 on the recommendation of the Conference of Commonwealth and State Ministers for the Arts, advises all levels of government on the development of library and related information services in Australia. In particular, the 12-member council works to develop a national information plan and to establish mechanisms to facilitate resource sharing in the field of library and related information services. In March 1985, the council released for comment a *National Plan for Library and Information Services*, which outlines a philosophy and a series of proposals for a national information plan.

The emphasis on cooperative activity in Australia is best seen in the development of national union catalogs. The National Library of Australia, as the largest central library and as part of its coordinating role, has operated national union catalogs of monographs, serials, newspapers, music, and materials for the handicapped. A number of smaller state and local union catalogs have also been developed.

Australia has several cooperative interlibrary networks on a national scale as well as other networks of significant size and importance. Both CAVAL in Victoria and the

Office of Library Co-operation in Sydney include the respective state library and university libraries in their membership. In cooperation with the Department of Health the National Library operates the MEDLINE system in Australia and offers services to libraries in New Zealand, Oceania, Southeast Asia, and China. All government and private schools in Australia have access to a catalog card service through the Australian School Catalogue Information Service. This shared cataloging system is managed by a board that includes representatives from each of the state and territory public education authorities.

Cooperative agreements on acquisitions operate at a local level among individual libraries or among libraries in a particular network. As resources for the development of library collections become scarcer because of continued budget restraints, far more determined effort on a national scale clearly will be needed to ensure that adequate resources are available for use in Australian libraries.

The Future

Libraries in Australia are actively involved in advances in electronic communications and library technology. Few libraries of any kind are now untouched by automated cataloging and online information retrieval systems, and there is increasing interest in the opportunities provided by telefacsimile transmission systems and other such developments. Major challenges for the future include providing more effective nationwide document delivery services; better services to specialist groups, including people with disabilities; the implementation of a nationwide program for the conservation of library materials, and more effective rationalization of collection building across the nation.

The key challenge, however, is the opportunity to influence national information planning in Australia. The current government has a commitment to develop an effective national information policy and plan for the country and has recently issued a discussion paper on the topic. Libraries are an essential element in information provision and are unlikely to have a better opportunity in the next generation to involve themselves in government action to achieve this goal.

Frankfurt Book Fair, 1986

Herbert R. Lottman

International Correspondent, *Publishers Weekly*

Indian summer in Frankfurt, for those who brought suitable clothing, provided something of a vacation environment for the thirty-eighth Frankfurt Book Fair, held October 1–6, 1986. Veteran fairgoers have watched that city become more hospitable each year, as shopping streets become pedestrian malls, the Main riverside becomes a park, and the big banks put up their not-unattractive skyscrapers in a downtown that is sometimes called Manhattan. "Our profession is emotional, and both optimism and pessimism are

Note: Adapted from *Publishers Weekly*, October 31, 1986, where the article was entitled "Frankfurt, 1986: A Low-Key but Profitable Fair."

contagious," remarked one of the Buchmesse veterans, Alfredo Machado of Brazil's Ré-cord, who thought that his North American colleagues were not looking very happy. But up and down the aisles of international Hall Four, more people were prepared to say that this fair was "the best ever" than "the worst."

It is almost ho-hum information: the book fair continues to grow. The number of exhibiting imprints was up to 6,922 (from 6,635 in 1985) and foreign participants were up to 5,021 (against 4,808). Importantly, the number of exhibitors with stands of their own was 4,942 (vs. 4,902). An estimated 320,000 titles were displayed in the 1,030,000 square feet of exhibition space. The largest exhibiting countries after the Federal Republic were the United Kingdom (705 individual exhibitors, 101 on collective stands), the United States (547), France (261), and Italy (260).

The fair management estimates that 120,000 visitors to the book fair spend at least one night in town. Since there are only about 15,000 beds in city limits, fairgoers fill all available hotel rooms within a 60-mile radius. American participation was somewhat smaller—attributed to a boycott by several American houses in protest against the scheduling of the fair during a major Jewish holiday. Fair director Peter Weidhaas told the German press that, in his opinion, the lower numbers could also be explained by economic factors and fears of "Khadafi and the effect of Chernobyl." But one of Frankfurt's top hotels reported only a single cancellation by an American specifically mentioning terrorism.

Security, in fact, was the major headache for fair organizers. There was the perennial threat to the Israeli collective stand, the concern for the safety of Americans abroad, the Arab extremist declaration of war against France, and lesser problems like the hostility of Germany's Serbo-Croatians to the Yugoslav regime. This year there was a new worry, with the Sikh extremist threat to India—for India was the star of the fair. But trouble, when it came, affected only the tiny Iranian stand in a remote corner of the ground floor of Hall Four, when regime opponents and partisans of Khomeini went from taunts to open combat, and the stand was shut down.

In his opening press conference Peter Weidhaas declared that the call for a boycott by American publishers had brought no results (although many more people than usual cut their stay short, leaving on Friday before the beginning of the Jewish holiday). "We, the Book Fair, have made our apologies for the clash of dates, which was unfortunately unavoidable. . . . Some of those affected have not accepted our apologies. For various reasons, we must quietly accept this fact."

There was almost no foreign echo of the U.S. concern. Only one European publisher seemed to have joined the protest, spectacularly. Milan's Sperling & Kupfer, a fiction and general nonfiction house owned 50 percent by Mondadori, brought no books to Frankfurt, and displayed a "WE ARE ANGRY" sign at its stripped booth with a notice signed by its president, Tiziano M. Barbieri.

The book fair organizers wanted to sponsor a celebration of Rosh Hashanah for fairgoers, but had to plan it with care, for neither the fair management nor Jewish guests wanted to offer a tempting target to terrorists. A special event was organized by Diane Doucet-Rosenstein, former head of the foreign department of C. H. Beck in Munich, who was at the fair to announce the opening of her own Munich-based literary agency and consultancy service called Interlingua. She had a friend in the fair's public relations chief, Helmut von der Lahr, and told him: "Can you imagine being alone on Christmas Eve, and far from home?" As it happened, Frankfurt was just inaugurating a Jewish Community Center and she promised fair participants that "all security measures are being taken by highly trained personnel." At least 150 persons participated;

some of them were non-Jewish Germans who wanted to manifest sympathy or solidarity.

Want to Buy a Company?

This thirty-eighth fair took place soon after the announcement of the acquisition of Doubleday by Germany's giant communications group Bertelsmann; during the fair Penguin made known its bid for NAL and Baker & Taylor acquired Feffer & Simons (a significant Frankfurt presence). In Europe, corporate raids affecting Bertelsmann and the Mondadori ownership were taking place.

One nice thing about a fair that brings together the top echelon of world publishing is that you can talk about things. Penguin's Peter Mayer buys NAL. Peter Mayer is right there, accessible at a dozen parties, to explain the move. He was saying, as he said when the Thomas group of trade imprints was acquired, that Penguin wasn't in the market for acquisitions, but was in a position to act when attractive properties became available. The companies he buys don't require management overhaul. He talked up the idea of "creative diversity" — having different imprints, hard and soft, in London and New York. The Bertelsmann people weren't ready to be questioned about their Doubleday acquisition.

It had been announced earlier in the year that the Elsevier fiction list, which included the lion's share of international bestsellers published in Dutch (with Mario Puzo, James Clavell, Jackie Collins . . .), had been taken over by a rising enterprise called Malherbe & Partners. Elsevier's remaining staff of 20 and its backlist of 1,000 titles went into the arrangement. A new imprint was born, De Boekerij, with canal-side headquarters in Amsterdam. And at the Frankfurt fair a new publishing director was introduced — Marijke Bartels, formerly of the Kluwer group (Bert Bakker, then Contact). She will preside not only over De Boekerij, but over separate imprints for children's books, high-level literature, nonfiction and Dutch literature. Bartels told *PW* that she realizes that she doesn't have a lifetime option on her blockbuster authors. "But the agents and publishers know that we are the biggest fiction publishers in the Netherlands, they know me, and they realize it's better to stay with a house that has earlier books by the same author." At the fair she and her managing director, René Malherbe, signed a two-book Sidney Sheldon contact with Mort Janklow.

American copyright holders were also affected by a change in the Nordic scene announced at the fair, as two fast-growing Finnish houses, Gummerus and Weilin + Göös, unveiled a Book of the Month Ltd. — they'll use this English-language logo to challenge the Great Finnish Book Club, the big club owned by the country's two largest publishers. On another scale, the Herbert Fleissner group of German trade imprints, which includes Langen Müller and Ullstein, announced acquisition of Switzerland's German-language Edition Sven Erik Bergh (a small imprint for fiction and music). Founder Bergh, who had earlier sold off his Swedish company, holds on to Bergh Publishing, Inc., in New York. Certainly there was more gossip, on the fairgrounds and at parties and dinners, about takeovers and their consequences than about terrorism. But neither subject seemed to slow down the *business* of the fair. "This year there's more to talk about than books," New York superagent Morton Janklow commented. "But books are being sold." He had brought as much good material as he had the year before, and even though many of his best customers for commercial fiction were changing hands or being raided, Janklow found no reluctance to buy.

A Low-Key but Profitable Fair

In many ways, noted Janklow, the fair is less essential than it used to be, because Europeans visit New York, because of telex. "I didn't have to come to Frankfurt to sell Sidney Sheldon. I could have talked to Michael Meller of Bertelsmann by phone." But Frankfurt remains important, says Janklow, for face-to-face contact and somewhat longer conversations than are possible back home.

Most of the leading players on the Frankfurt scene were saying that it was a quiet fair if a useful one, low-key but profitable. Often it was standing room only at the Agents and Scouts Center on the ground floor of the international pavilion. "I'm not going back home with six-figure deals, but I didn't have any six-figure deals to offer," reported New York agent Roslyn Targ. She found it a mid-list fair, with unexpected sales of titles such as *Sex Tips for Girls*, an S&S book by Cynthia Heimel, which was not new, and which had seemed too American to travel well (but publishers in Scandinavia, Italy, and Spain thought otherwise). In fiction, quality literature was in demand. (Don't get Targ wrong: she was also selling Belva Plain. But money was being made with the offbeat this year.) *PW* ran into a first-timer, Robert E. Roistacher of his own New York agency, loaded down with bound galleys of the only title he had brought to the fair. Before the fair was over he had sold it — *Hot Money: Peekaboo Finance and the Politics of Debt* by Thomas Naylor — to Mondadori of Italy and was close to closing with large houses in Britain and several European countries.

If the Frankfurt fair is no longer necessary to launch blockbuster fiction on international orbit — Janklow's phone and telex doing that job best — copublishing projects and illustrated and art books still need the kind of exposure the fair allows. Thus Canadian packager Madison Press Books used the fair to launch *Titanic Rediscovered* by Robert Ballard (leader of the expedition that discovered and explored the sunken ship), following a pre-Frankfurt sale to Warner. The campaign was carefully prepared, with a video and slide show on opening day at the posh Hessischer Hof hotel.

Even sober Springer-Verlag, the German-based scientific giant, came to the fair with what could be considered a typical Frankfurt book. Actually its *Vanishing Animals*, with a text by University of California professor Kurt Benirschke and startling illustrations by Andy Warhol, was already being published in English, French, and German by Springer itself, and if it does as well as expected, Jolanga L. von Hagen of New York's Springer-Verlag told *PW*, they'll do the Japanese version too. But Springer was quite prepared to sell rights for languages in which it doesn't publish. Another impressive book this year was in fact the result of a contract signed at the fair in 1984 between New York's Macmillan and the Jerusalem Publishing House. On opening day, Michael Weller of Mandarin Offset in Hong Kong brought copies of the *Illustrated Dictionary and Concordance of the Bible* to Shlomo Gafni at the Jerusalem Publishing House booth, and Gafni promptly handed one over to Macmillan's Charles Smith. Rights for Germany, France, Italy, and Scandinavia were discussed during fair week.

In the French compound of Hall Four, *PW* ran into a happy Tony Cartano of Presses de la Renaissance, part of the Belfond group. Prior to the fair he had acquired Pat Conroy's *The Prince of Tides* ($100,000, by auction) and was one of the publishers at a Frankfurt Conroy party hosted by Houghton Mifflin; at the fair he also acquired the memoirs of Sadat's widow on synopsis. He himself had brought a first novel to the fair — it had come in over the transom — based on the Soviets' shooting down of KAL flight 007; it sold before publication to Spain, Sweden, the Netherlands, and Denmark.

Everybody seemed to be busy. "Perhaps the talk at parties is about mergers," com-

mented Bertelsmann's Olaf Paeschke. "But not in the booths. There are plenty of good books to talk about this year." "It's like summer weather," explained Philippe Schuwer of France's Nathan. "Some summers are marvelous and some are terrible and you don't know why. This is a good fair. The paradox is that when printings decline, books get better, more specialized. Printings of 3,000–4,000 copies are becoming the usual thing all over the world."

A Successful German ABA

The Frankfurt fair is also Germany's equivalent of the annual American Booksellers Association trade exhibit, and the German pavilions at the fair were jammed with media people, authors being interviewed, booksellers and librarians, and the general public (the last category only after 2 P.M. daily). But trading in rights seemed unhectic, pleasantly so, to Eva Koralnik of the Ruth Liepman agency in Zurich. The feeling is that when attention is drawn by one or more big books, all the others on the list are neglected, and it didn't happen this time. The German domestic market was showing improvement, and German houses were willing and able to pay good advances. "Of course they need the big novels to finance the others," said Koralnik. Rainer Heumann of Mohrbooks, who also sells to Germany from Zurich, confirmed that his customers were optimistic about their prospects, and buying accordingly. And a publisher who sells in that market, Gerhard Beckmann of Zurich's Benziger, explained that sales had been rising all year. There are a number of healthy signs, such as the opening of first-class book stores in smaller cities and the abandoning of the tradition of publishing books twice a year—swamping review media as well as booksellers. On the other side, there is still a psychological price barrier, now 40 deutsche marks (about $20) for fiction, which makes it difficult to make money with translated novels from the expensive English-language area.

Overseas Book Sales News

For the first time in a long time, book sales were up in Japan. The increase was small, explained Toshiyuki Hattori of Kodansha, but publishers are hopeful. Certainly the Japanese were present in respectable numbers at this Frankfurt fair, and "eager to buy," reported Tom Mori of Tokyo's Tuttle-Mori agency. The Japanese snap up all the big books but also a considerable amount of category fiction—thrillers and horror notably. Mori described the procedure of his own team—which is the way most international agents work the fair. During the Frankfurt week Mori serves as a go-between, carrying American books to Japanese publishers. Back in Tokyo the following week, he sits at round-the-clock meetings with the publishers, and the week after that relays the Japanese offers to his U.S. principals.

Another country whose improved prospects affected rights transactions this year was Brazil. As Pedro Paulo de Sena Madureira of Editora Guanabara put it, the monetary reform of 1986 has become psychological reform, as investment in productive enterprises became feasible once again. Books had been doing well since the evaporation of the military regime, but 1986 saw what Sena Madureira described as an explosion. Brazil's giant TV chain, Globo, bought a publishing house—and that was taken as a sign. Book sales are growing, new publishing ventures are being started. Things are so

good that printing capacity can't keep up, Alfredo Machado of Récord told *PW*, and he is considering opening his own plant.

It was a less rosy story for Spanish America. At the Argentine collective stand, *PW* spoke with Javier Vergara of his own imprint, and Bonifacio del Carril of Emecé. On one hand, inflation has been saddled, down from 1,000 percent to an almost manageable 40 percent, which means that businesses can recover investment. But deflation reduces purchasing power. The market is healthy—but difficult, and the Argentinians don't expect next year to be better. Things look good only compared to Mexico and Venezuela, both hard hit by declining oil prices. Vergara played the Frankfurt fair cautiously, steering away from books requiring high advances. To break out of the isolated Latin American corral, Vergara considers the whole Spanish language as a single selling area, and puts "Barcelona/Buenos Aires/México/Santiago de Chile" on his covers; he'll soon open an office in Madrid for printing as well as distribution. Emecé already pools certain services with Barcelona's Plaza y Janés, including sharing scouting and translation costs, and runs a Mexican company for the Central American market.

Thumbs Up for Copublishing

Across the board, the copublishing business was looking up again. Paul Gottlieb of New York's Harry Abrams found the fair very active for him, which he explained by the fact that dollar prices suddenly didn't seem so high to the rest of the world. Charles Merullo, joint managing director of Macdonald, noted that the number of producers has declined, the cost of production per page is higher, sales are lower than they used to be— and still the makers of international packages are more optimistic than at any other time in the recent past. They are more selective, more creative, and getting better prices for their product. Some buyers of projects deplored the lack of originality in this year's offerings. Orbis's Julian Vinuales commented: "That's why so many rights are being exchanged; there are fewer original projects."

Exhibitors Large and Small

As in previous fairs, there were large national collective exhibitions organized by imprint or thematically, and some large publishing groups ran stands that were almost as large as these national ones. Distributors such as Feffer & Simons organized the space for individual houses, e.g., Crown, Bantam, and Farrar, Straus & Giroux. Large houses such as Simon & Schuster, Random House, Harper & Row, and Harcourt Brace Jovanovich staffed compounds of their own.

PW explored the Collins compound—one of Britain's largest, in the company of Alewyn Birch, group managing director-international. To keep the Frankfurt operation manageable, Birch had compiled a list of members of the Collins contingent, 51 names in all (in fact five additional people were present). They represented five divisions: general books; children's books; Grafton hardback and paperback lists; educational, reference, and professional; and special interests (including leisure time and how-to). Collins's chairman Ian Chapman was a busy member of the team, with George Craig, vice-chairman and group managing director. Birch explained that Collins sells more than it buys at Frankfurt, notably in visual books like the children's lines, special interest, and technical books in the educational division. There was a consensus among the

Collins editors that the fair seemed quieter – based on traffic in the aisles – and that this gave more freedom of movement to those doing business, and they were doing very good business.

How the fair grows with publishing lists could be seen in the case of a very small imprint, Economist Publications. The company began coming to Frankfurt a few years ago with a minimal stand and a few spin-off books (from the weekly *Economist* of London), such as the *The Economist Diary* and *The World in Figures. PW* talked to managing editor Penny Butler, who explained that her books are designed for direct mail, and then go to the trade through houses like Collins and Blackwell, or Gale Research and Facts on File in the United States. They keep many of their rights, as for *World Human Rights Guide* and *World Atlas of Elections*, and Frankfurt is where they try to sell them.

Speaking of small: Trade publishing allows one to start small and grow quickly, but you can also end big and want to be smaller. Thus Adam Helms up in Stockholm left the Bonnier group to launch Trevi 15 years ago (the anniversary was celebrated at a Frankfurt party). And *PW* ran into Per A. Sjögren, once head of Rabén & Sjögren and president of the Swedish Publishers Association, for a time of the International Publishers Association too. After his recent retirement he joined with a couple of younger book people in pocket-sized Askelin & Hägglund, with an office in the picturesque Old Town of Stockholm. Not too many books a year, Sjögren was telling old Frankfurt fair friends, but all of them hand-picked.

PW stopped at the booth of Mars Publishing House of Riyadh, Saudi Arabia, the brainchild of Egypt's most dynamic bookseller-importer, Ahmed Amin. Mars began as an extension of Amin's Cairo-based activity, and in ten years' time it has become Saudi Arabia's biggest publisher and book importer (the latter business still accounting for 70 percent of turnover). Mars now publishes some 50 books a year, with a backlist of 350 titles; the partners also claim to be the Arab world's leading publisher of children's books and even textbooks.

Although it was possible to spend a week in Frankfurt without meeting one, it should be said that authors are part of the fair, especially in the German ABA-like exhibition area. Fischer Verlag was hosting Golo Mann, Hoffmann & Campe had José Donoso, Houghton (as already noted) had Pat Conroy. For the first time, the Bertelsmann German clubs had a stand of their own – an experiment and strictly for PR, the clubs' Matthias Wegner explained. There *PW* spotted Isabel Allende under TV floodlights. In fact, the list of authors present at the fair ran into the hundreds.

Frankfurt's Indian Theme

In alternate years the Frankfurt fair comes with a theme, and this time it was India, a culture as well as a publishing country. There was an impressive list of literary and artistic events targeted to the German public and exhibitions of books published in India and books published elsewhere about India. India's own publishing community was given stand space in the separate pavilion devoted to things Indian, and one could take it all in while eating curry off paper plates and listening to sitar music. Why the India effort was unlikely to change the world was explained in a frank report in London's authoritative *The Bookseller*. India's best writers prefer to see print in London or New York "for a variety of reasons," wrote Tejeshwar Singh, "not the least of which are the exposure they get and the financial rewards they can expect." Singh found it ironic that Frankfurt di-

rector Weidhaas had financed translations into German of works from India's minority languages. "As far as I am aware, no reputable Indian publisher has published translations [into English] of the works of any of these authors." "We don't expect our event to change everything," Weidhaas told *PW*. "We just wanted to show that India has something to offer. . . . Now it's up to the Indians."

The Social Scene

There are Frankfurt rituals, like the S. Fischer Verlag buffet on the eve of the fair, held in the company's Frankfurt headquarters; at the tail end of the fair Lübbe gives a bash. In between, regular events include a late evening ballroom buffet thrown by author Heniz Konsalik and his partner in publishing, daughter Dagmar Stecher-Konsalik (Hestia Verlag) at the Frankfurter Hof; the equally swell Heyne Verlag Saturday night, also at the Frankfurter; the Reader's Digest Hessischer dinner—a dazzling sit-down affair—for U.K. and Europe publishers. This time it was the occasion for editor in chief John Zinsser to announce his retirement (at a good time for his peace of mind, for worldwide the company's book program was prospering).

German publishers often do their parties as stand-up lunches in off-fair premises (e.g., Hoffmann & Campe books at a Dominican cloister). The fair management invites foreign participants to an International Evening right inside Hall Four, with lobby space set up as a street fair, stands and carts for food and drinks, and musicians and circus performers in between. Bertelsmann's big Friday night bash is always one of the fair's hottest tickets. Most U.S. publisher parties are more modest, but one in particular draws the crème de la crème: the Harper & Row fair opener; everybody in that jampacked room was worth talking to.

Stand parties, too. One afternoon, *PW* sampled Dutch gin off the Meulenhoff stand, went on to plum brandy at Zagreb's Mladost, then up to the French Bordas group for genuine French champagne. The champagne came with a pitch for Bordas's house-originated coeditions, which included a remarkable one on the Lascaux cave paintings snapped up by Harry Abrams, Thames & Hudson, and Germany's Herder.

It hasn't taken the Chinese long to discover that the way to the book trade's heart is through its stomach, and so there was a Chinese party, tempting visitors with exotic dishes; this to commemorate the opening of a German branch of the China National Publications Import and Export Corporation at the Heidelberg headquarters of Springer-Verlag.

The big anniversary was Fisher's one-hundredth. Before becoming part of the Holtzbrinck group, S. Fischer was one of Germany's great literary houses, whose catalog included Franz Kafka, Hermann Hesse, Stefan Zweig, Thomas Mann, as well as Conrad, O'Neill, and Hemingway. Today's Fisher took over a large downtown theater for the event, which feted some of the founding family, Brigitte Fischer and husband Gottfried Berman-Fischer, now living in retirement in Tuscany. One of the fair's moving moments was the party thrown in an intimate Hessischer Hof setting by the Feltrinellis for the Fischers. "The past is here!" exclaimed Otto Lindhardt of Denmark's Lindhardt & Ringhof. For Inge Feltrinelli had also invited other publishing veterans, like Fritz Landshoff and H. M. Ledig-Rowohlt. (Fischer's present publisher, Monika Schoeller, daughter of the late Georg von Holtzbrinck, missed her own Tuesday night party to be with the Fischers at the Feltrinelli affair.)

The literary French imprint Christian Bourgois, part of the Presses de la Cité group, brought equally high-minded literary publishers together for a twentieth anniver-

sary dinner. (Just to take one letter of the alphabet, Bourgois has published Djuna Barnes, Max Beerbohm, Alban Berg, J. L. Borges, Piere Boulez, Paul and Jane Bowles, Richard Brautigan, Breyten Breytenbach, and William Burroughs.) Stockholm's Trevi, run by Solveig Nellinge with a staff of six, celebrated 15 years of successful publishing of international fiction.

Awards Presentation

The German book trade peace prize, worth DM 25,000, went to Wladyslaw Bartos-zewski, the Polish historian known for his leadership in Catholic aid to Jews in World War II and, more recently, for his support of Solidarity. The $3,000 Noma Award for Publishing in Africa, endowed by Japan's Kodansha, was announced at an Intercontinental rooftop affair; António Jacinto, poet and author from embattled Angola, was the winner.

Scheduling for Frankfurt

A large number of book trade events requiring the presence of participants from across the globe are scheduled each year to coincide with the Frankfurt fair — meetings of multinational publishing combines, for example, or of International Publishers Association executive bodies. It's now a tradition for the Motovun group of copublishers to breakfast together on the Frankfurt Sunday. Motovun — which takes its name from the Yugoslav hilltop village where members gather to exchange projects — is growing fast, thanks to the revival of the copublishing economy and to member-get-a-member tactics.

There were Chinese and Japanese participants this year along with the Europeans; the U.S. contingent included a group from W. H. Smith and guest observers from Facts on File, but American publishing is decidedly underrepresented in this organization, whose chairman is Edward Booher, former chairman of the McGraw-Hill Book Company. (Booher has been a consultant to the Holtzbrinck group in Stuttgart, and since the acquisition of Henry Holt and *Scientific American*, he is vice-chairman of both companies.) The 1987 summer meeting will be on a cruise ship sailing from Venice to Dubrovnik.

Each year on the morning before the opening of the fair the International Group of Scientific, Technical and Medical Publishers (STM) holds its general assembly in an Intercontinental ballroom. (Glancing down the list of companies present, from McGraw-Hill and Prentice-Hall to Bertelsmann, Elsevier, and Kluwer, an observer couldn't be blamed for thinking that this subdued and something less than glamorous gathering represented more publishing capital than would be brought together at any other time during fair week.) Opening the 1986 meeting, chairman Robert Duncan of Longman indicated that members had spent much of the year discussing the future of STM publishing, notably at a conference for heads of houses held at Gleneagles, Scotland. Duncan himself felt that the main business of STM as an organization is copyright protection. New members were elected to the Group Executive, including Sara Finnegan of Williams & Wilkins and Geoffrey Staines of France's InterEditions. Duncan stayed on as chairman, with Andrew H. Neilly, Jr., of John Wiley as vice-chairman.

They've already announced the date of the next STM assembly — October 6, 1987 — for, of course, the dates of the next Frankfurt Book Fair are also known — October 7–12. The question left open is: Will that be the beginning of the rainy season?

National Associations

American Library Association

50 E. Huron St., Chicago, IL 60611
312-944-6780

Regina U. Minudri

President

In 1986, the American Library Association (ALA) Council adopted a new mission statement for the association that reflects the library profession's concern with information issues in the 1980s, including the impact of new technology, increasing government restrictions, and a new attorney general's report on pornography. Other key areas of concern are literacy, professional recruitment and pay equity, legislation, and funding for libraries. The association continued a tradition of active member involvement with membership and conference registration at record highs.

Strategic Long-Range Plan

The strategic long-range plan approved by the ALA Council in 1986 includes the new mission statement and two additional priority areas of concern for the association. The plan represents the concerns of members as expressed in several membership surveys and numerous planning meetings conducted by membership groups, chapters, and ALA staff.

The new mission statement defines ALA's purpose: "to provide leadership for the development, promotion and improvement of library and information services and the profession of librarianship in order to enhance learning and ensure access to information for all."

The strategic long-range plan confirms ALA's commitment to several priority areas: access to information, legislation/funding, intellectual freedom, public awareness, and personnel resources. Two new priority areas are (1) library services, development, and technology and (2) ALA organizational support. The new priorities reflect the importance to ALA of providing guidelines and standards, research, and data about libraries and librarianship and of maintaining ALA's strengths as an association in such areas as financial stability and membership. A Planning Committee continues work on development of annual objectives, action plans, and budgets consistent with ALA priorities and goals.

Conference Highlights

"Saluting the Past, Charting the Future" was the theme for ALA's one-hundredth and fifth annual conference, held in New York. The conference attracted a record number of

16,318 members, exhibitors, and guests. Keynote speaker Anthony Burgess took a strong position on censorship, and William Carey, chief of the American Association for the Advancement of Science, discussed values and choice in a changing society. Rosabeth Moss Kanter, business leader, scholar, and author of *The Change Masters: Innovation and Entrepreneurship in the American Corporation*, focused on change in complex institutions.

More than 80 awards were presented. Two new awards are the Exhibition Catalogue Awards sponsored by the Rare Books and Manuscript Section of the Association for College and Research Libraries. Winners include "Renaissance Painting and Manuscripts, Treasures from the British Library," submitted by the J. Paul Getty Museum, and "Survivors, an Exhibtion of Rare Russian books," from the University of Illinois at Urbana-Champaign.

The Carroll Preston Baber Research Award of $10,000 was presented for the first time to Paula R. Moore, children's services coordinator at the Downer's Grove (Illinois) Public Library, and Leslie M. Edmonds, assistant professor at the University of Illinois Graduate School of Library and Information Science, for research into the effectiveness of children's use of online catalogs.

Three highly successful division conferences—the Association of College and Research Libraries held in Baltimore, the Public Library Association in St. Louis, and the American Association of School Librarians in Minneapolis—made it possible for many ALA members to participate in a national meeting for the first time.

Washington Report

Federal grants for needy college libraries and for new technology and joint-use projects as developed by the Association for College and Research Libraries and recommended by ALA were incorporated by Congress in a five-year extension and revision of the Higher Education Act. ALA President Beverly Lynch testified at two congressional hearings on the effects of drastic cuts in the Library of Congress budget on the nation's libraries and library users. Funds were later partially restored. Several witnesses testified for ALA at a congressional hearing held during National Library Week on a proposed White House Conference on Library and Information Services, access to government information, and the administration's zero budget for federal library and postal programs.

Issues

A special report published by ALA focused on the impact of new technology, government policy, and other forces that threaten public access to information. "What our citizens don't know can hurt them," ALA President Lynch said in releasing the report *Freedom and Equality of Access to Information* by a panel of librarians and other communications experts commissioned by ALA. Dan Lacey, former senior vice president, McGraw-Hill, chaired the panel, with Thomas J. Galvin, executive director of ALA, as vice chair.

More than 20 organizations joined with ALA to form a Coalition on Government Information to help ensure citizen access to government information and focus attention on recent efforts to limit such access. ALA members also led a campaign to reverse a Government Printing Office decision to eliminate dual distribution (paper and microfiche) of heavily used government publications.

The Committee on Intellectual Freedom issued a special alert to librarians on how to prepare for censorship attempts resulting from *The Report of the Attorney General's Commission on Pornography*.

A federal judge upheld a complaint against the Librarian of Congress charging that First Amendment rights of blind people were violated when he eliminated the braille edition of *Playboy*. ALA had joined the American Council of the Blind, the Blinded Veterans Association, and Playboy Enterprises in filing the complaint after Congress acted to reduce the appropriation for the blind and physically handicapped program in the amount it cost to publish *Playboy* in braille.

The Coalition for Literacy, a group of 11 national organizations founded and administered by ALA, reports that its "Volunteers against Illiteracy" drive has increased citizen awareness of functional illiteracy from 21.4 to 30 percent of the population in its first year. The theme for the campaign, created by the Advertising Council, is "The only degree you need is a degree of caring."

Leadership

Regina U. Minudri, director of the Berkeley (California) Public Library, took office as ALA's 1986–1987 president with the theme "Diversity: The Challenge to America's Libraries." Margaret E. Chisholm, director of the Graduate School of Library and Information Science at the University of Washington, Seattle, was elected ALA vice president/president-elect.

New staff appointments included Susan C. Odmark, as chief financial officer of ALA; Ann Carlson Weeks, as executive director of the American Association of School Librarians; Susan Roman, as executive director of the Association for Library Service to Children; Eleanor Jo Rodger, as executive director of the Public Library Association; and Emily I. Melton, as headquarters librarian.

Special Projects

"Are We to Be a Nation? The Making of the Federal Constitution" will be the focus of a traveling exhibit and support materials developed by ALA and the New York Public Library with a grant of $270,172 from the National Endowment for the Humanities. The exhibit, celebrating the bicentennial of the U.S. Constitution in 1987, will tour 30 public libraries in urban areas.

American library and book service professionals will be placed in jobs overseas for periods of several months to one year under a new Library/Book Fellows program administered by ALA with a grant of $243,754 from the United States Information Agency.

An ongoing series of statistical reports on the state of the nation's libraries — public, school, and academic — is being developed by ALA with an initial grant of $10,000 awarded by the Online Computer Library Center (OCLC). The first report will be released in spring 1988.

A new investment opportunity for libraries is the Public Library Trusteeship, established by two ALA divisions, the Public Library Association and American Association of Library Trustees. The program will enable libraries to earn higher rates of return on inactive and endowment funds through a cooperative approach to investing.

A survey to determine the nature and extent of nontaxed sources of revenue for public libraries will be conducted by ALA with a $30,000 grant from the H. W. Wilson Foundation.

ALA Publishing

ALA Publishing celebrated its centennial year by expanding its offerings in both print and video formats. A new Information Technology Publishing Section was established, building on the success of ALANET, ALA's electronic network, which has grown to more than 1,500 "mailboxes" in its first two years of operation. Joel M. Lee, former headquarters librarian and administrator of ALANET, was appointed head of the new section. ALA issued its first catalog of ALA videos and launched a new quarterly, *Library Video Magazine,* designed to broaden opportunities for continuing education and professional growth. "Booklist," which reviewed more than 6,000 books, published a special multimedia bibliography, "Ending Hunger." "Library Technology Reports" published a special update on optical disc technology. An expanded tenth edition of *Guide to Reference Books,* edited by Eugene Sheehy, was published. ALA Publishing became the exclusive U.S. distributor of Library Association, Ltd. (London), materials, making available noted publications such as *Walford's Guide to Reference Material.* ALA Publishing also assumed responsibility for production of the *Journal of Education for Librarianship* under contract with the Association for Library and Information Science Education.

Children and Young Adults

The American Association of School Librarians held its fourth national conference with the theme "Focus '86: The Curriculum and You." More than 3,100 school library media specialists, educators, and guests attended the five-day program in Minneapolis. Keynote speaker for the conference was Secretary of Education William J. Bennett. A status report and preview of new standards for school library media programs was presented.

ALA's Young Adult Services Division published "You Are Not Alone! Intellectual Freedom Issues and Library Services to Youth: A Packet of Materials" and *Selected Videos and Films for Young Adults: 1975–1985.* The division presented two regional workshops, funded by a grant from the National Endowment for the Humanities, to train teams of librarians to develop humanities programs in libraries for teenagers.

"Managers and Missionaries: Library Services to Children and Young Adults in the Information Age" was the theme for the twenty-eighth Allerton Institute, sponsored by ALA's three youth divisions—the Association for Library Service to Children, American Association of School Librarians, and Young Adult Services—with the University of Illinois Graduate School of Library and Information Science.

Newbery and Caldecott Medals

Patricia MacLachland and Chris Van Allsburg were awarded the John Newbery and Randolph Caldecott medals sponsored by ALA's Association for Library Service to Children. MacLachlan, author of *Sarah, Plain and Tall* (a Charlotte Zolotow book), won the 1986 Newbery Medal for the most distinguished contribution to American liter-

ature for children published in 1985. Harper & Row published the book. Van Allsburg, illustrator of *The Polar Express*, won the 1986 Caldecott Medal for the most distinguished American picture book for children published in 1985. Houghton Mifflin is the publisher. It is the second Caldecott Medal for Van Allsburg, who won in 1982 for his book *Jumanji*.

Membership

ALA membership reached an all-time high of 43,397, a 3 percent increase over 1985. Personal membership topped the 40,000 mark for the first time (40,280), and organizational membership showed a 5 percent increase, reversing a ten-year downward trend.

Both the Midwinter Meeting in Chicago and the annual conference in New York recorded the largest number of registrants in ALA's history. The Independent Librarians Exchange Round Table recruited 221 members in its first year. A new toll-free ALA Memberline gives members more ready access to the specialized expertise and resources of ALA headquarters staff.

National Library Week

Chrysler Chairman Lee Iacocca, Miami Dolphins quarterback Dan Marino, and boxing great Sugar Ray Leonard appeared on posters and public service advertisements urging Americans to "Get a head start at the Library." Full-page public service ads appeared in *Money* and *U.S. News & World Report* magazines. The 1987 theme is "Take Time to Read" in honor of the Year of the Reader proclaimed by the Library of Congress's Center for the Book and Congress. The year-long campaign will be introduced during National Library Week, April 5–11.

Selected Division/Office Highlights

"Energies for Transition" was the theme for the fourth national conference of the Association of College and Research Libraries held in Baltimore. The division began publication of *Rare Books and Manuscripts Librarianship*, a new semiannual journal.

The Association of Specialized and Cooperative Library Agencies began developing standards for library cooperatives and networks and for library service to patients in mental health facilities. It is also revising *Library Standards for Adult Correctional Institutions*.

The Public Library Association held its second national conference, "Public Libraries: Gateways to Growth," attended by more than 2,000 librarians and trustees in St. Louis.

The Reference and Adult Services Division published *Other Lives, Other Roads: Spanish-Language Books for Public Libraries*; and *Women's Legal Rights in the United States*. It also published *Notable Books, 1985* with assistance from the Carnegie Reading List Fund.

The Committee on Accreditation presented the Final Report of the ALA/U.S. Department of Education Accreditation Project at an annual conference program. Thirteen interested societies appointed liaisons to assist with follow-up activities.

The Office for Intellectual Freedom sponsored Banned Books Week '86—

Celebrating the Freedom to Read with the theme "The Worlds of Science and Technology—How Free?" in cooperation with the American Booksellers Association, the American Society of Journalists and Authors, the Association of American Publishers, and the National Association of College Stores.

The Office for Library Personnel Resources published *Academic and Public Librarians: Data by Race, Ethnicity and Sex* and two new *Topics in Personnel* kits on how to hire and pay equity. Conference hearings were held on recruitment concerns and plans laid for national recruitment efforts.

Society of American Archivists

600 S. Federal St., Suite 504, Chicago, IL 60605
312-922-0140

Donn C. Neal

Executive Director

The Society of American Archivists (SAA), founded in 1936, is a professional association of 2,500 individuals and 1,000 institutions interested in the identification, preservation, and use of archives, manuscripts, current records, machine-readable records, recordings, photographs, films, and maps. The society's membership includes persons affiliated with government, academic institutions, businesses, religious organizations, and associations. Although the society's geographic base is the United States and Canada, members in 60 countries make SAA an international organization.

SAA serves the archival profession in numerous ways. Through its annual meeting, publications program, workshops, and sections, SAA facilitates communication and cooperation among archivists and archival repositories. SAA also advances professional education and training, offers placement services, supports research dealing with archival problems, represents archivists in areas involving related professions, and acts as an advocate on matters affecting archivists.

A Year of Transition

For archivists, and for SAA in particular, 1986 was a year of transition. There was prolonged but inconclusive debate over the nomination of a new Archivist of the United States, and SAA's longtime executive director retired. In addition, the society itself passed the 50-year milestone with a festive annual meeting.

The society also continued to focus on several significant issues, including goals and priorities for the archival profession, certification of individual archivists, and continuing professional education for archivists.

Archivist of the United States

President Ronald Reagan nominated John Agresto, deputy director of the National Endowment for the Humanities, to be the first Archivist of the United States following

independence of the National Archives. Agresto, a political scientist, met with immediate and vigorous opposition from a broad coalition of nearly 20 scholarly, genealogical, archival, library, and historical organizations. Many individuals also expressed their opposition to Agresto, and numerous newspapers throughout the country took stands against him.

Agresto's opponents contended that he lacked the scholarly credentials, archival experience, and administrative perspective that the position demands. In addition, they questioned the role that politics seemed to play in his selection, since Secretary of Education William Bennett, for whom Agresto had worked, was his champion and since several candidates for the position (including Agresto) had been queried by the White House about their political affiliations.

Two rounds of hearings before the Senate Governmental Affairs Committee revealed widespread and growing resistance to Agresto and virtually no support for him among the groups of users of the National Archives. Many of those who opposed him cited the act establishing the independence of the National Archives, which directs that the Archivist be chosen "without regard to political affiliations and solely on the basis of professional qualifications." In October, the Senate committee declined to take action on Agresto's nomination, leaving him—and the National Archives—in limbo until 1987.

The opposition to Agresto, which the National Coordinating Committee for the Promotion of History helped to orchestrate, demonstrated how archivists and other scholars can work together when their common interests are involved. It remains to be seen if these groups can act together in pursuit of positive goals as well, but the Agresto affair has shown the importance of concerted action and the influence of those who care about archival issues.

SAA Affairs

In August 1986, Ann Morgan Campbell concluded 12 years as executive director of the society. Campbell was the first full-time professional director of SAA, and during her leadership the association grew enormously in membership, publications, services, and influence. Her successor is Donn C. Neal, an historian with ten years of experience working with consortia of colleges and universities.

The change in leadership in the SAA office coincided with the society's fiftieth annual meeting. This gala event was attended by approximately 1,100 archivists and others and was one of the society's most successful meetings, with more than 100 sessions. As usual, the society's new president (William L. Joyce, Princeton University) and vice president (Sue E. Holbert, Minnesota Historical Society) took office at the annual meeting.

The society also recognized three new fellows and announced a number of prizes and awards. The new fellows, chosen by SAA's Professional Standards Committee, are Lewis J. Bellardo, Georgia Historical Society, who was honored for his achievements and leadership in the area of state archives; Francis X. Blouin, Jr., Bentley Historical Library, University of Michigan, who was recognized for his activities to cultivate research in the archival profession; and Nancy A. Sahli, National Historical Publications and Records Commission, who was honored for the positive influence she has exerted in the areas of automation and teaching and as an archives specialist at the commission.

Prizes and awards include the following:

- *Waldo Gifford Leland Prize* for an outstanding published work in the field of archival history, theory, or practice to John Barton (Archives of Ontario) and Johanna Wellheiser (Metropolitan Toronto Library Board) for *An Ounce of Prevention*, published by the Toronto Area Archivists Group
- *C. F. W. Coker Prize* for outstanding achievement in archival description to Nancy A. Sahli (NHPRC) for *MARC for Archives and Manuscripts: The AMC Format* and Max J. Evans (Utah State Historical Society) and Lisa B. Weber (SAA staff) for *MARC for Archives and Manuscripts: A Compendium of Practice*
- *Fellows' Posner Award* for best article in *The American Archivist* to Joanne Yates (Massachusetts Institute of Technology) for "Internal Communications Systems in American Business Structures: A Framework to Aid Appraisal" (Spring 1985)
- *Sister M. Claude Lane Award* for outstanding work by a religious archivist to James M. O'Toole (University of Massachusetts)
- *Colonial Dames Scholarship* to Connie L. Cartledge

Goals and Priorities for the Archival Profession

Much of the society's attention continued to be on the work of its Committee on Goals and Priorities (CGAP), which published a monumental and well-received report, *Planning for the Archival Profession*, in 1985. To encourage implementation of the report's recommendations, CGAP identified major actors who could see these recommendations through to realization and singled out some of the highest priorities for the profession. Extending CGAP's work, the SAA Council selected five of these priorities as particularly useful in shaping the activities of the society and its constituent groups. These priorities include

1 Developing, implementing, and monitoring standards for establishing professional competence and for archival programs;
2 Training archivists to plan for the development of their programs and resources;
3 Developing comprehensive educational programs;
4 Promoting the development of coordinated and cooperative collecting strategies; and
5 Educating records creators about the benefits and obligations of preserving documents of enduring value.

Certification

For several years, SAA has been exploring the voluntary certification and recertification of individual archivists. During 1986, archivists continued to wrestle with the exact nature of the plan to be considered by the SAA Council in January 1987. A revised plan received widespread distribution and was discussed at meetings of numerous regional archival organizations and at the SAA annual meeting. The SAA council also conducted a membership poll on certification.

The purpose of certification is to establish the professional qualifications of prac-

ticing archivists, not those entering the field. The plan includes certification by petition during the initial two years of operation, then certification by examination of professional competence. Recertification would be possible through either the current examination or submission of evidence of continued archival experience and activities. An independent and financially self-supporting "academy" would administer the program after a start-up period.

Considerable debate continues over the philosophy and specific provisions of certification. Advocates assert that certification would create, raise, or make uniform standards of archival practice and would help to establish criteria for professional accomplishments. Opponents argue that educational standards should be strengthened first; that the program would absorb too much time, money, and energy; that too few archivists would pursue certification; and that certification is philosophically wrongheaded or excessively technical in nature. Rarely do differences of opinion run so deeply among archivists, and there is considerable uncertainty about the outcome of this issue.

Education

Supported by grants from NHPRC and the Mellon Foundation, SAA is engaged in an initiative to encourage, coordinate, standardize, and strengthen professional continuing education for archivists. With the leadership of an education officer, Timothy L. Ericson, SAA will support the development of the knowledge and skills of archivists, largely through advanced and specialized courses and workshops, new curricula, and new teaching materials. The society will also seek to coordinate its offerings with those of other organizations.

SAA's existing educational activities in conservation and automation continued to make their own contributions to archivists who must know basic preservation techniques, how to care for photographic materials, and how to use automation to exchange information about their collections.

Archival Census

The SAA Task Force on Institutional Evaluation completed the first phase of its work on an archival census, which collected and evaluated information in nine categories from nearly 600 repositories throughout the United States. A preliminary report of the findings [which is reprinted in the Library Research and Statistics Section of Part 4 of this volume] includes some median figures on finances, staff, holdings, facilities, and use.

The typical archives was founded about 15 years ago and has fewer than four employees, half of whom are professional archivists. Staff salaries average about $21,000 a year (out of a total budget of $83,000). The typical archives contain about 2,000 cubic feet of holdings in approximately 3,000 square feet of space. Archivists describe about 80 percent of these materials at the collection level but usually do not publish a guide. On average, 325 researchers use the repository annually.

The task force continues to work on refining, analyzing, and extending the census data and will publish further reports.

Special Libraries Association

1700 18th St. N.W., Washington, DC 20009
202-234-4700

Frank H. Spaulding

President

The theme of the seventy-seventh annual conference of the Special Libraries Association (SLA), "Excellence in the World of Information," served as the guide for all the association's services to its members and society in 1985-1986. Excellence will continue to be the association's theme in the current and succeeding years, for excellence can be the only goal for information professionals.

About SLA

The Special Libraries Association is the second largest library and information-related association in the United States and the third largest in the world. Its approximately 12,300 members are organized in 55 regional chapters throughout the United States, Canada, and Europe and in 29 subject/functional divisions. SLA members work in special libraries and information centers serving business, research, government, universities, newspapers, museums, and institutions that use or produce specialized information. SLA has a tradition of special support services and opportunities for modern information managers. Association members form an international network of information professionals with a common interest in meeting information needs and putting knowledge to work.

The officers of the Special Libraries Association (June 1986–June 1987) are president: Frank H. Spaulding, AT&T Bell Laboratories, Holmdel, New Jersey; president-elect: Emily R. Mobley, Purdue University Libraries, West Lafayette, Indiana; secretary: Laura J. Rainey, Rockwell International, Canoga Park, California; treasurer: Muriel B. Regan, Gosage Regan Associates, New York City; and executive director: David R. Bender.

SLA Membership Survey

In 1986 SLA conducted a survey of its membership to identify trends in special librarianship and information management. The survey questionnaire, consisting of 54 questions, was mailed to 4,480 individuals; 2,327 completed surveys were returned. The high response rate (51.9 percent) reflects the SLA members' concern for the organization. Following are some highlights of the findings:

- 55 percent of the membership is between the ages of 31 and 45.
- 85 percent of the membership is female.
- 82 percent of the members have a master's degree in library/information science, and 20 percent have a master's degree in a particular subject field.
- 76 percent of the respondents have five or more years in the information field.

However, more than 50 percent have held their current position less than three years.

- 49 percent of the membership is employed in a corporate library. The next largest employer is academic institutions, followed by nonprofit and government agencies.
- 36 percent of the respondents have budgets greater than $100,000.
- Just over half of the respondents pay their own membership dues.
- Close to 40 percent of the respondents have been members less than two years.
- Of those members who have contacted SLA headquarters in the past six months, 84 percent indicated that the contact was satisfactory.
- 95 percent of the chapters and 85 percent of the divisions offer educational programming.
- 88 percent of the chapters and 70 percent of the divisions have directories.
- April, May, and October are preferred months for continuing education activities.
- Software application, library management, and finance/budgeting are the most desired topics for continuing education activities.
- 40 percent of the membership would prefer to hold the annual conference in small, less expensive cities. However, almost one-third of the membership had no preference for type of city.
- More than one-third of the respondents indicated that division programming, career, and networking opportunities should be increased.
- *Special Libraries* was rated highest in value of the publications read.
- Library management/skills articles were of greatest importance, with software applications articles next in value.
- 80 percent of the membership is not familiar with the Government Relations Program.
- 50 percent of those surveyed indicated that they would use brochures and a handbook/guide to promote the profession/image.
- 77 percent of those surveyed agreed that the name "Special Libraries Association" accurately describes the makeup of the membership.

SLA Long-Range Plan

In 1986 the board of directors approved the first major change to the association's five-year long-range plan, which was approved in 1984. The six priorities in support of SLA goals approved in 1984 were continuing education, public relations, membership services, finances, graduate education and accreditation, and chapter/division programming. Four new priorities are now being addressed in the expanded long-range plan, recognizing other areas of concern facing special librarians and information managers: membership development and growth, government relations/information policies, research (applied), and organizational structure.

Some of SLA's key accomplishments since 1984 (in support of the original six priorities) are improved and expanded professional development courses, an active public

relations program, new membership services based on results of the membership needs assessment survey, increased revenue from both dues and nondues sources, active involvement in graduate library accreditation (currently assessing the knowledge and competencies needed by entry-level special librarians and library managers), and leadership training for chapter and division officers.

A slide/tape package highlighting the main elements of the long-range plan has been made available to all chapters and divisions as a planning tool in preparing their own unit long-range plan. The commitment to a strategic vision and a supportive, dynamic long-range plan enable SLA to build a stronger future for the library/information profession.

SLA Activities

Conference

A highly successful seventy-seventh annual conference was held in Boston in June 1986. Approximately 5,200 attendees and 227 exhibitors participated in 335 programs on the theme of "Excellence in the World of Information." The keynote speaker, Rosabeth Moss Kanter, spoke on "Change Masters: Keys to Successful Innovation." Julianne H. Prager discussed "The Creative Environment for Excellence," and a panel of experts presented their views on "Technological Innovations for Excellence." The theme of the 1987 conference will be "Global Information Access—Expanding Our World," to be held in Anaheim, California.

Institute

On October 19–22, 1986, SLA held its first State-of-the Art Institute, "Government Information: An Endangered Resource of the Electronic Age." The institute concentrated on seven topics: federal information flow, government publications, sources of federal information, threats to access, creating information, information and the economy, and the future. The two-and-one-half-day interactive learning experience combined lectures by experts in their field, group discussions, and study sessions, providing a unique forum for information professionals to gain new insights into the availability and use of government information. Steve Bell, anchorperson for ABC's "World News This Morning," was the keynote speaker. Proceedings of the institute are available from the association office. Plans are underway for a second State-of-the-Art Institute in 1987.

Professional Development

Professional development is a major service to special librarians, information managers, and other information professionals. The first of the four components of this program service is continuing education courses offered at both the annual conference and at the SLA Winter Meeting. In Boston more than 1,000 information professionals participated in the 23 courses offered. The most popular topics emphasized computer applications and analysis, budgeting techniques, fee for information service, and excellence in library management. At the 1986 Winter Meeting in Nashville, more than 150 participants enrolled in courses and workshops. In addition, regional continuing education courses are given in seven cities in the United States and Canada throughout the

year. The Middle Management Institute, a five-unit program designed to bridge the educational gap between graduate library school and the requirements of a midlevel position in library/information management, has had 14 graduates. The Employment Clearinghouse and the Career Advisory Service are offered to all interested professionals at the annual conference. The Professional Development Committee and staff are presently developing a proposed Executive Development Program.

Accreditation

SLA continues to take an active role in graduate library and information science program accreditation. At the June 1986 Committee on Accreditation meeting at the American Library Association Conference, SLA affirmed its support of the recommendation that an Inter-Association Advisory Committee on Accreditation be formed with representation of SLA as one of the interested associations and institutions.

Publications

SLA's serial publications, *Special Libraries* (quarterly) and *SpeciaList* (monthly), continue to offer subscribers the best and most current information on theories, trends, and events that influence the profession. The fall 1986 issue of *Special Libraries* was devoted to library education in the United States as SLA salutes the first 100 years of library education. Other nonserial publications issued by SLA in 1986 include *The Special Librarian as a Supervisor or Middle Manager*, the *SLA Triennial Salary Survey*, *Special Libraries: A Guide for Management*, and *Who's Who in Special Libraries*.

Government Relations

In 1986 a director of government relations and fund development was added to the SLA staff. This position was established as part of the association's long-range plan, in recognition of the growth of SLA's government relations activity, and to increase the association's visibility in Washington, D.C.

Major issues of concern in 1986 were Library of Congress budget cuts, Senate and House document availability, privatization of NTIS, copyright-Canada, and the Gramm-Rudman-Hollings bill. Government relations is an area of increasing professional interest for all information associations.

Public Relations

Public relations is a growing concern among SLA chapters and divisions. Among the press releases and brochures presenting the views and concerns of the special librarians to the general public in 1986 is the brochure "What's Your IQ? (Image Quotient)," prepared to help professionals understand better impression formation. In light of today's economic revolution with decreasing library budgets, a presidential task force is at work to determine "The Value of the Information Professional." Its results will be presented at the 1987 SLA annual conference.

Scholarship

L. Draffan of the University of Washington and Paul D. Otto, who will enter Columbia University, received SLA's $6,000 scholarships. Lorelei A. Tanji of the University of California, Los Angeles, and Lin Veronica Look, who will enter the University of California, Berkeley, received $3,000 stipends from SLA's Positive Action Program for Minority Groups. Beth Paskoff was awarded the $1,000 Institute for Scientific Information scholarship, and Kathleen L. Maciuszko received the $1,000 Plenum scholarship.

Awards

At the SLA Banquet and Awards Ceremony in Boston the following information leaders were honored:

Doris L. Schild, a retired librarian from IBM Systems Research Institute, New York, and Ann Strickland, retired governmental reference librarian, Tucson, Arizona, received the John Cotton Dana Award in recognition of their exceptional service to special librarianship.

Edward G. Strable, retired manager of Information Services with J. W. Thompson USA, Chicago, and Mary Elizabeth Gibbs Moore, Gibbs Moore Information Services, Greensboro, North Carolina, were installed as members of the SLA Hall of Fame for their outstanding contributions to the growth and development of SLA at the chapter, division, and association levels.

Mary McNierney Grant, director of the Center for Business Research at the C. W. Post Campus of Long Island University, was awarded the SLA Professional Award in recognition of her significant contributions to the field of special librarianship. Among Grant's contributions to the field is the *Directory of Business and Financial Services*, now in its eighth edition.

Vivian J. Arterbery, former library director for the Rand Corporation, Santa Monica, California; James B. Tchobanoff, section manager of the Technical Information Center, Pillsbury Company, Minneapolis, Minnesota; and David R. Bender, SLA executive director, received the SLA President's Award for their outstanding contributions to the SLA long-range plan, which have furthered the goals and objectives of SLA in the past year.

The H. W. Wilson Award for the Best Paper in *Special Libraries* in 1985 was presented to Samuel Demas.

Frederick Kilgour, chairman emeritus, Online Computer Library Center, Dublin, Ohio, was elected an honorary member of SLA for his outstanding and innovative contributions to librarianship and information management.

The board of directors, at its June 1986 meeting, approved the establishment of a Fellows Award. The award will be given to members recognized by their peers as outstanding leaders in the profession who have made a significant contribution to SLA. The fellows may be called upon to advise the association board, to prepare discussion material, and to alert the membership to issues and trends warranting action. The first fellows will be recognized at the 1987 Awards Banquet in Anaheim.

Association Structure

At the 1986 Winter Meeting in Nashville, Tennessee, the board of directors established a Special Committee on Association Structure. SLA has been operating within a structure

designed in 1973 that provided for chapters and subject divisions along with committees that advise the board of directors. The special committee is charged to find the best way to organize SLA to cover its present needs and perhaps 10 to 15 years of future needs.

The Future of SLA

The mission of the Special Libraries Association is to advance the leadership role of its members in putting knowledge to work in the "Information Society." By becoming information leaders, through the efforts and resources of an effective, member-driven association . . . by taking the initiative in acknowledging excellence both within and outside the association . . . by being confident in knowing the value of information and the value of the professional services we provide in our work . . . by taking a leadership role in intersociety cooperation . . . by supplying information leadership to government and industry as the information society changes and evolves . . . we plant ourselves on the most direct path toward that elusive, shining goal: excellence.

Association of Research Libraries

1527 New Hampshire Ave. N.W., Washington, DC 20036

Nicola Daval

Information Officer

The Association of Research Libraries (ARL) is an organization of 118 major research libraries in the United States and Canada. ARL is an effective advocate for research libraries in both the library and scholarly communities, as well as in government and the private sector. It serves as a forum for consideration of issues, conducts studies, and develops plans to promote coordinated, collective action among its member institutions as they adapt to change in the world of scholarship and information, to new technology developments, and to increasingly stringent economic conditions.

ARL held two membership meetings during 1986. The May meeting focused on "Research Libraries: Measurement, Management, Marketing," and the October meeting on "North American Collections Inventory (NCIP): Means to an End." Edited proceedings, *Minutes of the Meetings*, are available for purchase from the association.

The moratorium on new members initiated in October 1985 continued through 1986. The President's Task Force on Membership Criteria made an interim report to the membership in October. The final report and recommendations are expected in time for membership consideration in May 1987.

ARL operates an auxiliary unit, the Office of Management Studies (OMS), and, until 1986, also operated the Center for Chinese Research Materials (CCRM). In September 1986, CCRM separated from ARL to become an independent, nonprofit organization. CCRM was established in 1968 with a $500,000 grant from the Ford Foundation and the sponsorship of ARL and the Joint Committee on Contemporary China of the American Council of Learned Societies and the Social Science Research Council. Later funding was received from the Mellon Foundation and the National Endowment for the

Humanities. CCRM's purpose is to provide rare and valuable research materials and bibliographic services to librarians and scholars in the field of Chinese studies, gathered from East Asian libraries in the United States and abroad. The center, which is now located in suburban Virginia, will continue to provide materials and services to the scholarly community and to seek additional materials needed by the community.

ARL activities and programs during 1986 centered on the objectives of the ARL five-year plan, adopted by the membership in 1983. The objectives address scholarly communication, access to research materials, preservation, information policy, staffing needs of research libraries, and management. Highlights of the year included completion of the CONSER Abstracting and Indexing (A&I) Project, a new cooperative venture with the Library of Congress to convert the *National Register of Microform Masters*, expanded efforts to build a collections inventory, and ARL's continued effectiveness as an advocate for research libraries in the federal legislative arena.

Access to Research Materials

CONSER A&I Project

The CONSER Abstracting and Indexing Project, a joint project with the National Federation of Abstracting and Indexing Services, was completed during 1986. Begun in 1983, this landmark cooperative project among members of the information community had as its primary goal to provide a link between library catalogs and A&I citations by enriching the CONSER database with information about coverage by abstracting and indexing services. The project has been a resounding success for libraries, the A&I services, and individual scholars and users.

Eighty-five services participated in the project, supplying information on serials coverage in 136 different A&I products covering more than 117,000 entries. In excess of 130,000 notes (in MARC field 510) were added to almost 50,000 unique bibliographic records. These titles represent the core materials needed to support the majority of serial information requested by library patrons. The records were enhanced with their ISSNs, key titles, and abbreviated key titles. The enhanced records have been authenticated and distributed through MARC-Serials. The A&I services have received the standardized information and library entries to use in subsequent production of their title coverage lists. Maintenance procedures have been established, with coordination through the National Serials Data Program. Funding for the project came from the National Endowment for the Humanities, the Council on Library Resources, the H. W. Wilson Foundation, the Xerox Corporation, and the Faxon Company.

ARL Recon Project

The ARL Recon Project, which began in July 1985, is designed to enrich the North American database with the bibliographic records of monographs for all significant collections in U.S. and Canadian research libraries. During the first 18 months, ten coordinated projects were begun, and collaborative projects involving 20 libraries are planned in four priority areas. In addition to assisting libraries in developing plans for coordinated retrospective conversion projects, in the past months ARL has focused on establishing the ARL Recon Clearinghouse to help libraries convert their records effectively

and economically. To date, the clearinghouse has data on recon projects planned or underway in 44 libraries; it will be updated as reports of new activities are received.

Collections Inventory

By the end of 1986, approximately 85 percent of the ARL membership was participating or planning to participate in the North American Collections Inventory Project (NCIP). ARL is currently in the third phase of this project to develop an online inventory of North American research library collections. NCIP builds on the work of the Research Libraries Group (RLG) begun in 1979 and collaborative efforts of RLG and ARL since 1983 to develop a standard approach to describe and assess research library collections in specific subject areas covering the full range of scholarly interests. This approach has led to a database that provides information on the location of specific subject collections and relative collection strengths and language coverage. The database, managed by RLG, is available both online and in printed form.

The ARL Office of Management Studies is operating the project, providing training in completing the conspectus for staff members in ARL libraries and serving as distributor for conspectus materials for non-RLG libraries. Also during 1986, OMS began publishing a project newsletter, *NCIP News*, to keep library directors and collection development librarians current on the latest NCIP developments. Revisions to worksheets and development of supplemental guidelines for all subject divisions of the conspectus are scheduled for completion in 1987.

In response to strong Canadian interest in NCIP, OMS has held four training workshops for members of the Canadian Association of Research Libraries. In addition to participating in the North American Inventory, the Canadian association is working with the National Library of Canada (NLC) to develop a Canadian Collections Inventory. NLC is developing system software for the Canadian Collections Inventory.

Preservation

ARL has undertaken a cooperative project with the Library of Congress to convert the monographic records in the *National Register of Microform Masters* (NRMM) to machine-readable form. The three-year project, with funding from the Andrew W. Mellon Foundation and the National Endowment for the Humanities, is expected to result in the creation of more than 460,000 records for microform masters held by libraries, archives, publishers, and other producers. ARL and LC have signed an agreement detailing the responsibilities of each organization in regard to this project, and a request for proposal for the conversion has been prepared in accordance with the technical guidelines of the ARL Recon Project. Contractor evaluation and selection will take place in early 1987 and conversion of NRMM records should begin before summer 1987.

In a continuing effort to help ARL libraries improve their preservation efforts, OMS has developed a Preservation Planning self-study, funded by a grant from the National Endowment for the Humanities. The ten libraries that served as demonstration sites for the development of the self-study have completed their final reports. (These reports can be purchased from OMS.) OMS also received a supplemental grant from the National Endowment in 1986 to update and expand the *Manual* and *Resource Notebook* used by libraries in preservation studies.

Staffing for Research Libraries

ARL's commitment to improve staffing for research libraries encompasses both the preparation of new staff and the development of existing staff to meet changing demands. Following the success of its first Institute on Research Libraries for Library and Information Science Faculty, OMS conducted a second institute during summer 1986. Ten library school faculty members participated in the institute, which was sponsored by a grant from the Council on Library Resources, to examine developments in research libraries that have an impact on the preparation of professional librarians. Boston Public Library and the libraries of the Massachusetts Institute of Technology and Harvard and Boston universities participated by providing group briefings on operations and activities. This institute, like its 1984 predecessor, received high ratings from participants.

Also through OMS, ARL operates an extensive training program for staff members in ARL and other research libraries. Two new programs were introduced during 1986. The first was the Leadership Development Program, designed to assist in building commitment for future library development among senior managerial staff. The second new training initiative was a Management Institute for Assistant/Associate Directors in ARL Libraries. Following the model of the successful Management Institute for ARL Directors, this institute provided a model-based examination of three broad themes: strategic planning, organizational change, and the role and use of power and influence in academic and research libraries. The institute was extremely successful, and a second one is planned for 1987. OMS Analytical Skills Institutes continue to be popular among librarians, as are the Management Skills Institutes (at both the basic and advanced levels) and Special Focus Workshops, which are sponsored by individual libraries and cover such topics as team building, managing change, organizational problem solving, and negotiation skills.

Information Policy

As in years past, in 1986 ARL concentrated its activities in the legislative arena on issues of primary concern to research libraries. Key among these was the reauthorization of the Higher Education Act (HEA), which was adopted by Congress and signed by the president. Library provisions in Titles II and VI of the revised HEA include those recommended jointly by ARL and ALA. Funding for library programs in both titles amounts to $31 million for FY 1987. Other areas of concern in 1986 included privatization of the National Technical Information Service, the second five-year review of the library photocopying provisions of the copyright law, discriminatory pricing to North American libraries of foreign journal publications, and plans by the Government Printing Office to save money by ceasing distribution to depository libraries of paper copies of almost all congressional publications, including the *Congressional Record*, the *Federal Register*, and other key titles.

Two new groups were established to address ARL concerns in this area. The first, the ARL Committee on Government Policies, will monitor the wide range of legislative and federal government issues of importance to ARL and advise on positions and strategies for the association. The second group, the ARL Task Force on Government Information in Electronic Format, was formed to address issues on library access to government information in electronic format, including the encouragement of proposed pilot projects for dissemination of electronic information to depository libraries. ARL

has also joined the Coalition on Government Information, a group of 20 organizations initiated by ALA to focus national attention on all efforts to limit access to government information and to develop support for improvements in access to government information.

Management of Research Libraries

The ARL Office of Management Studies continued to provide support to research libraries seeking to improve their management and service capabilities through its program of assisted self-studies (e.g., collection analysis, preservation, public services) and its active publications program, as well as the activities already described. Of particular interest is the automation inventory of ARL member libraries, which includes information on automation status, equipment, and expenditures. The data are available in a published report and are being maintained in an online database.

Maintaining the integrity of statistical data collected by ARL has been a priority of the association for many years. Building on issues covered at the May 1986 ARL membership meeting, ARL has revised the survey form for the collection of 1985–86 ARL Statistics in an attempt to collect more consistent and comparable figures. Expenditures for materials and salaries have been disaggregated, as have figures for current serials received (purchased and nonpurchased), and for the first time figures were collected separately for law and medical libraries at ARL institutions. (The past practice of individual libraries regarding inclusion of law and/or medical library figures has not been changed, however.) The Committee on ARL Statistics also conducted its third Supplementary Statistics survey in 1986 as a means of refining and clarifying data elements and of exploring new categories of data before adding them to the annual statistical survey.

In addition to its annual statistical publications, *ARL Statistics, 1984–85* and *ARL Annual Salary Survey* (for 1985), ARL published *The Gerould Statistics, 1907/08–1961/62* in 1986, completing the series of historical data on ARL libraries. This study reproduces and analyzes the statistical series on university libraries first collected by James Thayer Gerould at the University of Minnesota in 1908 and continued by the Princeton University Library from 1920 to 1962. *The Gerould Statistics*, along with *Cumulated ARL University Library Statistics, 1962/63 through 1978/79* and the annual *ARL Statistics*, comprise the longest and most comprehensive data series on libraries available.

Scholarly Communication

In 1985, the ARL Task Force on Scholarly Information completed its report to the ARL membership, outlining perceptions held within the research library community about changes taking place in the scholarly communication system. The report, which was published as *The Changing System of Scholarly Communication*, reviews the rapidly changing environment in which participants in the scholarly communication system must function and focuses particularly on scholars, publishers, and the record of scholarship and its use.

Summary

Aware of its important role as a vital force in the library, research, and higher education communities, the Association of Research Libraries will continue its efforts to identify

and solve the problems common to large research libraries so that they may effectively serve the needs of students, faculty, and the research community in general. It will also continue its efforts to strengthen and extend the capacity of North American research libraries to provide the recorded information needed both now and in the future by the research community.

The Evolution of WHCLIST

Barbara Cooper

Past Chairperson,
White House Conference on Library and Information Services Taskforce

The White House Conference on Library and Information Services Taskforce (WHCLIST) was organized in November 1980 in Minneapolis under sponsorship of the National Commission on Libraries and Information Science. Its charter is contained in Resolution F-5 of the 1979 White House Conference on Library and Information Services, calling for a delegation to be established consisting of one lay and one professional member from each state, territory, and special delegation to the conference. The National Commission is to assist the ad hoc group with planning for the conference and in promoting implementation and follow-up of conference resolutions.

The Implementation Process

First and foremost among the strategies employed by WHCLIST to carry out its charge has been personal initiative. The strength of the group has grown out of a unique mix of elected lay and professional leaders who were chosen because of their high visibility within their states. Using their connections with associations and other delegates, they have been able to get things accomplished and with high enthusiasm.

Another strength came from the overall White House Conference process within the states and at the national level in the years before 1979. In 1975 the National Commission had introduced its landmark "Toward a National Program for Library and Information Services: Goals for Action," opening the discussion on desired — and sometimes controversial — goals for the future. Many state librarians and library leaders had used the preparatory activities to promote new programs and gain statewide support for them. The American Library Association, NCLIS, and other professional associations that had participated in preconference activities participated in the implementation phase, along with WHCLIST.

Progress

Annual Reports

Progress has been summarized annually by WHCLIST in the *Report from the States* (including noncontiguous areas and special delegations), available through ERIC. The first report was requested by NCLIS as a working paper for the 1980 organizational meeting of WHCLIST in Minneapolis. Since 1981 the reports have been produced by

New York State Regent Laura Chodos, with substantial assistance from Joseph Shubert and the New York State Library staff. The reports are narrative, not statistical. Prepared by WHCLIST delegates and state librarians, they give valuable insight into the uneven progress of follow-up activities such as new legislation, progress in interlibrary cooperation, public awareness campaigns, statewide lay support group formation, and expansion of services. They also stand as records of the accomplishments of state library agencies and other institutions in effecting some of the changes forecast by the early NCLIS study. The early grass-roots discussion of such complicated "turf" topics as interlibrary cooperation, multitype systems, and universal library cards has helped foster later acceptance and legal adoption.

Five-Year Review

At the five-year midpoint between 1979 and the hoped-for second conference within a decade, WHCLIST acted as a catalyst for a "Five-Year Review of Progress Made toward Implementation of the Resolutions Adopted at the 1979 White House Conference on Library and Information Services." This was presented at the fifth annual WHCLIST meeting September 6-8, 1984, in Evanston, Illinois. Copies are available from Mary Alice Hedge Reszetar, associate director of NCLIS, who produced the review. Although the document is an impressive record of issues that are still very much alive, it is proof that the most basic issues assigned to structure a conference will emerge and be dealt with through the national conference process: Great or good progress has been made toward implementing 55 of the 64 resolutions.

COSLINE

In late 1984, COSLINE, the Council of State Library Agencies in the Northeast, held a seminal regional conference to focus on the formation of a library advocacy constituency, especially of citizens in a statewide Friends group or citizens council. Elinor Hashim, then chairperson of NCLIS, was a COSLINE guest. She announced that on July 10, 1984, NCLIS had resolved to appoint a design group for a 1989 conference and to request commitment by the president and Congress for its planning and conduct. The *Library Journal* of June 1, 1985, contains articles by Hashim, former NCLIS chairperson Charles Benton, and the author, then WHCLIST chairperson, that describe this gathering of forces.

WHCLIST Evolves

These events set in motion the evolution of WHCLIST from a group that looked back to a group that needed to look ahead. The original 118 elected delegates were now to be augmented by "associate members," anyone who evinced an interest in working toward WHCLIST goals by paying dues of $10. At the five-year level, too, it was obvious that membership composed solely of participants in the 1979 conference was no longer possible. At the sixth annual conference in Princeton, New Jersey, in 1985, the makeup of the state delegations was further clarified to allow each state a voting delegation of six at the annual conference. These changes allowed WHCLIST to draw in those who believe in a White House Conference and to double the number of active workers by 1986.

Included in the WHCLIST network are state library agency heads who have always been a vital part of the network, whether or not they are members.

At this half-way point WHCLIST also confronted the question of whether a second conference was in fact needed in light of the many accomplishments of the first and of what had been required of the states to plan and produce the WHCLIS I preconference, including both state and federal funds. In a June 1986 position paper, Eileen Cooke, executive director of the ALA Washington Office, reviewed some of the results of WHCLIS I for the library community, including improved visibility for libraries in the new U.S. Department of Education and an increase from $5 million to $12 million in LSCA Title III (interlibrary cooperation) resulting from networking resolutions. This strong funding support continues; and issues of networking and resource sharing, access, telecommunications, and document delivery technology are still high on the list of concerns to be addressed by WHCLIS II. Literacy is another of today's programs that derived impetus for funding and action from 1979 resolutions.

Public awareness is, of course, one of the major hoped-for results of any White House conference. The WHC resolution ". . . to encourage and assist the formation and development of Friends of Library groups in the United States" has surely been implemented successfully. Locally, at the state level, and nationally, these groups (with leadership from library professionals) have done much since 1979 to help get new money for services, buildings, and automation. A recent survey by Friends of Libraries U.S.A., whose strong leadership is directly traceable to participation in WHCLIS I, indicates that in one year more than 600,000 Friends raised nearly $28 million for libraries. Thirty-five states now have statewide Friends or citizens councils. These groups form a great resource in conducting successful state legislative initiatives and library days. WHCLIST's *Report from the States* shows a growth in both organizational expertise and library funding at the state level that is surely more than coincidental.

Legislation

The results of WHCLIS I were impressive to library supporters in Congress. Senator Claibourne Pell of Rhode Island and Representative Bill Ford of Michigan introduced identical legislation in April 1985, calling for a second White House Conference. The target date had been set in 1979 Resolution F-3, which called for one every decade ". . . to establish the national information goals and priorities for the next decade, to assure effective transfer of knowledge to citizenry, and to accomplish this goal in light of accelerated changes in information technology and practices."

Working with ALA and the National Commission, WHCLIST undertook a two-year effort to secure congressional cosponsors and gain passage of the legislation. A significant number, 172 representatives and 50 senators, agreed to become cosponsors. WHCLIST's brochure, "Target Date: 1989," was distributed nationally and brought an estimated 700 responses from librarians, trustees, and Friends who wanted to keep in touch with those working to make WHCLIS II a reality. WHCLIST delegates testified at a House hearing in 1986, but a Senate hearing did not materialize and the companion bills expired with the Ninety-ninth Congress. WHCLIST will be undertaking a similar role when new legislation is introduced in 1987 and should be better prepared to ensure passage. It has also embarked on the additional role of creating a network of library associations and outside groups that should be involved in conference preparation, urg-

ing them to set up liaison members or committees to plan future programs and preconference activities.

WHCLIS II: Form and Scope

What would be accomplished by a second national conference, and what form would it take? Library and information services for productivity, literacy, and democracy were identified as overarching themes by the National Commission Preliminary Conference Design Group, which met a number of times during 1985 and presented its report to NCLIS in December 1985, outlining a focus and format for WHCLIS II. The group felt that all issues that might surface through local, state, and national activities could be addressed under these broad themes, which would continue to be timely as planning and legislation proceeded through authorization and funding.

Current legislation proposes that once again a national advisory committee would have the responsibility for planning and conducting the second conference. NCLIS would oversee this effort and appoint eight members of the advisory committee. In the political realm, the president would appoint ten members, the Speaker of the House five (no more than three of whom would be representatives), and the president pro tempore of the Senate five (no more than three senators). The Librarian of Congress and secretary of education would also be advisory committee members.

The Preliminary Conference Design Group report notes three alternatives for funding. Although monies for library programs are small in comparison to other federal categories, it seemed unrealistic to expect federal appropriations for the entire operation. It was also not realistic to expect NCLIS and its advisory committee to produce a national conference (with state components) that would have the impact of WHCLIS I, without federal funds and White House sponsorship. Therefore the design group favored a combination of federal, state, and private sources, with the federal commitment at $5 million and a fallback position of not less than the 1979 cost of $3.9 million. Lay support groups might be eager to help fund travel expenses, to take this burden from state agencies, and other sponsors might be found to participate in planning and funding.

The need for maximum flexibility in the states was recognized early on. No repetition of the fairly rigid 1979 state preconference format was envisioned, although many design group members felt it was an important opportunity for state library agencies to once again promote solutions to state funding needs and to mobilize new professional and lay supporters. Therefore, it was left to each state to decide how much effort it would put into capitalizing on national legislation.

Preconference Meetings

WHCLIST's annual meetings (in connection with national library legislative day and ALA annual and midwinter conferences) are now dedicated to examining the proposed themes of the second conference. The meetings format is designed for replication at the state level also. A September 1986 meeting in Phoenix, Arizona, focused on library and information services to enhance productivity. It resulted in a broad definition of serving business and enlarged the concept of reference. Reports on the most recent conferences (at Princeton and Phoenix), and information about the 1987 conference to be held in Williamsburg, Virginia, on August 27–29, may be secured from the current WHCLIST chairperson: Mary Kit Dunn, 901 Brookside Dr., Greensboro, North Carolina 27408.

American Society for Information Science

1424 16th St. N.W., Washington, DC 20036
202-462-1000

Linda Resnik

Executive Director

In 1986, the American Society for Information Science (ASIS) adopted as its nickname the "Information Society for the Information Age," emphasizing its position as the leading organization for professionals in information science and technology. With a renewed focus on education, networking, and professional interaction, as well as on its advisory role to other organizations and government leaders on the value of information professionals, ASIS launched several aggressive initiatives to broaden its reach and impact within the dynamic information industry.

ASIS serves its broad and diverse membership in numerous ways. Through publications and meetings, ASIS provides opportunities for all professionals to share details of their work, their problems, and their solutions with colleagues throughout the world. With educational and professional development seminars and workshops, members can maintain or upgrade their skills in new and emerging aspects of the information profession. ASIS maintains active placement and job listing services for its members and provides numerous forums for members to communicate and cooperate among themselves in areas of common interest.

History of ASIS

When founded in 1937 as the American Documentation Institute (ADI), the society consisted of scientific and professional organizations, foundations, and government agencies with an orientation toward solving information-related problems using a promising new medium: microfilm. At that time, microfilm offered the first practical alternative to paper documentation and represented an exponential increase in the amount of information that could be stored and transmitted. With its role in the use of microfilm to solve information storage problems, ADI leapt to the forefront of what has become the information industry.

During those early years, ADI was in the vanguard in such activities as developing microfilm readers, cameras, and services; working toward agreements to control photoduplication of copyrighted materials; establishing programs for storage and reproduction of auxiliary publications to support journal editors; and operating an Oriental scientific literature service during World War II.

Beginning in the early 1950s, ADI leadership recognized that greater opportunities for widespread impact on the blossoming information profession rested in an emphasis on the *science* of information, rather than on the specific *media* of information. Thus, ADI amended its bylaws to include individual members, as well as institutional members, and began to focus on the multidisciplinary realities of the dynamic information profession. The transformation was completed in 1968, when ADI changed its name to the American Society for Information Science.

Fiftieth Anniversary Celebration

In 1986, almost half a century after its inception, ASIS began planning to celebrate its fiftieth anniversary. The yearlong celebration will formally begin in fall 1987. Special activities, ranging from seminars and workshops to new publications to souvenirs and social events honoring the profession's pioneers, will mark the important milestone in the history of the information profession.

SIGs and Chapters

The foundation of many ASIS efforts are the chapters and special interest groups (SIGs) that have been created by the membership to represent it and its interests in several areas. More than 50 local and student chapters throughout the United States, Canada, Europe, and Asia have been chartered to serve the professional needs of individual members in specific geographic areas. Each of these chapters builds its own program of activities geared to the needs of its membership. During 1986, greater emphasis was placed on the professional development of the members and more continuing education workshops and seminars were offered.

With 23 SIGs, ASIS covers virtually every technology and subject area in which active developments are recorded for information storage and retrieval. As has been typical throughout their existence, the SIGs presented to their members news of the latest research efforts in the various fields of information science and technology and emphasized the potential applications of new developments.

ASIS Long-Range Planning

In 1986, ASIS reviewed and revised its long-term goals to establish a firmer foundation for the 1990s. After an extensive process, which included participation by hundreds of ASIS members, as well as chapters and SIGs, the following goals pertaining to ASIS programs were adopted:

- To provide an environment that will stimulate participation and interaction among professionals from various disciplines and types of organizations having interests in information.
- To encourage and support the growth of information professionals and their organizations.
- To increase the awareness, credibility, and influence of ASIS and information professionals among decision makers in industry, government, education, and the professions and within the general public.
- To provide expertise and leadership in addressing the issues of an "information society" and in developing informed policies on national and international information issues.
- To maintain a leadership role in promoting information research and development and ensuring that the results of research are disseminated and technology is effectively transferred.

Activities for Public and Professional Awareness

During 1986, ASIS phased in its new national promotion effort emphasizing that ASIS helps individuals and companies get the "information edge" — described by ASIS as knowledge, insight, and direction about the people, products, services, and developments affecting information access. ASIS members participated in numerous debates, workshops, and briefings for corporate, political, and governmental leaders on such issues as privatization of government services, privacy, freedom of information, the White House Conference on Libraries and Information Services, the Government Information Act, copyright, and other issues that can and will affect access to information.

ASIS officers participated in various meetings at which the presidential theme for 1986 — challenges to the profession — was discussed and debated. Throughout her term, Julie A. C. Virgo, 1986 ASIS president, challenged ASIS members and other information professionals to adopt more aggressive stances in positioning themselves as critical links in the information transfer process. Noting the proclivity of certain multinational corporations to acquire library and information-related companies, Virgo suggested that failure by today's information professionals to exert their leadership will lead to the creation of a new style of information management led by people trained more as businesspeople and less as information experts.

Near the end of 1986, Thomas H. Hogan took office as the 1987 ASIS president, emphasizing outreach as the important theme of his term. Hogan promised more aggressive ASIS efforts in membership recruitment and public involvement in information-related issues.

Awards

The Award of Merit is presented annually to an individual who has made a noteworthy contribution to the field of information science, including the expression of new ideas, the creation of new devices, the development of better techniques, and outstanding service to the profession of information science. The 1986 ASIS Award of Merit, the highest honor bestowed by ASIS on an information professional, was presented to Bernard M. Fry, professor emeritus at Indiana University. Fry was honored for his widely recognized accomplishments in library and information science education; government publications development; transborder flow of information; impact of copyright legislation; and the economic factors that affect scholarly communication.

Other 1986 ASIS award winners include Marta Dosa, professor, School of Information Studies, Syracuse University, Syracuse, New York — Outstanding Information Science Teacher; *Organizing Information: Principles of Data Base and Retrieval Systems*, by Dagobert Soergel, published by Academic Press — Best Information Science Book; and N. Bernard (Buzzy) Basch, president, Turner Subscriptions — Watson Davis Award, given annually to an individual or individuals for outstanding continuous service to the society.

Publications

ASIS continued its active publications program in 1986 with six new titles or volumes in continuing series. New titles include *Telecommunications Networks: Issues and Trends*, edited by Mary Ellen Jacob; *New Directions in Library and Information Science Educa-*

tion, by Jose-Marie Griffiths and Donald W. King; and *Toward Foundations of Information Science*, edited by Laurence B. Heilprin. The 12th edition of *Library and Reference Facilities in the Area of the District of Columbia*, compiled by Margaret Jennings and published for ASIS in cooperation with The Joint Venture, was introduced late in 1986. Also published in 1986 were Volume 21 of the prestigious *Annual Review of Information Science and Technology (ARIST)*, edited by Martha E. Williams, and Volume 23 of the *Proceedings of the ASIS Annual Meetings*.

In addition to monographs and other books, ASIS continued publication of two of the leading periodicals in the field of information science. The *Journal of the American Society for Information Science*, published for ASIS by John Wiley and Sons, is a fully refereed scholarly and technical publication. The *Bulletin of the American Society for Information Science*, published by ASIS, is a newsmagazine focusing on issues affecting the information science field, pragmatic management reports, opinions, and news of people and events in the information science community.

Conferences

ASIS sponsors two of the field's most highly respected meetings each year. In 1986, the fifteenth ASIS Mid-Year Meeting in Portland, Oregon, presented an intense view of the management of databases, including techniques for building, changing, and using databases. The forty-ninth ASIS Annual Meeting, "Shaping the Future: The Sky's the Limit," held in Chicago, offered more than 150 sponsored events that provided opportunities to see the many ways in which information professionals are shaping the future of technology and how that technology is shaping the future of information.

ASIS Officers

At the end of 1986, new officers took their seats on the ASIS board of directors. President-elect is Martha E. Williams, professor of information science at the University of Illinois, Urbana. N. Bernard (Buzzy) Basch, president of Turner Subscriptions in New York City, was elected to a three-year term as treasurer.

Membership

ASIS membership was approximately 4,000 in 1986. Among the members are information specialists from such fields as computer science, management, engineering, librarianship, chemistry, linguistics, and education. ASIS members continue to lead the information profession in the search for new and better theories, techniques, and technologies to improve access to information through storage and retrieval advances. As has been true for nearly 50 years, ASIS and its members are called upon to help determine new directions and standards for the development of information policies and practices.

The Future

As 1986 ended, ASIS leaders and members turned their attention to the growing importance of information professionals in an information-intense society. Plans for the cele-

bration of the society's fiftieth anniversary, a continuation of the long-range planning process, aggressive recruitment efforts, and expanded activity in the area of public affairs will occupy the time and energy of the ASIS membership in 1987.

Association of American Publishers

220 E. 23 St., New York, NY 10010
212-689-8920

2005 Massachusetts Ave. N.W., Washington, DC
202-232-3335

Judith Platt

Publications Director

The Association of American Publishers (AAP), formed in 1970 by a merger of the American Book Publishers Council and the American Educational Publishers Institute, is the voice of book publishing in the United States. AAP's membership was broadened in 1982 to include publishers of freestanding multimedia products, including computer software and online databases. The more than 300 firms belonging to the association are located in every region of the country and represent every segment of the industry. AAP member firms publish the vast majority of printed materials sold to American schools and colleges, libraries, and bookstores and through direct-to-consumer channels. Members publish books in every field—general trade, textbooks, reference, religious, scientific, technical, medical, professional and scholarly—in hardcover and paperback. They also produce journals, computer software, and a range of educational materials, including classroom periodicals, maps, globes, filmstrips, audio- and videotapes, test materials, and loose-leaf services.

The AAP's core program serves those member interests that transcend specific market concerns, including domestic and international copyright, postal rates and regulations, censorship, libel and other First Amendment concerns, tax and trade issues, library and education funding, and new technology. The association's six divisions focus on particular product lines or market areas: general trade, mass market paperbacks, elhi textbooks, college textbooks, professional and scholarly publications, and foreign markets for U.S. books. Each division has its own executive body, with an annually elected chairperson, which gives general direction to divisional activities. These activities and special projects focus on marketing, promotion, research, and member education.

AAP policy is set by a 16-member board of directors, elected by the membership for a four-year term, under the direction of a chairperson who serves for two years. The chief operating officer, the president, is responsible for managing the association within the framework and guidelines set by the board. On May 1, 1986, Ambassador Nicholas A. Veliotes took office as AAP president, replacing Townsend Hoopes, who retired in January 1986. The association maintains two offices, in New York and Washington, and employs 28 staff members.

Highlights of 1986 Activities

Management of the association changed hands with the retirement of Townsend Hoopes, who had served as AAP president since 1973. AAP Chairman Jeremiah Kaplan (Macmillan) announced in January that a seven-member search committee headed by Brooks Thomas (Harper & Row) had unanimously selected U.S. Ambassador to Egypt Nicholas A. Veliotes to succeed Hoopes. AAP Executive Vice President Thomas D. McKee served as acting president until Veliotes officially assumed office on May 1.

The association's sixteenth annual meeting was held March 2–5 at The Breakers Hotel, Palm Beach, Florida. Congressman William H. Gray III, chairman of the House Budget Committee, and Gordon Ambach, New York State Commissioner of Education, were featured speakers. A special luncheon program sponsored by the AAP Freedom to Read Committee included a talk by Ellen Levine, editor in chief of *Women's Day Magazine* and a member of the Attorney General's Commission on Pornography.

Chairman Jeremiah Kaplan announced that plans to close the New York office and move all operations to Washington had been shelved.

AAP's fifth Consolidated Divisional Meeting, which brought the individual annual meetings of the various divisions together in one place, was held in Washington, D.C., January 16–17, 1986.

AAP testified at Senate hearings in January, opposing legislation to extend the manufacturing clause of the Copyright Act, stating that "no other country in the world has a law which holds the creative rights of its own authors and publishers hostage to the happenstance of the place of manufacture." The clause expired on July 1, 1986, with no legislation passed to extend it.

A First Amendment case in which AAP was coplaintiff made history when the U.S. Supreme Court decided that a controversial Indianapolis city ordinance declaring pornography a violation of women's civil rights is unconstitutional.

Through its International Copyright Protection Group, AAP continued its fight against international piracy of U.S. copyrighted works, testifying before the House Ways and Means and Senate Finance committees.

After 14 months of planning, the Higher Education Division's new electronic ordering network, PUBNET, got underway with a pilot test.

A provisional *Standard for Preparation and Markup of Electronic Manuscripts*, the outgrowth of AAP's three-year Electronic Manuscript Project, was published and submitted for final review and approval by the National Information Standards Organization (Z39) for adoption as an American National Standard.

Publishers won a significant victory in their copyright enforcement action against Texaco. A federal judge ruled that the suit could continue, and could do so on a class-action basis. In another important court victory, a federal judge ruled that the importation and sale of overseas editions of books whose rights were held by U.S. publishers is copyright infringement.

On November 17 the American Book Awards were presented, the last to be given under AAP auspices.

Divisions

General Publishing Division

The General Publishing Division (GPD), chaired by Bruce Harris (Crown), represents some 120 publishers of fiction, nonfiction, children's literature, religious, and reference

books. Its programs, frequently carried out in conjunction with other AAP divisions, have three main objectives: to broaden the audience for books; to strengthen ties with the library and bookselling communities; and to improve publishers' management and marketing skills.

The division maintains close ties with the American Booksellers Association, the National Association of College Stores, and the American Library Association. Joint liaison committees with each of these associations meet on a regular basis to review shared concerns and seek solutions to common problems. During 1986, the GPD Executive Council established closer ties with P.E.N. in an effort to promote effective communication among all segments of the book community. A GPD subcommittee is currently looking into the new phenomenon of street book vending, to assess the extent of the problem and explore possible remedies.

The division is cooperating with the Center for the Book in the Library of Congress to develop projects in support of the "1987 Year of the Reader" campaign. GPD cosponsors, along with the AAP Paperback Publishing Division, the ALA, NACS, ABA, and the Center for the Book, the "I'd Rather Be Reading" promotional campaign. In June, GPD cosponsored, with the Paperback Publishing Division, an "Evening of Readings," which raised more than $75,000 to benefit the Literacy Volunteers of New York City.

GPD sponsors an informal series of "forum luncheons" on a range of subjects of interest to publishers. Among the areas covered in the 1986 series were effective publishing and marketing of children's books; supporting a sale force; the role of special sales; and profitable direct marketing.

The division publishes an annual *Exhibits Directory*, with a comprehensive list of the meetings and trade shows of various educational, library, technical, and scientific associations. The *Directory* is a valuable resource for publishers interested in exhibiting at these events.

Higher Education Division

The Higher Education Division (HED), chaired by Lisa Bayard (Holt, Rinehart & Winston), is concerned with all aspects of marketing, production, and distribution of textbooks for postsecondary education. A primary objective of the division is to keep open lines of communication between publishers and college bookstore managers, college faculty, and students. The division has a close working relationship with the National Association of College Stores.

For more than a year an HED task force has been working to create and develop PUBNET, a new electronic ordering system for college publishers. In May 1986, the HED Executive Council approved the implementation of PUBNET, and the first phase of the pilot program began late in 1986. The first publisher database went online on December 23, 1986.

Initially set up to serve the college textbook industry, this electronic data communications network is expected to eventually serve other segments of the publishing industry. PUBNET is accessible through a wide range of data entry devices, including asynchronous terminals, microcomputers, minicomputers, and mainframes. Its first application will be to perform three major functions for the college textbook industry: electronic order processing, electronic information distribution, and electronic mail. The program has 21 charter members; following its pilot test, it will be fully operational for the summer 1987 ordering schedule.

HED's effective public relations program, the AAP Student Service, strengthens ties with college students through a number of popular brochures, including *How to Get the Most Out of Your Textbook* and *How to Improve Your Reading Skills*. The division also publishes material for college bookstore managers and college faculty members, one of which is *Links*.

The Higher Education Division sponsors the popular AAP/WEST seminars for publishers west of the Rockies. The fall 1986 seminar, "College Publishing: Are We in Trouble," which focused on the subject of used books, proved so timely that a portion of it will be presented at the HED 1987 annual meeting in Princeton, New Jersey.

The division publishes the annual *AAP College Textbook Publishers Greenbook*, a directory of college textbook publishers and their customer service representatives, which has proven particularly valuable for college store managers.

HED sponsors a Publishers Center each year at the National Association of College Stores meeting and trade fair. The division also operates the AAP College Textbook Fiche Service, which, for a small annual fee, provides 400 college bookstore subscribers with microfiches, updated monthly, of some 55,000 textbook titles available from more than three dozen leading publishers.

International Division

The International Division (ID), chaired by Adrian Higham (John Wiley & Sons), was established in response to the growing importance of foreign markets for U.S. books to meet the challenge of an increasingly complex international marketplace. The division represents the whole range of AAP membership, both in size of house and type of publishing product, focusing on all issues affecting the marketing of U.S. books abroad.

Among the division's highest priorities are improving trade relations with the Third World; developing members' professional skills through seminars and workshops; developing and strengthening ties with those U.S. government agencies, including the United States Information Agency, the Department of State, and the Commerce Department, most concerned with promoting U.S. books abroad through overseas fairs and exhibits; fostering international respect for copyright; gathering and disseminating international sales statistics; and promoting U.S. publisher attendance and active participation at international bookfairs.

AAP activities in the international arena in 1986 included an exchange of delegations with the People's Republic of China in conjunction with the Beijing and Xian Book Fairs. International Division Chairman Adrian Higham, AAP President Nicholas Veliotes, and other AAP member publishers participated in high-level discussions with PRC officials in Beijing to stress the need for strong ties between U.S. and Chinese publishers, to encourage the increased availability of foreign exchange for book and journal purchases, and to stress the importance of early enactment of an effective Chinese copyright law.

AAP member publishers participated in Soviet-American talks on books and publishing held at the Frankfurt Book Fair, organized by the USIA as part of the president's U.S.-Soviet Exchange Initiative.

The ID's annual meeting, June 12–13, included presentations on the role of government in assisting the export publisher and reviews of the Asian, African, and Canadian markets.

The division again sponsored an International Visitors Center at the 1986 Ameri-

can Booksellers Association convention in New Orleans. Since it was inaugurated six years ago, the center has become increasingly popular, providing a place for overseas booksellers, publishers, and agents to meet with American publishing representatives. A directory of international sales and rights personnel attending ABA was distributed at the center.

Among the division's publications are statistical reports on international sales of mass market paperback books and materials on English for speakers of other languages.

Paperback Publishing Division

The Paperback Publishing Division (PPD), chaired by Susan Petersen (Ballantine/ Fawcett/Del Ray), is carrying out its mandate to promote paperback books as an indispensable component of educational and recreational reading in the United States, exploring new areas in marketing, production, and distribution.

The division works to enhance the market for paperback books, strengthen the lines of communication with booksellers and wholesalers, and provide a forum where mutual problems can be discussed and cooperative efforts made to solve them. The division maintains strong ties with the American Booksellers Association, the National Association of College Stores, the Independent Periodical Distributors Association, and the Council of Periodical Distributors Associations. PPD sponsored a very successful workshop in 1986 that brought publishers and representatives of the book wholesaler community together. Meetings with NACS representatives provided an opportunity to discuss ways of improving the marketing of paperback books in college stores.

An important legal victory was achieved in July 1986 in a lawsuit aimed at ending the illegal importation of overseas editions of books to which U.S. publishers hold the rights. The litigation, which was initiated in 1984 and coordinated by the Paperback Publishing Division, resulted in a ruling in federal court that the importation and sale of the British editions of books whose U.S. rights were held by the publisher-plaintiffs infringed the copyrights of all 18 books involved.

Headway was made in another area of concern to PPD members—"loose in the mail" books—with the issuance of new regulations by the U.S. Postal Service intended to streamline the procedure for getting these books back into the hands of their publishers.

The division sponsors two programs publicizing bestsellers: America's Top Ten—a monthly listing of bestselling backlist books; and Campus Paperback Bestsellers—a monthly listing of the ten bestselling books on college campuses.

"Book Previews," one of PPD's most popular programs, alerts college bookstore buyers to paperback titles that will be popular on campuses during the coming year. The program, which combines a slide presentation with live narrative, was expanded in 1986 to include children's books.

PPD is coordinating an effort to promote literacy ads in paperback books. In cooperation with the Coalition for Literacy, the ads focus community awareness on the high social costs of illiteracy.

PPD's Educational Marketing Committee sponsors a successful cooperative exhibits program that enables publishers to exhibit books at a number of trade shows for a fraction of the cost of an individual exhibit. The program, which began several years ago with two trade shows, will cover 12 shows in the 1986–1987 exhibit year.

The Professional and Scholarly Publishing Division

The Professional and Scholarly Publishing Division (PSP), chaired by Myer Kutz (John Wiley & Sons), is concerned with production, marketing, and distribution of technical, scientific, medical, and scholarly books and journals, loose-leaf services, and database publishing, produced primarily, although not exclusively, for the practicing engineer and scientist and the professional business community. The division monitors relevant federal funding for programs of concern to PSP members; works to facilitate the exchange of information through seminars on journal publishing, marketing, sales, new technology, and copyright; and maintains close ties with other professional associations such as the International Group of Scientific, Technical and Medical Publishers, the Society for Scholarly Publishing, and the American Medical Publishers' Association.

The tenth annual PSP awards were presented in January 1986 at the Consolidated Divisional Meeting in Washington, D.C. The R. R. Hawkins Award for the Outstanding Technical, Scientific or Medical Book for 1985 went to Van Nostrand Reinhold Company for *American Insects: A Handbook of the Insects of America North of Mexico*, by Ross H. Arnett, Jr., Ph.D. In addition, 33 other awards and honorable mentions were given for books, journals, loose-leaf publications, and microcomputer software.

During 1986, an extensive series of seminars and workshops were conducted by the Journals and Marketing committees. The division's other standing committees are Looseleaf, Database, Public Relations, and the PSP Awards Program.

School Division

The AAP School Division, chaired by Richard Peterson (Scott Foresman), is concerned with the production, marketing, and distribution of textbooks and other instructional materials for kindergarten through twelfth grade. The division's primary focus is on increasing funding for educational materials and simplifying textbook adoption procedures. It works to publicize the importance of instructional materials in the educational process, and, through its work with professional organizations, research groups, and the educational community, strives to enhance the image of the publishing industry. The division sponsors seminars and conferences on topics of concern to educators and publishers.

The School Division works closely with state boards of education, legislatures, departments of education, and other state organizations in areas of common concern, and sponsors legislative advocates in a number of states to put forward the views and represent the interests of member publishers.

School Division committees work to acquaint parents, educators, and others with the concerns of educational publishers through seminars and publications such as *Parent's Guide to More Effective Schools, Textbook Publishers and the Censorship Controversy, How a Textbook Is Made*, and *Standardized Testing*. Public service ads and radio spots are also part of the division's grass-roots public information campaign.

Now in its sixth year, the Education Research Awards competition has provided grants for graduate study to 15 doctoral students in education. Two of these grants were awarded in 1986.

The School Division also presents an annual Mary McNulty Award for service and commitment to educational excellence. The 1986 recipient was Alexander J. Burke, Jr., of McGraw-Hill.

The Critical Issues in Educational Publishing Committee sponsors an ongoing se-

ries of luncheon seminars on subjects of concern to educational publishers. The 1986 series included "Budgeting for Editors, Designers and Supervisors," "The Art of Negotiation," and "Testing."

In addition to its Executive Committee, standing committees of the division include Communications, Critical Issues in Educational Publishing, Research, Statistics, Testing, Textbook Specifications, and selected state committees.

Core Activities

Book Distribution Program

AAP's Book Distribution Program serves to keep publishers informed of current developments in book distribution and, working with a variety of organizations within and outside the book community, to promote the development of more efficient book distribution systems.

In 1986, the Book Distribution Program continued to represent AAP on the Network Advisory Committee to the Library of Congress (and other library organizations), on the Book Industry Systems Advisory Committee (BISAC), and in the area of standardization. Several draft American National Standards, including the AAP Standard for Preparation and Markup of Electronic Manuscripts, were received from the National Information Standards Organization (Z39) and circulated for review prior to casting AAP's ballot.

BISAC activity included the adoption of the Bookland EAN bar code, approval of a computer-to-computer format to indicate the items covered in a payment to a publisher, and development of a computer-to-computer format for order acknowledgment. The latter will be used in the PUBNET system (discussed earlier under Higher Education Division).

Several years ago the program initiated a meeting of international distribution specialists held in conjunction with the Frankfurt Book Fair. It will also chair the 1987 meeting.

Copyright Committee

The Copyright Committee, chaired by Myer Kutz (John Wiley & Sons), promotes and defends the proprietary rights of authors and publishers. The committee monitors copyright activity in the United States and worldwide, acts as an advisory body to the AAP board of directors in formulating policy on legislative issues involving copyright, and works with AAP's copyright counsel in the preparation of congressional testimony. One of the committee's primary objectives is to foster an awareness of the central role copyright plays in the artistic and commercial lives of the publishing industry. In pursuing its educational objectives, the committee sponsors workshops and seminars on various aspects of copyright. It recommends and coordinates enforcement activities, including litigation, and works closely with the AAP International Copyright Protection Group in efforts to combat international piracy. The committee maintains close contact with the U.S. Copyright Office.

A significant development in the AAP copyright enforcement action against Texaco occurred in June 1986 with a favorable ruling in federal court allowing the plaintiffs to pursue their suit and to do so on a class-action basis. (The six named plaintiffs are

suing on their own behalf and on behalf of some 600 other publishers whose works are entered in the Copyright Clearance Center.)

Another copyright court victory was achieved in the copyright infringement action against a California book importer (see Paperback Publishing Division section). The Copyright Committee also coordinated a suit against the U.S. Customs Service, challenging its classification of several art books (which enter the U.S. duty-free) as "bound lithographs" (which are subject to duty). The Customs Service reclassified all but one of the books in question after suit was filed, and AAP is pursuing reclassification of the remaining book.

The committee coordinated AAP action on a number of legislative issues, including proposals to extend the manufacturing clause of the copyright law beyond the scheduled expiration date of July 1, 1986. Although no legislation to extend the clause was enacted in the Ninety-ninth Congress, the committee will continue to follow this issue closely.

Another major legislative concern is possible U.S. adherence to the Berne Convention and the legislation required to implement such adherence. In March, the Copyright Committee recommended that AAP support U.S. accession to Berne, provided that such accession "does not become an inadvertent or backdoor means to change domestic copyright law in a manner that will impact upon the way American publishers do business or disrupt certain contractual relationships." In April, AAP testified to that effect at Senate hearings.

The committee also monitored legislation introduced to modify the work-for-hire provisions of the copyright law and prepared briefing documents for the AAP board pointing up the fallacies of arguments advanced in support of such legislation.

The Copyright Committee protested a proposed increase in Copyright Office fees, reasoning that any fee increase should be tied to an overall revision of the registration system—particularly elimination of the registration requirement as a condition for receiving statutory damages and attorney's fees. The fee-increase proposal was later withdrawn by the Copyright Office.

Freedom to Read Committee

The Freedom to Read (FTR) Committee, AAP's First Amendment advocacy group, is concerned with protecting and promoting those freedoms guaranteed by the First Amendment to the Constitution. Chaired by Erwin Glikes, publisher of the Free Press (Macmillan), the committee plays a major educational role to promote an understanding of and appreciation for First Amendment rights. The committee plays an active role in the judicial and legislative arenas, intervening in selected court cases, testifying before congressional committees and other panels, and issuing public statements to protest attempts to limit free communication. The committee works closely with organizations having similar concerns, notably the Office for Intellectual Freedom of the American Library Association.

Much of the committee's attention during 1986 was focused on the activities of the Attorney General's Commission on Pornography, whose controversial report was issued in July. AAP testified for a second time (the first testimony was given in June 1985) at commission hearings in New York in January. An FTR-sponsored program at the AAP annual meeting gave publishers an opportunity to hear commission member Ellen Levine. The committee also coordinated AAP's submission of statements by five au-

thors urging the commission to exercise restraint in dealing with literary areas protected by the First Amendment.

In a carefully limited amicus brief, AAP intervened in litigation against the commission brought by Playboy Enterprises, Inc. The AAP position, protesting as improper and unconstitutional the commission's action in sending a warning letter to certain publisher/distributors, was upheld in federal court.

Following careful study of the commission's report, the Freedom to Read Committee formulated recommendations to the AAP board of directors that resulted in November in board adoption of a six-point formal resolution expressing AAP's concern over major aspects of the commission's report and follow-up measures proposed by the attorney general that would encourage censorship and have a "chilling effect" on the publication and distribution of Constitutionally protected material.

A First Amendment case in which AAP was a coplaintiff made history when the Supreme Court upheld the plaintiffs' position that an Indianapolis city ordinance declaring pornography a violation of women's civil rights was overbroad and unconstitutional.

The Freedom to Read Committee and the ALA Office for Intellectual Freedom sponsored a timely program on "The Worlds of Science and Technology: How Free?" during the 1986 ALA midsummer meeting in New York.

The committee coordinated AAP's successful intervention on behalf of Simon & Schuster to reverse a lower court's misinterpretation of New Jersey's "Son of Sam" law. The committee has undertaken a broad study of these laws, which are intended to prevent criminals from profiting from book or movie rights sales of accounts of their crimes.

The Freedom to Read Committee helped coordinate publisher participation in a campaign to defeat an obscenity referendum in Maine. The referendum was rejected by a wide margin.

International Copyright Protection Group

Formed three years ago to combat the international theft of U.S. copyrighted works, the International Copyright Protection Group (ICPG) is composed of members of the Copyright Committee and the International Division. Under the chairmanship of Alexander J. Burke, Jr. (McGraw-Hill), the ICPG has mounted an effective campaign against international piracy. The group develops and exchanges current information on copyright enforcement and piracy overseas; creates and coordinates antipiracy strategies for the AAP membership; and directs lobbying efforts in Washington aimed at educating members of Congress and the administration to the serious threat posed by international piracy.

The ICPG coordinates publisher participation in the International Intellectual Property Alliance, a coalition of the copyright industries that AAP helped organize several years ago to lobby for administrative and legislative solutions to the piracy problem.

In February 1986, ICPG Chairman Alexander Burke appeared before the House Ways and Means Committee and asked Congress to take "every possible action," including denial of trade benefits, to end copyright piracy in the Dominican Republic. A new copyright law, which AAP helped draft, was enacted and signed by the president of the Dominican Republic on July 4, 1986—the culmination of three years of pressure exerted

by AAP on a country that had one of the worst piracy records in the Western Hemisphere.

AAP President Nicholas Veliotes testified on behalf of the International Intellectual Property Alliance before the Senate International Trade Subcommittee on May 14, calling on Congress to fund an all-out effort to end international piracy through the creation of an "Anti-Piracy Delta Force" in the Office of the U.S. Trade Representative.

The ICPG coordinated Alliance action in June 1986 petitioning the president to strip Indonesia of certain trade benefits because of its intransigence on the piracy issue. Working through the Alliance, the group achieved another resounding success in June, when the government of Singapore, which had been targeted as one of the most blatant pirate nations, indicated its intention to join the Universal Copyright Convention and agreed to enter into an interim bilateral arrangement with the United States that will afford copyright protection to U.S. works beginning in early 1987.

In July, the U.S. and Korean governments entered into an agreement calling for enactment by Korea of copyright laws covering all published materials, including software, to go into effect on July 1, 1987, and a commitment by Korea to join the Universal Copyright Convention.

The ICPG/Alliance educational campaign, which has created a heightened awareness of the importance of intellectual property, resulted in an important development with respect to forthcoming multilateral trade talks. In the face of strenuous opposition from several developing countries, in September 1986, a U.S. negotiating team successfully achieved inclusion of intellectual property rights protection on the agenda for the eighth round of GATT (General Agreement on Tariffs and Trade) talks. For the first time in history, the need to promote adequate and effective protection for patents, trademarks, and copyrights, will be an integral part of the GATT negotiations.

International Freedom to Publish Committee

AAP's International Freedom to Publish (IFTP) Committee is the only entity formed by a major publishers' group in any country for the specific purpose of defending and broadening the freedom of written communication wherever it is threatened. The committee monitors the status of human rights for publishers and authors, offering moral support and practical assistance when needed. Through correspondence and in testimony before congressional committees, the IFTP Committee communicates with lawmakers on human rights issues. The committee extends open invitations to foreign writers to visit the United States and contacts foreign authorities on behalf of writers and publishers who are denied basic freedoms. The committee works closely with such groups as Amnesty International, the Helsinki Watch, the Americas Watch, the Fund for Free Expression, and other human rights organizations. As John Macrae III (Henry Holt and Co.), chair of the committee, said in a special message to the AAP 1986 annual meeting: "Book publishing, which is one of the great peaceful means of educating the human race, cannot exist solely within national borders. The freedom of writers everywhere to express themselves as they wish and to make arrangements for the publication of their works throughout the world without fear or intimidation is a paramount concern of American publishers."

Roland Algrant (Hearst) took over the chairmanship of the committee in fall 1986.

During 1986, the committee sponsored a luncheon for writers from repressive countries who were in New York to attend the P.E.N. International Congress in January.

As part of its continuing effort to monitor free expression and aid persecuted writers, the committee fielded two fact-finding missions during 1986, one to South Africa and the other to Yugoslavia. The reports of these fact-finding missions were made available to other human rights groups.

New Technology Committee

The activities of the New Technology Committee are carried on by two virtually autonomous subcommittees: Software and Electronic Publishing.

The Software Subcommittee, chaired by Diane Litwin (John Wiley & Sons), studies and makes recommendations regarding the copyright law, procedures of the U.S. Copyright Office, U.S. Customs regulations, and postal rates as they apply to computer software. The subcommittee also sponsors workshops and seminars to assist AAP members who are publishing or contemplating publishing software. The subcommittee conducted two workshops in 1986: "Site Licensing for Software in a College Environment" and "The Effect of Reviews and Publicity on the Marketing of Elhi Software."

The Electronic Publishing Subcommittee, under the chairmanship of Nicholas Alter (University Microfilms International), has coordinated and directed AAP's three-year, $360,000 Electronic Manuscript Project culminating in January 1986 with the publication of the *AAP Standard for the Preparation and Markup of Electronic Manuscripts*. This was followed in June with the publication of four guidebooks to assist authors and editors in using the *AAP Standard*.

In fall 1986, the AAP board of directors approved establishment of an Electronic Publishing Special Interest Group (EPSIG), open to AAP members and nonmembers, to assist in the use of the *AAP Standard* and to serve as an information clearinghouse on the *Standard* and related products. With four membership categories, EPSIG offers a variety of benefits at various cost options.

The New Technology Committee also operates the Publishing Industry Electronic Mail Network, which, for a small subscription fee, provides a convenient electronic communications network for the industry.

Postal Committee

The Postal Committee monitors the activities of the U.S. Postal Service (USPS), formulates positions and prepares testimony on postal matters for congressional hearings, intervenes in proceedings before the Postal Rate Commission, and sees that publisher concerns and views on postal matters are heard in Congress and in the executive branch. The committee is chaired by Stephen Bair (Time-Life Books).

The Postal Committee joins with other mail users in support of measures that will keep the U.S. Postal Service viable and competitive.

Two proceedings are currently pending before the Postal Rate Commission. Both were initiated by the United Parcel Service, and each may adversely affect the rates paid by publishers to ship books. AAP has formed a coalition with other concerned organizations (the Parcel Shippers Association and the Mail Order Association of America) to protect the rights of publishers and other mailers in these proceedings.

Changes in Postal Service procedures have produced problems for some publishers in getting books delivered to consumers who have moved. The Postal Committee is working to have these procedures revised to ensure proper and timely forwarding of books sent via the mails.

As a result of long-term efforts by the AAP Postal Committee, the U.S. Postal Service issued new regulations governing procedures for the return of "loose in the mail" books and sound recordings. The new regulations, which go into effect January 1, 1987, streamline the procedure and improve USPS efficiency in getting these books back to their publishers.

Administrative Committees

The four administrative committees of AAP are described:

The Lawyers Committee, composed of both in-house and outside counsel of AAP member companies, meets quarterly to advise the association in such areas as libel and invasion of privacy, First Amendment, antitrust, product liability, insurance coverage, and others.

The Compensation Survey Committee coordinates and oversees preparation of the AAP *Survey of Compensation and Personnel Practices in the Publishing Industry.* The *Survey* provides member companies with information on salary and personnel practices in the industry, enabling them to make more informed decisions concerning compensation and fringe benefits. The *Survey*, prepared in collaboration with Sibson & Company, is published approximately every two years.

The Insurance Committee monitors the AAP group insurance plan. With more than 100 participating companies and annual premiums in excess of $6 million, the plan offers several options of coverage in life, medical, dental, liability, and eye care insurance. It provides good coverage and service at reasonable cost, and continues to be an important economic benefit to AAP members.

The Statistics Committee oversees the preparation of monthly and annual statistical reports published by AAP. The AAP financial report, which includes information on sales, operating costs, inventory turnover, and accounts receivable aging, is prepared by the Statistical Service Center, an independent consulting firm, under procedures guaranteed to protect confidentiality of financial data reported by individual houses.

Political Action Committee

The AAP Political Action Committee allows industry members to take an active part in the political process. The committee supports candidates for the House and Senate of both political parties who are responsive to and concerned about issues vital to publishers.

Awards

The 1986 American Book Awards were presented on November 17. Two awards were presented: *World's Fair* by E. L. Doctorow (Random House) and *Arctic Dreams* by Barry Lopez (Scribner's) were the winners in the fiction and nonfiction categories, respectively. This is the final year that the awards will be given under AAP auspices. On January 1, 1987, the awards program becomes an independent, tax-exempt organization, and resumes the name National Book Awards, the predecessor of the current program.

The Eleventh Annual Curtis G. Benjamin Award for Creative Publishing was pre-

sented to Simon Michael Bessie, copublisher of Cornelia and Michael Bessie Books and a member of the board of Harper & Row Publishers.

The School Division's Mary McNulty Award went to Alexander J. Burke, Jr., of McGraw-Hill Book Company.

The Professional and Scholarly Publishing Division's R. R. Hawkins Award went to Van Nostrand Reinhold Company for *American Insects: A Handbook of the Insects of America North of Mexico*, by Ross H. Arnett, Jr., Ph.D.

Publications

AAP Monthly Report is a newsletter published at the beginning of each month that covers a range of association activities and issues of concern to the industry. With a circulation of more than 2,000, the *Monthly Report* is a primary channel of communication with the membership.

The association also publishes *Industry Statistics Report* on sales and operating expenses; *Survey of Compensation and Personnel Practices in the Publishing Industry*; an annual *Exhibits Directory* with information on more than 300 meetings and trade shows of interest to publishers; a directory of college textbook publishers, *The Greenbook*; and a broad range of special divisional and other publications. A publications list is available from AAP on request.

American Booksellers Association

122 E. 42 St., New York, NY 10168

Bernard Rath

Executive Director

The American Booksellers Association was founded in November 1900 by six retail booksellers to represent the interests of their trade. The association has developed and expanded throughout its 85-year history; however, its essential objective has remained unchanged: to be an organization for, by, and about the retail bookseller. [For a list of the association's specific objectives, see the 1986 *Bowker Annual*, p. 204—*Ed.*]

As of this writing, the association's membership is constituted of 3,744 main stores and 689 branches; 344 individuals who are prospective booksellers; and 712 associate members whose ranks include publishers, wholesalers, sidelines manufacturers, and other suppliers. Foreign stores are eligible for membership, as are institutions, individuals who work in stores, and retired book people.

The association's staff of 26 works with budgeted gross revenues of $3,183,310. Its subsidiary, Booksellers Publishing, Inc., with a staff of seven, publishes the trade industry journal *American Bookseller* and generates gross revenues of $833,758. Elected officers for 1986–1987 are President J. Rhett Jackson of The Happy Bookseller, Columbia, South Carolina; Vice President Kim Browning of Dodds Bookshop, Long Beach, California; Secretary Andy Ross of Cody's Books, Berkeley, California; and Treasurer A. David Schwartz of Dickens Book, Ltd., Milwaukee, Wisconsin. The elected board of directors includes the four officers, along with an immediate past president and 13 di-

rectors. (Two vacancies on the board of directors remain unfilled for the balance of the current board's term.) Annual elections are held in the spring, and new officers and directors take office at the membership meeting held at the annual convention and trade show.

Bookselling Highlights of 1986

The year 1986 was an active one for retail bookselling on many fronts: industry involvement in the campaign against illiteracy, including the launch of the Give the Gift of Literacy campaign; continued involvement in fighting restrictive censorship legislation through the industry organization Media Coalition; increased discounting activity by national and regional chains; an increasing number of stores making the transition to computers for a variety of in-store tasks ranging from payroll to inventory control systems; and the purchase of the B. Dalton bookstore chain by Barnes and Noble bookstores, making Barnes and Noble the largest operator of bookstores nationwide and bringing further industry concentration in the hands of a few large chains. The American Booksellers Association has been active in all of these areas and concerns.

ABA Annual Convention

At the eighty-sixth annual ABA convention and trade show, held in New Orleans, the nationwide Give the Gift of Literacy campaign was launched with a press conference featuring heads of publishing houses, ABC news commentator Sam Donaldson, and the industry person most instrumental in wakening the publishing/bookselling community to the problem of illiteracy, Bette Fenton, B. Dalton's vice president of community relations. Give the Gift of Literacy, of which ABA, along with B. Dalton, is a prime sponsor, is a program in which participating booksellers agree to give counter space in their stores for a cylinder in which consumer donations to literacy organizations are collected. Information about the illiteracy problem in the United States is provided, as well as an 800 telephone number for consumers who wish to receive information about signing up for training as a literacy volunteer.

ABA's New Orleans convention received excellent reviews from convention-goers both for the facilities and location. Exhibitors expressed disappointment with the reported number of booksellers in attendance, although the same amount of business was recorded as in previous years. James Brown, who was the featured entertainer at the annual banquet, also promoted his book, *Godfather of Soul*. Breakfast speakers included Walter Cronkite, Carol Burnett, Pat Conroy, David Stockman, Beverly Sills, David Halberstam, Jose Aruego, Betsy Byars, and Richard Peck. Panel sessions of interest included such topics as "Literacy Promotion at the Local Level: A Training Workshop," "What to Do When the Censor Knocks: A Workshop and Update on Censorship Activities in 1986," "Planning Your Store's Second Five Years," "Making Your Store a Force in the Community," "1987 Comes Early: The Art of Stocking and Selling Calendars," "Religious Books: Their Place in the Trade Market," and "Third-World Communities: Bookselling and Publishing."

Book Shop 1986

The 1986 holiday gift books insert "Book*Shop" appeared in three publications — *Time*, the *New Yorker*, and the *New York Times* (outside the New York City metropolitan

area) — during a three-week period before Christmas. More than 800 bookstores nation-wide participated. The insert had eight pages and featured cover art by the noted illustrator Chris Van Allsburg. The consumer incentive offer was a limited edition bookplate featuring the insert's cover art.

Bookstore Merchandising Group

Activities of the ABA Bookstore Merchandising Group in 1986 included the following in-store promotions: All*Stars, Reading Rainbow, Halloween, and Poster Portfolio. All ABA member stores have the opportunity to participate in a new program launched under the direction of the Marketing Committee, the Personal Bookseller campaign — a program featuring ad slicks, bookmarks, and bags highlighting the concept of each store as the "personal bookseller" in the community. The logo and theme can be utilized in an in-store display.

Censorship

The area of restrictive censorship legislation continues to be one of strong concern to booksellers everywhere. The types of cases being brought are twofold: minors access legislation, which attempts to curb the sale of books and periodicals that are deemed sexually explicit to adults and more particularly to minors, and civil rights ordinances, which seek to redefine pornography as a form of sexual discrimination against women.

ABA was involved in fighting such legislation as a named plaintiff in a number of cases in 1986 through its participation in the industry organization Media Coalition. ABA's efforts were successful in the three courts in which it was a plaintiff — in a civil rights case in Indianapolis and in "minors access" cases in Virginia and Georgia. The substantial legal fees awarded to the plaintiffs have been set aside for use by Media Coalition as a reserve fund for legal efforts to challenge ordinances that may be unconstitutional and impinge on the rights of booksellers to conduct business.

ABA was a coplaintiff with *Playboy* magazine in seeking an injunction to stop the distribution of a letter from Attorney General Meese's Commission on Pornography to chain operators branding them as "pornographers" for continued sale of magazines such as *Playboy* and *Penthouse* and linking such magazines to violence triggered by pornography. A debate on the issues raised by the Meese Commission is one of the items on the agenda for the convention scheduled for Washington, D.C., in May 1987.

Other Legal Activities

As part of its effort to make the reading public aware of the attempts to restrict the right to read, ABA once again cosponsored, with the American Library Association and the National Association of College Stores, a Banned Books Week in September. Stores and libraries were mailed a packet of materials to be used in promotions and displays to call attention to the book banning issue.

Again, on the legal front, ABA lost in a court decision regarding the business operation of J. Ben Stark, a book importer. Stark was sued by U.S. publishers for violation of copyright for his importation of British books on which U.S. publishers held copyright. ABA filed a brief on Stark's behalf, citing first amendment and right to read arguments; however, the court ruled in favor of the U.S. publishers. No appeal was planned.

Among the news items affecting the retail book trade in 1986 was a long-awaited decision in the *NCBA* vs. *Hearst* suit, in favor of the plaintiffs, citing that Avon Books (a subsidiary of Hearst) was not cost-justified in granting an extra discount to chain operators as opposed to independent operators. Although Hearst was planning to appeal Judge Thelton Henderson's decision, the NCBA attorney, Bill Petrocelli, was confident that NCBA would win any appeal and was pressing for an out-of-court settlement. No decision was handed down in the separate *NCBA* vs. *Bantam* suit.

Booksellers Order Service

Among the disappointments of 1986 was the decision to close down the Booksellers Order Service (BOS), a subsidiary of the American Booksellers Association. BOS, an electronic ordering service and cooperative buying group, never realized the support among booksellers or publishers it needed to be financially viable. Continued operation would have required a tremendous infusion of cash to revise the necessary software. BOS ceased operations on November 30, 1986.

Plans for 1987

The long-awaited membership survey, to be conducted in 1987, will enable ABA to complete membership records for its database and provide the association with comprehensive statistical data regarding its membership. Convention planning is well along as this report is being prepared, with many speakers and special events planned, as well as a sold-out exhibit hall. Following the 1987 annual convention, the ABA staff will move to new office facilities in an office condominium being purchased by the association. With books expected to receive much publicity during the year, surely 1987 will be remembered as "The Year of the Reader."

Book Industry Study Group, Inc.

160 Fifth Ave., New York, NY 10010
212-929-1393

Susan Kranberg

Assistant Managing Agent

The Book Industry Study Group, Inc. (BISG), is a not-for-profit corporation with a membership of approximately 175 individuals and firms from the various sectors of the book industry: publishers, manufacturers, suppliers, wholesalers, retailers, librarians, industry associations, and others engaged in the development, production, and dissemination of books. The immediate purpose of BISG is to promote and support research in and about the industry, so that the various sectors will be better able to realize their professional and business objectives. The Group's ultimate goal is to increase readership, improve the distribution of books of all kinds, and expand the market for them.

BISG had its beginnings during the 1975 annual conference of the Book Manufacturers Institute when a small group of concerned publishers, manufacturers, and repre-

sentatives from several trade associations met to discuss the urgent need to improve the industry's research capability. This small group invited others to join it in sponsoring a seminal study of book information needs on which a future program could be based. BISG was incorporated as a not-for-profit corporation in February 1976, and its *Report on Book Industry Information Needs* was completed in April 1976. The report confirmed the feasibility of a program of major research studies by and about the industry.

Trade and professional associations, such as the Association of American Booksellers (ABA), the Association of American University Presses (AAUP), the Association of American Publishers (AAP), the Evangelical Christian Publishers Association, and the National Association of College Stores (NACS) have joined BISG and are cooperating with it. BISG is unique because its membership cuts across section lines and is concerned with the industry as a whole. In seeking support from and representing every sector of the industry, BISG has affirmed its belief in the interdependence of all segments and their common need to find ways to study and solve problems.

The 1986–1987 elected officers are Stephen Adams, Macmillan, chairman; Alexander J. Burke, Jr., McGraw-Hill, vice chairman; Seymour Turk, Book-of-the-Month Club, treasurer; and Robert W. Bell, Lehigh University Press, secretary. The board of directors is made up of the elected officers and Paul Alms, Rand McNally; DeWitt C. Baker, B & H Consulting; Lewis H. Brown, S. D. Warren; James Buick, Zondervan; Jerry Butler, R. R. Donnelley; Frank Farrell, Grolier; Steve Hill, Houghton Mifflin; Lawrence Hughes, Hearst; Peggy Langstaff, Ingram; Richard Morgan, Scott Foresman; Andrew H. Neilly, Jr., John Wiley; Joan Neumann, Research and Reference Library Agency; George Q. Nichols, National Publishing; Neil Perlman, Cahners; Bernard Rath, American Booksellers Association; and Jerome Rubin, Times Mirror. The four officers and Baker, Butler, Langstaff, and Perlman constitute the executive committee.

Activities, 1982–1987

Since 1977, BISG has published an annual statistical report, *Book Industry Trends (Trends)*, which has become the industry tool for business planning. *Trends* reviews and forecasts book sales, in units and dollars, by market segment and product classification for a ten-year period. The report also includes statistics on library acquisitions, consumer expenditures on books, and publishers' manufacturing expenditures. The eleventh edition will be published in June 1987 and will include data for 1982–1991. *Trends Update*, published four times a year, provides broad-based statistical analyses on diverse topics, including bookstore sales, paperbound versus hardcover sales, and publishers' manufacturing and operating expenditures.

In 1982, BISG published *Book Distribution in the United States: Issues and Perception*. This study, conducted by Arthur Andersen & Company, provides the first in-depth investigation of physical distribution problems facing the book industry in the 1980s since the Cheney report of the 1930s. Survey findings cover such areas as trends and opportunities for improvement, ordering, processing and reordering, physical movement of books, and inventory control and returns.

In 1982, BISG sponsored the first seminar that focused on *Book Industry Trends* statistics. Now an annual event, the Trends Seminar brings together leading industry executives and analysts to discuss emerging trends and opportunities in the book industry. The 1987 seminar will be held June 24 in New York City and will feature a special afternoon program, "Opportunities in Foreign Markets."

In 1984, BISG published the 1983 *Consumer Research Study on Reading and Book Purchasing*. The results of the study, conducted by Market Facts, Inc., and written by Research & Forecasts, Inc., provide both an update and an expansion of the landmark 1978 study. For the first time, the book-buying and reading habits of juveniles and the elderly have been analyzed as separate markets. Published in three separate volumes— *Adults, Juveniles*, and *The Elderly*—the study also includes a complete exploration of contemporary leisure-time activities that interfere with, or supplement, reading.

The Book Industry Systems Advisory Committee (BISAC), a committee of BISG, has been instrumental in developing voluntary standardized computer-to-computer communications formats in use throughout the industry and in expanding the acceptance of the International Standard Book Number (ISBN) and the Standard Address Number (SAN) within the publishing and bookselling communities. In 1985, BISAC approved a new machine-readable code for books known as the Bookland EAN. BISAC continued its promotion effort of the new bar code with the publication in 1986, in conjunction with BISG, of the *Machine-Readable Coding Guidelines for the Book Industry*. The report provides criteria to determine which machine-readable code to use and guidelines for printing scannable codes on book jackets and covers.

The Serials Industry Systems Advisory Committee (SISAC), another committee of BISG, was formed in 1983 to meet the need for computer-to-computer communications formats by journal publishers, subscription agents, librarians, and booksellers. SISAC has developed a serial issue and article identifier, which is being tested in a machine-readable format on the cover of journals. It is also developing computer-to-computer order and claim formats.

Future Projects

BISG is considering sponsoring a study of book sales in nonbook outlets to be started in FY 1987. It is also exploring the feasibility of collecting retail sales statistics by subject category on an ongoing basis. Also under consideration is the creation of a database to contain information on research studies relating to books that have been published or are in progress.

The Council of National Library and Information Associations

461 W. Lancaster Ave., Haverford, PA 19041
215-649-5251

Adele A. Lerner
Archivist, The New York Hospital–Cornell Medical Center

The impetus for the creation of the Council of National Library and Information Associations, Inc. (CNLIA), in 1942 came from the war effort and the need for cooperation to fulfill the growing information needs of the nation. Fourteen library associations joined together as a council, each with equal voting power and all with the same concerns. Since 1942, CNLIA has functioned as a forum in which library and information associations have discussed shared interests through the successive eras.

CNLIA Membership

As an umbrella group for national organizations, CNLIA has served as a vehicle for implementing projects of mutual benefit to its member associations. Through the years, its membership has grown to 20 associations and includes specialized groups as well as more generalized associations:

American Association of Law Libraries
American Library Association
American Society of Indexers
American Theological Library Association
Art Libraries Society/North America
Association of Christian Librarians
Association of Jewish Libraries
Catholic Library Association
Chinese-American Librarians Association
Church and Synagogue Library Association
Council of Planning Librarians
Library Binding Institute
Library Public Relations Council
Lutheran Library Association
Medical Library Association
Music Library Association
National Librarians Association
Society of American Archivists
Special Libraries Association
Theatre Library Association

CNLIA is mandated to serve as an alliance of organizations to discuss common concerns in information science and consider appropriate action. Each member association may appoint two delegates, called councilors, to represent it on the council and to attend the meetings, held in the spring and fall of each year. Large and small associations have equal privileges and can bring matters of significance to the attention of the full council. The council may initiate programs in accordance with its mandate, but no member association can be bound to any course of action or financial commitment except by choice of its own governing body. Association members who are not councilors may be appointed to serve on ad hoc committees to which they can bring their specialized knowledge.

Council Activities

CNLIA can speak with the united voice of the broadest spectrum of the information community. As such, it has promoted many projects in which its members have cooperated. Past projects include the establishment of the Universal Serials and Book Exchange, the Continuing Library Education Network and Exchange (CLENE), *Who's Who in Library and Information Services*, and the American National Standards Com-

mittee on Library, Information Sciences and Related Publishing Practice (ANSC Z39) of the National Standards Institute.

Past CNLIA committees exemplify the broad range of issues addressed by the council, including Library Service in Hospitals, Preservation of Materials, National Library Information Systems, Micro-Reproduction, and Library Education. With the aid of funds received from the National Endowment for the Humanities, the Committee on Specialized Cataloging produced three manuals for the cataloging of special materials under *Anglo-American Cataloging Rules 2*. These include *Cataloging of Graphic Materials* published by the Library of Congress.

Currently, the council has four committees in addition to the Nominating and Program committees. The Ad Hoc Committee on Copyright Law, Practice and Implementation continues to serve as a watch-dog on copyright issues for member associations. In view of the council's ongoing sponsorship of the *Bowker Annual* through its many editions, the Ad Hoc Advisory Committee to the *Bowker Annual* was reactivated in 1985. The committee has always acted as a conduit for ideas between CNLIA member associations and the editor of the *Bowker Annual*. Recently, this resulted in a number of special articles on archives and archival management in the 1985 edition, and in subsequent editions archival concerns will be an integral part of the book. Other suggested topics of interest to information associations include conservation, access to information, and library legislation.

In response to increased federal government involvement in the library and information field, in August 1986 CNLIA established a Joint Committee on Legislation. The committee's charge includes monitoring legislation and defining the legislative needs of member associations. The Joint Committee will serve as liaison between such large organizations as the Special Libraries Association and the American Library Association, both of which are actively involved with library legislation, and smaller members of CNLIA. The committee will alert member associations of pertinent issues, serve to focus necessary action, develop a list of potential speakers for legislative hearings, and generally facilitate communication regarding governmental matters relevant to CNLIA.

The CNLIA Joint Committee on Cooperation was established in May 1983 to ascertain the areas in which member associations can assist each other. The results of a member survey to identify specific association goals, major strengths, and problems indicated that both small and large associations need operational assistance at their headquarters. Suggestions were made involving cooperative purchasing of office materials, shared computer technology (people as well as hardware), and shared office space and staff. CNLIA publications also were recommended dealing with such topics as preservation of materials, fund raising, copyright, and association public relations and membership. Expertise was offered for convention planning, financial management, data processing service, and continuing education.

In accordance with its mandate, the council provides aid for programs promoting librarianship and information science. For example, CNLIA provides support for National Library Legislation Day, which annually brings together library advocates from all over the United States with members of Congress during National Library Week in the spring. CNLIA also sends observers to meetings of the National Commission on Libraries and Information Science and corresponds with the International Federation of Documentation, the International Council on Archives, and the International Federation of Library Associations and Institutions. CNLIA is particularly eager to assist in planning for the next White House Conference on Library and Information Services

(WHCLIS), having expressed to the WHCLIS Taskforce its support for professional association involvement in the formulation of national information goals.

CNLIA Meetings

The November 1984 biannual meeting of the full council addressed the need for advocacy for libraries, archives, and manuscript repositories. Larry J. Hackman, New York State Archivist, and Richard S. Halsey, representing the Citizen's Library Council of New York State, instructed the councilors on the techniques for the creation of a coalition and strategies for action. This topic was again taken up in November 1986. Sandy Morton, Director of the Special Libraries Association, Office of Government Relations and Fund Development, brought the CNLIA councilors up to date on legislative issues of interest to the library community. These include the need for passage of legislation for a White House conference and the problems relating to access to information. Morton shared hints for successful lobbying, stressing the importance of thanking legislators who have been supportive of library and information programs.

The May 1985 meeting dealt with effective public relations for associations. John Felton of the Public Relations Society of America discussed the effective use of print and nonprint media as a means of reaching potential association members. In May 1986 the program focused on the continuing education of these members. Wilma Jensen of the Lutheran Church Library Association, representing a small association, explained how, with few funds but much dedication, her group provided continuing education to professional and many nonprofessional volunteers who care for Lutheran Church collections. Kathy Warye of the Special Libraries Association showed the wide variety of continuing education experiences that a large, amply funded association can offer. Both presentations stressed the importance of professionalism in our field.

The Council of National Library and Information Associations is strengthened by a broad membership from the information community and welcomes new applications. Inquiries may be directed to the CNLIA Secretariat at 461 W. Lancaster Ave., Haverford, PA 19041.

Part 2
Legislation, Funding, and Grants

Legislation and Regulations
Affecting Libraries in 1986

Eileen D. Cooke
Director, Washington Office, American Library Association

Carol C. Henderson
Deputy Director, Washington Office, American Library Association

The year 1986 began with the Reagan administration's budget proposals not only to eliminate federal library programs for the fifth year in a row but also to rescind library funds already appropriated. In March, the pervasive Gramm-Rudman-Hollings (G-R-H) balanced budget and deficit control legislation caused 4.3 percent cuts in domestic programs. The results ranged from the pullback of some Library Services and Construction Act funds from the states, to higher postal rates, to the loss of Sunday and evening hours at the Library of Congress, to a proposal to charge the public for congressional documents. At year's end, however, library grant programs were back at pre–G-R-H funding levels or above; the Library of Congress was once more open evenings and Sundays, and a newly revised Higher Education Act authorized funds for high tech library equipment and for needy college libraries.

Administration efforts to restrict access to and privatize government information continued as evidenced by proposals to discontinue or contract out the National Technical Information Service. The Office of Management and Budget's information management authority, the Paperwork Reduction Act, was renewed. New national security guidelines would restrict release of unclassified but "sensitive" information. Continued rate increases for library telecommunications prompted a third joint Senate letter to the Federal Communications Commission.

Funding, FY 1986

Rescission Proposals

Together with his FY 1987 budget, President Reagan submitted to Congress on February 5 a large number of proposed rescissions and deferrals of funds already appropriated by Congress and signed into law for FY 1986, the fiscal year that began October 1, 1985. Included were proposed rescissions (or "unappropriations") of all funds for the Library Services and Construction Act Title II public library construction, LSCA VI library literacy programs, Higher Education Act Title II-B library training and research, and HEA II-C research library grants – a total of $34 million.

The required 45-legislative-day period for congressional review of the rescission proposals expired April 15, and funds were then released, but with the 4.3 percent Gramm-Rudman-Hollings cut that had taken effect March 1. The rescission request for LSCA II was of dubious legality, because during the FY 1982 LSCA impoundment controversy, the General Accounting Office had held that mandatory spending provisions

Table 1 / **Appropriations for Library and Related Programs, FY 1987**
(dollars in thousands)

Library Programs	FY 1986 Appropriation	FY1986 after 4.3% Sequester[1]	FY 1987 Budget	FY 1987 House	FY 1987 Senate	FY 1987 Appropriation
Education Consolidation & Improvement Chapter 2 (including school libraries)	$ 528,909	$ 506,200	$ 528,909	$ 544,909	$ 526,837	$ 529,337
GPO Superintendent of Documents	25,981	24,993	27,835	24,359	23,634	23,634
Higher Education Act Title II	7,000	6,699	0	deferred	7,000	7,000
Title II-A, College Libraries	0	0	0	deferred	0	0
Title II-B, Training & Research	1,000	957	0	deferred	1,000	1,000
Title II-C, Research Libraries	6,000	5,742	0	deferred	6,000	6,000
Library of Congress	230,125	221,136*	266,197	234,699	236,299	235,399
Library Services & Construction Act	120,500	115,318		130,000	125,500	125,500
Title I, Public Library Services	75,000	71,774		80,000	80,000	80,000
Title II, Public Library Construction	22,500	21,533		25,000	22,500	22,500
Title III, Interlibrary Cooperation	18,000	17,226		20,000	18,000	18,000
Title IV, Indian Library Services	(funded at 2% of appropriations for LSCA I, II, & III)					
Title VI, Library Literacy Programs	5,000	4,785	0	5,000	5,000	5,000
Medical Library Assistance Act	7,790	7,530	7,400	9,160	9,460	9,410
National Agricultural Library	11,272	10,778	11,421	10,936	10,936	10,936
National Commission on Libraries & Information Science	690	660	690	660	690	660
National Library of Medicine	50,018	47,743	49,008	52,428	52,628	52,428

Library-Related Programs

Adult Education Act	101,963	97,579	104,000	110,000	101,963	105,981
Bilingual Education	169,115	161,844	142,951	175,951	138,955	173,095
Corporation for Public Broadcasting[2]	214,000	214,000	130,000	214,000	238,000	228,000
ECIA Chapter I (ESEA I Disadvantaged Children)	3,688,163	3,529,572	3,688,163	3,999,163	3,889,163	3,944,163
Education for Handicapped Children (state grants)	1,215,550	1,163,282	1,135,145	1,300,000	1,408,000	1,338,000
HEA Title III, Developing Institutions	141,208	135,136	141,208	deferred	141,208	146,208
Title IV-C, College Work Study	592,500	567,023	400,000	deferred	592,500	592,500
Title VI, International Education	26,550	25,408	0	deferred	26,550	26,550
Indian Education Act	67,071	64,187	75,729	67,236	62,000	64,036
National Archives and Records Administration	97,363	93,176	101,321	101,321†	96,321	96,321
Center for Statistics (Department of Education)	8,747	8,371	12,000	8,747	8,747	8,747
National Endowment for the Arts	165,661	158,538	144,900	165,661	159,950	165,081
National Endowment for the Humanities	138,641	132,679	126,440	138,641	136,700	138,490
National Historical Publications and Records Commission	4,000	3,828	0	4,000†	4,000	4,000
National Institute of Education	50,831	48,628	58,231	deferred	54,831	54,831
Postal Revenue Forgone Subsidy	748,000	715,836	0	650,000	650,000	650,000
Postsecondary Education Improvement Fund	12,710	12,163	10,000	deferred	12,700	12,163
Public Telecommunications Facilities	24,000	22,968	0	23,000	18,000	20,500
Revenue Sharing	4,185,000	4,005,045	0	0	0	0
Science & Math Education	45,000	43,057	75,000	43,066	100,000	80,000
Women's Education Equity	6,000	5,741	0	6,000	1,000	3,500

* Includes $867,000 restored in a supplemental funding bill.
† Would be cut 9.75% under House-passed across-the-board cut.
1 Balanced Budget-Emergency Deficit Control Act (Gramm-Rudman-Hollings Amendment) required 4.3% cut as March 1, 1986.
2 CPB funded two years in advance.

such as those in LSCA II are unavailable to the administration for rescission. The 45-day delay itself caused problems for currently funded programs such as LSCA and HEA II. More than half the fiscal year had elapsed before funds were released. The Education Department had held up LSCA II funds for two states that had earlier received FY 1986 allocations.

G-R-H Sequester

The presidential sequester order mandated by the Gramm-Rudman-Hollings amendment (Balanced Budget and Emergency Deficit Control Act, PL 99-177) took effect March 1 in the absence of alternative deficit reduction actions by Congress and the president. The effect on nonexempt domestic programs was a 4.3 percent cut from FY 1986 appropriated levels. (See Table 1 for the dollar effects on library and related programs.)

About one-third of the states were required to "deobligate" some Library Services and Construction Act Titles I and III funds. This was apparently seen by the Department of Education as the lesser of two evils. The alternatives were to retrieve funds from states that had already received allocations, or impose a double cut on states that had not yet received allocations. The two states that had already received LSCA II allocations were told they could not use those funds pending congressional review of a proposed rescission. The number and/or amount of LSCA IV, VI, and Higher Education Act II-B and II-C grants were reduced to comply with the sequester order.

The 4.3 percent cut also affected all federal agency libraries, including the National Library of Medicine and the National Agricultural Library. For the Library of Congress, the 4.3 percent G-R-H cut came on top of a 3.5 percent cut in congressional appropriations. As a result, LC declared a fiscal emergency and announced, then implemented, a series of drastic reductions in LC staff, services, and hours. Also affected was congressional printing, as the Joint Committee on Printing proposed, but partially implemented, a plan for the public to pay for basic congressional documents.

Funding, FY 1987

For the fifth year in a row, the Reagan administration's FY 1987 budget proposed to eliminate the Library Services and Construction Act and the Higher Education Act Title II library grant programs. At congressional hearings, Chester Finn, Jr., the new assistant secretary for educational research and improvement, called the library programs "desirable but dispensable." Congress, however, in the words of the Senate Appropriations Committee (S. Rept. 99-408), "strongly reject[ed] the administration's attempt to eliminate this modest but important Federal share of library assistance which continues to have a major impact in leveraging support for the Nation's public and research libraries."

Funding for all the programs mentioned in this article was provided by H.J.Res. 738 (PL 99-500), at $576 billion the largest money bill ever passed, incorporating all the regular appropriations bills. After a difficult budget and appropriations process, Congress agreed on $80 million for LSCA I public library services, $22.5 million for LSCA II public library construction, $18 million for LSCA III interlibrary cooperation, an automatic 2 percent set-aside of Titles I, II and III funding for LSCA IV Indian library services, $5 million for LSCA VI library literacy programs, $1 million for HEA II-B library training and research, and $6 million for HEA II-C research library grants.

These amounts brought funding back to presequester levels and for LSCA I pro-

vided a 6.6 percent increase above that. House-passed funding levels provided an 11 percent increase above March 1 cut levels for LSCA II and III as well, but House-Senate conferees agreed to the Senate-passed levels. The House deferred all HEA funding pending completion of the reauthorization process; conferees took the Senate levels.

The National Commission on Libraries and Information Science was back in the administration's budget with $690,000, the presequester level, after having been proposed for zero the year before. The House passed $660,000, the postsequester level; the Senate took it back to $690,000, noting in its report (S. Rept. 99-408) "that the NCLIS had taken a particularly active role in developing library programs for the rapidly growing elderly population." Conferees, however, agreed on the lower number.

The National Agricultural Library received $10,936,000 as passed by both the House and Senate. The administration had requested $11,421,000. For FY 1986, $11,272,000 was appropriated; the March Gramm-Rudman-Hollings cut reduced that figure 4.3 percent, to $10,778,000. For the National Library of Medicine, $62,088,000 was provided, restoring the G-R-H cut plus a 7.5 percent increase. Of the total, $9,410,000 was for the Medical Library Assistance Act. (See also the section of this article on the Library of Congress.)

For the Government Printing Office Superintendent of Documents operation, FY 1987 funding was $23,634,000 as passed by the Senate, 5.4 percent below the presequester FY 1986 level of $24,993,000. The House-passed amount was $24,359,000. The House Appropriations Committee said the reduction would be accomplished partly by converting more depository library publications to microfiche.

The continuing resolution provided $650 million for postal revenue forgone as passed by the House and approved by the Senate Appropriations Committee. The U.S. Postal Service estimated that this amount would be enough to keep preferred postal rates at current levels through September 30, 1987. The president had recommended elimination of postal revenue forgone funding, which at the time the budget was submitted would have caused a 40 percent jump in the cost of a 2-pound library rate book package.

The administration requested an overall 10 percent cut in National Endowment for the Humanities funding and a much more severe cut (52 percent) for NEH Humanities Projects in Libraries. Congress brought NEH back almost to the presequester level. (The totals and selected programs are shown in Table 2.) The House Appropriations Committee in its report (H. Rept. 99-174) said it "will continue to allot funds for the various humanities disciplines including the media, museum, and library programs," and that it "commends the National Endowment for the Humanities for its program to

Table 2 / National Endowment for the Humanities Funding, FY 1987
(amounts in thousands)

Funding Category	FY 1986 Appropriation	FY 1986 after 4.3% Sequester	FY 1987 Reagan	FY 1987 House	FY 1987 Senate	FY 1987 Continuing Resolution
NEH total	$138,641	$132,679	$126,440	$138,641	$136,700	$138,490
Humanities Projects in Libraries	2,922	2,796	1,400	2,900	2,000	2,900
Office of Preservation	3,976	3,805	4,000	4,000	4,000	4,000
Challenge Grants	16,898	16,171	16,500	16,500	16,500	16,500

preserve rare books and encourage the Endowment to increase its emphasis on this valuable program."

The National Archives and Records Administration received $100,321,000, of which $4 million was for the grant programs of the National Historical Publications and Records Commission (NHPRC). The administration had recommended $101,321,000, with no funds for NHPRC. The House passed $105,321,000, adding $4 million for NHPRC, but also passed a 9.75 percent across-the board cut to the funding bill which included NARA. The Senate Appropriations Committee approved only $100,321,000, including NHPRC; conferees agreed to the Senate figure.

General revenue sharing, which provided $4,005,045,000 in unrestricted grants to local governments in FY1986, was neither reauthorized nor funded. Libraries received $75,950,000, or about 1.7 percent of revenue sharing funds in FY 1983. How much of this amount was substituted for former local support is unknown. In West Virginia, 22 percent of local support for public libraries came from revenue sharing; in Pennsylvania it was 14 percent. Public libraries may also be affected as localities search for funds to make up for revenue sharing dollars spent on other local services. (Table 1 shows funding details for these and other library and related programs.)

Balanced Budget and Deficit Control Act

The March 1 sequester or across-the-board cuts of 4.3 percent on nonexempt domestic programs was the first of a six-year deficit reduction schedule to balance the budget under the Gramm-Rudman-Hollings amendment (Balanced Budget and Emergency Deficit Control Act, PL 99-177). Each scheduled cut took place automatically in the absence of other deficit reduction action by Congress and the president.

However, in a 7–2 decision on July 7, the U.S. Supreme Court ruled the automatic trigger provision unconstitutional because it violated the Constitution's separation of powers requirements by granting executive branch powers to the comptroller general, a legislative branch officer. The comptroller general, as head of the General Accounting Office, had the final say in determining whether each year's G-R-H deficit reduction target had been met, and if not, how much spending would have to be cut.

Under a fallback provision in the law, Congress then ratified the March 1 cuts that would otherwise have been invalidated. The Senate passed legislation to amend G-R-H to give final authority over a sequester to the Office of Management and Budget, but the House did not act. Congress avoided the scheduled October sequester order through transition revenue from tax reform legislation and by passing a reconciliation measure that produced enough savings to meet the G-R-H target. Had such an across-the-board cut been necessary, nonexempt domestic programs were facing an estimated cut of 13.9 percent.

HEA Reauthorization

A five-year extension and amendment of the Higher Education Act was signed into law on October 17 (S. 1965, PL 99-498). It took three months of negotiations to resolve more than 500 differences between House and Senate HEA reauthorization bills. The

conference report (H. Rept. 99-861) on S. 1965 was adopted by the House on September 24 by a vote of 385–25, and by voice vote in the Senate on September 25. House-Senate differences in library-related provisions were resolved in a manner that preserved the essential elements of the recommendations made by the American Library Association and the Association of Research Libraries as embodied in the House-passed bill, HR 3700.

Title II, which includes the major HEA library provisions, was renamed "Academic Library and Information Technology Enhancement." Title II, Part A, grants for College Library Resources were targeted to the neediest academic libraries based on criteria developed by ALA's Association of College and Research Libraries. For II-A, $10 million was authorized for grants of between $2,000 and $10,000 depending on enrollment to libraries ranking below the norm in their institutional class when scored for both "materials expenditures/FTE student" and "volumes held/FTE student." Waivers of need criteria were allowed for no more than 5 percent of grantees for very unusual circumstances. Maintenance of effort requirements were continued. Limited funding will result in fewer, not smaller, grants to the most needy. Within three years of first funding for the revised II-A, the National Commission on Libraries and Information Science is to conduct an evaluation study of the II-A need criteria.

For II-B, $5 million was authorized to continue the Library Career Training, and Research and Demonstration programs, with funding to be split two-thirds for training and one-third for research. The unfunded II-B Special Purpose Grants were repealed in favor of the new II-D programs.

For II-C, $10 million was authorized to continue grants to major research libraries (Strengthening Research Library Resources). II-C was amended to permit institutions that do not otherwise qualify to provide additional documentation to demonstrate the national or international significance for scholarly research of the collection described in the grant proposal.

For II-D, $5 million was authorized for a new program, College Library Technology and Cooperation Grants, of competitive grants of at least $15,000 for up to three years with a one-third matching requirement. Grants could be used for technological equipment necessary to participate in networks for sharing of library resources, joint-use library facilities, resources, or equipment, and other special projects to utilize technology to enhance library services.

Under HEA Title VI, International Education Programs, $1 million was newly authorized for the acquisition, maintenance, preservation, and making available of periodicals published outside the United States. Library eligibility was continued or expanded for HEA III aid for developing institutions and HEA VII academic facilities construction and renovation.

HR 3700 was passed by the House on December 4, 1985, by a vote of 350–67; the Senate passed S. 1965 on June 3 by 93–1. The II-A need criteria was identical in the two versions, except that the House authorized $75,000 for the NCLIS evaluation. Conferees left the NCLIS study requirement intact, but dropped the authorization for funding. Conferees agreed with the House on a $1 million authorization for foreign periodicals; the Senate allowed the activity but had no authorization for funding.

Although both bills dropped the unfunded II-D National Periodical System study, the Senate put nothing in its place. In conference, the Senate agreed to the House II-D technology grants. Major differences in authorized levels of funding, or ceilings above which funding cannot rise, were resolved, as reflected in Table 3.

Table 3 / HEA Authorization Levels, FY 1987
(amounts in thousands)

Funding Category	Previous Authorization	Previous Funding	New FY 1987 Authorization		
			House	Senate	Conference Report
II-A college libraries	$35,000	$ 0	$12,500	$5,000	$10,000
II-B training, research	35,000	957	5,000	1,050	5,000
II-C research libraries	15,000	5,742	12,500	6,300	10,000
II-D library tech & coop.	–	–	5,000	–	5,000

Government Documents Access

One of the near casualties of the Gramm-Rudman-Hollings balanced budget measure was free public access to congressional bills, reports, public laws, and committee documents. The Joint Committee on Printing (JCP), in an effort to make required cuts in the congressional printing budget, announced in March that House and Senate document rooms would be closed to the public; purchase of documents from the Government Printing Office (GPO) would be the only alternative. That proposal died after the American Library Association and other groups protested that it would make timely participation in the legislative process dependent on the ability to pay.

The compromise solution in effect since June allows the public to obtain one free copy of bills and other congressional documents (up to six per visit) from the Senate Document Room, B-04 Hart Senate Office Building, Washington, D.C. 20510. Additional copies may be purchased from the Senate Document Room for two to three cents per page. Committee prints and hearing records are still available from committees but in much reduced supply. They may also be purchased from the Superintendent of Documents, Congressional Sales Office, Main GPO, Washington, D.C. 20402. An explanation of the revised procedures, "How to Purchase Congressional Publications," is available from either source.

Deficit reduction pressures and resultant budget cuts also prompted the Government Printing Office to announce that as of October 1 it would discontinue hard copy for all dual format (microfiche and paper) documents sent to depository libraries. The publications involved include such frequently consulted titles as the *Federal Register*, the *Code of Federal Regulations*, the *Congressional Record*, and all congressional hearings and reports. The plan caused considerable objection by librarians to the nature of the material, the short notice, and the lack of consultation. Joint Committee on Printing Chairman Senator Charles Mathias (R–Md.) instructed the GPO to put the plan on hold. JCP and GPO officials were still trying at year's end to determine how the GPO will make necessary budget savings without undermining the intent of the depository library program.

Library of Congress

For the Library of Congress, the Gramm-Rudman-Hollings cut of 4.3 percent on March 1 came on top of an earlier 3.5 percent cut in congressional appropriations, leaving LC with $18.3 million (or 8 percent) less in FY 1986 than in FY 1985. The result was a fiscal emergency requiring the elimination of 300 positions, reading rooms closed on Sundays and most evenings, and significantly fewer items purchased, cataloged, preserved, and made available to the blind. Media coverage of sit-ins and protests by LC users over

elimination of Sunday and evening hours, hearings by congressional appropriations subcommittees and the Joint Committee on the Library, including outspoken testimony by Librarian of Congress Daniel Boorstin, and testimony and letters from library associations and many librarians about the impact of LC cuts on library services throughout the country – all made the LC budget situation very visible.

On July 10, LC restored evening, Sunday, and holiday hours of service in the general reading rooms after four months of curtailed service. A supplemental funding bill (HR 4515, PL 99-349) restored $867,000 to LC's FY 1986 budget, $247,000 of which was directed by Congress to restore Sunday and evening hours. The added funding originated in a Senate amendment by Senator Robert Byrd (D–W. Va.). For FY 1987, LC received $235,399,000, considerably above the FY 1986 postsequester level of $221,136,000 (including supplemental funding), but still below the FY 1985 figure of $238,542,000. The House passed $234,699,000; the Senate passed $236,299,000. Congress also passed a three-year reauthorization of the American Folklife Center at the Library of Congress.

National Library Celebrations

The House Postsecondary Education Subcommittee held an April 8 library oversight hearing on the Office of Management and Budget Circular A-130, *Management of Federal Information Resources*, and its implications for access to government information; H.J.Res. 244, calling for a White House Conference on Library and Information Services in 1989; and the impact of administration budget proposals for federal library programs.

April 8 also brought 475 library supporters to Washington, D.C., for the annual Library Legislative Day of organized lobbying during National Library Week. Representative Major Owens (D–N.Y.) again called a special order on April 9 that prompted 22 House members to make one-minute speeches about libraries, many of them calling attention to the cuts at the Library of Congress.

Legislation and Presidential Proclamations on January 29 and April 22 designated 1986 as the Sesquicentennial Year of the National Library of Medicine (S.J.Res. 198, PL 99-231), and April 1986 as National School Library Month (S.J.Res. 52, PL 99-273). President Reagan, on December 3, proclaimed 1987 as the Year of the Reader, and invited librarians, among others, to observe this year with appropriate activities. The proclamation implemented H.J.Res. 671 (PL 99-494) passed by Congress in October at the request of Librarian of Congress Daniel Boorstin for LC's Center for the Book.

National Technical Information Service

The Office of Management and Budget requested that the Commerce Department study privatization alternatives for the National Technical Information Service, which provides for the centralized collection, announcement, and dissemination of U.S. government-sponsored research and development reports and translations of foreign technical literature. Numerous librarians were among those commenting on the issues raised by an April 28 *Federal Register* inquiry and at a July 30 open workshop.

Librarians questioned OMB's motives in requesting the privatization study, since NTIS already leases its database to commercial firms and covers its direct costs through such leasing and the selling of reports. Other questions raised were whether agencies

and foreign governments would continue to provide reports to a privatized operation and whether NTIS, if privatized, would continue to archive and make available specialized reports that sell only a few copies. A Commerce Department privatization task force evaluated comments and made recommendations. OMB's decision was to be incorporated into the president's FY 1987 budget.

Paperwork Reduction Act

The Paperwork Reduction Act of 1980 provided the Office of Management and Budget its authority to develop and supervise federal government information policies and activities and established OMB's Office of Information and Regulatory Affairs (OIRA). After OIRA had generated congressional criticism with its development of Circular A-130, *Management of Federal Information Resources*, and with its cost/benefit review process of federal agency regulations, the Paperwork Reduction Act had been allowed to expire. However, in a surprise move, and with no public hearings, the act was reauthorized for three years in Title VII of the FY 1987 omnibus funding bill (H.J.Res. 738, PL 99-500).

Postal Issues

Rates

Preferred postal rates changed three times in 1986. On January 1, rates were increased to the final step of the phased rate schedule leading to full attributable costs. On March 9, rates went up again due to a shortfall in funding coupled with Gramm-Rudman-Hollings cuts. A slight reduction on April 20 was due to an adjustment in the reconciliation legislation for FY 1986. A 2-pound, fourth-class library rate book package went from 54¢ in December 1985 to 67¢, then to 74¢, and back to 73¢, for a net increase of 35 percent.

Preferred Postal Rate Study

A congressionally mandated study of preferred postal rates conducted by the Postal Rate Commission (PRC) was presented to House and Senate postal authorizing committees at a joint hearing June 18. The least controversial of the recommendations was a proposed recalculation of the revenue forgone subsidy to avoid overstating the amount needed. This change alone would save an estimated $265.5 million.

The PRC further recommended that the revenue forgone appropriation be eliminated except for free mail for the blind and certain voting-rights mail. Coupled with this was a recommendation that Congress consider changing the law so that the PRC in proposing rates could take into account the public benefit of organizations eligible to use certain subclasses of mail. The PRC recommended eliminating publisher and distributor eligibility for the fourth-class library rate as too indirect a subsidy to libraries and schools. Other recommendations were to restrict the use of advertising in third-class nonprofit mail, and to use a much narrower definition of nonprofit "educational" organization in eligibility for preferred rates.

Budget Reconciliation

The only Postal Rate Commission study recommendation acted on by Congress was the recalculation of the method for computing the postal revenue forgone appropriation, which was included in the budget reconciliation measure (HR 5300) given final congressional approval October 17 and signed into law October 21 (PL 99-509). Preferred rate mail has been determined to be less expensive to handle than mail sent at the comparable unsubsidized rates. However, the U.S. Postal Service calculates the amount of revenue forgone subsidy needed by figuring what that mail would cost if it were going at the standard unsubsidized rates (rates that are based on the higher costs of handling unsubsidized mail). The recalculation is estimated to save $200 million in FY 1989; it takes effect then or in conjunction with the next general postal rate increase.

Presidential Libraries

New legislation signed into law May 27 (HR 1349, PL 99-323) will reduce taxpayer costs of presidential libraries and strengthen the role of the U.S. Archivist by requiring minimum standards set by the Archivist that future presidential libraries must meet. A presidential library donated to the government must have an endowment equal to at least 20 percent of the cost of building and equipping the facility, with larger endowments required for facilities more than 70,000 square feet and for additions or modifications. Previously, the government assumed the entire cost of maintaining such facilities once donated. The new requirements apply to all presidents after President Reagan.

Sensitive Information

New guidelines give federal agencies authority to restrict the release of a broad range of government information that is unclassified but considered "sensitive" because its disclosure or misuse could adversely affect national security or other federal government interests. The latter includes "the wide range of government or government-derived economic, human, financial, industrial, agricultural, technological, and law enforcement information, as well as the privacy or confidentiality of personal or commercial proprietary information provided to the U.S. Government by its citizens." NTISSP No. 2, National Policy on Protection of Sensitive, But Unclassified Information in Federal Government Telecommunications and Automated Information Systems, was signed October 29 by then National Security Adviser John Poindexter.

Tax Reform

A major legislative accomplishment of the Ninety-ninth Congress was passage of a sweeping tax reform bill, HR 3838. House and Senate gave final approval to a conference report (H. Rept. 99-841) of more than 1,800 pages on September 25 and 27, and the president signed it into law (PL 99-145) on October 22. The effects on libraries will not be clear for some time, but provisions of concern include loss of the itemized deduction for state and local sales taxes, reduction of the tax advantage to charitable giving through eliminating the temporary charitable deduction for nonitemizers, the lowering of tax rates and the consolidation of tax brackets, and changes in the way charitable

contributions of appreciated property are treated under the alternative (and newly increased) minimum tax.

Telecommunications

Telecommunications rates for library connections to nationwide bibliographic databases have continued to increase every few months, causing planning, paperwork, and cost problems. Although the Federal Communications Commission allowed new AT&T private line tariffs to take effect in April 1985, it is conducting a continuing investigation of the tariffs. Senate Communications Subcommittee member Larry Pressler (R–S.Dak.) delivered on May 2 a letter with 29 Senate signatures to FCC Chairman Mark Fowler on the problems that continuing cost increases cause for libraries. This was Pressler's third joint letter to the FCC on this issue. Fowler responded with a nine-page analysis on May 28.

WHCLIS II

House legislation calling for a White House Conference on Library and Information Services in 1989 came very close to passing late in the session, but H.J. Res. 244 was pulled in the press of year-end business. As of October 18 when Congress adjourned, H.J.Res. 244 had 172 cosponsors; S.J.Res. 112 had 50 cosponsors. The measures attracted substantial bipartisan support and are expected to be reintroduced early in 1987 in the new Congress.

Other Legislative and Regulatory Activity

The Japanese Technical Literature Act (S. 1073, PL 99-382) was enacted to increase the availability of Japanese technical literature in the United States, mainly through increased activity by the National Technical Information Service. The act includes a requirement for consultation with libraries. A new program, the VISTA Literacy Corps, was established by Congress in a reauthorization of the Domestic Volunteer Service Act (HR 4116, PL 99-551) and funded at $2 million for FY 1987. VISTA will expand its current literacy efforts by assigning more volunteers to literacy projects, which may be administered by a variety of nonprofit agencies, including libraries.

Congress allowed the manufacturing clause of the copyright law to lapse as scheduled on July 1, and the president transmitted to the Senate on June 20 the Berne Convention for the Protection of Literacy and Artistic Works. The House, but not the Senate, passed legislation (HR 4800 and HR 5686) to continue implementation of the Nairobi Protocol to the Florence Agreement. The protocol extends duty-free treatment among adhering countries to certain audio, visual, and microform materials. The Senate, but not the House, passed a bill (S. 786) to establish an Information Age Commission. Representative George Brown (D–Calif.) introduced the Government Information Act (HR 5412) to establish an independent Government Information Agency to incorporate NTIS and many government information collection and dissemination activities. No action was taken, but a revised version may be reintroduced in 1987.

Table 4 shows the status of legislation of interest to librarians at the end of the second session of the Ninety-ninth Congress.

Table 4 / Status of Legislation of Interest to Librarians
(99th Congress, 2nd Session, Convened January 21, 1986, Adjourned October 18, 1986)

Legislation	House Introduced	House Hearings	House Reported by Subcommittee	House Committee Report No.	House Floor Action	Senate Introduced	Senate Hearings	Senate Reported by Subcommittee	Senate Committee Report No.	Senate Floor Action	Conference Report	Final Passage	Public Law
Age Discrimination in Employment	HR 4154	X		756	X	HR 4154	X		none	X	none	X	99-592
Civil Service Retirement Credit	HR 2663			none	X	S 1800	X		none	X	none	X	99-638
Computer Fraud and Abuse Act	HR 4718	X	X	612	X	S 2281	X		432	X	none	X	99-474
Congressional Budget Resolution	HConRes 337	X		598	X	SConRes 120	X		264	X	664	X	
Copyright—Berne Convention						S 2904	X						
Copyright—Home Audio Recording	HR 2911					S 1739	X	X					
Copyright—Manufacturing Clause	HR 3465, 4696	X				S 1822	X		303, 322				
Effective Schools & Even Start Act	HR 4463	X	X	640	X								
Electronic Communications Privacy	HR 4952	X	X	647	X	S 2575		X	541	X	none	X	99-508
Federal Management Reorganization						S 2230	X		347				
Florence Agreement Protocol	HR 4800, 5686	X		581	X	S 1274				X			
Freedom of Information Act Amendments	HR 4862	X	X	832	X	S 150		X					
Government Information Agency	HR 5412												
Head Start, dependent care extension	HR 4421			545	X	S 2444			327	X	815	X	99-425

227

Table 4 / Status of Legislation of Interest to Librarians
(99th Congress, 2nd Session, Convened January 21, 1986, Adjourned October 18, 1986)
(cont.)

Legislation	House					Senate						Final Action	
	Introduced	Hearings	Reported by Subcommittee	Committee Report No.	Floor Action	Introduced	Hearings	Reported by Subcommittee	Committee Report No.	Floor Action	Conference Report	Final Passage	Public Law
Higher Education Act Extension	HR 3700	X	X	383	X	S 1965	X	X	296	X	861	X	99–498
Information Policy Institute or Commission	HR 744, 5515					S 786			505	X			
Japanese Technical Literature	HR 3831	X	X	618	X	S 1073			175	X	none	X	99–382
LC American Folklife Center	HR 4545	X		800	X	S 2673	X		none	X	none	X	99–473
Omnibus Budget Reconciliation	HR 5300			727	X	S 2706			348	X	1012	X	99–509
Paperwork Reduction Act reauth.						S 2887			none				

Presidential Libraries	HR 1349	X	125	S 1047	X	257	X	none	X	99-323
Public Lending Right Study Commission	HR 5571	X		S 658						
Revenue Sharing extension	HR 1400	X	610							
Tax Reform Act	HR 3838	X	426	HR 3838	X	313	X	841	X	99-514
WHCLIS II	HJRes 244	X		SJRes 112		none				
Year of the Reader (1987)	HJRes 671		none	SJRes 397	X		X	none	X	99-494
Appropriations										
Supplemental, FY 1986	HR 4515	X	510	HR 4515	X	301	X	649	X	99-349
Continuing Resolution, FY 1987	HJRes 738	X	831	HJRes 738	X	500	X	1005	X	99-500
Agriculture, FY 1987	HR 5177	X	686	HR 5177	X	438	X			
Commerce, State Department, FY 1987	HR 5161	X	669	HR 5161	X	425	X			
HUD, Independent Agencies, FY 1987	HR 5313	X	731	HR 5313	X	487	X	977	X	
Interior, FY 1987	HR 5234	X	714	HR 5234	X	397	X	1002	X	
Labor-HHS-Education, FY 1987	HR 5233	X	711	HR 5233	X	408	X		X	
Legislative, FY 1987	HR 5203	X	693	HR 5203	X	384	X	960	X	
Treasury, Postal, FY 1987	HR 5294	X	723	HR 5294	X	406	X	805	X	

For one free copy of bills, reports and laws, write: Senate Documentation Room, Hart Senate Office Building, Rm. B-04, Washington, D.C. 20510.

Legislation and Regulations Affecting Publishing in 1986

AAP Washington Staff*

Postal Issues

Revenue Foregone

The Ninety-ninth Congress approved $650 million for revenue foregone, allowing eligible nonprofit mailers to continue mailing at the present rate until October 1, 1987.

Funding beyond the current fiscal year, however, faces new obstacles as a result of a study by the Postal Rate Commission (PRC) undertaken at congressional request, discussing preferred mail rate eligibility. The PRC recommendations would adversely affect publishers who mail at the library rate, making them ineligible for library rate privileges. Noting that at present, the library rate may be used for promotional purposes, such as mailing free sample copies of books to college professors, the report states: "The principles adopted in the report for evaluating subsidy in terms of relation to the non-profits' purposes lead us to recommend that this eligibility, added to the law of 1976, be terminated." With the Senate going Democratic, it is unclear whether this study will receive the attention of Congress in 1987.

Postal Rate Commission Proceedings

Two proceedings pending before the Postal Rate Commission, both initiated by United Parcel Service (UPS), may potentially adversely affect the rates paid by publishers for the shipment of books.

UPS I

The first of the proceedings, initiated in August 1985, involves a generic study of the manner in which costs are attributed to various classes and subclasses of mail in the determination of rates. The narrow premise of this case is that rates for third- and fourth-class mail — which includes the book rate — are subsidized through revenues derived principally from first-class mail users. UPS has committed substantial resources to this case and is expected to launch a major assault designed to increase the allocation of costs to parcel shippers. At the same time, however, information has been developed suggesting that the costs of the parcel classes have been overstated. This allocation error, if rectified, might well serve to offset and possibly overcome any other changes in costing methodology that may be made as related to the parcel classes used by publishers.

In this proceeding, then, the AAP's position is both offensive and defensive. AAP formed a loose coalition with other organizations (Parcel Shippers Association and Mail Order Association of America). AAP is hopeful that this joint participation will enable it to share the cost burden and to present and defend AAP's positions more effectively. It is not expected that any determinations will be reached until mid-1987.

*Contributors to this article include the following members of the Washington professional staff of the Association of American Publishers: Richard P. Kleeman, Diane Rennert, and Carol A. Risher.

UPS II

The second of the proceedings, launched by UPS on August 30, 1986, involves a specific "complaint" that parcel post rates are below cost and must therefore be increased. This complaint may be subject to dismissal on jurisdictional grounds. If, however, the proceeding goes forward, it will be necessary for AAP to actively participate: Many publishers make use of the zoned parcel post rates; any increase in those rates would necessarily entail subsequent increases in the other rates for the other parcel classes (special rate fourth, library rate, and bound printed matter) used by publishers; and any increase in parcel post rates would, in any event, release constraints upon UPS rate levels, a service that is significantly used by publishers. AAP is hopeful that the newly formed parcel shippers coalition will also function in this proceeding.

General Postal Operations

Several problems of an operational nature have industrywide implications to publishers with which the AAP continues to deal.

Auctions

Under procedures adopted several years ago at the insistence of the AAP, the Postal Service is supposed to return books that become lost in the mail, to the publisher, if the publisher makes an appropriate request and if the book is demonstrably new. Otherwise, books as well as other products lost in the mail are sold at periodic public auctions. The existing Postal Service procedures are cumbersome and inefficient and are not working effectively. As a consequence, a significant number of books, potentially eligible for return to publishers, are being sold at auction. A gray market has developed in these books. The AAP persists in its efforts to secure improved postal service procedures and adherence by the Postal Service to its rules and will continue its efforts in this area until a satisfactory resolution is achieved.

Mail Forwarding

As the result of changes made by the Postal Service in its procedures, some publishers have experienced difficulties in effecting delivery of books to consumers who have moved. This problem particularly affects book club publishers. Both directly and through the Mailers Technical Advisory Committee (MTAC), AAP is attempting to persuade the Postal Service to revise its procedures in order to ensure the proper and timely forwarding of books sent via the mails.

General Rate Increases

The Postal Service has reported to the Board of Governors that a general rate increase is "unlikely" for the next 18 months to 2 years. Because there is a ten-month period between the filing of a rate increase and the implementation of new rates, this would indicate that we will not be confronting a new rate case before the latter part of 1987. The Postal Service's projection is based on the fact that it will show a moderate surplus ($350 million to $450 million) at the end of the current fiscal year. According to some postal analysts, however, the projection is on the optimistic side because of certain assumptions as to wage increases, COLA adjustments, and oil prices.

Tax Reform Law: Mostly Good News for Publishers

Following a journey through Congress that lasted almost two years, a major tax reform bill was signed into law. Of special interest to publishers is the lowering of the top tax rate on business profits from 46 to 34 percent. AAP was in the thick of the fight to retain deductibility for state and local taxes. The final version of the bill retains this deductibility for property and income taxes, but eliminates the deduction for sales taxes. The Senate/House Conference Committee chose this compromise as it sought to find revenues to support a lowered maximum individual rate of 28 percent. The AAP School Division, in response to the serious concern of educational publishers over the loss of the sales tax deductibility, will monitor the impact of this loss in the individual states and report periodically to the membership.

State Tax on Mail-Order Sales

Legislation was introduced in the first session of the Ninety-ninth Congress by Senator Mark Andrews (R–N.D.) that would require out-of-state mail-order businesses to collect and remit use taxes to a state, even if the seller had no business presence in the state. This legislation, which would pose serious problems for book clubs and other direct book marketers, is almost certain to reappear in the One-hundredth Congress. It has support from individual state governments, always looking for ways to increase their revenue base.

Copyright Legislation

Manufacturing Clause

On the legislative front, the major thrust of AAP efforts during the past year was to defeat legislation to extend the manufacturing clause of the Copyright Act. The manufacturing clause, prior to its expiration on July 1, 1986, required that most American-authored, preponderantly textual, books claiming U.S. copyright protection be manufactured in either the United States or Canada. Although AAP has always found the clause unnecessary and distasteful, sentiment in Congress was initially seen as strongly supporting extension of some form of the manufacturing clause; proposed extensions included an expansion of the clause to art books and deletion of the exemption for manufacture in Canada. Under the circumstances, AAP met with the printers and unions and negotiated a compromise bill that could bring publishers a step closer to phasing out the clause completely. The mood in Washington changed, however, when the administration weighed in heavily in April 1986 expressing strong opposition and threatening veto. The Congress adjourned October 18 without acting on any of the versions of the manufacturing clause extension legislation. The manufacturing clause remains a thing of the past.

U.S. Adherence to Berne

Another major legislative issue of continuing importance to AAP is U.S. adherence to the Berne Convention. In December 1985, AAP convened an open forum for members, to review the implications of Berne adherence for U.S. publishers and to identify those

portions of U.S. domestic copyright law that might have to be modified to allow the United States to join the Berne Convention. Private sector copyright interests in the United States generally support U.S. adherence to Berne, and the U.S. government supports this position as well. In March, AAP announced its decision to support U.S. accession to Berne provided that "accession does not become an inadvertent or backdoor means to change domestic copyright law in a manner that will impact upon the way American publishers do business or disrupt certain contractual relationships." In April, AAP testified to that effect before a Senate subcommittee.

First Amendment Developments

Major developments in the First Amendment area during 1986 were the issuance of the report of the attorney general's Commission on Pornography and several last-minute amendments to the federal Freedom of Information Act (FOIA), as part of the hastily enacted Omnibus Drug Act.

The AAP continued its active interest and participation in the activities of the Pornography Commission (see *Bowker Annual*, 1986, p. 229), not because AAP members publish pornography—they do not—but because of the potential excesses and intrusions into protected speech that such a study by such a group almost inevitably entail. The association gave testimony before the commission for a second time, with Heather Grant Florence (Bantam), then chairperson of the AAP Freedom to Read Committee, presenting her views and introducing to the 11 commissioners a censored author (James Landis, whose book, *The Sisters Impossible*, had been removed from school library shelves in Salisaw, Oklahoma).

Publishers attending their annual meeting in Florida heard a report by Ellen Levine, editor in chief of *Woman's Day*, on divisions within the commission as it approached the end of its deliberations. And the AAP intervened, in a carefully limited amicus brief, in litigation against the commission brought by Playboy Enterprises, Inc. The suit, which charged the commission with improper and unconstitutional threats to publishers and distributors of legitimate, constitutionally protected materials, was favorably decided: The letter in which the threat was contained was ordered withdrawn by a Washington, D.C., federal court.

Publishers welcomed the commission's decision holding that the printed word is virtually never pornographic, but found much else to cause them concern in the final report, issued in July. The AAP board of directors, in November, adopted the following six resolutions concerning the report, on recommendation of the association's Freedom to Read Committee:

1 We restate our members' unswerving support for the unfettered freedom to publish for the general adult reading audience, and (subject only to resolution 3 below), for adult readers' full freedom to obtain and read whatever they wish.

2 We reiterate our willingness to accept Constitutionally tested limitations on the availability of sexually explicit materials to young persons, and on the imposition of sexually explicit messages on nonconsenting adults.

3 We share the general repugnance to child pornography and support efforts to eliminate this abhorrent child abuse. To best achieve this desired goal, any legislative proposals should be focused on this issue and should not inhibit the dis-

semination of works having serious literary, artistic, scientific, or educational value.

4 We voice dismay at the apparent encouragement, expressed in a government-sponsored report, for widespread citizen action against Constitutionally protected materials that happen to be held in unfavorable regard by individuals or groups. Such a message can only give apparent government sanction to "self-help" by self-appointed vigilantes in an atmosphere already conducive to censorship.

5 We disapprove of the report's proposals to impose new legislation to curb sexually explicit materials involving adults and directed to adult audiences and to increase penalties under existing laws. We believe new legislation and restraints are unnecessary, and such efforts as the Justice Department's "Obscenity Strike Force" on federal, state, and local levels can only contribute to a growing climate of hostility to the sale or display of works of a controversial nature.

6 We strongly endorse the report's acknowledgment that "education" rather than "negative and reactive" measures is the preferred means of addressing the social concerns raised by the report.

After spending almost the whole year in discussion of possible amendments to the 1986 Freedom of Information Act without enacting any of them, Congress moved speedily and without public hearings to incorporate FOIA changes in the Omnibus Drug legislation. The changes enable federal authorities to withhold information about law enforcement efforts that might impair an ongoing investigation and clarify FOIA provisions dealing with fees and standards for waivers of fees for requesters of information (but without defining the term "media" as applied to such requesters). The changes, according to Senator Orrin Hatch (R-Utah), chairman of the Constitutional Subcommittee of the Senate Judiciary Committee, are designed to "considerably enhance the ability of federal law enforcement agencies such as the FBI and the Drug Enforcement Administration to combat crime, including drug offenses."

The U.S. Supreme Court in February, by a 6 to 3 vote, affirmed the decisions of two lower courts holding the Indianapolis pornography/women's civil rights ordinance unconstitutional. The decisions upheld the position taken by publisher-distributor members of the Media Coalition, a New York-based group whose individual members had challenged the ordinance as overbroad. (See also *Bowker Annual, 1986*, p. 229.)

A federal judge in August upheld a complaint against Daniel Boorstin, Librarian of Congress, charging that the First Amendment rights of the blind were violated by the elimination of brailled editions of *Playboy*. The suit, brought by the American Council of the Blind, the Blinded Veterans Association, Playboy Enterprises, and the American Library Association, contradicted Boorstin's understanding that, by eliminating $103,000 from the library's appropriation, Congress was in effect telling the Librarian to eliminate brailling of *Playboy*, an activity costing approximately that amount. A proposed appeal of the decision was subsequently dropped.

The Supreme Court was to decide early in 1987 whether to accept an appeal by the state of Virginia from a federal district court ruling, upheld in the Fourth Circuit U.S. Court of Appeals, that the state's "minors' access [i.e., access to bookstore materials] law" was excessively and unconstitutionally broad. Media Coalition members won a victory in the appellate court both on the substance of the case and on the state's obligation to reimburse the plaintiffs' attorney fees.

Legislation and Regulations Affecting the Information Industry in 1986

Kenneth B. Allen

Senior Vice President, Government Relations, Information Industry Association

The Ninety-ninth Congress of the United States is now history. Before it adjourned, a number of significant bills were enacted that will have a major impact on the information industry. In addition, several other bills were not enacted that are certain to be on the agenda of the One-hundredth Congress.

Right to Electronic Privacy

Perhaps the most significant piece of legislation affecting the information industry was the Electronic Communications Privacy Act of 1986 (PL 99-508). Enacted in the waning moments of the Ninety-ninth Congress, this law extends to electronic communications the same protections against interception and disclosure provided by federal law for first-class mail and voice telephone communications. Providers of electronic data services are prohibited, with certain exceptions, from disclosing the contents of data communications, and third parties, including the government, may not intercept or obtain such communications without a warrant, court order, or other legal process. This legislation is significant in that it establishes a new right to privacy for data communications that protects both the users and providers of such services.

Computer Crime

Legislation was also enacted to refine further the federal laws dealing with computer crime. The Computer Fraud and Abuse Act of 1986 (PL 99-474) extends the protection of federal statute to private computers where two or more states are involved in the criminal act and also establishes prohibitions on trafficking in computer passwords. The need for this legislation was demonstrated by the results of a survey, conducted jointly by the Information Industry Association and the Videotex Industry Association, regarding incidences of computer abuses.

Federal Information Policy

The Paperwork Reduction Act of 1980 established an Office of Information and Regulatory Affairs (OIRA) within the Office of Management and Budget to develop governmentwide information policies and procedures such as OMB Circular No. A-130, "Management of Federal Information Resources." During the Ninety-ninth Congress there was a major effort to abolish OIRA due to dissatisfaction with, among other things, its role in reviewing government regulations (a responsibility assigned to the office by President Reagan). After extensive negotiations, OIRA was reauthorized as part of the Omnibus Budget Reconciliation Act of 1986 (PL 99-509). In exchange for reauthorization, the administration agreed to certain changes in the law, including requiring that future OIRA administrators be subject to Senate confirmation. The same

law also expanded government computer procurement regulations (PL 89-306) to encompass hardware, software, and all related services. Previously, these regulations applied primarily to the acquisition of computer equipment.

Freedom of Information Act

A major initiative was undertaken to reach agreement among congressional staff, the media, business, and public interest groups on a comprehensive revision to the Freedom of Information Act (FOIA). Despite lengthy negotiations, this goal was unreachable. The comprehensive revision was dropped, and an FOIA amendment was introduced to strengthen the protection of business information provided to the federal government. Although this bill did not pass, the closing hours of the Congress saw other FOIA amendments tacked onto the Anti-Drug Abuse Act of 1986 (PL 99-507). A major concern to the information industry is that these amendments establish that information companies that are not considered traditional media organizations must pay higher fees for acquiring government records. Contradictory interpretations regarding the intent of these amendments were placed in the legislative history, and implementation must await issuance of regulations by the Office of Management and Budget.

Copyright

A major victory was achieved in the Ninety-ninth Congress with the expiration of the manufacturing clause of the Copyright Act after 95 years, despite extensive lobbying to extend it once again. Originally intended to protect the fledgling U.S. printing industry, the clause denied copyright protection to certain works by U.S. authors originally printed abroad. In addition to having outlived its usefulness, the manufacturing clause had been ruled illegal under the General Agreement on Tariffs and Trade and would have kept the United States from joining the international Berne Copyright Convention (the major international copyright agreement).

On June 18, 1986, President Reagan transmitted the Berne Convention to Congress along with a recommendation that the Senate give its advice and consent to accession. Outgoing Senator Charles ("Mac") Mathias (R-Md.) introduced S. 2904 to modify the U.S. law that stands in the way of accession to Berne. This Congress also enacted a resolution (PL 99-203) calling for a celebration in 1990 to commemorate the bicentennial of the passage of the first patent and copyright acts in 1790.

Telecommunications

During the Ninety-ninth Congress, the most significant piece of legislation dealing with telecommunications was the federal Telecommunications Policy Act of 1986 introduced by Senator Robert Dole (R-Kans.). This bill would have consolidated regulatory oversight of telecommunications deregulations in the Federal Communications Commission (FCC) and removed all such authority from the district court and the Department of Justice. Proponents argued that regulatory oversight would be more efficient because the FCC has resources and expertise not available to the other parties. Opponents expressed concern that the FCC might permit the telephone companies to enter into new lines of business without implementing safeguards to preserve a competitive marketplace. The bill died when Congress adjourned, but it is expected to be reintroduced.

Other Legislation That Will Be Back

A number of other bills that did not get enacted are expected to emerge during the One-hundredth Congress. Among these legislative proposals are a bill to create a 1989 White House Conference on Libraries and Information Science (ten years after the last such conference) and a bill to establish a National Commission on the Information Age. On another front, Senator Jesse Helms (R-N.C.) introduced a bill to regulate telephone services used for pornographic purposes (Dial-A-Porn). Information companies would be required to police their own networks for obscene and indecent messages. These and other legislative initiatives will be back on the agenda as the One-hundredth Congress continues to face the challenge of addressing the new issues emerging from the information age.

Funding Programs and Grant-Making Agencies

Council on Library Resources

1785 Massachusetts Ave. N.W., Washington, DC 20036
202-483-7474

Mary Thompson

Program Associate

The Council on Library Resources (CLR), an exempt privately operated foundation that conducts its own programs and also awards grants in its areas of interest, had its thirtieth anniversary in 1986. The council was founded in 1956 at the instance of the Ford Foundation, with a mandate "to aid in the solution of library problems; to conduct research in, develop and demonstrate new techniques and methods and to disseminate through any means the results thereof." Early concerns of CLR centered on basic research, such as the Barrow Laboratory investigations into causes of paper deterioration and techniques for making better paper, on emerging technologies that might be exploited to improve the operating performance of libraries, and on coordinated bibliographic control. Over the years, much attention has also been paid to programs designed to strengthen the management skills of the administrators of large research libraries, to improve professional education for academic librarians, to integrate the library more fully into the college curriculum, to promote improved and equitable access to the nation's research collections by all users, and to encourage international standards and program development. From the beginning, the council's program has concentrated on academic and research libraries because of their key role in collegiate instruction, their centrality to research and scholarship, and their fundamental importance to society.

CLR has no endowment; its programs and grants are made possible by the support the council obtains from other funding agencies. For the fiscal year ending June 30, 1986, CLR was funded by the National Endowment for the Humanities and ten private foundations: the Carnegie Corporation of New York, the Exxon Education Foundation, the Ford Foundation, the J. Paul Getty Trust, the William and Flora Hewlett Foundation, the Lilly Endowment, Inc., the Andrew W. Mellon Foundation, the Pew Memorial Trust, the Alfred P. Sloan Foundation, and the H. W. Wilson Foundation.

The council's board of directors consists of 22 individuals from academic institutions, research libraries, business, and the professions. In 1986, Herman B Wells, University Chancellor at Indiana University, retired from the board on which he had served since the council's inception in 1956, and was elected director emeritus. Fred C. Cole,

member of the board and CLR's second president, died in May 1986. He was also the Ford Foundation adviser who stimulated the discussions that led to the formation of the council. He remained closely tied to CLR, as a board member for 24 years and as president from 1967 to 1977.

CLR officers are Maximilian W. Kempner, chairman; Charles Churchwell, vice chairman; Warren J. Haas, president; Deanna Marcum, vice president; and Mary Agnes Thompson, secretary and treasurer.

Highlights of 1985–1986

Research

A much-expanded research program took shape after a period of planning and experiment, and the first major grant was made during 1986. The intent of the program is to encourage investigation of the effect of the "information revolution" on scholarship, research, and teaching. It is anticipated that CLR will assist a few universities as they address issues raised by the increasing growth of information technologies and underscored by economic forces and organizational change. In addition, a new series of grants available to individuals undertaking research on specific topics has been established, and periodic conferences to report on research activities are planned.

The first university center has been established at the University of California, Los Angeles, where most academic components of the university have begun to develop a university-based research program focused on the issues, problems, and needs for research with respect to long-range strategic planning for libraries and information resources in the research university of the future. The UCLA work is viewed by CLR as a prototype for other university efforts. The project is designed to (a) explore the effect of technology on the ways information resources will be used in the research university; (b) seek better understanding of the information requirements of individual disciplines; and (c) determine the role of information resources in the work of individual scholars, researchers, students, and teachers.

The results of the research and analytical studies to be undertaken in the next two or three years will help determine how the university should plan and organize to meet established requirements. A strategic plan for consideration by UCLA faculty and administrators will be constructed as the basis for the development and management of information resources at UCLA. A second objective, directly related to the first, is explicit testing of a process for academic strategic planning for information resources. The documentation of the process and the results will be made available to other institutions. Formal research projects of sufficient magnitude and importance to represent major contributions to the advancement of knowledge in this field will be identified by an advisory committee and disciplinary task forces. The research itself will be carried out under the direction of many UCLA faculty members. Published and internal reports will provide the basis for discussions with other institutions and individuals with parallel research projects.

The CLR Economics Seminar, an earlier research enterprise and a precursor of the expanded research program, culminated in the publication of *The Economics of Research Libraries*, by Martin M. Cummings, the project's director. The monograph synthesizes the reports and discussions that were part of the two-year program, which explored the response of universities to changing economic conditions and new demands for information resources.

Resources and Preservation

Preservation figured prominently in both staff effort and grant activity during 1986. The central element was the work of the Committee on Preservation and Access, which completed its assignment with the publication of the report *Brittle Books* in April 1986. The committee assessed the extent and importance of the problem of brittle books and concluded that concentrated attention over a long period of time is required if an important segment of recorded information is not to be lost.

Participants in a CLR-sponsored meeting in late March at Wye Plantation, Maryland, reviewed the recommendations of the committee and encouraged continuation and expansion of the effort. As a result, a Commission on Preservation and Access has been established and its operating costs funded for an initial period of three years by several universities and foundations (including CLR). A complementary National Advisory Council on Preservation, including representatives of organizations that have an interest in the success of preservation efforts, has been formed to help ensure effective communication between the commission itself and all who can contribute to meeting the responsibilities it has assumed.

The commission will work on behalf of the libraries and organizations that must, in the end, do the work of preservation. Simultaneously, it must be an effective agent for all who will provide the necessary financial support and intellectual assistance. Among its early tasks, the commission will be expected to

1 Develop a funding plan for the preservation of brittle books and develop a program to generate funds for use by participating libraries.
2 Establish the general conditions, policies, and procedures governing preservation work for those agencies interested in participating in the brittle books program.
3 Promote further development of a preservation information service by the Library of Congress and encourage the Advisory Council members to bring such information to the attention of their own organizations.
4 Encourage technical and other research on topics of importance to the brittle books program.
5 Establish a monitoring system to gather and analyze information about all aspects of preservation activity. Results of analytical work will help shape future methods and directions, will keep participants informed, and will be required in the preparation of reports to funding sources.
6 Monitor the performance of bibliographic systems to ensure that information required to manage the preservation effort and to promote access to products is readily available.
7 Ensure that access to preserved materials is efficient and supportive of research and scholarship.
8 Build and maintain effective communication with key organizations through the Advisory Council and promote participation in planning and operations by institutions and individuals committed to the cause of preservation.

The need to preserve library materials has received little general public attention. To raise awareness of the importance of the issue, a documentary film—sponsored by CLR, the Library of Congress, and the National Endowment for the Humanities (NEH)—is being produced for public television broadcast, probably in fall 1987. A

shorter version of the film will be made available for audiences in universities, public libraries, and schools and for other interested audiences. Funding for the film was provided by the Andrew W. Mellon Foundation, NEH, and CLR.

Because preservation is an international problem, CLR helped fund a conference for representatives from more than 30 national libraries, held in Vienna in April 1986. Participants considered the national and international aspects of preservation and the prospects for collaborative work.

To curtail preservation problems in the future, CLR continues to encourage efforts to have scholarly works published on acid-free paper. Building on earlier CLR work, a standard for permanent and durable uncoated paper has been established, and funding has been provided to develop a national standard for hardcover bindings.

Bibliographic Services

While CLR interest in bibliographic matters remains strong, the special Bibliographic Service Development Program (BSDP) is drawing to a close, as libraries and networks begin to implement system linkages. In early 1986, two new committees were established to manage the transition of the Linked Systems Project (LSP) to operational status. The LSP Policy Committee will address management issues that arise as implementation proceeds. The committee has approved agreements that will guide future development work and serve as the basis for the program's governance and financial structure. These agreements include a formal statement that the LSP protocols will be the protocols of the International Standards Organization/Open Systems Interconnection (ISO/OSI) and/or National Information Standards Organization (NISO) Committee Z39; a list, in order of priority, of work yet to be done in the context of LSP; and the assumptions and ground rules that will guide the exchange of authority and bibliographic data via the link. The LSP Technical Committee was established to monitor the implementation and performance of the LSP protocols, and will also encourage and expedite extended use of the protocols by sharing information and resources.

An Association of American Publishers project (partially funded by CLR) to create codes for manuscripts in electronic form completed the bulk of its work during 1986. A provisional standard was published and presented to ISO and NISO in 1986. The *Author's Guide*, the *Reference Manual on Electronic Manuscript Preparation and Markup*, the *Markup of Mathematical Formulas* guide, and the *Markup of Tabular Material* guide were also completed.

In January 1986, the council sponsored a conference to review the results of research undertaken by OCLC and Forest Press to investigate the effectiveness of the Dewey Decimal Classification (DDC) schedules and relative index as subject access enhancements to online catalogs. Participants concluded that the DDC may be useful in enhancing subject access under certain circumstances. The project also generated additional information concerning the ways in which users interact with online catalogs.

Access

Providing equitable access to information is one of the primary responsibilities of libraries. The council's activities in this arena are necessarily diffused; considerations pertinent to the goal of equitable access permeate every CLR activity. Special support from the Ford Foundation permits CLR to explore access-related issues on many fronts.

Several small grants were made in 1986 to permit exploration of technological approaches to enhancing access to information, to examine the quality and coverage of databases, and to measure the influence of library policies and procedures on access.

Meetings were held with librarians of historically black colleges to consider prospects for utilizing more fully technology-based information systems to improve their services. Similarly, public libraries were urged to assess the present and potential influence of computer-based information resources on services to users. In the final analysis, the goal of equitable access to information is an appropriate driving force behind collaborative undertakings of libraries. The success of all such ventures ultimately must be measured by how they improve services to users.

Librarianship and Librarians

The transition to the research library projected for the future will require librarians of diverse backgrounds and knowledge. How to prepare the new leadership is a persistent and still unanswered question. The council has supported program explorations and development in several library schools since the beginning of the decade. In 1986, CLR support for the University of Michigan library school's program designed to recruit distinctive students drew to a close as the university assumed responsibility for continuing the effort. The library and library school are working together to recruit students to academic librarianship and to provide a productive internship as an integral part of the educational program.

Plans have been made to continue the Senior Fellows program, an intensive academic session at UCLA for newly appointed library directors and senior library managers, for two more sessions in 1987 and 1989. UCLA and participants will assume an increasing proportion of the cost each year.

The University of Georgia Libraries and a group of libraries in the Chicago area (University of Chicago; University of Illinois, Chicago; and Northwestern University) began internship programs for staff who were recent library school graduates. The internships are designed to bring new librarians into closer contact with the complexities and opportunities of scholarship and university operations. In spring 1986, two additional internship program grants were awarded to the University of Missouri at Columbia and Columbia University.

The Faculty/Librarian Cooperative Research program, designed to encourage closer working relationships between teaching faculty and librarians, continues to expand. Ten awards were made in the two cycles of 1985–1986.

Major New Grants and Contracts, FY 1985–1986

American Film Foundation
Production of a documentary film on the preservation of
library materials $320,000

Gary W. Collins
Development of a plan for a Library of Congress optical
disc life determination program $15,000

Columbia University
Program for recent library school graduates $44,450

Robert M. Hayes
  Study of preservation costs and benefits $40,100
Library of Congress
  International conference on preservation of library materials $18,250
Louisiana State University
  Development of a curriculum for library systems analysts $52,000
National Information Standards Organization
  Development of a national standard for hardcover edition bindings $25,000
Research Libraries Group
  Analysis of the RLG conspectus as a collection management tool $10,000
  Creation of a national database of public records information $32,928
University of California, Los Angeles
  Research program $400,000
  Senior Fellows program $45,000
University of Illinois, Urbana
  Developing and evaluating online catalog interface enhancements $23,000
University of Missouri, Columbia
  Internships for recent library school graduates $73,205
University of Pittsburgh
  Study of roles of information managers in American universities $10,990

U.S. Department of Education Library Programs, 1986

Anne J. Mathews

Director, Library Programs

Office of Educational Research and Improvement
U.S. Department of Education
555 New Jersey Ave. N.W., Washington, DC 20208
202-357-6293

Library Programs (LP), one of five major components of the Office of Educational Research and Improvement, is responsible for administering the Library Services and Construction Act (LSCA, PL 98-480) and the Higher Education Act (HEA, PL 99-498) Title II grant funds. The main focus of Library Programs' efforts is on the efficient administration of the approximately $132.5 million appropriated annually by Congress through these acts. These monies account for only a small percentage of the total amount spent by libraries, but they have been a major stimulus for the development of libraries and library services in the United States. For this reason, Library Programs must be intellectually as well as financially responsible for the quality and usefulness of the projects funded.

Note: The following individuals assisted in writing and compiling data for this article: Dayna Buck, Robert Klassen, Trish Skaptason, Dorothy Kittel, Don Fork, Adrienne Chute, Clarence Fogelstrom, Frank Stevens, Louise Sutherland, Yvonne Carter, Carol Cameron, Beth Fine, and Sandy Milevski.

Library Programs includes the following tasks as part of its main goal of administering library program monies:

- To provide creative guidance to programs, based on the ongoing assessment of regional and national needs, and up-to-date knowledge of current trends in research and practice
- To collaborate within Library Programs, with other Department of Education units, and with national library associations to extend and enhance the impact of program monies
- To disseminate the results of the most effective programs
- To develop effective internal management, governance, planning, and self-evaluation
- To exercise national leadership in library issues

Library Services and Construction Act (LSCA, PL 98-480)

State-Administered Programs

The LSCA State Grant Program (Titles I, II, and III) encourages each state to identify its particular needs and to create programs, acquire resources, or improve services to meet those needs. The result in 1986 was that some 3,500 projects covering the entire spectrum of library concerns were funded with LSCA monies (Table 1). State-administered LSCA funds have a vast effect on library services throughout the country, allowing state and local libraries to reach increased numbers of people and provide them with improved library services.

The unique impact of the state grant awards for the improvement of statewide and local public library services under LSCA Titles I, II, and III has been characterized in the state reports as follows:

- Nearly 75 percent of the LSCA Title I program funds were used to provide library services to unserved or underserved areas. Special efforts were made to strengthen more than 160 major urban libraries.
- More than 25 percent of LSCA I program funds were used to support library services to an estimated 3 million disadvantaged persons, nearly 3 million limited English-speaking individuals, about 1 million blind and physically handicapped persons, and nearly 650,000 persons who have been institutionalized.
- More than 2,580 public library construction programs to remodel or build library facilities have been funded since the beginning of Title II appropriations.
- More than 50 percent of the LSCA III program funds were used to continue support of computerized bibliographic databases, both for current materials and for retrospective conversion of older materials. Generally, these funds are used to link state and local libraries with major nationwide bibliographic utilities, such as the Online Computer Library Center, Inc. (OCLC).

Some specific highlights of LSCA State-Administered Programs activities follow. (Due to the schedule for receiving state reports, FY 1985 figures, the latest available for most programs, are used to describe State-Administered Programs, unless otherwise noted.)

Table 1 / LSCA Titles I, II, and III, FY 1986

State	Title I	Title II	Title III
Totals	$70,339,000	$21,102,000	$16,881,000
Alabama	$ 1,195,607	$ 363,255	$ 285,332
Alaska	320,901	131,980	69,353
Arizona	946,519	297,467	224,333
Arkansas	784,395	254,583	184,301
California	6,530,564	1,774,544	1,603,169
Colorado	990,755	309,168	235,256
Connecticut	998,995	308,703	234,822
Delaware	352,320	140,291	77,611
District of Columbia	356,592	141,421	78,666
Florida	2,900,029	814,204	706,702
Georgia	1,640,753	481,104	395,757
Hawaii	455,877	167,684	103,182
Idaho	448,085	165,623	101,258
Illinois	3,084,019	862,873	752,134
Indiana	1,575,401	463,817	379,620
Iowa	929,928	293,079	220,237
Kansas	809,781	261,298	190,570
Kentucky	1,133,272	346,867	270,447
Louisiana	1,316,005	395,203	315,569
Maine	487,799	176,128	111,064
Maryland	1,280,564	385,828	306,817
Massachusetts	1,648,544	483,165	397,681
Michigan	2,474,740	701,708	601,688
Minnesota	1,241,605	375,523	297,197
Mississippi	848,741	271,603	200,190
Missouri	1,447,462	429,975	348,029
Montana	404,852	154,187	90,583
Nebraska	601,159	206,113	139,056
Nevada	425,463	159,639	95,672
New Hampshire	440,796	163,695	99,458
New Jersey	2,076,095	596,260	503,253
New Mexico	551,642	193,015	126,829
New York	4,639,639	1,274,361	1,136,254
North Carolina	1,727,218	503,976	417,107
North Dakota	371,171	145,278	82,266
Ohio	2,898,520	813,805	706,330
Oklahoma	1,031,977	320,072	245,435
Oregon	868,095	276,723	204,969
Pennsylvania	3,188,330	890,465	777,891
Rhode Island	440,293	163,562	99,334
South Carolina	1,018,404	316,482	242,084
South Dakota	375,696	146,474	83,383
Tennessee	1,375,324	410,894	330,216
Texas	4,166,091	1,149,100	1,019,324
Utah	606,688	207,576	140,421
Vermont	331,960	134,906	72,584
Virginia	1,596,514	469,402	384,833
Washington	1,281,318	386,027	307,004
West Virginia	693,153	230,448	161,772
Wisconsin	1,392,919	415,548	334,560
Wyoming	329,698	134,307	72,025
American Samoa	48,495	22,247	12,098
Guam	67,825	27,360	16,871
Puerto Rico	1,019,911	316,881	242,456
Trust Territories	70,515	28,072	17,535
Virgin Islands	65,512	26,748	16,300
Northern Mariana Islands	44,474	21,183	11,105

LSCA Title I

Blind and Physically Handicapped Persons

In FY 1985, LSCA Title I funds for library services to the blind and physically handicapped totaled approximately $4.5 million (Table 2). Although this represents an increase of only 1 percent in federal dollars committed to this program, increased state and local allocations resulted in an overall 12 percent increase from FY 1984 to FY 1985 funds supporting these library services. Trends in state reports indicate

- Acquisition of large-print books continues to increase.
- Radio reading services have increased.
- Automated services to the blind and physically handicapped are becoming common.
- Volunteers remain essential to nearly all programs.
- The special needs of blind and physically handicapped children are beginning to be recognized.

Services to State Institutionalized Persons

About 650,000 institutionalized people were reached by library services in FY 1985. As a result of ongoing state and local efforts, institutional libraries are gaining acceptance as a valuable support service. Federal funds for projects focus on specific institutionalized populations, rather than general support of the library facility.

In FY 1985, the federal dollar ($2.6 million) generated approximately 5.9 state and/or local dollars ($15.2 million) for a total of $17.8 million used to support library services for the institutionalized. This shows substantial commitment on the part of state and local authorities for this area of library service.

Trends in institutional libraries, as identified in state reports, include

- Literacy was a major programming category.
- The efforts of institutional librarians were recognized.
- Interlibrary loans increased.
- Networking among institutional librarians was more frequent in FY 1985 than in previous years.
- Computer literacy was emphasized.
- Health information was increasingly a program element in institutions.

Library Services to the Elderly

Access, education, information, management, and training were emphasized in public library projects for the elderly during 1985. The following trends in public library services for the elderly have been noted:

- Concerted efforts to make library services more accessible to the homebound
- Increased collection of large-print books
- Information projects in the areas of health, gardening, travel, and consumer education

Table 2 / LSCA Title I, Funds for the Blind and Physically Handicapped, FY 1985

State	Federal	State	Local	Total
Totals	$4,450,139	$13,330,719	—	$18,001,089
Alabama	32,904	75,158	—	108,062
Alaska	—	60,500	—	60,500
Arizona	29,310	256,205	—	285,515
Arkansas	73,482	94,497	—	767,979
California	81,691	1,234,509	—	1,316,200
Colorado	20,000	244,462	—	264,462
Connecticut	154,774	65,676	—	220,450
Delaware	16,991	87,316	—	104,307
District of Columbia	11,366	69,153	—	80,519
Florida	146,838	451,898	216,705	815,441
Georgia	76,550	731,481	—	808,031
Hawaii	10,000	249,223	3,526	262,749
Idaho	—	196,312	—	196,312
Illinois	43,037	—	—	43,037
Indiana	206,396	—	—	206,396
Iowa	9,111	42,889	—	52,000
Kansas	122,500	175,000	—	297,500
Kentucky	69,800	200,000	—	269,800
Louisiana	137,366	120,513	—	257,879
Maine	72,188	26,662	—	98,850
Maryland	78,956	160,750	—	239,706
Massachusetts	115,095	22,995	—	138,090
Michigan	503,960	111,376	—	615,336
Minnesota	12,633	491,168	—	503,801
Mississippi	43,037	88,486	—	131,523
Missouri	105,314	380,851	—	486,165
Montana	88,641	53,861	—	142,502
Nebraska	60,000	254,296	—	314,296
Nevada	—	17,348	—	17,348
New Hampshire	26,147	57,665	—	83,812
New Jersey	240,540	126,181	—	366,721
New Mexico	3,000	127,088	—	130,088
New York	338,282	981,281	—	1,319,563
North Carolina	48,891	533,200	—	582,091
North Dakota	90,587	9,000	—	99,587
Ohio	155,703	734,426	—	890,129
Oklahoma	25,179	—	—	25,179
Oregon	240,000	207,808	—	447,808
Pennsylvania	60,000	1,432,000	—	1,492,000
Rhode Island	65,073	154,381	—	219,454
South Carolina	64,803	186,523	—	251,326
South Dakota	195,932	—	—	195,932
Tennessee	256,620	288,507	—	545,127
Texas	—	934,978	—	934,978
Utah	106,637	177,540	—	284,177
Vermont	17,749	29,262	—	47,011
Virginia	61,000	59,000	—	120,000
Washington	49,000	601,704	—	650,704
West Virginia	11,503	174,222	—	185,725
Wisconsin	—	420,577	—	420,577
Wyoming	25,178	30,200	—	55,378
American Samoa	—	—	—	—
Guam	—	18,043	—	18,043
Puerto Rico	38,600	29,200	—	67,800
Trust Territories	—	—	—	—
Virgin Islands	—	—	—	63,123

- Emphasis on historical and cultural projects, including oral histories
- Volunteers and volunteer training continuing as an important aspect of public library services to older adults
- Public relations programs to help senior citizens become more aware of the services available to them

Public Library Construction (LSCA Title II)

In FY 1986, an appropriation of $21.1 million was available for the Library Services and Construction Act Title II program. During FY 1985, 34 states had received LSCA Title II funding to support 268 construction projects. This $15 million investment allowed 167 remodeling or renovation projects, 48 new buildings, and 27 other types of projects.

Since it was first authorized in 1964, the LSCA Title II program has obligated more than $264.6 million in federal funds, of which approximately $190.1 million was from LSCA, $50 million from the Emergency Job Act, and about $24.5 million from other federal sources (Table 3). Reports indicate that 2,850 public library construction projects have been funded under the LSCA Title II program through September 1985.

Interlibrary Cooperation (LSCA Title III)

In FY 1985, $17.6 million was allocated for interlibrary cooperation. Statewide and regional resource sharing continued to be a major project emphasis. Following are representative examples of state efforts to increase access to library materials.

In *Ohio*, plans for statewide resource sharing included analysis of the current status of regional resource sharing, identification of existing automated circulation systems, and recommendations to further develop and integrate them into the regional system.

In *Michigan*, LSCA Title III funds continued to support the development of regional and statewide holding lists of serials, distribute the Library of Michigan COM catalog, and develop a telefacsimile copier network.

In *Illinois*, the University of Illinois received funds for the development of a microcomputer interface to link public and academic library circulation systems. Projects to improve delivery of resources and information in Illinois included a grant to expand the facsimile transmission network. As a result of those efforts, interlibrary loan growth went from a 3 percent increase to a 17 percent increase during the first quarter of FY 1986.

In *California*, a statewide Networking Conference was held, in addition to a Second Binational Conference on Libraries across the border with Mexico. The University of California's Division of Library Automation was successful in the first phase of developing procedures to test radio communication of data among libraries by means of packet radio transmission.

Discretionary Programs

Two LSCA discretionary programs were also funded during FY 1986. Title IV, the Library Services for Indian Tribes and Hawaiian Natives Program, is funded through a 2 percent set aside from Titles I, II, and III. In 1986, awards totaling $2.2 million were granted to 185 Indian tribes and Hawaiian natives (Tables 4 and 5).

Table 3 / LSCA Title II, Construction, FYs 1965–1985

Fiscal Year	Number of Library Projects Approved	Funding by Source (in thousands)		
		Federal	Local and State*	Total
1965	363	$ 29,864	$ 62,851	$ 92,715
1966	364	29,778	62,483	92,261
1967	278	24,583	52,107	76,690
1968	284	27,429	66,137	93,566
1969	211	22,257	69,500	91,757
1970	65	5,095	16,989	22,084
1971	114	8,571	34,427	42,998
1972	131	9,533	30,646	40,179
1973	52	2,606	15,360	17,966
1974	99	10,787[a]	44,570	55,357
1975	65	4,048[b]	26,776	30,824
Total LSCA	2,026	$174,551	$481,846	$656,397
Appalachian Regional Development Act	—	14,300[c]	—	14,300
Subtotal	2,026	$188,851	$481,846	$670,697
1976[d]	11	1,606	938	2,544
1977	5	851	3,432	4,283
1978	13	2,094	1,021	3,115
1979	9	2,281	2,516	4,797
1980	7	1,626	4,307	5,933
1981	10	1,654	2,921	4,575
1982	3	551	209	760
Subtotal	58	$ 10,663	$ 15,344	$ 25,907
1983, 1984[e]	498	49,514	98,939	148,453
1985[f]	268	15,527	58,430	73,957
Total	2,850	$264,555	$654,539	$919,014

*Budgeted amounts as reported by states.
[a]1973 appropriation released in FY 1974.
[b]Carryover funds from FY 1973 appropriation not obligated in FY 1974.
[c]Funds from the Appalachian Regional Development Act (ARDA). LSCA-administered projects are listed separately. Since ARDA projects also include LSCA funds, the number of ARDA projects and local/state matching funds for these projects are included in the tables.
[d]Although LSCA federal funds were not available for projects from FY 1976, all projects approved between FYs 1976 and 1982 were administered under the LSCA administrative authority, but funded from other federal programs. Of the 58 projects approved since FY 1976, 49 received funds from the Appalachian Regional Development Act program in the amount of $9.2 million.
[e]The Emergency Jobs Act (PL 98-8) provided $50 million for library construction in FY 1983 to be administered under the LSCA Title II authority.
[f]The FY 1985 federal obligation of $15.5 million included $15 million from LSCA and the balance of $0.5 million from the Emergency Jobs Act Program.

Title VI, Library Literacy Program, was funded for the first time in FY 1986. This $5 million program provided $25,000 grants to 240 state or local public libraries to create or assist literacy training programs.

Some specific highlights of the LSCA Discretionary Programs follow. (FY 1986 funding figures are used to report on Discretionary Programs.)

Library Services for Indian Tribes and
Hawaiian Natives Program (LSCA Title IV)

One hundred and eighty-five Indian tribes and all Hawaiian natives benefited from the $2.2 million of FY 1986 funds granted from LSCA Title IV. The money was used in 29 states to build and renovate libraries, train library personnel, improve access to library

Table 4 / Title IV, Basic Grant Awards, FY 1986

State	No. of Awards	$ Amount
Alabama	1	$ 3,277
Alaska	26	117,972
Arizona	8	26,216
California	24	111,418
Colorado	1	3,277
Florida	2	6,554
Hawaii	1	552,750
Idaho	2	6,554
Iowa	1	3,277
Maine	3	9,831
Michigan	5	16,385
Minnesota	3	9,831
Mississippi	1	3,277
Missouri	1	3,277
Montana	7	22,939
Nebraska	3	9,831
Nevada	3	9,831
New Mexico	13	42,601
New York	3	9,831
North Carolina	1	3,277
North Dakota	3	9,831
Oklahoma	22	72,094
Oregon	2	6,554
Rhode Island	1	3,277
South Dakota	6	19,662
Utah	2	6,554
Washington	14	45,878
Wisconsin	6	19,594
Wyoming	1	3,277
Total	165*	$1,158,927

*Some awards serve more than one Indian tribe, for a total of 185 tribes.

Table 5 / Title IV, Special Projects Awards, FY 1986

State	Grantee	$ Amount
Arizona	Navajo Nation,	$143,580
	Navajo Nation	57,375
California	Morongo Band of Mission Indians	40,925
Florida	Miccosukee Tribe	51,668
Montana	Confederated Salish and Kootenai Tribe	40,208
New York	St. Regis Band of Mohawks	37,294
North Dakota	Three Affiliated Tribes	41,436
Oklahoma	Sac and Fox Tribe of Indians of Oklahoma	167,185
	Cherokee Nation	49,769
	Chickasaw Nation	39,737
	Delaware Tribe of Western Oklahoma	28,802
South Dakota	Rosebud Sioux Tribe	140,355
	Sisseton-Wahpeton Sioux Tribe	60,594
Utah	Ute Indian Tribe	42,840
Washington	Nisqually Indian Tribe	82,305
Wisconsin	Oneida Tribe of Indians	596
	Lac du Flambeau Tribe	27,404

services, and conduct surveys to better determine the library needs of tribal communities. Specific projects funded in FY 1986 include

- A $143,580 grant to the Navajo Nation to support two bookmobiles, establish ten collection points for books, and complete a library needs assessment.
- A $167,185 grant to the Sac and Fox tribe in Oklahoma to build a 2,200 square foot library in Stroud and to pay part of the salaries of the Sac and Fox Tribal Archives director and library aide.
- A $140,355 grant to the Rosebud Sioux tribe in South Dakota to held fund a van and extend the service hours of audiovisual materials.
- A $51,668 grant to the Miccosukee tribe in Florida to expand library programs for elderly persons and for preschoolchildren.

Alu Like, Inc., the grantee that assists Hawaiian natives, is a nonprofit organization that helps develop economic and social self-sufficiency among Hawaiian natives. Library improvement projects include an outreach program, employment and training for Hawaiians in library and information services, and strengthening collections of books about Hawaiian and Pacific peoples and their cultures.

Library Literacy Program (LSCA Title VI)

Title VI of the LSCA amendments of 1984 (PL 98-480) established a new discretionary grant program to provide support to state and local public libraries for literacy programs. This new Library Literacy Program was funded for the first time in FY 1986. Congress appropriated $5 million for the program in FY 1986, which was reduced to $4,785,000 under the Balanced Budget and Deficit Control Act of 1985 (PL 99-177).

The Library Literacy Program is the first federal library program under which state and local public libraries apply directly to the U.S. Department of Education and compete for grant awards. Under the program, state and local public libraries may apply for grants of up to $25,000 for literacy programs. State public libraries may use grant funds to coordinate and plan library literacy programs and to arrange for the training of librarians and volunteers to carry out such programs. Local public libraries may use grant funds to promote the use of the voluntary services of individuals, agencies, and organizations in providing literacy programs and to acquire library materials, use library facilities, and train volunteers for local literacy programs.

On September 30, 1986, 239 grants totaling $4,736.643 were awarded to 22 state libraries and 217 local public libraries. Approximately 100 literacy experts and librarians skilled in literacy activities participated in reviewing the 390 applications. Grants ranged in size from $1,500 to the maximum amount of $25,000. The average amount awarded was $19,818. Five of the grants to local public libraries are supporting joint projects that involve a total of 36 libraries. Projects in state public libraries emphasize training librarians and volunteers, as well as coordinating statewide literacy projects. Projects in local public libraries emphasize acquiring literacy materials, recruiting and training volunteers to be tutors, and promoting their literacy programs to reach the illiterate population in their communities. All projects planned coordinated efforts with literacy councils, schools, private agencies, and other literacy providers in the state or community. Grantees were also encouraged to coordinate their activities with those supported by Title I of the Library Services and Construction Act. (Table 6 lists the number of grants each state received under the Library Literacy Program in FY 1986.)

Table 6 / Title VI, Library Literacy Program

State	No. of Literacy Grants	Funds
Alabama	2	$ 36,360
Arizona	5	85,845
California	14	339,547
Colorado	5	106,708
Connecticut	2	44,000
Delaware	3	58,700
District of Columbia	1	25,000
Florida	9	168,293
Georgia	2	49,850
Hawaii	3	39,960
Illinois	7	151,601
Indiana	9	152,688
Iowa	2	50,000
Kansas	4	77,310
Kentucky	3	50,760
Louisiana	12	237,871
Maine	3	54,959
Maryland	2	50,000
Massachusetts	5	84,070
Michigan	13	263,546
Minnesota	2	49,525
Mississippi	8	108,115
Missouri	2	50,000
Montana	1	25,000
Nebraska	1	20,400
New Hampshire	1	25,000
New Jersey	13	297,400
New Mexico	1	5,000
New York	15	339,428
North Carolina	2	25,296
North Dakota	1	25,000
Ohio	5	74,868
Oklahoma	8	109,452
Oregon	4	99,986
Pennsylvania	13	254,938
Rhode Island	3	45,984
South Carolina	6	91,878
South Dakota	2	43,833
Tennessee	3	42,663
Texas	18	357,130
Utah	2	49,500
Vermont	1	19,000
Virginia	5	98,282
Washington	6	149,030
West Virginia	3	66,500
Wisconsin	7	136,367
Total	239	$4,736,643

Higher Education Act (HEA, PL 99-498)

Title II of the Higher Education Act has been the backbone of federal financial assist-ance to college and university libraries for two decades. With the enormous expansion of resources and demand on higher education libraries, Title II has been a vital element in helping college and university libraries preserve, acquire, and share resources and train and retrain personnel to improve services or use new technology. In 1986, HEA Title II was reauthorized and some parts rewritten to further accommodate change. De-scriptions of the individual programs follow.

College Library Resources Program (HEA II-A)

During its reauthorization in Congress in 1986, the Title II-A portion of the Higher Education Act was amended to award grants to institutions of higher education strictly on the basis of need. To date, no funds have been appropriated.

Library Career Training Program (HEA Title II-B)

The Library Career Training Program (Title II-B of the Higher Education Act) authorizes a program of federal financial assistance to institutions of higher education and other library organizations and agencies to assist in training persons in librarianship and to establish, develop, and expand programs of library and information science, including new techniques of information transfer and communications technology. Grants are made for fellowships and traineeships at the associate, bachelor, master, postmaster, and doctoral levels for training in librarianship. Grants may also be used to assist in covering the costs of institutes, or courses, to upgrade the competencies of persons serving in all types of libraries, information centers, or instructional materials centers offering library and information services, and those serving as educators. Table 7 shows the Library Career Training grants awarded in academic year 1985–1986.

Table 7 / HEA Title II-B, Library Career Training, Academic Year 1985–1986

Institution	Program Director	No.	Level	Amount
Alabama				
University of Alabama	James D. Rames	1	M	$ 8,000
Arizona				
University of Arizona	Margaret F. Maxwell	1	M	$ 8,000
Arkansas				
University of Central Arkansas	Selvin Royal/Judy Charter	1	M	$ 8,000
California				
California State University	Marilyn W. Greenberg	2	M	$16,000
San Jose State University	John Morlan	1	M	$ 8,000
University of California, Berkeley	Robert D. Harlan	1	M	$ 8,000
University of California, Los Angeles	Marcia J. Bates	4	D(2) M(2)	$40,000
Florida				
Florida State University	Harold Goldstein	3	M(2) D(1)	$28,000
Georgia				
Atlanta University	Lorene B. Brown	2	M	$16,000
Illinois				
Rosary College	Tze-Chung Li	1	M	$ 8,000
University of Chicago	Julie M. Hurd	2	D(2)	$24,000
University of Illinois	Leslie Edmonds	3	M(2) D(1)	$28,000
Indiana				
School of Library and Information Science	Herbert S. White	1	M	$ 8,000
Iowa				
University of Iowa	Carl F. Orgren	1	M	$ 8,000
Kentucky				
University of Kentucky	Timothy W. Sineath	1	M	$ 8,000

Table 7 / HEA Title II-B, Library Career Training, Academic Year 1985–1986 (*cont.*)

Institution	Program Director	No.	Level	Amount
Maryland				
University of Maryland	Claude E. Walston	1	M	$ 8,000
Massachusetts				
Simmons College	Robert Stueart	1	M	$ 8,000
Michigan				
University of Michigan	Robert Warner	3	D(1)	$28,000
Wayne State University	Peter Spyers-Derran	1	M(1)	$ 8,000
Mississippi				
University of Southern Mississippi	Onvak Bosherars, Jr.	1	M	$ 8,000
Missouri				
University of Missouri	Emma Jean McKinnin	1	M	$ 8,000
University of Missouri	Mary F. Lenox	2	M	$16,000
New Jersey				
Rutgers University	Betty J. Turock	4	M(2) D(2)	$40,000
New York				
Columbia University	Paul N. Banks	5	3M 2PM	$48,000
CUNY, Queens College	David Cohen	3	M	$24,000
Long Island University, C.W. Post Campus	Lucienne G. Maillet	2	M	$16,000
Saint John's University	Jovian Lang, OFM	1	M	$ 8,000
SUNY at Buffalo	George Bobinski	2	M(1)	
North Carolina				
North Carolina Central University	Benjamin Speller, Jr.	1	M	$ 8,000
Ohio				
Kent State University	Lubomyr Wynar	1	M	$ 8,000
Pennsylvania				
University of Pittsburgh	Blanche Woolls	4	M(2) D(2)	$40,000
South Carolina				
University of South Carolina	John Olsgaard	1	M	$ 8,000
Tennessee				
Vanderbilt University,	Edwin S. Gleaves	1	M	$ 8,000
Texas				
North Texas State University	Herman L. Totten	2	D(1) M(1)	$20,000
Texas Woman's University	Brooke E. Shield	1	D(1)	$12,000
University of Texas	Ronald Wyllys	1	M	$ 8,000
Washington				
University of Washington	Margaret Chisholm	2	M	$14,000
Wisconsin				
University of Wisconsin at Madison	Jane Robbins-Carter	1	D	$12,000
University of Wisconsin, at Milwaukee	Mohammed M. Aman	1	M	$ 8,000

Fellowship Program

In FY 1986, $612,000 was awarded for fellowships under HEA Title II. Thirty-nine library and information science education programs received 68 fellowship awards (14 doctoral, 3 postmaster's, and 51 master's programs). The order of priorities for fellowship training levels in FY 1986 was as follows: master, doctoral, and postmaster. Stipend levels varied, depending on the level of study and length of program, within a range of $3,500 to $6,000 per fellow plus dependency allowance as permitted. Additionally, grantee institutions received an institutional allowance equal to the amount of stipend per fellow. Table 8 reviews the fellowship program since it began in FY 1966.

Library Research and Demonstration Program (HEA Title II-B)

The Library Research and Demonstration Program (Title II-B of the Higher Education Act) authorizes the award of grants and contracts for research and demonstration projects related to the improvement of libraries, training in librarianship, and for the dissemination of information derived from these projects. A description of projects funded in FY 1985 with completion dates in 1987 follows.

*Libraries and Literacy Education ($148,037)
Project Directors: Jane Robbins-Carter and Douglas Zweizig, University of Wisconsin, Madison.

In FY 1979, the U.S. Department of Education awarded a contract to study the nature and extent of literacy programs among the nation's libraries. A new study will be conducted to update the findings of the earlier study; to assess the current status of libraries in literacy education; to determine or project an expanded role for libraries in literacy education; to identify and describe at least six exemplary literacy programs; and to assess the applications and effectiveness of new technology in literacy educational services.

*The Cooperative System for Public Library Data Collection, A Pilot Project ($54,423)
Project Director: Mary Jo Lynch, ALA, Research Office.

This project seeks to demonstrate a statistical data-gathering model by which state library agencies will standardize data collection practices for the nation's public libraries. Seventeen states are involved in the demonstration, which will lead to primary leadership at the state level, with the federal government serving in a coordinating and guidance role. Standardization of the data to be collected will enhance the reliability of the data and its expeditious collection. The project is cofunded by the Center for Education Statistics ($30,000) and Library Programs ($25,000 in FY 1985, and $17,787 in FY 1986).

*Issues in Library Research: Proposals for the Nineties ($304,339)
Project Directors: Sandra N. Milevski and Yvonne B. Carter, Library Programs, U.S. Department of Education.

This major research project of 18 months' duration was initiated and directed in-house by Library Programs to identify and explore issues and areas of the greatest future impact on the provision of library and information services. The expertise of both library and nonlibrary specialists will be solicited to enumerate broad topical areas and issues to serve as the basis for requests for field-initiated research proposals starting in FY 1987. Expected products of this research include commissioned overview papers for

Table 8 / Library Education Fellowship/Traineeship Program, Academic Years 1966–1986

Academic Year	No. of Institutions	Doctoral	Post-master	Master	Bachelor	Associate	Total	FY
1966/67	24	52	25	62	—	—	139	1966
1967/68	38	116	58	327	—	—	501	1967
1968/69	51	168	47	494	—	—	709	1968
1969/70	56	193	30	379	—	—	602	1969
1970/71	48	171	15	200	20	—	406	1970
1971/72	20	116	6	—	20*	—	142	1971
1972/73	15	39	3	20*	—	—	62	1972
1973/74	34	21	4	145 + 14*	—	20	204	1973
1974/75	50	21	3	168 + 3*	—	5	200	1974
1975/76	22	27	6	94	—	—	127	1975
1976/77	12	5	3	43	—	—	51	1976
1977/78	37	18	3	134	—	5	160	1977
1978/79	33	25	9	139	10	5	188	1978
1979/80	36	19	4	134	2	3	162	1979
1980/81	32	17	5	72	—	7	101	1980
1981/82	34	13	2	59	—	5	79	1981
1982/83	33	13	2	56	—	3	74	1982
1983/84	33	8	7	56	4	—	75	1983
1984/85	41	5	4	67	—	—	76	1984
1985/86	38	11	4	57	—	—	72	1985
1986/87	39	14	3	51	—	—	68	1986
Total		1,072	243	2,737 + 37	16 + 40	53	4,198	

*Indicates traineeships.

each of the topics identified, one or more real-time interactive international satellite teleconferences, videotapes of the teleconferences, commissioned research plans, and a final publication in book form.

*National Survey of Public Library Services to the Aging: Update 1986 ($22,674)
Project Director: Betty Turock, Rutgers University.

This project seeks (1) to update and amplify the 1971 national survey; (2) to identify and measure variables in library services to older adults, ascertain problem areas, and suggest modifications; and (3) to sponsor a symposium, "Public Library Services for Older Adults."

Table 9 shows the number of projects funded and the total funds obligated under the Library Research and Demonstration Program since 1967.

Strengthening Research Library Resources Programs (HEA Title II-C)

In authorizing the Strengthening Research Library Resources Program, Congress recognizes that the expansion of educational and research programs, together with the rapid increase in the production of recorded knowledge, places unprecedented demands on major research libraries by requiring programs and services beyond the financial capabilities of the individual and collective library budgets. Further, the nation's major research libraries are acknowledged as essential elements to advanced and professional education and research. (Major research libraries are defined as public or private nonprofit institutions having collections available to qualified users that make a significant contribution to higher education and research, that are broadly based, are unique in nature and contain material not widely available, are in substantial demand by researchers and scholars not connected with the institution, and of national or international significance for research.)

Table 9 / HEA Title II-B, Library Research and Demonstration, FYs 1967–1986

FY	Obligation	No. of Projects
1967	$ 3,381,052	38
1968	2,020,942	21
1969	2,986,264	39
1970	2,160,622	30
1971	2,170,274	18
1972	2,748,953	31
1973	1,784,741	24
1974	1,418,433	20
1975	999,338	19
1976	999,918	19
1977	995,193	18
1978	998,904	17
1979	990,563	12
1980	319,877	4
1981	239,954	12
1982	243,438	1
1983	237,643	4
1984	240,000	2
1985	360,000	3
1986	344,800	3
Total	$25,631,009	335

During the nine years of program operation, 797 applications have been received. Of these, 284 were funded, benefiting 270 institutions. A total of $52,494,264 has been awarded to further the purposes of the II-C program (Table 10).

Table 10 / Strengthening Research Library Program Funding, FYs 1977–1986

FY	Authorization	Budget Request	Appropriation	Awarded
1977	$10,000,000	–	–	–
1978	15,000,000	$5,000,000	$ 5,000,000	$ 4,999,966
1979	20,000,000	5,000,000	6,000,000	6,000,000
1980	20,000,000	6,000,000	6,000,000	5,992,268
1981	10,000,000	7,000,000	6,000,000	6,000,000
1982	15,000,000	6,000,000	5,760,000	5,760,000
1983	15,000,000	–	6,000,000	6,000,000
1984	15,000,000	–	6,000,000	6,000,000
1985	15,000,000	–	6,000,000	6,000,000
1986	15,000,000	–	5,742,000	5,742,000
Total			$52,502,000	$52,494,264

In FY 1986, 97 applications were received, requesting a total of $18,759,576. Thirty-eight top-ranking applications, benefiting 44 institutions, were reviewed and funded, using the entire amount appropriated ($6 million, minus the 4.3 percent reduction required by the Gramm-Rudman-Hollings Act, for a total of $5,742,000). Bibliographic control and access, which emerged as the major activity in the first year of the program, received 77 percent of the FY 1986 funds. Preservation projects accounted for 20 percent of the monies, with only 3 percent going for collection development (Tables 11 and 12). Table 13 summarizes Strengthening Research Library Program grant activity since FY 1978.

Table 11 / Strengthening Research Library Program Grant Awards by Major Activity, FY 1986

Institution	Bibliographic Control	Preservation	Collection Development	Total
American Antiquarian Society	$ 91,500	–	–	$ 91,500
American Museum of Natural History	–	$ 161,160	–	161,160
Art Institute of Chicago	79,327	–	–	79,327
Center for Research Libraries	–	139,214	–	139,214
Columbia University	188,595	22,950	–	211,545
Cornell University	74,630	2,826	–	77,456
Dartmouth College	208,709	25,500	–	234,209
Detroit Public Library	27,600	33,199	–	60,799
Duke University	170,242	–	–	170,242
Emory University	75,173	17,000	–	92,173
Folger Shakespeare Library	–	–	$124,968	124,968
Harvard University	69,278	170,665	–	239,943
Houston Academy of Medicine	62,209	10,679	–	72,888
Huntington Library	–	53,380	–	53,380

Table 11 / Strengthening Research Library Program Grant Awards
by Major Activity, FY 1986 *(cont.)*

Institution	Program Activity			
	Bibliographic Control	Preservation	Collection Development	Total
Indiana University	94,573	2,316	—	96,889
Johns Hopkins University	40,350	—	—	40,350
Massachusetts Institute of Technology	196,226	—	—	196,226
Missouri Botanical Garden	240,044	—	—	240,044
New York Public Library	62,596	33,394	39,728	135,718
Ohio State University	21,644	66,711	—	88,355
Princeton University	23,367	27,060	—	50,427
Stanford University	359,407	—	—	359,407
Stanford University, Hoover Institution	—	257,916	—	257,916
State Historical Society of Wisconsin	117,616	2,438	—	120,054
SUNY at Buffalo	94,996	—	—	94,996
University of California, Berkeley	250,023	—	—	250,023
University of California, Riverside	135,000	—	—	135,000
University of California, San Diego	156,121	14,769	25,521	196,411
University of Chicago	210,438	—	—	210,438
University of Illinois, Urbana	204,449	—	—	204,449
University of Kansas	102,140	—	—	102,140
University of Kentucky	96,694	56,628	—	153,322
University of Maryland	404,776	—	—	404,776
University of Minnesota	64,108	—	—	64,108
University of Missouri	133,665	17,862	—	151,527
University of Pittsburgh	132,000	—	—	132,000
University of Wisconsin, Madison	101,210	6,742	—	107,952
Washington State University	140,668	—	—	140,668
Total	$4,429,374	$1,122,409	$190,217	$5,742,000

An amendment regarding eligibility added in FY 1986 with the reauthorization of the Higher Education Act will affect the FY 1987 competition. It permits institutions that do not qualify under the criteria listed in the program regulations to provide additional information or documents to demonstrate the national or international significance for scholarly research of the particular collection described in the grant application.

College Library Technology and Cooperation Program (HEA II-D)

During its reauthorization in Congress in 1986, the Title II-D portion of the Higher Education Act was rewritten to award grants to institutions of higher education for technological equipment. This is an entirely new grant program that has not yet been funded. Further information about this and other federally supported programs is available upon request.

Table 12 / Strengthening Research Library Resources
Program Grants, FY 1986

Institution and Project Director	Grant Award	Project Description
American Antiquarian Society, Worcester, Mass. Alan Degutis	$ 91,500	To produce MARC cataloging of the microform set, *Early American Imprints: First Series* (Evans), published by Readex Microprint Corp., which includes the text of every available book, pamphlet, and broadside printed in the United States between 1640 and 1800.
American Museum of Natural History, New York, N.Y. Nina Root	161,160	To microfilm, restore, and conserve some 80 unique scientific and historic ledgers, scrapbooks, field diaries and notebooks, and specimen catalogs from scientific expeditions, fieldwork, and laboratory work.
Center for Research Libraries, Chicago Donald Simpson	139,214	To continue to microfilm CRL's newspaper files that relate to ethnic groups whose major migration to the United States took place in the late nineteenth and early twentieth centuries. CRL's newspaper files include more than 500 ethnic newspapers published in 38 languages.
Columbia University, New York, N.Y. Pat Battin	211,545	To catalog and preserve unique and rare titles from the Edwin R. A. Seligman Collection in the field of economics. Titles will be entered into Research Libraries Information Network (RLIN) and reported to the Edwin Seligman Collection project.
Cornell University, Ithaca, N.Y. Jan Kennedy Olsen	77,456	To establish a national repository for a comprehensive library collection on agriculture in China. Machine-readable catalog records would be created and entered into bibliographic databases available nationally and internationally.
Dartmouth College Library, Hanover, N.H. John James	234,209	To continue to increase accessibility and availability of materials from the theater and performing arts collections through preservation and the creation of machine-readable records and by entering these records into RLIN and OCLC.
Detroit Public Library, Detroit, Mich. Ronald Grantz	60,799	To preserve the historic photographic prints of the pioneer automotive photographer Nathan Lazarnick held in the National Automotive History Collection.
Duke University, Durham, N.C. Jerry D. Campbell	170,242	To conduct a project with North Carolina State University at Raleigh and the University of North Carolina at Chapel Hill to convert to machine-readable form their current serials records.
Emory University, Atlanta, Ga. Herbert F. Johnson	106,030	To conduct a project of retrospective conversion cataloging and preservation for a discrete collection of 16,977 titles of eighteenth-century imprints in philosophy and religion.
Folger Shakespeare Library, Washington, D.C. Philip Knachel	124,968	To collect materials that will complement and make more accessible the Folger's extensive and unique holdings in the fields of continental European Renaissance and early modern history and

**Table 12 / Strengthening Research Library Resources
Program Grants, FY 1986** *(cont.)*

Institution and Project Director	Grant Award	Project Description
		literature and in the field of English Renaissance manuscripts.
Harvard College, Cambridge, Mass. Sidney Verba	239,943	To improve bibliographic control of master film negative preparatory to listing and input into national databases, and to film 1 million pages of research materials too fragile or rare for lending.
Houston Academy of Medicine, Houston, Tex.	72,888	To catalog the Burbank-Fraser Collection of Arthritis, Rheumatism, and Gout, to enter the data into the OCLC network, to provide the cataloging worksheets to the University of Pittsburgh Falk Library, and to publicize the collection to historians, researchers, and libraries.
Huntington Library, San Marino, Calif. Daniel H. Woodward	53,380	To preserve and make available to scholars the Samuel L. M. Barlow letterbooks and Richard Bull's expanded version of James Granger's *Biographical History of England.*
Indiana University, Bloomington, Ind. David Fenske	96,889	To conserve and increase nationwide bibliographic access and availability of the extensive collection of operatic musical scores and recordings by cataloging significant additional materials and by taping opera recordings that are only available on 78 rpm discs.
Johns Hopkins University, Baltimore, Md. Susan Martin	40,350	To catalog each title in the Yale University Library Collection of German baroque literature on microfilm and to enter the bibliographic records into the RLIN database of the Research Libraries Group.
Massachusetts Institute of Technology, Cambridge, Mass. Jay Lucker	196,226	To continue to provide national access to the collection of scientific and technical publications issued by the institute from 1861 through 1974 by cataloging and adding full MARC records to OCLC; to bring under bibliographic control major archival and manuscript collections; and to produce finding aids.
Missouri Botanical Garden Library, St. Louis, Mo.	240,044	To enable the libraries of the Missouri Botanical Garden and the New York Botanical Garden to enter into the OCLC database full bibliographic records and/or locations for more than 80,000 titles, especially primary botanical research literature, including rare books, monographs, and serials.
New York Public Library, New York, N.Y. Edward Kasinec	135,718	To conserve, restore, catalog, and enhance NYPL's collection of imperial Russian political, social, and literary journals.
Ohio State University, Columbus, Ohio Jill Fatzer	88,355	To preserve and provide online bibliographic access to Ohio State University's unique collection of medieval and medieval tradition (thirteenth through twentieth century) Slavic Cyrillic manuscripts in microform in the Hilanden Research Library.

Table 12 / **Strengthening Research Library Resources
Program Grants, FY 1986** (cont.)

Institution and Project Director	Grant Award	Project Description
Princeton University, Princeton, N.J. Dorothy Pearson	50,427	To produce master preservation micro-film and to catalog and create machine-readable records for pamphlets, monographs, and serials, as well as posters, broadsides, and fliers that collectively document the socioeconomic and political life of Latin America.
Stanford University, Stanford, Calif. Cynthia Gozzi	359,407	To create and input into the RLIN data-base bibliographic records with multiple access points and Name Authority Cooperative (NACO) headings for Segment I and the supplement of the microfilm set *Goldsmiths'—Kress Library of Economic Literature.*
State Historical Society of Wisconsin, Madison, Wisc. Herbert Tepper	120,054	To complete the processing of the Cutter Pamphlet Collection into the current bound pamphlet collection. This involves basic conservation procedures, including refiling the acid-free folders, transfer of rare and scarce materials to the rare collection, and full cataloging of all the pamphlets on the OCLC system.
State University of New York (SUNY) at Buffalo, N.Y. Robert Bertholf	94,996	To sort, process, and produce MARC records for the Poetry Collection and input them into the RLIN database.
University of California, Berkeley, Calif. Joseph Rosenthal	205,023	To conduct a major retrospective con-version and catalog improvement project for records and monographs contained in the collection of the Ban-croft Library, a noncirculating rare book and special collections library.
University of California, Riverside, Calif. Nancy Douglas and George Slusser	135,000	To improve access to the Eaton Collec-tion of Science Fiction and Fantasy Literature through bibliographic control.
University of California, San Diego, La Jolla, Calif. Dorothy Gregor	196,411	To strengthen the Archive for New Poetry and to extend access to these materials to the international scholarly community through cataloging, preser-vation, and dissemination of informa-tion.
University of Chicago, Chicago, Ill. Martin Runkle	210,438	To continue an important cooperative venture with the Library of Congress. The project will provide retrospective conversion and original cataloging in machine-readable form for titles in science and technology drawn from the John Crerar Library of the University of Chicago.
University of Illinois—Urbana, Urbana, Ill. Carol Boast	204,449	To make uniformly accessible and available for interlibrary loan for the first time hard copy and microform versions of major series from agricultural experi-ment stations in every state and from the U.S. Department of Agriculture through series cataloging and series analytics in the OCLC database and indexing in the AGRICOLA and AGRIS databases.
University of Kansas Libraries, Lawrence, Kans. Sheryl Williams	102,140	To continue the cataloging of serials and ephemeral materials contained in the Wilcox Collection of Contemporary Political Movements.

**Table 12 / Strengthening Research Library Resources
Program Grants, FY 1986** (cont.)

Institution and Project Director	Grant Award	Project Description
University of Kentucky, Lexington, Ky. William Marshall	153,322	To continue to preserve an important portion of the Kentuckiana holdings of the University of Kentucky and to pro- vide intellectual access to the collection by continuing to place cataloged entries into the OCLC database and by dissem- inating information about the collection through a published guide.
University of Maryland, College Park, Md. Marietta A. Plank	404,776	To conduct a project in cooperation with the University of Delaware, Texas A&M University, and the New York State Library to provide machine-readable full cataloging records for Segment 2 of the microfilm collection *Goldsmiths'–Kress Library of Economic Literature*, which consists of 29,412 titles on 1,669 reels.
University of Minnesota, Minneapolis, Minn. Mary Frances Collins and Eugene Wiemers	64,108	To improve scholarly access to the extensive collection of Scandinavian holdings, consisting of approximately 1,100 serial titles dating from the early nineteenth century onward. Catalog data for 400 monographs will be en- tered into RLIN and typed records will be contributed to OCLC.
University of Missouri–Columbia Libraries, Columbia, Mo. Thomas Shaughnessy	151,572	To provide or improve cataloging of pre- 1800 cataloged titles in the Rare Book Collection and for pre-1800 titles to be transferred from the general stacks. Titles needing preservation will be treated or microfilmed.
University of Pittsburgh, Pittsburgh, Pa. Charles Aston and Ruth Carter	132,000	To complete the cataloging of the John A. Nietz Textbook Collection of pre-1900 American textbooks, one of the three largest in the United States, and to make records available in the OCLC online database. An index to the records will be produced, published, and made available.
University of Wisconsin, Madison, Wisc. D. Kaye Gapen	107,952	To create and add to the national OCLC and RLIN databases machine-readable records of the outstanding collection of 25,000 pieces of musical theater perfor- mance materials known as the Tams- Whitmark Collection; to clean, preserve, and store the physical documents; and to make films available on demand to the scholarly and performing communi- ties.
Washington State University, Pullman, Wash. John Guido	104,668	To enter cataloging data for approxi- mately two-thirds of the manuscripts and archives collections of the Washing- ton State University Libraries into the Western Library Network (WLN) data- base, following implementation of the USMARC format for manuscripts and archives by the WLN staff.

Table 13 / Strengthening Research Library Program Grant Summary, FYs 1978–1986

Fiscal Year	Bibliographic Control	Percent of Funding	Preservation	Percent of Funding	Collection Development	Percent of Funding	Total Funding
1978	$ 2,864,339	57	$ 1,340,554	27	$ 795,103	16	$ 4,999,996
1979	3,978,366	66	1,393,201	23	628,433	11	6,000,000
1980	4,345,765	73	805,383	13	841,120	14	5,992,268
1981	4,249,840	71	1,298,542	22	451,618	7	6,000,000
1982	4,042,549	70	1,521,258	27	196,193	3	5,760,000
1983	4,738,575	79	909,612	15	351,813	6	6,000,000
1984	4,526,772	76	1,044,973	17	428,255	7	6,000,000
1985	4,236,695	70	1,729,997	29	33,308	6	6,000,000
1986	4,429,374	77	1,122,409	20	190,217	3	5,742,000
Total	$37,412,275	71	$11,165,929	21	$3,916,060	8	$52,494,264

National Endowment for the Humanities
Support for Libraries, 1986

110 Pennsylvania Ave. N.W., Washington, DC 20506
207-786-0438

The National Endowment for the Humanities (NEH), an independent federal grant-making agency created by Congress in 1965, supports research, education, and public understanding in the humanities through grants to organizations, institutions, and individuals. According to the legislation that established the Endowment, the term "humanities" includes, but is not limited to, the study of archaeology, ethics, history, the history and criticism of the arts, the theory of the arts, jurisprudence, language (both modern and classical), linguistics, literature, philosophy, comparative religion, and those aspects of the social sciences that have humanities content and employ humanistic methods.

The Endowment's grant-making operations are conducted through five major divisions: (1) The Division of Research Programs provides support for the preparation for publication of important texts in the humanities, for the organization of collections and the preparation of reference materials, for the conduct of collaborative or coordinated research, and for the development of potential research through specific regrant programs. (2) The Division of Fellowships and Seminars, through several programs, provides stipends that enable individual scholars, teachers, and members of nonacademic professions to undertake study and research in the humanities that will enhance their capacity as teachers, scholars, or interpreters of the humanities and that will enable them to make significant contributions to thought and knowledge in the humanities. (3) The Division of Education Programs supports projects and programs through which institutions endeavor to renew and strengthen the impact of teaching in the humanities at all levels. (4) The Division of General Programs endeavors to fulfill the Endowment's mandate to foster public appreciation and understanding of the humanities. The division includes programs that assist institutions and organizations in developing humanities projects for presentation to general audiences, including adults and young adults. The division is composed of Museums and Historical Organizations, Media, Humanities Projects in Libraries, and the Public Humanities Program. Applications must meet published deadlines. (5) Finally, the Division of State Programs makes grants to citizens' committees in each state to provide support for local humanities projects, primarily directed toward general audiences.

In addition to support through each of the five divisions, support is also available to libraries through two offices, the Office of Preservation and the Office of Challenge Grants. The Office of Challenge Grants helps institutions to develop new and increased nonfederal, long-range sources of support in order to improve the quality of their humanities resources and activities and to strengthen their financial stability. The Office of Preservation supports training, technical development, and preservation activities in libraries and other repositories.

In FY 1986 new challenge grant offers of $4.84 million were made to 13 institutions, either wholly or partially for library support. These included two public libraries, nine colleges or universities, and two research libraries or historical organizations. Table 1 shows examples of grants in effect as of December 1986.

Table 1 / Examples of Current NEH Library Grants, December 1986

Recipient	Project Description	Amount
Office of Challenge Grants		
Brown University, Providence, RI	To establish an endowment to cover the costs of library acquisitions in certain subject areas in the humanities and for staff to catalog these holdings	$750,000
College of Idaho, Caldwell, ID	To support an endowment for increased library acquisitions in the humanities; an endowment for faculty development through such activities as research projects, seminars, attendance at conferences, and course development; and an endowed chair in the Department of English	$337,500
Denver Public Library, Denver, CO	To endow the purchase of acquisitions and the preservation of the library's special collections in its Western History Department. The grant will also spearhead a larger campaign to expand ongoing private support for the library	$370,000
Guilford College, Greensboro, NC	To augment an endowment for library acquisitions in the humanities; to provide partial support for library automation; and for renovation and the addition of a new wing for the library	$450,000
Homewood Public Library, Homewood, AL	To support the humanities-related portion of the costs to remodel a building originally designed as a church to serve as the new library facility	$90,000
Division of General Programs		
Tucson Public Library, Tucson, AZ	To support a series of reading and discussion programs using works in the Library of America series as texts to consider themes in works by major American writers	$206,605
American Library Association, Chicago, IL	To support a tour of facsimiles of the New York Public Library's exhibition on the drafting and ratification of the U.S. Constitution. The facsimiles will travel to 30 public libraries in an 18-month period	$270,172
University of California, Berkeley, CA	To support cataloging of 2,298 Japanese maps dating from the mid-seventeenth to the early twentieth century, including numerous woodcut and manuscript maps	$146,733
New York Library New York, NY	To support the accessioning of 20,000 linear feet of manuscripts and archives, thereby establishing basic bibliographic and physical control over the entire manuscript and archive collections of the New York Public Library	$250,000
Goshen College Goshen, IN	To support the cataloging on OCLC of 7,600 titles from a collection that documents the radical Reformation in Europe and the Mennonites in America	$75,000

Categories of Support

The NEH seeks to cooperate with libraries in strengthening the general public's knowledge and use of the humanities through its various programs. A description of these programs follows.

Division of General Programs

The single program within the division that supports libraries directly is Humanities Projects in Libraries, though other programs offer indirect support. The program encourages public, academic, or special libraries to plan and present humanities programs. Cooperative projects between public, academic, or special libraries and between libraries, museums, historical societies, and other cultural institutions are also encouraged. Programs may take place at locations other than the library, but the primary objective of using library resources to enhance the understanding and appreciation of the humanities must be evident in the design of any project.

Among the many possible ways applicants to Humanities Projects in Libraries might fulfill the Endowment's mandate to foster public understanding and appreciation of the humanities are the following: Investigate the history of systems of thought; explore language as a reflection of culture; pose a philosophical debate concerning fundamental human rights; trace the development of the origins of social, political, or religious systems or institutions; and examine central themes such as love, war, family, or work through literature that illustrates such themes. A variety of methods and formats may be employed for the exploration of topics within the disciplines of the humanities. Some formats that have proven useful include reading and discussion groups; lecture series; conferences; film series accompanied by discussion groups and supplementary readings; exhibitions of library material or small exhibitions subordinate to other program formats; and such written materials as anthologies devoted to specific themes, essays illuminating specific topics, annotated bibliographies, or reading lists.

Applicants are urged to consider carefully the most appropriate means of implementing their projects and to discuss them with Endowment staff. Projects should involve the active collaboration of scholars from the appropriate disciplines of the humanities during both the planning and presentation of programs. They should create an opportunity for thoughtful examination of scholarly work or dialogue between the scholarly community and the general public based on the existing collections of humanities resources of the library.

The division also encourages libraries to design out-of-school projects for groups of young people of high school or junior high school age. By involving youth in projects, libraries can help them to acquire and apply new knowledge and skills in the disciplines of the humanities. Projects for this age group are intended to encourage a lifelong interest in the humanities on the part of young people by introducing them to the range of resources and activities in the humanities that are available to them outside of school.

Division of Education Programs

Libraries may receive Division of Education Programs grants directly or be part of a college or university effort to strengthen teaching in the humanities. Direct grants to libraries are usually in support of humanities institutes at which elementary and second-

ary school teachers or college and university faculty use the library's resources as part of a program of study directed by recognized scholars. The Folger Shakespeare Library and the Newberry Library are recent grantees. The division also encourages applications for projects to foster greater cooperation between libraries and humanities departments on individual college and university campuses.

Division of Fellowships and Seminars

The division of Fellowships and Seminars' fellowship programs provide support for persons who wish to work individually; the division's seminar programs enable individuals to pursue their work and to exchange ideas in the collegial atmosphere of a community of scholars.

NEH fellowships provide opportunities for individuals to pursue independent study and research that will enhance their capacity as teachers, scholars, or interpreters of the humanities and that will enable them to make significant contributions to thought and knowledge in the humanities. These 6- to 12-month fellowships free people from the day-to-day responsibilities of teaching and other work for extended periods of uninterrupted investigation, reflection, and often writing. The programs are designed to support a range of people from those who have made significant contributions to the humanities to those at the beginning of their careers. Projects too may cover a range of activities from general study to specialized research.

Fellowships for University Teachers are for faculty members of departments and programs in universities that grant the Ph.D. and faculty members of postgraduate professional schools. The annual application deadline is June 1.

Fellowships for College Teachers and Independent Scholars are for faculty members of two-year, four-year, and five-year colleges, faculty members of departments and programs in universities that do not grant the Ph.D., individuals affiliated with institutions other than colleges and universities, and scholars and writers working independently. The annual application deadline is June 1.

Summer Stipends provide support for faculty members in universities and two-year, four-year, and five-year colleges and for others working in the humanities to pursue two consecutive months of full-time study or research. Applicants may propose projects that can be completed during the stipend period or that are part of a long-range endeavor. Each college and university in the United States may nominate three members of its faculty for the summer stipend competition. Nonfaculty college and university staff members are eligible for this program and may apply without nomination, provided that they have no teaching duties during the year of their application. The annual application deadline is October 1.

Summer Seminars for College Teachers provide opportunities to teachers in two-year, four-year, and five-year colleges and universities and to others who are qualified to do the work of the seminar and make a contribution to it. Participants, working under the direction of distinguished scholars and teachers at institutions with libraries suitable for advanced study, pursue research in their own fields or in fields related to their interests. The seminars last eight weeks and are broadly distributed throughout the country. Seminars have been held at independent research libraries such as the Newberry and Huntington. The annual application deadline is March 1.

Summer Seminars for Secondary School Teachers provide opportunities for teachers of grades 7 through 12 to work in their areas of interest with distinguished teachers

and committed scholars studying seminal works in the humanities systematically and thoroughly. The seminars last for four, five, or six weeks, depending on the individual seminar, and are held at institutions broadly distributed throughout the country. The annual application deadline is March 1.

Graduate Study Fellowships for Faculty at Historically Black Colleges and Universities are offered by the Endowment in response to President Reagan's initiative (Executive Order 12320) regarding historically black colleges and universities. These fellowships are intended to strengthen the teaching of the humanities at these colleges and universities by providing one year of support for teachers to work toward the completion of a doctoral degree in one of the disciplines of the humanities. The annual application deadline is March 15.

The *Travel to Collections Program* offers small grants to scholars who must travel to use research collections of libraries, archives, museums, and other repositories. Awards are made to help defray the costs of transportation, subsistence and lodging, reproduction and photoduplication, and associated research. Annual application deadlines are January 15 and July 15.

Younger Scholars Awards provide for secondary school and undergraduate students to carry out projects of research and writing in the humanities during the summer. Recipients work under the close supervision of a humanities scholar, and no academic credit may be taken for this work. The annual application deadline is November 1.

The Division of Research Programs

The Texts Program provides support for the preparation for publication of works that promise to make major contributions to the study of the humanities. The Editions category supports various stages of the preparation of authoritative and annotated editions of sources of significant value to humanities scholars and general readers. The Translations category supports the individual or collaborative efforts to translate into English works that provide insight into the history, literature, philosophy, and artistic achievements of other cultures and that make available the thought and learning of their civilizations. Grants in the Publication Subvention category assist the publication and dissemination of distinguished scholarly works in all fields of the humanities..

The Reference Materials Program provides support for projects that promise to facilitate research in the humanities by organizing essential resources for scholarship and by preparing finding aids and other reference materials that can improve scholarly access to information and collections. Grants in the Tools category support the creation of dictionaries, historical and linguistic atlases, encyclopedias, concordances, *catalogues raisonnés*, linguistic grammars, descriptive catalogs, databases, and other materials that serve to codify information essential to research in the humanities. In the Access category, the Endowment supports projects that promise to increase the availability of important research collections and other significant source material in all fields of the humanities through such activities as archival arrangement and description projects; bibliographies; records surveys; cataloging projects involving print, graphic, film, sound, and artifact collections; indices; foreign microfilming; and other guides to humanities documentation.

The Interpretive Research Program supports coordinated or collaborative projects of important, original research in all fields of the humanities. The Projects category supports research that will advance knowledge or deepen critical understanding of an

important topic in the humanities. In the Humanities, Science and Technology category, the Endowment supports research that uses the disciplines of the humanities to interpret, analyze, or evaluate science and technology and their meaning for and place in human affairs.

The Regrants Program awards funds to organizations that will then regrant those funds according to an effective and coherent plan improving the state of research in a particular area or topic in the humanities. The Conferences category supports conferences designed to advance the state of research in a field or topics of major importance in the humanities. Through grants in the Centers for Advanced Study category, the Endowment supports interrelated research efforts in well-defined subject areas at independent centers for advanced study, American research centers overseas, independent research libraries, and research museums. Through the Regrants for International Research category, the Endowment awards funds to national organizations and learned societies to enable American scholars to pursue research abroad, to attend or participate in international conferences, and to engage in collaborative work with foreign colleagues. Through Regrants in Selected Areas, the Endowment supports three kinds of regrants offered by the American Council of Learned Societies: ACLS fellowships, Grants-in-Aid, and Research Fellowships for Recent Recipients of the Ph.D.

Office of Challenge Grants

Libraries are eligible for support within the Endowment's Challenge Grants program, now (1986) in the tenth year of funding. By inviting libraries to appeal to a broader funding public, challenge grants assist them to increase long-term financial stability and capital support and thereby improve the quality of humanities activities and collections. To receive each federal dollar, a challenge grant recipient must raise $3 from new or increased nonfederal funding sources. Both federal and nonfederal funds may apply to a variety of expenditures supporting the humanities: acquisitions, conservation, renovation and construction, program development, equipment, and other managerial or program expenses related to the humanities.

Office of Preservation

The Office of Preservation addresses the problem of the physical deterioration of humanities resources, especially brittle books. Awards support cooperative microfilming, training in preservation administration, and the development of preservation techniques. The office also administers the U.S. Newspaper Program, which enjoys the cooperation of the Library of Congress. This program, already active in 26 states and territories, will establish a bibliographic database of some 300,000 newspaper titles and undertake microfilming where necessary to preserve extant print materials.

Division of State Programs

The Endowment annually makes grants to state humanities councils in the 50 states, the District of Columbia, Puerto Rico, and the U.S. Virgin Islands. The state councils, in turn, award regrants to institutions and organizations within each state according to guidelines and application deadlines determined by each council. Most grants are for projects that promote public understanding and appreciation of the humanities. Guide-

lines and application deadlines may be obtained by contacting the appropriate state council directly.

State Humanities Councils

Committee for the Humanities in Alabama
Walter Cox, Exec. Dir.
Box A-40, Birmingham-Southern College, Birmingham, AL 35254. 205-324-1314

Alaska Humanities Forum
Gary Holthaus, Exec. Dir.
943 W. Sixth Ave., Rm. 120, Anchorage, AK 99501. 907-272-5341

Arizona Humanities Council
Lorraine W. Frank, Exec. Dir.
918 N. Second St., Phoenix, AZ 85004. 602-257-0335

Arkansas Endowment for the Humanities
Jane Browning, Exec. Dir.
Remmel Bldg., Suite 102, 1010 W. Third St., Little Rock, AR 72201. 501-372-2672

California Council for the Humanities
James Quay, Exec. Dir.
312 Sutter St., Suite 601, San Francisco, CA 94108. 415-391-1474

Colorado Endowment for the Humanities
James Pierce, Exec. Dir.
1836 Blake St. #100, Denver, CO 80202. 303-292-4458

Connecticut Humanities Council
Bruce Fraser, Exec. Dir.
41 Lawn Ave., Wesleyan Sta., Middletown, CT 06457. 203-347-6888

Delaware Humanities Forum
Henry Hirschbiel, Exec. Dir.
2600 Pennsylvania Ave., Wilmington, DE 19806. 302-573-4410

D.C. Community Humanities Council
Francine Carey, Exec. Dir.
1341 G St. N.W., Suite 620, Washington, DC 20005. 202-347-1732

Florida Endowment for the Humanities
Ann Henderson, Exec. Dir.
Box 16989, Tampa, FL 33687-6989. 813-974-4094

Georgia Endowment for the Humanities
Ronald E. Benson, Exec. Dir.
1589 Clifton Rd. N.E., Emory University, Atlanta, GA 30322. 404-329-7500

Hawaii Committee for the Humanities
Annette M. Lew, Exec. Dir.
First Hawaiian Bank Bldg., 3599 Waialae Ave., Rm. 23, Honolulu, HI 96816. 808-732-5402

Association for the Humanities in Idaho
Thomas H. McClanahan, Exec. Dir.
Len B. Jordan Bldg., Rm. 300, 650 W. State St., Boise, ID 83720. 208-345-5346

Illinois Humanities Council
Robert J. Klaus, Exec. Dir.
618 S. Michigan Ave., Chicago, IL 60605. 312-939-5212

Indiana Committee for the Humanities
Kenneth L. Gladish, Exec. Dir.
1500 N. Delaware St., Indianapolis, IN 46202. 317-638-1500

Iowa Humanities Board
Donald Drake, Exec. Dir.
Oakdale Campus, University of Iowa, Iowa City, IA 52242. 319-353-6754

Kansas Committee for the Humanities
Marion Cott, Exec. Dir.
112 W. Sixth St., Suite 210, Topeka, KS 66603. 913-357-0359

Kentucky Humanities Council, Inc.
Ramona Lumpkin, Exec. Dir.
417 Clifton Ave., University of Kentucky, Lexington, KY 40506-0414. 606-257-5932

Louisiana Committee for the Humanities
Michael Sartisky, Exec. Dir.
1001 Howard Ave., Suite 4407, New Orleans, LA 70113. 504-523-4352

Maine Humanities Council
Dorothy Schwartz, Exec. Dir.
Box 7202, Portland, ME 04112. 207-773-5051

Maryland Humanities Council
Naomi F. Collins, Exec. Dir.
516 N. Charles St., #201, Baltimore, MD 21201. 301-837-1938

Massachusetts Foundation for the Humanities and Public Policy
David Tebaldi, Exec. Dir.
One Woodbridge St., South Hadley, MA 01075. 413-536-1385

Michigan Council for the Humanities
Ronald Means, Exec. Dir.
Nisbet Bldg., Suite 30, 1407 S. Harrison Rd., East Lansing, MI 48824. 517-355-0160

Minnesota Humanities Commission
Cheryl Dickson, Exec. Dir.
580 Park Square Ct., Sixth and Sibley Sts., St. Paul, MN 55101. 612-224-5739

Mississippi Committee for the Humanities
Cora Norman, Exec. Dir.
3825 Ridgewood Rd., Rm. 111, Jackson, MS 39211. 601-982-6752

Missouri Committee for the Humanities
Jackie Houck, Acting Exec. Dir.
Loberg Bldg., Suite 204, 11425 Dorsett Rd., Maryland Heights, MO 63043. 314-739-7368

Montana Committee for the Humanities
Margaret Kingsland, Exec. Dir.
Box 8036, Hellgate Sta., Missoula, MT 59807. 406-243-6022

Nebraska Committee for the Humanities
Sarah Rosenberg, Exec. Dir.
Lincoln Center Bldg., Suite 422, 215 Centennial Mall S., Lincoln, NE 68508. 402-474-2131

Nevada Humanities Committee
Judith Winzeler, Exec. Dir.
Box 8029, Reno, NV 89507. 702-784-6587

New Hampshire Council for the Humanities
Charles G. Bickford, Exec. Dir.
15 S. Fruit St., Concord, NH 03301. 603-224-4071

New Jersey Committee for the Humanities
Miriam L. Murphy, Exec. Dir.
73 Easton Ave., New Brunswick, NJ 08901. 201-932-7726

New Mexico Humanities Council
D. Nathan Sumner, Exec. Dir.
Onate Hall, Rm. 209, University of New Mexico, Albuquerque, NM 87131. 505-277-3705

New York Council for the Humanities
Jay Kaplan, Exec. Dir.
198 Broadway, 10th fl., New York, NY 10038. 212-233-1131

North Carolina Humanities Committee
Brent D. Glass, Exec. Dir.
112 Foust Bldg., UNC-Greensboro, Greensboro, NC 27412. 919-334-5325

North Dakota Humanities Council
Everett Albers, Exec. Dir.
Box 2191, Bismarck, ND 58502. 701-663-1948

Ohio Humanities Council
Charles C. Cole, Jr., Exec. Dir.
760 Pleasant Ridge Ave., Columbus, OH 43209. 614-231-6879

Oklahoma Foundation for the Humanities
Anita May, Exec. Dir.
Executive Terrace Bldg., 2809 Northwest Expressway, Suite 500, Oklahoma City, OK 73112. 405-840-1721

Oregon Committee for the Humanities
Richard Lewis, Exec. Dir.
418 S.W. Washington, Rm. 410, Portland, OR 97204. 503-241-0543

Pennsylvania Humanities Council
Craig Eisendrath, Exec. Dir.
401 N. Broad St., Philadelphia, PA
19108. 215-925-1005

**Fundacion Puertorriquena de las
Humanidades**
Arturo Morales Carrion, Exec. Dir.
Box S-4307, Old San Juan, PR 00904.
809-721-2087

**Rhode Island Committee for the
Humanities**
Thomas H. Roberts, Exec. Dir.
463 Broadway, Providence, RI 02909. 401-
273-2250

**South Carolina Committee for the
Humanities**
Leland Cox, Exec. Dir.
Box 6925, Columbia, SC 29260. 803-738-
1850

**South Dakota Committee on the
Humanities**
John Whalen, Exec. Dir.
Box 7050, University Sta., Brookings, SD
57007. 605-688-6113

Tennessee Committee for the Humanities
Robert Cheatham, Exec. Dir.
1001 18 Ave. S., Nashville, TN 37212.
615-320-7001

Texas Committee for the Humanities
James Veninga, Exec. Dir.
1604 Nueces, Austin, TX 78701. 512-473-
8585

Utah Endowment for the Humanities
Delmont Oswald, Exec. Dir.
10 W. Broadway, Broadway Bldg., Suite

900, Salt Lake City, UT 84101. 801-531-
7868

**Vermont Council on the Humanities and
Public Issues**
Victor R. Swenson, Exec. Dir.
Grant House, Box 58, Hyde Park, VT
05655. 802-888-3183

Virgin Islands Humanities Council
David Barzelay, Exec. Dir.
Market Sq., Conrad Bldg., No. 6 Torvet
Straede/4th fl., Suite 6, Box 1829, St.
Thomas, VI 00801. 809-774-4044

**Virginia Foundation for the Humanities
and Public Policy**
Robert C. Vaughan, Exec. Dir.
1939 Ivy Rd., Charlottesville, VA 22903.
804-924-3296

**Washington Commission for the
Humanities**
Hidde Van Duym, Exec. Dir.
Olympia, WA 98505. 206-866-6510

Humanities Foundation of West Virginia
Charles Daugherty, Exec. Dir.
Box 204, Institute, WV 25112. 304-768-
8869

Wisconsin Humanities Committee
Patricia Anderson, Exec. Dir.
716 Langdon St., Madison, WI 53706.
608-262-0706

Wyoming Council for the Humanities
Dennis Frobish, Exec. Dir.
Box 3972, University Sta., Laramie, WY
82071-3972. 307-766-6496

National Science Foundation Support for Research in Information Science and Technology, 1986

1800 G St. N.W., Washington, DC 20550
202-357-9572

Yi-Tzuu Chien, Acting Director

Division of Information, Robotics and Intelligent Systems

The National Science Foundation (NSF) is an independent agency of the federal government, established by Congress in 1950 to maintain the health and promote the progress of science in the United States. For many years, NSF has supported research in the vital areas of information science and technology through a division in the Directorate for Biological and Behavioral Sciences. In October 1986, recognizing the increasing need to advance research in information- and computer-related fields, NSF created a new Directorate for Computer and Information Science and Engineering (CISE), responsible for the coordination of all computer-related research programs in the foundation. The Division of Information, Robotics and Intelligent Systems (IRIS), one of the five divisions in CISE, has the broad responsibility of supporting research central to the progress of information science and technology, with an increasing emphasis toward the emerging areas of automation and machine intelligence.

Information, in the context of modern technologies, takes many forms: language, speech, images, and various types of signals or sensory data, including text, numbers, and symbols. The impact of information and the technologies developed to process information is most dramatically seen when vast amounts of data from different sources must be efficiently organized, accessed, and possibly combined to enhance the ability to work and live in a knowledge-intensive society. Research supported by the IRIS Division primarily focuses on how to provide the best computational structures and physical devices to facilitate the use of these information forms. The new division is currently organized to have four programs, which reflect the most critical elements of the field at the present time.

The Program in Knowledge and Database Systems explores the propagation of symbolic (information-bearing) structures and the dynamics of their propagation and utilization. It supports research to improve understanding of issues related to data organization, knowledge and information retrieval, methods of inference, and problem solving and decision making under uncertainty. Research topics include the use of natural language for information processing, knowledge acquisition and representation, and database management.

The Interactive Systems Program supports research fundamental to the design of systems that can assist or enable users to perform information-based work. It emphasizes problems of user-system interaction, including the exploration of novel input and output modalities and experimental methods applicable to these problems. Important thrusts are the development of logical structure of the user-system dialogue; cognitive and machine processes underlying the dialogue; methods of systematic dialogue and interface design; and the methodological problem of arriving at valid empirical generalizations about user-system interaction.

The Information Impact Program deals with the social and economic consequences of information technologies, emphasizing the changing structure of information indus-

tries and the projection of future organizational designs. Key thrusts include the development of methods and databases to understand and analyze social and economic processes affected by the computing and communications technologies, as well as issues relating to the markets for information and the health of information industries. The experimental application of new computing capabilities to improve the elaboration and testing of social and economic theory is also an important element of this program.

A new program in this division is Robotics and Machine Intelligence. It focuses on scientific and engineering research fundamental to the design of systems capable of implementing some of the characteristics of human intelligence, especially those related to information processing. An important goal of this program is to advance the knowledge required for the development of future automated systems to be used in a variety of environments, including factory, laboratory, office, library, and home. Key research thrusts include pattern recognition, image processing, computer vision, speech understanding, automated reasoning and problem-solving techniques, as well as machine planning of complex tasks that involve temporal and spatial relationships typically encountered in robotic or other autonomous systems.

The overall characteristic of this division is unique in that the research it supports is multidisciplinary and crosses departmental boundaries. Many projects deal with research that requires expertise in psychology, economics, mathematics, computer and information sciences, as well as several fields of engineering. The division also participates in a number of initiatives designed to improve the knowledge base and human resources for teaching and learning science and engineering. Computers, multiprocessors, and information networks are critical instruments for experimental information science and technology research. Thus the division seeks resources to meet such needs for those researchers whose work explores these new technologies.

Library-Related Research

Although the IRIS Division has expanded its scope of research to include a broad range of information science and technology, many of the research projects sponsored by the division have and will continue to have a significant impact on modern library science and related activities. A list of the FY 1986 research projects with relevance to library science follows.

Douglas P. Metzler, University of Pittsburgh, "An Expert System Approach to Syntactic Parsing and Information Retrieval," $115,220.

Robert N. Oddy, Syracuse University, "Representations for Anomalous States of Knowledge in Information Retrieval," $86,969.

William Shaw, University of North Carolina, "An Evaluation and Comparison of Term and Citation Indexing," $85,583.

Pranas Zunde, Georgia Institute of Technology, "A Study of Word Association Aids in Information Retrieval," $97,727.

Richard B. Hull, University of Southern California, "Investigation of Practical and Theoretical Aspects of Semantic Database Models," $69,815.

Jeffrey D. Ullman, Stanford University, "Implementation of Logical Query Languages for Databases," $121,222.

John DuBois, University of California, Los Angeles, "Information Transfer Constraints and Strategies in Natural Language Communication," $45,489.

Ray Jackendoff and Jane Grimshaw, Brandeis University, "Syntactic and Semantic Information in a Natural Language Lexicon," $98,507.

Wendy G. Lehnert, University of Massachusetts, Amherst, "Presidential Young Investigator Award: Natural Language Computing Systems," $10,000.

Kathleen R. McKeown, Columbia University, "Presidential Young Investigator Award: Natural Language Interfaces," $37,500.

Donald E. Nute, University of Georgia, "Discourse Representation for Natural Language Processing," $80,492.

Naomi Sager, New York University, "Language as a Database Structure," $198,800.

Sharon C. Salveter, Boston University, "Transportable Natural Language Database Update," $59,178.

David S. Touretzky, Carnegie-Mellon University, "Distributed Representations for Symbolic Data Structures," $63,584.

Robert C. Berwick, Massachusetts Institute of Technology, "Computational Properties of Natural Languages (Computer Research)," $25,000.

Ralph Grishman (in collaboration with Lynette Hirschman of Burroughs Corporation), New York University, "Industry/University Cooperative Research: Acquisition and Use of Semantic Information for Natural Language Processing (Computer Research)," $78,400.

Alan W. Biermann, Duke University, "Dialog Processing for Voice Interactive Problem Solving," $27,676.

Robert Rodman, North Carolina State University, "Dialogue Processing for Voice Interactive Problem Solving," $65,276.

Tefko Saracevic, Case-Western Reserve University, "Cognitive Aspects of Information Seeking and Retrieving," $90,561.

Gregory A. Holton, JBF Associates, Inc., "Development of an Intelligent Database Model," $40,000.

Richard S. Marcus, Massachusetts Institute of Technology, "Models for Supporting and Analyzing Computer-Mediated Retrieval," $121,040.

Zelig Harris, New York University, "Informational Representation in Survey Structures," $159,972.

Part 3
Library/Information Science Education, Placement, and Salaries

Library Education: A Centenary

Michael Buckland

Assistant Vice President for Library Plans and Policies, University of California

In 1887, Melvil Dewey founded the first library school in the United States at Columbia University. This important centenary has received suitable attention in recent library literature, giving cause to reflect on the changes in library services through the centuries.[1]

The pattern is clearly uneven: Online catalogs are new and different, yet the collection development policies outlined by Gabriel Naudé in 1627, three and a half centuries ago, are surprisingly contemporary. He advocated the inclusion of works by new, dissident writers, such as Copernicus, Galileo, and even those "thirty or forty writers of reputation [who] have declared themselves against Aristotle."[2] The professional literature of a century ago is still remarkably contemporary. The *Library Journal* of 1886 contains discussions of copyright, public access to government documents, education for librarianship, preservation and conservation, reduction of catalog costs through cooperative cataloging arrangements, improved subject access, lack of comparable pay for women, and a plea for more bibliographical instruction to balance the (then) current emphasis on library technology. This mixture of change and continuity suggests that different aspects of librarianship vary with respect to change.

Library Values

Library values include social values as they influence library policy and professional issues: the mission of library service, the principles of selection, and the librarian's attitude toward readers. These values underlie day-to-day priorities and decisions, especially the use of labor, the largest budget item.

Western library values have changed little in a century: They derive from stable cultural norms and, one hopes, will change little in the future. One could reasonably recommend Naudé's principles of book selection (but not his techniques: He recommended searching bookshops for printed sheets not yet folded and bound). Yet library values are not fixed and universal; what would be acceptable in San Francisco today may not be tolerable in Beijing or Tehran. Library provision acceptable now in Massachusetts might not have been acceptable in colonial times, or vice versa. Values can change but because of *cultural* forces rather than *time*.

Library Technology

Technology available for use in library services is concerned with the handling of physical things: paper, cardboard, microfilms, magnetic, optical, or other recording media. Technology is especially important for library service because libraries are concerned

with *recorded* knowledge. Librarians and library users are concerned with ideas, assertions, and evidence represented in text, images, and sound. However, they can only do so through text-bearing, image-bearing, and sound-bearing objects, such as books made of paper, images on cathode-ray tubes, sounds recorded on magnetic tape, and so on. Carbon paper, microfilm, and typewriters were available a century ago. Telephones, copying machines, and computers have been added to the options available. Information technology continues to develop additional media for bearing text and more powerful tools for handling text, a clear line of progress with time.

Library Science

A third category, distinguishable from library values and library technology, is "library science," in the sense of librarianship:

1 Information retrieval theory, the description and representation of recorded knowledge: indexing, cataloging, classification
2 Information-gathering behavior: user studies, bibliometrics, social epistemology, and knowledge utilization
3 Historical studies of books and of communication
4 Understanding of the nature of libraries and related information services.[3]

These aspects of "library science" have made some progress in the past century, but not much. The central issues are rooted in truly obscure aspects of human behavior, so progress will continue to be slow and difficult. Scholarly explanation may lag behind the intuition of those with the most practical experience. Much of the progress in the past century in these areas has been the refinement of earlier progress (e.g., cataloging principles) or concerned with relatively superficial symptoms of deeper phenomena (e.g., bibliometrics and citation studies).

In recent years librarianship has broadened in scope and extent. The scope is clearly extensive: libraries of all kinds, archives, databases, records management, and documentation in litigation, engineering, and bureaucracies. Whether or not all are considered part of "librarianship," they are all examples of retrieval-based information services with shared characteristics. At the least, library services can sensibly be viewed as part of a larger family of related activities, and library schools can be expected to become, by expansion, merger, or coalition, colleges of broader scope, with the master of library science degree as one important specialty within a range of programs.

The gradual maturing of library schools as academic departments in an academic environment also indicates a broader view of librarianship.[4] One conceptual, academic perspective would be to regard "information science" as having to do with representations of knowledge both abstractly ("texts") and concretely ("text-bearing objects"). Within it, librarianship has specialized in the handling (description, arrangement, access, and use) of text-bearing objects. For this, information retrieval is central, but needs to be studied in relation to the texts, to the text-bearing objects, to knowledge, and, indeed, to people, their beliefs, and their need for knowledge. This broader view reinforces considerations of economies of scope and of scale in the schools. The present pattern of a "library school" primarily concerned with awarding a "library degree" can be seen as a case of arrested development.

The Future

So long as the mission of libraries is to bring information to people, the curriculum of library education will remain fairly stable, containing the role of information in society and of library services; the needs, information-gathering behavior, and institutional contexts of groups to be served; theory and practice of information retrieval (cataloging, bibliography, etc.); and the managerial, political, and technological means most likely to be useful in developing and providing good library service. Areas that deal with library values will change the least and those dealing with library technology will change the most.

Meanwhile, improved library technology provides new opportunities to grapple with some old problems. Catalogs, bibliographies, and texts, all online, are already beginning to overcome some of the constraints imposed by the technology of cardboard and paper. One such barrier is the historic, but unhelpful, separation of catalogs from bibliographies[5]; another is the physical separation of the catalog record from the text it represents; a third is the need for the reader to travel to the library to read. New information technology is beginning to remove these three familiar impediments to good service.

The trend is to prove library services not only in libraries but wherever people happen to be. Yet old nontechnological problems remain: of knowing what to look for, of comprehending it, of deciding whether to believe it, and of ensuring that only those who should have access to information do have access to it. The liberating power of the new information technology can be expected to induce renewed attention to traditional, nontechnological concerns — so long as librarianship remains a service profession concerned with ideas as well as with records. Education for librarianship in the next century will depend on what librarians make of library services in the nearer future.

References

1. *Library Trends* 34, no. 3 (Winter 1986), which is devoted entirely to historical topics in library education; *Library Trends* 34, no. 4 (Spring 1986), which contains the papers, mainly on recent and current trends in library education, presented at the Library Education Centennial Symposium held at Columbia University on June 27-28, 1986, as well as an historical overview by Ed Holley, which will appear in the *ALA Yearbook of Library and Information Services, 1987*. Other material appears in the *Journal of Education for Library and Information Science* 26, nos. 3 and 4 (Winter and Spring 1986) and in *Special Libraries* 77, no. 4 (Fall 1986).
2. Gabriel Naudé. *Advice on Establishing a Library* (Berkeley: University of California Press, 1950), p. 24. Originally published as *Avis pour dresser une bibliothèque*, 1627.
3. This approach follows that of Patrick Wilson, "Bibliographical R&D," in *The Study of Information: Interdisciplinary Messages*, ed. by Fritz Machlup and Una Mansfield (New York: Wiley, 1983), pp. 389-397.
4. Michael K. Buckland, "The School, Its Faculty and Students," in *Changing Technology and Education for Librarianship and Information Science*, ed. by Basil Stuart-Stubbs (Greenwich, Conn.: JAI Press, 1985), pp. 117-127.
5. Raynard C. Swank, "Subject Catalogs, Classifications, or Bibliographies? A Review of Critical Discussions, 1876-1942," *Library Quarterly* 14 (October 1944): 1316-1332.

Accreditation: A Way Ahead

Committee on Accreditation, American Library Association

50 E. Huron St., Chicago, IL 60611

In 1984, Robert M. Hayes, dean, Graduate School of Library and Information Science, University of California, Los Angeles, developed a proposal to consider the involvement of associations other than the American Library Association in the accreditation of programs in library and information science education. The American Library Association and a number of other societies were involved in the project, which was funded by the U.S. Department of Education, over a two-year period. The ALA Committee on Accreditation received the final report of the project at the ALA annual conference in June 1986, and the report was presented to the ALA Executive Board at that time. The Committee on Accreditation is currently considering the implications of the following summary of the report.

Introduction

The Purpose of the Project

The stated purpose of this project was "To explore procedures and guidelines for participation of a variety of associations in the accreditation of programs of library and information science education." The project was undertaken by the American Library Association Committee on Accreditation ALA/COA on behalf of a variety of professional and educational groups concerned with the quality of educational programs leading to professional degrees in the field of library and information science. As the body formally recognized by the Council on Postsecondary Accreditation, the ALA has current responsibility for review and accreditation of such programs. However, there is need that the full range of concerns in the field, as represented by the several involved societies, be properly and adequately considered in the accreditation process. To date, except for the Canadian Library Association, for which there is an agreement that ALA will serve as its agent for accreditation, there is no formal participation of other interested societies. (Of course, there is informal participation, since the membership of ALA/COA as well as of site visit teams typically includes persons who have membership or affiliation with many interested societies.)

In order to involve other societies in the accreditation process for which ALA has current responsibility, at least two and possibly three things must be accomplished:

1 Procedures and interorganizational arrangements must be effected that will provide the basis for participation of multiple societies. These must provide means to deal with financial responsibilities, administration, and policy determination.

Note: This project was prepared for the U.S. Department of Education, Office of Educational Research and Improvement, Library Programs, with federal funds from the U.S. Department of Education under contract number 300-84-0134. The content of this report does not necessarily reflect the views or policies of the U.S. Department of Education nor does mention of trade names, commercial products, or organizations imply endorsement by the U.S. government.

2 Guidelines must be established by which the specific interests and concerns of each participating interested society will be recognized in the accreditation process.

3 The 1972 *Standards for Accreditation*, which provide the current basis for evaluation of programs, may need to be revised to reflect the interests of the participating interested societies, beyond the extent guidelines may be able to satisfy.

The purpose of the project presented in this report was to develop specific recommendations with respect to these two or three needs, as a joint effort of the ALA and a wide range of other interested societies.

The Organization of the Report

The report on the project consists of eight chapters and four appendices. The first chapter is this executive summary, which is intended to serve not only as an introduction to the report but as a freestanding document in itself, suitable for communication of the results to a large audience. The second chapter is a background paper, describing the current accreditation process and the role of the ALA Committee on Accreditation. Chapters 3 and 4 are concerned with procedural issues related to organization and financing of the accreditation process in the context of the involvement of multiple professional societies. Chapters 5 through 8 are concerned with substantive issues involved in the evaluation of educational programs in the field, with emphasis on the interests of participating societies. The appendices provide details of the current accreditation standards, currently accredited programs, a bibliography of relevant documents, and details about the participating societies and the persons who donated their time and energies to this project.

The Major Recommendations

Based on the reports of the several working groups, the Steering Committee has one major recommendation, the first, and a number of subsidiary ones that in large measure merely amplify the major one:

Recommendation 1. The American Library Association should take immediate initiative to invite other interested professional societies to join it in the formation of an Inter-Association Advisory Committee on Accreditation.

Recommendation 2. The American Library Association should commit sufficient funds, estimated at $25,000, as an augmentation of the budget of the Committee on Accreditation, to cover the first year of operational expenses for the recommended Inter-Association Advisory Committee on Accreditation, with expectation that in subsequent years those costs would be shared equitably by the participating societies.

Recommendation 3. The Inter-Association Advisory Committee on Accreditation should be charged with the following responsibilities:

- To review the final report on this project, to evaluate the several recommendations embodied in the reports of the working groups incorporated in it, and to select those which should be implemented.
- To identify the continuing costs involved in the implementation of the selected

recommendations, including the costs of the Inter-Association Advisory Committee itself.

- To identify the appropriate formula for sharing of the costs of the Inter-Association Advisory Committee among the participating societies in subsequent years.
- To identify potential sources for funding one-time costs involved in implementing other selected recommendations and to work with the Committee on Accreditation in developing and submitting proposals to those agencies.
- To cooperate with the Committee on Accreditation in the implementation of selected recommendations and advise the participating societies on the progress in implementation.
- To identify the appropriate formula for sharing of the continuing costs of accreditation among the participating societies.

Recommendation 4. It is recommended that, for the foreseeable future, accreditation should be focused on the first professional degree at the master's level.

Recommendation 5. It is recommended that the Inter-Association Advisory Committee on Accreditation should work closely with each of the participating professional societies in the development of policy statements and appropriate documents that identify the educational requirements, for both general and society-specific objectives, in forms that will assist the process of evaluation of programs for accreditation.

Recommendation 6. It is recommended that the 1972 *Standards for Accreditation* and associated or related guidelines continue to serve as the basis for accreditation, but that the Inter-Association Advisory Committee on Accreditation should establish, in cooperation with the Committee on Accreditation, a review process aimed at identifying the needs for additional guidelines and perhaps eventual replacement of the 1972 Standards.

History of the Project and Its Origins

The general history of accreditation in the field of librarianship has been well documented in the literature, but Chapter 2 of this report provides a brief review, together with a discussion of the current policies and procedures of the Committee on Accreditation of the American Library Association. These have worked well for many decades, and for the past 10 to 15 years they have been guided by the 1972 *Standards for Accreditation*.

But within the past few years, a number of actions have been taken by several interested societies, by the U.S. Department of Education and other governmental agencies, and by various schools of library and information science that provide evidence of the need for a critical examination of the process of accreditation. Most recently, there have been five specific activities that are of immediate relevance:

- The Special Libraries Association and the American Society for Information Science have each proposed development of standards for evaluation of education in these fields.
- The report, published in the *Journal of Medical Education*, concerning the academic health science library as potential manager of health science information,

identified educational needs that would represent major extensions of the requirements for professional practice in medical librarianship.

- The several open meetings held by ALA/COA each year have revealed increasing concern for improved guidelines and procedures for accreditation.
- The U.S. Department of Education contracted for a study, which was conducted by King Research, Inc., of the future directions for library education.
- The Association for Library and Information Science Education held an invitational conference, under sponsorship of the H. W. Wilson Foundation, Inc., to consider and develop a new program of accreditation for library and information science education.

The concerns of the several professional societies with evaluation of educational programs are, of course, long-standing. The Medical Library Association and the American Association of Law Libraries, for example, have instituted various forms of certification. Several of the societies have established "educational committees" to consider their specific requirements. And the ALA Committee on Accreditation has continually strived to develop better criteria for evaluation, with specific concern about meeting the needs of the full range of professional requirements. Indeed, the 1972 *Standards for Accreditation* make explicit reference to "the major documents and policy statements of relevant professional organizations" as the basis for evaluation of the goals of programs being evaluated.

The King Research study of future directions for library education was explicitly concerned with the means for accommodating specialization within the curricula of programs for library and information science education. Of special concern were issues related to new kinds of specialties and new institutional contexts. It reflected the general concern of the U.S. Department of Education with these issues, and provided a frame of reference for them to consider funding of this project.

As the immediate predecessor of this project, the conference convened by the Association for Library and Information Science Education (ALISE) has particular significance. First, it demonstrated the general importance with which the issues in accreditation are viewed by the several societies. Second, it resulted in a hearty, unanimous endorsement of the concept of cooperation in accreditation among the several professional societies involved. Third, it explored several potential models which could be considered for such intersociety cooperation:

- An umbrella organization in which ALA would continue to assume the major responsibility for accreditation, with other societies participating in the process.
- A separate organization to assume responsibility for the entire process of accreditation, acting on behalf of the societies represented by it.
- A federation of library and information science societies, which, as equal partners, would plan, participate, support, and join together in evaluating the accreditation of programs.

The societies that participated in that ALISE meeting concluded that the goals should be that of federation, with recognition that it will take time, money, effort, and commitment to get there, and with recognition that intermediate stages will be required to do so.

The ALISE meeting served not only as the starting point for the project presented in this report, but indeed it provided the forum within which, at its conclusion, it was announced that the continuation project would be undertaken, with funding by the U.S. Department of Education. The contract was formally signed; the project was initiated; and the societies represented at the ALISE meeting were asked to continue their participation.

Organization of the Project

The Participating Societies

The following interested societies were formally invited to participate in the project: American Association of Law Libraries, American Library Association, American Society for Information Science, Association for Library and Information Science Education, Association of Research Libraries, Canadian Library Association, Medical Library Association, and Special Libraries Association. Each society indeed agreed to participate, although during the progress of the project the American Association of Law Libraries decided to withdraw, with the view that its needs were adequately met by current accreditation practices, supplemented by its own processes of certification.

Other relevant societies were informed of the project and encouraged to participate: Society of American Archivists, Association of Records Managers and Administrators, and National Federation of Abstracting and Information Services. They did so primarily by observing the progress of the project, but with limited input to the discussion.

Each participating society nominated a person to serve as a member of the Steering Committee, which coordinated the work on the project and was responsible for this final report. Each participating society appointed representatives to the set of working groups that was focused on specific sets of issues.

Management Structure

The project involved three levels of responsibility: project management, the Steering Committee, and the working groups.

The office of the ALA Accreditation Officer was responsible for project management, including financial management, logistical arrangements, communications among the several other participating societies and persons, and arrangements for publication of the final report.

The Steering Committee was the focal point of the project. The membership included representatives from each of the participating societies and was headed by the chairman of the ALA/COA. The effect is that ALA had two members on the Steering Committee, but that seems appropriate for at least three reasons:

- ALA is by far the largest of the participating interested societies, with membership greater than the total of all the others.
- ALA was representing not only itself, but a number of constituent interests, such as those of school librarians and college and research librarians.
- ALA is the recognized agency for accreditation in the field of library and information science.

The Steering Committee was responsible for policy guidance for the project, for the final recommendations, and for preparation and submission of this final report.

The working groups clearly were the central means for accomplishing the objectives of the project. There were six of them, focused on the following areas of concern:

- Working Group 1: Organization of the Accreditation Process
- Working Group 2: Finance of the Accreditation Process
- Working Group 3: Guidelines for Program Goals and Objectives
- Working Group 4: Guidelines for Faculty
- Working Group 5: Guidelines for Curriculum
- Working Group 6: Guidelines for Society-Specific Objectives

Each Working Group was chaired by a current member of one of the participating societies.

Time Schedule

The project was initiated with the signing of the contract with the U.S. Department of Education at the end of the ALISE-sponsored conference, in October 1984. During the ensuing two months the Steering Committee and working groups for the project were appointed, and the background paper (Chapter 2 of the final report) was prepared and distributed to the participants.

The Steering Committee and working groups first met during the ALA Midwinter Meeting in January 1985 where charges to the working groups were developed. From then until the ALA annual conference in June 1985, the working groups were identifying issues within their respective areas of concern, identifying alternatives, and preparing for discussion and presentation at the ALA annual conference. During that meeting, there were both working group sessions and plenary sessions for presentation of results to date.

Between June 1985 and January 1986, the working groups focused their attention on development of draft recommendations for consideration by the Steering Committee at the ALA Midwinter Meeting in January 1986. The result of those efforts was the preparation of a set of draft reports, which then served as the basis for discussion during that meeting. Again, during that meeting, there were both working group sessions and plenary sessions for review of the draft reports and the recommendations to the Steering Committee contained in them.

The ensuing two months were devoted to the preparation of the final report, under the guidance of the Steering Committee, for submission to the U.S. Department of Education, in fulfillment of the contractual obligations of the project, and for distribution to the participating societies.

Throughout the project, the ALA Committee on Accreditation provided full and complete coverage of the objectives and progress of the project by presentation during the ALA/COA "open meetings" as part of the ALA meeting schedule. Beyond that, presentations were made during the ALISE conference held just before the ALA Midwinter Meeting of January 1986.

Summary of Reports of the Working Groups

Working Group 1: Organization of the Accreditation Process

The working group on the Organization of the Accreditation Process was charged with the following responsibilities:

1 To recommend an organizational model that will accommodate the participation of a number of library and information societies in the accreditation process.

2 To explore implications for procedural guidelines that will stem from the identification of an organizational model.

3 To recommend a mechanism for broadening the participation in the accreditation process by appropriate societies.

4 To prepare a report for the Steering Committee that describes the working group's methodology and explains its recommendations.

This working group in a very real sense was concerned with the most central issue of the project—the organizational mechanisms through which to involve several societies in the process of accreditation. The report is included as Chapter 3 of the final report on the project. It is indeed an excellent approach to a solution of the problems, and the overall recommendations from this working group were, as a result, heartily endorsed by the Steering Committee and form the main content of the final recommendations for the project.

To summarize, Working Group 1 recommended that other associations be invited to join with the American Library Association in governing the accreditation process. It recommends, as the essential preliminary, that an Inter-Association Advisory Committee on Accreditation should be formed to provide the formal means for initiating that involvement. That Advisory Committee would then take responsibility for planning and implementing the further steps. Specifically, it would provide the means by which potentially interested organizations could be invited to join in the planning; it would serve as the means for seeking subsidy for further stages; it would provide the means for communication with the Committee on Accreditation itself; it would provide the means for communication with the Council on Postsecondary Accreditation to ensure compliance with guidelines in further stages; it would define the level and type of programs to be accredited; it would recommend the criteria for membership on the Committee on Accreditation; it would set the schedule for further stages in development; and it would evaluate whether those stages had progressed effectively. In other words, this recommended Advisory Committee would provide the means for maintaining the momentum generated by the ALISE initiative and by this project through a formally established, continuing agency.

Working Group 1 recommends that the Advisory Committee orient its future planning toward change of the organization of accreditation in three stages:

1 Addition of representatives from other information profession associations to the Committee on Accreditation, to augment the present membership, which is, except for two public members, chosen to represent the American Library Association.

2 Change in the governance of the Committee on Accreditation to an "umbrella-form" organization, with the American Library Association continuing as the

responsible organization but serving as the agent for other participating societies.

3 Change to a federated structure, in which the several participating societies function as co-equal partners, at least with respect to policy formulation and accreditation decisions.

This staged approach to change provides the means for gradual transformation, with the possibility of pausing or even stopping at any stage when it appears that the objectives in involving the several societies have been adequately met. The judgments in that respect would be the responsibility of the Inter-Association Advisory Committee on Accreditation, with the decisions, of course, then made by the participating societies.

The working group makes recommendations concerning the selection of members of the Committee on Accreditation and its size. It also discusses some specific issues related to accreditation procedures, such as selection of site visit team members and the kinds and levels of programs to be accredited. The report from the working group then concludes with a tentative time schedule for transition from the current status through the three stages recommended, as listed above.

Working Group 2: Finance of the Accreditation Process

The working group on Finance of the Accreditation Process was basically charged to develop an equitable financing model for the associations and institutions participating in the accreditation process. Within that broad charge, the following specific questions were to be explored:

1 Is there an equitable scheme for prorating costs among the participating groups and societies?

2 What specific factors — such as size, membership, organizational budget, number of educational programs sponsored, etc. — should be involved in cost sharing and cost distribution?

3 What costs should be borne by the participating societies and groups, and what costs should be borne by the institutions?

4 Is there a cost break-even point?

In addition, the group was charged to review the present COA budget and attempt to identify additional costs that would result from adding a number of societies and groups; to identify possible sources of start-up funding, to estimate the amount needed, and for how long it should be available; and to estimate the ongoing costs to the constituent groups and societies after start-up funding is withdrawn.

This working group was concerned with perhaps the most difficult and sensitive of the issues involved in multisociety cooperation: Who is going to pay for it, and how much? Without question, while the professional concerns of the several societies may lead them to an interest in accreditation, their decisions concerning participation are likely to be governed by the budgetary implications. While the working group does not make explicit recommendations concerning the mechanism for funding, it does provide substantive data of great value in subsequent steps in evaluation by the proposed Advisory Committee.

Specifically, the working group report, presented as Chapter 4 of the final report on the project, provides an analysis of current costs of accreditation. The report estimates total costs per annum of over $1 million for just the programs currently covered by accreditation. Over half of that cost is borne by the schools being accredited, the great bulk of it in the time and effort involved in preparing self-studies and in the conduct of site visits. The remaining costs, with which the societies would be primarily concerned, total about $500,000 — half of it the cost of volunteer service on the Committee on Accreditation and on site visit teams. The core expenses — the direct and indirect costs of the Committee on Accreditation itself — are estimated at about $250,000. It is that final figure of $250,000 that would represent the financial commitment involved in participation in the process of accreditation. Of course, it is recognized that these estimates reflect the current situation and that participation of multiple societies in an expanded program will doubtless involve increased costs, which the working group report arbitrarily estimates at perhaps 10 percent.

The working group report presents alternative formulas for allocation of those costs, based on the experience of other cooperative arrangements. It concludes with the recommendation that the Inter-Association Advisory Committee determine, as a primary responsibility, what the funding needs will be. In fact, first among those would be the costs of the Advisory Committee itself, which the working group report estimates at $25,000 for the first year of operations.

In light of the estimates of costs to the institutions being accredited, the working group report concludes with the recommendation that every effort be made, by whatever may be the accrediting agency, to reduce the fiscal burden on those institutions.

Working Group 3: Guidelines for Program Goals and Objectives

The working group on Guidelines for Program Goals and Objectives was charged with the following tasks:

1 Clarify the role of goals and objectives in the accreditation process. In particular, should goals be defined by the program being accredited or by the larger information professions?
2 Clarify the role of goals and objectives in relation to curriculum.
3 Consider how general goals and objectives relate to society-specific goals and objectives (i.e., those defined by the information professions).
4 Clarify the desired *level* of goals and objectives — should they be very general and lofty or should they be very specific?

This working group drew heavily upon the statements regarding goals and objectives embodied in the 1972 *Standards for Accreditation* in dealing with its charges, finding them of continuing value and appropriate to involvement of multiple societies. Perhaps the most important implicit recommendation in the report of this working group, presented as Chapter 5 of the final report on the project, is that the participating societies themselves need to develop the "major documents and policy statements," to which the 1972 *Standards* refer as the basis for evaluating program goals and objectives. For the accrediting body to assist the schools and to apply such policy statements in accreditation decisions, the documents identifying them must exist.

Working Group 4: Guidelines for Faculty

The working group on Guidelines for Faculty was charged as follows:

1 Should there be guidelines of faculty competencies specific to society interests? If so, what?
2 Should there be guidelines relating to the size (i.e., number) of faculty? If so, what?
3 Should there be guidelines concerning general qualifications of faculty with respect to, for example, teaching competency; service to community, university, and profession; research productivity and research competency?
4 Should there be guidelines with respect to experience — academic, practice, counseling, other?
5 Should there be guidelines for professional development of faculty — need for retraining, updating, etc.?

This working group placed special emphasis on the institutional prerogatives and responsibilities. The view expressed is that the institution is "primarily responsible for establishing standards for faculty appointment, promotion, and tenure" and for operational policies relating to work load, leaves, and compensation.

The report of this working group, presented as Chapter 6 of the final report on the project, does discuss some general qualifications, drawing heavily upon the 1972 *Standards for Accreditation*. It discusses academic qualification, scholarship, experience, professional activity, community service, subject expertise, and teaching effectiveness as areas of essential competency whatever may be the assigned specializations. It then discusses the need for more specialized competencies related to specializations, concluding that participating societies need to suggest means for measuring effectiveness in their scope of interest.

Working Group 5: Guidelines for Curriculum

The working group on Guidelines for Curriculum was charged as follows:

1 What should be the *general approach* to curricular issues, on a continuum that runs from "sidestepping curricular definitions" to "a series of definitions, course descriptions, etc."?
2 What should be the approach to:

- Definition of "core curriculum/competencies," if any?
- Society-specific specializations?
- Specializations outside information science/librarianship?
- Quality determination and/or validation?
- Joint degree programs?
- Definition of the level at which the first degree is granted?

3 Categorize the spectrum of the information disciplines and define what our accreditation process covers. In particular, should it cover information management in other schools?

The report of this working group is presented in Chapter 7 of the final report on the project. It provides a most provocative and thorough analysis of the scope of the field, the content of academic programs, the nature and role of the "core curriculum," and the means for measuring quality. The analysis of the core knowledge requirements identifies three main categories of content which are worth repeating here:

> *Knowledge areas*, encompassing philosophy and background, environmental and contextual knowledge, and management knowledge.
>
> *Tool areas*, encompassing quantitative and analytical tools (such as statistics, research methods, systems analysis) and bibliographic and organizational tools (the traditional "core": cataloging and classification, reference, collection development, data and file structure, etc.)
>
> *Skill requirements*, encompassing communication skills, technological skills, and interpersonal skills.

The working group report includes a discussion of the problems involved in dealing with multiple specializations within a unified accreditation program. Of special concern in this respect is how to deal with undergraduate as well as graduate programs. It discusses three options: accreditation of programs, accreditation of specialties, and accreditation of schools. It recommends that these alternatives continue to be explored.

Working Group 6: Guidelines for Society-Specific Objectives

The working group on Guidelines for Society-Specific Objectives was charged as follows:

1 What are the unique needs of each society? In what areas do societies have goals specific and separate from the communal goals of the federation?

2 Who will decide what society goals are adopted by the profession?

3 How should these objectives be incorporated into the accreditation process?

4 Who will decide whether a program is meeting these objectives?

5 If a school offered itself for accreditation in an area of emphasis or concentration, what action, if any, will be taken to distinguish a general program accreditation from one for stated areas of emphasis? By what criteria are schools offering specializations accredited?

This final working group provided the means by which particular concerns of the participating societies would be discussed, without the constraints of identified categories, whether organizational or substantive. As the report, presented as Chapter 8 of the final report on the project, says, some of the societies – the Society of American Archivists and the American Society for Information Science, in particular – pointed out that degrees other than the MLS are appropriate means for entry to the field of their concern. Others were concerned about the relationship of accreditation to continuing education and their societal responsibilities in that respect. Of general concern was the means for developing and evaluating areas of emphasis within curricula and programs. The report concludes with reviews of the statements from various professional societies of their expectations.

In bringing together those policy statements, from at least some of the participating professional societies, this working group has again highlighted the importance of such documents to the accreditation process. As the 1972 *Standards* state, the goals of programs should be judged in the context of the "major documents and policy statements" of the professional societies. If nothing else, it is hoped that this project has alerted all of the societies involved to the necessity of creating and reviewing their own statements of policy in this respect.

Relationships among Working Group Reports

Given the fact that the several working groups arrived at the respective reports quite independently, there is a remarkable degree of consistency among them. In particular, the need for an Inter-Association Advisory Committee on Accreditation is emphasized in several of them. The need for the participating societies to develop policy statements that document their requirements for educational specialization is emphasized in several of them. The essential endorsement of the 1972 *Standards for Accreditation* as still a workable basis for accreditation decisions is evident throughout the reports of the four working groups concerned with substantive aspects.

There certainly are a few inconsistencies, both within the reports of individual working groups and among them. They appear to be minor and simply represent the nature of the process by which the work on this project was carried out.

Guide to Library Placement Sources

Margaret Myers

Director, Office for Library Personnel Resources
American Library Association

This year's guide updates the listing in the 1986 *Bowker Annual* with information on new services and changes in contacts and groups listed previously. The sources listed primarily give assistance in obtaining professional positions, although a few provide assistance with paraprofessional positions as well. The latter, however, tend to be recruited through local sources.

General Sources of Library Jobs

Library Literature

Classified ads of library vacancies and positions wanted are carried in many of the national, regional, and state library journals and newsletters. Members of associations can sometimes list position wanted ads free of charge in their membership publications. Listings of positions available are regularly found in *American Libraries, Chronicle of Higher Education, College & Research Libraries News, Library Journal, LJ/SLJ Hotline,* and *Wilson Library Bulletin.* (State and regional library association newsletters, state library journals, foreign library periodicals, and other types of periodicals carrying such ads are listed in later sections of this guide.)

Newspapers

The *New York Times* Sunday Week in Review section carries a special section of ads for librarian jobs in addition to the regular classifieds. Local newspapers, particularly the larger city Sunday editions, such as the *Washington Post* and *Los Angeles Times*, often carry job vacancy listings in libraries, both professional and paraprofessional.

Library Joblines

Library joblines or job hotlines give recorded telephone messages of job openings in a specific geographic area. Most tapes are changed once a week on Friday afternoon, although individual listings may sometimes be carried for several weeks. Although the information is fairly brief and the cost of calling is borne by the individual job seeker, a jobline provides a quick and up-to-date listing of vacancies which is not usually possible with printed listings or journal ads.

Most joblines carry listings for their state or region only, although some will occasionally accept out-of-state positions if there is room on the tape. While a few will list technician and other paraprofessional positions, the majority are for professional jobs only. When calling the joblines, one might occasionally find a time when the telephone keeps ringing without any answer; this will usually mean that the tape is being changed or there are no new jobs for that period. The classified section of *American Libraries* carries jobline numbers in each issue.

The following joblines are in operation: *Arizona State Library/Association* 602-278-1327; *Association of College and Research Libraries* 312-944-6795; *British Columbia Library Association* 604-263-0014 (British Columbia listings only); *California Library Association* 916-443-1222 for northern California and 213-629-5627 for southern California (identical lists); *California Media and Library Educators Association* 415-697-8832; *Colorado State Library* 303-866-6741 (Colorado listings only, includes paraprofessional); *Connecticut* 203-727-9675 (Connecticut jobs only); *Delaware Library Association* 800-282-8696 (in-state), 302-736-4748, ext. 69 (out-of-state); *Drexel University College of Information Studies* 215-895-1672; *State Library of Florida* 904-488-4532 (in-state listings only); *Library Jobline of Illinois* 312-828-0930, professional positions, 312-828-9198, support staff positions (cosponsored by the Special Libraries Association Illinois Chapter and Illinois Library Association); *Maryland Library Association* 301-685-5760; *Metropolitan Washington Council of Governments Library Council* (District of Columbia) 202-223-2272; *Michigan Library Association* 517-487-5617; *Midwest Federation of Library Associations* 317-926-8770 (also includes paraprofessional and out-of-state if room on tape; cosponsored by four state library associations—Illinois, Indiana, Minnesota, Ohio); *Missouri Library Association* 314-442-6590; *Mountain Plains Library Association* 605-677-5757, 800 number available to MPLA members, $20 to nonmembers (includes listings for the states of Arizona, Colorado, Kansas, Montana, Nebraska, Nevada, North and South Dakota, Utah, and Wyoming); *Nebraska* 402-471-2045 (during regular business hours); *New England Library Jobline* 617-738-3148 (New England jobs only); *New Jersey Library Association* 609-695-2121; *New York Library Association* 212-227-8483; *North Carolina State Library* 919-733-6410 (professional jobs in North Carolina only); *Oklahoma Jobline* (Oklahoma Department of Libraries) 405-521-4202 (5 P.M.–8 A.M., Monday through Friday and all weekend); *Oregon Library Association* 503-585-2232 (cosponsored by Oregon

Educational Media Association and Oregon State Library); *Pacific Northwest Library Association* 206-543-2890 (Alaska, Alberta, British Columbia, Idaho, Montana, Oregon, and Washington; includes both professional and paraprofessional and other library related jobs); *Pennsylvania Cooperative Jobline* 717-234-4646 (cosponsored by the Pennsylvania Library Association, Medical Library Association–Philadelphia and Pittsburgh groups, American Society for Information Science–Delaware Valley Chapter, and West Virginia Library Association; also accepts paraprofessional out-of-state listings); *Public Library Association (PLA) Jobline* 312-664-5627; *Special Libraries Association* 202-234-3632; *Special Libraries Association, New York Chapter* 212-214-4226; *Special Libraries Association, San Andreas–San Francisco Bay Chapter* 408-378-8854; *Special Libraries Association, Southern California Chapter* 818-795-2145; *Texas Library Association Job Hotline* 512-328-1518 (5:30 P.M. Friday through 8:00 A.M. Monday, weekends only); *Texas State Library Jobline* 512-463-5470 (Texas listings only); *University of South Carolina College of Library and Information Science* 803-777-8443; *Virginia Library Association Jobline* 703-370-7267 (Virginia libraries only); *University of Western Ontario School of Library and Information Science* 519-661-3543.

For those employers who wish to place vacancy listings on the jobline recordings, the following numbers can be called: *ACRL* 312-944-6780, ext. 286; *Arizona* 602-269-2535; *California* 916-447-8541; *Colorado* 303-866-6732; *District of Columbia* 202-223-6800, ext. 458; *Florida* 904-487-2651; *Illinois* 312-644-1896; *Maryland* 301-685-5760 (Monday or Wednesday, 10:00 A.M.–2:30 P.M.); *Missouri* 314-449-4627; *New York/ SLA* 212-880-9716; *North Carolina* 919-733-2570; *Oklahoma* 405-521-2502; *Oregon* 503-378-4502; *Pennsylvania* 717-233-3113; *PLA Jobline* 312-944-6780; *San Andreas–San Francisco/SLA* 415-642-2511; *Southern California/SLA* 818-354-4200; *Special Libraries Association* 202-234-4700; *Texas* 512-463-5475.

Write: *British Columbia Library Association*, Box 46378, Sta. G, Vancouver, BC., Canada V6R 4G6; *California Media and Library Educators Association*, 1575 Old Bayshore Highway, Suite 204, Burlingame, CA 94010; *Colorado State Library Jobline*, 201 E. Colfax, 3rd fl., Denver, CO 80203; *Connecticut Library Assn.*, 231 Capitol Ave., Hartford, CT 06106; *Delaware Library Association*, Box 843, Wilmington, DE 19899; *State Library of Florida*, R.A. Gray Building, Tallahassee, FL 32399-0251; *Library Jobline of Illinois*, Illinois Library Association, 425 N. Michigan Ave., Suite 1304, Chicago, IL 60611 ($20 fee/2 weeks); *Maryland Library Association*, 115 W. Franklin St., Baltimore, MD 21201; *Michigan Library Association*, 415 W. Kalamazoo St., Lansing, MI 48933 ($10 fee/week); *Mountain Plains Library Association*, c/o I.D. Weeks Library, Univ. of South Dakota, Vermillion, SD 57069; *Nebraska Job Hotline*, Library Commission, 1420 P St., Lincoln, NE 68510; *New England Library Jobline*, c/o James Matarazzo, GSLIS, Simmons College, 300 The Fenway, Boston, MA 02115; *New Jersey Library Association*, 116 W. State, Trenton, NJ 08608; *New York Library Association*, 15 Park Row #434, New York, NY 10038 ($10 fee/week for nonmembers); *Oregon Library Association JOBLINE*, Oregon State Library, Salem, OR 97310; *PNLA Jobline*, c/o Graduate School of Library & Information Sciences, University of Washington FM-30, Seattle, WA 98195; *Texas Library Association Job Hotline*, 3355 Bee Cave Road, Suite 603, Austin, TX 78746; *University of South Carolina, College of Library and Information Science*, Admissions & Placement Coordinator, Columbia, SC 29208 (no geographic restrictions); *Virginia Library Association Jobline*, 80 S. Early St., Alexandria, VA 22304; *University of Western Ontario* 519-661-3542. For the *Midwest*

Federation Jobline, employers should send listings to their own state association executive secretary or call 317-926-6561. There is a $10 fee for the first week and $5 per listing each week thereafter. Paraprofessional positions are also accepted.

Specialized Library Associations and Groups

The National Registry for Librarians, formerly housed in the Illinois State Job Service at 40 W. Adams St., Chicago, IL 60603 is no longer in operation. Referral service will still be carried out through state and local Job Service offices, but no independent registry will be maintained for librarians.

Advanced Information Management, 444 Castro St., Suite 503, Mountain View, CA 94041: Personnel agency that specializes in finding both temporary and permanent positions for people with all levels of library experience, from paraprofessional to professional, primarily in public and special libraries in the Bay Area, although there are plans to expand. A career counseling service is planned.

American Association of Law Libraries: 53 W. Jackson Blvd., Chicago, IL 60604, 312-939-4764: Placement service is available without charge for eight lines of copy, $2.50 per line for all lines of copy if more than eight lines are requested. Lists of openings and personnel available are published ten times per year in a newsletter distributed to membership. Applicants are referred to placement officers for employment counseling.

American Libraries, "Career LEADS EXPRESS," c/o Beverly Goldberg, 50 E. Huron St., Chicago, IL 60611: Advance galleys (3–4 weeks) of classified job listings to be published in next issue of *American Libraries*. Early notice of approximately 100 "Positions Open" sent about the seventeenth of each month; does not include editorial corrections and late changes as they appear in the regular *AL* LEADS section, but does include some "Late Job Notices." For each month, send $1 check made out to AL EXPRESS, self-addressed, standard business-size envelope (4 × 9), and 39¢ postage on envelope.

American Libraries, Consultants Keyword Clearinghouse (CKC), an *AL* service that helps match professionals offering library/information expertise with institutions seeking it. Published quarterly, *CKC* appears in the Career LEADS section of the January, April, June, and October issues of *AL*. Rates: $4/line—classified; $40/inch—display. Inquiries should be made to Beverly Goldberg, LEADS Editor, *American Libraries*, 50 E. Huron St., Chicago, IL 60611, 312-944-6780, ext. 326.

American Library Association, Association of College and Research Libraries, 50 E. Huron St., Chicago, IL 60611-2795, 312-944-6780, ext. 286: In addition to classified advertising each month in *College & Research Libraries News*, ACRL lists job openings in academic and research libraries in the Fast Job Listing Service, a monthly bulletin that announces positions one month before they appear in *C&RL News*, as well as positions that do not appear anywhere else because of early applications deadlines. $10 to ACRL members (indicate ALA/ACRL membership number); $15 to nonmembers. Renewable after six months.

Also available is the ACRL Jobline, a recorded telephone message updated each Friday. Call 312-944-6795 to hear the recording; 312-944-6780, ext. 286, to place a listing for a two-week period.

American Library Association, Office for Library Personnel Resources, 50 E. Huron St., Chicago, IL 60611, 312-944-6780: A placement service is provided at each an-

nual conference (June or July) and midwinter meeting (January). Request job seeker or employer registration forms prior to each conference. Persons not able to attend conference can register with the service and can also purchase job and applicant listings sent directly from the conference site. Information included when requesting registration forms. Handouts on interviewing, preparing a résumé, and other job seeking information are available from the ALA Office for Library Personnel Resources.

In addition to the ALA conference placement center, ALA division national conferences usually include a placement service.

American Library Association, ASCLA/SLAS State Library Consultants to Institutional Libraries Discussion Group, Institutional Library Mailed Jobline. Monthly compilation of job openings in institutional libraries throughout the United States and territories. Send self-addressed, stamped envelope(s) to Institutional Library Jobline, c/o S. Carlson, R.I. Department of State Library Services, 95 Davis St., Providence, RI 02908. Send job postings to same or call 401-277-2726. Listings will appear for one month unless resubmitted.

American Society for Information Science, 1424 16 St., N.W., #404, Washington, DC 20036, 202-462-1000: There is an active placement service operated at ASIS annual meetings (usually October) and midyear meetings (usually May) (locales change). All conference attendees (both ASIS members and nonmembers), as well as ASIS members who cannot attend the conference, are eligible to use the service to list or find jobs. Job listings are also accepted from employers who cannot attend the conference, interviews are arranged, and special seminars are given. Throughout the year, current job openings are listed in *ASIS JOBLINE*, a monthly publication sent to all members, and available to nonmembers on request. Seventeen of the ASIS chapters have placement officers who further assist members in finding jobs.

Art Libraries Society/North America (ARLIS/NA), c/o Exec. Dir., 3900 E. Timrod St., Tucson, AZ 85711, 602-881-8479: Art librarian and slide curator jobs are listed in the *ARLIS/NA UPDATE* (four times a year) and a job registry is maintained at society headquarters. (Any employer may list a job with the registry, but only members may request job information.)

Associated Information Managers, c/o Sheila Brayman, Exec. Dir., 1776 E. Jefferson St., Suite 442, Rockville, MD 20852, 301-231-7447: *AIM Career Exchange Clearinghouse* lists positions open and wanted on a biweekly basis in conjunction with the *AIM Network*. Position applicants send résumé and cover letter to AIM for forwarding to employers. Employers listing positions open may list their organization name and contact person and telephone number, or may request that AIM serve as the clearinghouse. Reference numbers for all listings will be assigned by AIM. Minimum salary level for all positions is $25,000. The *Career Exchange Clearinghouse* is open to AIM members only.

Association for Educational Communications & Technology, Placement and Referral Service, 1126 16 St., N.W., Washington, DC 20036, 202-466-4780: Positions available are listed in the association member newsletter *Access*. A referral service is available at no charge to AECT members only. A placement center operates at the annual conference, free to all conference registrants. In addition, there are two placement bulletin boards on TechCentral, AECT's electronic mail and information system—job opportunities and positions desired.

Black Caucus Newsletter, c/o George C. Grant, Rollins College, Campus Box 2654, Winter Park, FL 32789: Lists some job vacancy notices. Free to members; $4 to others. Published bimonthly.

C. Berger and Company, 130 W. Liberty Dr., Wheaton, IL 60187, 312-653-1115: CBC represents midwest clients in filling permanent positions in library or information management, supervision, or subject specialty areas. Professional and support personnel can also be supplied to special, academic, and public libraries on a temporary basis or in a maintenance capacity. Teams of qualified specialists and project management services are also available under contract.

Canadian Association of Special Libraries and Information Services/Ottawa Chapter Job Bank, c/o Coordinator, CASLIS, 13C Deerfield Dr., Nepean, Ont. K2G 3R7, Canada: Those looking for a job should send resume; employers with a job to list should call 613-237-3688.

Catholic Library Association, 461 W. Lancaster Ave., Haverford, PA 19041, 215-649-5250: Personal and institutional members of CLA are given free space (35 words) to advertise for jobs or to list job openings in *Catholic Library World* (ten per year). Others may advertise at $1 per printed line.

Center for the Study of Rural Librarianship, Clarion University of Pennsylvania, Clarion, PA 16214, 814-226-2383: *Rural Libraries Jobline*, monthly listing. Send $1 for each month listing is desired.

Council on Library/Media Technicians, c/o Shirley Daniels, Newsletter Editor, 5049 Eighth St., N.E., Washington, DC 20017: *COLT Newsletter* appears eleven times a year and will accept listings for library/media technician positions. However, correspondence relating to jobs cannot be handled.

Gossage Regan Associates, Inc., 15 W. 44 St., New York, NY 10036, 212-869-3348: Gossage Regan Associates works with library trustees, faculty search committees, or with library directors, systems heads, library search committees, chief executive officers of corporations or higher education institutions or other organizations to locate, screen, assess, and recommend candidates for library management positions such as directors, division heads, or information specialists. In the New York/New Jersey/Connecticut metropolitan area provides temporary librarians and information specialists, paraprofessionals and clericals to special, academic, and public libraries, for long and short-term assignments. GRA People, a Gossage Regan Associates' subsidiary, is a registered employment agency for permanent placement of library and information personnel.

GRAPEVINE, c/o Beverly Goldberg, *American Libraries*, 50 E. Huron St., Chicago, IL 60611: Online database of job openings on ALANET updated every Monday. Short-entry job alert, which includes job title, institution, date available, salary and contact person. Limited Boolean search flexibility. GRAPEVINE ads will not automatically appear in *American Libraries* LEADS; employers can choose one or both services. $25 for GRAPEVINE ad; $10 if also advertised with LEADS. Can be read on ALANET by typing > VINE at system level or from within the Units menu (ALANET4).

HBW Library Recruiters, 6352 Lakeshore Dr., Dallas, TX 75214, 214-826-6981 or 3304 North Utah, Oklahoma City, OK 73112, 405-947-1109: A firm of professional librarians that works exclusively for libraries and information centers seeking to fill executive positions. HBW will assist library boards, county administrators, city managers, faculty search committees, library directors, and personnel officers with the selection of key administrative and managerial staff. HBW will assist with the development of position guidelines and requirements, candidate lists, screening, credential checks and verification, and preliminary interviewing through final selections. There is no obligation for an exploratory discussion.

Information Exchange System for Minority Personnel (IESMP, Inc.), Box 90216, Washington, DC 20090: Nonprofit organization designed to recruit minority librarians for EEO/AA employers. *Informer*, quarterly newsletter. Write for membership categories, services, and fees.

Library Associates, 2600 Colorado Blvd., Suite 160, Santa Monica, CA 90404, 213-453-5583 or 5270: A consulting firm owned and operated by librarians; the agency will provide personnel on a temporary or contract basis to fill vacancies, substitute for regular staff, etc., in addition to providing expertise for such projects as automation, systems analysis, records retention and organization, cataloging, indexing/abstracting, thesauri construction, marketing strategy, and implementing marketing plans for vendors who sell information products.

Medical Library Association, 919 N. Michigan Ave., Suite 3208, Chicago, IL 60611, 312-266-2456: *MLA News* (10 issues per year, June/July and November/December combined issues) lists positions wanted and positions available in its "Employment Opportunities" column. The position available rate is $12.50 per line for nonmembers. Up to ten free lines for MLA members plus $10 per line over ten lines. Positions wanted rates $8.50 per line for nonmembers; $10 per line for members with 20 free lines. Advance mailings of "Employment Opportunities" may be requested for a period of six months. This service is available for a prepaid fee: MLA members, $15; nonmembers, $25. Also MLA offers placement service at annual conference each spring.

Online, Inc., c/o June Thompson, 11 Tannery Lane, Weston, CT 06883, 203-227-8466; Electronic Mail—TCU 202 (The Source), CLASS.ONLINE (ONTYME); TFHN (BRS); ALANET mailbox is ALA0795: Jobline is available for positions sought and positions available in the online/library field through the Online Chronicle (file 170) on DIALOG. All postings are free.

Professional Information Resources: The Vita Bank, Box 248, Buchanan Dam, TX 78609-0248, 512-793-6118 or 512-444-3097: The Vita Bank is a service that helps academic and research libraries identify library professionals with requisite skills to fill vacant positions. The information contained in the database and available for searching includes that relating to education, job background, specialities, and skills of approximately 2,000 academic and research library professionals throughout the United States and Canada. Libraries wishing to search The Vita Bank should contact PIR; the charge for a search is $200, for which libraries will receive computer-generated printouts of the credentials of individuals retrieved. Librarians wishing to be included in The Vita Bank should send current resume. Inclusion in the database is free.

Reforma, National Association to Promote Library Service to the Spanish-Speaking, Anita Peterson, Jobline Ed., Inglewood Public Library, 101 W. Manchester Blvd., Inglewood, CA 90301: A monthly jobline listing is compiled and sent to Reforma chapters for further dissemination to members.

Rhode Island Association Bulletin, Jobline, c/o Charlotte Schoonover, Kingston Free Library, 1329 Kingston Rd., Kingston, RI 02881: Jobline appears monthly in *RILA Bulletin*, listing positions in southeast New England, including paraprofessional and part-time jobs. Job seekers desiring copy of most recent monthly Jobline, send self-addressed, stamped envelope. Groups of envelopes may also be sent. To post a notice, contact C. Schoonover at above address.

Society of American Archivists, 600 S. Federal, Suite 504, Chicago, IL 60605, 312-922-0140: The *SAA Newsletter* is sent (to members only) six times annually and lists

jobs, as well as details of professional meetings and courses in archival administration. The "Employment Bulletin" is sent to members who pay a $12 subscription fee and alternates with the *Newsletter*.

Special Libraries Association, 1700 18 St., N.W., Washington, DC 20009, 202-234-4700: SLA maintains a telephone jobline, SpeciaLine, which is in operation 24 hours a day, seven days a week, 202-234-3632. Most SLA chapters have employment chairpersons who act as referral persons for employers and job seekers. Several SLA chapters have joblines. The Association's monthly newsletter *The SpeciaList*, carries classified advertising. SLA also offers a conference employment clearinghouse at the annual conference held in June.

Theresa M. Burke Employment Agency, 25 W. 39 St., New York, NY 10018, 212-398-9250: A licensed professional employment agency which has specialized for nearly 40 years in the recruitment of library and information personnel for academic, public, and special libraries. Presently the majority of openings are in special libraries in the New York metropolitan area and require subject backgrounds and/or specific kinds of experience. Fees are paid by the employer.

State Library Agencies

In addition to the joblines mentioned previously, some of the state library agencies issue lists of job openings within their areas. These include: Indiana (monthly on request); Iowa (*Joblist*, monthly); Massachusetts (*Massachusetts Position Vacancies*, monthly, sent to all public libraries in-state and to interested individuals on a one-time basis); Minnesota (*Position Openings in Minnesota and Adjoining States*, semimonthly, sent to public and academic libraries); Mississippi (job vacancy list, monthly); and Ohio (*Library Opportunities in Ohio*, monthly, sent to accredited library education programs and interested individuals upon request).

The North Carolina state library has an electronic bulletin board service that lists job openings in the state. It can be accessed in-state and nationally by Western Union Easylink system users (use NCJOBS).

On occasion when vacancy postings are available, state library newsletters or journals will list these, such as: Alabama (*Cottonboll*, bimonthly); Indiana (*Focus on Indiana Libraries*, 11 times/year); Kansas (*Kansas Libraries*, monthly); Louisiana (*Library Communique*, monthly); Missouri (*Show-Me Libraries*, monthly); Nebraska (*Overtones*, 10 times/year); New Hampshire (*Granite State Libraries*, bimonthly); North Carolina (*Flash Newsletter*, monthly); Utah (*Horsefeathers*, monthly); and Wyoming (*Outrider*, monthly).

Many state library agencies will refer applicants informally when vacancies are known to exist, but do not have formal placement services. The following states primarily make referrals to public libraries only: Alabama, California, Georgia, Idaho, Louisiana, South Carolina (institutional also), Tennessee, Vermont, and Virginia. Those who refer applicants to all types of libraries are Alaska, Delaware, Florida, Kansas, Maine, Maryland, Massachusetts, Mississippi, Montana, Nebraska, Nevada (largely public and academic), New Hampshire (public, school, and academic), New Mexico, North Dakota, Ohio, Rhode Island, South Dakota, Utah, West Virginia (public, academic, special), and Wyoming.

The following state libraries post library vacancy notices for all types of libraries on a bulletin board: California, Connecticut, Florida, Indiana, Michigan, Montana, Ohio,

Utah, and Washington. Addresses of the state agencies are found in the *Bowker Annual* or *American Library Directory*.

State and Regional Library Associations

State and regional library associations will often make referrals, run ads in association newsletters, or operate a placement service at annual conferences, in addition to the joblines sponsored by some groups. Referral of applicants when jobs are known is done by the following associations: Arkansas, Delaware, Hawaii, Louisiana, Michigan, Nevada, Pennsylvania, South Dakota, Tennessee, Texas, and Wisconsin. Although listings are infrequent, job vacancies are placed in the following association newsletters or journals when available: Alabama (*Alabama Librarian*, ten times/year); Arkansas (*Arkansas LA Newsletter*, six times/year); Connecticut (*Connecticut Libraries*, eleven times/year), Delaware (*Delaware Library Association Bulletin*, three times/year), District of Columbia (*Intercom*, eleven times/year); Indiana (*Focus on Indiana Libraries*, ten times/year); Iowa (*Catalyst*, six times/year); Kansas (*KLA Newsletter*, three times/year); Massachusetts (*Bay State Letter*, eight times/year); Minnesota (*MLA Newsletter*, ten issues/year); Missouri (bimonthly); Mountain Plains (*MPLA Newsletter*, bimonthly, lists vacancies and position wanted ads for individual and institutional members or area library school students); Nevada (*Highroller*, four times/year); New England (*NELA Newsletter*, six times/year); New Hampshire (*NHLA Newsletter*, six times/year); New Jersey (*NJLA Newsletter*, ten times/year); New Mexico (shares notices via State Library's *Hitchhiker*, weekly); New York (*NYLA Bulletin*, ten times/year); Rhode Island (*RILA Bulletin*, ten times/year); South Dakota (*Bookmarks*, bimonthly); Vermont (*VLA News*, Box 803, Burlington, VT 05402, ten issues/year); Virginia (*Virginia Librarian*, quarterly); and Wyoming (*Roundup*, three times/year).

At their annual conference the following associations have indicated some type of placement service although it may only consist of bulletin board postings: Alabama, Connecticut, Illinois, Indiana, Kansas, Louisiana, Maryland, Mountain Plains, New Jersey, New York, Oregon, Pacific Northwest, Pennsylvania, South Dakota, Tennessee, Texas, Vermont, and Wyoming.

The following associations have indicated they have no placement service at this time: Georgia, Middle Atlantic Regional Library Federation, Minnesota, Mississippi, Montana, Nebraska, Nevada, New Mexico, and North Dakota. State and regional association addresses are found in Part 6 of the *Bowker Annual*.

Library Education Programs

Library education programs offer some type of service for their current students as well as alumni. Most schools provide job hunting and résumé writing seminars. Many have outside speakers representing different types of libraries or recent graduates relating career experiences. Faculty or a designated placement officer offer individual advisory services or critiquing of résumés.

Of the ALA accredited programs, the following handle placement activities through the library school: Atlanta, British Columbia, Clarion, Columbia, Dalhousie, Drexel, Emory, Hawaii, Illinois, Louisiana, McGill, Michigan, Missouri, Pittsburgh, Pratt, Queens, Rhode Island, Rosary, Rutgers, St. John's, South Carolina, Syracuse, Tennessee, Texas-Austin, Toronto, Western Ontario, and Wisconsin-Madison.

The central university placement center handles activities for the following schools: California-Berkeley, North Carolina at Chapel Hill, and Peabody/Vanderbilt. However, in most cases, faculty in the library school will still do informal counseling regarding job seeking.

In some schools, the placement services are handled in a cooperative manner; in most cases the university placement center sends out credentials while the library school posts or compiles the job listings. Schools utilizing both sources include: Alabama, Albany, Alberta, Arizona, Atlanta, Brigham Young, Buffalo, Catholic, Chicago, Clarion, Emporia, Florida State, Indiana, Iowa, Kent State, Kentucky, Long Island, Maryland, Montreal, North Carolina-Greensboro, North Carolina Central, North Texas State, Northern Illinois, Oklahoma, Peabody/Vanderbilt, Pratt, Queens, St. John's, San Jose, Simmons, South Florida, Southern Connecticut, Southern Mississippi, Syracuse, Tennessee, Texas Woman's, UCLA, Washington, and Wisconsin-Milwaukee. Schools vary as to whether they distribute placement credentials free, charge a general registration fee, or request a fee for each file or credential sent out.

Schools that post job vacancy notices for review but do not issue printed lists are Alabama, Albany, Alberta, Arizona, Atlanta, British Columbia, Buffalo, Catholic, Chicago, Columbia, Emory, Florida State, Hawaii, Kent State, Louisiana, Maryland, McGill, Montreal, North Carolina at Chapel Hill, North Carolina-Greensboro, North Carolina Central, Northern Illinois, Oklahoma, Queens, St. John's, San Jose, Simmons, South Carolina, South Florida, Southern Mississippi, Syracuse (general postings), Tennessee, Texas Woman's, Toronto, Washington, Western Ontario and Wisconsin-Milwaukee.

Some schools also issue a printed listing of positions open which is distributed primarily to students and alumni and only occasionally available to others. The following schools issue listings free to students and alumni *only* unless indicated otherwise: Albany (weekly to SLIS grads registered with placement office); Brigham Young; California-Berkeley (alumni receive weekly out of state listings if registered; $45 fee for service, also a jobline, call 415-642-1716 to list positions); Clarion (free to students and with SASE to alumni); Drexel (job hotline listing local jobs only, 215-895-1672 — changed each Monday); Illinois (free in office; 8 issues by mail for $4 and 8 self-addressed, stamped no. 10 envelopes to alumni, $4 and 8 SASEs to nonalumni); Indiana (free for one year following graduation; alumni and others may send self-addressed stamped envelops); Iowa (weekly, $15/year for registered students and alumni); Long Island (listing from career services, $35/year includes handling résumé, seminars, etc.); Michigan (free for one year following graduation, all other grads, $15/year, 24 issues; $20 to others); Missouri (Library Vacancy Roster, monthly printout, 50¢ an issue, with minimum of 5 issues, to anyone); North Carolina at Chapel Hill (available by mail to alumni and students who pay $15 referral fee); North Texas State ($5/6 months, students and alumni); Peabody/Vanderbilt (students and alumni if registered for free); Pittsburgh (free for 6 months following graduation; other graduates $2/6 months; others $3/6 months); Pratt (alumni — weekly during spring, fall, and summer sessions; others — renew every 3 months); Rhode Island (monthly, $3/year); Rosary (*Placement News* every 2 weeks, free for 3 months following graduation — $15/year for students and alumni; $25 to others; *Placement News* is also on Lincolnet and can be accessed via telephone lines); Rutgers (subscription $4/6 months, $8/year — twice a month to anyone); Southern Connecticut (printed listing twice a month, free in office, mailed to students/alumni free); Syracuse (School Media — New York State Listings — $8 NYLA members; $12 nonmembers);

Texas-Austin (bimonthly placement bulletin free to alumni and students one year following graduation, $6/6 months or $11/year thereafter); UCLA (alumni—every 2 weeks by request, renew every 3 months); Wisconsin-Madison (subscription $8/year for 12 issues, to anyone). Western Ontario operates the SLIS Jobline which announces openings for professionals—call 519-661-3543; to list positions, call 519-661-3542. Wisconsin-Milwaukee sends copies of particular job announcements to graduates who are interested in the type and location of the job, who seem to meet the qualifications, and have registered with the school for this service. It also prepares a job database for access on microcomputers in both the school and the university library.

Employers often list jobs with schools only in their particular geographic area; some library schools give information in-person to nonalumni regarding their specific locale, but are *not* staffed to handle mail requests. Schools that allow librarians in their area to view listings are: Alabama, Albany, Alberta, Arizona, Brigham Young, British Columbia, Buffalo, California-Berkeley, Catholic, Chicago, Clarion, Columbia, Dalhousie, Drexel, Emory, Emporia, Florida State, Hawaii, Illinois, Indiana, Iowa, Kent State, Kentucky, Long Island, Louisiana, Maryland, McGill, Michigan, Missouri, Montreal, North Carolina at Chapel Hill, North Carolina Central, North Carolina-Greensboro, North Texas State, Northern Illinois, Oklahoma, Peabody/Vanderbilt, Pittsburgh, Pratt, Queens, Rhode Island, Rutgers, St. John's, San Jose, South Carolina, Southern California, Southern Connecticut, Southern Mississippi, Syracuse, Tennessee, Texas-Austin, Texas Woman's, Toronto, UCLA, Washington, Western Ontario, Wisconsin-Madison, and Wisconsin-Milwaukee.

A list of accredited program addresses is included elsewhere in Part 3 of the *Bowker Annual*. Individuals interested in placement services of other library education programs should contact the schools directly.

Federal Library Jobs

Consideration for employment in many federal libraries requires establishing civil service eligibility and being placed on the Office of Personnel Management (OPM) register maintained in Washington, D.C. Eligibility can be obtained by meeting specific education and/or experience requirements and submitting appropriate forms to OPM during designated "open" periods. Interested applicants should contact their local Federal Job Information/Testing Center (FJI/TC) periodically to find out when the next open period will be and to obtain the proper forms for filing. The FJI/TC is listed under "U.S. Government" in major metropolitan telephone directories.

Applications are evaluated for the grade(s) for which applicants are qualified and will accept. Information on beginning salary levels can be obtained from the FJI/TC. If one applies during an open period, a notice of results indicating the grades for which one is eligible or ineligible will be received. Eligibility remains in effect for one year unless an extension is requested. New or revised information regarding education and/or experience may be submitted at any time. Name and social security number should be included with any information or inquiry concerning eligibility on the register.

OPM encourages applicants to keep their file current to improve chances for employment. In addition, one should be specific regarding the conditions under which employment will be accepted. Failure to do so may result in missing consideration for positions in which one is genuinely interested.

The OPM office which maintains the register is one that refers names, not one that hires and, consequently, is unaware of actual vacancies until an agency requests candidates to fill them. As vacancies occur, applications are evaluated according to the agency's specific requirements. OPM will refer only the most highly qualified candidates to an agency for consideration.

In addition to filing the appropriate forms, applicants can attempt to make personal contact directly with federal agencies in which they are interested. Over half the vacancies occur in the Washington area. Most librarian positions are in three agencies — Army, Navy, and Veterans Administration. The Veterans Administration Library Network (VALNET) employs more than 350 professional librarians at 175 health care facilities located throughout the United States and Puerto Rico. Although most VALNET positions require training in medical librarianship, many entry-level GS-9 positions require no previous experience; GS-11/13 positions require experience specific to the duties of each vacancy. For a copy of the current vacancy list, telephone 202-389-2820 Monday through Friday, 8:00 A.M.–4:30 P.M. EST, or contact the closest VA Medical Center Library Service.

There are some "excepted" agencies which are not required to hire through the usual OPM channels. Although these agencies may require the standard forms, they maintain their own employee selection policies and procedures. Government establishments with positions outside the competitive civil service include Board of Governors of the Federal Reserve System, Central Intelligence Agency, Defense Intelligence Agency, Department of Medicine and Surgery, Federal Bureau of Investigation, Foreign Service of the United States, General Accounting Office, National Science Foundation, National Security Agency, Tennessee Valley Authority, U.S. Nuclear Regulatory Commission, U.S. Postal Service, Judicial Branch of the Government, Legislative Branch of the Government, U.S. Mission to the United Nations, World Bank and IFC, International Monetary Fund, Organization of American States, Pan American Health Organization, and United Nations Secretariat.

The Library of Congress, the world's largest and most comprehensive library, is an excepted service agency in the legislative branch and administers its own independent merit selection system. Job classifications, pay, and benefits are the same as in other federal agencies, and qualifications requirements generally correspond to those used by the U.S. Office of Personnel Management. The library does not use registers, but announces vacancies as they become available. A separate application must be submitted for each vacancy announcement. For most professional positions, announcements are widely distributed and open for a minimum period of 30 days. Qualifications requirements and ranking criteria are stated on the vacancy announcement. The Library of Congress Recruitment and Placement Office is located in Room LM-107 of the James Madison Memorial Building, 101 Independence Ave., S.E., Washington, DC 20540, 202-287-5627.

How to Get a Federal Job: A Guide to Finding and Applying for a Job with the United States Government Anywhere in the Country by Krandall Kraus (New York: Facts on File, 1986) lists general procedures, for finding a job with the government. The *Federal Times* and the Sunday *Washington Post* sometimes list federal library openings.

Additional General and Specialized Job Sources

Affirmative Action Register, 8356 Olive Blvd., St. Louis, MO 63132: The goal is to "provide female, minority, handicapped, and veteran candidates with an opportunity to

learn of professional and managerial positions throughout the nation and to assist employers in implementing their Equal Opportunity Employment programs." Free distribution of monthly bulletin is made to leading businesses, industrial and academic institutions, and over 4,000 agencies which recruit qualified minorities and women, as well as to all known female, minority, and handicapped professional organizations, placement offices, newspapers, magazines, rehabilitation facilities, and over 8,000 federal, state, and local government employment units with a total readership in excess of 3.5 million (audited). Individual mail subscriptions are available for $15 per year. Librarian listings are in most every issue. Sent free to libraries on request.

The Chronicle of Higher Education (published 48 times a year—two-week breaks in August and December, 1255 23 St., N.W., Washington, DC 20037): Publishes an average of 59 library positions per week, approximately 94 percent administrative and 6 percent faculty.

Education Information Service, Box 662, Newton Lower Falls, MA 02162: Instant Alert service for $29 will send individual 12 notices of domestic or overseas openings on same day EIS learns of opening. Also publishes periodic list of educational openings including librarian openings worldwide. Library jobs are small portion of this publication. Cost $7.

National Faculty Exchange, Indiana University-Purdue University at Fort Wayne, 2101 Coliseum Blvd. East, Fort Wayne, IN 46805: The program brokers exchange of faculty and staff at U.S. institutions. Librarians interested in participation should ascertain if their academic institution is a member.

School Libraries: School librarians often find that the channels for locating positions in education are of more value than the usual library ones, e.g., contacting county or city school superintendent offices. The *School Library Media Quarterly* (11:63-65, Fall 1982) contains a discussion under the "Readers' Queries" column on recommended strategies for seeking a position in a school library media center. Primary sources include university placement offices that carry listings for a variety of school system jobs and *local* information networks among teachers and library media specialists. A list of commercial teacher agencies may be obtained from the *National Association of Teachers' Agencies*, c/o Spears Teacher Placement Service, 1100 N. W. Loop 410, Suite 219, San Antonio, TX 78213, 512-344-6189.

Overseas

Opportunities for employment in foreign countries are limited, and immigration policies of individual countries should be investigated. Employment for Americans is virtually limited to U.S. government libraries, libraries of U.S. firms doing worldwide business, and American schools abroad. Library journals from other countries will sometimes list vacancy notices. Some persons have obtained jobs by contacting foreign publishers or vendors directly. Non-U.S. government jobs usually call for foreign language fluency.

Council for International Exchange of Scholars (CIES), Suite 300, 11 Dupont Circle, N.W., Washington, DC 20036, 202-939-5401: Administers U.S. government Fulbright awards for university lecturing and advanced research abroad; usually six to eight awards per year are made to specialists in library science. In addition, many countries offer awards in any specialization of research or lecturing for which specialists in library and information science may apply. Open to U.S. citizens with university or college

teaching experience. Applications and information may be obtained, beginning in April each year directly from CIES.

Department of Defense, Dependents Schools, 2461 Eisenhower Ave., Alexandria, VA 22331-1100: Overall management and operational responsibilities for the education of dependent children of active duty U.S. military personnel and DOD civilians who are stationed in foreign areas. Also responsible for teacher recruitment. For complete application brochure, write to above address.

Education Information Service, Box 662, Newton Lower Falls, MA 02162: Provides a monthly update on education overseas openings including librarians, media center directors, and audiovisual personnel. Also includes such openings in U.S. school/college libraries.

Instant Alert, 15 Orchard St., Wellesley Hills, MA 02181: Notifies clients of library openings overseas and in U.S. school and college libraries. Applicants indicate their specific requirements, and as fast as the service learns of a position which meets these requirements, a personal notice is mailed.

International Association of School Librarianship, Box 1486, Kalamazoo, MI 49005: Informal contacts might be established through this group.

International Schools Services, Box 5910, Princeton, NJ 08543, 609-452-0990: Private, nonprofit organization founded in 1955 to serve American schools overseas, other than Department of Defense schools. These are American elementary and secondary schools enrolling children of business and diplomatic families living away from their homeland. ISS seeks to register men and women interested in working abroad in education who meet basic professional standards of training and experience. Specialists, guidance counselors, department heads, librarians, supervisors, and administrators normally will need one or more advanced degrees in the appropriate field as well as professional experience commensurate with positions sought. ISS also publishes a comprehensive directory of overseas schools and a monthly newsletter, *News Links*, for those interested in the intercultural educational community. Information regarding these publications and other services may be obtained by writing to the above address.

Library/Book Fellows Program, c/o Robert Doyle, American Library Association, 50 E. Huron St., Chicago, IL 60611, 312-944-6780: ALA administers a grant from the U.S. Information Agency for a program which places American library and book service professionals in institutions overseas for periods of several months to one year. Assignments vary depending on projects requested by host countries. Persons with foreign language skills, technical expertise, and international interests or expertise are sought for a database of potential fellows.

Peace Corps, P301, 806 Connecticut Ave., N.W., Washington, DC 20526: Needs several librarians with work experience in medicine, agriculture, automated systems, cataloging, and technical service to rural areas. For brochure and application form, call toll-free 800-424-8580, ext. 93, or write to the above address.

U.S. Information Agency (USIA), U.S. Information Service overseas (USIS), seeks librarians with MLS and at least four years' experience for regional library consultant positions. Candidates must have proven administrative ability and skills to coordinate the overseas USIS library program with other information functions of USIS in various cities worldwide. Some practical work experience in at least one of the major functional areas of adult library services is required. Additional relevant experience might include cooperative library program development, community outreach, public affairs, project management, or personnel training. USIA maintains more than 132 libraries in more than 80 countries, 1 million books, and 400 local library staff worldwide. Libraries pro-

vide reference service and publications about the United States for foreign audiences. U.S. citizenship is required. Benefits include overseas allowances and differentials where applicable, vacation leave, term life insurance, and medical and retirement programs. Send standard U.S. government application (SF-171) to Special Services Branch, USIA, 301 Fourth St., S.W., Washington, DC 20547.

Overseas — Exchange Programs

International Exchanges: Most exchanges are handled by direct negotiation between interested parties. A few libraries have established exchange programs for their own staff. In order to facilitate exchange arrangements, the *IFLA Journal* (issued February, May, August, and November) provides a listing of persons wishing to exchange positions *outside* their own country. All listings must include the following information: full name, address, present position, qualifications (with year of obtaining), language, abilities, and preferred country/city/library and type of position. Send to International Federation of Library Associations and Institutions (IFLA) Secretariat, Box 95312, 2509 CH, The Hague, Netherlands.

A *Librarian's Directory of Exchange Programs/Study Tours/Funding Sources and Job Opportunities Outside of the U.S.* by Diane Stine (1982) lists additional information on groups that sponsor exchanges and contacts for possible positions abroad. Order from OLPR/ALA, 50 E. Huron, Chicago, IL 60611 for $1.50 *prepaid*. Also available from OLPR or the ALA International Relations Committee is a two-page "Checklist for Preparing for an International Exchange," prepared by the ALA IRC/IRRT.

Additional clearinghouses for information on exchanges are the following:

American Libraries, Professional Exchange, 50 E. Huron St., Chicago, IL 60611, 312-944-6780, ext. 326: Classified section for persons who wish to place ad if interested in trading jobs and/or housing on a temporary basis. Rate: $5/line. Inquiries should be made to Beverly Goldberg, LEADS Editor.

American Library Association, Association of College and Research Libraries, ACRL Exchange Librarian Program, 50 E. Huron St., Chicago, IL 60611, 312-944-6780: Maintains file of American and foreign academic libraries that might be interested in providing opportunity for librarians to work on their staff in an exchange arrangement, as a temporary replacement, or nonsalaried visitor.

ACRL/NEC (New England Chapter), c/o Jeremy Slinn, O'Neill Library, Boston College, 140 Commonwealth Ave., Chestnut Hill, MA 02169, 617-552-4470: A clearinghouse has been established to promote exchanges, particularly with foreign libraries. A listing of institutions willing to host exchanges in New England and abroad is maintained, but no specific job openings or placement services are provided.

Bureau for International Staff Exchange, c/o A. Hillier, College of Librarianship Wales, Llanbadarn Fawr, Aberystwyth, Dyfed SY23 3AS, Wales, Great Britain: Assists in two-way exchanges for British librarians wishing to work abroad and for librarians from the United States, Canada, E.E.C. countries, the Commonwealth, and as many other countries as possible who wish to work in Britain.

Using Information Skills in Nonlibrary Settings

A great deal of interest has been shown in "alternative careers" or in using information skills in a variety of ways in nonlibrary settings. These jobs are not usually found

through the regular library placement sources, although many library schools are trying to generate such listings for their students and alumni. Job listings that do exist may not call specifically for "librarians" by that title, so ingenuity may be needed to search out jobs where information management skills are needed. Some librarians are working on a free-lance basis by offering services to businesses, alternative schools, community agencies, legislators, etc.; these opportunities are usually not found in advertisements but created by developing contacts and publicity over a period of time. A number of information-brokering business firms have developed from individual free-lance experiences. Small companies or other organizations often need one-time service for organizing files or collections, bibliographic research for special projects, indexing or abstracting, compilation of directories, and consulting services. Bibliographic networks and online database companies are using librarians as information managers, trainers, researchers, systems and database analysts, online services managers, etc. Jobs in this area are sometimes found in library network newsletters or data processing journals. Librarians can be found working in law firms as litigation case supervisors (organizing and analyzing records needed for specific legal cases); with publishers as sales representatives, marketing directors, editors, and computer services experts; with community agencies as adult education coordinators, volunteer administrators, grants writers, etc. A listing of job titles are found in a three-page handout on "Alternative Career Directions for Librarians," available from OLPR/ALA, 50 E. Huron St., Chicago, IL 60611.

Classifieds in *Publishers Weekly* and *The Wall Street Journal* (especially the Tuesday edition) may lead to information-related positions. One might also consider reading the Sunday classified ad sections in metropolitan newspapers in their entirety to locate descriptions calling for information skills but under a variety of job titles. Directories such as *Information Sources, Library Resources Market Place, Information Industry Market Place*, and *An International Directory of Information Products and Services* might provide leads of possible organizations in which information skills can be applied. "Information Resource(s) Management – IRM" in the *Annual Review of Information Science and Technology*, vol. 17, 1982 (pp. 228–266) provides a listing of associations and journals involved with IRM, as well as an extensive bibliography on the topic.

The Directory of Fee-Based Information Services is an annual publication which lists information brokers, free-lance librarians, independent information specialists, and institutions which provide services for a fee. Individuals do not need to pay to have listings; 1987 directory is available for $28.95 prepaid plus $2 postage and handling (foreign postage, $5) from Burwell Enterprises, 5106 F.M. 1960 West, Suite 349, Houston, TX 77069 (713-537-9051). It is supplemented by *The Journal of Fee-Based Information Services* ($35, foreign postage, $5). The journal includes articles by, for, and about individuals and companies in the fee-based information field, book reviews, calendar of upcoming events, issue-oriented articles, and new listings for companies which will appear in subsequent annual editions of the *Directory*.

The Independent Librarians Exchange Round Table is a unit within the American Library Association as a networking source for persons who own their own information businesses, are consultants, work for companies providing support services to libraries or providing other information services outside traditional library settings. Dues are $5 in addition to ALA dues.

A growing number of publications are addressing opportunities for librarians in the broader information arena. *Mind Your Own Business: A Guide for the Information Entrepreneur* by Alice Sizer Warner (New York: Neal-Schuman, 1987; $24.95; ISBN

155570-014-4) describes planning for and managing an information business, including marketing, sales, and record-keeping. *Careers in Other Fields for Librarians . . . Successful Strategies for Finding the Job* by Rhoda Garoogian and Andrew Garoogian is a 1985 publication from ALA (ISBN 0-8389-0431-9; 171 pages, $12.95). Chapters discuss bridging traditional and nontraditional employment; opportunities in business, government, education, and entrepreneurship; and employment techniques (where to look for jobs, résumés and letters, interviewing). Of particular interest is the chapter describing the translation process of traditional library tasks and skills with new types of job responsibilities. Scattered throughout are sample job descriptions in other fields where information functions are found. *New Options for Librarians: Finding a Job in a Related Field*, edited by Betty-Carol Sellen and Dimity S. Berkner (New York: Neal-Schuman, 1984; $19.95; ISBN 0-918212-73-1) covers how to prepare for and initiate a job search and examines career possibilities in such areas as publishing, public relations, abstracting and indexing, association work, contract service companies, information management, and more. Included also is a survey of librarians working in related fields and an annotated bibliography. A summary of the survey is found in "Librarians in Alternative Work Places" *Library Journal* 110 (February 15, 1985): 108–110.

Careers in Information, edited by Jane F. Spivack (White Plains, N.Y.: Knowledge Industries, 1982) includes chapters on the work of information specialists, entrepreneurship in the information industry, and information professionals in the federal government, as well as guidance on finding a job, placements and salaries for the broader information field as well as librarianship. The results of a 1980 study funded by the National Science Foundation and carried out by the University of Pittsburgh School of Library and Information Science and King Research, Inc. is found in *The Information Professional: Survey of an Emerging Field*, by Anthony Debons et al. published in 1981 by Marcel Dekker. "Atypical Careers and Innovative Services in Library and Information Science," edited by Walter C. Allen and Lawrence W.S. Auld is an entire issue of *Library Trends* [32 (Winter 1984): 251-358], focusing on new directions potentially available to librarians and some of the implications for the changing role of the information professional

Infomediary, an international, professional quarterly journal which began in 1985, focuses on information brokerage, consulting and the entrepreneurial aspects of the library and information field. It is edited by Susan Klement and published by Elsevier/North Holland. Volume 2 (January 1986–December 1987) is DFL 300 or $121, including postage, and can be obtained from Elsevier Science Publishers, Journal Information Center, 52 Vanderbilt Ave., New York, NY 10017.

Other publications include the following: *What Else You Can Do with a Library Degree*, edited by Betty-Carol Sellen, is published by Neal-Schuman Publishers and Gaylord Brothers, Inc. (Box 4901, Syracuse, NY 13221) for $14.95 plus 25¢ postage; *The Information Brokers: How to Start and Operate Your Own Fee-Based Service* by Kelly Warnken (New York: Bowker, 1981, $24.94); and *Abstracting & Indexing Career Guide*, available for $15 from National Federation of Abstracting & Indexing Services, 112 S. 16 St., Suite 1207, Philadelphia, PA 19102.

Temporary/Part-Time Positions

Working as a substitute librarian or in temporary positions may be considered to be an alternative career path as well as an interim step while looking for a regular job. This

type of work can provide valuable contacts and experience. A description of a corps of temporary library workers who tackle all types of jobs through a business called Pro Libra Associates, Inc. (106 Valley St., South Orange, NJ 07079, 201-762-0070) can be found in *American Libraries* [12 (October 1981): 540541]. Similar agencies that hire library workers for part-time or temporary jobs might be found in other geographic areas, such as C. Berger and Company, 130 W. Liberty Dr., Wheaton, IL 60187 (312-653-1115) in the Chicago area and Gossage Regan Associates, Inc., 15 W. 44 St., New York, NY 10036 (212-869-3348) in the New York area; Library Associates, 2600 Colorado Blvd., Suite 160, Santa Monica, CA 90404 (213-453-5583 or 5270); and Advanced Information Management, 444 Castro St., Suite 503, Mountain View, CA 94041 (415-965-7799) in California. Part-time jobs are not always advertised, but often found by canvassing local libraries and leaving applications.

Job Hunting in General

Wherever information needs to be organized and presented to patrons in an effective, efficient, and service-oriented fashion, the skills of professional librarians can be applied, whether or not they are in traditional library settings. However, it will take considerable investment of time, energy, imagination, and money on the part of an individual before a satisfying position is created or obtained, in a conventional library or another type of information service. Usually, no one method or source of job-hunting can be used alone. *Finding a Position: Strategies for Library School Graduates* by Robert F. Delzell gives useful information on job searching procedures, what to expect from the employer, and what the employer expects from you. This is available as Occasional Paper No. 153 (April 1982) for $3 plus 50¢ postage from Publications Office, University of Illinois at Urbana-Champaign, 249 Armory Bldg., 505 E. Armory St., Champaign, IL 61820 (ISSN 0276-1769).

Public and school library certification requirements often vary from state to state; contact the state library agency for such information in a particular state. Certification requirements are summarized in *Certification of Public Libraries in the U.S.*, 3rd ed. 1979, from the ALA Library Administration and Management Association ($3). A summary of school library/media certification requirements by state is found in *Requirements for Certification* edited by Elizabeth H. Woellner and published annually by the University of Chicago Press. "School Library Media Certification Requirements: 1984 Update" by Ann Y. Franklin also provides a compilation in *School Library Journal*, vol. 30, January 1984, pp. 21–34. State supervisors of school library media services may also be contacted for information on specific states; the *Bowker Annual* contains a list of these contact persons.

Civil service requirements either on a local, county, or state level often add another layer of procedures to the job search. Some civil service jurisdiction require written and/ or oral examinations; others assign a ranking based on a review of credentials. Jobs are usually filled from the top candidates on a qualified list of applicants. Since the exams are held only at certain time periods and a variety of jobs can be filled from a single list of applicants (e.g., all Librarian I positions regardless of type of function), it is important to check whether the library falls under civil service procedures.

If one wishes a position in a specific subject area or in a particular geographic location, remember those reference skills to ferret information from directories and other tools regarding local industries, schools, subject collections, etc. Directories such

as the *American Library Directory, Subject Collections, Directory of Special Libraries and Information Centers, Directory of Health Sciences Libraries*, as well as state directories or other special subject areas can provide a wealth of information for job seekers. Some students have pooled resources to hire a clipping service for a specific time period in order to get classified librarian ads for a particular geographic area.

For information on other job-hunting and personnel matters, request a checklist of personnel materials available from the ALA Office for Library Personnel Resources, 50 E. Huron St., Chicago, IL 60611.

Placements and Salaries, 1985: No Surprises

Carol L. Learmont

Associate Dean, School of Library Service, Columbia University

Stephen Van Houten

Head, Cataloging Department, Library of Health Sciences,
University of Illinois, Chicago

Fifty-eight of the 63 eligible schools responded to all or part of the questionnaire for this 35th annual report on placements and salaries of graduates of ALA-accredited library school programs. Two western, one midwestern, one southeastern, and one northeastern school did not participate.

In 1985, the average beginning-level salary was $19,753, based on 1,493 known full-time permanent professional salaries. Salaries for 1985 improved over 1984, and for the third year the increase in the average beginning salary was higher than the increase in the cost of living. The 1985 salaries increased at the rate of 5 percent compared to 6 percent in 1984 and 7 percent in 1983.

In 1985, the average (mean) beginning salary for women was $19,651, a 5 percent increase over 1984; for men, $20,221, a 6 percent increase. The median salaries were $19,000 for all graduates; for women, only $19,000; and for men, only $19,400.

For new graduates with relevant prior experience, the average beginning salary was $21,267, up from $20,277 in 1984; without experience, $18,529, up from $17,408 in 1984. Twenty-four women and 13 men reported receiving salaries of $30,000 or more.

Placement officers report a critical shortage of children's and young adult specialists in schools and public libraries nationwide. Retirements and the decline in library school enrollments have created a market for graduates. The usual need for people with backgrounds in science, math, and languages persists.

There were 272 temporary professional placements reported in 1985 compared with 257 in 1984 and 242 in 1983. There is some evidence that one- and two-year intern programs may be the reason for the increase in the numbers and better salaries in this category.

Canadian salaries, once again, are given in U.S. dollar equivalents. The category Other Information Specialists includes a wide variety of nontraditional positions.

Note: Adapted from *Library Journal*, October 15, 1986.

Table 1 / Status of 1985 Graduates, Spring 1986*

	No. of Graduates			Not in Library Positions			Empl. Not Known			Permanent Prof. Placements			Temp. Prof. Placements			Nonprof. Library Placements			Total in Library Positions		
	Women	Men	Total	Women	Men	Total	Women	Men	Total	Women	Men	Total	Women	Men	Total	Women	Men	Total	Women	Men	Total
United States	2295	571	3062	243	73	317	374	85	645	1464	359	1829	134	34	169	80	20	102	1678	413	2100
Northeast	841	203	1172	60	14	74	154	47	325	547	120	670	51	15	67	29	7	36	627	142	773
Southeast	417	106	575	50	18	68	50	9	111	285	75	360	19	4	23	13	0	13	317	79	396
Midwest	609	159	773	68	16	85	112	21	135	381	107	488	27	10	37	21	5	28	429	122	553
Southwest	222	46	278	32	9	41	25	2	34	148	28	179	8	1	9	9	6	15	165	35	203
West	206	57	264	33	16	49	33	6	40	103	29	132	29	4	33	8	2	10	140	35	175
Canada	326	69	422	39	11	51	51	9	84	128	34	163	90	13	103	18	2	21	236	49	287
All Schools	2621	640	3484	282	84	368	425	94	729	1592	393	1952	224	47	272	98	22	123	1914	462	2387

*Includes placements undifferentiated by sex.

312

Placements

First-professional degrees were awarded to 3,484 graduates by the 58 schools reporting in 1985 (Table 1). In 1984, the 57 reporting schools awarded 3,529 first-professional degrees; in 1983, the 60 reporting schools awarded 3,494 first-professional degrees. In 1985, the average number of graduates of schools reporting was 60; in 1984 it was 62; in 1983 it was 58.

Table 1 shows permanent and temporary professional placements, as well as non-professional library placements, and totals for the three. These are library or information-related positions. Table 1 also shows the number of graduates reported who were not in library positions or whose employment status was unknown at the beginning of April 1986. Of these, 13 percent were known not to be in library positions compared to 12 percent in 1984 and 15 percent in 1983. In April 1986, the whereabouts of 21 percent were unknown compared with 19 percent in April 1985 and 21 percent in April 1984.

Of the 1985 graduates, 69 percent were known to be employed either in professional or nonprofessional positions in libraries or information-related work, as were 69 percent of the 1984 graduates and 64 percent of the 1983 graduates. Of the 1985 graduates, 57 percent were known to be employed in permanent professional positions, compared with 58 percent of the 1984 graduates and 53 percent of the 1983 graduates.

Employment distribution of 1,920 of the 3,484 graduates (55 percent) is shown in Tables 4, 5, and 12. In all, 1,992 permanent full-time professional placements were reported and 272 temporary professional placements. Of the 1,992 people finding permanent professional positions, 568 (29 percent) found jobs before graduation and 560 (28 percent) reported actively searching for less than 90 days for professional employment after getting their degrees.

There were 111 people (6 percent) who looked for three or four months, 73 (4 percent) who looked from four to six months, and 62 (3 percent) who looked for more than six months. A total of 368 people (18 percent) went back to their previous positions. Nothing is known about the length of time it took the 250 others (12 percent) to find employment.

In 1985, 4 percent of the graduates were in nonprofessional library and related positions (Table 1). This placement category has represented 4 percent of the total placements since 1979, and within the category 82 percent are women and 18 percent are men.

There was a slight increase in the percentage of both public and school library placements and a slight decrease in the percentages of College and University and Other Library Agencies placements in 1985. The percentage of placements by type of library and other information specialties in 1985 appears in Table 5, showing 72 placements undifferentiated by type of library or related work. There were 69 in 1984.

Comparison of U.S. and Canadian placements appears in Table 6. Table 7, showing Special Placements, is self-explanatory and gives a rough picture of hiring activity in various specialties in 1985.

Demand and Supply

A total of 64,042 listings of open library positions were reported received at 50 schools. The lowest number reported received was 100; the highest, 4,200. The listings were for

Table 2 / Placements and Salaries of 1985 Graduates—Summary by Region*

	Placements	Salaries			Low Salary			High Salary			Average Salary			Median Salary		
		Women	Men	Total	Women	Men	Total	Women	Men	Total	Women	Men	Total	Women	Men	Total
United States	1829	1144	268	1417	7450	9675	7450	43632	42000	43632	19763	20388	19872	19000	19500	19000
Northeast	670	426	85	513	7800	10500	7800	35000	38076	38076	20144	20848	20254	19320	20000	19500
Southeast	360	209	59	268	12000	13080	12000	43632	42000	43632	19482	20456	19696	18817	19000	19000
Midwest	488	288	73	361	7450	9675	7450	35000	40000	40000	18669	19464	18830	18000	18900	18000
Southwest	179	134	28	165	13000	16000	13000	32000	38200	38200	20499	20776	20467	19500	19800	19500
West	132	87	23	110	12000	16800	12000	31000	28000	31000	21061	20974	21043	21000	21000	21000
Canada	163	54	22	76	10950	9148	9148	29828	26939	29828	17278	18192	17542	17155	18246	17885
All Schools	1992	1198	290	1493	7450	9148	7450	43632	42000	43632	19651	20221	19753	19000	19400	19000

* Includes placements undifferentiated by sex.

positions at all levels, and many were duplicated in several places. In 1984, 52 schools reported receiving 67,941 listings. The average number reported received in 1985 was 1,281 compared with 1,307 in 1984 and 1,078 in 1983.

Thirty-five schools reported increases in position listings in 1985 over 1984. In 1984, 37 schools reported increases. Increases reported in 1985 ranged from 5 percent to 100 percent. The median was 10 percent. Eleven schools reported no significant change from 1984. Seven schools reported a decrease ranging from 5 percent to 40 percent. Forty-seven placement officers reported no major difficulty in placing 1985 graduates, and only two reported major difficulty. Four placement officers indicated that they had more difficulty placing graduates in 1985 than in 1984, 23 reported having less difficulty, and 27 reported about the same level of difficulty in both years.

There is a very strong demand for specialists in children's and young adult services in both public and school libraries. There is also a very strong demand for specialists in technical services, especially in cataloging and for people with strong systems backgrounds. Other specialties in demand were medical, law, government documents, records management, and science.

Undergraduate majors that make graduates especially attractive to employers are, as has been true for several years, any of the sciences (including computer science), math, foreign languages, and engineering. Music and business were also mentioned.

Salaries

The salary statistics reported include only salaries that were reported as full-time annual salaries. Variables such as vacations and other fringe benefits, which may be part of the total compensation, are excluded. Salaries do not reflect differences in hours worked per week. Such information might provide more precise comparability, but such data are probably beyond the needs of most library schools and of the profession. In any case, the validity of this analysis rests on comparable statistics collected since 1951.

All of the 58 reporting schools supplied some salary data. Not all schools could provide all the information requested, nor could they supply it for all employed graduates. Data for graduates in irregular placements, such as those for graduates from abroad returning to posts in their homeland, appointments in religious orders or elsewhere where remuneration is in the form of some combination of salary plus living, and all salaries for part-time employment, were excluded as best the authors can tell.

The exclusions were added to the number of salaries not known or not reported. As a result, there is known salary information for 1,493 of the 1985 graduates (1,198 women, 290 men, and 5 undifferentiated by sex). This represents 75 percent of the known placements and 43 percent of all graduates reported. These response ratios have remained fairly constant for the past few years.

In 1984 there was salary information on 76 percent of the known placements, representing 44 percent of the number of graduates reported. Salary data as reported by the 58 schools are contained in Tables 2 and 3 and summarized in Table 8. Salary figures are in U.S. dollars.

Average (Mean) Salaries

The average salary for all 1985 graduates was $19,753, an increase of $962 (5 percent) over the 1984 average of $18,791. The average salary for women was $19,651 and the

Table 3 / Placements and Salaries of 1985 Graduates*

Schools	Placements	Salaries Women	Salaries Men	Salaries Total	Low Salary Women	Low Salary Men	Low Salary Total	High Salary Women	High Salary Men	High Salary Total	Average Salary Women	Average Salary Men	Average Salary Total	Median Salary Women	Median Salary Men	Median Salary Total
Alabama	27	23	4	27	16000	19500	16000	24000	39208	39208	20749	27227	21709	21000	23000	21000
Albany	33	28	3	31	13000	11600	11600	31172	19731	31172	19137	16777	18909	18500	19000	18500
Alberta	6	6	0	6	13359	0	13359	29828	0	29828	18695	0	18695	16060	0	16060
Arizona	29	23	6	29	16762	16000	16000	32000	38200	38200	20484	22208	20841	19500	19248	19500
Atlanta	11	8	3	11	15160	17160	15160	24490	21804	24490	19606	18771	19378	18168	17348	18168
Brigham Young	19	11	6	17	15060	16800	15060	25550	28000	28000	19595	20447	19896	19000	19000	19000
British Columbia	26	0	0	0	0	0	0	0	0	0	0	0	0	0	0	0
Buffalo	19	14	4	19	15700	17947	15700	26900	22520	26900	19412	19117	19170	18500	18000	18403
California (Berk.)	29	20	7	27	15852	17004	15852	30000	26760	30000	21518	22536	21782	20700	23052	21600
California (L.A.)	33	23	4	27	18000	17500	17500	27000	21252	27000	22461	20188	22125	22200	21000	21860
Case Western	14	0	0	0	0	0	0	0	0	0	0	0	0	0	0	0
Chicago	14	6	1	7	17000	20500	17000	24300	20500	24300	19883	20500	19971	19000	20500	20000
Clarion	31	18	6	24	7800	14400	7800	22085	20070	22085	17450	17326	17419	17000	16450	17000
Columbia	44	24	9	33	15000	17500	15000	30000	28000	30000	20485	21253	20694	20000	20593	20500
Dalhousie	12	4	1	5	14600	14381	14381	19126	14381	19126	16908	14381	16403	16759	14381	16759
Drexel	62	36	13	49	14660	10500	10500	32000	29500	32000	20577	21560	20838	19200	21000	20000
Emory	34	21	10	31	16500	14000	14000	26061	22080	26061	19534	18198	19103	18500	18000	18500
Emporia	13	5	1	6	16082	23000	16082	21000	23000	23000	17970	23000	18809	17950	23000	17950
Florida State	47	11	0	11	15656	0	15656	22000	0	22000	18399	0	18399	18750	0	18750
Hawaii	13	10	0	10	12000	0	12000	30924	0	30924	19996	0	19996	18000	0	18000
Illinois	53	33	14	47	13500	14500	13500	25500	29000	29000	18664	19907	19034	18000	19500	18000
Indiana	99	49	11	60	7450	15167	7450	25570	34000	34000	17621	18976	17869	17000	17000	17000
Iowa	30	20	6	26	13002	16500	13002	34900	22100	34900	18538	19017	18648	17500	18000	18000
Kent State	63	36	12	48	13500	13900	13500	35000	27600	35000	19597	19077	19467	17763	18000	18000
Kentucky	31	10	2	12	14950	25000	14950	26000	26000	26000	18132	25500	19360	17000	25000	17500
Long Island	29	13	2	15	12000	17500	12000	28600	22000	28600	20456	19750	20362	20000	17500	20000
Louisiana State	29	19	9	28	13104	16000	13104	27000	26300	27000	18942	21461	19752	18000	22000	19000

Maryland	57	35	5	40	14000	15000	14000	34200	25400	34200	19872	19280	19798	19000	18500	19000
McGill	36	1	0	1	16790	0	16790	16790	0	16790	16790	0	16790	16790	0	16790
Michigan	70	49	9	58	12000	15900	12000	34000	40000	40000	19267	22667	19794	18800	21800	18900
Missouri	22	20	2	22	12200	18000	12200	23900	21600	23900	18488	19800	18607	17700	18000	17700
Montreal	16	7	8	15	14615	9148	9148	18250	26939	26939	16162	19623	18008	16026	20440	16790
North Carolina	45	31	11	42	13300	18000	13300	28000	42000	42000	18830	22052	19674	18500	19000	18500
N. C. Central	13	9	4	13	14894	19000	14894	22590	20000	22590	18822	19750	19108	18500	20000	18500
North Texas State	48	34	9	44	15000	16000	15000	27500	26000	27500	19639	19013	19406	19200	17800	19000
Oklahoma	12	6	2	9	15500	16500	14000	24500	20000	25000	20199	18250	19077	18500	16500	18500
Peabody	30	16	3	19	13000	13500	13000	25000	17000	25000	17824	15500	17457	17500	16000	17000
Pittsburgh	42	14	7	21	11372	16500	11372	23000	31200	31200	18582	21680	19615	19350	20670	21000
Pratt	7	5	0	6	20000	0	20000	25000	0	25000	21500	0	21375	21000	0	20750
Queens	24	9	3	12	16500	20624	16500	30000	28000	30000	23111	23875	23302	21000	23000	21000
Rhode Island	43	26	5	31	12300	15000	12300	31000	29400	31000	18862	20420	19113	18000	20000	18000
Rosary	37	22	1	23	10300	18000	10300	26000	18000	26000	18339	18000	18324	17500	18000	17900
Rutgers	70	53	12	65	14300	15500	14300	35000	35100	35100	22957	22183	22814	21000	20500	21000
St. Johns	17	9	6	15	18000	20000	18000	29000	25500	29000	22711	22217	22513	22500	21800	22000
Simmons	141	107	5	112	13500	17384	13500	30000	19500	30000	18984	18083	18944	18000	17532	18000
S. California	36	29	5	34	12000	17000	12000	27000	19000	27000	20966	17800	20500	21000	18000	20000
S. Connecticut	29	22	2	24	14400	17400	14400	32300	38076	38076	21725	27738	22226	21000	17400	21000
South Florida	11	9	2	11	13000	17000	13000	25650	40000	40000	20769	28500	22175	23000	17000	23000
S. Mississippi	28	21	6	27	12000	13080	12000	43632	21804	43632	19652	16912	19044	18000	16000	18000
Syracuse	22	13	3	16	16000	15000	16000	35000	28000	35000	20731	21000	20781	19000	20000	19000
Tennessee	18	2	0	2	17800	0	17800	20000	0	20000	18900	0	18900	17800	0	17800
Texas	63	46	9	56	13000	16800	13000	30250	30000	30250	20386	21094	20484	19448	20000	19500
Texas Woman's	27	25	2	27	13500	24000	13500	31825	27000	31825	21961	25500	22223	21500	24000	22000
Toronto	25	19	3	22	10950	16571	10950	21718	19929	21718	17090	18249	17248	18250	18246	18250
Washington	38	23	6	29	12400	18000	12400	31000	23700	31000	20428	20203	20382	20280	18420	20280
Western Ontario	42	17	10	27	13140	13140	13140	19710	19710	19710	17563	17411	17506	17885	17885	17885
Wisconsin (Mad.)	27	18	8	26	15000	15420	15000	21800	20500	21800	17653	17396	17574	17365	17000	17200
Wisconsin (Milw.)	46	30	8	38	11000	9675	9675	29000	25000	29000	19235	18272	19033	19800	19000	19689

*Includes placements undifferentiated by sex.

Table 4 / Placements by Type of Library*

Schools	Public			Elementary & Secondary			College & Univ.			Special			Other			Total		
	Women	Men	Total	Women	Men	Total	Women	Men	Total	Women	Men	Total	Women	Men	Total	Women	Men	Total
Alabama	7	0	7	8	2	10	4	1	5	4	1	5	0	0	0	23	4	27
Albany	7	0	7	7	1	8	8	0	8	4	1	5	4	1	5	30	3	33
Alberta	3	0	3	1	0	1	0	0	0	2	0	2	0	0	0	6	0	6
Arizona	8	1	9	2	0	2	8	4	12	5	1	6	0	0	0	23	6	29
Atlanta	3	1	4	0	0	0	3	1	4	2	1	3	0	0	0	8	3	11
Brigham Young	5	1	6	1	1	2	2	2	4	2	2	4	2	0	2	13	6	19
British Columbia	10	1	11	1	0	1	7	2	9	4	0	4	0	0	0	23	3	26
Buffalo	3	0	3	5	2	7	0	0	0	5	2	7	1	0	1	14	4	19
California (Berk.)	10	1	11	0	0	0	8	3	11	4	3	7	0	0	0	22	7	29
California (L.A.)	9	1	10	0	1	1	3	2	5	11	3	14	3	0	3	27	6	33
Case Western	3	0	3	0	0	0	3	1	4	3	4	7	0	0	0	9	5	14
Chicago	0	1	1	1	0	1	4	1	5	5	0	5	1	1	2	11	3	14
Clarion	13	4	17	5	0	5	3	5	8	1	0	1	0	0	0	22	9	31
Columbia	9	4	13	1	1	2	11	5	16	5	2	7	5	1	6	31	13	44
Dalhousie	2	0	2	2	0	2	3	1	4	4	0	4	0	0	0	11	1	12
Drexel	8	4	12	6	1	7	6	3	9	7	3	10	12	9	21	45	17	62
Emory	8	4	12	2	0	2	8	5	13	3	1	4	3	0	3	24	10	34
Emporia	1	0	1	7	1	8	1	0	1	2	0	2	0	1	1	11	2	13
Florida State	11	1	12	12	1	13	8	3	11	11	0	11	0	0	0	42	5	47
Hawaii	1	0	1	2	1	3	2	1	3	5	0	5	1	0	1	11	2	13
Illinois	11	5	16	2	1	3	16	7	23	10	1	11	0	0	0	39	14	53
Indiana	33	8	41	4	0	4	25	11	36	11	4	15	1	2	3	74	25	99
Iowa	6	3	9	4	0	4	9	4	13	4	0	4	0	0	0	23	7	30
Kent State	23	5	28	6	0	6	5	7	12	13	2	15	2	0	2	49	14	63
Kentucky	5	1	6	6	0	6	7	3	10	5	2	7	2	0	2	25	6	31
Long Island	8	3	11	4	1	5	5	0	5	6	2	8	0	0	0	23	6	29
Louisiana State	4	3	7	6	0	6	5	2	7	3	2	5	2	2	4	20	9	29

School																		
Maryland	12	2	14	5	0	5	5	3	8	28	2	30	0	0	0	50	7	57
McGill	9	1	10	1	0	1	8	0	8	11	3	14	2	0	2	31	5	36
Michigan	19	2	21	5	1	5	20	4	24	9	2	11	6	1	7	60	10	70
Missouri	2	0	2	7	0	7	5	1	6	4	1	5	1	0	1	20	2	22
Montreal	2	0	2	1	0	1	1	1	2	1	7	8	0	0	0	7	9	16
North Carolina	4	2	6	7	0	7	14	11	25	4	0	4	3	0	3	32	13	45
North Carolina Central	5	1	6	2	1	3	2	2	4	0	0	0	0	0	0	9	4	13
North Texas State	10	3	13	13	0	13	9	5	15	5	1	6	1	0	1	38	9	48
Oklahoma	0	1	1	6	0	6	2	1	3	0	1	1	1	0	1	9	2	12
Peabody	6	0	6	4	1	5	10	3	13	4	0	4	0	2	2	26	4	30
Pittsburgh	10	3	13	2	2	4	5	3	8	9	3	12	3	0	3	29	13	42
Pratt	2	0	3	0	0	0	0	0	0	2	1	3	1	0	1	5	1	7
Queens	6	3	9	2	0	2	2	1	3	6	2	8	1	1	1	18	6	24
Rhode Island	12	2	14	7	1	9	6	1	7	5	3	8	0	0	0	34	8	43
Rosary	11	2	13	7	0	8	5	0	5	6	2	8	0	1	3	32	5	37
Rutgers	19	5	24	6	1	6	4	6	10	23	1	25	3	0	0	57	13	70
St. Johns	3	0	4	1	1	2	2	3	5	4	1	5	0	0	0	11	6	17
Simmons	24	0	24	15	0	15	46	6	52	37	1	38	7	0	7	134	7	141
South Carolina	6	4	10	19	0	19	4	0	4	2	1	3	0	0	0	31	5	36
Southern Connecticut	8	0	8	11	1	11	2	1	3	4	0	4	0	0	0	27	2	29
South Florida	2	0	2	4	0	4	3	2	3	0	2	2	0	0	0	9	2	11
Southern Mississippi	3	3	6	11	0	11	4	2	6	2	0	2	4	0	4	22	6	28
Syracuse	2	1	3	3	1	4	7	2	9	1	2	1	1	0	1	17	5	22
Tennessee	3	1	4	2	0	2	4	1	5	4	0	6	4	1	5	14	4	18
Texas	15	2	18	10	0	10	13	3	16	9	3	12	0	0	0	53	9	63
Texas Woman's	8	1	9	12	1	12	3	0	3	3	0	3	1	0	1	25	4	27
Toronto	6	2	8	0	0	0	1	0	1	11	1	12	0	0	3	21	4	25
Washington	15	3	18	2	0	2	4	3	7	7	1	8	3	1	3	30	8	38
Western Ontario	11	3	14	5	0	5	4	2	6	8	2	10	2	3	4	29	12	42
Wisconsin (Madison)	8	1	9	4	0	4	5	6	11	1	0	1	1	2	2	18	9	27
Wisconsin (Milwaukee)	8	3	11	10	0	10	8	4	12	8	1	9	1	2	3	35	11	46
Total	**462**	**101**	**565**	**275**	**23**	**300**	**370**	**149**	**522**	**341**	**82**	**423**	**83**	**27**	**110**	**1592**	**393**	**1992**

*Includes placements undifferentiated by sex or type of library.

319

Table 5 / Placements by Type of Library, 1951–1985

Year	Public	School	College & Universities	Other Library Agencies*	Total
1951-1955**	2076 (33%)	1424 (23%)	1774 (28%)	1000 (16%)	6264
1956-1960**	2057 (33)	1287 (20)	1878 (30)	1105 (17)	6327
1961-1965	2876 (30)	1979 (20)	3167 (33)	1600 (17)	9622
1966-1970	4773 (28)	3969 (23)	5834 (34)	2456 (15)	17032
1971	999 (29)	924 (26)	1067 (30)	513 (15)	3503
1972	1117 (30)	987 (26)	1073 (29)	574 (15)	3751
1973	1180 (31)	969 (25)	1017 (26)	712 (18)	3878
1974	1132 (31)	893 (24)	952 (26)	691 (19)	3668
1975	994 (30)	813 (24)	847 (25)	714 (21)	3368
1976	764 (27.1)	655 (23.2)	741 (26.3)	657 (23.2)	2817
1977	846 (28.4)	673 (22.6)	771 (25.9)	687 (23.1)	2977
1978	779 (26.1)	590 (19.8)	819 (27.4)	798 (26.7)	2986
1979	778 (27.4)	508 (17.9)	716 (25.3)	835 (29.4)	2837
1980	659 (27.1)	473 (19.5)	610 (25.1)	687 (28.3)	2429
1981	642 (27.3)	451 (19.2)	556 (23.6)	704 (29.9)	2353
1982	588 (28.5)	358 (17.4)	505 (24.5)	612 (29.7)	2063
1983	501 (28.0)	308 (17.3)	424 (23.8)	552 (30.9)	1785
1984	548 (27.9)	284 (14.4)	551 (28.0)	583 (29.7)	1966
1985	565 (29.4)	300 (15.6)	522 (27.2)	533 (27.8)	1920

*From 1951 through 1966 these tabulations were for "special and other placements" in all kinds of libraries. From 1967 to 1979 these figures include only placements in library agencies that do not clearly belong to one of the other three groups; in the 1980 through 1985 reports these figures include the sum of responses to placements in special libraries and in other information specialties.

**Figures for individual years are reported in preceding articles in this series.

Table 6 / U.S. and Canadian Placements Compared
(Percents may not add to 100 because of rounding)

	Placements	Public Libraries	School Libraries	College & University Libraries	Special Libraries	Other Info. Specialties
All Schools*	1920	565 (29.4)	300 (15.6)	522 (27.2)	423 (22.0)	110 (5.7)
Women	1531	462 (30.2)	275 (18.0)	370 (24.2)	341 (22.3)	83 (5.4)
Men	382	101 (26.4)	23 (6.0)	149 (39.0)	82 (21.5)	27 (7.1)
U.S. Schools*	1764	515 (29.2)	289 (16.4)	492 (27.9)	369 (20.9)	99 (5.6)
Women	1405	419 (29.8)	265 (18.9)	346 (24.6)	300 (21.4)	75 (5.3)
Men	353	94 (26.6)	23 (6.5)	143 (40.5)	69 (19.5)	24 (6.8)
Canadian Schools*	156	50 (32.0)	11 (7.1)	30 (19.2)	54 (34.6)	11 (7.1)
Women	126	43 (34.1)	10 (7.9)	24 (19.0)	41 (32.5)	8 (6.3)
Men	29	7 (24.1)	0 (0.0)	6 (20.7)	13 (44.8)	3 (10.3)

*Includes placements undifferentiated by sex.

average for men was $20,221, a difference of $570 (Table 8). Table 9 shows the annual changes in average salaries since 1967, and includes a beginning salary index figure that may be compared with the Annual Cost of Living (COL) Index Report issued by the government.

The COL Index for 1985 was 322.2, an increase of 11.1 points over the 1984 figure of 311.1, a gain of 3.6 percent. The comparable increase in the beginning salary index was 13 points, only 1.9 points above the increase in the cost of living.

Salaries in 1985 in the category of average salaries for women ranged from a low of $7,450 to a high of $43,632, a difference of $36,182; for men, the range was $9,148 to $42,000, a $32,852 difference. In the 50 schools that reported average salaries for both

Table 7 / Special Placements*

	Women	Men	Total
Government jurisdictions (U.S. and Canada)			
State and provincial libraries	54	9	63
Other government agencies (except USVA hospitals)	36	8	44
National libraries	14	14	28
Armed Services libraries (domestic)	5	5	10
Overseas agencies (incl. Armed Services)	0	0	0
Library Science			
Advanced study	12	2	14
Teaching	8	3	11
Other			
Children's services (public libraries)	106	7	113
Children's services (school libraries)	107	5	112
Business, finance, industrial, corporate	84	16	100
Law	56	17	73
Medicine (incl. nursing schools)	46	7	53
Systems analysis; automation	28	24	52
Science and technology	30	15	45
Youth services (public libraries)	39	6	45
Audiovisual and media centers	39	4	43
Youth services (school libraries)	37	3	40
Information services (nonlibrary)	26	10	36
Social sciences	32	3	35
Rare books, manuscripts, archives	20	12	32
Research and development	22	4	26
Databases (publishing, servicing)	20	4	24
Hospitals (incl. USVA hospitals)	13	8	21
Art and museum	12	7	19
Communications industry (advertising, newspaper, etc.)	16	3	19
Free-lance	15	3	18
Historical agencies	14	4	18
Religion (seminaries, theological schools)	9	8	17
Government documents	8	6	14
Indexing	13	1	14
Bibliographic instruction	11	2	13
Theater, motion pictures, dance, music	8	5	13
Outreach activities and services	6	5	11
Records management	9	2	11
Technical writing	9	2	11
Networks and consortia	8	1	9
Architecture	4	2	6
Correctional institutions	4	2	6
Pharmaceutical	5	1	6
Professional associations	6	0	6
Bookstore	4	1	5
Maps	4	1	5
Genealogical	3	1	4
Library services to the handicapped	4	0	4
Children's services (other)	3	0	3
International agencies	1	1	2
International relations (incl. area studies)	1	1	2
Public affairs information specialist	2	0	2
Conservation/Preservation	1	0	1
Spanish-speaking centers	1	0	1
Total Special Placements	**1015**	**245**	**1260**

*Includes special placements in all types of libraries.

men and women, the women's average salary was higher in 22 schools; the men's average salary was higher in 28 schools. In 1984, the women's average salary was higher in 24 schools, and the men's in 31 schools.

Table 12 summarizes the salaries received in the different types of libraries and other information specialties. The average salary is higher for men (the difference ranging from $58 to $1,866) in all five categories.

Table 8 / Salary Data Summarized

	Women	Men	Total
Average (Mean) Salary	$19651	$20221	$19753
Median Salary	19000	19400	19000
Individual Salary Range	7450–43632	9148–42000	7450–43632

Table 9 / Average Salary Index: Starting Library Positions, 1967–1985

Year	Library Schools	Fifth-Year Graduates	Average Beginning Salary	Increase in Average	Beginning Index
1967	40	4030	$7305	—	—
1968	42	4625	7650	$355	105
1969	45	4970	8161	501	112
1970	48	5569	8611	450	118
1971	47	5670	8846	235	121
1972	48	6079	9248	402	127
1973	53	6336	9423	175	129
1974	52	6370	10000	617	137
1975	51	6010	10594	554	145
1976	53	5415	11149	555	153
1977	53	5467	11894	745	163
1978	62	5442	12527	633	171
1979	61	5139	13127	600	180
1980	63	4396	14223	1096	195
1981	65	4512	15633	1410	214
1982	64	4050	16583	950	227
1983	60	3494	17705	1122	242
1984	57	3529	18791	1086	257
1985	58	3484	19753	962	270

Median Salaries

The median salary for all graduates in 1985 was $19,000, an increase of $1,000 over the 1984 median of $18,000. The median for women was $19,000; for men, $19,400. Of the 50 schools reporting on both men and women, the median salary for women was higher in 22 schools; for men in 25; and the same in three.

Salary Ranges

A wide range between high and low individual salaries continued in 1985. Table 13 shows the effects of experience and of no experience on salary levels. For the purposes of the survey, prior experience, if known, consisted of work of a professional and/or subject nature of a year or more. In 1985, the range (Table 8) was from a low of $7,450 to a high of $43,632, a difference of $36,182. The lowest salary reported was in a college library and the highest in a school library.

In 1985, the range of high salaries reported was from $14,381 to $43,632, a difference of $29,251. The high range in 1984 was from $17,300 to $48,500, a difference of $31,200. In 1985, 25 schools (also 25 schools in 1984) showed high salaries of $30,000 or more.

In this category, 20 women and 10 men reported salaries over $30,000. The median

Table 10 / High Salaries by Type of Library

	Public			School			College & Univ.			Special			Other		
	Women	Men	Total	Women	Men	Total	Women	Men	Total	Women	Men	Total	Women	Men	Total
$10,000				1		1									
11,000														1	1
12,000															
13,000															
14,000				1		1	1		1	1	1	1			
15,000		2	2	1	1	2	1		1	1	1	2			
16,000	3	3	6	1		1	3	1	4	1	1	2	2		2
17,000	2	4	6				2	4	6	2	2	4		1	1
18,000	6	4	10	1		1	8	2	10	2	4	6	3		3
19,000	4	2	6	4	1	5	6	2	8	1	5	6	2	2	4
20,000	3	12	15	2	3	5	10	5	15	4		4	2	1	3
21,000	7	4	11	2	1	3	1	6	7	6	7	13	1		1
22,000	5	2	7	4	1	5	5	2	7	3	2	5	1	1	2
23,000	9	1	10	1	1	2	3	2	5	3		3	4	2	6
24,000	4		4	4	1	5	3	1	4	5	1	6	4	1	5
25,000	7	1	8	3		3	4	2	6	8	3	11		1	1
26,000	1		1	3		3	1	1	2	3	3	6	2		2
27,000		1	1	2	1	3	1	1	2	2	1	3			
28,000	1	1	2	1	1	2	1		1	1	1	2	1		1
29,000				3	1	4		1	1	2		2		1	1
30,000				3		3	1	1	2	1		1	1	1	2
31,000				2		2	1		1	1		1		1	1
32,000				3		3							1		1
33,000															
34,000				2		2	1		1	1		1			
35,000				1		1				2	1	3	2		2
36,000															
37,000															
38,000					1	1		1	1						
39,000								1	1						
40,000								1	1		1	1			
41,000															
42,000								1	1						
43,000				1		1									

high salary for all graduates was $29,000 (up from $28,000 in 1984); for women, $27,000 (down from $27,057 in 1984); for men, $25,450 (up from $24,000 in 1984). Distribution of high salaries by type of libraries is shown in Table 10, and a comparison is shown in Table 12.

In 1985, the category Special Libraries accounted for 27 percent of the 48 highest salaries (29 percent in 1984) and the category Other Information Specialties accounted for 13 percent (13 percent in 1984). School libraries accounted for 40 percent (36 percent in 1984); academic libraries accounted for 17 percent (14 percent in 1984); and public libraries had a 4 percent share (9 percent in 1984).

The positions were scattered geographically and included 23 states, the District of Columbia, and two provinces. California accounted for six positions, New York for three, Texas for four, and the rest for one or two each.

The lowest reported beginning-level salaries from each school ranged from $7,450 to $18,000. The 1984 range was $7,315 to $17,300. The median low salary was $13,500 ($13,860 in 1984) for all graduates. Fifty schools reported low salaries for both men and

women; of these, 40 reported that the lowest low salary was received by a woman; nine reported the lowest low salary was received by a man; one school reported that both received the same.

Public libraries accounted for 35 percent of the 54 lowest salaries reported (39 percent in 1984); academic libraries accounted for 31 percent (27 percent in 1984); special libraries accounted for 17 percent (16 percent in 1984); school libraries for 9 percent (16 percent in 1984); and Other Information Specialties for 7 percent (2 percent in 1984).

Thirty-one states, three provinces, Taiwan, and Israel were represented. New York led with six placements, followed by North Carolina with four, Pennsylvania and Texas with three each, and the rest with one or two.

Distribution of low salaries is shown in Tables 11 and 12.

Next Year

Placement officers at 25 schools predict little or no change in the number of job vacancy listings for the class of 1986. Twenty officers think that there will be increases ranging from 4 percent to 34 percent; six predict decreases ranging from 8 percent to 59 percent. Placement officers at 16 schools expect the same difficulty placing 1986 graduates as placing 1985 graduates; five expect more difficulty; and ten expect less.

Salaries for 1986 will be stronger according to 32 placement officers whose estimates ranged from $300 to over $5,000. Most estimates were in the $1,500–$2,500 range. Eighteen officers do not expect any significant increase.

Table 11 / Low Salaries by Type of Library

	Public			School			College & Univ.			Special			Other		
	Women	Men	Total	Women	Men	Total	Women	Men	Total	Women	Men	Total	Women	Men	Total
$ 7,000							2		2						
8,000															
9,000	1		1				1		1		1	1			
10,000				1	1	2							1		1
11,000	1		1							2		2		1	1
12,000	1		1	2		2	3		3	3		3			
13,000	11	3	14	1		1	4	2	6	1		1			
14,000	8		8	4		4	5	3	8	2	1	3	1		1
15,000	11	4	15	5	1	6	10	2	12	9	2	11			
16,000	8	7	15	6		6	14	5	19	6	3	9	1		1
17,000	2	6	8	6	1	7	5	9	14	7	5	12	3	1	4
18,000	3	3	6	7		7	6	7	13	8	4	12	3		3
19,000	1	4	5	4	1	5	2	1	3	6	6	12	5	2	7
20,000	1	5	6	2	3	5		1	1	2		2	3	2	5
21,000	2	3	5		1	1	3		3	4	6	10	3		3
22,000	1		1	1		1	1		1				2	1	3
23,000		1	1	2		2	1		1	1		1	1	2	3
24,000					1	1							1	1	2
25,000				4		4				2		2		1	1
26,000										1			1		1
27,000		1	1												
28,000	1		1		1	1				2		2			
29,000				2	1	3									
30,000													1	1	2
31,000														1	1

Table 12 / Comparison of Salaries by Type of Library

	Placements	Salaries Known			Low Salary			High Salary			Average Salary			Median Salary		
		Women	Men	Total	Women	Men	Total	Women	Men	Total	Women	Men	Total	Women	Men	Total
Public Libraries																
United States	515	341	73	416	9282	13080	9282	28537	28000	28537	18573	18649	18593	18300	18084	18300
Northeast	176	119	22	142	11372	15000	11372	25000	28000	28000	18532	19011	18622	18000	18084	18000
Southeast	88	51	18	69	12000	13080	12000	25000	25000	25000	18291	18011	18218	18168	17400	18000
Midwest	155	95	19	114	9282	13900	9282	25368	20900	25368	17581	17667	17595	17000	17500	17150
Southwest	50	40	8	49	13500	17800	13500	25000	27000	27000	19104	20246	19298	19300	19800	19400
West	46	36	6	42	15226	18000	15226	28537	23052	28537	21132	20221	21002	21000	19000	21000
Canada	50	20	4	24	13140	13140	13140	18980	18246	18980	16854	16461	16789	17148	16571	17148
All Schools	565	361	77	440	9282	13080	9282	28537	28000	28537	18477	18535	18495	18168	18000	18084
School Libraries																
United States	289	218	16	234	10300	10500	10300	43632	38076	43632	21499	22567	21572	21000	21000	21000
Northeast	92	64	10	74	12300	10500	10500	34200	38076	38076	20870	22297	21063	19250	20000	19731
Southeast	88	67	3	70	13000	20000	13000	43632	27200	43632	21346	23400	21434	21000	23000	21000
Midwest	58	47	1	48	10300	15900	10300	35000	15900	35000	20778	15900	20676	19689	15900	19150
Southwest	43	37	1	38	16500	24000	16500	32000	24000	32000	23323	24000	23341	22250	24000	22250
West	8	3	1	4	25000	28000	25000	30924	28000	30924	27158	28000	27369	25550	28000	25550
Canada	11	5	0	5	15330	0	15330	29828	0	29828	20741	0	20741	19710	0	19710
All Schools	300	223	16	239	10300	10500	10300	43632	38076	43632	21482	22567	21555	20500	21000	21000
College/Univ. Libraries																
United States	492	280	111	394	7450	9675	7450	31000	42000	42000	18311	20267	18837	18000	19000	18000
Northeast	150	86	27	114	7800	14400	7800	28000	30000	30000	18479	19740	18756	18000	18500	18000
Southeast	110	56	25	81	13000	13500	13000	27000	42000	42000	17991	20710	18830	18000	18500	18000
Midwest	153	88	39	127	7450	9675	7450	25000	40000	40000	17662	20440	18515	17500	20000	18000
Southwest	49	32	12	46	13000	16000	13000	31000	38200	38200	18642	19837	18774	18000	17800	18000
West	30	18	8	26	15060	17000	15060	30000	26760	30000	21083	20470	20894	20700	19000	20700
Canada	30	5	4	9	14965	13140	13140	17155	21900	21900	16279	16644	16441	16790	14381	16790
All Schools	522	285	115	403	7450	9675	7450	31000	42000	42000	18275	20141	18783	18000	19000	18000
Special Libraries																
United States	369	239	48	287	11000	14000	11000	35000	40000	40000	20832	21452	20936	20000	21000	20400
Northeast	172	119	15	134	14500	15000	14500	35000	35100	35100	21457	22272	21549	20900	19500	20891
Southeast	50	28	10	38	12000	14000	12000	26000	40000	40000	19411	23160	20398	19205	21804	20000
Midwest	83	48	10	58	11000	15413	11000	35000	21804	35000	20408	19069	20177	19000	18000	19000
Southwest	27	20	6	26	15000	16500	15000	27300	26000	27300	21092	21284	21136	20500	20804	20500
West	37	24	7	31	12000	16800	12000	31000	25440	31000	20025	20803	20201	20000	21000	20400

Table 12 / Comparison of Salaries by Type of Library (cont.)

	Placements	Salaries Known			Low Salary			High Salary			Average Salary			Median Salary		
		Women	Men	Total	Women	Men	Total	Women	Men	Total	Women	Men	Total	Women	Men	Total
Canada	54	20	9	29	11680	9143	9148	21718	22630	22630	17547	18205	17752	17885	18615	18250
All Schools	423	259	57	316	11000	9148	9148	35000	40000	40000	20579	20939	20644	20000	20440	20000
Other Libraries																
United States	99	57	17	74	16000	11600	11600	35000	31200	35000	22674	23266	22810	22000	23000	22500
Northeast	54	33	10	43	18000	11600	11600	35000	31200	35000	23886	23582	23816	23000	23000	23000
Southeast	11	6	1	7	17824	24500	17824	26000	24500	26000	21557	24500	21977	20400	24500	22500
Midwest	19	8	4	12	16000	17000	16000	24500	23000	24500	20225	20375	20275	19000	19000	19000
Southwest	6	4	1	5	18000	30000	17000	24000	30000	30000	20750	23700	22600	21000	30000	21000
West	9	6	1	7	18000	23700	18000	26000	23700	26000	21667	23700	21957	21000	23700	22000
Canada	11	4	3	7	10950	19710	10950	18250	19710	19710	14969	19710	17001	14615	19710	18250
All Schools	110	61	20	81	10950	11600	10950	35000	31200	35000	22168	22733	22308	21000	22500	22000

Table 13 / Effects of Experience on Salaries

	Salaries without Previous Experience (43 Schools)			Salaries with Previous Experience (52 Schools)		
	Women	Men	Total	Women	Men	Total
Number of Positions	331	89	422	473	124	600
Range of Low Salaries	$9282–22500	$9675–22520	$9282–21800	$7800–30000	$9148–40000	$7800–26000
Mean (Average)	15523	17007	15147	16851	19858	16596
Median	20500	13900	13104	12200	20000	12500
Range of High Salaries	$13000–30924	$16000–26000	$13000–30924	$16790–35000	$14381–42000	$17155–42000
Mean (Average)	22041	20528	22333	26557	26535	28317
Median	20500	21804	20000	23900	40000	40000
Range of Average Salaries	$13000–17543	$13405–18500	$13000–15992	$16060–20028	$14381–21675	$16217–20357
Mean (Average)	18525	18636	18529	21009	22314	21267
Median	20500	17481	16813	18671	28000	21509

The responses to a question about the perception of types of libraries that are notably increasing or decreasing in the number of positions are summarized as follows:

Type of Placement	No. of Schools Responding	
	Increase	Decrease
Public libraries	10	1
School libraries	19	3
Academic libraries	11	2
Special libraries	14	7
Other information specialties	0	1

Retirements are a major factor contributing to an increase in need, especially for children's and young adult services people in school and public libraries. This is now a major crisis. The improved economy in the United States is frequently cited as a factor in increased hiring. It is also clear that declining enrollments in library schools are now reflected in demand for trained people. Comments on the future reflect changes in regional economies. Canadian schools had no special predictions this year.

In 1985, 55 foreign students from 27 countries were reported among the graduates.

Accredited Library Schools

This list of graduate schools accredited by the American Library Association was issued in October 1986. A list of more than 300 institutions offering both accredited and non-accredited programs in librarianship appears in the thirty-ninth edition of the *American Library Directory* (R. R. Bowker, 1986).

Northeast: Conn., D.C., Mass., Md., N.J., N.Y., Pa., R.I.

Catholic University of America, School of Lib. and Info. Science, Washington, DC 20064. Raymond F. Vondran, Dean. 202-635-5085.

Clarion University, College of Lib. Science, Clarion, PA 16214. Ruth J. Person, Dean. 814-226-2271.

Columbia University, School of Lib. Service, New York, NY 10027. Robert Wedgeworth, Dean. 212-280-2292.

Drexel University, College of Info. Studies, Philadelphia, PA 19104. Guy Garrison, Dean. 215-895-2474.

Long Island University, C. W. Post Center, Palmer School of Lib. and Info. Science, Greenvale, NY 11548. Lucienne G. Maillet, Dean. 516-299-2855, 2856.

Pratt Institute, Grad. School of Lib. and Info. Science, Brooklyn, NY 11205. Nasser Sharify, Dean. 718-636-3702.

Queens College, City University of New York, Grad. School of Lib. and Info. Studies, Flushing, NY 11367. Thomas T. Surprenant, Dir. 718-520-7194.

Rutgers University, School of Communication, Info., and Lib. Studies, New Brunswick, NJ 08903. Patricia G. Reeling, Chpn. 201-932-7917.

St. John's University, Div. of Lib. and Info. Science, Jamaica, NY 11439. Mildred Lowe, Dir. 718-990-6200.

Simmons College, Grad. School of Lib.

and Info. Science, Boston, MA 02115. Robert D. Stueart, Dean. 617-738-2225.

Southern Connecticut State University, School of Lib. Science. and Instructional Technology, New Haven, CT 06515. Emanuel T. Prostano, Dean. 203-397-4532.

State University of New York at Albany, School of Info. Science and Policy, Albany, NY 12222. Richard S. Halsey, Dean. 518-442-5115.

State University of New York at Buffalo, School of Info. and Lib. Studies, Buffalo, NY 14260. George S. Bobinski, Dean. 716-636-2412.

Syracuse University, School of Info. Studies, Syracuse, NY 13244-2340. Jeffrey Katzer, Interim Dean. 315-423-2736.

University of Maryland, College of Lib. and Info. Services, College Park, MD 20742. Claude E. Walston, Dean. 301-454-5441.

University of Pittsburgh, School of Lib. and Info. Science, Pittsburgh, PA. 15260. Toni Carbo Bearman, Dean. 412-624-5230.

Southeast: Ala., Fla., Ga., Ky., La., Miss., N.C., S.C., Tenn.

Atlanta University, School of Lib. and Info. Studies, Atlanta, GA 30314. Lorene B. Brown, Dean. 404-681-0251, ext. 230.

Emory University, Div. of Lib. and Info. Management, Atlanta, GA 30322. A. Venable Lawson, Dir. 404-727-6840.

Florida State University, School of Lib. and Info. Studies, Tallahassee, FL 32306. F. William Summers, Dean. 904-644-5775.

Louisiana State University, School of Lib. and Info. Science, Baton Rouge, LA 70803. Kathleen M. Heim, Dean. 504-388-3158.

North Carolina Central University, School of Lib. and Info. Science, Durham, NC 27707. Benjamin F. Speller, Dean. 919-683-6485.

University of Alabama, Grad. School of Lib. Service, Tuscaloosa, AL 35487. James D. Ramer, Dean. 205-348-4610.

University of Kentucky, College of Lib. and Info. Science, Lexington, KY 40506-0027. Timothy W. Sineath, Dean. 606-257-8876.

University of North Carolina, School of Lib. Science, Chapel Hill, NC 27514. Evelyn H. Daniel, Dean. 919-962-8366.

University of North Carolina at Greensboro, Dept. of Lib. Science/ Educational Technology, Greensboro, NC 27412. Cora Paul Bomar, Acting Chair. 919-334-5100.

University of South Carolina, College of Lib. and Info. Science, Columbia, SC 29208. Fred W. Roper, Dean. 803-777-3858.

University of South Florida, School of Lib. and Info. Science, Tampa, FL 33620. John A. McCrossan, Dir. 813-974-3520.

University of Southern Mississippi, School of Lib. Service, Hattiesburg, MS 39406. Jeanine Laughlin, Dir. 601-266-4228.

University of Tennessee, Knoxville, Grad. School of Lib. and Info. Science, Knoxville, TN 37996-4330. Anne E. Prentice, Dir. 615-974-2148.

Vanderbilt University, George Peabody College for Teachers, Dept. of Lib. and Info. Science, Nashville, TN 37203. Edwin S. Gleaves, Chpn. 615-322-8050.

Midwest: Ill., Ind., Iowa, Kans., Mich., Minn., Mo., Ohio, Wis.

Emporia State University, School of Lib. and Info. Management, Emporia, KS 66801. Robert Grover, Dean. 316-343-1200.

Indiana University, School of Lib. and Info. Science, Bloomington, IN 47405. Herbert S. White, Dean. 812-335-2848.

Kent State University, School of Lib. Science, Kent, OH 44242. Rosemary R. Dumont, Dean. 216-672-2782.

Northern Illinois University, Dept. of Lib. Science, DeKalb, IL 60115. Cosette N. Kies, Chpn. 815-753-1733.

Rosary College, Grad. School of Lib. and Info. Science, River Forest, IL 60305. Richard Tze-chung Li, Dean. 312-366-2490.

University of Chicago, Grad. Lib. School, Chicago, IL 60637. Don R. Swanson, Acting Dean. 312-962-8272.

University of Illinois, Grad. School of Lib. and Info. Science, 1407 W. Gregory, 410 DKH, Urbana, IL 61801. Leigh Estabrook, Dean. 217-333-3280.

University of Iowa, Grad. School of Lib. and Info. Science. Iowa City, IA 52242. Carl F. Orgren, Dir. 319-353-3644.

University of Michigan, School of Lib. Science, Ann Arbor, MI 48109-1346. Richard M. Warner, Dean. 313-764-9376.

University of Missouri, Columbia, School of Lib. and Info. Science, Columbia, MO 65211. Mary F. Lenox, Dean. 314-882-4546.

University of Wisconsin-Madison, School of Lib. and Info. Studies, Madison, WI 53706. Jane B. Robbins-Carter, Dir. 608-263-2900.

University of Wisconsin-Milwaukee, School of Lib. and Info. Science, Milwaukee, WI 53201. Mohammed M. Aman, Dean. 414-963-4707.

Southwest: Ariz., Okla., Tex.

North Texas State University, School of Lib. and Info. Sciences, Denton, TX 76203. Dewey E. Carroll, Dean. 817-565-2445.

Texas Woman's University, School of Lib. and Info. Studies, Denton, TX 76204. Brooke E. Sheldon, Dean. 817-898-2602.

University of Arizona, Grad. Lib. School, Tucson, AZ 85719. Charles D. Hurt, Dir. 602-621-3565.

University of Oklahoma, School of Lib. and Info. Studies, Norman, OK 73019. Sylvia G. Faibisoff, Dir. 405-325-3921.

University of Texas at Austin, Grad. School of Lib. and Info. Science, Austin, TX 78712-1276. Ronald E. Wyllys, Dean. 512-471-3821.

West: Calif., Colo., Hawaii, Utah, Wash.

Brigham Young University, School of Lib. and Info. Sciences, Provo, UT 84602. Nathan M. Smith, Dir. 801-378-2977.

San Jose State University, Div. of Lib. and Info. Science, San Jose, CA 95192. James S. Healey, Dir. 408-277-2292.

University of California, Berkeley, School of Lib. and Info. Studies, Berkeley, CA 94720. Robert C. Berring, Dean. 415-642-1464.

University of California, Los Angeles, Grad. School of Lib. and Info. Science. Los Angeles, CA 90024. Robert M. Hayes, Dean. 213-825-4351.

University of Hawaii, Grad. School of Lib. Studies, Honolulu, HI 96822. Miles M. Jackson, Dean. 808-948-7321.

University of Washington, Grad. School of Lib. and Info. Science, Seattle, WA 98195. Margaret Chisholm, Dir. 206-543-1794.

Canada

Dalhousie University, School of Lib. Service, Halifax, N.S. B3H 4H8. Mary Dykstra, Dir. 902-424-3656.

McGill University, Grad. School of Lib. and Info. Studies, Montreal, P.Q. H3A 1Y1. Helen Howard, Dir. 514-392-5930.

Université de Montréal, Ecole de bibliothéconomie et des sciences de l'information, Montréal, P.Q. H3C 3J7. Richard K. Gardner, Dir. 514-343-6044.

University of Alberta, Faculty of Lib. Science, Edmonton, Alta. T6G 2J4. John G. Wright, Dean. 403-432-4578.

University of British Columbia, School of Lib., Archival, and Info. Studies, Van-

couver, B.C. V6T 1W5. Basil Stuart-Stubbs, Dir. 604-228-2404.

University of Toronto, Faculty of Lib. and Info. Science, Toronto, Ont. M5S 1A1. Ann H. Schabas, Dean. 416-978-3202.

University of Western Ontario, School of Lib. and Info. Science, London, Ont. N6G 1H1. Jean M. Tague, Dean. 519-661-3542.

Library Scholarship Sources

For a more complete list of scholarships, fellowships, and assistantships offered for library study, see *Financial Assistance for Library Education* published annually by the American Library Association.

American Library Association. (1) The David H. Clift Scholarship of $3,000 is given to a varying number of U.S. or Canadian citizens who have been admitted to accredited library schools. For information, write to: Staff Liaison, David H. Clift Scholarship Jury, ALA, 50 E. Huron St., Chicago, IL 60611; (2) the Louise Giles Minority Scholarship of $3,000 is given to a varying number of minority students who are U.S. or Canadian citizens and have been admitted to accredited library schools. For information, write to: Staff Liaison, Louise Giles Minority Scholarship Jury, ALA, 50 E. Huron St., Chicago, IL 60611; (3) the F. W. Faxon Scholarship of $3,000 is given to a U.S., Canadian, or foreign student who has been admitted to an accredited library school. Scholarship includes ten-week expenses-paid internship at F. W. Faxon in Westwood, Massachusetts. For information, write to: Staff Liaison, F. W. Faxon Scholarship, ALA, 50 E. Huron St., Chicago, IL 60611; (4) the ACRL Doctoral Dissertation Fellowship of $1,000 for a student who has completed all coursework in the area of academic librarianship; (5) the Samuel Lazerow Fellowship of $1,000 for a librarian currently working in acquisitions or technical services in an academic or research library. For information, write to: Pro-

gram Officer, ACRL/ALA, 50 E. Huron St., Chicago, IL 60611; (6) the Nihoff International West European Specialist Study Grant pays travel expenses, room, and board for a 10-day trip to the Netherlands and two other European countries for an ALA member. Selection based on proposal outlining purpose of trip. For information, write to Program Officer, ACRL/ALA, 50 E. Huron St., Chicago, IL 60611; (7) Bound-to-Stay Bound Books Scholarship of $1,500 for two students admitted to an ALA-accredited program who will work with children in a library for one year after graduation. For information, write to: Executive Director, ALSC/ALA, 50 E. Huron St., Chicago, IL 60611; (8) EBSCO/JMRT Scholarship of $1,000 for a U.S. or Canadian citizen and member of the ALA Junior Members Round Table. Based on financial need and professional goals. For information, write: Valerie Platz, 418 Tenth St. N.E., Washington, DC 20002; (9) LITA/CLSI Scholarship in Library and Information Technology of $1,500 for a student who may not have completed more than 12 hours toward a degree in library science before June 1, 1987. Foreign students may apply. For information, write to: LITA/ALA, 50 E. Huron St., Chicago, IL 60611.

American Association of Law Libraries.
(1) A varying number of scholarships of
a minimum of $1,000 for graduates of
an accredited law school who are degree
candidates in an accredited library
school; (2) a varying number of scholarships of varying amounts for library
school graduates working on a law degree, nonlaw graduates enrolled in an
accredited library school, and law librarians taking a course related to law
librarianship; (3) a stipend of $3,500
for an experienced minority librarian
working toward an advanced degree to
further a law library career. For information, write to: School and Grants
Committee, AALL, 53 W. Jackson,
Suite 703, Chicago, IL 60604.

American-Scandinavian Foundation. Fellowships and grants for 25 to 30 students, in amounts from $1,500 to
$7,500, for advanced study in Den-
mark, Finland, Iceland, Norway, or
Sweden. For information, write to: Exchange Div., American-Scandinavian
Foundation, 127 E. 73 St., New York,
NY 10021.

Association for Library and Information
Science Education. A varying number
of research grants of $2,500 (maximum)
for member of ALISE. For information, write to: Janet Phillips, Exec.
Secy., ALISE, 471 Park Lane, State
College, PA 16801.

Beta Phi Mu. (1) The Sarah Rebecca Reed
Scholarship of $1,500 each for a person
accepted in an ALA-accredited library
program; (2) the Frank B. Sessa Scholarship of $750 for a Beta Phi Mu mem-
ber for continuing education; (3) the
Harold Lancour Scholarship of $1,000
for graduate study in a foreign country
related to the applicant's work or
schooling. For information, write to:
Exec. Secy., Beta Phi Mu, Grad. School
of Lib. and Info. Science, Univ. of
Pittsburgh, Pittsburgh, PA 15260.

Canadian Library Association. (1) The
Howard V. Phalin-World Book Graduate Scholarship in Library Science of
$2,500; (2) the H. W. Wilson Scholar-
ship of $2,000; and (3) the Elizabeth
Dafoe Scholarship of $1,750 are given
to a Canadian citizen or landed immi-
grant to attend an accredited Canadian
library school. For information, write
to: Scholarships and Awards Committee, Canadian Lib. Assn., 151 Sparks
St., Ottawa, Ont. K1P 5E3, Canada.

Catholic Library Association. (1) Rev.
Andrew L. Bouwhuis Scholarship of
$1,500 for a person with a B.A. degree
who has been accepted in an accredited
library school. (Award based on financial need and proficiency.) (2) World
Book-Childcraft Awards: one scholarship of a total of $1,500 to be distrib-
uted among no more than four
recipients for a program of continuing
education. Open to CLA members only.
For information, write to: Scholarship
Committee, Catholic Lib. Assn., 461
W. Lancaster Ave., Haverford, PA
19401.

Church and Synagogue Library Association. Two Muriel Fuller Memorial
Scholarships of $60 each for a corre-
spondence course offered by the Univ.
of Utah Continuing Education Div.
Write to: CSLA, Box 1130, Bryn Mawr,
PA 19010.

Information Exchange System for Minority Personnel. Scholarship of $500, in-
tended for minority students, for
graduate study. For information, write
to: Dorothy M. Haith, Chpn., Clara
Stanton Jones School, Box 90216,
Washington, DC 20090.

Medical Library Association. (1) A scholarship of $2,000 for graduate study in
medical librarianship, with at least one-
half of the program yet to be completed; (2) two fellowships of $3,000,
plus $500 travel expenses, each for med-
ical librarians from outside the United
States and Canada to observe medical
libraries in the United States or Canada. Open to MLA members only. For

information, write to: Scholarship Committee, Medical Lib. Assn., Suite 3208, 919 N. Michigan Ave., Chicago, IL 60611.

The Frederic G. Melcher Scholarship (administered by Association of Library Service to Children, ALA). Two scholarships of $4,000 each for a U.S. or Canadian citizen admitted to an accredited library school who plans to work with children in school or public libraries. For information, write to: Exec. Secy., Assn. of Lib. Service to Children, ALA, 50 E. Huron St., Chicago, IL 60611.

Mountain Plains Library Association. Varying number of grants of $100 and $500 (maximum) each for residents of the association area. Open only to MPLA members with at least two years of membership. For information, write to: Joseph R. Edelen, Jr., MPLA Exec. Secy., Univ. of South Dakota Lib., Vermillion, SD 57069.

Natural Sciences and Engineering Research Council. (1) A varying number of scholarships of $11,600 each; and (2) a varying number of scholarships of varying amounts for postgraduate study in science librarianship and documentation for a Canadian citizen or landed immigrant with a bachelor's degree in science or engineering. For information, write to: Research Manpower Programs, Natural Sciences and Engineering Research Council, 200 Kent St., Ottawa, Ont. K1A 1H5, Canada.

REFORMA, the National Association to Promote Library Services to the Spanish-Speaking. A scholarship of $1,000 to attend an ALA-accredited program. For information, write to: Ron Rodriguez, Los Angeles Public Lib., 7400 E. Imperial Hwy., Box 7011, Downey, CA 90241.

Southern Regional Education Board. (1) A varying number of grants of varying amounts to cover in-state tuition for West Virginia residents for graduate or postgraduate study in an accredited library school; (2) a varying number of grants of varying amounts to cover in-state tuition for residents of West Virginia, Alabama, Mississippi, or South Carolina for postgraduate study in an accredited library school. For information, write to SREB, 1340 Spring St. N.W., Atlanta, GA 30309.

Special Libraries Association. (1) Two $6,000 scholarships for U.S. or Canadian citizens, accepted by an ALA-accredited library education- program, who show an aptitude for and interest in special libraries; (2) two $1,000 scholarships for U.S. or Canadian citizens with an MLS and an interest in special libraries who have been accepted in an ALA-accredited Ph.D. program. For information, write to: Scholarship Committee, SLA, 235 Park Ave. S., New York, NY 10003; (4) two scholarships of $3,000 each for minority students with an interest in special libraries. Open to U.S. or Canadian citizens only. For information, write to: Positive Action Program for Minority Groups, 1700 18th St. N.W., Washington, DC 20009.

Library Scholarship and Award Recipients, 1986

AALL Distinguished Service Award. For outstanding service to law librarianship. *Offered by*: American Association of Law Libraries. *Winner*: Julius J. Marke, Dir., St. John's University Law Library, Jamaica, N.Y.

AALL Law Library Publication Award. For outstanding achievement in creating

in-house user-oriented library materials. *Offered by*: American Association of Law Libraries. *Winner*: Case Western Reserve Law Library Staff for Computer Lab Manual & Bibliography/Pathfinder Series.

AASL Distinguished Library Service Award for School Administrators. For exemplary leadership in the development and support of library media programs at the building and district levels. *Offered by*: ALA American Association of School Librarians. *Winner*: William H. Phillips.

AASL/Baker & Taylor President's Award — $2,000. For demonstrating excellence and providing an outstanding national or international contribution to school librarianship and school library development. *Offered by*: ALA American Association of School Librarians. *Donor*: Baker & Taylor. *Winner*: Margaret Hayes Grazier.

AASL/Encyclopaedia Britannica National School Library Media Program of the Year Award. *Offered by*: American Association of School Librarians. *Winner*: District 108, Highland Park, Ill., Gerald Williams, Supt.

AASL/Follett Microcomputer in the Media Center Award. *Offered by*: American Association of School Librarians. *Winners*: Elizabeth M. Bankhead, Carole Martinez, and Robert J. Skapura.

AASL/SIRS Intellectual Freedom Award — $1,000. For a school library media specialist who has upheld principles of intellectual freedom. *Offered by*: ALA American Association of School Librarians and Social Issues Resources Series, Inc. *Winner*: Carolyn Kellerman.

ACRL Academic/Research Librarian of the Year Award — $2,000. For an outstanding national or international contribution to academic and research librarianship and library development. *Offered by*: ALA Association of College and Research Libraries. *Donor*: Baker & Taylor. *Winner*: Margaret Beckman.

ACRL Doctoral Dissertation Fellowship. For research in academic librarianship. *Offered by*: ALA Association of College and Research Libraries. *Winner*: Gemma S. DeVinney.

AIA/ALA-LAMA Library Buildings Award. *Offered by*: ALA Library Administration and Management Association. *Winner*: Not awarded in 1986.

ALA Equality Award — $500. For an outstanding contribution toward promoting equality between women and men in the library profession. *Donor*: Scarecrow Press. *Offered by*: American Library Association. *Winner*: Kay A. Cassell.

ALA Honorary Life Membership Award. *Offered by*: American Library Association. *Winner*: Elizabeth W. Stone.

ALA Map and Geography Honor Award. *Offered by*: ALA Map and Geography Round Table. *Winner*: David A. Cobb.

ALISE Doctoral Students Dissertation Awards — $400. To promote the exchange of research ideas between doctoral students and established researchers. *Offered by*: Association for Library and Information Science Education. *Winners:* Michael B. Eisenberg and Joanne R. Euster.

ALISE Research Grant Award — $1,500–$2,500. For a project that reflects ALISE goals and objectives. *Offered by*: Association for Library and Information Science Education. *Winner*: Not awarded in 1986.

ALISE Research Paper Competition — $500. For a research paper concerning any aspect of librarianship or information studies by a member of ALISE. *Offered by*: Association for Library and Information Science Education. *Winner*: Wayne Wiegand.

ALTA Literacy Award. For an outstanding contribution to the extirpation of illiteracy. *Offered by*: ALA American Li-

brary Trustee Association. *Winner*: Jim Edgar, Illinois State Libn. and Secretary of State.

ALTA Major Benefactors Honor Awards. *Offered by*: ALA American Library Trustee Association. *Winners*: F. W. Symmes Foundation (Greenville, S.C., County Library); Adele Dillard Pannill (posthumously) (Blue Ridge Regional Library, Va.); Mr. and Mrs. Raymond Schrader (Norelius Community Library, Lake View, Iowa); Mr. and Mrs. E. A. Norelius (Norelius Community Library); Mr. and Mrs. Frank Walker (Stockton, Kansas Public Library); Dr. and Mrs. C. W. Mehegan (Stillwell, Okla., Public Library); Jesse and Ruth Drew (posthumously) (Virginia Beach, Va., Public Library); Peggy Palmer Summers (posthumously) (Kinderhook Regional Library, Lebanon, Mo.); The Havre Clinic (Havre-Hill County Library, Havre, Mont.); The Kresge Foundation, Alfred H. Taylor, Jr., Pres. (Troy Public Library, Troy, Mich.).

ASCLA Exceptional Achievement Award. For recognition of leadership and achievement in the areas of library cooperation and state library development. *Offered by*: ALA Association of Specialized & Cooperative Library Agencies. *Winner*: Not awarded in 1986.

ASCLA Exceptional Service Award. For exceptional service to ASCLA or any of its component areas of service, namely, services to patients, the homebound, medical, nursing, and other professional staff in hospitals, and inmates; demonstrating professional leadership, effective interpretation of program, pioneering activity, or significant research or experimental projects. *Offered by*: ALA Association of Specialized & Cooperative Library Agencies. *Winner*: Sister Arleen M. Hynes, O.S.B.

ASIS Award of Merit. For an outstanding contribution to the field of information science. *Offered by*: American Society for Information Science. *Winner*: Bernard M. Fry.

ASIS Best Information Science Book. *Offered by*: American Society for Information Science. *Winner*: Dagobert Soergel for *Organizing Information: Principles of Data Base and Retrieval Systems*.

ASIS Best Information Science Teacher Award. *Offered by*: American Society for Information Science. *Winner*: Marta Dosa, Syracuse Univ.

ASIS Best *JASIS* Paper Award. For the best paper published in the *Journal of the American Society for Information Science. Offered by*: American Society for Information Science. *Winner*: Robert Fugman for "The 5-Axiom Theory of Indexing and Information Supply."

ASIS Best Student Paper. For the best paper by a student of information science that is not a doctoral dissertation. *Offered by*: American Society for Information Science. *Winner*: P. F. Anderson for "Technological and Non-Technological Gatekeepers: An Overview of the Literature."

Advancement of Literacy Award. *Offered by*: Public Library Association. *Winner*: New Readers Press.

Joseph L. Andrews Bibliographic Award. For a significant contribution to legal bibliographical literature. *Offered by*: American Association of Law Libraries (AALL). *Winner*: Paul Finkelman, Asst. Prof. of History, SUNY Binghamton.

Armed Forces Librarians Achievement Citation. For significant contributions to the development of armed forces library service and to organizations encouraging an interest in libraries and reading. *Offered by*: Armed Forces Librarians Section, ALA Public Library Association. *Winner*: Not awarded in 1986.

Baker & Taylor Conference Grants. *Of-*

fered by: ALA Young Adult Services Division. *Winners*: Audra L. Caplan and Paul J. Scaer.

Carrol Preston Baber Award — $10,000. For an innovative research project that will improve library services to a specific group of people. *Donor*: Eric Baber. *Offered by*: American Library Association. *Winners*: Leslie M. Edmonds and Paula R. Moore.

Beta Phi Mu Award — $500. For distinguished service to education for librarianship. *Offered by*: ALA Awards Committee. *Donor*: Beta Phi Mu Library Science Honorary Association. *Winner*: Agnes Lytton Reagan.

Blackwell North American Resources Section Scholarship Award (formerly National Library Service Resources Section Publication Award). Presented to the author/authors of an outstanding monograph, published article, or original paper on acquisitions pertaining to college or university libraries. *Offered by*: ALA Resources and Technical Services Division, Resources Section. *Donor*: Blackwell North America. *Winners*: William Hepfer, Stanley P. Hodge, Patricia A. McClung, Marcia Pankake, Beth J. Shapiro, John Whaley.

Bound to Stay Bound Books Scholarship. *Offered by*: Association for Library Service to Children. *Winner*: Sadako Kashiwagi.

Rev. Andrew L. Bouwhuis Scholarship — $1,500. For a person with a B.A. degree who has been accepted in an accredited library school. (Award is based on financial need and proficiency.) *Offered by*: Catholic Library Association. *Winner*: Patricia E. Mardeusz.

R. R. Bowker/Ulrich's Serials Librarianship Award. *Offered by*: ALA Resources and Technical Services Division. *Winner*: Ruth C. Carter.

CAPL Public Library Services Award. For outstanding service to Canadian public libraries. *Offered by*: Canadian Association of Public Libraries. *Winner*: Rita Cox.

CASLIS Award for Special Librarianship in Canada. *Offered by*: Canadian Association of Special Libraries and Information Services. *Winner*: Miriam Tees.

CIS/GODORT/ALA Documents to the People Award — $1,000. For effectively encouraging the use of federal documents in support of library services. *Offered by*: ALA Government Documents Round Table. *Donor*: Congressional Information Service, Inc. *Winner*: Judy E. Myers.

CLA Dafoe Scholarship — $1,750. For a Canadian citizen or landed immigrant to attend an accredited Canadian library school. *Offered by*: Canadian Library Association. *Winner*: Ryan Scott Schultz.

CLA Outstanding Service to Librarianship Award. *Offered by*: Canadian Library Association. *Winner*: Samuel Rothstein.

CLA Research & Development Award — $1,000. For theoretical and applied research that advances library and information science. *Offered by*: Canadian Library Association. *Winners*: Peter McNally, Alvin Schrader, Garth Homer.

CLR Grants. For a list of the recipients of CLR grants for the 1984–1985 academic year, see the report from the Council on Library Resources, in Part 2.

CSLA Award for Outstanding Congregational Librarian. For distinguished service to the congregation and/or community through devotion to the congregational library. *Offered by*: Church and Synagogue Library Association. *Winner*: Mary Field Schwarz, First Presbyterian Church Lib., St. Joseph, Mo.

CSLA Award for Outstanding Congregational Library. For responding in creative and innovative ways to the library's

mission of reaching and serving the congregation and/or the wider community. *Offered by*: Church and Synagogue Library Association. *Winner*: First Baptist Church Lib., La Crescenta, Calif.

CSLA Award for Outstanding Contribution to Librarianship. For providing inspiration, guidance, leadership, or resources to enrich the field of church or synagogue librarianship. *Offered by*: Church and Synagogue Library Association. *Winner*: Janelle A. Paris.

CSLA Distinguished Service Award for School Administrators. *Offered by*: Canadian School Library Association. *Winner*: Not awarded in 1986.

California State Library Minority Recruitment/Scholarship — Varying amounts. *Offered by*: Sponsor varies (as indicated in parentheses). *Winners*: Victoria Ann Sanders and Lorraine Lee Oback ($2,500 each/San Jose State Univ.); Regina Roberts ($5,000/ Sacramento Public Lib.); Irene Rocha and Sadako Kashiwagi ($2,500 each/ San Francisco Public Lib.); Patricia Oliverez ($1,880), Vicki Mata ($890), Angela Vu ($870), June Hayashi ($1,080), and Dung Truong ($580) (San Jose Public Lib.); Margaret Guerrero ($5,000/Palm Springs Public Lib.); Leigh Ho Piper ($2,500/Los Angeles County Public Lib.); Charles B. Wilke and Christopher Deane ($2,500 each/ Los Angeles Public Lib.); Alice Perez ($5,000/Riverside City/County Public Lib.); Linda E. Brooks ($2,500/ Oakland Public Lib.); Kathryn Eileen Pudlock and Lori Norine Curtis ($2,500 each/Univ. of California, Los Angeles); and Lin Veronica Look ($5,000/Univ. of California, Berkeley).

Francis Joseph Campbell Citation. For an outstanding contribution to the advancement of library service to the blind. *Offered by*: Section on Library Service to the Blind and Physically Handicapped of the Association of Specialized and Cooperative Library Agencies. *Winner*: Robert G. Levy.

Canadian Library Trustees Merit Award. For exceptional service as a trustee in the library field. *Offered by*: Canadian Library Trustees Association. *Winner*: Anne Hart.

Canebsco Periodical Award. For excellence in a Canadian school library media periodical as a vehicle for the professional development of school library media personnel. *Offered by*: Canadian School Library Association. *Winner*: Christine Spring-Gifford, ed., *Learning Resources Journal*, Calgary, Alta., Canada.

Carnegie Reading List Grants. *Offered by*: ALA Publishing Committee. *Winners*: *Booklist*: $3,000 for four children's bibliographies; $1,050 for special bibliographies and reviews on vocational-technical materials; $2,000 for five special adult book lists; Young Adult Services Division of the American Library Association (ALA): $520 for *High Interest/Low Reading Level Booklist* and $1,500 for *Best Books for Young Adults and Selected Films for Young Adults* lists; ALA Association for Library Service to Children: $1,500 for *Notable Children's Materials* list; and ALA Reference and Adult Services Division: $1,344 for *Notable Books* list.

James Bennett Childs Award. For a distinguished contribution to documents librarianship. *Offered by*: ALA Government Documents Round Table. *Winner*: Francis J. Buckley, Jr..

David H. Clift Scholarship — $3,000. For a worthy student to begin a program of library education at the graduate level. *Offered by*: ALA Awards Committee, Standing Committee on Library Education. *Winners*: Carol Lynn Thompson and Nanette Clark Cardon.

C. F. W. Coker Prize. For outstanding achievement in the area of archival de-

scription. *Offered by*: Society of American Archivists. *Winners*: Nancy A. Sahli for *MARC for Archives and Manuscripts: The AMC Format* and Max J. Evans and Lisa B. Weber for *MARC for Archives and Manuscripts: A Compendium of Practice*.

Cunningham Fellowship — $3,500. A six-month grant and travel expenses in the United States and Canada for a foreign librarian. *Offered by*: Medical Library Association. *Winner*: Frances L. Bluhdorn, Head Libn., Royal Prince Alfred Hospital, Camerdown, New South Wales, Australia..

Colonial Dames Scholarships. *Offered by*: Society of American Archivists. *Winner*: Connie L. Cartledge.

John Cotton Dana Award. For exceptional support and encouragement of special librarianship. *Offered by*: Special Libraries Association. *Winners*: Doris L. Schild and Ann Strickland.

John Cotton Dana Library Public Relations Award. *Offered by*: American Library Association. *Winners*: *Public Library Category*: Alameda County Library System, Hayward, Calif.; Atlanta-Fulton Public Library, Atlanta, Ga.; Brown County Library, Green Bay, Wisc.; Carlsbad City Library, Carlsbad, Calif.; Duluth Public Library, Duluth, Minn.; Miami-Dade Public Library System, Miami, Fla.; Ralph Ellison Library, Oklahoma City, Okla.; St. Paul Public Library, St. Paul, Minn.; Westbank Community Library, Austin, Tex. *State Library Category*: New Hampshire: Concord, N.H.; Kentucky Dept. for Libraries and Archives, Frankfort, Ky. *Special Library Category*: Brisco Library, Univ. of Texas Health Science Center, San Antonio, Tex.; Food & Nutrition Information Center, National Agriculture Library, Beltsville, Md. *Service Library Category*: Chanute Air Force Base Library, Chanute AFB, Ill. *Consortia Category*:

Serra Cooperative Library System, San Diego, Calif.; Ohio Council of Library Information Services, Cleveland, Ohio. *College or University Library Category*: Reeves Memorial Library, Seton Hill College, Greensburg, Pa. *School Library Category*: Newport Harbor High School Library Media Center, Newport Beach, Calif.

Watson Davis Award. For a significant long-term contribution to the American Society for Information Science. *Offered by*: American Society for Information Science. *Winner*: N. Bernard Basch.

Dartmouth Medal. For achievement in creating reference works of outstanding quality and significance. *Offered by*: ALA Reference and Adult Services Division. *Winner*: *International Encyclopedia of Education: Research and Studies* (Pergamon).

Melvil Dewey Medal. For recent creative professional achievement of a high order, particularly in library management, library training, cataloging and classification, and the tools and techniques of librarianship. *Offered by*: ALA Awards Committee. *Donor*: Forest Press. *Winner*: Richard De Gennaro.

Janet Doe Lectureship — $250. *Offered by*: Medical Library Association. *Winner*: Virginia Holtz for "Measures of Excellence: The Search for the Gold Standard."

Miriam Dudley Bibliographic Instruction Award. For leadership in academic library instruction. *Offered by*: American Library Association. *Winner*: Virginia Tiefel.

Ida and George Eliot Prize — $100. For an essay published in any journal in the preceding calendar year that has been judged most effective in furthering medical librarianship. *Donor*: Login Brothers Books. *Offered by*: Medical Library Association. *Winner*: M. Sandra Wood, ed., *Cost Analysis, Cost Re-*

covery, Marketing and Fee-Based Services.

FLRT Achievement Award. For leadership or achievement in the promotion of library and information service and the information profession in the federal community. *Offered by*: Federal Librarians Round Table. *Winner*: Not awarded in 1986.

Facts on File Award—$1,000. For a librarian who has made current affairs more meaningful to adults. *Offered by*: ALA Reference and Adult Services Division. *Winner*: Not awarded in 1986.

Frederick Winthrop Faxon Scholarship—$3,000. *Offered by*: American Library Association. *Winner*: Christopher Edward Marhenke.

Fellows' Posner Prize. For the best article in the *American Archivist Journal. Offered by*: Society of American Archivists. *Winner*: Joanne Yates for "Internal Communications Systems in American Business Structures: A Framework to Aid Appraisal" (Spring 1985).

Gale Research Company Financial Development Award—$2,500. *Offered by*: American Library Association. *Donor*: Gale Research Co. *Winner*: Not awarded in 1986.

Louise Giles Minority Scholarship—$3,000. For a worthy student who is a U.S. or Canadian citizen and is also a member of a principal minority group. *Offered by*: ALA Awards Committee, Office for Library Personnel Resources Advisory Committee. *Winners*: Jacqueline Angelia Simpson and Marcia Michelle Martin.

Murray Gottlieb Prize—$100. For the best unpublished essay submitted by a medical librarian on the history of some aspect of health sciences or a detailed description of a library exhibit. *Donor*: Ralph and Jo Grimes. *Offered by*: Medical Library Association. *Winner*: Not awarded in 1986.

Grolier Award for Research in School Librarianship in Canada—$1,000. For theoretical or applied research that advances the field of school librarianship. *Offered by*: Canadian Library Trustees Association. *Winner*: Not awarded in 1986.

Grolier Foundation Award—$1,000. For an unusual contribution to the stimulation and guidance of reading by children and young people through high school age, for continuing service, or one particular contribution of lasting value. *Offered by*: ALA Awards Committee. *Donor*: Grolier Foundation. *Winner*: Isabel Schon.

Grolier National Library Week Grant. *Offered by*: ALA National Library Week Committee. *Winner*: South Carolina Association of School Librarians.

Philip M. Hamer Award. For outstanding work by an editor of a documentary publication. *Offered by*: Society of American Archivists. *Winner*: Not awarded in 1986.

Frances Henne Award. *See* Voice of Youth Advocates Research Grant.

ISI Information Science Doctoral Dissertation Scholarship—$1,000. *Offered by*: Institute for Scientific Information and the American Society for Information Science. *Winner*: Elizabeth Liddy (Syracuse Univ).

ISI Scholarship—$1,000. For beginning doctoral candidates in library/information science. *Offered by*: Special Libraries Association. *Donor*: Institute for Scientific Information. *Winner*: Beth Paskoff.

John Phillip Imroth Memorial Award for Intellectual Freedom—$500. For a notable contribution to intellectual freedom and remarkable personal courage. *Offered by*: ALA Intellectual Freedom Round Table. *Donor*: Intellectual Freedom Round Table. *Winner*: Thomas J. Mills.

Information Industry Association Entre-

preneur of the Year Award. *Offered by*:
Information Industry Association.
Winner: James Kollegger, pres., EIC/
Intelligence.
Information Industry Association Hall of
Fame Award. For leadership and inno-
vation in furthering the progress of the
information industry. *Offered by*: In-
formation Industry Association. *Win-
ner*: Neil Hirsch, pres., Telerate.
Intellectual Freedom Round Table State
Program Award. *Offered by*: ALA In-
tellectual Freedom Round Table. *Win-
ner*: Indiana Library Association.
JMRT Professional Development Grant.
See 3M/JMRT Professional Develop-
ment Grant.
J. Morris Jones–World Book Encyclope-
dia–ALA Goal Award. *See* World Book
Encyclopedia–ALA Goal Award.
Knowledge Industry Publications, Inc.,
Award. For outstanding library litera-
ture. *Offered by*: American Library As-
sociation. *Winners*: *Libraries in
American Periodicals before 1876: A
Bibliography with Abstracts and an In-
dex*. comp. by Larry J. Barr, Haynes
McMullen, and Steven G. Leach, ed. by
Haynes McMullen (McFarland and
Co., 1983).
LITA/CLSI Scholarship in Library and
Information Technology. *Offered by*:
ALA Library and Information Technol-
ogy Association. *Winner*: Not awarded
in 1986.
LITA/Gaylord Award for Achievement in
Library and Information Technology.
For distinguished leadership, notable
development or application of technol-
ogy, superior accomplishments in
research or education or original contri-
butions to the literature of the field. *Offered by*: Library and Information
Technology Association. *Winner*: Not
awarded in 1986.
LRRT Research Award—$500. To encour-
age excellence in library research. *Offered by*: ALA Library Research Round

Table. *Winners*: Peter Hernon and
Charles R. McClure for "Unobtrusive
Testing of Library Reference Services:
An Experimental Approach."
Harold Lancour Scholarship—$1,000.
For graduate study in a foreign country
related to the applicant's work or
schooling. *Offered by*: Beta Phi Mu.
Winner: John V. Richardson, Jr.
Sister M. Claude Lane Award. For out-
standing work by a religious archivist.
Offered by: Society of American Archi-
vists. *Winner*: James M. O'Toole, Univ.
of Massachusetts.
Samuel Lazerow Fellowship—$1,000. For
outstanding contributions to acquisi-
tions or technical services in an academic or research library. *Offered by*:
ALA Association of College and Research Libraries and the Institute for
Scientific Information. *Winner*: Not
awarded in 1986.
Waldo Gifford Leland Prize. For an outstanding published work in the archival
field. *Offered by*: Society of American
Archivists. *Winners*: John Barton and
Johanna Wellheiser for *An Ounce of
Prevention*.
Joseph W. Lippincott Award—$1,000.
For distinguished service to the profession of librarianship, such service to in-
clude outstanding participation in the
activities of professional library associ-
ations, notable published professional
writing, or other significant activity on
behalf of the profession and its aims.
Offered by: ALA Awards Committee.
Donor: Joseph W. Lippincott. *Winner*:
Elizabeth W. Stone.
MLA Minority Scholarship—$2,000. For
a minority student entering an ALA-
accredited library school. *Offered by*:
Medical Library Association. *Winner*:
Joy E. Summers.
MLA President's Award. For an outstanding contribution to medical librarian-
ship. *Offered by*: Medical Library
Association. *Winner*: Irwin H. Pizer,

University Libn., Library of Health Sciences, Univ. of Illinois at Chicago.
John P. McGovern Award Lectureship—$500. *Offered by*: Medical Library Association. *Winner*: Sherry Turkle, Assoc. Prof., Science, Technology, and Society, M.I.T., for "Computers and the Human Spirit."
Margaret Mann Citation. For outstanding professional achievement in the area of cataloging the classification. *Offered by*: ALA Resources and Technical Services Division/Cataloging and Classification Section. *Winner*: Jean Weihs.
Allie Beth Martin Award—$2,000. For an outstanding librarian. *Offered by*: ALA Public Library Association. *Donor*: Baker & Taylor. *Winner*: Suzanne D. Sutton.
Frederic G. Melcher Scholarship—$4,000. For young people who wish to enter the field of library service to children. *Offered by*: ALA Association for Library Service to Children. *Winners*: Nora M. Carson and Carrie Yuen-Lo.
Margaret E. Monroe Library Adult Services Award. *Offered by*: ALA Reference and Adult Services Division. *Winner*: Helen H. Lyman.
Isadore Gilbert Mudge Citation. For a distinguished contribution to reference librarianship. *Offered by*: ALA Reference and Adult Services Division. *Winner*: Sylvia G. Mechanic.
Gerd Muehsam Memorial Award. For the best paper on a subject related to art or visual resources librarianship. *Offered by*: Art Libraries Society of North America. *Winner*: Alison Chipman.
Martinus Nijhoff International West European Specialist Study Grant. *Offered by*: Association of College and Research Libraries. *Winner*: Frederick C. Lynden.
Marcia C. Noyes Award—$250 and travel expenses to MLA annual meeting. For an outstanding contribution to medical librarianship. *Offered by*: Medical Library Association. *Winner*: Ursula Poland, Libn. and Prof. of Medical Library Science, Albany Medical College, Albany, N.Y.
Eunice Rockwell Oberly Award. For the best bibliography in agriculture or related sciences. *Offered by*: ALA Association of College and Research Libraries. *Winner*: Not awarded in 1986.
Eli M. Obloler Memorial Award. *Offered by*: ALA Intellectual Freedom Round Table. *Winner*: Lawrence W. Levy.
Shirley Olofson Memorial Award. For individuals to attend their second annual conference of ALA. *Offered by*: ALA Junior Members Round Table. *Winners*: Hope L. Baugh, Colleen M. Conway, Nancy L. Snauffer.
Howard V. Phalin-World Book Graduate Scholarship in Library Science—$2,500 (maximum). For a Canadian citizen or landed immigrant to attend an accredited library school in Canada or the United States. *Offered by*: Canadian Library Association. *Winner*: Clare Beghtol.
Esther J. Piercy Award. For contribution to librarianship in the field of technical services by younger members of the profession. *Offered by*: ALA Resources and Technical Services Division. *Winner*: Not awarded in 1986.
Plenum Scholarship Award—$1,000. For graduate study leading to a doctorate in library or information science. *Offered by*: Special Libraries Association. *Donor*: Plenum Publishing Corporation. *Winner*: Kathleen L. Maciuszko.
Herbert W. Putnam Award—$500. A grant-in-aid for an American librarian of outstanding ability for travel, writing, or any other use that might improve his or her service to the profession. *Offered by*: American Library Association. *Winner*: Not awarded in 1986.
Putnam Publishing Group Award—$400. To attend the ALA annual conference. *Offered by*: ALA Association for Library Service to Children. *Donor*: Put-

nam Publishing Group. *Winners*: Andrea Howe, Carla J. Kozak, Nancy J. Short, Blaine Victor.

Sarah Rebecca Reed Scholarship—$1,500. For study at an ALA-accredited library school. *Offered by*: Beta Phi Mu. *Winner*: Cynthia Rasely. *Runner-up* ($500) Tina B. Bixler.

Reference Service Press Award. *Offered by*: ALA Reference and Adult Services Division. *Winners*: Harold W. Tuckett, Jr., and Carla Stoffle.

Rittenhouse Award—$200. For the best unpublished paper on medical librarianship submitted by a student enrolled in, or having been enrolled in, a course for credit in an ALA-accredited library school, or a trainee in an internship program in medical librarianship. *Donor*: Rittenhouse Medical Bookstore, *Offered by*: Medical Library Association. *Winner*: Not awarded in 1986.

Frank Bradway Rogers Information Advancement Award—$500. For an outstanding contribution to knowledge of health science information delivery. *Donor*: Institute for Scientific Information. *Offered by*: Medical Library Association. *Winner*: Naomi C. Broering.

SLA Hall of Fame. For an extended and sustained period of distinguished service to the Special Libraries Association in all spheres of its activities. *Offered by*: Special Libraries Association. *Winners*: Edward G. Strable and Mary Elizabeth Gibbs Moore.

SLA Honorary Member. For a nonmember's contribution to SLA or to special librarianship. *Offered by*: Special Libraries Association. *Winner*: Frederick Kilgour.

SLA Minority Stipends—$3,000. For students with financial need who show potential for special librarianship. *Offered by*: Special Libraries Association. *Winners*: Lorelei A. Tanji and Lin V. Look.

SLA President's Award. For an SLA member in recognition of a notable or important contribution to SLA. *Offered by*: Special Libraries Association. *Winners*: Vivian J. Arterbery, James B. Tchobanoff, David R. Bender.

SLA Professional Award. For a member's contribution to the work of SLA or to special librarianship. *Offered by*: Special Libraries Association. *Winner*: Mary McNierney Grant.

SLA Scholarships—$6,000. For students with financial need who show potential for special librarianship. *Offered by*: Special Libraries Association. *Winners*: George L. Draffan and Paul D. Otto.

Margaret B. Scott Award of Merit. For an outstanding school librarian. *Offered by*: Canadian School Library Association. *Winners*: Grace Funk and Gerry Brown.

Margaret B. Scott Memorial Award—$400. For the development of school libraries in Canada. *Offered by*: Canadian School Library Association and Ontario Library Association. *Winners*: Joan Heaton, Joan Kerrigan, Edward Somerville.

Frank B. Sessa Scholarship—$750. For continuing education of a Beta Phi Mu member. *Offered by*: Beta Phi Mu. *Winner*: Connie Champlin.

John Sessions Memorial Award. For significant efforts to work with the labor community. *Offered by*: ALA Reference and Adult Services Division. *Winner*: Martin P. Catherwood Lib., Cornell Univ., Ithaca, N.Y.

3M/JMRT Professional Development Grant. To encourage professional development and participation of new librarians in ALA and JMRT activities. To cover expenses for recipients to attend ALA conferences. *Offered by*: ALA Junior Members Round Table. *Winners*: Cheryl A. Bernero, Elena C. Carvajal, Heleni M. Pedersoli.

Trustee Citations. For distinguished service to library development whether on the local, state, or national level. *Offered by*: ALA American Library

Trustee Association. *Donor*: ALA. *Winners*: John H. Robertson and Amanda L. Williams.

Voice of Youth Advocates Research Grant—$500. *Offered by*: ALA Young Adult Services Division. *Winner*: Not awarded in 1986

Whitney-Carnegie Fund Grants. *Offered by*: ALA Publishing Committee. *Winners*: C. J. Nyman for an *Evaluation of Reference Services: Methodologies and Reviews* ($1,500); W. Bernard Lukenbill for a study of *Youth Literature: An Interdisciplinary Guide to North American Research Studies, 1930–1985* ($1,500); Thomas L. Hart for a *Bibliography of School Library Media Statutes, Regulations and Publications* ($2,500).

H. W. Wilson Co. Award—$500. For the best paper published in *Special Libraries*. *Offered by*: Special Libraries Association. *Winner*: Samuel Demas.

H. W. Wilson Co. Scholarship—$2,000. Available to Canadian citizen or landed immigrant for pursuit of studies at an accredited Canadian library school. *Offered by*: Canadian Library Association. *Winner*: Judith Osborne.

H. W. Wilson Library Periodical Award—$500. To a periodical published by a local, state, or regional library, library group, or library association in the United States or Canada that has made an outstanding contribution to librarianship. *Offered by*: ALA Awards Committee. *Donor*: H. W. Wilson Co. *Winner*: *ALKI: The Washington Library Association Journal*, V. Louise Saylor, ed.

H. W. Wilson Library Staff Development Grant—$2,500. *Offered by*: ALA Awards Committee. *Winner*: Louisville Free Public Library for "Improving Patron Relations," William H. Ptasek, dir., Mary V. Somerville, project dir.

Justin Winsor Prize. *Offered by*: ALA Library History Round Table. *Winner*: Ronald Blazek for "Adult Education and Economic Opportunity in the Gilded Age: The Library, the Chautauqua, and the Railroads in DeFuniak Springs, Florida."

World Book–Childcraft Awards—$1,000. For continuing education in school or children's librarianship; distributed among no more than four recipients (candidates must be members of Catholic Library Association). *Offered by*: Catholic Library Association. *Winner*: Kathleen Suchy.

World Book Encyclopedia–ALA Goal Award—$5,000. To support programs that recognize, advance, and implement the goals and objectives of the American Library Association. *Donor*: World Book-Childcraft International, Inc. *Winners*: American Association of School Librarians, Association for Library Service to Children, and Young Adult Services Division of the American Library Association, and the Univ. of Illinois Graduate School of Library and Information Science for "Missionaries and Managers: Library Services to Children & Young Adults in the Information Age"; Intellectual Freedom Committee (C. James Schmidt, chair) for a workshop to coordinate national reporting of censorship incidents and strategies.

Part 4
Research and Statistics

Library Research and Statistics

Research on Libraries and Librarianship in 1986

Mary Jo Lynch

Director, ALA Office for Research (OFR)

As 1986 drew to a close, the library community learned that the Department of Education's Library Programs Office was initiating a new project entitled "Topics in Library Research—Proposals for the Nineties." The official fact sheet announced that the purpose of this project was

> to identify and explore issues and areas of the greatest future impact on the provision of library information services by tapping the expertise of specialists from both the library and non-library communities; to identify significant components of the broad issue areas for further development as research plans; to disseminate the results to the profession in order to elicit field-initiated projects in those areas.

In late October 1986, leaders in the library field selected a small group of experts to identify and discuss topics of importance to library and information science. Papers on selected topics will serve as the basis of a series of seminars and for informal discussions between the Library Programs Office and major library/information science research funders to ensure complementary research. The Library Programs Office may also commission research proposals with its own funds in the future.

Academic Libraries

Of the three major ALA library divisions that held national conferences in 1986, research was most prominent at the fourth national conference of the Association of College and Research Libraries (ACRL) in April, where one of the five theme sessions focused on research in the format of a dialogue between experienced researchers and new researchers. This session was well attended and enthusiastically received, but the rest of the conference contained little research. A review of the conference proceedings by Larry Hardesty in the September 1987 issue of *College and Research Libraries* notes that of the 60 papers presented at the conference, only 7 presented research. Although "learn about research" rated only fourth as a major goal of those attending the conference, one of the two major announced goals of ACRL conferences is "to promote study, research, and publication relevant to academic and research librarianship." ACRL has been working on this problem for several years.

The approach taken by 1984–1985 ACRL President Sharon Rodgers was to appoint

an Ad Hoc Task Force on Research. That group, chaired by Dorothy Anderson of UCLA, sponsored a very successful clinic for new researchers at the 1985 conference. One result of that event was the formation of a Discussion Group on Research within ACRL, which sponsored a second clinic at the 1986 Chicago conference focusing on "Designing a Research Study."

Another step toward increasing the importance of research in ACRL was the appointment of a standing Committee on Research in 1986. Chaired by Thomas Kirk, the committee explored how ACRL might develop a research agenda.

An important force in promoting research among academic librarians is the Council on Library Resources (CLR). CLR's Faculty/Librarian Cooperative Research program was the topic of a special meeting organized by the Library Research Round Table (LRRT) and cosponsored by ACRL at the 1986 annual conference. This program on "Linking Theory with Practice" featured presentations by four teams whose work has been funded by CLR.

The council is also supporting work of a very different character in the expanded research program announced in 1985. CLR's 1986 annual report reminds the reader that the intent of the program is "to encourage investigation of the effect of the 'information revolution' on scholarship, research and teaching." It was anticipated that CLR "will assist a few universities as they address issues raised by the increasing growth of information technologies and underscored by economic forces and organizational change."

Within that framework, grants would also be given to individuals undertaking research on specific topics. The first grant made under that program was given in 1985–1986 to the University of California, Los Angeles, and managed by Robert Hayes, dean of the Graduate School of Library and Information Science. The project, viewed by CLR as a prototype for other university efforts, is designed

- To explore the effect of technology on the ways information resources will be used in a research university;
- To seek better understanding of the information requirements of individual disciplines; and
- To determine the role of information resources in the work of individual scholars, researchers, students, and teachers.

An invitational conference, attended by representatives of a few selected academic institutions, was held in Malibu, California, in September to discuss the work done at UCLA and its implications for strategic planning on other campuses.

Public Libraries

ALA's Public Library Association (PLA) also held a national conference in 1986 that included two program sessions on research. At a program labeled "Current Research in Public Libraries," Richard Rubin, a doctoral student at the University of Illinois Graduate School of Library and Information Science, reported on a study of different methods used to measure in-house use of library materials. The study was done by the Illinois Library Research Center at the request of and with the financial support of the Coalition for Library Research — a group organized by Herbert Goldhor. Six of the 18 member libraries were included in the study. In addition, three branches in Dallas and three in Minneapolis contributed data, as did three small public libraries in Illinois. Rubin's

report was published in November as *Inhouse Use of Materials in Public Libraries* (Monograph 18, University of Illinois Graduate School of Library and Information Science).

A second meeting, sponsored by the PLA Research Committee, was titled "Answers for Managers: New Data for Decision Making." This program featured presentations by both the manager requesting the research and the librarian who carried it out in three different libraries. The reports were followed by a frank discussion of the use of research results in making decisions.

Data for decision making were also the topic of an article on "Output Measures: Myths, Realities, and Prospects" by Charles McClure, Douglas Zweizig, Nancy Van House, and Mary Jo Lynch in the summer 1986 issue of *Public Libraries*. The four researchers serve on the study team for the Public Library Development Program (PLDP), which will include a revision of *Output Measures for Public Libraries*.

According to a progress report presented at a meeting at the national conference, PLDP, which started in August 1985, is right on schedule (as this article goes to press). At midwinter 1987, the study team will present the completed manuscripts for two publications to PLA's New Standards Task Force: a revised planning manual, to be called *A Planning and Role Setting Manual for Public Libraries*, and the second edition of *Output Measures for Public Libraries*. Also due at midwinter is a report on the design for a public library data service that will collect data on input measures, community measures, and output measures so that libraries engaged in planning and measurement can compare themselves with other libraries. The manuscripts will be published in June 1987. The data service will be tested in 1987 and inaugurated in 1988.

In September 1986, questionnaires were mailed to select public libraries in the ALA Survey of Public Library Services. This project, a collaborative effort of the Office for Research (OFR), the Public Information Office (PIO), and the Public Library Association, will gather data in two areas: (1) how libraries and the business community work together, and (2) the public library services and concerns of greatest interest to the media. Data on libraries and business will help PIO develop a kit to assist libraries in developing promotions and programs to involve the business community. Data on topics of interest to the media will help PIO, PLA, and OFR respond to representatives of the nation's press who telephone ALA with questions.

Future research on public library concerns was announced in October when the H. W. Wilson Foundation awarded $30,000 to ALA for a survey of nontax sources of revenue for public libraries. The survey will ask a stratified random sample of libraries to indicate sources of income other than local, state, or federal tax dollars by indicating the amount of money received from such sources as interest, contracts, gifts, fines, and fees. Special attention will be given to services for which public libraries charge fees, the categories of persons to whom fees are charged, the amount of revenue received from fees, and the uses made of that revenue. Design work will be completed in spring 1987, the survey will be conducted in the fall 1987, and a report will be published by ALA in early 1988.

School Librarianship

The national conference of the American Association of School Librarians (AASL), held in Minneapolis at the end of September 1986, included a program on research in school library media issues organized by AASL's Research Committee. Three literature

reviews were presented, covering research on promoting reading, developing information skills, and helping teachers to teach. The focus of those reviews was on two questions: "What do we know?" and "What do we need to know?" In addition, the meeting included ten poster sessions where research in progress or recently completed was displayed.

Personnel Issues

The *ALA Survey of Librarian Salaries, 1986* was published in June 1986. This is the third report in a series started by the Office for Research and the Office for Library Personnel Resources in 1982 that reports salaries scheduled and paid to librarians in 13 positions in public and academic libraries.

Another publication of interest to those concerned with library personnel is the long-awaited report of the study on professional competencies conducted by King Research, Inc., for the U.S. Department of Education, *New Directions in Library and Information Science Education* by José-Marie Griffiths and Donald W. King, published by Knowledge Industry Publications, Inc. This 465-page volume includes a wealth of information about the project. Twelve separate reports, available from King Research, provide lists of competencies for specific types of information professionals.

Technical Services

Two summaries of work in the area of technical services were published in 1986. Sheila Intner's "Library Research" column in Volume 11, Number 2, of the *RTSD Newsletter* summarized research during the last four years on topics identified in an article by Elaine Svenonius in the March 1981 issue of *Library Resources and Technical Services*. In that article Svenonius lists questions on indexing, classification, and cataloging that needed answering and suggested methodologies for investigating the issues she had identified. Intner reviews research on these topics reported recently in her columns.

A summary of work-in-progress on technical services questions is contained in the premier issue of the "Annual Review of OCLC Research: July, 1985–June, 1986." This handsome pamphlet from the OCLC Offices of Research and Technical Planning describes work underway in those two units. The bulk of the report consists of page-long summaries of projects in the Office of Research whose function it is to carry out mission-oriented research that will help OCLC and its members store, access, and use information more efficiently and effectively. The Office of Technical Planning focuses on the evaluation of new technologies to determine their importance to OCLC and its members.

Projects currently underway in the OCLC Office of Research cover such topics as "Automated Title Page Cataloging," "Dewey Decimal Classification Online Project," "Class Disperson between the LC Classification and the DDC," "Electronic Information Delivery Online Systems (EIDOS)," "Nonfiction Book Use by Public Library Users," and "OCOC CD-ROM Retrieval System."

ALA Conference Programs

The ALA annual conference in New York featured numerous meetings on research. ALA's Library Research Round Table sponsored its annual Research Forum series

where recent research results were presented and discussed. ACRL sponsored a full morning program organized by the new Research Discussion Group. Billed "Research Clinic II: Designing a Research Study," the program was a follow-up to the very successful Research Clinic I organized by the Ad Hoc Research Development Committee for the 1985 annual conference. The Monday morning clinic combined lecture and small-group discussion to help researchers develop a basic framework for carrying out a research study.

A second full morning program on research was presented by the Young Adult Services Division's Research Committee and cosponsored by the Research Committee of the American Association of School Librarians. "Searching for Solutions: Using Research Findings to Improve Library Service to Children and Young Adults" featured small-group discussions on six specific topics in addition to general sessions.

In 1986, the Library History Round Table (LHRT) and the Library Research Round Table (LRRT) joined forces to sponsor a "Research Paper Awards Program" where the annual awards of both groups could be presented. LHRT honored the Justin Winsor Prize Essay written by Ronald Blazek of Florida State University on "Adult Education and Economic Opportunism in the Gilded Age: The Library, the Chautauqua and the Railroads in DeFuniak Springs, Florida." LRRT presented its Research Development Award to Charles McClure and Peter Hernon for "Unobtrusive Testing of Library Reference Services: An Experimental Approach." This paper builds on previous work by the authors and will appear as a chapter in their book, *Unobtrusive Testing and Library Reference Service*, to be published by Ablex in 1987.

Awards

Also announced at ALA was the first project to win the Carroll Preston Baber Research Award—a new award established in 1985 to encourage innovative research that will lead to improvements in library services to specific groups of people through new uses of technology. The project, which will investigate the use of online catalogs by children, was designed by Leslie Edmonds, an assistant professor at the University of Illinois Graduate School of Library and Information Service, and Paula Moore, children's services coordinator at Downer's Grove (Illinois) Public Library.

Earlier in 1986, ACRL announced the winner of its Doctoral Dissertation Fellowship, which was presented at the New York conference. Gemma DeVinney of the State University of New York, Buffalo, won a citation and $1,000 contributed by the Institute for Scientific Information (ISI) for a proposal to study "The 1965–75 Faculty Status Movement as a Professionalization Effort with Social Movement Characteristics: A Case Study of the State University of New York."

Even earlier in 1986 was the presentation of awards at the Midwinter 1986 meeting of the Association for Library and Information Science Education (ALISE). John Richardson, winner of the Research Paper Award, read his paper on "Paradigmatic Shifts in Teaching of Government Publications, 1895-1985." Also making presentations were the two winners of the Doctoral Students' Dissertation Awards. Marion Paris received the award for her dissertation, which tried to determine the reasons behind the recent closing of four library schools. Danny Wallace won for a study of "The Relationship between Journal Productivity and Obsolescence in a Subject Literature."

Presenting reports on work that won the Research Grant Awards in 1985 were two teams of researchers: Peter Hernon and Charles McClure reported on "Unobtrusive Testing of Reference Service for U.S. Government Publications in Academic and Research

Libraries," and Kathleen Garland and Galen Rike reported on their study of "The Relationship between Scholarly Productivity and Selected Institution-Level Variables: A Study of Library and Information Science Faculty Teaching in ALA-Accredited Programs."

Also presented at the 1986 ALISE meeting were plans for future work supported by Research Grant Awards. Ellen G. Detlefsen presented plans for a joint study with I. H. Frieze and J. Olson comparing graduates with the MLS and those with the MBA in such areas as career development, family life, and job satisfaction. Kathleen Heim described her proposed work on the role of library and information science faculty in state and national policy formulation.

Statistics

Since 1965, a major source of national statistics on libraries has been the National Center for Education Statistics (NCES), operated first within the Office for Education in the Department of Health, Education, and Welfare and then within the Office for Educational Research and Improvement (OERI) of the Department of Education. In 1985, during a reorganization of OERI, NCES became the Center for Statistics. In 1986, Congress mandated another name change, and the center is now called the Center for Education Statistics.

Before those several name changes took place, the Office of the Assistant Secretary for Educational Research and Improvement asked the National Academy of Sciences to undertake an evaluation of NCES because of a concern that NCES had lost the confidence of both data providers and data users. In January 1985, a Panel to Evaluate the National Center for Education Statistics was established under the Committee on National Statistics of the National Research Council. In fall 1986, its report was published as *Creating a Center for Education Statistics: A Time for Action*. This report was highly critical of almost all aspects of the center. Clearly, libraries have not been alone in their unhappiness with it.

Almost at the same time, the library community saw proof of positive change at the center. At the national conference of the American Association of School Librarians in late September, a summary of "early tabulations" of data from the national survey of public and private school library media centers conducted in fall 1985 was distributed. In addition to the summary, approximately 40 tables were made available to leaders in the school library field. The most recent previous survey of this topic had been done in 1978 with results published in 1981. This prompt dissemination of results represents a real change of direction for the center and bodes well for the publication of a complete report promised for 1987.

Similar improvements seem likely with college and university statistics. A summary report of the 1985 HEGIS survey of academic libraries was ready for distribution early in 1987. Institutional data will not be produced by the center, but tapes are available with documentation much improved from that of earlier HEGIS surveys. The form used in 1985 has already been improved for use in 1988 as part of the new Integrated Post-Secondary Education System (IPEDS). Staff at the center worked closely with the ALA Office for Research and the new ACRL Committee on Academic Library Statistics. That committee used the draft IPEDS form and the annual questionnaire from the Association of Research Libraries (ARL) to design a survey sent in October to non-ARL university libraries and to a sample of academic libraries known as the "ACRL 100."

This collaboration is part of ACRL's efforts to help librarians reduce the labor involved in filling out diverse forms for the many agencies that ask for statistics.

In 1985, it was announced that the Center for Statistics and the Library Programs units of the Office for Educational Research and Improvement were jointly funding a contract with ALA's Office for Research for a pilot project to develop "A Cooperative System for Public Library Data Collection." Seventeen state library agencies are now part of the pilot. Representatives from most of these states came to a March 1986 workshop in Chicago where all aspects of the proposed system were discussed and existing problems with state-level data collection were aired. One result of the workshop was a revised list of items and instructions that states will incorporate into their data collection forms for FY 1986 data. Data from public libraries in all 17 states will go to the center in machine-readable form. Fourteen of those states will send microcomputer discs in a Lotus 1-2-3 format developed by the Ohio State Library.

The pilot project will be concluded in March 1987 with a technical report that will include specifications for multistate data tables to be published in 1988 and recommendations on how to expand the pilot to include all 50 states. The Office for Research will continue to work with the center until that data report is published and will seek funding to expand the 17-state pilot into a 50-state system. Several additional states have already indicated interest in contributing 1987 data.

At the 1986 annual conference in New York, the Online Computer Library Center (OCLC) announced an initial $10,000 grant that will enable ALA to launch a regular series of statistical reports on the state of the nation's libraries. The reports will be designed to provide information for the public, media, and policymakers who affect library support, as well as for librarians.

In its first year, the project will convene a panel of ALA member experts representing all types of libraries to propose a set of key indicators that will become the basis for regular reports on the nation's libraries. An initial publication scheduled for June 1987 will present existing data on the key indicators. A plan will be developed for additional library and consumer research to meet identified gaps in current data collection.

Selected Characteristics of the U.S. Population

W. Vance Grant

Specialist in Education Statistics, Education Information Office
Office of Educational Research and Improvement,
U.S. Department of Education

Item	Number	Percent
Total U.S. population (July 1, 1986)[1]	241,489,000	100.0
Resident population, 50 states and D.C.	240,941,000	99.8
Armed forces overseas	548,000	0.2
Resident population, Puerto Rico, and the outlying areas of the U.S. (July 1, 1985)[2]	3,682,700	—

Item	Number	Percent
U.S. population, 5 years old and over, including armed forces overseas (July 1, 1985)[3]	221,246,000	100.0
5–9 years	16,822,000	7.6
10–14 years	17,103,000	7.7
15–19 years	18,587,000	8.4
20–24 years	21,207,000	9.6
25–64 years	118,997,000	53.8
65 years and over	28,530,000	12.9
Public and private school enrollment (fall 1985)[4]	57,460,000	100.0
Elementary and secondary schools	45,213,000	78.7
Public	39,513,000	68.8
Private	5,700,000	9.9
Institutions of higher education	12,247,000	21.3
Public	9,479,000	16.5
Private	2,768,000	4.8
Educational attainment of the population 25 years old and over (March 1985)[5]		
Total	143,524,000	100.0
With 4 or more years of college	27,808,000	19.4
With 1 to 3 years of college	23,406,000	16.3
With 4 years of high school or more	106,080,000	73.9
With less than 4 years of high school	37,444,000	26.1
Population residing in and outside metropolitan areas (July 1, 1986)[6]	236,158,000	100.0
Nonmetropolitan areas	56,435,000	23.9
Metropolitan areas	179,723,000	76.1
In central cities	74,476,000	31.5
Outside central cities	105,247,000	44.6
Employment status of the population[7]	182,935,000	—
Total noninstitutional population 16 years old and over (October 1986)		
Civilian labor force[8]	118,482,000	100.0
Employed[8]	110,240,000	93.0
Unemployed[8]	8,242,000	7.0
Estimated enrollment and teaching staff (fall 1986)[9]	61,050,000	100.0
Elementary and secondary schools	47,950,000	78.5
Enrollment	45,400,000	74.4
Teachers	2,550,000	4.2
Institutions of higher education	13,100,000	21.5
Enrollment	12,400,000	20.3
Senior instructional staff[10]	700,000	1.1

Note: Because of rounding, details may not add to totals.

[1]Estimates of the Bureau of the Census, *Current Population Reports*, Series P-25, No. 996.
[2]Estimates of the Bureau of the Census, *Current Population Reports*, Series P-25, No. 997.
[3]Estimates of the Bureau of the Census, *Current Population Reports*, Series P-25, No. 985.
[4]Data from the *Digest of Education Statistics*, 1987 edition, Center for Education Statistics, U.S. Department of Education. The statistics for private elementary and secondary schools are estimates.
[5]Unpublished data from the Education and Social Stratification Branch, Bureau of the Census.
[6]Estimates of the Bureau of the Census, *Current Population Reports*, Series P-25, No. 976.
[7]Data from the Bureau of Labor Statistics, published in the December 1986 issue of *Economic Indicators*.
[8]Seasonally adjusted.
[9]These estimates from the Center for Education Statistics include full-time and part-time staff and students.
[10]Excludes junior instructional staff, such as graduate and teaching assistants.

Number of Libraries in the United States and Canada

Statistics are from the thirty-ninth edition of the *American Library Directory* (*ALD*) edited by Jaques Cattell Press (R. R. Bowker, 1986). In addition to listing and describing more than 36,899 individual libraries, the thirty-ninth edition of *ALD* lists more than 350 library networks, consortia, and other cooperative library organizations, including processing and purchasing centers and other specialized organizations. Data are exclusive of elementary and secondary school libraries. The directory does not list public libraries with holdings of fewer than 500 volumes. Law libraries with fewer than 10,000 volumes are included only if they specialize in a specific field.

Libraries in the United States

A. Public libraries 8,865
Public libraries
with branches 1,365
Public library branches 6,350
Total public libraries
(including branches) 15,215*
B. Junior college libraries 1,285
Departmental 82
Medical 3
Religious 3
University and college 2,113
Departmental 1,501
Law 208
Medical 262
Religious 135
Total academic libraries . . . 5,592*

C. Armed forces
Air force 117
Medical 15
Army 155
Law 1
Medical 38
Navy 136
Medical 22
Total armed forces
libraries 484*
D. Government libraries 1,237
Law 428
Medical 223
Total government libraries . 1,237*
E. Special libraries 5,466*
F. Law libraries 635*
G. Medical libraries 2,058*

Note: Numbers followed by an asterisk are added to find "Total libraries counted" for each of the three geographic areas (United States, U.S.-administered regions, and Canada). The sum of the three totals is the "Grand total of libraries listed" in the *ALD* (shown in the Summary). For details on the count of libraries, see the preface to the thirty-ninth edition of the *ALD-Ed.*

H. Religious libraries 788*
    Total law (including
    academic, armed forces,
    and government)   1,272
    Total medical (including
    academic, armed forces,
    and government)   2,599
    Total religious (including
    academic)   926
    Total special (including
    all law, medical,
    and religious)   10,263
    Total libraries
    counted (*)   31,475

Libraries in Regions Administered by the United States

A. Public libraries   8
    Public libraries with
    branches   2
    Public library branches   17
    Total public libraries
    (including branches) 27*
B. Junior college libraries   5
    University and college
    libraries   25
    Departmental   15
    Law   2
    Total academic
    libraries 47*
C. Armed forces
    Air force   1
    Army   1
    Navy   4
    Total armed forces 6*
D. Government libraries   8
    Law   5
    Medical   1
    Total government
    libraries 8*
E. Special libraries 7*

F. Medical libraries 4*
    Total libraries
    counted (*)   99

Libraries in Canada

A. Public libraries   800
    Public libraries with
    branches   144
    Public library branches   919
    Total public libraries
    (including branches) 1,863*
B. Junior college libraries   105
    Departmental   42
    Medical   1
    Religious   2
    University and college   153
    Departmental   211
    Law   17
    Medical   28
    Religious   19
    Total academic
    libraries 578*
C. Government libraries 286*
    Law   14
    Medical   3
D. Special libraries 962*
E. Law libraries 52*
F. Medical libraries 199*
G. Religious libraries 20*
    Total libraries
    counted (*)   3,960

Summary

Total of U.S. libraries   31,475
Total of libraries administered
    by the United States   99
Total of Canadian libraries   3,960
Grand total of libraries listed . . .   35,534

Public and Academic Library
Acquisition Expenditures, 1985–1986

Every two years until 1983 and annually since then, the R. R. Bowker Company has compiled statistics on library acquisition expenditures from information reported in the *American Library Directory* (*ALD*). The statistics given here are based on information from the thirty-ninth edition of the directory (1986). In most cases, the statistics reflect expenditures for the 1985–1986 period. The total number of public libraries listed in the thirty-ninth edition of *ALD* is 8,865; the total number of academic libraries is 5,592.

Understanding the Tables

Number of libraries includes only those libraries in *ALD* that reported annual acquisition expenditures (8,571 public libraries; 3,532 academic libraries). Libraries that reported annual income but not expenditures are not included in the count. Academic libraries include university, college, and junior college libraries. Special academic libraries, such as law and medical libraries, that reported acquisition expenditures separately from the institution's main library are counted as independent libraries.

Total acquisition expenditures for a given state is always greater than the sum of the categories of expenditures. This is because the total acquisition expenditures amount also includes the expenditures of libraries that did not itemize by category.

Figures in *categories of expenditures* columns represent only those libraries that itemized expenditures. Libraries that reported a total acquisition expenditure amount but did not itemize are only represented in the total acquisition expenditures column.

Unspecified includes monies reported as not specifically for books, periodicals, audiovisual, microform, or binding (e.g., library materials). This column also includes monies reported for categories in combination, for example, audiovisual *and* microform. When libraries report only total acquisition expenditures without itemizing by category, the total amount is not reflected as unspecified.

Table 1 / Public Library Acquisition Expenditures

State	Number of Libraries	Total Acquisition Expenditures	Categories of Expenditure			
			Books	Other Print Materials	Periodicals	Manuscripts & Archives
Alabama	119	$ 5,984,690	$ 2,820,433	$ 64,767	$ 282,946	$ 700
Alaska	29	2,658,851	1,447,577	2,300	298,463	—
Arizona	75	5,879,838	4,142,482	430	618,155	11,000
Arkansas	43	1,845,616	1,236,224	13,513	183,410	—
California	193	48,940,047	34,054,422	473,227	5,926,082	8,305
Colorado	114	6,805,753	4,644,341	234,703	720,375	4,000
Connecticut	159	8,789,921	5,308,147	73,834	1,476,902	200
Delaware	25	1,415,836	594,138	109	120,988	—
District of Columbia	3	25,633,492	963,579	—	154,913	—
Florida	124	15,984,581	9,533,635	41,491	2,156,258	572
Georgia	54	6,719,531	4,159,449	20,425	412,348	—
Hawaii	2	2,323,775	1,657,063	—	386,053	—
Idaho	93	1,789,941	824,298	—	92,948	—
Illinois	566	29,202,941	16,692,751	161,040	2,780,145	5,012
Indiana	216	12,304,613	7,861,770	76,249	1,064,181	4,984
Iowa	480	6,115,588	3,731,594	34,039	512,729	—
Kansas	291	6,062,573	4,099,437	92,753	573,202	1,000
Kentucky	119	6,499,830	3,648,761	11,411	311,881	—
Louisiana	64	7,887,408	3,676,246	37,563	567,033	—
Maine	174	2,410,588	1,252,792	924	157,269	—
Maryland	29	11,484,851	8,619,975	254,567	769,743	—
Massachusetts	323	17,037,177	7,873,167	29,400	1,813,940	1,700
Michigan	354	23,291,234	11,830,881	120,333	2,080,218	—
Minnesota	127	10,618,111	6,308,473	120,784	709,358	—
Mississippi	49	2,775,065	1,685,399	4,656	227,016	—
Missouri	114	6,940,708	4,658,557	14,912	915,093	—
Montana	78	1,323,382	746,952	8,312	86,760	—
Nebraska	209	3,233,778	1,323,074	2,906	191,044	—
Nevada	23	1,522,666	1,116,183	61	165,840	—
New Hampshire	219	2,376,001	1,606,293	15,691	129,392	393
New Jersey	288	43,751,901	11,576,205	221,934	1,925,880	200
New Mexico	47	2,337,027	740,281	—	124,462	—
New York	678	64,004,852	49,855,020	591,157	4,760,421	20,158
North Carolina	125	12,465,553	7,981,918	26,132	979,524	732
North Dakota	43	1,104,620	642,398	490	73,445	—
Ohio	241	33,816,409	19,899,847	83,293	3,391,482	4,512
Oklahoma	86	5,298,978	2,953,327	19,091	506,848	—
Oregon	92	6,972,138	3,192,045	37,740	471,301	—
Pennsylvania	425	17,483,149	10,508,030	55,114	2,016,609	200
Rhode Island	47	2,079,423	1,353,001	534	216,176	6,000
South Carolina	39	4,296,222	3,022,786	2,927	411,420	—
South Dakota	68	1,512,625	725,572	25,408	131,494	—
Tennessee	117	8,104,220	4,720,226	63,889	1,271,089	50
Texas	400	31,286,896	19,543,420	691,674	3,840,316	1,077
Utah	45	3,325,129	1,916,782	62,683	209,392	500
Vermont	148	1,220,581	687,164	4,013	101,540	—
Virginia	89	15,149,839	9,982,011	65,108	1,313,326	689
Washington	70	12,410,188	9,011,654	261,099	1,288,987	—
West Virginia	75	2,986,136	1,771,358	9,279	214,640	—
Wisconsin	323	10,707,779	5,213,383	96,100	677,363	550
Wyoming	25	1,836,827	1,034,486	129,926	132,988	500
Pacific Islands	1	80,000	60,000	5,000	12,000	—
Puerto Rico	2	219,049	192,537	—	16,263	—
Virgin Islands	1	78,188	43,338	—	30,000	—
Total U.S.	8,571	600,218,127	370,657,861	5,799,589	55,543,515	223,523
Estimated Percent of Acquisition			69.23	1.08	10.37	.04

Table 1 / Public Library Acquisition Expenditures (cont.)

Categories of Expenditure

AV Materials	AV Equipment	Microform	Conservation	Binding	Machine-Readable Materials	Unspecified	Database Fees
$ 477,444	$ 57,075	$326,598	$ 50,000	$ 92,155	$ 13,567	$ 381,285	$ 20,500
323,638	79,415	242,020	8,250	43,745	2,200	6,000	34,786
247,617	5,350	57,538	—	107,360	15,900	631,366	42,640
43,749	235	59,624	830	22,304	400	5,669	31,683
3,086,655	119,051	710,462	7,488	522,663	173,179	3,426,981	431,532
168,681	35,909	65,864	100	114,677	53,462	35,554	33,734
521,592	32,521	146,143	—	99,423	3,043	67,102	102,067
42,799	2,559	3,296	—	990	—	12,400	7,039
90,000	—	—	—	—	—	—	—
870,291	27,958	225,101	825	172,057	818	26,707	40,615
302,686	98,838	59,050	441	57,027	7,198	31,051	250
263,572	1,511	3,117	—	12,459	—	—	—
46,136	4,960	8,946	400	18,255	4,546	2,431	5,623
2,244,733	191,507	452,324	827	329,188	31,432	5,847,114	466,868
1,079,504	143,952	242,966	1,000	120,450	1,560	156,068	60,197
356,970	59,685	53,610	—	71,967	21,103	71,203	92,861
139,316	27,123	59,624	300	78,755	33,453	218,973	70,008
224,942	27,266	67,432	—	40,376	1,170	61,798	79,370
222,636	43,189	43,527	912	68,804	3,275	5,401	7,432
29,389	3,653	18,794	5,600	43,892	100	15,047	44,309
988,208	24,994	76,251	—	89,697	7,180	22,730	1,970
773,713	56,519	362,201	14,523	118,971	15,195	380,973	68,987
979,439	60,560	165,653	6,109	204,733	14,150	1,252,468	225,357
649,842	36,056	129,081	21,552	104,267	71,979	23,016	285,157
187,752	11,396	28,224	1,153	36,267	1,320	5,012	4,582
436,185	61,692	121,941	2,000	96,918	39,376	122,671	83,629
28,326	9,299	2,322	—	7,044	1,965	27,794	33,544
102,785	22,259	69,108	—	37,232	1,161	5,716	47,589
5,775	4,875	21,218	50	5,214	3,300	3,126	675
58,035	8,030	30,345	1,425	23,281	6,702	55,113	644
739,023	131,124	334,326	4,935	166,631	62,840	25,861,463	98,244
44,582	4,811	5,071	—	19,876	70	150	56,623
2,392,795	142,413	604,330	17,863	406,647	65,522	457,869	192,888
757,131	156,149	185,298	31,877	170,042	42,300	560,713	88,413
75,959	12,500	11,600	—	4,650	2,000	5,250	32,000
2,990,070	120,257	655,079	14,843	517,730	80,528	112,053	477,423
261,088	47,717	104,306	991	66,580	9,296	20,216	117,378
89,744	19,983	44,163	1,000	38,571	69,000	34,028	82,841
662,550	58,659	475,664	17,623	198,471	23,116	1,034,498	198,908
176,740	12,752	30,030	988	30,079	—	1,100	1,852
207,179	17,284	22,769	530	43,480	1,000	36,031	25,813
169,814	9,624	31,652	300	14,593	750	7,517	179,832
345,030	18,941	148,347	2,500	92,260	—	112,692	52,078
2,360,122	226,343	404,573	13,797	676,446	79,927	850,875	150,159
239,151	76,762	43,113	—	67,704	31,852	8,601	79,539
29,596	11,421	8,867	500	9,008	2,000	5,297	—
841,013	99,053	329,217	4,800	142,983	192,662	433,278	222,647
993,660	25,462	87,891	—	88,764	161	39,520	224,251
222,749	26,435	14,067	—	28,211	1,544	124,575	70
679,297	65,283	69,819	1,793	96,294	7,879	889,040	196,457
104,891	6,496	38,035	2,400	23,831	11,277	15,171	11,190
—	—	—	—	—	—	—	—
—	—	—	—	—	—	—	—
4,850	—	—	—	—	—	—	—
33,886,665	3,022,955	8,108,613	286,221	7,551,403	1,319,283	43,510,706	5,429,187
6.32	.56	1.51	.05	1.41	.24	8.13	1.01

Table 2 / Academic Library Acquisition Expenditures

State	Number of Libraries	Total Acquisition Expenditures	Categories of Expenditure			
			Books	Other Print Materials	Periodicals	Manuscripts & Archives
Alabama	60	$ 12,462,961	$ 5,535,775	$ 37,105	$ 5,083,692	$ 171
Alaska	11	2,598,001	1,173,528	–	743,885	–
Arizona	30	11,913,232	4,373,071	9,723	5,610,974	2,000
Arkansas	33	6,849,416	2,501,041	–	2,610,652	–
California	261	94,907,805	41,059,957	672,658	34,094,382	39,396
Colorado	54	11,101,880	5,247,664	32,680	3,752,834	1,000
Connecticut	69	19,461,680	5,428,082	2,824,167	5,001,635	359,900
Delaware	10	3,557,697	1,786,089	20,465	1,388,148	5,000
District of Columbia	25	14,326,999	6,510,165	–	4,650,115	30,100
Florida	97	22,924,063	7,284,980	165,033	9,121,328	–
Georgia	75	54,188,346	5,172,323	21,939	6,235,430	800
Hawaii	14	3,137,961	1,277,069	4,900	1,279,493	–
Idaho	9	2,476,579	943,967	3,144	1,210,615	–
Illinois	133	39,433,700	14,809,571	691,855	15,232,305	5,595
Indiana	66	17,286,610	6,699,868	175,073	7,709,302	1,124
Iowa	56	12,048,116	3,959,895	6,619	5,357,108	71,955
Kansas	55	8,911,207	3,878,578	12,120	3,765,039	400
Kentucky	51	10,629,255	4,000,201	50,282	4,474,045	6,191
Louisiana	42	13,917,672	5,519,343	29,239	5,667,046	1,308
Maine	28	3,980,644	1,522,007	1,707	1,614,860	6,000
Maryland	54	14,423,780	4,816,234	56,007	5,394,095	700
Massachusetts	126	42,707,980	14,397,239	240,288	14,079,835	17,406
Michigan	102	26,176,568	7,093,684	74,900	10,056,093	503
Minnesota	56	11,465,651	4,494,117	268,191	4,296,687	5,516
Mississippi	50	7,103,827	2,070,898	800	2,865,636	22,539
Missouri	90	17,259,114	5,528,896	222,694	7,651,402	2,114
Montana	15	2,423,572	729,427	–	1,338,967	2,000
Nebraska	36	6,526,061	2,228,719	21,398	3,359,874	350
Nevada	10	2,335,922	822,556	–	1,028,539	–
New Hampshire	27	5,109,565	2,094,291	10,577	2,551,975	–
New Jersey	65	18,561,694	6,086,577	256,368	4,748,671	1,545
New Mexico	31	5,014,857	1,405,225	9,150	1,801,583	–
New York	224	73,153,868	24,836,324	632,665	26,231,691	30,247
North Carolina	129	30,034,781	11,778,045	191,303	11,619,167	26,253
North Dakota	17	2,781,059	995,317	5,000	1,272,170	–
Ohio	158	36,030,214	14,257,043	57,372	15,144,787	15,675
Oklahoma	50	10,375,350	2,505,692	46,727	4,644,766	1,000
Oregon	42	10,228,313	2,989,678	3,874	4,485,142	–
Pennsylvania	185	39,766,297	13,222,838	144,762	15,655,336	38,607
Rhode Island	14	5,228,581	2,305,470	17,127	2,305,382	–
South Carolina	55	10,331,061	3,281,800	55,739	3,467,423	1,200
South Dakota	19	2,507,035	921,944	214,991	946,941	–
Tennessee	68	13,027,941	4,396,121	266,300	5,839,299	10,737
Texas	175	59,081,314	26,175,464	114,481	21,212,056	55,395
Utah	16	4,790,917	716,545	3,000	1,686,439	15,000
Vermont	22	3,364,001	1,345,076	3,646	1,523,194	30,500
Virginia	81	24,810,976	7,696,285	70,127	9,047,121	14,664
Washington	51	14,955,510	4,517,690	10,559	6,589,924	12,616
West Virginia	30	6,176,055	1,977,208	54,775	2,524,357	1,000
Wisconsin	74	19,013,442	8,174,205	182,294	6,382,102	3,400
Wyoming	8	3,172,053	1,625,670	–	1,354,819	–
Pacific Islands	4	241,002	79,835	–	74,000	–
Puerto Rico	25	4,944,636	2,647,201	11,000	1,467,828	–
Virgin Islands	2	164,800	94,500	1,600	53,000	–
Total U.S.	3,532	1,001,662,596	353,987,840	8,222,574	364,153,901	841,935
Estimated Percent of Acquisition			40.45	.94	41.61	.10

Table 2 / Academic Library Acquisition Expenditures (cont.)

Categories of Expenditure

AV Materials	AV Equipment	Microform	Conservation	Binding	Machine-Readable Materials	Unspecified	Database Fees
$ 185,471	$ 100,253	$ 199,487	$ 1,250	$ 549,154	$ 4,743	$ 84,446	$ 132,750
50,644	—	52,639	—	82,668	—	192,943	63,781
197,869	103,623	162,284	1,000	449,691	7,980	19,275	51,350
116,930	96,173	151,155	2,250	202,287	7,581	12,934	64,575
1,121,586	550,522	2,279,765	81,742	4,677,516	151,203	3,498,748	941,107
274,245	25,241	212,812	9,726	435,881	147,988	96,568	149,784
111,257	21,745	714,254	700	563,337	2,200	335,705	139,957
11,870	6,021	47,628	6,912	170,536	21,770	3,725	30,500
207,560	151,192	350,357	23,700	476,596	32,633	85,400	223,641
574,235	252,017	528,680	200	879,096	37,962	780,636	245,842
262,945	212,959	895,237	6,403	677,822	41,198	35,258,444	166,162
72,116	35,170	91,225	4,600	194,821	1,500	5,295	6,490
31,698	66,596	10,634	—	64,741	—	22,643	37,140
895,953	619,694	546,839	5,600	1,397,555	71,860	557,791	461,730
151,722	192,520	198,244	10,400	761,357	5,980	238,021	133,937
253,752	155,230	301,631	1,785	560,496	8,729	153,571	108,765
97,336	57,187	88,993	—	357,881	9,657	28,199	78,094
168,288	89,342	166,523	22,088	433,458	34,505	234,678	239,667
105,419	31,532	226,902	8,850	691,319	28,874	18,305	345,632
40,421	63,363	39,883	2,500	121,279	4,915	18,207	42,482
341,754	146,615	601,572	550	515,364	63,132	413,252	103,556
634,015	338,921	1,917,863	54,800	2,056,984	155,901	352,426	523,142
335,717	260,191	355,622	7,200	852,006	68,643	78,582	215,565
255,947	262,827	147,315	12,000	571,586	24,675	201,394	170,804
155,096	37,948	215,823	—	245,189	959	27,225	22,300
372,344	141,525	323,254	19,129	663,979	63,101	655,238	237,315
25,899	10,150	20,489	500	67,920	12,000	23,743	44,689
95,613	78,452	47,881	673	259,521	100	38,233	143,345
78,134	9,967	—	—	91,476	565	24,203	151
45,125	36,252	74,757	—	137,913	14,710	48,275	15,948
253,294	153,611	214,521	—	525,165	23,632	330,841	204,272
116,584	43,106	30,825	9,362	237,129	29,895	142,275	57,961
952,897	514,595	1,024,237	266,627	2,739,485	172,247	1,586,494	747,377
1,100,505	508,296	935,734	2,000	1,116,047	76,891	304,943	287,819
39,976	22,119	67,165	100	62,631	475	129,926	131,275
675,823	320,283	574,237	34,770	1,352,248	25,794	196,996	384,024
99,322	59,711	243,534	15,304	271,903	31,880	921,083	117,240
130,782	106,242	196,925	—	341,936	54,466	22,928	267,088
618,688	343,836	643,903	5,863	1,808,140	60,111	1,840,571	432,656
15,795	36,912	69,917	2,700	260,682	5,000	19,275	100,865
130,125	66,050	145,977	1,414	299,145	28,616	68,435	87,187
52,836	7,626	29,364	—	77,895	31,590	43,874	62,623
205,727	137,987	204,818	8,499	640,184	3,725	158,649	271,199
1,276,819	565,134	1,387,943	13,272	1,670,598	169,314	1,068,379	525,005
99,269	40,079	57,661	6,000	129,385	51,100	15,000	59,548
43,334	5,571	52,716	2,000	95,983	21,275	15,377	80,006
464,685	76,820	933,984	33	871,760	29,769	159,218	315,857
339,056	364,504	266,902	50	516,182	2,606	292,538	267,117
179,074	66,184	237,443	—	145,150	23,280	43,050	68,060
529,737	151,015	323,461	9,039	481,907	36,601	391,169	237,806
24,402	6,400	8,668	—	72,326	12,000	—	31,144
25,000	3,000	15,000	—	—	—	27,667	8,500
265,034	213,387	52,327	19,200	114,400	—	58,000	38,000
500	—	5,000	—	7.500	2,500	—	200
16,281.124	8,349,118	19,007,654	696,991	36,318,227	1,994,825	54,734,190	10,527,665
1.86	.95	2.17	.08	4.15	.23	6.25	1.20

Price Indexes for School and Academic Library Acquisitions

Kent Halstead

Research Economist

U.S. Department of Education, Office of Educational Research and Improvement
555 New Jersey Ave. N.W., Washington, DC 20208

The School Price Index (SPI) and the Higher Education Price Index (HEPI) report changes in the prices of goods and services purchased by elementary and secondary schools (SPI) and colleges and universities (HEPI) for their current operations.[1] Of relevance to the library community are the components of the indexes that report price changes in new acquisitions. These data can be used to project estimated future funding required to offset anticipated price increases. Also, past expenditures can be compared with price movements to ascertain whether spending has kept pace with price level changes. A decline in constant dollars means that the library's acquisitions budget has lost real purchasing power.

The Indexes and Database

Tables 1 and 2 show prices and indexes of new acquisitions for school and academic libraries. In both tables, the Library Acquisitions Price Index (LAPI) is a weighted aggregative index number with "fixed," or "constant," weights, often referred to as a "market basket" index. The LAPI measures price change by repricing each year and comparing the aggregate costs of the library materials bought by institutions in the base year. For college and university libraries the base year for establishing the market basket weights is 1971–1972; for elementary and secondary schools the 1973–1974 buying pattern has been used. Because the academic index was first published nearly a decade earlier, its composition is not as sophisticated as the index for schools.

Both the amount and quality of the various items that compose the acquisitions market basket must remain constant so that only the effects of price changes are reflected. Weights are changed infrequently — only when there is clear evidence of a shift in the relative *amounts* of various items purchased, or when new items are introduced. Institutions with substantially different buying patterns may wish to construct a tailored composite index using weights based on their own budget proportions. However, once established for a selected base year, the weights must be held constant.

The indexes for each acquisitions category (books, periodicals, and so on) are calculated with FY 1975 as the base. This means that current prices are expressed as a percentage of prices for 1975. An index of 110 means that prices have increased 10 percent since the base year. The index may be converted to any desired base period by dividing each index number to be converted by the index for the desired base period.

Sources of the price series are listed in the tables. Prices for library materials are generally quoted for the calendar year. The corresponding fiscal years are also listed for budget year identifications.

Table 1 / Average Prices and Indexes for Elementary and Secondary School Library Acquisitions, FYs 1975–1986

Hardcover Books / Mass Market Paperback Books

Year Calendar	Year Fiscal	Hardcover Elementary[1] Av. Price	Hardcover Elementary[1] Index	Hardcover Secondary[2] Av. Price	Hardcover Secondary[2] Index	Hardcover Total Index[3]	Paperback Elementary[1] Av. Price	Paperback Elementary[1] Index	Paperback Secondary[2] Av. Price	Paperback Secondary[2] Index	Paperback Total Index[3]
1974	1975	$5.01	100.0	$14.09	100.0	100.0	$ .98	100.0	$1.28	100.0	100.0
1975	1976	5.82	116.2	16.19	114.9	115.6	1.07	109.2	1.46	114.1	111.5
1976	1977	5.87	117.2	17.20	122.1	119.5	1.22	124.5	1.60	125.0	124.7
1977	1978	6.64	132.5	18.03	128.0	130.4	1.41	143.9	1.71	133.6	139.1
1978	1979	6.59	131.5	20.10	142.7	136.8	1.47	150.0	1.91	149.2	149.6
1979	1980	7.13	142.3	22.80	161.8	151.5	1.48	151.0	2.06	160.9	155.7
1980	1981	8.21	163.9	23.57	167.3	165.5	1.65*	168.4	2.50	195.3	181.0
1981	1982	8.29	165.5	26.63	189.0	176.5	1.79	182.7	2.65	207.0	194.1
1982	1983	8.87	177.1	30.34	215.3	195.1	2.02	206.2	2.95	230.4	217.6
1983	1984	9.70	193.7	31.19	221.4	206.7	2.24	228.7	3.13	244.5	236.1
1984	1985	10.11	201.9	29.82	211.6	206.5	2.28	232.8	3.38	264.0	247.5
1985	1986	9.89	197.5	31.44	223.2	209.6	2.67	272.5	3.59	280.4	276.3

U.S. Periodicals / Audiovisual Materials

Year Calendar	Year Fiscal	Elementary[4] Av. Price	Elementary[4] Index	Secondary[5] Av. Price	Secondary[5] Index	Total Index[6]	Microfilm[7] Av. Price	Microfilm[7] Index	16mm Film[8] Av. Price	16mm Film[8] Index	Videocassettes Av. Price	Videocassettes Index	Filmstrip[9] Av. Price	Filmstrip[9] Index
1974	1975	$3.72	100.0	$11.43	100.0	100.0	$.1060*	100.0	$11.55	100.0	—	—	$63.76	100.0
1975	1976	4.69	126.1	14.36	125.6	125.8	.1190	106.0	12.85	111.3	—	—	73.91	115.9
1976	1977	5.32	143.0	15.24	133.3	137.4	.1335*	125.9	12.93	111.9	—	—	58.41	91.6
1977	1978	5.82	156.5	16.19	141.6	147.9	.1475*	139.2	13.95	120.8	—	—	76.26	119.6
1978	1979	6.34	170.4	17.26	151.0	159.1	.1612	152.1	12.56	108.7	—	—	62.31	97.7
1979	1980	6.70	180.1	18.28	159.9	168.4	.1750*	165.1	13.62	117.9	—	—	65.97	103.5
1980	1981	7.85	211.0	19.87	173.8	189.4	.1890*	178.3	12.03	104.2	$ 7.58	103.6	67.39	105.7
1981	1982	8.56	230.1	21.83	191.0	207.4	.2021	190.7	16.09	139.3	14.87	203.2	71.12	111.5
1982	1983	9.90	266.1	23.93	209.4	233.2	.2184	205.1	15.01	129.9	10.47	143.1	81.62	128.0
1983	1984	11.49	308.8	26.43	231.3	263.9	.2274	214.6	15.47	133.9	11.04	150.9	79.57	124.8
1984	1985	12.21	328.2	27.90	244.2	279.5	.2450	231.2	16.93	146.5	8.44	115.4	85.76	134.5
1985	1986	13.31	357.8	26.41	231.3	284.3	.2612	246.5	16.50	142.8	10.24	140.0	83.50	131.0

Table 1 / Average Prices and Indexes for Elementary and Secondary School Library Acquisitions, FYs 1975–1986 (cont.)

| Year | | Audiovisual Materials (cont.) | | | | | Library Acquisitions Price Index[11] | Free Textbooks to Students[12] | | | | |
| Calendar | Fiscal | Prerecorded Cassette Tape | | Multimedia Kits | | Total Index[10] | | Hardbound | | Paperbound | | Total Index[12] |
		Av. Price	Index	Av. Price	Index			Av. Price	Index	Av. Price	Index	
1974	1975	$10.76	100.0	$100.00	NA	100.0	100.0	$3.74	100.0	$1.81	100.0	100.0
1975	1976	10.32	95.9	140.25	NA	113.3	115.5	4.10	109.6	2.08	114.9	110.6
1976	1977	12.08	112.3	93.63	NA	96.3	114.4	4.67	124.9	2.27	125.4	125.0
1977	1978	10.63	98.8	93.65	NA	117.7	128.6	5.23	139.8	2.40	132.6	138.4
1978	1979	12.57	116.8	117.38	NA	101.1	128.8	5.78	154.5	2.70	149.2	153.5
1979	1980	12.58	116.9	85.70	NA	106.7	140.0	6.12	163.6	2.87	158.6	162.7
1980	1981	9.34	86.8	92.71	NA	103.6	149.8	6.42	171.7	3.05	168.5	171.1
1981	1982	12.48	116.0	46.99	NA	120.7	161.2	6.64	177.5	3.23	178.5	177.7
1982	1983	10.47	99.8	57.52	NA	126.6	179.3	7.11	190.1	3.56	196.7	191.4
1983	1984	11.23	104.4	Discontinued		125.6	187.9	7.80	208.6	3.75	207.2	208.3
1984	1985	9.99	92.9			131.1	192.2	8.40	224.6	4.05	223.8	224.4
1985	1986	8.99	83.6			128.7	194.8	—a	243.6	—a	231.9	241.3

*Estimates

†Price series for free hardbound and paperbound textbooks, 1974–1984, was substantially altered in 1985.

1 Juvenile book category (age 8 or younger, fiction).

2 All book categories. The price for all book categories is considerably higher than the price of books selected for school libraries. However, the price trend for all books is considered parallel and is used as a proxy for a school library book price series, which is not available.

3 Weighted average: elementary (K–6) books, 53 percent; secondary (7–12) books, 47 percent. Weights based on data reported in the National Center for Education Statistics, Statistics of Public School Library Media Centers, 1973–1974.

4 Children's periodicals (approx. 175 titles).

5 General interest periodicals (approx. 75 titles).

6 Weighted average: elementary (K–6) periodicals, 42 percent; secondary (7–12) periodicals, 58 percent. Weights based on data reported in the National Center for Education Statistics, Statistics of Public School Library Media Centers, 1973–1974.

7 Average price per foot, 35mm positive microfilm.

8 Average cost per minute, color purchase.

9 Average cost of filmstrip set (cassette).

10 Weighted average: 16mm film, 31.4 percent; videocassettes, 0.6 percent; filmstrips, 32.5 percent; prerecorded tapes, 9.6 percent; multimedia kits, 25.9 percent. Based on industry sales data from Survey of 1975 Educational Media Sales, Associa-

11 Weighted average: hardcover books, 56 percent; paperback books, 3 percent; periodicals, 9 percent; microfilm, 2 percent; audiovisual materials, 30 percent. Weights based on data reported in the National Center for Education Statistics, Statistics of Public School Library Media Centers, 1973–1974.

12 Weighted average: hardbound textbooks, 81 percent; softbound textbooks, 19 percent. Weights based on data for 1974 reported in Trends in Textbook Markets — Status Reports, Paine Webber Mitchell & Hutchins, Inc., New York.

aChange in database invalidates comparisons of current year price to previous series.

Sources: Prices of hardcover books, and of mass market paperback books before 1980, are based on books listed in the Weekly Record of Publishers Weekly for the calendar year with an imprint for the same year (usually cited as preliminary data). After 1980 data on mass market paperbacks are taken from Paperbound Books in Print. Not included in the hardcover category are government documents and certain multivolume encyclopedias. The average prices are compiled by the R. R. Bowker Company. Prices of U.S. periodicals are compiled by Norman B. Brown and Jane Phillips. Prices of microfilm are compiled by Imre T. Jarmy from the Directory of Library Reprographic Services: A World Guide and supplemental data. Prices of audiovisual materials are compiled by David B. Walch based on information derived from selected issues of Choice, School Library Journal, and Booklist. Prices of hardbound and softbound textbooks are from J. Kendrick Noble, Jr., Trends in Textbook Markets—Status Report, prepared for the Book Industry Study Group, Inc., published by Paine Webber Mitchell & Hutchins, Inc., New York. All prices, except for textbook prices, are published in Part 4 of The Bowker Annual of Library and Book Trade Information.

Table 2 / Average Prices and Indexes for College and University Library Acquisitions, FYs 1975–1986

Year		U.S. Hardcover Books		U.S. Periodicals		Foreign Monographs[1]		Library Acquisitions Price Index[3]
Calendar	Fiscal	Av. Price	Index[2]	Av. Price	Index[2]	Av. Price	Index[2]	
1974	1975	$14.09	100.0	$34.55	100.0	$ 6.42	100.0	100.0
1975	1976	16.19	114.9	38.94	112.7	7.59	118.3	114.7
1976	1977	17.20[a]	122.1	41.85	121.1	7.91	123.2	122.0
1977	1978	18.03	128.0	45.14	130.6	8.89	138.5	130.4
1978	1979	20.10	142.7	50.11	145.0	9.41	146.6	144.0
1979	1980	22.80	161.8	57.23	165.6	11.52	179.5	165.6
1980	1981	23.57	167.3	67.81	196.3	13.05	203.3	181.4
1981	1982	26.88	190.8	73.89	213.9	13.84	215.6	201.5
1982	1983	30.34	215.3	78.04	225.9	11.91	185.5	214.3
1983	1984	29.00[b]	221.4	82.47	238.7	12.09	188.3	221.6
1984	1985	29.96	228.7	86.10	249.2	11.78	183.5	229.7
1985	1986	31.19	238.1	92.32	267.2	11.66	181.6	238.4

[1] All hardcover books, paperbacks, and pamphlets purchased during the fiscal year by the Library of Congress from approximately 100 foreign countries.

[2] Indexes are not fixed-weight indexes; they reflect changes in the type and mix of books and periodicals from year to year. The fiscal year index refers to average price in the previous calendar year due to the normal time delay between published date and purchase.

[3] Weighted average based on the estimated proportion of the total acquisitions budget expended for each category. Weights used — U.S. hardcover books, 55 percent; U.S. periodicals, 30 percent; and foreign monographs, 15 percent.

[a] In 1976, *Publishers Weekly* reported a book price of $17.39 for an 18-month period (1976–1977). An adjusted value of $17.20 for calendar year 1976 was determined from the trend line.

[b] New price series introduced. FY 1984 index based on 1984 series price of $31.19.

Source: Prices of hardcover books, 1974–1982, are published in *The Bowker Annual of Library & Book Trade Information,* R. R. Bowker, New York, based on books listed in the Weekly Record section of *Publishers Weekly* for the calendar year with an imprint for the same year. Not included are mass market paperbacks, government documents, and certain multivolume encyclopedias. Prices of hardcover books purchased by colleges and universities, 1983–present, are reported by Kathryn A. Soupiset, Trinity College, from book reviews appearing in *Choice.* U.S. periodicals are priced by the F. W. Faxon Co. and reported by F. F. Clasquin in an October issue of *Library Journal.* Foreign monographs are priced according to an unpublished price series prepared by the Library of Congress.

363

Library Buildings, 1986

Bette-Lee Fox

AV/Bibliographic Editor, *Library Journal*

Ann Burns

Assistant Editor, *Library Journal*

Frances G. Duckett

Assistant Editor, *Library Journal*

The topsy-turvy aspect of library construction continues for the third year with additions and renovations outpacing new construction by almost two to one. Yet the total project costs for the 118 additions and renovations ($59,206,517) is only 65 percent of the total project costs for the 69 new buildings ($90,951,900). And the total costs for both categories ($150,158,417) is the third highest in the last ten years.

The "Projects in Progress" feature debuted in the December 1985 issue of *PW* has netted major results: 61 completed projects (which appear in Tables 1–9 with an asterisk) and 472 projects underway in 1986 (see Tables 10–12), an increase of 19.5 percent over 1985, when 395 public and academic projects were listed. Table 10 shows square foot estimates of the projects and projected construction costs. Tables 11 and 12 list the individual projects and give the stage of progress of each. (The year following the library name represents the estimated year of completion.)

Large individual projects of note: the Tufts University Health Sciences Library (part of a $21 million building), the University of Iowa Law Library, Ames ($15,107,470), and the University of Alaska, Fairbanks ($13,200,000). Public projects include the new Central Library of the Irving Public Library, Texas, and the George Memorial Library in Richmond, Texas (both over $8,000,000), the Naperville Public Library, Illinois ($6,243,333), and the Atlantic City Free Public Library, New Jersey ($4,732,280), and the addition and renovation project at the Enoch Pratt Free Library in Baltimore ($3,750,000).

Funding from local governments still supports the bulk of the projects, amounting to $110,207,217 in 1986. Federal funds are half of gift funds, and state funds actually increased to the third highest in the last six years (the 1982 figure is misleading because two state agency projects alone accounted for almost $20,000,000).

Note: Adapted from *Library Journal*, December 1986.

Table 1 / Public Library Buildings: A Six-Year Cost Summary

	Fiscal 1981	Fiscal 1982	Fiscal 1983	Fiscal 1984	Fiscal 1985	Fiscal 1986
Number of new bldgs.	82	92	54	48	99	69
Number of ARRs[1]	76	76	42	63	125	118
Sq. ft. new bldgs.	1,134,748	2,058,429	835,211	800,252	852,831	1,051,757
Sq. ft. ARRs	954,106	737,707	369,351	523,963	1,227,063	1,186,451
NEW BLDGS.						
Construction cost	$64,658,453	$107,890,141	$48,761,130	$64,370,118	$52,799,143	$67,798,317
Equipment cost	9,059,027	14,580,451	6,426,618	6,451,298	6,585,913	9,211,025
Site cost	3,265,157	3,556,109	2,741,248	1,622,534	4,085,764	3,476,461
Other costs	7,167,009	13,219,164	6,018,787	6,397,740	5,728,714	10,466,097
Total—Project cost	86,019,599	141,893,227	63,947,783	78,841,690	70,583,649	90,951,900
ARRs—Project cost	55,388,161	38,147,095	18,769,475	30,762,934	69,256,835	59,206,517
NEW & ARR PROJECT COST	$141,407,760	$180,040,322	$82,717,258	$109,604,624	$139,840,484	$150,158,417
FUND SOURCES						
Federal, new bldgs.	$18,269,728	$11,922,851	$4,401,647	$2,274,957	$9,803,398	$6,367,559
Federal, ARRs	4,105,877	5,497,522	1,046,490	2,227,355	8,086,819	4,541,545
Federal, total	$22,375,605	$17,420,373	$5,448,137	$4,502,312	$17,890,217	$10,909,104
State, new bldgs.	$3,537,248	$23,532,309	$8,175,330	$4,340,803	$4,139,433	$1,863,277
State, ARRs	1,343,174	1,049,493	3,160,159	2,784,153	1,607,519	7,054,676
State, total	$4,880,422	$24,581,802	$11,335,489	$7,124,956	$5,746,952	$8,917,953
Local, new bldgs.	$57,099,210	$87,920,271	$47,544,033	$71,043,181	$47,914,637	$67,449,000
Local, ARRs	43,598,892	24,626,721	10,640,891	22,921,592	49,096,264	42,758,217
Local, total	$100,698,102	$112,546,992	$58,184,924	$93,964,773	$97,010,901	$110,207,217
Gift, new bldgs.	$5,699,152	$20,143,884	$3,957,736	$1,169,101	$8,766,333	$15,299,620
Gift, ARRs	6,366,551	2,736,493	3,171,935	2,838,892	10,490,099	4,979,443
Gift, total	$12,065,703	$22,880,377	$7,129,671	$4,007,993	$19,256,432	$20,279,063
TOTAL FUNDS USED	$140,109,832	$175,995,668	$82,098,221	$109,600,034	$139,904,502	$150,313,337

[1] Additions, Remodelings, and Renovations

Table 2 / New Public Library Buildings, 1986

Community	Pop. in M	Code	Project Cost	Const. Cost	Gross Sq. Ft.	Sq.Ft. Cost	Equip. Cost	Site Cost	Other Costs	Volumes	Reader Seats	Federal Funds	State Funds	Local Funds	Gift Funds	Architect
ARIZONA																
Apache Junction	15	M	$738,218	$601,818	10,800	$55.72	$64,865	Owned	71,535	30,000	83	0	0	0	0	Enyart, Lawrence
CALIFORNIA																
* Bakersfield[1]	57	B	2,234,450	2,000,000	18,336	109.08	106,450	Leased	128,000	60,000	120	0	0	0	2,234,450	Milazzo & Associates
* Thornton[2]	2	B	427,666	366,545	2,775	132.09	31,801	12,000	17,320	12,000	36	0	0	427,666	0	Morris & Wenell
CONNECTICUT																
East Hampton[3]	9	M	1,527,500	1,215,772	11,940	101.82	121,859	44,000	145,869	30,000	79	0	200,000	1,300,000	27,500	Centerbrook Architects
Simsbury	22	M	2,790,500	2,235,000	21,300	104.93	252,000	Owned	303,500	110,000	140	0	199,683	2,590,817	0	Malmfeldt Associates
FLORIDA																
* Clearwater	30	B	1,224,178	944,808	15,000	62.99	175,000	Owned	104,370	50,000	75	0	0	1,224,178	0	Williams Architects
GEORGIA																
Douglasville	75	B	1,426,592	915,997	21,000	43.61	120,345	Owned	390,250	70,000	158	425,000	512,898	488,694	0	Tapp, William R., Jr.
Greensboro	12	M	590,894	424,162	8,600	49.32	113,010	10,000	43,722	38,000	50	0	368,000	54,900	167,994	Tuten, John A.
Unadilla	3	B	164,919	115,371	2,100	54.94	20,000	Owned	29,548	10,105	21	125,000		21,668	18,251	Robisch, Charles J.
ILLINOIS																
Chicago	40	B	1,770,000	1,050,000	13,000	80.77	210,000	235,000	275,000	100,000	103	0	0	1,770,000	0	Chicago Bureau of Arch
* Mackinaw	2	M	220,000	131,000	5,800	22.59	0	70,000	19,000	15,000	12	88,000	0	116,000	16,000	Lontai, Adam
Naperville	67	M	6,243,333	4,190,629	63,312	66.19	447,900	Owned	1,604,804	175,000	419	184,800	0	6,058,533	0	Cedarholm, Charles
Shorewood	10	M	719,660	590,095	15,000	39.34	33,565	55,000	41,000	36,000	52	250,000	0	456,660	13,000	Healy, Snyder, Bender
INDIANA																
Clayton	5	M	254,925	201,026	4,200	47.86	27,931	10,548	15,420	17,905	24	0	0	244,925	10,000	Curry, Robert E.
* Hammond	23	B	1,682,278	1,084,467	9,300	116.61	393,175	Owned	204,636	33,500	70	100,000	0	1,582,278	0	Carow, Jay
* Indianapolis	50	B	1,311,084	1,074,064	13,000	82.62	134,420	27,600	75,000	70,000	87	0	0	1,311,084	0	McGuire & Shook
* Indianapolis	45	B	1,108,509	896,784	11,100	80.79	94,983	45,000	71,742	55,000	86	254,962	0	853,547	0	Gibson, Ed & Assocs.
KANSAS																
* Garden City	30	M	1,650,000	1,200,000	31,000	38.71	190,000	124,000	136,000	160,000	67	0	0	850,000	800,000	L.C.B. Assocs.
* Kansas City	173	B	4,204,000	3,000,400	45,830	65.47	566,900	Owned	636,700	200,000	263	0	0	4,204,000	0	Buchanan Architects
Plainville	3	M	312,249	243,986	4,382	55.68	40,730	Owned	27,533	12,000	40	0	0	0	312,249	Keller, Ralph J.
MASSACHUSETTS																
Milford[4]	25	M	2,751,100	2,228,459	25,446	87.58	251,721	79,000	191,920	109,000	116	512,200	0	2,143,800	95,100	Prout, Donald, Assocs.

Location	No.	Type														Name
MINNESOTA																
Aurora	4	M	320,000	212,854	3,200	66.52	78,553	Owned	28,593	20,000	29	160,000	160,000	0	0	Hildenbrand & Wirtanen
Blaine	182	S	751,309	646,344	12,500	51.71	51,784	Owned	53,181	0	0	0	0	751,309	0	Lindberg, Glen
Circle Pines	18	B	589,539	471,497	6,320	74.60	70,969	Owned	47,073	30,000	53	0	0	589,539	0	Lindberg, Glen
Eden Prairie	36	B	1,587,335	927,860	10,133	91.57	132,839	285,000	241,636	50,000	52	0	0	1,587,335	0	Parker, Leonard, Assocs.
Fergus Falls	13	M	1,324,000	1,025,000	12,700	80.71	140,000	82,000	77,000	75,000	68	200,000	0	1,040,000	84,000	Foss Assocs.
Wadena	8	M	348,387	230,713	4,010	57.53	69,934	Owned	47,740	18,900	22	173,177	0	165,210	10,000	Silvernail, Brooke
NEBRASKA																
York[5]	15	M	1,676,426	922,162	18,127	50.87	129,803	375,000	249,461	50,000	80	0	0	0	1,676,426	Cannon, James L.
NEW JERSEY																
Atlantic City[6]	40	M	4,732,280	3,308,000	30,000	110.27	600,000	504,000	320,280	120,000	170	0	0	4,732,280	0	Blumberg/Gruen Assocs.
Braddock	25	B	401,550	310,584	5,000	62.11	24,589	Owned	66,377	25,000	34	390,000	0	11,550	0	Churchill, Alexander
NEW MEXICO																
Belen	10	M	555,000	418,000	8,950	46.70	15,000	79,500	42,500	66,000	54	0	0	540,000	15,000	Vigil, Claudio
NEW YORK																
Indian Lake	1	M	174,657	130,401	2,720	47.94	20,006	Owned	24,250	11,500	32	69,151	62,500	31,006	12,000	Claek, William J.
Rochester	23	B	342,000	287,000	3,800	75.53	40,000	Owned	15,000	15,000	34	0	11,300	330,700	0	Wulff, David H.
NORTH CAROLINA																
Kannapolis	30	M	1,073,274	818,128	15,000	54.54	120,844	Owned	134,302	55,000	139	0	100,000	473,274	500,000	Murray, Martin L.
Maxton	5	B	230,208	181,058	3,994	45.33	31,250	Owned	17,900	12,000	30	0	40,000	122,000	68,208	Sawyer, John R.
NORTH DAKOTA																
* Garrison	2	M	250,000	158,000	2,002	78.92	50,000	Owned	42,000	16,000	17	64,150	0	185,850	0	Anderson, Robert
OKLAHOMA																
Madill	3	MS	94,800	87,000	3,900	22.31	3,000	Owned	4,800	20,000	8	0	0	20,000	100,000	Kennedy, Jo
Tecumseh	6	B	487,400	413,000	8,000	51.63	40,000	Owned	34,400	20,000	40	0	17,400	470,000	0	Price & Reaves
OREGON																
Clatskanie	5	M	121,000	70,000	2,496	28.05	22,000	23,000	6,000	11,000	24	51,000	0	0	70,000	Lillich, Morris
Newport[7]	8	M	850,000	650,000	7,700	84.42	50,000	Owned	150,000	45,000	52	850,000	0	0	0	Sherwood, Carl R.
RHODE ISLAND																
Glocester[a]	8	M	321,629	280,228	4,660	60.14	17,491	Owned	23,910	21,000	50	0	137,500	73,818	110,311	Robbins, Alden S.
SOUTH CAROLINA																
Chester	30	M	1,070,114	769,332	15,000	51.29	150,808	82,469	67,505	70,000	112	100,287	40,000	750,000	179,827	Williams, Frank
* Columbia	60	B	1,043,931	774,693	18,000	43.04	139,223	45,000	85,015	110,000	64	0	0	1,043,931	0	Carlisle Assocs.
* Eastover	5	B	171,870	122,912	2,583	47.59	21,497	14,336	12,525	17,765	35	0	0	171,870	0	Davis, Curt

Table 2 / New Public Library Buildings, 1986 (cont.)

Community	Pop. in M	Code	Project Cost	Const. Cost	Gross Sq. Ft.	Sq.Ft. Cost	Equip. Cost	Site Cost	Other Costs	Volumes	Reader Seats	Federal Funds	State Funds	Local Funds	Gift Funds	Architect
TEXAS																
Grapevine[9]	25	M	1,534,423	1,295,778	15,000	86.39	53,227	Owned	185,418	64,170	71	133,437	0	1,360,619	40,367	Hatfield Halcomb
Hitchcock[10]	8	M	314,980	260,696	5,898	44.20	9,500	31,750	13,034	41,000	22	125,000	0	0	189,980	Mackey, Rodney
*Houston	36	B	1,193,097	931,960	8,886	104.88	103,300	Owned	157,837	34,000	65	1,075,000	0	118,097	0	Molina & Assocs.
*Houston	42	B	1,304,250	988,000	11,000	89.82	200,000	38,250	78,000	50,000	87	0	0	1,304,250	0	Marshall, James, AIA
*Houston	44	B	1,604,276	1,264,276	16,000	79.01	130,000	113,000	97,000	80,000	143	0	0	1,604,276	0	McKittrick, Richardson ...
Humble	54	B	771,691	609,691	10,137	60.15	107,000	Owned	55,000	55,000	98	0	0	771,691	0	Bailey, Ray
*Irving[11]	150	MS	8,438,000	6,596,000	180,000	36.64	985,000	Owned	857,000	400,000	300	0	0	8,438,000	0	Meier, Frank L.
*Navasota	7	M	476,272	273,276	8,312	32.88	61,347	50,000	91,649	25,000	58	100,000	0	300,000	76,272	Albright, Dave
Paint Rock	1	M	37,576	37,176	1,232	30.18	250	Owned	150	10,000	9	0	0	0	37,576	Cardinal Homes
*Richmond	195	MS	8,405,393	6,768,310	77,365	87.49	447,118	460,000	729,965	175,000	223	199,518	0	188,089	8,017,786	Wedemeyer, Ronald
*Weslaco	25	M	1,744,767	1,098,731	25,371	43.31	458,643	Owned	187,393	75,000	190	300,000	0	1,444,767	0	Hobart, Gene P.
VIRGINIA																
*Clarksville	7	B	59,397	40,000	2,400	16.67	19,397	Owned	0	9,300	43	0	5,433	719	53,245	Edgerton....Simmons
*Falls Church	33	B	3,715,644	2,380,171	25,000	95.20	237,422	375,408	722,643	125,000	204	0	0	3,715,644	0	Mills, Claggett & Wenning
*Newport News	185	B	1,024,000	870,000	13,000	66.92	116,000	15,000	23,000	60,000	60	0	0	1,024,000	0	Forrest Coile Assocs.
*Reston	40	B	3,856,090	2,842,932	30,000	94.76	366,090	Owned	647,068	150,000	212	0	0	3,856,090	0	LBC&W
*Richmond	23	B	667,000	572,000	8,000	71.50	58,000	Owned	37,000	45,000	45	0	0	667,000	0	Hardwicke Johnson
*Richmond	21	B	176,000	95,559	1,700	56.21	49,576	Owned	30,865	15,000	23	0	0	176,000	0	none
*Rocky Mount	36	M	467,318	359,318	9,600	37.43	0	80,000	28,000	70,000	45	132,440	0	308,691	27,943	Dewberry & Davis
*Rustburg[12]	47	MS	905,000	803,000	12,500	6.42	75,000	Owned	27,000	75,000	72	227,000	0	678,000	0	Architectural Partners
WASHINGTON																
Ocean Park	2	B	241,310	167,364	3,200	52.30	29,089	40,000	4,857	15,000	n/a	0	0	221,310	20,000	Rowe, Ron G.
Renton	60	B	1,509,500	1,172,000	15,000	78.13	150,000	62,500	125,000	85,000	155	0	0	1,509,500	0	Mithun Bowman Emrich
WEST VIRGINIA																
*Alum Creek	4	B	60,135	52,716	1,250	42.17	5,164	Leased	2,255	6,000	24	30,000	5,000	0	25,135	Goff, Jerry
*Hannan	2	M	30,379	26,147	640	40.86	3,073	Leased	1,159	4,000	20	14,500	1,500	3,379	11,000	Goff, Jerry
*Ronceverte	2	M	66,638	51,067	1,250	40.85	5,584	7,500	2,487	6,000	24	32,937	2,063	31,638	0	Goff, Jerry
WISCONSIN																
Glendale	28	M	480,000	317,000	15,000	21.13	125,000	0	38,000	110,000	85	0	0	200,000	280,000	Burgener, Dennis

Table 3 / Public Library Buildings: Additions and Renovations, 1986

Community	Pop. in M	Code	Project Cost	Const. Cost	Gross Sq.Ft.	Sq.Ft. Cost	Equip. Cost	Site Cost	Other Costs	Volumes	Reader Seats	Federal Funds	State Funds	Local Funds	Gift Funds	Architect
ALABAMA																
*Cullman	62	M	$20,000	$17,661	606	$29.14	0	Owned	$2,339	5,000	8	$10,000	0	$10,000	0	Freeman, R. Mack
Gadsden	103	M	380,614	270,379	3,680	103.42	$68,235	Owned	42,000	20,000	35	215,000	$16,963	148,651	0	Cannon-Nance
Guntersville	30	M	143,976	127,737	2,362	54.08	0	Owned	16,239		0	64,000	0	74,976	$5,000	Strickland, Roberts . . .
ALASKA																
Talkeetna	1	M	83,500	73,500	1,152	63.80	6,000	Owned	4,000	10,000	28	0	75,000	8,500	0	Perrin, Rick
CALIFORNIA																
Oceanside	50	B	208,666	63,872	3,000	21.29	101,204	Leased	43,590	20,000	36	0	0	144,794	63,872	Oremem Assocs.
*San Diego	20	B	549,000	370,000	2,800	132.14	74,000	Owned	105,000	35,000	34	0	0	399,000	150,000	Lareau, Dick . . .
San Jose	84	B	869,994	719,994	9,836	73.20	150,000	Owned	0	70,000	71	0	0	869,994	0	Stewart, Carl
Santa Monica[13]	12	B	1,084,592	922,643	8,435	109.38	62,949	Owned	99,000	15,000	50	199,100	0	875,492	10,000	Daniel, W. Gayle . . .
Vallejo	4	B	150,000	98,750	2,500	39.50	40,250	Owned	11,000	30,000	40	0	0	150,000	0	Tyrrell, Paul
COLORADO																
Bayfield[14]	3	M	7,139	6,289	1,776	5.34	0	Owned	850	15,000	20	3,355	0	3,584	200	Lynch, Jay
Fairplay[15]	2	B	11,799	2,000	787	2.54	8,400	Owned	1,399	3,500	12	5,400	0	6,399	0	Collins, Michael
*Longmont[16]	65	M	107,981	70,638	1,200	58.86	31,369	Owned	5,974	120,000	132	50,463	0	57,518	0	Miller, Jerry
Stratton[16]	1	M	24,502	14,048	723	19.43	2,233	7,800	420	15,000	12	18,750	0	0	5,752	Mack, John
CONNECTICUT																
Columbia[17]	4	M	555,181	384,482	4,800	80.10	43,743	59,000	67,956	24,000	31	0	157,300	315,000	82,881	Breen, Edward
Durham[18]	5	M	845,148	565,201	7,200	78.50	138,800	65,000	76,147	35,000	62	0	200,000	466,148	179,000	King, Charles A.
Hartford	17	B	145,454	127,850	5,400	23.68	0	Owned	17,604	24,000	46	39,150	33,292	73,012	0	Vance, James & Assocs.
Norwich	39	M	106,000	60,000	4,000	15.00	35,000	Owned	11,000	100,000	120	22,000	0	84,000	0	Interdesign
FLORIDA																
*Lakeland	64	M	2,009,000	1,738,959	36,674	47.42	127,071	Owned	142,970	127,000	300	200,000	0	1,809,000	0	Furr, Michael B. . . .
GEORGIA																
Albany	110	MS	2,271,518	1,796,474	40,753	44.08	324,554	Owned	150,490	155,000	162	125,000	587,000	1,559,518	0	Maschke, David M.G.
IDAHO																
Jerome	8	M	111,069	103,969	2,535	41.01	0	Owned	7,100	40,000	30	51,000	0	51,000	9,069	Pea, Wayne
Pocatello	50	M	4,031	3156	500	6.31	875	0	0	115,000	61	1,645	0	2,386	0	none
Twin Falls	29	M	4,859	4,859	250	19.43	0	Owned	0	150,000	100	2,350	0	2,509	0	none
ILLINOIS																
*Crystal Lake	19	M	2,208,000	1,475,000	26,650	55.34	202,000	256,000	275,000	110,000	155	0	250,000	1,913,000	45,000	LaRoi Architects Ltd.
Dixon	16	M	78,500	39,500	426	92.72	25,000	Owned	14,000	87,000	120	0	39,250	36,750	2,500	McLane, John
Dundee	35	M	425,992	207,128	10,045	20.62	94,393	Owned	124,471	43,750	50	155,967	0	270,025	0	Burnidge, Cassell . . .
Granite City	37	M	138,419	105,135	2,550	41.23	21,500	Owned	11,784	140,000	90	55,367	0	83,052	0	FGM Architects
Niles	53	M	1,105,500	940,000	14,090	66.71	100,000	Owned	65,500	140,000	141	0	250,000	855,500	0	Orput Assocs.
Park Forest[19]	26	M	121,200	100,50	39,000	2.57	16,000	Owned	4,700	120,000	94	30,300	0	90,900	0	none

Table 3 / Public Library Buildings: Additions and Renovations, 1986 (cont.)

Community	Pop. in M	Code	Project Cost	Const. Cost	Gross Sq. Ft.	Sq.Ft. Cost	Equip. Cost	Site Cost	Other Costs	Volumes	Reader Seats	Federal Funds	State Funds	Local Funds	Gift Funds	Architect
INDIANA																
*Carmel	33	M	2,900,000	1,795,048	32,000	56.09	867,748	Owned	237,204	100,000	180	0	0	2,900,000	0	Pecsok, Jelliffe...
East Chicago	40	M	1,492,966	1,200,237	26,800	44.78	174,482	Owned	118,247	150,000	85	0	0	1,492,966	0	Bittner & Detella
*Fortville[20]	6	M	671,025	405,089	7,738	52.35	42,538	120,000	103,398	56,000	58	257,000	0	414,025	0	Randall, Parke...
Linton	4	M	6,200	6,200	1,235	5.02	0	Owned	0	7,000	20	0	0	5,000	1,200	none
Mentone	4	M	43,717	39,542	2,638	14.99	2,875	Owned	1,300	1,840	0	19,700	0	24,017	0	Scearce, Donald
Muncie[21]	80	M	233,928	200,473	11,350	17.66	146,600	Owned	33,455	100,000	64	60,450	0	173,478	0	Gooden Assocs.
*Nappanee[22]	9	M	2,834,358	815,384	12,900	63.20	53,483	85,000	1,787,374	55,000	100	160,550	0	2,785,692	48,666	Holdeman, Robert L.
*New Carlisle	4	M	551,179	415,020	6,000	69.17		Owned	82,676	30,000	30	0	0	390,629	0	Pecsok, Jelliffe,...
IOWA																
Elk Horn	1	M	11,362	10,000	748	15.19	662.00	Owned	0	3,266	17	0	0	11,132	230	none
Somers[23]	1	M	18,964	12,152	1,320	9.20	6,812	0	0	4,000	15	0	0	2,000	16,964	none
KANSAS																
*Oskaloosa	2	M	59,363	53,763	1,036	51.89	2,000	Owned	3,600	10,000	24	23,000	0	10,363	26,000	Hicks & Assocs.
Paola	7	M	197,938	160,373	3,460	46.35	6,745	17,500	13,320	80,000	56	50,382	0	50,441	97,115	Koupal, Howard,...
Troy	9	M	15,123	15,123	1,000	15.12	0	Leased	0	27,000	20	0	0	9,054	6,069	none
Wichita	32	B	82,501	45,006	2,716	16.57	34,345	0	3,150	11,000	20	0	0	82,501	0	Sanders, Tom
KENTUCKY																
Lexington	38	B	31,808	15,105	13,000	1.16	16,703	Leased	0	60,000	38	0	0	31,808	0	none
Louisville	240	B	231,348	173,665	8,090	21.46	0	0	57,683	31,000	40	115,718	0	115,630	0	Louis & Henry, Inc.
MARYLAND																
*Baltimore	750	M	3,750,000	3,000,000	12,000	250.00	250,000	0	500,000	1,350,000	n/a	0	2,777,000	750,000	223,000	Ayers-Saint...
*Crisfield[24]	4	B	240,000	194,000	2,100	92.38	33,190	Owned	12,810	25,000	30	150,000	0	90,000	0	Ciancitto, Ardis...
MASSACHUSETTS																
Ipswitch[25]	12	M	192,500	147,500	2,000	73.75	28,000	Owned	17,000	20,000	12	0	0	164,500	28,000	Notter, Finegold...
Millville[26]	2	M	130,317	58,674	1,928	30.43	9,103	55,000	7,540	2,970	74	6,585	0	57,020	18,534	none
Norfolk[27]	68	M	430,000	345,000	7,418	46.51	45,000	Owned	40,000	20,000	50	0	48,178	430,000	0	Design Partnership...
Sandwich	12	M	940,000	790,000	17,000	46.47	60,000	Owned	90,000	90,000	300	167,460	0	712,540	60,000	Gill, Grattan
MINNESOTA																
Heron Lake	2	M	25,838	2,174	3,200	.68	1,164	22,500	0	10,000	25	0	0	214	25,624	none
Hutchinson[28]	14	B	706,758	587,728	10,611	55.39	75,340	Owned	43,690	27,600	60	0	0	706,758	0	Korngiebel Architecture
Windom[29]	5	M	68,500	21,000	3,348	6.27	2,500	45,000	0	17,000	25	0	0	53,500	15,000	none
MISSISSIPPI																
Hernando[30]	3	MS	405,333	327,046	6,000	54.51	56,873	Owned	21,414	80,350	57	219,333	0	165,000	21,000	Godbold, Hansen...
Jackson	444	MS	2,900,000	1,891,411	63,680	29.70	860,050	Owned	148,539	156,000	254	0	200,000	2,700,000	0	Cooke-Douglass...
MISSOURI																
Rock Port	9	M	136,000	54,000	4,500	12.00	20,000	60,000	2,000	50,000	13	0	0	135,000	1,000	none

MONTANA

City																Architect
Butte	35	M	34,256	28,295	1,430	19.78	3,584	Owned	2,377	90,000	100	14,256	0	20,000	0	Gottland, Harold
*Havre[31]	18	M	591,029	294,346	12,800	23.00	22,323	250,000	24,360	95,000	40	84,710	42,000	0	464,319	Springer Group . . .
NEBRASKA																
Crawford[32]	3	M	78,376	53,376	2,500	21.35	0	25,000	0	18,500	22	38,886	0	39,490	0	none
Lyman	1	M	8,083	8,083	3,750	2.16	0	0	0	9,000	0	4,649	0	3,434	0	none
Yutan[33]	1	M	18,000	17,200	1,024	16.80	800	0	0	10,000	16	9,000	0	9,000	0	none
NEW HAMPSHIRE																
Conway	8	M	248,632	198,175	4,000	49.54	33,463	Owned	16,994	n/a	7	181,500	0	1,000	66,132	Jawitz & Tambling
NEW YORK																
Addison	3	M	3,350	3,350	5,000	.67	0	Owned	0	20,000	5	0	1,675	1,675	0	not reported
Burnt Hills	12	M	8,000	8,000	5,760	1.39	0	Owned	0	25,000	32	4,000	0	4,000	0	none
Cheektowaga	110	MS	34,032	29,755	450	66.12	4,277	Owned	0	n/a	n/a	0	8,000	26,032	0	Bryon, Chester L.
Cold Spring	10	M	126,824	104,385	2,160	48.32	12,000	0	10,439	2,000	48	14,000	23,580	30,774	8,470	Smith, Peter
Corning	26	M	6,600	6,600	40,000	.15	600	Owned	0	120,000	75	0	3,300	1,378	0	not reported
Dundee	1	M	2,756	0	4,000		2,756	Owned	0	15,260	31	93,750	1,378	0	0	Sautter, M. & R. Brewer
Elma	10	M	189,018	152,854	4,000	38.21	17,949	0	18,215	40,000	70	0	18,000	0	9,000	Renaldo, James
Fishkill	16	M	362,784	315,265	4,485	70.30	34,275	Owned	13,244	25,115	55	0	64,000	68,268	298,784	Battoglia Assocs.
Gowanda	3	B	42,941	36,301	n/a	n/a		Owned	6,640	n/a	24	0	20,000	22,941	0	Rogers, Trevor W.
Granville	5	M	3,865	3,865	170	22.73		Owned	0	n/a	30	0	1,875	0	1,990	not reported
Harrison	23	M	1,045,958	774,709	14,770	52.45	154,633	Owned	116,616	130,500	75	0	40,000	886,066	119,892	Aaron Cohen Assocs.
Katonah	15	M	8,000	8,000	19,500	.41	0	25,000	0	60,000	150	0	4,000	0	4,000	not reported
Liverpool	50	M	1,105,000	840,000	10,500	80.00	75,000	0	165,000	110,000	150	101,000	275,000	729,000	0	Sargent, D. Kenneth
New York (Brnx)	51	B	196,800	196,800	16,486	11.94	0	0	0	50,000	84	0	64,930	131,870	0	not reported
New York (Brnx)	27	B	283,200	283,200	12,283	23.06	0	0	3,540	30,000	72	0	141,600	141,600	0	Gibbons, Kenneth
Scarsdale	18	M	17,830	14,290	19,500	.73	5,535	Owned	0	118,000	139	0	8,000	9,830	0	not reported
Schenectady	21	B	87,202	81,667	2,918	27.99	3,065	Owned	0	4,000	4	0	15,578	71,624	0	not reported
Scio	2	M	12,165	9,100	700	13.00	0	Owned	0	5,400	n/a	0	6,082	6,082	0	Bentley, Roger
Wellsville	6	M	101,287	101,287	41,000	2.47		Owned	0	85,000	n/a	0	50,643	50,643	0	not reported
Whitesboro	22	M	1,142,000	935,520	10,000	93.55	111,780	Owned	94,700	70,000	66	0	82,000	1,060,000	0	McDonald, David
NORTH CAROLINA																
Durham[34]	20	B	260,441	214,342	8,500	25.22	11,618	20,000	14,481	30,000	50	12,993	0	247,448	0	Hackney, Sears, & Assocs.
NORTH DAKOTA																
*Hazen	20	B	45,000	45,000	2,200	20.45	0	0	0	10,000	20	22,500	0	22,500	0	not reported
OKLAHOMA																
Bixby	7	B	276,397	238,966	5,280	45.26	12,477	Owned	24,954	20,500	34	0	16,959	276,397	0	HTB Architects
Carnegie	6	M	84,155	1,925	35,136	.05	n/a	n/a	n/a	11,902	53	0	17,763	19,682	45,588	not reported
Norman	80	MS	3,250,471	2,183,460	50,000	43.67	699,048	163,363	204,600	200,000	300	0		3,232,708	0	Graves, Boynton . . .
OREGON																
*Klamath Falls	58	MS	20,735	n/a	31,204	n/a	n/a	n/a	n/a	200,000	116	10,000	735	10,000	0	Pence, Nina
La Grande	12	M	31,105	31,105	392	79.34	0	Owned	0	50,000	40	14,692	0	16,413	0	none
Newberg[35]	19	M	1,595,000	1,177,250	17,700	66.51	120,000	125,000	172,750	88,000	95	176,000	37,000	1,097,000	285,000	Danielson, Richard D.
Seaside	5	M	131,000	126,000	5,000	25.20	5,000	0	5,000	22,000	40	54,000	0	60,000	5,000	Miller, Jim

Table 3 / Public Library Buildings: Additions and Renovations, 1986 (cont.)

Community	Pop. in M	Code	Project Cost	Const. Cost	Gross Sq. Ft.	Sq.Ft. Cost	Equip. Cost	Site Cost	Other Costs	Volumes	Reader Seats	Federal Funds	State Funds	Local Funds	Gift Funds	Architect
RHODE ISLAND																
Charlestown[36]	5	M	300,450	233,422	4,956	47.10	38,268	Owned	28,760	6,000	46	0	150,225	0	150,225	Monroe, Kevin S.
N. Providence[37]	29	M	2,500,000	1,800,000	37,000	48.64	224,000	300,000	176,000	115,200	168	0	1,250,000	1,250,000	0	Castellucci Galli Corp.
Tiverton[38]	7	B	61,568	52,880	1,166	45.35	2,629	0	6,059	13,000	12	30,000	0	4,268	27,300	Almy Assocs.
SOUTH CAROLINA																
Landrum	7	B	134,429	104,160	1,950	53.42	19,339	Owned	10,930	50,000	60	17,500	10,000	23,532	83,397	Hollis & Crocker
Seneca	7	B	254,105	212,970	7,519	28.32	29,074	Owned	12,061	30,000	74	50,000	0	204,105	0	Sample, William H.
Union[39]	31	M	537,986	464,175	8,000	58.02	41,820	Owned	31,991	50,000	42	204,857	50,000	37,624	245,505	Gaulden, F. Earle
SOUTH DAKOTA																
Faulkton[40]	3	M	62,000	27,244	3,075	8.86	10,656	24,000	100	16,000	12	31,000	0	26,000	5,000	none
Sioux Falls	90	M	11,350	9,166	190	48.24	1,184	0	1,000	146,000	12	5,675	0	0	5,675	Fritzel, Kroeger . . .
TEXAS																
* Big Lake	5	M	179,787	156,955	4,000	39.23	7,832	Owned	15,000	34,000	50	0	0	179,787	0	Meek, Jack
Highlands	10	B	169,514	139,019	2,700	51.49	30,495	Owned	0	19,000	35	0	0	169,514	0	Harris County . . .
Iowa Park	6	M	468,708	381,198	5,742	66.39	49,928	n/a	37,582	18,000	45	100,000	0	20,000	490,000	Daugherity & Glover
Memphis	6	M	200,000	173,377	3,956	43.83	24,014	Owned	2,609	25,000	26	0	0	0	200,000	Odom, J.A.
Orange	24	M	312,302	274,730	2,100	131.00	15,279	Owned	22,293	n/a	n/a	100,000	0	173,302	39,000	Page Southerland Page
Texas City	43	M	1,311,000	996,000	21,000	47.43	230,000	0	85,000	120,000	132	150,000	0	1,161,000	0	Reed & Clements
VIRGINIA																
* Kenbridge	6	B	66,720	19,689	3,132	6.29	16,981	25,250	4,800	14,370	15	10,500	4,370	0	51,850	Edgerton Assocs.
Lexington[41]	37	MS	1,247,496	690,528	15,000	46.04	79,956	250,000	227,012	80,000	80	115,642	0	370,000	761,854	Shertz, Franklin . . .
* South Hill[42]	14	B	75,000	63,000	1,350	46.66	5,000	0	7,000	4,000	24	24,000	0	0	51,000	Edgerton Assocs.
Suffolk	48	MS	909,297	484,248	15,000	32.28	40,758	330,000	54,291	100,000	150	120,542	0	788,755	0	Warner & Barnes Assocs.
WASHINGTON																
Bellingham	46	M	3,215,246	2,361,532	42,548	55.50	449,604	Owned	404,110	250,000	194	0	0	3,215,246	0	LaTourelle & Assocs.
Colfax	17	MS	427,332	314,473	18,095	17.37	62,859	0	50,000	100,000	48	0	0	427,332	0	Miller, Nelson T.
WEST VIRGINIA																
Pineville	9	BS	128,568	111,190	2,400	46.33	10,015	Leased	7,363	11,000	40	0	12,000	116,568	0	SEM Partners, Inc.
WISCONSIN																
* Adams[43]	15	M	151,287	121,233	5,058	23.97	14,103	Owned	15,951	18,440	36	103,430	0	30,496	17,361	Mid-State Assocs., Inc.
Marshfield	30	M	1,222,246	934,506	19,500	48.00	94,726	84,000	109,014	150,000	147	0	0	888,303	333,943	Miller, Robert
* Palmyra	2	M	250,420	214,131	5,703	37.55	11,871	Owned	24,418	14,500	30	73,438	0	119,500	57,482	DeQuardo & Assocs.
Sauk City	12	M	186,000	162,000	2,200	73.64	0	20,000	4,000	30,000	30	90,000	0	96,000	0	Loveland, Gary
* Withee[44]	2	M	113,473	90,762	2,940	30.87	10,000	4,224	8,487	10,000	45	0	0	103,473	10,000	Volovsek, Richard
WYOMING																
Lyman	2	B	179,281	158,843	3,300	48.13	12,938	Owned	7,500	15,000	20	0	0	179,281	0	Holland-Pasker & Assocs.

References

1. Project built and donated by local developer; only library expense: large monthly lease.
2. Post-modern design, eight chimney skylights, redwood lattice arches.
3. Multipurpose center includes senior center and pre-school day care.
4. $79,000 gift for adjacent children's park; town birthplace of Mrs. Melvil Dewey.
5. Project money from local estate & earned interest on investments.
6. Skylights over reading areas; glass-enclosed atrium connects to government facility.
7. Ceramic fireplace mural interior focal point; demonstration of area artists and craftspeople.
8. Financed by mortgage from Farmers Home Administration.
9. Children's reading loft with mural; skylighted lobby accentuates 25-foot circulation desk.
10. Texas Library Association's Library Project of the Year, 1986.
11. Includes 26,000 sq. ft. basement and two-floor (72,000 sq. ft.) addition to existing parking structure.
12. Part of $1.2 million project with schools.
13. Glass walls integrate facade of Cultural Heritage Landmark with children's "environment" and amphitheater, community room, art exhibit area.
14. 1910 building made energy-efficient.
15. Floor of remodeled 1874 courthouse.
16. Former church, historical building.
17. 19th century farmhouse.
18. $34,123 donated in services; 80 volunteers worked 86 days to paint and finish all surfaces.
19. 25% energy cost saving anticipated from heating and air conditioning renovation.
20. Greenhouse and glass area joining children's and outdoor activity areas.
21. 1904 building, in National Register of Historic Places.
22. Renovation surrounds 1936 structure on three sides; includes architect-donated stained glass window.
23. Labor done by volunteers.
24. Skylight over children's reading pit.
25. Phase I of project had zero impact on tax rate.
26. Former funeral home renovated by Blackstone Valley Regional Vocational Technical High School.
27. New entrances and elevation maintain New England vernacular style of former Grange Hall.
28. Carnegie Building; National Registry of Historic Places.
29. Railroad ticket counter used as check-out; 1950s mural provides color scheme.
30. Renovated department store.
31. Building donated by Le Havre Medical Association.
32. Building and site donated by members of Christian Scientist Church.
33. Building built for Fire Hall and Village Hall in late 1920s.
34. 1940 building in historic black neighborhood; made handicapped accessible.
35. Adaptive remodel of Carnegie Building.
36. Energy-efficient features: passive solar trombe wall and provision for day lighting.
37. Part of skating rink converted into two-story space for library; includes center for visually and hearing impaired.
38. Building used as library for over 100 years.
39. Designed to complement Carnegie Building, first one in South Carolina; includes copper roof exactly duplicating original.
40. Former grocery store.
41. Renovated 1920s automobile dealership; twin towers and lancet windows.
42. Shelving built and installed by local high school students.
43. Former Hudson car showroom and garage; only public library in county.
44. Former school built in 1890; historic landmark.

Table 4 / Public Library Buildings Not Previously Reported

Community	Pop. in M	Code	Project Cost	Const. Cost	Gross Sq. Ft.	Sq.Ft. Cost	Equip. Cost	Site Cost	Other Costs	Volumes	Reader Seats	Federal Funds	State Funds	Local Funds	Gift Funds	Architect
Valley Falls, (1985) KS	2	M	$25,186	$8,786	535	$16.42	$3,400	$13,000	0	9,000	20	0	0	$25,186	0	none
Ipswich, MA (1985)	16	M	192,500	147,500	2,000	73.75	28,000	Owned	17,000	55,000	20	0	0	164,500	28,000	Notter, Finegold, Alexander
Almond, NY (1985)	1	M	4,000	4,000	7,500	.53	0	Owned	0	10,000	n/a	0	2,000	2,000	0	Cornell, Bruce
Belfast, NY (1985)	2	M	6,000	6,000	1,100	5.45	0	Owned	0	8,0000	n/a	0	3,000	3,000	0	none
Elmira, NY (1985)	98	M	6,000	6,000	60,000	.10	0	Owned	0	455,196	n/a	0	3,000	3,000	0	none
Fillmore, NY (1985)	1	M	3,570	3,362	1,835	1.83	208	Owned	0	9,134	n/a	0	1,785	1,785	0	Cox, Donald
Fort Plain, NY (1985)	3	M	89,257	74,680	1,228	60.81	4,985	Owned	9,592	6,000	0	51,008	0	1,500	36,749	Owens, Theodore
Hornell, NY (1985)	10	M	12,000	0	4,800	0	12,000	Owned	0	55,000	n/a	0	6,000	6,000	0	none
Horseheads, NY (1985)	7	M	10,362	10,362	6,290	1.65	0	Owned	0	45,000	n/a	0	5,181	5,181	0	none
New Lebanon, NY (1985)	3	M	17,132	16,132	550	29.33	1,000	Owned	0	8,500	6	0	4,701	12,431	0	Murad, Tony
New York, NY (1985)	37	B	300,730	270,893	16,364	16.55	0	Owned	29,837	11,336	108	0	150,365	150,365	0	none
Riverhead, NY (1985)	24	M	58,554	54,901	22,380	2.45	0	Owned	3,653	120,000	n/a	0	22,500	36,054	0	Scheiner, Robert
Schenectady, NY (1985)	21	B	230,563	182,314	3,000	60.77	14,074	31,250	2,925	20,000	24	0	61,418	169,145	0	Cullen, James
West Islip, NY (1985)	30	M	27,400	27,400	20,000	1.37	0	Owned	0	150,000	131	0	6,000	21,400	0	none
Sallisaw, OK (1985)[45]	6	M	185,689	169,189	3,564	47.47	12,500	Owned	4,000	17,000	39	75,000	0	50,000	60,689	Lane, Frank
Troy, PA (1985)	26	MS	375,498	329,360	7,750	42.50	8,340	Owned	37,798	60,000	36	160,254	0	215,244	0	Kostecky, John M., Jr.
Smithfield, RI (1985)[46]	9	M	197,967	174,367	5,100	34.19	7,200	Owned	16,400	60,000	23	83,792	10,000	7,526	96,649	Mosher Associates
Houston, TX (1985)	90	B	2,146,680	1,142,500	13,246	86.25	261,293	371,000	371,887	55,000	106	0	0	2,146,680	0	White Budd VanNess
Everett, WA	15	B	98,268	44,121	1,500	29.41	24,857	Owned	29,290	6,000	15	29,290	0	68,978	0	none

References

45. Old railroad depot.
46. 1908 schoolhouse; time-capsule blackboard (with signatures and messages) discovered during construction; resealed as is.

Table 5 / Academic Libraries, 1976–1986

	1976	1977	1978–79	1980	1981	1982	1983	1984	1985	1986
New Libraries	15	6	38	14	19	20	8	12	12	13
Additions	5	5	8	2	0	9	1	6	4	2
Additions plus Renovation	8	7	22	11	11	6	11	8	8	7
TOTALS	28	18	66	27	30	35	20	26	24	22
Combined Additions and Additions plus Renovation	13	12	30	13	11	15	12	14	12	9
Percentage of Combined A and R	46.42	66.66	45.45	48.15	36.66	42.85	60.00	53.85	50.00	40.90

Table 6 / New Academic Libraries, 1986

Name of Institution	Project Cost	Gross Area	Assignable	Non-Assignable	Sq.Ft. Cost	Building Cost	Equipment Cost	Book Capacity	Seating Capacity	Architect
University of Iowa Law Library, Ames	$15,107,470	103,916	81,662	22,254	$18.28	$1,900,000	$1,900,000	n/a	700	Birkerts, Gunnar
Health Sciences Lib.,[1] Tufts Univ., Boston	n/a	59,635	44,411	15,224	n/a	n/a	100,000	171,990	514	Bertrand ... Warnecke, John
Texas Woman's Univ., Denton	10,000,000	135,000	107,000	28,000	55.29	7,464,651	1,693,800	725,000	860	Hendricks & Walls
Albany Law School, N.Y.	6,300,000	53,000	43,500	9,500	103.74	5,500,000	350,000	320,000	450	Mendel, Mesick...
Willamette University, Salem, Ore.	n/a	63,000	58,000	5,000	80.29	5,058,000	669,000	250,000	625	Wofford, Theodore
* Taylor University, Upland, Ind.	5,567,000	61,000	50,000	11,000	73.77	4,500,000	1,067,000	210,000	450	Troyer, Le Roy & Assocs.
Univ. of South Florida, Sarasota	n/a	67,979	58,000	9,979	71.87	4,885,510	n/a	77,000	315	Harvard ... Architects Collab.
* Austin College, Sherman, Tex.	n/a	68,821	51,037	17,784	66.84	4,600,000	450,000	238,750	655	Malone, Tom
Lee Coll. & Church of God Sch. of Theology, Cleveland, Tenn.	2,751,000	43,500	39,200	4,300	58.30	2,536,000	215,000	180,000	425	Rardin & Carroll
Sch. of Marine & Atmospheric[2] Science, University of Miami, Fla.	n/a	17,000	15,650	1,350	125.21	2,128,570	76,878	80,000	110	Abramovitz-Harris-Kingsland
* University of Oklahoma, Norman	1,700,000	13,000	11,000	2,000	84.62	1,100,000	120,000	80,000	175	Kaighn Assocs. & Bauer, Stark
Aguadilla Regional College, P.R.	800,678	n/a	26,000	n/a	n/a	n/a	100,000	64,560	383	Quiñones, Pablo
Health Science Center, University of Tennessee, Memphis	n/a	61,075	43,625	17,450	n/a	n/a	n/a	200,000	200	Gassner, Nathan

[1] Library part of 135,000 gross square foot, $21 million Center for Health Communications
[2] One wing of Science/Administration building

Table 7 / Academic Libraries: Additions and Renovations, 1986

Name of Institution		Project Cost	Gross Area	Assignable	Non-Assignable	Sq.Ft. Cost	Building Cost	Equipment Cost	Book Capacity	Seating Capacity	Architect
University of Alaska, Fairbanks	Total	$13,200,000	91,616	n/a	n/a	$104.45	$9,569,447	$867,000	1,100,000	848	GDM & Assocs.
	New	n/a	69,616	n/a	n/a	n/a	n/a	n/a	n/a	n/a	
	Renovated	n/a	22,000	n/a	n/a	n/a	n/a	n/a	n/a	n/a	
Lehigh University, Bethlehem, Pa.	Total	10,800,000	117,000	87,000	30,000	73.66	8,618,000	800,000	n/a	900	Warner Burns Toan Lunde
	New	n/a	77,000	58,000	19,000	107.37	8,268,000	730,000	n/a	600	
	Renovated	n/a	40,000	29,000	11,000	8.75	350,000	70,000	n/a	300	
Wesleyan University, Middletown, Ct.	Total	10,000,000	116,000	103,000	13,000	69.61	8,075,000	800,000	799,375	680	Perry, Dean, Rogers
	New	6,806,000	42,000	39,000	3,000	131.90	5,540,000	515,720	210,050	268	
	Renovated	3,194,000	74,000	64,000	10,000	34.26	2,535,000	284,280	589,325	412	
* Florida Atlantic Univ., Boca Raton	Total	7,678,598	164,224	150,824	13,400	43.30	7,111,855	566,743	800,000	1,321	Spillis Candela
	New	6,578,598	86,268	80,677	5,591	70.27	6,061,855	516,743	400,000	694	
	Renovated	1,100,000	78,956	70,147	8,809	13.30	1,050,000	50,000	400,000	627	
* Bucknell Univ., Lewisburg, Pa.	Total	7,496,436	137,282	121,187	16,095	46.69	6,410,305	611,750	575,000	1070	Shepley Bulfinch
	New	5,491,687	72,210	64,784	7,426	66.58	4,807,729	393,000	373,570	675	
	Renovated	2,003,749	65,072	56,403	8,669	24.63	1,602,576	218,750	201,430	395	
Medical College of Wisconsin, Milwaukee	Total	115,000	1,800	1,800	0	n/a	n/a	91,000	25,000	16	MCW Engineering Dept.
	New	65,000	600	600	0	n/a	n/a	41,000	22,000	0	
	Renovated	50,000	1,200	1,200	0	n/a	n/a	50,000	3,000	16	
* Midwestern State Univ., Wichita Falls, Tex.	Total	4,236,511	99,867	70,721	29,146	40.92	4,086,511	150,000	500,000	1,000	Harper Perkins
	New	3,409,391	44,867	31,117	13,750	72.65	3,259,391	150,000	n/a	n/a	
	Renovated	827,120	55,000	39,604	15,396	15.04	827,120	0	n/a	n/a	

377

Table 8 / Academic Libraries: Additions Only, 1986

Name of Institution	Project Cost	Gross Area	Assignable	Non-Assignable	Sq.Ft. Cost	Building Cost	Equipment Cost	Book Capacity	Seating Capacity	Architect
Albertson LRC, Univ. of Wisconsin-Stevens Point	$7,200,000	87,000	60,000	27,000	$68.97	$6,000,000	$1,200,000	370,000	400	Strang Partners
Doane College, Crete, Neb.	626,291	11,484	11,000	484	48.40	55,872	70,419	200,000	302	Dawson, Robert

Table 9 / Academic Libraries: Renovations Only, 1986

Name of Institution	Project Cost	Gross Area	Assignable	Non-Assignable	Sq.Ft. Cost	Building Cost	Equipment Cost	Book Capacity	Seating Capacity	Architect
Iowa State University, Ames	$3,500,000	226,218	169,921	56,297	n/a	n/a	$1,000,000	1,513,000	2,200	Herbert, Charles
Oklahoma Christian College, Oklahoma City	1,100,000	30,000	n/a	n/a	33.33	1,000,000	100,000	150,000	350	Tredway & Goto
*Creighton University, Omaha, Neb.	762,000	22,000	n/a	n/a	15.27	336,000	426,000	201,000	200	Daly, Leo A.
*University of California, Irvine	595,614	n/a	18,807	n/a	n/a	516,000	79,614	0	189	Rossetti Assocs.
SUNY College at New Paltz	n/a	8,511	6,638	1,873	46.90	399,151	n/a	0	200	Mendel, Mesick . . .
*Northwestern University, Evanston, Ill.	86,235	917	917	0	52.97	48,577	31,591	0	0	Baker & Assocs.

Table 10 / Library Projects in Progress, 1986

Stages of Project	PUBLIC			ACADEMIC		
	No. of Projects	Construction Cost Projected	Gross Square Feet	No. of Projects	Construction Cost Projected	Gross Square Feet
Pre-design stage:						
1. Preliminary investigation	25	$8,148,300	134,340	0	0	0
2. Program filed	11	7,460,548	168,478	3	$26,840,000	681,531
3. Project funded	18	30,869,325	376,993	0	0	0
4. Architect selected	15	11,861,000	170,967	1	14,120,000	122,000
Design stage:						
5. Design stage in progress	96	151,332,221	1,852,899	16	108,973,800	1,081,348
6. Construction documents completed	48	54,209,318	566,936	6	30,845,000	377,299
7. Bidding complete	10	5,430,420	76,149	0	0	0
8. Contracts awarded	185	197,201,874	2,803,693	38	152,948,355	2,073,425
TOTALS	**408**	**$466,513,006**	**6,150,455**	**64**	**$333,727,155**	**4,335,603**

Table 11 / Public Library Projects in Progress, 1986*

NAME OF LIBRARY	STAGES†							
	1	2	3	4	5	6	7	8
ALABAMA								
Alexander City P.L. [1987]		✓	✓					
Andalusia P.L. [1988]	✓	✓	✓	✓				
Arab P.L. [1987]	✓	✓	✓	✓	✓			
Auburn P.L. [1987]	✓	✓	✓	✓	✓			
Smithfield Branch, Birmingham [1987]	✓	✓	✓	✓	✓			
Boaz P.L. [1987]	✓				✓			
Carrollton P.L. [1986]								✓
Cullman Cty. P.L. [1987]	✓	✓	✓	✓	✓	✓		
Eufaula Carnegie Library [1986]	✓	✓	✓	✓	✓	✓	✓	
Eufaula Carnegie Library [?]	✓	✓	✓	✓	✓	✓	✓	✓
Eva P.L. [1986]	✓	✓	✓	✓	✓	✓	✓	✓
Fairfield P.L. [1987]	✓	✓	✓	✓	✓	✓	✓	✓
Florence-Lauderdale P.L. [1987]	✓	✓	✓	✓	✓			
Gadsden P.L. [1987]	✓	✓	✓	✓	✓	✓	✓	✓
Emma Knox Kenan P.L., Geneva [1986]	✓	✓	✓	✓	✓	✓	✓	✓
Gulf Shores P.L. [1987]	✓	✓	✓	✓	✓	✓	✓	✓
Clyde Nix P.L., Hamilton [?]	✓	✓	✓	✓	✓	✓	✓	✓
Homewood P.L. [1987]	✓	✓	✓	✓	✓	✓	✓	✓
Huntsville-Madison Cty. [1987]	✓	✓	✓	✓	✓	✓	✓	✓
Irondale P.L. [1987]				✓	✓	✓		
Jacksonville P.L. [1987]								✓
Montrose-Crescenta Br., Montrose [1986]	✓	✓	✓	✓				
Oceanside P.L. [1989]	✓	✓	✓	✓	✓			
Ontario Branch [1986]	✓	✓	✓	✓	✓	✓	✓	
Parlier Branch Library [1987]	✓	✓	✓	✓	✓	✓	✓	✓
San Ramon City, Pleasant Hill [1987]	✓							
Redwood City P.L. [1988]	✓	✓	✓	✓	✓	✓		

NAME OF LIBRARY	STAGES							
	1	2	3	4	5	6	7	8
Monroeville Cty. P.L. [1986]	✓	✓	✓	✓	✓	✓	✓	✓
Oneonta P.L. [1986]	✓	✓	✓	✓		✓	✓	✓
Saraland P.L. [1987]	✓	✓	✓	✓				
Sheffield P.L. [1987]	✓			✓				
ARIZONA								
Glendale P.L. [1987]	✓	✓	✓	✓	✓	✓	✓	
Dobson Ranch Branch, Mesa [1987]	✓							✓
Cholla Branch, Phoenix [1988]	✓							
Scottsdale P.L. [1987]	✓	✓	✓	✓	✓	✓	✓	✓
Scottsdale P.L. [?]	✓	✓	✓	✓	✓	✓	✓	
Tucson P.L. [1989]	✓	✓	✓					
CALIFORNIA								
Beale Memorial, Bakersfield [1987]	✓	✓	✓	✓	✓	✓	✓	✓
Beverly Hills Branch [1989]	✓	✓				✓		
City of Cerritos P.L. [1986]	✓	✓	✓	✓	✓	✓	✓	✓
Costa Mesa Branch [1987]	✓	✓	✓	✓	✓	✓	✓	✓
El Segundo P.L. [?]	✓	✓	✓	✓				
Fremont Main, Hayward [1988]	✓	✓	✓	✓				
Pleasanton Library, Hayward [1987]	✓	✓	✓	✓				
Heritage Park Regional, Irvine [1987]	✓	✓	✓					
Florence Riford Lib. Ctr., La Jolla [1988]	✓	✓	✓	✓	✓			
Crown Valley Br., Laguna Niguel [1987]	✓	✓	✓	✓	✓	✓	✓	✓
Merchant's Walk Lib., Marietta [?]				✓	✓	✓		
Candler Cty. Lib., Metter [1987]	✓			✓	✓	✓	✓	
M. Vinson Memorial, Milledgeville [1986]	✓	✓	✓	✓	✓	✓	✓	✓
Monroe-Walton Cty. Lib. [1987]	✓	✓	✓	✓	✓	✓	✓	
Jasper Cty. Lib., Monticello [1987]	✓	✓	✓	✓	✓	✓	✓	
C.D. Perry Memorial, Nashville [1987]								✓

Linda Vista Branch, San Diego [1987]	✓	✓	✓	✓		✓			Newnan-Coweta Cty. P.L. [1987]					✓			
North Park Branch, San Diego [1986]	✓	✓	✓	✓				✓	Norcross P.L. [1988]	✓	✓	✓					
Otay Mesa Branch, San Diego [1986]	✓	✓	✓	✓	✓	✓	✓	✓	Irwin County, Ocilla [1987]							✓	✓
Wadsworth Memorial, Tracy [1987]	✓	✓	✓	✓	✓	✓	✓	✓	Peachtree City P.L. [1987]	✓	✓	✓	✓	✓	✓	✓	✓
South Whittier Lib., Whittier [?]				✓	✓				Peachtree Corners P.L. [1988]	✓	✓	✓					
Willowbrook Library [1987]				✓		✓			Pembroke P.L. [1987]	✓	✓	✓	✓	✓	✓	✓	✓
Woodland P.L. [1986]	✓	✓	✓	✓	✓	✓	✓	✓	Richmond Hill P.L. [1986]	✓	✓	✓	✓	✓	✓	✓	✓
COLORADO									Sara Hightower Regional, Rome [1988]	✓	✓	✓	✓	✓			
P.S. Miller Lib., Castle Rock [1987]						✓			Rossville P.L. [1986]	✓	✓	✓	✓	✓	✓	✓	✓
Idaho Springs P.L. [1986]	✓	✓	✓	✓	✓	✓	✓	✓	St. Mary's Library [1988]	✓	✓						
Werner Lib., Steamboat Springs [1987]	✓	✓	✓	✓	✓				Snellville P.L. [1987]	✓	✓	✓	✓	✓			
San Miguel Cty., Telluride [1987]	✓	✓	✓	✓				✓	W.H. Stanton Lib., Social Circle [1987]				✓				✓
CONNECTICUT									Hancock Cty. Lib., Sparta [?]	✓							
Lucy Robbins Welles, Newington [1987]	✓	✓	✓	✓		✓	✓	✓	Statesboro Regional [1987]	✓	✓	✓	✓	✓	✓	✓	✓
DISTRICT OF COLUMBIA									Sue Kellogg, Stone Mountain [1987]	✓	✓	✓	✓	✓			
Shepherd Park Branch [1988]			✓	✓					Mountain Park, Stone Mountain [1987]	✓	✓	✓	✓	✓			
FLORIDA									Margaret Jones Lib., Sylvester [1987]	✓	✓	✓	✓	✓	✓	✓	✓
Casselberry Central Branch [1988]		✓	✓	✓	✓				Thomson-McDuffie Cty. [1987]					✓			
Crescent City P.L. [1987]	✓	✓	✓	✓	✓	✓			Coastal Plain Regional, Tifton [1987]							✓	✓
Volusia Cty., Daytona Beach [1987]							✓		Dade Cty. P.L., Trenton [1988]	✓	✓						
Deland P.L. [1988]	✓	✓	✓	✓	✓				Reid H. Cofer Lib., Tucker [1987]	✓	✓	✓	✓	✓			
Northwest Branch, Lake Mary [1987]	✓	✓	✓	✓			✓		Oconee Cty. Lib., Watkinsville [1987]	✓	✓	✓	✓	✓	✓		
Forest City/Wekiva, Longwood [1987]	✓	✓	✓	✓			✓		Piedmont Reg. Lib., Winder [1987]	✓	✓	✓	✓	✓	✓		
Marco Island Branch, Naples [1987]	✓	✓	✓	✓	✓	✓			**IDAHO**								
Pasco County HQ, New Port Richey [1987]						✓	✓	✓	Camas Cty. District, Fairfield [1986]				✓		✓		✓
East Branch, Oviedo [1987]	✓	✓	✓	✓			✓		Filer P.L. [1987]	✓	✓	✓	✓	✓	✓		
Palm Harbor Library [1987]		✓	✓	✓	✓				Ketchum Community Lib. [1986]								✓
North Branch, Sanford [1987]	✓	✓	✓	✓			✓		Prairie Free Lib., Mountain Home [1986]		✓	✓					✓
Tarpon Springs Library [1986]	✓	✓	✓	✓	✓	✓	✓	✓	Salmon P.L. [1987]	✓			✓	✓			

*In Tables 11 and 12, the year following the library name represents the estimated year of completion.
†See Table 10 for a description of Stages 1–8.

Table 11 / Public Library Projects in Progress, 1986* (cont.)

NAME OF LIBRARY	STAGES 1	2	3	4	5	6	7	8
GEORGIA								
Northwest Branch, Albany [1987]		✓						
Southside Branch, Albany [1988]		✓						
Victoria Evans Memorial, Ashburn [1988]	✓	✓		✓				
Barnesville-Lamar Cty. [1987]	✓	✓	✓	✓	✓	✓	✓	✓
Buford P.L. [1988]	✓	✓	✓					
Sequoyah Regional System, Canton [?]		✓						
Cartersville-Bartow Cty. [1988]	✓	✓		✓				
Euharlee Library, Cartersville [1987]	✓	✓	✓	✓	✓	✓	✓	✓
Cave Spring P.L. [1987]	✓	✓	✓	✓	✓	✓	✓	✓
Chamblee Library [1987]	✓	✓	✓	✓	✓			
Tessie W. Norris Lib., Cochran [1986]	✓	✓	✓	✓	✓	✓	✓	✓
Commerce P.L. [1986]	✓	✓	✓	✓	✓	✓	✓	✓
Cordele-Crisp Carnegie Lib. [1987]	✓	✓	✓	✓	✓	✓	✓	✓
Cornelia-Habersham Cty. P.L. [1987]	✓	✓	✓	✓	✓	✓		
Ida Hilton P.L., Darien [1987]	✓	✓	✓	✓	✓	✓	✓	✓
Scott Candler Library, Decatur [1986]	✓	✓	✓	✓	✓	✓	✓	✓
Duluth P.L. [1988]	✓	✓	✓	✓				
Eatonton-Putnam Cty. Lib. [1987]						✓	✓	✓
Fortson P.L., Hampton [1987]	✓	✓	✓	✓	✓	✓	✓	✓
Hart Cty. Library, Hartwell [?]	✓							
Wayne Cty. Lib., Jesup [1987]	✓	✓	✓	✓	✓	✓		
Clayton Cty. Lib., Jonesboro [1987]	✓	✓	✓	✓	✓	✓		
Camden Cty. Library, Kingsland [1988]	✓	✓	✓	✓				
Lawrenceville P.L. [1989]	✓	✓	✓					
Lilburn P.L. [1988]	✓	✓	✓					
Bruce St. Sch., Lithonia [1987]	✓	✓		✓	✓	✓		
Loganville City Library [?]	✓	✓		✓				
Morgan Cty. Lib., Madison [1988]	✓	✓		✓				

NAME OF LIBRARY	STAGES 1	2	3	4	5	6	7	8
ILLINOIS								
Ida P.L., Belvidere [1987]			✓	✓	✓	✓	✓	✓
Berkeley P.L. [1986]	✓	✓	✓	✓	✓	✓	✓	✓
Glenwood-Lyrwood, Glenwood [1986]	✓	✓	✓	✓	✓	✓	✓	✓
Warren-Newport P.L., Gurnee [1986]	✓	✓	✓	✓	✓	✓	✓	✓
Hillside P.L. [1987]	✓	✓		✓	✓	✓	✓	✓
Jerseyville Free Library [1987]	✓	✓	✓	✓	✓	✓	✓	✓
Joliet P.L. [1988]	✓	✓	✓	✓				
Filger Library, Minonk [1986]	✓	✓	✓	✓	✓	✓	✓	✓
Green Hills P.L., Palos Hills [1986]	✓	✓	✓	✓	✓	✓	✓	✓
Lakeview Branch, Peoria [1987]	✓	✓	✓	✓	✓	✓	✓	✓
Rolling Meadows Library [1987]	✓	✓	✓	✓	✓	✓	✓	✓
Bryan-Bennett Library, Salem [1986]	✓	✓	✓	✓	✓	✓	✓	✓
Utica P.L. [?]			✓	✓	✓	✓	✓	✓
Warrenville P.L. District [1987]	✓	✓	✓	✓	✓	✓	✓	✓
Wauconda Township [1987]	✓	✓	✓	✓	✓	✓	✓	✓
Wilmette P.L. District [1987]	✓	✓	✓	✓	✓	✓	✓	✓
Woodridge P.L. [1986]	✓	✓	✓	✓	✓	✓	✓	✓
Woodstock P.L. [1987]	✓	✓	✓	✓	✓	✓	✓	✓
INDIANA								
Charlestown-Clark Cty. P.L. [1986]	✓	✓	✓	✓	✓	✓	✓	✓
Bartholomew Cty. Lib., Columbus [1987]	✓	✓	✓	✓	✓	✓	✓	✓
Wright-Hageman P.L., Edinburgh [1986]	✓	✓	✓	✓	✓	✓	✓	✓
Franklin P.L. [1988]	✓	✓	✓	✓				
White River Lib., Franklin [1988]	✓	✓	✓	✓	✓	✓	✓	✓
Hartford City P.L. [1987]	✓	✓	✓	✓	✓	✓	✓	✓
Huntingdon City-Township P.L. [1987]	✓	✓	✓	✓	✓	✓	✓	✓
West Indianapolis Branch [1986]	✓	✓						✓
Tippecanoe Cty. P.L., Lafayette [1988]	✓	✓		✓			✓	

KANSAS, **KENTUCKY**, **LOUISIANA** (left column) — **MASSACHUSETTS** (continued), **MICHIGAN** (right column)

Library	✓	✓	✓	✓	✓	✓
Noblesville-Southeastern P.L. [1986]	✓	✓	✓	✓	✓	✓
Plainfield P.L. [1986]				✓		
Scott County P.L., Scottsburg [1986]			✓		✓	✓
KANSAS						
Johnston P.L., Baxter Springs [1986]		✓	✓	✓	✓	✓
Bradford Memorial, El Dorado [1987]		✓	✓	✓	✓	✓
Goddard P.L. [1986]	✓	✓	✓	✓	✓	✓
Sheridan Cty. Library, Hoxie [1986]		✓	✓	✓	✓	✓
Kingman Carnegie Library [1986]			✓	✓	✓	✓
Leavenworth P.L. [1986]	✓	✓	✓	✓	✓	✓
Lackman Branch, Lenexa [1986]	✓	✓	✓	✓	✓	✓
Louisburg P.L. [1987]		✓	✓	✓	✓	
Minneola City Library [1987]	✓	✓		✓		
Russell P.L. [1987]		✓	✓			
KENTUCKY						
Danville-Boyle Cty. P.L. [1988]	✓	✓	✓	✓	✓	✓
Powell Cty. P.L., Stanton [1986]	✓	✓	✓	✓	✓	✓
LOUISIANA						
Bienville Parish, Arcadia [1987]	✓	✓	✓	✓	✓	✓
Lee Road Branch, Covington [1987]			✓	✓		
St. Tammany Parish, Covington [1987]		✓	✓	✓	✓	
Folsom Branch Library [1987]			✓	✓		
Grand Isle Branch [1987]	✓	✓	✓	✓	✓	✓
Jefferson Parish, Harvey [1988]	✓	✓	✓	✓	✓	✓
Claiborne Parish, Homer [1987]	✓		✓	✓	✓	
Rosedale Branch, Jefferson [1986]		✓	✓	✓	✓	✓
St. James Parish, Lutcher [1987]			✓	✓	✓	✓
Madisonville Branch Lib. [1987]				✓		
Mandeville Branch Library [1987]				✓		
Metairie Road Branch, Metairie [1988]	✓	✓	✓	✓	✓	✓
Broadmoor Branch, New Orleans [1988]	✓	✓	✓	✓	✓	✓
Pearl River Branch [1987]				✓		
Slidell Branch Library [1987]				✓		
Lafourche Parish, Thibodaux [1987]	✓	✓	✓	✓	✓	✓
Live Oak Branch, Waggaman [1988]	✓	✓	✓	✓	✓	✓
Winn Parish Library, Winnfield [1986]			✓	✓	✓	✓

Library	✓	✓	✓	✓	✓	✓
Boston P.L. [1988]	✓	✓	✓	✓	✓	✓
Kirstein Business Branch, Boston [1990]						✓
McKim Bldg., Boston [1991]			✓	✓	✓	✓
Jonathan Bourne P.L., Bourne [1987]	✓		✓	✓	✓	✓
Boylston P.L. [?]				✓	✓	
Bridgewater P.L. [?]						
Canton P.L. [?]	✓					✓
Charlestown Serv. Bldg. [1991]		✓		✓	✓	✓
Eldredge P.L., Chatham [1989]		✓	✓			✓
Chelmsford P.L. [?]	✓					✓
Chilmark P.L. [1988]	✓	✓	✓	✓	✓	✓
Eastham P.L. [1988]	✓	✓	✓	✓	✓	✓
Franklin P.L. [1988]	✓		✓	✓	✓	✓
Lincoln P.L. [?]	✓	✓	✓	✓	✓	✓
Reuben Hoar Lib., Littleton [1988]	✓	✓	✓	✓	✓	✓
Mashpee P.L. [1987]	✓	✓	✓	✓	✓	✓
Milton P.L. [1987]	✓	✓	✓	✓	✓	✓
Newton Free Library [1989]	✓	✓	✓	✓	✓	✓
Stevens Memorial, North Andover [1988]	✓	✓	✓	✓	✓	✓
Norton P.L. [1988]	✓	✓	✓	✓	✓	✓
Plymouth P.L. [?]	✓	✓	✓	✓	✓	✓
Rockland Memorial Library [1988]	✓	✓	✓	✓	✓	✓
Wellfleet P.L. [1987]	✓	✓	✓	✓	✓	✓
West Bridgewater P.L. [1988]	✓	✓	✓	✓	✓	✓
G.A.R. Memorial, West Newbury [?]	✓	✓		✓	✓	✓
West Roxbury Branch [1988]	✓	✓	✓	✓	✓	✓
West Tisbury P.L. [?]	✓	✓	✓	✓	✓	✓
J.V. Fletcher Lib., Westford [1988]	✓	✓	✓	✓	✓	✓
Whitman P.L. [?]	✓	✓	✓	✓	✓	✓
Fiske P.L., Wrentham [?]	✓	✓	✓	✓	✓	✓
MICHIGAN						
Bessemer P.L. [1986]	✓	✓	✓	✓	✓	✓
Constantine Twnshp. Lib. [1987]	✓	✓	✓	✓	✓	✓
Dundee Branch [1987]		✓	✓	✓	✓	✓
Elk Rapids District Library [1986]	✓	✓	✓	✓	✓	✓
Surrey Twnshp. P.L., Farwell [1986]	✓	✓	✓	✓	✓	✓

Table 11 / Public Library Projects in Progress, 1986* (cont.)

NAME OF LIBRARY	STAGES 1	2	3	4	5	6	7	8
MARYLAND								
Annapolis Area Library [1986]	✓	✓	✓	✓	✓	✓	✓	
Annapolis Library HQ [1989]	✓							
So. Maryland Reg., Charlotte Hall [1988]	✓	✓	✓	✓	✓	✓		
Spauldings Branch, District Hgts. [1986]								✓
Edgewater Library [1989]	✓	✓						
Cecil County HQ, Elkton [1987]								✓
Howard Cty. Lib., Ellicott City [1986]	✓	✓	✓	✓	✓	✓	✓	✓
Federalsburg Branch [1986]	✓	✓	✓	✓	✓	✓	✓	✓
Northeast Branch, Hampstead [1988]	✓	✓	✓	✓	✓			✓
Havre de Grace Branch [1987]								✓
Calvert Cty. P.L., Lusby [1987]	✓	✓	✓	✓	✓	✓		
Millersville Branch [1991]	✓							
Southern Branch, Prince Frederick [1988]						✓		
Somerset Cty., Princess Anne [1987]	✓	✓	✓	✓	✓			
Provinces Branch, Severn [1986]	✓	✓	✓	✓	✓	✓	✓	✓
Severna Park Branch [1989]	✓							
Northwest Branch, Taneytown [1988]	✓	✓	✓	✓	✓			
Baltimore Cty. P.L., Towson [1987]	✓	✓	✓	✓	✓			
Walkersville Branch [1989]	✓	✓	✓	✓	✓			
MASSACHUSETTS								
Jones Library, Amherst [1989]	✓							
Memorial Hall Library, Andover [1987]	✓	✓	✓	✓	✓	✓	✓	✓
Stevens P.L., Ashburnham [1987]				✓	✓			
Ayer Library [?]	✓							
Bellingham P.L. [1988]	✓							
Boston P.L. [1987]	✓	✓	✓	✓	✓	✓	✓	✓
Boston P.L. [1988]	✓	✓						

NAME OF LIBRARY	STAGES 1	2	3	4	5	6	7	8
Holly Township [1987]	✓	✓	✓	✓		✓	✓	✓
Hall-Fowler Memorial, Ionia [1986]	✓	✓	✓	✓	✓	✓	✓	✓
Jackson District Library [1987]	✓	✓	✓	✓	✓	✓	✓	✓
W. Alice Chapin Memorial, Marion [1986]	✓	✓	✓	✓	✓	✓	✓	✓
Monroe Cty. Library [1986]	✓	✓	✓	✓	✓	✓	✓	
Pigeon District Library [1986]		✓	✓	✓			✓	✓
Romeo District Library [1987]	✓	✓	✓	✓	✓	✓	✓	
Vicksburg Community Library [1987]	✓	✓	✓	✓	✓	✓	✓	✓
Henika P.L., Wayland [?]	✓	✓	✓	✓	✓	✓	✓	✓
Ypsilanti District Library [1986]	✓	✓	✓	✓	✓	✓	✓	✓
MINNESOTA								
Bemidji P.L. [?]	✓							
Cloquet P.L. [1987]						✓		
Forest Lake P.L. [?]	✓	✓	✓	✓				
International Falls P.L. [?]	✓							
Kasson P.L. [?]	✓							
Rush City P.L. [1987]	✓	✓	✓		✓			
Stillwater P.L. [1987]	✓	✓	✓		✓	✓		
MISSISSIPPI								
Okolona Carnegie P.L. [1986]	✓	✓	✓	✓	✓	✓	✓	
Pascagoula City Library [1986]	✓	✓	✓	✓	✓	✓	✓	✓
MISSOURI								
Henry Cty. Lib., Clinton [1986]	✓	✓	✓		✓			
Summers Memorial Lib., Kebanon [1987]	✓	✓	✓		✓		✓	
Barry-Lawrence Reg., Monett [?]	✓	✓	✓	✓	✓		✓	
MONTANA								
Hamilton P.L. [1986]	✓	✓	✓		✓	✓		
Big Horn Cty. Lib., Hardin [1987]	✓	✓	✓	✓	✓	✓	✓	✓

Laurel P.L. [1988]

Mineral County P.L., Superior [1986]

NEBRASKA

Gordon P.L. [1986]

NEVADA

Bunkerville Library [?]

Elko County Library [1987]

Green Valley Lib., Henderson [1987]

Indian Springs Library [1986]

Clark Cty. Lib. District, Las Vegas [1986]

Las Vegas Library [1988]

Rainbow Library, Las Vegas [1988]

Spring Valley Lib., Las Vegas [1985]

Sunrise Library, Las Vegas [1987]

West Las Vegas Library [?]

Mt. Charleston Library [1987]

Moapa Valley Library, Overton [1987]

Washoe Cty. Library, Reno [1987]

Washoe Cty. Library, Reno [1987]

Sandy Valley Library [1987]

Silver Springs Branch [?]

West Wendover Branch [1987]

NEW JERSEY

Hillsborough P.L., Belle Mead [1988]

Newark P.L. [1987]

Nutley P.L. [1989]

Roseland Free P.L. [1987]

W. Deptford P.L., Thorofare [1988]

Westfield Memorial Lib. [1988]

NEW MEXICO

Alamogordo P.L. [1986]

Hatch P.L. [?]

Hobbs P.L. [1987]

Santa Fe P.L. [1986]

Socorro P.L. [1988]

Noble P.L. [1986]

Pryor P.L. [1986]

Tonkawa P.L. [?]

Maxwell Park Library, Tulsa [1986]

OREGON

Bandon P.L. [1986]

Manzanita Branch [1987]

RHODE ISLAND

Coventry P.L. [1988]

East Greenwich Free Library [?]

Providence P.L. [1988]

N. Smithfield P.L., Slatersville [1988]

West Warwick P.L. System [1989]

SOUTH CAROLINA

Beaufort County Library [1988]

Laurens County Library [?]

Sumter County Library [1986]

TEXAS

Allen P.L. [1988]

Southwest Branch, Arlington [1986]

Carnegie Library, Ballinger [1986]

Bedford P.L. [1987]

Cedar Hill P.L. [1986]

Corrigan P.L. [1986]

Crosby Branch Library [1987]

Dallam-Hartley Cty. Lib., Dalhart [1986]

North Oak Cliff Branch, Dallas [1986]

Renner Frankford Branch, Dallas [1986]

Dickinson P.L. [1987]

Eagle Pass P.L. [198¢]

Ennis P.L. [1987]

Fort Worth P.L. [1986]

Longview P.L. [1987]

McKinney Memorial P.L. [1987]

Mesquite Main Library [1987]

Table 11 / Public Library Projects in Progress, 1986* (cont.)

NAME OF LIBRARY	STAGES 1	2	3	4	5	6	7	8
NEW YORK								
Brooklyn P.L. [1987]								✓
Community Free Library, Holley [1987]	✓	✓	✓	✓	✓	✓	✓	✓
Nioga Library System, Lockport [1986]	✓	✓	✓	✓	✓	✓	✓	✓
North Tonawanda P.L. [1987]	✓	✓	✓	✓	✓	✓	✓	✓
Pleasant Valley Free Library [1986]	✓	✓	✓	✓	✓	✓	✓	✓
Prospect Free Library [1987]	✓	✓	✓	✓	✓	✓	✓	✓
Ransomville Free Library [1987]	✓	✓	✓	✓	✓	✓	✓	✓
Highland Branch, Rochester [1986]	✓	✓	✓	✓	✓	✓	✓	✓
Irondequoit P.L., Rochester [1986]	✓	✓	✓	✓	✓	✓	✓	✓
South Avenue Branch, Rochester [1987]	✓	✓	✓	✓	✓	✓	✓	✓
Onondaga Cty. P.L., Syracuse [1988]			✓	✓	✓	✓	✓	✓
NORTH CAROLINA								
Newport P.L. [?]	✓	✓	✓	✓	✓	✓	✓	
Ashe Cty. Lib., West Jefferson [1987]	✓	✓	✓	✓	✓	✓	✓	✓
OHIO								
Bluffton-Richland P.L., Bluffton [1986]	✓	✓	✓	✓	✓	✓	✓	✓
Bucyrus P.L. [1987]	✓	✓	✓	✓	✓	✓		

NAME OF LIBRARY	STAGES 1	2	3	4	5	6	7	8
Paris P.L. [1987]								✓
Plano P.L. [1988]				✓	✓			
Round Rock P.L. [1987]			✓	✓	✓			
Cortez Branch, San Antonio [1987]	✓	✓	✓	✓	✓			
Pan American Br., San Antonio [1987]	✓	✓	✓	✓	✓			✓
1000 Oaks-El Sendero, S. Antonio [1987]	✓	✓	✓	✓	✓	✓	✓	
Evelyn Meador Branch, Seabrook [1987]	✓	✓	✓	✓	✓	✓	✓	
Blanche K. Werner P.L., Trinity [1987]	✓	✓	✓					✓
Nicholas P. Simms Lib., Waxahachie [?]	✓	✓						
Collingworth Cty. Lib., Wellington [1988]	✓	✓	✓	✓	✓			
UTAH								
Kaysville City Library [1986]			✓					✓
VERMONT								
Brooks Memorial, Brattleboro [1986]	✓	✓	✓	✓	✓	✓	✓	
VIRGINIA								
Eastern District Branch, Bluefield [1986]	✓	✓	✓	✓	✓	✓	✓	✓
Pohick Regional, Burke [1986]	✓	✓	✓	✓	✓	✓	✓	✓
Hampton P.L. [1986]	✓	✓	✓	✓	✓	✓	✓	✓

Portage District HQ, Garrettsville [1987]	✓	✓	✓	✓	✓	✓	✓	✓
Schiappa Memorial, Steubenville [1986]	✓	✓	✓	✓	✓	✓	✓	✓
Streetsboro Branch Library [1988]	✓	✓	✓	✓				
Worthington P.L. [1986]								✓
OKLAHOMA								
Buffalo P.L. [1986]			✓					✓
Robt. Williams P.L., Durant [1987]					✓			
Hobart P.L. [1987]	✓	✓	✓	✓	✓	✓		
Miami P.L. [1987]	✓	✓	✓	✓	✓			
Midwest City P.L. [1987]	✓	✓	✓	✓	✓	✓	✓	✓
Moore P.L. [1987]	✓	✓	✓	✓	✓	✓	✓	✓
Hancock P.L. [1987]	✓	✓		✓	✓			
Hillsboro P.L. [1987]	✓	✓	✓	✓	✓	✓		
Hudson P.L. [?]	✓							
Johnson Creek P.L. [?]	✓							
Manitowoc P.L. [1986]	✓	✓	✓	✓	✓	✓	✓	✓
Menomonie P.L. [1986]								✓
Oconomowoc P.L. [1986]	✓	✓	✓	✓	✓	✓	✓	✓
Plymouth P.L. [?]	✓			✓	✓			
Portage Free Library [?]	✓							

Madison County Library [1986]	✓	✓	✓	✓	✓	✓	✓	✓
West Avenue Br., Newport News [1986]	✓	✓	✓	✓	✓	✓	✓	✓
Victoria P.L. [?]	✓				✓			✓
Virginia Beach P.L. [1987]	✓	✓	✓	✓	✓	✓	✓	✓
WISCONSIN								
Beloit P.L. [1991]	✓			✓				
Bloomer P.L. [1987]		✓	✓	✓	✓	✓		
Hildebrand Memorial, Boscobel [?]	✓							
Burlington P.L. [1987]	✓	✓	✓	✓	✓	✓	✓	✓
Clintonville P.L. [?]	✓			✓	✓			
Memorial P.L., Dodgeville [?]		✓	✓	✓	✓			
Shawano City-Cty. Library [?]	✓							
Stoughton P.L. [?]	✓	✓						
Verona P.L. [?]		✓			✓			
Waukesha P.L. [1987]	✓	✓	✓	✓	✓	✓	✓	✓
Winneconne P.L. [1990]	✓							
WYOMING								
Little Snake River Valley, Baggs [1986]								✓
Fulmer P.L., Sheridan [1986]	✓	✓	✓	✓	✓	✓	✓	✓

Table 12 / Academic Library Projects in Progress, 1986

NAME OF LIBRARY	STAGES							
	1	2	3	4	5	6	7	8
ARKANSAS								
Ouachita Bapt. Univ., Arkadelphia [1987]					✓			
CALIFORNIA								
Grad. Theological Union, Berkeley [1986]							✓	✓
California State Univ., Chico [1987]				✓	✓	✓		
California State Univ., Northridge [1989]				✓	✓			
Univ. of California-Davis [1990]	✓	✓	✓	✓	✓	✓		
Univ. So. California, Los Angeles [1986]	✓	✓	✓	✓	✓	✓	✓	✓
Univ. So. California, Los Angeles [1987]	✓	✓	✓	✓	✓	✓		
Cal State Polytechnic, Pomona [1988]	✓	✓	✓	✓	✓	✓		
Univ. of California-San Francisco [1990]	✓	✓	✓	✓	✓			
Cal State-Stanislaus, Turlock [1988]	✓	✓	✓	✓	✓			
CONNECTICUT								
So. Connecticut State, New Haven [1986]	✓	✓	✓	✓	✓	✓	✓	✓
Yale Medical Ctr., New Haven [1989]	✓	✓	✓	✓	✓			
FLORIDA								
Univ. of Florida, Gainesville [1986]	✓							✓
Florida Intl. Univ., North Miami [1988]	✓	✓	✓	✓	✓	✓	✓	✓
Rollins College, Winter Park [1987]	✓	✓	✓	✓	✓	✓	✓	✓
ILLINOIS								
So. Illinois Univ., Carbondale [1987]	✓	✓	✓	✓	✓	✓	✓	✓

NAME OF LIBRARY	STAGES							
	1	2	3	4	5	6	7	8
MISSOURI								
Univ. of Missouri-Columbia [1988]	✓	✓	✓	✓	✓	✓	✓	✓
Maryville College, St. Louis [1987]	✓	✓	✓	✓	✓	✓		
St. Louis College of Pharmacy [1987]	✓	✓	✓	✓	✓	✓	✓	✓
St. Louis Univ. [1986]								✓
NEW MEXICO								
Univ. of New Mexico, Albuquerque [1986]	✓	✓	✓	✓	✓	✓		✓
NEW YORK								
John Jay Coll. of Criminal Justice, New York [1988]				✓				
Avery Fisher Ctr., New York University [1987]	✓	✓	✓	✓	✓	✓	✓	✓
SUNY at Purchase [1986]	✓	✓	✓	✓	✓	✓	✓	✓
Rochester Inst. of Technology [1988]	✓			✓				
Eastman Sch. of Music, Univ. of Rochester [1988]				✓	✓			
Univ. of Rochester Medical Ctr. [1987]	✓	✓	✓	✓	✓	✓	✓	✓
NORTH CAROLINA								
Univ. of N.C.-Wilmington [1987]	✓	✓	✓	✓	✓	✓	✓	✓
OHIO								
Walsh College, Canton [1986]	✓	✓	✓	✓	✓	✓	✓	✓

Institution	1	2	3	4	5	6	7
Univ. of Illinois at Chicago [?]	✓	✓	✓	✓			
Concordia College, River Forest [1988]	✓	✓	✓				
INDIANA							
Univ. of Evansville [1986]							✓
DePauw Univ., Greencastle [1987]	✓	✓	✓	✓	✓		✓
Ball State Univ., Muncie [1986]	✓	✓	✓	✓			✓
Indiana Univ. at South Bend [1988]	✓	✓	✓	✓	✓		
IOWA							
Coe College, Cedar Rapids [1988]	✓	✓	✓	✓			
Clarke College, Dubuque [1986]	✓	✓	✓	✓	✓	✓	✓
KANSAS							
Wichita State Univ. [1988]	✓	✓	✓	✓			✓
KENTUCKY							
Univ. of Louisville [1988]	✓	✓					
MAINE							
Univ. of Maine, Farmington [1986]							✓
Univ. of Maine, Orono [1986]	✓	✓	✓			✓	✓
MARYLAND							
St. Mary's College, St. Mary's City [1989]	✓	✓	✓	✓	✓		
MICHIGAN							
Hope College, Holland [1987]	✓	✓	✓				✓
MINNESOTA							
Univ. of Minnesota, Minneapolis [1994]	✓	✓					
Univ. of Minnesota, Minneapolis [1988]	✓	✓					
College of St. Benedict, St. Joseph [1986]	✓	✓	✓	✓	✓	✓	✓
Macalester College, St. Paul [1988]	✓	✓	✓	✓	✓		✓
Cedarville College [1987]	✓	✓	✓	✓	✓		✓
Case Western Reserve, Cleveland [1986]	✓	✓	✓	✓	✓	✓	✓
Northeastern Ohio Univs., Coll. of Medicine, Rootstown [1987]	✓	✓	✓	✓	✓		✓
Franciscan Univ. of Steubenville [1987]	✓						✓
PENNSYLVANIA							
Lafayette College, Easton [1987]	✓	✓	✓	✓	✓	✓	✓
SOUTH CAROLINA							
Newberry College [1986]	✓	✓	✓	✓	✓	✓	✓
TENNESSEE							
Tennessee Tech Univ., Cookeville [1989]			✓				
Maryville College [1986]	✓	✓					✓
Univ. of Tennessee, Knoxville [1987]	✓	✓	✓	✓	✓	✓	✓
TEXAS							
Texas A&M Univ., Galveston [1986]	✓	✓	✓	✓	✓	✓	✓
Texas College of Ostepathic Medicine, Fort Worth [1986]	✓	✓	✓	✓	✓	✓	✓
Texas Southern Univ., Houston [1987]	✓	✓	✓	✓	✓	✓	✓
VERMONT							
Vermont Law School, S. Royalton [1988]	✓	✓	✓	✓			
VIRGINIA							
Randolph-Macon Coll., Ashland [1987]	✓	✓	✓	✓	✓	✓	✓
Washington Coll., Fredericksburg [1989]	✓	✓	✓	✓	✓	✓	✓
Davis & Elkins College [1989]			✓	✓			
WISCONSIN							
Univ. of Wisconsin-Madison [1990]	✓	✓				✓	

389

Archival Census: First Analysis

Society of American Archivists

600 S. Federal St., Suite 504, Chicago, IL 60605
312-922-0140

In summer 1985, many U.S. archival institutions responded to the Census of Archival Repositories being carried out by the Society of American Archivists' (SAA) Task Force on Institutional Evaluation. Paul Conway, Gerald R. Ford Library archivist, who is processing the data, furnished the *SAA Newsletter* this summary report. (Conway will present a longer report at the SAA annual meeting in Chicago, including a description of how different types of archives vary from the composite picture in the summary report.) Several task force members assisted in data analysis, and the opinions expressed do not necessarily represent the views of the society. Nevertheless, SAA expects readers to be stimulated by this first view of the census returns. Comments on this article and on the census are encouraged. For information on obtaining a copy of the data on tape or floppy disk, contact SAA headquarters.

A typical archives in the United States today was founded in the early 1970s and functions with fewer than four employees, half of whom are professional archivists. Staff members in this typical repository are paid an average of $21,000 per year, have an anual budget of $83,000, and have custody of 2,000 cubic feet of archival materials in a building of about 3,000 square feet. Archivists describe 80 percent of their holdings at the collection level but do not publish a guide. About 325 researchers visit the reading room each year, relying more on a card catalog for access than on any other kind of finding aid.

These median figures are just some of the patterns emerging from responses to the Society of American Archivists' first Census of Archival Repositories in the United States. The nine-section questionnaire, asking for available information on a wide range of responsibilities and activities, generated over 300 analytical variables from 52 questions. What follows is a summary of certain key measures, arranged into four sections: (1) a general profile, (2) finances and staff, (3) physical facilities and holdings, and (4) description and research use. All but the first two tables exclude the National Archives in Washington, D.C., and any repositories unable to answer the specific questions.

Analysis of census returns is the culmination of a three-year effort by the society's Task Force on Institutional Evaluation, chaired by Mary Jo Pugh. Building on previous, more limited surveys in the United States and Canada, the task force benefited from the work of the society's Task Force on Standard Reporting Practices and advice from the staff of the Institute for Social Research at the University of Michigan. Census responses form the core of a nationwide database of comparable measures of all types of archival repositories. This project complements and reinforces the task force's guidelines on self-evaluation, published in the SAA booklet *Evaluation of Archival Institutions*.

The census elicited a good response, considering the complexity of the questionnaire. Of 1,252 questionnaires mailed, 549 were returned, for a response rate of almost 44 percent. The mailing was a combination of SAA's individual and institutional membership rolls. The distribution of responses to the census very nearly matches the distri-

Note: Reprinted with permission of the Society of American Archivists from the *SAA Newsletter*, March 1986.

bution of the mailing list by region and type of repository, allowing for qualified generalizations within the limits of the mailing list. Any conclusions should be tempered by the realization that nothing in this world is absolute, especially survey research.

A Profile of Responses

The basic identification requested from each repository confirms the broad portrait of archival resources of which most of us are aware: archives are concentrated in the mid-Atlantic and midwestern states; there was a phenomenal growth in the number of repositories in the 1960s and 1970s, but growth has leveled off in the 1980s; and there is a tremendous variety of types of institutions calling themselves archives.

Archives in every state in the nation responded to the census. Table 1 illustrates the distribution of respondents in six regions of the United States, roughly coinciding with the composition of regional archival organizations. A comparison of the regional distribution of survey respondents with the regional distribution of the full mailing list shows that responses are slightly weighted in favor of the southern and Mountain states, and slightly against the mid-Atlantic states.

The first question asked respondents to check the category that best described their type of institution. Answers to this question are summarized in Table 2.

Table 1 / Regional Distribution

Region	Respondents	
	Percent	No.
New England	11	61
Mid-Atlantic	26	140
South	19	103
Midwest	28	154
Mountain	6	34
Pacific	10	54
Total responses		549

Table 2 / Type of Repository

Type	Respondents	
	Percent	No.
Federal government	5	26
State government and historical society	12	60
Local government and historical society	9	52
College and university	37	206
Business	6	33
Religious organizations	19	103
Special subjects	9	50
Museum archives	3	19
Total responses		549

The census asked respondents to indicate the year in which their repository was established and the founding year of the parent institution to which they belong. The overall responses to these questions show a brief spurt in repository development during the depression — probably stemming in part from the WPA records survey — and the phenomenal growth of archives since 1960. Sixty-seven percent of responding repositories were founded since 1961. Regionally, the same patterns apply, but there are some differences in the "takeoff point" in the last two decades.

The census confirmed that parent institutions are slow to care for their archives. Overall more than half the responding archives were founded more than 60 years after the parent. Even more striking, of those repositories founded since 1961, more than 70 percent belong to institutions founded before 1900. Generally, parents view archives as history, not as an ongoing administrative service. Only 44 percent reported having any records management responsibilities.

Finances and Staff

Slightly more than half of all respondents have separately identifiable budgets. Program and salary costs for the remaining 42 percent are subsumed into the operating budgets of parent institutions. The average financial resources for all repositories able to report a figure is $325,000. However, almost 95 percent of the responding institutions have total budgets under $1 million. By excluding the few big-budget archives (more than $1.2 million) from the tally, the budget average drops to under $168,000.

Table 3 is the total budget figure divided into four relatively arbitrary categories designed simply to illustrate the clustering of responses. Half of all repositories able to report a figure have budgets under $83,000, and nearly a quarter have budgets less than $25,000.

Given the labor-intensive nature of most archival work, staff resources are an important indicator of the wealth of an institution. The questionnaire did not provide definitions for staff categories, but merely requested totals for the repository as a whole and the division by "professional" and "other." A general lack of consensus on just what a "professional" archivist is will prohibit firm conclusions about the structure of archival staffs until related survey questions on training and experience are considered. Nevertheless, the reported total staff averages eight to nine people nationwide, including the director, three to four "professional" archivists, and "other" clerical and technical assistants. Half of all archives reported having total staffs under 3.5, only two of whom

Table 3 / Total Financial Resources

Resource Amount	Respondents	
	Percent	No.
$100–$25,000	22	70
$25,001–$100,000	31	101
$100,001–$1 million	41	134
$1 million or more	6	19
Total responses		324

are "professional" archivists. Table 4 shows the distribution of the total number of staff in responding repositories.

The use of volunteer labor is a widespread practice in archives. Overall, 232 archives reported an average of seven volunteer assistants—nearly equal to the reported paid staff averages. Many volunteers may be less than full-time workers and some smaller archives may be fully volunteer organizations. When the analysis is limited to repositories making use of both volunteers and paid staff, the average drops to five people, still a significant figure. Half of the archives have fewer than three volunteer assistants.

Indeed, salary data are about the only information consistently gathered in past SAA surveys. Most recently, David Bearman's 1982 survey placed the average archivist's salary at $21,419. While the primary goal of this census was not to obtain individual salary differentials, data on the high, low, and average salaries at the repository level (including directors) were gathered for comparative purposes. Table 5 shows the distribution of reported average salaries according to SAA membership dues categories.

Obviously, explaining salary distribution is a complex matter. One of the more intriguing comparative questions is the relation of salaries to staff size. Are archivists in larger repositories paid more, on the average, than staff in smaller institutions?

The short answer is no! Average salary figures are distributed in almost equal proportions from the smallest to the largest archives. The pattern is the same for reported lowest salary. Archives look much alike on the low end of the salary range. Not so on

Table 4 / Total Number of Staff

| | Respondents | |
No. of Staff	Percent	No.
1	17	86
1.5–3	33	165
3.5–10	31	154
10.5–30	13	69
30.5–156	6	29
Total responses		503

Table 5 / Average Salary

| | Respondents | |
Salary Amount	Percent	No.
$1,200–$15,000	17	48
$15,001–$22,000	44	126
$22,501–$30,000	31	91
$30,001–$47,553	8	24
Total responses		289

the high end—which one may fairly assume represents the salary of the director. Over 35 percent (117) of the responding repositories reported that the highest salary exceeded $30,000, the average high salary being $27,900. Most significantly, there is a striking correlation between the size of a repository's staff and the director's salary. Archives with more than ten employees have a director paid more than $30,000 in 72 percent of the cases, whereas only 18 percent of the directors in archives with three or fewer employees make that much.

Facilities and Holdings

Archival buildings are small and densely packed. While the nationwide average total floor space available is 19,000 square feet, half of the responding repositories are smaller than 3,000 square feet. Table 6 shows the distribution of responses in four basic groups.

Only half of all respondents reported having adequate space to carry out the functions specified in their mission statements. Most archival materials are stored on site. Fewer than 20 percent of all respondents reported having access to offsite storage facilities. Of these only half had more than 1,000 square feet at their disposal.

Responses to questions on available equipment paint a disturbing picture. Although 72 percent reported having an in-house fire *detection* system, less than half have a fire *suppression* system extending beyond the random extinguisher in the corner. Archival security in a typical building means closed stacks and burglar alarms. But only 60 percent of reporting repositories have a humidity-controlled environment.

The survey questionnaire apparently asked for a daunting amount of detail on the nature and quantity of each repository's holdings. One purpose for generating 65 variables in eight questions was to minimize the problems of comparing unrelated data while exploring the composition of archival materials. The single most striking conclusion from this avalanche of data is also the most obvious: If archives are anything, they are an incredible melange of documents, books, audiovisual items, and all manner of artifacts. Any effort to create a homogeneous picture from the reported holdings is bound to be an ongoing process. Only a summary can be given here.

Only two-thirds of all archives were able to respond to the most basic question on total volume. Of those that did, the overall average is just over 11,000 cubic feet. Yet half of all archives providing total figures have holdings under 2,000 cubic feet; only 10 percent have more than 9,000 cubic feet in custody. Table 7 is the distribution of this figure into four categories.

Table 6 / Total Floor Space (square feet)

Square Feet	Percent	No.
40–1,000	24	105
1,001–10,000	50	219
10,001–50,000	20	86
50,001–923,102	6	25
Total responses		435

Table 7 / Total Volume of Holdings (cubic feet)

	Respondents	
Cubic Feet	Percent	No.
6–500	22	81
501–5,000	46	168
5,001–50,000	27	99
50,001–137,000	5	17
Total responses		365

Description and Research Use

A major purpose of the census was to gather raw data on the percentage of holdings described at various levels (collection, series, file) and in various formats (guides, catalogs, inventories) and to link this information with research use. Archivists had as much difficulty completing this section as any part of the questionnaire. Only half of the respondents were able to give a figure on the percentage of holdings described at the collection level. Table 8 divides this total response into five parts. Overall, these archivists have described an average of 80 percent of their holdings at the collection level; 60 percent at the series level; and 45 percent at the file level.

The repository guide has traditionally been viewed as an essential component of a mature archival program. Recently, the value of the guide to organize holdings internally and to develop research use has come under increased scrutiny. The census returns show that, nationwide, only 20 percent of all respondents have published a guide. Ten archives reported publishing their guides more than 15 years ago. Fifty-nine percent of all respondents have neither a formally published guide nor an informally compiled in-house guide. Instead, most archives rely on a card catalog for access to holdings. Sixty-two percent of all respondents make use of a card catalog to describe at least some of their holdings. Closer comparison of the responses to several questions on description will be necessary to sort out how archives balance the strengths and limitations of different formats.

**Table 8 / Total Percent of Holdings at
the Collection Level**

	Respondents	
Percent of Holdings	Percent	No.
1–20	6	18
21–40	4	12
41–60	12	34
61–80	14	40
81–100	64	185
Total responses		286

Table 9 / Total Number of Researchers

No. of Researchers	Respondents	
	Percent	No.
2–50	22	76
51–350	30	107
351–1,000	20	71
1,001–37,434	28	100
Total responses		354

However, the adequacy of archival description is not keeping people from the reading rooms. Nationwide, each archives provides reference services to more than 1,400 researchers per year. Beneath this average figure, however, is the wild variance in research use summed up in Table 9. Only 64 percent of all respondents were able to provide a total figure for the number of uses. Half of these archives have fewer than 325 researchers visit each year. Nearly one quarter of the archives can barely keep dust off the reference tables — having fewer than 50 researchers. At the other end of the spectrum, 28 percent of those responding provide some level of reference service to more than 1,000 people each year. A clearer understanding of this diversity must await the comparison of types of researchers and types of archival institutions.

Response patterns from SAA's first nationwide archival census add substance to the skeleton of images developed by the task forces on Archives and Society and Goals and Priorities and by the commentary of many concerned archivists. As a whole, archives have too little money, staff, and space and are taxed with too much material and too many researchers for the resources available. Beneath average impoverishment, however, is a rich variance that needs to be explained.

Census data will soon be available in a machine-readable format. One strength of the data set is the flexibility it provides in linking information on archival functions and activities with the resources available to carry them out. It will allow comparisons by type of repository, size of staff or holdings, total financial resources, and many other important measures. The analyses that emerge over the next few years should be the products of many archivists with many concerns and points of view.

Adult Literacy Programs: Services, Persons Served, and Volunteers

Center for Statistics, U.S. Department of Education, Office of Educational Research and Improvement, Washington, DC 20208
202-254-7351

A recent survey of adult literacy programs was conducted by the Center for Statistics (CS) through its Fast Response Survey System (FRSS). The survey was requested by the Adult Literacy Initiative created by President Reagan in 1983 to coordinate literacy activities, promote awareness and volunteerism, and collaborate with and build on exist-

ing literacy efforts. The Adult Literacy Initiative needed data to support a number of activities, including promoting awareness of the problem of adult illiteracy through a National Awareness Campaign, promoting the coordination of literacy resources in the public and private sectors, and encouraging volunteerism through the Federal Employee Literacy Training (FELT) program and similar efforts. The survey collected information on the literacy services provided by the programs, the number of persons served, and the use and training of volunteers. Such literacy programs as correctional and military programs and those provided by businesses were not included in the survey. This report focuses on differences between adult education and local adult literacy programs.

Survey Results

Highlights

In spring 1985, adult literacy instruction was provided by an estimated 2,900 adult education programs, offered through school districts, community colleges, and adult learning centers. In addition, an estimated 1,300 local adult literacy programs (LALPs) were offered by volunteer groups, community-based organizations, other private literacy organizations, and libraries. About two-thirds of the programs used volunteers. About half of adult education programs and almost all LALPs used volunteers.

Services Provided

There is considerable discussion within the adult literacy field as to what levels of training should be encompassed by the term "literacy instruction." An estimated 23 million Americans are below the eighth-grade reading level, which is generally considered "functional literacy." Basic literacy and pre-general educational development (GED) services are directed toward these individuals. However, an additional 40 million adults are considered "marginally competent," with skills below the twelfth-grade level; GED services are designed to serve this group.

The programs participating in the survey indicated which of five instructional services each provided (Table 1).

- Basic literacy instruction (below fourth-grade) was provided by the highest proportion of programs (86 percent).
- GED (from the ninth grade through high school equivalency) and pre-GED (grades 5 through 8) were offered by two-thirds of the programs.
- English as a second language (ESL), both oral and written, was available in 58 percent of programs.
- ESL, oral only, was provided by about one-fourth of the programs.

Adult education programs and LALPs differed in the proportion of programs providing each instructional service. GED and pre-GED instruction were available much more frequently in adult education programs than LALPs, while oral and written ESL were available slightly more often in LALPs. Overall, adult education programs offered more of these five services than LALPs: an average of 3.3 services compared with 2.3. (Similar differences are found when programs are categorized by volunteer use or volun-

Table 1 / Instructional Services Provided by Adult Literacy Programs, by Program Characteristic: 50 States and D.C., Spring 1985

Program Characteristic	Number of Programs	Percent of Programs Providing Instructional Services					Average Number of Services per Program
		Basic Literacy[a]	Pre-GED[b]	GED[c]	ESL,[d] Oral Only	ESL, Oral and Written	
Total	4,180	86	66	66	24	58	3.0
Type of program							
Adult education programs	2,890	88	77	83	27	55	3.3
Local adult literacy programs	1,290	81	40	26	18	64	2.3
Use of volunteers							
Do not use volunteers	1,490	81	72	79	21	44	3.0
Use volunteers	2,690	89	62	58	26	66	3.0
Service area							
Urban	1,030	88	62	60	29	68	3.1
Suburban	780	81	56	59	22	68	2.9
Rural	1,910	87	72	72	20	44	2.9
Combined area[e]	460	89	67	63	35	78	3.3

[a]Basic literacy includes instruction in reading, writing, and computation below fourth-grade level.

[b]Pre-GED includes instruction at grades 5 through 8.

[c]GED (general educational development) is instruction at the ninth grade through the high school equivalency diploma.

[d]ESL (English as a second language) is provided at all levels to those whose native language is not English.

[e]Programs were asked to indicate which of the following *best* described their service areas: urban, suburban, or rural. Those that checked more than one category are reported as serving combined areas.

Note: Percents do not total to 100 because respondents could indicate more than one type of instruction.

teer management. Both of these variables are related to program type in that more LALPs use volunteers and more are managed by volunteers, or a volunteer board, when compared with adult education programs.)

Most programs employed more than one instructional setting, including classes, group tutoring, and individual tutoring. About three-fourths of all programs offered instruction through individual tutoring, while over half made group tutoring and classes available (Table 2). Individual tutoring was more prevalent in LALPs (93 percent) than in adult education programs (65 percent). However, more adult education programs than LALPs provided group tutoring and far more provided classes. These findings reflect the fact that adult education programs are often provided in school districts and community colleges and tend to provide a more formal type of instruction.

Persons Served

An estimated 729,000 persons received instruction during a one-month period in spring 1985 (Table 3). (Responding programs were asked to provide the "number of clients/ students served in the past month.") The majority (about 605,000) obtained instruction through adult education programs, while the rest were served by LALPs. Although the average number of persons served per program was 175, half of the programs served 50 or fewer. Adult education programs served a larger average number of persons (210) than LALPs (96). More were served in urban areas (260,000) than in either suburban or rural areas, although there were only about half as many programs in urban areas as there were in rural areas.

Almost one-third of the programs had waiting lists of persons wishing to receive instruction. There were about 76,000 people on waiting lists nationally. Per program, the average number of people on the waiting list was 61. A higher proportion of LALPs had waiting lists.

Volunteers

Nearly two-thirds of all the programs used volunteers, and an additional 15 percent plan to do so in the next two years (Table 4). LALPs used volunteers more frequently than adult education programs (94 percent compared with 51 percent). This difference will probably decrease in the next two years, however, since an additional 21 percent of adult education programs plan to start using volunteers.

Volunteers were employed in a variety of capacities, most of them directly related to instruction (Table 5):

- One-to-one tutoring (92 percent of programs using volunteers)
- Teaching small groups (39 percent)
- Teacher's aides (34 percent)
- Teaching classes (8 percent)

Over one-fourth of the programs used volunteers in other roles. These roles included program management, screening and matching clients and volunteers, training volunteers, publicity and outreach, fund raising, clerical duties, and odd jobs.

Adult education programs and LALPs were generally similar in their use of volun-

Table 2 / Type of Instruction Provided by Adult Literacy Programs, by Program Characteristic: 50 States and D.C., Spring 1985

Program Characteristic	Number of Programs	Percent of Programs Offering Type of Instruction		
		Individual Tutoring	Group Tutoring	Classes
Total	4,180	74	59	60
Type of program				
Adult education programs	2,890	65	66	77
Local adult literacy programs	1,290	93	44	23
Use of volunteers				
Do not use volunteers	1,490	51	53	80
Use volunteers	2,690	87	63	49
Service area				
Urban	1,030	80	60	54
Suburban	780	66	54	58
Rural	1,910	72	60	65
Combined area*	460	83	61	57

*Programs were asked to indicate which of the following best described their service areas: urban, suburban, or rural. Those that checked more than one category are reported as serving combined areas.

Note: Percents do not total to 100 because respondents could indicate more than one type of instruction.

Table 3 / Number of Persons Receiving Instructional Services and Numbers on Waiting Lists,* by Program Characteristic: 50 States and D.C., Spring 1985

Program Characteristic	Total Number of Persons Served (in thousands)	Average Number of Persons Served per Program	Percent of Programs with a Waiting List	Average Number of Persons on Waiting Lists
Total	729	175	30	61
Type of program				
Adult education programs	605	210	17	103
Local adult literacy programs	124	96	59	34
Use of volunteers				
Do not use volunteers	188	127	14	191
Use volunteers	541	202	39	36
Service area				
Urban	260	255	47	56
Suburban	153	196	29	31
Rural	171	90	20	99
Combined area†	145	313	36	30

*Numbers represent a one-month period in spring 1985.

†Programs were asked to indicate which of the following best described their service areas: urban, suburban, or rural. Those that checked more than one category are reported as serving combined areas.

Note: Averages exclude programs reporting no persons served during the reporting period.

Table 4 / Use of Volunteers by Adult Literacy Programs, by Program Characteristic: 50 States and D.C., Spring 1985

Program Characteristic	Percent of Programs That Use Volunteers	Percent of Programs That Plan to Use Volunteers in the Next Two Years*	Total Number of Volunteers (in thousands)	Average Number of Volunteers per Program	Total Number of Teaching/ Tutoring Volunteers (in thousands)
Total	64	15	107	40	90
Type of program					
Adult education programs	51	21	25	18	23
Local adult literacy programs	94	2	82	68	67
Program management					
Not volunteer–managed	51	21	34	25	31
Volunteer–managed	89	4	73	58	59
Service area					
Urban	72	11	39	54	34
Suburban	63	16	18	38	16
Rural	58	19	25	23	20
Combined area†	79	11	25	68	20

*Only programs that do not use volunteers were asked if they plan to use volunteers in the next two years.

†Programs were asked to indicate which of the following best described their service areas: urban, suburban, or rural. Those that checked more than one category are reported as serving combined areas.

Note: Averages exclude programs reporting no volunteers.

Table 5 / Roles of Volunteers in Adult Literacy Programs, by Program Characteristic: 50 States and D.C., Spring 1985

Program Characteristic	Number of Programs	Percent of Programs Using Volunteers in Roles						
		One-to-One Tutoring	Teaching Small Groups	Teaching Classes	Teacher Aides	Transportation	Child Care	Other*
Total	2,690	92	39	8	34	10	7	28
Type of program								
Adult education programs	1,470	89	38	8	47	10	8	18
Local adult literacy programs	1,220	96	40	8	18	10	5	40
Program management								
Not volunteer – managed	1,420	91	38	10	45	9	7	19
Volunteer – managed	1,270	93	39	6	20	11	7	38
Service area								
Urban	740	95	47	9	28	5	5	30
Suburban	490	90	39	6	35	11	7	32
Rural	1,100	89	31	7	34	13	8	24
Combined area†	370	97	45	12	42	9	7	31

*Other uses of volunteers include program management, screening and matching volunteers and clients, training or supervising volunteers, clerical work, odd jobs, etc.

†Programs were asked to indicate which of the following *best* described their service areas: urban, suburban, or rural. Those that checked more than one category are reported as serving combined areas.

Note: Percents do not total to 100 because respondents could indicate more than one type of volunteer role.

Table 6 / Barriers to the Use of Volunteers by Adult Literacy Programs, by Program Characteristic: 50 States and D.C., Spring 1985

Program Characteristic	Number of Programs	Percent of Programs Indicating Barriers					
		Personnel for Training Volunteers	Materials for Training Volunteers	Materials for Students	People to Volunteer	Facilities for Training or Teaching	Other Barrier*
Total	4,180	36	19	11	59	12	29
Type of program							
Adult education programs	2,890	39	23	12	61	11	26
Local adult literacy programs	1,290	29	9	8	55	13	34
Use of volunteers							
Do not use volunteers	1,490	38	25	11	60	13	25
Use volunteers	2,690	35	15	11	58	11	30
Service area							
Urban	1,030	36	17	12	59	14	34
Suburban	780	38	19	9	62	17	26
Rural	1,910	37	20	10	58	8	25
Combined area†	460	26	17	15	57	16	33

*Other barriers include need for funding, personnel to manage a volunteer program, and lack of qualified volunteers.

†Programs were asked to indicate which of the following best described their service areas: urban, suburban, or rural. Those that checked more than one category are reported as serving combined areas.

Note: Percents do not total to 100 because respondents could indicate more than one type of barrier.

teers, except that far more adult education programs used volunteers as teacher's aides than did LALPs (perhaps because a higher proportion of adult education programs provided classes), while more LALPs used volunteers in the other roles described.

At the time this survey was conducted, an estimated 107,000 volunteers served in these programs (Table 4). The majority of these, about 82,000, were providing services through LALPs. About 80 percent of the volunteers were teaching or tutoring; again, most of these were serving in LALPs. LALPs averaged 68 volunteers per program, with 56 of the volunteers teaching or tutoring. Adult education programs reported markedly fewer volunteers per program: an average of 18 volunteers, of whom 17 were teaching or tutoring.

Barriers to Using Volunteers

Asked about barriers to using volunteers, or using more volunteers, programs indicated (Table 6):

- A lack of people to volunteer (59 percent)
- A lack of personnel to train volunteers (36 percent)
- A lack of materials for training volunteers (19 percent)

Over one-fourth of the programs identified other barriers. These included a variety of responses mentioned by small numbers of programs, such as the need for funding, staff to coordinate a volunteer program, and volunteers with special qualifications (e.g., certification to teach).

A higher proportion of adult education programs than LALPs cited the need for people to volunteer and the need for personnel to train volunteers.

Volunteer Training

Almost all (96 percent) of the programs using volunteers for teaching or tutoring provided training for them. Of these programs, 86 percent provided preservice training in 1983–1984, an average of 13 hours of training. In-service training was provided at two-thirds of the programs in 1983–1984, with an average of 9 hours.

In about four-fifths of the programs, training was conducted by program staff or other volunteers (Table 7). About one-third of the programs used a national literacy organization; this was twice as common among LALPs when compared with adult education programs. A relatively small proportion (11 percent) of programs used outside consultants for training.

The materials utilized by the most programs in their volunteer training were the Laubach Literacy Action materials (59 percent) and in-house materials (43 percent). About one-third of the programs used materials from Literacy Volunteers of America. (Laubach Literacy Action and Literacy Volunteers of America are two of the largest national volunteer literacy organizations, with member groups nationwide.) More LALPs than adult education programs had Laubach materials, while more adult education programs than LALPs relied on in-house materials.

About three-fourths of the programs with volunteer teachers or tutors observed the volunteers to ensure the quality of instruction (Table 8). Fifty-two percent observed volunteers more than once a month, and 21 percent did so less than once a month. More

Table 7 / Who Trains Adult Literacy Volunteers, by Program Characteristic: 50 States and D.C., Spring 1985

Program Characteristic	Number of Programs	Percent of Programs Indicating Category of Trainer			
		Program Staff or Volunteers	National Literacy Organization	Outside Consultant	No Training Provided
Total	2,600	79	36	11	4
Type of program					
Adult education programs	1,400	82	24	14	5
Local adult literacy programs	1,210	74	49	8	1
Program management					
Not volunteer – managed	1,350	83	25	16	5
Volunteer – managed	1,250	74	47	6	2
Service area					
Urban	730	78	39	13	2
Suburban	470	80	43	7	1
Rural	1,050	77	31	11	6
Combined area*	350	84	35	13	2

*Programs were asked to indicate which of the following *best* described their service areas: urban, suburban, or rural. Those that checked more than one category are reported as serving combined areas.

Note: Percents do not total to 100 because respondents could indicate more than one category of instruction.

Table 8 / Observation of Volunteers by Adult Literacy Programs, by Program Characteristic: 50 States and D.C., Spring 1985

Program Characteristic	Number of Programs	Percent of Programs Observing Volunteers			Number of Programs Observing Volunteers	Percent of Programs Whose Volunteers Are		
		More Than Once a Month	Less Than Once a Month	Not at All		Observed by Paid Staff	Observed by Volunteers	Observed by Both Paid Staff and Volunteers
Total	2,600	52	21	27	1,909	75	16	8
Type of program								
Adult education programs	1,400	71	21	9	1,278	89	6	5
Local adult literacy programs	1,210	30	22	48	631	48	37	16
Program management								
Not volunteer – managed	1,350	67	21	12	1,189	88	5	7
Volunteer – managed	1,250	35	22	43	720	55	35	10

Note: Because of rounding, percents may not total to 100.

Table 9 / Ratings of Effectiveness of Teaching/Tutoring Volunteers, by Program Characteristic: 50 States and D.C., Spring 1985

Program Characteristic	Number of Programs	Percent of Programs Indicating Rating				
		Excellent	Good	Fair	Poor
Total	2,600	40	51	7	2
Type of program					
Adult education programs	1,400	35	53	10	3
Local adult literacy programs	1,210	45	50	4	*
Program management					
Not volunteer – managed	1,350	35	53	10	3
Volunteer – managed	1,250	45	50	5	*

*Less than 1 percent.

Note: Because of rounding, percents may not total to 100.

adult education programs than LALPs conducted observations of volunteers (about 90 percent compared with about 50 percent). Adult education programs and LALPs also differed in the frequency of observation. Almost three-fourths of adult education programs observed volunteers more than once a month compared with 30 percent of LALPs.

Ratings of Volunteer Effectiveness

Programs using volunteers for teaching or tutoring were asked to rate the effectiveness of these volunteers (Table 9). Forty percent of the programs rated the volunteers as excellent, 51 percent as good, 7 percent as fair, and 2 percent as poor. A higher proportion of LALPs (45 percent) rated volunteers as excellent compared with adult education programs (35 percent).

Survey Background

In May 1985, questionnaires were mailed to a national probability sample of 900 adult literacy programs. The sample was drawn from the database of Contact Literacy, Inc., which maintains a national listing of literacy resources. To the extent that this database is complete, the estimates in this report reflect such programs nationwide. (Available information indicates that the Contact database is a relatively complete listing.)

About 11 percent (97) of the sampled programs were found out of the scope of this survey; many of these had closed, or did only diagnostic testing or referral, or provided materials. The response rate among eligible programs was 97 percent. All statements of comparison made in the text are significant at the 95 percent confidence level. Standard errors for selected items are presented in Table 10 as a general guide to the precision of numbers in the tables.

The survey was performed under contract with Westat, Inc., using the Fast Response Survey System. Westat's project director was Elizabeth Farris, and the survey manager was Mary Collins. Douglas Wright was the CS project officer for this survey. FRSS was established by CS to collect quickly, and with minimum burden on respondents, small quantities of data needed for education planning and policy.

For information about this survey or the Fast Response Survey System, contact Helen MacArthur, Office of Educational Research and Improvement, Center for Statistics. For single copies of this bulletin, contact the Information Services office at the same address, or telephone 202-254-6057.

Table 10 / Standard Errors of Selected Items

Item	Estimate	Standard Error
Percent of programs providing:		
Basic literacy, all programs	86.0	1.4
GED, all programs	65.8	1.2
Average number of services per program:		
All programs	3.0	.05
Adult education programs	3.3	.05
Local adult literacy programs	2.3	.08
Percent of programs offering:		
Individual tutoring, all programs	74.1	1.4
Classes, all programs	60.4	1.8
Average number of clients per program:		
All programs	174.9	13.3
Adult education programs	209.7	16.6
Local adult literacy programs	96.4	12.3
Percent of programs using volunteers:		
All programs	64.4	1.2
Adult education programs	51.0	1.6
Local adult literacy programs	94.3	1.2
Percent of programs that are volunteer-managed:		
All programs	34.1	1.5
Adult education programs	15.9	1.5
Local adult literacy programs	74.8	2.7
Average number of volunteers per program:		
All programs	40.4	3.5
Adult education programs	17.6	1.5
Local adult literacy programs	67.5	6.2
Percent of programs using volunteers for one-to-one tutoring, all programs	92.1	1.5
Percent of programs indicating these barriers to the use of volunteers:		
Personnel to train volunteers, all programs	35.7	1.3
People to volunteer, all programs	58.9	1.8
Percent of programs rating volunteers as excellent:		
All programs	39.7	2.0
Adult education programs	34.6	2.9
Local adult literacy programs	45.4	3.0

Book Trade Research and Statistics

Book Title Output and Average Prices: 1986 Preliminary Figures

Chandler B. Grannis
Contributing Editor, *Publishers Weekly*

U.S. book title output appears to have been between about 50,000 and 51,000 in 1986 — possibly a little more — to judge from preliminary data compiled by the R. R. Bowker Company. Average prices of books appear, on the whole, to have increased modestly compared with the previous year, according to the preliminary computations. Additional compilation of 1986 data was going on as this issue of *The Bowker Annual* was going to press, and final figures for 1986 will be published in *Publishers Weekly* late in summer 1987.

The 1985 book output, according to final Bowker figures, came to just more than 50,000, a decline of about 1.5% from the 1984 total of 51,058 — which was 4.3% below the 1983 total of 53,380, an all-time record in the Bowker calculations.

Two Bowker sources are used in compiling the title counts and price averages. The database of Bowker's *Weekly Record/American Book Publishing Record* (*WR/ABPR*) supplies the figures for hardcover and trade paperbacks. The new entries in the annual *Paperbound Books in Print* (*PBIP*) index provide the title counts and price averages of mass market paperbacks.

For hardcover books and trade paperbacks, the *WR/ABPR* database provide information both for brand-new books and new editions; it also includes data about imports and translations. None of this breakdown information is available from the *PBIP* database.

Table 1, which shows overall title counts by subject category, does not separate hardcover books from trade paperbacks, but combines the figures. It should be especially noted that the column headed "All Hard & Paper" combines the figures for hardcover books, trade paperbacks, and mass market paperbacks.

Table 2 shows mass market paperback output totals by category.

Table 3 provides title counts of trade paperbacks — that is, paperbacks other than mass market — by category. Table 4 reports import totals by category, and Table 5 gives a partial enumeration of translations, according to the languages from which the books are translated. The final report for 1986 hopefully will include a more comprehensive count of titles and figures on additional languages of origin.

The price-average tables show, in Table A, hardcover prices per volume, and in

Note: Adapted from *Publishers Weekly*, March 13, 1987.

Table 1 / American Book Title Production, 1984–1986

Category*	1984 All Hard & Paper	1985 (final) Hard & Trade Paper			1985 (final) All Hard & Paper	1986 Preliminary Hard & Trade Paper			1986 Preliminary All Hard & Paper
		Books	Editions	Totals		Books	Editions	Totals	
Agriculture	507	450	79	529	536	371	70	441	445
Art	1,838	1,392	150	1,542	1,545	1,170	143	1,313	1,316
Biography	2,098	1,604	270	1,874	1,953	1,435	222	1,657	1,729
Business	1,696	1,142	350	1,492	1,518	994	324	1,318	1,349
Education	1,052	885	188	1,073	1,085	720	113	833	841
Fiction	5,413	2,290	291	2,581	5,105	2,192	320	2,512	4,877
General Works	3,021	2,549	270	2,819	2,905	1,681	226	1,907	1,970
History	2,257	1,913	383	2,296	2,327	1,567	337	1,904	1,936
Home Economics	1,306	999	128	1,127	1,228	714	83	797	894
Juveniles	3,128	3,183	191	3,374	3,801	3,200	152	3,352	3,812
Language	670	519	99	618	632	439	106	545	562
Law	1,406	1,036	307	1,343	1,349	781	293	1,074	1,077
Literature	2,006	1,669	260	1,929	1,964	1,492	275	1,767	1,800
Medicine	3,554	2,925	618	3,543	3,570	2,225	465	2,690	2,731
Music	387	277	78	355	364	217	65	282	292
Philosophy, Psychology	1,554	1,220	227	1,447	1,559	1,079	208	1,287	1,369
Poetry, Drama	1,164	1,075	75	1,150	1,166	977	54	1,031	1,056
Religion	2,482	2,211	329	2,540	2,564	1,942	247	2,189	2,212
Science	3,236	2,808	481	3,289	3,304	2,086	471	2,557	2,570
Sociology, Economics	7,794	6,285	1,112	7,397	7,441	5,562	864	6,426	6,471
Sports, Recreation	1,299	876	129	1,005	1,154	684	119	803	962
Technology	2,639	2,079	405	2,484	2,526	1,715	359	2,074	2,110
Travel	551	366	90	456	465	313	89	402	412
TOTAL	51,058	39,753	6,510	46,263	50,070	33,556	5,605	39,161	42,793

Note: Figures for mass market paperbound book production are based on entries in Paperbound Books in Print. Other figures are from the Weekly Record (American Book Publishing Record) database. The heading "Books" refers to brand-new titles; "Editions" refers to new or revised editions.

Table 2 / Paperbacks Other Than Mass Market, 1984–1986

Category	1984 Totals	1985			1986 Preliminary		
		New Books	New Edns.	Totals	New Books	New Edns.	Totals
Fiction	518	365	71	436	287	70	357
Nonfiction	14,649	12,520	2,383	14,903	10,356	2,059	12,415
TOTAL	15,167	12,885	2,454	15,339	10,643	2,129	12,772

Table 3 / Mass Market Paperbound Titles

Category	1984 Final	1985 Final	1986 Prelim.
Agriculture	2	7	4
Art	3	3	3
Biography	75	79	72
Business	22	26	31
Education	5	12	8
Fiction	2,663	2,524	2,365
General Works	66	86	63
History	25	31	32
Home Econ.	83	101	97
Juveniles	257	427	460
Language	23	14	17
Law	6	6	3
Literature	57	35	33
Medicine	29	36	41
Music	3	9	10
Philos., Psych.	85	112	82
Poetry, Drama	9	16	25
Religion	14	24	23
Science	53	15	13
Sociol., Econ.	45	44	45
Sports, Recr.	181	149	159
Technology	85	42	36
Travel	12	9	10
TOTAL	**3,803**	**3,807**	**3,632**

Table A-1, hardcover prices excluding volumes priced at $81 or more — that is, eliminating the relatively few extremely high unit prices that would skew the averages. Table B covers mass market price averages. Table C deals with the other paperbacks, giving also an indication of relative output by category. Table D, a hand-produced compilation, is based on the prices of books advertised in the Fall Announcement numbers of *PW* in three broad areas of mainly retail and public or university library interest.

Most of the tables accompanying this report show breakdowns into 23 subject categories, long used as a convenient standard for book industry and library statistics. These categories represent Dewey Decimal Classifications as follows: Agriculture, 630–639, 712–719; Art, 700–711, 720–779; Biography (Dewey numbers not used here); Business, 650–659; Education, 370–379; General Works, 000–099; History, 900–909, 930–999; Home Economics, 640–649; Juveniles; Language, 400–499; Law, 340–349; Literature, 800–810, 813–820, 823–899; Medicine, 610–619; Music, 780–789; Philosophy, Psychology, 100–199; Poetry, Drama, 811, 812, 821, 822; Religion, 200–299; Science, 500–599; Sociology, Economics, 300–339, 350–369, 380–399; Sports, Recreation, 790–799; Technology, 600–609, 620–629, 660–699; Travel, 910–919.

Table 4 / Imported Titles, 1984–1986: Hardbound and Trade Paperbound Only

Category	1984 Totals	1985 Books	1985 Edns.	1985 Totals	1986 Prelim. Books	1986 Prelim. Edns.	1986 Prelim. Totals
Agriculture	103	101	17	118	86	3	89
Art	61	157	9	166	139	6	145
Biography	240	188	28	216	133	20	153
Business	140	120	26	196	115	15	130
Education	190	207	4	211	174	5	179
Fiction	164	155	16	171	148	13	161
General Works	268	312	17	329	241	19	260
History	324	348	47	395	231	35	266
Home Econ.	41	36	5	41	27	4	31
Juveniles	69	87	5	92	88	4	92
Language	179	200	16	216	177	19	196
Law	158	147	23	170	110	24	134
Literature	238	246	21	267	197	15	212
Medicine	508	531	67	598	447	47	494
Music	54	64	6	70	46	5	51
Philosophy, Psychology	211	257	10	267	195	15	210
Poetry, Drama	174	203	17	220	177	8	185
Religion	160	153	20	173	100	7	107
Science	1,032	1,121	121	1,242	803	122	925
Sociology, Economics	1,373	1,421	138	1,559	1,150	115	1,265
Sports, Recreation	137	95	12	107	78	9	87
Technology	454	364	55	419	439	54	493
Travel	61	56	5	61	30	8	38
TOTAL	6,337	6,669	680	7,349	5,331	572	5,903

Table 5 / Translations into English from Principal Languages, 1984–1986: Hardbound and Trade Paperbound Only

	FRENCH	GERMAN	RUSSIAN	SPANISH	ITALIAN	JAPANESE	DUTCH	LATIN	HEBREW	SWEDISH	DANISH	YIDDISH	NORWEGIAN	ARABIC	FINNISH	OTHER	TOTAL
1984 Final	355	425	181	97	97	64	38	42	28	21	27	10	4	16	10	N/A	1,439
1985 Final	416	369	182	86	92	59	40	30	29	28	17	15	13	8	5	N/A	1,389
1986 Prelim.	382	359	139	74	83	104	40	32	39	22	24	11	8	16	3	N/A	1,336

Note: "Total" covers only the languages listed here.

Table A / Average Per-Volume Prices of Hardcover Books, 1977 and 1984–1986*

Category	1977 Prices	1984 Vols.	1984 Prices	1985 Vols.	1985 Prices	1986 Prelim. Vols.	1986 Prelim. Total	1986 Prelim. Prices
Agriculture	$16.24	359	$34.92	368	$36.77	311	$ 11,760.13	$37.81
Art	21.24	1,114	33.03	908	35.15	776	26,369.03	33.98
Biography	15.34	1,408	22.53	1,298	22.20	1,138	25,560.40	22.46
Business	18.00	1,116	26.01	1,040	28.84	938	28,448.46	30.32
Education	12.95	580	24.47	602	27.28	446	11,430.78	25.62
Fiction	10.09	1,989	14.74	1,800	15.29	1,772	29,000.38	16.36
General Works	30.99	1,602	35.61	1,632	37.91	1,203	44,588.04	37.06
History	17.12	1,432	27.53	1,506	27.02	1,239	34,404.06	27.76
Home Economics	11.16	655	15.70	594	17.50	419	7,970.71	19.02
Juveniles	6.65	2,398	10.02	2,529	9.95	2,558	26,891.81	10.51
Language	14.96	410	22.97	347	28.68	293	8,960.43	30.58
Law	25.04	925	43.88	955	41.70	746	35,825.33	48.02
Literature	15.78	1,243	23.57	1,181	24.53	1,118	28,415.30	25.41
Medicine	24.00	2,836	40.65	2,798	44.36	2,063	98,314.39	47.65
Music	20.13	232	27.79	238	28.79	181	5,856.59	32.35
Philosophy, Psychology	14.43	895	29.70	895	28.11	799	23,173.87	29.00
Poetry, Drama	13.63	599	26.75	563	22.14	495	11,736.70	23.71
Religion	12.26	1,118	17.76	1,100	19.13	932	20,117.38	21.58
Science	24.88	2,535	46.57	2,556	51.19	1,935	103,698.10	53.59
Sociology, Economics	29.88	5,066	33.35	4,761	33.33	4,095	121,605.78	29.69
Sports, Recreation	12.28	623	20.16	530	23.43	426	10,031.35	23.54
Technology	23.61	1,797	45.80	1,693	50.37	1,501	79,695.95	53.09
Travel	18.44	252	21.31	210	24.66	177	4,112.30	23.23
TOTAL	$19.22	31,184	$29.99	30,104	$31.46	25,561	$797,967.27	$31.21

*From *Weekly Record* listings of domestic and imported books.

417

Table A-1 / Average Per-Volume Prices of Hardcover Books,
Eliminating All Volumes Priced at $81 or More, 1983–1986

Category	1983 Prices	1984 Vols.	1984 Prices	1985 Vols.	1985 Prices	1986 Prelim. Vols.	1986 Prelim. Total	1986 Prelim. Prices
Agriculture	$27.76	333	$28.85	337	$29.99	289	$ 9,252.03	$32.01
Art	26.77	1,041	28.90	868	30.35	752	23,084.58	30.69
Biography	19.77	1,393	20.91	1,282	20.81	1,128	24,338.40	21.57
Business	24.02	1,103	24.74	1,024	27.27	915	25,566.16	27.94
Education	21.32	576	21.81	598	24.02	445	11,335.78	25.47
Fiction	14.14	1,987	14.49	1,799	15.24	1,766	27,940.38	15.82
General Works	26.12	1,530	26.97	1,561	29.05	1,154	36,059.64	31.24
History	23.85	1,401	23.89	1,487	25.41	1,223	32,197.06	26.32
Home Economics	14.53	654	15.53	591	17.11	416	7,699.21	18.50
Juveniles	9.15	2,394	9.75	2,529	9.95	2,556	26,602.82	10.40
Language	25.26	406	22.96	343	27.61	288	8,408.43	29.19
Law	30.25	854	31.60	888	35.87	677	24,809.83	36.64
Literature	21.31	1,230	21.69	1,169	23.46	1,107	26,779.30	24.19
Medicine	33.02	2,601	33.93	2,505	36.29	1,776	65,052.13	36.62
Music	24.06	240	25.01	236	27.72	178	5,591.64	31.41
Philosophy, Psychology	25.08	880	25.22	886	27.34	792	22,155.87	27.97
Poetry, Drama	19.39	588	19.32	554	20.90	493	11,301.70	22.92
Religion	15.93	1,111	16.30	1,096	18.88	927	18,598.43	20.06
Science	36.49	2,265	37.71	2,232	40.06	1,620	65,048.57	40.15
Sociology, Economics	24.83	4,977	25.48	4,689	27.91	4,045	114,478.48	28.30
Sports, Recreation	10.07	618	19.27	525	21.36	425	9,281.35	21.83
Technology	34.16	1,629	35.77	1,507	38.60	1,294	50,956.49	39.37
Travel	18.36	248	18.92	207	22.07	177	4,112.30	23.23
TOTAL	$24.15	30,059	$24.66	28,913	$26.57	24,443	$650,650.58	$26.61

Table B / Average Per-Volume Prices of Mass Market Paperbacks, 1984-1986

Category	1984 Prices	1985 Vols.	1985 Prices	1986 Prelim. Vols.	1986 Prelim. Total	1986 Prelim. Prices
Agriculture	$2.85	7	$5.76	4	$24.35	$6.09
Art	8.28	3	9.80	3	29.40	9.80
Biography	4.45	79	4.81	72	378.10	5.25
Business	4.91	26	7.57	31	239.45	7.72
Education	5.15	12	6.07	8	50.70	6.34
Fiction	3.02	2,524	3.24	2,365	8,249.05	3.49
General Works	4.58	86	4.64	63	316.05	5.02
History	3.77	31	5.38	32	166.85	5.21
Home Economics	4.94	101	5.65	97	609.25	6.28
Juveniles	2.31	427	2.71	460	1,246.25	2.70
Language	5.55	14	4.28	17	96.80	5.69
Law	5.11	6	6.62	3	13.40	4.46
Literature	3.62	35	4.76	33	169.35	5.13
Medicine	5.01	36	6.65	41	296.80	7.24
Music	5.28	9	5.67	10	42.05	4.20
Philosophy, Psychology	4.38	112	4.22	82	416.05	5.07
Poetry, Drama	5.10	16	4.88	25	144.65	5.78
Religion	3.87	24	3.21	23	97.45	4.24
Science	3.55	15	4.83	13	78.45	6.03
Sociology, Economics	4.42	44	4.76	45	248.65	5.53
Sports, Recreation	4.06	149	3.80	159	643.70	4.04
Technology	8.61	42	12.29	36	443.60	12.32
Travel	5.86	9	4.93	10	50.15	5.02
TOTAL	$3.41	3,807	$3.63	3,632	$14,050.55	$3.87

Table C / Average Per-Volume Prices of Trade Paperbacks, 1977 and 1984-1986

Category	1977 Prices	1984 Vols.	1984 Prices	1985 Vols.	1985 Prices	1986 Prelim. Vols.	1986 Prelim. Total	1986 Prelim. Prices
Agriculture	$5.01	131	$27.05	198	$9.50	115	$1,508.53	$13.11
Art	6.27	671	13.13	593	14.04	492	7,495.78	15.23
Biography	4.91	560	15.09	536	10.78	475	5,555.99	11.69
Business	7.09	506	17.10	425	16.83	348	6,322.45	18.16
Education	5.72	433	12.84	440	12.98	351	4,870.87	13.87
Fiction	4.20	696	8.95	726	13.66	700	5,954.12	8.50
General Works	6.18	1,286	14.32	1,123	19.13	628	14,443.04	22.99
History	5.81	744	13.49	729	14.08	608	8,818.62	14.50
Home Economics	4.77	544	9.40	513	9.22	358	3,503.87	9.78
Juveniles	2.68	412	5.94	767	5.20	721	4,232.18	5.86
Language	7.79	219	11.60	252	13.25	241	3,446.85	14.30
Law	10.66	371	17.61	339	18.46	277	4,761.57	17.18
Literature	5.18	652	11.70	694	14.04	614	8,196.58	13.34
Medicine	7.63	651	15.78	698	16.01	567	11,193.91	19.74
Music	6.36	136	12.53	113	12.20	94	1,364.45	14.51
Philosophy, Psychology	5.57	540	13.64	523	13.25	459	6,246.25	13.60
Poetry, Drama	4.71	511	8.88	550	8.86	501	5,025.10	10.03
Religion	3.68	1,314	9.32	1,373	9.30	1,197	11,128.02	9.29
Science	8.81	589	16.22	677	19.78	550	12,840.34	23.34
Sociology, Economics	6.03	2,481	17.72	2,402	16.30	2,139	36,258.09	16.95
Sports, Recreation	4.87	467	11.40	447	10.66	354	4,026.05	11.37
Technology	7.97	692	21.11	722	21.08	510	13,790.20	27.03
Travel	5.21	274	9.88	235	10.48	214	2,373.10	11.08
TOTAL	$5.93	14,880	$13.86	15,075	$13.98	12,513	$183,355.96	14.65

Table D / Average and Median Prices, Three Categories: *PW* Fall Announcement Ads, 1982–1986

Novels*	Avg.	Med.	Biography**	Avg.	Med.	History***	Avg.	Med.
1986—305 vols/53 pubs.	$17.13	$16.95	1986—125 vols/53 pubs.	$22.28	$19.95	1986— 73 vols/24 pubs.	$28.99	$24.95
1985—219 vols/49 pubs.	$16.53	$16.95	1985—137 vols/60 pubs.	$22.09	$19.50	1985—179 vols/70 pubs.	$24.25	$25.00
1984—172 vols/42 pubs.	$16.46	$15.95	1984—134 vols/60 pubs.	$21.75	$18.95	1984—149 vols/79 pubs.	$24.77	$22.50
1983—214 vols/42 pubs.	$15.27	$14.95	1983—150 vols/62 pubs.	$20.74	$18.50	1983—172 vols/51 pubs.	$21.90	$20.00
1982—177 vols/41 pubs.	$14.75	$14.95	1982—140 vols/62 pubs.	$20.43	$18.95	1982—152 vols/64 pubs.	$22.88	$19.50

*Not Mystery, Western, SF, Light Romances.

**Includes memoirs and letters.

***Includes pictorial history but not Art books.

Book Sales Statistics:
Highlights from AAP Annual Survey, 1985

Chandler B. Grannis

Contributing Editor, *Publishers Weekly*

Book sales receipts by American publishers came to almost $9.88 billion in 1985, according to estimates and data compiled by the Association of American Publishers. The total was 8.3% higher than the 1984 figure. Publishers' sales in 1986, to judge from trend reports by AAP, passed the $10 billion mark, though the margin of increase was not known at the time this edition of *The Bowker Annual* went to press. (The annual AAP report is usually issued in late spring or very early summer and reprinted immediately in *Publishers Weekly*.)

A glance at Table 1 (reprinted from the July 19, 1986 issue of *Publishers Weekly*) shows that 1985 was a notably good year for the entire trade book group, in which net sales receipts by publishers increased 17.3% over 1984. Publishers' audiovisual and other media business increased overall by 14%. Elementary and high school text materials sold 13% above the 1984 level; and most other categories increased in the range of 6% to 8%. Book club, mail-order, college text, subscription-reference and mass market (rack-sized book) sales gained more modestly. Only in sales of Bibles and liturgical materials was a dollar decline recorded.

Changes in the patterns of publishing cause some adjustment in industry statistics. An example is suggested by the footnote to the adult paperbound figures in the adult trade group: this group of paperbacks includes the sales of full-size ("non-rack-sized") books by mass market publishers, whose other sales are included in the "mass market paperback rack-sized" category. The *non*-rack-sized titles brought in $113.5 million in 1982, $174.7 million in 1984, and $170.2 million in 1985.

In very round percentage figures, combined elhi, college, and standardized-tests publishers account for around 29% of the industry's receipts; the trade group, for 20%; professional categories, for 16%; mass market and book clubs each for about 7%; mail order for about 6%; and subscription-reference and religious, each about 5%.

Book industry estimates are compiled from several sources, including actual reports and projections; different authorities produce different estimates. Other than AAP, the prime compiler of book sales statistics is the Book Industry Study Group, Inc. Reporting for the BISG, John P. Dessauer, the leading industry statistician, estimates total publishers' receipts in 1985 at more than $10.9 billion and projects a 1986 total of more than $11.9 billion. Dessauer also estimates unit sales (numbers of copies of books); his 1986 estimate is more than 2.2 billion, a year's increase of less than 2%. Roughly speaking, book publishing—not in terms of consumer expenditures, but in publishers' receipts (which, of course, are less)—is either an $11 billion or a $12 billion industry.

Table 1 / Estimated Book Publishing Industry Sales, 1972, 1977, 1982, 1984-1985
(Millions of Dollars)

Category	1972 $	1977 $	1982 $	1982 % Change from 1977	1984 $	1984 % Change from 1982	1985 $	1985 % Change from 1984	1985 % Change from 1982	1985 % Change from 1977
Trade (total)	444.8	887.2	1355.5	52.8	1695.8	25.1	1988.7	17.3	46.7	124.2
Adult hardbound	251.5	501.3	671.6	34.3	833.4	24.1	995.9	19.5	48.3	98.7
Adult paperbound*	82.4	223.7	452.0	102.1	582.1	28.8	656.6	12.8	45.3	193.5
Juvenile hardbound	106.5	136.1	180.3	32.5	208.2	15.5	250.7	20.4	39.0	84.2
Juvenile paperbound	4.4	26.1	51.5	97.3	72.1	40.0	85.5	18.6	66.0	227.6
Religious (total)	117.5	250.6	390.0	55.6	461.7	18.4	455.0	-1.5	16.7	81.6
Bibles, testaments, hymnals, and prayer books	61.6	116.3	163.7	40.8	182.0	11.2	174.7	-4.0	6.7	50.2
Other religious	55.9	134.3	226.2	68.4	279.7	23.7	280.3	0.2	23.9	108.7
Professional (total)	381.0	698.2	1230.5	76.2	1458.1	18.5	1561.0	7.1	26.9	123.6
Technical and scientific	131.8	249.3	431.4	73.0	526.4	22.0	561.7	6.7	30.2	125.3
Business and other professional	192.2	286.3	530.6	85.3	589.1	11.0	630.3	7.0	18.8	120.2
Medical	57.0	162.6	268.5	65.1	342.6	27.6	369.0	7.7	37.4	126.9
Book clubs	240.5	406.7	590.0	45.1	660.9	12.0	686.7	3.9	16.4	68.8
Mail-order publications	198.9	396.4	604.6	52.5	573.9	-5.1	603.7	5.2	4.3	52.3
Mass market paperback rack-sized	250.0	487.7	665.5	36.5	732.9	10.1	761.5	3.9	14.4	56.1
University presses	41.4	56.1	122.9	119.1	139.3	13.3	147.8	6.1	20.3	163.5
Elementary and secondary text	497.6	755.9	1051.5	39.1	1310.7	24.7	1481.1	13.0	40.9	95.9
College text	375.3	649.7	1142.4	75.8	1279.0	12.0	1325.0	3.6	16.0	103.9
Standardized tests	26.5	44.6	69.7	56.3	85.8	23.1	92.2	7.5	32.3	106.7
Subscription reference	278.9	294.4	396.6	34.7	465.2	17.3	486.6	4.6	22.7	65.3
AV and other media (total)	116.2	151.3	148.0	-2.2	175.0	18.2	199.5	14.0	34.8	31.9
Elhi	101.2	131.4	130.1	-1.0	152.3	17.1	173.9	14.2	33.7	32.3
College	9.2	11.6	7.9	-31.9	8.8	11.4	9.9	12.6	25.3	-14.7
Other	5.8	8.3	10.0	20.5	13.9	39.0	15.7	13.0	57.0	89.2
Other sales	49.2	63.4	77.1	21.6	83.1	7.8	89.7	8.0	16.3	41.5
Total	3017.8	5142.2	7844.3	52.5	9121.4	16.3	9878.5	8.3	25.9	92.1

*Includes non-rack-sized sales by mass market publishers of $113.5 million in 1982, $174.7 million in 1984, and $170.2 million in 1985.
Source: Association of American Publishers 1985 Annual Statistics.

U.S. Book Exports, Imports, and International Title Output

Chandler B. Grannis

Contributing Editor, *Publishers Weekly*

U.S. book exports in 1985 dropped 8.9% below those of 1984, while book imports increased 14.8%, according to the Department of Commerce. Omitting shipments valued below $500, the 1985 export total was $591,166,181. The import total, omitting shipments valued below $250, came to $564,159,820. Imports have been increasing in dollar value since 1980 and, according to Department of Commerce figures just released, are actually moving ahead of exports; for the first six months of 1986, exports totaled $292.5 million and imports were $309.4 million.

The ratio of exports to imports, as noted by *PW* in September 1985, was about 67 to 33 in 1982, and 57 to 43 in 1984. The 1985 ratio was roughly 51 to 49. And for the first half of 1986, the ratio is reversed — about 49 to 51. This trend has, of course, been the subject of much concern, discussion, and action by book industry leaders and organizations, and some government agencies.

Not known are the effects the omission of small shipments from Department of Commerce data collection may have on actual totals of book exports and imports. The shipments include undoubtedly large numbers of book club and mail order transactions, single or other small shipments to individuals and institutions, and small orders handled through retailers.

The figures shown in Tables 1–4 have been extracted and arranged, with some added computations, from lengthy printouts of Department of Commerce data. This "raw" material has once again been supplied to *PW* by William S. Lofquist, printing and publishing specialist at the department's International Trade Administration. The material is public information available for the industry's use, but the department, since the early 1980s, has not had funds to publish it, as was once done in the Department of Commerce's quarterly, *Printing and Publishing*. Mr. Lofquist, however, continues to publish his industry analyses, partly in the *Book Research Quarterly*, edited by John P. Dessauer at the University of Scranton.

The information provided in Tables 1 and 2 has always been arranged under very broad headings. Much the largest category of exports, for example, is a catch-all labeled "Books Not Specially Provided For," which, before 1983, was even more comprehensive, since it included mass market paperbacks. Among imports, about 88% of the dollar value appears as "Other Books."

Tables 3 and 4 show more shifts in the ranking of countries doing book business with the United States. Export data show declines in purchases by four out of the top five customers for U.S. books. The increase in sales to China is dramatic, but not unexpected. Among sources of books, the increase for Sweden is startling. U.S. use of foreign book production services is reflected obviously in several of the import figures.

Table 5 is an extract from the book title output table in the *UNESCO Yearbook*; only the principal book-producing countries have been selected here. The yearbook is a massive compendium of many kinds of information about book and periodical publishing, translations, libraries, education, and other cultural activity around the world.

Note: Adapted from *Publishers Weekly*, September 19, 1986, where the article was entitled "U.S. Exports, Imports, UNESCO Reports."

Table 1 / U.S. Book Exports, 1984–1985
Shipments Valued over $500

	1984 $	1985 $	% Change	1984 units	1985 units	% Change
Bibles, Testaments and Other Religious Books (2703020)	$32,616,369	$30,229,735	−7.3	39,917,993	39,266,888	−1.6
Dictionaries and Thesauruses (2703040)	5,287,873	4,284,676	−19.0	1,065,146	694,651	−34.8
Encyclopedias (2703060)	27,091,095	26,888,675	−.7	5,747,777	4,953,897	−13.8
Textbooks, Workbooks and Standardized Tests (2703070)	108,914,225	107,413,027	−1.4	19,984,105	17,774,326	−11.1
Technical, Scientific, and Professional Books (2703080)	153,979,796	140,460,968	−8.8	33,721,126	29,149,797	−13.6
Paperbound Mass Market Books (2704020)	48,013,579	46,567,173	−3.0	40,759,120	36,565,112	−10.3
Books Not Specially Provided for (2704040)	257,680,035	220,935,095	−14.3	108,621,812	89,167,869	−17.9
Children's Picture and Coloring Books (7375200)	9,171,050	9,323,953	+1.7	—	—	—
Total Exports	$642,754,022	$591,166,181	−8.9	—	—	—

Source for Tables 1, 2, and 3: Department of Commerce; compiled by the writer from printouts supplied by William S. Lofquist, Industry Specialist (Printing and Publishing), International Trade Administration.

Table 2 / U.S. Book Imports, 1984–1985
Shipments Valued over $250

	1984 $	1985 $	% Change	1984 units	1985 units	% Change
Bibles, Prayerbooks (270520)	$8,105,846	$9,781,475	+20.7	9,641,586	8,840,492	-8.3
Books, Foreign Language (2702540)	30,264,284	33,483,433	+10.6	18,504,722	24,016,684	+29.8
Books, Not Specially Provided for, wholly or in part the work of an author who is a U.S. domiciliary (2702560)	17,020,190	16,036,054	-5.8	57,493,924	56,219,149	-2.2
Other Books (2702580)	426,004,940	491,852,127	+15.5	393,509,167	450,116,467	+14.4
Children's Picture and Coloring Books (7375200)	10,332,542	13,006,731	+25.9	—	—	—
Total Imports	$491,527,202	$564,159,820	+14.8	—	—	—

Table 3 / U.S. Book Imports: Principal Countries, 1984–1985
Shipments Valued over $250

	1984 $	1985 $	% Change
United Kingdom	$135,444,093	$130,930,198	−3.3
Japan	79,307,764	94,340,686	+19.0
Canada	84,177,657	87,398,155	+3.8
Italy	32,038,953	50,383,025	+57.3
Hong Kong	28,956,169	36,445,299	+25.9
West Germany	20,314,134	25,547,406	+25.8
Singapore	12,244,877	12,308,701	+0.5
Belgium	7,789,270	12,009,476	+54.2
Netherlands	12,489,829	10,581,900	−15.3
Sweden	1,627,995	10,258,010	+530.2
France	6,772,656	9,335,737	+37.8
China, Taiwan	6,825,878	7,377,550	+8.1
Mexico	6,592,940	7,030,761	+6.6
Switzerland	6,598,625	6,687,723	+1.4
Rep. of Korea	4,461,730	4,846,738	+8.6
Israel	4,113,101	4,598,969	+11.8
*Total	$491,527,202	$564,159,820	+14.8

*Includes figures for the countries not specifically listed here.

Table 4 / U.S. Book Exports: Principal Countries, 1984–1985
Shipments Valued over $500

	1984 $	1985 $	% Change
Canada	$259,676,622	$240,348,325	−8.1
United Kingdom	86,049,986	67,648,757	−22.2
Australia	54,041,856	57,732,102	+4.6
Japan	30,888,319	34,803,278	−14.3
Netherlands	23,147,174	21,793,469	−6.0
West Germany	11,047,863	13,696,873	+21.2
Mexico	7,532,170	12,347,720	+63.6
Singapore	10,232,829	10,689,036	+4.3
India	7,958,715	9,916,504	+24.6
Ireland	19,592,693	8,597,071	−56.1
France	7,730,374	7,993,249	+.8
South Africa Rep.	12,639,329	7,268,164	−42.7
China, People's Rep.	1,335,271	5,578,657	+317.8
Saudi Arabia	9,114,172	5,374,887	−41.0
Hong Kong	7,916,572	5,077,053	−37.4
Venezuela	3,761,108	4,647,802	+23.6
Italy	3,880,909	4,620,411	+13.1
Switzerland	4,536,765	4,571,590	+.2
Philippine Rep.	4,086,622	4,540,179	+11.1
New Zealand	6,069,166	4,430,987	−29.2
*Total	$642,754,822	$591,166,181	−8.9

*Includes figures for the countries not specifically listed here.

Table 5 / Title Output: Principal Book-Producing Countries, 1981–1983

	1981	1982	1983
Africa			
Nigeria	1,150	1,666	1,495
North America			
Cuba	1,438	1,640	1,917
Mexico	2,954	2,818	—
*United States	48,793	46,930	53,380
South America			
Argentina	4,251	4,962	4,216
Chile	918	—	1,326
Colombia	7,671	—	—
Venezuela	4,200	—	—
Brazil	—	19,179	—
Asia			
China, People's Rep.	22,920	—	31,602
Hong Kong	4,367	3,560	5,681
India	11,562	10,649	—
Indonesia	—	5,488	5,731
Iran	1,385	2,994	4,835
Israel	1,990	1,892	—
Japan	42,217	42,977	—
Korea, Rep. of	25,747	30,436	35,512
Malaysia	2,356	2,801	—
Pakistan	1,600	—	—
Singapore	1,783	1,530	1,927
Sri Lanka	2,352	1,951	—
Thailand	4,498	5,645	6,819
Turkey	4,793	6,440	6,869
Vietnam	1,495	—	—

	1981	1982	1983
Europe			
Albania	1,043	1,149	997
Austria	6,214	6,736	—
Belgium	9,736	8,041	8,065
Bulgaria	5,036	5,070	4,924
Czechoslovakia	10,493	10,519	9,574
Denmark	8,563	10,189	9,460
Finland	8,227	7,436	8,594
France	37,308	42,186	37,576
East Germany	5,979	5,938	6,175
West Germany	56,568	58,592	58,489
Hungary	8,810	8,836	8,469
Italy	13,457	12,926	13,718
Netherlands	13,939	13,324	—
Norway	—	5,175	5,540
Poland	10,435	9,814	8,789
Portugal	6,714	9,139	8,647
Romania	7,242	6,702	—
Spain	29,625	32,138	—
Sweden	8,582	8,509	8,036
Switzerland	10,544	11,405	—
United Kingdom	42,972	48,029	50,981
Yugoslavia	11,088	10,535	10,931
Oceania			
Australia	6,793	2,358	—
New Zealand	2,499	—	2,944
U.S.S.R			
U.S.S.R. totals	83,007	80,674	82,589
Byelorussia	3,189	2,923	3,264
Ukraine	8,450	8,239	8,882

Source: *UNESCO Statistical Yearbook 1985*, Table 7.6, except U.S. figures, supplied by R. R. Bowker Co. data services.

*Not included in U.S. figures are publications of state and local governments, some institutions, company reports, proceedings, lab manuals, yearbooks, U.S. Government Printing Office publications, and university theses. However, the books of university presses, religious denominations and other nonprofit publishers are included.

British Book Production, 1986

The number of books published in the United Kingdom in 1986 was again a record. *The Bookseller* recorded an issued total of 57,845 titles in 1986 against 52,994 in 1985 (Table 1). The latest total was made up of 44,174 new titles — 7 percent more than in 1985 — and 13,671 reprints and new editions (including paperbacks) — 16.5 percent up. Overall, where the 1984 increase was under 1 percent and the 1985 increase under 3 percent, the 1986 leap is over 9 percent.

Table 2 shows 40 years of like-with-like comparison — subject always to the accuracy of publishers' notifications to J. Whitaker & Sons, Ltd. This year, 1987, will see a change in method which, despite the much improved efficiency and punctuality of notifying publishers, is likely to lead to an understatement of output. As an example of past practice, in 1986 all books notified in 1986 were included, *plus* those published in 1985 but not notified until early 1986. In the future the criteria will be stricter: only those books notified and listed in 1987 will be included in the 1987 total. It is hoped that the much diminished number of laggard publishers will diminish yet further.

The present extent of understatement — the problem was briefly noted at the half-year stage in the July 12, 1986 issue — is indicated by the 57,845 total in Table 1 against the total of 52,496 in Table 3, the 1986 full classification table, compiled on a strict calendar year basis.

Table 1 / Comparison of Book Production by Subject, 1985 and 1986

	1985	1986	+ or −
Art	1,300	1,637	+337
Biography	1,796	2,002	+206
Chemistry and physics	731	866	+135
Children's books	4,410	4,642	+232
Commerce	1,628	1,877	+249
Education	1,292	1,241	−51
Engineering	1,826	1,880	+54
Fiction	5,846	6,108	+262
History	1,916	2,197	+281
Industry	516	493	−23
Law and public administration	1,800	1,956	+156
Literature	1,671	1,666	−5
Medical science	3,655	3,760	+105
Natural sciences	1,190	1,553	+363
Political science	3,917	4,233	+316
Religion	1,992	2,622	+630
School textbooks	1,824	2,297	+473
Sociology	1,151	1,242	+91
Travel and guidebooks	1,120	1,212	+92
Total new books	41,254	44,174	+2,920
Total new editions	11,740	13,671	+1,931
Overall total	52,994	57,845	+4,851

Note: Adapted from *The Bookseller* (12 Dyott St., London WC1A 1DF, England), January 2, 1987, where the article is entitled "Output — The Rise Goes On."

Table 2 / Title Output, 1947–1986

Year	Total	Reprints & New Editions
1947	13,046	2,441
1948	14,686	3,924
1949	17,034	5,110
1950	17,072	5,334
1951	18,066	4,938
1952	18,741	5,428
1953	18,257	5,523
1954	18,188	4,846
1955	19,962	5,770
1956	19,107	5,302
1957	20,719	5,921
1958	22,143	5,971
1959	20,690	5,522
1960	23,783	4,989
1961	24,893	6,406
1962	25,079	6,104
1963	26,023	5,656
1964	26,154	5,260
1965	26,358	5,313
1966	28,883	5,919
1967	29,619	7,060
1968	31,470	8,778
1969	32,393	9,106
1970	33,489	9,977
1971	32,538	8,975
1972	33,140	8,486
1973	35,254	9,556
1974	32,194	7,852
1975	35,608	8,361
1976	34,434	8,227
1977	36,322	8,638
1978	38,766	9,236
1979	41,940	9,086
1980	48,158	10,776
1981	43,083	9,387
1982	48,307	10,360
1983	51,071	12,091
1984	51,555	11,309
1985	52,994	11,740
1986	57,845	13,671

Inevitably, Table 1, the accompanying comparison table, shows rises in almost every main category, with religion showing an increase of no less than 630 titles, or 32 percent. And—if greater title output is indeed a barometer of greater public interest and response—it is good to see output of both children's books and fiction well ahead of the 1985 figures.

The figures are not subject to any unusual rise in U.S.-originated titles through stockholding distributors: these in fact showed a marginal decline, and represent about 27 percent of the total.

Table 3 / Book Title Output, 1986

Classification	December 1986				January–December 1986			
	Total	Reprints & New Editions	Trans.	Ltd. Editions	Total	Reprints & New Editions	Trans.	Ltd. Editions
Aeronautics	11	1	—	—	213	57	—	—
Agriculture and forestry	35	9	—	—	448	85	5	—
Architecture	38	5	—	—	383	76	4	—
Art	105	13	6	1	1,505	194	28	7
Astronomy	12	2	1	—	120	26	2	—
Bibliography	106	21	—	—	747	136	3	1
Biography	141	39	4	—	1,842	556	65	4
Chemistry and physics	113	15	—	—	811	169	11	—
Children's books	155	27	9	—	4,510	930	119	4
Commerce	206	62	—	—	1,683	465	—	1
Customs	17	—	—	—	182	53	16	1
Domestic science	51	22	—	1	866	175	7	2
Education	135	18	—	—	1,093	145	7	—
Engineering	221	64	2	—	1,649	390	43	—
Entertainment	55	18	—	—	589	99	26	—
Fiction	362	190	18	1	6,002	2,806	288	11
General	117	24	1	—	1,087	149	11	1
Geography	86	52	—	—	585	144	3	1
Geology	29	6	2	—	253	34	10	—
History	250	44	8	3	1,947	388	76	5
Humor	17	3	1	—	293	46	2	—
Industry	57	15	—	—	414	93	9	—
Language	56	9	2	—	732	147	4	—
Law and public administration	207	47	3	—	1,678	418	10	2
Literature	152	31	13	—	1,546	282	83	1
Mathematics	101	20	—	—	722	132	6	—
Medical science	383	61	2	—	3,374	646	18	—
Military science	11	5	—	—	238	51	2	1
Music	34	7	—	—	437	87	9	—
Natural sciences	176	21	4	—	1,369	175	22	1
Occultism	48	26	2	—	548	298	32	—
Philosophy	53	6	—	—	660	165	55	—
Photography	12	—	—	—	165	17	1	—
Plays	39	13	4	—	315	93	35	—
Poetry	91	6	18	5	751	94	85	30
Political science	393	87	4	—	3,822	730	91	—
Psychology	78	9	—	—	818	180	14	—
Religion	201	35	23	—	2,268	411	190	—
School textbooks	178	13	—	—	1,836	258	—	—
Science, general	4	—	—	—	99	18	1	—
Sociology	112	10	2	—	1,132	128	20	—
Sports	47	11	—	—	713	169	8	—
Stockbreeding	27	4	1	—	295	76	3	1
Trade	37	12	—	—	512	147	1	—
Travel and guidebooks	86	45	—	—	1,113	457	11	—
Wireless and television	22	6	—	—	131	46	—	—
Totals	4,867	1,134	130	11	52,496	12,441	1,436	74

Number of Book Outlets in the United States and Canada

The *American Book Trade Directory* has been published by the R. R. Bowker Company since 1915. Revised annually, it features lists of booksellers, wholesalers, periodicals, reference tools, and other information about the U.S. book market as well as markets in Great Britain and Canada. The data provided in Tables 1 and 2 for the United States and Canada, the most current available, are from the 1986 edition of the directory.

The 23,648 stores of various types shown in Table 1 are located in approximately 6,300 cities in the United States, Canada, and regions administered by the United States. All "general" bookstores are assumed to carry hardbound (trade) books, paperbacks, and children's books; special effort has been made to apply this category only to bookstores for which this term can properly be applied. All "college" stores are assumed to carry college-level textbooks. The term "educational" is used for outlets handling school textbooks up to and including the high school level. The category "mail order" has been confined to those outlets that sell general trade books by mail and are not book clubs; all others operating by mail have been classified according to the kinds of books carried. The term "antiquarian" covers dealers in old and rare books. Stores handling only secondhand books are classified by the category "used." The category "paperback" represents stores with more than 80 percent of their stock in paperbound books. Other stores

Table 1 / Bookstores in the United States (and Canada)*

Antiquarian	1,293	(82)	Office supply	82	(11)
Mail order antiquarian	708	(25)	Paperback†	732	(34)
College	3,005	(167)	Religious	3,848	(248)
Department store	586	(107)	Remainders	12	(3)
Drugstore	21	(4)	Rental	2	(0)
Educational	113	(18)	Science-technology	39	(6)
Exporter-importer	20	(1)	Special‡	2,101	(151)
Foreign language	122	(25)	Stationer	122	(33)
General	6,391	(983)	Used	1,070	(72)
Gift shop	150	(17)			
Juvenile	215	(41)	*Totals*		
Law	42	(3)	Bookstores	21,568	(2080)
Mail order (general)	316	(14)	Bookstore chain headquarters	1,283	(135)
Medical	36	(1)	Bookstore chain branches	5,796	(624)
Museum store and			Independent bookstores	14,489	(1321)
art gallery	387	(29)			
Newsdealer	155	(5)			

*In Tables 1 and 2, the Canadian figure for each category is in parentheses following the U.S. figure.
†This figure does not include paperback departments of general bookstores, department stores, stationers, drugstores, or wholesalers handling paperbacks.
‡"Special" includes stores specializing in subjects other than those specifically given in the list.

Table 2 / Wholesalers in the United States (and Canada)

Total listed	1210	(163)
General wholesalers	926	(128)
Paperback wholesalers*	284	(35)

*This figure is the total of all wholesalers who indicated in the survey that at least 51% of total volume was accounted for by paperbound sales.

with paperback departments are listed under the major classification ("general," "department store," "stationer," etc.), with the fact that paperbacks are carried given in the entry. A bookstore that specializes in a subject to the extent of 50 percent of its stock has that subject designated as its major category.

Book Review Media Statistics

Number of Books Reviewed by Major Book-Reviewing Publications, 1985–1986

	Adult		Children's		Young Adult		Total	
	1985	1986	1985	1986	1985	1986	1985	1986
Booklist[1]	4,239	3,913	1,468	1,621	1,560	1,378	7,930	7,484
Bulletin of the Center for Children's Books	—	—	450	440	385	360	825	800
Chicago Sun Times	1,000	800	200	250	—	—	1,200	1,150
Chicago Tribune	659	860	200	200	—	—	859	1,060
Choice[2]	6,439	6,197	—	—	—	—	6,784	6,197
Horn Book	9	5	278	301	110	53	497	359
Kirkus Services[3]	4,000	4,000	—	—	—	—	4,000	4,000
Library Journal	4,138	3,975	—	—	—	—	4,138	3,975
Los Angeles Times	2,625	2,600	125	125	—	—	2,750	2,725
New York Review of Books	338	400	—	—	—	—	338	400
New York Times Sunday Book Review[4]	2,250	2,250	250	250	—	—	2,500	2,500
Publishers Weekly[5]	5,300	5,242	600	1,200	—	—	5,900	6,442
School Library Journal	25	204	2,419	1,937	250	574	2,694	2,715
Washington Post Book World	1,757	2,377	191	163	—	—	1,948	2,540

[1]All figures are for a 12-month period from September 1 to August 31; 1985 figures are for September 1, 1984–August 31, 1985. Totals include reference and subscription books. In addition, Booklist publishes reviews of nonprint materials—926 in 1985 and 846 in 1986—and of special bibliographies—more than 4,000 each year.

[2]All figures are for a 12-month period beginning September and ending July/August; 1985 figures are for September 1985–August 1986. Total for 1985 includes 345 nonprint materials; total for 1986 includes 391 nonprint materials.

[3]Adult figures include both adult and juvenile books.

[4]Adult figure includes paperbacks reviewed in "New and Noteworthy" column.

[5]Includes reviews of paperback originals and reprints.

Prices of U.S. and Foreign Published Materials

Rebecca T. Lenzini

Vice President and Director, Academic Information Services, The Faxon Company

15 Southwest Park, Westwood, MA 02090
617-329-3350

The year 1986 was one of modest increases in average prices of most published materials with the exception of hardcover books. All categories of materials indexed in this report continued to outstrip the 1986 Consumer Price Index increase of 1.9% by a significant margin. U.S. periodicals posted an average increase of 8.9% over 1985 prices, with an average subscription price of $65.00 (an increase of $5.30 over the 1985 average price of $59.70). Preliminary 1987 results show U.S. periodicals increasing 9.9% over 1986 prices (10.3% if Soviet translations are included). The changes in the indexes for the principal categories of U.S. materials published in 1986 are as follows.

U.S. Materials	Index Change	Percent Change
Consumer Price Index*	3.4	1.9
Periodicals	21.5	8.9
Hardcover books	− 1.3	− .76
Academic books	8.6	5.9
College books	12.2	7.1
Mass market paperbacks	9.4	6.9
(Higher priced) paperbacks	11.2	4.8

*Adjusted to base year 1977

A three-year summary of the percent change in these same categories follows.

U.S. Materials	Percent Change		
	1984	1985	1986
Consumer Price Index*	3.2	3.6	1.9
Periodicals	9.4	8.6	8.9
Hardcover books	− 4.4	4.8	− .76
Academic books	2.2	4.7	5.9
College books	3.3	4.1	7.1
Mass market paperbacks	8.0	5.3	6.9
(Higher priced) paperbacks	18.4	− 3.1	4.8

*Adjusted to base year 1977.

U.S. Published Materials

Average prices and price indexes of U.S. periodicals are shown in Table 1 and of U.S. hardcover books in Table 2. Until 1985, Table 2 contained data on U.S. serials services; however, this index was temporarily suspended while the ALA/RTSD Library Materials Price Index Committee studied its scope and usefulness. Now that the committee's studies have been concluded, the index will be resumed beginning with the 1988 edition of *The Bowker Annual*, barring any unforseen difficulties.

Table 1 / U.S. Periodicals: Average Prices and Price Indexes, 1983–1986*

(Index Base: 1977 = 100)

Subject Area	1977 Average Price	1983 Average Price	1983 Index	1984 Average Price	1984 Index	1985 Average Price	1985 Index	1986 Average Price	1986 Index
U.S. periodicals:									
excluding Soviet translations**	$24.59	$50.23	204.3	$54.97	223.5	$59.70	242.8	$65.00	264.3
including Soviet translations**	33.42	65.74	196.7	72.47	216.8	80.78	241.7	87.38	261.5
Agriculture	11.58	21.27	183.7	24.06	207.8	26.05	225.0	28.71	247.9
Business and economics	18.62	35.67	191.6	38.87	208.8	44.41	238.5	47.15	253.2
Chemistry and physics	93.76	207.94	221.8	228.90	244.1	238.43	254.3	264.05	281.6
Children's periodicals	5.82	11.49	197.4	12.21	209.8	13.31	228.7	13.76	236.4
Education	17.54	31.36	178.8	34.01	193.9	37.81	215.6	40.47	230.7
Engineering	35.77	73.18	204.6	78.70	220.0	84.38	235.9	92.66	259.0
Fine and applied arts	13.72	25.17	183.5	26.90	196.1	27.03	197.0	28.28	206.1
General interest periodicals	16.19	26.43	163.2	27.90	172.3	26.41	163.1	26.95	166.5
History	12.64	22.43	177.5	23.68	187.3	25.55	202.1	26.04	206.0
Home economics	18.73	35.68	190.5	37.15	198.3	41.04	219.1	45.59	243.4
Industrial arts	14.37	28.83	200.6	30.40	211.6	35.09	244.2	39.75	276.6
Journalism and communications	16.97	37.39	220.3	39.25	231.3	46.08	271.5	47.54	281.1
Labor and industrial relations	11.24	29.22	260.0	29.87	265.7	34.75	309.2	37.14	330.4
Law	17.36	29.66	170.9	31.31	180.4	35.13	202.4	36.44	209.9
Library and information sciences	16.97	36.72	216.4	38.85	228.9	40.66	239.6	42.82	252.3
Literature and language	11.82	21.19	179.3	23.02	194.8	24.18	204.6	25.21	213.3
Mathematics, botany, geology, and general science	47.13	97.26	206.4	106.56	226.1	116.93	248.1	129.95	275.7
Medicine	51.31	112.72	219.7	125.57	244.7	137.92	268.8	151.77	295.8
Philosophy and religion	10.89	20.21	185.6	21.94	201.5	24.30	223.1	24.85	228.2
Physical education and recreation	10.00	19.07	190.7	20.54	205.4	23.72	237.2	24.78	247.8
Political science	14.83	28.97	195.3	32.43	218.7	32.72	220.6	35.19	237.3
Psychology	31.74	59.31	186.9	69.74	219.7	76.34	240.5	83.71	263.7
Sociology and anthropology	19.68	40.54	206.0	43.87	222.9	50.87	258.5	56.31	286.1
Soviet translations**	175.41	341.04	194.4	381.86	217.7	453.47	258.5	483.09	275.4
Zoology	33.69	70.74	210.0	78.35	232.6	90.75	269.4	102.83	305.2
Total number of periodicals:									
excluding Soviet translations**	3,218	3,671		3,731		3,731		3,731	
including Soviet translations**	3,418	3,881		3,942		3,942		3,942	

*Compiled by Judith G. Horn and Rebecca T. Lenzini. For further comments see *Library Journal*, April 15, 1986, "Price Indexes for 1986: U.S. Periodicals," by Judith G. Horn. Note that Table 1 uses a one-year (1977), rather than a three-year (1977–1979), base, conforming to the practice of the Bureau of Labor Statistics and making these price indexes comparable to the consumer price indexes. For average prices for years prior to 1983, see previous editions of the *Bowker Annual*.

**The category Soviet Translations was added in 1986. Data for U.S. periodicals including Soviet translations are based on the total group of titles included in the indexes of this table; data for U.S. periodicals excluding Soviet translations are based on the total group of titles minus the Soviet translation titles.

Table 2 / U.S. Hardcover Books: Average Prices and Price Indexes, 1983–1986*
(Index Base: 1977 = 100)

Categories with Dewey Decimal Numbers	1977 Average Price	1983 (final) Volumes	1983 (final) Average Price	1983 (final) Index	1984 (final) Volumes	1984 (final) Average Price	1984 (final) Index	1985 (final) Volumes	1985 (final) Average Price	1985 (final) Index	1986 (preliminary) Volumes	1986 (preliminary) Average Price	1986 (preliminary) Index
Agriculture (630–639; 712–719)	$16.24	395	$33.39	205.6	359	$34.92	215.0	368	$36.77	226.4	311	$37.81	232.8
Art (700–711; 720–779)	21.24	1,180	33.79	159.1	1,114	33.03	155.5	908	35.15	165.5	776	33.98	160.0
Biography	15.34	1,540	22.40	146.0	1,408	22.53	146.9	1,298	22.20	144.7	1,138	22.46	146.4
Business (650–659)	18.00	1,152	27.72	154.0	1,116	26.01	144.5	1,040	28.84	160.2	938	30.33	168.5
Education (370–379)	12.95	617	21.56	166.5	580	24.47	189.0	602	27.28	210.7	446	25.63	197.9
Fiction	10.09	2,072	14.29	141.6	1,989	14.74	146.1	1,800	15.29	151.5	1,772	16.37	162.2
General Works (000–099)	30.99	1,582	37.45	120.8	1,602	35.61	114.9	1,632	37.91	122.3	1,203	37.06	119.6
History (900–909; 930–999)	17.12	1,612	24.96	145.8	1,432	27.53	160.8	1,506	27.02	157.8	1,239	27.77	162.2
Home Economics (640–649)	11.16	713	16.62	148.9	655	15.70	140.7	594	17.50	156.8	419	19.02	170.4
Juveniles	6.65	2,524	9.73	146.3	2,398	10.02	150.7	2,529	9.95	149.6	2,558	10.51	158.0
Language (400–499)	14.96	379	23.80	159.1	410	22.97	153.5	347	28.68	191.7	293	30.58	204.4
Law (340–349)	25.04	1,196	39.09	156.1	925	43.88	175.2	955	41.70	166.5	746	48.02	191.8
Literature (800–810; 813–820; 823–889)	15.78	1,264	23.63	149.7	1,243	23.57	149.4	1,181	24.53	155.4	1,118	25.42	161.1
Medicine (610–619)	24.00	3,270	39.84	166.0	2,836	40.65	169.4	2,798	44.36	184.8	2,063	47.66	198.6
Music (780–789)	20.13	270	25.77	128.0	232	27.79	138.1	238	28.79	143.0	181	32.36	160.8
Philosophy, Psychology (100–199)	14.43	1,024	25.73	178.3	895	29.70	205.8	895	28.11	194.8	799	29.00	201.0
Poetry, Drama (811; 812; 821; 822)	13.63	675	22.42	164.5	599	26.75	196.3	563	22.14	162.4	495	23.71	174.0
Religion (200–299)	12.26	1,257	16.74	136.5	1,118	17.76	144.9	1,100	19.13	156.0	932	21.59	176.1
Science (500–599)	24.88	2,878	47.03	189.0	2,535	46.57	187.2	2,556	51.19	205.7	1,935	53.59	215.4
Sociology, Economics (300–339; 350–369; 380–399)	29.88	5,717	43.34	145.0	5,066	33.35	111.6	4,761	33.33	111.5	4,095	29.70	99.4
Sports, Recreation (790–799)	12.28	693	20.05	163.3	623	20.16	164.2	530	23.43	190.8	426	23.55	191.8
Technology (600–609; 620–629; 660–699)	23.61	2,046	41.14	174.2	1,797	45.80	194.0	1,693	50.37	213.3	1,501	53.10	224.9
Travel (910–919)	18.44	286	21.65	117.4	252	21.31	115.6	210	24.66	133.7	177	23.23	126.0
Total	$19.22	34,342	$31.19	162.3	31,184	29.99	156.0	30,104	$31.46	163.7	25,561	$31.22	162.4

*Compiled by Dennis E. Smith and Sue Plezia, University of California, from data supplied by the R. R. Bowker Company. Price indexes in Tables 2 and 6 are based on books recorded in the R. R. Bowker Company's *Weekly Record* (cumulated in the *American Book Publishing Record*). The 1986 preliminary figures include items listed during 1986 with an imprint date of 1986. Final data for previous years include items listed between January of that year and June of the following year with an imprint date of the specified year. Conventional rounding was used in the calculations of average prices.

Periodical Prices

The year 1986 marks the second year in which the U.S. Periodicals Price Index has been produced by the Faxon Company in cooperation with ALA/RTSD Library Materials Price Index Committee. Periodical subscription prices for 1986 were obtained from Faxon's online price file. They are publishers' list prices in effect for the 1986 subscription year for U.S. college and university libraries. The prices are supplied directly to Faxon by the publishers, and any Faxon discounts and service charges are not included.

Several changes to the full periodical indexes were implemented in 1986 with the approval of the Library Materials Price Index Committee. Most importantly, the publication date of the full report (which appears in *Library Journal*) was moved forward from July/August to April 15 of each year. The earlier publication date became possible with the change from manual to automated production that accompanied the transfer of responsibility for maintaining the index to Faxon. Hopefully, the April publication date will increase the usefulness of the index for library budgeting purposes.

Because of the earlier publication of the full report, the traditional reporting of preliminary figures at ALA Midwinter was discontinued in 1985. Instead, summary results for each calendar year are now distributed in February. The committee is now working to provide these data to libraries as early as possible in each calendar year, through the ALA network, ALANET.

Beginning with 1986, a new category, Soviet Translations, is being included in the U.S. Periodicals Price Index as reflected in Table 1. This category was previously included in the Serials Services Price Index; all publications included in the category were found to meet the ANSI standard criteria for inclusion in the periodical index. Readers also will find a new index sorted by Library of Congress classification codes within the full report. This index appears for the first time in the 1986 report and will be continued each year.

Book Prices

Table 3, North American Academic Books, is compiled from data supplied from the approval plans of three major agencies noted in the table's footnote for the information of the reader. The average increase in this category posted in 1985–1986 over 1984–1985 was 5.9%; the average price reported was $33.66, an increase of $1.89 from the previous average of $31.77. Those readers interested in the methodology used in compiling this report are referred to "Reporting Book Prices" by the compiler, Dora Biblarz, Arizona State University, published in the summer 1986 issue of *Book Research Quarterly* (vol. 2, no. 2).

Table 4 lists the average prices of U.S. college books as taken from reviews appearing in *Choice*. (The number of titles reviewed in *Choice* for 1986 was 3% less than in 1985. This may be because the *Choice* staff was lacking an editor for seven months of the calendar year, although there is no clear evidence of this.) Compiler Kathryn A. Soupiset, Trinity University, notes that titles with a price of $500 or greater were excluded, as were microforms, continuations, parts of sets, and government documents. Additional information and tables appear in a separate article published in the March 1987 issue of *Choice*.

Caution is advised in using the data in Table 5, which provides price indexes for mass market paperbacks by subject class. Several subject classes that make up the survey

(text continues on page 443)

Table 3 / North American Academic Book Price Index, 1983/84–1985/86*
(Index Base: 1979/80 = 100)

Subject	LC Class	1979/80		1983/84			1984/85			1985/86			
		Number of Titles	Overall Average	Number of Titles	Overall Average	Index	Number of Titles	Overall Average	Index	Number of Titles	Overall Average	Percent Increase	Index
Agriculture	S	1,275	$22.80	1,135	$35.03	153.6	1,365	$35.94	157.6	1,156	$39.65	10.3	173.9
Anthropology	GN	688	18.23	505	25.31	138.8	603	26.75	146.7	608	28.81	7.7	158.0
Botany	QK	428	30.06	362	44.10	146.7	442	46.45	154.5	367	52.44	12.9	174.5
Business and economics	H	6,980	18.92	8,202	26.24	138.7	8,954	26.87	142.0	7,959	29.31	9.1	154.9
Chemistry	QD	950	43.44	884	57.61	132.6	959	64.10	147.6	897	71.43	11.4	164.4
Education	L	2,682	14.37	2,209	20.70	144.1	2,528	21.29	148.2	1,994	23.26	9.3	161.9
Engineering and technology	T	5,277	28.83	5,922	42.06	145.9	6,155	43.41	150.6	5,342	47.11	8.5	163.4
Fiction and children's literature	PZ	572	11.47	723	14.88	129.7	915	15.81	137.8	1,066	16.56	4.7	144.4
Fine and applied arts	M–N	4,846	21.82	3,921	30.18	138.3	4,246	30.54	140.0	3,883	32.34	5.9	148.2
General works	A	322	22.71	263	30.18	132.9	241	36.96	162.7	211	39.79	7.7	175.2
Geography	G	554	23.22	523	36.48	157.1	520	33.02	142.2	473	36.54	10.7	157.4
Geology	QE	475	31.59	537	43.86	138.8	603	42.46	134.4	555	47.35	11.5	149.9
History	C–D–E–F	5,713	18.95	4,927	25.82	136.3	5,778	25.25	133.2	5,766	27.14	7.5	143.2
Home economics	TX	492	16.71	401	21.72	130.0	476	22.95	137.3	537	22.28	-2.9	133.3
Industrial arts	TT	111	16.14	132	19.84	122.9	135	17.53	108.6	105	18.00	2.7	111.5
Law	K	1,122	19.82	1,079	29.83	150.5	1,139	30.90	155.9	1,075	35.43	14.7	178.8

Subject	LC class	No.	Price	No.	Price	Index	No.	Price	Index	No.	Price	% change	Index
Library and information science	Z	774	21.82	778	29.69	136.1	902	30.51	139.8	753	33.95	11.3	155.6
Literature and language	P	8,823	15.43	9,072	21.54	139.6	10,543	22.03	142.8	10,329	23.62	7.2	153.1
Math and computer science	QA	2,281	24.62	3,970	27.78	112.8	4,683	28.91	117.4	3,525	32.86	13.7	133.5
Medicine	R	6,636	26.02	7,475	37.44	143.9	8,319	39.92	153.4	8,015	42.47	6.4	163.2
Military and naval science	U–V	599	18.14	771	23.95	132.0	968	24.46	134.8	981	25.85	5.7	142.5
Philosophy and religion	B	3,319	15.63	3,734	21.10	135.0	4,427	21.86	139.9	3,719	25.06	14.6	160.3
Physical education and recreation	GV	1,391	12.43	869	16.81	135.2	867	16.88	135.8	886	17.96	6.4	144.5
Physics and astronomy	QB	1,114	35.63	1,228	44.07	123.7	1,493	47.14	132.3	1,449	51.96	10.2	145.8
Political science	J	2,861	17.25	2,726	24.73	143.4	3,001	25.02	145.0	2,566	27.36	9.4	158.6
Psychology	BF	1,752	18.84	1,587	27.93	148.2	1,640	28.69	152.3	1,379	31.67	10.4	168.1
Science (general)	Q	313	22.85	340	31.78	139.1	388	32.34	141.5	362	34.61	7.0	151.5
Sociology	HM	4,851	16.87	3,824	23.63	140.1	4,083	24.47	145.1	3,698	25.91	5.9	153.6
Zoology	QH	2,982	32.70	3,222	45.43	138.9	3,676	47.11	144.1	3,335	53.32	13.2	163.1
Average for all subjects		70,183	$21.98	71,321	$30.34	138.0	80,049	$31.77	144.5	72,991	$33.66	5.9	153.1
Canadian history		348	$9.17	300	$15.52	169.2	415	$16.87	184.0	465	$15.97	-5.3	174.2
Canadian literature		540	5.37	470	8.16	152.0	672	8.11	151.0	668	8.14	0.4	151.6

*Compiled by Dora Biblarz, Arizona State University, from data collected from approval plan statistics supplied by Baker & Taylor, Coutts Library Services, and Blackwell/North America. Baker & Taylor and Blackwell/North America used a fiscal year from July 1 to June 30. Coutts Library Services used a fiscal year from June 1 to May 31 from 1979/80 to 1982/83; in 1983/84 Coutts changed its fiscal year to February 1 to January 31.

This table covers titles published or distributed in the United States and Canada. Baker & Taylor figures include continuations (series, serials, and sets) and paperbacks of 48 pages or less. "General Supplementary" and "Extracurricular" (nonacademic) categories are included by Baker & Taylor in 1979/80 but excluded beginning with 1980/81.

Table 4 / U.S. College Books: Average Prices and Price Indexes, 1984–1986*
(Index Base for all years: 1978 = 100. 1985 also indexed to 1984; 1986 also indexed to 1985)

Choice Subject Categories	1978 Number of Titles	1978 Average Price per Title	1984 Number of Titles	1984 Average Price per Title	1984 Prices Indexed to 1978	1985 Number of Titles	1985 Average Price per Title	1985 Prices Indexed to 1978	1985 Prices Indexed to 1984	1986 Number of Titles	1986 Average Price per Title	1986 Prices Indexed to 1978	1986 Prices Indexed to 1985
General	47	$15.25	13	$30.92	202.8	17	$36.65	240.3	118.5	9	$32.22	211.3	87.9
Humanities	92	16.14	40	27.90	172.9	27	23.93	148.3	85.8	33	31.64	196.0	132.2
Art	315	26.60	322	39.28	147.7	298	46.46	174.7	118.3	278	45.43	170.8	97.8
Photography[1]	—	—	37	33.11	—	42	37.19	—	112.3	28	37.46	—	100.7
Communication arts	71	14.03	64	23.50	167.5	64	23.81	169.7	101.3	35	25.46	181.5	106.9
Classical studies[2]	—	—	9	—	—	9	27.67	—	—	84	35.58	—	128.6
Language and literature	97	13.38	71	23.51	175.7	93	24.25	181.2	103.1	93	26.87	200.8	110.8
Linguistics[3]	22	15.07	20	22.10	146.6	17	39.29	260.7	177.8	—	—	—	—
Classical[4]	18	13.41	19	23.32	173.9	18	26.72	199.3	114.6	—	—	—	—
English and American	834	12.42	602	23.11	186.1	635	22.65	182.4	98.0	609	23.40	188.4	103.3
Germanic	51	12.35	45	19.33	156.5	47	23.17	187.6	119.9	39	20.54	166.3	88.6
Romance	101	12.27	84	21.24	173.1	110	20.98	171.0	98.8	102	23.28	189.7	111.0
Slavic	46	13.22	44	21.27	160.9	33	24.21	183.1	113.8	32	25.63	193.9	105.9
Other	67	13.03	35	26.69	204.8	52	28.40	218.0	106.4	53	22.81	175.1	80.3
Performing arts	16	15.07	11	21.27	141.1	17	22.00	146.0	103.4	7	27.14	180.1	123.4
Dance	21	12.95	17	24.88	192.1	14	32.36	249.9	130.1	9	28.22	217.9	87.2
Film	80	15.70	60	22.85	145.5	68	26.60	169.4	116.4	60	28.42	181.0	106.8
Music	138	15.10	113	26.85	177.8	146	26.86	177.9	100.0	141	31.43	208.1	117.0
Theater	34	13.84	49	26.63	192.4	55	27.04	195.4	101.5	35	28.09	203.0	103.9
Philosophy	197	14.21	153	25.32	178.2	147	28.67	201.8	113.2	141	30.04	211.4	104.8
Religion	300	11.98	193	20.54	171.5	187	23.74	198.2	115.6	191	26.14	218.2	110.1
Total Humanities	2,500	14.86	1,979	26.12	175.8	2,079	27.89	187.7	106.8	1,970	29.11	195.9	104.4
Science and technology	102	21.31	187	33.48	157.1	153	36.36	170.6	108.6	136	36.15	169.6	99.4
History of science and technology	85	17.37	89	30.96	178.2	89	29.87	172.0	96.5	76	34.18	196.8	114.4
Astronautics and astronomy	22	23.78	19	28.11	118.2	21	28.52	119.9	101.5	20	26.40	111.0	92.6
Biology	231	23.67	91	42.21	178.3	91	41.96	177.3	99.4	94	39.27	165.9	93.6
Botany[1]	—	—	41	43.07	—	32	51.53	—	119.6	36	47.28	—	91.8
Zoology[1]	—	—	64	35.50	—	41	38.15	—	107.5	33	38.52	—	101.0

	(1)	(2)	(3)	(4)	(5)	(6)	(7)	(8)	(9)	(10)	(11)	(12)	(13)
Chemistry	95	28.59	29	59.34	207.6	28	55.93	195.6	94.3	16	53.69	187.8	96.0
Earth science	84	29.99	48	49.48	165.0	46	45.59	152.0	92.1	47	50.36	167.9	110.5
Engineering	241	25.75	172	43.04	167.1	154	51.30	199.2	119.2	157	55.52	215.6	108.2
Health sciences	92	14.88	115	25.04	168.3	90	28.09	188.8	112.2	127	29.76	200.0	105.9
Information and computer science	53	20.37	101	29.80	146.3	81	31.77	156.0	106.6	81	34.77	170.7	109.4
Mathematics	70	22.54	59	32.61	144.7	46	35.26	156.4	108.1	43	42.86	190.2	121.6
Physics	47	28.77	21	36.57	127.1	16	36.63	127.3	100.2	21	50.10	174.1	136.8
Sports and physical education	73	10.32	65	17.57	170.3	46	18.87	182.8	107.4	28	25.25	244.7	133.8
Total Sciences	1,195	22.77	1,101	35.08	154.1	934	38.11	167.4	108.6	915	40.27	176.9	105.7
Social and behavioral sciences	156	16.37	188	24.73	151.1	177	25.97	158.6	105.0	137	28.00	171.0	107.8
Anthropology	102	16.97	104	29.70	175.0	131	28.98	170.8	97.6	104	32.97	194.3	113.8
Business, management, and labor	136	14.36	164	28.69	199.8	190	27.33	190.3	95.3	175	30.62	213.2	112.0
Economics	242	17.65	333	27.77	157.3	354	29.58	167.6	106.5	303	32.83	186.0	111.0
Education	129	12.48	81	22.28	178.5	71	23.20	185.9	104.1	71	24.75	198.3	106.7
History, geography, and travel	116	16.26	59	25.53	157.0	66	27.52	169.2	107.8	91	38.01	233.8	138.1
Ancient (including archaeology)[4]	67	21.79	41	31.54	144.7	46	28.85	132.4	91.5	—	—	—	—
Africa	38	16.34	29	27.86	170.5	22	28.95	177.2	103.9	40	32.43	198.5	112.0
Asia and Oceania	78	19.03	69	28.42	149.3	58	31.17	163.8	109.7	68	33.81	177.7	108.5
Europe	308	16.52	275	28.88	174.8	300	30.87	186.9	106.9	299	32.81	198.6	106.3
Latin America and the Caribbean	47	15.82	32	26.81	169.5	42	28.79	182.0	107.4	44	35.32	223.3	122.7
Middle East and North Africa	40	16.80	26	28.15	167.6	31	30.42	181.1	108.1	44	31.95	190.2	105.0
North America	275	16.08	272	24.85	154.5	316	25.59	159.1	103.0	327	28.43	176.8	111.1
Political Science	281	14.74	437	25.82	175.2	442	27.26	184.9	105.6	551	28.60	194.0	104.9
Psychology	142	15.39	186	26.92	174.9	138	29.75	193.3	110.5	137	31.92	207.4	107.3
Sociology	280	14.69	219	24.19	164.7	220	26.41	179.8	109.2	192	27.20	185.2	103.0
Total Social and Behavioral Sciences	2,437	15.98	2,515	26.62	166.6	2,604	27.94	174.8	105.0	2,583	30.51	190.9	109.2
Total (excluding reference)	6,179	16.83	5,608	28.11	167.0	5,634	29.63	176.1	105.4	5,477	31.64	188.0	106.8
Reference	453	34.15	591	47.50	139.1	553	47.00	137.6	98.9	528	51.63	151.2	109.9
Grand Total	6,632	$18.02	6,199	$29.96	166.3	6,187	$31.19	173.1	104.1	6,005	$33.40	185.3	107.1

*Compiled by Kathryn A. Soupiset, Trinity University, from book reviews appearing in Choice during the calendar year indicated. The cooperation of the Choice editorial staff is gratefully acknowledged. Additional information about these data appears in the March 1987 issue of Choice.

[1] Began appearing as a separate section in September 1983.
[2] Began appearing as a separate section in December 1985.
[3] Incorporated into Language and Literature in December 1985.
[4] Incorporated into Classical Studies in December 1985.

Table 5 / U.S. Mass Market Paperbacks: Average Price and Price Indexes, 1983–1986*

(Index Base: 1981 = 100)

	1981	1983 (final)			1984 (final)			1985 (final)			1986 (preliminary)		
	Average Price	Total Volumes	Average Price	Index	Total Volumes	Average Price	Index	Total Volumes	Average Price	Index	Total Volumes	Average Price	Index
Agriculture	$2.54	7	$5.09	200.4	2	$2.85	112.2	7	$5.76	226.8	4	$6.09	239.8
Art	5.49	6	4.63	84.3	3	8.28	150.8	3	9.80	178.5	3	9.80	178.5
Biography	3.82	49	4.63	121.2	72	4.45	116.4	79	4.81	125.9	72	5.25	137.4
Business	4.63	8	5.02	108.4	23	4.92	106.3	26	7.57	163.5	31	7.72	166.7
Education	3.96	6	5.54	139.9	5	5.15	130.1	12	6.07	153.3	8	6.34	160.1
Fiction	2.47	2,838	2.87	116.2	2,498	3.03	122.7	2,524	3.24	131.2	2,365	3.49	141.3
General Works	3.63	48	5.32	146.6	59	4.58	126.2	86	4.63	127.5	63	5.02	138.3
History	3.53	25	4.42	125.2	21	3.77	106.8	31	5.34	151.3	32	5.21	147.6
Home Economics	4.35	77	4.69	107.8	81	4.95	113.8	101	5.65	129.9	97	6.28	144.4
Juvenile	1.79	223	2.24	125.1	220	2.31	129.1	427	2.71	151.4	460	2.71	151.4
Language	3.42	20	3.42	100.0	20	5.56	162.6	14	4.28	125.1	17	5.69	166.4
Law	3.09	2	2.95	95.5	6	5.12	165.7	6	6.62	214.2	3	4.47	144.7
Literature	3.42	32	3.97	116.1	54	3.63	106.1	35	4.76	139.2	33	5.13	150.0
Medicine	3.66	31	5.18	141.5	33	5.01	136.9	36	6.65	181.7	41	7.24	197.8
Music**	5.68**	2	5.45	96.0	3	5.28	93.0	9	5.68	100.0	10	4.21	74.1
Philosophy, Psychology	2.84	90	4.34	152.8	90	4.38	154.2	112	4.22	148.6	82	5.07	178.5
Poetry, Drama	3.22	18	4.91	152.5	10	5.11	158.7	16	4.88	151.6	25	5.79	179.8
Religion	2.70	22	3.86	143.0	15	3.87	143.3	24	3.22	119.3	23	4.24	157.0
Science	4.45	17	4.26	95.7	54	3.55	79.8	15	4.83	108.5	13	6.03	135.5
Sociology, Economics	3.43	43	4.25	123.9	44	4.42	128.9	44	4.77	139.1	45	5.53	161.2
Sports, Recreation	3.05	171	3.46	113.4	189	4.06	133.1	149	3.80	124.6	159	4.05	132.8
Technology	4.20	47	4.02	95.7	81	8.61	205.0	42	12.29	292.6	36	12.32	293.3
Travel	3.23	18	9.93	307.4	10	5.86	181.4	9	4.93	152.6	10	5.02	155.4
Total	$2.65	3,800	$3.13	118.1	3,593	$3.41	128.7	3,807	$3.62	136.6	3,632	$3.87	146.0

*Compiled by Dennis E. Smith and Sue Plezia, University of California, from data supplied by the R. R. Bowker Company. Average prices of mass market paperbacks are based on listings of mass market titles in *Paperbound Books in Print*. Conventional rounding was used in the calculations of average prices.

**1982 is used as the index base for Music.

continue to be limited in size. For example, "Art" consists of only three books and shows no increase whatsoever. Other areas limited in size include agriculture and law. Table 6 focuses on higher priced trade paperbacks.

Nonprint Media Prices

Table 7 lists prices of U.S. nonprint media. Compiler David Walch, California Polytechnic State University, notes that after taking a rather substantial jump, the "rental cost per minute" for 16mm films declined in 1986, which may reflect a market substantially impacted by the precipitous growth of the video market. Although the "purchase cost per minute" for 16mm films was up slightly, the overall average cost of a 16mm film showed a much larger increase, due primarily to the increasing length of films. (The average length of a given educational film has shown an increase of approximately 36% over a ten-year period.) The per minute purchase price of video has decreased to the lowest level in the history of the index, which may be atrributable to sharpened competition resulting from the popularity and availability of the medium.

Foreign Published Materials

British Prices

Prices for British academic books, as reported in Table 10, are based on price information from the B. H. Blackwell database. Because the Library Materials Price Index Committee used the Blackwell database for the first time in 1985, that year has become the base for subsequent indexes.

A total of 9,428 titles were indexed for 1986 reflecting an average price of £22.09. The price per title increased 15.8% over 1985. Compiler Curt Holleman, Southern Methodist University, notes that if this inflationary increase is added to the average loss in value of the dollar compared to the pound over 1985 (13.2%) and the increase in British title production (4.2%), American libraries had to pay 36.6% more to keep up with British academic book production in 1986 than in 1985.

German Prices

Prices for German books as reported in Tables 11, 12, and 13 are compiled from *Buch und Buchhandel in Zahlen*. Readers should note that the indexes are based on average prices unadjusted for title production. The Library Materials Price Index Committee is continuing its investigation in the feasibility of producing a German Academic Book Price Index that could be used in a manner similar to the U.S. Academic Book Price Index.

Hardcover and scholarly paperback books (Table 13) show a marked decrease from the 13.0% rate of increase shown for 1984 production. The 1985 rate of increase is 5.6% with an average price of 43.96 Deutsch Marks. However, paperbacks (Table 12) posted a gain of 9.4% in 1985 (compared to 3.9% the year before), which resulted in an 8.3% combined increase rate for the two categories as shown in Table 11. Compiler Steven Thompson, Brown University, notes that the average annual market exchange rate was

(*text continues on page 446*)

Table 6 / U.S. Trade (Higher Priced) Paperback Books: Average Prices and Price Indexes, 1983–1986*

(Index Base: 1977 = 100)

	1977 Average Price	1983 (final)			1984 (final)			1985 (final)			1986 (preliminary)		
		No. of Books	Average Price	Index	No. of Books	Average Price	Index	No. of Books	Average Price	Index	No. of Books	Average Price	Index
Agriculture	$5.01	153	$13.89	277.2	131	$27.05	539.9	198	$ 9.50	189.6	115	$13.12	261.9
Art	6.27	609	13.24	211.2	671	13.12	209.3	593	14.04	223.9	492	15.24	243.1
Biography	4.91	485	11.35	231.2	560	15.09	307.3	536	10.78	219.6	475	11.70	238.3
Business	7.09	411	16.02	226.0	506	17.10	241.2	425	16.83	237.4	348	18.17	256.3
Education	5.72	398	11.27	197.0	433	12.84	224.5	440	12.98	226.9	351	13.88	242.7
Fiction	4.20	499	7.32	174.3	696	8.95	213.1	726	13.66	325.2	700	8.51	202.6
General Works	6.18	1,035	11.89	192.4	1,286	14.32	231.7	1,123	19.13	309.5	628	23.00	372.2
History	5.81	603	12.40	213.4	744	13.49	232.2	729	14.08	242.3	608	14.50	249.6
Home Economics	4.77	505	8.87	186.0	544	9.40	197.1	513	9.22	193.3	358	9.79	205.2
Juveniles	2.68	397	4.76	177.6	412	5.94	221.6	767	5.20	194.0	721	5.87	219.0
Language	7.79	250	11.01	141.3	219	11.61	149.0	252	13.25	170.1	241	14.30	183.6
Law	10.66	383	13.69	128.4	371	17.61	165.2	339	18.46	173.2	277	17.19	161.3
Literature	5.18	599	10.24	197.7	652	11.70	225.9	694	14.04	271.0	614	13.35	257.7
Medicine	7.63	640	14.32	187.7	651	15.78	206.8	698	16.01	209.8	567	19.74	258.7
Music	6.36	129	11.21	176.3	136	12.53	197.0	113	12.20	191.8	94	14.52	228.3
Philosophy, Psychology	5.57	424	11.48	206.1	540	13.64	244.9	523	13.25	237.9	459	13.61	244.3
Poetry, Drama	4.71	498	7.85	166.7	511	8.88	188.5	550	8.86	188.1	501	10.03	213.0
Religion	3.68	1,090	8.05	218.8	1,314	9.32	253.3	1,373	9.30	252.7	1,197	9.30	252.7
Science	8.81	629	17.44	198.0	589	16.22	184.1	677	19.78	224.5	550	23.35	265.0
Sociology, Economics	6.03	2,411	12.53	207.8	2,481	17.72	293.9	2,402	16.30	270.3	2,139	16.95	281.1
Sports, Recreation	4.87	434	9.94	204.1	467	11.40	234.1	447	10.66	218.9	354	11.37	233.5
Technology	7.97	731	18.18	228.1	692	21.11	264.9	722	21.08	264.5	510	27.04	339.3
Travel	5.21	259	9.26	177.7	274	9.88	189.6	235	10.48	201.2	214	11.09	212.9
Total	$5.93	13,572	$11.79	198.8	14,880	$13.86	233.7	15,075	$13.98	235.8	12,513	$14.65	247.0

*See footnote to Table 2.

Table 7 / U.S. Nonprint Media: Average Prices and Price Indexes, 1981–1986*
(Index Base: 1977 = 100)

Category	1977 Average Price	1981 Average Price	1981 Index	1982 Average Price	1982 Index	1983 Average Price	1983 Index	1984 Average Price	1984 Index	1985 Average Price	1985 Index	1986 Average Price	1986 Index
16mm Films													
Rental cost per minute	$1.23	$1.65	134.1	$1.61	130.9	$1.82	148.0	$1.81	147.2	$2.15	174.8	$ 2.00	162.6
Purchase cost per minute	13.95	16.09	115.3	15.01	107.6	15.47	110.9	16.93	121.4	16.50	118.3	16.85	120.8
Cost of film	308.85	343.79	111.3	432.35	140.0	423.87	137.2	470.65	152.4	475.07	153.8	507.19	164.2
Length per film (min.)	22.1	21.4	—	28.7	—	27.4	—	27.8	—	28.8	—	30.1	—
Videocassettes													
Purchase cost per minute	7.58**	14.87	196.2	10.47	138.1	11.04	145.6	8.44	111.3	10.24	135.1	7.44	98.2
Cost of video	271.93**	322.54	118.6	337.40	124.1	320.16	117.7	333.38	122.6	333.94	122.8	274.54	101.0
Length per video (min.)	—					29.0		39.5		32.6		36.9	
Filmstrips													
Cost of filmstrip	18.60	25.40	136.6	29.14	156.7	28.60	153.8	33.04	177.6	32.41	174.2	34.13	183.5
Cost of filmstrip set	72.26	71.12	98.4	81.62	113.0	79.57	110.1	85.76	118.7	83.50	115.6	85.33	118.1
Number of film-strips per set	4.1	2.8	—	2.8	—	2.8	—	2.6	—	2.6	—	2.5	—
Number of frames per filmstrip	64.2	71.4	—	67.8	—	70.7	—	67.0	—	66.7	—	65.9	—
Sound Recordings													
Average cost per cassette	10.63	12.48	117.4	10.74	101.0	11.23	105.6	9.99	94.0	8.99	84.6	10.61	99.8

*Compiled by David B. Walch, California Polytechnic State University, from selected issues of Choice, School Library Journal, and Booklist.

**1980 is used as the base year for videocassettes.

Table 8 / U.S. Library Microfilm: Average Rates and Index Values, 1981–1985*
(Index Base: 1978 = 100)

Year	Negative Microfilm (35mm)			Positive Microfilm (35mm)		
	Average Rate/Exposure	Index Value	Change in Index	Average Rate/Foot	Index Value	Change in Index
1978	$0.0836	100.0	+ 0.0	$0.1612	100.0	+ 0.0
1981	0.0998	119.4	19.4	0.2021	125.4	25.4
1982	0.1067	127.6	8.3	0.2184	135.5	10.1
1983	0.1110	131.6	3.9	0.2274	141.1	5.6
1984	0.1250	149.5	17.9	0.2450	152.0	10.9
1985	0.1290	154.3	4.8	0.2612	162.0	10.0

*Compiled by Imre T. Jarmy, Library of Congress, from data secured from the staff of the 50 indexed libraries. Data for 1986 were not available at presstime.

Table 9 / Selected U.S. Daily Newspapers: Average Subscription Rates and Index Values, 1981–1985*
(Index Base: 1978 = 100)

Year	Average Rate	Index Value	Change in Index
1978	$76.4391	100.0	+ 0.0
1981	98.5521	128.9	28.9
1982	103.6382	135.6	6.7
1983	107.4728	140.6	5.0
1984	109.5210	143.3	2.7
1985	111.3121	145.6	2.3

*Compiled by Imre T. Jarmy, Library of Congress, from data secured from indexed newspapers and, when necessary, by examining the final issue of a title for the year. Data were compiled for the 133 titles surveyed in the continental United States, Alaska, and Hawaii. Data for 1986 were not available at presstime.

2.4613 Deutsch Marks per U.S. dollar in 1985, as reported by the Bureau of Statistics, International Monetary Fund.

Latin American Prices

The data reported for Latin American books (Table 14) reflects the widely divergent collection profiles of seven large research libraries, some of which aim for comprehensive coverage in all countries, although others acquire selectively in only a few. The total number of books acquired by the reporting libraries ranges from 23 for Surinam to 6,986 for Brazil, and the average cost from $6.97 (Honduras, 224 units) to $17.26 (Surinam, 23 units). As in previous years, prices and price changes fluctuate substantially from one country to another and one year to another. Compiler David Block, Cornell University, is presently investigating alternative methodologies for compilation of the index, with the cooperation of the Library Materials Price Index Committee and the Seminar on the Acquisition of Latin American Library Materials (SALALM).

Readers should note that, aside from collecting profiles, other variables account for the striking divergencies in Table 14: (a) levels of development of the book trade in the more than 25 countries, (b) the lack of meaningful list prices in most countries, (c) a high rate of inflation, (d) currency revaluation, (e) shipping, handling, service, and

Table 10 / British Academic Books: Average Prices and Price Indexes, 1985-1986*
(Index Base: 1985 = 100)

Subject Category	1985 No. of Titles	1985 Average Price £	1986 No. of Titles	1986 Average Price £	Index
General works	29	30.54	41	48.36	158.3
Fine arts	329	21.70	324	21.44	98.8
Architecture	97	20.68	119	21.70	104.9
Performing arts	246	15.35	210	17.91	116.7
Humanities	1,978	16.56	1,909	19.10	115.3
Literary texts (excluding fiction)	570	9.31	408	10.12	108.7
Literary criticism	438	14.82	395	17.85	120.4
Law	188	24.64	273	26.06	105.8
Library science and book trade	78	18.69	99	20.91	111.9
Mass communications	38	14.20	67	15.34	108.0
Social sciences	953	18.11	1,077	21.88	120.8
Military science	83	17.69	96	19.43	109.8
Sports and recreation	44	11.23	67	11.77	104.8
Applied social sciences	791	16.13	833	18.57	115.1
Criminology	45	11.45	49	14.63	127.8
Applied interdisciplinary social sciences	254	14.17	300	16.11	113.7
General science	43	13.73	51	29.00	211.2
Biological sciences	353	27.75	359	30.40	109.5
Pure sciences	438	30.19	450	31.95	105.8
Computer sciences	150	20.14	179	22.60	112.2
Interdisciplinary technical fields	38	26.14	56	23.87	91.3
Technology	556	34.02	617	39.10	114.9
Food and home economics	38	23.75	58	25.46	107.2
Medicine	746	22.71	783	25.69	113.1
Dentistry	20	19.39	22	18.10	93.3
Nursing	71	8.00	66	10.50	131.3
Agriculture and forestry	78	23.69	74	28.98	122.3
Animal husbandry and veterinary medicine	34	20.92	40	22.46	107.4
Natural resources and conservation	58	22.88	81	25.61	111.9
*Total***	9,049	19.07	9,428	22.09	115.8

*Compiled by Curt Holleman, Southern Methodist University, from data supplied by Chris Tyzack of B.H. Blackwell and Peter H. Mann of Loughborough University of Technology. The committee uses 1985 as the base year because that is the first year that the BHB database was used as the source of prices.
**Includes other small categories not listed in this table.

binding charges not consistently reflected in the reported costs, (f) changes in the scope of dealer coverage, and (g) inconsistencies in reporting practices.

U.S. Purchasing Power Abroad

Beginning with the fourth quarter of 1985 and continuing through 1986, U.S. libraries witnessed a sharp downturn in the value of the U.S. dollar against foreign currencies. This rapid weakening of the dollar has had a substantial impact on library budgets and the extent to which libraries can continue to maintain their current foreign materials collection strategies. The compounding effect of two years of rapid decline is evidenced in the following statistical comparison, which suggests that German, Dutch, and Japanese publications have been most affected, although France and the United Kingdom follow closely. (Exchange rates are expressed in U.S. dollar terms and are based on nom-

(*text continues on page 451*)

Table 11 / German Books: Average Prices and Price Indexes, 1983–1985*
(Index Base: 1977 = 100)

	1977 Average Price	1983 Average Price	1983 Index	1984 Average Price	1984 Index	1984 % Increase	1985 Average Price	1985 Index	1985 % Increase
General, library science, college-level textbooks	DM68.47	DM63.39	92.6	DM61.67	90.1	−2.7	DM73.02	106.6	18.4
Religion, theology	23.21	25.06	108.0	27.82	119.9	11.0	29.01	125.0	4.3
Philosophy, psychology	26.67	24.45	91.7	29.02	108.8	18.7	25.83	96.9	−11.0
Law, administration	33.92	53.94	159.0	59.65	175.9	10.6	59.12	174.3	−0.9
Social sciences, economics, statistics	25.97	31.86	122.7	35.57	137.0	11.6	35.42	136.4	−0.4
Political and military science	22.91	33.97	148.3	28.96	126.4	−14.7	29.72	129.7	2.6
Literature and linguistics	27.79	30.72	110.5	34.86	125.4	13.5	34.57	124.4	−0.8
Belles lettres	6.57	9.39	142.9	10.28	156.5	9.5	11.49	174.9	11.8
Juveniles	9.07	8.72	96.1	8.43	92.9	−3.3	11.76	129.7	39.5
Education	16.50	22.77	138.0	23.31	141.3	2.4	33.57	203.5	44.0
School textbooks	10.88	15.17	139.4	—	—	—	—	—	—
Fine arts	49.70	46.34	93.2	54.57	109.8	17.8	46.94	94.4	−14.0
Music, dance, theater, film, radio	28.04	27.44	97.9	30.65	109.3	11.7	29.44	105.0	−3.9
History, folklore	38.79	35.24	90.8	40.56	104.6	15.1	36.18	93.3	−10.8
Geography, anthropology, travel	32.20	31.62	98.2	32.56	101.1	3.0	32.52	101.0	−0.1
Medicine	50.29	68.26	135.7	65.83	130.9	−3.6	69.42	138.0	5.5
Natural sciences	93.45	120.08	128.5	121.48	130.0	1.2	136.16	145.7	12.1
Mathematics	28.98	46.64	160.9	43.30	149.4	−7.2	37.51	129.4	−13.4
Technology	42.45	62.31	146.8	61.12	144.0	−1.9	58.65	138.2	−4.0
Touring guides and directories	21.78	33.10	152.0	35.91	164.9	8.5	37.73	173.2	5.1
Home economics and agriculture	25.10	25.09	100.0	25.61	102.0	2.1	24.88	99.1	−2.9
Sports and recreation	18.99	19.28	101.5	22.60	119.0	17.2	21.80	114.8	−3.5
Miscellaneous	11.30	15.65	138.5	18.48	163.5	18.1	18.65	165.0	0.9
Total	DM21.87	DM27.93	127.7	DM30.06	137.4	7.6	DM32.57	148.9	8.3

*This is a combined index for numbered paperback books (Taschenbucher) and for bound volumes and scholarly paperbacks (andere Tital). The indexes are tentative and based on average prices unadjusted for title production. Figures for 1985 were compiled by Steven E. Thompson, Brown University, from *Buch und Buchhandel in Zahlen* (Frankfurt, 1986). The category for school textbooks (Schulbucher) has been dropped from the *Buch und Buchhandel in Zahlen* charts. The index year 1977 has been adopted to conform to the year used in the U.S. Government's Consumer Price Index.

Information Note: The average annual market exchange rate for 1985 was 2.4613 Deutsch Marks per U.S. dollar, as reported by the U.S. Bureau of Statistics, International Monetary Fund, in its periodical *International Financial Statistics.*

Table 12 / German Paperback Books: Average Prices and Price Indexes, 1983–1985*

(Index Base: 1977 = 100)

	1977 Average Price	1983 Average Price	1983 Index	1984 Average Price	1984 Index	1985 Average Price	1985 Index
General, library science, college-level textbooks	DM6.47	DM16.39	253.3	DM13.53	209.1	DM13.70	211.7
Religion, theology	7.03	9.19	130.7	9.70	138.0	10.82	153.9
Philosophy, psychology	8.06	10.98	136.2	11.03	136.8	11.98	148.6
Law, administration	8.95	11.47	128.2	11.42	127.6	13.38	149.5
Social sciences, economics, statistics	10.02	11.80	117.8	11.67	116.5	12.87	128.4
Political and military science	8.24	10.15	123.2	11.20	135.9	12.21	148.2
Literature and linguistics	8.36	10.98	131.3	13.45	160.9	11.26	134.7
Belles lettres	4.89	7.22	147.6	7.35	150.3	8.15	166.7
Juveniles	4.77	6.45	135.2	6.66	139.6	6.89	144.4
Education	10.88	10.37	95.3	10.92	100.4	11.31	104.0
School textbooks	2.52	4.20	166.7	—	—	—	—
Fine arts	10.28	11.65	113.3	11.70	113.8	12.76	124.1
Music, dance, theater, film, radio	8.11	10.43	128.6	10.13	124.9	11.65	143.6
History, folklore	8.35	11.22	134.4	12.07	144.6	12.87	154.1
Geography, anthropology, travel	6.82	11.72	171.8	12.45	182.6	12.51	183.4
Medicine	10.42	10.85	104.1	9.38	90.0	11.23	107.8
Natural sciences	10.85	13.34	122.9	14.63	134.8	15.45	142.4
Mathematics	15.00	14.83	98.9	14.07	93.8	12.07	80.5
Technology	20.63	11.93	57.8	11.40	55.3	13.13	63.6
Touring guides and directories	7.11	9.13	128.4	8.98	126.3	11.00	154.7
Home economics and agriculture	6.77	9.04	133.5	9.47	139.9	9.78	144.5
Sports and recreation	6.81	9.76	143.3	10.78	158.3	10.74	157.7
Miscellaneous	5.00	8.94	178.8	9.55	191.0	10.53	210.6
Total	DM6.69	DM8.69	129.9	DM9.03	135.0	DM9.88	147.7

*The indexes are tentative and based on average prices unadjusted for title production. Figures for 1985 were compiled by Steven E. Thompson, Brown University, from *Buch und Buchhandel in Zahlen* (Frankfurt, 1986). The category for school textbooks (Schulbucher) has been dropped from the *Buch und Buchhandel in Zahlen* charts. The index year 1977 has been adopted to conform to the year used in the U.S. Government's Consumer Price Index.

Information Note: The average annual market exchange rate for 1985 was 2.4613 Deutsch Marks per U.S. dollar, as reported by the U.S. Bureau of Statistics, International Monetary Fund, in its periodical *International Financial Statistics.*

Table 13 / German Hardcover and Scholarly Paperback Books:
Average Prices and Price Indexes, 1983–1985*
(Index Base: 1977 = 100)

	1977 Average Price	1983 Average Price	1983 Index	1984 Average Price	1984 Index	1985 Average Price	1985 Index
General, library science, college-level textbooks	DM82.28	DM74.27	90.3	DM77.80	94.6	DM89.26	108.5
Religion, theology	27.67	28.50	103.0	32.33	116.8	33.29	120.3
Philosophy, psychology	40.38	31.24	77.4	47.38	117.3	39.24	97.2
Law, administration	37.50	59.95	159.9	64.57	172.2	66.42	177.1
Social sciences, economics, statistics	32.20	37.93	117.8	45.99	142.8	42.61	132.3
Political and military science	27.85	42.41	152.3	35.92	129.0	36.27	130.2
Literature and linguistics	40.90	41.18	100.7	55.18	134.9	53.42	130.6
Belles lettres	7.48	11.81	157.9	13.96	186.6	15.36	205.3
Juveniles	12.86	9.89	76.9	9.19	71.5	14.83	115.3
Education	18.19	25.07	137.8	27.65	152.0	39.82	218.9
School textbooks	10.98	15.46	140.8	—	—	—	—
Fine arts	58.51	54.04	92.4	63.40	108.4	52.57	89.8
Music, dance, theater, film, radio	37.89	39.68	104.7	45.01	118.8	41.22	108.8
History, folklore	49.82	48.48	97.3	54.24	108.9	48.85	98.1
Geography, anthropology, travel	34.76	34.70	99.8	37.14	106.8	36.77	105.8
Medicine	61.55	78.81	128.0	76.59	124.4	80.58	130.9
Natural sciences	131.28	138.55	105.5	141.29	107.6	156.24	119.0
Mathematics	32.83	49.30	150.2	54.66	166.5	43.38	132.1
Technology	45.39	65.87	145.1	64.20	141.4	60.81	134.0
Touring guides and directories	22.94	34.94	152.3	39.06	170.3	38.92	169.7
Home economics and agriculture	31.49	33.60	106.7	32.50	103.2	30.94	98.3
Sports and recreation	24.55	25.39	103.4	29.80	121.4	29.65	120.8
Miscellaneous	11.71	21.53	183.9	22.95	196.0	20.39	174.1
Total	DM27.68	DM36.79	132.9	DM41.62	150.4	DM43.96	158.8

*See footnote to Table 12.

Table 14 / Latin American Books: Number of Copies and Average Cost of Books Purchased by Seven Selected U.S. Libraries, FYs 1985–1986**

	Number of Books		Average Cost		% (+ or −) in cost over 1985
	FY 1985	FY 1986	FY 1985	FY 1986	
Argentina	7,128	6,069	$9.28*	$10.15	9.3
Bolivia	1,298	1,146	7.90	9.00	14.0
Brazil	9,454	6,986	8.33	7.71	−7.5
Chile	2,183	2,206	12.89*	10.92	−15.3
Colombia	2,705	3,686	11.94	11.54	−3.3
Costa Rica	579	566	12.72	15.01	18.0
Cuba	464	317	8.70	10.27	18.1
Dominican Republic	1,313	896	13.69	12.45	−9.0
Ecuador	1,591	1,304	10.07	10.60	5.3
El Salvador	415	318	10.30	11.80	14.5
Guatemala	297	309	17.01	12.40	−27.1
Guyana	20	40	7.35	9.41	28.0
Haiti	314	133	9.45	11.98	26.8
Honduras	598	224	6.19	6.97	12.7
Jamaica	319	94	7.23*	8.79	21.5
Mexico	4,026	4,126	9.25	10.77	16.5
Nicaragua	375	273	11.24	13.47	19.8
Panama	122	105	14.03	11.55	−17.7
Paraguay	507	504	9.29	9.22	−0.7
Peru	2,990	2,891	8.78	7.89	−10.2
Puerto Rico	515	122	7.73	6.99	−9.6
Surinam	30	23	12.15	17.26	42.1
Trinidad	36	40	17.02	16.70	−1.9
Uruguay	1,844	1,491	15.51*	12.13	−21.8
Venezuela	2,654	1,968	12.25	11.73	−4.3
Other Caribbean	2,080	501	10.74	11.92	11.0

*Includes some binding costs.
**Compiled by David Block, Seminar on the Acquisition of Latin American Library Materials (SALALM), Acquisition Committee, from reports on the number and cost of current monographs purchased by the libraries of Cornell University, University of Florida, University of Illinois, Library of Congress, University of Minnesota, University of Texas, and University of Wisconsin.

inal New York closing quotations for interbank payments of listed currencies of the Chase Manhattan Bank, as of close of business, January 31, 1986 and December 31, 1986 as well as those same dates in 1985. Readers interested in quotations for earlier years are referred to earlier volumes of *The Bowker Annual*.)

Country	Jan. 31, 1985	Dec. 31, 1985	%Change	Jan. 31, 1986	Dec. 31, 1986	%Change
Canada	.7544	.7157	−5.1	.6982	.7241	+3.8
France	.1034	.1327	+28.3	.1366	.1568	+14.8
United Kingdom	1.1271	1.442	+27.9	1.4120	1.4825	+4.9
Germany	.3159	.4068	+28.8	.4188	.5199	+24.1
Japan	.00395	.004986	+25.3	.0052	.0063	+21.5
Netherlands	.2795	.3604	+28.9	.3707	.4603	+24.2
Spain	.0057	.006494	+12.3	.0066	.0076	+15.2

Using the Price Indexes

In planning future budgets, libraries are encouraged to monitor industry trends as well as those affecting currency conversion. To assist with these efforts, the ALA/RTSD Library Materials Price Index Committee sponsors the preparation and publication of

Tables 1–14. The price indexes, designed to measure the rate of price change of newly published materials against those of earlier years on the national level, are useful for comparing with local purchasing patterns. They reflect retail prices, not the cost to a particular library, and were never intended to be a substitute for information that a library might collect about its own purchases.

The prices on which the indexes are based do not include discounts, vendor service charges, or other service charges. These variables naturally affect the average price for library materials paid by a particular library; however, as studies have shown, this does not necessarily mean that the rate of increase in prices paid by a particular library is significantly different from the rate of increase shown by the price indexes. The Library Materials Price Index Committee is interested in pursuing correlation of individual library's prices with national prices and would like to be informed of any studies undertaken. In addition, the committee welcomes interested parties to its meetings at ALA's annual and midwinter sessions.

Libraries using the U.S. prices indexes, or any other index, should not be misled by overall or general rates of increase or decrease. The rates for specific subject classes must be analyzed in relation to an individual library's purchasing pattern.

As in the past three years, the data in Tables 1–14 were compiled on a personal computer that computes to 15 decimal places. As a result, users may encounter discrepancies with data reported in previous years.

The current members of the Library Materials Price Index Committee are Rebecca T. Lenzini (chairperson), Dora Biblarz, Steven E. Thompson, Curt Holleman, Kathryn Hammell, and Marilyn Fletcher. Consultants to the committee and members of the Subcommittee for Index Production are Kathryn Soupiset, David B. Walch, Imre Jarmy, Mary Elizabeth Clack, Dennis E. Smith, and David Block.

Part 5
Reference Information

Bibliographies

The Librarian's Bookshelf

Olha della Cava

Librarian, School of Library Service Library
Columbia University, New York

This bibliography is intended as a buying and reading guide for individual librarians and as a selection tool for staff library collections. A few of the titles listed are core titles that any staff development collection might contain, but most are titles published since 1984 with an emphasis on continuing education. Bibliographic tools that most libraries are likely to have for day-to-day operations have been excluded from this list. Three key areas of professional concern — online catalogs, library automation, and microcomputers in libraries — also are omitted, because they are treated in the "High Technology Bibliography," which immediately follows "The Librarian's Bookshelf."

Books

General Works

Advances in Librarianship. Vol. 13. Ed. by Wesley Simonton. Orlando, FL: Academic Press, 1984. $57.60

ALA World Encyclopedia of Library and Information Services. 2nd ed. Ed. by Robert Wedgeworth. Chicago: American Library Association, 1986. $165.

ALA Yearbook of Library and Information Services, 1986. Vol. 11. Ed. by Roger Parent. Chicago: American Library Association, 1986. $70.

American Library Directory, 1986. 39th ed. 2 vols. New York: R. R. Bowker. 1986. $129.95.

American Library Laws. 5th ed. Ed. by Alex Ladenson. Chicago: American Library Association, 1984. $110.

Bowker Annual of Library and Book Trade Information, 1987. 32nd ed. New York: R. R. Bowker, 1987. $89.95.

Bowman, Mary Ann. *Library and Information Science Journals and Serials: An Analytical Guide.* Westport, CT: Greenwood Press, 1985. $29.95.

Crawford, Walt. *Technical Standards: An Introduction for Librarians.* White Plains, NY: Knowledge Industry, 1986. $36.50.

Dowlin, Kenneth E. *The Electronic Library: The Promise and the Process.* New York: Neal-Schuman, 1984. $24.95.

Encyclopedia of Library and Information Science. New York: Marcel Dekker, 1968–1986. Vols. 1–40. $55 per vol.

Foskett, D. J. *Pathways for Communcation: Books and Libraries in the Information Age.* London: Bingley, 1984 (U.S. dist. by Shoe String Press, Hamden, CT). $19.50.

Harrod's Librarians' Glossary of Terms Used in Librarianship, Documentation and the Book Crafts and Reference

Books. 5th ed. Rev. and updated by Ray Prytherch. Aldershot, Hampshire, England; Brookfield, VT: Gower, 1984. (U.S. dist. by Lexington Books, Lexington, MA). $71.50.

Libraries and Information Science in the Electronic Age. Ed. by Hendrik Edelman. Philadelphia: ISI Press, 1986. $39.95.

Libraries in the Age of Automation: A Reader for the Professional Librarian. White Plains, NY: Knowledge Industry, 1986. $36.50.

Library Forms Illustrated Handbook. Ed. by Elizabeth Futas. New York: Neal-Schuman, 1984. $75.

Library Science Annual 1986, Vol. 2. Ed. by Bohdan S. Wynar. Littleton, CO: Libraries Unlimited, 1986. $37.50.

Purcell, Gary R., with Gail Ann Schlachter. *Reference Sources in Library and Information Services: A Guide to the Literature.* Santa Barbara, CA: ABC-Clio, 1984. $45.

Tayyeb, R., and K. Chandna. *A Dictionary of Acronyms and Abbreviations in Library and Information Science.* 2nd ed. Ottawa: Canadian Library Association, 1985. $20.

Academic and Research Libraries

ACRL Statistics 1982–83: A Compilation of Statistics from the 117 Members of the Association of Research Libraries. Washington, DC: Association of Research Libraries, 1984. $10.

Access to Scholarly Information: Issues & Strategies. Ed. by Sul H. Lee. Ann Arbor, MI: Pierian Press, 1985. $24.50.

Adams, Roy J. *Information Technology & Libraries: A Future for Academic Libraries.* London; Dover, NH: Croom Helm, 1986. $29.

Association of College and Research Libraries. National Conference (Fourth, 1986, Baltimore). *Energies for Transition.* Ed. by Danuta A. Nitecki. Chicago: Association of College and Research Libraries, ALA, 1986. $30.

Austerity Management in Academic Libraries. Ed. by John F. Harvey and Peter Spyers-Duran. Metuchen, NJ: Scarecrow Press, 1984. $25.

Cronin, Mary J. *Performance Measurement for Public Services in Academic and Research Libraries.* Washington, DC: Association of Research Libraries, Office of Management Studies, 1985. $15.

Cummings, Martin Marc. *The Economics of Research Libraries.* Washington, DC: Council on Library Resources, 1986. $5.

Financing Information Services: Problems, Changing Approaches, and New Opportunities for Academic and Research Libraries. Ed. by Peter Spyers-Duran and Thomas W. Mann, Jr. Westport, CT: Greenwood Press, 1985. $29.95.

IT: Resource Strategies for Academic Libraries: Proceedings of a Conference Held by the Centre for Library and Information Management and the IT Working Group of the Council of Polytechnic Librarians, 29 November, 1983. Ed. by Lesley Gilder. Loughborough, England: Centre for Library and Information Management, Loughborough University, 1984. £9.

Issues in Academic Librarianship: Views and Case Studies for the 1980's and 1990's. Ed. by Peter Spyers-Duran and T. W. Mann, Jr. Westport, CT: Greenwood Press, 1985. $29.95.

Kantor, Paul B. *Objective Performance Measures for Academic and Research Libraries.* Washington, DC: Association of Research Libraries, 1984. $25.

Moran, Barbara B. *Academic Libraries: The Changing Knowledge Centers of Colleges and Universities.* Washington, DC: Association for the Study of Higher Education, 1984. $7.50.

SPEC Kits. Washington, DC: Association

of Research Libraries. 1973– . Nos. 1– . $10 for members, $20 for non-members. (Recent kits have been on such topics as bibliographic instruction, end-user searching services, microcomputer software policies, and barcoding of collections.)

Standing Conference of National and University Libraries. *Issues Facing Academic Libraries: A Review. Papers Prepared for a Meeting of SCONUL Council Together with Summaries of Discussions.* London: SCONUL, 1985. Price unknown.

Stubbs, Kendon L. *Quantitative Criteria for Academic Research Libaries.* Chicago: Association of College and Research Libraries, ALA, 1984. $19.

Trochim, Mary Kane. *Measuring the Circulation Use of a Small Academic Library Collection: A Manual.* Washington, DC: Office of Management Studies, Association of Research Libraries, 1985. $40.

Universities, Information Technology and Academic Libraries: The Next Twenty Years. Ed. by Robert M. Hayes. Norwood, NJ: Ablex, 1985. $29.95.

Administration and Personnel

Bloomberg, Marty. *Introduction to Public Services for Library Technicians.* 4th ed. Littleton, CO: Libraries Unlimited, 1985. $35.

Boss, Richard W. *Telecommunications for Library Management: Strategies for Cost-effective Management.* White Plains, NY: Knowledge Industry, 1985. $36.50.

Bumbarger, William, B. *Operation Function Analysis—Do It Yourself Productivity Improvement.* New York: Van Nostrand Reinhold, 1984. $24.95.

Bunch, Allan. *The Basics of Information Work.* London: Bingley, 1984 (U.S. dist. by Shoe String Press, Hamden, CT). £8.75.

Clark, Philip M. *Microcomputer Spreadsheet Models for Libraries.* Chicago: American Library Association, 1985. $24.95.

Conroy, Barbara. *Improving Communication in the Library.* Phoenix, AZ: Oryx Press, 1986. $25.

Costing and the Economics of Library and Information Services. Ed. by Stephen A. Roberts. London: Aslib, 1984. Price unknown.

Daily, Jay Elmwood. *Staff Personality Problems in the Library Automation Process: A Case in Point.* Littleton, CO: Libraries Unlimited, 1985. $28.50.

Handbook of Library Training Practice. Ed. by Ray Prytherch. Aldershot, Hampshire, England; Brookfield, VT: Gower, 1986 (U.S. dist. by Lexington Books, Lexington, MA). $68.95.

Issues in Library Management: A Reader for the Professional Librarian. White Plains, NY: Knowledge Industry, 1984. $27.50.

Jones, K. H. *Conflict and Change in Library Organizations: People, Power and Service.* London: Bingley, 1984 (U.S. dist. by Shoe String Press, Hamden, CT). $12.50.

Kesner, Richard M. *Microcomputer Applications in Libraries: A Management Tool for the 1980s and Beyond.* Westport, CT: Greenwood Press, 1984. $29.95.

Kirby, John. *Creating the Library Identity: A Manual of Design.* Aldershot, Hampshire, England; Brookfield, VT: Gower, 1985 (U.S. dist. by Lexington Books, Lexington, MA). $53.

Kohl, David F. *Acquisitions, Collection Development, and Collection Use: A Handbook for Library Management.* Santa Barbara, CA: ABC-Clio, 1985. $35.

_____. *Administration, Personnel, Buildings, and Equipment: A Handbook for Library Management.* Santa Barbara, CA: ABC-Clio, 1985. $35.

_____. *Cataloging and Catalogs: A Handbook for Library Management.* Santa Barbara, CA: ABC-Clio, 1986. $35.

_____. *Circulation, Interlibrary Loan, Patron Use, and Collection Maintenance: A Handbook for Library Management.* Santa Barbara, CA: ABC-Clio, 1985. $35.

_____. *Library Education and Professional Issues: A Handbook for Library Management.* Santa Barbara, CA: ABC-Clio, 1986. $35.

Management Strategies for Libraries: A Basic Reader. Ed. by Beverly P. Lynch. New York: Neal-Schuman, 1985. $35.

Martin, Lowell Arthur. *Organizational Structure of Libraries.* Metuchen, NJ: Scarecrow Press, 1984. $14.50.

Performance Evaluation: A Management Basic for Librarians. Ed. by Jonathan A. Lindsey. Phoenix, AZ: Oryx Press, 1986. $35.

Plate, Kenneth H. *Library Manager's Workbook: Problem-Solving in the Supervision of Information Service Personnel.* Studio City, CA: Pacific Information, 1985. $24.50.

Rawles, Beverly A. *Working with Library Consultants.* Hamden, CT: Shoe String Press, 1984. $14.50.

Riggs, Donald E. *Strategic Planning for Library Managers.* Phoenix, AZ: Oryx Press, 1984. $27.50.

Roberts, Stephen A. *Cost Management for Library and Information Services.* Stoneham, MA; Kent, UK: Butterworths, 1985. $27.

Schauer, Bruce P. *The Economics of Managing Library Services.* Chicago: American Library Association, 1986. $24.

T.I.P. Kit: Topics in Personnel. Chicago: Office for Library Personnel Resources, ALA, 1982– . $10. (Recent kits have been on such topics as humanizing the workplace, writing library job descriptions, and employee selection and minimum qualifications for librarians.)

Trumpeter, Margo C. *Basic Budgeting Practices for Librarians.* Chicago: American Library Association, 1985. $25.

White, Herbert S. *Library Personnel Management.* White Plains, NY: Knowledge Industry, 1985. $36.50.

Archives, Preservation, and Special Collections

Archival Choices: Managing the Historical Record in an Age of Abundance. Ed. by Nancy E. Peace. Lexington, MA: Lexington Books, 1984. $23.

Cook, Michael. *Archives and the Computer.* 2nd ed. Stoneham, MA; Kent, UK: Butterworths, 1986. $49.95.

Haas, Joan K. *Appraising the Records of Modern Science and Technology: A Guide.* Cambridge, MA: MIT Press, 1985 (U.S. dist. by Society of American Archivists, Chicago, IL). Price unknown.

Hedstrom, Margaret. *Archives & Manuscripts: Machine-readable Records.* Chicago: Society of American Archivists, 1984. $8.

Kesner, Richard M. *Automation for Archivists and Records Managers: Planning and Implementation Strategies.* Chicago: American Library Association, 1984. $27.50.

Library Preservation Program: Models, Priorities, Possibilities: Proceedings of a Conference, April 29, 1983, Washington, D.C. Ed. by Jan Merrill-Oldham and M. Smith. Chicago: American Library Association, 1985. $8.95.

Makepeace, Chris E. *Ephemera: A Book on Its Collection, Conservation, and Use.* Aldershot, Hampshire, England; Brookfield, VT: Gower, 1985 (U.S. dist. by Lexington Books, Lexington, MA). $32.50.

Middleton, Bernard C. *The Restoration*

of Leather Bindings. Rev. ed. Chicago: American Library Association, 1984. $25.

A Modern Archives Reader: Basic Readings on Archival Theory and Practice. Ed. by Maygene F. Daniels and Timothy Walch. Washington, DC: National Archives and Records Service, 1984. $14.

Morris, John. *The Library Disaster Preparedness Handbook.* Chicago: American Library Association, 1986. $20.

Rare Books: Trends, Collections, Sources. Ed. by Alice D. Schreyer. New York: R. R. Bowker, 1984. $49.95.

Saffady, William. *Micrographics.* 2nd ed. Littleton, CO: Libraries Unlimited, 1985. $28.

Stielow, Frederick J. *The Management of Oral History Sound Archives.* Westport, CT: Greenwood Press, 1986. $35.

Bibliographic Instruction

Adams, Mignon, S., and Jacquelyn M. Morris. *Teaching Library Skills for Academic Credit.* Phoenix, AZ: Oryx Press, 1985. $29.50.

Bibliographic Instruction and the Learning Process: Theory, Style and Motivation. Ed. by Carolyn A. Kirkendall. Ann Arbor, MI: Pierian Press, 1984. $8.95.

The Bibliographic Instruction Clearinghouse: A Practical Guide. Prepared by the Clearinghouse Committee, Bibliographic Instruction Section, ACRL. Ed. by Kathleen Coleman. Chicago: ACRL/American Library Association, 1984. $12 for nonmembers ($9 to members).

Fjallbrant, Nancy, and I. Malley. *User Education in Libraries.* 2nd rev. ed. London: Bingley, 1984 (U.S. dist. by Shoe String Press, Hamden, CT). $19.50.

Increasing the Teaching Role of Academic Libraries. Ed. by Thomas G. Kirk. San Francisco: Jossey-Bass, 1984. $8.95.

Jay, M. Ellen. *Building Reference Skills in the Elementary School.* Hamden, CT: Library Professional Publications, 1986. Price unknown.

Katz, William A. *Your Library: A Reference Guide.* 2nd ed. New York: Holt, Rinehart & Winston, 1984. $19.95.

Kohl, David F. *Reference Services and Library Instruction.* Santa Barbara, CA: ABC-Clio, 1985. $35.

Kuhlthau, Carol Collier. *Teaching the Library Research Process: A Step-by-Step Program for Secondary School Students.* West Nyack, NY: Center for Applied Research in Education, 1985. $22.95.

Malley, Ian. *The Basics of Information Skills Teaching.* London: Bingley, 1984 (U.S. dist. by Shoe String Press, Hamden, CT). £8.75.

Marketing Instruction Services: Applying Private Sector Techniques to Plan and Promote Bibliographic Instruction: Papers Presented at the Thirteenth Library Instruction Conference Held at Eastern Michigan University, May 3 & 4, 1984. Ed. by Carolyn A. Kirkendall. Ann Arbor, MI: Pierian Press, 1986. $19.50.

Teaching Librarians to Teach: On-the-job Training for Bibliographic Instruction Librarians. Ed. by Alice S. Clark and Kay F. Jones. Metuchen, NJ: Scarecrow Press, 1986. $18.50.

User Instruction in Academic Libraries: A Century of Selected Readings. Comp. by Larry L. Hardesty et al. Metuchen, NJ: Scarecrow Press, 1986. Price unknown.

Wolf, Carolyn E. *Basic Library Skills.* 2nd ed. Jefferson, NC: McFarland, 1986. $12.95.

Children's and Young Adult Services and Materials

Carlson, Ann D. *Early Childhood Literature-sharing Programs in Li-*

braries. Hamden, CT: Shoe String Press, 1985. $19.50.

Children's Periodicals of the United States. Ed. by R. Gordon Kelly. Westport, CT: Greenwood Press, 1984. $49.95.

The Elementary School Library Collection: A Guide to Books and Other Media, Phases 1-2-3. 14th ed. Williamsport, PA: Brodart, 1984. $69.95.

Gillespie, John Thomas. *Best Books for Children, Preschool through the Middle Grades*. 3rd ed. New York: R. R. Bowker, 1985. $34.50.

Lima, Carolyn W. *A to Z: Subject Access to Children's Picture Books*. 2nd ed. New York: R. R. Bowker, 1985. $34.50.

Only the Best Is Good Enough: The Woodfield Lectures in Children's Literature, 1978-1985. Ed. by Margaret Fearn. London: Rossendale, 1985. Price unknown.

Reflections on Literature for Children. Ed. by Francelia Butler and Richard Rotert. Hamden, CT: Library Professional Publications, 1984. $29.50.

Schon, Isabel. *A Hispanic Heritage, Series II: A Guide to Juvenile Books about Hispanic People and Cultures*. Metuchen, NJ: Scarecrow Press, 1985. $13.50.

Wehmeyer, Lillian Biermann. *The School Librarian as Educator*. 2nd ed. Littleton, CO: Libraries Unlimited, 1984. $22.50.

Whitehead, Robert J. *A Guide to Selecting Books for Children*. Metuchen, NJ: Scarecrow Press, 1984. $20.

Collection Development

Curley, Arthur. *Building Library Collections*. 6th ed. Methuchen, NJ: Scarecrow Press, 1985. $28.75.

Guide for the Development and Management of Test Collections: With Special Emphasis on Academic Settings. Chicago: Education and Behavioral Sciences Section, ACRL/ALA, 1985. $12.

Haka, Clifford H. *A Guidebook for Shelf Inventory Procedures in Academic Libraries*. Washington, DC: Office of Management Studies, Association of Research Libraries, 1985. $15.

Hall, Blaine H. *Collection Assessment Manual for College and University Libraries*. Phoenix, AZ: Oryx Press, 1985. $36.50.

Hoffmann, Frank W. *Popular Culture and Libraries*. Hamden, CT: Shoe String Press, 1984. $29.50.

Library and Information Science and Archive Administration: A Guide to Building up a Basic Collection for Library Schools. Comp. by J. Stephen Parker. Paris: General Information Programme and UNISIST, UNESCO, 1984. Price unknown.

Microforms in Libraries: A Manual for Evaluation and Management. Comp. by Committees of the Reproduction of Library Materials Section and Resources Section, Resources and Technical Services Division, American Library Association. Ed. by Francis Spreitzer. Chicago: American Library Association, 1985. $12.50.

Selection of Library Materials in the Humanities, Social Sciences and Sciences. Ed. by Patricia A. McClung. Chicago: American Library Association, 1985. $49.

Spiller, David. *Book Selection: An Introduction to Principles and Practice*. 4th ed. London: Bingley, 1986 (U.S. dist. by Shoe String Press, Hamden, CT). £14.75.

Comparative and International Librarianship

Ahmad, Nazir. *University Library Practices in Developing Countries*. London, Boston: Routledge & Kegan Paul, 1984, $45.

Aspects of African Librarianship: A Collection of Writings. Comp. and ed. by Michael Wise. London, New York: Mansell, 1985. $35.

Australian Academic Libraries in the Seventies: Essays in Honour of Dietrich Borchardt. Ed. by Harrison Bryan and John Horacek. St. Lucia: University of Queensland Press, 1984. $30.

Castelyn, Mary. *A History of Literacy and Libraries in Ireland: The Long Traced Pedigree.* Aldershot, Hampshire, England; Brookfield, VT: Gower, 1984 (U.S. dist. by Lexington Books, Lexington, MA). $29.

Citizen Participation in Library Decision-Making: The Toronto Experience. Ed. By John Marshall. Metuchen, NJ: Scarecrow Press, 1985. $25.

Davies, Helen. *Libraries in West Africa: A Bibliography.* 3rd ed. Oxford: Zell, 1984. Price unknown.

Fifty Years of Librarianship in India: Past, Present and Future, Seminar Papers, 29th All India Library Conference. Comp. by P. B. Mangla and J. L. Saradana. New Delhi: Indian Library Association, 1984. RS100.

International Librarianship Today and Tomorrow: A Festschrift for William J. Welsh. Comp. by Joseph W. and Mary S. Price. Munich, New York: Saur, 1985. $32.50.

Librarianship in the Muslim World, 1984. Vol. 2. Ed. by Anis Khurshid and M. K. Sherwani. Karachi, Pakistan: Islamic Library Information Centre, Library and Information Department, University of Karachi, 1985. $13.

Library and Information Science in France: A 1983 Overview. Ed. by William Vernon Jackson and Benjamin Whitten. Austin: University of Texas, Graduate School of Library and Information Science, 1984. $13.50.

Library Work for Children and Young Adults in the Developing Countries: Proceedings of the IFLA/UNESCO

Pre-session Seminar in Leipzig, GDR, 10-15 August, 1981. Ed. by Genevieve Patte and Sigrun K. Hannesdottir. New York: Saur, 1984. $28.

Nahari, Abdulaziz Mohamed. *The Role of National Libraries in Developing Countries, with Special Reference to Saudi Arabia.* London, New York: Mansell, 1984. $32.

Parker, J. Stephen. *UNESCO and Library Development Planning.* London: Library Association, 1985. £39.50.

Proceedings of the First Soviet-American Library Seminar: May 4-6, 1979, Washington, DC. Ed. by Jean E. Lowrie. Chicago: American Library Association, 1984. $27.50.

Rochester, Maxine K. *Foreign Students in American Library Education: Impact on Home Countries.* Westport, CT: Greenwood Press, 1986. $35.

University Libraries in Developing Countries: Structure and Function in Regard to Information Transfer for Science and Technology. Ed. by Anthony J. Loveday and Gunter Gattermann. New York: Saur, 1985. $20.

van Swigchem, P. J. *IFLA and the Library World: A Review of the Work of IFLA, 1981-1985.* The Hague: IFLA, 1985. Dfl. 20.

Copyright

Miller, Jerome K. *The Copyright Directory, Vol. 1: General Information.* Friday Harbor, WA: Copyright Information Services, 1985. $18.

Modern Copyright Fundamentals: Key Writings on Technological and Other Issues. Ed. by Ben H. Weil and Barbara Friedman Polansky. New York: Van Nostrand Reinhold, 1985. $34.50.

Strong, William S. *The Copyright Book: A Practical Guide.* 2nd ed. Cambridge, MA: MIT Press, 1984. $13.95.

Document Delivery and Fee-Based Services

Burwell, Helen P. *Directory of Fee-based Information Services, 1985.* Houston, TX: Burwell Enterprises, 1985. $24.95.

Education for Librarianship and Information Management

Asp, William G., et al. *Continuing Education for the Library Information Professions.* Hamden, CT: Library Professional Publications, 1985. $25.

Changing Technology and Education for Librarianship and Information Science. Ed. by Basil Stuart-Stubbs. Greenwich, CT: JAI Press, 1985. $47.50.

Continuing Education: Issues and Challenges, Papers from the Conference Held at Moraine Valley Community College, Palos Hills, Illinois, U.S.A., August 13–16, 1985. Ed. by Esther E. Horne. New York: Saur, 1985. $38.

Cronin, Blaise. *The Transition Years: New Initiatives in the Education of Professional Information Workers.* London: Aslib, 1984. £10.

Education for Professional Librarians. Ed. by Herbert S. White. White Plains, NY: Knowledge Industry, 1986. $36.50.

Financial Assistance for Library Education: Academic Year 1985–1986. Chicago: American Library Association, $1.

Griffiths, José-Marie. *New Directions in Library and Information Science Education.* White Plains, NY: Knowledge Industry, 1986. $45.

Information Technology in the Library-Information School Curriculum: An International Conference. Ed. by Chris Armstrong and Stella Keenan. Aldershot, Hampshire, England; Brookfield, VT: Gower, 1985. $53.95.

International Guide to Library and Information Science Education. Ed. by Josephine R. Fang and Paul Nauta. New York: Saur, 1985. $46.

Indexing and Abstracting

Austin, Derek. *PRECIS: A Manual of Concept Analysis and Subject Indexing.* 2nd ed. London: British Library, 1984. £8.50.

Brenner, Everett H. *Indexing and Searching in Perspective.* Philadelphia: National Federation of Abstracting and Information Services, 1985. Price unknown.

Dykstra, Mary. *PRECIS: A Primer.* London: British Library, Bibiographic Services Division, 1985. Price unknown.

Lancaster, F. Wilfrid. *Vocabulary Control for Information Retrieval.* 2nd ed. Arlington, VA: Information Resources Press, 1986. Price unknown.

Milstead, Jessica L. *Subject Access Systems: Alternatives in Design.* Orlando, FL: Academic Press, 1984. $28.

Wellisch, Hans H. *Indexing and Abstracting, 1977–1981: An International Bibliography.* Santa Barbara, CA: ABC-Clio, 1984. $45.

Information and Society

Alliance for Excellence: Librarians Respond to "A Nation at Risk": Recommendations and Strategies from Libraries and the Learning Society. Washington, DC: U.S. Department of Education, Office of Educational Research and Improvement, Center for Libraries and Education Improvement, GPO, 1984. Price unknown.

Cleveland, Harlan. *The Knowledge Executive: Leadership in an Information Society.* New York: Truman Talley Books, 1985. $18.95.

Cordell, Arthur J. *The Uneasy Eighties: The Transition to an Information Society.* Ottawa: Science Council of Canada, 1985. $7.

Hernon, Peter. *Public Access to Government Information: Issues, Trends and Strategies.* Norwood, NJ: Ablex, 1984. $49.50.

The Information Economy in the U.S.: Its Effect on Libraries and Library Networks: Proceedings of the Library of Congress Network Advisory Committee Meeting, November 14-16, 1984. Washington, DC: Network Development and MARC Standards Office, Library of Congress, 1985. $7.50.

Libraries and the Learning Society: Papers in Response to "A Nation at Risk." Ed. by Richard M. Dougherty et al. Chicago: American Library Association, 1984. $9.

Rogers, A. Robert. *The Library in Society.* Littleton, CO: Libraries Unlimited, 1984. $28.50.

The Study of Information: Interdisciplinary Messages. Ed. by Fritz Machlup and Una Mansfield. New York: Wiley, 1984. $30.

The Use of Information in a Changing World: Proceedings of the Forty-second FID Congress Held in The Hague, the Netherlands, 24-27 September 1984. Ed. by A. van der Laan and A. A. Winters. Amsterdam, New York: Elsevier, North-Holland, 1984. $53.75.

Information Management and Technology

Information Comes of Age: Proceedings of the Annual Conference of the Institute of Information Scientists, University of Kent at Canterbury, July 1984. London: Rossendale, 1985. £15.

Information Management: From Strategies to Action. Ed. by Blaise Cronin. Medford, NJ: Learned Information, 1985. Price unknown.

Information Technology and Information Use: Towards a Unified View of Information and Information Technology. Ed. by Peter Ingwersen et al. London: Taylor Graham, 1986. £37.

Marsterson, William A. J. *Information Technology and the Role of the Librarian.* London; Dover, NH: Croom Helm, 1986. $32.50.

Poole, Herbert L. *Theories of the Middle Range.* Norwood, NJ: Ablex, 1985. $29.50.

Soergel, Dagobert. *Organizing Information: Principles of Data Base and Retrieval Systems.* Orlando, FL: Academic Press, 1985. $51.50.

Toward Foundations of Information Science. Ed. by Laurence B. Heilprin. White Plains, NY: Knowledge Industry, 1985. $34.95.

Intellectual Freedom

American Library Association. Commission on Freedom and Equality of Access to Information. *Report of the Commission on Freedom and Equality of Access to Information.* Chicago: American Library Association, 1986. Price unknown.

The First Freedom Today: Critical Issues Relating to Censorship and Intellectual Freedom. Ed. by Robert B. Downs and R. E. McCoy. Chicago: American Library Association, 1984. $40.

Geller, Evelyn. *Forbidden Books in American Public Libraries, 1876-1939: A Study in Cultural Change.* Westport, CT: Greenwood Press, 1984. $29.95.

Right to Information: Legal Questions and Policy Issues. Ed. by Jana Varlejs. Jefferson, NC: McFarland, 1984. $9.95.

Schexnaydre, Linda, and Nancy Burns. *Censorship: A Guide for Successful Workshop Planning.* Prepared under the sponsorship of Emporia State University, School of Library and Information Management. Phoenix, AZ: Oryx Press, 1984. $18.50.

Library and Archival Security

Lincoln, Alan J. *Crime in the Library: A Study of Patterns, Impact and Security.* New York: R. R. Bowker, 1984. $29.95.

Security for Libraries: People, Buildings, Collections. Ed. by Marvine Brand.

Chicago: American Library Association, 1984. $12.

Library and Information Science Research

Alley, Brian. *Librarian in Search of a Publisher: How to Get Published in the Library and Information Field*. Phoenix, AZ: Oryx Press, 1986. $18.50.

Brockman, John R. *Academic Library Management Research: An Evaluative Review*. Loughborough, England: Centre for Library and Information Management, Department of Library and Information Studies, Loughborough University, 1984. Price unknown.

Librarian/Author: A Practical Guide on How to Get Published. Ed. by Betty-Carol Sellen. New York; Neal-Schuman, 1985. $24.95.

Nagasankara Rao, Dittakavi. *Research Methodology in Library and Information Science: A Selected Bibliography*. Monticello, IL: Vance Bibliographies, 1984. $2.25.

Powell, Ronald R. *Basic Research Methods for Librarians*. Norwood, NJ: Ablex, 1985. $29.50.

Swisher, Robert, and Charles McClure. *Research for Decision Making: Methods for Librarians*. Chicago: American Library Association, 1984. $20.

Library Automation

See the "High Technology Bibliography," following in Part 5.

Library Buildings and Space Planning

Dahlgren, Anders. *Planning the Small Public Library Building*. Chicago, IL: Library Administration and Management Association, American Library Association, 1985. $5.

Fraley, Ruth A. *Library Space Planning: How to Assess, Allocate, and Reorgan-ize Collections, Resources and Physical Facilities*. New York: Neal-Schuman, 1985. $35.

Library History

Balbi, Adriano. *A Statistical Essay on the Libraries of Vienna and the World*. Trans. by Larry Barr and Janet L. Barr. Jefferson, NC: McFarland, 1986. $25.95.

Beckman, Margaret. *The Best Gift: A Record of the Carnegie Libraries in Ontario*. Toronto: Dundurn Press, 1984. $29.85.

Benidt, Bruce Weir. *The Library Book: Centennial History of the Minneapolis Public Library*. Minneapolis, MN: Minneapolis Public Library and Information Center, 1984. $19.95.

Buzas, Ladislaus. *German Library History, 800–1945*. Trans. by William D. Boyd. Jefferson, NC: McFarland, 1986. $55.

Carrier, Esther Jane. *Fiction in Public Libraries, 1900–1950*. Littleton, CO: Libraries Unlimited, 1985. $27.50.

Christ, Karl. *Handbook of Medieval Library History*. Rev. by Anton Kern. Trans. and ed. by Theophil M. Otto, Metuchen, NJ: Scarecrow Press, 1984. $35.

Dickson, Paul. *The Library in America: A Celebration in Words and Pictures*. New York: Facts on File, 1986. $35.

Harris, Michael H. *The History of Libraries in the Western World*. Compact textbook ed. Metuchen, NJ: Scarecrow Press, 1984. $15.

Kaser, David. *Books and Libraries in Camp and Battle: The Civil War Experience*. Westport, CT: Greenwood Press, 1984. $27.95.

Korey, Marie Elena. *The Wolf Years: The Renascence of the Library Company of Philadelphia, 1952–1984*. Philadelphia: The Company, 1984. Price unknown.

Molz, Redmond Kathleen. *National Plan-*

ning for Library Service, 1935–1975. Chicago: American Library Association, 1984. $28.50.

Radford, Neil A. *The Carnegie Corporation and the Development of American College Libraries, 1928–1941.* Chicago: American Library Association, 1984. $29.95.

Richards, Pamela S. *Scholars and Gentlemen: The Library of the New-York Historical Society, 1804–1982.* Hamden, CT: Archon Books, 1984. $17.50.

Wallace, Danny P. *The User Friendliness of the Library Catalog.* Champaign: University of Illinois, Graduate School of Library and Information Science, 1984. $3.

Library Profession and Professionals

Adams, Marie. *Professionalism: A Continuing Process.* London: Association of Assistant Librarians, 1985. £3.50.

Benge, Roland C. *Confessions of a Lapsed Librarian.* Metuchen, NJ: Scarecrow Press, 1984. $16.

Caputo, Janette S. *The Assertive Librarian.* Phoenix, AZ: Oryx Press, 1984. $19.50.

Dale, Doris C. *A Directory of Oral History Tapes of Librarians in the United States and Canada.* Chicago: American Library Association, 1986. $15.

Downs, Robert B. *Perspectives on the Past: An Autobiography.* Metuchen, NJ: Scarecrow Press, 1984. $17.

Garoogian, Rhoda. *Careers in Other Fields for Librarians: Successful Strategies for Finding the Job.* Chicago: American Library Association, 1985. $12.95.

Gurnsey, John. *The Information Professions in the Electronic Age.* London: Bingley, 1985 (U.S. dist. by Shoe String Press, Hamden, CT). £12.50.

Heim, Kathleen M. *On Account of Sex.* Chicago: American Library Association, 1984. $25.

Irvine, Betty Jo. *Sex Segregation in Librarianship: Demographic and Career Patterns of Academic Library Administrators.* Westport, CT: Greenwood Press, 1985. $29.95.

Kilgour, Frederick G. *Collected Papers of Frederick G. Kilgour.* 2 vols. Comp. by Patricia A. Becker and Ann T. Dodson. Dublin, OH: OCLC, 1984. $57.50.

Kraske, Gary E. *Missionaries of the Book: The American Library Profession and the Origins of United States Cultural Diplomacy.* Westport, CT: Greenwood Press, 1985. $35.

Lynch, Mary Jo, M. Meyers, and J. Guy. *ALA Survey of Librarian Salaries, 1986.* Chicago: American Library Association, 1986. $40.

New Options for Librarians: Finding a Job in a Related Field. Ed. by Betty-Carol Sellen and D. S. Berkner. New York: Neal-Schuman, 1984. $19.95.

Prentice, Ann E. *Professional Ethics and Librarians.* Phoenix, AZ: Oryx Press, 1985. $32.50.

Stokes, Roy B. *Henry Bradshaw, 1831–1886.* Metuchen, NJ: Scarecrow Press, 1984. $22.50.

Tallman, Johanna E. *Check Out a Librarian.* Metuchen, NJ: Scarecrow Press, 1985. $15.

Wiegand, Wayne A. *The Politics of an Emerging Profession: The American Library Association, 1876–1917.* Westport, CT: Greenwood Press, 1986. $39.95.

Library Public Relations

Burgess, Dean, et al. *Getting It Passed: Lobbying for Libraries.* Chicago: American Library Association, LAMA Public Relations Section, 1984. $9.

Franklin, Linda C. *Display and Publicity Ideas for Libraries.* Jefferson, NC: McFarland, 1985. $14.95.

Great Library Promotion Ideas: JCD Library Public Relations Award Winners

and Notables 1984. Ed. by Ann Heidbreder Eastman and Roger H. Parent. Chicago: American Library Association, 1984. $12.50.

Kirby, John. *Creating the Library Identity: A Manual of Design.* Aldershot, Hampshire, England; Brookfield, VT: Gower, 1985 (U.S. dist. by Lexington Books, Lexington, MA). $53.95.

Marketing for Libraries and Information Agencies. Ed. by Darlene E. Weingand. Norwood, NJ: Ablex, 1984. $24.50.

Nagasankara Rao, Dittakavi. *Publicity and Public Relations in Libraries: A Selected Bibliography.* Monticello, IL: Vance Bibliographies, 1985. $2.25.

Microcomputers in Libraries

See the "High Technology Bibliography," following in Part 5.

Networks, Interlibrary Cooperation, and Resource Sharing

Bibliographic Services and User Needs. Comp. and ed. by Paul Peterson. Washington, DC: Council on Library Resources, 1984. $10.

Boucher, Virginia. *Interlibrary Loan Practices Handbook.* Chicago: American Library Association, 1984. $20.

Gadsen, S. R. *The Administration of Interlending by Microcomputer.* Boston Spa, England: British Library, 1984. £9.50.

Key Issues in the Networking Field Today: Proceedings of the Library of Congress Network Advisory Committee Meeting, May 6-8, 1985. Washington, DC: Network Development and MARC Standards Office, Library of Congress, 1985. Free.

Linking: Today's Libraries, Tomorrow's Technologies: Report of the Bibliographic and Communications Network Pilot Project. Ottawa: National Library of Canada, 1984. Free.

Local Area Networks and Libraries: The Los Angeles Chapter of ASIS Seminar Proceedings. Ed. by Wendy Culotta et al. Studio City, CA: Pacific Information, 1985. $28.50.

Maciuszko, Kathleen L. *OCLC: A Decade of Development, 1967-1977.* Littleton, CO: Libraries Unlimited, 1984. $54.

Morris, Leslie R. *Interlibrary Loan Policies Directory.* 2nd ed. Chicago: American Library Association, 1984. $27.50.

Smith, Jewell, and Sara Parker. *Library Cooperation.* Chicago: Library Administration and Management Association/ALA, 1984. $1.

Toward a Common Vision in Library Networking: Proceedings of the Library of Congress Network Advisory Committee Meeting, December 9-11, 1985. Washington, DC.: Network Development and MARC Standards Office, Library of Congress, 1986. Free.

Nonprint Materials

AVMP Audio Video Market Place, 85-86. New York: R. R. Bowker, 1985. $49.95.

Daniel, Evelyn H. *Media and Microcomputers in the Library: A Selected Annotated Resource Guide.* Phoenix, AZ: Oryx Press, 1984, $24.95.

Educational Media and Technology Yearbook, 1986. Vol. 12. Ed. by Elmwood E. Miller. Littleton, CO: Libraries Unlimited, 1986. $47.50.

The Equipment Directory of Audio-visual, Computer and Video Products, 1986-87. 32nd ed. Fairfax, VA: International Communications Industries Association, 1986. Price unknown.

Fothergill, Richard. *Non-book Materials in Libraries: A Practical Guide.* 2nd ed., London: Bingley, 1984 (U.S. dist.

by Shoe String Press, Hamden, CT). $23.

Intner, Sheila S. *Access to Media: A Guide to Integrated, Online Bibliographic Systems.* New York: Neal-Schuman, 1984. $35.

Napier, Paul A. *Index to Micrographics Equipment Evaluations.* 2nd ed. Westport, CT: Meckler, 1985. $35.

Teague, Sidney J. *Microform, Video and Electronic Media Librarianship.* Stoneham, MA; Kent, UK: Butterworths, 1985. £15.

Weihs, Jean Riddle. *Accessible Storage of Nonbook Materials.* Phoenix, AZ: Oryx Press, 1984. $19.50.

Online Catalogs

See the "High Technology Bibiography," following in Part 5.

Periodicals and Serials

Advances in Serials Management: a Research Annual. Vol. 1. Ed. by M. Tuttle. Greenwich, CT: JAI Press, 1986. $56.50.

Library Serials Standards: Development, Implementation, Impact: Proceedings of the Third Annual Serials Conference. Ed. by Nancy Jean Melin. Westport, CT: Meckler, 1984. $35.

Ott, Jean. *Serials Accessioning Manual.* Washington, DC: Serial Record Division, Library of Congress, 1985. $10.

Projects and Procedures for Serials Administration. Comp. and ed. by Diane Stine. Ann Arbor, MI: Pierian Press, 1985. Price unknown.

Thomas, Nancy G. *Notes for Serials Cataloging.* Littleton, CO: Libraries Unlimited, 1986. $17.50.

Public Libraries

Ballard, Thomas. *Knowin' All Them Things That Ain't So: Managing To-*

day's Public Library. Champaign: University of Illinois, Graduate School of Library and Information Science, 1985. $3.50.

Childers, Thomas. *Information and Referral: Public Libraries.* Norwood, NJ: Ablex, 1984. $37.50.

Durrance, Joan C. *Armed for Action: Library Response to Citizen Information Needs.* New York: Neal-Schuman, 1984. $29.95.

Houghton, Tony. *Bookstock Management in Public Libraries.* London: Bingley, 1985 (U.S. dist. by Shoe String Press, Hamden, CT). £10.50.

Lilore, Doreen. *The Local Union in Public Libraries.* Hamden, CT: Shoe String Press, 1984. $19.50.

Nauratil, Marcia J. *Public Libraries and Nontraditional Clienteles: The Politics of Special Services.* Westport, CT: Greenwood Press, 1985. $27.95.

Public Libraries and the Challenges of the Next Two Decades. Ed. by Alphonse F. Trezza. Littleton, CO: Libraries Unlimited, 1985. $35.

Public Libraries: Re-appraisal and Restructuring. Ed. by Clint Harris and Brian Clifford. London: Rossendale, 1985. £10.

Rosenberg, Philip. *Cost Finding for Public Libraries: A Management Handbook.* Chicago: American Library Association, 1985. $9.

Sager, Donald J. *Managing the Public Library.* White Plains, NY: Knowledge Industry, 1984. $34.50.

Shavit, David. *Federal Aid and State Library Agencies: Federal Policy Implementation.* Westport, CT: Greenwood Press, 1985. $27.95.

Shoham, Snunith. *Organizational Adaptation by Public Libraries.* Westport, CT: Greenwood Press, 1984. $29.95.

Shuman, Bruce A. *River Bend Revisited: The Problem Patron in the Library.* Phoenix, AZ: Oryx Press, 1984. $22.50.

Webb, Terry. *Reorganization in the Public Library.* Phoenix, AZ: Oryx Press, 1984. $35.

Weingand, Darlene E. *The Organic Public Library.* Littleton, CO: Libraries Unlimited, 1984. $23.50.

Reference Services and Online Searching

Borgman, Christine L. *Effective Online Searching: A Basic Text.* New York: Marcel Dekker, 1984. $27.50.

Gilreath, Charles L. *Computerized Literature Searching: Research Strategies and Databases.* Boulder, CO: Westview, 1984. $22.

Hede, Agnes A. *Reference Readiness: A Manual for Librarians and Students.* 3rd ed. Hamden, CT: Shoe String Press, 1984. $15.

Hillard, James M. *Where to Find What: A Handbook to Reference Service.* 2nd rev. ed. Metuchen, NJ: Scarecrow Press, 1984. $22.50.

Humphrey, Susanne M. *Databases: A Primer for Retrieving Information by Computer.* Englewood Cliffs, NJ: Prentice-Hall, 1986. $29.95.

Katz, Bill. *Reference and Online Services Handbook.* Vol. II. New York: Neal-Schuman, 1985. $39.95.

Klingensmith, Patricia J., and Elizabeth E. Duncan. *Easy Access to DIALOG, ORBIT, and BRS.* New York: Marcel Dekker, 1984. $49.75.

Li, Tze-chung. *An Introduction to Online Searching.* Westport, CT: Greenwood Press, 1985. $27.95.

Managing Online Reference Services. Ed. by Ethel Auster. New York: Neal-Schuman, 1986. $35.

Markey, Karen. *Subject Searching in Library Catalogs: Before and after the Introduction of Online Catalogs.* Dublin, OH: OCLC, 1984. $21.

Murfin, Marjorie E. *Reference Service: An Annotated Bibliographic Guide*

Supplement, 1976–1982. 2nd ed. Littleton, CO: Libraries Unlimited, 1984, $35.

Neway, Julie M. *Information Specialist as Team Player in the Research Process.* Westport, CT: Greenwood Press, 1985. $29.95.

Numeric Databases. Ed. by Ching-chih Chen and Peter Hernon. Norwood, NJ: Ablex, 1984. $29.95.

Olle, James Gordon H. *A Guide to Sources of Information in Libraries.* Aldershot, Hampshire, England; Brookfield, VT: Gower, 1984 (U.S. dist. by Lexington Books, Lexington, MA). $33.95.

Online Catalogs, Online Reference: Converging Trends. Proceedings of a Library and Information Technology Association Preconference Institute, June 23–24, 1983, Los Angeles. Ed. by Brian Aveney and Brett Butler. Chicago: American Library Association, 1984. $25.

Online Database Search Services Directory: A Reference and Referral Guide to Libraries, Information Firms, and Other Sources Providing Computerized Databases. Ed. by John Schmitteroth, Jr., and Doris Morris Maxfield. Detroit, MI: Gale Research, 1984– . $75.

Online Searching: The Basics, Settings & Management. Ed. by Joann H. Lee. Littleton, CO: Libraries Unlimited, 1984. $23.50.

Printed Reference Material. 2nd ed. Ed. by Gavin Higgens. London: Library Association, 1984. $55.

Pritchard, Eileen. *Literature Searching in Science, Technology and Agriculture.* Westport, CT: Greenwood Press, 1984. $29.95.

Robinson, Judith Schiek. *Subject Guide to U.S. Government Reference Sources.* Littleton, CO: Libraries Unlimited, 1985. $40.

Sears, Jean L. *Using Government Publications.* 2 vols. Phoenix, AZ: Oryx Press, 1985. $67.50.

Slavens, Thomas P. *Reference Interviews, Questions, and Materials.* 2nd ed. Metuchen, NJ: Scarecrow Press, 1985. $15.

Stevens, Rolland E. *Reference Work in the University Library.* Littleton, CO: Libraries Unlimited, 1986. $37.50.

Yates, Rochelle. *A Librarian's Guide to Telephone Reference Service.* Hamden, CT: Library Professional Publications, 1986. $19.50.

School Libraries/Media Centers

Anderson, Pauline. *Library Media Leadership in Academic Secondary Schools.* Hamden, CT: Shoe String Press, 1985. $16.50.

Baker, D. Philip. *The Library Media Program and the School.* Littleton, CO: Libraries Unlimited, 1984. $19.50.

Behavior Management in the School Library Media Center. Ed. by Thomas L. Hart. Chicago: American Library Association, 1985. $12.50.

Edsall, Marian S. *Practical PR for School Library Media Centers.* New York: Neal-Schuman, 1984. $19.95.

Hackman, Mary H. *Library Media Skills and the Senior High School English Program.* Littleton, CO: Libraries Unlimited, 1985. $23.50.

Instruction in School Library Media Center Use (K–12). 2nd ed. Ed. by Thomas L. Hart. Chicago: American Library Association, 1985. $15.

Kulleseid, Eleanor. *Beyond Survival to Power for School Library Media Professionals.* Hamden, CT: Shoe String Press, 1985. $20.

Media Librarianship. Ed. by John W. Ellison. New York: Neal-Schuman, 1985. $29.95.

Microcomputer Information for School Media Centers. Ed. by Nevada Wallis Thomason. Metuchen, NJ: Scarecrow Press, 1985. $25.

Miller, Inabeth. *Microcomputers in School Library Media Centers.* New York: Neal-Schuman, 1984. $19.95.

Naumer, Janet N. *Media Center Management with an Apple II.* Littleton, CO: Libraries Unlimited, 1984. $16.50.

Nickel, Mildred L. *Steps to Service: A Handbook of Procedures for the School Library Media Center.* Rev. ed. Chicago: American Library Association, 1984. $9.95.

Raddon, Rosemary. *Planning Learning Resource Centres in Schools and Colleges.* Aldershot, Hampshire, England; Brookfield, VT: Gower, 1984 (U.S. dist. by Lexington Books, Lexington, MA). £15.

School Library Media Annual, 1985. Vol. 3. Ed. by Shirley L. Aaron and Pat R. Scales. Littleton, CO: Libraries Unlimited, 1985. $35.

Thomason, Nevada W. *Circulation Systems for School Library Media Centers: Manual to Microcomputers.* Littleton, CO: Libraries Unlimited, 1985. $23.50.

Turner, Philip M. *Helping Teachers Teach: A School Library Media Specialist's Role.* Littleton, CO: Libraries Unlimited, 1985. $18.50.

Wilkens, Lea-Ruth C. *Supporting K–5 Reading Instruction in the School Library Media Center.* Chicago: American Library Association, 1984. $12.50.

Services for Special Groups

Casey, Genevieve M. *Library Services for the Aging.* Hamden, CT: Shoe String Press, 1984. $18.50.

Dalton, Phyllis I. *Library Service to the Deaf and Hearing Impaired.* Phoenix, AZ: Oryx Press, 1985. $39.50.

Glover, Peggy D. *Library Services for the Woman in the Middle.* Hamden, CT: Library Professional Publications, 1985. $20.

Revised Standards and Guidelines of Service for the Library of Congress Network of Libraries for the Blind and Physically Handicapped, 1984. Chi-

cago: ALA, Association of Specialized and Cooperative Library Agencies, 1984. $12.

Special Libraries

Arny, Linda Ray. *The Search for Data in the Physical and Chemical Sciences.* New York: Special Libraries Association, 1984. $17.

Bailey, Martha J. *The Special Librarian as a Supervisor or Middle Manager.* 2nd ed. Washington, DC: Special Libraries Association, 1986. $18.95.

Bryant, E. T. *Music Librarianship: A Practical Guide.* 2nd ed. Metuchen, NJ: Scarecrow Press, 1985. $32.50.

Cost Analysis, Cost Recovery, Marketing, and Fee-based Services: A Guide for the Health Sciences Librarian. Ed. by M. Sandra Wood. New York: Haworth Press, 1985. $29.95.

Directory of Special Libraries and Information Centers in U.S.A. and Canada. 9th ed. 3 vols. Ed. by Brigitte Darnay. Detroit, MI: Gale Research, 1985. $555.75 for 3 vols.

Farrell, Barbara. *Guide for a Small Map Collection.* 2nd ed. Ottawa: Association of Canadian Map Libraries, 1984. $16.

Ferguson, Elizabeth. *Special Libraries at Work.* Hamden, CT: Shoe String Press, 1984. $21.50.

Information and Special Libraries in 2009: Informed Speculations. Ed. by Judy Genesen and David E. King. Chicago: Special Libraries Association, Illinois Chapter, 1984. $10.

Keaveney, Sydney Starr. *Contemporary Art Documentation and Fine Arts Libraries.* Metuchen, NJ: Scarecrow Press, 1986. $17.50.

Manual of Business Library Practice. 2nd ed. Ed. by Malcolm J. Campbell. London: Bingley, 1985 (U.S. dist. by Shoe String Press, Hamden, CT). $19.50.

Medical Librarianship in the Eighties and Beyond: A World Perspective. Ed. by Fiona Mackay Picken and M. C. Kahn. London, New York: Mansell, 1986. $58.

Mount, Ellis. *University Science and Engineering Libraries.* 2nd ed. Wesport, CT: Greenwood Press, 1985. $35.

Museum Librarianship. Ed. by John C. Larsen. Hamden, CT: Library Professional Publications, 1985. $18.50.

A Reader in Art Librarianship. Ed. by Philip Pacey. Munich, New York: Saur, 1985. $48.

Roper, Fred Wilburn. *Introduction to Reference Sources in the Health Sciences.* 2nd ed. Chicago: Medical Library Association, 1984. $27.

SLA Triennial Salary Survey. Washington, DC: Special Libraries Association, 1986. $25.

Welch, J. *Searching the Medical Literature: A Guide to Printed and Online Sources.* London: Chapman and Hall, 1985 (U.S. dist. by Sheridan House, White Plains, NY). $32.50.

White, Herbert S. *Managing the Special Library: Strategies for Success within the Larger Organization.* White Plains, NY: Knowledge Industry, 1984. $36.50.

Technical Services

Bloomberg, Marty. *Introduction to Technical Services for Library Technicians.* 5th ed. Littleton, CO: Libraries Unlimited, 1985. $20.

Crawford, Walt. *MARC for Library Use: Understanding the USMARC Formats.* White Plains, NY: Knowledge Industry, 1984. $28.50.

Library Technical Services: Operations and Management. Ed. by Irene P. Godden. Orlando, FL: Academic Press, 1984. $32.

Reed-Scott, Jutta. *Issues in Retrospective Conversion: Report of a Study Conducted for the Council on Library Re-*

sources. Washington, DC: Council on Library Resources, 1984. $3.

Retrospective Conversion: From Cards to Computer. Ed. by Anne G. Adler and Elizabeth A. Baber. Ann Arbor, MI: Pierian Press, 1984. $39.50.

Retrospective Conversion: Report of a Meeting Sponsored by the Council on Library Resources, July 16-18, 1984, Wayzata, Minnesota. Comp. and ed. by Dorothy Gregor. Washington, DC: Council on Library Resources, 1984. $6.

Technical Services: Acquisitions

Guidelines for Handling Library Orders for In-print Monographic Publications. 2nd ed. Comp. by the Resources and Technical Services Division, Resources Section, Bookdealer-Library Relations Committee, American Library Association. Chicago: American Library Association, 1984. $3.

Issues in Acquisitions: Programs and Evaluations. Ed. by Sul H. Lee. Ann Arbor, MI: Pierian Press, 1984. $24.50.

Library Acquisition Policies and Procedures. 2nd ed. Ed. by Elizabeth Futas. Phoenix, AZ: Oryx Press, 1984. $38.50.

Magrill, Rose Mary, and D. J. Hickey. *Acquisitions Management and Collection Development in Libraries*. Chicago: American Library Association, 1984. $18.

Pemberton, J. Michael. *Policies of Audiovisual Producers and Distributors: A Handbook for Acquisition Personnel*. Metuchen, NJ: Scarecrow Press, 1984. $27.50.

Publishers and Librarians: A Foundation for Dialogue: Proceedings of the Forty-second Conference of the Graduate Library School, May 13-15, 1983. Ed. by Mary Biggs. Chicago: University of Chicago Press, 1984. $12.

Technical Services: Cataloging and Classification

Akers' Simple Library Cataloging. 7th ed. Completely revised and rewritten by Arthur Curley and Jana Varleijs. Metuchen, NJ: Scarecrow Press, 1984. $16.50.

Burger, Robert H. *Authority Work: The Creation, Use, Maintenance, and Evaluation of Authority Records and Files*. Littleton, CO: Libraries Unlimited, 1985. $23.50.

Castonguay, Russell. *A Comparative Guide to Classification Schemes for Local Government Documents Collections*. Westport, CT: Greenwood Press, 1984. $35.

Cataloging Government Documents: A Manual of Interpretation for AACR2. Ed. by Bernadine A. Hoduski. Documents Cataloging Committee, Government Documents Round Table. Chicago: American Library Association, 1984. $49.

Cataloging Special Materials: Critiques and Innovations. Ed. by Sanford Berman. Phoenix, AZ: Oryx Press, 1986. $32.50.

Chan, Lois Mai. *Library of Congress Subject Headings: Principles and Application*. 2nd ed. Littleton, CO: Libraries Unlimited, 1986. $45.

Cochrane, Pauline Atherton. *Redesign of Catalogs and Indexes for Improved Online Subject Access: Selected Papers of Pauline A. Cochrane*. Phoenix, AZ: Oryx Press, 1985. $45.

Cole, Jim E. *Notes Worth Noting: Notes Used in AACR2 Serials Cataloging*. Ann Arbor, MI: Pierian Press, 1984. $12.50.

Dodd, Sue A., and Ann M. Sandberg-Fox. *Cataloging Microcomputer Files: A Manual of Interpretations for AACR2*. Chicago: American Library Association, 1985. $25.

Foundations of Cataloging: A Sourcebook. Ed. by Michael Carpenter and

Elaine Svenonius. Littleton, CO: Libraries Unlimited, 1985. $27.50.

Greenberg, Alan M., and C. R. McIver. *LC and AACR 2: An Album of Cataloging Examples Arranged by Rule Number.* Metuchen, NJ: Scarecrow Press, 1984. $19.50.

Hafter, Ruth. *Academic Librarians and Cataloging Networks: Visibility, Quality Control, and Professional Status.* Westport, CT: Greenwood Press, 1986. $29.95.

Harriman, Robert. *Newspaper Cataloging Manual.* CONSER/USNP ed. Washington, DC: Serial Record Division, Library of Congress, 1984– Price unknown.

Hoffman, Herbert H. *Small Library Cataloging.* 2nd ed. Metuchen, NJ: Scarecrow Press, 1986. $18.50.

Hunter, Eric J. *Computerized Cataloging.* London: Bingley, 1985 (U.S. dist. by Shoe String Press, Hamden, CT). $19.50.

LC Rule Interpretations of AACR2, 1978–1985. Comp. by Sally C. Tseng. 2nd cumulated ed. Metuchen, NJ: Scarecrow Press, 1985. Price unknown.

Manheimer, Martha L. *OCLC: An Introduction to Searching and Input.* 2nd ed. New York: Neal-Schuman, 1986. $17.95.

Milstead, Jessica L. *Subject Access Systems: Alternatives in Design.* Orlando, FL: Academic Press, 1984. $22.

Olson, Nancy B. *Cataloging of Audiovisual Materials: A Manual Based on AACR2.* 2nd ed. Mankato, MN: Minnesota Scholarly Press, 1985. $34.50.

Photographic Cataloging Manual. Prepared by the American Museum of Natural History. New York: The Museum, Department of Library Services, 1984. $10.

Salinger, Florence A., and Eileen Zagon. *Notes for Catalogers: A Sourcebook of Examples from Use with AACR2.* White Plains, NY: Knowledge Industry, 1985. $34.50.

Shaw, Sarah J., and Lauralee Shiere. *Sheet Music Cataloging and Processing: A Manual.* Madison, WI: Music Library Association, 1984. $11.75.

Subject and Information Analysis. Comp. by Eleanor D. Dym. New York: Marcel Dekker, 1985. Price unknown.

Theory of Subject Analysis: A Sourcebook. Ed. by Lois Mai Chan et al. Littleton, CO: Libraries Unlimited, 1985. $36.

White-Hensen, Wendy. *Archival Moving Image Materials: A Cataloging Manual.* Washington, DC: Motion Picture, Broadcasting and Recorded Sound Division, Library of Congress, 1984. $15.

Periodicals

The list of journals that follows may be viewed as a core collection in a professional library or may be used by librarians as a selection tool for personal subscriptions. Titles used primarly as acquisition tools have been omitted.

ACRL-BIS Newsletter
ALA Washington Newsletter
American Archivist
American Libraries
Audiovisual Librarian
Behavioral and Social Sciences Librarian
Book Research Quarterly
Business Information Review
Cataloging and Classification Quarterly
Collection Building
Collection Management
College and Research Libraries
Community and Junior College Libraries
Conservation Administration News
Current Research in Library and Information Science
Database
Database Alert
Database End-User
Government Information Quarterly
Health Libraries Review
IFLA Journal
The Indexer

Infomediary
Information and Referral
Information Development
Information Processing and Management
Information Technology and Libraries
Information Today
International Library Review
International Review of Children's Literature and Librarianship
Journal of Academic Librarianship
Journal of Education for Librarianship
Journal of Library Administration
Journal of Library History, Philosophy and Comparative Librarianship
Library Acquisitions: Practice and Theory
Library and Archival Security
Library and Information Science Research
Library Currents
Library Hi Tech
Library Hi Tech News
Library Hotline
Library Journal
Library Management

Library of Congress Information Bulletin
Library Quarterly
Library Resources and Technical Services
Library Technology Reports
Library Trends
Microfilm Review
Newsletter on Intellectual Freedom
Online
Online Libraries and Microcomputers
Online Review
Public Computing
Public Library Quarterly
The Reference Librarian
RQ
RSR (Reference Services Review)
Rare Book and Manuscript Librarianship
School Library Media Quarterly
Science and Technology Libraries
Serials Librarian
Serials Review
SLJ (School Library Journal)
Special Libraries
Top of the News
Wilson Library Bulletin

High Technology Bibliography

Arthur Downing

Head, Bibliographic Services Unit
New York Academy of Medicine Library
2 E. 103 St., New York, NY 10029

Many of the monographs published since the last edition of this annotated bibliography seem to share the theme of management. Consequently, in the list that follows one will find a manual for managing an automation project, a handbook for training staff, sources for developing policies on the use of microcomputers, collections of library policy statements, and other volumes that address the evolving role of the information professional. In addition, the widespread use of microcomputers has led to the publication of works encouraging more sophisticated applications through downloading and networking.

Identifying trends in the periodical literature becomes especially difficult, as every year the volume of published material increases and new areas of interest in library automation continue to branch out. Nevertheless, it would be impossible to overlook the growing attention microcomputing receives in the literature, due to the acquisition of microcomputers by all types of libraries. Microcomputer users' columns and software

reviews are now common features in general interest library periodicals. In addition, the abundance of articles describing local achievements (sometimes called "how we did it" articles), which in the past had centered around the installation of an online catalog, are now more often sharing an experience with the application of commercially available software (usually dBase III) to library functions.

The various disc technologies represent an area of potential growth in publication equal to that of microcomputing. Although only a few years ago the terms "videodisc" and "optical digital disc" were unknown to most librarians, already columns, newsletters, and journals are devoted to the use of these technologies in the library. In fact, "CD-ROM" was one of the few high technology terms added as a cross-reference to the index *Library Literature* in 1986.

Books

This bibliography is intended as a practical tool for a general audience, and works that only seem useful to a limited group of readers, such as those written with a very technical approach, have been excluded. The selection process involved the compilation of a core list of titles based on favorable reviews from a variety of professional journals (see the appendix to this bibliography), followed by an examination of each work. The absence of particular titles from the list may be attributed to the application of the guidelines, or more likely, the unfortunate delay in the appearance of book reviews.

The first section — Books, 1980 through Late 1985 — consists of items from the last two editions of this bibliography that are still in print at this writing. The basic citations have been updated, and the complete annotations may be found in earlier editions of the *Bowker Annual*. The second section — Books, Late 1985 through 1986 — lists monographs that became available for consideration after the publication of the last edition of the bibliography. The actual span of coverage begins approximately with the fourth quarter of 1985.

Books, 1980 through Late 1985

Overview or Miscellaneous

Automated Circulation: An Examination of Choices, Edited by Joseph R. Matthews and Kevin E. Hegarty. Chicago: American Library Association, 1984. 140 pp. no index. $15 pap. ISBN 0-8389-0402-5.

Boss, Richard. *Automating Library Acquisitions: Issues and Outlook.* Professional Librarian Series. White Plains, NY: Knowledge Industry Publications, 1982. 135 pp. bibliog. index. appendix. $27.50 pap. ISBN 0-86729-006-4.

Cable for Information Delivery: A Guide for Librarians, Educators and Cable Professionals. Edited by Brigitte L. Kenney. White Plains, NY: Knowledge Industry Publications, 1983. 172 pp. bibliog. illus. index. appendix. $34.50; $27.50 pap. ISBN 0-86729-056-0; pap. 0-86729-055-2.

Carter, Ruth C., and Scott Bruntjen. *Data Conversion.* Professional Librarian Series. White Plains, NY: Knowledge Industry Publications, 1983. 169 pp. bibliog. index. appendix. $34.50; $27.50 pap. ISBN 0-86729-047-1; pap. 0-86729-046-3.

Crossroads: Proceedings of the First National Conference of the Library and Informa- tion Technology Association. September 17–21, 1983. Library and Information Tech- nology Series No. 1. Chicago: American Library Association, 1984. 261 pp. no index. $40 pap. ISBN 0-8389-3307-6.

Dowlin, Kenneth E. *The Electronic Library: The Promise and the Process.* New York: Neal-Schuman, 1983. 199 pp. illus. index. appendix. $35 pap. ISBN 0-918212-75-8.

Fosdick, Howard. *Computer Basics for Librarians and Information Specialists.* Arlington, VA: Information Resources Press, 1981. 203 pp. bibliog. index. $22.50. ISBN 0-87815-034-X.

Hagler, Ronald, and Peter Simmons. *The Bibliographic Record and Information Tech- nology.* Chicago: American Library Association, 1982. 346 pp. index. appendix. $27.50 ISBN 0-8389-0370-3.

Information Technology: Critical Choices for Library Decision-Makers. Books in Li- brary and Information Science No. 40. Edited by Allen Kent and Thomas J. Galvin. New York: Dekker, 1982. 477 pp. index. appendix. $59.75. ISBN 0-8247-1737-6.

Kesner, Richard M. *Automation for Archivists and Records Managers: Planning and Implementation Strategies.* Chicago: American Library Association, 1984, 222 pp. bib- liog. index. appendix. notes. $27.50. ISBN 0-8389-0406-8.

Library Automation as a Source of Management Information: Clinic on Library Appli- cations of Data Processing (19th, 1982). Edited by F. Wilfrid Lancaster. Urbana: Uni- versity of Illinois, 1983. 200 pp. index. $15. ISBN 0-87845-068-8.

Professional Competencies—Technology and the Librarian. Edited by Linda C. Smith. Clinic on Library Applications of Data Processing, 1983. Urbana: Graduate School of Library and Information Science, University of Illinois, 1984. 138 pp. index. $15. ISBN 0-87845-070-X.

Readings in Technology. Edited by Nancy Viggiano. New York: Special Libraries Asso- ciation, 1984. 195 pp. no index. $16.50 pap. ISBN 0-87111-297-3.

Reynolds, Dennis. *Library Automation: Issues and Applications.* New York: R. R. Bowker, 1985. 615 pp. index $37.50. ISBN 0-8352-1489-3.

Rosenberg, Kenyon C., with the assistance of Paul T. Feinstein. *Dictionary of Library and Educational Technology,* 2nd ed. rev. and expanded. Littleton, CO: Libraries Un- limited, 1983. 185 pp. bibliog. $24.50 ISBN 0-87287-396-X. Updated version of *Media Equipment: A Guide and Dictionary.*

Saffady, William. *Introduction to Automation for Librarians.* Chicago: American Li- brary Association, 1983. 304 pp. bibliog. illus. index. $35. ISBN 0-8389-0386-X.

_____. *Micrographics,* 2nd ed. Library Science Text Series. Littleton, CO: Libraries Unlimited, 1985. 254 pp. illus. index. $28. ISBN 0-87287-453-2.

_____. *Video-Based Information Systems: A Guide for Education, Business, Li- brary and Home Use.* Chicago: American Library Association, 1985. 240 pp. illus. in- dex. $30 pap. ISBN 0-8389-0429-4.

Serials Automation for Acquisition and Inventory Control. Edited by William Gray

Potter and Arlene Farber Sirkin. Chicago: American Library Association, 1981. 181 pp. bibliog. index. appendix. $15. ISBN 0-8389-3267-3.

Government Publications

New Technology and Documents Librarianship. Proceedings of the Third Annual Library Government Documents Information Conference. Edited by Peter Hernon. Westport, CT: Meckler, 1983. 107 pp. bibliog. $35. ISBN 0-930466-64-0.

Library Systems and Planning for Automation

Boss, Richard. *Library Manager's Guide to Automation,* 2nd ed. White Plains, NY: Knowledge Industry Publications, 1984. 169 pp. bibliog. index. appendix. $36.50; $27.50 pap. ISBN 0-86729-052-8; pap. 0-86729-051-X.

Corbin, John. *Developing Computer-Based Library Systems.* Phoenix, AZ: Oryx (A Neal-Schuman Professional Book), 1981. 226 pp. bibliog. index. appendix. $36. ISBN 0-912700-10-6.

Library Systems Evaluation Guide. 8 vols. Powell, OH: James E. Rush Associates, 1983–1986. about 250 pp. each. bibliog. index. appendix. individual volumes available separately. contact publisher for price. ISBN 0-912803-00-2 (set). Series includes volumes on public service, acquisition, management services, interlibrary loan, cataloging, serials control, circulation control, and integrated systems.

Matthews, Joseph R. *Choosing an Automated Library System: A Planning Guide.* Chicago: American Library Association, 1980. 119 pp. bibliog. index. $12.50 pap. ISBN 0-8389-0310-X.

————. *Directory of Automated Library Systems.* Library Automation Planning Guides No. 2. New York: Neal-Schuman, 1985. 217 pp. indexes. $34.95 pap. ISBN 0-918212-0.

A Reader on Choosing an Automated Library System. Edited by Joseph R. Matthews. Chicago: American Library Association, 1983. 390 pp. index. $35. ISBN 0-8389-0383-5.

Sager, Donald J. *Public Library Administrator's Planning Guide to Automation.* OCLC Library, Information and Computer Science Series No. 2. Dublin, OH: OCLC, 1983. 144 pp. bibliog. index. $12.50 pap. ISBN 0-933418-43-4.

Tedd, Lucy. *An Introduction to Computer-Based Library Systems,* 2nd ed. New York: Wiley, 1984. 262 pp. appendixes. index. $34.95. ISBN 0471-26285-A.

Microcomputers

The Application of Mini- and Micro-Computers in Information Documentation and Libraries. Contemporary Topics in Information Transfer, Vol. 3. $77. Edited by Carl Keren and Linda Perlmutter, New York: North-Holland, 1983. 801 pp. index. ISBN 0-444-86767-8.

Clark, Philip M. *Microcomputer Spreadsheet Models for Libraries: Preparing Documents, Budgets and Statistical Reports.* Chicago: American Library Association, 1985. 118 pp. illus. index. $24.95 pap. ISBN 0-8389-0403-3.

Costa, Betty, and Marie Costa. *A Micro Handbook for Small Libraries and Media Centers.* 2nd ed. Littleton, CO: Libraries Unlimited, 1986. 220 pp. bibliog. index. illus. appendixes. $23.50. ISBN 0-87287-523-3.

Dewey, Patrick R. *Public Access Microcomputers: A Handbook for Librarians.* White Plains, NY: Knowledge Industry Publications, 1984. 150 pp. bibliog. index. illus. appendixes. $34.50; $27.50 pap. ISBN 0-86729-086-2; pap. 0-86729-085-4.

Media and Microcopmputers in the Library: A Selected Annotated Bibliograhy. Edited by Evelyn H. Daniel and Carol Notowitz. Phoenix, AZ: Oryx, 1984. 157 pp. index. appendix. $27.50. ISBN 0-89774-117-X.

Microcomputers in Libraries. Edited by Ching-Chih Chen and Stacey E. B. Bressler. Applications in Information Management and Technology Series. New York: Neal-Schuman, 1982. 259 pp. bibliog. illus. index. $35. pap. ISBN 0-918212-61-8.

Micros at Work: Case Studies of Microcomputers in Libraries. Compiled by Jim Milliot. White Plains, NY: Knowledge Industry Publications, 1985. 148 pp. bibliog. index. appendixes. $36.50; $28.50 pap. ISBN 0-86729-117-6; pap. 0-86729-116-8.

Miller, Inabeth. *Microcomputers in School Library Media Centers.* New York: Neal-Schuman, 1984. 182 pp. bibliog. index. appendix. $24.95. ISBN 0-918212-51-0.

Naumer, Janet Noll. *Media Center Management with an Apple II.* Littleton, CO: Libraries Unlimited, 1984. 236 pp. index. illus. appendix. $19.50. pap. ISBN 0-87287-392-7.

Troutner, Joanne. *The Media Specialist, the Microcomputer and the Curriculum.* Littleton, CO: Libraries Unlimited, 1983. 197 pp. bibliog. index. appendix. $19.50. ISBN 0-87287-367-6.

Walton, Robert A. *Microcomputers: A Planning and Implementation Guide for Librarians and Information Professionals.* Phoenix, AZ: Oryx, 1983. 96 pp. bibliog. index. illus. appendix. $27.50. ISBN 0-89774-099-1.

Woods, Lawrence A., and Nolan F. Pope. *Librarian's Guide to Microcomputer Technology and Applications.* White Plains, NY: Published for the American Society for Information Science by Knowledge Industry Publications, 1983. 209 pp. bibliog. index. appendix. $34.50; $27.50 pap. ISBN 0-87629-045-5; pap. 0-87629-044-7.

Online Public Access Catalogs

Crawford, Walt. *MARC for Library Use: Understanding the USMARC Formats.* White Plains, NY: Knowledge Industry Publications, 1984. 222 pp. bibliog. glossary. index. appendixes. $36.50; $28.50 pap. ISBN 0-86729-120-6; pap. 0-86729-119-2.

Fayen, Emily Gallup. *The Online Catalog: Improving Public Access to Library Materials.* White Plains, NY: Knowledge Industry Publications. 1983. 148 pp. bibliog. index. appendixes. $34.50; $27.50 pap. ISBN 0-87629-054-4; pap. 0-87629-053-6.

Hildreth, Charles R. *Online Public Access Catalogs: The User Interface.* OCLC Library, Information and Computer Science Series. Dublin, OH: OCLC, 1982. 263 pp. bibliog. index. appendix. $18 pap. ISBN 0-933418-34-5.

Intner, Sheila S. *Access to Media: A Guide to Integrating and Computerizing Catalogs.* New York: Neal-Schuman, 1984. 301 pp. $37.50. index. glossary. appendixes. ISBN 0-918212-88-X.

Markey, Karen. *Subject Searching in Library Catalogs: Before and after the Introduction of Online Catalogs.* OCLC Library, Information and Computer Science Series No. 4. Dublin, OH: OCLC, 1984. 176 pp. bibliog. index. illus. appendixes. $21 pap. ISBN 0-933418-54-X.

Matthews, Joseph R. *Public Access to Online Catalogs,* 2nd ed. Library Automation Planning Guides No. 1. New York: Neal-Schuman, 1985. 497 pp. bibliog. glossary. index. $35 pap. ISBN 0-918212-89-8.

Online Catalogs, Online Reference: Converging Trends. (Proceedings of a Library and Information Technology Association Institute Meeting, June 23-24, 1983, Los Angeles). Library and Information Technology Series No. 2. Edited by Brian Aveney and Brett Butler. Chicago: American Library Association, 1984. 211 pp. no index. $20 pap. ISBN 0-8389-3308-4.

Public Access to Library Automation. Edited by J. L. Divilbliss. Clinic on Library Applications of Data Processing; 1980. Urbana: Graduate School of Library and Information Science, University of Illinois, 1981. 128 pp. illus. index. $10. ISBN 0-87845-065-3.

Using Online Catalogs: A Nationwide Survey. Edited by Joseph R. Matthews, Gary S. Lawrence, and Douglas K. Ferguson. New York: Neal-Schuman, 1983. 255 pp. $35 pap. ISBN 0-918212-76-6.

Online Searching

Chen, Ching-Chih, and Susanna Schweizer. *Online Bibliographic Searching: A Learning Manual.* Applications in Information Management and Technology Series. New York: Neal-Schuman, 1981. 227 pp. bibliog. illus. index. appendix. $24.95 pap. ISBN 0-918212-59-6.

Hartner, Elizabeth P. *An Introduction to Automated Literature Searching.* Books in Library and Information Science, Vol. 36. New York: Dekker, 1981. 145 pp. bibliog. index. appendix. $29.75 pap. ISBN 0-8247-1293-5.

Li, Tze-Chung. *An Introduction to Online Searching.* Contributions in Librarianship and Information Science No. 50. Westport, CT: Greenwood, 1984. 289 pp. bibliog. index. $27.95. ISBN 0-313-24274-7. ISSN 0084-9243.

Meadow, Charles T., and Pauline Atherton Cochrane. *Basics of Online Searching.* Information Science Series; A Wiley Interscience Publication. New York: Wiley, 1981. 245 pp. illus. index. appendix. $26.95. ISBN 0-471-05283-3.

Numeric Databases. Edited by Ching-Chih Chen and Peter Hernon. Norwood, NJ: Ablex, 1984. 332 pp. bibliog. index. illus. $37.50 pap. ISBN 0-89391-247-6.

Online Search Strategies. Professional Librarian Series. Edited by Ryan E. Hoover. White Plains, NY: Knowledge Industry Publications, 1982. 345 pp. bibliog. index. appendix. $37.50; $29.50 pap. ISBN 0-86729-005-6; pap. 0-86729-004-8.

Books, Late 1985 through 1986

Overview or Miscellaneous

Annual Review of Information Science and Technology. Vol. 20. Edited by Martha E. Williams. White Plains, NY: Knowledge Industry Publications for the American Society for Information Science, 1985. 360 pp. bibliog. index. $52.50. ISBN 0-86729-175-3. ISSN 0066-4200. Each year the progress and issues surrounding a selected group of general subjects are comprehensively discussed in review articles by noted authors. Among the sections composing this volume are "Information Delivery Systems" (treating videotex, teletext, cable, and satellite media), "Database Management Systems," "Expert Systems," and "Online Public Access Catalogs." Includes a cumulative keyword index for volumes 1–20.

ASIS '85: Proceedings of the 48th ASIS Annual Meeting. October 20–24, 1985. Edited by Carol A. Parkhurst. ASIS Proceedings, Vol. 22. White Plains, NY: Knowledge Industry Publications for the American Society for Information Science, 1985. index. $22.50 pap. ISBN 0-87629-176-1. ISSN 0044-7870. This collection of presented papers and abstracts offers a thought-provoking glimpse into state-of-the-art applications of library and information technology. The papers are grouped into five categories: (1) distribution, communication, and hardware, (2) databases – organization and access, (3) information products and services, (4) management, policy, and politics, (5) human factors – man-machine interface. The 82 contributions cover a wide field of subjects, but among the most intriguing are document delivery by satellite, videotex, a talking terminal for the blind, computer-aided instruction, and expert systems.

Crawford, Walt. *Technical Standards: An Introduction for Librarians.* Professional Librarian Series. White Plains, NY: Knowledge Industry Publications, 1986. 299 pp. appendix. bibliog. glossary. index. $36.50; $28.50 pap. ISBN 0-86729-192-3; 0-86729-191-5. Crawford brings to light the types of technical standards that operate inside and beyond the library, then surveys the development process of standards on the national and international levels. In the second half of the book he briefly summarizes the standards applicable to libraries and publishers. These cover topics ranging from the highly technical (such as synchronous signaling rates) to the formats for book spines. This book is not meant as a substitute for the actual standards, but rather as a guide to an otherwise perplexing and increasingly unavoidable field.

Reference and Online Services Handbook: Guidelines, Policies and Procedures for Librarians, Volume II. Edited by Bill Katz. New York: Neal-Schuman, 1986. 602 pp. index. $39.95. ISBN 0-918212-74-X. The editor has assembled a collection of materials contributed through a sampling of academic and public libraries. Reprinted in a standard type are 29 online policy statements, 16 user guides that explain or promote online searching services, 4 sets of instructions for using an online catalog, and 6 statements on microcomputer hardware and software, including a user agreement form.

School Library Media Annual 1985, Volume 3. Edited by Shirley L. Aaron and Pat R. Scales. Littleton, CO: Libraries Unlimited, 1985. 450 pp. $40. ISBN 0-87287-475-3. Included in this sourcebook are several valuable sections such as an annotated list of microcomputer software, compiled from recommendations by students and teachers. Review articles in the "Trends and Forecasts" section deal with telecommunications, interactive video (with a lengthy bibliography), and the use of microcomputers in elementary schools. Also contains a list of secondary schools using OCLC.

Tracy, Joan I. *Library Automation for Library Technicians: An Introduction.* Metuchen, NJ: Scarecrow Press, 1986. 163 pp. bibliog. glossary. index. $16. ISBN 0-8108-1865-5. "This book is intended for the person who plans to seek a position as a technician in a library with automated systems and the technicians employed in a library that has automated systems or will be installing them." The author begins with several chapters that describe the overall role of automation in library activities, then focuses on specific applications to the acquisitions, serials control, circulation, and related support functions. The clear presentation, effective use of illustrations, and the elementary level of the material allow for use in a variety of situations, such as training new employees or acquainting staff with the operations of other library departments.

Library Systems and Planning for Automation

Automated Library Systems in ARL Libraries. Systems and Procedures Exchange Center, Kit No. 126. Washington, DC: Office of Management Studies, Association of Research Libraries, 1986. 108 pp. $20 pap.; $10 for ARL members. ISSN 0160-3582. In the tradition of ARL SPEC Kits, this publication primarily consists of reproductions of actual planning and policy documents in use at ARL member libraries. The documents included in this kit are concerned with prepurchase or design decisions, staff responsibilities for operating the system, and organizational changes related to system implementation. Updates SPEC Kit No. 90, 1983.

Barcoding of Collections in ARL Libraries. Systems and Procedures Exchange Center, Kit No. 124. Washington, DC: Office of Management Studies, Association of Research Libraries, 1986. 118 pp. $20 pap.; $10 for ARL members. ISSN 0160-3582. A report of a survey of 88 ARL libraries on the barcoding systems used at their institutions. Following a presentation of the survey results, materials contributed by the respondents document decision processes with regard to equipment, training, staffing, and maintenance.

Corbin, John. *Managing the Library Automation Project.* Phoenix, AZ: Oryx, 1985. appendixes. bibliog. glossary. index. $35. ISBN 0-89774-151-X. "The purpose of this book is to provide a practical handbook and guide for the librarian untrained in systems development, and perhaps even unfamiliar with computers, who is nonetheless responsible for developing an automated library system." Corbin offers a reasonably thorough, methodical approach to the complicated process of acquiring and installing an automated system. Among the topics treated are selecting the appropriate system, writing a Request for Proposal (RFP), site preparation, data conversion, system acceptance, and staff education. Corbin focuses on effective organization and developing an effective approach to decision making. Appendixes contain sample job descriptions, an equipment inventory list, and a sample RFP. A revised edition of the author's *Developing Computer Based Library Systems* (1983).

Grosch, Audrey N. *Distributed Computing and the Electronic Library: Micros to Superminis.* Professional Librarian Series. White Plains, NY: Knowledge Industry Publications, 1985. 205 pp. appendix. bibliog. glossary. index. $36.50; pap. $28.50. ISBN 0-86729-145-1; pap. 0-86729-144-3. "This volume is intended as a basic source for librarian and information specialists who need to acquire some background in the current state of distributed systems for libraries or information centers." The current state of affairs from the perspective of the library is represented by the results of a survey (296 responses) on the type of systems in use, applications, networking activities, and user

satisfaction. Later chapters describe the available systems, then profile the major vendors and trends in the United States and abroad. The appendixes include a directory of installed systems at 92 libraries (with brief notes on each) and a directory of library hardware and software suppliers.

Microcomputers

Downloading/Uploading Online Databases and Catalogs: Proceedings of the Congress for Librarians, February 18, 1985, St. John's University, NY. Library Hi Tech Special Studies Series No 1. Edited by Bella Hass Weinberg and James A. Benson. Ann Arbor, MI: Pierian Press, 1985. 136 pp. appendixes, bibliog. glossary. index. $24.50 pap. ISBN 0-87650-195-1. By adding supplementary materials to the conference proceedings, the editors have almost created a primer for librarians investigating the field of database downloading. The volume begins with an effective introduction to the terminology. Subsequent papers are grouped into four sections covering hardware, software, applications, and copyright considerations. The section on applications describes projects undertaken by libraries to compile bibliographies and manage downloaded bibliographic databases. A glossary and comprehensive bibliography (380 citations) complete this exceptional work.

Local Area Networks: The Los Angeles Chapter of ASIS Seminar Proceedings. Edited by Wendy Culotta, Zorana Ercegovac, and Dana Roth. Studio City, CA: Pacific Information, 1985. 174 pp. bibliog. index. $28.50 pap. ISBN 0-913203-12-2. Broader in scope than the title suggests, this set of proceedings presents the views and experiences of the conference participants concerning wide area networks, local area networks, and the future of networking in general. The volume consists of presented papers and the discussions of three different panels, composed of users, vendors, and systems designers.

Microcomputer Software Policies in ARL Libraries. Systems and Procedures Exchange Center, Kit No. 123. Washington, DC: Office of Management Studies, Association of Research Libraries, 1986. 114 pp. $20; $10 to ARL members. ISSN 0160-3582. The first section presents the results of a survey of the members of the Association of Research Libraries concerning their policies on the acquisition and circulation of software. Following this discussion are reprints of seven acquisition and collection development policies, five user and circulation policies, along with the reports of two task forces.

Van Young, Sayre. *MicroSource: Where to Find Answers to Questions about Microcomputers.* Littleton, CO: Libraries Unlimited, 1986. 250 pp. bibliog. indexes. $22.50. ISBN 0-87287-527-X. In his own words the author sought "to prepare a pathfinder of information for librarians faced with building a collection in an entirely new subject, keeping in mind the questions I had asked when entering the microcomputer world." Based on actual reference questions he collected, Van Young constructed a sourcebook and core bibliography targeted primarily to medium-sized school and public libraries. Chapters offer sources to consult for purchasing hardware and software, locating free and easy materials, understanding telecommunications, and the full range of topics of interest to the beginner. He begins each chapter with a set of reference questions, introduces the topic, then lists possible sources while noting the advantages and disadvantages of each.

Online Searching

End-User Searching Services. Systems and Procedures Exchange Center, Kit No. 122. Washington, DC: Office of Management Studies, Association of Research Libraries, 1986. 112 pp. bibliog. $20 pap.; $10 for ARL members. ISSN 0160-3582. The contributed policy statements are grouped into the following areas: grant proposal for an end user program (one document); program descriptions including goals, objectives, and staff responsibilities (five); publicity fliers (four); instructional tools, such as point-of-use material, worksheets, flip charts, and formal guides (nine); and program evaluation materials (six).

Feinglos, Susan J. *MEDLINE: A Basic Guide to Searching.* MLA Information Series. Chicago: Medical Library Association, 1985. appendixes. bibliog. index. $20 pap. ISBN 0-912176-16-9. Feinglos has skillfully organized an introduction to searching MEDLINE on the systems of the National Library of Medicine, DIALOG, and Bibliographic Retrieval Services. While not intended to replace the more detailed manuals supplied by the vendors, this work provides comprehensive treatment of all relevant areas: database contents, indexing policies, handling MeSH, performing a search interview, and many others. Particular attention is paid to the formulation of efficient search strategies with six sample strategies worked out in detail. Clear examples supporting the text are abundant. A glossary and a 12-part appendix complete this valuable guide, which has information to offer novices and experienced users.

Managing Online Reference Services. Edited by Ethel Auster. New York: Neal-Schuman, 1986. 408 pp. bibliog. indexes. $35 pap. 0-918212-93-6. Auster gathered outstanding articles published between 1975 and 1984 as background material for both planners and current managers. The material is organized around eight topics: overall planning, selecting online services, training staff, marketing, financial considerations, evaluation of the service, use of a microcomputer, and the impact of online services. Each section contains an introduction, followed by three to four articles and a bibliography. The high standards for inclusion applied by the compiler are apparent in this partial list of contributors: Marcia Bates, Pauline Atherton Cochrane, Walt Crawford, F. W. Lancaster, Mary Jo Lynch, Carol Tenopir, and Martha E. Williams.

Periodicals

No attempt has been made to examine all pertinent journal articles or to derive a list of the "best." The sheer number of articles published in 1986 makes this an impossible task. Instead, this section cites significant review articles, supplements and special issues of journals, superior columns, and journals that regularly publish items of interest and high quality. Once again, the guiding principle has been to list publications of practical value for a general audience of librarians.

Overview or Miscellaneous

Information Technology and Libraries. Quarterly. Edited by William Gray Potter. American Library Association, 50 E. Huron St., Chicago, IL 60611. 1968– . $25. ISSN 0730-9295. The official publication of the Library and Information Technology Association. Although the discussion is more often handled from a scholarly perspective than a practical one, the articles are informative, well researched, authoritative, and

timely. Contributions in 1986 deal with policies for microcomputers in libraries, expert systems, electronic imaging, health risks involved with photocopiers, and quality control in OCLC.

"Library Computing: A Special Supplement to *Library Journal* and *School Library Journal.*" May 1986 and November 1986. Beginning with the November 1986 issue, separate editions of this semiannual supplement were produced for each journal. "Designed to provide basic and introductory articles on various aspects of library automation." Topics discussed during the year include online searching in a high school, purchasing and installing a telephone system, creating databases with students, online remote public access to the library, and electronic bulletin boards operated by libraries, including a directory of systems now operating or scheduled to be implemented.

Library Hi-Tech. Quarterly. Edited by C. Edward Wall. Pierian Press, Box 1808, Ann Arbor, MI 48106. Summer 1983– . Institutions $45; individuals $25. ISSN 0737-8831. Excellent articles with a broad range of appeal, due to the variety of subject matter and the understandable presentations. Topics covered during 1986 include electronic document delivery, CD-ROM, online public access catalogs, gateway services, and laser discs. Updated by *Library Hi-Tech News.* Discounts available on combined subscriptions.

Library Technology Reports: Authoritative Information on Library Systems, Equipment and Supplies. Bimonthly. Edited by Howard S. White. American Library Association, 50 E. Huron St., Chicago, IL 60611. 1965– . $155. ISSN 0024-2586. Each issue is in fact a monograph devoted to a review of products in a particular field of technology. Recent subjects include automated circulation systems, private branch exchange (PBX) telephone systems, electronic news gathering television cameras, microcomputer circulation systems, and word processing software packages. The research is consistently thorough and reliable in this outstanding guide.

Optical Information Systems (formerly *Videodisc and Optical Disc*). Bimonthly. Edited by Judith Paris Roth. Meckler Publishing Corp., 11 Ferry Lane W., Westport, CT 06880. 1981– . $95. ISSN 0886-5809. The content and style of the articles vary considerably—some focus on specific, technical topics, yet many others serve as important introductions and reference guides. In 1986 special issues appeared on optical systems in health care, a directory of organizations working with CD-ROM technology, a glossary of CD-ROM terminology, and an overview of optical publishing. Each issue contains a calendar of upcoming events, and an ongoing report tracks the progress of videodisc projects in the public and private sectors. Companion newsletter is *Optical Information Systems Update.*

"Perspectives on Telecommunication: Principles, Developments, Prospects." Edited by Lois F. Lunin and Larry L. Learn. *Journal of the American Society for Information Science* 6 (November 1986): 401–35. The editor states her purpose to be the creation of a tutorial to help the general reader understand the fundamentals of telecommunication. Beyond achieving this basic goal, the series of papers that compose this special section also provide insight into the regulatory environment surrounding the industry, the evolution of information networks, teleprocessing, international communications, and the future of the technology.

"Role of Computers in Sci-Tech Libraries." Edited by Ellis Mount. *Science and Technology Libraries* 6 (Summer 1986). The first article in this special issue summarizes the 160

responses to a questionnaire on the use of microcomputers in sci-tech libraries. Specifically the questionnaire treated hardware purchases, local applications, levels of user access, and problems encountered. Another contribution compares the use of online and print sources, based on experiences in an academic library. Remaining articles describe particular applications: a UNIX-based catalog, statistics generated from a library computer, and the use of a microcomputer for multiple functions in a special library.

Swora, Tamara, and Audrey Fischer. "Technical Services in 1984 and 1985: Micrographics, Optical Disk Technology and Fair Use." *Library Resources and Technical Services* 30 (July/September 1986): 183–217. The scope of this review article is consistent with the title. The authors not only discuss new publications but also the work of conferences, the progress toward technical standards, and other relevant events.

Wilson Library Bulletin. 10/yr. Edited by Milo Nelson. H. W. Wilson, 950 University Ave., Bronx, NY 10452. 1914–   . $35. ISSN 0043-5651. In the last few years this general interest publication has been adding significant coverage of automation, especially online searching. It is particularly noteworthy for the regular columns: "School Library Technology," "Online Update," "Microcomputing," "Cutting Edge," and "Using Software."

Library Systems and Planning for Automation

Matthews, Joseph R. "Growth and Consolidation: The 1985 Automated Library System Marketplace." *Library Journal* 111 (April 1, 1986): 25–37. "The progress and pitfalls experienced by the automated library system marketplace during 1985 are reviewed in this annual article." Matthews profiles industry activity in four areas: turnkey systems, software developed by libraries, microcomputer software, and COM catalogs. The fascinating text is interwoven with a series of tables and charts depicting the number of customers with installed systems by turnkey and software vendors, market share of 1985 installations, size of systems by number of terminals, and a vendor directory arranged by the function of the system.

Microcomputers

Library Software Review. Bimonthly. Edited by Nancy Melin Nelson. Meckler Publishing Corp., 11 Ferry Lane W., Westport, CT 06880. 1982–   . $69. ISSN 0742-5759. Generally contains six to ten articles that describe new applications for, or personal experiences with, commercially available programs of interest to information professionals, a lengthy review of featured software, a series of shorter reviews, and a special interest column for Apple computer users. Optical systems also received attention in 1986.

Mason, Robert M. "Mason on Micros." See issues of *Library Journal.* A column that incorporates news with evaluation, advice, and philosophy. In 1986, subjects include improvements in word processing software, support for hardware and software, and advances in compact discs. Pleasurable and informative reading.

Microcomputers for Information Management: An International Journal for Library and Information Services. Quarterly. Edited by Ching-chih Chen. Ablex Publishing Corp., 355 Chestnut St., Norwood, NJ 07648. $65 institutions; $29.50 individuals.

ISSN 0742-2342. At first glance one might judge this journal as being too technical, scholarly, or international in coverage to offer much to the average librarian. Through closer examination one will encounter superb introductions to new technology and useful presentations of local accomplishments. Recent issues discuss expert systems for reference work, the use of Pro-Cite to create a serials database, and file management using MS-DOS. The editor appears to be achieving his goal "to highlight new trends and developments, while not losing sight of the basic library and information management applications."

Online Searching

Database: The Magazine of Database Reference and Review. Bimonthly. Edited by Helen A. Gordon. Online, 11 Tannery Lane, Weston, CT 06883. 1978– . $78. ISSN 0162-4105. Typical issues of this essential publication may contain a mixture of database profiles and comparisons, detailed tips on searching, guides to the online literature, plus a collection of dependably worthwhile columns. "Caduceus" offers expert insight into the searching of biomedical files. "Silver Disk" reports on new developments in the field of laser/optical technologies. Items of special note appearing in 1986 are a two-part description of full-text newspaper files with a chart outlining the strengths of 57 titles in more than 150 subject areas, and half of a four-part series (the remainder appearing in *Online*) composing a directory of laser disc files.

Online: The Magazine of Online Information Systems. Bimonthly. Edited by Helen A. Gordon. Online, 11 Tannery Lane, Weston, CT 06883. 1978– . $78. ISSN 0146-5422. Each issue contains a wealth of material for the online searcher looking to explore new databases, sharpen searching skills, or keep current with new products. Broader in scope than its title may suggest, coverage regularly includes microcomputer software along with optical/digital technologies. Shares some of the excellent columns ("Caduceus," "Hardcopy," and "The Silver Disk") with its companion journal, *Database*.

"Perspectives on Online Searching." Edited by Lois F. Lunin and Donald T. Hawkins. *Journal of the American Society for Information Science* 37 (July 1986): 179–270. A 20-year overview of the development of the online database industry. Discusses natural language processing methods, end user searching, gateway retrieval systems, and an outlook toward the future. Includes a lengthy bibliography.

Tenopir, Carol. "Online Databases." See issues of *Library Journal*, generally the first issue of the month. An excellent two-page column that concentrates on a single issue. In 1986 the author addressed CD-ROM databases, user reaction to a laser disc bibliographic searching system, and online searching in elementary and secondary schools. Each column is carefully written, thoroughly researched, and contains an amount of information equal to that of a feature article in other periodicals.

Appendix

Sources consulted for book reviews include the following:

Bulletin of the Medical Library Association
College and Research Libraries

Database
Information Technology and Libraries
Journal of Academic Librarianship
Library Hi-Tech News
Library Journal
Library Science Annual
Online
RQ
Special Libraries
Wilson Library Bulletin

Basic Publications for the Publisher and the Book Trade

Jean Peters

Librarian, R. R. Bowker Company

Bibliographies of the Book Trade

Gottlieb, Robin. *Publishing Children's Books in America, 1919-1976: An Annotated Bibliography.* New York: Children's Book Council, 1978. pap. $10.

Lee, Marshall. *Bookmaking: The Illustrated Guide to Design/Production/ Editing.* New York: R. R. Bowker, 1980. $44.95. Bibliography is divided into four parts: Part 1 covers books and includes a general bibliography as well as extensive coverage of books on all technical aspects of bookmaking; Part 2 lists periodicals; Part 3 lists films, filmstrips, etc.; Part 4 lists other sources.

The Reader's Adviser: A Layman's Guide to Literature. 13th ed. New York: R. R. Bowker, 1986. $195 (Vols. 1-3); $75 each vol. Vol. 1. *The Best in American and British Fiction, Poetry, Essays, Literary Biography, Bibliography, and Reference,* edited by Fred Kaplan. Vol. 2. *The Best in American and British Drama and World Literature in English*

Translation, edited by Maurice Charney. Vol. 3. *The Best in the Reference Literature of the World,* edited by Paula Kaufman. Forthcoming 1988: Vol. 4. *The Best in the Literature of Philosophy and World Religions,* edited by William Reese. Vol. 5. *The Best in the Literature of Science, Technology, and Medicine,* edited by Paul T. Durbin.

Tanselle, G. Thomas. *Guide to the Study of United States Imprints.* 2 vols. Cambridge, MA: Belknap Press of Harvard University Press, 1971. $80. Includes sections on general studies of American printing and publishing as well as studies of individual printers and publishers.

Trade Bibliographies

American Book Publishing Record Cumulative, 1876-1949: An American National Bibliography. 15 vols. New York: R. R. Bowker, 1980. $1,995.

American Book Publishing Record Cu-

mulative, 1950–1977: An American National Bibliography. 15 vols. New York: R. R. Bowker, 1979. $1,995.

American Book Publishing Record Cumulative, 1876–1982. New York: R. R. Bowker. Microfiche $999.

American Book Publishing Record Five-Year Cumulatives. New York: R. R. Bowker, 1960–1964 Cumulative. 5 vols. $150. 1965–1969 Cumulative. 5 vols. $150. 1970–1974 Cumulative. 4 vols. $150. 1975–1979 Cumulative. 5 vols. $175. 1980–1984 Cumulative. 5 vols. $199. Annual vols.: 1978, $59; 1979, $59; 1980, $59; 1981, $82.50; 1982, $82.50; 1983, $82.50; 1984, $89.95; 1985, $110; 1986, $110.

Books in Print. 6 vols. New York: R. R. Bowker, ann. $225. fiche $550.

Books in Print Supplement. New York: R. R. Bowker, ann. $119.

Books in Series in the United States. 4th ed. New York: R. R. Bowker, 1984. 6 vols. $325.

British Books in Print. New York: R. R. Bowker, 1985. $249.95 (plus duty where applicable).

Canadian Books in Print, edited by Marian Butler. Toronto: University of Toronto Press, ann. $70.

Canadian Books in Print: Subject Index, edited by Marian Butler. Toronto: University of Toronto Press, ann. $55.

Cumulative Book Index. New York: H. W. Wilson. Monthly with bound semi-annual and larger cumulations. Service basis.

El-Hi Textbooks in Print. New York: R. R. Bowker, ann. $75.

Forthcoming Books. New York: R. R. Bowker. $95 a year. Bimonthly supplement to *Books in Print.*

Large Type Books in Print. New York: R. R. Bowker, 1985. $59.

On Cassette: A Comprehensive Bibliography of Spoken Word Audio Cassettes. New York: R. R. Bowker, 1986. $59.95.

Paperbound Books in Print. New York: R. R. Bowker. Spring, 1986, 3-vol. set $110. Fall, 1986, 3-vol. set $110.

Publishers' Trade List Annual. New York: R. R. Bowker, ann. 4 vols. $149.95.

Reginald, Robert, and Burgess, M. R. *Cumulative Paperback Index, 1939–59.* Detroit: Gale, 1973. $58.

Small Press Record of Books in Print, edited by Len Fulton. Paradise, CA: Dustbooks, 1985. $29.95.

Subject Guide to Books in Print. 4 vols. New York: R. R. Bowker, ann. $159.95.

Subject Guide to Forthcoming Books. New York: R. R. Bowker. $65 a year.

Book Publishing

Education and Practice

Bailey, Herbert S., Jr. *The Art and Science of Book Publishing.* Austin: University of Texas Press, 1980. pap. o.p.

Biggs, Mary. *Publishers and Librarians: A Foundation for Dialogue.* Chicago: University of Chicago Press, 1984. pap. $5.95.

Bodian, Nat G. *Book Marketing Handbook: Tips and Techniques for the Sale and Promotion of Scientific, Technical, Professional, and Scholarly Books and Journals.* New York: R. R. Bowker, 1980. $59.95.

_____. *Book Marketing Handbook, Volume Two: 1,000 More Tips and Techniques for the Sale and Promotion of Scientific, Technical, Professional, and Scholarly Books and Journals.* New York: R. R. Bowker, 1983. $59.95.

_____. *Copywriter's Handbook: A Practical Guide for Advertising and Promotion of Specialized and Scholarly Books and Journals.* Philadelphia: ISI, 1984. pap. $19.95.

Brownstone, David M. *The Dictionary of Publishing.* New York: Van Nostrand Reinhold, 1982. $21.95.

Carter, Robert A. *Trade Book Marketing: A Practical Guide.* New York: R. R. Bowker, 1983. pap. $19.95.

Dessauer, John P. *Book Publishing: What It Is, What It Does.* New York: R. R. Bowker, 1981. $29.95. pap. $15.95.

Glaister, Geoffrey. *Glaister's Glossary of the Book: Terms Used in Paper-Making, Printing, Bookbinding, and Publishing.* 2nd ed., completely rev. Berkeley: University of California Press, 1979. $75.

Grannis, Chandler B. *Getting into Book Publishing.* New York: R. R. Bowker, 1983. Pamphlet, one free; in bulk 75¢ each.

_____, ed. *What Happens in Book Publishing.* 2nd ed. New York: Columbia University Press, 1967. $40.

Greenfeld, Howard. *Books: From Writer to Reader.* New York: Crown, 1976. pap. $4.95.

Gross, Gerald. *Editors on Editing.* Rev. ed. New York: Harper & Row, 1985. $24.45. pap. $12.95.

Huenefeld, John. *The Huenefeld Guide to Book Publishing.* Bedford, MA: Huenefeld Co., 1986. $185.

Mora, Imre. *Publisher's Practical Dictionary in 20 Languages.* Munich: K. G. Saur, 1984. $65.

Peters, Jean, ed. *Bookman's Glossary.* 6th ed. New York: R. R. Bowker, 1983. $24.95.

Powell, Walter W. *Getting into Print: The Decision-making Process in Scholarly Publishing.* Chicago: University of Chicago Press, 1985. $19.95.

Poynter, Dan. *The Self-Publishing Manual: How to Write, Print and Sell Your Own Book.* Santa Barbara, CA: Para Publishing, 1986. $14.95.

Richards, Pamela Spence. *Marketing Books and Journals to Western Europe.* Phoenix, AZ: Oryx, 1985. pap. $22.50.

Analysis, Statistics, Surveys

Altbach, Philip G., Arboleda, Amadio A., and Gopinathan, S., eds. *Publishing in the Third World: Knowledge and Development.* Portsmouth, NH: Heinemann Educational Books, 1985. $35.

Altbach, Philip G., and Rathgeber, Eva-Marie. *Publishing in the Third World: Trend Report and Bibliography.* New York: Praeger, 1980. $39.95.

Arthur Andersen & Co. *Book Distribution in the U.S.: Issues and Perceptions.* New York: Book Industry Study Group, 1982. $60.

Association of American Publishers 1985 Industry Statistics. New York: Association of American Publishers, 1986. Nonmemb. $300.

Association of American Publishers. *1987 Survey of Compensation and Personnel Practices in the Publishing Industry.* Prepared and Conducted by Sibson & Co., Inc. New York: Association of American Publishers, 1987. Available only to AAP members. Price not set.

Bowker Annual of Library and Book Trade Information. New York: R. R. Bowker, ann. $89.95.

Center for Book Research. *1985 Library Acquisition Survey.* New York: Association of American Publishers, 1985. pap. $45 to AAP members; $150 to nonmembers.

Compaine, Benjamin. *The Book Industry in Transition: An Economic Analysis of Book Distribution and Marketing.* White Plains, NY: Knowledge Industry Publications, 1978. $29.95.

_____, ed. *Who Owns the Media? Concentration of Ownership in the Communications Industry.* 2nd ed. White Plains, NY: Knowledge Industry Publications, 1982. $45.

Coser, Lewis A., Kadushin, Charles, and Powell, Walter W. *Books: The Culture and Commerce of Publishing.* New York: Basic Books, 1982. $19.

Dessauer, John P. *Book Industry Trends 1986.* New York: Book Industry Study Group, 1986. $150.

_____. *Trends Update* (monthly). Ex-

pands upon statistics in the annual compilation and explains forecasting techniques. $240 a year. $25 single copy.

Fox, Mary F., ed. *Scholarly Writing and Publishing: Issues, Problems, and Solutions.* Boulder, CO: Westview, 1985. $30. pap. $15.

Gedin, Per. *Literature in the Marketplace.* Trans. by George Bisset. Woodstock, NY: Overlook, 1977. $12.95.

Geiser, Elizabeth, and Dolin, Arnold, eds. *The Business of Book Publishing.* Boulder, CO: Westview, 1985. $38.75.

Graubard, Steven R., ed. *Reading in the 1980s.* New York: R. R. Bowker, 1983. $19.95.

Kozol, Jonathan. *Illiterate America.* Garden City, NY: Doubleday, 1985. $35. pap. $15.95.

Long, Elizabeth. *The American Dream and the Popular Novel.* Boston: Routledge & Kegan Paul, 1985. $22.50.

Machlup, Fritz, and Leeson, Kenneth W. *Information through the Printed Word: The Dissemination of Scholarly, Scientific, and Intellectual Knowledge,* 4 vols. Vol. 1. *Book Publishing.* Vol. 2. *Journals.* Vol. 3. *Libraries.* Vol. 4. *Books, Journals, and Bibliographic Services.* New York: Praeger, 1978. Vol. 1, $42.95; Vol. 2, $42.95; Vol. 3, $40.95; Vol. 4, $42.95.

1983 Consumer Research Study on Reading and Book Purchasing. New York: Book Industry Study Group, 1984. 3 vols. $5,000.

Shatzkin, Leonard. *In Cold Type: Overcoming the Book Crisis.* Boston: Houghton Mifflin, 1983. pap. $8.95.

Walters, Ray. *Paperback Talk.* Derived from the author's column "Paperback Talk" and articles contributed by him to *The New York Times Book Review.* With an introduction by Ian and Betty Ballantine. Chicago: Academy Chicago Publishers, 1985. $19.95. pap. $9.95.

Whiteside, Thomas. *The Blockbuster Complex.* Middletown, CT: Wesleyan University Press. Dist. by Columbia University Press, 1981. $17.50.

History

Bruccoli, Matthew J. *The Fortunes of Mitchell Kennerley, Bookman.* San Diego: Harcourt Brace Jovanovich, 1986. $24.95.

Bussy, R. Kenneth. *Two Hundred Years of Publishing: A History of the Oldest Publishing Company in the United States, Lea & Febiger, 1785–1985.* Philadelphia: Lea & Febiger, 1985. $12.50.

Carpenter, Kenneth E., ed. *Books and Society in History: Papers of the ACRL Rare Books and Manuscripts Preconference June 1980, Boston, Mass.* New York: R. R. Bowker, 1983. $29.95.

Cave, Roderick. *The Private Press.* New York: R. R. Bowker, 1983. $59.95.

Cerf, Bennett. *At Random: The Reminiscences of Bennett Cerf.* New York: Random House, 1977. $12.95.

Crider, Allen Billy. *Mass Market Publishing in America.* Boston: G. K. Hall, 1982. $36.50.

Davis, Kenneth C. *Two-Bit Culture: The Paperbacking of America.* Boston: Houghton Mifflin, 1984. $18.95. pap. $9.95.

Dennison, Sally. [*Alternative*] *Literary Publishing: Five Modern Histories.* Iowa City: University of Iowa Press, 1984. $12.95. pap. $9.95.

Dzwonkoski, Peter, ed. *American Literary Publishing Houses, 1900–1980: Trade and Paperback.* Detroit: Gale, 1986. (Dictionary of Literary Biography, vol. 46). $176.

Hall, Max. *Harvard University Press: A History.* Cambridge, MA: Harvard University Press, 1986. $20.

Haydn, Hiram. *Words & Faces.* New York: Harcourt Brace Jovanovich, 1974. $8.95.

Joyce, Donald F. *Gatekeepers of Black Culture: Black-owned Book Publishing in the United States.* Westport, CT: Greenwood Press, 1983. $29.95.

Madison, Charles. *Jewish Publishing in America.* New York: Hebrew Publishing Co., 1976. $15.

Morpurgo, J. E. *Allen Lane: King Penguin.* New York: Methuen, 1980. $25.

Norrie, Ian. *Mumby's Publishing and Bookselling in the Twentieth Century.* 6th ed. London: Bell & Hyman, 1982. Dist. by R. R. Bowker. $35.

Regnery, Henry. *Memoirs of a Dissident Publisher.* New York: Harcourt Brace Jovanovich, 1979. $12.95.

Schwed, Peter. *Turning the Pages: An Insider's Story of Simon and Schuster, 1924–1984.* New York: Macmillan, 1984, $17.95.

Silverman, Al, ed. *The Book of the Month: Sixty Years of Books in American Life.* Boston: Little, Brown, 1986. $17.95.

Stern, Madeleine B. *Books and Book People in 19th-Century America.* New York: R. R. Bowker, 1978. $29.95.

————. *Publishers for Mass Entertainment in Nineteenth Century America.* Boston: G. K. Hall, 1980. $29.50.

Tebbel, John. *Between Covers: The Rise and Transformation of Book Publishing in America.* New York: Oxford University Press, 1987. $24.95.

————. *A. History of Book Publishing in the United States.* 4 vols. Vol. 1. *The Creation of an Industry, 1630–1865.* Vol. 2. *The Expansion of an Industry, 1865–1919.* Vol. 3. *The Golden Age between Two Wars, 1920–1940.* Vol. 4. *The Great Change, 1940–1980.* New York: R. R. Bowker, 1972, 1975, 1978, 1981. $39.95 each.

Book Design and Production

Grannis, Chandler B. *The Heritage of the Graphic Arts.* New York: R. R. Bowker, 1972. o.p.

Lee, Marshall. *Bookmaking: The Illustrated Guide to Design and Production.* 2nd ed. New York: R. R. Bowker, 1980. $44.95.

Mintz, Patricia Barnes. *Dictionary of Graphic Arts Terms: A Communication Tool for People Who Buy Type & Printing.* New York: Van Nostrand Reinhold, 1981. $23.95.

Rice, Stanley. *Book Design: Systematic Aspects.* New York: R. R. Bowker, 1978. $19.95.

————. *Book Design: Text Format Models.* New York: R. R. Bowker, 1978. $19.95.

White, Jan. *Editing by Design.* 2nd ed. New York: R. R. Bowker, 1982, pap. $29.95.

Williamson, Hugh. *Methods of Book Design: The Practice of an Industrial Craft.* 3rd ed. New Haven, CT: Yale University Press, 1983. $45. pap. $13.95.

Wilson, Adrian. *The Design of Books.* Layton, UT: Gibbs M. Smith, 1974. pap. $10.95.

Bookselling

Manual on Bookselling: How to Open and Run Your Own Bookstore. 3rd ed. New York: American Booksellers Association, 1980. Dist. by Harmony Books. $12.95.

White, Ken. *Bookstore Planning and Design.* New York: McGraw-Hill, 1982. $49.50.

Censorship

de Grazia, Edward, comp. *Censorship Landmarks.* New York: R. R. Bowker, 1969. o.p.

The First Freedom Today: Critical Issues Relating to Censorship and Intellectual Freedom, edited by Robert B. Downs and Ralph F. McCoy. Chicago: American Library Association, 1984. $40.

Gregorian, Vartan. *Censorship: Five Hundred Years of Conflict*. New York: Oxford University Press, 1984. $32.50.

Haight, Anne Lyon. *Banned Books*. 4th ed., updated and enlarged by Chandler B. Grannis. New York: R. R. Bowker, 1978. o.p.

Hentoff, Nat. *The First Freedom: The Tumultuous History of Free Speech in America*. New York: Delacorte, 1980. $11.95. Dell. pap. $2.50.

Hurwitz, Leon. *Historical Dictionary of Censorship in the United States*. Westport, CT: Greenwood Press, 1985. $55.

Jenkinson, Edward B. *Censors in the Classroom: The Mind Benders*. Carbondale, IL: Southern Illinois University Press, 1982. pap. $3.50.

Copyright

Johnston, Donald F. *Copyright Handbook*. 2nd ed. New York: R. R. Bowker, 1982. $29.95.

Strong, William S. *The Copyright Book: A Practical Guide*. Cambridge, MA: MIT Press, 1984. $13.95.

Editing

Barzun, Jacques. *Simple and Direct: A Rhetoric for Writers*. New York: Harper & Row, 1985. $14.50. pap. $6.95.

Bernstein, Theodore. *The Careful Writer*. New York: Atheneum, 1965. pap. $10.95.

The Chicago Manual of Style, 13th rev. ed. Chicago: University of Chicago Press, 1982. $35.

Fowler, H. W. *Dictionary of Modern English Usage*. 2nd rev. ed. New York: Oxford University Press, 1983. pap. $8.95.

Jordan, Lewis. *The New York Times Manual of Style and Usage*. New York: Times Books, 1982. pap. $5.95.

Plotnik, Arthur. *The Elements of Editing: A Modern Guide for Editors and Jour-*

nalists. New York: Macmillan, 1982. $9.50. pap. $4.95.

Skillin, Marjorie E., and Gay, Robert M. *Words into Type*. Rev. ed. Englewood Cliffs, NJ: Prentice-Hall, 1974. $34.95.

Strunk, William, Jr., and White, E. B. *The Elements of Style*. 3rd ed. New York: Macmillan, 1979. $6.95. pap. $2.25.

Zinsser, William. *On Writing Well: An Informal Guide to Writing Nonfiction*. 2nd ed. New York: Harper & Row, 1985. $12.45.

Editors, Agents, Authors

Appelbaum, Judith, and Evans, Nancy. *How to Get Happily Published*. New York: NAL, 1982. $6.95.

Berg, A. Scott. *Max Perkins: Editor of Genius*. New York: Washington Square Press, 1983. pap. $5.95.

Commins, Dorothy Berliner. *What Is an Editor? Saxe Commins at Work*. Chicago: University of Chicago Press, 1978. pap. $5.95.

Curtis, Richard. *How to Be Your Own Literary Agent*. Boston: Houghton Mifflin, 1983. $12.95. pap. $7.95.

Dill, Barbara. *The Journalist's Handbook on Libel and Privacy*. New York: Free Press, 1986. $19.95.

Henderson, Bill, ed. *The Art of Literary Publishing: Editors on Their Craft*. Yonkers, NY: Pushcart, 1980. $15.

Meyer, Carol. *Writer's Survival Manual: The Complete Guide to Getting Your Book Published*. New York: Crown, 1982. $13.95. Bantam, 1984, pap. $3.95.

Unseld, Siegfried. *The Author and His Publisher*. Chicago: University of Chicago Press, 1980. $15.

Electronic Publishing

Bove, Tony. *The Art of Desktop Publishing: Using Personal Computers to Pub-*

lish It Yourself. New York: Bantam, 1986. $18.95.

Compaine, Benjamin. *Understanding New Media: Trends and Issues in Electronic Distribution of Information.* Cambridge, MA: Ballinger, 1984. $29.95.

Greenberger, Martin, ed. *Electronic Publishing Plus: Media for a Technological Future.* White Plains, NY: Knowledge Industry Publications, 1985. $45.

Neustadt, Richard M. *The Birth of Electronic Publishing: Legal and Economic Issues in Telephone, Cable and Over-the-Air Teletext and Videotext.* White Plains, NY: Knowledge Industry Publications, 1982. $32.95.

Roth, Stephen F. *The Computer Edge.* New York: R. R. Bowker, 1985. $24.95.

Spigai, Frances, and Sommer, Peter. *Guide to Electronic Publishing: Opportunities in Online and Viewdata Services.* White Plains, NY: Knowledge Industry Publications, 1982. $95.

Stultz, Russell A. *Writing and Publishing on Your Microcomputer.* Plano, TX: Wordware Publishing, 1984. pap. $13.95.

Book Trade Directories and Yearbooks

American and Canadian

American Book Trade Directory, 1986. New York: R. R. Bowker, ann. $129.95.

Chernofsky, Jacob L., ed. *AB Bookman's Yearbook.* 2 vols. Clifton, NJ: AB Bookman's Weekly, ann. $15. free to subscribers to *AB Bookman Weekly.*

The Community of the Book: A Directory of Selected Organizations and Programs, compiled by Carren O. Kaston; edited and with an introduction by John Y. Cole. Washington, DC: Library of Congress, 1986. free.

Fulton, Len, and Ferber, Ellen. *Directory of Poetry Publishers, 1985–86.* Paradise, CA: Dustbooks, 1985. pap. $9.95.

Kim, Ung Chon. *Policies of Publishers.* Metuchen, NJ: Scarecrow, 1982. pap. $16.50.

Literary Agents of North America Marketplace 1986. New York: Author Aid-Research Associates, 1986. $19.95.

Literary Market Place, 1987, with Names & Numbers. New York: R. R. Bowker, ann. $75.

Publishers Directory, edited by Linda S. Hubbard. Detroit: Gale, 1986. $250.

Publishers, Distributors, & Wholesalers of the United States: A Directory. New York: R. R. Bowker, 1986. $75.

Foreign and International

International Directory of Little Magazines and Small Presses 1986–87. Paradise, CA: Dustbooks. ann. $29.95.

International ISBN Directory. Berlin: International ISBN Agency, 1987. Dist. by R. R. Bowker. $149.95.

International Literary Market Place 1987–88. New York: R. R. Bowker. $110.

Publishers' International Directory. 2 vols. New York: K. G. Saur, 1986. $175.

Taubert, Sigfred, ed. *The Book Trade of the World.* Vol. I. *Europe and International Sections.* Vol. II. *U.S.A., Canada, Central and South America, Australia and New Zealand.* Vol. III. *Asia.* Vol. IV. *Africa.* New York: K. G. Saur. Vol. I, 1972, $70; Vol. II, 1976, $70; Vol. III, 1980, $70; Vol. IV, 1984, $70.

UNESCO Statistical Yearbook, 1985. Lanham, MD: Unipub, 1985 pap. $58.

Newspapers and Periodicals

Directory of Small Magazine-Press Editors and Publishers, edited by Len Fulton and Ellen Ferber. Paradise, CA: Dustbooks, 1985. $14.95.

Editor and Publisher International Year Book. New York: Editor and Publisher. ann. 1986. $60.

IMS-Ayer Directory of Publications, 1986. Fort Washington, PA: IMS ann. $110.

Irregular Serials and Annuals: An International Directory. New York: R. R. Bowker, 1986. $149.95

Magazine Industry Market Place: The Directory of American Periodical Publishing. New York: R. R. Bowker, 1987. $59.95.

New Serial Titles 1950–1970. New York: R. R. Bowker, 1973. 4 vols. o.p. Available on microfilm, $100; or xerographic reprint, $250.

Sources of Serials: An International Publisher and Corporate Author Directory to Ulrich's and Irregular Serials. New York: R. R. Bowker, 1981. $65.

Standard Periodical Directory, edited by Patricia Hagood. New York: Oxbridge Communications, 1985. $225.

Ulrich's International Periodicals Directory. 2 vols. New York: R. R. Bowker, 1986. $142.45.

Working Press of the Nation: Newspapers, Magazines, Radio and TV, and Internal Publications. Chicago: National Research Bureau, ann. 5 vols. $250.

Periodicals

AB Bookman's Weekly (weekly including yearbook). Clifton, NJ: AB Bookman's Weekly. $60.

American Book Publishing Record (monthly). New York: R. R. Bowker. $65.

The American Bookseller (monthly). New York: American Booksellers Association. $24.

Book Research Quarterly. New Brunswick, NJ: Transaction Periodicals Consortium. Individuals $30; institutions $50.

BP Report: On the Business of Book Publishing (weekly). White Plains, NY: Knowledge Industry Publications. $275.

EPB: Electronic Publishing Business (monthly). New York: Electronic Publishing Ventures. $95.

Electronic Publishing Review (quarterly). Medford, NJ: Learned Information, Inc. $68.

Publishers Weekly. New York: R. R. Bowker. $89.

Scholarly Publishing: A Journal for Authors & Publishers (quarterly). Toronto: University of Toronto Press. $37.50

Small Press: The Magazine for Independent/In-house/Desktop Publishing (bimonthly). Westport, CT: Meckler. $23.95.

Weekly Record. New York: R. R. Bowker. $75. A weekly listing of current American book publications, providing complete cataloging information.

Z39 American National Standards for Information Sciences (April 1986)

American National Standards Institute (ANSI), Inc.
1430 Broadway, New York, NY 10018

The American National Standards Institute (ANSI) is the coordinator of America's voluntary standards system—a federation of standards writing organizations, commerce and industry, and public and consumer interests. It also serves as a clearinghouse and information center for American National Standards and international standards. ANSI maintains an inventory of all 8,000 American National Standards and the 6,000 standards promulgated by the International Organization for Standardization (ISO)

and the International Electrotechnical Commission (IEC). In addition, it obtains or stocks standards of the 89 national standardizing bodies of other countries that cooperate within ISO.

The American National Standards that follow were developed by American National Standards Committee Z39 on library and information sciences and related publishing practices, now the National Information Standards Organization (Z39). (For more than 40 years, Z39 has developed voluntary consensus standards that facilitate the exchange and use of information and contribute to more efficient information services.) These American National Standards cover many aspects of library science, publishing, and information services, such as information transfer, forms and records, identification systems, publication formats, transliteration, and preservation of materials. These standards address the application of both traditional and new technologies to information services. All of them may be obtained at the prices noted from the American National Standards Institute.

Z39.1-1977 *Periodicals: Format and Arrangement*, $6.00. Applicable to periodicals, serials, and monographs, this standard is intended to guide and assist editors and publishers in organizing bibliographic information so that their publications can be more readily identified and used.

*Z39.2-1985 *Bibliographic Information Interchange*, $6.00. Specifies requirements for a generalized interchange format that will accommodate data describing all forms of material susceptible of bibliographic description and related data. The standard describes a generalized structure designed specifically for exchange of data between processing systems and may be used for the communication of records in any media.

Z39.4-1984 *Basic Criteria for Indexes*, $7.00. Provides guidelines and a uniform vocabulary for use in the preparation and evaluation of indexes. Seeks to deal with the principles of indexing regardless of the type of material indexed or the indexing method (manual or mechanical) used. Includes a definition of an index, a discussion of the nature and variety of indexes, and recommendations regarding the preparation, organization, and style of indexes in general.

*Z39.5-1985 *Abbreviation of Titles of Publications*, $6.00. Contains recommendations applicable to serial publications of all types and to many nonserial publications, including monographs and proceedings of meetings. They are intended to guide and assist authors, editors, librarians, and others working in various areas of information transfer activity in preparing unique, unambiguous abbreviations within a specific frame of reference for the titles of publications cited in footnotes, references, and bibliographies.

*Z39.6-1983 *Trade Catalogs*, $5.00. This standard is intended to assist in producing trade catalogs that will contain the maximum amount of necessary information in a form that can be used most easily. To aid manufacturers and distributors in achieving greater economy in artwork, layout, and production of trade catalogs and in their use; to improve the value, reliability, and usefulness of trade catalogs as a continuing reference for users; and to serve as a checklist for the prevention of omissions and oversights.

*Z39.7-1983 *Library Statistics*, $11.00. Pertaining to public, college and university, and school and special libraries, these recommendations are intended to guide and assist statisticians, librarians, and researchers in the behavioral sciences in collecting, organizing, and interpreting library-related statistical data and similar information.

---

*These standards include Library of Congress Cataloging in Publication Data.

Z39.8-1977 (R1982) *Compiling Book Publishing Statistics*, $5.00. Defines methods of recording and classifying statistics for nonperiodical books and pamphlets (including government publications, textbooks, theses, offprints, art collections, and some computer printouts in visible typography) published in the United States and available to the public.

Z39.9-1979 (R1984) *International Standard Serial Numbering*, $5.00. Defines the structure and use of a standard code for the unique identification of serial publications (both print and nonprint). Also designates a national code authority for administration of the code.

Z39.10-1971 (R1977) *Directories of Libraries and Information Centers*, $5.00. Lists recommendations for the compilation of library and information center directories so that the essential information will be presented in the most suitable and efficient form.

Z39.11-1972 (R1978) *System for the Romanization of Japanese*, $5.00. Establishes a system for the Romanization of the Japanese written language. Covers writings in classical Chinese by Japanese authors as well as other works in classical Chinese where the text as published or written incorporates Japanese "reading marks" (*kunten*) or is accompanied by material in Japanese integral to the bibliographic unit.

Z39.12-1972 (R1984) *System for the Romanization of Arabic*, $5.00. Provides a system for the Romanization of Arabic designed primarily to render Arabic personal, corporate, and place-names, as well as the titles and other indicia of Arabic publications, documents, etc., into the Roman alphabet in a way that will make it possible for persons using such Romanized material to reconstruct, if required, the original Arabic writing. This standard should be particularly useful for the compilation of library catalogs, bibliographies, and lists of names, in addition to the citation of Arabic publications in books, journal articles, etc.

Z39.13-1979 (R1984) *Describing Books in Advertisements, Catalogs, Promotional Materials, and Book Jackets*, $5.00. Provides guidance to publishers and distributors in the advertising and promotion of books to the trade, institutions, educators, and the consumer. Specifies bibliographic elements recommended for inclusion in a particular advertising medium for a particular market.

Z39.14-1979 *Writing Abstracts*, $6.00. Assists authors, editors, and staffs of access services in preparing useful abstracts to help readers and users of machine-based bibliographic services (such as online searching and SDI alerting, including systems employing full-text searching) to identify quickly and accurately the basic content of a document, determine its relevance to their interests, and decide whether they need to read the document in its entirety. This new revision incorporates helpful changes and additions from the International Standard on Abstracts for Publications and Documentation, ISO 214-1976.

*Z39.15-1980 *Title Leaves of a Book*, $5.00. Specifies the information which should be shown on the title leaves of a book and the manner in which such information should be presented to enable publishers and editors to produce title leaves that facilitate their use by bibliographers, librarians, and researchers.

Z39.16-1979 (R1985) *Preparation of Scientific Papers for Written or Oral Presentation*, $6.00. Guidelines to aid scientists in all disciplines to prepare papers that will have a high probability of being accepted for publication and of being noticed, read, and completely understood. Though directed primarily to authors, some recommenda-

*These standards include Library of Congress Cataloging in Publication Data.

tions are useful to journal editors. Covers content, style, organization, illustrations, tables, references, etc.

Z39.18-1974 *Guidelines for Format and Production of Scientific and Technical Reports*, $6.00. Establishes format and production guidelines for scientific and technical reports intended for dissemination. It may be applied, in whole or in part, to other types of documents such as letter reports, technical memoranda, and manuals.

*Z39.19-1980 *Guidelines for Thesaurus Structure, Construction, and Use*, $6.00. Presents rules and conventions for the structure, construction, and maintenance of a thesaurus of terms. A thesaurus so constructed and maintained will provide operators and users of an information storage and retrieval system with a systematic means for controlling the indexing and searching vocabulary.

*Z39.20-1983 *Criteria for Price Indexes for Library Materials*, $5.00. Provides criteria for developing price indexes to measure periodic changes in the average list price of certain library materials, divided into subject categories when useful, as follows: hardcover trade and technical books, paperback books, periodicals, serial services, and rates for library-produced microfilm.

*Z39.21-1980 *Book Numbering*, $5.00. Coordinates and standardizes the use of book numbers so that a standard book number identifies one title, from one specific publisher, and is unique to that title or edition.

*Z39.22-1981 *Proof Corrections*, $7.00. This standard lists proofreaders' marks commonly employed by proofreaders in the United States for general copy. Also included are sections on definitions, use of symbols, and queries and special directions.

*Z39.23-1983 *Standard Technical Report Number (STRN)*, $5.00. To facilitate bibliographic retrieval of technical reports, this standard outlines a numbering system to be administered by the National Technical Information Service, which will coordinate the assignment of code numbers and maintain a registry. The standard specifies the alphanumeric format to be used.

Z39.24-1976 *System for the Romanization of Slavic Cyrillic Characters*, $5.00. Provides systems for the Romanization of the Slavic Cyrillic letters used in Russian and five major Slavic languages: Ukrainian, Byelorussian, Serbian, Macedonian, and Bulgarian. These systems use a minimum number of diacritical marks so as to facilitate the Roman letter representation of the Cyrillic letters in either manual or machine conversion where they may be used.

Z39.25-1975 *Romanization of Hebrew*, $6.00. For the use of scholars, journalists, religious functionaries, librarians, cartographers, teachers, and publishers, this standard presents four styles of a system for Romanizing the Hebrew alphabet, with guidelines for selecting the one most appropriate to the purpose. Both the General-Purpose and More Exact styles assume Israeli pronunciation and are English-language oriented; the Narrow Transliteration and Keypunch-Compatible systems are for use when full reversibility is required.

*Z39.26-1981 *Advertising of Micropublications*, $5.00. This standard, for the advertising of microform publications, applies to printed advertisements, catalogs, circulars, brochures, and other promotional vehicles through which publishers of microform material communicate with present and potential customers. It lists the types of information that should be supplied to enable prospective purchasers to evaluate the product.

*These standards include Library of Congress Cataloging in Publication Data.

*Z39.27-1984 *Structure for the Representation of Names of Countries, Dependencies, and Areas of Special Sovereignty for Information Interchange*, $5.00. Provides a structure for the identification, naming, and coding of the basic geopolitical entities of the world, without overlap.

Z39.29-1977 *Bibliographic References*, $16.00. Details preparation of human-readable bibliographic references for use as bibliography, end-of-work-reference, or for use in abstracting and indexing publications. Input to computer system excluded from its scope, but output of bibliographic references from a computer system (example, printouts) included. Encompasses all common print materials, providing they are uniquely identifiable and accessible: books, journal articles, technical reports, conference proceedings, patents, dissertations (published and unpublished), newspaper articles, laws, manuscripts, maps, printed music, letters, films, sound recordings, microforms, and computer programs.

*Z39.30-1982 *Order Form for Single Titles of Library Materials in 3-Inch by 5-Inch Format*, $6.00. Provides for a form for ordering single titles of print (monographic and serial) and nonprint materials. Form may be 3 × 5 inches, or 3 × 10 inches, or enlarged to meet specific needs. It may be prepared by typewriter, by computer, or by hand.

Z39.31-1976 (R1983) *Format for Scientific and Technical Translation*, $5.00. Specifies the format for presenting written or printed scientific and technical (S&T) translations. It applies to all translations of S&T materials. It does not apply to the preparation of abstracts in one language from material in another language.

*Z39.32-1981 *Information on Microfiche Headings*, $6.00. Provides micropublishers and other microfiche users with a set of specifications as to the categories of information to be included in headings. This standard recommends further categories of information that may be given when they apply and space permits.

Z39.33-1977 (R1982) *Development of Identification Codes for Use by the Bibliographic Community*, $5.00. Guidelines for modification of existing and development of new identification code standards. General considerations for the development of codes are given, along with code design, format, composition, and code identifier. Requires registration by an authorized code authority, while use-constructed derivative codes do not.

Z39.34-1977 (R1983) *Synoptics*, $6.00. Defined as a concise form, for publication in primary journals, of a full paper simultaneously published in a journal or available in some other form. Discusses related present and planned usages, citation requirements, recommended length and style, various types and availabilities of backup full papers, and referencing practices. Examples included.

Z39.35-1979 *System for the Romanization of Lao, Khmer, and Pali*, $6.00. Designed for rendering the titles, names (personal, corporate, and place), and other indicia of Lao, Khmer, and Pali publications, documents, etc., into the Roman alphabet. The Pali portions cover this language when written in any of the following scripts: Devanagari, Sinhalese, Burmese, Thai, Bengali, Khmer, Lao, Tua Tham/A, Tua Tham/B, and Northern Thai. Romanization derived from the standard can also be used to reconstruct the original script in most cases. Useful for compilation of library catalogs, bibliographies, and lists of names and for the citation of publications in books, journal articles, and the like.

*These standards include Library of Congress Cataloging in Publication Data.

Z39.37-1979 *System for the Romanization of Armenian*, $5.00. Designed to render Armenian names (personal, corporate, place) and titles and other indicia of Armenian publications, documents, etc., into the Roman alphabet. Romanizations derived from this standard are also usable, with some exceptions, in reconstructing Armenian script. Equivalencies, based on Classical and East Armenian, comprehend both Classical and Reformed orthography.

Z39.39-1979 *Compiling Newspaper and Periodical Publishing Statistics*, $5.00. Methods of recording and classifying statistics on paid, nonpaid, and controlled circulation newspapers and periodical publications, whether originally issued in print or microform. For general interest, consumer, special business, technical, agricultural, and academic newspapers and periodicals, house organs, newsletters, entertainment guides, journals, etc. Covers circulation, number of issues, supplements, and subject group classifying. Useful for libraries, information centers, all who produce, handle, sell, purchase, or disseminate newspapers and periodicals, as well as researchers and statisticians who collect, organize, or analyze such data.

Z39.40-1979 *Compiling U.S. Microform Publishing Statistics*, $5.00. Methods of recording and classifying publishing statistics for microforms, whether originally issued in print or microform. Statistics for original format (book, collection, dissertation, microfiche, microfilm, etc.) and present format (roll film, microfiche, micropaque, etc.). Standards for presentation of subject content. Intended to help librarians and micropublishers quantify microform publishing statistics in a way compatible with standards on other publishing statistics. Companion to ANSI Z39.39-1979, Compiling Newspaper and Periodical Publishing Statistics, and ANSI Z39.8-1977, Compiling Book Publishing Statistics.

*Z39.41-1979 *Book Spine Formats*, $5.00. Specifies the information which should be shown on the spine of a book and the manner in which it should be displayed, so that designers and publishers can produce spine formats that will facilitate the locating of books by librarians, scholars, and others. The standard also includes rules for the use of edge-titles.

*Z39.42-1980 *Serial Holdings Statements at the Summary Level*, $7.00. Establishes rules and punctuation for preparing consistent, standardized records of the bibliographic units of serials located at a particular library or institution. Such serial holdings statements will be at the summary (i.e., least specific) level of detail. Identifies specific data areas, data elements, and punctuation, and provides guidance on formatting and displaying data elements.

*Z39.43.-1980 *Identification Code for the Book Industry*, $5.00. Provides a unique numeric identification for each address of each organization, in or served by the book industry, that is engaged in repetitive transactions with other members of this group, in order to facilitate communications among them.

*Z39.44-1986 *Serials Holdings Statements*, $12.00. Establishes rules for preparing consistent, standardized records for all serials in all physical forms. Data areas, data elements, and punctuation to be used in holdings statements are identified and specifications provided for displaying the data elements. Both automated and manual systems are accommodated. Potential applications include serial check-in functions, inventory operations, and union list activities.

*Z39.45-1983 *Claims for Missing Issues of Serials*, $6.00. Describes the data ele-

ments to be included in claims for missing issues of serial publications and the order in which they are to appear.

*Z39.46-1983 *Patent Documents—Identification of Bibliographic Data*, $5.00. Covers a list of approximately 50 distinct pieces of bibliographic data widely used on the first page of patent documents or in patent gazettes and identified through INID Codes or Numbers. Included are data for document identification, filing, priority, publication, technical information, and international patent conventions.

*Z39.47-1985 *Extended Latin Alphabet Coded Character Set for Bibliographic Use*, $8.00. Establishes both the 7-bit and 8-bit code values for the computer codes for characters used in bibliographic work when handling non-English items. The character set is primarily intended for the interchange of bibliographic information among data processing systems and within message transmission systems.

*Z39.48-1984 *Permanence of Paper for Printed Library Materials*, $5.00. Sets the criteria for permanence of uncoated paper so that it should last several hundred years without significant deterioration; identifies the specific qualities of such paper; specifies test requirements; and considers applications and uses.

*Z39.49-1985 *Computerized Book Ordering*, $18.00. Establishes fixed- and variable-length formats for the computerized ordering of books and is intended for anyone who buys or sells books and has access to a computer. The fixed-length format is intended for communication with magnetic tape. The variable-length format allows greater flexibility and lower cost for online communications.

Development and Approval of Z39 Standards

The American National Standards in the preceding list were developed by the National Information Standards Organization (Z39). They were prepared by volunteer Standards Committees — which draw on expert opinion from a variety of disciplines — are reviewed on a regular basis, and revised if necessary. NISO's voting membership, which participates in the formal review and approval of these standards, includes the following organizations:

Academic Press
American Association of Law Libraries
American Chemical Society
American Library Association
American Psychological Association
American Society for Information Science
American Society of Indexers
American Theological Library Association
Aspen Systems Corporation
Association of American Publishers

*These standards include Library of Congress Cataloging in Publication Data.

Association of American University Presses
Association of Information and Dissemination Centers
Association of Jewish Libraries
Association of Research Libraries
Blue Bear Group, Inc.
Book Manufacturers Institute, Inc.
CAPCON Library Network
Catholic Library Association
Colorado Alliance of Research Libraries
Cooperative College Library Center
Council of Biology Editors
Council of National Library and Information Associations
EBSCONET
F. W. Faxon Company, Inc.
INCOLSA
Information Handling Services
Information Industry Association
Information Workstation Group
Library Binding Institute
Library Corporation
Library of Congress
Medical Library Association
Music Library Association
National Agricultural Library
National Archives and Records Service
National Bureau of Standards, Information Resources and Services Division
National Commission on Libraries and Information Science
National Federation of Abstracting and Information Services
National Library of Medicine
Oceana Publications, Inc.
OCLC, Inc.
OHIONET
PALINET
Philips Subsystems and Peripherals, Inc.
Pittsburgh Regional Library Center
Reference Technology, Inc.
Research Libraries Group, Inc.
Society for Scholarly Publishing
Society for Technical Communication
Special Libraries Association

SUNY/OCLC Network

U.S. Department of Commerce, National Technical Information Service (NTIS)

U.S. Department of Commerce, Printing and Publishing Division

U.S. Department of Defense

U.S. Department of Energy, OSTI

U.S. ISBN Maintenance Agency

Waldenbooks

H. W. Wilson Company

Ready Reference

Publishers' Toll-Free Telephone Numbers

Ann Niles

Assistant College Librarian, Carleton College Library, Northfield, MN 55057

Toll-free telephone numbers in publishing continue to proliferate . Publishers often list their toll-free telephone number in catalogs, advertisements, and blurbs. Many list 800 numbers in *Publishers Trade List Annual, Books in Print*, and *Literary Market Place*. Toll-free numbers are useful to rush order books for reserve; to determine whether a title is still in print, available in paperback or hardbound, the expected date of publication, the number of copies of a book in stock, and the current price of a title; to request a list of the individual titles in a series or a recent catalog; to determine whether a new edition is in preparation or a series has been completed; to verify a change in the title of a work or the availability of a foreign edition in the United States; to claim standing and firm orders; and to reconcile problems with orders and accounts. Because it is usually more efficient to telephone than to write, this list is offered again as a ready reference feature.

Publisher	City/State	Toll-Free No.
A.R.E. Press	Virginia Beach, VA	800-368-2727
ABC-Clio Information Services	Santa Barbara, CA	800-422-2546
ACS Publications	San Diego, CA	800-843-6666
AFCEA International Publishers	Burke, VA	800-336-4583
APL Press	Rockville, MD	800-592-0050
ASQC Quality Press	Milwaukee, WI	800-952-6587
Abbeville Press	New York, NY	800-227-7210
Abelard-Schuman Jr. Books	New York, NY	800-242-7737
Abilene Christian University Press	Abilene, TX	800-527-0575
Abingdon Press	Nashville, TN	800-251-3320
Abradale Press Books	New York, NY	800-345-1359
William Abrahams Books	New York, NY	800-526-0275
Harry N. Abrams	New York, NY	800-345-1359
Academic Press	Orlando, FL	800-321-5068
Academy Architecture	New York, NY	800-221-7945
Accent Books	Denver, CO	800-525-5550
Accent Publications	Scituate, MA	800-525-5550
Access Press	Los Angeles, CA	800-638-6460
Achievement House	Danbury, CT	800-551-1133
Acorn Books	New York, NY	800-257-5755

Publisher	City/State	Toll-Free No.
Acropolis Books	Washington, DC	800-621-5199
Adama Books	New York, NY	800-672-6672
Adler & Adler Publishers	Bethesda, MD	800-253-3677
Adler's Foreign Books	Evanston, IL	800-235-3771
Ad-Lib Publications	Fairfield, IA	800-624-5893
Advanced Dungeons & Dragons	Lake Geneva, WI	800-558-5977
Agape	Carol Stream, IL	800-323-1049
Agency for Instructional Technology	Bloomington, IN	800-457-4509
AgriData Resources	Milwaukee, WI	800-558-9044
Agrinde Publications	New York, NY	800-251-4000
Albatross Publishing House	New York, NY	800-223-2584
Alemany Press	Hayward, CA	800-227-2375
Aletheia Books	Frederick, MD	800-692-6300
Alfraguera	Northvale, NJ	800-526-0107
Alfred Publishing Co.	Sherman Oaks, CA	800-292-6122
Allen & Unwin	Winchester, MA	800-547-8889
Allyn & Bacon	Newton, MA	800-526-4799
Alphabet Press	Natick, MA	800-462-1252
Altea	Northvale, NJ	800-526-0107
The Alternate Source	Lansing, MI	800-253-3200
American Association for Medical Transcription	Modesto, CA	800-982-2182
American Association on Mental Deficiency	Washington, DC	800-424-3688
American Bible Society	New York, NY	800-543-8000
American Chemical Society	Washington, DC	800-424-6747
American College of Laboratory Animal Medicine	Hershey, PA	800-321-5068
American Correctional Association	College Park, MD	800-222-5646
American Council on Education	Washington, DC	800-257-5755
The American Educational Trust	Washington, DC	800-368-5788
American Geophysical Union	Washington, DC	800-424-2488
American Guidance Service	Circle Pines, MN	800-328-2560
American Institute of Physics	New York, NY	800-247-7497
American Institute of Small Business	Minneapolis, MN	800-328-2906
American Law Institute	Philadelphia, PA	800-253-6387
American Library Association	Chicago, IL	800-545-2433
American Mathematical Society	Providence, RI	800-556-7774
American Medical Association	Chicago, IL	800-621-8335
American Numismatic Association	Colorado Springs, CO	800-367-9723
American Nurses Association	Kansas City, MO	800-368-5643
American Phytopathological Society	St. Paul, MN	800-328-7560
American Polygraph Association	Severna Park, MD	800-272-8037
American Psychiatric Press	Washington, DC	800-368-5777

Publisher	City/State	Toll-Free No.
American Society for Information Science	Washington, DC	800-248-5474
American Society for Civil Engineers	New York, NY	800-548-2723
American Society of Clinical Pathologists Press	Chicago, IL	800-621-4142
American Sports Communications	New York, NY	800-526-0275
American Technical Publishers	Alsip, IL	800-323-3471
American Travel Publications	Carlsbad, CA	800-227-7346
American Veterinary Publications	Santa Barbara, CA	800-235-6947
Amnesty International USA	New York, NY	800-251-4000
Amphoto	New York, NY	800-526-3641
Anaheim Publishing Co	Belmont, CA	800-831-6996
Ancestry	Salt Lake City, UT	800-531-1790
Anchor Bible	New York, NY	800-645-6156
Anchor Press	New York, NY	800-645-6156
John Mackenzie Anderson	Cincinnati, OH	800-732-2663
Robert D. Anderson	Sacramento, CA	800-222-3030
Anderson Publishing Co.	Cincinnati, OH	800-543-0883
Anderson World Books	Mountain View, CA	800-227-8318
Andrews, McMeel & Parker	Fairway, KS	800-826-4216
Annual Reviews	Palo Alto, CA	800-523-8635
Antioch Publishing Co.	Yellow Springs, OH	800-543-2397
Apollo Book	Poughkeepsie, NY	800-431-5003
Apollo Books (MN)	Winona, MN	800-328-8963
Apollo Editions	New York, NY	800-242-7737
Applause Theatre Book Publications	New York, NY	800-242-7737
Appleton & Lange	East Norwalk, CT	800-423-1359
Arbit Books	Milwaukee, WI	800-558-6908
Architectural Book Publishing Co.	Stamford, CT	800-526-7626
Argus Communications	Allen, TX	800-527-4748
Ariel Press	Columbus, OH	800-336-7769
Arista Corp.	New York, NY	800-227-1606
Arlington House	New York, NY	800-526-4264
Arno Press	New York, NY	800-242-7737
Art for Children	New York, NY	800-645-6156
Art Institute of Chicago	Chicago, IL	800-621-2736
Art Trade Press	Detroit, MI	800-521-0707
Artabras	New York, NY	800-227-7210
Artech House	Dedham, MA	800-225-9977
Ash-Kar Press	San Francisco, CA	800-227-1516
Ashton-Tate Publishing Group	Torrance, CA	800-437-4329
Aslib	Detroit, MI	800-521-0707
Aspen Systems Corp.	Rockville, MD	800-638-8437
Associated Booksellers	Bridgeport, CT	800-232-2224
Association for Library Service to Children	Chicago, IL	800-545-2433

Publisher	City/State	Toll-Free No.
Association of College and Research Libraries	Chicago, IL	800-545-2433
Association of Commonwealth Universities	Detroit, MI	800-521-0707
Atheneum	New York, NY	800-257-5755
Atlantic Monthly Press Books	Boston, MA	800-343-9204
Auerbach Publishers	Pennsauken, NJ	800-843-0460
Augsburg Publishing House	Minneapolis, MN	800-328-4648
Aura Books	Los Angeles, CA	800-843-6666
Automobile Quarterly Publications	Princeton, NJ	800-523-0236
Aviation Book Co.	Glendale, CA	800-423-2708
Axcess Software	Tempe, AZ	800-292-3687
BE Publications	Bridgeport, CT	800-826-8692
BLOC Development Corp.	Miami Beach, FL	800-231-1149
BMH Books	Winona Lake, IN	800-348-2756
BUC International Corp.	Fort Lauderdale, FL	800-327-6929
Backcountry Publications	Woodstock, VT	800-635-5009
Baha'i Publishing Trust	Wilmette, IL	800-323-1880
Baker Book House	Grand Rapids, MI	800-253-7283
Ballantine Books	New York, NY	800-638-6460
Ballinger Publishing Co.	Cambridge, MA	800-242-7737
Balsam Press	New York, NY	800-526-7626
Bantam Books	New York, NY	800-323-9872
Barbacoa Press	Kansas City, MO	800-255-0513
Barbour & Co.	Westwood, NJ	800-221-2648
Barnes & Noble Books	New York, NY	800-242-7737
Richard W. Baron Publishing Co.	New York, NY	800-526-0275
Barre Publishing Co.	New York, NY	800-526-4264
Barron's Educational Series	Woodbury, NY	800-645-3476
Basic Books	New York, NY	800-242-7737
Basic Reference Library	Guilford, CT	800-243-6532
Battelle Press	Columbus, OH	800-526-7254
Beacon Press	Boston, MA	800-242-7737
Bear & Co.	Santa Fe, NM	800-932-3277
Beau Bayou Publishing Co.	Lafayette, LA	800-624-0466
Beaufort Books	New York, NY	800-526-7626
Bedford Books	New York, NY	800-221-7945
Peter Bedrick Books	New York, NY	800-242-7737
Beginner Books	New York, NY	800-638-6460
Behrman House	New York, NY	800-221-2755
Belding Books	Portland, OR	800-452-3032
Bell and Howell	Wooster, OH	800-321-9881
Matthew Bender & Co.	New York, NY	800-833-3630
Bennett & McKnight Publishing Co.	Peoria, IL	800-447-0682
Robert Bentley	Cambridge, MA	800-423-4595
Benziger	New York, NY	800-257-5755
Bergh Publishing Group	Indianapolis, IN	800-526-0275

Publisher	City/State	Toll-Free No.
Bergwell Educational Software	Uniondale, NY	800-645-1737
Bergwell Productions	Garden City, NY	800-645-1737
Berkley Publishing Group	New York, NY	800-223-0510
Berlitz Publications	New York, NY	800-257-5755
Cornelia & Michael Bessie Books	New York, NY	800-242-7737
Bethany House Publishers	Minneapolis, MN	800-328-6109
Bethel Publishing Co.	Elkhart, IN	800-348-7657
Bibli O'Phile	New York, NY	800-255-1660
Bicycle Books	San Francisco, CA	800-526-7626
Bilingual Books	Seattle, WA	800-228-4078
Billboard Books	New York, NY	800-526-3641
Bishop Graphics	Westlake Village, CA	800-222-5808
Blacksmith Corp.	Southport, CT	800-531-2665
Basil Blackwell	New York, NY	800-242-7737
Blackwell Scientific Publications	Boston, MA	800-325-4177
John F. Blair Publisher	Winston-Salem, NC	800-222-9796
Blood-Horse	Lexington, KY	800-354-9207
Blue Jay	New York, NY	800-221-7945
Blue Mountain Arts	Boulder, CO	800-525-0642
Board of Publication, LCA	Philadelphia, PA	800-367-8737
Clark Boardman Co.	New York, NY	800-221-9428
Edward Marshall Boehm	Trenton, NJ	800-257-9410
Bonanza Books	New York, NY	800-526-4264
Books by Cooks	New York, NY	800-334-8128
Books in Focus	New York, NY	800-242-7737
Books on Demand	Ann Arbor, MI	800-521-0600
Books on Tape	Newport Beach, CA	800-626-3333
Bounty Books	New York, NY	800-526-4264
R. R. Bowker Co.	New York, NY	800-521-8110
Bowmar/Noble Publishers	Oklahoma City, OK	800-654-8608
Marion Boyars Publishers	New York, NY	800-526-7626
Bradbury Press Books	Scarsdale, NY	800-257-5755
Brady Communications Co.	Bowie, MD	800-638-0220
Branchemco	Jacksonville, FL	800-874-5990
Breakthrough Publications	Briarcliff, NY	800-824-5000
Brentwood Communications Group	Columbus, GA	800-334-8861
Brethren Press	Elgin, IL	800-323-8039
Breton Publishers	Boston, MA	800-343-2204
Bridgebooks	Philadelphia, PA	800-523-1631
Brigham Young University Press	Provo, UT	800-453-3235
Broadman Press	Nashville, TN	800-251-3225
Broadway Play Publishing	New York, NY	800-752-9782
Brodart Co.	Williamsport, PA	800-233-8467
Paul H. Brookes Publishing Co.	Baltimore, MD	800-638-3775
Brooks/Cole Engineering	Wadsworth, CA	800-354-9706
Brooks/Cole Publishing Co.	Monterey, CA	800-354-9706
Broude Brothers, Ltd., Music	New York, NY	800-225-3197

Publisher	City/State	Toll-Free No.
Brownlow Publishing Co.	Fort Worth, TX	800-433-7610
Buckeye Press	Columbus, GA	800-241-8981
Bull Publishing Co.	Palo Alto, CA	800-526-7626
Bureau of National Affairs	Washington, DC	800-862-4636
Business Publications	Plano, TX	800-323-4560
Business Research Services	Lombard, IL	800-325-8720
Butterworth Publishers	Stoneham, MA	800-325-4177
CBP Press	St. Louis, MO	800-351-2665
CBS Educational and Professional Publications	New York, NY	800-227-2754
C. C. Publications	Tigard, OR	800-547-4800
CIBA Medical Education Division	West Caldwell, NJ	800-631-1181
COM Press	Wentworth, NH	800-221-0419
CRC Press	Boca Raton, FL	800-272-7737
C. S. S. of Ohio	Lima, OH	800-537-1030
Caedmon	New York, NY	800-223-0420
Cajun Publishing	New Iberia, LA	800-551-3076
Calbre Press	Northbrook, IL	800-323-0037
California College Publishing	National City, CA	800-221-7374
Callaghan & Co.	Wilmette, IL	800-323-1336
Cambridge Book Co.	New York, NY	800-221-4764
Cambridge University Press	New York, NY	800-872-7423
Campbell's List	Maitland, FL	800-624-2232
Canter & Associates	Santa Monica, CA	800-262-4347
Capitol Publications	Arlington, VA	800-847-7772
Carcanet	New York, NY	800-242-7737
Career Publishing	Orange, CA	800-854-4014
CareerTrack Publications	Boulder, CO	800-334-1018
Carolina Biological Supply Co.	Burlington, NC	800-334-5551
Caroline House	Naperville, IL	800-245-2665
Carolrhoda Books	Minneapolis, MN	800-328-4929
Carroll and Graf Publishers	New York, NY	800-982-8319
Cassell Communications	Fort Lauderdale, FL	800-351-9278
Castle Books	Secaucus, NJ	800-526-7257
Catholic Publishers	Nashville, TN	800-251-4000
Cavendish, Marshall Corp.	Freeport, NY	800-821-9881
Celestial Arts Publishing Co.	Berkeley, CA	800-841-2665
Centennial Press	Lincoln, NE	800-228-4078
Irena Chalmers Cookbooks	New York, NY	800-334-8128
Changing Times Education Service	St. Paul, MN	800-328-1452
Chariot Books	Elgin, IL	800-323-7543
Charismatic Renewal Services	South Bend, IN	800-348-2227
Chartwell Books	Secaucus, NJ	800-526-7257
Chatsworth Press	Chatsworth, CA	800-262-7367
Chatterbox Voice Learning Systems	Boulder, CO	800-531-5314
Chicago Historical Society	Chicago, IL	800-621-2736
Childrens Press	Chicago, IL	800-621-1115

Publisher	City/State	Toll-Free No.
Chilton Book Co.	Radnor, PA	800-345-1214
Christian Activity Products	Grand Rapids, MI	800-253-7283
Christian Books Publishing House	Gardiner, ME	800-228-2665
Christian Publishing Service	Tulsa, OK	800-826-5992
Christian Science Publishing Co.	Boston, MA	800-225-7090
Citadel Press	Secaucus, NJ	800-572-6657
Clarion Books	New York, NY	800-225-3362
Cliff Notes	Lincoln, NE	800-228-4078
Close Up Foundation	Arlington, VA	800-336-5479
Cold Spring Harbor Laboratory	Cold Spring Harbor, NY	800-843-4388
Collamore Press	New York, NY	800-257-5755
Collector Books	Paducah, KY	800-626-5420
College Hill Press	San Diego, CA	800-343-9204
College Press Publishing Co.	Joplin, MO	800-641-7148
College Skills Center	Baltimore, MD	800-638-1010
College Survival	Rapid City, SD	800-528-8323
Collier Books	New York, NY	800-257-5755
Collier-Macmillan International	New York, NY	800-257-5755
Colophon Books	New York, NY	800-242-7737
Colorado School of Mines	Golden, CO	800-446-9488
Columbia Pictures Publications	Miami, FL	800-327-7643
Colwell Systems	Champaign, IL	800-248-7000
The Comedy Center	Wilmington, DE	800-441-7098
Communication Networks	Richmond, VA	800-882-4800
Communications Channels	Atlanta, GA	800-241-9834
Communications Library	White Plains, NY	800-248-5474
CompCare Publications	Minneapolis, MN	800-328-3330
Computer Information	San Diego, CA	800-528-3665
Computer Science Press	Rockville, MD	800-242-7737
Concordia Publishing House	St. Louis, MO	800-325-3040
The Conference Board	New York, NY	800-872-6273
Congdon & Weed	New York, NY	800-221-7945
Congressional Information Service	Bethesda, MD	800-638-8380
Consumer Guide/Publications International	Skokie, IL	800-526-4264
Contemporary Focus Paperbacks	Guilford, CT	800-243-6532
Continental Press	Elizabethtown, PA	800-233-0759
Continuum Publishing Co.	New York, NY	800-242-7737
David C. Cook Publishing Co.	Elgin, IL	800-323-7543
Cornell Maritime Press	Centreville, MD	800-638-7641
Council Oak Books	Tulsa, OK	800-526-7626
Countryman Press	Woodstock, VT	800-635-5009
Covenant Press	Chicago, IL	800-621-1290
Crain Books	Chicago, IL	800-323-4900
Crawford Press	Topeka, KS	800-255-3502
Creative Computing Press	New York, NY	800-932-0017
Creative Homeowner Press	Upper Saddle River, NJ	800-631-7795

Publisher	City/State	Toll-Free No.
Creative Teaching Press	Huntington Beach, CA	800-732-1548
Crestwood House	Mankato, MN	800-535-4393
Criterion	New York, NY	800-242-7737
Crittenden Publishing	Novato, CA	800-421-3483
Cross River Press	New York, NY	800-227-7210
Crossroad/Continuum	New York, NY	800-257-5755
Thomas Y. Crowell	New York, NY	800-242-7737
Thomas Y. Crowell Jr. Books	New York, NY	800-638-3030
Crowell-Collier Press	New York, NY	800-257-5755
Crown Publishers	New York, NY	800-526-4264
Cy De Cosse	Minnetonka, MN	800-328-3895
D & S Publishers	Clearwater, FL	800-237-9707
DATA	San Diego, CA	800-854-7030
DAW Books	New York, NY	800-526-0275
DOK Publishers	East Aurora, NY	800-458-7900
Da Capo Press	New York, NY	800-221-9369
Dance Magazine	New York, NY	800-331-1750
The Dartnell Corp.	Chicago, IL	800-621-5463
Datamost	Chatsworth, CA	800-692-1649
Datar Publishing Co.	Crestwood, MO	800-633-8378
F. A. Davis	Philadelphia, PA	800-523-4049
John Day	New York, NY	800-242-7737
Dealer's Choice Books	Tampa, FL	800-238-8288
Decbooks	Bedford, MA	800-343-8322
B. C. Decker	St. Louis, MO	800-325-4177
Marcel Dekker	New York, NY	800-228-1160
Delacorte Press	New York, NY	800-645-6156
Delgren Books	Tucson, AZ	800-528-4923
Dell Publishing Co.	New York, NY	800-932-0070
The Delmar Co.	Charlotte, NC	800-438-1504
Delmar Publishers	Albany, NY	800-833-3350
Delorme Publishing Co.	Freeport, ME	800-227-1656
Delta Books	New York, NY	800-645-6156
Dembner Books	New York, NY	800-223-2584
Denison Library Book Service	Minneapolis, MN	800-328-3831
Denison Music Co.	Minneapolis, MN	800-328-3831
T. S. Denison & Co.	Minneapolis, MN	800-328-3831
Deseret Book Co.	Salt Lake City, UT	800-453-3876
Desert Publications	Boulder, CO	800-824-7888
Andre Deutsch	New York, NY	800-526-0275
Devin-Adair	Greenwich, CT	800-251-4000
DeVore & Sons	Wichita, KS	800-835-1051
Dexter & Westbrook	Baldwin, NY	800-645-6505
Dial Books for Young Readers	New York, NY	800-526-0275
Dial Press	New York, NY	800-645-6156
Dialogue House Library	New York, NY	800-221-5844
Digital Press	Bedford, MA	800-343-8322

Publisher	City/State	Toll-Free No.
Dillon Press	Minneapolis, MN	800-328-8322
Directories Publishing Co.	Clemson, SC	800-222-4531
The Distributors	South Bend, IN	800-348-5200
Dodd, Mead & Co.	New York, NY	800-251-4000
Dog-Masters Systems	Agoura Hills, CA	800-351-1700
Dolphin Books	New York, NY	800-645-6156
The Donning Co. Publishers	Norfolk, VA	800-446-8572
Dormac	Beaverton, OR	800-547-8032
Dorset House Publishing Co.	New York, NY	800-342-6657
Dorsey Professional Books	Homewood, IL	800-323-4560
Doubleday & Co.	New York, NY	800-645-6156
Dover Publications	Mineola, NY	800-223-3130
Dow Jones-Irwin	Homewood, IL	800-323-4560
Drawing Board Computer Supplies, Division	Hartford, CT	800-243-3207
Drivers License Guide Co.	Redwood City, CA	800-227-8827
Dryden Press	Hinsdale, IL	800-323-7437
Dungeons & Dragons	Lake Geneva, WI	800-558-5977
Dun's Marketing Service	New York, NY	800-526-0651
Duquesne University Press	Pittsburgh, PA	800-221-3845
Dushkin Publishing Group	Guilford, CT	800-243-6532
E. P. Dutton	New York, NY	800-526-0275
Dutton Children's Books	New York, NY	800-526-0275
Dynamic Publications	Silver Spring, MD	800-255-1777
EBSCO Industries	Birmingham, AL	800-633-6088
EDC Publishing	Tulsa, OK	800-331-4418
EIC/Intelligence	New York, NY	800-223-6275
EMC Corp.	St. Paul, MN	800-328-1452
ERA/CCR Corp.	Nyack, NY	800-845-8402
ESP	Jonesboro, AR	800-643-0280
East Woods Press	Charlotte, NC	800-438-1242
Eastman Kodak Co.	Rochester, NY	800-242-7737
Ecco Press	New York, NY	800-223-2584
Economics Press	Fairfield, NJ	800-526-2554
The Economy Co.	Oklahoma City, OK	800-654-8608
Editions Berlitz	New York, NY	800-257-5755
Editorial Caribe	Miami, FL	800-222-5342
Educational Activities	Baldwin, NY	800-645-3739
Educational Design	New York, NY	800-221-9372
Educational Ministries	Brea, CA	800-221-0910
Educational Service	Stevensville, MI	800-253-0763
Educators Publishing Service	Cambridge, MA	800-225-5750
Wm. B. Eerdman's Publishing Co.	Grand Rapids, MI	800-253-7521
Elek-Tek	Chicago, IL	800-621-1269
Empire Books	New York, NY	800-242-7737
Encore Editions	New York, NY	800-257-5755
Encyclopaedia Britannica Educational Corp.	Chicago, IL	800-554-9862

Publisher	City/State	Toll-Free No.
Encyclopaedia Britannica	Chicago, IL	800-554-9862
Endless Quest	Lake Geneva, WI	800-558-5977
Eurasia Press	New York, NY	800-242-7737
Euromonitor Publications	Detroit, MI	800-521-0707
Europa Publications	Detroit, MI	800-521-0707
M. Evans & Co.	New York, NY	800-526-0275
Faber & Faber	Winchester, MA	800-242-7737
Fachinformationszentrium (FIZ)	New York, NY	800-247-7497
Facts & Comparisons	New York, NY	800-242-7737
Facts on File	New York, NY	800-322-8755
Falcon Books	Layton, UT	800-421-8714
Family Circle Books	New York, NY	800-247-2904
Fantasy Forest	Lake Geneva, WI	800-558-5977
Farm Journal Books	Philadelphia, PA	800-237-1212
W. D. Farmer	Atlanta, GA	800-225-7526
Farrar, Straus & Giroux	New York, NY	800-242-7737
Fawcett Book Group	New York, NY	800-638-6460
The Faxon Company	Westwood, MA	800-225-6055
Federal Document Retrieval	Washington, DC	800-368-1009
Frederick Fell Publishers	Hollywood, FL	800-526-7626
Festival	Nashville, TN	800-251-3320
Fielding Publications	New York, NY	800-631-1199
Film Communicators	North Hollywood, CA	800-423-2400
Films	New York, NY	800-242-7737
Fliptrack Learning Systems	Glen Ellyn, IL	800-222-3547
Florida Bar Continuing Legal Educational Publications	Tallahassee, FL	800-874-0005
Forest Publishing	Lake Forest, IL	800-323-9442
Reginald Bishop Forster Associates	Sacramento, CA	800-328-5091
Fortress Press	Philadelphia, PA	800-367-8737
Forward Movement Publications	Cincinnati, OH	800-543-1813
Foundation Center	New York, NY	800-424-9836
Fountain Publishing Co.	New York, NY	800-242-7737
Foxfire Press	New York, NY	800-526-0275
Charles Franklin Press	Edmonds, WA	800-992-6657
Free City	New York, NY	800-242-7737
Free Press	New York, NY	800-257-5755
Eleanor Friede	New York, NY	800-257-5755
Frost and Sullivan	New York, NY	800-242-7737
Fulcrum	Golden, CO	800-992-2908
Funk & Wagnalls Co.	New York, NY	800-242-7737
GP Coursework	Columbia, MD	800-638-3838
Gale Research	Detroit, MI	800-521-0707
Galilee Books	New York, NY	800-645-6156
Gallaudet College Press	Washington, DC	800-672-6720
Gallery Books	New York, NY	800-932-0070
Garden Way Publishing Co.	Charlotte, VT	800-242-7737
Geneva Press	Philadelphia, PA	800-523-1631

Publisher	City/State	Toll-Free No.
Genova	Davison, MI	800-521-7488
Geological Society of America	Boulder, CO	800-472-1988
C. R. Gibson Co.	Norwalk, CT	800-243-6004
Ginn & Co.	Lexington, MA	800-848-9500
Glencoe Publishing Co.	Encino, CA	800-257-5755
Peter Glenn Publications	New York, NY	800-223-1254
Global Engineering Documents	Santa Ana, CA	800-854-7179
Global Studies	Guilford, CT	800-243-6532
Globe Book Co.	New York, NY	800-221-7994
Globe Pequot Press	Chester, CT	800-243-0495
David R. Godine	Boston, MA	800-242-7737
Golden-Lee Books	Brooklyn, NY	800-221-0960
Gollehon Press	Grand Rapids, MI	800-262-4947
Good Apple	Carthage, IL	800-435-7234
Good Books	Intercourse, PA	800-762-7171
Good Money Publications	Worcester, VT	800-535-3551
Goodheart-Willcox Co.	South Holland, IL	800-323-0440
Gospel Advocate Co.	Nashville, TN	800-251-8446
Gospel Publishing House	Springfield, MO	800-641-4310
Grand Rapids International	Grand Rapids, MI	800-253-5465
Graphic Arts Center Publishing Co.	Portland, OR	800-452-3032
Great American Cooking School	New York, NY	800-334-8128
Great Game Products	Bethesda, MD	800-426-3748
Great Plains National Instructional Television Library	Lincoln, NE	800-228-4630
Great Plains Software	Fargo, ND	800-345-3276
Stephen Greene Press/Lewis Publisher	New York, NY	800-526-0275
Greenhaven Press	St. Paul, MN	800-231-5163
Greenwich Press	Trumbull, CT	800-243-4246
Greenwillow Books	New York, NY	800-631-1199
Gregg Press	Boston, MA	800-343-2806
Grove Press	New York, NY	800-638-6460
Grove's Dictionaries of Music	New York, NY	800-221-2123
M. Grumbacher	New York, NY	800-346-3278
Grune & Stratton	Orlando, FL	800-468-8671
Gryphon House	Mt. Rainier, MD	800-638-0928
Guilford Press	New York, NY	800-221-3966
HP Books	Tucson, AZ	800-528-4923
Hadley School for the Blind	Winnetka, IL	800-323-4238
Hafner Press	New York, NY	800-257-5755
G. K. Hall & Co.	Boston, MA	800-343-2806
Hammond	Maplewood, NJ	800-526-4953
Handy Folio Music Co.	Minneapolis, MN	800-328-3831
Happiness Unlimited Publications	Virginia Beach, VA	800-525-5018
Harcourt Brace Jovanovich	San Diego, CA	800-543-1918

Publisher	City/State	Toll-Free No.
Harfax	New York, NY	800-242-7737
Harmony Books	New York, NY	800-526-4264
Harper and Row Publishers	New York, NY	800-242-7737
Harper Forum Books	New York, NY	800-242-7737
Harris Publishing Co.	Twinsburg, OH	800-321-9136
Harrison Co.	Norcross, GA	800-241-3561
Harrison House	Tulsa, OK	800-331-3647
Harvard Business School Press	Boston, MA	800-242-7737
Harvest Books	New York, NY	800-543-1918
Harvest House Publishers	Eugene, OR	800-547-8979
Hastings House, Publishers	New York, NY	800-526-7626
Hawthorne	New York, NY	800-526-0275
Hazelden Foundation	Center City, MN	800-328-9000
Hearst General Books	New York, NY	800-631-1199
Heartquest	Lake Geneva, WI	800-558-5977
Heartsong Books	Minneapolis, MN	800-328-6109
D. C. Heath & Co.	Lexington, MA	800-428-8071
William S. Hein & Co.	Buffalo, NY	800-828-7571
Heinle & Heinle Publishers	Boston, MA	800-225-3782
Hemisphere Publications	New York, NY	800-526-0275
Herald House	Independence, MO	800-821-7550
Herald Press	Scottdale, PA	800-245-7894
Hero Games	Charlottesville, VA	800-325-0479
Hewlett-Packard Co.	Santa Clara, CA	800-367-4772
Hideaways International	Littleton, MA	800-843-4433
Hill & Wang	New York, NY	800-242-7737
Hillside	New York, NY	800-526-0275
History of Science Society	Philadelphia, PA	800-341-1522
Hi-Time Publishing Corp.	Milwaukee, WI	800-558-2292
Holman Bible Publishers	Nashville, TN	800-251-3225
Home Planners	Farmington Hills, MI	800-521-6797
Home Vision	Chicago, IL	800-323-4222
Homestead Book	Seattle, WA	800-426-6777
Hope Publishing Co.	Carol Stream, IL	800-323-1049
Horizon Publishers & Distributors	Bountiful, UT	800-453-0812
The Horn Book	Boston, MA	800-325-1170
Houghton Mifflin Co.	Boston, MA	800-225-3362
Hubbard Scientific	Northbrook, IL	800-323-8368
Hudson River Library	New York, NY	800-257-5755
Human Resources Development Press	Amherst, MA	800-822-2801
Humanics	Atlanta, GA	800-874-8844
Humanities Press	Atlantic Highlands, NJ	800-221-3845
Hunter Books	Kingwood, TX	800-231-3024
Huntington House	Lafayette, LA	800-572-8213
ICS Books	Harrisburg, PA	800-732-3669
IEEE Computer Society Press	Washington, DC	800-272-6657

Publisher	City/State	Toll-Free No.
IHRDC	Boston, MA	800-327-6756
IMS Press	Fort Washington, PA	800-523-5884
IPS Information Processing Supplies	Burr Ridge, IL	800-323-5569
ISI Press	Philadelphia, PA	800-523-1850
IWP Publishing	Menlo Park, CA	800-843-6666
Ibis Publishing	Charlottesville, VA	800-582-0026
Icarus Press	South Bend, IN	800-242-7737
Icon	New York, NY	800-242-7737
Image Books	New York, NY	800-645-6156
Imported Publications	Chicago, IL	800-345-2665
Incentive Publications	Nashville, TN	800-421-2830
Independence Press	Independence, MO	800-821-7550
Institute for Economic Research	Fort Lauderdale, FL	800-327-6720
Institute for Palestine Studies	Washington, DC	800-874-3614
Institute for the Study of Human Knowledge	Cambridge, MA	800-222-4745
Institute of Early American History & Culture	Williamsburg, VA	800-223-2584
Institute of Modern Languages	Silver Spring, MD	800-242-7737
Institute of Physics (England)	New York, NY	800-247-7497
Instrumentalist Co.	Northfield, IL	800-323-5559
Insurance Achievement	Baton Rouge, LA	800-535-3042
Intel Corp.	Santa Clara, CA	800-548-4725
Inter/Face Associates	Middletown, CT	800-433-1116
International Association of Milk	Ames, IA	800-525-5223
International Aviation Publishers	Riverton, WY	800-443-9250
International Center for Creative Thinking	New Rochelle, NY	800-828-8285
International Fire Service Training Association	Stillwater, OK	800-654-4055
International Publications Service	Philadelphia, PA	800-821-8312
International Specialized Book Services	Portland, OR	800-547-7734
International Video Entertainment	Woodland Hills, CA	800-423-7455
Interport USA	Portland, OR	800-233-5729
Interstate Printers & Publications	Danville, IL	800-843-4774
Inter-Varsity Press	Downers Grove, IL	800-843-7225
Interweave Press	Loveland, CO	800-272-2193
Investor Publications	Cedar Falls, IA	800-553-1789
Investrek Publishing	Huntington Beach, CA	800-334-0854
Iron Crown Enterprises	Charlottesville, VA	800-325-0479
Richard D. Irwin	Homewood, IL	800-323-4560
Israel Physical Society	New York, NY	800-247-7497
Ivory Tower Publishing Co.	Watertown, MA	800-322-5016
JA Micropublishing	Eastchester, NY	800-227-2477
JFJ Publishing	San Francisco, CA	800-227-3190

Publisher	City/State	Toll-Free No.
Jalmar Press	Rolling Hills Estates, CA	800-662-9662
Jamestown Publications	Providence, RI	800-872-7323
Janus Book Publishers	Hayward, CA	800-227-2375
Jefferson Law Books	Cincinnati, OH	800-543-0883
Jerusalem Bible	New York, NY	800-645-6156
Jesuit Historical Institute	Chicago, IL	800-621-1008
Johnson Institute	Minneapolis, MN	800-231-5165
Johnson Reference Books	Alexandria, VA	800-851-2665
Johnson Reprint Co.	New York, NY	800-543-1918
Joint Center for Political Studies	Washington, DC	800-323-5277
Jones & Bartlett Publishers	Boston, MA	800-832-0034
Bob Jones University Press	Greenville, SC	800-845-5731
Josephson/Kluwer Legal Education Centers	Culver City, CA	800-421-4577
Joshua Town Publishing Associates	Lyme, CT	800-242-7737
Journey Books	Elgin, IL	800-323-7543
Jove Publications	New York, NY	800-223-0510
Judson Press	Valley Forge, PA	800-331-1053
Jury Verdict Research Institute	Solon, OH	800-321-6910
K-Dimensions Publishers	Decatur, GA	800-241-4702
KC Publications	Las Vegas, NV	800-626-9673
KET	Lexington, KY	800-354-9067
Joan Kahn	New York, NY	800-221-7945
Kalmbach Publishing	Milwaukee, WI	800-558-1544
Kampmann and Co.	New York, NY	800-526-7626
Kar-Ben Copies	Rockville, MD	800-452-7236
Kaypro Corp.	Del Mar, CA	800-452-9776
J. J. Keller Associates	Neenah, WI	800-558-5011
Kent Publishing Co.	Boston, MA	800-354-9706
Kent State University Press	Kent, OH	800-242-7737
Key Book Service	Bridgeport, CT	800-243-2790
Key Curriculum Project	Berkeley, CA	800-338-7638
Keystone Publications	New York, NY	800-223-0935
Neil A. Kjos Music Co.	San Diego, CA	800-854-1592
Kluwer Law Books Publishers	New York, NY	800-821-4526
Knapp Press	New York, NY	800-526-4264
Alfred A. Knopf	New York, NY	800-638-6460
Knowledge Industry Publications	White Plains, NY	800-248-5474
John Knox Press	Atlanta, GA	800-334-6580
Kodansha International	New York, NY	800-242-7737
Kregel Publications	Grand Rapids, MI	800-253-5465
Lane Publishing Co.	Menlo Park, CA	800-227-7346
Larousse & Co.	New York, NY	800-526-0275
Seymour Lawrence	New York, NY	800-526-0275
Lawyers Cooperative Publishing	Rochester, NY	800-527-0430
Lea & Febiger	Philadelphia, PA	800-433-3850
Learning Process Center	National City, CA	800-221-7374

Publisher	City/State	Toll-Free No.
Learning Publications	Holmes Beach, FL	800-222-1525
Learning Well	Roslyn Heights, NY	800-645-6564
Learning Works	Santa Barbara, CA	800-235-5767
Leaven Press	Kansas City, MO	800-821-7926
Lederer Enterprises	Asheville, NC	800-258-7160
Hal Leonard Publishing Corp.	Milwaukee, WI	800-558-4774
Lerner Publications Co.	Minneapolis, MN	800-328-4929
Lewis Publishers	Chelsea, MI	800-525-7894
Lexington Books	Lexington, MA	800-428-8071
Peter Li	Dayton, OH	800-531-3456
Library of America	New York, NY	800-631-3577
Light & Life Press	Winona Lake, IN	800-348-2513
Light Impressions Corp.	Rochester, NY	800-828-6216
Liguori Publications	Liguori, MO	800-325-9521
Limelight Editions	New York, NY	800-242-7737
Linch Publishers	Winter Park, FL	800-327-7055
Linden Publishing Co.	Fresno, CA	800-345-4447
Lineal Publishing Co.	Fort Lauderdale, FL	800-222-4253
J. B. Lippincott	Philadelphia, PA	800-242-7737
Lippincott Junior Books	New York, NY	800-242-7737
Little, Brown & Co.	Boston, MA	800-343-9204
Liveright Publishing Corp.	New York, NY	800-233-4830
Llewellyn Publications	St. Paul, MN	800-843-6666
Lodestar Books	New York, NY	800-526-0275
Lomond Publications	Mt. Airy, MD	800-443-6299
Lothrop, Lee & Shepard Books	New York, NY	800-631-1199
Loyola University Press	Chicago, IL	800-621-1008
Robert B. Luce	Bridgeport, CT	800-243-2790
MTI Teleprograms	Deerfield, IL	800-621-2131
Macmillan Publishing Co.	New York, NY	800-257-5755
MacRae's Blue Book	New York, NY	800-622-7237
Madrona Press	Austin, TX	800-624-1739
Magickal Childe	New York, NY	800-843-6666
Ralph Maltby Enterprises	Newark, OH	800-848-8358
Management Information Source	Portland, OR	800-626-8257
Mangold	Northvale, NJ	800-526-0107
Manor Health Care Corp.	Silver Spring, MD	800-637-1400
Mansell Publishing	Bronx, NY	800-367-6770
Richard Marek Books	New York, NY	800-221-7945
Market Data Retrieval	Westport, CT	800-243-5538
Marquis Who's Who	Wilmette, IL	800-621-9669
Master Book Publishers	San Diego, CA	800-621-0852
Masterco Press	Ann Arbor, MI	800-443-0100
Masterworks Publishers	Friday Harbor, WA	800-445-1313
Mastery Education Corp.	Watertown, MA	800-225-3214
Math House	Glen Ellyn, IL	800-222-3547
Matrix Software	Big Rapids, MI	800-622-4070

Publisher	City/State	Toll-Free No.
Matvest Media	Minneapolis, MN	800-547-5570
Mayflower Books	New York, NY	800-932-0070
McCutchan Publishing Corp.	Berkeley, CA	800-227-1540
McDonnell Douglas Information Systems Group	St. Louis, MO	800-325-1087
McGraw-Hill Book Co.	New York, NY	800-628-0004
McRel Laboratory	New York, NY	800-242-7737
Media Materials	Baltimore, MD	800-638-1010
Media Press	Chatsworth, CA	800-262-7367
Medical Economics Books	Oradell, NJ	800-223-0581
Medical Manor Books	Philadelphia, PA	800-343-8464
Mentor Books	New York, NY	800-526-0275
Meridian Books	New York, NY	800-526-0275
Merriam-Webster	Springfield, MA	800-828-1880
Charles E. Merrill Publishing Co.	Westerville, OH	800-848-6205
Frank Merriwell	Syosset, NY	800-645-6337
Mesorah Publications	Brooklyn, NY	800-637-6724
The Michie Co. Law Publishers	Charlottesville, VA	800-446-3410
Micro Information Publishers	Prior Lake, MN	800-328-0196
Microlytics	East Rochester, NY	800-828-6293
Microsystems Press	New York, NY	800-932-0017
Midway Reprints	Chicago, IL	800-621-2736
Milady Publishing Corp.	New York, NY	800-223-8055
Milford Null Modem	Malvern, PA	800-345-2121
Miller Accounting Publishers	San Diego, CA	800-543-1918
Minerva Press	New York, NY	800-242-7737
Minnesota Historical Society Press	St. Paul, MN	800-647-7827
Mitchell Publishing	Santa Cruz, CA	800-435-2665
Modern Curriculum Press	Cleveland, OH	800-321-3106
Money Market Directories	Charlottesville, VA	800-446-2810
Montezuma Micro	Dallas, TX	800-527-0347
Moody Press	Chicago, IL	800-621-5111
Thomas More Press	Chicago, IL	800-835-8965
Morgan-Rand Publications	Philadelphia, PA	800-354-8673
Morrison-Peterson Publishers	Kailua, HI	800-528-3665
William Morrow & Co.	New York, NY	800-631-1199
C. V. Mosby Co.	St. Louis, MO	800-325-4177
Mother Earth News	Henderson, NC	800-438-0238
Motorbooks International Publishers	Osceola, WI	800-826-6600
Mountain Missionary Press	Harrisville, NH	800-367-1888
John Muir Publications	Santa Fe, NM	800-223-2584
Multnomah Press	Portland, OR	800-547-5890
Mike Murach & Associates	Fresno, CA	800-221-5528
Museum of Modern Art	New York, NY	800-343-9204
Museum of Western Art	Denver, CO	800-525-7047
Music Sales Corp.	New York, NY	800-431-7187

Publisher	City/State	Toll-Free No.
S. D. Myers	Akron, OH	800-321-9580
NEC Home Electronics USA	Wood Dale, IL	800-632-7638
NILS Publishing Co.	Chatsworth, CA	800-423-5910
Nassau Press	Princeton, NJ	800-526-0275
National Assessment of Educational Progress	Princeton, NJ	800-223-0267
National Association for Education of Young Children	Washington, DC	800-424-2460
National Association of Home Builders	Washington, DC	800-368-5242
National Association of Social Workers	Silver Spring, MD	800-638-8799
National Bureau of Economic Research	Cambridge, MA	800-621-2736
National Center for Constitutional Studies	Salt Lake City, UT	800-522-6227
National Center for State Courts	Williamsburg, VA	800-446-8952
National Clearinghouse for Bilingual Education	Arlington, VA	800-647-0123
National Council for International Visitors	Washington, DC	800-523-8101
National Fire Protection Association	Quincy, MA	800-344-3555
National Forensics Center	Lawrenceville, NJ	800-526-5177
National Health Publishing	Owings Mills, MD	800-446-2221
National Information Center for Educational Media	Albuquerque, NM	800-421-8711
National Law Publishing	Owings Mills, MD	800-446-2221
National League for Nursing	New York, NY	800-847-8480
National Learning Corp.	Syosset, NY	800-645-6337
National Museum of Canada	Chicago, IL	800-621-2736
National Nursing Review	Los Altos, CA	800-221-4093
National Practice Institute	Minneapolis, MN	800-328-4444
National Public Radio	Washington, DC	800-253-0808
National Publications of the Black Hills	Rapid City, SD	800-843-8892
National Register Publishing Co.	Wilmette, IL	800-323-6772
National Society for the Study of Education	Chicago, IL	800-621-2736
National Society to Prevent Blindness	New York, NY	800-221-3004
National Textbook Co.	Lincolnwood, IL	800-323-4900
National Tour Association	Lexington, KY	800-682-8886
National Underwriter Co.	Cincinnati, OH	800-543-0874
Natural History Press	New York, NY	800-645-6156
Navpress	Colorado Springs, CO	800-525-7151
Nazareth Books	New York, NY	800-645-6156

Publisher	City/State	Toll-Free No.
Thomas Nelson	Nashville, TN	800-251-4000
The New American Library	New York, NY	800-526-0275
New Boundary Design	Chanhassen, MN	800-328-6795
New Classics Library	Gainesville, GA	800-336-1618
New Directions Publishing Corp.	New York, NY	800-223-2584
New Horizon Press	Far Hills, NJ	800-257-5755
New Leaf Press	Green Forest, AZ	800-643-9535
New Readers Press	Syracuse, NY	800-448-8878
New York Academy of Sciences	New York, NY	800-843-6927
New York Graphic Society Books	Boston, MA	800-343-9204
New York Zoetrope	New York, NY	800-242-7546
Newberry Library Publications	Chicago, IL	800-621-2736
Newbury House Publishers	Rowley, MA	800-242-7737
Newmarket Press	New York, NY	800-257-5755
Nightingale Paperbacks	Boston, MA	800-343-2806
Ursula Nordstrom Books	New York, NY	800-242-7737
Norse Press	Sioux Falls, SD	800-843-1300
North Light Publishers	Fairfield, CT	800-543-4644
North River Press	Croton-on-Hudson, NY	800-251-4000
Northland Press	Flagstaff, AZ	800-346-3257
Northwestern Press	Minneapolis, MN	800-328-3831
Northwestern University Traffic Institute	Evanston, IL	800-323-4011
Jeffrey Norton Publishers	Guilford, CT	800-243-1234
W. W. Norton & Co.	New York, NY	800-223-2584
Obelisk	New York, NY	800-526-0275
Ohara Publications	Burbank, CA	800-423-2874
Ohio University Press	Athens, OH	800-242-7737
Oil Daily	Washington, DC	800-368-5803
Old Golf Shop	Cincinnati, OH	800-227-8700
Oliver-Nelson	Nashville, TN	800-251-4000
101 Productions	San Francisco, CA	800-621-0851
Open Court Publishing Co.	La Salle, IL	800-435-6850
Orbis Books	Maryknoll, NY	800-258-5838
Oriental Institute	Chicago, IL	800-621-2736
Ken Orr & Associates	Topeka, KS	800-255-2459
Oryx Press	Phoenix, AZ	800-457-6799
Ken Osbeck Publications	Grand Rapids, MI	800-253-5465
Osborne/McGraw-Hill	Berkeley, CA	800-227-0900
Our Sunday Visitor	Huntington, IN	800-348-2440
Outdoor Bible Series	New York, NY	800-645-6156
Outlet Book Co.	New York, NY	800-526-4264
Overlook Press	New York, NY	800-631-3577
Oxford University Press	New York, NY	800-458-5833
Oxmoor House	Birmingham, AL	800-242-7737
P. A. R.	Providence, RI	800-556-7277
PC Press	New York, NY	800-932-0017

Publisher	City/State	Toll-Free No.
PSG Publishing Co.	Littleton, MA	800-225-5020
PSI Research	Milpitas, CA	800-228-2275
PWS Publications	Boston, MA	800-354-9706
Pacific Press Publishers Association	Boise, ID	800-447-7377
Pacific Search Press	Seattle, WA	800-858-0628
Paganiniana Publications	Neptune, NJ	800-631-2188
Paideia Press	Grand Rapids, MI	800-253-7283
Paladin Press	Boulder, CO	800-351-1700
A. N. Palmer Co.	Schaumburg, IL	800-323-9563
Pan American Navigation Service	Van Nuys, CA	800-423-5932
Pantheon	New York, NY	800-638-6460
Paper Birch Press	Ashland, WI	800-336-5666
Para Research	Gloucester, MA	800-843-6666
Paraclete Press	Orleans, MA	800-451-5006
Parenting Press	Seattle, WA	800-992-6657
Parents Anonymous	Los Angeles, CA	800-421-0353
Parents Magazine Press	New York, NY	800-526-0275
B. A. Pargh Co.	Nashville, TN	800-227-1000
Parish Life Press	Philadelphia, PA	800-367-8737
Parnassus Press	Oakland, CA	800-225-3362
Pasha Publications	Arlington, VA	800-424-2908
Patchwork Publications	Las Vegas, NV	800-634-6268
Pathway Press	Cleveland, TN	800-251-7216
Peachtree Publishers	Atlanta, GA	800-241-0113
Pegasus	Indianapolis, IN	800-257-5755
Pelican Books	New York, NY	800-631-3577
Penguin Books	New York, NY	800-631-3577
Peregrine Smith Books	Layton, UT	800-421-8714
Perennial Library	New York, NY	800-242-7737
Perma Bound Books	Jacksonville, IL	800-637-6581
Permanent Press	Sag Harbor, NY	800-221-0960
Thomas W. Perrin	Rutherford, NJ	800-321-7912
Peters Corp.	Santa Fe, NM	800-621-5884
Peterson's Guides	Princeton, NJ	800-225-0261
Pflaum Press	Dayton, OH	800-543-4383
Phoenix Books	Chicago, IL	800-621-2736
Phoenix Publishing	Canaan, NH	800-843-6666
Physician's Record Co.	Berwyn, IL	800-323-9268
Pick Publications	Southfield, MI	800-247-1559
Picture Book Studio, USA	Natick, MA	800-462-1252
Pilgrimage Press	Cincinnati, OH	800-543-0883
Pilot Publications	Ocala, FL	800-521-2120
Piper Books	New York, NY	800-225-3362
Plenum Publishing	New York, NY	800-221-9369
Plume Books	New York, NY	800-526-0275
Pomegranate Artbooks	Corte Madera, CA	800-227-1428

Publisher	City/State	Toll-Free No.
Pope John Center	St. Louis, MO	800-533-8095
Clarkson N. Potter Books	New York, NY	800-526-4264
Power Books	Old Tappan, NJ	800-631-1970
Predicasts	Cleveland, OH	800-321-6388
Prentice Hall	Englewood Cliffs, NJ	800-562-0245
Presbyterian & Reformed Publishing House	Grand Rapids, MI	800-253-7283
Price/Stern/Sloan Publishers	Los Angeles, CA	800-421-0892
Princeton Architectural Press	Princeton, NJ	800-334-0854
Print Media Services	Elk Grove, IL	800-323-8899
Pritchett & Hull Associates	Atlanta, GA	800-241-4925
Pro Serve Corp. of Sarasota	Sarasota, FL	800-237-9222
Professional Education Systems	Eau Claire, WI	800-826-7155
Professional Resource Exchange	Sarasota, FL	800-443-3364
Prometheus Books	Buffalo, NY	800-421-0351
Proscenium Publishers	New York, NY	800-242-7737
Psychohistory Press	New York, NY	800-521-7004
Psychological Assessment Resources	Lutz, FL	800-331-8378
Public Media	Chicago, IL	800-323-4222
Public Utilities Reports	Arlington, VA	800-368-5001
Publishers Group West	Emeryville, CA	800-982-8319
Puffin Books	New York, NY	800-631-3577
Pushcart Press	Wainscott, NY	800-223-2584
Putnam Publishing Group	New York, NY	800-847-5515
QED Information Services	Wellesley, MA	800-343-4848
Quadrangle Books	New York, NY	800-242-7737
Quality Books	Lake Bluff, NY	800-323-4241
Quality Education Data	Denver, CO	800-525-5811
Quantum Press	New York, NY	800-645-6156
Que Corp.	Indianapolis, IN	800-428-5331
Queue	Bridgeport, CT	800-232-2224
Quill Trade Paperbacks	New York, NY	800-631-1199
Quinlan Press	Boston, MA	800-551-2500
Quintessence Publishing Co.	Chicago, IL	800-621-0387
R. C. Publications	Bethesda, MD	800-222-2654
Raintree Publishers	Milwaukee, WI	800-558-7264
Rand McNally & Co.	Chicago, IL	800-323-4070
Randall Book Co.	Sandy, UT	800-453-1356
Randall House Publications	Nashville, TN	800-251-5762
Random House	New York, NY	800-638-6460
Rapture	New York, NY	800-526-0275
Rawson Associates	New York, NY	800-257-5755
Reader's Digest Association	Pleasantville, NY	800-431-1726
Reader's Digest Press	New York, NY	800-638-6460
Realtors National Marketing	Chicago, IL	800-621-7035
Record Research	Menomonee Falls, WI	800-521-0707

Publisher	City/State	Toll-Free No.
Redwood Records	Oakland, CA	800-227-2400
Regal Books	Ventura, CA	800-235-3415
Regency	Nashville, TN	800-251-4000
Regents Publishing Co.	New York, NY	800-822-8202
Reiss Publishing	New York, NY	800-526-0275
Research Publications	Phoenix, AZ	800-528-0559
Research Publications	Woodbridge, CT	800-732-2477
Resource Applications	Baltimore, MD	800-826-1877
Resource Publications	San Jose, CA	800-228-2028
Retail Reporting Bureau	New York, NY	800-251-4545
Fleming H. Revell Co.	Old Tappan, NJ	800-631-1970
Reward Paperbacks	Englewood Cliffs, NJ	800-562-0245
Reynal & Co.	New York, NY	800-631-1199
Richardson & Snyder	New York, NY	800-526-0275
Rittenhouse Book Distributors	King of Prussia, PA	800-345-6425
Riverdale Systems Design	Riverdale, NY	800-622-4070
Riverside Publishing Co.	Boston, MA	800-225-3362
Riverwood Publications	New York, NY	800-526-0275
Rizzoli International Publications	New York, NY	800-433-1238
Rodale Press	Emmaus, PA	800-527-8200
Roscoe Pound-American Trial Lawyers Association	Washington, DC	800-424-2725
Roth Publishing	Great Neck, NY	800-327-0295
Fred B. Rothman & Co.	Littleton, CO	800-457-1986
Royal House Publishing Co.	Beverly Hills, PA	800-222-3360
Running Press Book Publishers	Philadelphia, PA	800-428-1111
Russel Sage Foundation	New York, NY	800-242-7737
Rutledge Books	New York, NY	800-526-4264
Rynd Communications	Owings Mills, MD	800-446-2221
SRA—Science Research Associates	Chicago, IL	800-621-0476
William H. Sadlier	New York, NY	800-221-5175
Sadlier-Oxford	New York, NY	800-221-5175
Sage Books	Athens, OH	800-242-7737
Salem Press	Englewood Cliffs, NJ	800-221-1592
Sales Success Press	Newport Beach, CA	800-772-1172
Salesman's Guide	New York, NY	800-223-1797
Sammis Publishing Corp.	New York, NY	800-526-4264
Howard W. Sams & Co.	Indianapolis, IN	800-428-7267
Santillana Publishing Co.	Northvale, NJ	800-526-0107
K. G. Saur Verlag	New York, NY	800-521-0707
Saybrook	Old Saybrook, CT	800-233-4830
Scala Art Books	New York, NY	800-242-7737
Schirmer Books	New York, NY	800-257-5755
Scholarly Resources	Wilmington, DE	800-772-8937
School Aid Co.	Danville, IL	800-447-2665
School Zone Publishing Co.	Grand Haven, MI	800-253-0564
Scott Publications	Livonia, MI	800-458-8237

Publisher	City/State	Toll-Free No.
Scott Publishing Co.	New York, NY	800-242-7737
Scribner Book Co.	New York, NY	800-257-5755
Scribner Library Paperbacks	New York, NY	800-257-5755
Charles Scribner's Sons	New York, NY	800-257-5755
Scripture Press Publications	Wheaton, IL	800-323-9409
Seabury Books	Minneapolis, MN	800-242-7737
Second Chance Press	Sag Harbor, NY	800-221-0960
Sentinel Publishing Co.	Lubbock, TX	800-858-4062
Sentry Editions	New York, NY	800-225-3362
Seven Locks Press	Cabin John, MD	800-251-4000
Shambhala Publications	Boulder, CO	800-638-6460
Harold Shaw Publishers	Wheaton, IL	800-742-9782
Shawnee Printing Co.	Shawnee, OK	800-654-4166
Shepard's/McGraw-Hill	Colorado Springs, CO	800-525-2474
Shipley Associates	Bountiful, UT	800-343-0009
M. Shonken Communications	New York, NY	800-227-1617
Showcase Publishing Co.	Fairfield, CA	800-526-0275
Sierra Club Books	San Francisco, CA	800-638-6460
Elisabeth Sifton Books	New York, NY	800-631-3577
Signet Books	New York, NY	800-526-0275
Signet Classics	New York, NY	800-526-0275
Signs of the Times Publishing Co.	Cincinnti, OH	800-543-1925
Silver Burdett	Morristown, NJ	800-631-8081
Simmons-Boardman Books	Omaha, NE	800-228-9670
Simon & Schuster	New York, NY	800-223-2336
Slack	Thorofare, NJ	800-257-8290
M. Ismail Sloan	Lynchburg, VA	800-221-5724
Gibbs M. Smith	Layton, UT	800-421-8714
W. H. Smith Publishers	New York, NY	800-932-0070
Smithsonian Books	Washington, DC	800-223-2584
Social Issues Resources Series	Boca Raton, FL	800-327-0513
Society for Teachers of Family Medicine	Kansas City, MO	800-821-2512
Society for Visual Education	Chicago, IL	800-621-1900
SoftCorp	Clearwater, FL	800-255-7526
Software Directions	Randolph, NJ	800-346-7638
Somerset Press	Carol Stream, IL	800-323-1049
Sotheby's Publications	Hagerstown, MD	800-242-7737
South-Western Publishing Co.	Cincinnati, OH	800-543-0487
Spectrum Books	Englewood Cliffs, NJ	800-562-0245
Spire Books	Old Tappan, NJ	800-631-1970
Spizzirri Publishing Co.	Medinah, IL	800-325-9819
Springer-Verlag	New York, NY	800-526-7254
Springflower Books	Minneapolis, MN	800-328-6109
Springhouse Corp.	Springhouse, PA	800-346-7844
Squadron Signal Publications	Carrollton, TX	800-527-7427
St. Luke's Press	Memphis, TN	800-524-5554

Publisher	City/State	Toll-Free No.
St. Martin's Press	New York, NY	800-221-7945
St. Mary's Press	Winona, MN	800-533-8095
Stackpole Books	Harrisburg, PA	800-732-3669
Standard Publishing	Cincinnati, OH	800-543-1301
Robert A. Stanger Co.	Shrewsbury, NJ	800-631-2291
Stanton & Lee Publishers	Madison, WI	800-356-4600
Starblaze Editions	Norfolk, VA	800-446-8572
Star-Gate Enterprises	Orinda, CA	800-824-2222
Starkey Laboratories	Eden Prairie, MN	800-328-8602
Steck-Vaughn Co.	Austin, TX	800-531-5015
Steinway & Sons	Long Island City, NY	800-223-6017
Stillpoint	Walpole, NH	800-526-0275
Stockton Press	New York, NY	800-221-2123
Stoeger Publishing Co.	South Hackensack, NJ	800-631-0722
Storey Communications	Pownal, VT	800-441-5700
Story House Corp.	Charlottesville, NY	800-847-2105
Stratford Press	Los Angeles, CA	800-242-7737
Lyle Stuart	Secaucus, NJ	800-572-6657
Stubs Publications	New York, NY	800-223-7565
Sunburst Communications	Pleasantville, NY	800-431-1934
Sunflower Books	New York, NY	800-932-0070
Sunset Books	Menlo Park, CA	800-227-7346
Swallow Press	Athens, OH	800-242-7737
Swansea Press	Philadelphia, PA	800-792-6732
Sweet Publishing Co.	Fort Worth, TX	800-531-5220
Sybex	Berkeley, CA	800-227-2346
Sycamore Island Books	Boulder, CO	800-824-7888
Symbol of Excellence Publishers	Birmingham, AL	800-231-0503
Systems Impact Co.	Washington, DC	800-822-4636
T.I.S.	Bloomington, IN	800-367-4002
TAB Books	Blue Ridge Summit, PA	800-233-1128
TEL Publishers	Rockford, IL	800-835-5835
TFH Publications	Neptune, NJ	800-631-2188
TSC Computer	Boston, MA	800-225-3362
TSR	Lake Geneva, WI	800-558-5977
TSR Hobbies	Lake Geneva, WI	800-638-6460
Taft Corp.	Washington, DC	800-424-3761
Taking Sides	Guilford, CT	800-243-6532
Truman M. Talley	New York, NY	800-526-0275
J. P. Tarcher	Los Angeles, CA	800-225-3362
Taunton Press	Newtown, CT	800-243-7252
Taurus	Northvale, NJ	800-526-0107
Tax Analysts	Arlington, VA	800-336-0439
Taylor & Francis	Philadelphia, PA	800-821-8312
Taylor & Ng	Fairfield, CA	800-227-4090
Teacher's College Press	New York, NY	800-242-7737
Teaching Resources Corp.	Hingham, MA	800-527-4747

Publisher	City/State	Toll-Free No.
Tech Ed Publishing	Tempe, AZ	800-323-3133
Technical Data Corp.	Boston, MA	800-343-7745
Technology Marketing Corp.	Norwalk, CT	800-243-6002
Technomic Publishing Co.	Lancaster, PA	800-233-9936
Teleometrics International	The Woodlands, TX	800-527-0406
Telshore Publishing Co.	Marshfield, MA	800-343-9707
Temporal Acuity Products	Bellevue, WA	800-426-2673
Ten Speed Press	Berkeley, CA	800-841-2665
Thames & Hudson	New York, NY	800-223-2584
Thompson Publishing Group	Washington, DC	800-424-2959
Thorndike Press	Thorndike, ME	800-223-6121
Three M Publishing	St. Paul, MN	800-328-1449
Ticknor & Fields	New York, NY	800-225-3362
Tidewater Publishers	Centreville, MD	800-638-7641
Time-Life Books	Alexandria, VA	800-343-9204
Times Books	New York, NY	800-242-7737
Times Mirror Magazines and Book Division	New York, NY	800-526-0275
Todd & Honeywell	Great Neck, NY	800-233-3361
Joan Toggitt	West Caldwell, NJ	800-922-0808
Tor	New York, NY	800-221-7945
Torah Aura Productions	Los Angeles, CA	800-238-6724
Torchbooks	New York, NY	800-242-7737
Training Resource Corp.	Harrisburg, PA	800-222-9909
Treasure Chest Publications	Tucson, AZ	800-223-5369
Tree Communications	New York, NY	800-242-7737
Treehouse Paperbacks	Englewood Cliffs, NJ	800-562-0245
Triad Publishing Co.	Gainesville, FL	800-874-7777
Trimark Publishing Co.	New Castle, DE	800-874-6275
Trinet	Parsippany, NJ	800-874-6381
Troll Associates	Mahwah, NJ	800-526-5289
Trophy	New York, NY	800-242-7737
Twayne Publishers	Boston, MA	800-343-2806
Twenty-Third Publications	Mystic, CT	800-321-0411
Tyndale House Publishers	Wheaton, IL	800-323-9400
U.S. Catholic Conference	Washington, DC	800-235-8722
U.S.-China Peoples Friendship Association	Washington, DC	800-368-5883
UMI Research Press	Ann Arbor, MI	800-521-0600
Ultralight Publications	Hummelstown, PA	800-441-7527
Frederick Ungar Publishing Co.	New York, NY	800-242-7737
Unicorn Books	New York, NY	800-526-0275
Unilaw Library	Norfolk, VA	800-446-8572
Unipub	Lanham, MD	800-233-0506
Unique Publications	Burbank, CA	800-332-3330
University Books	Secaucus, NJ	800-572-6657
University Microfilms International	Ann Arbor, MI	800-521-0600

Publisher	City/State	Toll-Free No.
University of Arkansas Press	Fayetteville, AR	800-242-7737
University of California	Berkeley, CA	800-822-6657
University of Chicago Press	Chicago, IL	800-621-2736
University of Illinois Press	Champaign, IL	800-242-7737
University of Missouri Press	Columbia, MO	800-242-7737
University of Notre Dame Press	Notre Dame, IN	800-242-7737
University of Oklahoma Press	Norman, OK	800-242-7737
University of Pittsburgh Press	Pittsburgh, PA	800-242-7737
University of Utah Press	Salt Lake City, UT	800-662-0062
University of Washington Press	Seattle, WA	800-441-4115
University Press of Kentucky	Lexington, KY	800-242-7737
University Publications of America	Frederick, MD	800-692-6300
The Upper Room	Nashville, TN	800-251-3320
VC Publishing	Hudson, FL	800-472-9336
Vadore Publishing Co.	Dix Hills, NY	800-645-1112
Valley of the Sun	Malibu, CA	800-421-6603
Venture Economics	Wellesley Hills, MA	800-521-8110
Veterinary Medicine Publishing Co.	Lenexa, KS	800-255-6864
Victor Books	Wheaton, IL	800-323-9409
Video Forum	Guilford, CT	800-243-1234
Video Travel	Williamsport, PA	800-828-6888
Viking Press	New York, NY	800-631-3577
Villard Books	New York, NY	800-638-6460
Vintage Trade Books	New York, NY	800-638-6460
Virago	New York, NY	800-645-6156
Visual Education Association	Springfield, OH	800-543-5947
Voluntad Publishers	Lincolnwood, IL	800-323-4900
Voyager Books	New York, NY	800-543-1918
Wadsworth Health Sciences	Monterey, CA	800-354-9706
Wadsworth Publishing Co.	Belmont, CA	800-354-9706
J. Weston Walch Publishers	Portland, ME	800-341-6094
Frank R. Walker Co.	Chicago, IL	800-631-7795
Wallace-Homestead Book Co.	Lombard, IL	800-323-2596
Walterick Publishers	Kansas City, KS	800-255-4097
William K. Walthers	Milwaukee, WI	800-558-5478
Warne	New York, NY	800-631-3577
Warner Books	New York, NY	800-638-6460
Warner Press	Anderson, IN	800-428-6427
Warren, Gorham & Lamont	New York, NY	800-922-0066
Wasatch Education Systems	Salt Lake City, UT	800-624-1732
Washington Square Press	New York, NY	800-223-2336
Watson-Guptill Publications	New York, NY	800-526-3641
Franklin Watts	Danbury, CT	800-672-6672
Weber Systems	Chesterland, OH	800-851-6018
Samuel Weiser	York Beach, ME	800-843-6666
Wesleyan University Press	Middleton, CT	800-242-7737
West Publishing Co.	St. Paul, MN	800-328-9352

Publisher	City/State	Toll-Free No.
Westcliffe Publishers	Englewood, CO	800-523-3692
Westin Communications	Woodland Hills, CA	800-421-1893
Westminster Press	Philadelphia, PA	800-523-1631
Westmoreland Museum of Art	Greensburg, PA	800-242-7737
Whatever Publishers	Mill Valley, CA	800-227-3900
Whitaker House	Springdale, PA	800-245-2422
White Dove Publishing Co.	San Diego, CA	800-621-0852
Whitney Library of Design	New York, NY	800-526-3641
Whole World Publishing	Deerfield, IL	800-323-4305
Oliver Wight, Ltd. Publications	Essex Junction, VT	800-343-0625
Wildwood Publications	Traverse City, MI	800-447-7367
John Wiley & Sons	New York, NY	800-526-5368
Wiley-Interscience	New York, NY	800-526-5368
Wiley Professional Books	Somerset, NJ	800-526-5368
Williams & Wilkins	Baltimore, MD	800-638-0672
Willow Creek Press	Oshkosh, WI	800-341-7770
H. W. Wilson Co.	Bronx, NY	800-367-6770
B. L. Winch & Associates/Jalmar Press	Rolling Hills Estates, CA	800-662-9662
Windfall Books	New York, NY	800-645-6156
Windsor Publications	Woodland Hills, CA	800-423-5761
Wine Appreciation Guild	San Francisco, CA	800-242-9462
Winn Books	Seattle, WA	800-426-4150
Winston Press	Minneapolis, MN	800-328-5125
Harry Winston	New York, NY	800-223-2305
Winston-Derek Publications	Nashville, TN	800-826-1888
Wolcotts	Paramount, CA	800-421-2220
Woman's Press	New York, NY	800-544-1016
Wonder-Treasure Books	Los Angeles, CA	800-421-0892
Woodcraft Supply Co.	Woburn, MA	800-225-1153
Word Among Us Press	Washington, DC	800-638-8539
Word Books	Waco, TX	800-433-3340
Wordware Publishing Co.	Plano, TX	800-231-7467
Workman Publishing Co.	New York, NY	800-722-7202
World Book	Chicago, IL	800-621-8202
Wright Group	San Diego, CA	800-523-2371
Writers and Readers Publishing	New York, NY	800-223-2584
Writer's Digest Books	Cincinnati, OH	800-543-4644
Year Book Medical Publishers	Chicago, IL	800-621-9262
Yours Truly	Westminster, CA	800-845-7076
Zebra Books	New York, NY	800-221-2647
Charlotte Zolotow Books	New York, NY	800-242-7737

How to Write a Letter to Your Legislator

American Library Association, 110 Maryland Ave. N.E., Washington, DC 20002

The most frequently used, correct forms of address are:

To your Senator	*To your Representative*
The Honorable (*full name*)	The Honorable (*full name*)
United States Senate	U.S. House of Representatives
Washington, DC 20510	Washington, DC 20515

"Sincerely yours" is in good taste as a complimentary close. Remember to sign your given name and surname. If you use a title in your signature, be sure to enclose it in parentheses.

Forms similar to the above, addressed to your state capital, are appropriate for your state representatives and senators.

Where possible use your official letterhead. If this is not in order, and you write as an individual, use plain white bond paper, and give your official title following your signature as a means of identification and to indicate your competency to speak on the subject.

Do's

1 Your legislators like to hear opinions from home and want to be kept informed of conditions in the district. Base your letter on your own pertinent experiences and observations.

2 If writing about a specific bill, describe it by number or its popular name. Your legislators have thousands of bills before them in the course of a year and cannot always take time to figure out to which one you are referring.

3 They appreciate intelligent, well-thought-out letters that present a definite position, even if they do not agree.

4 Even more important and valuable to them is a concrete statement of the reasons for your position—particularly if you are writing about a field in which you have specialized knowledge. Representatives have to vote on many matters with which they have had little or no firsthand experience. Some of the most valuable information they receive comes from facts presented in letters from people who have knowledge in the field.

5 Short letters are almost always best. Members of Congress receive many, many letters each day, and a long one may not get as prompt a reading as a brief statement.

6 Letters should be timed to arrive while the issue is alive. Members of the committee considering the bill will appreciate having your views while the bill is ripe for study and action.

7 Don't forget to follow through with a thank-you letter.

Note: "How to Write a Letter to Your Legislator" is reprinted with the permission of the American Library Association Washington office.

Don'ts

1 Avoid letters that merely demand or insist on votes for or against a certain bill or that say what vote you want but not why. A letter with no reasoning, good or bad, is not very influential.

2 Threats of defeat at the next election are not effective.

3 Boasts of how influential the writer is are not helpful.

4 Do not ask for a vote commitment on a particular bill before the committee in charge of the subject has had a chance to hear the evidence and makes its report.

5 Form letters or letters that include excerpts from other letters on the same subject are not as influential as a simple letter drawing on your own experience.

6 Congressional courtesy requires legislators to refer letters from nonconstituents to the proper offices, so you should generally confine your letter writing to members of your state's delegation or members of the committee specifically considering the bill.

7 Do not engage in letter-writing overkill. Quality, not quantity, is what counts.

Distinguished Books

Notable Books of 1986

This is the fortieth year in which this list of distinguished books has been issued by the Notable Books Council of the Reference and Adult Services Division of the American Library Association.

Atwood, Margaret. *The Handmaid's Tale.* Houghton. $16.95.

Baker, Will. *Mountain Blood.* University of Georgia Press. $14.95.

Beschloss, Michael R. *Mayday: Eisenhower, Khrushchev, and the U-2 Affair.* Harper. $19.95.

Carillo, Charles. *Shepherd Avenue.* Atlantic. $15.95.

Carter, Angela. *Saints and Sinners.* Viking. $13.95.

Charyn, Jerome. *Metropolis: New York as Myth, Marketplace, and Magical Land.* Putnam. $18.95.

Critchfield, Richard. *Those Days: An American Album.* Doubleday/Anchor. $19.95.

Denby, Edwin. *The Complete Poems.* Random. $16.45; pap. $7.95.

Dubus, Andre. *The Last Worthless Evening.* Godine. $15.95.

Duras, Marguerite. *The War: A Memoir.* Translated from the French by Barbara Bray. Pantheon. $13.95.

Erdrich, Louise. *The Beet Queen.* Holt. $16.95.

Goldberg, Vicki. *Margaret Bourke-White: A Biography.* Harper. $25.45.

Grooms, Red. *Red Grooms: A Retrospective, 1956–1984.* Abrams/Pennsylvania Academy of Fine Arts. $29.95.

Henley, Patricia. *Friday Night at Silver Star: Stories.* Graywolf. pap. $7.50.

Hersh, Seymour M. *"The Target Is Destroyed": What Really Happened to Flight 007 and What America Knew about It.* Random. $17.95.

Hochschild, Adam. *Half the Way Home: A Memoir of Father and Son.* Viking. $15.95.

Hugo, Richard. *The Real West Marginal Way: A Poet's Autobiography.* Norton. $19.95.

Ishiguro, Kazuo. *An Artist of the Floating World.* Putnam. $15.95.

Jhabvala, Ruth Prawer. *Out of India.* Morrow. $16.95.

Lopez, Barry. *Arctic Dreams: Imagination and Desire in a Northern Landscape.* Scribner. $22.95.

McFadden, Cyra. *Rain or Shine: A Family Memoir.* Knopf. $16.95.

Malone, Michael. *Handling Sin.* Little, Brown. $17.95.

Maslow, Jonathan Evan. *Bird of Life, Bird of Death: A Naturalist's Journey through a Land of Political Turmoil.* Simon & Schuster. $17.95.

Mathiessen, Peter. *Men's Lives: The Surfmen and Baymen of the South Fork.* Random. $29.95.

Mehta, Ved. *Sound-Shadows of the New World.* Norton. $17.95.

Parfit, Michael. *South Light: A Journey to the Last Continent.* Macmillan. $16.95.

Pratt, Charles W. *In the Orchard.* Tidal Press. $22.00.

Price, Reynolds. *Kate Vaiden.* Atheneum. $16.95.

Rivabella, Omar. *Requiem for a Woman's Soul.* Translated from the Spanish by Paul Riviera and Omar Rivabella. Random. $14.95.

Rosengarten, Theodore. *Tombee: Portrait of a Cotton Planter; with the Journal of Thomas B. Chaplin (1822–1890).* Morrow. $22.95.

Roszak, Theodore. *The Cult of Information: The Folklore of Computers and the True Art of Thinking.* Pantheon. $17.95.

Rush, Norman. *Whites.* Knopf. $14.95.

Shipler, David K. *Arab and Jew: Wounded Spirits in a Promised Land.* Times Books. $22.50.

Sperber, A. M. *Murrow: His Life and Times.* Freundlich. $25.00.

Stone, Robert. *Children of Light.* Knopf. $17.95.

Szulc, Tad. *Fidel: A Critical Portrait.* Morrow. $19.95.

Taylor, Peter. *A Summons to Memphis.* Knopf. $15.95.

Best Young Adult Books of 1986

Each year a committee of the Young Adult Services Division of the American Library Association compiles a list of best books for young adults selected on the basis of young adult appeal. These titles must meet acceptable standards of library merit and provide a variety of subjects for different tastes and a broad range of reading levels. *School Library Journal (SLJ)* also provides a list of best books for young adults. The 1986 list was compiled by the Baltimore-Washington Young Adult Review Committee, made up of public and school librarians in the greater Baltimore-Washington area, and was published in the December 1986 issue of the journal. The following list combines the titles selected for both lists. The notation ALA or *SLJ* following the price indicates the source of each selection.

Allen, Benedict. *Who Goes Out in the Midday Sun?* Viking. $18.95. *SLJ.*

Angelou, Maya. *All God's Children Need Traveling Shoes.* Random. $15.95. ALA, *SLJ.*

Appel, Allen. *Time After Time.* Carroll & Graf. $17.95. ALA.

Archer, Jules. *The Incredible Sixties: The Stormy Years that Changed America.* Harcourt. $16.95. ALA, *SLJ.*

Arnosky, Jim. *Flies in the Water, Fish in the Air: A Personal Introduction to Fly Fishing.* Lothrop. $11.75. ALA, *SLJ.*

Atwood, Margaret. *The Handmaid's Tale.* Houghton. $16.95. ALA.

Avi. *Wolf Rider.* Bradbury. $12.95. ALA.

Bess, Clayton. *Tracks.* Houghton. $12.70. ALA.

Birnbaum, Louis. *Red Dawn at Lexington.* Houghton. $18.95. *SLJ.*

Blume, Judy. *Letters to Judy: What Your Kids Wish They Could Tell You.* Putnam. $17.95. ALA.

Bodanis, David. *The Secret House.* Simon & Schuster. $18.95. ALA.

Boissard, Janine. *A Time to Choose.* Little. $15.95. *SLJ.*

Branscum, Robbie. *The Girl.* Harper. $10.89. ALA.

Brooks, Bruce. *Midnight Hour Encores.* Harper. $13.95. ALA.

Brooks, Terry. *Magic Kingdom for Sale—Sold.* Ballantine/Del Rey. $16.95. ALA.

Callahan, Steven. *Adrift: Seventy-Six*

Days Lost at Sea. Houghton. $15.95. ALA, *SLJ.*

Calvert, Patricia. *Yesterday's Daughter.* Scribner. $11.95. ALA.

Caras, Roger. *Mara Simba: The African Lion.* Holt. $15.95. ALA.

Card, Orson Scott. *Speaker for the Dead.* Tor. $15.95. ALA.

Cash, Johnny. *Man in White.* Harper. $13.95. *SLJ.*

Cohen, Susan, and Daniel Cohen. *A Six-Pack and a Fake I.D.: Teens Look at the Drinking Question.* Evans. $11.95. ALA.

Collier, James Lincoln. *When the Stars Begin to Fall.* Delacorte. $14.95. ALA.

Cooney, Caroline. *Don't Blame the Music.* Pacer/Putnam. $13.95. ALA.

Crutcher, Chris. *Stotan!* Greenwillow. $10.25. ALA.

Dahl, Roald. *Going Solo.* Farrar. $12.95. ALA.

Dana, Barbara. *Necessary Parties.* Harper/Zolotow. $14.89. ALA.

Dann, Patty. *Mermaids.* Clarion/Ticknor & Fields. $13.95. ALA.

Derby, Pat. *Visiting Miss Pierce.* Farrar. $12.95. ALA.

Doctorow, E. L. *World's Fair.* Random. $17.95. *SLJ.*

Fante, John. *1933 Was a Bad Year.* Black Sparrow. $8.50. ALA.

Fine, Judylaine. *Afraid to Ask: A Book for Families to Share about Cancer.* Lothrop. $12.88; pap. $6.95. ALA.

Finnegan, William. *Crossing the Line: A Year in the Land of Apartheid.* Harper. $22.95. ALA.

Gingher, Marianne. *Bobby Rex's Greatest Hits.* Atheneum. $15.95. ALA.

Gino, Carol. *Rusty's Story.* Bantam. pap. $3.95. *SLJ.*

Gordon, Sol. *When Living Hurts.* Union of American Hebrew Congregations. pap. $8.95. *SLJ.*

Greenberg, Joanne. *Simple Gifts.* Holt. $15.45. ALA.

Greene, Constance C. *The Love Letters of J. Timothy Owen.* Harper. $11.89. ALA.

Grunwald, Lisa. *Summer.* Knopf. $15.95. ALA.

Guy, David. *Second Brother.* NAL. $6.95. ALA.

Hall, Lynn. *The Solitary.* Scribner. $11.95. ALA.

Hambly, Barbara. *Dragonsbane.* Ballantine/Del Rey. pap. $3.50. ALA, *SLJ.*

Hill, Susan. *The Woman in Black.* Godine/Harper. $15.95. ALA.

Hitchcock, Barbara, compiler. *Sightseeing: A Space Panorama.* Knopf. $24.95. *SLJ.*

Hunter, Mollie. *Cat, Herself.* Harper. $11.89. ALA.

James, Bill. *The Bill James Historical Baseball Abstract.* Villard. $24.95. *SLJ.*

Jones, Diana Wynne. *Howl's Moving Castle.* Greenwillow. $10.25. ALA.

Jones, Douglas C. *Roman.* Holt. $15.45. *SLJ.*

Keegan, John, and Richard Holmes. *Soldiers: A History of Men in Battle.* Viking. $22.95. *SLJ.*

Kerr, M. E. *Night Kites.* Harper. $10.89. ALA.

Koertge, Ron. *Where the Kissing Never Stops.* Atlantic. $14.45. ALA.

Korman, Gordon. *Son of Interflux.* Scholastic. $12.95. ALA.

Kress, Nancy. *Trinity and Other Stories.* Bluejay. $15.95. *SLJ.*

Lasky, Kathryn. *Pageant.* Four Winds. $12.95. ALA.

Le Vert, John. *The Flight of the Cassowary.* Atlantic. $14.95. ALA.

Levoy, Myron. *Pictures of Adam.* Harper. $12.89. ALA.

Lopez, Barry. *Arctic Dreams: Imagination and Desire in a Northern Landscape.* Scribner. $22.95. ALA.

Mahy, Margaret. *The Catalogue of the Universe.* McElderry. $11.95. ALA.

Mandela, Winnie. *Part of My Soul Went with Him*. Norton. $14.95; pap. $4.95. ALA.

Mathabane, Mark. *Kaffir Boy*. Macmillan. $19.95. *SLJ*.

Mazer, Harry. *When the Phone Rang*. Scholastic. $11.95. ALA.

Meeting the Winter Bike Rider. Dell. pap. $3.50. ALA.

Miller, Helen Hill. *Captains from Devon: The Great Elizabethan Seafarers Who Won the Oceans for England*. Algonquin. $16.95. *SLJ*.

Moll, Richard. *The Public Ivys*. Viking. $18.95. ALA.

Naylor, Phyllis Reynolds. *The Keeper*. Atheneum. $13.95. ALA.

Okomoto, Jean Davies. *Jason's Women*. Atlantic. $13.95. ALA.

Parini, Jay. *The Patch Boys*. Holt. $15.95. ALA.

Patent, Dorothy Hinshaw. *The Quest for Artificial Intelligence*. Harcourt. $13.95. ALA.

Pei, Lowry. *Family Resemblances*. Knopf. $16.95. ALA, *SLJ*.

Pekkanen, John. *Donor: How One Girl's Death Gave Life to Others*. Little. $16.95. *SLJ*.

Ramati, Alexander. *And the Violins Stopped Playing: A Story of the Gypsy Holocaust*. Franklin Watts. $15.95. ALA.

Rinaldi, Ann. *Time Enough for Drums*. Holiday House. $12.95. ALA.

Rostkowski, Margaret I. *After the Dancing Days*. Harper. $13.89. ALA.

Rylant, Cynthia. *A Fine White Dust*. Bradbury. $11.95. ALA.

Sanders, Scott R. *Bad Man Ballad*. Bradbury. $13.89. ALA.

Spiegelman, Art. *Maus: A Survivor's Tale*. Pantheon. $8.95. ALA.

Strieber, Whitley, and James Kunetka. *Nature's End: the Consequences of the Twentieth Century*. Warner. $17.95. *SLJ*.

Sullivan, Jack, ed. *Penguin Encyclopedia of Horror and the Supernatural*. Viking. $29.95. ALA.

Thompson, Julian. *A Band of Angels*. Scholastic. $12.95. ALA.

Townsend, Sue. *The Adrian Mole Diaries*. Grove/Random. $14.95. ALA.

Voigt, Cynthia. *Izzy, Willy-Nilly*. Atheneum. $14.95. ALA.

Wilford, John. *Riddle of the Dinosaurs*. Knopf. $22.95. ALA.

Willey, Margaret. *Finding David Dolores*. Harper. $10.89. ALA.

Winters, Nathan B. *Architecture Is Elementary: Visual Thinking through Architectural Concepts*. Gibbs M. Smith. $19.95. *SLJ*.

Wirths, Claudine G., and Mary Bowman-Kruhm. *I Hate School: How to Hang in and When to Drop Out*. Crowell. $11.89. ALA.

Zerman, Melvyn Bernard. *Taking on the Press: Constitutional Rights in Conflict*. Crowell. $11.89. ALA, *SLJ*.

Zolotow, Charlotte, ed. *Early Sorrows: Ten Stories of Youth*. Harper. $12.89. ALA.

Best Children's Books of 1986

A list of notable children's books is selected each year by the Notable Children's Books Committee of the Association for Library Service to Children of the American Library Association (ALA). The committee is aided by suggestions from school and public children's librarians throughout the United States. The book review editors of *School Library Journal (SLJ)* also compile a list each year, with full notations, of best books for

children. The following list is a combination of ALA's Notable Children's Books of 1986 and *SLJ*'s selection of "Best Books 1986," published in the December 1986 issue of *SLJ*. The source of each selection is indicated by the notation ALA or *SLJ* following each entry. [See "Literary Prizes" in Part 5 for Newbery, Caldecott, and other award winners — *Ed*.]

Alcock, Vivien. *The Cuckoo Sister.* Delacorte. $14.95. ALA, *SLJ*.

Alexander, Lloyd. *The Illyrian Adventure.* Dutton. $12.58. ALA.

Andrews, Jan. *The Very Last First Time.* Illustrated by Ian Wallace. Atheneum. $11.95. ALA.

Archer, Jules. *The Incredible Sixties: The Stormy Years that Changed America.* Harcourt. $16.95. *SLJ*.

Arnosky, Jim. *Flies in the Water, Fish in the Air: A Personal Introduction to Fly Fishing.* Lothrop. $11.75. ALA, *SLJ*.

Ashabranner, Brent. *The Children of the Maya: A Guatemalan Indian Odyssey.* Photographs by Paul Conklin. Dodd. $12.95. ALA, *SLJ*.

Bauer, Marion Dane. *On My Honor.* Clarion. $11.95. ALA, *SLJ*.

Brooks, Bruce. *Midnight Hour Encores.* Harper. $13.89. *SLJ*.

Brown, Laurene Krasny, and Marc Brown. *Dinosaurs Divorce: A Guide for Changing Families.* Atlantic. $13.95. *SLJ*.

Browne, Anthony. *Piggybook.* Knopf. $10.99. *SLJ*.

Bunting, Eve. *The Mother's Day Mice.* Illustrated by Jan Brett. Clarion/Ticknor & Fields. $12.95. *SLJ*.

Cameron, Ann. *More Stories Julian Tells.* Illustrated by Ann Strugnell. Knopf. $10.95. ALA, *SLJ*.

Carrick, Carol. *What Happened to Patrick's Dinosaurs?* Illustrated by Donald Carrick. Clarion. $12.95. ALA, *SLJ*.

Daly, Niki. *Not so Fast, Songololo.* Atheneum/McElderry. $12.95. *SLJ*.

Duder, Tessa. *Jellybean.* Viking. $11.95. ALA.

Ernst, Lisa Campbell. *Up to Ten and*

Down Again. Lothrop. $10.88. *SLJ*.

Fine, Judylaine. *Afraid to Ask: A Book for Families to Share about Cancer.* Lothrop. $12.88; pap. $6.95. ALA.

Fisher, Leonard Everett. *Ellis Island: Gateway to the New World.* Holiday. $12.95. *SLJ*.

Fleischman, Paul. *Rear-View Mirrors.* Harper. $10.89. *SLJ*.

Fleischman, Sid. *The Whipping Boy.* Illustrated by Peter Sis. Greenwillow. $11.75. ALA, *SLJ*.

Fox, Paula. *The Moonlight Man.* Bradbury. $12.95. ALA, *SLJ*.

Frank, Rudolph. *No Hero for the Kaiser.* Translated from the German by Patricia Crampton. Illustrated by Klaus Steffens. Lothrop. $13.00. ALA.

Fritz, Jean. *Make Way for Sam Houston.* Illustrated by Elise Primavera. Putnam. $12.95; pap. $4.95. ALA, *SLJ*.

Garner, Alan. *A Bag of Moonshine.* Illustrated by Patrick James Lynch. Delacorte. $16.95. ALA.

Gehrts, Barbara. *Don't Say a Word.* Translated from the German by Elizabeth D. Crawford. Atheneum/McElderry. $11.95. ALA.

Giblin, James Cross. *Milk: The Fight for Purity.* Crowell. $11.89. ALA.

Glenn, Mel. *Class Dismissed II: More High School Poems.* Photographs by Michael Bernstein. Clarion/Ticknor & Fields. $12.95. *SLJ*.

Goffstein, M. B. *Our Snowman.* Illustrated by author. Harper/Zolotow. $11.89. ALA.

Goor, Ron, and Nancy Goor. *Pompeii: Exploring a Roman Ghost Town.* Photographs by Ron Goor. Crowell. $11.89. *SLJ*.

Grifalconi, Ann. *The Village of Round*

and Square Houses. Illustrated by author. Little. $14.95. ALA, *SLJ.*

Griffith, Helen V. *Georgia Music.* Illustrated by James Stevenson. Greenwillow. $11.88. ALA, *SLJ.*

Hansen, Joyce. *Which Way Freedom!* Walker. $12.85. ALA.

Harris, Joel Chandler. *Jump!: The Adventures of Brer Rabbit.* Adapted by Van Dyke Parks and Malcolm Jones. Illustrated by Barry Moser. Harcourt. $14.95. ALA, *SLJ.*

Harvey, Brett. *My Prairie Year.* Based on the diary of Elenore Plaisted. Illustrated by Deborah Kogan Ray. Holiday. $11.95. ALA.

Hayes, Sarah. *This Is the Bear.* Illustrated by Helen Craig. Lippincott. $11.89. *SLJ.*

Hest, Amy. *The Purple Coat.* Illustrated by Amy Schwartz. Four Winds. $12.95. ALA.

Hoban, Tana. *Shapes, Shapes, Shapes.* Photographs by author. Greenwillow. $11.88. *SLJ.*

Hurd, Thacher. *The Pea Patch Jig.* Illustrated by author. Crown. $10.95. *SLJ.*

Hutchins, Pat. *The Doorbell Rang.* Greenwillow. $11.88. ALA.

Hutton, Warwick. *Moses in the Bulrushes.* Atheneum/McElderry. $12.95. ALA.

Jones, Diana Wynne. *Howl's Moving Castle.* Greenwillow. $10.25. ALA.

Kellogg, Steven, reteller. *Pecos Bill.* Illustrated by reteller. Morrow. $12.88. *SLJ.*

Khalsa, Dayal Kaur. *Tales of a Gambling Grandma.* Potter. $10.95. ALA.

Kitzinger, Sheila. *Being Born.* Photographs by Lennart Nilsson. Grosset & Dunlap. $14.95. ALA.

Konigsburg, E. L. *Up from Jericho Tel.* Atheneum. $12.95. ALA.

Kuklin, Susan. *Thinking Big: The Story of a Young Dwarf.* Photographs by author. Lothrop. $10.88. *SLJ.*

Lauber, Patricia. *Volcano: The Eruption*

and Healing of Mount St. Helens. Bradbury. $14.95. ALA, *SLJ.*

Lobel, Arnold. *The Random House Book of Mother Goose.* Random. $14.99. ALA, *SLJ.*

MacDonald, Suse. *Alphabatics.* Bradbury. $15.95. ALA, *SLJ.*

McKissack, Patricia C. *Flossie the Fox.* Illustrated by Rachel Isadora. Dial. $10.63. *SLJ.*

McLaughlin, Molly. *Earthworms, Dirt, and Rotten Leaves: An Exploration.* Illustrated by Robert Shetterly. Atheneum. $12.95. ALA.

McMillan, Bruce. *Counting Wildflowers.* Lothrop. $11.88. ALA.

McNulty, Faith. *Peeping in the Shell.* Illustrated by Irene Brady. Harper. $10.89. ALA.

Martin, Bill, Jr., and John Archambault. *White Dynamite and Curly Kidd.* Illustrated by Ted Rand. Holt. $11.45. *SLJ.*

Meltzer, Milton. *Poverty in America.* Morrow. $11.75. *SLJ.*

Menotti, Gian Carlo. *Amahl and the Night Visitors.* Illustrated by Michele Lemieux. Morrow. $14.88. ALA, *SLJ.*

Naylor, Phyllis Reynolds. *The Keeper.* Atheneum. $13.95. ALA.

Nelson, Theresa. *The 25¢ Miracle.* Bradbury. $13.95. *SLJ.*

Ormerod, Jan. *The Story of Chicken Licken.* Lothrop. $13.00. ALA.

Patent, Dorothy Hinshaw. *Buffalo: The American Bison Today.* Photographs by William Munoz. Clarion/Ticknor & Fields. $12.95. *SLJ.*

Peck, Richard. *Blossom Culp and the Sleep of Death.* Delacorte. $14.95. ALA.

Prelutsky, Jack, selector. *Read-Aloud Rhymes for the Very Young.* Illustrated by Marc Brown. Knopf. $14.99. *SLJ.*

Ride, Sally, with Susan Okie. *To Space and Back.* Lothrop. $14.96. ALA, *SLJ.*

Rogasky, Barbara, reteller. *The Water of Life.* Illustrated by Trina Schart Hyman. Holiday. $14.95. *SLJ.*

Rostkowski, Margaret I. *After the Dancing Days*. Harper. $13.89. ALA.

Rylant, Cynthia. *A Fine White Dust*. Bradbury. $11.95. ALA, *SLJ*.

_____. *Night in the Country*. Illustrated by Mary Szilagyi. Bradbury. $12.95. *SLJ*.

Savage, Deborah. *A Rumor of Otters*. Houghton. $12.95. ALA, *SLJ*.

Sewall, Marcia. *The Pilgrims of Plymouth*. Illustrated by author. Atheneum. $14.95. *SLJ*.

Shura, Mary Frances. *The Josie Gambit*. Dodd. $10.95. ALA.

Simon, Seymour. *The Sun*. Morrow. $12.88. ALA.

Sleator, William. *The Boy Who Reversed Himself*. Dutton. $12.95. *SLJ*.

Smith, Doris Buchanan. *Return to Bitter Creek*. Viking. $11.95. ALA, *SLJ*.

Stanley, Diane. *Peter the Great*. Four Winds. $13.95. ALA.

Stevenson, James. *When I Was Nine*. Greenwillow. $11.88. ALA.

Voigt, Cynthia. *Come a Stranger*. Atheneum. $14.95. *SLJ*.

Watkins, Yoko Kawashima. *So Far from the Bamboo Grove*. Lothrop. $10.25. ALA, *SLJ*.

Wells, Rosemary. *Max's Christmas*. Dial. $7.89. ALA, *SLJ*.

Williams, Vera B. *Cherries and Cherry Pits*. Greenwillow. $11.88. ALA.

Worth, Valerie. *Small Poems Again*. Illustrated by Natalie Babbitt. Farrar. $6.95. ALA.

Yorinks, Arthur. *Hey, Al*. Pictures by Richard Egielski. Farrar. $12.95. ALA.

Yue, Charlotte, and David Yue. *The Pueblo*. Illustrated by authors. Houghton. $12.95. *SLJ*.

Zelinsky, Paul O., reteller. *Rumpelstiltskin*. Illustrated by reteller. Dutton. $12.58. ALA, *SLJ*.

Zerman, Melvyn Bernard. *Taking on the Press: Constitutional Rights in Conflict*. Crowell. $11.89. *SLJ*.

Ziefert, Harriet. *A New Coat for Anna*. Illustrated by Anita Lobel. Knopf. $10.99. ALA.

Bestsellers of 1986:
Hardcover Fiction and Nonfiction

Daisy Maryles

Executive Editor, *Publishers Weekly*

Although several new sales records were set by the 1986 group of hardcover bestsellers, these books did not in most cases surpass the figures achieved by the top-selling 1985 hardcovers. Once again, in 1986 five hardcovers went over the million mark; and 12 books over the 500,000 line (compared to 13 in 1985). But in fiction, only 15 went over 200,000 units sold, down from the 19 that achieved that sales level in 1985. What did not change much was the number of fiction bestsellers with reported sales of more than 100,000 — 42 in 1986, 43 in 1985.

The competition for placement among the nonfiction bestsellers of the year was the stiffest ever. For the first time, a 300,000-copy sale did not guarantee a spot among the top 15. But again, in the 200,000-copy range and over 100,000, the 1986 group of non-

Note: Adapted from *Publishers Weekly*, March 13, 1987.

fiction leaders performed much the same as 1985 bestsellers — 23 sold more than 200,000 and 51 were over 100,000 in 1986; in 1985, 21 and 50 went over 200,000 and 100,000 respectively.

Even without surpassing the 1985 record, the sales performance of the 1986 bestsellers is impressive and far outstrips the unit sales figures of *PW* annual bestsellers of past years. A look at just the leaders on the 1986 hardcover lists demonstrates how high some books and authors have soared. In the case of Stephen King, his 1,206,266 sales by the end of the year for *It* are considerably higher than his previous hardcover sales record, achieved by *Pet Sematary*, 657,741 in 1983. A collaboration with Peter Straub, *The Talisman*, made it to *only* 880,287 in 1984. And the number 1 nonfiction title, *Fatherhood* by Bill Cosby, set a record as the fastest-selling hardcover book in U.S. publishing history — its unit sales of 2.4 million as of the end of 1986 were the highest of any book on *PW*'s annual bestseller charts; the previous highest grosser was Richard Bach for *Jonathan Livingston Seagull*, which sold 1,815,000 copies during 1972. It's hard to believe that back in 1979 Robert Ludlum made it to the top of the list with sales of 250,000 (in 1986, his latest hit had sales of more than 657,000).

Although first novels enjoyed a good run in 1985 — four claim sales of more than 100,000 copies — new novelists enjoyed an even better run in 1985, when three first efforts made it to the top 15. Fourteen of the 15 top 1986 fiction bestsellers were by people who have been on these end-of-the-year lists before — the only new name is Pat Conroy, certainly no debutant. There were almost no surprise subjects on the nonfiction list either — humor, fitness, biographies, and bestselling nonfiction veterans dominated. The only new subject category among the nonfiction bestsellers was sports, with one hit among the top 15 and two more among the runners-up.

All the figures for the top hardcover bestsellers, including runners-up, are based on sales figures supplied by publishers. We asked them to give us figures that reflect only 1986 U.S. trade sales — that is, sales to bookstores, wholesalers, and libraries only — not book club, overseas, and direct mail sales.

"Sales," as used on these lists, refers to books shipped and billed in calendar year 1986. Publishers were, however, asked to reflect returns made through January 30, 1987. Still, in many cases, the 1986 sales figures include books still on bookstore and wholesaler shelves and/or books on the way back to the publishers' warehouses, as well as books planned for return that may not yet have been counted.

The Million Mark

Five books soared over the million mark in 1986 and — as noted earlier — one even went over two million. Distribution in mass market outlets, aggressive promotion, and widespread discounting seem to combine in these cases to push a book to the seven-figure point.

In the case of the two fiction high rollers, their ability to sell well over the 750,000 mark was never a question. But that extra push? According to Viking sales director Brenda Marsh, King always gets maximum distribution and the advance was first set at 850,000, until customer demand brought the pre-pub in-print figure to 1,000,000. Success was helped, she said, by better-than-usual reviews for King; by the sheer size of the book (1,152 pages); and by the "super-sensational marketing campaign" that capitalized on the book's catchy title. Advance order easels, posters, streamers, ceiling signs, buttons for store employees were all part of an "It" kit sent to booksellers. The point-of-

purchase material carried such claims as "We're making *IT* big," "Don't leave this store without *IT*," and "*IT* is here."

Putnam's *Red Storm Rising*, with sales of 1,025,020, was Tom Clancy's second book. His first, *The Hunt for Red October*, was the first novel ever published by Naval Institute Press and its sales of more than 295,000 in 1985 were enough to place it at number 13 on that year's annual list. According to Putnam publisher Christine Schillig, Clancy's second book was simply "the right book with the right author at the right moment." She called *Red Storm Rising* a breakout book that reached a "huge audience of men who never before bought a book." The enormous public attention received by the author's first book and the fact that it was adopted as a favorite by Washington military and government critics (Reagan himself claimed to have read and loved it) made it possible for Clancy to tap the male fascination with military stories and high-tech weaponry.

Paul Bresnick, the Dolphin editor who came up with the idea of getting actor Bill Cosby to write a book on fathering, offers his winning formula in much the same terms: "It was the right idea at the right time with the right author." Bresnick adds one more given—"the book delivered." He points to the actor's immense popularity on the number 1 television sitcom and new sensibilities about parenting as factoring significantly into the book's success. Its publication right before Father's Day was a natural for giving the book momentum. Sales were also helped by wide distribution to outlets more traditionally reserved for paperbacks. All the 2,000-plus outlets of Kroeger's had 30-copy floor displays of the book ("We were the second hardcover to get this treatment, *Elvis and Me* was the first," says Bresnick) as did all K Mart locations. The price point of $14.95 was a "super idea," noted Bresnick. "Since we anticipated aggressive discounting, we thought it was important that the customer get change from a $10 bill when buying *Fatherhood*." He emphasized the importance of the chains and the discounting marketplace in taking a book to the level achieved by the Cosby title. But major success was never in doubt; the book had 1,000,000 in print before publication and there was a record-breaking first serialization in *Good Housekeeping* at $45 a word.

The second nonfiction million-copy bestseller, *Fit for Life*, is a holdover from the previous year, when sales of 574,000 put it on the number 4 spot for the year-end list. Its phenomenal success continued in 1986, with unit sales that reached 1,350,252 in a 12-month time span. It had a short-lived run as the fastest-selling hardcover bestseller, to be overtaken almost immediately by *Fatherhood*. But unlike the other "millionaires," *Fit for Life*'s success wasn't evident from the onset. It went out with a mere 50,000-copy first printing, and despite its $50,000 ad budget, three-week author tour to 15 cities and a strong advance sale, was initially slow to get on the bestseller list. The house commitment, demonstrated by full-page ads in the *New York Times*, the enthusiasm of Merv Griffin (who lost weight on the diet regimen) and the authors' appearance on "Donahue," sent the book over the top.

Supermarket Sales

Bantam's track record for getting a nonfiction title over the million-copy sale threshold has been well demonstrated—*His Way* with 1986 sales of 1,005,000 is its third hardcover in two years to make it into seven figures (*Iacocca* and *Yeager* were the other two). Publisher Linda Grey pointed to the single most important factor shared by all three megabestsellers—"Each chronicled extraordinary lives—a subject larger than life where the

interest of the public transcends traditional levels and draws people to bookstores who usually don't buy books, especially hardcovers." Sinatra's attempts to bring litigation to stop author Kitty Kelley from writing her book certainly contributed to the book's pre-pub notoriety. It went out with a 525,000 first printing, the largest initial hardcover printing in Bantam's history. Exceptional sales in Southern California supermarkets and wide distribution in Duane Reade drugstores in the East were just a few of the indicators for the book's success in nontraditional outlets for hardcovers. Grey points to first serialization in *People* ("a perfect launching pad") as being instrumental in creating the "frenzy" for the book right from the start.

One book that didn't sell a million copies in 1986 but did hit that figure if you add on the sales achieved in the first month or so of 1987 was *The Rotation Diet* from Norton. The book was the bestselling hardcover in Norton's 60-plus years, and it added a new dimension to the concept of selling hardcovers in the supermarket. Author Martin Katahn, director of the Vanderbilt weight management program, was looking for volunteers to test his diet theory outlined in the book. An ad in a Nashville paper attracted more than 1,200 volunteers instead of the hoped-for 25; local radio and television coverage offered to give the essentials of the diet free on the air. Soon almost 70,000 people were on the diet. A friend of the author's, an executive in the food service business, arranged for all the area Kroeger's supermarkets to merchandise "Rotation Diet specials," with official weigh-ins, weekly diet plans, and shopping lists. Nashville papers were covering the phenomenon, even reporting at one point that the city was running out of vegetables. This same kind of promotion was expanded in supermarkets across the country. There were even corporate sponsors for the book; in Tulsa, billboards from competing corporations offered a penny a pound per employee for United Way.

The Fiction Bestsellers

Six of the novelists that were among the 1985 top 15 fiction bestsellers are back again this year with more crowd pleasers, including Stephen King, Tom Clancy, Jackie Collins, Danielle Steel, Louis L'Amour, and Lawrence Sanders. Robert Ludlum and Jeffrey Archer were on the 1984 end-of-the-year list; John le Carré was high up in 1983; Judith Krantz and Ken Follett made it onto the 1982 list; James Clavell led the 1981 list; and Clive Cussler and Barbara Taylor Bradford have had previous spots on the runners-up list. For Pat Conroy, this was his breakout book, but his previous books did rack up mass market sales and have been made into successful movies. Clearly, there was no room among the top spots for an author with no previous track record.

The number 3 fiction bestseller, James Clavell's *Whirlwind*, enjoyed the number 1 spot for five of the last seven weeks of 1986 and is still among the weekly bestsellers; yet, it was one of the books singled out in bookseller surveys as a "keen disappointment," perhaps a reflection of large quantities on hand despite strong sales.

Pat Conroy was the most talked-about author at the 1985 ABA Convention and booksellers were eagerly anticipating selling *The Prince of Tides*, number 9 on the 1986 list with sales of about 297,000. It made it onto *PW*'s weekly list prior to official publication date and went up as high as number 5 during its 18-week tenure. It, too, was cited by some booksellers as disappointing; others noted that it was among the books they were most successfully handselling.

Robert Ludlum seems to go from strength to strength. An actor and theatrical producer who at 40 decided to change careers, Ludlum came out with his first book, *The*

Scarlatti Inheritance, in 1971, but it took him until 1973 to crack these year-end lists with *The Matlock Paper* in the number 8 spot. His newest, *The Bourne Supremacy*, is his bestselling hardcover to date. Jackie Collins, too, had her bestselling hardcover with *Hollywood Husbands*, which racked up 517,000 copies, enough for the number 5 position. Back in 1983, *Hollywood Wives* landed on the number 9 spot with sales of 226,505; in 1985, *Lucky* was number 7 with sales of about 386,000.

This is the fourth year in a row that Louis L'Amour has had a hardcover bestseller among the top 15, a perfect batting average considering that *Last of the Breed* is only his fourth hardcover original. Danielle Steel, too, is a regular on these lists, at least since 1981. In 1986, she racked up enough sales of *Wanderlust* to give her the number 6 position. She did better in 1985 when she had two among the top 10 — *Secrets* in the number 6 spot and *Family Album*, at number 9.

Krantz also boasts a perfect bestselling record. Each of her four books has made it onto these annual lists; her latest, *I'll Take Manhattan*, selling the best with about 400,000 copies, giving her the number 4 slot. Five of John le Carré's appearances on these charts were in the number 4 position, the last for *The Little Drummer Girl* with sales of more than 400,000 copies in 1983. His sales have slipped a bit, as *A Perfect Spy* reached number 10 based on sales of 285,600. On the other hand, Jeffrey Archer went up a few notches with sales of 278,000 for *A Matter of Honor*, in the number 11 spot, compared with his last bestseller appearance, *First Among Equals*, number 14 in 1984 with sales of 226,000. *The Eighth Commandment*, number 13 on the 1986 list, is Lawrence Sanders's twenty-first novel. His first novel, *The Anderson Tapes*, was published in 1970, and his publisher estimates that his books have sold in excess of 25 million copies and are published in 15 languages.

The Fiction Runners-Up

The second tier of fiction bestsellers includes several first novels — even one by President Reagan's daughter — as well as bestseller veterans and a number of science fiction books; among them four of the first five volumes of the Mission Earth series by L. Ron Hubbard.

The fiction runners-up are:

16 *Seasons of the Heart* by Cynthia Freeman (Putnam, 3/86; *175,798* sold in 1986)

17 *Lake Wobegon Days* by Garrison Keillor (Viking, 9/85; *175,248*)

18 *Foundation and Earth* by Isaac Asimov (Doubleday, 10/86; *170,000*)

19 *Through a Glass Darkly* by Karleen Koen (Random, 9/86; *165,244*)

20 *A Taste for Death* by P. D. James (Knopf, 11/86; *162,869*)

21 *The Golden Cup* by Belva Plain (Delacorte, 10/86; *160,239*)

22 *Flight of the Intruder* by Stephen Coonts (Naval Institute Press, 9/86; *156,824*)

23 *Mordant's Need: The Mirror of Her Dreams* by Stephen R. Donaldson (Del Rey Hardcover, 11/86; *140,000*)

24 *Garden of Eden* by Ernest Hemingway (Scribners, 5/86; *137,662*)

25 *The Songs of Distant Earth* by Arthur C. Clarke (Del Rey Hardcover, 5/86; *135,000*)

26 *Regrets Only* by Sally Quinn (Simon & Schuster, 8/86; *131,000*)

27 *Suspects* by William Caunitz (Crown, 8/86; *121,000*)

28 *Homefront* by Patti Davis (Crown, 3/86; *118,000*)

29 *Break In* by Dick Francis (Putnam, 3/86; *115,655*)

30 *Fortune of Fear, Volume 5* by L. Ron Hubbard (Bridge Publications, 10/86; *111,638*)

In 1985, 12 fiction titles with sales of more than 100,000 didn't make our top 30 list. In 1986, there were only six such titles: *Magic Kingdom for Sale — Sold!* by Terry Brooks (Del Rey Hardcover); *The Good Mother* by Sue Miller (Harper & Row): *Nobody Lives Forever* by John Gardner (Putnam); and three other titles by L. Ron Hubbard all published by Bridge — *An Alien Affair, Volume 4, The Enemy Within, Volume 3* and *Black Genesis: Fortress of Evil, Volume 2*.

Nonfiction Leaders

One title *PW* had expected to see place among the nonfiction books that sold in the six figures was David Stockman's *The Triumph of Politics: Why the Reagan Revolution Failed*, especially because of its pre-publication printing of 360,000 copies and a 10-week run on *PW*'s bestseller list. Harper & Row, which paid about $2.4 million for the book, declined to share any figures on it, stating this was company policy for this title. The question of how much of its price tag the book has earned out will continue to be the subject of much conjecture.

Seasoned authors were also a common characteristic of the nonfiction top 15, with such names as Dr. Seuss, Jeff Smith, Robert Schuller, Andy Rooney, James Herriot, and Leo Buscaglia. Entertainment figures like Frank Sinatra, Bill Cosby, and Carol Burnett were author and/or subjects of three other top sellers. And football's bad boy Jim McMahon made it to the list with what may be one of the first football biographies to achieve that goal.

Men Who Hate Women and the Women Who Love Them, Bantam's self-help guide "for men and women caught up in misogynistic relationships" by psychologist Dr. Susan Forward is the only nonfiction top seller not by or about a well-known name. However, Forward, in the number 13 spot, is a recognized name in her field and has a two-hour daily ABC radio program.

Jeff Smith, star of the very successful national public television series *The Frugal Gourmet*, had an excellent 1986 run in print, with two books among the top 15, *The Frugal Gourmet Cooks with Wine* at number 7 and *The Frugal Gourmet*, number 12. The latter was number 8 on last year's list of top nonfiction movers. Morrow's third title among the top 15 was one of the 1985 bestsellers that sold more than 100,000 copies that year.

Theodor Seuss Geisel, better known to his younger fans as Dr. Seuss, wrote his first book specifically for adults, *You're Only Old Once*. Sales went over the 655,000 mark, enough to land it on the number 5 spot, the same position captured in 1984 for his children's title, *The Butter Battle Book*, which had 423,405 sales that year.

Andrew Rooney once again scored, with *Word for Word*. In 1984, he made the number 4 spot for *Pieces of My Mind*, which garnered sales that year of 425,000; two years earlier he had two books on the year-end list: *And More by Andy Rooney* at number 3 with sales of more than 510,000 and *A Few Minutes with Andy Rooney*, number 7

with sales that year of about 306,000. Veterinarian James Herriot had two winners last year, *James Herriot's Dog Stories* at number 10 and *The Christmas Day Kitten*, number 17. His first appearance on these lists was back in 1972 with *All Things Bright and Beautiful*, number 8 with sales of 187,563.

"Televangelist" Robert Schuller makes a fourth appearance in four years on these lists; he had the number 5 spot in 1985 for *The Be-Happy Attitudes*, with sales of 525,000. Leo Buscaglia's philosophy of "caring and sharing" continues to be popular and his latest book, *Bus 9 to Paradise*, rounds out the nonfiction top 15 — the same spot he achieved in 1985 with *Loving Each Other*.

The Nonfiction Runners-Up

Many books on the list that follows would have earned a spot among the top 15 in previous years, considering that in 1985 the number 15 nonfiction bestseller had sales of more than 219,000; about 215,000 was enough in 1984; and 185,000 in 1983. The books that follow, too, include many familiar names and themes; however, politics and business titles seem to have fared less well than in previous years.

16 *A Day in the Life of America* by Rick Smolan and David Cohen, project directors (Collins, 10/86; *300,000* copies sold in 1986)

17 *The Christmas Day Kitten* by James Herriot (St. Martin's, 10/86; *260,000*)

18 *Rock Hudson* by Sara Davidson (Morrow, 7/86)

19 *One Knee Equals Two Feet (and Everything Else You Need to Know about Football)* by John Madden with Dave Anderson (Villard, 9/86; *230,368*)

20 *When All You've Ever Wanted Isn't Enough: The Search for a Life that Matters* by Harold Kushner (Summit Books, 4/86; *212,000*)

21 *The Rice Diet Report* by Judy Moscovitz (Putnam, 3/86; *209,083*)

22 *The Reckoning* by David Halberstam (Morrow, 10/86; *208,385*)

23 *Dreamgirl: My Life as a Supreme* by Mary Wilson (St. Martin's, 10/86; *205,000*)

24 *Weight Watchers Favorite Recipes* (NAL Books, 12/86; *199,386*)

25 *Pat Nixon: The Untold Story* by Julie Nixon Eisenhower (Simon & Schuster, 11/86; *188,000*)

26 *Jane Fonda's New Workout & Weight-Loss Program* by Jane Fonda (Simon & Schuster, 7/86; *163,000*)

27 *Necessary Losses* by Judith Viorst (Simon & Schuster, 4/86; *158,000*)

28 *And So It Goes* by Linda Ellerbee (Putnam, 5/86; *155,053*)

29 *Snake: The Candid Autobiography of Football's Most Dangerous Renegade* by Ken Stabler and Berry Stainback (Doubleday, 9/86; *150,000*)

30 *My Daddy Was a Pistol and I'm a Son of a Gun* by Lewis Grizzard (Villard, 10/86; *145,951*)

There were also 21 more nonfiction titles that sold more than 100,000 copies in 1986 without making the top 30 list, two more than the 19 books that fared the same

way in 1985. They include: *The Story of English* by Robert McCrum, William Cran, And Robert MacNeil (Elisabeth Sifton Books/Viking); *Ford: The Men and the Machine* by Robert Lacey (Little, Brown); *Unlimited Power* by Anthony Robbins (Simon & Schuster); *Yeager: An Autobiography* by General Chuck Yeager and Leo Janos (Bantam); *New Good Housekeeping Cookbook* by the editors of *Good Housekeeping* (Morrow); *Dancing on My Grave* by Gelsey Kirkland with Greg Lawrence (Doubleday); *Enter Talking* by Joan Rivers with Richard Meryman (Delacorte Press); *Across China* by Peter Jenkins (Morrow); *Mayflower Madam: The Secret Life of Sydney Biddle Barrows* by Sydney Biddle Barrows with William Novak (Arbor House); *I, Tina* by Tina Turner (Morrow); *America's Date with Destiny* by Pat Robertson (Nelson); *Iacocca: An Autobiography* by Lee Iacocca with William Novak (Bantam); *Paul Prudhomme's Louisiana Kitchen* by Paul Prudhomme (Morrow); *Medical Makeover* by Robert Giller (Morrow); *Wiseguy: Life in a Mafia Family* by Nicholas Pileggi (Simon & Schuster); *The Great Getty* by Robert Lenzer (Crown); *The Search for Signs of Intelligent Life in the Universe* by Jane Wagner (Harper & Row); *No Laughing Matter* by Joseph Heller and Speed Vogel (Putnam); *Made in Japan: Akio Morita and Sony* by Akio Morita with Edwin M. Reingold and Mitsuko Shimomura (E. P. Dutton); *Marilyn* with text by Gloria Steinem and photographs by George Barris (Henry Holt and Co.); and *LIFE: The First Fifty Years* by the editors of *Life* (Little, Brown).

PW's 1986 Hardcover Bestsellers

Fiction

1 *It* by Stephen King. Viking (Published Sept. 15, 1986); 1,206,266 copies sold in 1986
2 *Red Storm Rising* by Tom Clancy. Putnam (Aug. 7, 1986); 1,025,020
*3 *Whirlwind* by James Clavell. Morrow (Nov. 10, 1986)
4 *The Bourne Supremacy* by Robert Ludlum. Random House (March 15, 1986); 657,054
5 *Hollywood Husbands* by Jackie Collins. Simon & Schuster (Oct. 15, 1986); 517,000
6 *Wanderlust* by Danielle Steel. Delcorte Press (July 25, 1986); 502,234
7 *I'll Take Manhattan* by Judith Krantz. Crown (May 15, 1986); 418,000
8 *Last of the Breed* by Louis L'Amour. Bantam (July 1, 1986); 400,000
9 *The Prince of Tides* by Pat Conroy. Houghton Mifflin (Oct. 21, 1986); 297,000
10 *A Perfect Spy* by John le Carré. Knopf (May 15, 1986); 285,600
11 *A Matter of Honor* by Jeffrey Archer. Linden Press (July 11, 1986); 278,000

Note: Rankings on these lists are determined by sales figures provided by publishers; the numbers reflect reports of copies "shipped and billed" only and should not be regarded as net sales figures, since publishers do not yet know what their final returns will be.
*Sales figures were submitted to *PW* in confidence, for use only in placing the titles in their correct positions on a specific list.

*12 *Lie Down with Lions* by Ken Follett. Morrow (Jan. 31, 1986)

13 *The Eighth Commandment* by Lawrence Sanders. Putnam (June 5, 1986); 251,745

14 *Act of Will* by Barbara Taylor Bradford. Doubleday (June 20, 1986); 205,000

15 *Cyclops* by Clive Cussler. Simon & Schuster (Jan. 30, 1986); 183,000

Nonfiction

1 *Fatherhood* by Bill Cosby. Doubleday (Published May 23, 1986); 2,400,000 copies sold in 1986

2 *Fit for Life* by Harvey and Marilyn Diamond. Warner Books (June 12, 1985); 1,350,252

3 *His Way: The Unauthorized Biography of Frank Sinatra* by Kitty Kelley. Bantam (Oct. 15, 1986); 1,005,000

*4 *The Rotation Diet* by Martin Katahn. Norton (May 6, 1986)

5 *You're Only Old Once* by Dr. Seuss. Random House (March 2, 1986): 655,304

*6 *Callanetics: Ten Years Younger in Ten Hours* by Callan Pinckney. Morrow (Sept. 1984)

*7 *The Frugal Gourmet Cooks with Wine* by Jeff Smith. Morrow (Oct. 16, 1986)

8 *Be Happy—You Are Loved!* by Robert H. Schuller. Thomas Nelson (Sept. 23, 1986); 380,292

9 *Word for Word* by Andrew A. Rooney. Putnam (Nov. 16, 1986); 375,601

10 *James Herriot's Dog Stories* by James Herriot. St. Martin's (June 2, 1986); 375,000

11 *McMahon!: The Bare Truth about Chicago's Brashest Bear* by Jim McMahon with Bob Verdi. Warner Books (Nov. 1986); 360,950

*12 *The Frugal Gourmet* by Jeff Smith. Morrow (July 1984)

13 *Men Who Hate Women and the Women Who Love Them* by Dr. Susan Forward and Joan Torres. Bantam (Sept. 1986); 330,000

14 *One More Time* by Carol Burnett. Random House (Oct. 21, 1986); 329,167

*15 *Bus 9 to Paradise* by Leo Buscaglia. Morrow/Slack (Feb. 14, 1986)

Literary Prizes, 1986

ASCAP-Deems Taylor Awards. *Offered by:* American Society of Composers, Authors, and Publishers. *Winners:* Jack Chambers for *Milestones—The Music and Times of Miles Davis* (Beech Tree); Michael Forsyth for *Buildings for Music* (MIT); Nelson George for *Where Did Our Love Go?* (St. Martin's); Philip Gossett for *Anna Bolena and the Artistic Maturity of Gaetano Donizatti* (Oxford); John Edward Hasse for *Ragtime* (Schirmer); Peter Ostwald for *Schu-*

mann—*The Inner Voice of a Musical Genius* (Northeastern Univ.); Nancy Reich for *Clara Schumann—The Artist and the Woman* (Cornell Univ.); Martin Williams for *Jazz Heritage* (Oxford).

Academy of American Poets Fellowship Award. For distinguished poetic achievement. *Winner:* Irving Feldman.

Jane Addams Children's Book Award. For a book promoting the cause of peace, social justice, and world community. *Offered by:* Women's International League for Peace and Freedom and the Jane Addams Peace Association. *Winner:* Milton Meltzer for *Ain't Gonna Study War No More* (Harper).

Nelson Algren Award. For a work of fiction in progress. *Offered by:* PEN American Center. *Winner:* Mary La Chapelle for "Three Stories" (unpublished).

American Academy and Institute of Arts and Letters Awards in Literature. *Winners:* Russell Banks, Frederick Busch, Robert A. Caro, Robert Kelly, Barry Lopez, David Mamet, Marsha Norman, Lore Segal.

American Academy in Rome Fellowship in Literature. *Offered by:* American Academy and Institute of Arts and Letters. *Winner:* Richard Kenney.

American Book Awards. *Winners:* (fiction) E. L. Doctorow for *World's Fair* (Random House); (nonfiction) Barry Lopez for *Arctic Dreams* (Scribners).

American Printing History Association Award. For distinguished contribution to the study of the history of publishing and printing. *Winner:* G. Thomas Tanselle.

American Society of Journalists and Authors Author of the Year Award. *Winner:* John McPhee.

Ana Award, *Winner:* John Bryson for *Evil Angels* (Viking).

Hans Christian Andersen Medals. *Winners:* Robert Ingpen and Patricia Wrightson.

Associated Writing Programs Award. For book-length manuscript to be published by a university press. *Winner:* (novel) Kenn Robbins for *The Buttermilk Bottoms* (Univ. of Iowa Press).

Association of Logos Bookstores Book Awards. For excellence in religious publishing. *Winners:* (fiction) Garrison Keillor for *Lake Wobegon Days* (Viking); (nonfiction) Robert Bellah et al. for *Habits of the Heart: Individualism and Commitment in American Life* (Univ. of California); (religious inspirational) Mike Mason for *The Mystery of Marriage* (Multnomah); (religious scholarly) Jaroslav Pelikan for *Jesus Through the Centuries* (Yale Univ.).

Association of Logos Bookstores Award. *Winner:* Peter Spier for *The Book of Jonah* (Doubleday).

Australian Book Awards. *Winners:* (book of the year) Thurley Fowler for *The Green Wind* (Rigby); (junior book of the year) Mary Steele for *Arkwright* (Hyland); (picture book of the year) Terry Denton for *Felix and Alexander* (Oxford): (South Australian Festival Award) Ivan Southall for *The Long Night Watch* (Methuen).

Australian Council Book Award. *Winner:* (book of the year) Peter Carey for *Illywhacker* (Univ. of Queensland).

Australian Literature Society Gold Medal Award. *Winner:* Thea Astley.

Bancroft Prizes—$4,000 each. For books of exceptional merit and distinction in American history, American diplomacy, and the international relations of the United States. *Offered by:* Columbia University. *Winners:* Kenneth T. Jackson for *Crabgrass Frontier: The Suburbanization of the United States* (Oxford); Jacqueline Jones for *Labor of Love, Labor of Sorrow: Black Women, Work and the Family from Slavery to the Present* (Basic).

Banta Award. For literary achievement by a Wisconsin author. *Offered by:* Wis-

consin Library Association. *Winner:* Lorine Niedecker for *From This Condensery: The Complete Writing of Lorine Niedecker* (Jargon Society).

Mildred L. Batchelder Award. For an American publisher of a children's book originally published in a foreign language in a foreign country and subsequently published in English in the United States. *Winner:* Rudolf Frank for *No Hero for the Kaiser* (Lothrop).

Bay Area Book Reviewers Association. *Winners:* (fiction) Molly Giles for *Rough Translations* (Univ. of Georgia); (poetry) August Kleinzahler for *Storm over Hackensack* (Moyer Bell); (arts and letters) Paul Robinson for *Opera and Ideas* (Harper); (history and social issues) Carolyn Wakeman and Yue Daiyun for *To the Storm* (Univ. of California): (translation) Stephen Mitchell for *Sonnets to Orpheus* by Rainer Maria Rilke (Simon & Schuster).

Bay Area Book Reviewers Association Publishers Award. *Winner:* Yoshiko Uchida for *The Happiest Ending* (Atheneum).

Before Columbus Foundation American Book Awards. For literary achievement by people of various ethnic backgrounds. *Winners:* Miguel Algarin for *Time's Now* (Arte Publico); Helen Barolini, ed. for *The Dream Book: An Anthology of Writing by Italian American Women* (Schocken); Natasha Borovsky for *A Daughter of the Nobility* (Holt); Raymond Federman for *Smiles on Washington Square* (Thunder's Mouth); Linda Hogan for *Seeing Through the Sun* (Univ. of Massachusetts); Susan Howe for *My Emily Dickinson* (North Atlantic); Jeff Hannusch (a.k.a. Almost Slim) for *I Hear You Knockin'* (Swallow); Cherrie Moraga and Gloria Anzaldua, eds. for *This Bridge Called My Back: Writings by Radical Women of Color* (Kitchen Table: Women of Color); Toshio Mori for

Yokahama California (Univ. of Washington); Anna Lee Walters for *The Sun Is Not Merciful* (Firebrand); Terence Winch for *Irish Musicians/American Friends* (Coffee House); *(lifetime achievement award)* Hisaye Yamamoto.

Curtis G. Benjamin Award for Creative Publishing. *Winner:* Simon Michael Bessie.

Bennett Award. *Winner:* Nadine Gordimer.

Bibliographical Society of America Research Fellowships. For scholars undertaking research associated with the history of the book trade and publishing. *Offered by:* Bibliographical Society of America. *Winners:* Georgia B. Bumgardner for *The History of the Illustration of American Literature to 1865* (American Antiquarian Society); John A. Emerson for *An Unknown Ninth Century Gradual and Antiphonal from Southern France, Albi, Bibliothèque municipale, MS 44: A Paleographical, Liturgical, and Musical Study* (Univ. of California); Joel J. Gold for *The Battle of the Shorthand Books, 1635–1800* (Univ. of Kansas); Michael Gullick for *English and French Medieval Manuscripts in Medieval Bindings pre-1225 in U.S.A. Collections* (Camberwell School of Art and Crafts, London); Leslie K. Howsam for *The Victorian Bestseller: Production, Packaging, and Distribution of Scriptures by the British and Foreign Bible Society, 1804–1864* (York University, Toronto); David Chalmers Hunter for *English Song Books of the Early Eighteenth Century: Their Contents, Publication, and Description* (Louisiana State Univ.): Richard S. Peterson for editing *Envies Scourge, and Vertues Honour* (Univ. of Connecticut); William S. Peterson for *A Bibliography of Sir John Betjeman* (Univ. of Maryland); William P. Stoneman for *Anglo-Saxon Manuscripts in North American Collections*

(Victoria College, Univ. of Toronto); Steven N. Zwicker for *Polemic and History: The English Translation of Tacitus's "Annals" (1698)* (Washington Univ.).

Irma Simonton Black Award. For unified excellence of a story line, language, and illustration in a published work for young children. *Offered by:* Bank Street College of Education. *Winner:* Sandra Boynton for *Chloe and Maude* (Little, Brown).

James Tait Black Memorial Prizes (Great Britain). For the best biography and the best novel of the year. *Offered by:* University of Edinburgh. *Winners:* (biography) David Nokes for *Jonathan Swift: A Hypocrite Reversed* (Oxford); (novel) Robert Edric for *Winter Garden* (Deutsch).

Bologna Children's Book Fair Prizes (Italy). *Offered by:* Bologna Trade Fair Promotion Agency. *Winners:* (graphics–children's) *One Morning* (G. C. Press-Japan); (graphics–youth) *Der Hut des Kaminfegers* (BVD Basilius-Switzerland); (junior critics) *Peter and the Wolf* (Sauerlander-Switzerland).

Booker Prize for Fiction. *Offered by:* Book Trust (Great Britain). *Winner:* Kinglsey Amis for *The Old Devils* (Hutchinson).

British Columbia Book Prize for Poetry. *Winner:* Joe Rosenblatt for *Poetry Hotel* (McClelland & Stewart).

Boston Globe–Horn Book Awards. For excellence in text and illustration. *Winners:* (fiction) Zibby Oneal for *In Summer Light* (Viking Kestrel); (nonfiction) Peggy Thomson for *Auks, Rocks and the Odd Dinosaur: Inside Stories from the Smithsonian's Museum of Natural History* (Crowell); (illustration) Molly Bang for *The Paper Crane* (Greenwillow).

John Nicholas Brown Prize. *Offered by:* Medieval Academy of America. *Winner:* Bernard F. Reilly for *The Kingdom of Leon Castilla under Queen Urraca, 1109–1126* (Princeton Univ.).

John Burroughs Medal. *Winner:* Gary Paul Nabhan for *Gathering the Desert* (Univ. of Arizona).

Witter Bynner Foundation Prize for Poetry. *Offered by:* American Academy and Institute of Arts and Letters. *Winner:* C. D. Wright.

CLA Book of the Year (Canada). *Offered by:* Canadian Library Association. *Winner:* Cora Taylor for *Julia* (Western Producer Prairie Books).

Caldecott Medal. For the artist of the most distinguished picture book. *Offered by:* R. R. Bowker Company. *Winner:* Richard Egielski for *Hey, Al* (Farrar, Straus).

John W. Campbell Award. For an author whose first professional story was published in the preceding two years. *Offered by:* World Science Fiction Convention. *Winner:* David Brin.

John W. Campbell Memorial Award. For an outstanding science fiction novel. *Offered by:* Center for the Study of Science Fiction. *Winner:* Melissa Scott.

Canada-Australia Literary Award. *Offered by:* Australian Council. *Winner:* Jack Hodgins.

Canada Council Children's Literature Prizes. *Winners:* (text) Cora Taylor for *Julia* (Western Producer Prairie Books); Robert Soulieres for *Casse-tete Chinois* (Editions Pierre Tisseyre); (illustration) Terry Gallagher for *Murdo's Story: A Legend from Northern Manitoba* (Pemmican Publications); Roger Pare for *L'Alphabet* (Editions La Courte Echelle).

Canada Council Governor General's Literary Awards. *Winners—English-Language Books:* (fiction) Margaret Atwood for *The Handmaid's Tale* (McClelland & Stewart); (poetry) Fred Wah for *Waiting for Saskatchewan* (Turnstone); (drama) George F. Walker for *Criminals in Love* (Playwrights Can-

ada); (nonfiction) Ramsay Cook for *The Regenerators: Social Criticism in Late Victorian English Canada* (Univ. of Toronto); *French-Language Works*: (fiction) Fernand Ouellette for *Lucie ou un midi en novembre* (Boreal Express); (poetry) Andre Roy for *Action Writing* (Les Herbes Rouges); (drama) Maryse Pelletier for *Duo pour voix obstinées* (VLB Editeur); (nonfiction) François Ricard (*La litterature contre elle-même* (Boreal Express).

Canada Council Translation Prizes. For the best translation in English and French. *Winners:* (English into French) Michelle Robinson for *Louis Riel: la fin d'un rêve* (Editions Pierre Tisseyre); (French into English) Yvonne M. Klein for *Lesbian Triptych* (Women's Press).

Carey-Thomas Awards. For a distinguished project of book publishing. *Offered by:* R. R. Bowker Company. *Winners:* Elisabeth Sifton Books/ Viking Press; (honor citations) Clarkson N. Potter/Crown for *Fra Angelico* by Jacqueline and Maurice Guillaud; Univ. of Nebraska/Joslyn Art Museum for *Karl Bodmer's America*; (special citation) Ecco Press.

Carnegie Medal (Great Britain). For an outstanding book for children. *Offered by:* British Library Association. *Winner:* Kevin Crossley-Holland for *Storm* (Heinemann).

Casey Awards. *Offered by: Spitball Baseball Magazine. Winner:* Bill James for *The Bill James Historical Baseball Abstract* (Villard).

Catholic Book Awards. For an outstanding religious book. *Winners:* (adult) Donal Dor for *Spirituality and Justice* (Orbis); (professional and educational books) James A. Coriden, Thomas J. Green, Donald E. Heintschel, eds. for *The Code of Canon Law* (Paulist); (quality of design and production) Alzina Stone Dale for *The Art of G. K. Chesterton* (Loyola Univ.).

Catholic Press Association. *Winners:* (children's) Thomas L. Weck for *Back-Back and the Lima Bear* (Winston-Derek); (youth) Matthew Lancaster for *Hang Toughf* (Paulist).

Child Study Children's Book Committee Book Award. *Winner:* Beverley Naidoo for *Journey to Jo'burg* (Lippincott).

Gilbert Chinard Prize. For a distinguished scholarly book or manuscript in the history of Franco-American relations. *Offered by:* Institut Français de Washington and the Society for French Historical Studies. *Winner:* Carl J. Ekberg for *Colonial Ste. Genevieve: An Adventure on the Mississippi Frontier* (Patrice Press).

Cholmondeley Award (Great Britain). For contributions to poetry. *Offered by:* Society of Authors. *Winners:* Lawrence Durrell, James Fenton, Selima Hill.

Christopher Book Awards. For books that affirm the highest values of the human spirit. *Winners:* Barry Lopez for *Arctic Dreams: Imagination and Desire in a Northern Landscape* (Scribners); Theresa Saldana for *Beyond Survival* (Bantam); Christopher Collier and James Lincoln Collier for *Decision in Philadelphia: The Constitutional Convention of 1787* (Random House); Pablo Galdamez for *Faith of a People: The Life of a Basic Christian Community in El Salvador* (Orbis); Mark Mathabane for *Kaffir Boy: The True Story of a Black Youth's Coming of Age in Apartheid South Africa* (Macmillan); Lou Ann Walker for *A Loss for Words: The Story of Deafness in a Family* (Harper); James M. Washington, ed. for *A Testament of Hope: The Essential Writings of Martin Luther King, Jr.* (Harper); Alan Neame, trans. for *Through the Gospel with Dom Helder Camara* (Orbis); Harold S. Kushner for *When All You've Wanted Isn't Enough: The Search for a Life That Matters* (Summit); (special award) Elie Wiesel;

(children's) Marion Walker Doren for *Borrowed Summer* (Harper); Mel Glenn for *Class Dismissed II: More High School Poems* (Clarion); Amy Hester for *The Purple Coat* (Four Winds): Barbara Sameuls for *Duncan and Dolores* (Bradbury).

Fred Cody Memorial Award. *Offered by:* Bay Area Book Reviewers Association. *Winner:* Wright Morris.

Columbia University Translation Center Awards. For excellence in translation. *Winners:* (Arab League Translation Award) James Kenneson for *Fountain and Tomb* by Naguib Mahfouz; (Van de Bovenkamp-Armand G. Erpf Awards) Frank Hugus for *The Bell in Macedonia* by Knud H. Thomsen and Diana der Hovanessian and Marzbed Margossian for *Land of Fire* by Eghishe Charents; (Robert Payne Award) Charles G. Hanzlicek and Dana Hobova for *Mirroring: Selected Poems of Vladimir Holan*; (Dutch Translation Award) Rod Jellema for *Country Fair: Poems from Friesland since 1945*; (Greek Translation Award) James Stone for *The Bones: Selected Poems, 1972–82* by Jannis Kondos; (Soros Translation Award) Eszter Molnar for *Sinbad's Autumn Journey* by Gyula Krudy; (Max Hayward Award) Paul F. Schmidt for *The King of Time* by Velimir Khlebnikov; (Translation Center Awards) John Jacobs for *The Fables of Odo of Cheriton*; (Thornton Niven Wilder Prizes) Talat Sait Halman for translations into Turkish, Julia Hartwig and Artur Miedzyrzecki for translations into Polish; and Zhu Wan for translations into Chinese; (gold medal) Robert Payne (posthumous).

Common Wealth Award. For distinguished service in literature. *Winner:* John Ashbery.

Commonwealth Club of California. To honor the finest works of literature by California authors. *Offered by:* Commonwealth Club of California.

Winners—Gold Medal: (fiction) Cecile Pineda for *Face* (Viking); (nonfiction) Spiro Kostof for *A History of Architecture* (Oxford): (*Silver Medal*) Amy Hempel for *Reasons to Live* (Knopf); T. Coraghessian Boyle for *Greasy Lake and Other Stories* (Viking); Ann Stanford for *The Countess of Forli* (Orirana); (poetry) W. S. Di Piero for *Early Light* (Univ. of Utah); (Californiana) Thomas Albright for *Art in the San Francisco Bay Area, 1945–1980* (Univ. of California): (notable contribution to publishing) Walter A. Nelson-Rees for *John O'Shea, 1876–1956* (WIM); (children's) Meghan Collins for *The Willow Maiden* (Dutton).

Duff Cooper Memorial Prize (Great Britain). For a distinguished book on history, biography, politics, or poetry. *Winner:* Alan Crawford for *C. R. Ashbee: Architect, Designer and Romantic Socialist* (Yale Univ.).

De la Torre Bueno Prize. *Offered by:* Dance Perspectives Foundation. *Winner:* Jennifer Dunning for *But First a School* (Viking).

C. J. Dennis Award. *Winner:* John Landy for *Close to Nature* (Curry O'Neil, Ross).

Bill Duthie Booksellers' Choice Award. *Winner:* Cameron Young, Ken Seabrook, et al. for *The Forests of British Columbia* (Whitecap).

Editors' Book Award. *Winner:* David Bosworth for *From My Father, Singing* (Univ. of Pittsburgh).

Elliott Prize. For a first article in the field of medieval studies. *Offered by:* Medieval Academy of America. *Winner:* Margot E. Fassler for "Who Was Adam of St. Victor? The Evidence of the Sequence Manuscripts" (*Journal of the American Musicological Society* 37).

Robert Waldo Emerson Award. *Offered by:* Phi Beta Kappa. *Winner:* Benjamin I. Schwartz for *The World of Thought in Ancient China* (Belknap)..

Evans Biography Award. *Winner:* Paul Andrew Hutton for *Phil Sheridan and His Army* (Univ. of Nebraska).

Hubert Evans Nonfiction Prize. *Winner:* Bruce Hutchison for *The Unfinished Country* (Douglas & McIntyre).

Geoffrey Faber Memorial Prize (Great Britain). *Winner:* David Scott for *A Quiet Gathering* (Bloodaxe).

Eleanor Farjeon Award. *Winner:* Judith Elkin.

Faulkner Award for Fiction. *Offered by:* PEN American Center. *Winner:* Peter Taylor for *The Old Forest and Other Stories* (Doubleday).

Dorothy Canfield Fisher Children's Book Award. For a children's book by a distinguished Vermont author selected by Vermont schoolchildren. *Offered by:* Vermont Department of Libraries and Vermont Congress of Parents and Teachers. *Winner:* Robert Kimmel Smith for *The War with Grandpa* (Delacorte).

E. M. Forster Award. *Offered by:* American Academy and Institute of Arts and Letters. *Winner:* Julian Barnes.

Miles Franklin Award. *Winner:* C. K. Koch for *The Doubleman* (Chatto & Windus).

George Freedley Memorial Award. *Offered by:* Theatre Library Association. *Winners:* Margot Peters for *The Life of Mrs. Patrick Campbell* (Knopf) and Marie Koller for *The Theater Duke Georg II of Saxe-Meiningen and the German Stage* (Stanford Univ.).

Douglas Southall Freeman Literary Award. *Winner:* James A. Ramage for *Rebel Raider: The Life of General John Hunt Morgan* (Univ. of Kentucky).

Friends of American Writers Award. *Winners:* Charles Dickinson for *Crows* (Knopf); Mary Morris for *The Bus of Dreams* (Houghton Mifflin); (children's) Tom Townsend for *Where the Pirates Are* (Eakin); Whitley Strieber for *Wolf of Shadows* (Knopf).

Friends of the Chicago Public Library. *Winners:* (fiction) Jan Novak for *The Willys Dream Kit* (Harcourt); (nonfiction) Franz Schulze for *Mies Van der Rohe* (Univ. of Chicago); (children's) Betty Bates for *Thatcher Payne-in-the-Neck* (Holiday).

Fulcrum American Writing Award. *Winner:* Linda Hasselstrom *Going Over East* (Fulcrum).

Christian Gauss Award. For an outstanding book in the field of literary scholarship or criticism. *Offered by:* Phi Beta Kappa. *Winner:* Maynard Mack for *Alexander Pope: A Life* (Norton).

Georgia Children's Book Award. *Offered by:* University of Georgia College of Education. *Winner:* Betty Miles for *The Secret Life of the Underwear Champ* (Knopf); (picture storybook) Michael Hague for *The Unicorn and the Lake* by Marianna Mayer (Dial).

Tony Godwin Award. For an American or British editor (in alternate years) to spend six weeks working at a publishing house in the other's country. *Offered by:* Harcourt. *Winner:* Kathleen Anderson.

Golden Kite Awards. *Offered by:* Society of Children's Book Writers. *Winners:* (fiction) Patricia MacLachlan for *Sarah, Plain and Tall* (Harper); (nonfiction) Rhoda Blumberg for *Commodore Perry in the Land of the Shogun* (Lothrop).

Golden Spur Awards. *See* Western Writers of America Spur Awards.

Edgar Graham Memorial Prize. *Winners:* Penelope Francks for *Technology and Agricultural Development in Pre-War Japan* (Yale Univ.); Ronald J. Herring for *Land to the Tiller: The Political Economy of Agrarian Reform in South Asia* (Yale Univ.).

Kate Greenaway Medal (Great Britain). For distinguished illustration of a book for children. *Offered by:* British Library Association. *Winner:* Juan Wijngaard

for *Sir Gawain and the Loathly Lady* by Selina Hastings (Walker).

Eric Gregory Trust Awards (Great Britain). For poets under the age of 30. *Offered by:* Society of Authors. *Winners:* Mick North, Lachlan Mackinnon, Oliver Reynolds, Stephen Romer.

Guardian Fiction Award. *Winner:* Anne Tilling for *Henry's Leg* (Viking Kestrel).

Roderick Haig-Brown Regional Prize. *Winner:* Donald Graham for *Keepers of the Light* (Harbour).

Sarah Josepha Hale Award. For a writer of distinction who reflects the literary tradition of New England. *Offered by:* Friends of the Richards Library, Newport, N.H. *Winner:* Robert Coles.

Haskins Medal. For a distinguished book in the field of medieval studies by a scholar in the United States or Canada. *Offered by:* Medieval Academy of America. *Winner:* William Roach for *The Third Continuation by Manessier*, fifth volume, *The Continuations of the Old French "Perceval" of Chretien de Troyes* (American Philosophical Society).

R. R. Hawkins Award. For the most outstanding book of the year from the fields of science, medicine, technology, and business. *Offered by:* Association of American Publishers Professional and Scholarly Publishing Division. *Winner:* Jane Goodall for *The Chimpanzees of Gombe* (Belknap).

Florence Roberts Head Memorial Award. For an outstanding book about the Ohio scene. *Offered by:* Ohioana Library Association. *Winner:* Grace Goulder Izant for *Hudson's Heritage* (Kent State Univ.).

Heinemann Award (Great Britain). For a genuine contribution to literature. *Offered by:* Royal Society of Literature. *Winner:* Brian Moore for *Black Robe* (Cape).

Drue Heinz Literature Prize. For an outstanding collection of unpublished short fiction. *Offered by:* University of Pittsburgh Press and the Howard Heinz Endowment. *Winner:* Rick De Marinis for *Under the Wheat* (Univ. of Pittsburgh).

Ernest Hemingway Foundation Award. *Offered by:* PEN American Center. For a work of first fiction by an American. *Winner:* Alan Hewat for *Lady's Time* (Harper).

Ritz Paris Hemingway Award. *Winner:* Marguerite Duras for *The Lover* (Pantheon).

Sidney Hillman Foundation Prize. For an outstanding work on civil liberties, race relations, social and economic welfare, or world understanding. *Offered by:* Sidney Hillman Foundation of the Amalgamated Clothing and Textile Workers Union. *Winner:* Joseph Lelyveld for *Move Your Shadows: South Africa, Black and White* (Times Books).

Historical Novel Prize (Great Britain). *Winner:* Michael Weston for *The Cage* (Bodley Head).

Clarence L. Holte Literary Award. *Winner:* John Hope Franklin for *George Washington Williams: A Biography* (Univ. of Chicago).

Amelia Frances Howard-Gibbon Award (Canada). For the illustrator of an outstanding book. *Offered by:* Canadian Library Association, Canadian Association of Children's Librarians. *Winner:* Ken Nutt for *Zoom Away* (Groundwood).

Hugo Awards. *See* World Science Fiction Convention.

Ingersoll Prizes in Literature and Humanities. *Winners:* (T. S. Eliot Award) V. S. Naipaul; (Richard Weaver Award) Robert Nisbet.

International Reading Association Children's Book Award. For a first or second book of fiction or nonfiction by an author of promise. *Winner:* Pam Conrad for *Prairie Songs* (Harper).

Iowa School of Letters Award. For short fiction. *Offered by:* Iowa Arts Council Writers Workshop and the University of Iowa Press. *Winner:* Daniel O'Brien for *Eminent Domain* and Russell Working for *Resurrections.*

Washington Irving Children's Book Choice Awards. (fiction) Rosemary Wells for *Peabody* (Dial/Dutton); (nonfiction) Bernard Evslin for *Hercules* (Morrow).

Joseph Henry Jackson Award. *Offered by:* San Francisco Foundation. *Winner:* Jane Hirshfield for *Of Gravity and Angels* (work in progress).

Jerusalem Prize (Israel). *Winner:* J. M. Coetzee.

Juniper Prize. For an outstanding manuscript of original English poetry. *Offered by:* University of Massachusetts Press. *Winner:* Lynda Hull.

Jane Heidinger Kafka Prize. For an outstanding work of fiction by an American woman. *Offered by:* University of Rochester English Department and Writer's Workshop. *Winner:* Ursula Le Guin for *Always Coming Home* (Harper).

Sue Kaufman Prize. For a first work of fiction. *Offered by:* American Academy and Institute of Arts and Letters. *Winner:* Cecile Pineda.

Robert F. Kennedy Book Award. For works that reflect Robert Kennedy's purposes. *Winners:* Anthony Lukas for *Common Ground* (Knopf) and Robert Morrell for *Reaping the Whirlwind* (Knopf).

Coretta Scott King Award. For a work that promotes the cause of peace and brotherhood. *Offered by:* American Library Association Social Responsibilities Round Table. *Winners:* Mildred Pitts Walker for *Justin and the Best Biscuits in the World* (Lothrop); (illustrator) Jerry Pinkney for *Half a Moon and One Whole Star* by Crescent Dragon-Wagon (Macmillan).

Robert Kirsch Award. For an outstanding body of work by an author from the West or featuring the West. *Offered by: Los Angeles Times. Winner:* Kay Boyle.

Roger Klein Award for Editing. *Offered by:* PEN American Center. *Winner:* Anne Freedgood.

Janusz Korczak Award. *Offered by:* Anti-Defamation League of B'Nai B'rith. *Winners:* Alice Miller for *Thou Shalt Not Be Aware: Society's Betrayal of the Child* (Farrar, Straus); (children's) Irene Awret for *Days of Honey: The Tunisian Boyhood of Rafael Uzan* (Schocken).

Gordon J. Laing Prize. *Winner:* Paul Ricoeur for *Time and Narrative, Vol. 1* (Univ. of Chicago).

Lamont Poetry Selection. *Offered by:* Academy of American Poets. *Winner:* Jane Shore for *The Minute Hand* (Univ. of Massachusetts).

Evelyn Sibley Lampman Award. For a significant contribution to children's literature in the Pacific Northwest area. *Offered by:* Oregon Library Association. *Winner:* Irene Brady.

Harold Morton Landon Translation Award. *Offered by:* American Academy and Institute of Arts and Letters. *Winner:* William Arrowsmith for Eugenio Montale's *The Storm and Other Things* (Norton).

Allen Lane Award. *Offered by:* Australian Council. *Winner:* John Bryson for *Evil Angels* (Viking).

Peter I. B. Lavan Younger Poets Awards. *Offered by:* Academy of American Poets. *Winners:* Rita Dove, Rodney Jones, Timothy Steele.

Locus Awards. *Offered by:* Locus Publications. *Winners:* (anthology) Harlan Ellison, ed. for *Medea: Harlan's World* (Bantam); (artist) Michael Whelan; (collection) Stephen King for *Skeleton Crew* (Putnam); (fantasy novel) Roger Zelazny for *Trumps of Doom* (Arbor); (first novel) Carl Sagan for *Contact* (Simon & Schuster); (nonfiction/reference) Algis Budrys for *Benchmarks: Galaxy Bookshelf* (Southern Illinois

Univ.): (publisher) Ballantine/Del Rey; (science fiction novel) David Brin for *The Postman* (Bantam)..

Los Angeles Times Book Awards. To honor literary excellence. *Winners:* (biography) Maynard Mack for *Alexander Pope: A Life* (Norton): (current interest) Joseph Lelyveld for *Move Your Shadow: South Africa, Black and White* (Times Books); (fiction) Margaret Atwood for *The Handmaid's Tale* (Houghton Mifflin); (history) Geoffrey Hosking for *The First Socialist Society: A History of the Soviet Union from Within* (Harvard Univ.); (poetry) Derek Walcott for *Collected Poems, 1948–1984* (Farrar, Straus).

Maud Hart Lovelace Book Award. *Offered by:* Friends of the Minnesota Valley Regional Library. *Winner:* Barbara Dana for *Zucchini* (Harper).

James Russell Lowell Prize. For an outstanding literary or linguistic study, a critical edition, or a critical biography. *Offered by:* Modern Language Association of America. *Winner:* Joel Fineman for *Shakespeare's Perjured Eye: The Invention of Poetic Sensitivity in the Sonnets* (Univ. of California).

Walter and Lillian Lowenfels Criticism Award. *Offered by:* Before Columbus Foundation. *Winner:* Michael Feingold for *Close Your Eyes and Think of England* (*Village Voice*).

Dorothy McKenzie Award. For service on behalf of children. *Offered by:* Southern California Council on Literature. *Winner:* Caroline Feller Bauer.

Lenore Marshall/Nation Award. For an outstanding book of poems published in the United States. *Offered by: The Nation* and the New Hope Foundation. *Winner:* Howard Moss for *New Selected Poems* (Atheneum).

Emil/Kurt Maschler Award. *Winner:* Allan Ahlberg, illus. by Janet Ahlberg for *The Jolly Postman* (Collins).

Somerset Maugham Awards (Great Britain). For young British authors to gain

experience in foreign countries. *Offered by:* Society of Authors. *Winners:* Patricia Ferguson for *Family Myths and Legends* (Deutsch); Adam Nicolson for *Frontiers* (Weidenfeld & Nicolson); Tim Parks for *Tongues of Flame* (Heinemann).

Howard R. Marraro Prize. *Winners:* Teodolinda Barolini for *Dante's Poets: Textuality and Truth in the Comedy* (Princeton Univ.): Glauco Cambon for *Michelangelo's Poetry: Fury of Form* (Princeton Univ).

Frederic G. Melcher Award. For work that makes a significant contribution to religious liberalism. *Offered by:* Unitarian Universalist Association. *Winner:* Edward Harrison for *Masks of the Universe* (Macmillan).

Kenneth W. Mildenberger Prize. For an outstanding research publication in the field of teaching foreign languages and literature. *Winner:* Jack C. Richards for *The Context of Language Teaching* (Cambridge Univ.).

Mitchell Prizes. For an outstanding book on the history of art. *Winners:* John Rewald for *Cezanne: A Biography* (Abrams) and Thomas E. Crowe for *Painters and Public Life in Eighteenth-Century Paris* (Yale Univ.).

Modern Language Association of America Prize for Independent Scholars. *Winner:* Edward J. Brunner for *Splendid Failure: Hart Crane and the Making of "The Bridge"* (Univ. of Illinois).

Frank Luther Mott-Kappa Tau Alpha Award. For the best researched book dealing with the media. *Offered by:* National Journalism Scholarship Society. *Winner:* Roy Hoopes for *Ralph Ingersoll: A Biography* (Atheneum).

NSW Premier's Literary Awards. *Winners:* Helen Garner for *Postcards from Surfers* (McPhee Gribble/Penguin); George Munster for *A Paper Prince* (Viking/Penguin); Phillip Pepper and Tess de Araugo for *The Kurnai of Gippsland, Vol. I* (Hyland House); Robert Gray for

Selected Poems (Angus & Robertson); James Aldridge for *The True Story of Spit McPhee* (Viking/Penguin).

National Arts Club Gold Medal of Honor for Literature. *Winner:* Robertson Davies.

National Book Critics Circle Awards. *Winners:* (biography/autobiography) Theodore Rosengarten for *Tombee: Portrait of a Cotton Planter* (Morrow); (criticism) Joseph Brodsky for *Less Than One: Selected Essays* (Farrar, Straus); (fiction) Reynolds Price for *Kate Vaiden* (Atheneum); (general nonfiction) John W. Dower for *War without Mercy: Race and Power in the Pacific War* (Pantheon); (poetry) Edward Hirsch for *Wild Gratitude* (Knopf); (citation for excellence in reviewing) Richard Eder.

National Jewish Book Awards. *Winners:* (biography) Jehuda Reinharz for *Chaim Weizmann: The Making of a Zionist Leader* (Oxford); (fiction) Arnost Lustig for *The Unloved: From the Diary of Perla S.* (Arbor); (holocaust) Raul Hilberg for *The Destruction of the European Jews: Revised and Definitive Edition* (Holmes and Meier); (Israel) Steven L. Spiegel for *The Other Arab-Israeli Conflict: Making America's Middle East Policy from Truman to Reagan* (Univ. of Chicago); (Jewish history) Robert Liberles for *Religious Conflict in Social Context: The Resurgence of Orthodox Judaism in Frankfurt am Main, 1838–1877* (Leo Baeck Institute/Greenwood); (Jewish thought) David Hartman for *A Living Covenant: The Innovative Spirit in Traditional Judaism* (Free Pr.); (scholarship) Michael Fishbane for *Biblical Interpretation in Ancient Israel* (Oxford); (visual arts) Carol Herselle Krinsky for *Synagogues of Europe: Architecture, History, Meaning* (Architectural History Foundation/MIT); (literature) Linda Atkinson for *In Kindling Flame: The Story of*

Hannah Senesh, 1921–1944 (Lothrop); (illustrated books) Robert Andrew Parker for *Brothers* by Florence B. Freedman (Harper).

Nebula Awards. For outstanding works of science fiction. *Offered by:* Science Fiction Writers of America. *Winners:* (novel) Orson Scott Card for *Ender's Game* (Tor Books); (Grand Master Award) Arthur C. Clarke.

Nene Award. For an outstanding children's book selected by Hawaii's schoolchildren. *Offered by:* Hawaii Association of School Librarians and the Hawaii Library Association Children's and Youth Section. *Winner:* Stephen Manes for *Be a Perfect Person in Just Three Days* (Houghton Mifflin).

Neustadt International Prize for Literature. *Winner:* Max Frisch.

New Options Political Book Award: *Winner:* Marilyn French for *Beyond Power: Of Women, Men and Morals* (Summit).

New York Academy of Sciences Awards. For quality books about science for children. *Winners:* (older category) Sara Stein for *The Evolution Book* (Workman); (younger category) Satoshi Kitamura for *When Sheep Cannot Sleep: The Counting Book* (Farrar, Straus).

New York Times Best Illustrated Children's Book Awards. *Winners:* Donald Crews for *Flying* (Greenwillow); Arthur Geisert for *Pigs from A to Z* (Houghton Mifflin); Red Grooms for *Rembrandt Takes a Walk* by Mark Strand (Clarkson N. Potter); Yohji Izawa for *One Morning* by Canna Funakoshi (Picture Book Studio); Michael McCurdy for *The Owl Scatterer* by Howard Norman (Atlantic Monthly); Petra Mathers for *Molly's New Washington Machine* by Laura Geringer (Harper); William Steig for *Brave Irene* (Farrar, Straus); Chris Van Allsburg for *The Stranger* (Houghton Mifflin); Robert Van Nutt for *The Ugly Duckling* by Hans Christian Andersen

(Knopf); Vera B. Williams for *Cherries and Cherry Pits* (Greenwillow).

John Newbery Medal. For the most distinguished contribution to literature for children. *Donor:* ALA Association for Library Service to Children. *Medal contributed by:* Daniel Melcher. *Winner:* Sid Fleischmann for *The Whipping Boy* (Greenwillow).

Nobel Prize for Literature. For the total literary output of a distinguished writer. *Offered by:* Swedish Academy. *Winner:* Wole Soyinka, Nigerian poet.

Noma Award for Publishing in Africa (Japan). *Winner:* Antonio Jacinto for *Sobre viver em Tarrafal de Santiago* (Instituto do Livro do Disco, Luanda).

Scott O'Dell Award for Historical Fiction. *Winner:* (children's) Patricia MacLachlan for *Sarah, Plain and Tall* (Harper).

Ohioana Books Awards. To honor Ohio authors. *Offered by:* Ohioana Library Association. *Winners:* (biography) Freda Postle Koch for *Colonel Coggeshall: The Man Who Saved Lincoln* (Poko Pr.); (fiction) Hugh Nissenson for *The Tree of Life* (Harper); Nancy Pelletier for *The Rearrangement* (Macmillan); (history) Donald A. Hutslar for *The Architecture of Migration* (Ohio Univ.).

Olive Branch Awards. *Winners:* Gwynne Dwyer for *War* (Crown); William J. Broad for *Star Warriors* (Simon & Schuster).

George Orwell Award. *Offered by:* National Council of Teachers of English. *Winners:* Neil Postman for *Amusing Ourselves to Death: Public Discourse in the Age of Show Business* (Elisabeth Sifton/Viking).

PEN Publisher Citation. *Winner:* Harry Ford.

PEN Translation Prizes. For an outstanding book-length translation into English. *Winners:* (poetry) Dennis Tedlock for *Popul Vuh: The Mayan Book of Creation* (Simon & Schuster); (prose)

Barbara Bray for *The Lover* by Marguerite Duras (Pantheon).

Pacific Northwest Booksellers Association Book Awards. *Winners:* Alex Hancock for *Into the Light* (Creative Arts); Barry Lopez for *Arctic Dreams* (Scribners); Robert Pyle for *Wintergreen* (Scribners); Kim Stafford for *Having Everything Right* (Confluence); James Welch for *Fool's Crow* (Viking); Ellen Wheat for *Jacob Lawrence* (Univ. of Washington).

Maxwell Perkins Prize. *Offered by:* Charles Scribner's Sons. *Winner:* Gabrielle Burton for *Heartbreak Hotel* (Scribners).

James D. Phelan Award. *Winner:* Sallie Tisdale for *Harvest Moon* (work in progress).

Phi Beta Kappa Science Award. *Winner:* Fred L. Whipple for *The Mystery of Comets* (Smithsonian Institution).

Edgar Allan Poe Awards. For outstanding mystery, crime, and suspense writing. *Offered by:* Mystery Writers of America. *Winners:* (critical biographical work) Peter Lewis for *John le Carre* (Ungar); (fact crime) Natalie Robins and Steven M. L. Aronson for *Savage Grace* (Morrow); (first novel) Jonathan Kellerman for *When the Bough Breaks* (Atheneum); (novel) L. R. Wright for *The Suspect* (Viking); (paperback original) Warren Murphy for *Pigs Get Fat* (NAL); (grandmaster award for lifetime achievement) Ed McBain (Evan Hunter); (children's) Patricia Windsor for *The Sandman's Eyes* (Delacorte).

Poggioli Award. *Offered by:* PEN American Center. For an outstanding translation. *Winner:* Ned Condini for *Poems by Mario Luzi*.

Present Tense/Joel H. Cavior Literary Awards. *Awarded by:* American Jewish Committee. To honor authors and translators of works that reflect humane Jewish values. *Winners:* (biography/autobiography) Jehuda Reinharz for *Chaim Weizmann: The Making of a*

Zionist Leader (Oxford); (fiction) William Herrick for *That's Life* (New Directions); (general nonfiction) Charles Silberman for *A Certain People: American Jews and Their Lives Today* (Summit); (history) Michael R. Marrus for *The Unwanted: European Refugees in the Twentieth Century* (Oxford); (religious thought) Robert Alter for *The Art of Biblical Poetry* (Basic); (lifetime achievement) Irving Howe.

Prix Fémina (France). For an outstanding novel. *Winner:* Rene Belletto for *L'Enfer* (POL).

Prix Fémina Étranger (France). *Winner:* Torgny Lindgren for *Bethsabee* (Actos Sud).

Prix Goncourt (France). For a work of imagination in prose, preferably a novel, exemplifying youth, originality, *esprit*, and form. *Winner:* Michel Host for *Valet de Nuit* (Grasset).

Prix Médicis (France). To honor experimental fiction written in French. *Winner:* Pierre Combescot for *Les Funerailles de la Sardine* (Grasset).

Prix Médicis Essai. *Winner:* Julian Barnes for *Le Perroquet de Flaubert* (Stock).

Prix Médicis Etranger (France). For the best foreign novel translated into French. *Winner:* John Hawkes for *Adventures in the Skin Trade* (Seuil).

PSP Awards. For the most outstanding books in the fields of science, medicine, technology, and business. *Offered by:* Professional and Scholarly Publishing Division, Association of American Publishers. *Winners:* (architecture and urban planning) Michael J. Bednar for *The New Atrium* (McGraw-Hill); (business, management, and economics) William J. Baumol for *Superfairness: Applications and Theory* (MIT); (health sciences) Sidney I. Landau, ed. for *International Dictionary of Medicine and Biology* (Wiley); (humanities) Joan Peyser for *The Orchestra: Origins and Transformations* (Scribners); (law) Nicholas N. Kittrie and Eldon D. Wedlock, Jr., eds. for *The Tree of Liberty: A Documentary History of Rebellion and Political Crime in America* (Johns Hopkins); (life sciences) Steven L. Hilty and William L. Brown for *A Guide to the Birds of Colombia* (Princeton Univ); (physical sciences) Paul E. Hodge for *Galaxies* (Harvard Univ.); (social and behavioral sciences) James R. Beniger for *The Control Revolution: Technological and Economic Origins of the Information Society* (Harvard Univ); (technology and engineering) Joseph E. Shigley and Charles R. Mischke, eds. for *Standard Handbook of Machine Design* (McGraw-Hill).

Pulitzer Prizes in Letters. To honor distinguished works by American writers, dealing preferably with American themes. *Winners:* (biography) Elizabeth Frank for *Louise Bogan: A Portrait* (Knopf); (fiction) Larry McMurtry for *Lonesome Dove* (Simon & Schuster); (general information) Joseph Lelyveld for *Move Your Shadow: South Africa, Black and White* (Times Books); J. Anthony Lukas for *Common Ground: A Turbulent Decade in the Lives of Three American Families* (Knopf); (history) Walter A. McDougal for *Heavens and the Earth: A Political History of the Space Age* (Basic); (poetry) Henry Taylor for *The Flying Change* (Louisiana State Univ.).

QPB New Voice Award. *Winner:* Vikram Seth for *The Golden Gate* (Random).

Rea Award. For an outstanding short story. *Winner:* Cynthia Ozick.

Trevor Reese Memorial Prize (Great Britain). *Winner:* C. A. Bayly for *Rulers, Townsmen, and Bazaars: North Indian Society in the Age of British Expansion, 1770–1870* (Cambridge Univ.).

Regina Medal. For excellence in the writing of literature for children. *Offered by:* Catholic Library Association. *Winner:* Betsy Byars.

Howard U. Ribalow Prize. To honor the best work of fiction on a Jewish theme.

Offered by: Hadassah Magazine. *Winner:* Lore Segal for *Her First American* (Knopf).

Richard and Hilda Rosenthal Foundation Award. For a work of fiction that is a considerable literary achievement though not necessarily a commercial success. *Offered by:* American Academy and Institute of Arts and Letters. *Winner:* Richard Powers.

David H. Russell Award. *Winner:* Frederic G. Cassidy, ed. for *Dictionary of American Regional English* (Harvard Univ.).

St. Louis Literary Award. *Winner:* Saul Bellow.

Saddleman Lifetime Achievement Award. *Offered by:* Western Writers of America. *Winner:* Jack Scheaffer.

School Library Media Specialists of Southeastern New York Award. For an outstanding contribution to children's literature. *Winners:* Alice Provensen and Martin Provensen.

Delmore Schwartz Memorial Poetry Award. *Offered by:* New York University College of Arts and Science. *Winner:* Brenda Hillman.

Virginia McCormick Scully Literary Award. *Winner:* Louise Erdrich for *Love Medicine* (Holt).

Seal Books Award (Canada). For an outstanding first novel. *Winner:* Jo Anne Williams Bennett for *Downfall People* (McClelland & Stewart/Seal Books).

Mina P. Shaughnessy Prize. For an outstanding research publication in the field of teaching English language and literature. *Offered by:* Modern Language Association of America. *Winner:* Robert Scholes for *Textual Power: Literary Theory and the Teaching of English* (Yale Univ.).

W. H. Smith & Son Literary Award (Great Britain). For a significant contribution to literature. *Winner:* Doris Lessing for *The Good Terrorist* (Cape).

W. H. Smith/Books in Canada Award. For an outstanding first novel. *Winner:* Wayne Johnson for *The Story of Bobby O'Malley* (Oberon).

John Ben Snow Prize. *Winner:* Don R. Gerlach for *Proud Patriot: Philip Schuyler and the War of Independence, 1775–1783* (Syracuse Univ.).

John Ben Snow Foundation Prize ($750). *Winner:* Hans S. Pawlisch for *Sir John Davies and the Conquest of Ireland: A Study in Legal Imperialism* (Cambridge Univ.).

Society of Midland Authors Awards. For outstanding books about the Midwest or by midwestern authors. *Winners:* (biography) Franz-Schulze for *Mies van der Rohe* (Univ. of Chicago); (fiction) Donald Bodey for *F.N.G.* (Viking); (nonfiction) Frank Gonzalez-Crussi for *Notes of an Anatomist* (Harcourt); (poetry) Andrew Hudgins for *Saints and Strangers* (Houghton Mifflin); (children's) Pam Conrad for *Prairie Songs* (Harper).

South Australian Festival Awards. *Offered by:* Australian Council. *Winners:* (fiction) Helen Garner for *The Children's Bach* (McPhee Gribble/Penguin); (nonfiction) Ron Gibbs for *A History of Prince Alfred College* (Peacock); (poetry) Robert Gray for *Selected Poems* (Angus & Robertson).

South Australian Government Biennial Literature Prize. *Offered by:* Australian Council. *Winner:* Helen Garner for *The Children's Bach* (McPhee Gribble/Penguin).

Southern California Council on Literature for Children and Young People Award. *Winner:* (fiction) Mary V. Carey for *A Place for Allie* (Dodd); (illustration) Don Wood for *The Napping House* (Harcourt Brace Jovanovich); (nonfiction) Edwin Krupp and Robin Rector Krupp for *The Comet and You* (Macmillan).

Southwestern Booksellers Association Texas Literary Awards. *Winners:* (fiction) Larry McMurtry for *Lonesome Dove* (Simon & Schuster); (nonfiction)

Darwin Payne for *Owen Wister: Chronicler of the West, Gentleman of the East* (Southern Methodist Univ.).

Agnes Lynch Starrett Poetry Prize. *Offered by:* University of Pittsburgh Press. *Winner:* Robey Wilson, Jr., for *Kingdoms of the Ordinary* (Univ. of Pittsburg).

Jean Stein Award. *Offered by:* American Academy and Institute of Arts and Letters. *Winner:* Gregory Corso.

Aiken Taylor Award. For modern American poetry. *Winner:* Howard Nemerov.

Texas Bluebonnet Award. *Offered by:* Texas Association of School Librarians and Children's Round Table of the Texas Library Association. *Winner:* Betty Ren Wright for *The Dollhouse Murders* (Holiday).

Theatre Library Association Award. For the outstanding book in the field of motion pictures and broadcasting. *Winners:* Richard Abel for *French Cinema: The First Wave, 1915-1929* (Princeton Univ.) and Richard Schickel for *D. W. Griffith: An American Life* (Simon & Schuster).

Betty Trask Award (Great Britain). *Offered by:* Society of Authors. *Winners:* Tim Parks for *Tongues of Flame* (Heinemann); Patricia Ferguson for *Family Myths and Legends* (Deutsch).

Harold D. Vursell Memorial Award. *Offered by:* American Academy and Institute of Arts and Letters. *Winner:* Gretel Ehrlich.

Washington Post/Children's Book Guild Nonfiction Award. *Winner:* Kathryn Lasky.

Washingtonian Book Award. *Winners:* Evan Thomas and Walter Isaacson for *The Wise Men: Six Friends and the World They Made* (Simon & Schuster).

Victorian Fellowship of Australian Writers Awards. *Winners:* Peter Carey for *Illywhacker* (Univ. of Queensland); Christina Stead for *Ocean Story* (Penguin).

Victorian Premier's Literary Awards. *Winners:* (Australian Studies Award) D. J. Mulvaney and J. H. Calaby for *So Much That Is New: Baldwin Spenser—1860-1929* (Melbourne Univ.); (drama) Janis Balodis for *Too Young for Ghosts* (Currency); (fiction) John Bryson for *Evil Angels* (Penguin); Peter Carey for *Illywhacker* (Univ. of Queensland); (poetry) Rhyll McMaster for *Washing the Money* (Angus & Robertson); John A. Scott for *St. Clair* (Univ. of Queensland).

Wattie Book of the Year (New Zealand). *Offered by:* Book Publishers Association of New Zealand. *Winner:* Witi Imimaera for *The Matriarch* (Heinemann).

Richard M. Weaver Award for Scholarly Letters. *Winner:* Andrew Lytle.

Western States Book Awards. *Winners:* (creative nonfiction) Anita Sullivan for *The Seventh Dragon: The Riddle of Equal Temperament* (Metamorphous); (fiction) Clarence Major for *My Amputations* (Fiction Collective); (poetry) Mary Barnard for *Time and the White Tigress* (Breitenbush).

Western Writers of America Spur Awards. *Winners:* (historical novel) John Byrne Cooke for *The Snowblind Moon* (Simon & Schuster); (nonfiction) Paul Andrew Hutton for *Phil Sheridan and His Army* (Univ. of Nebraska); (novel) Larry McMurtry for *Lonesome Dove* (Simon & Schuster); (children's) Pam Conrad for *Prairie Songs* (Harper).

Whitbread Literary Awards (Great Britain). For literature of merit that is readable on a wide scale. *Offered by:* Booksellers Association of Great Britain. *Winners:* (novel) Kazuo Ishiguro for *An Artist of the Floating World* (Faber); (first novel) Jim Crace for *Continent* (Heinemann); (poetry) Peter Reading for *Stet* (Secker): (biography) Richard Mabey for *Gilbert White* (Century); (children's) Andrew Taylor for *The Coal House* (Collins).

William Allen White Children's Book Award. *Winner:* Mary Downing Hahn for *Daphne's Book* (Clarion).

Whiting Writers Awards. *Winners:* John Ash, Hayden Carruth, Kent Haruf, Denis Johnson, Darryl Pinckney, Padgett Powell, Mona Simpson, Frank Stewart, Ruth Stone, August Wilson.

Walt Whitman Award. For an American poet who has not yet published a book of poems. *Winner:* Chris Llewellyn for *Fragments from the Fire* (Viking/Penguin); (citation of merit) Stanley Kunitz.

Ethel Wilson Prize for Fiction. *Winner:* Keath Fraser for *Foreign Affairs* (Stoddart).

Laurence L. Winship Book Award. For a book having some relation to New England. *Offered by: Boston Globe. Winner:* Diane Korzenik for *Drawn to Art* (Univ. Press of New England).

George Wittenborn Memorial Award. For excellence of content and physical design of an art book, exhibition catalog, and/or periodical published in North America. *Offered by:* Art Libraries Society of North America. *Winners:* Yale Univ. Press for *The Société Anonyme and the Dreier Bequest at Yale University: A Catalogue Raisonné*, ed. by Robert L. Herbert, Eleanor S. Apter, and Elise K. Kenney; Univ. of Chicago Press and Dumbarton Oaks for *The Mosaics of San Marco in Venice* by Otto Demus; Univ. of Nebraska Press and Joslyn Art Museum for *Karl Bodmer's America*; Kevin Osborn for *Vector Rev*; and MIT Press for *Herbert Bayer: The Complete Work*, by Arthur A. Cohen.

World Fantasy Convention Awards. *Winners:* (anthology/collection) Robin McKinley, ed. for *Imaginary Lands* (Ace); (novel) Dan Simmons for *Song of Kali* (Bluejay); (life achievement) Avram Davidson.

World Science Fiction Convention Hugo Awards. For outstanding science fiction writing. *Winners:* (nonfiction) Tom Weller for *Science Made Stupid* (Houghton Mifflin); (novel) Orson Scott Card for *Ender's Game* (Tor Books).

Yale Series of Younger Poets. For a first volume of poetry by a previously unpublished poet under forty. *Winner:* Julie Agoos for *Above the Land* (Yale Univ.).

Yale University Press Board of Governors Award. *Winner:* Thomas E. Crow for *Painters and Public Life in Eighteenth-Century Paris* (Yale Univ.).

Young Hoosier Book Award. For a book selected by Indiana schoolchildren. *Offered by:* Indiana Media Educators. *Winners:* (grades 4–6) Joan Carris for *When the Boys Ran the House* (Lippincott); (grades 6–8) Lois Duncan for *Stranger with My Face* (Little, Brown).

Morton Dauwen Zabel Award for Criticism. *Offered by:* American Academy and Institute of Arts and Letters. *Winner:* Philip Whalen.

Part 6
Directory of Organizations

Directory of Library and Related Organizations

National Library and Information-Industry Associations, United States and Canada

American Association of Law Libraries

53 W. Jackson Blvd., Chicago, IL 60604
312-939-4764

Object

"To promote librarianship, to develop and increase the usefulness of law libraries, to cultivate the science of law librarianship, and to foster a spirit of cooperation among members of the profession." Established 1906. Memb. 4,100. Dues (Active) $65; (Inst.) $65; (Assoc.) $65 & $125; (Student) $10. Year. June 1 to May 31.

Membership

Persons officially connected with a law library or with a law section of a state or general library, separately maintained. Associate membership available for others.

Officers (June 1986–June 1987)

Pres. Laura N. Gasaway, Univ. of North Carolina Law Lib., Van Hecke-Wettach Bldg. 064A, Chapel Hill, NC 27514; *V.P./Pres.-Elect.* Albert O. Brecht, Univ. of Southern California Law Lib., University Park, Los Angeles, CA 90089-0072; *Secy.* Gitelle Seer, Dewey, Ballantine, Bushby, Palmer & Wood, 140 Broadway, New York, NY 10005; *Treas.* Alan Holoch, Villanova Univ. Law Lib. Garey Hall, Villanova, PA 19085; *Immediate Past Pres.* Robert C. Berring, Univ. of California, School of Law (Boalt Hall), Berkeley, CA 94720.

Executive Board (1986–1987)

Carolyn P. Ahearn; Barbara L. Golden; Penny A. Hazelton; Patrick E. Kehoe; Kamla J. King; Donna M. Tuke.

Committee Chairpersons (1986–1987)

Awards. Lynn Foster, Univ. of Arkansas Law Lib., 400 W. Markham, Little Rock, AR 72201.
CONELL. Co-Chpns. Judy Dimes-Smith, Howard Univ. School of Law, 2900 Van Ness St. N.W., Washington, DC 20008; Colleen L. McCarroll, Sonnenschein, Carlin, Nath & Rosenthal, 8000 Sears Tower, 233 S. Wacker Dr., Chicago, IL 60606.
Committee on Committees. Vivian Campbell, Georgetown Univ. Law Cen-

ter, 600 New Jersey Ave. N.W., Washington, DC 20001.

Constitution and Bylaws. Mark E. Estes, Holme Roberts & Owen, 1700 Broadway, Suite 1800, Denver, CO 80290.

Copyright. Marlene C. McGuirl, Lib. of Congress Law Lib., 101 Independence Ave. S.E., Washington, DC 20540.

Council of Chapter Presidents Coord. Kathleen Larson, U.S. Dept. of Justice, Civil Rights Lib. Rm. 7618, Tenth & Pennsylvania Ave. N.W., Washington, DC 20530.

Database Relations—Academic. Joyce Saltalamachia, New York Law School Lib., 57 Worth St., New York, NY 10013.

Database Relations—Private. Helen P. Burwell, Hutcheson & Grundy, 3300 Citicorp Center, Houston, TX 77002.

Directory of Law Libraries. Eds. Anne H. Butler, Alston & Bird, 35 Broad St., Suite 1200, Atlanta, GA 30335; Randall T. Peterson, John Marshall Law School Lib., 315 S. Plymouth Ct., Chicago, IL 60604; Bardie C. Wolfe, Jr., St. Thomas Univ. Law Lib., 16400 N.W. 32 Ave., Miami, FL 33167.

Education. Patricia G. Strougal, Alston & Bird, 1200 C & S National Bank Bldg., Atlanta, GA 30335.

Educational Director. Margaret A. Leary, Univ. of Michigan Law Lib., S-180 Legal Research Bldg., 801 Monroe St., Ann Arbor, MI 48109-1210.

Elections. Francis R. Doyle, Loyola Univ. Law Lib., One E. Pearson St., Chicago, IL 60611.

Exchange of Duplicates. Carmen Brigandi, Supreme Court Lib.–Syracuse, 500 Court House, Syracuse, NY 13202.

Financial Advisory. Joyce Malden, Municipal Reference Lib., 1004 City Hall, Chicago, IL 60602.

Index Of Periodical Literature Advisory. Gary L. Stromme, Pacific Gas & Electric Co. Law Lib., Box 7442, San Francisco, CA 94120.

Index to Foreign Legal Periodicals. Ed. Thomas H. Reynolds, Univ. of California, School of Law Lib. (Boalt Hall), Berkeley, CA 94720.

Index to Foreign Legal Periodicals Advisory. Lance E. Dickson, Louisiana State Univ. Law Lib., Baton Rouge, LA 70803-1010.

Law Library Journal Advisory. Byron D. Cooper, Univ. of Detroit Law Lib., 651 E. Jefferson Ave., Detroit, MI 48226.

Law Library Journal Ed. Richard A. Danner, Duke Univ. Law Lib., Durham, NC 27706.

Legal Information Service to the Public. Michael S. Miller, Maryland State Law Lib., Courts of Appeal Bldg., 361 Rowe Blvd., Annapolis, MD 21401.

Legislation and Legal Developments. Joanne A. Zich, American Univ. Law Lib., 4400 Massachusetts Ave. N.W., Washington, DC 20016.

Location of Headquarters. Harry S. Martin, III, Harvard Univ. Law Lib., Langdell Hall, Cambridge, MA 02138.

Membership. Martha C. Byrnes, U.S. Supreme Court Lib., Washington, DC 20543.

Memorials. George Skinner, Univ. of Arkansas, School of Law Lib., Fayetteville, AR 72701.

Minorities. William James, Univ. of Kentucky Law Lib., Lexington, KY 40506.

National Legal Resources. Roy M. Mersky, Univ. of Texas, Tarlton Law Lib., 727 E. 26 St., Austin, TX 78705.

Newsletter. MaryLu Linnane, DePaul Univ. Law Lib., 25 E. Jackson Blvd., Chicago, IL 60604.

Nominations. Kathleen M. Carrick, Case Western Reserve Univ., Law Lib., 11075 East Blvd., Cleveland, OH 44106.

Placement. Barbara Gontrum, Univ. of Maryland, Thurgood Marshall Law Lib., 20 N. Paca St., Baltimore, MD 21201.

Public Relations. Barbara N. Greenspahn.

Publications. Frank G. Houdek, Southern Illinois Univ., School of Law Lib., Carbondale, IL 62901.

Publications Series Advisory. Susan Weinstein, Univ. of Denver, Westminster Law Lib., 1900 Olive St. LTLB, Denver, CO 80220.

Relations with Publishers and Dealers. Bruce S. Johnson, Coleman Karesh Law Lib., Univ. of South Carolina, Columbia, SC 29208.

Scholarships and Grants. Donald J. Dunn, Western New England College of Law Lib., 1215 Wilbraham Rd., Springfield, MA 01119.

Standards. Robert J. Nissenbaum, Cleveland State Univ., Cleveland Marshall College of Law, 1801 Euclid Ave., Cleveland, OH 44115.

Statistics. Anita L. Morse, Univ. of Wisconsin Law Lib., Madison, WI 53706.

Special-Interest Section Chairpersons 1986–1987

Academic Law Libraries. Peter Schanck, Univ. of Kansas Law Lib., Green Hall, Lawrence, KS 66045.

Automation and Scientific Development. S. Patricia Rempel, Univ. of Alberta, Edmonton, Alta. T6G 2H5, Canada.

Contemporary Social Problems. Scott B. Pagel, Columbia Univ. Law Lib., 435 W. 116 St., New York, NY 10027.

Foreign, Comparative, and International Law. Linda L. Thompson, World Bank Law Lib., 1818 H St. N.W., Washington, DC 20433.

Government Documents. Sally Holterhoff, Valparaiso Univ. Law Lib., Valparaiso, IN 46383.

Micrographics and Audi-Visual. Michael Klepper, Univ. of Virginia Law Lib., Charlottesville, VA 22901.

On-Line Bibliographic Services. Patricia S. Callahan, Univ. of Pennsylvania, 3400 Chestnut St., Philadelphia, PA 19104.

Private Law Libraries. Nuchine Nobari, Davis Polk & Wardwell, One Chase Manhattan Plaza, New York, NY 10005.

Readers' Services. Martha W. Rush, College of William & Mary, Marshall-Wythe Law Lib., Williamsburg, VA 23185.

State, Court and County Law Libraries. Kai-Yun Chiu, Baltimore Bar Lib., 618 Court House W., Baltimore, MD 21202.

Technical Services. Merle J. Slyhoff, Univ. of Pennsylvania, 3400 Chestnut St., Philadelphia, PA 19104.

Special-Interest Section Council Chair. Sandra S. Coleman, Harvard Univ. Law Lib., Langdell Hall, Cambridge, MA 02138.

Representatives

ABA (American Bar Association). Laura N. Gasaway.

American Correctional Institutions. Carl Romalis.

American Library Association. Sandra S. Coleman.

American Library Association. Committee on Cataloging. Lee W. Leighton.

American Library Association. Committee on Interlibrary Loan. Marjorie E. Crawford.

American National Standards Institute Committee Z-39. Robert J. Nissenbaum.

American National Standards Institute Committee PH5. Larry B. Wenger.

American Society for Information Science. James L. Hoover.

Association for Library and Information Science Education. Penny A. Hazelton.

Association of American Law Schools. Robert C. Berring.

Association of Legal Administrators. Jill Sidford; Donald G. Ziegenfuss.

British-Irish Association of Law Libraries. David A. Thomas.

Canadian Association of Law Libraries. Frances H. Hall.
Council of National Library and Information Associations. James L. Hoover; William H. Jepson.
International Association of Law Libraries. Igor I. Kavass.
International Federation of Library Associations. Robert C. Berring.
Library of Congress. Roy M. Mersky.
Library of Congress Network Advisory. Robert L. Oakley.

Library of Congress Special Committee on Foreign Class K Schedule. Thomas H. Reynolds.
National Association of Secretaries of State. Judith Meadows.
Special Libraries Association. Virginia Wise.
U.S. Copyright Office. Marlene C. McGuirl.
U.S. Congress Ad Hoc Committee on Depository Library Access to Data Base. Steve Margeton.

American Library Association

Executive Director, Thomas J. Galvin
50 E. Huron St., Chicago, IL 60611
312-944-6780

Object

The American Library Association is an organization for librarians and libraries with the overarching objective of promoting and improving library service and librarianship and providing lifelong learning services to all. Memb. (Indiv.) 40,280; (Inst.) 3,117. Dues (Indiv.) 1st year, $33; renewing memb., $65; (Nonsalaried Libns.) $23; (Trustee & Assoc. Membs.) $29; (Student) $16; (Foreign Indiv.) $39; (Inst.) $70 & up (depending upon operating expenses of institution).

Membership

Any person, library, or other organization interested in library service and librarians.

Officers

Pres. Regina U. Minudri, Dir., Berkeley Public Lib., 2090 Kittredge St., Berkeley, CA 94704; *Pres.-Elect.* Margaret E. Chisholm, Dir., School of Lib. and Info. Science, Univ. of Washington, 133 Suzzallo Lib., FM-30, Seattle, WA 98195; *Treas.* Patricia Glass Schuman, Pres.,

Neal-Schuman Publishers, 23 Leonard St., New York, NY 10013; *Exec. Dir. (Ex officio)* Thomas J. Galvin, ALA Headquarters, 50 E. Huron St., Chicago, IL 60611.

Executive Board

Past Pres. Beverly P. Lynch, Univ. Libn., Univ. of Illinois, Box 8198, Chicago, IL 60680. Other members: Arthur Curley (1987); Lucille C. Thomas (1987); Elizabeth D. Futas (1988); David P. Snider (interim 1988); Margaret L. Crist (1989); Carla J. Stoffle (1989); Patricia Wilson Berger (1990); Duane F. Johnson (1990).

Endowment Trustees

Lillian M. Bradshaw (1987); Albert W. Daub (1988); Richard M. Dougherty (1989).

Divisions

See the separate entries that follow: American Assn. of School Libns.; American Lib. Trustee Assn.; Assn. for Lib. Service

to Children; Assn. of College and Research Libs.; Assn. of Specialized and Cooperative Lib. Agencies; Lib Administration and Management Assn.; Lib. and Info. Technology Assn.; Public Lib. Assn.; Reference and Adult Services Div.; Resources and Technical Services Div.; Young Adult Services Div.

Publications

ALA Handbook of Organization and Membership Directory 1985-1986 (ann.).
ALA Yearbook (ann.; $65).
American Libraries (11 per year; memb.).
Booklist (22 issues; $51).
Choice (11 issues; $110).

Round Table Chairpersons

(ALA staff liaison is given in parentheses.)
Continuing Library Education Network and Exchange. William G. Asp, Office of Lib. Development and Service, 440 Capitol Sq., 550 Cedar St., St. Paul, MN 55101 (Elaine K. Wingate).
Ethnic Materials Information Exchange. Edith Maureen Fisher, Univ. of California-San Diego, Univ. Lib., C-075-R, La Jolla, CA 92093 (Jean E. Coleman).
Exhibits. Roger J. Long, McGregor Suscription Service, 2 S. Seminary, Mt. Morris, IL 61504 (Walter Brueggen).
Federal Librarians. Isabelle G. Mudd, Box 1061, Fairbanks, AK 99707 (Anne A. Heanue).
Government Documents. Philip Van de Voorde, 152 Parks Lane, Iowa State Univ., Ames, IA 50011 (Elaine K. Wingate).
Independent Librarians. Margaret J. Bennett, Pro Libra Assocs., 106 Valley St., South Orange, NJ 07079 (Margaret Myers).

Intellectual Freedom. Barbara Jones, Lib. Dir., Univ. of Northern Iowa, Cedar Falls, IA 50614 (to be appointed).
International Relations. Henriette D. Avram, Asst. Libn. for Processing, Lib. of Congress, Washington, DC 20540 (Elaine K. Wingate).
Junior Members. Bobbi Walters, 1406 Corte de Primavera, Thousand Oaks, CA 91360 (Patricia Scarry).
Library History. Robert S. Martin, Special Collections, Hill Memorial Lib., Louisiana State Univ., Baton Rouge, LA 70803 (Emily I. Melton).
Library Instruction. Marilyn P. Barr, Ritner Children's Branch, 2407 S. Broad St., Philadelphia, PA 19148 (Jeniece Guy).
Library Research. Peter Hernon, Simmons College Grad. School of Lib. Science, Boston, MA 02115 (Mary Jo Lynch).
Map and Geography. Donna P. Koepp, Spencer Research Lib., Univ. of Kansas, Lawrence, KS 66045 (Elaine K. Wingate).
Social Responsibilities. Gail P. Warner, Whitman County Lib., S. 102 Main St., Colfax, WA 99111 (Jean E. Coleman).
Staff Organizations. Janet Woody, 6010 Pollard, Richmond, VA 23226 (Elaine K. Wingate).

Committee Chairpersons

Access to Information, Freedom and Equality of (Special). J. Dennis Day, Dir., Public Lib., 209 E. Fifth S., Salt Lake City, UT 84111 (Thomas J. Galvin).
Accreditation (Standing). Robert B. Croneberger, Dir., Carnegie Lib., Pittsburgh, PA 15213 (Elinor Yungmeyer).
"American Libraries"—Editorial Advisory Committee for (Standing). Glenn E. Estes, Grad. School of Lib. and Info. Science, Univ. of Tennessee, Knoxville, TN 37996 (Arthur Plotnik).

Awards (Standing). Patricia Breivik, Auraria Lib., Lawrence at 11th St., Denver, CO 80204 (Elaine K. Wingate).

Chapter Relations (Standing). Dinah E. Lindauer, 81 Marion Ave., Merrick, NY 11566 (Patricia Scarry).

Coalition on Government Information (Ad hoc). Nancy C. Kranich, Dir., Public and Administrative Services, New York Univ. Libs., New York, NY 10012 (Eileen D. Cooke).

Committee on Committees. Margaret E. Chisholm, Dir., School of Lib. and Info. Science, 133 Suzzallo Lib., FM30, Univ. of Washington, Seattle, WA 98195 (Miriam L. Hornback).

Conference Program (Standing). *San Francisco, 1987*. Regina U. Minudri, Dir., Public Lib., 2090 Kittredge St., Berkeley, CA 94704. *New Orleans, 1988*. Margaret E. Chisholm, Dir., School of Lib. and Info. Science, Univ. of Washington, 133 Suzzallo Lib., FM 30, Seattle, WA 98195.

Constitution and Bylaws (Standing). Joseph J. Mika, Dir., Lib. Science Program, Wayne State Univ., Detroit, MI 48202 (Miriam L. Hornback).

Council Orientation (Special, Council). Stefan B. Moses, California Lib. Assn., 717 K St., Suite 300, Sacramento, CA 95814-3477 (Miriam L. Hornback).

Instruction in the Use of Libraries (Standing). Karen S. Seibert, Davis Lib. 080A, Univ. of North Carolina, Chapel Hill, NC 27514 (Andrew M. Hansen).

Intellectual Freedom (Standing, Council). Judith A. Drescher, Memphis-Shelby County Lib., 1850 Peabody Ave., Memphis, TN 38104 (Judith F. Krug).

International Relations (Standing, Council). Amanda S. Rudd, 5100 N. Marine Dr. #6A, Chicago, IL 60608 (Thomas J. Galvin).

Legislation (Standing, Council). Christie D. Vernon, 205 Lindsay Landing, Yorktown, VA 23692 (Eileen D. Cooke).

Library Education (Standing, Council). Jana Varlejs, Univ. of Wisconsin, School of Lib. and Info. Studies, Madison, WI 53706 (Margaret Myers).

Library Outreach Services, Office for (Standing, Advisory). Susan C. Luevano, 1551 El Portal Dr., La Habra, CA 90631 (Jean E. Coleman).

Library Personnel Resources, Office for (Standing, Advisory). Kathleen M. Heim, Grad. School of Lib. and Info. Science, Louisiana State Univ., Rm. 267-Coats Hall, Baton Rouge, LA 70803 (Margaret Myers).

Mediation, Arbitration, and Inquiry, Staff Committee on (Standing). Roger H. Parent, ALA Headquarters, 50 E. Huron St., Chicago, IL 60611.

Membership (Standing). John K. Mayeski, Ryan Lib., Kearney State College, Kearney, NE 68849 (Patricia Scarry).

Minority Concerns (Standing, Council). Ann K. Randall, City College Lib., 5th fl., 333 N. Academic Center, New York, NY 10031 (Jean E. Coleman).

National Library Week (Standing). Susan S. DiMattia, 44 Chatham Rd., Stamford, CT 06903 (Linda Wallace).

Organization (Standing, Council). Jane Anne Hannigan, 24 Starview Dr., Neshanic, NJ 08853 (Roger H. Parent).

Pay Equity (Standing, Council). Michele Leber, 1805 Crystal Dr., 911-5, Arlington, VA 22202 (Margaret Myers).

Planning (Standing, Council). Thomas E. Alford, Asst. City Libn., Public Lib., 630 W. Fifth St., Los Angeles, CA 90071 (Roger H. Parent).

Professional Ethics (Standing, Council). Jeanne M. Isacco, County Public Lib., 300 N. Roxboro St., Durham, NC 27702 (Judith F. Krug).

Program Evaluation and Support (Standing, Council). Richard A. Olsen, Adams Lib., Rhode Island College, 600 Mt. Pleasant Ave., Providence, RI 02908 (Susan C. Odmark).

Publishing (Standing, Council). Susan

Brynteson, Dir. of Libs., Univ. of Delaware, Newark, DE 19717-5267 (Gary Facente).

Realities Implementation (Ad hoc). Virginia H. Mathews, V.P., Shoe String Press, 995 Sherman Ave., Box 4327, Hamden, CT 06514 (Eileen D. Cooke).

Research (Standing). Charles R. Martell, Asst. Lib. Dir., California State Univ., Sacramento, CA 95819 (Mary Jo Lynch).

Resolutions (Standing, Council). Patricia H. Mautino, Oswego County BOCES, County Rte. 64, Mexico, NY 13114 (Miriam L. Hornback).

Standards (Standing). Helen Lloyd Snoke, School of Lib. Science, Univ. of Michigan, 580 Union Dr., Ann Arbor, MI 48109 (Mary Jo Lynch).

Women in Librarianship, Status of (Standing, Council). Betty-Carol Sellen, Brooklyn College Lib., Brooklyn, NY 11210 (Margaret Myers).

Joint Committee Chairpersons

American Correctional Association — ASCLA Committee on Institution Libraries. Brenda Vogel, 1122 Bellemore Rd., Baltimore, MD 21201 (ACA); Gary Long (ALA/ASCLA).

American Federation of Labor/Congress of Industrial Organization — ALA, Library Service to Labor Groups, RASD. Susan Kamm, Box 26467, Los Angeles, CA 90026 (ALA); Jim Auerbach, Dept. of Educ., 815 16th St. N.W., Rm. 407, Washington, DC 20006 (AFL/CIO).

Anglo-American Cataloging Rules, Common Revision Fund. Gary Facente, Assoc. Exec. Dir. for Publishing (ALA); Laurie Bowes, Canadian Lib. Assn., 151 Sparks St., Ottawa, Ont. K1P 5E3, Canada (CLA); Joyce Butcher, British Lib., 2 Sheraton St., London W1V 4BH, England ([British] Lib. Assn.).

Anglo-American Cataloging Rules, Joint Steering Committee for Revision of. Helen F. Schmierer, 5550 S. Dorchester, Apt. 408, Chicago, IL 60637 (ALA).

Association for Educational Communications and Technology — AASL. Thomas L. Hart, School of Lib. Science, Florida State Univ., Tallahassee, FL 32306 (AASL).

Association for Educational Communications and Technology — ACRL. Colette A. Wagner, LaGuardia Community College Lib., Long Island City, NY 11101 (ACRL).

Association of American Publishers — ALA. Regina U. Minudri, Dir., Public Lib., 2090 Kittredge St., Berkeley, CA 94704. (ALA); To be appointed (AAP).

Association of American Publishers — RTSD. Susan H. Vita, 3711 Taylor St., Chevy Chase, MD 20815 (ALA); Dedria Bryfonski, Gale Research Co., Book Tower, Detroit, MI 48226 (AAP).

Children's Book Council — ALA. Ann Kalkhoff, 220 Berkeley Place, #1D, Brooklyn, NY 11217 (ALA); Margery Cuyler, Holiday House, 18 E. 53 St., New York, NY 10022 (CBC).

Society of American Archivists — ALA Joint Committee on Library-Archives Relationships. Frederick J. Stielow, Hornbake Bldg., Univ. of Maryland, College Park, MD 20742 (ALA); To be appointed (SAA).

American Library Association
American Association of School Librarians

Executive Director, Ann Carlson Weeks
50 E. Huron St., Chicago, IL 60611
312-944-6780

Object

The American Association of School Librarians is interested in the general improvement and extension of library media services for children and young people. AASL has specific responsibility for: planning of program of study and service for the improvement and extension of library media services in elementary and secondary schools as a means of strengthening the educational program; evaluation, selection, interpretation, and utilization of media as it is used in the context of the school program; stimulation of continuous study and research in the library field and to establish criteria of evaluation; synthesis of the activities of all units of the American Library Association in areas of mutual concern; representation and interpretation of the need for the function of school libraries to other educational and lay groups; stimulation of professional growth, improvement of the status of school librarians, and encouragement of participation by members in appropriate type-of-activity divisions; conduct activities and projects for improvement and extension of service in the school library when such projects are beyond the scope of type-of-activity divisions, after specific approval by the ALA Council. Established in 1951 as a separate division of ALA. Memb. 5,878.

Membership

Open to all libraries, school library media specialists, interested individuals, and business firms with requisite membership in ALA.

Officers

Pres. Marilyn L. Miller, Manning Hall 025A, School of Lib. Science, Univ. of North Carolina, Chapel Hill, NC 27514; *1st V.P./Pres.-Elect.* Karen A. Whitney, Agua Fria Union H.S. Dist., 530 Riley Dr., Avondale, AZ 85323; *2nd V.P.* E. Blanche Woolls, 270 Tennyson Ave., Pittsburgh, PA 15213; *Rec. Secy.* Donald C. Adcock, School Dist. #41, 793 N. Main St., Glen Ellyn, IL 60137.

(Address correspondence to the executive director).

Board of Directors

Past Pres. Shirley L. Aaron, Professor, Florida State Univ., School of Lib. & Info. Studies, Tallahassee, FL 32306; *Exec. Dir.* Ann Carlson Weeks, ALA, 50 E. Huron, Chicago, IL 60611; *Regional Dirs.* Region I: Charles White, 12 Maple Row, Bethel, CT 06801 (1988); Region II: Sue Albertson Walker, 6065 Park Ridge Dr., E. Petersburg, PA 17520 (1989); Region III: Jacqueline G. Morris, 5225 Leone Pl., Indianapolis, IN 46226 (1987); Region IV: Connie Champlin, 312 S. 56 St., Omaha, NE 68134 (1988); Region V: Pat R. Scales, 101 Westminster Dr., Greenville, SC 29605 (1987); Region VI: Retta Patrick, RD#1, Box 74C-1, Roland, AR 72135 (1989); Region VII: M. Maggie Rogers, Northwest Regional Educational Laboratory 300 S.W. Sixth Ave., Portland, OR 97204 (1988); *Regional Dirs. from Affiliate Assembly:* Winona Jones (AA chpn., 1987); Merrilyn Ridgeway (1988); Patricia Meier (1987); *NPSS Chpn.* Mark C. Hillsamer; *SS Chpn.* Elsie

L. Brumback; *SLMES Chpn.* Aileen Helmick; *Ex officio, Ed., School Library Media Quarterly.* Marilyn W. Greenberg (1988); *Councilor.* Helen Lloyd Snoke.

Publication

School Library Media Quarterly (q.; memb.; nonmemb. $30). *Ed.* Marilyn W. Greenberg, Div. Curriculum & Instruction, California State Univ., 5151 State University Dr., Los Angeles, CA 90032.

Committee Chairpersons

Program Coordinating. Shirley L. Aaron, Professor, Florida State Univ., School of Lib. & Info. Studies, Tallahasee, FL 32306.

Unit Group I – Organizational Maintenance

Unit Head. Jane Bandy Smith, 77 E. Andrews Dr. N.W., Apt. 221, Atlanta, GA 30305.
Bylaws. Phyllis Van Orden, 2281 Trescott Dr., Tallahassee, FL 32312.
Conference Program Planning – San Francisco, 1987. Mary D. Lankford, Irving Independent School Dist., 820 O'Connor Rd., Irving, TX 75061.
Local Arrangements – San Francisco, 1987. Betty McDavid, Lib. Media Processing, Mt. Diablo Unified School Dist., 1026 Mohr Lane, Concord, CA 94518.
Membership. Joanne Troutner, 3002 Roanoke Circle, Lafayette, IN 47905.
Nominating – 1987 Election. O. Mell Busbin, Box 411, Boone, NC 28607.
Policy and Procedures Handbook Development. Diane A. Ball, 2410 Fairmont Ave., Dayton, OH 45419.
Resolutions. E. Blanche Woolls, 270 Tennyson Ave., Pittsburgh, PA 15213.

Standards. Christina Carr Young, National Commission on Lib. & Info. Science, GSA Bldg., Seventh & D Sts., S.W., Suite 3122, Washington, DC 20024.

Unit Group II – Organizational Relationships

Unit Head. Daniel A. Barron, School of Lib. & Info. Science, Univ. of South Carolina, Columbia, SC 29208.
American Association of School Administrators (liaison). To be appointed.
American University Press Services, Inc. (advisory). Mary Oppman, 7740 Oak Ave., Gary, IN 46403.
Association for Educational Communications and Technology – AASL (joint). Thomas L. Hart, Professor, School of Lib. Science, Florida State Univ., Tallahassee, FL 32306.
Association for Supervision and Curriculum Development (liaison). M. Ellen Jay, 12754 Turquoise Terr., Silver Spring, MD 20904.
Legislation. Phyllis Land Usher, 2305 W. Washington St., Indianapolis, IN 46222.
Liaison. Judith F. Davie, 2515-A Patriot Way, Greensboro, NC 27408.
National Association of Secondary School Principals (liaison). To be appointed.
National Congress of Parents and Teachers (liaison). To be appointed.
National Council for the Social Studies (liaison). To be appointed.
National Council of Teachers of English (liaison). To be appointed.
National Council of Teachers of Mathematics (liaison). To be appointed.

Unit Group III – Media Personnel Development

Unit Head. William E. Hug, 399 Ponderosa Dr., Athens, GA 30605.

Continuing Education. Jacqueline C. Mancall, 2088 Harts Lane, Miquon, PA 19452.

Evaluation of School Library Media Programs. Gerald G. Hodges, 1725 Dover St., Iowa City, IA 52240.

Intellectual Freedom. Frances McDonald, Rte. 1, Box 173, Kasota, MN 56040.

International Relations: Darlene Shiverdecker, Walnut Hills H.S., 3250 Victory Pkwy., Cincinnati, OH 45215.

Leadership Enhancement. Jerry R. Wicks, 1359 W. Thorndale Ave., Chicago, IL 60660.

Networking. Roger S. Ashley, 3211 Kernway, Bloomfield Hills, MI 48013.

Professional Development. Library Education. Henry C. DeQuin, School of Lib. Science, Northern Illinois Univ., DeKalb, IL 60115.

Public Relations. Bernice L. Yesner, 16 Sunbrook Rd., Woodbridge, CT 06525.

Research. David V. Loertscher, 401 W. Brooks, Rm. 123, Univ. of Oklahoma, Norman, OK 73019.

School Library Media Month. Lucille C. Thomas, 1184 Union St., Brooklyn, NY 11225.

Unit Group IV—Media Program Development

Unit Head. Thomas L. Hart, Florida State Univ., School of Lib. Science, Tallahassee, FL 32306-2048.

Accessing Instructional Materials and Information. Rosalind E. Miller, 442 Milligan Dr., Stone Mountain, GA 30083.

Early Childhood Education. M. Ellen Jay, 12754 Turquoise Terr., Silver Spring, MD 20904.

Library Media Skills Instruction. Carol C. Kuhlthau, 402 Franklin Rd., North Brunswick, NJ 08902.

Materials Selection. Dona Helmer, Box 196650, Anchorage, AK 99519-6650.

Microcomputer/Online Programs for

School Library Media Centers. Doris Masek, 6815 N. Algonquin Ave., Chicago, IL 60646.

School Media Programs in Vocational/ Technical Schools. Wilma Bates, Weaver Educational Center, 300 S. Spring St., Greensboro, NC 27401.

Standardization of Access to Library Media Resources. Charles T. Harmon, 1725 Dover St., Iowa City, IA 52240.

Student Involvement in the Media Center Program. Carolyne C. Burgman, Bluford School, 1901 Tuscaloosa St., Greensboro, NC 27401.

Video Communications. Blanche G. Browne, 1042 Mason Woods Dr. N.E., Atlanta, GA 30329.

Unit Group V—Public Information

Unit Head. Dale W. Brown, Public Schools, 3801 W. Braddock Rd., Alexandria, VA 22302.

Awards. Dawn H. Heller, 516 S. Ashland, La Grange, IL 60525.

AASL Distinguished Library Service Award for School Administrators Selection, AASL/SIRS. Wilma Bates, Weaver Educational Center, 300 S. Spring St., Greensboro, NC 27401.

Intellectual Freedom Award Selection, AASL/SIRS. Gene D. Lanier, Dept. of Lib. & Info. Studies, East Carolina Univ., Greenville, NC 27834-4353.

Microcomputer in the Media Center Award Selection, AASL/Follett Software Co. Beverly Bashia, Dir. of Media Serv., Merrillville H.S., Merrillville, IN 46410.

National School Library Media Program of the Year Award Selection, AASL/ EB. Pat R. Scales, 101 Westminister Dr., Greenville, SC 29605.

President's Award Selection, AASL/ Baker & Taylor. Paula K. Montgomery, 17 E. Henrietta St., Baltimore, MD 21230.

Special Committee Chairpersons

Interdivisional Concerns. Carolyn L. Cain, 406 Whitcomb Dr., Madison, WI 53711.

Planning and Budget. Hugh Durbin, 4240 Fairoaks Dr., Columbus, OH 43214.

Publications Advisory. Eleanor R. (Betty) Kulleseid, Bank Street College of Education, 610 W. 112 St., New York, NY 10025.

Section Chairpersons

Non-Public Schools Section (NPSS). Mark C. Hillsamer, St. Albans School, Massachusetts & Wisconsin Sts. N.W., Washington, DC 20016.

School Library Media Educators Section (SLMES). Aileen Helmick, 318 Johnson, Warrensburg, MO 64093.

Supervisors Section (SS). Elsie L. Brumback, 304 Tweed Circle, Cary, NC 27511.

Representatives

ALA Appointments Committee. Karen A. Whitney.

ALA San Francisco Conference (1987) Program Committee. Marilyn L. Miller.

ALA Legislation Assembly. Phyllis Land Usher.

ALA Membership Promotion Task Force. Joanne Troutner (1987).

ALA Planning and Budget Assembly. Hugh Durbin.

Education U.S.A. Advisory Board. To be appointed.

Freedom to Read Foundation. Frances McDonald (1987).

International Association of School Librarianship. Don Adcock.

Library Education Assembly. Henry C. DeQuin; Jacqueline C. Mancall; Aileen Helmick.

National Association of State Educational Media Professionals. To be appointed.

RTSD/CCS Cataloging of Children's Materials Committee. To be appointed.

American Library Association
American Library Trustee Association

Executive Director, Sharon L. Jordan
50 E. Huron St., Chicago, IL 60611
312-944-6780

Object

The development of effective library service for all people in all types of communities and in all types of libraries; it follows that its members are concerned as policymakers with organizational patterns of service, with the development of competent personnel, the provision of adequate financing, the passage of suitable legislation, and the encouragement of citizen support for libraries. Open to all interested persons and organizations. Organized 1890. Became an ALA division 1961. Memb. 1,658. (For dues and membership year, see ALA entry.)

Officers (1986–1987)

Pres. Kay Vowvalidis, 100 Deer Path Rd., Ozark, AL 36360; *1st V.P./Pres.-Elect.* Gloria Glaser, 60 Sutton Place S., Apt. 8C-S, New York, NY 10022; *2nd V.P.* Norma Buzan, 3057 Betsy Ross Dr., Bloomfield Hills, MI 48013; *Secy.* Patricia F. Turner.

Board of Directors

Councilor. Deborah Miller; *Past Pres.* Herbert A. Davis; *Council Administrator.* Mary Arney (1987); Jeanne Davies (1987); Lila Milford (1987); Charles E. Reid (1987); Aileen R. Schrader (1987). *Regional V.P.* Phillip G. James (1988); Norman Kelinson (1988); Esther Lopato (1987); Pat Nixon (1987); Jane M. Norcross (1988); John Parsons (1988); Dorothe C. Peterson (1987); Irving C. Portman (1987); Sharon A. Saulmon (1987). *Ex officio. PLA Past Pres.* Patrick O'Brien; *Ed. ALTA Newsletter.* Nancy Stiegemeyer; *ALTA Exec. Dir.* Sharon L. Jordan.

Publication

The ALTA Newsletter (6 per year; free to members). *Ed.* Nancy Stiegemeyer, 215 Camellia Dr., Cape Girardeau, MO 63701.

Committee Chairpersons

Action Development. Joanne C. Wisener, 860 19th Place, Yuma, AZ 85364.
ALTA Financial Development. James Hess, 91 Farms Rd. Circle, East Brunswick, NJ 08816.
ALTA Planning Committee. Norma Buzan, 3057 Betsy Ross Dr., Bloomfield Hills, MI 48013.
Awards. Charles E. Reid, 620 West Dr., Paramus, NJ 07652.
Budget. Gloria Glaser, 60 Sutton Place S., Apt. 8 C-S, New York, NY 10022.
Common Concerns (ALTA/PLA Joint Committee). Co-Chpns. Herbert A. Davis (ALTA), Box 108, Brooklandville, MD 21022; Annalee M. Bundy (PLA), Providence Pub. Lib., 150 Empire St., Providence, RI 02903.

Conference Program and Evaluation. Co-Chpns. Mary Arney, 3646 Charlotte, Kansas City, MO 64109; Judith M. Baker, 6260 Victoria, Oak Forest, IL 60452.
Financial Development. Co-Chpns. Jess L. Gardner, 175 Idle Hour Dr., Lexington, KY 40502; Norman Kelinson, 1228 Coffelt Ave., Bettendorf, IA 52722.
Intellectual Freedom. Robert Delzell, 1655 S. Marion, Apt. 103-B, Springfield, MO 65807.
Legislation. Co-Chpns. Wayne Moss, 5329 Boulevard Place, Indianapolis, IN 46203; Jerome L. Brill, 38 McElroy St., West Islip, NY 11795. *White House Conference Implementation (Legislation Subcommittee).* Barbara D. Cooper, 936 Intracoastal Dr., Apt. 6-D, Fort Lauderdale, FL 33304.
Library Investment (ALTA/PLA Joint Committee). Norman Kelinson, 1228 Coffelt Ave., Bettendorf, IA 52722.
Membership (Task Force). Gloria Glaser, 60 Sutton Place S., Apt. 8 C-S, New York, NY 10022.
Nominating. Joanne C. Wisener, 860 19th Place, Yuma, AZ 85364.
Publications. Robert L. Faherty, 6811 Lamp Post Lane, Alexandria, VA 22306.
Publicity. Co-Chpns. Gloria Dinerman, 82 Fordham, Colonia, NJ 07067; Allan Kahn, 2265 Glenkirk Dr., San Jose, CA 95124.
Resolutions. John Parsons, Skyline Plaza, 2013-N, 3701 S. George Mason Dr., Falls Church, VA 22041.
Specialized Outreach Services. Co-Chpns. Marguerite W. Yates, 190 Windemere Rd., Lockport, NY 14094; Arthur Kirschenbaum, 750 S. 26 Place, Arlington, VA 22202.
Trustee Citations, Jury on. Athalie Kirschenbaum, 750 S. 26 Place, Arlington, VA 22202.

Representatives

ALA Legislative Assembly. Wayne Moss.
ALA Membership Promotion Task Force. Gloria Glaser.
ALA Planning and Budget Assembly. Gloria Glaser.
ASCLA Decade of Disabled Persons Committee. Arthur Kirschenbaum.

FOLUSA. Minnie-Lou Lynch.
Freedom to Read Foundation. Madeleine Grant.
Office for Library Outreach Services. Arthur Kirschenbaum.
PLA Board of Directors. Herbert A. Davis.
PLA New Standards Task Force. Virginia Young.

American Library Association
Association for Library Service to Children

Executive Director, Susan Roman
50 E. Huron St., Chicago, IL 60611
312-944-6780

Object

Interested in the improvement and extension of library services to children in all types of libraries. Responsible for the evaluation and selection of book and nonbook material for, and the improvement of techniques of, library services to children from preschool through the eighth grade or junior high school age, when such materials or techniques are intended for use in more than one type of library. Founded 1901. Memb. 3,330. (For information on dues, see ALA entry.)

Membership

Open to anyone interested in library services to children.

Officers (July 1986–July 1987)

Pres. Gail M. Sage, Coord. of Children's Services, Sonoma County Lib., Third & E Sts., Santa Rosa, CA 95404; *V.P.* Jane Botham, 2579 Maryland Ave., Milwaukee, WI 53211; *Past Pres.* Margaret A. Bush, Grad. School of Lib. and Info. Science,

Simmons College, 300 The Fenway, Boston, MA 02115.
(Address correspondence to the executive director.)

Directors

Julie A. Cummins; Judith F. Davie; Eliza T. Dresang; Marilyn Berg Iarusso; Barbara Immroth; Jill L. Locke; Barbara T. Rollock; Susan Roman; Ellen M. Stepanian.

Committee Chairpersons

Priority Group I: Child Advocacy

Consultant. Roslyn Beitler, 3601 Connecticut Ave. N.W., Apt. 719, Washington, DC 20008 (1988).
Boy Scouts of America (Advisory). Margo Daniels, Patrick Henry Lib., 101 Maple Ave. E., Vienna, VA 22180.
Legislation. Joan M. Blumenstein, 8371 Sunnybrook Circle, Buena Park, CA 90621.
Liaison with Mass Media. Ann Maczuga, 3501 W. Pasadena, Phoenix, AZ 85019.

Liaison with National Organizations Serving the Child. Marjorie Jones, Junior Literary Guild, 245 Park Ave., New York, NY 10167.

Priority Group II: Evaluation of Media

Consultant. Phyllis J. Van Orden, 2281 Trescott Dr., Tallahassee, FL 32312.

Film Evaluation. Rita Hoffman, 6647 N. Talman, Chicago, IL 60645.

Filmstrip Evaluation. Randall Enos, Ramapo Catskill Lib. System, 619 North St., Middletown, NY 10990.

Notable Children's Books. Sara Miller, 52-6 Foxwood Dr., Pleasantville, NY 10570.

Recording Evaluation. Janet J. Gilles, 33260 Linden, Solon, OH 44139.

Selection of Children's Books from Various Cultures. Janice A. Yee, Santa Clara County Lib., 1095 N. 7 St., San Jose, CA 95112.

Priority Group III: Professional Development

Consultant. Helen Mae Mullen, Coord., Office of Work with Children, Free Lib. of Philadelphia, Logan Sq., Philadelphia, PA 19103.

Arbuthnot Honor Lecture. Elizabeth Watson, Youth Lib., 610 Main St., Fitchburg, MA 01420.

Education. Margaret Bush, Grad School of Lib. & Info. Science, Simmons College, 300 The Fenway, Boston, MA 02115.

Managing Children's Services (Discussion Group). Mary B. Bauer, 1026 Edgewood Ave., Silver Spring, MD 20901; Eva-Maria Lusk, Children's Services Coord., Spokane Public Lib., W. 906 Main Ave., Spokane, WA 99201.

Putnam Publishing Group Award. Craighton Hippenhammer, 1058 Hill-stone Rd., Cleveland Heights, OH 44121.

Scholarships. Melcher and Bound to Stay Bound. Gertrude Herman.

State and Regional Leadership (Discussion Group). To be appointed.

Teachers of Children's Literature (Discussion Group). Elizabeth F. Howard, 919 College Ave., Pittsburgh, PA 15232; Elizabeth M. Rosen, SLIS, Western Michigan Univ., Kalamazoo, MI 49008.

Priority Group IV: Social Responsibilities

Consultant. Amy Kellman, 211 Castlegate Rd., Pittsburgh, PA 15221.

Intellectual Freedom. Lucy Marx, Free Public Lib., Fourth & York Sts., Louisville, KY 40203.

International Relations. Mildred Lee, Sonoma County Office of Education, 410 Fiscal Dr., Rm. 111E, Santa Rosa, CA 95401.

Library Service to Children with Special Needs. Steven Herb, Dauphin County Lib. System, 101 Walnut St., Harrisburg, PA 17101.

Preschool Services and Parent Education. Caroline Feller Bauer, 6892 Seaway Circle, Huntington Beach, CA 92648.

Social Issues in Relation to Materials and Services for Children (Discussion Group). Joanne R. Long, 334 Woodland Rd., Madison, NJ 07940; Anitra T. Steele, Mid-Continent Public Lib., 15616 E. 24 Hwy., Independence, MO 64050.

Priority Group V: Planning and Research

Consultant. Mary C. Paulus, 120 Harry Lane, Owings Mills, MD 21117.

Caldecott Medal Calendar Committee. Mae Benne, 331 N.W. 53, Seattle, WA 98107.

Collections of Children's Books for Adult

Research (Discussion Group). Mary Beth Dunhouse, 140 Clarendon St., Apt. 1408, Boston, MA 02116.

Local Arrangements—San Francisco, 1987. Effie Lee Morris, 66 Cleary Ct. #1009, San Francisco, CA 94109.

Membership. Starr Latronica, 2626 Ashby Ave. #2, Berkeley, CA 94705.

National Planning of Special Collections. Nan Sturdivant, 2139 E. 55 Ct., Tulsa, OK 74105.

Nominating—1987. Beth Greggs, 800 Lynwood Ave. N.E., Renton, WA 98056.

Organization and Bylaws. Frances V. Sedney, Harford County Lib., 100 Pennsylvania Ave., Bel Air, MD 21014.

Program Evaluation and Support. Gail Sage, Sonoma County Lib., Santa Rosa, CA 95404.

Publications Committee. Adele Fasick, 4351 Bloor St. W., Unit 40, Etobicoke, Ont. M9C 2A4, Canada.

Research and Development. Leslie Edmonds, GSLIS, 410 David Kinley Hall, 1407 W. Gregory, Urbana, IL 61801.

"Top of the News" Editorial, Joint ALSC/ YASD. Joni Bodart, School of Lib. and Info. Management, Emporia State Univ., 1200 Commercial, Emporia, KS 66801.

Priority Group VI: Award Committees

Consultant. Bette J. Peltola, 4109 N. Ardmore, Milwaukee, WI 53211.

Mildred L. Batchelder Award Selection— 1987. Alice P. Naylor, Rte. 1, Box 36-A, Zionville, NC 28698.

Mildred L. Batchelder Award Selection— 1988. Ginny Moore Kruse, 1708 Regent St., Madison, WI 53705.

Caldecott Award—1987. Kay Vandergrift, 24 Starview Dr., Neshank, NJ 08853.

Caldecott Award—1988. Betty Peltola, 4109 N. Ardmore Ave., Milwaukee, WI 53211.

Newbery Award—1987. Trevelyn Jones, School Library Journal, 245 W. 17 St., New York, NY 10011.

Newbery Award—1988. Mary Burns, 11 Joanne Dr., Framingham Center, MA 01701.

Representatives

ALA Planning and Budget Assembly. Gail Sage.

ALA Legislation Assembly. Joan M. Blumenstein.

ALA Library Education Assembly. Margaret Bush.

ALA San Francisco (1987) Conference Program. Jane Botham.

RTSD/CCS Cataloging of Children's Materials. Mary Beth Dunhouse; Adeline W. Wilkes.

Liaison with Other National Organizations

American Association for Gifted Children. Naomi Noyes.

Association for Childhood Education International. Doris Robinson.

Association for Children and Adults with Learning Disabilities. Clara Bohrer.

Big Brothers and Big Sisters of America. Helen Mullen.

Boys Clubs of America. Jane Kunstler.

Camp Fire Inc. Anitra T. Steele.

Child Welfare League of America. Ethel Ambrose.

Children's Defense Fund. Effie Lee Morris.

Children's Theatre Association. Margaret Tassia.

Day Care and Child Development Council of America. James W. Hoogstra.

Four-H Programs, Extension Service. Elizabeth Simmons.

Freedom to Read Foundation. Lucy Marx.

Girl Scouts of America. Margo M. Daniels.

Girls Club of America. To be appointed.

International Reading Association. Clara Bohrer.

National Association for the Education of Young Children. Toni Bernardi.

National Association for the Perpetuation and Preservation of Storytelling. Elizabeth Simmons.

National Multiple Sclerosis Society. Melanie Myers.

National Story League. To be appointed.

Parents Without Partners. Lucy Marx.

Puppeteers of America. Darrell Hildebrandt.

Reading Is Fundamental. Kathleen Roedder.

Salvation Army. Doris Robinson.

Young Men's Christian Association. To be appointed.

Young Women's Christian Association. To be appointed.

American Library Association
Association of College and Research Libraries

Executive Director, JoAn S. Segal
50 E. Huron St., Chicago, IL 60611
312-944-6780

Object

The mission of the Association of College and Research Libraries (ACRL) is to foster the profession of academic and research librarianship and to enhance the ability of academic and research libraries to serve effectively the library and information needs of current and potential library users. This includes all types of academic libraries — community and junior college, college, and university — as well as comprehensive and specialized research libraries and their professional staffs. Founded 1938. Memb. 9,900. (For information on dues, see ALA entry.)

Publications

ACRL Publications in Librarianship (formerly *ACRL Monograph Series*) (occasional). *Ed.* Arthur P. Young, Univ. of Rhode Island, Kingston, RI 02881.

Choice (11 per year; $100); *Choice Reviews on Cards* ($160). *Ed.* Patricia E. Sabosik, 100 Riverview Center, Middletown, CT 06457.

College and Research Libraries (6 per year; memb.; nonmemb. $35). *Ed.* Charles R. Martell, Jr., California State Univ. at Sacramento Lib., 2000 Jed Smith Dr., Sacramento, CA 95819.

College and Research Libraries News (11 per year; memb.; nonmemb. $15). *Ed.* George M. Eberhart, ACRL headquarters.

Rare Books and Manuscripts Librarianship (2 per year; $20). *Ed.* Ann S. Gwyn, Johns Hopkins Univ. Lib., Baltimore, MD 21218.

Officers (July 1986–July 1987)

Pres. Hannelore B. Rader, Univ. of Wisconsin-Parkside, Kenosha, WI 53141; *V.P./Pres.-Elect.* Joanne R. Euster, Rutgers Univ., Alexander Lib., New Brunswick, NJ 08903; *Past Pres.* Sharon A. Hogan, Louisiana State Univ. Lib., Baton Rouge, LA 70803.

Board of Directors

Dirs.-at-Large. Bob D. Carmack (1987); Alexandra Mason (1987); W. Lee Hisle (1988); Edward J. Jennerich (1988); Anne Commerton (1989); Mary Sue Ferrell (1989); Rochelle Sager (1989); Anne K. Beaubien (1990); Melvin R. George (1990); Elizabeth M. Salzer (1990); *Chair, Budget and Finance Committee.* Patricia A. Wand (1988).

Section Chairpersons

Anthropology and Sociology. Gregory A. Finnegan, Dartmouth College, Baker Lib., Hanover, NH 03755.
Art. Janice Woo, Columbia Univ., Avery Lib., New York, NY 10027.
Asian and African. David L. Easterbrook, Univ. of Illinois at Chicago Lib., Chicago, IL 60680.
Bibliographic Instruction. Betsy Baker, Northwestern Univ. Lib., 1935 Sheridan Rd., Evanston, IL 60201.
College Libraries. Arthur H. Miller, Jr., Lake Forest College Lib., Lake Forest, IL 60045.
Community and Junior College Libraries. Imogene I. Book, Denmark Technical College Lib, Denmark, SC 29042.
Education and Behavioral Sciences. Jean T. Thompson, Univ. of Wisconsin–Madison Memorial Lib., 728 State St., Madison, WI 53706.
Law and Political Science. Peter B. Allison, Tamiment Institute, Bobst Lib., 70 Washington Sq. S., New York, NY 10012-1091.
Rare Books and Manuscripts. Donald Farren, Univ. of Maryland, McKeldin Lib., College Park, MD 20742.
Science and Technology. Sheila Grant Johnson, Oklahoma State Univ. Lib., Stillwater, OK 74078.
Slavic and East European. Miranda Beaven, Univ. of Minnesota, Wilson Lib., Minneapolis, MN 55455.

University Libraries. Donna Goehner, Illinois State Univ., Milner Lib., Normal, IL 61761-0900.
Western European Specialists. Anna H. Perrault, Louisiana State Univ. Lib., Baton Rouge, LA 70803.
Women's Studies. Lori Goetsch, Michigan State Univ. Lib., East Lansing, MI 48824-1073; Susan Searing, Univ. of Wisconsin, 112A Memorial Lib., 728 State St., Madison, WI 53706.

Discussion Groups

Black Studies Librarianship. Willie Mae Dawkins, Univ. of Wisconsin–Parkside Lib., Kenosha, WI 53141; Steven C. Newsome, Banneker-Douglas Museum, 84 Franklin St., Annapolis, MD 21401.
English and American Literature. John B. Dillon, Univ. of Wisconsin, 278E Memorial Lib., 728 State St., Madison, WI 53705.
Extended Campus Library Services. Mary Joyce Pickett, Illinois Institute of Technology, Galvin Lib., 35 W. 33 St., Chicago, IL 60616.
Fee Based Information Service Centers in Academic Libraries. Anne K. Beaubien, Univ. of Michigan, 205 Hatcher Grad. Lib., Ann Arbor, MI 48109-1205.
Heads of Public/Readers Services. Rochelle Sager, Adelphi Univ., Swirbul Lib., South Ave., Garden City, NY 11530.
Librarians of Library Science Collections. Alma Dawson, Louisiana State Univ. Lib., Rm. 263 Coates Hall, Baton Rouge, LA 70803-3920.
Microcomputer Services in Academic Libraries. Peggy Seiden, Carnegie-Mellon Univ., Hunt Lib., Pittsburg, PA 15213.
Personnel Administrators and Staff Development Offices of Large Research Libraries. Constance Corey, Arizona State Univ. Lib., Tempe, AZ 85287; Valerie Pena, Univ. of Pennsylvania, Van Pelt Lib., Philadelphia, PA 19104.

Public Relations in Academic Libraries. Beth Mullaney, Hunter College Lib., 695 Park Ave., New York, NY 10021.

Research. Melena Rowan, BRS Information Technology, 1200 Rte. 7, Latham, NY 12110.

Undergraduate Librarians. Wilma Reid Cipolla, SUNY Buffalo, Univ. Libs., 432 Capen Hall, Buffalo, NY 14260.

Commitee Chairpersons

Academic Library Statistics Committee. Kent Hendrickson, Univ. of Nebraska–Lincoln Libs., Lincoln, NE 68588-0410.

Academic or Research Librarian of the Year Award. Dale B. Canelas, Univ. of Florida Libs., 212 Lib. West, Gainesville, FL 32611.

Academic Status Committee. Keith M. Cottam, Univ. of Wyoming Libs., Laramie, WY 82070.

Appointments (1986) and Nominations (1987). Kathleen Gunning, Univ. of Houston Libs., Houston, TX 77035.

Appointments (1987) and Nominations (1988). Jordan M. Scepanski, California State Univ. Lib., Long Beach, 1250 Bellflower Blvd., Long Beach, CA 90840.

Audiovisual. Peggy Johnson, Univ. of Minnesota, St. Paul Campus Lib., St. Paul, MN 55104.

"Books for College Libraries—Third Edition" (ad hoc advisory). Richard Johnson, State Univ. of New York, College at Oneonta, Milne Lib., Oneonta, NY 13820.

Budget and Finance. Patricia A. Wand, Univ. of Oregon Lib., Eugene, OR 97403.

Conference Program Planning Committee, San Francisco, 1987. Hannelore B. Rader, Univ. of Wisconsin–Parkside, Kenosha, WI 53141.

Conference Program Planning Committee, New Orleans, 1988. Joanne R. Eus-

ter, Rutgers Univ., Alexander Lib., New Brunswick, NJ 08903.

Constitution and Bylaws. Wilson D. Snodgrass, Southern Methodist Univ., Central Univ. Libs., Box 1505, Dallas, TX 75275.

Continuing Education Courses Advisory. Thomas A. Tollman, Univ. of Nebraska at Omaha Lib., Omaha, NE 68182-0237.

Copyright. Mary Lee Sweat, Loyola Univ. Lib., 6363 St. Charles Ave., New Orleans, LA 70118.

Doctoral Dissertation Fellowship. Donald F. Joyce, Tennessee State Univ., Downtown Campus Lib., Tenth and Chalotte Ave., Nashville, TN 37203.

Samuel Lazerow Fellowship for Research in Acquisitions or Technical Services. Pam Cenzer, Univ. of Florida Libs., Gainesville, FL 32611.

Legislation. Fay Zipkowitz, Univ. of Rhode Island Grad. School of Lib. and Info. Studies, Kingston, RI 02881.

Membership. Elizabeth M. Salzer, Santa Clara Univ., Michel Orradre Lib., Santa Clara, CA 95053.

Performance Measures for Academic Libraries. Virginia Tiefel, Ohio State Univ. Libs., 1858 Niel Ave. Mall, Columbus, OH 43210.

Planning. Sharon J. Rogers, George Washington Univ. Lib., 2130 H St. N.W., Washington, DC 20052.

President's Program Planning Committee, San Francisco, 1987. Paul E. Birkel, Univ. of San Francisco, Gleeson Lib., San Francisco, CA 94117.

Professional Association Liaison. Jacquelyn M. Morris, Occidental College, Clapp Lib., 1600 Campus Rd., Los Angeles, CA 90041.

Professional Education. Joan Repp, Bowling Green State Univ., Jerome Lib., Bowling Green, OH 43403.

Publications. Ruth J. Person, Clarion Univ. of Pennsylvania, College of Lib. Science, Clarion, PA 16214-1232.

Research. Thomas Kirk, Berea College, Hutchins Lib., Berea, KY 40404.

Standards and Accreditation. Leslie A. Manning, Univ. of Colorado at Colorado Springs Lib., Box 7150, Colorado Springs, CO 80933.

Representatives

American Association for the Advancement of Science. Arleen N. Somerville.

American Association for the Advancement of Science, Consortium of Affiliates for International Programs. Arleen N. Somerville.

American Council on Education. Sharon J. Rogers.

ALA Committee on Appointments. Hannelore B. Rader.

ALA Committee on Professional Ethics. Mary Reichel.

ALA Conference Program Planning Committee (San Francisco, 1987). Hannelore B. Rader.

ALA Conference Program Planning Committee (New Orleans, 1988). Joanne R. Euster.

ALA Legislation Assembly. Fay Zipkowitz.

ALA Membership Promotion Task Force. Elizabeth M. Salzer.

ALA Planning and Budget Assembly. Hannelore B. Rader.

ASCLA Decade of Disabled Persons, Committee on the. Cay Thomas.

Association for Asian Studies, Committee on East Asian Libraries. Tze-chung Li.

Cataloging in Publications for Audiovisual Materials Interdivisional Group. Peggy Johnson.

Documentation Abstracts, Inc. Donald E. Riggs.

Freedom to Read Foundation. Evan Ira Farber.

LC Cataloging in Publication Advisory Group. Sue Ulrich Golden.

RTSD Committee on Cataloging: Description and Access. Ellen Waite.

RTSD Preservation of Library Materials Section. Victoria Steele.

American Library Association
Association of Specialized
and Cooperative Library Agencies

Executive Director, Sandra M. Cooper
50 E. Huron St., Chicago, IL 60611
312-944-6780

Object

To represent state library agencies, specialized library agencies, and multitype library cooperatives. Within the interest of these types of library organizations, the Association of Specialized and Cooperative Library Agencies has specific responsibility for:

1. Development and evaluation of goals and plans for state library agencies, specialized library agencies, and multitype library cooperatives to facilitate the implementation, improvement, and exten-

sion of library activities designed to foster improved user services, coordinating such activities with other appropriate ALA units.

2. Representation and interpretation of the role, functions, and services of state library agencies, specialized library agencies, and multitype library cooperatives within and outside the profession, including contact with national organizations and government agencies.

3. Development of policies, studies, and activities in matters affecting state library

agencies, specialized library agencies, and multitype library cooperatives relating to (a) state and local library legislation, (b) state grants-in-aid and appropriations, and (c) relationships among state, federal, regional, and local governments, coordinating such activities with other appropriate ALA units.

4. Establishment, evaluation, and promotion of standards and service guidelines relating to the concerns of this association.

5. Identifying the interests and needs of all persons, encouraging the creation of services to meet these needs within the areas of concern of the association, and promoting the use of these services provided by state library agencies, specialized library agencies, and multitype library cooperatives.

6. Stimulating the professional growth and promoting the specialized training and continuing education of library personnel at all levels of concern of this association and encouraging membership participation in appropriate type-of-activity divisions within ALA.

7. Assisting in the coordination of activities of other units within ALA that have a bearing on the concerns of this association.

8. Granting recognition for outstanding library service within the areas of concern of this association.

9. Acting as a clearinghouse for the exchange of information and encouraging the development of materials, publications, and research within the areas of concern of this association.

Memb. 1,393.

Board of Directors

Pres. Bridget Later Lamont, Dir., State Lib., Rm. 275, Centennial Bldg., Springfield, IL 62756; *V.P./Pres.-Elect.* Lorraine Schaeffer Summers, 505 Live Oak Plantation Rd., Tallahassee, FL 32312; *Past Pres.* Gail J. McGovern, Cons., California State Lib., 1001 Sixth St., Suite 300, Sacramento, CA 95814; *Div. Councillor,* Donna O. Dziedzic (1989); *Dirs.-at-Large.* Sandra M. Ellison (1987); Elliot Shelkrot (1987); Bruce E. Daniels (1988); Patricia E. Klinck (1988); *Sec. Reps.* Darrell L. Batson, LSSPS chpn. (1987); Barbara A. Webb, LSSPS (1987); Nancy L. Zussy, SLAS chpn. (1987); Joan Neumann, Multi-LINCS chpn; *Ex officio (nonvoting).* Mary Redmond, *Interface ed.* (1988); Organization and Bylaws Committee chpn. To be appointed; *Exec. Dir.* Sandra M. Cooper.

Publications

Bibliotherapy Forum Newsletter (q.; $5 memb.; $7 nonmemb.). *Newsletter Coord.* Lethene Parks, 8250 State Rd. N. 302, Gig Harbor, WA 98335.

Interface (q.; memb.; nonmemb. $10). *Ed.* Mary Redmond, State Lib., Legislative and Government Service, Cultural Education Center, Albany, NY 12230.

Committees

Awards. To be appointed.

Awards Program Review (ad hoc task force). Barratt Wilkins, State Libn., State Lib., Gray Bldg., Tallahassee, FL 32399-0250.

Budget and Finance. Lorraine Schaeffer Summers, 505 Live Oak Plantation Rd., Tallahassee, FL 32312.

Conference Program Coordination. Dottie R. Hiebing, Regional Lib. Co-op. V, Mill Run S., Suite 105, 59 Ave at the Common, Schrewsbury, NJ 07701-4515.

Conference Program — President's Program (1987) (ad hoc). Janice Beck Ison, Exec. Dir., Lincoln Trail Lib. System,

1704 W. Interstate Dr., Champaign, IL 61821.

Continuing Education. To be appointed.

Decade of Disabled Persons (ad hoc). Donna Benson, Rte. 1, Box 933, Allentown, NJ 08501.

Exceptional Achievement Award Jury. Frank V. Van Zanten, Mid-Hudson Lib. System, 103 Market St., Poughkeepsie, NY 12601.

Exceptional Service Award Jury. To be appointed.

"Interface" Advisory. Helen Morgan Moeller, Lib. Consultant, State Lib., Gray Bldg., Tallahassee, FL 32399-0250.

Legislation. Nancy L. Zussy, State Libn., State Lib., AJ-11, Olympia WA 98504.

Membership Promotion. To be appointed.

Nominating (1987). Laura G. Johnson, Indianapolis–Marion County Public Lib., 40 E. St. Clair St., Box 211, Indianapolis, IN 46206.

Organization and Bylaws. Nominating (1988). To be appointed.

Planning. Gail J. McGovern, State Lib., 1001 Sixth St., Suite 300, Sacramento, CA 95814.

Publications. To be appointed.

Research. Ruth M. Katz, Dir. of Academic Lib. Services, Joyner Lib., East Carolina Univ., Greenville, NC 27834.

Standards for Multiple Library Cooperatives and Networks (ad hoc subcommittee). Janice Beck Ison, Exec. Dir., Lincoln Trail Lib. System, 1704 W. Interstate Dr., Champaign, IL 61821.

Standards for Residents of Mental Health Facilities (ad hoc subcommittee). Kathleen O. Mayo, Institutional Consultant, State Lib., Gray Bldg., Tallahassee, FL 32399-0250.

Standards Review. Ann Joslin, Assoc. Dir., Lib. Development, State Lib., 325 W. State St., Boise, ID 83702.

Representatives

ALA Conference Program — San Francisco, 1987. Bridget Later Lamont; *New Orleans, 1988.* Lorraine Schaeffer Summers.

ALA Government Documents Round Table (GODORT). To be appointed.

ALA International Relations Assembly. To be appointed.

ALA Legislation Assembly. Nancy L. Zussy (1987).

ALA Library Education Assembly. To be appointed.

ALA Membership Promotion Task Force. To be appointed.

American Correctional Association. Brenda Vogel (1987).

Association for Radio Reading Services, Inc. To be appointed.

Chief Officers of State Library Agencies (COSLA). Sandra M. Cooper.

Freedom to Read Foundation. Judith R. Farley (1987).

Interagency Council on Library Resources for Nursing. Frederic C. Pachman (1987).

PLA Development Program. Sandra M. Ellison (1987).

RTSD/CCS Cataloging: Description and Access Committee. To be appointed.

Section Chairpersons

Libraries Serving Special Populations (LSSPS). Darrell L. Batson, Lib. Administrator, Metro Jail Lib., c/o 1401 E. Flamingo Rd., Las Vegas, NV 89119.

Multitype Library Networks and Cooperatives Section (Multi-LINCS). Joan Neumann, Exec. Dir., METRO, 57 Willoughby St., Brooklyn, NY 11201.

State Library Agency Section (SLAS). Nancy L. Zussy, State Libn., State Lib., AJ-11, Olympia, WA 98504.

American Library Association
Library Administration and Management Association

Executive Director, John W. Berry
50 E. Huron St., Chicago, IL 60611
312-944-6780

Object

"The Library Administration and Management Association provides an organizational framework for encouraging the study of administrative theory, for improving the practice of administration in libraries, and for identifying and fostering administrative skill. Toward these ends, the division is responsible for all elements of general administration which are common to more than one type of library. These may include organizational structure, financial administration, personnel management and training, buildings and equipment, and public relations. LAMA meets this responsibility in the following ways:

1. Study and review of activities assigned to the division with due regard for changing developments in these activities.

2. Initiating and overseeing activities and projects appropriate to the division, including activities involving bibliography compilation, publication, study, and review of professional literature within the scope of the division.

3. Synthesis of those activities of other ALA units which have a bearing upon the responsibilities or work of the division.

4. Representation and interpretation of library administrative activities in contacts outside the library profession.

5. Aiding the professional development of librarians engaged in administration and encouragement of their participation in appropriate type-of-library divisions.

6. Planning and development of those programs of study and research in library administrative problems which are most needed by the profession."

Established 1957.

Officers

Pres. Betty W. Bender; *V.P./Pres.-Elect.* Ann Heidbreder Eastman; *Past Pres.* Ronald G. Leach; *Exec. Dir.* John W. Berry.

(Address correspondence to the executive director.)

Board of Directors

Dirs. Adele W. Combs; A. Michael Deller; Robert A. Daugherty; Jane W. Greenfield; David Kaser; Janis C. Keene; Nathaniel H. Puffer; *Dirs.-at-Large.* Dale S. Montanelli; Susan E. Stroyan; *Councilor.* Carolyn A. Snyder; *Ex officio.* Anders C. Dahlgren; Margaret Chartrand; Suzanne K. Metzger; Robert F. Moran, Jr.; Sandra J. Pfahler; Kay K. Runge; Peter R. Young; *Committee Organizer.* Dallas Y. Shaffer.

Publication

LAMA Magazine Library Administration & Management (q.; memb. and subscription $25 U.S., $35 foreign). *Ed.* Donald E. Riggs, 2120 E. Knoll Circle, Mesa, AZ 85203.

Committee Chairpersons

Budget and Finance, Rodney M. Hersberger, California State College, 9001 Stockdale Hwy., Bakersfield, CA 93309.

Editorial Advisory Board. Patricia M. Paine, 3915 Benton St. N.W., Washington, DC 20007.

Governmental Affairs. Nancy L. Zussy, Washington State Lib., Bldg. AJ-11, Olympia, WA 98504.

Membership. Carol F. L. Liu, 162-20 Ninth Ave., #9C, Whitestone, NY 11357.

Organization. Dallas Y. Shaffer, PGCMLS, 7414 Riverdale Rd., New Carrollton, MD 20784.

Orientation. Nancy A. Davenport, Lib. of Congress, Washington, DC 20540.

Program. James G. Neal, E505 Pattee Lib., Penn State Univ., University Park, PA 16802.

Publications. Gail A. Schlachter, Ref. Serv. Press, 3540 Wilshire Blvd., Suite 310, Los Angeles, CA 90010.

Recognition of Achievement. Frank J. Dempsey, Arlington Heights Memorial Lib., 500 N. Dunton Ave., Arlington Heights, IL 60004.

Small Libraries Publications. Anders C. Dahlgren, 2706 Post Rd., Madison, WI 53713.

Special Conferences and Programs Committee. Barton M. Lessin, 206 Park Lib., Central Michigan Univ., Mt. Pleasant, MI 48859.

Discussion Group Chairpersons

Asst.-to-the-Dir. Rosie L. Albritton, 104 Ellis Lib., Univ. of Missouri–Columbia, Columbia, MO 65201.

Middle Management. Barbara J. Henn, MPS, Indiana Univ. Libs., Bloomington, IN 47405.

Women Administrators. Cindy L. Brennan, Dir., Public Lib., 421 N.E. Franklin St., Camas, WA 98607.

Section Chairpersons

Buildings and Equipment Section. Davis Kaser, School of Lib. & Info. Science, Indiana Univ. Libs., Bloomington, IN 47405.

Fund Raising and Financial Development Section. Nathaniel H. Puffer, Libs. for College Development, Univ. of Delaware, Newark, DE 19717-5267.

Library Organization and Management Section. Adele W. Combs, Northwestern Univ. Lib., 1935 Sheridan Rd., Evanston, IL 60201.

Personnel Administration Section. Jane W. Greenfield, Evanston Public Lib., 1703 Orrington, Evanston, IL 60201.

Public Relations Section. A. Michael Deller, Livonia Public Lib., 32901 Plymouth Rd., Livonia, MI 48150.

Statistics Section. Janis C. Keene, Tulsa City–County Lib., 400 Civic Center, Tulsa, OK 74103.

Systems and Services Section. Robert A. Daugherty, Circulation Dept., Univ. of Illinois at Chicago, Box 8198, Chicago, IL 60680.

Task Force on Feasibility of Establishing an International Relations Committee. Donna L. McCool, Washington State Univ. Libs., Pullman, WA 99163.

Task Force on Membership Involvement. Anne Rimmer, Main Lib., C-2, Indiana Univ., Bloomington, IN 47405.

Task Force on Membership Services Reps. William G. Jones, Univ. of Illinois at Chicago, Box 8198, Chicago, IL 60680.

Task Force on Non-Library Management Associations. Matthew J. Simon, Queens College Lib., 65-30 Kissena Blvd., Flushing, NY 11367.

Task Force on the Report of the Commission on Freedom and Equality of Access to Information. David R. Smith, Consultant, 130 Holly Rd., Hopkins, MN 55343.

Task Force to Analyze Needs ands Interests of LAMA Organizational Members Robert H. Rohlf, Hennepin County Lib., Admin. Office, 12601 Ridgedale Dr., Minnetonka, MN 55343.

American Library Association
Library and Information Technology Association

Executive Director, Donald P. Hammer
50 E. Huron St., Chicago, IL 60611
312-944-6780

Object

"The Library and Information Technology Association provides its members and, to a lesser extent, the information dissemination field as a whole, with a forum for discussion, an environment for learning, and a program for action on all phases of the development and application of automated and technological systems in the library and information sciences. Since its activities and interests are derived as responses to the needs and demands of its members, its program is flexible, varied, and encompasses many aspects of the field. Its primary concern is the design, development, and implementation of technological systems in the library and information science fields. Within that general precept, the interests of the division include such varied activities as systems development, electronic data processing, mechanized information retrieval, operations research, standards development, telecommunications, networks and collaborative efforts, management techniques, information technology and other aspects of audiovisual and video cable communications activities, and hardware applications related to all of these areas. Although it has no facilities to carry out research, it attempts to encourage its members in that activity.

Information about all of these activities is disseminated through the division's publishing program, seminars and institutes, exhibits, conference programs, and committee work. The division provides an advisory and consultative function when called upon to do so.

It regards continuing education as one of its major responsibilities and through the above channels it attempts to inform its members of current activities and trends, and it also provides retrospective information for those new to the field."

Officers

Pres. Raymond DeBuse, 6601 Shinckle Rd. N.E., Olympia, WA 98506; *V.P.* William Gray Potter, Hayden Lib., Arizona State Univ., Tempe, AZ 85287; *Past Pres.* Lois M. Kershner, Project Dir., Peninsula Libs. Automated Network, 25 Tower Rd., Belmont, CA 94002.

Directors

Officers. Brian Aveney (1987); Michael Gorman (1987); Ernest A. Muro (1987); Louella Wetherbee (1987); *Councillors.* Charles Husbands (1988); George Abbott (1988); Joan Maier McKean (1988); Bonnie K. Juergens (1989); *Ex officio. Bylaws and Organization Committee Chpn.* Jo-Ann Michalak (1986); *Exec. Dir.* Donald P. Hammer.

Publications

Information Technology and Libraries (ITAL, formerly JOLA) (q.; memb.; nonmemb. $35; single copies $7.50). *Ed.* William G. Potter, Hayden Lib., Arizona State Univ., Tempe, AZ 85287. For information or to send manuscripts, contact the editor.

LITA Newsletter (4 per year; memb.). *Ed.* Walt Crawford, The Research Libs. Group, Inc., Jordan Quadrangle, Stanford, CA 94305.

Committee Chairpersons

Budget Review. Lois M. Kershner, Project Dir., Peninsula Libs. Automated Network, 25 Tower Rd., Belmont, CA 94002.

Bylaws and Organization. Jo-Ann Michalak, 271 Hillman Lib., Univ. of Pittsburgh, Pittsburgh, PA 15260.

Education. Helen Spalding, Assoc. Dir. of Libs., Univ. of Missouri–Kansas City, 5100 Rockhill Rd., Kansas City, MO 64100.

Emerging Technologies. Lois M. Kershner, Project Dir., Peninsula Libs. Automated Network, 25 Tower Rd., Belmont, CA 94002.

ITAL Editorial Board. William G. Potter, Hayden Lib., Arizona State Univ., Tempe, AZ 85287.

Legislation and Regulation. Roberta Rand, OCLC, 250 W. First St., Suite 330, Claremont, CA 91711.

LITA/CLSA Scholarship Subcommittee. Arlene G. Taylor, Asst. Professor, Univ. of Chicago, 1100 E. 57 St., Chicago, IL 60637.

LITA/Gaylord Award. To be appointed.

Membership. Dale Flecker, Associate Univ. Libn. for Planning and Systems, Harvard Univ., Widener Lib., Cambridge, MA 02138.

Nominating. Frank P. Grisham, Exec. Dir., SOLINET, Atlanta, GA 30361.

Planning. William Gray Potter, Hayden Lib., Arizona State Univ., Tempe, AZ 85287.

Program Planning. Bruce A. Miller, NOTIS, Northwestern Univ. Lib., 1935 Sheridan Rd., Evanston, IL 60201.

Publications. Val Morehouse, Consultant, North Dakota State Lib., Capitol Grounds, Bismarck, ND 58505.

Representation in Machine-Readable Form of Bibliographic Information, RTSD/LITA/RASD (MARBI). Nolan Pope, 360 Memorial Lib., 728 State St., Madison, WI 53706.

Technical Standards for Library Automation (TESLA). Dorothy McPherson, Univ. of California, Div. of Lib. Automation, 186 University Hall, Berkeley, CA 94720.

Video Tutorial Project Subcommittee (a subcommittee of Publications Committee). Barry Baker, Asst. Dir. for Technical Services, Univ. of Georgia Libs., Athens, GA 30602.

Interest Group Chairpersons

Artificial Intelligence/Expert Systems. Kris Ecklund, Reference Collection Coord., California State Univ. Libs., Northridge, CA 91330.

Authority Control, LITA/RTSD. Catherine M. Thomas, Central Lib. C-075-K, Univ. of California–San Diego, La Jolla, CA 92093.

COM Catalogs. (No chair).

Consultant/User. (No chair).

Distributed Systems. Marietta A. Plank, Univ. of Maryland Libs., McKeldin Lib, College Park, MD 20742.

Electronic Mail/Electronic Publishing. Barbara Cohen, CLSI, 1220 Washington St., West Newton, MA 02165.

Human/Machine Interface. Ellen E. England, Asst. Administrative Analyst, Bibliographic Unit, Div. of Lib. Automation, Univ. of California, 186 University Hall, Berkeley, CA 94720.

Library Microcomputer Templates. Monica Ertel, Libn., Apple Computer Corp., 20650 Valley Green Dr., Cupertino, CA 95014.

Microcomputer Users. Sally S. Small, Assoc. & Head Libn., Berks Campus Lib., Penn State Univ., R.D. #5 Tulpehocken Rd., Box 2150, Reading, PA 19609.

On-line Catalogs. Joan Frye Williams, Inlex, Box 1934, Monterey, CA 93942.

Optical Information Systems. Anita Anker, MINITEX, S-33 Wilson Lib., 309 19th Ave. S., Univ. of Minnesota, Minneapolis, MN 55455.

Programmers/Analysts. Michele I. Dale-

hite, Florida Center for Lib. Automation, 2002 N.W. 13 St., #202, Gainesville, FL 32609.

Retrospective Conversion, LITA/RTSD. Donna Struthers, OCLC, 6565 Frantz Rd., Dublin, OH 43017.

Serials Automation. Linda Miller, APLO, Rm. 642 LM, Lib. of Congress, Washington, DC 20540.

Telecommunications. J. J. Hayden, IN-COLSA, 1100 W. 42 St., Indianapolis, IN 46208.

Vendor/User. Paul B. Lagueux, Sales Rep. Lib. System Div., GEAC Computers, Inc., 515 N. Washington St., Alexandria, VA 22314.

Video and Cable Utilization. Mary Ellen Ritz, Libn., Lib. Dist., Buena Park, CA 90620.

American Library Association
Public Library Association

Executive Director, Eleanor J. Rodger
50 E. Huron St., Chicago, IL 60611
312-944-6780

Object

The Public Library Association will advance the development and effectiveness of public library service and public librarians. The following objectives represent priority actions for PLA:

1. To raise the awareness of public librarians about the issues related to free and equal access to information.

2. To develop a coordinated program for continuing education which includes conference programming, preconferences, regional workshops, and publications.

3. To provide a Public Library Information Service for inquiries on public library issues.

4. To initiate, support, and disseminate information on new research projects on public library service or management.

5. To develop and implement a public relations program at the national level to increase awareness of the diverse nature and value of public library services.

6. To provide public libraries with planning and evaluation tools and to advocate and encourage the utilization of these tools.

7. To ensure that ALA and other units within ALA keep literacy as a high priority.

8. To develop a strategic plan to address public library funding issues.

9. To develop a plan to assist PLA in addressing member interests regarding distinct constituencies by the public library.

Organized 1944. Memb. 5,600.

Membership

Open to all ALA members interested in the improvement and expansion of public library services to all ages in various types of communities.

Officers (1986–1987)

Pres. Kathleen Mehaffey Balcom, Downers Grove Public Lib., 1050 Curtiss St., Downers Grove, IL 60515; *V.P.* Susan S. Goldberg, Tucson Public Lib., Box 17470, Tucson, AZ 85726-7470; *Past Pres.* Patrick O'Brien, Dallas Public Lib., 1515 Young St., Dallas, TX 75201.

Board of Directors (1986–1987)

Officers: Carol Ann Desch; J. Dennis Day, Linda Howard Mielke; Sarah A. Long; Dorothy S. Puryear; *Sec. Reps.*

AEPS Pres. Ann L. Scales; *AFLS Pres.* Katherine P. Sites; *CIS Pres.* Cheryl M. McCoy; *MLS Pres.* Patricia M. Hogan; *PLSS Pres.* Izabela M. Cieszynski; *SMLS Rep.* Terry L. Weech; *Ex officio. PLA/ ALA Membership Rep.* Linda P. Elliott; *Past Pres. ALTA.* Herbert P. Davis; *PLA/ ALA Councilor.* Rosemary S. Martin; *Public Libraries Ed.* Kenneth D. Shearer, Jr.; *Exec. Dir.* Eleanor J. Rodger.

Publications

Public Libraries (q.; memb.; nonmemb. $18). *Ed.* Kenneth D. Shearer, Jr., 1205 LeClair St., Chapel Hill, NC 27514.

Public Library Reporter (occas.) *Ed.* varies. Standing orders or single order available from Order Dept., ALA, 50 E. Huron St., Chicago, IL 60611.

Section Heads

Alternative Education Programs (AEPS). Daniel H. Gann.

Armed Forces Librarians (AFLS). Peggy K. Mann.

Community Information (CIS). Jane I. Light.

Metropolitan Libraries (MLS). Joan Collett.

Public Library Systems (PLSS). S. Jane Ulrich.

Small & Medium Sized Libraries Section (SMLS). Marilyn L. Hinshaw.

Committee and Task Force Chairpersons

Affiliates Network. Matthew C. Kubiak, West Florida Regional Lib., 200 W. Gregory, Pensacola, FL 32501-4878.

Audiovisual. Phil Scott Parson, Lincoln Trail Libs. System, 1704 W. Interstate Dr., Champaign, IL 61821.

Budget and Finance. Susan S. Goldberg, Tucson Public Lib., Box 17470, Tucson, AZ 85726-7470.

Bylaws and Organization. LaDonna T. Kienitz, Newport Beach Public Lib.,

856 San Clemente Dr., Newport Beach, CA 63475.

Cataloging Needs of Public Libraries. Janice M. DeSirey, Hennepin County Lib., 12601 Ridgedale Dr., Minnetonka, MN 55343.

Common Concerns (ALTA/PLA Joint Committee). Herbert P. Davis (ALTA), Box 108, Brooklandville, MD 21022; Annalee M. Bundy (PLA), Providence Public Lib., 150 Empire St., Providence, RI 02903.

Cost Finding. Linda Howard Mielke, Clearwater Public Lib. System, 100 N. Osceola Ave., Clearwater, FL 33515.

Division Program—San Francisco 1987. Mary Jo Detweiller, 9113 Main St., Manassas, VA 22110.

Division Program—New Orleans 1988. Elizabeth Martinez Smith, Orange County Public Lib., 431 City Dr., Orange, CA 92668-9990.

Education of Public Librarians. Dottie Hiebing, Regional V Lib. Cooperative, 59 Ave. of the Common, Suite 106, Shrewsbury, NJ 07701.

Goals, Guidelines, and Standards for Public Libraries. David R. Smith, 130 Holly Rd., Hopkin, MN 55343.

Intellectual Freedom. Monteria Hightower, 325 22nd Ave. E., Seattle, WA 98112.

International Relations. Robert H. Rohlf, Hennepin County Lib., 12601 Ridgedale Dr., Minnetonka, MN 55343.

Legislation. Patricia Olsen Wilson, Rochester Hills Public Lib., 210 W. University Dr., Rochester, MI 48063.

Library Investment (ALTA/PLA Joint Committee). Norman Kelinson, 12238 Caffelt Ave., Bettendorf, IA 52722.

Marketing of Public Library Services. Judith B. Wagner, Schaumburg Township Public Lib., 32 W. Library Lane, Schaumburg, IL 60194.

Allie Beth Martin Award. John Allyn Moorman, Oak Lawn Public Lib., 9427 S. Raymond Ave., Oak Lawn, IL 60453.

Membership. Linda P. Elliott, Oak Lawn Public Lib., 9427 S. Raymond Ave., Oak Lawn, IL 60453.

Multilingual Library Service. Vladimir F. Wertsman, 330 W. 55 St., Apt. 3G, New York, NY 10019.

New Standards Task Force. Karen J. Krueger, Arrowhead Lib. System, 17 N. Franklin St., Janesville, WI 53545.

1988 National Conference. Donald J. Sager, Milwaukee Public Lib., 814 W. Wisconsin Ave., Milwaukee, WI 53233.

1988 National Conference Evaluation Subcommittee. Darlene E. Weingand, Univ. of Wisconsin–Madison, 220 Lowell Hall, 610 Langdon, Madison, WI 53703.

1988 National Conference Exhibits Subcommittee. William H. Roberts, Forsyth County Public Lib., 660 W. Fifth St., Winston-Salem, NC 27101.

1988 National Conference Local Arrangements Subcommittee. Robert B. Croneberger, Carnegie Lib. of Pittsburgh, 4400 Forbes Ave., Pittsburgh, PA 15213-4080.

1988 National Conference Preconference Subcommittee. Jo Ellen Flagg, Kanawha County Public Lib., 123 Capitol St., Charlestown, WV 25301.

1988 National Conference Program Subcommittee. Sarah A. Long, Multnomah County Lib., 801 S.W. Tenth Ave., Portland, OR 97205.

1988 National Conference Public Relations Subcommittee. Sue Fontaine, Queens Borough Public Lib., 89-11 Merrick Blvd., Jamaica, NY 11432.

1988 Nominating Committee. Charles W. Robinson, Baltimore County Public Lib., 320 York Rd., Towson, MD 21204.

1987 Nominating Committee. Douglas P. Hindmarsh, Utah State Lib., 2150 S. 300 West, Suite 16, Salt Lake City, UT 84115.

Orientation. Claudia Sumler, North County Branch, Anne Arundel County Public Lib., 1010 Eastway, Glen Burnie, MD 21061.

Planning Process. Margaret T. Shea, Rhode Island Dept. of Lib. Service, 95 Davis St., Providence, RI 02908.

"Public Libraries/News" Advisory Board. Mary Jane Anderson, Answers Unlimited, Inc., 1618 Elder Lane, Northfield, IL 60093.

Publications. Claudya B. Muller, Suffolk Cooperative Lib., 627 N. Sunrise Service Rd., Bellport, NY 11713.

Research. Joan Coachman Durrance, School of Lib. Science, Univ. of Michigan, 580 Union Dr., Ann Arbor, MI 48109.

Service to Children. Mary K. Chelton, Virginia Beach Public Lib., Municipal Center, Virginia Beach, VA 23456.

Technology in Public Libraries. Carol F. Liu, 162-20 Ninth Ave., 9C, Whitestone, NY 11357.

Technology in Public Libraries Bibiliographic Network Subcommittee. Linda G. Bills, 6318 Bannister, Dublin, OH 43017.

Technology in Public Libraries Awareness Subcommittee. Robert D. Newhard, 24451 Ward St., Torrance, CA 90505-6516.

White House Conference Planning. Donald J. Napoli, South Bend Public Lib., 122 W. Wayne St., South Bend, IN 46601.

American Library Association
Reference and Adult Services Division

Executive Director, Andrew M. Hansen
50 E. Huron St., Chicago, IL 60611
312-944-6780

Objectives

The Reference and Adult Services Division is responsible for stimulating and supporting in every type of library the delivery of reference/information services to all groups, regardless of age, and of general library services and materials to adults. This involves facilitating the development and conduct of direct service to library users, the development of programs and guidelines for service to meet the needs of these users, and assisting libraries in reaching potential users.

The specific responsibilities of RASD are:

1. Conduct of activities and projects within the division's areas of responsibility.

2. Encouragement of the development of librarians engaged in these activities, and stimulation of participation by members of appropriate type-of-library divisions.

3. Synthesis of the activities of all units within the American Library Association that have a bearing on the type of activities represented by the division.

4. Representation and interpretation of the division's activities in contacts outside the profession.

5. Planning and development of programs of study and research in these areas for the total profession.

6. Continuous study and review of the division's activities.

Formed by merger of Adult Services Division and Reference Services Division, 1972. Memb. 5,469. (For information on dues, see ALA entry.)

Officers (1986–1987)

Pres. Elizabeth F. Stroup, 29 Hickory Ave., Takoma Park, MD 20912; *V.P./Pres.-Elect.* Charles A. Bunge, Univ. of Wisconsin-Madison, 600 N. Park St., Madison, WI 53706; *Secy.* Pamela Sieving, 2690 Apple Way, Ann Arbor, MI 41804.

Directors

Sheila T. Dowd; Mary Lou Goodyear; Olive James; Marcia J. Myers; Glenda S. Neely; Rebecca Whitaker; *Councilor.* Danuta A. Nitecki; *Past Pres.* Rebecca Kellogg; *Ex officio. History Sec. Chpn.* Raymond S. Wright III; *Machine-Assisted Reference Sec.* Sarah M. Pritchard; *Ed. RASD Update.* Constance R. Miller; *Ed. RQ.* Kathleen M. Heim; *Council of State and Regional Groups Chpn.* Bruce A. Adams; *Exec. Dir.* Andrew M. Hansen.

(Address general correspondence to the executive director.)

Publications

RASD Update (q.; memb.; nonmemb. $6). *Ed.* Constance R. Miller, Univ. of Illinois at Chicago, Science Lib., Box 7656, Chicago, IL 60680.

RQ (q.; memb.; nonmemb. $25). *Ed.* Kathleen M. Heim, Louisiana State Univ., School of Lib. and Info. Science, Coates Hall, Rm. 267, Baton Rouge, LA 70803.

Section Chairpersons

History. Raymond S. Wright III, Patron Service, Genealogical Lib., 35 N.W. Temple St., Salt Lake City, UT 84150.

Machine-Assisted Reference (MARS). Sarah M. Pritchard, 1708 Noyes Lane, Silver Spring, MD 20910.

Committee Chairpersons

Adult Library Materials. Phyllis K. Woodward, Lake County Public Lib., 1919 W. 81 St., Griffith, IN 46319. *Multilingual Subcommittee.* Sylva N. Manoogian, Foreign Languages Dept., Los Angeles Public Lib., 630 W. Fifth St., Los Angeles, CA 90071.

"Adult Services in Action" Advisory. To be appointed.

Adults, Library Service to. Suzanne D. Sutton, Bloomfield Township Public Lib., 1099 Lone Pine Rd., Bloomfield, MI 48013.

AFL/CIO-ALA (RASD) Joint Committee on Library Service to Labor Groups. Susan Kamm, Box 26467, Los Angeles, CA 90026.

Aging Population, Library Service to an. Celia H. Hales, 2025 Bradley St. #209, Maplewood, MN 55117.

Bibliography. Larayne J. Dallas, 6815-B Thorncliffe Dr., Austin, TX 78731.

Business Reference. Mary Gaylord, 6600 Alpha Dr. #211, Kent, OH 44240.

Catalog Use. Mary Ellen Larson, E108B Pattee Lib., Penn State Univ., University Park, PA 16802.

Conference Program (1987). John Y. Cole, 7206 Lenhart Dr., Chevy Chase, MD 20815.

Conference Program (1988). David F. Kohl, 2575 Forest Ave., Boulder, CO 80302.

Cooperative Reference Service. Barbara Scheele, Brooklyn College Lib., Brooklyn, NY 11210.

Dartmouth Medal. Bruce D. Bonta, Pattee Lib., Penn State Univ., University Park, PA 16802.

Evaluation of Reference and Adult Services. Marjorie E. Murfin, Ohio State Univ. Libs., Info. Services Dept., 185 Neil Ave. Mall, Columbus, OH 43210.

Executive. Elizabeth F. Stroup, 29 Hickory Ave., Takoma Park, MD 20912.

Facts on File. James Warner Granade, Rte. 1, Box 432, Gordonsville, VA 22942.

Fee-Based Reference Services. Jerome A. Lom, 215 Marengo Ave., Forest Park, IL 60130.

Interlibrary Loan. Christopher Wright, 15 Second St. N.E., Washington, DC 20002.

Legislation. Alice E. Wilcox, H/SS Reference Dept., O. M. Wilson Lib., University of Minnesota, 309 19th Ave. S., Minneapolis, MN 55455.

Membership. Carolyn M. Mulac, Interlibrary Loan, Chicago Public Lib., 425 N. Michigan Ave., Chicago, IL 60611.

Margaret E. Monroe Library Adult Services Award. Kenneth L. Ferstl, 1505 Victoria Dr., Denton, TX 76201.

Isadore Gilbert Mudge Citation. Barbara Cunningham, Eastern Shore Regional Lib., Box 4148, Salisbury, MD 21801.

Nominating (1987). Virginia Boucher, 845 Lincoln Pl., Boulder, CO 80302.

Nominating (1988). Nancy H. Marshall, Univ. Lib., College of William & Mary, Earl Gregg Swem Lib., Williamsburg, VA 23185.

Notable Books Council (1987). Dorothy Nyren, Brooklyn Public Lib., Grand Army Plaza, Brooklyn, NY 11238.

Notable Books Council (1988). Diane Gordon Kadanoff, Nowell Public Lib., 64 South St., Nowell, MA 02061.

Organization. Glenda S. Neely, Ekstrom Lib., Univ. of Louisville, Louisville, KY 40292.

Planning. Rebecca Kellogg, College of Arts and Sciences, Modern Languages 347, Univ. of Arizona, Tucson, AZ 85721.

Professional Development. Helen T. Burns, Free Lib. of Philadelphia OWA/YA, Logan Sq., Philadelphia, PA 19103-1152.

Publications. James H. Sweetland, 4105 N. Bartlett Ave., Milwaukee, WI 53211.

Reference Intern/Exchange Project (ad hoc). To be appointed.

Reference Service Press Award. Deborah C. Masters, 4317 N. Fourth St., Apt 301, Arlington, VA 22203.

Reference Services to Children and Young Adults. Neel Parikh, 3027 Richmond Blvd., Oakland, CA 94611.

Reference Sources (1987). James R. Kuhlman, Social Sciences Dept., Univ. of Georgia Libs., Athens, GA 30602.

Reference Sources (1988). Linda Samataro, 3649 Taliluna Ave., G-3, Knoxville, TN 37919.

Reference Sources for Small and Medium-sized Libraries. (5th ed.) ad hoc. Kevin M. Rosswurm, Mount Vernon Public Lib., 28 S. First Ave., Mount Vernon, NY 10550. *Co-Chpn.* Fr. Jovian P. Lang, OFM.

Reference Tools Advisory. La Verne Z. Coan, 2439 Cabot Rd., Canton, MI 48118.

RQ Editorial Advisory Board. Kathleen M. Heim, Louisiana State Univ., School of Lib. and Info. Science, Coates Hall, Rm. 267, Baton Rouge, LA 70803.

John Sessions Memorial Award. Barbara A. Genco, Office of New Books Selection, Brooklyn Public Lib., Grand Army Plaza, Brooklyn, NY 11238.

Spanish-Speaking, Library Service to the. Robert Caban, 2897 Royal Path Ct., Decatur, GA 30030.

Speakers and Consultants Directory. Dana C. Rooks, Univ. of Houston Libs., 4800 Calhoun, Houston, TX 77004.

Standards and Guidelines. Joanne Harrar, McKeldin Lib., Univ. of Maryland, College Park, MD 20742.

Wilson Indexes. Peter W. McCallion, Materials Acquisitions Office, New York Public Lib., 455 Fifth Ave., New York, NY 10016.

Discussion Group Chairs

Adult Materials and Services. Charlotte C. Clarke, Ramsey County Public Lib., Administration Offices, 1910 W. County Rd. B, Roseville, MN 55113.

Business Reference Services. Gerald L. Gill, Carrier Lib., James Madison Univ., Harrisonburg, VA 22807.

Interlibrary Loan. Venita Jorgensen, Interlibrary Loan Dept., Tomas Rivera Lib., Box 5900, Univ. of California, Riverside, CA 92517.

Multilingual Services and Materials. William E. McElwain, Foreign Language Sec., Chicago Public Lib., 78 E. Washington, Chicago, IL 60602.

Performance Standards for Reference/Information Librarians. Irene Hurlbert, Reference Dept., Central Univ. Lib., Univ. of California–San Diego, La Jolla, CA 92093.

Reference Services in Large Research Libraries. Virginia Parr, Reference Dept., Memorial Lib. #33, Univ. of Cincinnati, Cincinnati, OH 45221.

Reference Services in Medium-sized Research Libraries. Linda S. Sammataro, Reference Dept., Main Lib., Univ. of Tennessee, Knoxville, TN 37996-1000.

Women's Materials and Women Library Users. Donna Lynn Nerboso, 69-10 Yellowstone Blvd., Apt. 418, Forest Hills, NY 11375.

Representatives

ALA Legislation Assembly. Alice Wilcox, 315 Townes Lane, Wayzata, MN 55391.

ALA Legislation Committee (ad hoc Copyright Subcommittee). Mary U. Hardin, 1501 Locust St., Norman, OK 73069.

ALA Library Instruction Round Table.

Dennis Clark Hamilton, 3743 Meru Lane, Santa Barbara, CA 93105.

ALA Membership Promotion Task Force. Carolyn M. Mulac, Interlibrary Loan, Chicago Public Lib., 425 N. Michigan Ave., Chicago, IL 60611.

ASCLA "Let's Talk About It" Project. Marilyn H. Boria, Emhurst Public Lib., 211 Prospect, Elmhurst, IL 60126.

Coalition of Adult Education Organizations. Andrew M. Hansen, ALA, 50 E. Huron St., Chicago, IL 60611.

Freedom to Read Foundation. Neel Parikh, 3027 Richmond Blvd., Oakland, CA 94611.

RTSD CCS: Committee on Cataloging: Description and Access. To be appointed.

American Library Association
Resources and Technical Services Division

Executive Director, William I. Bunnell
50 E. Huron St., Chicago, IL 60611
312-944-6780

Object

The division is responsible for the following activities: "acquisition, identification, cataloging, classification, reproduction, and preservation of library materials; the development and coordination of the country's library resources; and those areas of selection and evaluation involved in the acquisition of library materials and pertinent to the development of library resources. Any member of the American Library Association may elect membership in this division according to the provisions of the bylaws." Established 1957. Memb. 5,818. (For information on dues, see ALA entry.)

Officers (June 1986–June 1987)

Pres. Judith P. Cannan, 4106 Duvawn St., Alexandria, VA 22310; *V.P./Pres.-Elect.* Marion T. Reid, Assoc. Dir. for Technical Services, Louisiana State Univ. Libs., Baton Rouge, LA 70803-3300.

(Address correspondence to the executive director.)

Directors

Officers: *Council of Regional Groups Chpn.* Jennifer Younger, 4175 Cherokee Dr., Madison, WI 53711; *RTSD Councillor.* Paul H. Mosher (1987); *Exec. Dir.* William I. Bunnell; *Past Pres.* Marcia Tuttle; *Dirs.-at-Large.* Nancy J. Williamson (1989); Jean G. Cook (1988); *Council of Regional Groups V. Chpn./Chpn.-Elect.* Dorothy Keeton McKowen; *LRTS Ed.* Elizabeth Tate (1987); *RTSD Newsletter Ed.* Thomas W. Leonhardt; *RTSD Planning and Research Committee Chpn.* John R. James (1986); *RTSD Sec. Chpns.* Marlene Sue Heroux (SS); Doris H. Clack (CCS); Jack Pontius (RLMS); Gail A. Kennedy (RS); Margaret Byrnes (PLMS); *LC Liaison.* Henriette D. Avram; *Parliamentarian.* Edward Swanson.

Publications

Library Resources and Technical Services (q.; RTSD memb. or $30). *Ed.* Elizabeth Tate, 11415 Farmland Dr., Rockville, MD 20852.

RLMS Circular (irreg., dist. free at annual

conferences). *Ed.* Douglas K. Freeman, Univ. of Tennessee Lib., Automated Processing Dept., Knoxville, TN 37916.
RLMS Microfile (irreg., prices vary.). *Issued by* Lib. of Congress Photoduplication Services, Washington, DC 20540. *Ed.* Douglas K. Freeman, Univ. of Tennessee Lib., Automated Processing Dept., Knoxville, TN 37916.
RTSD Newsletter (8 per year; memb. or $12). *Ed.* Thomas W. Leonhardt, Asst. Dir. for Technical Services, Univ. of Oregon Lib., Eugene, OR 97403.

Section Chairpersons

Cataloging and Classification Section (CCS). V. Chpn. Robert P. Holley, Asst. Dir., Technical Services, Marriott Lib., Univ. of Utah, Salt Lake City, UT 84112.
Council of Regional Groups (CRG). V. Chpn. Dorothy Keeton McKowen, 7625 Summit Lane, Lafayette, IN 47905.
Preservation of Library Materials Section (PLMS). V. Chpn. Jan Merrill-Oldham, 60 S. River Rd., Coventry, CT 20540.
Reproduction of Library Materials Section (RLMS). V. Chpn. Tamara Swora, Asst. Preservation Microfilming Officer and Optical Disk Print Pilot Operations Mgr., Preservation Microfilming Office, Lib. of Congress L7-G05, Washington, DC 20540.
Resources Section (RS). V. Chpn. William Z. Schenck, Collection Development Libn., Univ. of Oregon Lib., Eugene, OR 97403.
Serials Section (SS). V. Chpn. Jean W. Farrington, 414 Thayer Rd., Swarthmore, PA 19081.

Committee Chairpersons

Audiovisual. Bruce Johnson, 7397 Hickory Log Circle, Columbia, MD 21045.

Budget and Finance. Arnold Hirshon, 916 Hedgelawn Dr., Richmond, VA 23235.
Catalog Form and Function. Randall L. Ericson, 7 College Hill Rd. Clinton, NY 13323.
Character Set Task Force (ad hoc subcommittee). Charles Payne, 5807 Blackstone, Chicago, IL 60637.
Commercial Technical Services. Asa Pieratt, Head, Central Processing, Univ. of Delaware Libs., Newark, DE 19717-5267.
Conference Program—San Francisco, 1987. Judith P. Cannan, 4106 Duvawn St., Alexandria, VA 22310.
Conference Program—New Orleans, 1988. Marion T. Reid, Assoc. Dir. for Technical Services, Louisiana State Univ. Libs., Baton Rouge, LA 70803-3300.
Duplicates Exchange Union. Susan Davis, Head, Serial Records, Lockwood Lib., Univ. of Buffalo, Buffalo, NY 14260.
Education. John R. Kaiser, 1136 S. Atherton St., State College, PA 16801.
International Relations. Ann Thompson, Univ. of Cincinnati Libs., #33 Mail Location, Cincinnati, OH 45221-0033.
Legislative. Charlene Renner, Univ. Libs., FM 25, Univ. of Washington, Seattle, WA 98195.
LRTS Editorial Board. Elizabeth L. Tate, 11415 Farmland Dr., Rockville, MD 20852.
Membership. Sally Voth Rausch, Indiana Univ. Libs., Bloomington, IN 47401.
Nominating. Joe A. Hewitt, Davis Lib. 080-A, Univ. of North Carolina, Chapel Hill, NC 27514.
Organization and Bylaws. Marcia Tuttle, Serials Dept., Davis Lib. 080-A, Univ. of North Carolina, Chapel Hill, NC 27514.
Esther J. Piercy Award Jury. Judith N. Kharbas, Univ. of Rochester Libs., Rochester, NY 14627.
Planning and Research. John R. James,

Dartmouth College Lib., Hanover, NH 03755.

Preservation Microfilming. Cecelia L. Shores, Head, Acquisitions Dept., Center for Research Libs., 6050 S. Kenwood, Chicago, IL 60637.

Program Evaluation and Support. Marion T. Reid, Assoc. Dir. for Technical Services, Louisiana State Univ. Libs., Baton Rouge, LA 70803-3300.

Publications. Beth J. Shapiro, Assoc. Dir. for Readers Services, Michigan State Univ. Libs., East Lansing, MI 48824-1048.

Publisher/Vendor-Library Relations. Gay D. Donnelly, Head, Acquisitions Dept., Ohio State Univ. Libs., Columbus, OH 43210.

Representation in Machine-Readable Form of Bibliographic Information, RTSD/LITA/RASD (MARBI). Nolan F. Pope, 360 Memorial Lib., 728 State St., Univ. of Wisconsin, Madison, WI 53706.

Technical Services Costs. Heide Lee Hoerman, Asst. Dean for Technical Services, Renne Lib., Montana State Univ., Bozeman, MT 59717-0022.

Representatives

ALA Freedom to Read Foundation Board. Karin A. Trainer (1987).

ALA Government Documents Round Table. Judy Myers (1987).

ALA Legislation Assembly. Charlene Renner (1987).

ALA Membership Promotion Task Force. Sally Voth Rausch (1987).

CONSER Advisory Group. Suzanne Striedieck (1988).

Joint Advisory Committee on Nonbook Materials. Katha D. Massey, (1987); Verna Urbanski (1988).

Joint Steering Committee for Revision of AACR2. Helen F. Schmierer (1989).

National Information Standards Organization (NISO): Standards Committee Z39 on Library Work, Documentation, and Related Publishing Practices. Sally H. McCallum (1987); *Alternate.* Arnold Hirshon (1987).

National Institute for Conservation. Merrily Smith (1988).

American Library Association
Young Adult Services Division

Executive Director, Evelyn Shaevel
50 E. Huron St., Chicago, IL 60611
312-944-6780

Object

"Interested in the improvement and extension of services to young people in all types of libraries; has specific responsibility for the evaluation, selection, interrelation and use of books and nonbook materials for young adults except when such materials are intended for only one type of library."

Established 1957. Memb. 3,000. (For information on dues, see ALA entry.)

Membership

Open to anyone interested in library services to young adults.

Officers (July 1986–July 1987)

Pres. Marion Hargrove, YA Specialist, Prince George's County Memorial Lib., Bowie, MD 20782; *V.P./Pres-Elect.* Vivian Wynn, Cuyahoga County Public

Lib., Maple Heights Regional, 5225 Library Lane, Maple Heights, OH 44137; *Past Pres.* Joan L. Atkinson, Univ. of Alabama, Grad. School of Lib. Science, Box 6242, University, AL 35486.

Directors

Gerald G. Hodges; Gayle Keresey; Elizabeth O'Donnell; Roger Sutton; Deborah Taylor; Linda Waddle; Mary Elizabeth Wendt.

Committee Chairpersons

Audiovisual Producers and Distributors Liaison. Co-Chpns. Jean Kreamer, Univ. Media Center, Univ. of Southwestern Louisiana, Box 40396, Lafayette, LA 40396; Louise Spain, New York Public Lib., Donnell Lib., 20 W. 53 St., New York, NY 10019.

Author Award Feasibility. Rhonna Goodman, Asst. Coord., METRO, 57 Willoughby St., Brooklyn, NY 11201.

Best Books for Young Adults. Betty Carter, Univ. of Houston, College of Education, Houston, TX 77004.

Budget and Finance. Margaret J. Harris, Maple Heights Regional Lib., 5225 Library Lane, Maple Heights, OH 44137.

Computer Applications to Young Adults Services. Leslie S.J. Farmer, San Domenico School, 1500 Butterfield Rd., San Anselmo, CA 94960.

Education. Joy L. Lowe, Louisiana Tech. Univ., Box 3061, Ruston, LA 71272.

High-Interest/Low-Literacy Level Materials Evaluation. Barbara Lynn, Olathe South H.S., 1640 E. 151 St., Olathe, KS 66062.

Intellectual Freedom. Pamela Klipsch, Hayner Public Lib., Alton, IL 62002.

Leadership Training. Vivian Wynn, Cuyahoga County Public Lib., Maple

Heights Regional, 5225 Library Lane, Maple Heights, OH 44137.

Legislation. Linda K. Miller, 833 Lundvall, Rockford, IL 61108.

Library of Congress, Advisory Committee to the National Library Service for the Blind and Physically Handicapped. Patricia Muller, Virginia Lib., Arlington County Public Lib., 1015 Quincy St., Arlington, VA 22201.

Local Arrangements—San Francisco 1987. Judith G. Flum, Alameda County Lib., Hayward, CA 94545; Leslie S. J. Farmer, San Domenico School, 1500 Butterfield Rd., San Anselmo, CA 94960.

Long-Range Planning. Mary Elizabeth Wendt, 502 Tenth St, Brooklyn, NY 11215.

Media Selection and Usage. Ellen V. LiBretto, Queens Borough Public Lib., Jamaica, NY 11432.

Membership Promotion. Penny Parker, Enoch Pratt Free Lib., Baltimore, MD 21229.

National Organizations Serving the Young Adult Liaison. Carl R. Keehn, Prince George's County Memorial Lib., Laurel Branch, 507 Seventh St., Laurel, MD 20707.

Nominating. Barbara Newmark-Kruger, Westchester Lib. System, Elmsford, NY 10953.

Organization and Bylaws. Elizabeth M. O'Donnell, Manchester City Lib., Manchester, NH 03104.

Program Planning Clearinghouse and Evaluation. Gayle Keresey, East Arcadia School, Riegelwood, NC 28456.

Publications. Susan Berlin, Cuyahoga County Public Lib., 4510 Memphis Ave., Cleveland, OH 44144.

Publishers' Liaison. Barbara Newmark-Kruger, Westchester Lib. System, Elmsford, NY 10523.

Research. Lesley S. J. Farmer, San Domenico School, 1500 Butterfield Rd., San Anselmo, CA 94960.

Selected Films for Young Adults. Jennifer Jung Gallant, 482 Dover Center Rd., Bay Village, OH 44140.

"Top of the News" Editorial. Joni Bodart, School of Lib. and Info. Management, Emporia State Univ., 1200 Commercial St., Emporia, KS 66801.

YASD/Baker and Taylor Conference Grant. Carolyn Rowe Hale, Free Lib. of Philadelphia, Philadelphia PA 19144.

Young Adults with Special Needs. Marilee Foglesong, Warner Lib., Tarrytown, NY 10591.

Youth Participation. Christy Tyson, Spokane Public Lib., W. 906 Main Ave., Spokane, WA 99201.

Discussion Group Chairpersons

Booktalking. Joni Bodart, School of Lib. and Info. Management, Emporia State Univ., 1200 Commercial St., Emporia, KS 66801.

Computer Application for Young Adult Services. Lesley S. J. Farmer, San Domenico School, 1500 Butterfield Rd., San Anselmo, CA 94960.

Library Educators for Young Adult Services and Materials. To be appointed.

Young Adult Specialists. Julia Losinski, Prince George's County Memorial Lib., 6532 Adelphi Rd., Hyattsville, MD 20782.

Representatives

ALA Appointments Committee. Vivian Wynn.

ALA Budget Assembly. Vivian Wynn.

ALA Legislation Assembly. Marilee Foglesong.

ALA Library Education Assembly. Joy L. Lowe.

ALA Membership Promotion Task Force. Penny Parker.

ALA San Francisco Conference (1987) Program Committee. Marion Hargrove.

Freedom to Read Foundation. Pamela Klipsch.

American Merchant Marine Library Association

(Affiliated with United Seamen's Service)
Director, Sally-Ann Coash
One World Trade Center, Suite 1365, New York, NY 10048
212-775-1033

Object

Provides ship and shore library service for American-flag merchant vessels, the Military Sealift Command, the Coast Guard, and other waterborne operations of the U.S. government.

Officers

Chpn. of the Bd. Hoyt Haddock; *Pres.* Thomas J. Smith; *Treas.* Hubert Carr; *Secy.* Capt. Franklin K. Riley.

Trustees

W. J. Amoss; Ralph R. Bagley; Mildred M. Berg; Hubert Carr; Nicholas Cretan; Maj. Gen. H. R. DelMar; John I. Dugan; Arthur W. Friedberg; Hoyt S. Haddock; Capt. Robert E. Hart; James J. Hayes; Rear Admiral Thomas A. King; George F. Lowman; Thomas Martinez; Mace G. Mavroleon; Frank X. McNerney; Andrew Rich; Capt. Franklin K. Riley; George J. Ryan; Thomas J. Smith; Richard T. Soper; Anthony J. Tozzoli; Rev. James R. Whittemore; Vice Admiral Paul Yost, Jr.

Honorary Trustees

Rebekah T. Dallas; Charles Francis.

American Society for Information Science

Executive Director, Linda Resnik
1424 16th St. N.W., #404, Washington, DC 20036
202-462-1000

Object

The American Society for Information Science provides a forum for the discussion, publication, and critical analysis of work dealing with the design, management, and use of information systems and technology. Memb. (Indiv.) 3,400; (Student) 480; (Inst.) 100. Dues (Indiv.) $75; (Student) $20; (Inst.) $350 and $550.

Officers

Pres. Thomas Hogan, Learned Info., Medford, NJ 08055; *V.P./Pres.-Elect.* Martha Williams, Univ. of Illinois, CSL, 1101 W. Springfield, Urbana, IL 61801; *Treas.* N. Bernard Basch, The Turner Subscription Agency, 116 E. 16 St., New York, NY 10003; *Past Pres.* Julie Virgo, The Carroll Group, Chicago, IL, 60611.

(Address correspondence to the executive director.)

Board of Directors

Chapter Assembly Dir. Dan Robbins; *SIG Cabinet Dir.* Carol Wasserman Diener; *Dirs.-at-Large.* Trudi Bellardo; Marjorie Hlava; Edward J. Kazlauskas; Lois Lunin; Ann Prentice; Gerard Salton.

Publications

Annual Review of Information Science and Technology. Available from Elsevier Science Publishers.
Bulletin of the American Society for Information Science. Available directly from ASIS.

Collective Index to the Journal of the American Society for Information Science (vol. 1, 1950–vol. 25, 1974). Available from John Wiley & Sons, 605 Third Ave., New York, NY 10016.
DataBase Directory Service 1985–1986. Available from Knowledge Industry Publications.
Journal of the American Society for Information Science; formerly *American Documentation.* Available from John Wiley & Sons, 605 Third Ave., New York, NY 10016.
Key Papers in the Design and Evaluation of Information Systems. Ed. Donald W. King. Available from Greenwood Press.
Library and Reference Facilities in the Area of the District of Columbia.
Proceedings of the ASIS Annual Meetings. Available from Learned Information.

Committee Chairpersons

Awards and Honors. Helen Manning, Texas Instruments, Inc., Box 1443, MS 695, Houston, TX 77001.
Budget and Finance. N. Bernard Basch, Pres., The Turner Subscription Agency, 116 E. 16 St., New York, NY 10003.
Conferences and Meetings. Ron Hock, Mgr., New England Region, Dialog Info. Services, 5 Cambridge Center; Cambridge, MA 02142.
Constitution and Bylaws. Charles Sargent, Lib., Texas Tech Univ. Health Sciences Center, Lubbock, TX 79430.
Education. Marianne Cooper, Grad. School of Lib. and Info. Science, Queens College, Flushing, NY 11367.
Executive. Tom Hogan, Pres., Learned

Information, Inc., 143 Old Marlton Pike, Medford, NJ 08055.

International Relations. Claude Walston, Univ. of Maryland, CLIS, 4340 Leeds Hall Dr., Olney, MD 20832.

Marketing. Pauline Smillie, 597 Hansell Rd., Wynnewood, PA 19096.

Membership. W. David Penniman, AT&T Bell Labs., 600 Mountain Ave., Murray Hill, NJ 07974.

Nominations. Julie Virgo, V.P., The Carroll Group, 875 N. Michigan Ave., Suite 3311, Chicago, IL 60611.

Professionalism. Joe Ann Clifton, Litton

Industries, 5500 Canoga Ave., Woodland Hills, CA 91365.

Public Affairs. Sarah Kadec, 2833 Gunarette Way, Silver Spring, MD 20906.

Publications. Nancy Roderer, 3515 Legation St., Washington, DC 20015.

Research. Jeffrey Katzer, Professor, Syracuse Univ. School of Info. Studies, Syracuse, NY 13244.

Standards. Mary Ellen Jacob, OCLC Inc., 6565 Frantz Rd., Dublin, OH 43017.

American Theological Library Association

Executive Secretary, Simeon Daly, O.S.B.
St. Meinrad School of Theology, Archabbey Library
St. Meinrad, IN 47577

Object

"To bring its members into close working relationships with each other, to support theological and religious librarianship, to improve theological libraries, and to interpret the role of such libraries in theological education, developing and implementing standards of library service, promoting research and experimental projects, encouraging cooperative programs that make resources more available, publishing and disseminating literature and research tools and aids, cooperating with organizations having similar aims, and otherwise supporting and aiding theological education." Founded 1947. Memb. (Inst.) 160; (Indiv.) 480. Dues (Inst.) $75-$400,, based on total library expenditure; (Indiv.) $15-$80, based on salary scale. Year. May 1-April 30.

Member of the Council of National Library and Information Associations.

Membership

Persons engaged in professional library or bibliographical work in theological or religious fields and others who are interested in the work of theological librarianship.

Officers (June 1986–June 1987)

Pres. Stephen Lee Peterson, Yale Divinity School Lib., 409 Prospect St., New Haven, CT 06510; *V.P./Pres.-Elect.* Rosalyn Lewis, United Methodist Publishing House, 201 Eighth Ave. S., Lib. Rm. 122, Nashville, TN 37202; *Past Pres.* Sara J. Myers, Ira J. Taylor Lib., Iliff School of Theology, 2201 S. University Blvd., Denver, CO 80210; *Treas.* Robert A. Olsen, Jr., Libn., Brite Divinity School, Texas Christian Univ., Fort Worth, TX 76129.

Board of Directors

Diane Choquette; Leslie R. Galbraith; Alice M. Kendrick; James Overbeck; Eugene McCleod; William Miller.

Publications

Newsletter (q.; memb. or $10).
Proceedings (ann.; memb. or $20).
Religion Index One (formerly *Index to Religious Periodical Literature, 1949–date*).
Religion Index Two: Multi-Author Works.
Research in Ministry: An Index to Doctor of Ministry Project Reports.

Committee Chairpersons

ATLA Newsletter. Donn Michael Farris, Ed., Divinity School Lib., Duke Univ., Durham, NC 27706.
ATLA Representative to the Council of National Library and Information Associations. Paul A. Byrnes, 69 Tiemann Place, Apt. 44, New York, NY 10027.
Archivist. Gerald W. Gillette, Presbyterian Historical Society, 425 Lombard St., Philadelphia, PA 19147.
Bibliographic Systems. Clifford Wunderlich, Box 1225, Cambridge, MA 02238.
Collection Evaluation and Development.

Roger Loyd, Bridwell Lib., Perkins School of Theology, Southern Methodist Univ., Dallas, TX 75275.
Nominating. Dorothy Parks, Vanderbilt Univ., Divinity Lib., 419 21st Ave. S., Nashville, TN 37240.
Oral History. David Wartluft, Lutheran Theological Seminary, 7301 German Ave., Philadelphia, PA 19119.
Periodical Indexing Board. Norman Kansfield, Libn., Colgate Rochester/ Bexley Hall/Crozer Divinity School, 1100 S. Goodman St., Rochester, NY 14620.
Preservation Board. Co-Chpns. John A. Bollier, Sterling Memorial Lib., Rm. 118, 120 High St., New Haven, CT 06511; Charles Willard, Dir., Speer Lib., Princeton Theological Seminary, Princeton, NJ 08540.
Program. Cecil White, 161 Delores St., #5, San Francisco, CA 94103.
Publication. Ellis O'Neal, Jr., Andover Newton Theological School, Newton Centre, MA 02159.
Reader Services. Christine Wenderoth, Columbia Theological Seminary, 701 Columbia Dr., Decatur, GA 30031.
Relationship with Learned Societies. Simeon Daly, ATLA.
Statistician and Liaison with ALA Statistics Coordinating Committee. Simeon Daly, ATLA.

ARMA International

Executive Director, Lou Snyder
4200 Somerset Dr., Suite 215, Prairie Village, KS 66208
913-341-3808

Object

"To promote a scientific interest in records and information management; to provide a forum for research and the exchange of ideas and knowledge; to foster professionalism; to develop and promulgate workable standards and practices; and to furnish a source of records and information management guidance through education and publications."

Membership

Membership application is available through ARMA Headquarters. Annual

dues are $55 for national affiliation. Chapter dues vary from city to city. Membership categories are chapter member ($55 plus chapter dues), student member ($10), and member-at-large.

Officers

Pres. and CEO. Harry L. Ludwig, III, Contel Corp., 245 Perimeter Center Pkwy., Box 105194, Atlanta, GA 30348; *Exec. V.P.* John Moss Smith, Atomic Energy of Canada, Ltd., 275 Slater St., Ottawa, Ont. K1A 0S4, Canada; *Secy.-Treas.* David O. Stephens, United Energy Services Corp., Box 1616, Reading, PA 19603-1616; *Past Pres. and Chpn. of the Board.* Helen Brook Dowd, LeBoeuf, Lamb, Leiby and MacRae, 520 Madison Ave., New York, NY 10022.

Board of Directors (1986–1987)

Regional V.P.s. Region I. Philip K. Albert, Sr., Johns Hopkins Univ./APL, Johns Hopkins Rd., Laurel, MD 20707; *Region II.* Manker R. Harris, 12 Trailridge Lane, Springfield, IL 62704; *Region III.* Wendy Shade, Bell & Hawell Records Management, 3661 N.E. Expressway, Doraville, GA 30340; *Region IV.* Brian A. Solberg, 3M Co., Bldg. 220-10W, St. Paul, MN 55144; *Region V.* Ann E. H. Tofft, 4822, Rockwood Dr., Houston, TX 77004; *Region VI.* Allan H. Mawhinney, Box 1273, Long Beach, CA 90801; *Region VII.* Mary Lou Oliva, Merck & Co., Inc., Box 2000, Rahway, NJ 07065; *Region VIII.* James Allin Spokes, Records Management, Manitoba Hydro, Box 815, Winnipeg, Man. R3C 2P4, Canada; *Region IX.* Robert N. Allerding, 61 Somerset Rd., Deleware, OH 43015; *Region X.* Dorris M. Schneider, Records Manager, SAIF Corp., 400 High St. S.E., Salem, OR 97312.

Publication

Records Management Quarterly. Ed. Ira Penn, Box 4580, Silver Spring, MD 20904.

Committee Chairpersons

Archives. Ivan L. Waite, Box 15307, Civic Center Sta., Kansas City, MO 64109.
Audit/Budget/Compensation. David O. Stephens, Gilbert/Commonwealth, Box 1498, Reading, PA 19603.
Awards/Nominating. Helen Brook Dowd, LeBouef, Lamb, Leiby and MacRae, 520 Madison Ave., New York, NY 10022.
Conferences. Mariyana L. Stamey, City of Sarasota, Box 1058, Sarasota, FL 33578.
Education. Marilyn Wilkins, Eastern Illinois Univ., Business Education and Office Management, Charleston, IL 61920.
ELF Project. Martin Richelsoph, 2824 E. Clarendon, Phoenix, AZ 85016.
Industry Action. Jean Crary Brown, Univ. of Delaware Archives, 78 E. Delaware Ave., Newark, DE 19716.
Legislative and Regulatory Affairs—U.S. Donald S. Skupsky, Information Requirements Clearinghouse, 3801 E. Florida, Suite 4, Denver, CO 80210.
Legislative and Regulatory Affairs—Canada. Ted Hnatiuk, Imperial Oil, Ltd., Corporate Records and Archives, 111 St. Clair Ave. W., Toronto, Ont. M5W 1K3, Canada.
Long Range Planning. Waymon Underwood, Credit Life Insurance, One S. Limestone St., Springfield, OH 45501.
1987 Program Chairperson. Carl E. Weise, Rockwell International Corp.,

600 Grant St. (PC80), Pittsburgh, PA 15219.

Scholarship. Zona Beloungea, Manufacturers Bank, 411 W. LaFayette, Detroit, MI 48226.

Standards. Robert B. Austin, Austin Assocs., Prentice Point Suite 500, 5299 DTC Blvd., Englewood, CO 80111.

Technical Research. Pat Vice, Boise Cascade Corp., One Jefferson Sq., Boise, ID 83728.

Teller. Terry Starchich, Electronic Realty Assoc., Box 2974, Shawnee Mission, KS 66201.

Art Libraries Society of North America (ARLIS/NA)

Executive Director, Pamela J. Parry
3900 E. Timrod St., Tucson, AZ 85711
602-881-8479

Object

"To promote art librarianship and visual resources curatorship, particularly by acting as a forum for the interchange of information and materials on the visual arts." Established 1972. Memb. 1,250. Dues (Inst.) $75; (Indiv.) $45; (Business Affiliate) $75; (Student) $20; (Retired/unemployed) $30; (Sustaining) $175; (Sponsor) $500. Year. Jan.–Dec. 31.

Membership

Open and encouraged for all those interested in visual librarianship, whether they be professional librarians, students, library assistants, art book publishers, art book dealers, art historians, archivists, architects, slide and photograph curators, or retired associates in these fields.

Officers (Feb. 1987–Feb. 1988)

Chpn. Jeffrey Horrell, Dartmouth College, Sherman Art Lib., Hanover, NH 03755; *V. Chpn.* Ann Abid, Cleveland Museum of Art Lib., 11150 East Blvd., Cleveland, OH 44106; *Secy.* Helene Roberts, Fogg Art Museum, Fine Arts Lib., Cambridge, MA 02138; *Treas.* William Dane, Newark Public Lib., Art and Music Dept., 5 Washington St., Newark, NJ 07101; *Exec. Dir.* Pamela J. Parry, 3900 E. Timrod St., Tucson, AZ 85711; *Past chpn.* Susan Craig, Univ. of Kansas, Art Lib., Lawrence, KS 66045.

(Address correspondence to the executive director.)

Committees

(Direct correspondence to headquarters.)
AAT Advisory.
Cataloging Advisory.
Conference.
Development.
International Relations.
Membership.
Gerd Muehsam Award.
Nominating.
Professional Development.
Publications.
Standards.
Travel Award.
Wittenborn Award.

Executive Board

The chairperson, past chairperson, chairperson-elect, secretary, treasurer, and four regional representatives (East, Midwest, West, and Canada).

Publications

ARLIS/NA Update (q.; memb.).
Art Documentation (q.; memb.).
Handbook and List of Members (ann.; memb.).
Occasional Papers (price varies).
Miscellaneous others (request current list from headquarters).

Chapters

Arizona; Central Plains; DC-Maryland-Virginia; Delaware Valley; Kentucky-Tennessee; Michigan; Mid-States; New England; New Jersey; New York; Northern California; Northwest; Ohio; Southeast; Southern California; Texas; Twin Cities; Western New York.

Asian/Pacific American Librarians Association

President, Asha Capoor, Director, Technical Services, Baker & Taylor
652 E. Main St., Bridgewater, NJ 08807-0920

Object

"To provide a forum for discussing problems and concerns of Asian/Pacific American librarians; to provide a forum for the exchange of ideas by Asian/Pacific American librarians and other librarians; to support and encourage library services to the Asian/Pacific American communities; to recruit and support Asian/Pacific American librarians in the library/ information science professions; to seek funding for scholarships in library/ information science schools for Asian/ Pacific Americans; and to provide a vehicle whereby Asian/Pacific American librarians can cooperate with other associations and organizations having similar or allied interests." Founded 1980; incorporated 1981; affiliated with ALA 1982. Dues (Inst.) $25; (Indiv.) $10; (Students and Unemployed Librarians) $5.

Membership

Open to all librarians/information specialists of Asian/Pacific descent working in U.S. libraries/information centers and other such related organizations and to others who support the goals and purposes of APALA. Asian/Pacific Americans are defined as those who consider themselves Asian/Pacific Americans. They may be Americans of Asian/Pacific descent, Asian/Pacific people with the status of permanent residency, or Asian/ Pacific people living in the United States.

Officers (June 1986–June 1987)

Pres. Asha Capoor, Dir., Technical Services, Baker & Taylor, 652 E. Main St., Bridgewater, NJ 08807-0920; *V.P./Pres.-Elect.* Betty L. Tsai, Technical Services Libn., Bucks County Community College, Newton, PA 18940; *Treas.* Erlinda J. Regner, Chicago Public Lib., 425 N. Michigan, Chicago, IL 60614; *Secy.* Jack Tsukamoto, Periodicals Libn., Ball State Univ., Muncie, IN 47306.

Advisory Committee

The president, immediate past president, vice president/president-elect, secretary, treasurer, chairpersons of the regional chapters, and an elected representative of the standing committees.

Publications

APALA Newsletter (q.; memb.). *Ed.* Sharad Karkhanis, Kingsborough Com-

munity College Lib., Oriental Blvd., Brooklyn, NY 11235.
Membership Directory.

Committee Chairpersons

Constitution and Bylaws. Connie Rebadavia, Head, Science and Technology team, Alexander Lib., Rutgers Univ., New Brunswick, NJ 08903.
Membership. Chiou-Sen Chen, Serials Acquisitions Libn., Alexander Lib., Rutgers Univ., New Brunswick, NJ 08903.
Publicity and Program. Augurio Collantes, Hostos Community College/CUNY, 500 Grand Concourse, Bronx, NY 10451.
Recruitment and Scholarship. Ichiko Morita, Automated Processing Dept., Ohio State Univ., 1858 Neil Ave., Columbus, OH 43210.

Associated Information Managers

Executive Director, Sheila Brayman
1776 E. Jefferson St., Suite 470S, Rockville, MD 20852
301-231-7447

Object

To advance information management as a profession and to promote information management as an executive function by improving recognition of its applicability as a strategic and tactical tool in achieving organizational and executive effectiveness. AIM provides the meeting ground for the professionals responsible for meeting the present and future information needs of their organizations within the information management context. Established January 1981. Memb. (Indiv.) 600; (Corporate) 23.

Membership

Corporate planners, vice presidents of communication and marketing, administration managers, on-line users, data processing, telecommunications, librarianship, records management, office automation, and management information systems (MIS) personnel. Its primary focus is on the management of these information activities and on making the total information base supportive of management and the decision-making process.

Board of Directors made up of leading information professionals in industry, academia, and government. Dues (Corporate) sustaining $3,000, supporting $1,000, contributing $500; (Regular) $85; (Foreign) $120; (Student) $35.

Board of Directors

Chpn. Donald A. Marchand, Dir., Inst. of Info. Management, Technology and Policy, Univ. of South Carolina; *V. Chpn.* Forest Woody Horton, Jr., Management Consultant; *Secy.-Treas.* Molly A. Wolfe, Pres., Knowledgeware Systems, Inc.; *Past Chpn.* Herbert R. Brinberg, Pres. and CEO, Wolters Samson U.S. Corp.; Christopher Burns, Pres., Christopher Burns, Inc.; Ramona C. T. Crosby, Supv., Info. and Computer Services, Stauffer Chemical Co.; A. Jackson Forster, Pres., INFOTECH; M. Robert Kelly, V.P., Inter-America Research Assocs.; Rhoda R. Mancher, Assoc. Dir., Info. Resources Management, U.S. Dept. of the Navy; Reed Phillips, Dir., Info. Resources Management, U.S. Dept of Commerce; Arthur H. Schneyman, Mgr., Administrative Sys-

tems and Management Consultants, Mobil Corp.; Melinda J. Scott, Mgr., Main Hurdman; E. Norman Sims, Dir., Office of Info. Services, Council of State Governments; Robert O. Stanton, Mgr., Libs. and Info. Services, AT&T Bell Laboratories; *Exec. Dir.* Sheila Brayman.

Publications

AIM Network (bi-weekly; free to membs.). Newsletter.

AIM 1985 Membership Profile Survey (memb. $15; nonmemb. $25).
Marketing Yourself in Your Organization, by Morton Meltzer (memb. $9.95; nonmemb. $14.95).
Partners in Fact: Information Managers/ Information Company Executives Talk (memb. $14.95; nonmemb. $19.95).
Who's Who in Information Management (ann.; nonmemb. $50).

Association for Federal Information Resources Management (AFFIRM)

Executive Vice Chairperson, John W. Coyle
U.S. Department of the Interior, Washington, DC 20240
202-343-4281

Object

"Founded in 1979, AFFIRM is an organization of professionals associated to promote and advance the concept and practice of information resources management (IRM) in the government of the United States. AFFIRM carries out its goal through providing a forum for professionals in IRM to exchange ideas, exploring new techniques to improve the quality and use of federal information systems and resources, advocating effective application of IRM to all levels of the federal government, enhancing the professionalism of IRM personnel, and interacting with state and local government on IRM issues."

Membership

Regular membership is extended to professionals currently or formerly employed by the federal government in some capacity related to IRM. Persons who do not qualify for regular membership may join as associate members. The following component disciplines of IRM are represented: automatic data processing; library and technical information; paperwork management; privacy, freedom of informa-

tion, and information security; records and statistical data collection; telecommunications; and other related areas. Dues (Regular Memb.) $20; (Assoc. Memb.) $30.

Officers (July 1986–June 1987)

Chpn. Carol Becker, Dept. of State; *V. Chpn./Chpn.-Elect.* John Coyle, Dept. of the Interior; *V. Chpn., Finance.* Richard Green, Dept. of Health and Human Services; *V. Chpn., Admin.* Pamela Tyler, Veterans Administration.

Committee Chairpersons

Membership. Jessica Rickenbach.
Newsletter. Sarah Kadec.
Organizational Liaison. Marvin Gordon.
Publicity. Leon Transeau.

Meetings.

AFFIRM holds monthly luncheon-speaker meetings at the George Washington University's Marvin Center on 21 St. N.W. AFFIRM also sponsors an annual one-day seminar in Information Resources Management, usually in the autumn.

Association for Information and Image Management

(Formerly National Micrographics Association)
Executive Director, Bettie Alexander Steiger
1100 Wayne Ave., Silver Spring, MD 20910
301-587-8202

Object

To serve the professional and trade members of the Association in promoting education on and applications for information and imaging technologies which facilitate the effective storage, transfer, retrieval, and processing of images and information. Founded 1943. Membs. 8,100. Dues (Indiv.) $75. Year July 1–June 30.

Officers (May 1986–Apr. 1987)

Pres. James E. Weldon, Micro Design Div., Bell & Howell Co., 857 W. State St., Hartford, WI 53027; *V.P./Pres.-Elect.* Gary W. Pack, Datagraphix Inc., Box 82449, 5C-3910, San Diego, CA 92138; *Treas.* John A. Lacy, Eastman Kodak, 343 State St., Rochester, NY 14650.

(Term of office coincides with the Annual Conference & Exposition.)

Publications

FYI/IM Newsletter (mo.).
Journal of Information and Image Management (mo.; memb.). *Ed.* Ellen T. Meyer. Book reviews and product reviews included. Ads accepted.

Association for Library and Information Science Education

(Formerly Association of American Library Schools)
Executive Secretary, Janet Phillips
471 Park Lane, State College, PA 16803-3208
814-238-0254

Object

"To advance education for librarianship." Founded 1915. Memb. 680. Dues (Inst.) $250; (Assoc. Inst.) $150; (Indiv.) $25; (Assoc. Indiv.) $20. Year. Sept. 1986–Aug. 1987.

Membership

Any library school with a program accredited by the ALA Committee on Accreditation may become an institutional member. Any faculty member, administrator, librarian, researcher, or other individual employed full time may become a personal member.

Any school that offers a graduate degree in librarianship or a cognate field but whose program is not accredited by the ALA Committee on Accreditation may become an associate institutional member. Any retired or part-time faculty member, student, or other individual employed less than full time may become an associate personal member.

Officers (Feb. 1987–Jan. 1988)

Pres. Kathleen M. Heim, School of Lib. and Info. Science, Louisiana State Univ., Baton Rouge, LA 70803; *Past Pres.* Ann Prentice, Grad. School of Lib. Science, Univ. of Tennessee, Knoxville, TN 37996-4330; *V.P./Pres.-Elect.* Leigh S. Estabrook, Univ. of Illinois Grad. School of

Lib. and Info. Science, Urbana, IL 61801. Tel. 217-333-3280; *Secy.-Treas.* Norman Horrocks, Scarecrow Press, Box 4167, Metuchen, NJ 08840.

(Address correspondence to the executive secretary.)

Directors

Thomas Childers, College of Info. Studies, Drexel Univ., Philadelphia, PA 19104; June Lester Engle, Div. of Lib. and Info. Management, Emory Univ., Atlanta, GA 30322; Adele Fasick, Univ. of Toronto, Faculty of Lib. and Info. Science, Toronto, Ont. M5S 1A1, Canada.

Publications

ALISE Library and Information Science Education Statistical Report (ann.) $25.

Journal of Education for Library and Information Science ($5 per year; $30 domestic; $40 foreign).

Committee Chairpersons

Conference. J. Michael Pemberton, Grad. School of Lib. and Info. Science, Univ. of Tennessee, Knoxville, TN 37996-4330.

Continuing Education. Ruth Person, College of Lib. Science, Clarion Univ., Clarion, PA 16214.

Editorial Board. Charles D. Patterson, School of Lib. and Info. Science, Louisiana State Univ., Baton Rouge, LA 70803.

Governmental Relations. Nasser Sharify, Grad. School of Lib. and Info. Science, Pratt Institute, Brooklyn, NY 11205.

Nominating. Robert Wedgeworth, School of Lib. Service, Columbia Univ., New York, NY 10027.

Research. Nancy Van House, School of Lib. and Info. Studies, Univ. of California, Berkeley, CA 94720.

Representatives

ALA SCOLE. Thomas Childers (Drexel).

IFLA. Kathleen M. Heim (Louisiana); Mohammed M. Aman (Wisconsin-Milwaukee); Josephine Fang (Simmons).

Association of Academic Health Sciences Library Directors

Secretary-Treasurer, Karen L. Brewer
Basic Medical Sciences Library, Northeastern
Ohio Universities College of Medicine,
State Route 44, Rootstown, OH 44272
216-325-2511

Object

"To promote, in cooperation with educational institutions, other educational associations, government agencies, and other non-profit organizations, the common interests of academic health sciences libraries located in the United States and elsewhere, through publications, research, and discussion of problems of mutual interest and concern, and to advance the efficient and effective operation of academic health sciences libraries for the benefit of faculty, students, administrators, and practitioners."

Membership

Regular membership is available to non-profit educational institutions operating a school of health sciences that has full or provisional accreditation by the Association of American Medical Colleges. Annual dues $50. Regular members shall be represented by the chief administrative of-

ficer of the member institution's health sciences library.

Associate membership (and nonvoting representation) is available to organizations having an interest in the purposes and activities of the association.

Officers (Nov. 1986–Nov. 1987)

Pres. Shelley Bader, Himmelfarb Health Sciences Lib., George Washington Univ. Medical Center, 2300 Eye St. N.W., Washington, DC 20037; *Pres.-Elect.* Nina W. Matheson, Welch Medical Lib., Johns Hopkins Univ. School of Medicine, 1900 E. Monument St., Baltimore, MD 21205; *Secy.-Treas.* Karen L. Brewer, Basic Medical Sciences Lib., Northeastern Ohio Universities College of Medicine, State Rte. 44, Rootstown, OH 44272; *Past Pres.* Lucretia McClure, Edward G. Miner Lib., School of Medicine and Dentistry, Univ. of Rochester, 601 Elmwood Ave., Rochester, NY 14642.

Board of Directors (Nov. 1986–Nov. 1987)

Officers; Rachael Goldstein, Health Sciences Lib., Columbia Univ., 701 W. 168 St., New York, NY 10032; Erica Love, Medical Center Lib., Univ. of New Mexico, Albuquerque, NM 87109; Gerald J. Oppenheimer, Archivist, Health Sciences Lib., Univ. of Washington SB-55, Seattle, WA 98195; Richard Lyders, Data Mgr., Houston Academy of Medicine, Texas Medical Center Lib., Jesse H. Jones Lib. Bldg., Houston, TX 77030; David Curry, Health Sciences Lib., Univ. of Iowa, Iowa City, IA 52242; Alison Bunting, UCLA Biomedical Lib., Center for the Health Sciences, Los Angeles, CA 90024.

Association of Christian Librarians

Executive Secretary, L. Alan Brock
Box 4, Cedarville, OH 45314
513-766-2211

Object

" . . . to meet the needs of evangelical Christian librarians serving in institutions of higher learning. The Association shall promote high standards of professionalism in library work as well as projects that encourage membership participation in serving the academic library community." Founded 1956. Memb. (Indiv.) 301. Dues (Indiv.) $16–37, based on salary scale. Year. Conference to Conference (2nd week in June).

ACL is a member of the Council of National Library and Information Associations.

Membership

A full member shall be a Christian librarian subscribing to the purposes of the corporation who is affiliated with an institution of higher learning. Associate members include those who are in agreement with the purposes of the corporation but who are *not* affiliated with institutions of higher learning or who are nonlibrarians.

Officers (June 1986–June 1987)

Pres. David Wright, Ironside Memorial Lib., Bryan College, Dayton, TN 37321;

V.P. David Twiest, Vernon Strombeck Lib., Trinity Western Univ., Langley, B.C. V3A 1MB, Canada; *Secy.* Mary Lou Hovda, McAlister Lib., Northwestern College, Roseville, MN 55113; *Treas.* Stephen Brown, Cedarville College Lib., Cedarville, OH 45314; *Past Pres.* Clyde Root, Pentecostal Research Lib., Lee College, Cleveland, TN 37311; *Pub. Rel. Dir.* John Witmer, Dallas Theological Seminary, Dallas, TX 75204.

Board of Directors

Douglas Butler; Fayetta Davis; Bea Flinner; Lorene Francen; Dennis Read.

Publications

The Christian Librarian (q.; memb. or $16).
The Christian Periodical Index.

Committee Chairpersons

ACL Representative to the Council of National Library and Information Associations. Dorsey Reynolds, Valley Forge Christian College, Charlestown Rd., Phoenixville, PA 19460.
Archivist. Jan Bosma, Cedarville College, Cedarville, OH 45314.
Bible College Section. Nancy J. Olson, Great Lakes Bible College, Box 40060, Lansing, MI 48901.
Christian Librarian. Ronald Jordahl, Ed., Prairie Bible Institute, Three Hills, Alta. T0M 2A0, Canada.
Christian Periodical Index. Douglas J. Butler, Ed., Asbury College, Wilmore, KY 40390.
Liberal Arts Section. Douglas J. Butler, Asbury College, Wilmore, KY 40390.
Program. William F. Abernathy, Asbury College, Wilmore, KY 40390.
Seminary Section. David C. McClain, Baptist Bible College & Seminary, Clarks Summit, PA 18411.

Association of Jewish Libraries

c/o National Foundation for Jewish Culture
122 E. 42 St., Rm. 408, New York, NY 10017

Object

"To promote the improvement of library services and professional standards in all Jewish libraries and collections of Judaica; to serve as a center of dissemination of Jewish library information and guidance; to encourage the establishment of Jewish libraries and collections of Judaica; to promote publication of literature which will be of assistance to Jewish librarianship; and to encourage people to enter the field of librarianship." Organized 1966 from the merger of the Jewish Librarians Association and the Jewish Library Association. Memb. 700. Dues (Inst.) $25; (Student/retired) $18. Year. July 1–June 30.

Officers (June 1986–June 1988)

Pres. Edith Lubetski, Hedi Steinberg Lib., Stern College, Yeshiva Univ., 245 Lexington Ave., New York, NY 10016-4699; *Past Pres.* Hazel B. Karp, Hebrew Academy of Atlanta Lib., 880 Somerset Dr. N.W., Atlanta, GA 30327; *V.P./Pres.-Elect.* Marcia Posner, Judaica Lib. Consultant, Federation of Jewish Philanthropies Lib., 130 E. 59 St., New York, NY 10022; *V.P. Membership.* David J. Gilner, Hebrew Union College Lib., 3101 Clifton Ave., Cincinnati, OH 45220; *Treas.* Sharona R. Wachs, 1000 Washington Ave., Albany, NY 12203-1927; *Corres. Secy.* Esther Nussbaum, Ramaz Upper School Lib., 60 E. 78 St., New York, NY

10021; *Rec. Secy.* Annette Levy, Jewish Federation Libs., 801 Percy Warner Blvd., Nashville, TN 37205; *Publns. Coord.* Ralph R. Simon, Sindell Lib., Temple Emanu El, 2200 S. Green Rd., Cleveland, OH 44121.

(Address correspondence to the president.)

Publications

AJL Newsletter (q.). *Ed.* Irene S. Levin, 48 Georgia St., Valley Stream, NY 11580.

Judaica Librarianship (2 per year). *Co-eds.* Marcia Posner and Bella Hass Weinberg, 19 Brookfield Rd., New Hyde Park, NY 11040.

Divisions

Research and Special Library Division (R&S). Pres. Linda P. Lerman, Lib. of the Jewish Theological Seminary of America, 3080 Broadway, New York, NY 10027-9985.

Synagogue, School and Center Division (SSC). Pres. Sue Barancik, Temple Adath B'nai Israel, 3600 Washington Ave., Evansville, IN 47715.

Association of Librarians in the History of the Health Sciences

President, Dorothy Whitcomb
Health Sciences Library, University of Wisconsin, Madison, WI 53706
608-262-2402

Object

To serve the professional interests of librarians, archivists, and other specialists actively engaged in the librarianship of the history of the health sciences by promoting an exchange of information and by improving standards of service, by identifying and making contact with persons similarly engaged, providing opportunities to meet on appropriate occasions, issuing a newsletter and such other materials as may seem appropriate to the association's interests, and by cooperating with other similar organizations in projects of mutual concern.

Membership

Voting members shall be actively engaged in librarianship of the history of health sciences. Nonvoting membership shall be open to people interested in the concerns of the association.

Officers (May 1986–May 1987)

Pres. Dorothy Whitcomb, Health Sciences Lib., Univ. of Wisconsin, Madison, WI 53706; *Secy.-Treas.* Janet Kubinec-Sutton, c/o HQ, V Corps, Surgeon, APO New York, NY 09097; *Ed.* Lisabeth Holloway, 58 W. Tulpehocken St., Philadelphia, PA 19144.

Steering Committee

Victoria Steele, Biomedical Lib., Center for Health Sciences, UCLA, Los Angeles, CA 90024; Elizabeth White, Houston Academy of Medicine Lib., Texas Medical Center, Houston, TX 77030; Deborah Woolverton, Medical and Chirurgical Faculty of Maryland, 1211 Cathedral St., Baltimore, MD 21201.

Committees

Ad Hoc Committee on Genre Terms. Nancy Zinn, Lib., Univ. of California-

San Francisco, San Francisco, CA 94143.

Publications. Glen Jenkins, Cleveland Health Sciences Lib., 11000 Euclid Ave., Cleveland, OH 44106.

Publications

Watermark (q.; memb.; nonmemb. $15). *Ed.* Lisabeth Holloway, 58 Tulpehocken St., Philadelphia, PA 19144.

Association of Research Libraries

Executive Director, Shirley Echelman
1527 New Hampshire Ave. N.W., Washington, DC 20036
2202-232-2466

Object

To initiate and develop plans for strengthening research library resources and services in support of higher education and research. Established 1932 by the chief librarians of 43 research libraries. Memb. (Inst.) 118. Dues (ann.) $5,790. Year. Jan.–Dec.

Membership

Membership is institutional.

Officers (Oct. 1986–Oct. 1987)

Pres. Herbert F. Johnson, Emory Univ. Lib., Atlanta, GA 30322; *V.P.* Elaine F. Sloan, Indiana Univ. Libs., Bloomington, IN 47401; *Past Pres.* Anne Woodsworth, Univ. of Pittsburgh Libs., Pittsburgh, PA 15260.

Board of Directors

David Bishop, Univ. of Georgia Libs.; Richard E. Chapin, Michigan State Univ. Lib.; Peter Freeman, Univ. of Alberta Lib.; Charles E. Miller, Florida State Univ. Lib.; Margaret Otto, Dartmouth College Libs.; Joseph Rosenthal, Univ. of California, Berkeley Lib.; Martin D. Runkle, Univ. of Chicago Lib.; Merrily Taylor, Brown Univ. Lib.

Publications

ARL Annual Salary Survey (ann.; $15).
The ARL Index and Quantitative Relationships in the ARL. Kendon Stubbs ($5).
ARL Minutes (s. ann.; $15 each).
ARL Newsletter (approx. 5 per year; $15).
ARL Statistics (ann.; $15).
Cataloging Titles in Microform Sets. Report based on a study conducted for ARL in 1980 by Information Systems Consultants, Inc., Richard W. Boss, Principal Investigator ($12).
Cumulated ARL University Library Statistics, 1962–1963 through 1978–1979. Compiled by Kendon Stubbs and David Buxton ($15).
The Gerould Statistics, 1907/08–1961/62. A compilation of data on ARL libraries, begun in 1908 by James Thayer Gerould, and later continued as the "Princeton University Library Statistics." Compiled by Robert Molyneux ($25).
Microform Sets in U.S. and Canadian Libraries. Report of a Survey on the Bibliographic Control of Microform Sets contributed by the Association of Research Libraries Microform Project ($12).
Objective Performance Measures for Academic and Research Libraries, by Paul B. Kantor ($25).
Our Cultural Heritage: Whence Salvation? Louis B. Wright; The Uses of the

Past, Gordon N. Ray; remarks to the 89th membership meeting of the association ($3).

Plan for a North American Program for Coordinated Retrospective Conversion. Report of a study conducted by the Association of Research Libraries, prepared by Jutta Reed-Scott ($15).

76 United Statesiana. Seventy-six works of American scholarship relating to America as published during two centuries from the Revolutionary Era of the United States through the nation's bicentennial year. Edited by Edward C. Lathem, dist. by the Univ. of Virginia Press ($7.50; $5.75 paper).

13 Colonial Americana. Edited by Edward C. Lathem, dist. by the Univ. of Virginia Press ($7.50).

Committee Chairpersons

ARL Statistics. Herbert F. Johnson, Emory Univ. Lib., Atlanta, GA 30322.

Bibliographic Control. Joseph Rosenthal, Univ. of California, Berkeley Libs., Berkeley, CA 94720.

Collection Development. Robert C. Miller, Notre Dame Univ. Libs., Notre Dame, IN 46556.

Government Policies. James F. Wyatt, Univ. of Rochester Libs., Rochester, NY 14627.

Management of Research Library Resources. Joan Chambers, Univ. of California, Riverside Libs., Riverside, CA 92517.

Nominations. Elaine F. Sloan, Indiana Univ. Lib., Bloomington, IN 47401.

Preservation of Research Library Materials. David C. Weber, Stanford Univ. Libs., Stanford, CA 94305.

Task Force Chairpersons

Government Information in Electronic Format. D. Kaye Gapen, Univ. of Wisconsin Libs., Madison, WI 53706.

President's Task Force on Membership Criteria. Anne Woodsworth, Univ. of Pittsburgh Libs., Pittsburgh, PA 15260.

Scholarly Communication. Charles B. Osburn, Univ. of Alabama Libs., University, AL 35486.

ARL Membership in 1986

Nonuniversity Libraries

Boston Public Lib.; Canada Institute for Scientific and Technical Info.; Center for Research Libs.; Linda Hall Lib.; Lib. of Congress; National Agricultural Lib.; National Lib. of Canada; National Lib. of Medicine; New York Public Lib.; New York State Lib.; Newberry Lib.; Smithsonian Institution Libs.

University Libraries

Alabama; Alberta; Arizona; Arizona State; Boston; Brigham Young; British Columbia; Brown; California (Berkeley); California (Davis): California (Irvine); California (Los Angeles); California (Riverside); California (San Diego); California (Santa Barbara); Case Western Reserve; Chicago; Cincinnati; Colorado; Colorado State; Columbia; Connecticut; Cornell; Dartmouth; Delaware; Duke; Emory; Florida; Florida State; Georgetown; Georgia; Georgia Institute of Technology; Guelph; Harvard; Hawaii; Houston; Howard; Illinois; Indiana; Iowa; Iowa State; Johns Hopkins; Kansas; Kent State; Kentucky; Laval; Louisiana State; McGill; McMaster; Manitoba; Maryland; Massachusetts; Massachusetts Institite of Technology; Miami; Michigan; Michigan State; Minnesota; Missouri; Nebraska; New Mexico; New York; North Carolina; North Carolina State; Northwestern; Notre Dame; Ohio State; Oklahoma; Oklahoma State; Oregon; Pennsyl-

vania; Pennsylvania State; Pittsburgh; Princeton; Purdue; Queen's (Kingston, Canada); Rice; Rochester; Rutgers; Saskatchewan; South Carolina; Southern California; Southern Illinois; Stanford; SUNY (Albany); SUNY (Buffalo); SUNY (Stony Brook); Syracuse; Temple; Tennessee; Texas; Texas A & M; Toronto; Tulane; Utah; Vanderbilt; Virginia; Virginia Polytechnic; Washington; Washington State; Waterloo; Wayne State; Western Ontario; Wisconsin; Yale; York.

Association of Visual Science Librarians

c/o Laurel Gregory, Science-Optometry Librarian
Pacific University, The Library, Forest Grove, OR 97116

Object

"To foster collective and individual acquisition and dissemination of visual science information, to improve services for all persons seeking such information, and to develop standards for libraries to which members are attached." Founded 1968. Memb. (U.S.) 51; (foreign) 13.

Officer

Chpn. Laurel Gregory, Science-Optometry Libn., Pacific Univ., Forest Grove, OR 97116.

Publications

Opening Day Book Collection — Visual Science.
PhD Theses in Physiological Optics (irreg.).
Standards for Visual Science Libraries.
Union List of Vision-Related Serials (irreg.).

Meetings

Annual meeting held in December in connection with the American Academy of Optometry; mid-year mini meeting with the Medical Library Association.

Beta Phi Mu

(International Library Science Honor Society)
Executive Secretary, Blanche Woolls
School of Library and Information Science
University of Pittsburgh, Pittsburgh, PA 15260

Object

"To recognize high scholarship in the study of librarianship and to sponsor appropriate professional and scholarly projects." Founded at the University of Illinois in 1948. Memb. 20,500.

Membership

Open to graduates of library school programs accredited by the American Library Association who fulfill the following requirements: complete the course requirements leading to a fifth-year or other advanced degree in librarianship with a scholastic average of 3.75 where A equals 4 points. This provision shall also apply to planned programs of advanced study beyond the fifth year that do not culminate in a degree but that require full-time study for one or more academic years; receive a letter of recommendation from their respective library schools attesting to their

demonstrated fitness of successful professional careers. Former graduates of accredited library schools are also eligible on the same basis.

Officers (1986–1987)

Pres. Edward G. Holley, Dean Emeritus and Professor, School of Lib. Science, Univ. of North Carolina, Chapel Hill, NC 27514; *V.P./Pres.-Elect.* Elaine F. Sloan, Dean of Lib. Services, Univ. Libs., Indiana Univ., Bloomington, IN 47405; *Past Pres.* H. Joanne Harrar, Dir. of Libs., Univ. of Maryland, College Park, MD 20742; *Treas.* Dennis K. Lambert, Collection Development Center, The Milton S. Eisenhower Lib., The Johns Hopkins Univ., Baltimore, MD 21218; *Exec. Secy.* Blanche Woolls, Professor, School of Lib. and Info. Science, Univ. of Pittsburgh, Pittsburgh, PA 15260; *Admin. Secy.* Mary Y. Tomaino, School of Lib. and Info. Science, Univ. of Pittsburgh, Pittsburgh, PA 15260.

Directors

Elaine R. Goldberg, Liverpool Public Lib., Tulip and Second Sts., Liverpool, NY 13088 (1987); Mary E. Jackson, Univ. of Pennsylvania, Van Pelt Lib., Philadelphia, PA 19104 (1987); Mary C. Chobot, 4950 Andrea Ave., Annandale, VA 22003 (1988); Marianna Markowetz, 814 A. 57 St., West Allis, WI 53214 (1988); Gordon N. Baker, Lib./Media Specialist, Edwin S. Kemp Elementary School, 10990 Folsom Rd., Hampton, GA 30228 (1989); John V. Richardson, Jr., Assoc. Professor, Grad. School of Lib. and Info. Science, Univ. of California–Los Angeles, Los Angeles, CA 90024 (1989); *Dir.-at-Large.* Betty J. Turock, Asst. Professor, School of Communication, Info. and Lib. Studies, Rutgers Univ., New Brunswick, NJ 08903 (1988).

Publication

Newsletter (bienn.). Beta Phi Mu sponsors a modern Chapbook series. These small volumes, issued in limited editions, are intended to create a beautiful combination of text and format in the interest of the graphic arts and are available to members only.

Chapters

Alpha. Univ. of Illinois, Grad. School of Lib. and Info. Science, Urbana, IL 61801; *Beta.* Univ. of Southern California, School of Lib. Science, University Park, Los Angeles, CA 90007; *Gamma.* Florida State Univ., School of Lib. Science, Tallahassee, FL 32306; *Delta* (Inactive). Loughborough College of Further Education, School of Libnshp., Loughborough, England; *Epsilon.* Univ. of North Carolina, School of Lib. Science, Chapel Hill, NC 27514; *Zeta.* Atlanta Univ., School of Lib. and Info. Studies, Atlanta, GA 30314; *Theta.* Pratt Institute, Grad. School of Lib. and Info. Science, Brooklyn, NY 11205; *Iota.* Catholic Univ. of America, School of Lib. and Info. Science, Washington, DC 20064; Univ. of Maryland, College of Lib. and Info. Services, College Park, MD 20742; *Kappa.* Western Michigan Univ., School of Libnshp., Kalamazoo, MI 49008; *Lambda.* Univ. of Oklahoma, School of Lib. Science, Norman, OK 73019; *Mu.* Univ. of Michigan, School of Lib. Science, Ann Arbor, MI 48109; *Nu.* Columbia Univ., School of Lib. Service, New York, NY 10027; *Xi.* Univ. of Hawaii, Grad. School of Lib. Studies, Honolulu, HI 96822; *Omicron.* Rutgers Univ., Grad. School of Lib. and Info. Studies, New Brunswick, NJ 08903; *Pi.* Univ. of Pittsburgh, School of Lib. and Info. Science, Pittsburgh, PA 15260; *Rho.* Kent State Univ., School of Lib. Science, Kent, OH 44242; *Sigma.* Drexel Univ., School of Lib. and Info.

Science, Philadelphia, PA 19104; *Tau.* State Univ. of New York at Geneseo, School of Lib. and Info. Science, College of Arts and Science, Geneseo, NY 14454; *Upsilon.* Univ. of Kentucky, College of Lib. Science, Lexington, KY 40506; *Phi.* Univ. of Denver, Grad. School of Libnshp. and Info. Mgmt., Denver, CO 80208; *Pi Lambda Sigma.* Syracuse Univ., School of Info. Studies, Syracuse, NY 13210; *Chi.* Indiana Univ., School of Lib. and Info. Science, Bloomington, IN 47401; *Psi.* Univ. of Missouri, Columbia, School of Lib. and Info. Sciences, Columbia, MO 65211; *Omega.* San Jose State Univ., Div. of Lib. Science, San Jose, CA 95192; *Beta Alpha.* Queens College, City College of New York, Grad. School of Lib. and Info. Studies, Flushing, NY 11367; *Beta Beta.* Simmons College, Grad. School of Lib. and Info. Science, Boston, MA 02115; *Beta Delta.* State Univ. of New York–Buffalo, School of Info. and Lib. Studies, Buffalo, NY 14260; *Beta Epsilon.* Emporia State Univ., School of Lib. Science, Emporia, KS 66801; *Beta Zeta.* Louisiana State Univ., Grad. School of Lib. Science, Baton Rouge, LA 70803; *Beta Eta.* Univ. of Texas at Austin, Grad. School of Lib. and Info. Science, Austin, TX 78712; *Beta Theta.* Brigham Young Univ., School of Lib. and Info. Science, Provo, UT 84602; *Beta Iota.* Univ. of Rhode Island, Grad. Lib. School, Kingston, RI 02881; *Beta Kappa.* Univ. of Alabama, Grad. School of Lib. Service, University, AL 35486; *Beta Lambda.* North Texas State Univ., School of Lib.

and Info. Science, Denton, TX 76203; Texas Woman's Univ., School of Lib. Science, Denton, TX 76204; *Beta Mu.* Long Island Univ., Palmer Grad. Lib. School, C.W. Post Center, Greenvale, NY 11548; *Beta Nu.* St. John's Univ., Div. of Lib. and Info. Science, Jamaica, NY 11439; *Beta Xi.* North Carolina Central Univ., School of Lib. Science, Durham, NC 27707; *Beta Omicron.* Univ. of Tennessee, Knoxville, Grad. School of Lib. and Info. Science, Knoxville, TN 37916; *Beta Pi.* Univ. of Arizona, Grad. Lib. School, Tucson, AZ 85721; *Beta Rho.* Univ. of Wisconsin-Milwaukee, School of Lib. Science, Milwaukee, WI 53201; *Beta Sigma.* Clarion State College, School of Lib. Science, Clarion, PA 16214; *Beta Tau.* Wayne State Univ., Div. of Lib. Science, Detroit, MI 48202; *Beta Upsilon.* Alabama A & M Univ., School of Lib. Media, Normal, AL 35762; *Beta Phi.* Univ. of South Florida, Grad. Dept. of Lib., Media and Info. Studies, Tampa, FL 33620; *Beta Psi.* Univ. of Southern Mississippi, School of Lib. Service, Hattiesburg, MS 39406; *Beta Omega.* Univ. of South Carolina, College of Libnshp., Columbia, SC 29208; *Beta Beta Gamma.* Rosary College, Grad. School of Lib. and Info. Science, River Forest, IL 60305; *Beta Beta Delta.* Europe, Univ. of Cologne; *Beta Beta Epsilon.* Univ. of Wisconsin, Madison, Lib. School, Madison, WI 53706; *Beta Beta Zeta.* Univ. of North Carolina, Greensboro, Dept. of Lib. Science/Educational Technology, Greensboro, NC 27412.

Bibliographical Society of America

Executive Director, Irene Tichenor
Box 397, Grand Central Sta., New York, NY 10163
718-638-7957

Object

"To promote bibliographical research and to issue bibliographical publications." Organized 1904. Memb. 1,400. Dues. $30. Year. Calendar.

Officers (Jan. 1986–Jan. 1988)

Pres. G. Thomas Tanselle, Guggenheim Memorial Foundation, 90 Park Ave., New York, NY 10016; *V.P.* Marjorie G. Wynne; *Treas.* R. Dyke Benjamin, Lazard Freres and Co., One Rockefeller Plaza, New York, NY 10020; *Secy.* Joan M. Friedman, Yale Center for British Art, 2120 Yale Sta., New Haven, CT 06520.

Council

(1987) Roland Folter; Paul Needham; Katharine F. Pantzer; W. Thomas Taylor; (1988) John Bidwell; J. William Matheson; Roger E. Stoddard; Roderick D. Stinehour; (1989) William P. Barlow, Jr.; Ralph W. Franklin; Richard G. Landon; Bernard M. Rosenthal.

Publication

Papers (q.; memb.) *Eds.* John Lancaster and Ruth Mortimer, Box 776, Williamsburg, MA 01096.

Committee Chairpersons

Fellowship Program. Richard G. Landon, Thomas Fisher Lib., Univ. of Toronto, Toronto, Ont. M5S 1A5, Canada.
Publications. Paul Needham, J. Pierpont Morgan Lib., 29 E. 36 St., New York, NY 10016.

Canadian Association for Information Science
(L'Association Canadienne des Sciences de L'Information)

P.O./C.P. 6174, Sta./Succ. J,
Ottawa, Ont. K2A, 1T2, Canada
613-225-3781

Object

Brings together individuals and organizations concerned with the production, manipulation, storage, retrieval, and dissemination of information with emphasis on the application of modern technologies in these areas. CAIS is dedicated to enhancing the activity of the information transfer process, utilizing the vehicles of research, development, application, and education, and serving as a forum for dialogue and exchange of ideas concerned with the theory and practice of all factors involved in the communication of information. Dues (Inst.) $150; (Regular) $50; (Student) $25.

Membership

Institutions and all individuals interested in information science and who are in-

volved in the gathering, the organization, and the dissemination of information (computer scientists, documentalists, information scientists, librarians, journalists, sociologists, psychologists, linguists, administrators, etc.) can become members of the Canadian Association for Information Science.

Officers
(Nov. 1, 1985–Aug. 31, 1987)

Pres. Sally Grande, Home Oil Co., 2300 Home Oil Tower, Calgary, Alta. T2P 2Z5. Tel. 403-232-7035; *V.P./Pres.-Elect.* Michael Ridley, MacMaster Univ., Hamilton, Ont., Canada. Tel. 416-9140 ext. 2326; *Secy.-Treas.* Marjorie Melick, Algonquin College Resource Centre, 1385 Woodroffe Ave., Nepean, Ont. K2G 1V8. Tel. 618-727-7694; *Publications Dir.* Ethel Auster, FLIS, Univ. of Toronto, 140 St.

George St., Toronto, Ont. M5S 1A1. Tel. 416-978-7098; *Membership Dir.* Maggie Weaver, 84 Shaftesbury Ave., Toronto, Ont. M4T 1A5; *Past Pres.* Gilles Deschatelets, Univ. of Montreal, Box 6128, Montreal, P.Q. H3C 3J7.

Board of Directors

Ottawa Chapter. Bonnie Bullock; *Montreal Chapter.* John O'Shaughnessy; *Quebec Chapter.* Jean Morel; *Atlantic Chapter.* Michael Shepherd; *Toronto Chapter.* Felicity Pickup; *CAIS West Chapter.* Helen Mayoh.

Publications

The Canadian Conference of Information Science; Proceedings (ann.).
The Canadian Journal of Information Science (q.).

Canadian Library Association

Executive Director, Jane Cooney
200 Elgin St., Ottawa, Ont. K2P 1L5, Canada
613-232-9625

Object

To develop high standards of librarianship and of library and information service. CLA develops standards for public, university, school, and college libraries and library technician programs; offers library school scholarship and book awards; carries on international liaison with other library associations; makes representation to government and official commissions; offers professional development programs; and has supported intellectual freedom research. Founded in Hamilton in 1946, CLA is a nonprofit voluntary organization governed by an elected council and board of directors. Memb. (Indiv.) 3,700; (Inst.) 800. Dues (Indiv.) $65 &

$100, depending on salary; (Inst.) from $65 up, graduated on budget basis. Year. July 1–June 30.

Membership

Open to individuals, institutions, and groups interested in librarianship and in library and information services.

Officers (1986–1987)

Pres. Ken Jensen, Asst. Chief Libn., Regina Public Lib., 2311 12th Ave., Regina, Sask. S4P 0N4; *1st V.P./Pres.-Elect.* William Converse, Chief Libn., Univ. of Winnipeg, 515 Portage Ave., Winnipeg,

Man. R3B 2E9; *2nd V.P.* Lorraine McQueen, Chief, Union Catalogue Div., National Lib. of Canada, 395 Wellington St., Ottawa, Ont. K1A 0N4; *Treas.* Iain Bates, Univ. Libn., Acadia Univ., Wolfville, N.S. B0P 1X0; *Past Pres.* Beth Miller, Coord., Cooperative Work Study Program, School of Lib. and Info. Science, Elborn College, Univ. of Western Ontario, London, Ont. N6G 1H1.

Board of Directors

Officers, division presidents.

Council

Officers; division presidents; councillors, including representatives of ASTED and provincial/regional library associations.

Councillors-at-Large

To June 30, 1987: Karen Adams, Jean Dirksen; to June 30, 1988: Elizabeth Beeton, Paul Wiens; to June 30, 1989: Jane Beaumont, Derek R. Francis.

Publications

Canadian Library Journal (6 issues; memb. or nonmemb. subscribers, Canada $36, U.S. $40 (Can.), International $45 (Can.).
CM: Canadian Materials for Schools and Libraries (6 per year, $30).

Division Chairpersons

Canadian Association of College and University Libraries. Madge MacGown, Education Area Coord., Herbert T. Coutts Lib., Univ. of Alberta, Edmonton, Alta. T6G 2G5.
Canadian Association of Public Libraries. Stan Smith, Chief Libn., Surrey Public Lib., 14245 56th Ave., Surrey, B.C. V3W 1J2.
Canadian Association of Special Libraries and Information Services. Carol Smale, Asst. Chief, Location Div., National Lib. of Canada, 395 Wellington St., Ottawa, Ont. K1A 0N4.
Canadian Library Trustee Association. Lorraine Williams, 10 Elfindale Crescent, North York, Ont. M2J 1B5.
Canadian School Library Association. Susan Traill, School Lib. Consultant, Manitoba Education, 404 1181 Portage, Winnipeg, Man. R3G 0T3.

Association Representatives

Association pour l'avancement des sciences et des techniques de la documentation (ASTED). Diane Paradis, Dir.-Gen, ASTED, 7243 rue Saint-Denis, Montreal, P.Q. H2R 2E3.
Atlantic Provinces Library Association. Elizabeth Hamilton, Harriet Irving Lib., Univ. of New Brunswick, Fredericton, N.B.
British Columbia Library Association. Linda Hale, 1816 E. 35 Ave., Vancouver, B.C. V5P 1B6.
Library Association of Alberta. Duncan Rand, Chief Libn., Lethbridge Public Lib., 810 Fifth Ave. S., Lethbridge, Alta. T1J 4C4.
Manitoba Library Association. Jim Blanchard, Libn., Canadian Grain Commission, 1001-303 Main St., Winnipeg, Man. R3C 3G7.
Ontario Library Association. Penny McKee, Aurora Public Lib., 56 Victoria St., Aurora, Ont. L4G 1R2.
Quebec Library Association. Rosemary Lydon, Head Libn., Westmount Public Lib., 4574 Sherbrooke St. W., Montreal, P.Q. H3Z 1G1.
Saskatchewan Library Association. Linda Fritz, Native Law Centre Lib., Univ. of Saskatchewan, 159 Diefenbaker Crescent, Saskatoon, Sask. S7M 0W0.

Catholic Library Association

Executive Director, Matthew R. Wilt
461 W. Lancaster Ave., Haverford, PA 10941
215-649-5250

Object

The promotion and encouragement of Catholic literature and library work through cooperation, publications, education, and information. Founded 1921, Memb. 3,250. Dues $35-$500. Year. July 1986-June 1987.

Officers (April 1985-April 1987)

Pres. Mary A. Grant, St. John's Univ., Jamaica, NY 11439; *V.P./Pres.-Elect.* Irma C. Godfrey, Lib. Consultant, Archdiocese of St. Louis, St. Louis, MO 63109; *Past Pres.* Sister Mary Dennis Lynch, SHCJ Rosemont College, Rosemont, PA 19010.

(Address general correspondence to the executive director.)

Executive Board

Officers; Irma C. Godfrey (1985-1987), Lib. Consultant, Archdiocese of St. Louis, St. Louis, MO 63109; Sister Chrysantha Rudnik, CSSF (1981-1987), Felician College, Chicago, IL 60659; Gayle E. Salvatore (1981-1987), Brother Martin H.S., New Orleans, LA 70122; Sister Barbara Anne Kilpatrick, RSM (1983-1989), St. Vincent de Paul School, Nashville, TN 37208; Reverend Kenneth O'Malley, CP (1983-1989), Catholic Theological Union, Chicago, IL 60615; Sister Jean Bostley, SSJ (1985-1991), St. Joseph's Central H.S. Lib., Pittsfield, MA 01201; Arnold Rzepecki (1985-1991), Sacred Heart Seminary College Lib., Detroit, MI 48206.

Publications

Catholic Library World (6 issues; memb. or $35).

The Catholic Periodical and Literature Index (subscription).

Representatives

ALA Resources and Technical Services Division, Cataloging. Tina-Karen Weiner Forman, Los Angeles Lib., Univ. of California, 405 Hilgard Ave., Los Angeles CA 90024.

American Theological Library Association. Rev. Kenneth O'Malley, Catholic Theological Union, Chicago, IL 60615.

Catholic Press Association. John T. Corrigan, CFX, CLA Headquarters, 461 W. Lancaster Ave., Haverford, PA 19041.

Council of National Library and Information Associations (CNLIA). John T. Corrigan, CFX, CLA Headquarters, 461 W. Lancaster Ave., Haverford, PA 19041; Brother De Sales Pergola, OSF, St. Francis Prep School, Fresh Meadows, NY 11365.

National Information Standards Organization (Z-39). John T. Corrigan, CFX, CLA Headquarters, 461 W. Lancaster Ave., Haverford, PA 19041.

Society of American Archivists. Rev. Harry Culkin, Cathedral College of the Immaculate Conception, Douglaston, NY 11362.

Special Libraries Association. Mary Jo DiMuccio, Sunnyvale Public Lib., Sunnyvale, CA 94087.

Section Chairpersons

Academic Librarians. Gorman Duffett, Hiram College, Hiram, OH 44234.

Archives. Warren Willis, U.S. Catholic Conference, Washington, DC 20005.

Children's Libraries. Marland L. Schrauth, St. Alphonsus School, Minneapolis, MN 55429.

High School Libraries. Sister Louis Bertrand, IHM, Archbishop Wood H.S. for Girls, Warminster, PA 18974.

Library Education. Raymond Vondran, The Catholic Univ. of America, Washington, DC 20064.

Parish/Community Libraries. Patricia Leiper, St. Anthony Parish, Sacramento, CA 95831.

Round Table Chairpersons

Cataloging and Classification Round Table. Tina-Karen Wiener Forman, Los Angeles Lib., Univ. of California, 405 Hilgard Ave., Los Angeles, CA 90024.

Committee Chairpersons

Ad Hoc Committee on Grants and Development. Brother Emmett Corry, OSF, St. John's Univ., Jamaica, NY 11439.

Advisory Council. Irma C. Godfrey, Lib. Consultant, Archdiocese of St. Louis, St. Louis, MO 63109.

Catholic Library World Editorial. Sister Jean R. Bostley, SSJ, St. Joseph Central H.S., Pittsfield, MA 01201.

The Catholic Periodical and Literature Index. Sister Mary Ellen Lampe, St. Mary's College, Orchard Lake, MI 48033.

Constitution and Bylaws. Thomas J. Neihengen, Gordon Technical H.S., Chicago, IL 60618.

Elections. Sister Thomas Marie Callahan, St. Ignatius Loyola School, New York, NY 10028.

Finance. Irma C. Godfrey, Lib. Consultant, Archdiocese of St. Louis, St. Louis, MO 63109.

Membership. Eleanora Baer, St. Louis, MO 63144.

Nominations. Kelly Fitzpatrick, Mount St. Mary's College, Emmitsburg, MD 21727.

Program Coordinator. John T. Corrigan, CFX, CLA Headquarters, 461 W. Lancaster Ave., Haverford, PA 19041.

Public Relations. Martha Ogilvie Klein, Laguna Hills, CA 92653.

Publications. Richard Fitzsimmons, The Pennsylvania State Univ., Dunmore, PA 18512.

Regina Medal. Sister Mary Arthur Hoagland, IHM, West Philadelphia Catholic H.S. for Boys, Philadelphia, PA 19139.

Scholarship. Josephine Riis Fang, Simmons College, Boston, MA 02115.

Chief Officers of State Library Agencies

Barbara Weaver, Director
New Jersey Department of Education, Division of State Library CN520,
185 W. State St., Trenton, NJ 08625
609-292-6200

Object

The object of COSLA is to provide "a means of cooperative action among its state and territorial members to strengthen the work of the respective state and territorial agencies. Its purpose is to provide a continuing mechanism for dealing with the problems faced by the heads of these agencies which are responsible for state and territorial library development."

Membership

The Chief Officers of State Library Agencies is an independent organization of the men and women who head the state and

territorial agencies responsible for library development. Its membership consists solely of the top library officers of the 50 states and one territory, variously designated as state librarian, director, commissioner, or executive secretary.

Officers (1986–1987)

Chpn. Barbara Weaver, Dir., New Jersey Dept. of Educ., Div. of State Lib. CN520, 185 W. State St., Trenton, NJ 08625. Tel. 609-292-6200; *V. Chpn.* Thomas F. Jaques, State Libn., Louisiana State Lib., Box 131, Baton Rouge, LA 70821; *Secy.* J. Gary Nichols, Maine State Lib., State

House Sta. #64, Augusta, ME 04333; *Treas.* Richard M. Cheski, State Libn., State Lib. of Ohio, 65 S. Front St., Columbus, OH 43215; *ALA Affiliation.* Sandra Cooper, ALA, Exec. Dir., ASCLA.

Directors

Officers; immediate past chpn.; two elected members: J. B. Forsee, Dir., Div. of Public Lib. Services, 156 Trinity Ave S.W., Atlanta, GA 30303; Nancy L. Zussy, State Libn., Washington State Lib., A.J. 11, Olympia, WA 98504.

Chinese-American Librarians Association

Executive Director, Amy Seetoo Wilson
c/o University Microfilms, Ann Arbor, MI 48106
800-521-0600

Object

"(1) To enhance communications among Chinese-American librarians as well as between Chinese-American librarians and other librarians; (2) to serve as a forum for discussion of mutual problems and professional concerns among Chinese-American librarians; (3) to promote Sino-American librarianship and library services; and (4) to provide a vehicle whereby Chinese-American librarians may cooperate with other associations and organizations having similar or allied interest."

Membership

Membership is open to everyone who is interested in the association's goals and activities. Memb. 400. Dues (Regular) $15; (Student and Nonsalaried) $7.50; (Inst.) $45; (Permanent) $150.

Officers (July 1986–June 1987)

Pres. Marjorie H. Li, Rutgers Univ. Libs., New Brunswick, NJ 08903; *V.P./Pres.-Elect.* Irene Yeh, Stanford Univ., Stanford, CA 94305; *Treas.* Eugenia Tang, Texas A&M Univ. Lib., College Station, TX 77843; *Exec. Dir.* Amy Seetoo Wilson, Univ. Microfilms International, Ann Arbor, MI 48106.

Publications

Journal of Library and Information Science (2 per year; memb. or $15).
Membership Directory (memb.)
Newsletter (3 per year; memb., nonmemb. $10/yr).

Committee Chairpersons

Annual Program. Irene Yeh.
Awards. Hwa-wei Lee.

Constitution and Bylaws. Stella Chiang.
Finance. Chang-chien Lee.
Long-Range Strategic Planning Task Force. Lena Yang.
Membership. Sheila Lai.
Nominating. William Wan.
Public Relations. Amy Seetoo Wilson.
Publications. Margaret Fung.

Mid-West. In-lan W. Li, John Marshall Law School Lib., Chicago, IL 60604.
Northeast. Diana Shih, American Museum of Natural History, Central Park W. at 79 St., New York, NY 10024.
Southwest. Elizabeth Tsai, Texas Woman's Univ., Denton, TX 76204.

Chapter Chairpersons

California. Julia Tung, Hoover Institute, Stanford Univ., Stanford, CA 94305.
Mid-Atlantic. Margaret Wang, Serials Dept., Univ. of Delaware, Newark, DE 19711.

Journal Officers

Margaret C. Fung, Exec. Ed., Box 31, Tyngsboro, MA 01879. *Newsletter Ed.* Diana Shih, American Museum of Natural History, Central Park W. at 79 St., New York, NY 10024.

Church and Synagogue Library Association

Executive Secretary, Dorothy J. Rodda
Box 1130, Bryn Mawr, PA 19010

Object

"To act as a unifying core for the many existing church and synagogue libraries; to provide the opportunity for a mutual sharing of practices and problems; to inspire and encourage a sense of purpose and mission among church and synagogue librarians; to study and guide the development of church and synagogue librarianship toward recognition as a formal branch of the library profession." Founded 1967. Dues (Contributing) $100; (Inst.) $75; (Affiliated) $35; (Church or Synagogue) $23; (Indiv.) $12. Year. July 1986–June 1987.

Officers (July 1986–June 1987)

Pres. Sally-Bruce McClatchey, 3355 Ridgewood Rd. N.W., Atlanta, GA 30327; *1st V.P./Pres.-Elect.* Janelle Paris, 253 Normal Park Rd., Huntsville, TX 77340; *2nd V.P. (Conference).* Naomi

Kauffman, 1411 Schwenkmill Rd., Perkasie, PA 18944; *3rd V.P. (Membership).* Charlotte Sanford, 383 Col. Ledyard Hey., Ledyard, CT 06339; *Treas.* Smith Gooch, 3507 Monte Vista N.E., Albuquerque, NM 87106; *Past Pres.* Marilyn Demeter, 3145 Corydon Rd., Cleveland Heights, OH 44118; *Publns. Dir. and Bulletin Ed.* William H. Gentz, 300 E. 34 St., Apt. 9C, New York, NY 10016.

Executive Board

Officers; committee chairpersons.

Publications

A Basic Book List for Church Libraries: Annotated Bibliography ($3.95).
Church and Synagogue Libraries (bi-mo.; memb. or $15, Can. $18). *Ed.* William H. Gentz. Book reviews, ads, $175 for full-page, camera-ready ad, one-time rate.

Church and Synagogue Library Resources: Annotated Bibliography ($3.95).

CSLA Guide No. 1, Setting Up a Library: How to Begin or Begin Again ($3.50).

CSLA Guide No. 2, rev. 2nd ed. *Promotion Planning All Year 'Round* ($4.95).

CSLA Guide No. 3, rev. ed. *Workshop Planning* ($6.50).

CSLA Guide No. 4, rev. ed. *Selecting Library Materials* ($3.95).

CSLA Guide No. 5. Cataloging Books Step by Step ($4.95).

CSLA Guide No. 6. Standards for Church and Synagogue Libraries ($4.95).

CSLA Guide No. 7. Classifying Church or Synagogue Library Materials ($3.95).

CSLA Guide No. 8. Subject Headings for Church or Synagogue Libraries ($4.95).

CSLA Guide No. 9. A Policy and Procedure Manual for Church and Synagogue Libraries ($3.95).

CSLA Guide No. 10. Archives in the Church or Synagogue Library ($4.95).

CSLA Guide No. 11. Planning Bulletin Boards for Church and Synagogue Libraries ($6.95).

CSLA Guide No. 12. Getting the Books Off the Shelves: Making the Most of Your Congregation's Library ($6.95).

CSLA Guide No. 13. The ABC's of Financing Church and Synagogue Libraries: Acquiring Funds, Budgeting, Cash Accounting ($5.95).

CSLA Guide No. 14. Recruiting and Training Volunteers for Church and Synagogue Libraries ($5.95).

The Family Uses the Library. Leaflet (10¢; $7/100).

Helping Children Through Books: Annotated Bibliography ($5.95).

Know Your Neighbor's Faith: An Annotated Interfaith Bibliography ($3.95).

Religious Books for Children: An Annotated Bibliography ($5.95).

The Teacher and the Library—Partners in Religious Education. Leaflet (10¢; $7/100).

Committee Chairpersons

Awards. Patricia Pearl.

Chapters. Fay W. Grosse.

Constitution and Bylaws. Lois Seyfrit.

Continuing Education. Claudia Hannaford.

Library Services. Doris Metzler.

Nominations and Elections. Patricia Tabler.

Council of National Library and Information Associations

461 W. Lancaster Ave., Haverford, PA 19041
215-649-5251

Object

To provide a central agency for cooperation among library/information associations and other professional organizations of the United States and Canada in promoting matters of common interest.

Membership

Open to national library/information associations and organizations with related interests of the United States and Canada. American Assn. of Law Libs.; American Lib. Assn.; American Society of Indexers;

American Theological Lib. Assn.; Art Libs. Society/North America; Assn. of Christian Libs., Inc.; Assn. of Jewish Libs.; Catholic Lib. Assn.; Chinese–American Libns. Assn.; Church and Synagogue Lib. Assn.; Council of Planning Libns.; Lib. Binding Institute; Lib. Public Relations Council; Lutheran Lib. Assn.; Medical Lib. Assn.; Music Lib. Assn.; National Libns. Assn.; Society of American Archivists; Special Libs. Assn.; Theatre Lib. Assn.

Officers (July 1986–June 1987)

Chpn. Norma Yueh, Ramapo College of New Jersey Lib., Mahwah, NJ 07430; *V. Chpn.* Christine Hoffman, Manhattan School of Music Lib., 120 Claremont Ave., New York, NY 10027; *Secy.-Treas.* Mildred Lowe, Dir., Div. of Lib. and Info. Science, St. John's Univ., Grand Central and Utopia Pkwys., Jamaica, NY 11439.

(Address correspondence to chairperson at 461 W. Lancaster Ave., Haverford, PA 19041.)

Directors

Anne Hartmere, The Architects Collaborative, 46 Brattle St., Cambridge, MA 02138; Dorothy J. Rodda (July 1985–June 1987). Exec. Dir., Church and Synagogue Lib. Assn., Box 1130, Bryn Mawr, PA 19010; Jane E. Stevens (July 1985–June 1988), 410 Riverside Dr., New York, NY 10025.

Council of Planning Librarians, Publications Office

1313 E. 60 St., Chicago, IL 60637-2897

Object

To provide a special interest group in the field of city and regional planning for libraries and librarians, faculty, professional planners, university, government, and private planning organizations; to provide an opportunity for exchange among those interested in problems of library organization and research and in the dissemination of information about city and regional planning; to sponsor programs of service to the planning profession and librarianship; to advise on library organization for new planning programs; and to aid and support administrators, faculty, and librarians in their efforts to educate the public and their appointed or elected representatives to the necessity for strong library programs in support of planning. Founded 1960. Memb. 170. Dues (Inst.) $45; (Indiv.) $25; (Student) $5. Year. July 1–June 30.

Membership

Open to any individual or institution that supports the purpose of the council, upon written application and payment of dues to the treasurer.

Officers (1986–1987)

Pres. Mary D. Ravenhall, City Planning and Landscape Architecture Lib., Univ. of Illinois, Urbana, IL 61801; *V.P./Pres.-Elect.* Katherine G. Eaton, 1631 E. 24 Ave., Eugene, OR 97403; *Past Pres.* Lynne DeMerritt, Libn., Municipal Research and Services Center of Washington Lib., 4719 Brooklyn Ave. N.E., Seattle, WA 98105; *Secy.* Anne McGowan, Lib. Mgr., Wyoming Dept. of Economic Planning and Development, Herschler Bldg., Cheyenne, WY 82002; *Treas.* M. Kay Mowery, State Information and Reference

Center, California State Lib., Box 942837, Sacramento, CA 94237; *Memb.-at-Large.* Elizabeth D. Byrne, Environmental Design Lib., 210 Wuster Hall, Univ. of California, Berkeley, CA 94720; *Ed., Bibliography Series.* Patricia Coatsworth, Merriam Center Lib., 1313 E. 60 St., Chicago, IL 60637.

Publications

CPL Bibliographies (approx. 24 published per year) may be purchased on standing order or by individual issue. Catalog sent upon request. The following is only a partial list of publications.

No. 154. *Industrial Transformation, Economic Development, and Regional Planning.* Nancey Leigh-Preston ($10).

No. 155. *Electronic Banking: An Annotated Bibliography, 1978–1983.* Sybil A. Boudreaux and Marilyn L. Hankel ($15).

No. 156. *Fifteen Years of Community-Based Development: An Annotated Bibliography, 1968–1983.* Chris Tilly et al. ($15).

No. 157. *Management Science Applications to Academic Administration: An Annotated Bibliography.* Gregory P. White ($12).

No. 162. *Nonmetropolitan Growth in the United States: A Bibliography.* Barney Warf ($8).

No. 164. *Hospitals and Urban Neighborhoods: Bases for Joint Planning and Community Development.* Shawn V. LaFrance ($8).

Council on Library Resources, Inc.

1785 Massachusetts Ave. N.W., Washington, DC 20036
202-483-7474

Object

A private operating foundation, the Council seeks to assist in finding solutions to the problems of libraries, particularly academic and research libraries. In pursuit of this aim, the Council conducts its own projects, makes grants to and contracts with other organizations and individuals, and calls upon many others for advice and assistance with its work. The Council was established in 1956 by the Ford Foundation, and it now receives support from a number of private foundations and other sources. Current program emphases include research and analysis, enhancing, preserving, and extending access to library resources; bibliographic services; the management of libraries; and professional education.

Membership

The Council's membership and board of directors is limited to 25.

Officers

Chpn. Maximilian Kempner; *V. Chpn.* Charles Churchwell; *Pres.* Warren J. Haas; *V.P.* Deanna B. Marcum; *Secy-Treas.* Mary Agnes Thompson.

(Address correspondence to headquarters.)

Publications

Annual Report.
CLR Recent Developments.

Educational Film Library Association

Executive Director, Marilyn Levin
45 John St., Suite 301, New York, NY 10038
212-227-5599

Object

"To promote the production, distribution and utilization of educational films and other audiovisual materials." Incorporated 1943. Memb. 1,800. Dues (Inst.) $175; (Commercial organizations) $265; (Indiv.) $45; (Students and Retirees) $25. Year. July–June.

Officers

Pres. Bill Howie, Media Services, Southern Methodist Univ., Dallas, TX 75275; *Pres.-Elect.* Judith Gaston, Dir., Univ. Film & Video, Univ. of Minnesota, 3300 University Ave. S.E, Minneapolis, MN 55414; *Past-Pres.* Michael Miller, Head, Avery Fisher Center for Music & Media, Bobst Lib., New York Univ., 70 Washington Sq. S., New York, NY 10012; *Secy.* Sue Owens, Coord., AV Services, Instructional Materials Center, State Education Bldg., Little Rock, AR 72201; *Treas.* Ron MacIntyre, AV Libn., South Dakota State Lib., 800 N. Illinois, Pierre, SD 57501.

Board of Directors

Maureen Gaffney, Dir., Media Center for Children, 3 W. 29 St., New York, NY 10001; Lillian Katz, Head, Media Services, Port Washington Public Lib., 245 Main St., Port Washington, NY 11050; Kathryn Lamont, Marketing Admin., Films Inc., 5547 N. Ravenswood Ave., Chicago, IL 60640-1190; Laurie Caplane, V.P. Marketing, Citibank, 641 Lexington Ave., 15th fl., New York, NY 10043; Roberta Davis, V.P., Morgan Guaranty Trust, 23 Wall St., New York, NY 10015; Mary Banta, Head, Network Technical Services, Wayne County Intermediate School Dist., 33500 Van Born Rd., Wayne, MI 48184; Sharon K. Chaplock, Dir., Audiovisual Center, Milwaukee Public Museum, 800 W. Wells St., Milwaukee, WI 53233; Mark L. Richie, Dir., Burlington County AVA Center, 122 High St., Mount Holly, NJ 08060; Gregory Chiampou, Analyst–Corporate Planning, NBC, Rm. 2250 W, 30 Rockefeller Plaza, New York, NY 10112; *Counsel.* Marshall Beil, Esq., Rambar & Curtis, 19 W. 44 St., New York, NY 10036.

Publications

American Film and Video Festival Program Guide (ann.).
EFLA Bulletin (q.) *Ed.* Joel Kanoff.
EFLA Evaluations (2 per year). *Ed.* Judith Trojan.
Sightlines (q.). *Ed.* Judith Trojan.
Write for list of other books and pamphlets.

Federal Library and Information Center Committee (FLICC)

Executive Director, James P. Riley
Library of Congress, Washington, DC 20540
202-287-6055

Object

The Committee makes recommendations on federal library and information policies, programs, and procedures to federal agencies and to others concerned with libraries and information centers.

The Committee coordinates cooperative activities and services among federal libraries and information centers and serves as a forum to consider (1) issues and policies that affect federal libraries and information centers, (2) needs and priorities in providing information services to the government and to the nation at large, (3) efficient and cost-effective use of federal library and information resources and services.

Furthermore, the Committee promotes (1) improved access to information, (2) continued development and use of the Federal Library and Information Network (FEDLINK), (3) research and development in the application of new technologies to federal libraries and information centers, (4) improvements in the management of federal libraries and information centers, and (5) relevant education opportunities. Founded 1965.

Membership

Libn. of Congress, Dir. of the National Agricultural Lib., Dir. of the National Lib. of Medicine, representatives from each of the other executive departments, and representatives from each of the following agencies: the National Aeronautics and Space Admin., the National Science Foundation, the Smithsonian Institution, the U.S. Supreme Court, U.S. Info. Agency, the Veterans Admin., the Na-

tional Archives and Records Service, the Administrative Offices of the U.S. Courts, the Defense Technical Info. Center, the Govt. Printing Office, the National Technical Info. Service, and the Office of Scientific and Technical Info. Ten additional voting member agencies shall be selected on a rotating basis by the permanent members of the Committee from the three branches of government, independent agencies, boards, committees, and commissions. These rotating members will serve two-year terms. In addition to the permanent representative of DOD, one nonvoting member shall be selected from each of the three services (U.S. Army, U.S. Navy, U.S. Air Force). These service members, who will serve for two years, will be selected by the permanent Dept. of Defense member from a slate provided by the Federal Lib. and Info. Center Committee. The membership in each service shall be rotated equitably among the special service, technical, and academic and school libraries in that service. DOD shall continue to have one voting member in the committee. The DOD representative may poll the three service members for their opinions before reaching a decision concerning the vote. One representative from each of the following agencies is invited as an observer to committee meetings: General Accounting Office, General Services Admin., Joint Committee on Printing, Natl. Commission on Libs. and Info. Science, and the Office of Management and Budget.

Officers

Chpn. Ruth Ann Stewart; *Exec. Dir.* James P. Riley, Federal Lib. and Info.

Center Committee, Lib. of Congress, Washington, DC 20540.

(Address correspondence to the executive director.)

Publications

Annual Report (Oct.).
FEDLINK Technical Notes (bi-mo.).
FLICC Newsletter (q.).

The Federal Publishers Committee (FPC)

Chairperson, Robin A. Atkiss
Rm. 329-D, 200 Independence Ave. S.W., Washington, DC 20201
202-472-7257

Object

To foster and promote cost-effective publications management in the federal government in all aspects of publishing, including planning, marketing, writing, graphic design, printing, promotion, mailing, storage, inquiry response, and clearinghouse dissemination and all the costs associated with these functions.

Membership

Membership is available to persons in the federal government agencies involved in publishing, publishing personnel from organizations such as the Joint Committee on Printing, Government Printing Office, National Technical Info. Service, National Commission on Libs. and Info. Sci-

ence, and the Lib. of Congress, and to publishing personnel in independent establishments and government corporations such as the Veterans Admin., U.S. Trade Commission, and the U.S. Postal Service. There are 662 members at the present time. Meetings are held monthly during business hours.

Officers (1986–1987)

Chpn. Robin A. Atkiss; *Secy.* Marilyn Marbrook.

Committee Chairpersons

Administration. Sandra Smith.
Task Force Activity. June Malina.

Information Industry Association

President, Paul G. Zurkowski
555 New Jersey Ave. N.W., Suite 800, Washington, DC 20001
202-639-8262

Membership

For details on membership and dues, write to the association headquarters. Memb. More than 460.

Staff

Pres. Paul G. Zurkowski; *Senior V.P., Government Relations.* Kenneth Allen; *Dir., Government Relations.* David Pey-

ton; *V.P., Marketing Admin.* Alison Caughman; *Dir., Marketing.* Michael Atkin; *Dir., Membership Development.* Judith Angerman; *Dir. of Meetings.* Linda Cunningham; *Senior V.P., Operations and Divs.* Ted Caris; *Controller.* Shad Ahmad; *Exec. Dir., Financial Information Services.* Robert Bartolotta; *Dir., Member Services.* Martha Gillis; *Dir., Publications.* Barbara Van Gorder.

Board of Directors

Chair. Carl M. Valenti, Dow Jones Information Services; *Chair-Elect.* Daniel M. Sullivan, Frost & Sullivan, Inc.; *Past Chair.* Robert S. November, American Banker/Bond Buyer; Peter Marx, Goulston & Storrs; Paul Massa, Congressional Information Services; Marsha Carow, Harcourt Brace Jovanovich; Daniel H. Carter, Walter Ulrich Consulting; Robert J. Eckenrode, NYNEX Corp.; Joseph J. Fitzsimmons, University Microfilms International; Peter R. Genereaux, I. P. Sharp Assocs., Ltd.; William Giglio, McGraw-Hill; Lois Granich, PsychINFO; James H. Holly, Times Mirror Videotex Services; John A. Jenkins, BNA Electronic Media Div.; James P. McGinty, Dun & Bradstreet Corp.; L. John Rankine, IBM; Gary G. Reibsamen, NewsNet; Jack Simpson, Mead Data Central; Fran Spigai, Database Services, Inc.

Division Chairpersons

Database and Publishing. Art Elias, Biosciences Information Service.

Financial Information Services. Richard J. Cowles, Telerate Systems Inc.
Videotex. James H. Holly, Times Mirror Videotex Services.

Council Chairpersons

Business Operations. Vernon H. L. Tyerman, Pacific Telesis Corp.
Public Policy and Government Relations. Stephen D. Pfleiderer, Prentice-Hall Information Services.
Technology and Innovation. Vacant.

Publications

Artificial Intelligence: Reality or Fantasy? The Business of Information Report (1983).
Compensation Practices in the Information Industry: A Survey of Benefits and Salaries.
How to Succeed in the Electronic Information Marketplace.
The Information Executive's Guide to Intellectual Property Rights.
The Information Millenium: Alternative Futures (1986).
Information Sources (1987).
So You Want to Be a Profitable Database Publisher (1983).
Strategic Marketing: Techniques, Technologies and Realities in the Information Industry.

International Council of Library Association Executives

Willine Mahoney
Illinois Library Association
H25 N. Michigan Ave., Chicago, IL 60611

Object

"To provide an opportunity for the exchange of information, experience, and opinion on a continuing basis through discussion, study and publication; to promote the arts and sciences of educational association management; and to develop and encourage high standards of profes-

sional conduct." Conducts workshops and institutes; offers specialized education.

Membership

Membership is available to chief paid executives engaged in the management of library associations. Founded 1975. Dues $25. Year. July 1–June 30.

Officers (July 1986–June 1987)

Pres. Willine Mahoney, Illinois Lib. Assn., 425 N. Michigan Ave., Chicago, IL 60611; *Pres.-Elect.* Mary Ann Gessner, Michigan Lib. Assn., 415 W. Kalamazoo, Lansing, MI 48933; *Secy.-Treas.* Raymond Means, Nebraska Lib. Assn., Creighton Univ., 2500 California St., Omaha, NE

68178; *Past Pres.* Abigail Studdiford, New Jersey Lib. Assn., 116 W. State St., Trenton, NJ 08608.

Board of Directors (July 1986–June 1987)

Officers; Margaret Bauer, 2941 N. Front St., Harrisburg, PA 17101; Sherylynn Aucoin, Box 131, Baton Rouge, LA 70821.

Meetings

Two meetings are held annually in conjunction with those of the American Library Association in January and June. Elections are held during the June meeting.

Lutheran Church Library Association

122 Franklin Ave., Minneapolis, MN 55404
612-870-3623
Executive Director, Wilma Jensen
(Home address: 3620 Fairlawn Dr., Minnetonka, MN 55345
612-473-5965)

Object

"To promote the growth of church libraries by publishing a quarterly journal, *Lutheran Libraries*; furnishing booklists; assisting member libraries with technical problems; and providing meetings for mutual encouragement, assistance, and exchange of ideas among members." Founded 1958. Memb. 1,800. Dues $15, $25, $100, $500, $1,000. Year. Jan.–Jan.

Officers (Jan. 1987–Jan. 1988)

Pres. Mary Jordan, First Lutheran Church Lib., 309 E. Third St. N., Newton, IA 50208; *V.P./Pres.-Elect.* Ron Klug, 1115 S. Division St., Northfield, MN 55057; *Secy.* Barbara Aslakson,

Prince of Peace Lutheran Church, 8115 State Hwy. 7, St. Louis Park, MN 55426; *Treas.* Jane Johnson, 2930 S. Hwy. 101, Wayzata, MN 55291.

(Address correspondence to the executive director.)

Executive Board

Linda Beck; Bernita Kennen, Sonja Nelson; Fins Peterson; Carl Weller; Robert Wiederaenders.

Publication

Lutheran Libraries (q.; memb., nonmemb. $10). *Ed.* Ron Klub, 1115 S. Division St., Northfield, MN 55057.

Committee Chairpersons

Advisory. Anders Hanson, 4480 Parklawn Ave., Apt. 211, Edina, MN 55435.

Budget. Rev. Carl Manfred, 5227 Oaklawn Ave., Minneapolis, MN 55436.

Council of National Library and Information Assns. Wilma W. Jensen, Exec. Dir., and Mary A. Huebner, Libn., Concordia College, 171 White Plains Rd., Bronxville, NY 10708.

Library Services Board. Juanita Carpenter, Libn., Rte. 1, Prior Lake, MN 55372.

Membership. Betty LeDell, Libn., Grace Lutheran of Deephaven, 15800 Sunset Dr., Minnetonka, MN 55343.

Publications Board. Rod Olson, Augsburg Publishing House, 426 S. Fifth, Box 1209, Minneapolis, MN 55440.

Medical Library Association

Executive Director, Raymond A. Palmer
919 N. Michigan Ave., Suite 3208, Chicago, IL 60611
312-266-2456

Object

The Medical Library Association (MLA) was founded in 1898 and incorporated in 1934. MLA's major purposes are: (1) to foster medical and allied scientific libraries, (2) to promote the educational and professional growth of health science librarians, and (3) to exchange medical literature among the members. Through its programs and publications, MLA encourages professional development of its membership, whose foremost concern is the dissemination of health sciences information for those in research, education, and patient care.

Membership

MLA has 1,366 institutional members and 3,777 individual members. Institutional members are medical and allied scientific libraries. Institutional member dues are based on the number of subscriptions (subscriptions up to 199 – $100; 200 – 299 – $135; 300–599 – $165; 600–999 – $200; 1,000 + – $235). Individual MLA members are people who are (or were at the time membership was established) engaged in professional library or bibliographic work in medical and allied scientific libraries or people who are interested in medical or allied scientific libraries. Annual dues for individual members are $75, with special membership categories for emeritus, associate, student, life, and sustaining members.

Officers

Pres. Judith Messerle, St. Louis Univ., Medical Center Lib., 1402 S. Grand Blvd., St. Louis, MO 63104; *Pres.-Elect.* Holly Shipp Buchanan, NKC Hospitals, Inc., Corporate Info. Resources, Box 35070, Louisville, KY 40232; *Past Pres.* Jean K. Miller, Lib., Health Science Center at Dallas, Univ. of Texas, 5323 Harry Hines Blvd., Dallas, TX 75235.

Directors

Gary D. Byrd (1984–1987); June Fulton (1984–1987); Frances Groen (1984–1987); Jane Lambremont (1984–1987); Jacqueline D. Bastille (1985–1988); Richard A. Lyders (1985–1988); Sherilynne S.

Fuller (1986–1989); J. Michael Homan (1986–1989); Rosanne Labree (1986–1989); Raymond A. Palmer (*Ex officio*).

Publications

Bulletin of the Medical Library Association (q.; $75).
Current Catalog Proof Sheets (w.; $96).
Handbook of Medical Library Practice, 4th ed., vol. 1 ($22.50).
Hospital Library Management ($67.50).
Introduction to Reference Sources in the Health Sciences ($27).
MEDLINE: A Basic Guide to Searching ($16 membs.; $20 nonmembs.).
MLA Directory (ann.; $35).
MLA News (10 times per year; $30).

Standing Committee Chairpersons

Awards Committee. Faith Van Toll, Shiffman Medical Lib., Wayne State Univ., 4325 Brush St., Detroit, MI 48201. *Janet Doe Lectureship Subcommittee.* Ursula H. Poland; Gerald J. Oppenheimer; Irwin H. Pizer. *Ida and George Eliot Prize Subcommittee.* Brett A. Kirkpatrick; Nancy Fabrizio; Debra S. Ketchell. *Murray Gottlieb Prize Subcommittee.* James A. Parrish; Dana M. McDonald; Sherry L. Montgomery. *Rittenhouse Award Subcommittee.* Katherine Ann Branch; Janet D. Carter; Valerie K. Smith. *Frank Bradway Bogers Information Advancement Award Subcommittee.* June Glaser; Linda A. Watson; Sandra K. Millard.
Bulletin Consulting Editors Panel. Susan Crawford, School of Medicine Lib., Washington Univ., 4580 Scott Ave., St. Louis, MO 63110.
Bylaws Committee. Lucretia McClure, Edward G. Miner Lib., School of Medicine/Dentistry, Univ. of Rochester, 601 Elmwood Ave., Rochester, NY 14652.

Certification Committee. Cynthia Butler, Biomedical Lib., Univ. of California, Irvine, Box 19556, Irvine, CA 92713.
Committee on Committees. Holly Shipp Buchanan, NKC Hospitals, Inc., Corporate Info. Resources, Box 35070, Louisville, KY 40232.
Continuing Education Committee. Jacqueline D. Doyle, Health Sciences Lib., Good Samaritan Medical Center, Box 2989, Phoenix, AZ 85062.
Editorial Committee for MLA News. Robert A. Pisciotta, McGoogan Lib. of Medicine, Univ. of Nebraska Medical Center, 42nd and Dewey Ave., Omaha, NE 68105.
Editorial Committee for the Bulletin. M. Sandra Wood, George T. Harrell Lib., Milton S. Hershey Medical Center, Pennsylvania State Univ., Box 850, Hershey, PA 17033.
Editorial Panel for Certification and Registration Examination. Fred W. Roper, School of Lib. Science, Univ. of North Carolina, Manning Hall 026A, Chapel Hill, NC 27514.
Elections Committee. Holly Shipp Buchanan, NKC Hospitals, Inc., Corporate Info. Resources, Box 35070, Louisville, KY 40232.
Exchange Committee. Beth Weil, Biology Lib., 3503 Life Sciences Bldg., Univ. of California, Berkeley, CA 94720.
Executive Committee. Judith Messerle, Medical Center Lib., St. Louis Univ., 1402 S. Grand, St. Louis, MO 63104.
Finance Committee. Gary Byrd, Health Sciences Lib., Univ. of North Carolina, Chapel Hill, NC 27514.
Governmental Relations Committee. Valerie Florance, Welch Medical Lib., Johns Hopkins Univ., 1900 E. Monument St., Baltimore, MD 21205.
Grants and Scholarship Committee. Elaine Graham, UCLA Biomedical Lib., Center for the Health Sciences, Pacific Southwest Regional Medical Lib. Service, Los Angeles, CA 90024.

Health Sciences Library Technicians Committee. Ruth Makinen, Bio-Medical Lib., Univ. of Minnesota, 505 Essex St. S.E., Minneapolis, MN 55455.

International Cooperation Committee. Julie Johnson McGowan, School of Medicine Lib., Univ. of South Carolina, Veteran's Administration Medical Center, Columbia, SC 28208.

Joseph Leiter NLM/MLA Lectureship Committee. Lois Ann Colaianni, National Lib. of Medicine, 8600 Rockville Pike, Bethesda, MD 20209.

Membership Committee. Julie Ann Kesti, PSRMLS/Biomedical Lib., UCLA Center for the Health Sciences, Los Angeles, CA 90024.

MLA/NLM Liaison Committee. Gary D. Byrd, Health Sciences Lib., Univ. of North Carolina, Chapel Hill, NC 27514.

1987 National Program Committee. Carol G. Jenkins, Health Sciences Lib., Univ. of Maryland, S.E. Atlantic RMLS, 111 S. Greene St., Baltimore, MD 21201.

1988 National Program Committee. Mary M. Horres, Biomedical Lib. C-075-B, Univ. of California, San Diego, La Jolla, CA 92093.

Nominating Committee. Holly Shipp Buchanan, NKC Hospitals, Inc., Corporate Info. Resources, Box 35070, Louisville, KY 40232.

Oral History Committee. Suzanne Grefsheim, Health Sciences Lib., Univ. of Maryland, 111 S. Greene St., Baltimore, MD 21201.

Program and Convention Committee. Ruth Holst, Medical Lib., Columbia Hospital, 2025 E. Newport, Milwaukee, WI 53211.

Publication Panel. Joan S. Zenan, Savitt Medical Lib., Univ. of Nevada, Reno, NV 89557.

Publishing and Information Industries Relation Committee. Daniel T. Richards, Health Sciences Lib., Columbia Univ., 701 W. 168 St., New York, NY 10032.

Status and Economic Interests of Health Sciences Library Personnel Committee. Bernie Todd-Smith, Werner Health Science Lib., Rochester General Hospital Lib., 1425 Portland Ave., Rochester, NY 14621.

Ad Hoc Committees

Ad Hoc Committee on Appointment of Fellows and Honorary Members. Jean K. Miller, Lib., Health Science Center at Dallas, Univ. of Texas, 5323 Harry Hines Blvd., Dallas, TX 75235.

Ad Hoc Committee to Develop a Code of Ethics. Alice A. Brand, Professional Lib., Menninger Foundation, Box 829, Topeka, KS 66601.

Music Library Association

Box 487, Canton, MA 02021
617-828-8450

Object

"To promote the establishment, growth, and use of music libraries; to encourage the collection of music and musical literature in libraries; to further studies in musical bibliography; to increase efficiency in music library service and administration." Founded in 1931. Memb. about 1,700.

Dues (Inst.) $46; (Indiv.) $32; (Student) $16. Year. Sept. 1–Aug. 31.

Officers

Pres. Lenore Coral, Music Lib., Cornell Univ., Lincoln Hall, Ithaca, NY 14853-4101; *Past Pres.* Geraldine Ostrove, Music Div., Lib. of Congress, Washington, DC

20540; *Rec. Secy.* Ruth Henderson, Music Lib., City College, CUNY, New York, NY 10031; *Treas.* Sherry L. Vellucci, Talbott Lib., Westminster Choir College, Princeton, NJ 08540. *"Notes" Ed.* Michael Ochs, Music Lib., Harvard Univ., Cambridge, MA 02138; *Exec. Secy.* Linda Solow Blotner, 203 Deercliff Rd., Avon, CT 06001.

Members-at-Large

Marsha Berman, Music Lib., Univ. of California–Los Angeles, Los Angeles, CA 90024; James B. Coover, Music Lib., Baird Hall, SUNY, Amherst, NY 14260; John E. Druesedow, Jr., Music Lib., Duke Univ., Durham, NC 27707; Ida Reed, Music Lib., Hill Hall, Univ. of North Carolina–Chapel Hill, Chapel Hill, NC 27514; John H. Roberts, Van Pelt Lib., Univ. of Pennsylvania, Philadelphia, PA 19104; Richard P. Smiraglia, School of Lib. Service, Columbia Univ., 516 Butler Lib., New York, NY 10027.

Special Officers

Convention Mgr. Martin A. Silver, Music Lib., Univ. of California, Santa Barbara, CA 93106.
Placement. Laura Dankner, Music Lib., Loyola Univ., New Orleans, LA 70118.
Publicity. Dawn R. Thistle, Music Lib., College of the Holy Cross, Worcester, MA 01610.

Publications

MLA Index Series (irreg.; price varies according to size).
MLA Newsletter (q., free to memb.).
MLA Technical Reports (irreg.; price varies according to size).
Music Cataloging Bulletin (mo.; $18).
Notes (q.; inst. subscription $42); nonmemb. subscription $28).

Committee Chairpersons

Administration. H. Ross Wood, Music Lib., Wellesley College, Wellesley, MA 02181.
Awards. Publications. Joseph M. Boonin, Jerona Music Corp., 81 Trinity Place, Hackensack, NJ 07601; *Walter Gerboth Award.* Mary Wallace Davidson, Sibley Music Lib., Eastman School of Music, Rochester, NY 14606.
Bibliographic Control. Joan Swanekamp, Sibley Music Lib., Eastman School of Music, Rochester, NY 14606.
Development. Karen Nagy, Music Lib., Braun Arts Center, Stanford Univ., Stanford, CA 94305.
Education. Ann McCollough, Sibley Music Lib., Eastman School of Music, ·Rochester, NY 14606.
Finance. Richard P. Smiraglia, School of Lib. Service, Columbia Univ., 516 Butler Lib., New York, NY 10027.
Legislation. Margaret Welk Cundiff, Special Materials Cataloging—Music, Lib. of Congress, Washington, DC 20540.
Nominating. Judith Kaufman, Lib. W2510, SUNY at Stony Brook, Stony Brook, NY 11794.
Preservation. Jerry C. McBride, Music Lib., Middlebury College, Middlebury, VT 05753.
Program 1988. Gordon Theil, Music Lib., Univ. of California–Los Angeles, Los Angeles, CA 90024.
Public Libraries. Norma Jean Lamb, Buffalo and Erie County Public Lib., Lafayette Sq., Buffalo, NY 14203.
Publications. Susan T. Sommer, Collections Specialist–Music, New York Public Lib., 111 Amsterdam Ave., New York, NY 10023.
Reference and Public Service. Bonnie Jo Dopp, Martin Luther King Memorial Lib., 901 G St. N.W., Washington, DC 20001.
Resource Sharing and Collection Development. David Fenske, Indiana Univ., Music Lib., Bloomington, IN 47401.

National Association of Government Archives and Records Administrators (NAGARA)

Executive Director, Bruce W. Dearstyne
New York State Archives
10A75 Cultural Education Center, Albany, NY 12230
518-473-8037

Object

Founded in 1984, the Association is successor to the National Association of State Archives and Records Administrators, which had been established in 1974. NAGARA is a growing nationwide association of local, state, and federal archivists and records administrators, and others, interested in improved care and management of government records. NAGARA promotes public awareness of government records and archives management programs, encourages interchange of information among government archives and records management agencies, develops and implements professional standards of government records and archival administration, and encourages study and research into records management problems and issues. NAGARA is an affiliate of the Council of State Governments.

Membership

State archival and records management agencies are NAGARA's sustaining members, but individual membership is open to local governments, federal agencies, and to any individual or organization interested in improved government records programs.

Officers

Pres. William S. Price, North Carolina Div. of Archives and History; *V.P.* John Burns, California State Archives; *Secy.* M. Liisa Fagerlund, Utah State Archives and Records Service; *Treas.* Roy Tryon, Delaware Bureau of Archives and Records Management.

Publications

Clearinghouse (q.; free to memb.).
Information Clearinghouse Needs of the Archival Profession (report).
Preservation Needs in State Archives (report).

National Librarians Association

Executive Director, Peter Dollard
Box 586, Alma, MI 48801

Object

"To promote librarianship, to develop and increase the usefulness of libraries, to cultivate the science of librarianship, to protect the interest of professionally qualified librarians, and to perform other functions necessary for the betterment of the profession of librarians, rather than as an association of libraries." Established 1975. Memb. 300. Dues $20 per year; $35 for 2 years; (Students, Retired, and Unemployed Libns.) $10. Year. July 1–June 30.

Membership

Any person interested in librarianship and libraries who holds a graduate degree in library science may become a member upon election by the executive board and payment of the annual dues. The executive board may authorize exceptions to the degree requirements to applicants who present evidence of outstanding contributions to the profession. Student member-ship is available to those graduate students enrolled full time at any accredited library school.

Publication

The National Librarian (q.; 1 year $15, 2 years $28, 3 years $39). *Ed.* Peter Dollard.

Society for Scholarly Publishing

Secretary-Treasurer, Constance B. Kiley
American Geophysical Union, 2000 Florida Ave. N.W., Washington, DC 20009
202-328-3555

Object

To draw together individuals involved in the process of scholarly publishing. This process requires successful interaction of the many functions performed within the scholarly community. SSP provides the leadership for such interaction by creating the opportunities for the exchange of information and opinions among scholars, editors, publishers, librarians, printers, booksellers, and all others engaged in scholarly publishing.

Membership

Open to all with an interest in scholarly publishing and information dissemination. There are three categories of membership: individual, $40, contributing, $150; sustaining (organizational), $300. Dues are on a calendar year basis.

Officers
(July 1, 1986–June 30, 1988)

Pres. G. William Teare, Jr., Printing Industries of America, 1730 N. Lynn St., Arlington, VA 22209; *V.P.* Ann Reinke Strong, New England Journal of Medicine, 1440 Main St., Waltham, MA 02254; *Secy.-Treas.* Constance B. Kiley, Waverly Press, Mt. Royal & Guilford Aves., Baltimore, MD 21202.

Board of Directors

William Begell, Hemisphere Publishing Co., 79 Madison Ave., New York, NY 10016; Mary Curtis, Wiley-Interscience Journals, 605 Third Ave., New York, NY 10158; Margaret Foti, Cancer Research, West Bldg., Rm. 30, Temple Univ. School of Medicine, Philadelphia, PA 19140; Christopher Johnson, Capital City Press, Box 546, Montpelier, VT 05602; William Kaufmann, William Kaufmann Inc., Los Altos, CA; Shirley Echelman, Assn. of Research Libs., Washington, DC; Richard Rowson, Duke Univ. Press, Chapel Hill, NC; Barbara Janson, Janson Publications Inc., Providence, RI; Robert Shirrell, Univ. of Chicago Press, Chicago, IL; Hans Rutimann, Modern Language Assn., 62 Fifth Ave., New York, NY 10011; *Administrator.* Alice O'Leary, SSP, 2000 Florida Ave. N.W., Washington, DC 20009. 202-328-3555.

Committee Chairpersons

Annual Meeting Program. John Pugsley; Bradley Hundley.
Budget and Finance. Mark Mandelbaum.
Education. Vicki Sullivan.
Executive. G. William Teare, Jr.
Meetings. Skip McAfee.
Membership. Margaret O'Hara.
Nominations and Awards. Constance Greaser.

Planning. Ann Strong.
Publications. Maryanne M. Soper.

Meetings

An annual meeting is conducted each year in either May or June. The location changes each year. Additionally, SSP conducts three seminars throughout the year.

Society of American Archivists

Executive Director, Donn C. Neal
600 S. Federal St., Suite 504, Chicago, IL 60605
312-922-0140

Object

"To promote sound principles of archival economy and to facilitate cooperation among archivists and archival agencies." Founded 1936. Memb. 4,000. Dues (Indiv.) $45–$75, graduated according to salary; (Assoc.) $40, domestic; (Student) $30 with a two-year maximum on student membership; (Inst.) $65; (Sustaining) $150.

Officers (1986–1987)

Pres. William L. Joyce, Firestone Lib., Princeton Univ., Princeton, NJ 08544; *V.P.* Sue E. Holbert, Minnesota Historical Society, 1500 Mississippi St., St. Paul, MN 55101; *Treas.* Anne Diffendal, Nebraska State Historical Society, Lincoln, NE 68506.

Council

Francis X. Blouin, Jr.; Paul I. Chestnut; Richard J. Cox; Linda Edgerly; Anne R. Kenney; Eva Moseley; Trudy Huskamp Peterson; Victoria Irons Walch; Joan N. Warnow.

Staff

Exec. Dir. Donn C. Neal; *Membership Asst.* Bernice E. Brack; *System Admin.* Sylvia Burck; *Managing Ed.* William Burck; *Publns. Asst.* Al Correa; *Office Asst.* Diane Mobley; *Program Coord.* Patricia Palmer; *Meeting Mgr.* Toni Pedroza; *Publns. Asst.* Troy Sturdivant; *Program Officer.* Lisa Weber.

Publications

The American Archivist (q.; $30). *Ed.* Julia M. Young; *Managing Ed.* William Burck, 600 S. Federal, Suite 504, Chicago, IL 60605. Books for review and related correspondence should be addressed to the editor. Rates for B/W ads: full-page, $250; half-page, $175; outside back cover, $350; half-page minimum insertion; 10% discount for four consecutive insertions: 15% agency commission.

SAA Newsletter (6 per year; memb.). *Ed.* William Burck. Rates for B/W ads: full-page, $300; half-page, $175; quarter-page, $90; eighth-page, $50; 10% discount for six consecutive insertions; 15% agency commission.

Special Libraries Association

Executive Director, David R. Bender
1700 18th St. N.W., Washington, DC 20009
202-234-4700

Object

"To provide an association of individuals and organizations having a professional, scientific, or technical interest in library and information science, especially as these are applied in the recording, retrieval, and dissemination of knowledge and information in areas such as the physical, biological, technical and social sciences, the humanities, and business; and to promote and improve the communication, dissemination, and use of such information and knowledge for the benefit of libraries or other educational organizations. Organized 1909. Memb. 12,500. Dues (Sustaining) $300; (Indiv.) $75; (Student) $15. Year. Jan.–Dec. and July–June.

Officers (June 1986–June 1987)

Pres. Frank H. Spaulding, AT&T Bell Laboratories, Rm. 3D 203, Crawfords Corner Rd., Holmdel, NJ 07733; *Pres.-Elect.* Emily R. Mobley, Purdue Univ. Libs., Stewart Center, West Lafayette, IN 47907; *Div. Cabinet Chpn.* Ellen Steininger, Burson-Marstellar Lib., One East Wacker Dr., Chicago, IL 60601; *Div. Cabinet Chpn-Elect.* Ruth K. Seidman, U.S. Air Force, Geophysics Laboratory Research Lib., AFGL/SULL, Hanscom AFB, MA 01731; *Chapter Cabinet Chpn.* Julie A. Macksey, Upjohn Co., Corporate Lib. 267-2, 301 Henrietta St., Kalamazoo, MI 49001; *Chapter Cabinet Chpn-Elect.* M. Hope Coffman, Charles S. Draper Laboratory, Tech. Information Center, MSH74, 555 Technology Sq., Cambridge, MA 02139; *Treas.* Muriel B. Regan, Gossage Regan Assocs., 15 W. 44 St., New York, NY 10036; *Past Pres.* H. Robert

Malinowsky, Univ. of Illinois-Chicago Lib., Box 8198, Chicago, IL 60680.

Directors

Lou B. Parris (1984–1987), Exxon Products Research Co., Box 2189, Houston TX 77001; Laura J. Rainey (1984–1987), Rockwell International, Rocketdyne Div., 6633 Canoga Ave., Canoga Park, CA 91304; Jane I. Dysart (1985–1988), Royal Bank of Canada, Info. Resources, Royal Bank Plaza, Toronto, Ont. M5J 2J5, Canada; Edwina H. Pancake (1985–1988), Univ. of Virginia, Science & Engineering Lib., Clark Hall, Charlottesville, VA 22903; Catherine Scott (1986–1989), Museum Reference Center, A & I 2235, Smithsonian Institution, Washington, DC 20560; Judith J. Field (1986–1989), Minnesota Reference Lib., 645 State Office Bldg., St. Paul, MN 45155.

Publications

Special Libraries (q.) and *SpeciaList* (mo.). Cannot be ordered separately ($48 for both; add $5 for postage outside the U.S. including Canada). *Ed.* Elaine Hill.

Committee Chairpersons

Association Office Operations. Frank H. Spaulding, AT&T Bell Laboratories, Lib. Operations Rm. 3D201-A, Holmdel, NJ 07733.

Awards. Vivian J. Arterbery, Rand Corp. Lib., 1700 Main St., Santa Monica, CA 90406.

Bylaws. Barbara Sanduleak, American Society of Metals, Info. Service, Metals

Info., Metals Park, OH 44073.

Cataloging. Dorothy McGarry, Univ. of California–Los Angeles, Physical Sciences/Technology, 8251 Boelter Hall, Los Angeles, CA 90024.

Committee on Committees. Janet Rigney, Council Foreign Relations, 58 E. 68 St., New York, NY 10021.

Conference Program. Susan J. Shepherd, Merck & Co., Inc., Kelco Div., 8355 Aero Dr., San Diego, CA 92123.

Consultation Services. Mary Bonhomme, Cabot Corp., Info. Communication, 1020 W. Park Ave., Kokomo, IN 46901.

Copyright Law Implementation. Laura N. Gasaway, Univ. of North Carolina Law Lib., Van Hecke-Wettach Bldg., 064-A, Chapel Hill, NC 27514.

Finance. Muriel B. Regan, Gossage Regan Assocs., 15 W. 44 St., New York, NY 10036.

Government Relations. Catherine A. Jones. U.S. Lib. of Congress, Congressional Resource Service, Washington, DC 20540.

Long-Range Planning. Jane Dysart, Royal Bank of Canada, Info. Resources, Royal Bank Plaza, Toronto, Ont., M5J 2J5, Canada.

Networking. Bette Dillehay, A. H. Robbins Co. Lib., 1407 Cummings Dr., Richmond, VA 22320.

Nominating. David E. King, Libn., Standard Education Corp., 200 W. Monroe St., Chicago, IL 60606.

Positive Action Program for Minority Groups. Marlene H. Tebo, Univ. of California–Davis, Physical Science Lib., Davis, CA 95616.

Professional Development. Co-Chairs.

Joseph A. Canose, AT&T Bell Laboratories, Library Network, Crawfords Corner Rd., Holmdel, NJ 07733; William H. Fisher, Univ. of California, Los Angeles, Grad. School of Lib. and Info. Science, Los Angeles, CA 90024.

Public Relations. N. Bernard Basch, Turner Subscription Agency, 116 E. 16 St., New York, NY 10003.

Publications. Malcolm C. Hamilton, Harvard Univ., John F. Kennedy School of Government, 79 John F. Kennedy St., Cambridge, MA 02138.

Publisher Relations. Mary D. Burchill, Univ. of Kansas, School Law/Lib., Green Hall, Lawrence, KS 66045.

SLA Scholarship. Eleanor A. Maclean, McGill Univ., Blacker Wood Lib. of Zoology and Ornithology, 3459 McTavish St., Montreal, Que. H3A 1Y1, Canada.

Standards. Diane D. Worden, Upjohn Co., 7284-126-8, 301 Henrietta St., Kalamazoo, MI 49001.

Statistics. William H. Fisher, Univ. of California–Los Angeles, Grad. School of Info. Science, Los Angeles, CA 90024.

Student Relations Officer. Ollye G. Davis, Clark College, South Center Student/Public Policy, 240 Brawley Dr., Atlanta, GA 30314.

Tellers. Ellen Newman Cook, U.S. Dept. of Interior, Information Technology Center, 18th & C Sts. N.W., Washington, DC 20240.

H. W. Wilson Company Award. Linda C. Smith, Univ. of Illinois, GSLIS/410 David Kinley Hall, 1407 W. Gregory, Urbana, IL 61801.

Theatre Library Association

Secretary-Treasurer, Richard M. Buck
111 Amsterdam Ave., New York, NY 10023

Object

"To further the interests of collecting, preserving, and using theatre, cinema, and performing arts materials in libraries, museums, and private collections." Founded 1937. Memb. 500. Dues (Indiv.) $20; (Inst.) $25. Year. Jan. 1–Dec. 31, 1987).

Officers (1986–1987)

Pres. Mary Ann Jensen, Curator, William Seymour Theatre Collection, Princeton Univ. Lib., Princeton, NJ 08544; *V.P.* Martha Mahard, Asst. Curator, Harvard Theatre Collection, Cambridge, MA 02138; *Secy.-Treas.* Richard M. Buck, Asst. to the Chief, Performing Arts Research Center, The New York Public Lib. at Lincoln Center, 111 Amsterdam Ave., New York, NY 10023; *Rec. Secy.* Lois E. McDonald, Assoc. Curator, The Eugene O'Neill Theatre Center, 305 Great Neck Rd., Waterford, CT 06385.

(Address correspondence, except *Broadside* and *PAR*, to the secretary-treasurer. Address *Broadside* correspondence to Alan J. Pally, General Lib. and Museum of the Performing Arts, New York Public Lib. at Lincoln Center, 111 Amsterdam Ave., New York, NY 10023.

Address *PAR* correspondence to Barbara N. C. Stratyner, 265 Riverside Dr., New York, NY 10025.)

Executive Board

Officers; Elizabeth Burdick; Maryann Chach; Geraldine Duclow; John W. Frick; Brigitte Kueppers; Audree Malkin; James Poteat; Louis Rachow; Anne G. Schlosser; Don Stowell, Jr.; Richard Wall; Wendy Warnken; *Ex officio.* Barbara Naomi Cohen Stratyner; Alan J. Pally; *Honorary.* Marguerite McAneny; Paul Myers.

Publications

Broadside (q.; memb.)
Performing Arts Resources (ann.; memb.).

Committee Chairpersons

Awards. Martha Mahard.
Nominations. Elizabeth Burdick.
Program and Special Events. Richard M. Buck.
Publications. Martha Mahard, pro. tem.

Universal Serials and Book Exchange (USBE), Inc.

Managing Director, Claude L. Hooker
3335 V St. N.E., Washington, DC 20018
202-636-8723

Object

"To promote the distribution and interchange of books, periodicals, and other scholarly materials among libraries and other educational and scientific institutions of the United States and between them and libraries and institutions of other countries." Organized 1948. Year. Jan. 1–Dec. 31.

Membership

Membership in USBE is open to any library that serves a constituency and is an institution or part of an institution or organization. The USBE corporation includes a representative from each member library.

Board of Directors

Pres. Martin Runkle, Dir., Univ. of Chicago Lib., 1100 E. 57 St., Chicago, IL 60637; *V.P./Pres.-Elect.* Pat Molholt, Assoc. Dir. of Libs, Rennselaer Polytechnic Institute, Troy, NY 12180-3590; *Treas.* Agnes M. Griffen, Dir., Dept. of Public Libs., Montgomery County Government, Rockville, MD 20850; *Past Pres.* Murray S. Martin, Libn., Tufts Univ., Medford, MA 02155.

Members of the Board

Peter H. Bridge, Chief, Exchange & Gift Div., Library of Congress, Washington, DC 20540; Joyce D. Gartrell, Head, Serials Cataloging Dept., Columbia Univ. Libs., New York, NY 10027; Charlotta Hensley, Asst. Dir. for Technical Services, Univ. of Colorado Libs., Boulder, CO 80309; Sharon A. Hogan, Dir. of Libs., Louisiana State Univ., Baton Rouge, LA 70803-3300; Ellen Hoffman, Dir. of Libs., York Univ., 4700 Keele St., Downsview, Ont. M3J 2R2, Canada; Patricia A. Smith, Head, Acquisitions Dept., Colorado State Univ. Libs., Ft. Collins, CO 80523.

Publications

7,000 Most Available Titles. Microfiche listing of core serials collection.
USBE/NEWS. Monthly catalog and newsletter.
Subjects catalogs (Irreg.).

State, Provincial, and Regional Library Associations

The associations in this section are organized under three headings: United States, Canada, and Regional associations. Both the United States and Canada are represented under Regional associations. Unless otherwise specified, correspondence is to be addressed to the secretary or executive secretary in the entry.

United States

Alabama

Memb. 1,403. Founded 1904. Term of Office. Apr. 1986–Apr. 1987. Publication. *The Alabama Librarian* (9 per year). *Ed.* Betty Bryce, 1216 Indian Hill Circle, Tuscaloosa 35406.

Pres. Betty Clark, Birmingham Public Lib., 2100 Park Place, Birmingham 35203. Tel. 205-226-3656; *Pres.-Elect.* Pauline Williams, Univ. of Montevallo, Carmichael Lib., Sta. 102, Montevallo 35115. Tel. 205-665-6102; *2nd V.P.* Mary Maud McCain, 2020 Melinda Dr., Birmingham 35214. Tel. 205-841-3642; *Secy.* Kathy Vogel, 122 Plateau Rd., Montevallo 35115. Tel. 205-991-6600; *Treas.* Nancy Donahoo, Box 690, Columbiana 35051; *Past Pres.* Betty Ruth Goodwyn, Rte. 1 Box 405U, Helena 35080. Tel. 205-967-2090; *ALA Chapter Councillor.* Joan

Atkinson, Grad. School of Lib. Service, Univ. of Alabama, Box 6242, University 35486.

Address correspondence to Nancy Donahoo, Box 690, Columbiana 35051.

Alaska

Memb. 432. Term of Office. Mar. 1986–Mar. 1987. Publication. *Sourdough* (ann.).

Pres. Diana Brenner, Anchorage Museum of History and Art, 121 W. Seventh Ave., Anchorage 99501. Tel. 907-264-4326; *Secy.* Amy Waite, Fairbanks North Star Borough Public Libs., 1215 Cowles St., Fairbanks 99701. Tel. 907-452-5177; *Treas.* Rita Dursi, Arctic Environmental Information and Data Center, 707 A St., Anchorage 99501. Tel. 907-279-4523.

Address correspondence to the association c/o President Diane Brenner, 517 W. 12 Ave., Anchorage 99501.

Arizona

Memb. 989. Term of Office. Nov. 1986–Oct. 1987. Publication. *ASLA Newsletter* (mo.). *Ed.* Donald E. Riggs, Lib., Arizona State Univ. Libs., Tempe 85287.

Pres. Karen Whitney, Agua Fria H.S. 530 E. Riley Dr., Avondale 85323. Tel. 602-932-4250; *V.P./Pres.-Elect.* Linda Saferite, Scottsdale Public Lib., 3839 Civic Centre Plaza, Scottsdale 85251. Tel. 602-994-2454; *Secy.* Eleanor Ferrall, Hayden Lib., Arizona State Univ., Tempe 85285. Tel. 602-965-3258. *Treas.* Michael Ryan, Mesa Public Lib., 64 E. First St., Mesa 85201.

Address correspondence to the president.

Arkansas

Memb. 975. Term of Office. Sept. 1986–Sept. 1987. Publications. *Arkansas Libraries* (q.); *ALA Newsletter* (irreg.).

Pres. Leo Clougherty, 2204 N. Arthur, Little Rock 72207. Tel. 501-661-5981; *Exec. Dir.* Frank Ivey, Arkansas Lib. Assn., Penthouse, Boyle Bldg., 103 W. Capitol, Little Rock 72201.

Address correspondence to the executive director.

California

Memb. (Indiv.) 3,050; (Inst.) 178; (Business) 70. Term of Office. Jan. 1–Dec. 31, 1987. Publication. *The CLA Newsletter* (mo.).

Pres. John K. Kallenberg, Fresno County Lib.; *V.P./Pres.-Elect.* Halbert Watson, Pomona Public Lib.; *Past Pres.* Holly Millard, Metropolitan Cooperative Lib. System, Altadena; *Treas.* Ernest Siegel, Contra Costa County Lib., Pleasant Hill; *ALA Chapter Councillors.* Gilbert W. McNamee, San Francisco (to July 1987); and Betty J. Blackman, California State Univ., Dominguez Hills (to July 1991).

Colorado

Term of Office. Oct. 1986–Oct. 1987. Publication. *Colorado Libraries* (q.). *Ed.* Ingrid Schierling, Box 7507, Colorado Springs 80933.

Pres. Lucy Schweers, Michener Lib., Univ. of Northern Colorado, Greeley 80639; *Pres.-Elect.* William A. (Bill) Murray, Media Services, Aurora Public Schools, 875 Peoria St., Aurora 80011; *Exec. Dir.* Christine Hamilton-Pennell, Colorado Lib. Assn., Box 9365, Denver 80209. Tel. 303-722-3540; *Past Pres.* Brenda Hawley, Pikes Peak Lib. Dist., Box 1579, Colorado Springs 80901.

Address correspondence to the executive director.

Connecticut

Memb. 800. Term of Office. July 1, 1986–June 30, 1987. Publication. *Con-*

necticut Libraries (11 per year). *Ed.* David Kapp, 4 Llynwood Dr., Bolton 06040.

Pres. Elizabeth Kirkpatrick, Wethersfield Public Lib., 515 Silas Deane Hwy., Wethersfield 06109. Tel. 203-563-5348; *V.P./Pres.-Elect.* Susan Bullock, Meriden Public Lib., 105 Miller St., Meriden 06450. Tel. 203-238-2344; *Treas.* Mary Balmer, 54 Stone Pond Dr., Tolland 06084. Tel. 203-872-0267; *Exec. Secy.* Jeanne Simpson, Connecticut Lib. Assn., State Lib., 231 Capitol Ave., Hartford 06106. Tel. 203-278-6685.

Delaware

Memb. (Indiv.) 294; (Inst.) 12. Term of Office. Apr. 1986–Apr. 1987. Publication. *DLA Bulletin* (3 per year).

Pres. Susan Jamison, Corbit-Calloway Memorial Lib., Second & High Sts., Odessa 19730. Tel. 302-378-8838; *V.P./Pres.-Elect.* Mark Titus, Concord Pike Lib., 3406 Concord Pike, Wilmington 19803; *Secy.* Margaret Welshmer, Univ. of Delaware Libs., Newark 19717-5267; *Treas.* Lisa Beamer, Newark Free Lib., Newark 19711; *Past. Pres.* Jacqueline Paul, Delaware Law School, Widener Univ., Wilmington 19803. Tel. 302-478-5280.

Address correspondence to the Delaware Lib. Assn., Box 1843, Wilmington 19899.

District of Columbia

Memb. 1,000. Term of Office. May 1986–Apr. 1987. Publication. *INTERCOM* (mo.). *Ed.* Mary Feldman.

Pres. Jacque-Lynne Schulman, 5964 Ranleigh Manor Dr., McLean, VA 22101. Tel. 301-496-5511; *Pres.-Elect.* Molly Raphael, 3002 Ordway St. N.W., Washington, DC 20008. Tel. 202-244-1499; *Treas.* Andrew Lisowski, 7813 Wintercress Lane, Springfield, VA 22152. Tel. 703-866-9762; *Secy.* Janine Reid, The Faxon

Co., 450 Spring Park Place, Suite 100, Herndon, VA 22070. Tel. 703-471-5880.

Florida

Memb. (Indiv.) 1,000; (In-state Inst.) 80; (Out-of-state Inst.) 90. Term of Office. July 1, 1986–June 30, 1987.

Pres. Lydia M. Acosta, Univ. of Tampa, 401 W. Kennedy Blvd., Tampa 33606; *V.P./Pres.-Elect.* John D. Hales, Jr., Suwanne River Regional Lib., 207 Pine Ave., Live Oak 32060; *Secy.* Julia A. Woods, Florida International Univ., 11243 N. Kendall, Miami 33176; *Treas.* Thomas L. Reitz, Seminole Community College Lib., 1333 Gunnison Ave., Orlando 33204.

Address correspondence to Marjorie Stealey, executive secretary, Florida Lib. Assn., 1133 W. Morse Blvd., Suite 201, Winter Park 32789.

Georgia

Memb. 922. Term of Office. Oct. 1985–Oct. 1987. Publication. *Georgia Librarian.* *Ed.* James Dorsey, Emanuel Jr. College, Swainsboro 30401.

Pres. Wanda J. Calhoun, Augusta Regional Lib., 902 Greene St., Augusta 30902. Tel. 404-724-1871; *1st V.P./Pres.-Elect.* Glenda Anderson, Research Lib., City of Savannah, Box 1027, City Hall, Rm. 402, Savannah 31402; *2nd V.P.* Ralph E. Russell, Univ. Libn., Georgia State Univ., 100 Decatur St., Atlanta, 30303-3081; *Treas.* Gerald C. Becham, Troup-Harris-Coweta Regional Lib., 500 Broome St., LaGrange 30240; *Secy.* Julius Ariail, Georgia Southern College Lib., Box 8074, Statesboro 30460; *Exec. Secy.* Ann W. Morton, Box 833, Tucker 30084. Tel. 404-934-7118.

Address correspondence to the president.

Hawaii

Memb. 425. Term of Office. Mar. 1986–Mar. 1987. Publications. *Hawaii Library Association Journal* (ann.); *Hawaii Library Association Newsletter* (6 per year); *HLA Membership Directory* (ann.); *Directory of Libraries and Information Sources in Hawaii and the Pacific Islands* (irreg.).

Pres. DeEtta Wilson, Head Libn., Windward Community College, 45-720 Keaahala Rd., Kaneohe 96744. Tel. 808-235-7435; *V.P.* Rex Frandsen, Archivist, B.Y.U.–Hawaii, Box 1836, B.Y.U., Hawaii, Laie 96762; *Secy.* Sally Morgan, Head Libn., Kailua Public Lib., 239 Kuulei Rd., Kailua 96734; *Treas.* Raymond Fujii, Regional Libn., Kaneohe Regional Lib., 45-202 Hikiwale St., Kaneohe 96744.

Address correspondence to the president.

Idaho

Memb. (Indiv.) 446; (Inst.) 24. Term of Office. Oct. 4, 1986–Oct. 3, 1987. Publication. *The Idaho Librarian* (q.). *Ed.* Gregg Sapp.

Pres. Adrien Taylor, Boise State Univ. Lib., 1910 University Dr., Boise 83725. Tel. 208-385-1621; *V.P./Pres.-Elect.* Jerry Glenn, 594 Gemini, Rexburg 83440. Tel. 208-356-6054; *Secy.* Sandra Glover, Boise Public Lib., 715 S. Capitol Blvd., Boise 83702. Tel. 208-384-4078.

Illinois

Memb. 4,000. Term of Office. Jan. 1987–Jan. 1988. Publication. *ILA Reporter* (6 per year).

Pres. Carla Funk, American Medical Assn., 535 N. Dearborn St., Chicago 60610-4377. Tel. 312-645-4863; *V.P./Pres.-Elect.* Marlene Deuel, Poplar Creek Public Lib. Dist., 1405 S. Park Blvd.,

Streamwood 60103. Tel. 312-837-6800; *Treas.* Lois Pausch, Univ. of Illinois–Urbana/Champaign, Math Lib., Altgeld Hall, 1409 W. Green St., Urbana 61801. Tel. 217-244-0143; *Exec. Dir.* Willine C. Mahoney.

Address correspondence to Willine C. Mahoney, Executive Director, ILA, 425 N. Michigan Ave., Suite 1304, Chicago 60611. Tel. 312-644-1896.

Indiana

Memb. (Indiv.) 1,130; (Inst.) 231. Term of Office. May 1986–May 1987. Publication. *Focus on Indiana Libraries* (10 per year). *Ed.* Beth Steele, ILA/ILTA Exec. Office, 310 N. Alabama, Suite A, Indianapolis 46204; *Indiana Libraries* (q.). *Ed.* Danny Callison, School of Lib. and Info. Science, Indiana Univ., Bloomington 47401. Tel. 812-335-5113.

Pres. Jean Gnat, IUPUI Science Engineering Lib., Box 647, Indianapolis 46223. Tel. 317-274-0493; *V.P.* Patricia Schaeffer, Muncie Public Lib., 405 S. Tara Lane, Muncie 47304; *Secy.* Kathy Ann Crouse, Tipton County Public Lib., 127 E. Madison, Tipton 46072; *Treas.* Ellie Puliknda, Kokomo Public Lib., 220 N. Union, Kokomo 46901. Tel. 317-457-3242; *Exec. Dir.* Joyce M. Martello, 310 Alabama, Suite A, Indianapolis 46204. Tel. 317-636-6613.

Iowa

Memb. 1,642. Term of Office. Jan. 1987–Jan. 1988. Publication. *The Catalyst* (bi-mo.). *Ed.* Naomi Stovall, Iowa Lib. Assn., 823 Insurance Exchange Bldg., Des Moines 50309. Tel. 515-243-2172.

Pres. Lorna Truck, Public Lib. of Des Moines, Des Moines 50309. Tel. 515-243-4102.

Address correspondence to Iowa Lib. Assn.

Kansas

Memb. 1,000. Term of Office. July 1, 1986–June 30, 1987. Publications. *KLA Newsletter* (q.); *KLA Membership Directory* (ann.).

Pres. Robert Grover, School of Lib. and Info. Management, Emporia State Univ., Emporia 66801. Tel. 316-343-1200 Ext. 203; *Exec. Secy.* Leroy Gattin, SCKLS, 901 N. Main, Hutchinson 67501. Tel. 363-663-2501; *V.P./Pres.-Elect.* Max Leek, Dorothy Bramlage Public Lib., Junction City 66441; *Secy.* Paul J. Hawkins, SCKLS, 901 N. Main, Hutchinson 67501; *Treas.* Marcella Ratzlaff, Hutchinson Public Lib., Hutchinson 67501.

Address correspondence to the president or executive secretary.

Kentucky

Memb. 1,146. Term of Office. Oct. 1986–Oct. 1987. Publication. *Kentucky Libraries* (q.).

Pres. Patty B. Grider, Hart County Public Lib., Box 337, E. Third St., Munfordville 42765. Tel. 502-524-1953; *V.P./Pres.-Elect.* Linda Perkins, Kenwood Elem., 7420 Justan, Louisville 40214. Tel 502-454-8283; *Secy.* Jean Almand, Science Lib., Western Kentucky Univ., Bowling Green 42101. Tel. 502-745-6264. *Exec. Secy.* Vacant.

Address correspondence to the association, Box 8168, Paducah 42002-8168. Tel. 502-443-7365, Ext. 302.

Louisiana

Memb. (Indiv.) 1,313; (Inst.) 80. Term of Office. July 1986–June 1987. Publication. *LLA Bulletin* (q.).

Pres. Sue Hill, 6780 Nellie Ave., Baton Rouge 70805. Tel. 504-647-9499; 504-355-2713; *1st V.P.* Julia Avant, Rte. 2, Box 112-A, Downsville 71234. Tel. 318-255-1920; *2nd V.P.* Richard Reid, 1414 Louisi-

ana Ave., Lake Charles 70601. Tel. 318-437-5715; *Secy.* Bobbie Scull, 1089 Sinclair Dr., Baton Rouge 70815. Tel. 504-388-4400. *Parliamentarian.* Ian Claiborne, Box 461, New Roads 70760. Tel. 504-343-9758. *Exec. Dir.* Sharilynn Aucoin, Box 131, Baton Rouge 70821. Tel. 504-342-4928.

Address correspondence to executive director.

Maine

Memb. 722. Term of Office. (*Pres., V.P.*) Spring 1986–Spring 1988. Publications. *Downeast Libraries* (4 per year); *Maine Memo* (mo.).

Pres. Edna Mae Bayliss, Box 282, Readfield 04355; *V.P.* Reta Schreiber, Bangor Public Lib., 145 Harlow St., Bangor 04401; *Secy.* Rita P. Bouchard, State Law and Legislative Lib., State House, Sta. 43, Augusta 04333; *Treas.* Nann Hilyard, Auburn Public Lib., Auburn 04210.

Address correspondence to Maine Lib. Assn., c/o Maine Municipal Assn., Local Government Center, Community Dr., Augusta 04330. Tel. 207-623-8429.

Maryland

Memb. 1,100. Term of Office. July 1, 1986–June 30, 1987. Publication. *The CRAB.*

Pres. Suzanne Hill, Catonsville Community College, Learning Resource Center, 800 S. Rolling Rd., Catonsville 21228. Tel. 301-455-4585; *1st V.P.* Norma Hill, Howard County Public Lib., 10375 Little Patuxent Pkwy., Columbia 21044. Tel. 301-997-8000; *Secy.* Marilyn Borgendale, U/MD Health Sciences Lib., 111 S. Greene St., Baltimore 21201; *Treas.* John G. Ray, III, Loyola/Notre Dame Lib., 200 Winston Ave., Baltimore 21212; *Exec. Secy.* Robert Greenfield, 115 W. Franklin St., Baltimore 21201. Tel. 301-685-5760.

Address correspondence to the Maryland Lib. Assn., 115 W. Franklin St., Baltimore 21201.

Massachusetts

Memb. (Indiv.) 800; (Inst.) 100. Term of Office. July 1985–June 1987. Publications. *Bay State Librarian* (2 per year); *Bay State Letter* (8 per year).

Pres. Susan Flannery, Reading Public Lib., 64 Middlesex Ave., Reading 01867; *V.P.* Linda Wright, Bridgewater Public Lib., Bridgewater 02324; *Secy.* Susan Theriault, Leominster Public Lib., 30 West St., Leominster 01453; *Treas.* Ann Haddad, Falmouth Public Lib., Falmouth 02540; *Past. Pres.* Constance Clancy, South Hadley Lib. System, South Hadley 01075; *Exec. Secy.* Paula M. Bozoian, Massachusetts Lib. Assn., Box 556, Wakefield 01880. Tel. 617-438-0779.

Michigan

Memb. (Indiv.) 2,200; (Inst.) 150. Term of Office. Oct. 1987–Oct. 1988. Publication. *Michigan Librarian Newsletter* (10 per year).

Pres. Margaret Auer, Dir. of Libs., Univ. of Detroit, Detroit 48221; *Treas.* Jule Fosbender, Adrian Public Lib., 141-43 E. Maumee St., Adrian 49221; *Exec. Dir.* Marianne Gessner, Michigan Lib. Assn., 415 W. Kalamazoo, Lansing 48933. Tel. 517-487-6868.

Address correspondence to the executive director.

Minnesota

Memb. 900. Term of Office. (*Pres. & V.P.*) Jan. 1, 1987–Dec. 31, 1987; (*Secy.*) Jan. 1, 1985–Dec. 31, 1986; (*Treas.*) Jan. 1, 1986–Dec. 31, 1987. Publication. *MLA Newsletter* (10 per year).

Pres. Janice Feye-Stukas, Specialist/Consultant, Office of Lib. Development and Services, St. Paul; *V.P./Pres.-Elect.* Mona Carmack, Dir., Great River Regional Lib., St. Cloud 56301; *ALA Chapter Councillor.* Laura Landers, Deputy Dir., Hennepin County Lib., 12601 Ridgedale Dr., Minnetonka 55343; *Secy.* Anita Anker, MINITEX, 30 Wilson Lib., Univ. of Minnesota, Minneapolis, 55455; *Treas.* Edward Swanson, 1065 Portland Ave., St. Paul 55104.

Address correspondence to Pamela Towne, Administrative Secy., Minnesota Lib. Assn., North Regional Lib., Minneapolis Public Lib., 1315 Lowry Ave. N., Minneapolis 55411. Tel. 612-521-1735.

Mississippi

Memb. 1,200. Term of Office. Jan. 1987–Dec. 1987. Publication. *Mississippi Libraries* (q.).

Pres. Pamela Lambert, Drawer L, Richton 39476; *V.P./Pres.-Elect.* Jane Bryan, 1823 Presley, #484, Pascagoula 39567; *Secy.* Harriet Gray, 2 Briar Lane, Vicksburg 39180; *Treas.* JoEllen Ostendorf, 5036 Stanton Dr., Jackson 39211; *Exec. Secy.* Bernice L. Bell, MLA Office, Box 470, Clinton 39056.

Missouri

Memb. 1,200. Term of Office. Oct. 1986–Sept. 1987. Publication. *MO INFO* (6 per year).

Pres. Valerie Darst, 626 Taylor St., Moberly 65270. Tel. 816-263-5473; *V.P./Pres.-Elect.* Kent Oliver, 100 W. Broadway, Columbia 65203. Tel. 314-443-3161; *Secy.* Jan Sanders, 2020 W. Murray, Springfield 65807. Tel. 417-881-2840; *Treas.* Ken Rohrbach, 410 W. Springfield, Union 63084. Tel. 314-583-3224.

Address correspondence to Jean Ann McCartney, Executive Coordinator, Missouri Library Assn., Parkade Plaza, Suite 9, Columbia MO 65203.

Montana

Memb. 400. Term of Office. June 1, 1985–May 31, 1987. Publication. *Library Focus, the Newsletter of the Montana Library Association* (4–6 per year).

Pres. Lawrence Maxwell, 1920 Monroe, Butte 59701; *V.P./Pres.-Elect.* Bunny Morrison, MLA Box 954, Bozeman 59711; *Secy.* Judith Meadows, State Law Lib. of Montana, Justice Bldg., 215 N. Sanders, Helena 59620-3004.

Address correspondence to MLA, Box 954, Bozeman 59711.

Nebraska

Memb. 1,000. Term of Office. Oct. 1986–Oct. 1987. *NLA Quarterly.*

Pres. Judy Johnson, 218 S. 29 St., Lincoln 68510; *V.P.* Dee Yost, 724 E. Seventh St., Hastings 68901; *Past. Pres.* Thomas Boyle, 2050 Hazel St., Fremont 68025; *Secy.* Elizabeth Keefe, 1707 Childs Rd., Bellevue 68005; *Treas.* Rod Wagner, NLC, 1420 P St., Lincoln 68508; *Exec. Secy.* Ray Means, 678 Parkwood Lane, Omaha 68132. Tel. 402-556-0903 (h), 402-280-2217 (w).

Address correspondence to the executive secretary.

Nevada

Memb. 300. Term of Office. Jan. 1, 1987–Dec. 31, 1987. Publication. *Highroller* (4 per year).

Pres. Carol Madsen, Elko County Lib., 720 Court St., Elko 89801. Tel. 702-738-3066; *Pres.-Elect.* Danna Sturm, Douglas County Lib., Box 337, Minden 89423. Tel. 702-782-9841. *Exec. Secy.* Susan Conway, Serials Dept., Univ. of Nevada–Reno, Reno 89557. Tel. 702-784-6569; *Treas.* Joyce Cox, Reno Business College, 140 Washington St., Reno 89503. Tel. 702-323-4145; *Past Pres.* Anne Hawkins, Washoe County Lib., Box 2151, Reno 89505. Tel. 702-785-4012.

Address correspondence to the executive secretary.

New Hampshire

Memb. 420. Term of Office. June 1986–June 1987. Publication. *NHLA Newsletter* (bi-mo.).

Pres. Lydia M. Torr, Meredith Public Lib., Box 808, Meredith 03253; Tel. 603-279-4303; *V.P./Pres.-Elect.* Robert Fitzpatrick, Lamson Lib., Plymouth State College, Plymouth 03264; *Secy.* Deborah Wilcox, New Hampshire College, 2500 N. River Rd., Manchester 03104; *Treas.* Ellen Hardsog, Derry Public Lib., Derry 03038.

Address correspondence to the president.

New Jersey

Memb. 1,700. Term of Office. May–Apr. Publications. *New Jersey Libraries* (q.); *New Jersey Libraries Newsletter.* (mo.).

Pres. Marc Eisen, East Orange Public Lib., 21 S. Arlington Ave., East Orange 07018; *V.P./Pres.-Elect.* Thomas Alrutz, Newark Public Lib., Box 630, Newark 07102; *Past Pres.* Penny Brome, Dir., Cranford Public Lib., 224 Walnut Ave., Cranford 07016; *Treas.* Sara Eggers, Old Bridge Public Lib., Old Bridge 08857; *Exec. Dir.* Abigail Studdiford, New Jersey Lib. Assn., 116 W. State St., Trenton 08608. Tel. 609-394-8032.

Address correspondence to the executive director, NJLA Office, Trenton 08608. Tel. 609-394-8032.

New Mexico

Memb. 658. Term of Office. Apr. 1986–Apr. 1987. Publication. *New Mexico Library Association Newsletter.* Ed. Daryl Black, 3258 Calle de Molina, Santa Fe 87501.

Pres. Cherrill M. Whitlow, 2702 Morrow Rd. N.E., Albuquerque 87106; *1st*

V.P. Harris M. Richard, San Juan Community College, 4601 College Blvd., Farmington 87401; *2nd V.P.* Karen Watkins, New Mexico State Lib., 325 Don Gaspar, Santa Fe 87503; *Secy.* Betty Reynolds, 704 Neel Ave. N.W., Socorro 87801; *Treas.* Denis Roark, 2206 Mills Dr., Roswell 88201.

New York

Memb. 3,200. Term of Office. Oct 1986–Oct. 1987. Publication. *NYLA Bulletin* (10 per year). *Ed.* Richard Johnson.

Pres. Helen Flowers, Bay Shore H.S., 155 Third Ave., Bay Shore 11706; *1st V.P.* Julie Cummings, Monroe County Lib. System, 115 South Ave., Rochester 14604; *2nd V.P.* Richard Panz, Finger Lakes Lib. System, 314 N. Cayuga St., Ithaca 14850; *Exec. Dir.* Nancy W. Lian, CAE, New York Lib. Assn., 15 Park Row, Suite 434, New York 10038. Tel. 212-227-8032.

Address correspondence to the executive director.

North Carolina

Memb. 2,011. Term of Office. Oct. 1985–Oct. 1987. Publication. *North Carolina Libraries* (q.). *Ed.* Frances Bradburn, Central Regional Education Center, Box 549, Knightdale 27545.

Pres. Pauline F. Myrick, Box 307, Carthage 28327. Tel. 919-947-2976; *1st. V.P./Pres.-Elect.* Patsy Hansel, Asst. Dir., Cumberland County Public Lib., Box 1720, Fayetteville 28302. Tel. 919-483-8600; *2nd V.P.* Rose Simon, Dir. of Libs., Salem College, Winston-Salem 27108. Tel. 919-721-2649; *Secy.* Dorothy W. Campbell, Asst. Professor, School of Lib. and Info. Science, North Carolina Central Univ., 905 Jerome Rd., Durham 27713; *Treas.* Nancy Clark Fogarty, Jackson Lib., Univ. of North Carolina, Greensboro 27412; *Dir.* Arial Stephens, Thornton Lib., Box 339, Oxford 27565; *Dir.*

Benjamin Speller, Jr., Dean, School of Lib. and Info. Science, North Carolina Central Univ., Durham 27707.

North Dakota

Memb. (Indiv.) 469; (Inst.) 46. Term of Office. Oct. 1986–Oct. 1987. Publication. *The Good Stuff* (q.).

Pres. Neil V. Price, Dept. of Lib. Science, Box 8174, UND Sta., Grand Forks 58202. Tel. 701-777-3003; *V.P./Pres.-Elect.* Betty Gard, Chester Fritz Lib., Univ. of North Dakota, Grand Forks 58202; *Secy.* Lorraine Ettl, Lib. of Health Science, Univ. of North Dakota, Grand Forks 58202; *Treas.* Mary Jane Chaussee, Veterans Memorial Public Lib., 520 Ave. A East, Bismarck 58501.

Ohio

Memb. (Indiv.) 2,168; (Inst.) 270. Term of Office. Oct. 1986–Oct. 1987. Publications. *Ohio Library Association Bulletin* (3 per year); *Ohio Libraries; Newsletter of the Ohio Library Association* (9 per year).

Pres. Steven Hawk, Akron Summit County Public Lib., 55 S. Main St., Akron 44326. Tel. 216-762-7621; *V.P./Pres.-Elect.* Kathy East, Public Lib. of Columbus and Franklin County, 28 S. Hamilton Rd., Columbus 43213. Tel. 614-864-8050. *Secy.* Susan K. Barrick, Grove City Public Lib., Grove City 43123.

Oklahoma

Memb. (Indiv.) 1,001; (Inst.) 51. Term of Office. July 1, 1986–June 30, 1987. Publication. *Oklahoma Librarian* (bi-mo.).

Pres. Donna Skvarla, Oklahoma Dept. of Libs., 200 N.E. 18, Oklahoma City 73105; *V.P./Pres.-Elect.* Susan McVey, Oklahoma Dept. of Libs., 300 N.E. 18, Oklahoma City 73105; *Secy.* Patricia Zachary, 402 W. Nebraska, Walters 73572; *Treas.* Stephen Skidmore, Ponca City

Lib., 515 E. Grand, Ponca City 74601; *Exec. Secy.* Kay Boies, 300 Hardy Dr., Edmond 73013. Tel. 405-348-0506.

Oregon

Memb. (Indiv.) 600; (Inst.) 65. Term of Office. Apr. 1986–Apr. 1987. Publication. *Oregon Library Association News* (mo.). *Ed.* Gary Sharp, North Bend Public Lib., 1925 McPherson, North Bend 97459.

Pres. June. M. Knudson, Hood River County Lib., 502 State St., Hood River 97031. Tel. 503-386-2535; *V.P./Pres.-Elect.* Carolyn Peake, 6 Adams Ct., Lake Oswego 97034. Tel. 503-636-7628; *Secy.* Michael K. Gaston, Siuslaw Public Lib., Box A, Florence 97439. Tel. 503-997-3132; *Treas.* Maureen Seaman, c/o Oregon Grad. Center, 19600 N.W. Von Neumann Dr., Beaverton 97006. Tel. 503-690-1060.

Pennsylvania

Memb. 1,700. Term of Office. Nov. 1986–Oct. 1987. Publication. *PLA Bulletin* (8 per year).

Pres. James Hecht, Hoyt Lib., 248 Wyoming Ave., Kingston 17804. Tel. 717-287-2013; *Exec. Dir.* Margaret D. Bauer, Pennsylvania Lib. Assn., 2941 N. Front St., Harrisburg 17110. Tel. 717-233-3113.

Address correspondence to the association, 2941 N. Front St., Harrisburg 17110.

Puerto Rico

Memb. 450. Term of Office. Apr. 1986–Apr. 1988. Publications. *Boletin* (s. ann.); *Cuadernos Bibliotecológicos* (irreg.); *Informa* (mo.); *Cuadernos Bibliográficos* (irreg.).

Pres. Sylvia M. de Olmos; *Pres.-Elect.* Digna Escalera.

Address correspondence to the Sociedad de Bibliotecarios de Puerto Rico, Apdo. 22989, UPR Sta., Rio Piedras 00931.

Rhode Island

Memb. 541. Term of Office. Nov. 1986–Nov. 1987. Publication. *Rhode Island Library Association Bulletin. Ed.* Linda Walton.

Pres. Jonathan S. Tryon, Univ. of Rhode Island Grad. School of Lib. and Info. Studies, Kingston 02881. Tel. 401-792-2878; *V.P./Pres.-Elect.* Catherine Mello Aldes, East Providence Public Lib., 41 Grove Ave., East Providence 02914. Tel. 401-434-1136; *Secy.* Marguerite E. Horn, Brown Univ., Rockefeller Lib., Box A, Providence 02912; *Treas.* Douglas A. Pearce, Warwick Public Lib., 600 Sandy Lane, Warwick 02886. Tel. 401-739-5440; *Memb.-at-Large.* Peter E. Bennett, Providence Public Lib., 150 Empire St., Providence 02905. Tel. 401-521-7722; *NELA Councillor.* Janet A. Levesque, Cumberland Public Lib., 1464 Diamond Hill Rd., Cumberland 02864. Tel. 401-333-2552; *ALA Councillor.* Carol DiPrete, Roger Williams College Lib., Old Ferry Rd., Bristol 02809; *Past Pres.* Roberta A. E. Cairns, East Providence Public Lib., 41 Grove Ave., East Providence 02914. Tel. 401-434-2719.

Address correspondence to the secretary.

St. Croix

Memb. 48. Publications. *SCLA Newsletter* (q.); *Studies in Virgin Islands Librarianship* (irreg.).

Pres. Wallace Williams, Florence A. Williams Public Lib., 49–50 King St., Christianstead, St. Croix 08820; *V.P.* (To be appointed); *Secy.* Liane Forbes; *Treas.* Sylvania Golphen.

South Carolina

Memb. 712. Term of Office. Oct. 1986–Oct. 1987. Publications. *The South Carolina Librarian* (s. ann.). *Ed.* Katina P. Strauch, College of Charleston, Charles-

ton 29424; *News and Views of South Carolina Library Association* (bi-mo.). *Ed.* Michael Freeman, Thomas Cooper Lib., Univ. of South Carolina, Columbia 29208.

Pres. Barbara Williams-Jenkins, South Carolina State College, Orangeburg 29117. Tel. 803-536-7045; *V.P./Pres.-Elect.* Suzanne Krebsbach, McNair Law Firm, Box 11390, Columbia 29211. Tel. 803-799-9800; *2nd V.P.* Daniel D. Koenig, Piedmont Technical College, Greenwood 29646. Tel. 803-223-8357; *Secy.* Dorothy Flood, Robert Scott Small Lib., College of Charleston, Charleston 29409. Tel. 803-792-8006; *Treas.* Dennis L. Bruce, Spartanburg County Lib., Box 2409, Spartanburg 29304-2409. Tel. 803-596-3507.

South Dakota

Memb. (Indiv.) 505; (Inst.) 62. Term of Office. Sept. 1986–Sept. 1987. Publication. *Bookmarks* (bi-mo.). *Ed.* Donna Fisher, 3811 Brookside Dr., Rapid City 57706.

Pres. Jim Dertien, Sioux Falls Public Lib., 201 N. Main Ave., Sioux Falls 57102. Tel. 605-339-7115; *V.P./Pres.-Elect.* Ellen Hall, Presentation College Lib., 1500 N. Main St., Aberdeen 57401; *Secy.* Beverly Birkeland, Box 55, Faith 57626; *Treas.* Jane Larson, Vermillion Public Lib., 18 Church St., Vermillion 57069; *ALA Councillor.* Sandra Norlin, Brookings Public Lib., 515 Third St., Brookings, 57006; *MPLA Rep.* Jean Diggins, Rapid City Public Lib., 610 Quincy St., Rapid City 57197.

Tennessee

Memb. 1,047. Term of Office. Apr. 1986–Apr. 1987. Publication. *Tennessee Librarian* (q.).

Pres. James Donald Craig, Univ. Libn., Andrew Todd Lib., Middle Tennessee State Univ. Murfreesboro 37132. Tel. 615-

898-2772; *V.P./Pres.-Elect.* Julia G. Boyd, Dir., Upper Cumberland Regional Lib., 208 E. Minnear St., Cookeville 38501. Tel. 615-526-4016; *Treas.* Thomas A. Aud, Dir., Jackson/Madison County Lib., 433 E. Lafayette, Jackson 38301. Tel. 901-423-0225; *Exec. Secy.* Betty Nance, Box 120085, Nashville 37212. Tel. 615-297-8316.

Address correspondence to the executive secretary.

Texas

Memb. (Indiv.) 4,400; (Inst.) 100. Term of Office. Apr. 1986–Apr. 1987. Publications. *Texas Library Journal* (q.); *TLAcast* (mo.).

Pres. Joe F. Dahlstrom, Box 1187 HSU Sta., Abilene 79698; *Exec. Dir. (Continuing).* Ada M. Howard, TLA Office, 3355 Bee Cave Rd., Suite 603, Austin 78746. Tel. 512-328-1518.

Address correspondence to the executive director.

Utah

Memb. 600. Term of Office. (*Pres. & V.P.*) Mar. 1986–Mar. 1987. Publication. *HATU Newsletter* (q.).

Pres. Cathleen Partridge, Hercules Aerospace, Mailstop 8, Box 98, Magna 84044. Tel. 801-251-2544; *1st V.P.* Nathan Smith, Brigham Young Univ. 5042 HBLL, Provo 84602. Tel. 801-378-2976; *2nd V.P.* Mary Southwell, Weber County Lib., 2464 Jefferson, Ogden 84401. Tel. 801-399-8152; *Exec. Secy.* Gerald A. Buttars, Utah State Lib., 2150 S. 300 W., Salt Lake City 84115. Tel. 801-533-5875.

Vermont

Memb. 384. Term of Office. Jan. 1987–Dec. 1987. Publication. *VLA News* (10 per year).

Pres. Milton Crouch, Bailey Howe Lib., Univ. of Vermont, Burlington

05405; *V.P./Pres.-Elect.* Valerie Welch, Stowe Free Lib., Box 1080, Stowe 05672; *Secy.* Claire Buckley, South Burlington Community Lib., 500 Dorset St., South Burlington 05401; *Treas.* Sally Reed, Ilsley Lib., Middlebury 05753; *ALA Councillor.* Linda Hay, Box 32, Westminster 05159; *NELA Rep.* Gail Abbott Furnas, Windsor Public Lib., 43 State St., Windsor 05809.

Address correspondence to the president.

Virginia

Memb. 1,300. Term of Office. Jan. 1, 1987–Dec. 31, 1987. Publication. *Virginia Librarian* (q.); *Ed.* Izabela Cieszynski, Newport News Public Lib., 2400 Washington Ave., Newport News 23607.

Pres. Lynn Scott Cochrane, VPI & SU, Newman Lib., Blacksburg 24061. *V.P./Pres.-Elect.* Pat Paine, Fairfax County Public Lib., 11215 Waples Mill Rd., Fairfax 22030; *Secy.* Stephen Matthews, Box 1233, Middleburg 22117; *Treas.* Judith Segel, Arlington County Public Lib., 1015 N. Quincy St., Arlington 22201; *ALA Councillor.* Caroline Arden, The Catholic Univ., Grad. Lib. Dept., 5999 Ninth St. N., Arlington 22205; *Exec. Dir.* Deborah M. Trocchi, Publishers' Services, 80 S. Early St., Alexandria 22304. Tel. 703-370-6020.

Address correspondence to the executive director.

Washington

Memb. 1,000. Term of Office. August 1, 1985–July 31, 1987. Publication. *Alki* (3 per year).

Pres. Irene C. Heninger, Dir., Kitsap Regional Lib., 1301 Sylvan Way, Bremerton 98310. Tel. 206-377-7601; *V.P./Pres.-Elect.* Tom Mayer, SnoIsle Regional Lib., Box 148, Marysville 98270. Tel. 206-339-1711.

Address correspondence to the Washington Lib., 1232 143rd Ave. S.E., Bellevue 98007.

West Virginia

Memb. (Indiv.) 563; (Inst.) 95. Term of Office. Dec. 1986–Nov. 1987. Publication. *West Virginia Libraries.*

Pres. Ernest R. Kallay, Jr., Marion County Public Lib., 321 Monroe St., Fairmont 26554. Tel. 304-366-1210; *1st V.P.* James Fields, Cabell County Public Lib., 455 Ninth St. Plaza, Huntington 25701. Tel. 304-523-9451; *2nd V.P.* Linda J. Mullins, Drain-Jordan Lib., West Virginia State College, Institute 25112. Tel. 304-766-3116; *Secy.* Charles A. Julian, Learning Resources Center, West Virginia Northern Community College, College Square, Wheeling 26003. Tel. 304-233-5900 ext. 240; *Treas.* Dave Childers, West Virginia Lib. Commission, Cultural Center, Capitol Complex, Charleston 25305; *ALA Councillor.* Judy K. Rule, Cabell County Public Lib., 455 Ninth St. Plaza, Huntington 25701.

Address correspondence to the president.

Wisconsin

Memb. 1,600. Term of Office. Jan. 1987–Dec. 1987. Publications. *WLA Newsletter* (6 per year); *WLA Journal* (ann.).

Pres. William J. Wilson, McMillan Memorial Lib., 490 E. Grand Ave., Wisconsin Rapids 54494. Tel. 715-423-1040. *V.P./Pres.-Elect.* Heather Eldred, Wisconsin Valley Lib. System, 400 First St., Wausau 54401. Tel. 715-847-5550.

Address correspondence to the association, 1922 University Ave., Madison 53705. Tel. 608-231-1513.

Wyoming

Memb. (Indiv.) 440; (Inst.) 12; (Subscribers) 24. Term of Office. Sept.

1986–Sept. 1987. Publication. *Wyoming Library Roundup* (tri-mo.). *Ed.* Linn Rounds, Wyoming State Lib., Cheyenne 82002.

Pres. Lynnette Anderson, Casper College Lib., 125 College Dr., Casper 82601; *V.P.* Sandra Donovan, Laramie County Community College, Cheyenne 82007; *Exec. Secy.* Kay Nord, Box 304, Laramie 82070. Tel. 307-745-8662.

Address correspondence to the executive secretary.

Canada

Alberta

Memb. 529. Term of Office. July 1–June 30. Publication. *Letter of the L.A.A.* (6 per year). *Ed.* Marge Gamble, Box 1830, Strathmore T0J 3H0.

Pres. Duncan Rand, Lethbridge Public Lib., 810 Fifth Ave. S., Lethbridge T1J 4C4: *1st V.P.* Peter Freeman, Cameron Lib., Univ. of Alberta, Edmonton T5G 2J8; *Treas.* Rowena Lunn, Box 1830, Strathmore T0J 3H0; *Past Pres.* Ron Peters, S.A.I.T., 1301 16th Ave. N.W., Calgary T5G 2J8; *Exec. Secy.* Carol O'Hanlon, 7444 182nd St., Edmonton T5T 2G7.

Address correspondence to the president, Box 1357, Edmonton T5J 2N2.

British Columbia

Memb. 486. Term of Office. Mar. 1986–Mar. 1987. Publication. *The Reporter* (6 per year). *Ed.* Brian Owen.

Pres. Linda Hale; *Secy.* Denise Bonin; *Treas.* Ann Turner.

Address correspondence to the president, BCLA, Box 35187, Sta. E. Vancouver V6M 4G4.

Manitoba

Memb. 300. Term of Office. Spring 1987–Spring 1988. Publications. *Mani-toba Library Association Bulletin* (q.); *Newsline* (mo.).

Pres. Patricia Bozyk Porter, Box 176, Winnipeg Centennial Lib., Winnipeg R3C 2G9.

Address correspondence to the president.

Ontario

Memb. Over 3,000. Term of Office. Nov. 1986–Nov. 1987. Publications. *Focus* (bi-mo.); *The Reviewing Librarian* (q.); *Inside OLA* (mo.).

Pres. Gerda Molson, Niagara-on-the-Lake Public Lib., Box 430, Niagara-on-the-Lake L0S 1J0. Tel. 416-468-2023; *1st V.P.* Gerry Meek, Thunder Bay Public Lib., 285 Red River Rd., Thunder Bay P7B 1A9. Tel. 807-344-3585; *2nd V.P.* Peter Rogers, 145 Violet Dr., Stoney Creek, L8E 3J2; *Treas.* Larry Peterson, Metropolitan Toronto Reference Lib., 789 Yonge St., Toronto M4W 2G8. Tel. 416-393-7026; *Exec. Dir.* Larry Moore.

Address correspondence to Ontario Lib. Assn., 100 Richmond St. E., Suite 300, Toronto M5C 2P9. Tel. 416-363-3388.

Quebec

Memb. (Indiv.) 160; (Inst.) 45; (Commercial) 5. Term of Office. May 1986–May 1987. Publications. *ABQ/QLA Bulletin; QASL Newsletter.*

Pres. Rosemary E. Lydon, Westmount Public Lib., 4574 Sherbrooke St. W., Westmount H3Z 1G1. Tel. 514-937-2486; *Secy.-Treas.* Charlotte MacLaurin, Concordia Univ., Norris Lib., 1455 de Maisonneuve W., Montreal H3G 1M8; *Exec. Secy.* Geraldine Rose, Quebec Lib. Assn., Box 2216, Dorval H9S 5J4. Tel. 514-631-7616.

Saskatchewan

Memb. 200. Term of Office. July 1986–June 1987. Publication. *Saskatche-*

wan Library Association. Forum (5 per year).

Pres. Brett Balon, Systems Div., City of Regina, Box 1790, Regina, S4P 3C8; *1st V.P./Pres-Elect.* Ernest Ingles, Lib., Univ. of Regina, Regina S4S 0A2; *2nd V.P.* Terri Tomchyshyn; *Secy.* Moninder Sohal; *Treas.* June Sinclair Smith.

Address correspondence to the association, Box 3388, Regina S4P 3H1. Tel. 306-586-3089.

Regional

Atlantic Provinces: N.B., Nfld., N.S., P.E.I.

Memb. (Indiv.) 525. Term of Office. May 1986–May 1987. Publication. *APLA Bulletin* (bi-mo).

Pres. Richard Ellis; *Pres.-Elect.* Joy Tillotson; *V.P. Nova Scotia.* Jerry Miner; *V.P. Prince Edward Island.* Susanne Manovill; *V.P. New Brunswick.* Ken Moore; *V.P. Newfoundland.* George Beckett; *Secy.* Susanne Sexty; *Treas.* Elaine Toms; *Past Pres.* Elizabeth Hamilton; *V.P. Memb.* Susan Collins.

Address correspondence to Atlantic Provinces Lib. Assn., c/o School of Lib. Service, Dalhousie Univ., Halifax, N.S. B3H 4H8.

Middle Atlantic: Del., D.C., Md., N.J., W.Va.

Term of Office. June 1986–July 1987.

Pres. Lucy Cocke, Dir., Mount Vernon College Lib., 2100 Foxhall Rd. N.W., Washington, DC 20007. Tel. 202-331-3475; *V.P.* Sandra S. Stephan, Div. of Lib. Development and Services, Maryland State Dept. of Educ., Baltimore, MD 21201. Tel 301-333-2118; *Secy.* Jane Hukill, Dir., Delaware Campus Lib., Widener Univ., Box 7139, Concord Pike, Wilmington, DE 19803. Tel. 302-478-

3000; *Treas.* Richard Parsons, Admin. Asst. to the Dir., Baltimore County Public Lib., 320 York Rd., Towson, MD 21204. Tel. 301-296-8500.

Address correspondence to the president.

Midwest: Ill., Ind., Minn., Ohio

Term of Office. Oct. 1983–Oct. 1987.

Pres. Walter D. Morrill, Dir., Duggan Lib., Hanover College, Box 287, Hanover, IN 47243. Tel. 812-866-2151; *V.P.* James L. Wells, Dir., Washington County Lib., 3825 Lake Elmo Ave. N., Lake Elmo, MN 55042; *Secy.* Patricia Llerandi, Schaumburg Township Lib., 32 W. Library Lane, Schaumburg, IL 60194. Tel. 312-885-3373; *Treas.* A. Chapman Parson, Exec. Dir., Ohio Lib. Assn./Ohio Lib. Trustees Assn., 40 S. Third St., Columbus, OH 43212.

Address correspondence to the president, Midwest Federation of Lib. Assns.

Mountain Plains: Ariz, Colo., Kans., Mont., Nebr., Nev., N. Dak., S. Dak., Utah, Wyo.

Memb. (Indiv.) 647; (Inst.) 97. Term of Office. Sept. 1986–Oct. 1987. Publications. *MPLA Newsletter* (bi-mo.). *Ed. and Adv. Mgr.* Jim Dertien, Sioux Falls Public Lib., 201 N. Main Ave., Sioux Falls, SD 57102; *Membership Directory* (ann.).

Pres. Duane Johnson, Kansas State Lib., State Capitol, Topeka, KS 66612. Tel. 913-296-3296; *V.P./Pres.-Elect.* Sara Parker, Montana State Lib., 1515 E. Sixth Ave., Helena, MT 59620; *Secy.* Jean Johnson, Coe Lib., Univ. of Wyoming, Laramie, WY 82071; *Exec. Secy.* Joe Edelen, I.D. Weeks Lib., Univ. of South Dakota, Vermillion, SD 57069. Tel. 605-677-6082.

New England: Conn., Mass., Maine, N.H., R.I., Vt.

Term of Office. Oct. 1986–Oct. 1987. Publications. *NELA Newsletter* (6 per year). *Ed.* Frank Ferro, 35 Tuttle Place, East Haven, CT 06512.

Pres. Diane Tebbetts, Univ. of New Hampshire Lib., Durham, NH 03824. Tel. 603-862-1540; *V.P./Pres.-Elect.* Christine Kardokas, Worcester Public Lib., Salem Sq., Worcester, MA 01608. Tel. 617-799-1726; *Secy.* Michael York, Univ. of New Hampshire at Manchester, 220 Hackett Hill Rd., Manchester, NH 03102. Tel. 603-668-0700; *Treas.* Cynthia Arnold, Lincoln Academy Lib., Box 382, Newcastle, ME 04553. Tel. 207-563-3596; *Dirs.* Carolyn Noah, Worcester Public Lib., Salem Sq., Worcester, MA 01608. Tel. 617-799-1671; Betsy Wilkens, Windsor Public Lib., 323 Broad St., Windsor, CT 06095. Tel. 203-688-6433; *Exec. Secy.* Paula M. Bozoian, New England Lib. Assn., Box 421, Wakefield, MA 01880. Tel. 617-438-7179.

Address correspondence to the executive secretary at association headquarters.

Pacific Northwest: Alaska, Idaho, Mont., Oreg., Wash., Alberta, B.C.

Memb. (Active) 982; (Subscribers) 220. Term of Office (Pres., 1st V.P.) Oct. 1, 1986–Sept. 30, 1987. Publication. *PNLA Quarterly.* Ed. Kappy Eaton, 1631 E. 24 Ave., Eugene, OR 97403.

Pres. Peggy Cummings Forcier, Oregon St. Lib. Foundation, State Lib. Bldg., Salem, OR 97310-0642. Tel. 503-378-5082; *1st V.P.* B. J. Busch, Univ. of Alberta Lib. 8734 116th St., Edmonton, Alta. T6G 1P7, Canada; *2nd V.P.* Audrey Kolb, Alaska State Lib., 1215 Cowles St., Fairbanks, AK 99701; *Secy.* Karen Hatcher, Univ. of Montana Lib., 510 Arbor Dr., Missoula, MT 59802; *Treas.* Ralph Delamarter, Deschutes County Lib., 507 N.W. Wall St., Bend, OR 97701.

Address correspondence to the president.

Southeastern: Ala., Fla., Ga., Ky., La., Miss., N.C., S.C., Tenn., Va., W. Va.

Memb. 2,000. Term of Office. Oct. 1986–Oct. 1988. Publication. *The Southeastern Librarian* (q.).

Pres. Charles E. Beard, Dir., Irvine Sullivan Ingram Lib., West Georgia College, Carrollton, GA 30118. Tel. 404-834-1368; *V.P./Pres.-Elect.* George R. Stewart, Dir., Birmingham Public Lib., 2100 Park Place, Birmingham, AL 35203; *Secy.* Gail Lazenby, Asst. Dir., Cobb County Public Lib. System, 30 Atlanta St., Marietta, GA 30060; *Treas.* James E. Ward, Dir., Crisman Memorial Lib., Box 4146, David Lipscomb College, Nashville, TN 37203; *Exec. Secy.* Claudia Medori, SELA, Box 987, Tucker, GA 30085. Tel. 404-939-5080.

Address correspondence to SELA, executive secretary.

State Library Agencies

The state library administrative agencies listed in this section have the latest information on state plans for the use of federal funds under the Library Services and Construction Act. The name of the director, address, and telephone number are given for each state agency.

Alabama

Blaine Dessey, Dir., Alabama Public Library Service, 6030 Monticello Dr., Montgomery 36130. Tel. 205-277-7330.

Alaska

Karen Crane, Dir., Alaska State Lib., Dept. of Educ., Box G, Juneau 99811-0571. Tel. 907-465-2910.

Arizona

Sharon G. Turgeon, Dir., Dept. of Lib., Archives, and Public Records, 1700 W. Washington, State Capitol, Phoenix 85007. Tel. 602-255-4035.

Arkansas

John A. (Pat) Murphey, Jr., State Libn., Arkansas State Lib., One Capitol Mall, Little Rock 72201. Tel. 501-371-1526.

California

Gary E. Strong, State Libn., California State Lib., Box 942837, Sacramento 94237-0001. Tel. 916-445-2585 or 4027.

Colorado

Asst. Commissioner, Colorado State Lib., 201 E. Colfax, Denver 80203. Tel. 303-866-6733.

Connecticut

Richard Akelroyd, State Libn., Connecticut State Lib., 231 Capitol Ave., Hartford 06106. Tel. 203-566-4192.

Delaware

Frances West, Secy., Dept. of Community Affairs, Box 1401, 156 S. State St., Dover 19903. Tel. 302-736-4456.

Louise E. Wyche, Dir., Delaware Div. of Libs., Dept. of Community Affairs, Box 639, Dover 19901. Tel. 302-736-4748.

District of Columbia

Hardy R. Franklin, Dir., D.C. Public Lib., 901 G. St. N.W., Washington 20001. Tel. 202-727-1101.

Florida

Barratt Wilkins, State Libn., State Lib. of Florida, R. A. Gray Bldg., Tallahassee 32201. Tel. 904-487-2651.

Georgia

Joe B. Forsee, Dir., Div. of Public Lib. Services, 156 Trinity Ave. S.W., Atlanta 30303. Tel. 404-656-2461.

Hawaii

Bartholomew A. Kane, Asst. Superintendent/State Libn., Office of Lib. Services, Research and Evaluation Services Sec., 465 S. King St., Rm. B-1, Honolulu 96813. Tel. 808-548-5585 or 86, 87, 88.

Idaho

Charles A. Bolles, State Libn., Idaho State Lib., 325 W. State St., Boise 83702. Tel. 208-334-5124.

Illinois

Bridget L. Lamont, Dir., Illinois State Lib., Centennial Memorial Bldg., Springfield 62756. Tel. 217-782-2994.

Indiana

C. Ray Ewick, Dir., Indiana State Lib., 140 N. Senate Ave., Indianapolis 46204. Tel. 317-232-3692.

Iowa

John Montag, Dir., State Lib. of Iowa, Historical Bldg., Des Moines 50319. Tel. 515-281-4113.

Kansas

Duane F. Johnson, State Libn., Kansas State Lib., 3rd fl., State Capitol, Topeka 66612. Tel. 913-296-3296.

Kentucky

James A. Nelson, State Libn. and Commissioner, Kentucky Dept. for Libs. and Archives, Box 537, Frankfort 40602. Tel. 502-875-7000.

Louisiana

Thomas F. Jaques, State Libn., Louisiana State Lib., Box 131, Baton Rouge 70821. Tel. 504-342-4923.

Maine

J. Gary Nichols, State Libn., Maine State Lib., State House Sta. 64, Augusta 04333. Tel. 207-289-3561.

Maryland

Nettie B. Taylor, Asst. State Superintendent for Libs., Div. of Lib. Development and Services, Maryland State Dept. of Educ., 200 W. Baltimore St., Baltimore 21201. Tel. 301-659-2000.

Massachusetts

Roland R. Piggford, Dir., Massachusetts Bd. of Lib. Commissioners, 648 Beacon St., Boston 02215. Tel. 617-267-9400.

Michigan

James W. Fry, State Libn., Lib. of Michigan, Box 30007, Lansing 48909. Tel. 517-373-1593.

Minnesota

William G. Asp, Dir., Office of Lib. Development and Services, Minnesota Dept. of Educ., 440 Capitol Sq. Bldg., 550 Cedar St., St. Paul 55101. Tel. 612-296-2821.

Mississippi

David M. Woodburn, Dir., Mississippi Lib. Commission, 1221 Ellis Ave., Box 10700, Jackson 39209-0700. Tel. 601-359-1036.

Missouri

Richard Miller, Acting State Libn., Missouri State Lib., Box 387, Jefferson City 65102. Tel. 314-751-2751.

Montana

Sara Parker, State Libn., Montana State Lib., 1515 E. Sixth Ave., Helena 59620. Tel. 406-444-3115.

Nebraska

John L. Kopischke, Dir., Nebraska Lib. Commission, Lincoln 68508. Tel. 402-471-2045.

Nevada

Jean Kerschner, State Libn., Nevada State Lib., Capitol Complex, Carson City 89710. Tel. 702-885-5130.

New Hampshire

Shirley Adamovich, Commissioner of the Dept. of Libs., Arts, and Historical Resources, New Hampshire State Lib., 20 Park St., Concord 03301. Tel. 603-271-2392; Matt Higgins, State Libn. Tel. 603-271-2339.

New Jersey

Barbara F. Weaver, Asst. Commissioner for Education/State Libn., Div. of State Lib., Archives and History, 185 W. State St., Trenton 08625-0520. Tel. 609-292-6201.

New Mexico

Virginia Hendley, State Libn., New Mexico State Lib., 325 Don Gaspar St., Santa Fe 87503. Tel. 505-827-3804.

New York

Joseph F. Shubert, State Libn./Asst. Commissioner for Libs., New York State Lib., Rm. 10C34, C.E.C., Empire State Plaza, Albany 12230. Tel. 518-474-5930.

North Carolina

Jane Williams, Acting Dir./State Libn., Dept. of Cultural Resources, Div. of State Lib., 109 E. Jones St., Raleigh 27611. Tel. 919-733-2570.

North Dakota

Margaret Stefanak, State Libn., North Dakota State Lib., Liberty Memorial Bldg., Capitol Grounds, Bismarck 58505. Tel. 701-224-2492.

Ohio

Richard M. Cheski, Dir., State Lib. of Ohio, 65 S. Front St., Columbus 43266-0334. Tel. 614-462-7061.

Oklahoma

Robert L. Clark, Jr., Dir., Oklahoma Dept. of Libs., 200 N.E. 18 St., Oklahoma City 73105-3298. Tel. 405-521-2502.

Oregon

Wesley A. Doak, State Libn., Oregon State Lib., Salem 97310. Tel. 503-378-4367.

Pennsylvania

Elliot L. Shelkrot, State Libn., State Lib. of Pennsylvania, Box 1601, Harrisburg 17105. Tel. 717-787-2646.

Rhode Island

Fay Zipkowitz, Dir., Rhode Island Dept. of State Lib., 95 Davis St., Providence 02908. Tel. 401-277-2726.

South Carolina

Betty E. Callaham, Dir., South Carolina State Lib., 1500 Senate St., Box 11469, Columbia 29211. Tel. 803-734-8666.

South Dakota

Jane Kolbe, State Libn., South Dakota State Lib. and Archives, 800 Governors Dr., Pierre 57501. Tel. 605-773-3131.

Tennessee

State Libn. and Archivist, Tennessee State Lib. and Archives, 403 Seventh Ave. N., Nashville 37219. Tel. 615-741-2451.

Texas

Dorman H. Winfrey, Dir. and Libn., Texas State Lib., Box 12927, Capitol Sta., Austin 78711. Tel. 512-463-5460.

Utah

Russell L. Davis, Dir., Utah State Lib., 2150 S. 300 W., Suite 16, Salt Lake City 84115. Tel. 801-533-5875.

Vermont

Patricia E. Klinck, State Libn., State of Vermont, Dept. of Libs., c/o State Office Bldg., Post Office, Montpelier 05602. Tel. 802-828-3265.

Virginia

Ella Gaines Yates, State Libn., Virginia State Lib., Richmond 23219. Tel. 804-786-2332.

Washington

Nancy Zussy, State Libn., Washington State Lib. AJ-11, Olympia 98504-0111. Tel. 206-753-2915.

West Virginia

Frederic J. Glazer, Dir., West Virginia Lib. Commission, Science and Cultural Center, Charleston 25305. Tel. 304-348-2041.

Wisconsin

Leslyn M. Shires, Asst. Superintendent, Div. for Lib. Services, Wisconsin Dept. of Public Instruction, 125 S. Webster St., Madison 53707. Tel. 608-266-2205.

Wyoming

Wayne H. Johnson, State Libn., Wyoming State Lib., Barnett Bldg., Cheyenne 82002. Tel. 307-777-7283.

American Samoa

Sailautusi Avegalio, Federal Grants Mgr., Dept. of Educ., Box 1329, Pago Pago 96799, Tel. 633-5237.

Guam

Magdalena S. Taitano, Libn., Nieves M. Flores Memorial Lib., 254 Martyr St., Agana 96910. Tel. 671-472-6417.

Northern Mariana Islands (Commonwealth of the)

Dir. of Lib. Services, Commonwealth of the Northern Mariana Islands, Saipan 96950. Tel. 6534.

Pacific Islands (Trust Territory of the)

Harold Crouch, Chief of Federal Programs, Dept. of Educ., Trust Territory of the Pacific Islands, Saipan, Mariana Islands 96950. Tel. 9448.

Puerto Rico

Awilda Aponte Roque, Secy., Dept. of Educ., Apartado 859, Hato Rey 00919. Tel. 809-751-5572

Virgin Islands

Henry C. Chang, Dir., Libs. and Museums, Bureau of Libs., Museums, and Archaelogical Services, Dept. of Conservation and Cultural Affairs, Government of the Virgin Islands, Box 390, Charlotte Amalie, St. Thomas 00801. Tel. 809-774-3407; St. Croix 809-773-5715.

State School Library Media Associations

Unless otherwise specified, correspondence to an association listed in this section is to be addressed to the secretary or executive secretary named in the entry.

Alabama

Alabama Lib. Assn., Div. of Children's and School Libns. Memb. 720. Term of Office. Apr. 1986–Apr. 1987. Publication. *Alabama Librarian* (mo.).

Chpn. Emily Mitchell, Lib. Media Specialist, Crumley Chapel Elementary, 2201 Pershing Rd., Birmingham 35214. Tel. 205-798-2871; *Chpn.-Elect.* Kathryn Harrison, Lib. Media Specialist, Randolph School, 1005 Drake Ave., Huntsville 35802. Tel. 205-881-1701; *Secy.* Bobbie Carter, Lib. Media Specialist, Huntington Place Elementary, 14 Candlewood Dr., Northport 35476. Tel. 205-339-1773.

Alaska

[See entry under State, Provincial, and Regional Library Associations — *Ed.*]

Arizona

School Lib. Media Div., Arizona State Lib. Assn. Memb. 440. Term of Office. Nov. 1986–Oct. 1987. Publication. *ASLA Newsletter*.

Pres. Patti Hulet, MacArthur Elementary, 1852 E. First Pl., Mesa 85203. Tel. 602-833-7143; *Pres.-Elect.* Ellen Ramsey, Amphitheater H.S., 125 W. Yavapai, Tucson 85705. Tel. 602-293-0300; *Secy.* Virginia Hecht, Tucson Unified School Dist., 2025 E. Winsett St., Tucson 85719. Tel. 602-628-2364; *Treas.* Dick Trzicky, Gilbert Jr. H.S., Drawer #1, 1016 N. Burk, Gilbert 85234. Tel. 602-892-6908.

Address correspondence to the president.

Arkansas

School Lib. Div., Arkansas Lib. Assn. Memb. 334. Term of Office. Oct. 1986–Oct. 1987.

Chpn. Lee Annette Buck, Amboy Elementary School, 2400 W. 58, North Little Rock 72118. Tel. 501-753-4381; *V. Chpn.* Cassandra Barnett, Levertt Elementary School, Fayetteville 72701. Tel. 501-442-6061; *Secy.* Bevery Redford; *Treas.* Selvin Royal.

California

California Media and Lib. Educators Assn. (CMLEA), Suite 204, 1575 Old Bayshore Hwy., Burlingame 94010. Tel. 415-692-2350. Job Hotline. Tel. 415-697-8832. Memb. 1,250. Term of Office. June 1986–May 1987. Publication. *CMLEA Journal* (bi-ann.).

Pres. Larry Pierce, Dir. Educational Media Dept., Rowland Unified School Dist., 1830 Nogales St., Rowland Heights 91748; *Pres.-Elect.* Virginia Kalb, Dir. Media Services, Montebello Unified School Dist., 123 S. Montebello Blvd., Montebello 90640; *Secy.* Kay Niemeyer, Coord. School Lib. Resources, San Diego County Office of Education, 6401 Linda Vista Rd., San Diego 92111-7399; *Treas.* Norman Bixby, Lib. Media Specialist, Sonora H.S., 401 S. Palm St., La Habra 90631; *Business Office Secy.* Nancy D. Kohn, CMLEA, 1575 Old Bayshore Hwy., Burlingame 94010.

Colorado

Colorado Educational Media Assn. Memb. 680. Term of Office. Feb.

1986–Feb. 1987. Publication. *The Medium* (mo.).

Pres. Marjorie Brown, 1140 Judson, Boulder 80303; *Exec. Secy.* Terry Walljasper, Colorado Educational Media Assn., Box 22814, Wellshire Sta., Denver 80222.

Address correspondence to the executive secretary.

Connecticut

Connecticut Educational Media Assn. Term of Office. May 1986–May 1987. CEMA videotape "The School Library Media Specialist—A Continuing Story," available in ½″ ($35) or ¾″ Umatic ($40).

Pres. Roy Temple, 21 Hillcrest Ave., New Britain 06053. Tel. 203-224-9909; *V.P.* Harriet Selverstone, 31 Bonnie Brook Rd., Westport 06880. Tel. 203-226-6236; *Secy.* Marsha DuBeau, Brandy Hill Rd., Vernon 06066. Tel. 203-875-0626; *Treas.* Calvin Fish, 33 School St., Coventry 06238. Tel. 203-742-1737.

Address correspondence to Anne Weimann, Administrative Secy., 25 Elmwood Ave., Trumbull 06611. Tel. 203-372-2260.

Delaware

Delaware School Lib. Media Assn., Div. of Delaware Lib. Assn. Memb. 92. Term of Office. Apr. 1986–Apr. 1987. Publications. *DSLMA Newsletter* (irreg.); column in *DLA Bulletin* (3 per year).

Pres. Alice Thornton, Chistiana H.S., Salem Church Rd., Newark 19713. Tel. 302-454-2239; *V.P./Pres.-Elect.* Doris Brewer, Gunning Bedford Middle School, Delaware City 19706; *Secy.-Treas.* Mary Farnell, Frederick Douglass Intermediate School, Seaford 19973.

District of Columbia

D.C. Assn. of School Libns. Memb. 175. Term of Office. Aug. 1986–July 1987. Publication. *Newsletter* (4 per year).

Pres. Andre Y. Edwards, 1226 Jackson St. N.E., Washington 20017. Tel. 202-673-7385; *Corres. Secy.* Brenda C. Warley, Johnson Jr. H.S., Bruce & Robinson Sts. S.E., Washington 20020. Tel. 202-767-7110.

Address correspondence to the corresponding secretary.

Florida

Florida Assn. for Media in Education, Inc. Memb. 1,350. Term of Office. Oct. 1986–Oct. 1987. Publication. *Florida Media Quarterly.*

Pres. Donna Baumbach, 8625 Port Said St., Orlando 32817. Tel. 305-671-4746; *Pres.-Elect.* Jerry Barkholz, 12408 N. 52 St., Tampa 33617; *V.P.* Bette Moon, 603 Gulf Shore Dr., Destin 32541; *Secy.* Helen Tallman, 7601 S.W. 94 Ave., Miami 33173; *Treas.* Helen Jones, Rte. 1, Box 260, Leesburg 32748; *Parliamentarian.* Mary Alice Hunt, 1603 Kolopakin Nene, Tallahassee 32301.

Address correspondence to the association executive, Mary Margaret Rogers, Box 13119, Tallahassee 32317.

Georgia

School Lib. Media, Div. of the Georgia Lib. Assn. Term of Office. Oct. 1985–Oct. 1987.

Chpn. Joanne Lincoln, Professional Lib., Atlanta Public Schools, 2930 Forrest Hill Dr. S.W., Atlanta 30315. Tel. 404-761-5411.

Address correspondence to the chairperson.

Hawaii

Hawaii Assn. of School Libns. Memb. 225. Term of Office. June 1986–May 1987.

Pres. Pamela Yoshimoto, Farrington H.S., 1564 N. King St., Honolulu 96817.

Tel. 808-841-3331 ext. 59; *V.P./Pres.-Elect.* Diane Matsuoka, Waipahu H.S., 94-1211 Farrington Hwy., Waipahu 96797. Tel. 808-677-0550.

Address correspondence to the association, Box 23019, Honolulu 96822.

Idaho

Educational Media Div. of the Idaho Lib. Assn. Term of Office. Oct. 1986–Oct. 1988. Publication. Column in *The Idaho Librarian* (q.).

Chpn. Ken Worthington, Wood River H.S., Box 948, Hailey 83333. Tel. 208-788-3481; *Secy.* Marie Scharnhorst, Genessee 83832.

Address correspondence to the chairperson.

Illinois

Illinois Assn. for Media in Education (IAME), Sec. of the Illinois Lib. Assn. Memb. 590. Term of Office. Jan. 1987–Dec. 1987. Publication. IAME *News for You* (q.). *Ed.* Charles Rusiewski, 207 E. Chester, Nashville 62263.

Pres. Fran Corcoran, Dist 62, 777 Algonquin Rd., Des Plaines 60016. Tel. 312-824-1136.

Address correspondence to the president.

Indiana

Assn. for Indiana Media Educators. Memb. 950. Term of Office. (*Pres.*) May 1, 1986–Apr. 30, 1987. Publication. *Indiana Media Journal.*

Pres. Darrell Swarens, Box 731, Terre Haute 47808; *Exec. Secy.* Lawrence Reck, School of Education, Indiana State Univ., Terre Haute 47809. Tel. 812-237-2926.

Address correspondence to the executive secretary.

Iowa

Iowa Educational Media Assn. Memb. 550. Term of Office. Apr. 1986–Apr. 1987. Publication. *Iowa Media Message* (q.). *Ed.* Donald Rieck, Iowa State Univ., Media Resource Center, 121 Pearson Hall, Ames 50011.

Pres. Richard Valley, Decorah Senior H.S., Claiborne Dr., Decorah 52101; Tel. 319-382-3643; *V.P./Pres.-Elect.* Leon Maxson, Southern Prairie Area Education Agency, R.R. 5, Box 55, Ottumwa 52501; *Secy.* Shirley Yeries, R.R. 2, Oxford 52322; *Treas.* Don Powell, 212 Alpha N.W., Bondurant 50035; *Dirs.* (1987) Karlene Garn, Tom Hoffman, Larry McLain; (1988) Leah Hiland, Janet Summers, Tom Youngblut; (1989) Jeanne Dugdale, Mark Henderson, Susan Schrader.

Address correspondence to the president.

Kansas

Kansas Assn. of School Libns., Memb. 700. Term of Office. July 1986–June 1987. Publication. *KASL Newsletter* (s.ann.).

Pres. Pauline Means, Wichita South H.S., L.M.C., 701 W. 33 St., South Wichita 67217. Tel. 316-522-2233 ext. 42; *V.P./Pres.-Elect.* Mary Jo Reed, Dir. of Media Services, Salina Public Schools, 119 E. Mulberry, Salina 67401. Tel. 913-823-2246; *Treas.* Carol Fox, El Dorado H.S., El Dorado 67042. Tel. 316-321-3721; *Secy.* Betsy Losey, Roosevelt Elementary School, 2000 MacArthur, Hays 67601. Tel. 913-625-2565; *Busn. Mgr.* Kay Mounkes, Westridge Middle School, 9300 Nieman, Shawnee Mission 66214. Tel. 913-888-5214 ext. 14.

Address correspondence to the business manager.

Kentucky

Kentucky School Media Assn. Memb. 500. Term of Office. Oct. 1986–Oct. 1987. Publication. *KSMA Newsletter.*
Pres. Jeannie Pridgen, 2200 Richmond Rd. #412, Lexington 40502. Tel. 606-299-4817; *Pres.-Elect.* Maude Teegarden, Box 121, Brooksville 41004; *Secy.* Joyce Hahn, 342 Stoneybrook Dr., Lexington 40503; *Treas.* Hertha Smith, 8883 Valley Circle, Florence 41042.

Louisiana

Louisiana Assn. of School Libns., c/o Louisiana Lib. Assn., Box 131, Baton Rouge 70821. Memb. 384. Term of Office. July 1, 1986–June 30, 1987.
Pres. Marvene Dearman, 1471 Chevelle Dr., Baton Rouge 70806. Tel. (off.) 504-357-6464; (home) 504-925-8767.

Maine

Maine Educational Media Assn. Memb. 234. Term of Office. Oct. 1986–May 1987. Publication. *Mediacy* (q.).
Pres. Doris V. Chapman, 32 Anson Rd., Portland 04102. Tel. 207-772-1694; *Pres.-Elect.* Jo Coyne, South Portland H.S., 637 Highland Ave., South Portland 04106; *V.P.* Abigail Garthwaith, Asa Adams School, Orono 04473; *Secy.* Lorraine Stickney, Gorham H.S., 41 Morrill Ave., Gorham 04038; *Treas.* Alice Douglas, Morse H.S., Bath 04530.
Address correspondence to the president.

Maryland

Maryland Educational Media Organization. Term of Office. Oct. 1986–Oct. 1987. Publication. *Memorandum* (q.).
Pres. Toni Negro, Montgomery County Public Schools 850 Hungerford Dr., Rockville 20850; *Pres.-Elect.* Josephine Campa, 7708 Granada Dr., Bethesda 20817; *Secy.* Celeste Brecht, 4725 Salterforth Pl., Ellicot City 21043; *Treas.* Cheryl Gerring, 33T Ridge Rd., Greenbelt 20770.
Address correspondence to the president.

Massachusetts

Massachusetts Assn. for Educational Media. Memb. 400. Term of Office. June 1, 1986–May 31, 1987. Publication. *Media Forum* (q.).
Pres. Carolyn B. Markuson, Brookline Public Schools, 115 Greenough St., Brookline 02146. Tel. 617-730-2656; *V.P./ Pres.-Elect.* Bruce R. Oldershaw, Springfield College, 263 Alden St., Springfield 01109. Tel. 413-788-3113; *Secy.* Theresa Maffeo, Lynnfield Jr. High, Lynnfield 01940; *Treas.* Dana Pierce, Austin Middle School, East Freetown 02717.
Address correspondence to Charles W. Adams, Executive Secretary, 569 Main St., Hanover 02339. Tel. 617-878-3194.

Michigan

Michigan Assn. for Media in Education (MAME). Term of Office. One year.
Pres. Burton H. Brooks, Box 211, Grand Haven 49417. Tel. 616-842-0300; *Secy.* Marian West, 2222 Fuller #1008 A, Ann Arbor 48105. Tel. 313-663-5907; *Treas.* Annette Walker, Fenton Middle School, 404 W. Ellen, Fenton 48430. Tel. 313-629-4189; *Past Pres.* Roger Ashley, 3211 Kernway Dr., Bloomfield Hills 48013; *V.P. Special Interest Div.* Ricki Chowning, 465 Kenowa, Casnovia 49318. Tel. 616-675-5334; *V.P. Regions.* Jane Humble, 30 N. West St., Hillsdale 49242. Tel. 517-437-4313.
Address correspondence to the president, MAME, c/o Univ. of Michigan,

3334 School of Education, Ann Arbor 48109.

Minnesota

Minnesota Educational Media Organization. Memb. 1,000. Term of Office. (*Pres.*) May 1986–May 1987 (other offices 2 years in alternating years). Publication. *Minnesota Media.*

Pres. Bill Fredell, 408 Quarry Lane, Stillwater 55082. Tel. 612-439-5795; *Pres.-Elect.* Tim Eklund, Rte. 1, Park Rapids 56470; *Past Pres.* Helen Rudie, 307 Sixth Ave. S., Moorhead 56560; *Secy.* Mary Sack, R.R. 3, Box 41, New Richland 56072.

Mississippi

Mississippi Assn. of Media Educators. Memb. 76. Term of Office. Mar. 1986–Mar. 1987. Publication. *MAME* (newsletter, bi-ann.).

Pres. Curtis Kynerd, Hinds Junior College, Box 21, Raymond 39154; *V.P./Pres.-Elect.* Savan Wilson, Univ. of Southern Mississippi, Southern Sta., Box 5146, Hattiesburg 39402; *V.P. Membership.* Barbara Clayton, 1054 Voorhees Ave., Jackson 39209; *Secy.* Jim Gavette, Jackson State Univ., 515 Sykes Rd., Apt. D-7, Jackson 39212; *Newsletter Ed.* Brockford Gordon, Jackson State Univ., 505 Winter St., Jackson 39204.

Missouri

Missouri Assn. of School Libns. Memb. 850. Term of Office. June 1, 1986–May 31, 1987. Publications. *MASL Newsletter* (4 per year). *Ed.* Mary Reinert, Rte. 4, Box 147, Nevada 64772. *MASL Journal* (2 per year). *Ed.* Floyd Pentlin, 520 Grover, Warrensburg 64093.

Pres. George Ann Fisher, 801 Hillcrest, Butler 64730. Tel. 816-679-3652; *Secy.*

Carol Stockton, Rte. 2, Paris 65275; *Treas.* Anna Seewoester, Rte. 3, Nevada 64772.

Address correspondence to the president.

Montana

Montana School Lib. Media, Div. of Montana Lib. Assn. Memb. 170. Term of Office. June 1986–June 1987.

Pres. Patricia Jarvi, Box 998, Whitefish 59937.

Address correspondence to the president.

Nebraska

Nebraska Educational Media. Assn. Memb. 350. Term of Office. July 1, 1986–June 30, 1987. Publication. *NEMA News* (4 per year). *Ed.* Dick Allen, 1420 P St., Lincoln 68508.

Pres. Gene Schneberger, 1700 W. Stolley Park Rd., Grand Island 68801. Tel. 308-382-1804; *Pres.-Elect.* La Jean Price, 1225 Idylwild Dr., Lincoln 68504. Tel. 402-467-4451; *Secy.* Eunice Parrish, Tecumseh H.S., Box 338, Tecumseh 68450. Tel. 402-335-3328; *Treas.* Mary Lou Bayless, 4215 S. 20, Omaha 68107. Tel. 402-733-1707.

Address correspondence to the president.

Nevada

Nevada Assn. of School Libns. Memb. 41. Term of Office. Jan. 1, 1987–Dec. 31, 1987.

Pres. Lee Diane Gordon, Eldorado H.S., 1139 N. Linn Lane, Las Vegas 89110. Tel. 702-799-7230.

New Hampshire

New Hampshire Educational Media Assn. Memb. 225. Term of Office. June

1986–June 1987. Publication. *Online* (ir-reg.).

Pres. Jan Druke, Pittsfield H.S., Pittsfield 03263. Tel. 603-435-6701; *V.P.* Maureen Cullen, Winnacunnet H.S., Hampton 03842; *Treas.* Lucille Noel, Simonds Elementary School, Sutton 03221; *Rec. Secy.* Marion Pierce, Merrimack Valley H.S., Penacook 03303; *Corres. Secy.* Joyce Kendall, Fall Mt. Regional H.S., R.R. 1, Alstead 03602.

Address correspondence to the president.

New Jersey

Educational Media Assn. of New Jersey (EMAnj). (Organized Apr. 1977 through merger of New Jersey School Media Assn. and New Jersey Assn. of Educational Communication and Technology.) Memb. 1,000. Term of Office. June 1986–June 1987. Publications. *Signal Tab* (newsletter, mo.); *Emanations* (journal, 2 per year).

Pres. Dudy Schindler, R.D. 3, Box 77, Boonton 07005. Tel. 201-334-2027; *V.P.* Carol Kuhlthau, 402 Franklin Rd., North Brunswick 08902; *Rec. Secy.* Marjorie Horowitz, 10 Prospect Ave., Montclair 07042; *Corres. Secy.* Sharron Knauss, 242-C Stonybrook, 801 Cooper St., Deptford 08096; *Treas.* Robert Bonardi, 41 Walnut Hill Lane, Freehold 07728.

Address correspondence to the president.

New Mexico

New Mexico Lib. Assn., School Libs. Children and Young Adult Services Div. Memb. 222. Term of Office. Apr. 1987–Apr. 1988.

Chpn. Grace Stamper, Springer School Dist., Springer 87729.

Address correspondence to the chairperson.

New York

School Lib. Media Sec./New York Lib. Assn., 15 Park Row, Suite 434, New York 10038. Tel. 212-227-8032. Memb. 700. Term of Office. Oct. 1986–Oct. 1987. Publications. Participates in *NYLA Bulletin* (mo. except July and Aug.); *SLMSgram* (s. ann.).

Pres. Constance Richardson, Lib. Media Specialist, Pittsford Mendon H.S., Pittsford 14534. Tel. 716-385-6750 ext. 362; *1st V.P./Pres.-Elect.* James Bennett, Lib. Media Specialist, Shoreham-Wading River H.S., Rte. 25A, Shoreham 11786. Tel. 516-929-8500 ext. 237; *2nd V.P.* Jean Perry, Lib. Media Specialist, Bayport-Blue Point School Dist., Sylvan Ave. School, Bayport 11705; *3rd V.P.* Anne M. Sidwell, Coord., Oswego County BOCES School Lib. System, County Rte. 64, Mexico 13114; *Secy.* Sheryl Egger, Coord. of Libs., West Irondequoit Central School, Cooper Rd., West Irondequoit 14617; *Treas.* Ethel A. Keefer, Elmira City School Dist., Southside H.S., 777 S. Main St., Elmira 14904. Tel. 607-737-7448 ext. 24; *Past Pres.* Yvonne D. Hodson, Lib. Media Specialist/Resource Teacher Gifted and Talented, Olmstead School, 716 W. Delavan, Buffalo 14222. Tel. 716-885-1166; *Bur. of School Libs. Liaison.* Robert Barron, Chief, Bureau of School Libs., State Education Dept., Rm. 676, Education Bldg. Annex, Albany 12234; *Div. of Lib. Development Liaison.* Joseph Mattie, Assoc., Div. of Lib. Development, 10B41 Cultural Education Center, Empire State Plaza, Albany 12230.

Address correspondence to the president or secretary.

North Carolina

North Carolina Assn. of School Libns. Memb. 900. Term of Office. Oct. 1985–Oct. 1987.

Chpn. Helen Tugwell, Regional School Media Programs Coord., Region 5, North

Central Regional Education Center, Box 21889, 1215 Westover Terr., Greensboro 27420. Tel. 919-379-5764; *Chpn.-Elect.* Carol Southerland, Media Specialist, South Lenoir High, Deep Run 28525; *Secy.-Treas.* Martha Davis, Media Specialist, Smith H.S., 2407 S. Holden Rd., Greensboro 27407.

Address correspondence to the chairperson, 2002 Brickhaven Dr., Greensboro 27407.

North Dakota

North Dakota Lib. Assn., School Lib. Media Sec. Memb. 59. Term of Office. One year. Publication. *The Good Stuff* (q.).

Pres. Edna Boardman, 515 16 St. S.W., Minot 58701. Tel. 701-857-4534; *Secy.* Maureen Halvorson, 200 Second Ave. S.E., Jamestown 58401.

Address correspondence to the president.

Ohio

Ohio Educational Lib. Media Assn. Memb. 1,200. Term of Office. Jan. 1987–Dec. 1987. Publication. *Ohio Media Spectrum* (q.).

Pres. Sharyn Van Epps, Madeira H.S., 7465 Loannes Dr., Cincinnati 45243. Tel. 513-891-8222.

Oklahoma

Oklahoma Assn. of School Lib. Media Specialists. Memb. 250. Term of Office. July 1, 1986–June 30, 1987. Publications. School Library News column in *Oklahoma Librarian* (q.); Library Resources section in *Oklahoma Educator* (mo.).

Chpn. Anne Masters, Norman Public Schools, 131 S. Flood, Norman 73069. Tel. 405-360-0220; *V. Chpn./Chpn.-Elect.* Pat Cunningham, Tuttle Public Schools, Box B, Tuttle 73089; *Secy.* Mary Anne

Driver, Irving Middle School, 1920 E. Alameda, Norman 73069; *Treas.* Nancy Pelton, Parkland Elementary, 2201 S. Cornwall, Yukon 73099; *Past Chpn.* Barbara Rather, Union Public Schools, 5656 S. 129 E. Ave., Tulsa 74134.

Oregon

Oregon Educational Media Assn. Memb. 650. Term of Office, Oct. 1, 1986–Sept. 30, 1987. Publication. *INTERCHANGE.*

Pres. Jim Hayden; *Pres.-Elect.* Carol Abbott; *Past-Pres.* Mary Kerns; *Exec. Secy.* Sherry Hevland, 16695 S.W. Rosa Rd., Beaverton 97007.

Pennsylvania

Pennsylvania School Libns. Assn. Memb. 1,300. Term of Office. July 1, 1986–June 30, 1988. Publications. *Learning and Media* (4 per year); *027.8* (4 per year).

Pres. Margaret R. Tassia, Millersville Univ., Millersville 17551. Tel. 717-872-3630; *V.P./Pres.-Elect.* Diana Murphy, 135 Wiltshire Circle, Monroeville 15146; *Secy.* Rebecca Frost, 2422 Riverview Ave., Bloomsburg 17815; *Treas.* Maggie McCaskey, 1515 Pennsylvania Ave., Paoli 19301; *Past Pres.* Sharon Nardelli, The Baldwin School, Morris & Montgomery Aves., Bryn Mawr 19010. Tel. 215-525-2700.

Address correspondence to the president.

Rhode Island

Rhode Island Educational Media Assn. Memb. 263. Term of Office. June 1986–June 1987. Publication. *RIEMA* (newsletter, 9 per year).

Pres. Roland B. Mergener, Dir. Audiovisual Dept., Rhode Island College, 24 Oak Grove Blvd., North Providence 02911; *Pres.-Elect.* Linda Aldridge, Libn., Bristol H.S., Bristol 02809. Tel.

401-253-4000; *Secy.* Carol Driver, Lib., Charleston Elementary School, Carolina 02812; *Treas.* Arlene Luber, Media Specialist, East Providence School Dept., 2 Jackson Walkway, Providence 02903.

Address correspondence to the president.

South Carolina

South Carolina Assn. of School Libns. Memb. 600. Term of Office. May 1986–May 1987. Publication. *Media Center Messenger* (5 per year).

Pres. Ann T. White, Spartanburg School District 3, Box 267, Glendale 29346. Tel. 803-579-3330; *V.P./Pres.-Elect.* Ida Williams, 4240 Donovan Dr., Columbia 29210. Tel. 803-798-3130.

Address correspondence to the association, Box 2442, Columbia 29202.

South Dakota

South Dakota School Lib. Media Assn., Sec. of the South Dakota Lib. Assn. and South Dakota Education Assn. Term of Office. Oct. 1986–Oct. 1987.

Pres. Barbara B. Swift, Libn. K–12, Webster Public Schools, 421 E. Ninth Ave., Webster 57274. Tel. 605-345-4059; *Secy.-Treas.* Dorothy Iverson, Wakonda H.S., Box 268, Wakonda 57073. Tel. 605-267-2645.

Address correspondence to the president.

Tennessee

Tennessee Education Assn., School Lib. Sec. Term of Office. May 1986–May 1987.

Chpn. Pam Parman, Maryville H.S., Maryville 37801. Tel. 615-982-1132. *Chpn./Chpn.-Elect.* Deborah Davis, Denmark Elementary School, 980 Denmark Rd., Denmark 38391.

Address correspondence to the chairperson.

Texas

Texas Assn. of School Libns. Memb. 2,020. Term of Office. Apr. 1986–Apr. 1987. Publication. *Media Matters* (3 per year).

Chpn. Betty Hamilton, 911 E. Oak, Brownfield 79316. Tel. 806-637-7521 (w), 806-637-4213 (h); *Chpn.-Elect.* Elizabeth Polk, 9317 Springdale Rd., Austin 78754; *Secy.* Barbara Brooks, 6 Spring Valley Circle, Longview 75605; *Councillor.* Jo Ann Truitt, 1905 N.W. 12 St., Amarillo 79107.

Address correspondence to an officer or to TASL, 3355 Bee Cave Rd., Austin 78746. Tel. 512-328-1518.

Utah

Utah Educational Lib. Media Assn. Memb. 280. Term of Office. Mar. 1987–Mar. 1988. Publication. *UELMA Newsletter* (6 per year).

Pres. Karen Berner, Farrer Junior H.S., 100 N. 600 E., Provo 84601. Tel. 801-373-3504; *Pres.-Elect.* JaDene Denniston, Millville Elementary School, 67 S. Main, Millville 84326. Tel. 801-752-7162; *Secy.-Treas.* Kathleen Kouba, Mt. Ogden Middle School, 3260 Harrison Blvd., Ogden 84403. Tel. 801-399-3456.

Address correspondence to the association, Box 25355, Salt Lake City 84125.

Vermont

Vermont Educational Media Assn. Memb. 140. Term of Office. May 1986–May 1987. Publication. *VEMA News* (q.).

Pres. Regina Bellstrom, Box 15, Townshend 05353. Tel. 802-365-4071; *Pres.-Elect.* Joan Sabens, East Montpelier Elementary School, East Montpelier 05651. Tel. 802-223-7936; *Secy.* Juanita Platts, Morristown Elementary School, Morrisville 05661. Tel. 802-888-3101; *Treas.* Carol Kress, Mt. Abraham H.S., Bristol 05443. Tel. 802-453-2333.

Address correspondence to the president.

Virginia

Virginia Educational Media Assn. (VEMA). Term of Office. Nov. 1986–Nov. 1987.

Pres. Vykuntapathi Thota, Box 5002-N, Virginia State Univ., Petersburg 23803. Tel. 804-520-6271; *Pres.-Elect.* Nancy Vick, 420B Winston St., Farmville 23901. Tel. 804-392-4341; *Secy.* Phyllis Garland, 3125 Lynnhaven Dr., Virginia Beach 23451. Tel. 804-499-7686; *Treas.* Helen DeWell, 8513 Claypool Rd., Richmond 23236. Tel. 804-796-5984; *Exec. Dir.* Richard J. Kubalak, 1426 N. Quincy St., Arlington 22207. Tel. 703-558-2307.

Address correspondence to the president.

Washington

Washington Lib. Media Assn. Memb. 800. Term of Office. Jan. 1, 1987–Dec. 31, 1987. Publications. *The Medium* (3 per year). *Ed.* Sharon Quesnell. *The Newsletter* (irreg.)

Pres. Eileen Andersen, 2100 Electric #335, Bellingham 98226. Tel. 206-676-6481; *V.P./Pres.-Elect.* Carol J. Hoyt, 6347 137th N.E. #267, Redmond 98052. Tel. 206-485-0452; *Secy.* Patricia McLaren, 309 Orchid, Cashmere 98815. Tel. 509-782-2914; *Treas.* Barbara J. Baker, Box 1413, Bothell 98041. Tel. 206-485-0258; *Past Pres.* Nancy Graf, 1815 W. 17 Ave., Kennewick 99336. Tel. 509-375-9671.

Address correspondence to the president.

West Virginia

West Virginia Educational Media Assn. Memb. 350. Term of Office. Apr. 1987–Apr. 1988. Publication. *WVEMA Newsletter* (q.).

Pres. Eleanor Terry, Assoc. Professor of Educational Media, Marshall Univ., Huntington 25701. Tel. 304-696-2330; *V.P./Pres.-Elect.* Debra Hickman, Media Specialist, Glenwood Schools, Rte. 1 Box 460, Princeton 24740. Tel. 304-425-2445; *Treas.* Kathleen Kawecki, School Services Specialist, WNPB-TV, 191 Scott Ave., Morgantown 26507; *Rec. Secy.* Barbara Aguirre, Libn., Southern West Virginia Community College, Logan 25601; *Memb. Chpn.* Tom Blevins, Dir., Learning Resources, Bluefield State College, Bluefield 24701; *Past Pres.* Earl Nicodemus, Assoc. Professor of Education, Box 239, West Liberty State College, West Liberty 26074.

Address correspondence to the president.

Wyoming

Wyoming School Lib. Media Assn. Memb. 50. Term of Office. Sept. 1986–Sept. 1987.

Chpn. Don Ingalls, Sheridan H.S., Sheridan 82801. Tel. 307-672-2495.

State Supervisors of School Library Media Services

Alabama

Hallie A. Perry, Educational Specialist, Library Media Services, 111 Coliseum Blvd., Montgomery 36193. Tel. 205-261-2746.

Alaska

B. Jo Morse, Alaska State Lib., School Lib. Media Coord., 650 W. International Airport Rd., Anchorage 99518. Tel. 907-561-1132.

Arizona

Linda Edgington, Education Program Specialist, State Dept. of Educ., 1535 W. Jefferson, Phoenix 85007. Tel. 602-255-5391.

Arkansas

Betty J. Morgan, Specialist, Lib. Services, Arkansas Dept. of Educ., State Educ. Bldg., Rm. 301B, Little Rock 72201. Tel. 501-371-1861.

California

John Church, Mgr., Reference Services, State Dept. of Educ., 721 Capitol Mall, Sacramento 95814. Tel. 916-322-0494.

Colorado

Nancy M. Bolt, Asst. Commissioner, Colorado State Lib., 201 E. Colfax Ave., Denver 80203. Tel. 303-866-6732.

Boyd E. Dressler, Supv., Curriculum and Instruction Project, Colorado Dept. of Educ., 201 E. Colfax Ave., Denver 80203. Tel. 303-866-6748.

John Hempstead, Supv. of School Media Services, Dept. of Educ., 201 E. Colfax Ave., Denver 80203. Tel. 303-866-6730.

Connecticut

Robert G. Hale, Senior Coord., Learning Resources and Technology Unit, and Instructional Television Consultant; Betty B. Billman, Lib. Media Consultant, Learning Resources and Technology Unit; and Dorothy M. Headspeth, Info. Specialist, Learning Resources and Technology Unit; State Dept. of Educ., Box 2219, Hartford 06145. Tel. 203-566-2250.

Delaware

Richard L. Krueger, Lib. Specialist, State Dept. of Public Instruction, John G. Townsend Bldg., Box 1402, Dover 19903. Tel. 302-736-4692.

District of Columbia

Marie Haris, Acting Supervising Dir., Dept. of Lib. Science, Public Schools of the District of Columbia, Wilkinson Administrative Annex, Pomeroy Rd. & Erie St. S.E., Washington 20020. Tel. 202-767-8643.

Florida

Sandra W. Ulm, Administrator, School Lib. Media Services, Florida Dept. of Educ., 303 Winchester Bldg. A, Tallahassee 32399. Tel. 904-488-8184.

Georgia

Nancy V. Paysinger, Dir., Media Services Unit, Div. of Instructional Media, Georgia Dept. of Educ., Suite 2054, Twin Towers E., Atlanta 30334. Tel. 404-656-2418.

Hawaii

Patsy Izumo, Dir., Multimedia Services Branch, State Dept. of Educ., 641 18th Ave., Honolulu 96816. Tel. 808-732-5535.

Idaho

Rudy H. Leverett, Coord., Educational Media Services, State Dept. of Educ., Len B. Jordan Bldg., 650 State St., Boise 83720. Tel. 208-334-2113.

Illinois

Marie Rose Sivak, Program Consultant, Lib. Media Services and Gifted Education, State Bd. of Educ., 100 N. First St., Springfield 62777. Tel. 217-782-3810.

Indiana

Phyllis Land Usher, Senior Officer, Center for School Improvement and Perfor-

mance, Indiana Dept. of Educ., Indianapolis 46204. Tel. 317-927-0296.

Iowa

Betty Jo Buckingham, Consultant, Education Media, State Dept. of Public Educ., Grimes State Office Bldg., Des Moines 50319-0146. Tel. 515-281-3707.

Kansas

June Saine Level, Lib. Media Consultant, Educational Assistance Sec., Kansas State Dept. of Educ., 120 E. Tenth St., Topeka 66612. Tel. 913-296-3434.

Kentucky

Judy L. Cooper, Program Mgr. for School Media Services, State Dept. of Educ., 1830 Capitol Plaza Tower, Frankfort 40601. Tel. 502-564-2672.

Louisiana

James S. Cookston, State Supv. of School Libs., State Dept. of Educ., Box 44064, Education Bldg., Rm. 319-A, Baton Rouge 70804. Tel. 504-342-3464.

Maine

Walter J. Taranko, Coord., Media Services, Maine State Lib., LMA Bldg., State House Sta. 64, Augusta 04333. Tel. 207-289-2956.

Maryland

Paula Montgomery, Chief, School Media Services Branch, Div. of Lib. Development and Services, State Dept. of Educ., 200 W. Baltimore St., Baltimore 21201. Tel. 301-659-2125.

Massachusetts

Harold Raynolds, Jr., Commissioner of Education, Dept. of Educ., 1385 Hancock St., Quincy 02169. Tel. 617-770-7300.

Michigan

Jeffrey P. Johnson, Deputy State Libn., Lib. of Michigan, Box 30007, 735 E. Michigan Ave., Lansing 48909. Tel. 517-373-1593.

Minnesota

Robert H. Miller, Supv., Media and Technology Unit, State Dept. of Educ., Capitol Square Bldg., St. Paul 55101. Tel. 612-296-6114.

Mississippi

Joan P. Haynie, State Dept. of Educ., Educational Media Services, Box 771, Jackson 39205. Tel. 601-359-3770.

Missouri

Carl Sitze, Asst. Dir. of School Supv., Dept. of Elementary and Secondary Education, Box 480, Jefferson City 65102. Tel. 314-751-7754.

Montana

Margaret Rolando, Lib. Media Specialist, Office of Public Instruction, Rm. 106, State Capitol, Helena 59620. Tel. 406-444-2979.

Nebraska

Jack Baillie, Administrative Asst., State Dept. of Educ., Box 94987, 301 Centennial Mall S., Lincoln 68509. Tel. 402-471-3567.

Nevada

Christine Huss, Technology Consultant, State Dept. of Educ., Capitol Complex, Carson City 89710. Tel. 702-885-3136.

New Hampshire

Susan C. Snider, Consultant, Lib. Media Services, State Dept. of Educ., Div. of Instructional Services, 101 Pleasant St., Concord 03301. Tel. 603-271-2367.

New Jersey

Anne Voss, Coord., School and College Media Services, State Dept. of Educ., State Lib., CN 520, Trenton 08625. Tel. 609-984-3292.

New Mexico

Mary Jane Vinella, Lib./Media Consultant, Dept. of Educ., Education Bldg., Santa Fe 87501-2786. Tel. 505-827-6573.

New York

Robert E. Barron, Chief, Bur. of School Lib. Media Programs, State Educ. Dept., Albany 12234. Tel. 518-474-2468.

North Carolina

Elsie L. Brumback, Asst. State Superintendent, Dept. of Public Instruction, Raleigh 27603-1712. Tel. 919-733-3170.

North Dakota

Patricia Herbel, Dir., Elementary Education, Dept. of Public Instruction, State Capitol, Bismarck 58505. Tel. 701-224-2488.

Ohio

James A. Brown, Jr., Lib./Media Consultant, State Dept. of Educ., 65 S. Front St., Rm. 1005, Columbus 43266-0308. Tel. 614-466-2407.

Oklahoma

Barbara Spriestersbach, Administrator; Clarice Roads, Asst. Administrator; Betty Riley, Bettie Estes, and Linda Cowen, Coords.; Lib. and Learning Resources Div., State Dept. of Educ., 2500 N. Lincoln Blvd., Oklahoma City 73105. Tel. 405-521-2956.

Oregon

Don G. Erickson, Coord., Instructional Technology Unit, Oregon Dept. of Educ., 700 Pringle Pkwy. S.E., Salem 97310. Tel. 503-378-6405.

James W. Sanner, Specialist, Instructional Technology, Oregon Dept. of Educ., 700 Pringle Pkwy. S.E., Salem 97310. Tel. 503-378-6405.

Pennsylvania

Doris M. Epler, Div. of School Lib. Media, State Dept. of Educ., Box 911, 333 Market St., Harrisburg 17108. Tel. 717-787-6704.

Rhode Island

Richard Harrington, Coord. Grant Programs, State Dept. of Educ., 22 Hayes St., Providence 02908. Tel. 401-277-2617.

South Carolina

Margaret W. Ehrhardt, Lib./Media Consultant, State Dept. of Educ., Rutledge Bldg., Rm. 810, Columbia 29201. Tel. 803-734-8398.

South Dakota

James O. Hansen, State Superintendent, Div. of Education, Richard F. Kneip Bldg., 700 Governors Dr., Pierre 57501. Tel. 605-773-3243.

Tennessee

Betty Latture, State Dir. of Lib. Services, Rm. 116, Cordell Hull Bldg., Tennessee

Dept. of Educ., Nashville 37219. Tel. 615-741-5813.

Texas

Mary R. Boyvey, Dir., Lib. Media Program, Texas Education Agency, 1701 N. Congress, Austin 78701-1494. Tel. 512-463-9660.

Utah

Bruce Griffin, Assoc. Superintendent, Curriculum and Instruction Div., State Office of Educ., 250 E. Fifth St., Salt Lake City 84111. Tel. 801-533-5660.

Kenneth Neal, Coord., Informational Technologies, Curriculum and Instruction Div., State Office of Educ., 250 E. Fifth St., Salt Lake City 84111. Tel. 801-533-5573.

Vermont

School Lib./Media Consultant (to be appointed), Vermont Dept. of Educ., Montpelier 05602. Tel. 802-828-3111.

Virginia

Gloria K. Barber, Supv. of School Libs. and Info. Technology, Dept. of Educ., Box 6Q, 101 N. 14 St., Richmond 23219. Tel. 804-225-2958.

Washington

Nancy Motomatsu, Supv., Learning Resources Services, Office of State Superintendent of Public Instruction, Old Capitol Bldg., Olympia 98504. Tel. 206-753-6723.

West Virginia

Jeanne Moellendick, Coord., Lib./Media and Technology, c/o West Virginia State Dept. of Educ., Capitol Complex, Bldg. 6, Rm. 337, Charleston 25305. Tel. 304-348-7826.

Wisconsin

Dir., Bur. for Instructional Media and Technology (to be appointed), State Dept. of Public Instruction, Box 7841, Madison 53707. Tel. 608-266-1965.

Wyoming

Jack Prince, Coord., Instructional Resources, Wyoming Dept. of Educ., Hathaway Bldg., Cheyenne 82002. Tel. 307-777-6225.

American Samoa

Emma S. Fung Chen Pen, Program Dir., Office of Lib. Services, Dept. of Educ., Box 1329, Pago Pago 96799. Tel. 633-1181/1182.

Northern Mariana Islands (Commonwealth of the) (CNMI)

Ruth L. Tighe, Libn., Northern Marianas College, Box 1250, Saipan, CM 96950.

Pacific Islands (Trust Territory of)

Tamar A. Jordan, Public Libn., Government of the Republic of the Marshall Islands, Dept. of Interior and Outer Islands, Majuro, Marshall Islands 96960.

Puerto Rico

Jesús López Colón, Dir., Public Lib. Div., Dept. of Educ., Box 759, Hato Rey 00919. Tel. 809-753-9191; 754-0750.

Virgin Islands

Fiolina B. Mills, State Dir., Div. of Media Lib. Services, Virgin Islands Dept. of Educ., Box 6640, St. Thomas 00801. Tel. 809-774-3725.

International Library Associations

Inter-American Association of Agricultural Librarians and Documentalists

IICA-CIDIA, 7170 Turrialba, Costa Rica

Object

"To serve as liaison among the agricultural librarians and documentalists of the Americas and other parts of the world; to promote the exchange of information and experiences through technical publications and meetings; to promote the improvement of library services in the field of agriculture and related sciences; to encourage the improvement of the professional level of the librarians and documentalists in the field of agriculture in Latin America."

Officers

Pres. Orfila Márquez, CENIAP/ FONAIAP, Maracay, Venezuela; *V.P.* Nitzia Barrantes, UPEB, Panama; *Exec. Secy.* Ana María Paz de Erickson, c/o CATIE, Turrialba, Costa Rica.

Publications

AIBDA Actualidades (irreg., 5 per year).
Boletín Especial (irreg.).
Boletín Informativo (q.).

Diccionario Histórico del Libro y de la Biblioteca (U.S. price: Memb. $15 including postage; nonmemb. $20 including postage).
Páginas de Contenido: Ciencias de la Información (q.).
Proceedings. Cuarta Reunión Interamericana de Bibliotecarios y Documentalistas Agrícolas, Mexico, D.F., April 8–11, 1975 (U.S. price: Memb. $5 including postage; nonmemb. $10 including postage).
Proceedings. Quinta Reunión Interamericana de Bibliotecarios y Documentalistas Agrícolas, San José, Costa Rica, April 10–14, 1978 (U.S. price: Memb. $10 plus postage; nonmemb. $15 plus postage).
Proceedings. Tercera Reunión Interamericana de Bibliotecarios y Documentalistas Agrícolas, Buenos Aires, Argentina, April 10–14, 1972 (U.S. price: $10 including postage). Out of print. Available in Microfiche. (Price U.S. $10).
Revista AIBDA (2 per year; Memb. $12 including postage; nonmemb. $25 including postage).

International Association of Agricultural Librarians and Documentalists

c/o J. van der Burg, Acting Secy.-Treas.
PUDOC, Jan Kophuis, Box 4, 6700 AA Wageninger, The Netherlands

Object

"The Association shall, internationally and nationally, promote agricultural library science and documentation as well as the professional interest of agricultural librarians and documentalists." Founded 1955. Memb. 634. Dues (Inst.) $40; (Indiv.) $20.

Officers

Pres. E. J. Mann, England; *V.P.s* P. J. Wortley, England; H. Haendler, Ger-

many; *Secy.-Treas. (Acting)* Jan van der Burg, The Netherlands; *Ed.* Susan C. Harris, Colombia.

Executive Committee

L. Gregorio, Philippines; E. Herpay, Hungary; C. Joling, FAO; J. Kennedy Olsen, USA; Metcalfe, CABI; N.W.

Posnett, U.K.; J. M. Schippers, The Netherlands; H. Schmid, Austria; A. T. Yaikova, USSR; representatives of national associations of agricultural librarians and documentalists.

Publications

Quarterly Bulletin of the IAALD (memb.).

International Association of Law Libraries

c/o The University of Chicago, Law School Library,
1121 E. 60 St., Chicago, IL 60637, USA

Object

"To promote on a cooperative, non-profit, and fraternal basis the work of individuals, libraries, and other institutions and agencies concerned with the acquisition and bibliographic processing of legal materials collected on a multinational basis, and to facilitate the research and other uses of such materials on a worldwide basis." Founded 1959. Memb. over 550 in 48 countries.

Officers (1986–1989)

Pres. Adolf Sprudzs, The University of Chicago, Law School Lib., 1121 E. 60 St., Chicago, IL 60637; *1st V.P.* John Rodwell, Kensington, Australia; *2nd V.P.* Yoshiro Tsuno, Tokyo, Japan; *Secy.* Timothy Kearley, Champaign, Illinois; *Treas.* Ivan Sipkov, Washington, DC.

Board Members (1986–1989)

Katalin Balázs-Veredy, Hungary; Marga Coing, Fed. Rep. of Germany; David Combe, USA; Sng Yok Fong, Rep. of Singapore; Igor I. Kavass, USA; Arno Liivak, USA; Velma Newton, Barbados;

Joachim Schwietzke, Fed. Rep. of Germany.

Services

1. The dissemination of professional information through the *International Journal of Legal Information*, through continuous contacts with formal and informal national groups of law librarians and through work within other international organizations, such as IFLA.
2. Continuing education through the one-week IALL Seminars in International Law Librarianship periodically.
3. The preparation of special literature for law librarians, such as the *European Law Libraries Guide*, and of introductions to basic foreign legal literature.
4. Direct personal contacts and exchanges between IALL members.

Publication

International Journal of Legal Information (3 per year). *Ed.-in-Chief.* Ivan Sipkov, 4917 Butterworth Pl. N.W., Washington, DC 20016.

International Association of Metropolitan City Libraries

c/o W. M. Renes, City Librarian,
Dienst Openbare Bibliotheek, Bilderdijkstraat 1-3, 2513 CM Den Haag, The Netherlands

Object

"The Association was founded to assist the worldwide flow of information and knowledge by promoting practical collaboration in the exchange of books, exhibitions, staff, and information." Memb. 97.

Officers

Pres. Constance B. Cooke, Dir. of Libs., Queens Borough Public Lib., 89-11 Merrick Blvd., Jamaica, NY 11432; *Secy.-Treas.* W. M. Renes, City Libn., Dienst Openbare Bibliotheek, Bilderdijkstraat 1-3, 2513 CM Den Haag, The Netherlands;

Past Pres. Sten Cedergren, Dir. and City Libn., Goteborg, Sweden. (Address correspondence to the secretary-treasurer.)

Annual Conference

1987, Paris, France.

Publications

Annual International Statistics of City Libraries (INTAMEL).
Review of the Three Year Research and Exchange Programme 1968–1971.
Subject Departments in Public Libraries (Budapest 1983).

International Association of Music Libraries, Archives and Documentation Centres (IAML)

c/o Neil Ratliff, Secretary-General
Music Library, Hornbake 3210,
University of Maryland, College Park, MD 20742, USA
301-454-6903

Object

To promote the activities of music libraries, archives, and documentation centers and to strengthen the cooperation among them; to promote the availability of all publications and documents relating to music and further their bibliographical control; to encourage the development of standards in all areas that concern the association; and to support the protection and preservation of musical documents of the past and the present. Memb. 1,800.

Board Members (1986–1989)

Pres. Maria Calderisi Bryce, National Lib. of Canada, 395 Wellington St., Ottawa, Ont. K1A 0N4, Canada; *Past Pres.* Anders Lönn, Musikaliska akademiens bibliotek, Box 16 326, S-103 26 Stockholm, Sweden; *V.Ps.* Bernard Huys, Bibliothèque Royale de Belgique, 4 blvd. de l'Empereur, B-1000 Brussels, Belgium; Catherine Massip, 7 rue de l'Aigle, La Garenne-Colombes F-92250, France; Svetlana Sigida, Moscow State Conservatoire, ul. Gerzena 13, Moscow K9, USSR; Malcolm Turner, British Lib., Music Lib., Great Russell St., London WC1B 3DG, England; *Secy.-Gen.* Neil Ratliff, Music Lib., Hornbake 3210, Univ. of Maryland, College Park, MD 20742, USA; *Treas.* Don L. Roberts, Music Lib., Northwestern Univ., Evanston, IL 60201, USA.

Publication

Fontes Artis Musicae (4 per year; memb.). *Ed.* Brian Redfern, 15 Tudor St., Canning Hanson Park, Birmingham B18 4DG, England.

Professional Branches

Broadcasting and Orchestra Libraries. Lucas van Dijck, Nederlandse omroep stichting, Music Lib., Box 10, NL-1200 JB Hilversum, The Netherlands.

Libraries in Music Teaching Institutions. Robert Jones, Univ. of Illinois at Urbana-Champaign, Rm. 321, Univ. Lib., Urbana, IL 61801, USA.

Music Information Centers. Rogier Starreveld, Donemus, Paulus Potterstraat 14, NL-1071 CZ Amsterdam, The Netherlands.

Public Libraries. Bent Christiansen, Nobisvej 7, 3460 Birkerød, Denmark.

Research Libraries. Susan T. Sommer, Special Collections—Music, New York. Public Lib., 111 Amsterdam Ave., New York, NY 10023, USA.

Commission and Committee Chairpersons

Bibliography Commission. Joachim Jaenecke, Staatsbibliothek Preussischer Kulturbesitz, Musikabteilung, Potsdamer Strasse 33, D-100 Berlin 30, Fed. Rep. of Germany.

Cataloguing Commission. Lenore Coral, Music Lib., Lincoln Hall, Cornell Univ., Ithaca, NY 14853, USA.

Constitution Committee. Heinz Werner, Berliner Stadtbibliothek, Breite Strasse 32-34, DDR-106 Berlin, German Dem. Rep.

Publications Committee. Catherine Massip, 7 rue de l'Aigle, La Garenne-Colombes F-92250, France.

Service and Training Commission. Marsha Berman, Music Lib., Univ. of California, Los Angeles, CA 90024, USA.

US Branch

Pres. Don Roberts, Music Lib., Northwestern Univ., Evanston, IL 60201; *Secy.-Treas.* Charles Lindahl, Eastman School of Music, Sibley Music Lib., Rochester, NY 14604.

UK Branch

Pres. Malcolm Jones, Birmingham Central Lib., Birmingham B33 3HG, England; *Gen. Secy.* Anna Smart, The Lib., Royal Northern College of Music, 124 Oxford Rd., Manchester M13 9RD, England; *Treas.* Rosemary G. Hughes, West Glamorgan County Lib., Adult Lending Services, Clifton Row, Swansea, West Glamorgan, Wales.

Publication (UK Branch)

BRIO (2 per year; memb.). *Ed.* Ian Ledsham, Barber Institute of Fine Arts, Music Lib., Univ. of Birmingham, Box 363, Birmingham B15 2TS, England.

International Association of Orientalist Librarians (IAOL)

c/o Secretary-Treasurer, William S. Wong,
Assistant Director of General Services and
Professor of Library Administration,
University Library, University of Illinois at Urbana-Champaign,
1408 W. Gregory Dr., Urbana, IL 61801, USA

Object

"To promote better communication among Orientalist librarians and libraries, and others in related fields, throughout the world; to provide a forum for the discussion of problems of common interest; to improve international cooperation among institutions holding research resources for Oriental Studies." The term Orient here specifies the Middle East, East Asia, and the South and Southeast Asia regions.

Founded in 1967 at the 27th International Congress of Orientalists (ICO) in Ann Arbor, Michigan. Affiliated with the International Federation of Library Associations and Institutions (IFLA) and International Congress for Asian and North African Studies (formerly ICO).

Officers

Pres. Warren M. Tsuneishi; *Secy.-Treas.* William S. Wong; *Ed.* Om P. Sharma.

Publication

International Association of Orientalists Librarians Bulletin (s. ann., memb.).

International Association of School Librarianship

c/o Executive Secretary, Jean Lowrie,
Box 1486, Kalamazoo, MI 49005, USA

Object

"To encourage the development of school libraries and library programs throughout all countries; to promote the professional preparation of school librarians; to bring about close collaboration among school libraries in all countries, including the loan and exchange of literature; to initiate and coordinate activities, conferences, and other projects in the field of school librarianship." Founded 1971. Memb. (Indiv.) 800; (Assn.) 19.

Officers and Executive Board

Pres. Michael Cooke, Aberystwyth, Wales; *V.P.* John G. Wright, Edmonton, Alta., Canada; *Treas.* Donald Adcock, Glen Ellyn, Illinois, USA; *Exec. Secy.* Jean Lowrie, Kalamazoo, Michigan, USA; *Dirs.* David Elaturoti, Nigeria; Ann Parry, Sydney, Australia; Shirley Coulter, Nova Scotia, Canada; Oddvar Walmsness, Asker, Norway; Mieko Nagakura, Kanagawa, Japan; Joyce Wallen, Jamaica, West Indies; Peter Mwathi, Nairobi, Kenya; Wong Kim Song, Kuala Lumpur, Malaysia.

Publications

Getting Started: A Bibliography of Ideas and Procedures.

IASL Conference Proceedings (ann.).

IASL Monograph Series.

IASL Newsletter (q.).

Indicators of Quality for School Library Media Programs.

Persons to Contact for Visiting School Libraries/Media Centers, 4th ed.

American Memberships

American Assn. of School Libs.; Hawaii School Lib. Assn.; Illinois Assn. for Media in Education; Louisiana Assn. of School Libns.; Maryland Educational Media Organization; Michigan Assn. for Media in Education; Oregon Educational Media Assn; Virginia Educational Media Assn.

International Association of Sound Archives

c/o Helen Harrison, Media Librarian, Open University
Library, Walton Hall, Milton Keynes MK7 6AA, England

Object

IASA is a UNESCO-affiliated organization established in 1969 to function as a medium for international cooperation between archives and other institutions that preserve recorded sound documents. This association is involved with the preservation, organization, and use of sound recordings; techniques of recordings and methods of reproducing sound; the international exchange of literature and information; and in all subjects relating to the professional work of sound archives.

Membership

Open to all categories of archives, institutions, and individuals who preserve sound recordings or have a serious interest in the purposes or welfare of IASA.

Officers (1984–1987)

Pres. Ulf Scharlau, Süddeutscher Rundfunk, Schallarchiv/Bandaustausch, Neckarstrasse 230, D-7000 Stuttgart, Fed. Rep. of Germany; *V.Ps.* Peter Burgis, Asst. Director, National Film and Sound Archive, Canberra City, ACT Australia; D. G. Lance, Curator of Audiovisual Records, Australian War Memorial, Box 345, Canberra City, ACT 2601, Australia; Dietrich Lotichius, Leiter das Schallarchivs, Norddeutscher, Rundfunk, Rothenbaumchaussee 132, D-2000 Hamburg 13, Fed. Rep. of Germany; *Ed.* Dietrich Schüller, Phonogrammarchiv der Österreichischen Akademie der Wissenschaften, Liebiggasse 5, A-1010 Wien, Austria; *Secy. Gen.* Helen Harrison, Media Libn., Open Univ. Lib., Walton Hall, Milton Keynes MK7 6AA, England; *Treas.* Anna Maria Foyer, Sveriges Riksradio, Radioarkivet, S 10510 Stockholm, Sweden.

Publications

An Archive Approach to Oral History, by David Lance (1978).
Directory of Members, second edition, compiled by Grace Koch (1982. ISBN 0 946475 00 8).
Phonographic Bulletin (journal. ISSN 02533-004X). Index issues 1–40, 1971–1984.
Selection in Sound Archives, edited by Helen Harrison (1984. ISBN 0 94675 02 4).
Sound Archives: A Guide to Their Establishment and Development, edited by David Lance (1983. ISBN 0 946475 01 6).

International Council on Archives

Secretariat, 60 rue des Francs-Bourgeois,
F-75003 Paris, France

Object

"To establish, maintain, and strengthen relations among archivists of all lands, and among all professional and other agencies or institutions concerned with the custody, organization, or administration of archives, public or private, wherever located." Established 1948. Memb. 750 (representing 125 countries and territories). Dues (Indiv.) $30; (Inst.) $50; (Archives Assns.) $50 or $100; (Central Archives Directorates) $230 or $115 minimum, computed on the basis of GNP and GNO per capita.

Officers

Pres. Hans Booms; *V.Ps.* Angeline Kamba, Jean Favier; *Exec. Secy.* C. Kesckeméti; *Treas.* Klaus Oldenhage. (Address all correspondence to the executive secretary.)

Publications

ADPA—Archives and Automation (ann. 250 FB or U.S. $9 memb.; subscriptions to M. Jean Pieyns, Archives de l'Etat, rue Pouplin, 8, B-4000 Liege, Belgium).

Archivum (ann.; memb. or subscription to KG Saur Verlag, Possenbacker Str. 2, Postfach 71 1009, D-8 Munich 71, Fed. Rep. of Germany).

Guide to the Sources of the History of Nations (Latin American Series, 10 vols. pub.; African Series, 10 vols. pub.; Asian Series, 10 vols. pub.; Asian Series, 4 vols. pub.).

ICA Bulletin (s. ann.; memb., or U.S. $5).

Microfilm Bulletin (subscriptions to Centro Nacional de Microfilm, serrano 115, Madrid 6, Spain).

List of other publications available upon request to ICA secretariat, Paris, France.

International Federation for Documentation

Box 90402, 2509 LK The Hague, Netherlands

Object

To group internationally organizations and individuals interested in the problems of documentation and to coordinate their efforts; to promote the study, organization, and practice of documentation in all its forms; and to contribute to the creation of an international network of information systems.

Program

The program of the federation includes activities for which the following committees have been established: Central Classification Committee (for UDC); Research on the Theoretical Basis of Information; Linguistics in Documentation; Information for Industry; Education and Training; Classification Research; Terminology of Information and Documentation; Patent Information and Documentation; Social Sciences Documentation; Informetrics. It also includes the BSO Panel (Broad System of Ordering).

Officers

Pres. Michael W. Hill, Assoc. Dir., The British Lib. Science, Technology and In-

dustry, 25 Southampton Bldgs., Chancery Lane, London WC1A 2AW, United Kingdom; *V.Ps.* S. Fujiwara, Kanagawa Univ., Research Institute on Information and Knowledge, 3 chome 27, Rokkakubashi, Kanagawaku, Yokohama, Japan 221; A. I. Mikhailov, VINITI, Baltijskaja ul. 14, Moscow A219, USSR; M. H. Wali, Dir., National Lib. of Nigeria, PMB 12626, Lagos, Nigeria; *Treas.* P. P. Canisius, Dir., Bundesanstalt für Strassenwesen (BASt), Brüderstrasse 53, D-5060 Bergisch Gladback 1, Fed. Rep. of Germany; *Councillors.* J. R. P. Alvarez Ossorio, Madrid, Spain; T. Földi, Budapest, Hungary; E. Jirsa, Prague, Czechoslovakia; Ritva T. Launo, Helsinki, Finland; R. Ogwang-Ameny, Kampala, Uganda; J. Arias Ordoñez, Bogota, Colombia; T. S. Rajagopalan, New Delhi, India; W. L. Renaud, The Hague, Netherlands; M. Ristić, Belgrade, Yugoslavia; Vania M. Rodrigues Hermes de Araújo, Brasilia, Brazil; E. V. Smith, Ottawa, Canada; M. Thomas, Paris, France; *Belgian Memb.* J.-E. Humblet, Genval, Belgium; *Secy.-Gen.* Stella Keenan, The Hague, Netherlands; *Pres. FID/CLA*, R. A. Gietz, Buenos Aires, Argentina; *Pres. FID/CAO.* B. L. Burton, Hong Kong. (Address all correspondence to the secretary-general.)

Publications

FID Annual Report (ann.).
FID Directory (bienn.).
FID News Bulletin (mo.) with supplements on document reproduction (q.).
FID Publications (ann.).
International Forum on Information and Documentation (q.).
Newsletter on Education and Training Programmes for Information Personnel (q.).
R & D Projects in Documentation and Librarianship (bi-mo.).
Proceedings of congresses; Universal Decimal Classification editions; manuals; directories; bibliographies on information science, documentation, reproduction, mechanization, linguistics, training, and classification.

Membership

Approved by the FID Council; ratification by the FID General Assembly.

American Membership

U.S. Interim National Committee for FID.

International Federation of Film Archives

Secretariat, Coudenberg 70, B-1000 Brussels, Belgium

Object

"To facilitate communication and cooperation between its members, and to promote the exchange of films and information; to maintain a code of archive practice calculated to satisfy all national film industries, and to encourage industries to assist in the work of the Federation's members; to advise its members on all matters of interest to them, especially the preservation and study of films; to give every possible assistance and encouragement to new film archives and to those interested in creating them." Founded in Paris, 1938. Memb. 76 (in 56 countries).

Executive Committee (June 1985–June 1987)

Pres. Anna Lena Wibom, Sweden; *V.Ps.* Hector Garcia Mesa, Cuba; Wolfgang

Klaue, DDR; Sam Kula, Canada; *Secy. Gen.* Guido Cincotti, Italy; *Treas.* Raymond Borde, France. (Address correspondence to B. Van der Elst, executive secretary, at headquarters address.)

Committee Members

Eileen Bowser, USA; Robert Daudelin, Canada; David Francis, UK; PK Nair, India; Eva Orbanz, Fed. Rep. of Germany.

Publications

Annual Bibliography of FIAF Members' Publications.
Bibliography of National Filmographies.
Cinema 1900-1906, An Analytical Study.
Film Cataloging.
Film Preservation (available in English or French).
Glossary of Filmographic Terms in English, French, German, Spanish, and Russian.

Guidelines for Describing Unpublished Script Materials.
Handbook for Film Archives (available in English or French).
International Directory to Film & TV Documentation Sources.
International Index to Film Periodicals (cumulative volumes).
International Index to Film Television Periodicals (microfiche service).
International Index to Television Periodicals (cumulative volumes).
The Preservation and Restoration of Colour and Sound in Films.
Proceedings of the FIAF Symposiums; 1977: L'Influence du Cinema Sovietique Muet Sur le Cinema Mondial/The Influence of Silent Soviet Cinema on World Cinema; 1978: Cinema 1900-1906; 1980: Problems of Selection in Film Archives.
Study of the Usage of Computers for Filmcataloguing.

International Federation of Library Associations and Institutions (IFLA)

c/o The Royal Library, Box 95312,
2509 CH The Hague, Netherlands

Object

"To promote international understanding, cooperation, discussion, research, and development in all fields of library activity, including bibliography, information services, and the education of library personnel, and to provide a body through which librarianship can be represented in matters of international interest." Founded 1927. Memb. (Lib. Assns.) 171; (Inst.) 823; (Aff.) 156; 123 countries.

Officers and Executive Board

Pres. Hans-Peter Geh, Württembergische Landesbibliothek, Stuttgart, Fed. Rep. of Germany; *1st V.P.* Henriette Avram, Lib. of Congress, Washington, DC, USA; *2nd V.P.* Engelsina V. Pereslegina, All-Union State Lib. of Foreign Literature, Moscow, USSR; *Treas.* Anthony J. Evans, Loughborough Univ. of Technology, Loughborough, UK; *Exec. Bd.* P. B. Mangla, Delhi Univ. Campus, Delhi, India; P. J. Th. Schoots, City Lib., Rotterdam, Netherlands; M. Törngren, Stockholms Stadsbibliothek, Stockholm, Sweden; R. Wedgeworth, School of Lib. Service, Columbia Univ., New York, New York, USA; *Ex officio Memb.* I.H. Pizer, Chpn. Professional Bd., Univ. of Illinois, Chicago, Illinois, USA; *Secy. Gen.* Margreet Wijnstroom, IFLA headquarters;

Programme Officer, IFLA International Programme for Universal Bibliographic Control. Barbara Jover, c/o Reference Div., British Lib., London, UK; *Programme Officer, IFLA International Programme for UAP.* Stephen Vickers, c/o British Lib., Lending Div., Boston Spa, Wetherby, West Yorkshire, UK; *Dir., IFLA Office for International Lending.* M. B. Line, c/o British Lib. Lending Div., Boston Spa, Wetherby, West Yorkshire, UK: *Publications Officer.* W. R. H. Koops, Univ. Libn., Groningen, Netherlands; *Professional Coord.* A. L. van Wesemael, IFLA headquarters; *Programme Development Officer.* A. Wysocki, IFLA headquarters.

Publications

IFLA Annual.
IFLA Directory (bienn.).
IFLA Journal (q.).

IFLA Professional Reports.
IFLA Publications Series.
IM Newsletter (s. ann.).
International Cataloguing (q.).
UAP Newsletter (s. ann.).

American Membership

American Assn. of Law Libs.; American Lib. Assn.; Art Libs. Society of North America; Assn. for Lib. and Info. Science Education; Assn. for Population Planning/Family Planning Libs.; Assn. of Research Libs.; International Assn. of Law Libs.; International Assn. of Orientalist Libns.; International Assn. of School Libns.; Medical Lib. Assn.; Special Libs. Assn. *Institutional Membs.* There are 128 libraries and related institutions that are institutional members or affiliates of IFLA in the United States (out of a total of 823), and 61 Personal Affiliates (out of a total of 156).

International Organization for Standardization

ISO Central Secretariat
1 r. de Varembé, Case postale 56, CH-1211 Geneva 20, Switzerland

Object

To promote the development of standards in the world in order to facilitate the international exchange of goods and services and to develop mutual cooperation in the spheres of intellectual, scientific, technological, and economic activity.

Officers

Pres. I. Yamashita, Japan; *V.P.* D. G. Spickernell, UK; *Secy.-Gen.* Lawrence D. Eicher.

Technical Work

The technical work of ISO is carried out by over 180 technical committees. These include:

TC 46 — Documentation (Secretariat, DIN Deutsches Institut for Normung, 4-10, Burggrafenstr., Postfach 1107, D-1000 Berlin 30). Scope: Standardization of practices relating to libraries, documentation and information centers, indexing and abstracting services, archives, information science, and publishing.

TC 37 — Terminology (Principles & Coordination) (Secretariat, Osterreisches

Normungsinstitut, Leopoldgasse 4, A-1020 Vienna, Austria). Scope: Standardization of methods for creating, compiling, and coordinating terminologies.

TC 97—Information Processing Systems (Secretariat, American National Standards Institute, ANSI, 1430 Broadway, New York, NY 10018, USA). Scope: Standardization, including terminology, in the field of information processing systems, including but not limited to, personal computers and office equipment.

Publications

Activities Report (ann.).
Bulletin (mo.).
Catalogue (ann.).
Liaisons.
Member Bodies.
Memento (ann.).

Foreign Library Associations

The following list of regional and national foreign library associations is a selective one. For a more complete list with detailed information, see *International Guide to Library, Archival, and Information Science Associations* by Josephine Riss Fang and Alice H. Songe (R. R. Bowker, 1980). The *Guide* also provides information on international associations, some of which are described in detail under "International Library Associations" (immediately preceding this section). A more complete list of foreign and international library associations also can be found in *International Literary Market Place* (R. R. Bowker), an annual publication.

Regional

Africa

International Assn. for the Development of Documentation, Libs., and Archives in Africa, *Secy.* Zacheus Sunday Ali, Box 375, Dakar, Senegal.

Standing Conference of African Lib. Schools, c/o School of Libns., Archivists & Documentalists, Univ. of Dakar, B. P. 3252, Dakar, Senegal.

Standing Conference of African Univ. Libs., Eastern Area (SCAULEA), c/o Univ. Lib., Univ. of Nairobi, Kenya.

Standing Conference of African Univ. Libs., Western Area (SCAULWA), c/o M. Jean Aboghe-Obyan, Bibliotheque Universitaire, Univ. Omar Bongo, Libreville, Gabon.

Standing Conference of Eastern, Central, and Southern African Libns., c/o Tanzania Lib. Assn., Box 2645, Dar-es-Salaam, Tanzania.

The Americas

Asociación de Bibliotecas Universitarias, de Investigación e Institucionales del Caribe (Assn. of Caribbean Univ., Research and Institutional Libs.), *Exec. Secy.* Oneida R. Ortiz, Apdo. Postal S. Estacion de la Universidad, San Juan, PR 00931.

Asociación Latinoamericana de Escuelas de Bibliotecología y Ciencias de la Información (Latin American Assn. of Schools of Lib. and Info. Science), Colegio de Bibliotecología, Universidad Nacional Autónoma de México, México 20, D. F., Mexico.

Seminar on the Acquisition of Latin American Lib. Materials, SALALM

Secretariat, *Exec. Secy.* Suzanne Hodgman, Memorial Lib., Univ. of Wisconsin-Madison, Madison, WI 53706.

Asia

Congress of Southeast Asian Libns. (CONSAL), *Chpn.* Serafin Quiason, c/o National Lib. of the Philippines, T. M. Kalaw St., Manila, Philippines 2801.

British Commonwealth of Nations

Commonwealth Lib. Assn. (COMLA), c/o *Hon. Exec. Secy.* Joan E. Swaby, Box 40, Mandeville, Manchester, Jamaica, West Indies.

Standing Conference on Lib. Materials on Africa (SCOLMA), c/o *Secy.* P. M. Larby, Institute of Commonwealth Studies, 27-28 Russell Sq., London WC1B 5DS, England.

Europe

LIBER (Ligue des Bibliothèques Européenes de Recherche), Assn. of European Research Lib., c/o H.-A. Koch, Staats-und Universitätsbibliothek, Postfach 330160, D-2800 Bremen 33, Federal Republic of Germany.

Nordisk Videnskabeligt Bibliotekarforbund — NVBF (Scandinavian Assn. of Research Libns.), c/o Førstebibliotekar Ulla Jensen, I.D.E. Danish Institute of International Exchange, Amaliegade 38, DK 1256 Copenhagen K, Denmark.

National

Argentina

Asociación Argentina de Bibliotecas y Centros de Información Científicos y Técnicos (Argentine Assn. of Scientific and Technical Libs. & Info. Centers), Santa Fe 1145, Buenos Aires. *Exec. Secy.* Olga E. Veronelli.

Australia

Australian School Lib. Assn., c/o *Secy.* Box 287, Alderley, Qld. N.S.W. 4051.

LASIE (Lib. Automated Systems Info. Exchange), *Pres.* Dorothy Peake, Box 602, Lane Cove, N.S.W. 2066.

Lib. Assn. of Australia, *Exec. Dir.* Jennifer Adams, 376 Jones St., Ultimo, N.S.W. 2007.

The School Lib. Assn. of New South Wales, c/o *Secy.* Box 80, Balmain N.S.W. 2041.

State Libns.' Council of Australia, *Chpn.* Robert Sharman, State Libn., State Lib. Service of Western Australia, Box 8232, Perth Sterline St., Western Australia 6000.

Austria

Österreichische Gesellschaft für Dokumentation und Information — ÖGDI (Austrian Society for Documentation and Info.), *Exec. Secy.* Bruno Hofer, c/o ON, Österreichisches Normungsinstitut, Heinestrasse 38, POB 130, A-1021 Vienna.

Verband Österreichischer Volksbüchereien und Volksbibliothekare (Assn. of Austrian Public Libs. & Libns.), *Chpn.* Franz Pascher; *Secy.* Heinz Buchmüller, Langegasse 37, A-1080 Vienna.

Vereinigung Österreichischer Bibliothekare — VÖB (Assn. of Austrian Libns.), *Pres.* Ferdinand Baumgartner, c/o Österreichische Nationalbibliothek, Josefsplatz 1, A-1015 Vienna.

Belgium

Archives et Bibliothèques de Belgique/ Archief-en Bibliotheekwezen in België (Archives and Libs. of Belgium), *Exec. Secy.* T. Verschaffel, Bibliothèque Roy-

ale Albert I, 4 bd. de l'Empereur, B-1000 Brussels.

Association Belge de Documentation-ABD/Belgische Vereniging voor Documentatie-BVD (Belgian Assn. for Documentation), Box 110, 1040 Brussels 26. *Pres.* Van Siriaeys Luc.

Institut d'Enseignement Superieur Social de l'Etat, Sec. Bibliothecaires–Documentalistes (State Institute of Higher Social Education, Libn., and Documentalist Section), Rue de l'Abbaye 26, B-1050 Brussels.

Vereniging van Religieus-Wetenschappelijke Bibliothécarissen (Assn. of Theological Libns.), Minderbroederstr. 5, B-3800 St. Truiden. *Exec. Secy.* K. Van de Casteele, Spoorweglaan 237, B-2610 Wilrijk.

Vlaamse Vereniging voor Bibliotheek, Archief, en Documentatiewezen — VVBAD (Flemish Assn. of Libns., Archivists, and Documentalists), *Pres.* F. Heymans; *Secy.* F. Franssens, Goudbloemstraat 10, 2008 Antwerpen.

Bolivia

Asociación Boliviana de Bibliotecarios (Bolivian Lib. Assn.), *Pres.* Efraín Virreira Sánchez, Casilla 992, Cochabamba.

Brazil

Associação dos Arquivistas Brasileiros (Assn. of Brazilian Archivists), Praia de Botafogo 186, Sala B-217, CEP 22253 Rio de Janeiro, RJ. *Pres.* Lia Temporal Malcher.

Federação Brasileira de Associações de Bibliotecários (Brazilian Federation of Libns. Assns.), c/o. *Pres.* May Brooking Negrão, Rua Avanhandava, 40–cj. 110, Bela Vista, CEP 01306 São Paulo.

Bulgaria

Bulgarian Union of Public Libs., ul. Alabin, Sofia.

Sekciylna na Bibliotechnite Rabotnitsi pri Zentrainija Komitet na Profesionalniya Suyuz na Rabotnicite ot Poligrafičeskata Promišlenost i Kulturnite Instituti (Lib. Sec. at the Trade Union of the Workers in the Polygraphic Industry and Cultural Institutions), c/o Cyril and Methodius National Lib. Blvd., Tolbuhin. *Pres.* Stefan Kancev.

Canada

Association Canadienne de Science de l'Information (Canadian Assn. for Info. Science), Box 6174, Sta. J., Ottawa, Ont. K2A IT2.

Association Canadienne des Écoles des Bibliothécaires (Canadian Assn. of Lib. Schools), *Pres.* L. J. Amey, School of Lib. Service, Dalhousie Univ., Halifax, N.S. B3H 4H8.

Association pour l'avancement des sciences et des techniques de la documentation (ASTED, Inc.), *Dir.-Gen.* Lise Brousseau, 7243 rue Saint-Denis, Montréal P.Q. H2R 2E3.

Canadian Council of Lib. Schools (Conseil Canadien des Ecoles de Bibliothéconomie) (CCLS/CCEB), *Chair.* John G. Wright, Dean, Faculty of Lib. Science, Univ. of Alberta, Edmonton, Alberta T6G 2J4.

Canadian Lib. Assn., *Exec. Dir.* Jane Cooney, 200 Elgin St., 6th fl., Ottawa, Ont. K2P 1L5. (For detailed information on the Canadian Lib. Assn. and its divisions, see "National Library and Information-Industry Associations, United States and Canada"; for information on the library associations of the provinces of Canada, see "State, Provincial, and Regional Library Associations.")

La Société bibliographique du Canada

(The Bibliographical Society of Canada), *Secy.-Treas.* W. P. Stoneman, Victoria College, Univ. of Toronto, Toronto, Ont. M5S 1K7.

Chile

Colegio de Bibliotecarios de Chile, A. G. (Chilean Lib. Assn.), *Pres.* Soledad Fernández–Corugedo E., *Secy.* Miriam Angulo Fuentes, Casilla 3741, Santiago.

China (People's Republic of)

Library Assn. of China, c/o National Central Lib., 43 Nan Hai Rd., Taipei, *Exec. Dir.* Cheng–Luang Lin.
Zhongguo Tushuguan Xuehui (China Society of Lib. Science—CSLS), *Secy.-Gen.* Liu Deyuan, 7 Wenjinjie, Beijing (Peking).

Colombia

Asociación Colombiana de Bibliotecarios—ASCOLBI (Colombian Assn. of Libns.), Apdo. Aéreo 30883, Bogotá, D.E.
Asociación de Egresados de la Escuela Interamericana de Bibliotecologia—ASEIBI (International Lib. School Grad. Assn.), Apdo. Aéreo 1307, Medellin.

Costa Rica

Asociación Costarricense de Bibliotecarios (Assn. of Costa Rican Libns.), Apdo. Postal 3308, San José.

Cyprus

Kypriakos Synthesmos Vivliothicarion (Lib. Assn. of Cyprus), c/o Pedagogical Academy, Box 1039, Nikosia. *Secy.* Paris G. Rossos.

Czechoslovakia

Ústřední knihovnická rada ČSR (Central Lib. Council of the Czechoslovak Socialist Republic), *Chief, Dept. of Libs.* Marie Sedláčková, c/o Ministry of Culture of CSR, Valdštejnská 10, 118 11 Praha 1-Malá Strana.
Zväz slovenských knihovníkov a informatikov (Assn. of Slovak Libns. and Documentalists), *Pres.* Vít Rak; *Exec. Secy.* Elena Sakálová, Michalská 1, 814 17 Bratislava.

Denmark

Arkivforeningen (The Archives Society), *Exec. Secy.* Anna Thestrup, Rigsarkivet, Rigsdagsgarden 9, DK-1218 Copenhagen K.
Danmarks Biblioteksforening (Danish Lib. Assn.), *Pres.* Bent Sørensen, Trekronergade 15, DK-2500 Valby-Copenhagen.
Danmarks Forskningsbiblioteksforening (Danish Research Lib. Assn.), *Pres.* Mette Stockmarr, Danmarks Laererhøjskoles Bibliotek, Emdrupvej 101, DK-2400 Copenhagen NV.
Danmarks Skolebiblioteksforening (Assn. of Danish School Libs.), *Exec. Secy.* Niels Jacobsen, Norrebrogade 159, DK-2200 Copenhagen N.
Dansk Musikbiblioteksforening, Dansk sektion of AIBM (Danish Assn. of Music Libs., Danish Sec. of AIBM), c/o *Secy.,* Irlandsvej 90, DK-2300 Copenhagen K.

Dominican Republic

Asociación Dominicana de Bibliotecarios—ASODOBI (Dominican Lib. Assn.), c/o Biblioteca Nacional, Plaza de la Cultura, Santo Domingo. *Pres.* Prospero J. Mella Chavier; *Secy.-Gen.* Hipólito González C.

Ecuador

Asociación Ecuatoriana de Bibliotecarios—AEB (Ecuadorian Lib. Assn.), *Exec. Secy.* Elizabeth Carrion, Casa de la Cultura Ecuatoriana, Casilla 87, Quito.

Egypt

See United Arab Republic.

El Salvador

Asociación de Bibliotecarios de El Salvador (El Salvador Lib. Assn.), c/o *Secy.-Gen.* Edgar Antonio Pérez Borja, Urbanización Gerardo Barrios Polígono, "B" No. 5, San Salvador, C.A.

Ethiopia

Ye Ethiopia Betemetshaft Serategnoch Mahber (Ethiopian Lib. Assn. — ELA), *Exec. Secy.* Befekadu Debela, Box 30530, Addis Ababa.

Finland

Kirjastonhoitajaliitto–Bibliotekarieförbundet r.y. (Finnish Libns. Assn.), *Exec. Secy.* Jouko Lieko, Järnvägsmannagatan, Rautatieläisenkatu 6, SF–00520 Helsinki.

Suomen Kirjastoseura-Finlands Biblioteksförening (Finnish Lib. Assn.), *Secy.-Gen.* Maija Berndtson, Museokatu 18 A, SF-00100 Helsinki 10.

Tieteellisten Kirjastojen Virkailijat-Vetenskapliga Bibliotekens Tjänstemannaförening r.y. (Assn. of Research and Univ. Libns.), *Exec. Secy.* Kirsti Janhunen, Akavatalo, Rautatieläisenkatu 6, SF–0052 Helsinki.

Tietopalveluseura-Samfundet för Informationstjänst i Finland (Finnish Society for Info. Services), c/o *Pres.* Ritva

Launo, The State Alcohol Monopoly of Finland (ALKO), Helsinki.

France

Association des Archivistes Français (Assn. of French Archivists), *Pres.* Mlle. R. Cleyet-Michaud; *Exec. Secys.* Mme. M. P. Arnauld and Mme. E. Gautier-Desuaux, 60 r. des Francs-Bourgeois, F-75141 Paris, Cedex 03.

Association des Bibliothécaires Français (Assn. of French Libns.), *Exec. Secy.* Jacqueline Dubois, 65 rue de Richelieu, F-75002 Paris.

Association des Bibliothèques Ecclésiastiques de France (Assn. of French Theological Libs.), *Exec. Secy.* Jean–Marie Barbier, 6 rue du Regard, F-75006 Paris.

Association Française des Documentalistes et des Bibliotécaires Spécialisés — ADBS (Assn. of French Info. Scientists and Special Libns.), *Exec. Secy.* Serge Cacaly, 5, Av. Franco-Russe, 75007 Paris.

German Democratic Republic

Bibliotheksverband der Deutschen Demokratischen Republik (Lib. Assn. of the German Democratic Republic), c/o *Exec. Dir.* Klaus Plötz, Hermann-Matern-Str. 57, DDR-1040 Berlin.

Germany (Federal Republic of)

Arbeitsgemeinschaft der Kunstbibliotheken (Working Group of Art Libs.), c/o Bibliothek des Zentralinstituts für Kunstgeschichte in München, Meiserstr. 10, D-8000 Munich 2.

Arbeitsgemeinschaft der Spezialbibliotheken (Assn. of Special Libs.), *Chpn.* Walter Manz, Zentralbibliothek der Kernforschungsanlage Jülich GmbH, Postfach 1913, D-5170 Jülich 1.

Deutsche Gesellschaft für Dokumentation e.V. — DGD (German Society for Docu-

mentation), *Scientific Secy.* Hilde Strohl-Goebel, Westendstr. 19, D-6000 Frankfurt am Main 1.

Deutscher Bibliotheksverband e.V. (German Lib. Assn.), *Secy.* Ursula Schumacher, Bundesallee, 184/185, D-1000 Berlin 31.

Verband der Bibliotheken des Landes Nordrhein-Westfalen (Assn. of Libs. in the Federal State of North Rhine-Westphalia), *Chpn.* Hartwig Lohse, Ltd. Bibliotheksdirektor, Universitätsbibliothek Bonn, Vorsitzender, Adenaverallee 39–41, 5300 Bonn 1.

Verein der Bibliothekare an Öffentlichen Bibliotheken e.V.—VBB (Assn. of Libns. at Public Libs.), *Chpn.* Birgit Dankert; *Secy.* Katharina Boulanger, Postfach 1324, D-7410 Reutlingen 1.

Verein der Diplom-Bibliothekare an wissenschaftlichen Bibliotheken (Assn. of Graduated Libns. at Academic Libs.), *Chpn.* Helga Schwarz, c/o Deutsches Bibliotheksinstitut, Bundesallee 184/185, D-1000 Berlin 31.

Verein deutscher Archivare—VdA (Assn. of German Archivists), *Chpn.* Hermann Rumschöttel, Generaldirektion der Staatlichen Archive Bayerns, Schönfeldstr. 5, Postfach 22 02 40, D-8000 Munich 22.

Verein Deutscher Bibliothekare e.V.—VDB (Assn. of German Libns.), *Pres.* Ltd. Bibliotheksdirektor Yorck Haase; *Secy.* Bibliotheksrat Gerhard Haass, Landes- und Hochschulbibliothek, Schloss, D-6100 Darmstadt.

Ghana

Ghana Lib. Assn., *Exec. Secy.* D. B. Addo, Box 4105, Accra.

Great Britain

See United Kingdom.

Guatemala

Asociación Bibliotecológica Guatemalteca (Lib. Assn. of Guatemala), c/o *Dir.*, 18 Avenida "A," 4-04 Zona 15 V.H.I., Guatemala, C.A.

Guyana

Guyana Lib. Assn. (GLA), *Secy.* Wenda Stephenson, c/o National Lib., Box 10240, 76/77 Main St., Georgetown.

Hong Kong

Hong Kong Lib. Assn., *Chpn.* Malcolm Quinn, c/o Box 10095, G.P.O. Hong Kong.

Hungary

Magyar Könyvtárosok Egyesülete (Assn. of Hungarian Libns.), *Pres.* I. Billédi; *Secy.* D. Kovács, Úri U. 54–56, H–1014 Budapest.

Tájékoztatási Tudományos Tanács—MTESZ/TTT (Info. Science Council), c/o Pál Gágyor, Kossuth tér 6-8 Budapest 1055.

Iceland

Bókavarðafélag Islands (Icelandic Lib. Assn.), *Pres.* Erla Jónsdóttir, Box 7050, 127 Reykjavík.

India

Indian Assn. of Special Libs. and Info. Centres (IASLIC), *Gen. Secy.* S. K. Kapoor, P-291, CIT Scheme 6M, Kankurgachi, Calcutta 700 054.

Indian Lib. Assn. (ILA), *Pres.* T. S. Rajagopalan; *Secy.* C. P. Vashishth, A/40–41, No. 201, Ansal Bldgs., Dr. Mukerjee Nagar, Delhi 110 009.

Indonesia

Ikatan Pustakawan Indonesia — IP1 (Indonesian Lib. Assn.), *Pres.* Mastini Hardjo Prakoso; *Secy.* Soemarno HS, Jalan Merdeka Selatan 11, Jakarta-Pusat.

Iran

Iranian Lib. Assn., *Exec. Secy.* M. Niknam Vazifeh, Box 11-1391, Tehran.

Iraq

Iraqi Lib. Assn., *Exec. Secy.* N. Kamal-al-Deen, Box 4081, Baghdad-Adhamya.

Ireland (Republic of)

Cumann Leabharlann Na h-Éireann (Lib. Assn. of Ireland), *Pres.* I. O'Deirg; *Hon. Secy.* W. P. Smith, 53 Uppr. Mount St., Dublin 2.

Cumann Leabharlannaith Scoile — CLS (Irish Assn. of School Libns.), Headquarters: The Lib., Univ. College, Dublin 4. *Exec. Secy.* Sister Mary Columban, Loreto Convent, Foxrock Co., Dublin.

Italy

Associazione Italiana Biblioteche — AIB (Italian Libs. Assn.), *Secy.* G. Lazzari, Casella Postale 2461, 00100 Rome A-D.

Associazione Nazionale Archivistica Italiana — ANAI (National Assn. of Italian Archivists), *Secy.* Antonino Lombardo, Via di Ponziano 15, 00152 Rome.

Ivory Coast

Association pour le Développement de la Documentation des Bibliothèques et Archives de la Côte d'Ivoire (Assn. for the Development of Documentation, Libs., and Archives of the Ivory Coast), c/o Bibliothèque Nationale, B.P. 20915 Abidjan.

Jamaica

Jamaica Lib. Assn. (JLA), *Secy.* Gloria E. Salmon, Box 58, Kingston 5.

Japan

Information Science and Technology Assn., Japan (INHOSTA), *Pres.* Yukio Nakamura; *Dir. and Secy.-Gen.* Tsunetaka Ueda, Sasaki Bldg., 5-7 Koisikawa 2-chome, Bunkyoku, Tokyo 112.

Nihon Toshokan Kyôkai (Japan Lib. Assn. — JLA), *Secy.-Gen.* Hitoshi Kurihara, 1-10, Taishido 1-chome, Setagayaku, Tokyo 154.

Senmon Toshokan Kyôgikai — SENTOKYO (Japan Special Libs. Assn). *Exec. Dir.* Yoshitaro Tanabe, c/o National Diet Lib., 1-10-1 Nagata-cho, Chiyodaku, Tokyo 100.

Jordan

Jordan Lib. Assn. (JLA), *Pres.* Farouk Moaz; *V.P.* Izzat Zahidah; *Secy.* Ismail Al-Dabbas; *Treas.* Ali Turki, Box 6289, Amman.

Korea (Democratic People's Republic of)

Lib. Assn. of the Democratic People's Republic of Korea, *Secy.* Li. Geug, Central Lib., Box 109, Pyongyang.

Korea (Republic of)

Hanguk Tosogwan Hyophoe (Korean Lib. Assn.), *Exec. Secy.* Dae Kwon Park, 100-177, 1-Ka, Hoehyun-Dong, Choong-Ku, CPO Box 2041, Seoul.

Laos

Association des Bibliothécaires Laotiens (Laos Lib. Assn.), Direction de la Bibliothèque Nationale, Ministry of Education, Box 704, Vientiane.

Lebanon

Lebanese Lib. Assn. (LLA), *Pres.* L. Hanhan, Saab Medical Lib., AUB, Beirut.

Malaysia

Persatuan Perpustakaan Malaysia—PPM (Lib. Assn. of Malaysia), *Secy.* Ahmad Ridzuan, Box 12545, 50782 Kuala Lumpur.

Mauritania

Association Mauritanienne des Bibliothécaires, des Archivistes et des Documentalistes—AMBAD (Mauritanian Assn. of Libns., Archivists, and Documentalists), *c/o Pres.* Oumar Diouwara, Dir., National Lib., Nouakchott.

Mexico

Asociación de Bibliotecarios de Institución es de Enseñanza Superior e Investigación—ABIESI (Assn. of Libns. of Higher Education and Research Institutions), *Pres.* Elsa Barberena, Apdo. Postal 5-611, México 5, D.F.
Asociación Mexicana de Bibliotecarios, A.C. (Mexican Assn. of Libns.), *Pres.* Rosa Maria Fernández de Zamora, Apdo. 27-651, 06760, Mexico, D.F.
Colegio Nacional de Bibliotecarios—CNB (Mexico National College of Libns.), *Pres.* Eduardo Salas Estrada, Apdo. Postal 20-697, 01000 Mexico, D.F.

Netherlands

Nederlandse Vereniging van Bibliothecarissen, Documentalisten en Literatuuronderzoekers—NVB (Dutch Lib. Assn.), p/a Mw. H. J. Krikke-Scholten, Nolweg 13 d, 4209 AW Schelluinen.
UKB—Samenwerkingsverband van de Universiteits- en Hogeschoolbibliotheken, van de Koninklijke Bibliotheek en van de Bibliotheek, van de Koninklijke Nederlandse Akademie van Wetenschappen (Assn. of Univ. Libs., the Royal Lib., and the Lib. of the Netherlands Academy of Arts and Sciences), *Exec. Secy.* J. L. M. van Dijk, c/o Bibliotheek Rijksuniversiteit Limburg, Postbus 616, 6200 MD Maastricht.
Vereniging van Archivarissen in Nederland—VAN (Assn. of Archivists in the Netherlands), *Exec. Secy.* J. A. M. Y. Bos-Rops, Postbus 11645, 2502 AP Den Haag.
Vereniging voor het Theologisch Bibliothecariaat (Assn. of Theological Libns.), *Exec. Secy.* R. T. M. Van Dijk, Postbus 289, 6500 AG Nijmegen.

New Zealand

New Zealand Lib. Assn. (NZLA), *Pres.* M. Wooliscroft, 20 Brandon St., Box 12-212, Wellington 1.

Nicaragua

Bibliotecas Universitarias de Nicaragua, *Coord.* Elba Lucía Reyes; *Secy.* Sidar María, Biblioteca de la Universidad Centroamericana (UCA), Managua.

Nigeria

Nigerian Lib. Assn. (NLA), c/o *Hon. Secy.* E. O. Ejiko, P.M.B. 12655, Lagos.

Norway

Arkivarforeningen (Assn. of Archivists), *Secy.-Treas.* Kari Benedictow, Postboks 10, Kringsja, N-0807 Oslo 8.

Norsk Bibliotekforening — NBF (Norwegian Lib. Assn.), *Secy.-Treas.* G. Langeland, Malerhaugveien 20, N-0661 Oslo 6.

Norsk Fagbibliotekforening — NFF (Norwegian Assn. of Special Libs.), Malerhaugveien 20, N-0661 Oslo 6.

Pakistan

Pakistan Lib. Assn. (PLA), *Exec. Secy.* A. H. Siddiqui, c/o Pakistan Institute of Development Economics, Univ. Campus, Box 1091, Islamabad.

Society for the Promotion & Improvement of Libs. (SPIL), *Pres.* Hakim Mohammed Said, Al-Majeed, Hamdard Centre, Nazimabad, Karachi-18.

Panama

Asociación Panameña de Bibliotecarios (Panamanian Assn. of Libns.), *Pres.* Amelia L. de Barakat, Estafeta Universitaria, Apdo, 10808, Republic of Panama.

Papua New Guinea

Papua New Guinea Lib. Assn. (PNGLA), *Pres.* Margaret Obi; *V.P.* Ursula Pawe; *Secy.* Haro Raka; *Treas.* Lewis Kusso-Aless; *Pubns. Mgr.* Maria Teka, Box 5368, Boroko, PNG.

Paraguay

Asociación de Bibliotecarios Universitarios del Paraguay — ABUP (Paraguayan Assn. of Univ. Libns.), c/o Zayda Caballero, Head, Escuela de Bibliotecología, Universidad Nacional de Asunción, Casilla de Correo, 1408 Asunción, Paraguay.

Peru

Agrupación de Bibliotecas para la Integración de la Información Socio-Económica — ABIISE (Lib. Group for the Integration of Socio-Economic Info.), *Dir.* Betty Chiriboga de Cussato, Apdo. 2874, Lima 100.

Asociación Peruana de Archiveros (Assn. of Peruvian Archivists), Archivo General de la Nación, C. Manuel Cuadros s/n., Palacio de Justicia, Apdo. 3124, Lima 100.

Asociación Peruana de Bibliotecarios (Assn. of Peruvian Libns.), *Exec. Secy.* Amparo Geraldino de Orban, Apdo. 3760, Lima.

Philippines

Assn. of Special Libs. of the Philippines (ASLP), *Pres.* Paul M. de Vera, c/o The National Lib., Rm. 301, T. M. Kalaw, Manila.

Philippine Lib. Assn., Inc. (PLAI), *Pres.* Angelica A. Cabanero, Box 2926, Manila.

Poland

Stowarzyszenie Bibliotekarzy Polskich — SBP (Polish Libns. Assn.), *Pres.* Stefan Kubów; *Gen. Secy.* Andrzej Jopkiewicz, ul. Konopczyńskiego 5/7, 00-953 Warsaw.

Portugal

Associação Portuguesa de Bibliotecários, Arquivistas e Documentalistas (Portuguese Assn. of Libns., Archivists, and Documentalists), *Exec. Secy.* Jorge Resende, Rua Ocidental ao Campo Grande, 83 1751 Lisbon.

Rhodesia

See Zimbabwe.

Romania (Socialist Republic of)

Asociatia Bibliotecarilor din Republica Socialista Romania (Association des Bibliothecaires de la République Socialiste de Roumanie), *Pres.* G. Botez, Biblioteca Centrala de Stat, Strada Ion Ghica 4, 7001 8 Bucharest.

Scotland

See United Kingdom.

Senegal

Commission des Bibliothèques de l'ASD-BAM, Association Sénégalaise pour le Développement de la Documentation, des Bibliothèques, des Archives et des Musées (Senegal Assn. for the Development of Documentation, Libs., Archives, and Museums), *Gen. Secy.* Aïssatou Wade, B.P. 375, Dakar.

Sierra Leone

Sierra Leone Lib. Assn. (SLLA), c/o *Secy.* L. Hunter, Medical Lib., Connaught Hospital, Freetown.

Singapore

Congress of Southeast Asian Libns. (CONSAL), *Chpn.* Mrs. Hedwig Anuar, c/o National Lib., Stamford Rd., Singapore 0617.
Lib. Assn. of Singapore (LAS), *Hon. Secy.*, c/o National Lib., Stamford Rd., Singapore 0617.

South Africa

African Lib. Assn. of South Africa (ALASA), *Hon. Secy./Treas.* G. K. Motshologane, c/o Lib., Univ of the North, Private Bag X1112, Sovenga 0727.

Spain

Instituto de Información y Documentación en Ciencia y Tecnologia (ICYT), *Secy.* Milagros Villarreal de Benito, Joaquín Costa, 22, 28002 Madrid 6.

Sri Lanka

Sri Lanka Lib. Assn. (SLLA), *Pres.* W. B. Dorakumbura; *Gen. Secy.* J. V. Fernando, c/o Organisation of Professional Centre, 275/75, Bauddhaloka Mawatha, Colombo 7.

Sudan

Sudan Lib. Assn. (SLA), *Exec. Secy.* Mohamed Omar, Box 1361, Khartoum.

Sweden

Svenska Arkivsamfundet (The Swedish Archival Assn.), c/o Riksarkivet, Box 12541, S-102 29 Stockholm.
Svenska Bibliotekariesamfundet – SBS (Swedish Assn. of Univ. and Research Libs.), c/o *Secy.* Margareta Lagerman, Patentverkets bibliotek, Box 5055, S-10242 Stockholm.
Sveriges Allmänna Biblioteksförening – SAB (Swedish Lib. Assn.), *Pres.* B. Martinsson, Box 200, S-22100 Lund.
Sveriges Vetenskapliga Specialbiblioteks Förening – SVSF (Assn. of Special Research Libs.), *Pres.* Anders Ryberg; *Secy.* Birgitta Fridén, c/o Utrikesdepartementets bibliotek, Box 16126, S-10323 Stockholm.
Tekniska Litteratursällskapet – TLS (Swedish Society for Technical Documentation), *Secy.* Birgitta Levin, Box 5073, S-10242 Stockholm 5.
Vetenskapliga Bibliotekens Tjänsteman-

naförening – VBT (Assn. of Research Lib. Employees), *Pres.* Anders Schmidt, Lund Univ. Lib., Box 3, S-22100 Lund.

Switzerland

Schweizerische Vereinigung für Dokumentation/Association Suisse de Documentation – SVD/ASD (Swiss Assn. of Documentation), *Secy.-Treas.* W. Bruderer, BID GD PTT, CH-3030 Berne.

Vereinigung Schweizerischer Archivare – VSA (Assn. of Swiss Archivists), c/o Schweizerisches Bundesarchiv, Archivstrasse 24, CH 3001 Bern.

Vereinigung Schweizerischer Bibliothekare/Association des Bibliothécaires Suisses/Associazione dei Bibliotecari Svizzeri – VSB/ABS (Assn. of Swiss Libns.), *Exec. Secy.* W. Treichler, Hallwylstrasse 15, CH-3003 Bern.

Tanzania

Tanzania Lib. Assn., *Chpn.* T. E. Mlaki, Box 2645, Dar-es-Salaam.

Tunisia

Association Tunisienne des Documentalistes, Bibliothécaires et Archivistes (Tunisian Assn. of Documentalists, Libns., and Archivists), *Exec. Secy.* Mohamed Abdeljaoved, 43 rue de la Liberté, Le Bardo.

Turkey

Türk Kütüphaneciler Derneği – TKD (Turkish Libns. Assn.), *Exec. Secy.* Çiğdem Türkân, Headquarters, Elgün Sokaği 8/8, 06440 Kizilay, Ankara.

Uganda

Uganda Lib. Assn. (ULA), *Chpn.* P. W. Songa; *Secy.* L. M. Ssengero, Box 5894, Kampala.

Uganda Schools Lib. Assn. (USLA), *Exec. Secy,* J.W. Nabembezi, Box 7014, Kampala.

Union of Soviet Socialist Republics

USSR Lib. Council, *Pres.* N. S. Kartashov, Lenin State Lib., 3 Prospect Kalinina, 101 000 Moscow.

United Arab Republic

Egyptian School Lib. Assn. (ESLA), *Exec. Secy.* M. Salem, 35 Algalaa St., Cairo.

United Kingdom

ASLIB (The Assn. for Info. Management), *Dir.* Dennis A. Lewis, Information House, 26/27 Boswell St., London WC1N 3JZ.

Assn. of British Theological and Philosophical Libs. (ABTAPL), *Hon. Secy.* Alan Jesson, Bible Society's Lib., c/o University Lib., West Rd., Cambridge CB3 9DR.

Bibliographical Society, *Hon. Secy.* M. M. Foot, British Lib., Humanities and Social Sciences, Great Russell St., London WC1B 3DG.

British and Irish Assn. of Law Libns. (BIALL), *Hon. Secy.* D. M. Blake, Libn., Harding Law Lib., Univ. of Birmingham, Box 363, Birmingham B15 2TT.

The Lib. Assn., *Chief Exec.* George Cunningham, 7 Ridgmount St., London WC1E 7AE.

Private Libs. Assn. (PLA), *Hon. Secy.* Frank Broomhead, 16 Brampton Grove, Kenton, Harrow, Middlesex HA3 8LG.

School Lib. Assn. (SLA), *Chpn.* Jean Watts; *Exec. Secy.* Valerie Fea, Liden Lib., Barrington Close, Liden, Swindon, Wiltshire SN3 6HF.

Scottish Lib. Assn. (SLA), Motherwell

Business Centre, Coursington Rd., Motherwell ML1 1PW. *Exec. Secy.* R. Craig.

Society of Archivists (SA), *Hon. Secy.* A. J. E. Arrowsmith, Suffolk Record Office, County Hall, Ipswich IP4 2JS.

The Standing Conference of National and Univ. Libs. (SCONUL), *Exec. Secy.* A. J. Loveday, Secretariat and Registered Office, 102 Euston St., London NW1 2HA.

Welsh Lib. Assn., *Hon. Secy.* Dwynwen Roberts, Clwyd Lib. and Museum Service, County Civic Centre, Mold, Clwyd CH7 6NW.

Uruguay

Agrupación Bibliotecológica del Uruguay—ABU (Lib. and Archive Science Assn. of Uruguay), *Pres.* Luis Alberto Musso, Cerro Largo 1666, Montevideo.

Venezuela

Colegio de Bibliotecólogos y Archivólogos de Venezuela—COL-BAV (Assn. of Venezuelan Libns. and Archivists), *Exec. Secy.* Zunilde Nuñez de Rojas, Apdo. 6283, Caracas 101.

Wales

See United Kingdom.

Yugoslavia

Društvo Bibliotekara Bosne i Hercegovine—DB BiH (Lib. Assn. of Bosnia and Herzegovina), *Exec. Secy.* Amra Rešidbegović, Obala 42, YU-71000 Sarajevo.

Društvo Bibliotečkih Radnika Srbije (Society of Lib. Workers of Serbia), *Chair.* Dragan Ćirović; *Exec. Secy.* Ljiljana Popović, Skerlićeva 1, YU-11000 Belgrade.

Hrvatsko Bibliotekarsko Društvo—HBD (Croatian Lib. Assn.), *Pres.* Dora Sečić; *Exec. Secy.* Daniela Živković, National and Univ. Lib., Marulićev trg 21, YU-41000 Zagreb.

Sojuz na Društvata na Bibliotékarite na SR Makedonija (Union of Libns. Assn. of Macedonia), Bul. "Goce Delčev" br. 6, Box 566, YU-91000 Skopje.

Zveza Bibliotekarskih Društev Slovenije—ZBDS (Society of the Lib. Assns. of Slovenia), *Exec. Secy.* Mirko Popović, Turjaška 1, YU-61000 Ljubljana.

Zaire

Association Zairoise des Archivistes, Bibliothecaires, et Documentalistes—AZABDO (Zairian Assn. of Archivists, Libns., and Documentalists), *Exec. Secy.* Mulamba Mukunya, Box 805, Kinshasa XI.

Zambia

Zambia Lib. Assn. (ZLA), Box 32839, Lusaka.

Zimbabwe

Zimbabwe Lib. Assn.—ZLA, *Hon. Secy.* D. M. Thorpe, Box 3133, Harare.

Directory of Book Trade and Related Organizations

Book Trade Associations, United States and Canada

For more extensive information on the associations listed in this section, see the annual issues of the *Literary Market Place* (Bowker).

Advertising Typographers Assn. of America, Inc., RD 3, Box 643, Stockton, NJ 08559. *Exec. Secy.* Walter A. Dew, Jr. Tel. 201-782-4055.

American Booksellers Assn., Inc., 122 E. 42 St., New York, NY 10168. Tel. 212-867-9060. *Exec. Dir.* Bernard Rath; *Publications Dir.* Ginger Curwen; *Conventions and Meetings Dir.* Victoria Stanley; *Pres.* J. Rhett Jackson, The Happy Bookseller, Columbia, South Carolina; *V.P.* Kim Browning, Dodds Bookshop, Long Beach, California; *Secy.* Andy Ross, Cody's Books, Berkeley, California; *Treas.* A. David Schwartz, Dickens Books, Ltd., Milwaukee, Wisconsin.

American Institute of Graphic Arts, 1059 Third Ave., New York, NY 10021. Tel. 212-752-0813. *Pres.* Bruce Blackburn; *Dir.* Caroline W. Hightower.

American Medical Publishers Assn. *Pres.* John F. Dill, Year Book Medical Publishers, Inc., 35 E. Wacker Dr., Chicago, IL 60601. Tel. 312-726-9733; *Pres.-Elect.* Joseph M. Braden, J. B. Lippincott Co., Washington Sq., Philadelphia, PA 19105. Tel. 215-238-4477; *Secy.-Treas.* Braxton D. Mitchell, Urban & Schwarzenberg, Inc., 7 E. Redwood St., Baltimore, MD 21202. Tel. 301-539-2550.

American Printing History Assn., Box 4922, Grand Central Sta., New York, NY 10163. *Pres.* John Hench; *V.P. for Programs.* Barbara Paulson; *V.P. for Publications.* Frederic C. Beill, III; *V.P. for Membership.* Virginia Smith; *Secy.* Mrs. Allen T. Hazen; *Treas.* Pat Taylor; *Ed., Printing History.* Renee Weber; *Ed., The APHA Newsletter.* Stephen Saxe.

American Society of Indexers, Inc., 1700 18 St. N.W., Washington, DC 20009. *Pres.* Ben-Ami Lipetz, Woodward Rd., Box 434, Nassau, NY 12123. Tel. 518-766-3014; *Secy.* Eileen Mackesy, 171 Cypress Ave., Bogota, NJ 07603; *Treas.* Carolyn S. Bridgers, R.D. #3, Box 357, West Lake Rd., Oswego, NY 13126. Tel. 315-343-6815.

American Society of Journalists and Authors, 1501 Broadway, Suite 1907, New York, NY 10036. *Pres.* Dodi Schultz; *Exec. V.P.* Glen Evans; *V.Ps.* Seli Groves, Roberta Roesch; *Exec. Secy.* Alexandra Cantor; *Secy.* Janice Hopkins Tanne; *Treas.* Ivan B. Berger. Tel. 212-997-0947.

American Society of Magazine Photographers (ASMP), 205 Lexington Ave., New York, NY 10016. Tel. 212-889-9144. *Exec. Dir.* Patrice Garrison; *Pres.*

Helen Marcus; *Admin. Dir.* Lucy Farnsworth.

American Society of Picture Professionals, Inc., Box 5283, Grand Central Sta., New York, NY 10163. *National Pres.* Grace Evans; *National Secy.* John Schultz.

American Translators Assn., 109 Croton Ave., Ossining, NY 10562. Tel. 914-941-1500. *Pres.* Patricia Newman; *Pres.-Elect.* Karl Kummer; *Secy.* Deanna Hammond; *Treas.* Lloyd Vandersall; *Staff Administrator.* Rosemary Malia.

Antiquarian Booksellers Assn. of America, Inc., 50 Rockefeller Plaza, New York, NY 10020. Tel. 212-757-9395. *Pres.* Edwin Glaser; *V.P.* Michael Ginsberg; *Secy.* Peter Stern; *Treas.* Raymond Wapner; *Administrative Asst.* Janice M. Farina.

Assn. of American Publishers, 220 E. 23 St., New York, NY 10010. Tel. 212-689-8920. *Pres.* Nicholas Veliotes; *Sr. V.P.* Thomas D. McKee; *V.P. School Div.* Donald A. Eklund; *Dirs.* Parker B. Ladd, Saundra L. Smith; *Washington Office.* 2005 Massachusetts Ave. N.W., Washington, DC 20036. Tel. 202-232-3335; *Sr. V.P.* Richard P. Kleeman; *Dirs.* Diane G. Rennert, Carol A. Risher; *Chpn.* Jeremiah Kaplan, Macmillan Publishing Co.; *V. Chpn.* Charles R. Ellis, Elsevier Science Publishing Co.; *Secy.* Alberto Vitale, Time, Inc.; *Treas.* Donald L. Fruehling, McGraw-Hill Book Co.

Assn. of American University Presses, One Park Ave., New York, NY 10016. Tel. 212-889-6040. *Pres.* John Gallman, Dir., Indiana Univ. Press; *Exec. Dir.* Frances Gendlin. Address correspondence to the executive director or to Hollis A. Holmes, Membership Services Manager.

Assn. of Book Travelers, c/o *Pres.* Conrad Heintzelman, Box 308, Brightwaters, NY 11718. Tel. 516-666-0177; *Treas.* Donald Guerra; *Secy.* Robert Evans.

Address correspondence to the president.

Assn. of Canadian Publishers, 70 The Esplanade, 3rd fl., Toronto, Ont. M5E 1R2, Canada. Tel. 416-361-1408. *Pres.* Harald Bohne; *V.P.* Ann Wall; *Secy.* Carolyn MacGregor; *Exec. Dir.* Marcia George. Address correspondence to the executive director.

Assn. of Jewish Book Publishers, House of Living Judaism, 838 Fifth Ave., New York, NY 10021. *Pres.* Bernard I. Levinson. Address correspondence to the president.

Assn. of the Graphic Arts, 5 Penn Plaza, New York, NY 10117-0305. Tel. 212-279-2100. *Pres.* William Dirzulaitis; *Dir., Government Affairs.* John J. Liantonio; *V.P.* Gary J. Miller. *Office Mgr.* Barbara Cleamons.

Bibliographical Society of America. *See* "National Library and Information–Industry Associations, United States and Canada," earlier in Part 6 — *Ed.*

Book Industry Study Group, Inc., 160 Fifth Ave., New York, NY 10010. Tel. 212-929-1393. *Chpn.* Stephen Adams; *V. Chpn.* Alexander J. Burke, Jr., *Treas.* Seymour Turk; *Secy.* Robert W. Bell; *Managing Agent.* SKP Associates. Address correspondence to Susan Kranberg.

Book Manufacturers Institute, 111 Prospect St., Stamford, CT 06901. Tel. 203-324-9670. *Pres.* Stephen P. Snyder, Pres., Alpine Press/Courier; *Exec. V.P.* Douglas E. Horner. Address correspondence to the executive vice president.

Book Publicists of Southern California, 6430 Sunset Blvd., Suite 503, Hollywood, CA 90028. Tel. 213-461-3921. *Pres.* Irwin Zucker; *V.P.* Sol Marshall; *Secy.* Suzy Mallery; *Treas.* Nina Mills.

Book Week Headquarters, Children's Book Council, Inc., 67 Irving Place, New York, NY 10003. Tel. 212-254-2666. *Pres.* John Donovan; *Chpn.* *1987.* Stephen Roxburgh, Farrar, Straus

& Giroux, 19 Union Sq. W., New York, NY 10003. Tel. 212-741-6900.

The Bookbinders' Guild of New York, c/o *Secy.* Barbara Miller, Simon & Schuster, 1230 Ave. of the Americas, New York, NY 10020; *Pres.* Joel P. Moss, A. Horowitz and Sons, 300 Fairfield Rd., Box 1308, Fairfield, NJ 07006; *Treas.* Eugene Sanchez, Macmillan Publg. Co., 115 Fifth Ave., New York, NY 10010; *V.P.* Ray Franzino, Murray Printing Co., 60 E. 42 St. New York, NY 10017.

Bookbuilders of Boston, Inc., c/o *Pres.* Marianne Perlak, Harvard Univ. Press, 79 Garden St., Cambridge, MA 02138. Tel. 617-495-2667; *1st V.P.* Dixie Clarke; *2nd V.P.* Paula Carroll; *Treas.* Nancy Saglen.

Bookbuilders West, 170 Ninth St., San Francisco, CA 94103. *Pres.* Rebecca Cobb, R. R. Donnelley and Sons Co., 535 Middlefield Rd., No. 180, Menlo Park, CA 94025. Tel. 415-853-0705.

Canadian Book Publishers' Council, 45 Charles St. E., 7th fl., Toronto, Ont. M4Y 1S2, Canada. Tel. 416-964-7231. *Pres.* F. C. Larry Muller, Scholastic-TAB Publications; *1st V.P.* Brian E. Hickey, Harlequin Book Publg. Div.; *2nd V.P.* John Champ, Houghton Mifflin; *Secy.-Treas.* Allan Reynolds, Addison Wesley Publishers Ltd.; *Exec. Dir.* Jacqueline Hushion; *Member Organizations.* The School Group, The College Group, The Trade Group.

Canadian Booksellers Assn., 49 Laing St., Toronto, Ont. M4L 2N4, Canada. Tel. 416-469-5976. *Convention Mgr.* Irene Read. *Exec. Dir.* Serge Lavoie.

Chicago Book Clinic, 100 E. Ohio St., Suite 630, Chicago, IL 60611. Tel. 312-951-8254. *Pres.* Norman Baugher; *Exec. V.P.* Mercedes Bailey; *Treas.* Joseph Meinike; *Secy.* Pamela Teisler; *Admin. Dir.* Anthony Cheung; *V.P. Educ.* Judith Biss; *V.P. Memb.* Brad Heywood; *V.P. Oper.* Mario Fidanzi.

Chicago Publishers Assn., c/o *Pres.* Robert J. R. Follett, Follett Corp., 1000 W. Washington Blvd., Chicago, IL 60607. Tel. 312-666-4300.

The Children's Book Council Inc., 67 Irving Place, New York, NY 10003. Tel. 212-254-2666. *Pres.* John Donovan; *V.P.* Paula Quint; *Chpn.* George M. Nicholson, Dell Publishing Co./Delacorte Press, One Dag Hammarskjold Plaza, 245 E. 47 St., New York, NY 10017. Tel. 212-605-3000.

Christian Booksellers Assn., Box 200, 2620 Venetucci Blvd., Colorado Springs, CO 80901. Tel. 303-576-7880. *Pres.* William R. Anderson.

Connecticut Book Publishers Assn., c/o *Pres.* Alex M. Yudkin, Associated Booksellers, 147 McKinley Ave., Bridgeport, CT 06606. Tel. 203-366-5494; *Secy.* Barbara O'Brien; *Treas.* John Atkins.

The Copyright Society of the U.S.A., New York Univ. School of Law, 40 Washington Sq. S., New York, NY 10012. Tel. 212-598-2280. *Pres.* Theodora Zavin; *Secy.* Harold S. Klein; *Asst.* Kate McKay.

Council on Interracial Books for Children, Inc., 1841 Broadway, New York, NY 10023. Tel. 212-757-5339. *Pres.* Harriett Brown; *V.Ps.* Albert V. Schwartz, Frieda Zames; *Marketing Coord.* Melba Kgositsile; *Secy.* Rose Johnson.

Evangelical Christian Publishers Assn., Box 2439, Vista, CA 92083. Tel. 619-941-1636. *Exec. Dir.* C. E. (Ted) Andrew.

Graphic Artists Guild, 30 E. 20 St., Rm. 405, New York, NY 10003. Tel. 212-777-7353. *Pres.* Regina Ortenzi.

Guild of Book Workers, 521 Fifth Ave., 17th fl., New York, NY 10175. Tel. 212-757-6454. *Pres.* J. Franklin Mowery.

Information Industry Assn. *See* "National Library and Information-Industry Associations, United States and Canada," earlier in Part 6 — *Ed.*

International Assn. of Printing House Craftsmen, Inc., 7599 Kenwood Rd., Cincinnati, OH 45236. Tel. 513-891-0611. *Pres.* James Lower; *Exec. V.P.* Patricia A. Milligan.

International Copyright Information Center (INCINC), Assn. of American Publishers, 2005 Massachusetts Ave. N.W., Washington, DC 20036. Tel. 202-232-3335. *Dir.* Carol A. Risher.

International Standard Book Numbering U.S. Agency, 245 W. 17 St., New York, NY 10011. Tel. 212-337-6971, 6972, 6973, 6974, 6975. *Dir.* Emery Koltay; *Coord.* Beatrice Jacobson; *Officers.* Peter Simon, Ernest Lee, Isaura Perez, Lenore Cumberbatch.

JWB Jewish Book Council, 15 E. 26 St., New York, NY 10010. Tel. 212-532-4949. *Pres.* Abraham Kremer; *Dir.* Paula Gribetz Gottlieb.

Library Binding Institute, 150 Allens Creek Rd., Rochester, NY 14618. Tel. 716-461-4380. *Exec. Dir.* Sally Grauer; *Counsel.* Dudley A. Weiss; *Technical Consultant.* Werner Rebsamen.

Magazine and Paperback Marketing Institute (MPMI), 2947 Felton Rd., Norristown, PA 19401. Tel. 215-279-4153. *Exec. V.P.* Don DeVito.

Metropolitan Lithographers Assn., 21 E. 73 St., New York, NY 10021. Tel. 212-772-1027. *Pres.* Edmund Denburg; *Exec. Dir.* Wendy G. Glickstein.

Midwest Book Travelers Assn., c/o *Pres.* Mike Brennan, 1939 Highland Ave., Wilmette, IL 60091. Tel. 312-256-2807; *V.P.* Mary Rowles; *Secy.* Mary McCarthy; *Treas.* Jim Appolonio.

Minnesota Book Publishers Roundtable. *Pres.* Chip Wood, Univ. of Minnesota Press, Minneapolis, MN 55414; *V.P.* Judy Galbraith, Free Spirit Publishing Co., Minneapolis, MN 55401; *Secy.-Treas.* Brad Vogt, The Liturgical Press, Collegeville, MN 56321. Tel. 612-363-2538. Address correspondence to secretary-treasurer.

National Assn. of College Stores, 528 E. Lorain St., Box 58, Oberlin, OH 44074. Tel. 216-775-7777. *Pres.* Peter C. Vanderhoef, Univ. of Iowa, Iowa Book and Supply Co., 8 S. Clinton, Box 2030, Iowa City, IA 52244; *Exec. Dir.* Garis F. Distelhorst.

National Council of the Churches of Christ in the U.S.A., Div. of Education and Ministry, Rm. 704, 475 Riverside Dr., New York, NY 10115-0050. Tel. 212-870-2271. *Assoc. Gen. Secy.* To be appointed.

National Micrographics Assn. *See* Association for Information and Image Management, under "National Library and Information–Industry Associations, United States and Canada," earlier in Part 6 — *Ed.*

New Mexico Book League, 8632 Horacio Place N.E., Albuquerque, NM 87111. Tel. 505-299-8940. *Exec. Dir.* Dwight A. Myers; *Pres.* Lawrence Clark Powell; *V.P.* Marc Simmons; *Treas.* C. Rittenhouse; *Ed.* Carol A. Myers.

New York Rights and Permissions Group, c/o *Chpn.* Dorothy McKittrick Harris, Reader's Digest General Books, 260 Madison Ave., New York, NY 10016. Tel. 212-850-7048.

Northern California Booksellers Assn., c/o *Exec. Dir.* Melissa Mytinger, 2454 Telegraph Ave., Berkeley, CA 94704. Tel. 415-845-9033; *Pres.* Neal Coonerty, Bookshop Santa Cruz, 1547 Pacific Ave., Santa Cruz, CA 95060. Tel. 408-423-0900.

Periodical and Book Assn. of America, Inc., 120 E. 34 St., New York, NY 10016. Tel. 212-689-4952. *Exec. Dir.* Michael Morse; *Pres.* Gerald Rothberg; *V.P.* David Zentner; *Gen. Counsel.* Lee Feltman.

Periodical Distributors of Canada, c/o *Pres.* Cliff Connelly, Teck News Agency, Ltd., 5 Kirkland St., Box 488, Kirkland Lake, Ont. P2N 3J6, Canada. Tel. 705-567-3318; *V.P.* Paul Benjamin,

Benjamin News Reg'd, 0160 Jean-Milot St., LaSalle, Que. H8R 1X7, Canada. Tel. 514-364-1780; *Secy.-Treas.* Richard Bramall, Vancouver Magazine Service Ltd., 2500 Vauxhall Place, Richmond, B.C. V6V 1Y8, Canada. Tel. 604-278-4841.

Philadelphia Book Clinic. *Secy.-Treas.* Thomas Colaiezzi, Lea & Febiger, 600 Washington Sq., Philadelphia, PA 19106. Tel. 215-925-8700.

Pi Beta Alpha, 215 Eisenhower Dr., Bloomington, IL 61701. Tel. 309-828-8140. *Pres.* Robert Wakeham; *Pres.-Elect.* Thomas Richards; *V.P.* Cathie McNiel; *Dir. Memb. Loan Fund.* Glen Mallory; *Exec. Secy.* Larry Efaw..

Printing Industries of Metropolitan New York, Inc. *See* Assn. of the Graphic Arts.

Proofreaders Club of New York, c/o *Pres.* Allan Treshan, 38-15 149 St., Flushing, NY 11354.

Publishers' Ad Club, c/o *Secy.* Allison Gray, Crown Publishers, 225 Park Ave. S., New York, NY 10003. Tel. 212-254-1600; *Pres.* Caroline Barnett, Denhard & Stewart, 122 E. 42 St., New York, NY 10017. Tel. 212-481-3200; *V.P.* Ken Atkatz, Franklin Spier, 650 First Ave., New York, NY 10016. Tel. 212-679-4441; *Treas.* Jerry Younger, New York Times Book Review, 229 W. 43 St., New York, NY 10036. Tel. 212-556-1375.

Publishers' Alliance, c/o *Secy.* James W. Millar, Box 3, Glen Ridge, NJ 07028. Tel. 201-429-0169.

Publishers' Library Marketing Group. For information contact Donne Forrest, Dutton/Dial/Lodestar, 2 Park Ave., New York, NY 10016. Tel. 212-725-1818.

Publishers' Publicity Assn., c/o *Pres.* Jill Danzig, 321 W. 78 St., New York, NY 10024. Tel. 212-874-2342; *V.P.* Arlynn Greenbaum, John Wiley & Sons, 605 Third Ave., New York, NY 10158. Tel. 212-850-6259; *Secy.* Sally Williams,

Bantam Books, 666 Fifth Ave., New York, NY 10103. Tel. 212-554-9644; *Treas.* Anne Maitland, Pocket Books, 1230 Ave. of the Americas, New York, NY 10020. Tel. 212-246-2121.

The Religion Publishing Group, c/o *Secy.* Robin White Goode, Guideposts Books, 757 Third Ave., New York, NY 10017. Tel. 212-371-6431; *Pres.* Robert T. Heller, Doubleday, 245 Park Ave., New York, NY 10167. Tel. 212-984-7235.

Research and Engineering Council of the Graphic Arts Industry, Inc., Box 639, Chadds Ford, PA 19317. Tel. 215-388-7394. *Pres.* Frank E. Schaeffer; *1st V.P.-Secy.* Allan B. Dry; *2nd V.P.-Treas.* Joseph Fasolo; *Managing Dir.* Fred. M. Rogers.

Société de Developpement du Livre et du Périodique, 1151 r. Alexandre-DeSeve, Montreal, P.Q. H2L 2T7, Canada. Tel. 514-524-7528. *Prés.* Guy Saint-Jean; *Directrice Générale.* Louise Rochon; Association des Editeurs Canadiens; *Prés.* Carole Levert; Association des Libraries du Québec, *Prés.* Gérald G. Caza; Société Canadienne Française de Protection du Droit d'Auteur, *Prés.* Pierre Tisseyre; Société des Editeurs de Manuels Scolaires du Quebéc, *Prés.* Hervé Foulon.

Society of Authors' Representatives, Inc., 39½ Washington Sq. S., New York, NY 10012. Tel. 212-228-9740. *Pres.* Carl Brandt; *Exec. Secy.* Georgie Lee.

Society of Photographer and Artist Representatives, Inc. (SPAR), 1123 Broadway, Rm. 914, New York, NY 10010. Tel. 212-924-6023. *Pres.* Anita Green; *1st V.P.* Nancy Slome; *2nd V.P.* Judith Shepherd; *Treas.* Morris Kirchoff; *Secy.* Susan Miller.

Society of Photographers in Communication. *See* American Society of Magazine Photographers (ASMP).

Southern California Booksellers Assn., Box 2606, Beverly Hills, CA 90213.

Pres. Ed Fitzpatrick, Vroman's Bookstore, 695 E. Colorado Blvd., Pasadena, CA 91101. Tel. 818-449-5320; *V.P.* Adri Butler, Pacific Bookstore, 515 Wilshire Blvd., Santa Monica, CA 90401. Tel. 213-451-5746; *Secy.* Sandra Patterson, Paseo Book Co., 370 N. Lantana #13, Camarillo, CA 93010; Tel. 805-987-0300; *Treas.* Alan Kishbaugh, Publisher's Rep., 8136 Cornett Dr., Los Angeles, CA 90046. Tel. 213-654-3399.

Technical Assn. of the Pulp and Paper Industry (TAPPI), Technology Park/Atlanta, Box 105113, Atlanta, GA 30348. Tel. 404-446-1400. *Pres.* William H. Griggs; *V.P.* Vincent A. Russo; *Exec. Dir./Treas.* W. L. Cullison.

West Coast Bookmen's Assn., 27 McNear Dr., San Rafael, CA 94901. *Secy.* Frank G. Goodall. Tel. 415-459-1227

Women's National Book Assn., 160 Fifth Ave., New York, NY 10010. Tel. 212-675-7805, c/o *National Pres.* Cathy Rentschler, 60 W. 66 St. 16A, New York, NY 10023. Tel. 212-588-8400 ext. 257; *V.P./Pres.-Elect.* Marie Cantlon, 8 Whittier Place, 21-A, Boston, MA 02114; *Secy.* Suzanne Lavoie, Two Friars Lane, Mill Valley, CA 94941; *Treas.* Susan B. Trowbridge, Addison-Wesley Publishing Co., Reading, MA 01867; *Past Pres.* Sandra K. Paul, SKP Associates, 160 Fifth Ave., New York, NY 10010; *National Committee Chairs: Pannell Award Chpn.* Ann Heidbreder Eastman, Newman Lib., Virginia Polytechnic Institute and State Univ., Blacksburg, VA 24061; *70th Anniversary.* Claire Friedland, 36 E. 36 St., New York, NY 10016. Tel. 212-685-6205; *Bookwoman Ed.* Barbara Stratyner, 265 Riverside Dr. 7C, New York, NY 10025. Tel. 212-222-2172; *Book Review Ed.* Jane Williamson, Farnsworth Rd., Colchester, VT 05446; *Corres. Membership Chpn.* Patricia Hodge, RSM, Lib. Dir., Caldwell College, Caldwell, NJ 07006. Tel. 201-228-4424 ext. 314; *Publicity.* Marilyn Abel, 325 E. 64 St., New York, NY 10021. Tel. 212-879-6850; *UN/NGO Rep.* Sally Wecksler, 170 West End Ave., New York, NY 10023. Tel. 212-787-2239; *Chapter Presidents: Binghamton.* Jeannette C. Lee, 8 Pine St., Binghamton, NY 13901. Tel. 607-723-6626 (home); *Boston.* Marie Cantlon, Independent Acquisitions Ed., 8 Whittier Place, Boston, MA 02114. Tel. 617-720-3992; *Detroit.* Ruth Edberg, 924 S. Woodward #101, Royal Oak, MI 48067. Tel. 313-548-6783; *Los Angeles.* Sol Marshall, Pres., Creative Editorial Service, 8210 Varna Ave., Van Nuys, CA 91402. Tel. 818-988-2334; *Nashville.* Carolyn C. Daniel, Libn., McGavock H.S., 3150 McGavock Pike, Nashville, TN 37214. Tel. 615-889-7000 ext. 259; *New York.* Anna Marie Muskelly, 3555 Bruckner Blvd., Bronx, NY 10461; *San Francisco.* Mary Dunn-Bury, San Bruno Park School Dist., 500 Acacia Ave., San Bruno, CA 94066. Tel. 415-589-5900; *Washington, DC/Baltimore, MD.* Mary Levering, NLS/BPH, Lib. of Congress, Washington, DC 20542. Tel. 202-287-6115.

International and Foreign Book Trade Associations

For Canadian book trade associations, see the preceding section, "Book Trade Associations, United States and Canada." For a more extensive list of book trade organizations outside the United States and Canada, with more detailed information, consult *International Literary Market Place* (R. R. Bowker), which also provides extensive lists of major bookstores and publishers in each country.

International

Antiquarian Booksellers Assn., Suite 2, 26 Charing Cross Rd., London WC2H, 0DG, England.

International Booksellers Federation (IBF), Grünangergasse 4, A-1010 Vienna 1, Austria. *Pres.* Peter Meili; *Secy.-Gen.* Gerhard Prosser.

International League of Antiquarian Booksellers, c/o *Pres.* Hans Bagger, Kron–Prinsens–Gade 3, 114 København, Denmark.

International Publishers Assn., 3 av. de Miremont, CH-1206 Geneva, Switzerland. *Secy.-Gen.* J. Alexis Koutchoumow.

National

Argentina

Cámara Argentina de Editores de Libros (Council of Argentine Book Publishers), Talcahuano 374, p. 3, Of. 7, Buenos Aires 1013.

Cámara Argentina de Publicaciones (Argentine Publications Assn.), Reconquista 1011, p. 6, 1003 Buenos Aires. *Pres.* Augustin dos Santos.

Cámara Argentina del Libro (Argentine Book Assn.), Av. Belgrano 1580, p. 6, 1093 Buenos Aires. *Pres.* Jaime Rodriguez.

Federación Argentina de Librerías, Papelerías y Actividades Afines (Federation of Bookstores, Stationers, and Related Activities), Balcarce 179/83, Rosario, Santa Fe. *Pres.* Isaac Kostzer.

Australia

Assn. of Australian Univ. Presses, c/o Univ. of Western Australia Press, Nedlands, WA 6009. *Pres.* V. S. W. Greaves.

Australian Book Publishers Assn., 161 Clarence St., Sydney, N.S.W. 2000. *Dir.* Jan Noble.

Australian Booksellers Assn., Box 1032, North Richmond, Victoria 3121. *Dir.* J. Stephens.

Austria

Hauptverband der graphischen Unternehmungen Österreichs (Austrian Master Printers Assn.), Grünangergasse 4, A-1010 Vienna 1. *Pres.* Komm.-Rat. Dr. Dkfm. Willi Maiwald; *Gen. Secy.* Dr. Hans Inmann.

Hauptverband des österreichischen Buchhandels (Austrian Publishers and Booksellers Assn.), Grünangergasse 4, A-1010 Vienna. *Gen. Secy.* Gerhard Prosser.

Osterreichischer Verlegerverband (Assn. of Austrian Publishers), Grünangergasse 4, A-1010 Vienna. *Gen. Secy.* Gerhard Prosser.

Verband der Antiquare Österreichs (Austrian Antiquarian Booksellers Assn.), Grünangergasse 4, A-1010 Vienna. *Gen. Secy.* Gerhard Prosser.

Belgium

Association des Editeurs Belges (Belgian Publishers Assn. of French-language

Books), 111 av. du Parc. B-1060 Brussels.

Cercle Belge de la Librairie (Belgian Booksellers Assn.), rue de la Chasse Royale 35, 1160 Brussels.

Groupe des Editeurs de Livre de la CEE — GELC (Assn. of Book Publishers of the European Community), 111 Av. du Parc, 1060 Brussels. *V.P.* J. J. Schellens.

Syndicat Belge de la Librairie Ancienne et Moderne (Belgian Assn. of Antiquarian and Modern Booksellers), r. du Chêne 21, B-1000 Brussels.

Vereniging ter Bevordering van het Vlaamse Boekwezen (Assn. for the Promotion of Flemish Books), Frankrijklei 93, B-2000 Antwerp. *Secy.* A. Wouters. Member organizations: Algemene Vlaamse Boekverkopersbond; Uitgeversbond-Vereniging van Uitgevers van Nederlandstalige Boeken at the same address; and Bond-Alleenverkopers van Nederlandstalige Boeken (Book Importers), Bijkoevelaan 12, B 2110 Wijnegem. *Pres.* M. Kluwer.

Bolivia

Cámara Boliviana del Libro (Bolivian Booksellers Assn.), Box 682, La Paz. *Pres. Lic.* Javier Gisbert.

Brazil

Associação Brasileira de Livreiros Antiquarios (Brazilian Assn. of Antiquarian Booksellers, Rua do Rosario 155, 2° p., Rio de Janeiro RJ. *Pres.* Walter Geyerhahn.

Associação Brasileira do Livro (Brazilian Booksellers Assn.), Av. 13 de Maio 23, andar 16, Rio de Janeiro. *Dir.* Alberjano Torres.

Cámara Brasileira do Livro (Brazilian Book Assn.), Av. Ipiranga 1267, andar 10, São Paulo. *Secy.* Jose Gorayeb.

Sindicato Nacional dos Editores de Livros (Brazilian Book Publishers Assn.), Av.

Rio Branco 37, 15 andar, Salas 1503/6 e 1510/12, 20097 Rio de Janeiro. *Gen. Secy.* Berta Ribeiro.

Bulgaria

Darzhavno Sdruzhenie "Bulgarska Kniga i Pechat" (Bulgarian Book and Printing State Assn.), 11, Slaveykov Sq., Sofia 1000.

Burma

Burmese Publishers Union, 146 Bogyoke Market, Rangoon.

Chile

Cámara Chilena del Libro, Av. Bulnes 188, Santiago. *Secy.* A. Newman.

Colombia

Cámara Colombiana de la Industria Editorial (Colombian Publishers Council), Cr. 7a, No. 17–51, Of. 409–410, Apdo. áereo 8998, Bogota. *Exec. Dir.* Hipólito Hincapié.

Czechoslovakia

Ministerstvo Kultury CSR, Odbor Knižni Kultury (Ministry of Culture CSR, Dept. for Publishing and Book Trade), Staré Mésto, námesti Perštyně, 1, 117 65 Prague 1.

Denmark

Danske Antikvarboghandlerforening (Danish Antiquarian Booksellers Assn.), Box 2184, DK-1017 Copenhagen.

Danske Boghandlerforening (Danish Booksellers Assn.), Boghandlernes Hus, Siljangade 6, DK-2300 Copenhagen S. *Secy.* Elisabeth Brodersen.

Danske Forlaeggerforening (Danish Publishers Assn.), Kobmagergade 11, DK-1150 Copenhagen K. *Dir.* Erik V. Krustrup.

Finland

Kirja-ja Paperikauppojen Liitto ry (Finnish Booksellers and Stationers Assn.), Box 17 (Martinkyläntie 45), 01721 Vantaa, SF. *Secy.* Olli Eräkivi.

Suomen Antikvariaattiyhdistys Finska Antikvariatforeningen (Finnish Antiquarian Booksellers Assn.), P. Makasiininkatu 6, Helsinki 13.

Suomen Kustannusyhdistys (Publishers Assn. of Finland), Merimiehenkatu 12 A6, SF-00150, Helsinki. *Secy.-Gen.* Unto Lappi.

France

Editions du Cercle de la Librairie (Circle of Professionals of the Book Trade), 30, rue Dauphine, F-75263 Paris, Cedex 06. *Dir.* Pierre Fredet.

Fédération Française des Syndicats de Libraires (French Booksellers Assn.), 259 rue St.-Honoré, F-75001 Paris. *Pres.* Bernard Bollenot.

Office de Promotion de l'Edition Française (Promotion Office of French Publishing), 35, rue Grégoire-de-Tours, F-75279 Paris, Cedex 06. *Managing Dir.* Pierre-Dominique Parent; *Secy.-Gen.* Marc Franconie.

Syndicat National de la Librairie Ancienne et Moderne (SLAM), 4 rue gitle-Coeur, F-75006, Paris. *Pres.* Jeanne Laffitte.

Syndicat National de l'Edition (French Publishers Assn.), 35, rue Grégoire-de-Tours, 75279 Paris, Cedex 06. *Pres.* A. Pain; *Secy.* G. Ründ; *Dir.* Pierre Fredet.

Syndicat National des Importateurs et Exportateurs de Livres (National French Assn. of Book Importers and Exporters), 35, rue Grégoire-de-Tours 75279 Paris, Cedex 06.

German Democratic Republic

Börsenverein der Deutschen Buchhändler zu Leipzig (Assn. of GDR Publishers and Booksellers in Leipzig), Gerichtsweg 26, DDR-7010 Leipzig.

Germany (Federal Republic of)

Börsenverein des Deutschen Buchhandels (German Publishers and Booksellers Assn.), Grosser Hirschgraben 17-21, Box 100442, D-6000 Frankfurt am Main 1. *Secy.* Hans-Karl von Kupsch.

Bundesverband der Deutschen Versandbuchhändler e.V. (National Federation of German Mail-Order Booksellers), An der Ringkirche 6, D-6200 Wiesbaden. *Dirs.* Stefan Rutkowsky; Kornelia Wahl.

Landesverband der Buchhändler und Verleger in Niedersachsen e.V. (Provincial Federation of Booksellers and Publishers in Lower Saxony), Hausmannstr. 2, D-3000 Hannover 1, *Managing Dir.* Wolfgang Grimpe.

Presse-Grosso — Verband Deutscher Buch-, Zeitungs-und Zeitschriften-Grossisten e.V. (Federation of German Wholesalers of Books, Newspapers, and Periodicals), Classen-Kappelmann-Str. 24, D-5000 Cologne 41. *Mgr.* Hans Ziebolz.

Verband Bayerischer Verlage und Buchhandlungen e.V. (Bavarian Publishers and Booksellers Federation), Thierschstr. 17, D-8000 Munich 22. *Secy.* F. Nosske.

Verband Deutscher Antiquare e.V. (German Antiquarian Booksellers Assn.), Unterer Anger 15, D-8000 Munich 40.

Verband Deutscher Bühnenverleger e.V. (Federation of German Theatrical Publishers and Drama Agencies), Bismarckstr. 17, D-1000 Berlin 12.

Ghana

Ghana Booksellers Assn., Box 7869, Accra.

Great Britain

See United Kingdom.

Greece

Syllogos Ekdoton Vivliopolon (Publishers and Booksellers Assn. of Athens), 54 Themistocleus St., Gr-106 81, Athens. *Pres.* D. Pandeleskos; *Secy.* Stephanos Patakis.

Hong Kong

Hong Kong Booksellers and Stationers Assn., Man Wah House, Kowloon.

Hungary

Magyar Könyvkiadók és Könyvterjesztök Egyesülése (Hungarian Publishers and Booksellers Assn.), Vörösmarty tér 1, H-1051 Budapest. *Pres.* András Petró; *Secy. Gen.* Ferenc Zöld.

Iceland

Iceland Publishers Assn., Laufasvegi 12, 101 Reykjavik. *Pres.* Eyjólfur Sigurdsson, c/o Bókhladan, Glaesibae, 104 Reykjavík.

India

All-India Booksellers and Publishers Assn., 17L Connaught Circus, Box 328, New Delhi 11001. *Pres.* A. N. Varma.
Bombay Booksellers and Publishers Assn., c/o Bhadkamkar Marg, Navjivan Cooperative Housing Society, Bldg. 3, 6th fl., Office 25, Bombay 400 008. *Exec. Secy.* U. S. Manikeri.

Booksellers and Publishers Assn. of South India, c/o Affiliated East–West Press Private Ltd., Box 1056, Madras 600 010.
Delhi State Booksellers and Publishers Assn., c/o The Students' Stores, Box 1511, 100 006 Delhi. *Pres.* Devendra Sharma.
Federation of Indian Publishers, 18/1-C Institutional Area, New Delhi 110 067. *Pres.* Asoke Ghosh; *Hon. Gen. Secy.* Anand Bhushan.
Indian Assn. of Univ. Presses, Calcutta Univ. Press, Calcutta. *Secy.* Salil Kumar Chakrabarti.

Indonesia

Ikatan Penerbit Indonesia (IKAPI) (Assn. of Indonesian Book Publishers), Jalan Kalipasir 32, Jakarta Pusat 10330. *Pres.* Azmi Syahbuddin.

Ireland (Republic of)

CLE: The Irish Book Publishers' Assn., Book House Ireland, 65 Middle Abbey St., Dublin 1. *Admin.* Clara Clark.

Israel

Book and Printing Center of the Israel Export Institute, Box 50084, 29 Hamered St., 68 125 Tel Aviv. *Dir.* Tova Krim.
Book Publishers Assn. of Israel, Box 20123, 29 Carlebach St., Tel Aviv. *Chpn.* Racheli Eidelman; *International Promotion and Literary Rights Dept. Dir.* Lorna Soifer; *Exec. Dir.* Arie Friedler.

Italy

Associazione Italiana Editori (Italian Publishers Assn.), Via delle Erbe 2, I-20121 Milan. *Secy.* Achille Ormezzano.
Associazione Librai Antiquari d'Italia

(Antiquarian Booksellers Assn. of Italy), Via Jacopo Nardi 6, I-50132 Florence. *Pres.* Vittorio Soave.
Associazione Librai Italiani (Italian Booksellers Assn.), Piazza G. G. Belli 2, I-00153 Rome.

Jamaica

Booksellers Assn. of Jamaica, c/o B. A. Sangster, Sangster's Book Stores, Ltd., Box 366, 97 Harbour St., Kingston.

Japan

Antiquarian Booksellers Assn. of Japan, 29 San-ei-cho, Shinjuku-ku, Tokyo 160.
Books-on-Japan-in-English Club, Shinnichibo Bldg., 2-1 Sarugaku-cho 1-chome, Chiyoda-ku, Tokyo 101.
Japan Book Importers Assn., Rm. 612, Aizawa Bldg., 20-3, Nihonbashi 1-chome, Chuo-ku, Tokyo 103. *Secy.* Mitsuo Shibata.
Japan Book Publishers Assn., 6 Fukuromachi, Shinjuku-ku, Tokyo 162. *Pres.* Toshiyuki Hattori; *Exec. Dir.* Sadaya Murayama; *Secy.* Masaaki Shigehisa.
Japan Booksellers Federation, 1-2 Surugadai, Kanda, Chiyoda-ku, Tokyo 101.
Textbook Publishers Assn. of Japan (Kyokasho Kyokai), 20-2 Honshiocho Shinjuku-ku, Tokyo 160. *Secy.* Masae Kusaka.

Kenya

Kenya Publishers Assn., Box 72532, Nairobi. *Secy.* J. M. B. Clarke.

Korea (Republic of)

Korean Publishers Assn., 105-2, Sagandong, Chongno-ku, Seoul 110. *Pres.* In-kyu Lim; *V.Ps.* Byung-il Kwoun; Nak-jun Kim; Byung-seok Chun.

Luxembourg

Confédération du Commerce Luxembourgeois-Groupement Papetiers-Libraires (Confederation of Retailers, Group for Stationers and Booksellers), 23, Centre Allée-Scheffer, Luxembourg. *Pres.* Raymond Daman; *Secy.* Robert Steines.

Malaysia

Malaysian Book Publishers Assn., 399A, Jalan Tuanku Abdul Rahman, 50100 Kuala Lumpur. *Hon. Secy.* Johnny Ong.

Mexico

Instituto Mexicano del Libro A.C. (Mexican Book Institute), Paseo de la Reforma 95-603, Dept. 1024, México 4 D.F., C.P. 06030. *Secy.-Gen.* Isabel Ruiz González.

Morocco

Librairie-Papeterie, 344 Ave. Mohammed V, Rabat. *Contact* Kalila Wa Dimna.

Netherlands

Koninklijke Nederlandse Uitgeversbond (Royal Dutch Publishers Assn.), Keizersgracht 391, 1016 EJ Amsterdam. *Secy.* R. M. Vrij.
Nederlandsche Vereeniging van Antiquaren (Antiquarian Booksellers Assn. of the Netherlands), Nieuwe Spiegelstra. 33-35, 1017-DC Amsterdam. *Pres.* Mrs. C. F. M. van der Peet-Schelfhout.
Nederlandse Boekverkopersbond (Booksellers Assn. of the Netherlands), Waalsdorperweg 119, 2597-HS The Hague. *Pres.* J. van der Plas; *Exec. Secy.* A. Coyajee.
Vereeniging ter bevordering van de belangen des Boekhandels (Dutch Book

Trade Assn.), Frederiksplein 1, Box 5475, 1007 AL Amsterdam. *Secy.* M. van Vollenhoven-Nagel.

New Zealand

Book Publishers Assn. of New Zealand, Inc., Box 44146, Point Chevalier, Auckland 2. *Pres.* R. Stagg; *Dir.* Gerard Reid.
Booksellers Assn. of New Zealand, Inc., Box 11-377, Wellington. *Dir.* Kate Fortune.

Nigeria

Nigerian Booksellers Assn., Box 3168, Ibadan. *Pres.* W. Adegbonmire.
Nigerian Publishers Assn., c/o P.M.B. 5164, Ibadan. *Pres.* Bankole O. Bolodeoku.

Norway

Norsk Antikvarbokhandlerforening (Norwegian Antiquarian Booksellers Assn.), Ullevalsveien 1, 0165 Oslo 1.
Norsk Musikkforleggerforening (Norwegian Music Publishers Assn.), Box 822 Sentrum, N–0104 Oslo 1.
Norske Bok og Papiransattes Forbund (Norwegian Book Trade Employees Assn.), Øvre Vollgate 15, 0158 Oslo 1. *Contact.* Magda Sørevik.
Norske Bokhandlerforening (Norwegian Booksellers Assn.), Øvre Vollgate 15, 0158 Oslo 1. *Dir.* Olav Gjerdene.
Norske Forleggerforening (Norwegian Publishers Assn.), Øvre Vollgate 15, Oslo 1. *Dir.* Paul M. Rothe.

Pakistan

Pakistan Publishers and Booksellers Assn., YMCA Bldg., Shahra-e-Quaide-Azam, Lahore.

Paraguay

Cámara Paraguaya del Libro (Paraguayan Publishers Assn.), Casilla de Correo 1705, Asunción.

Peru

Cámara Peruana del Libro (Peruvian Publishers Assn.), Jirón Washington 1206, of. 507–508, Lima 100. *Pres.* Andrés Carbone O.

Philippines

Philippine Book Dealers Assn., MCC Box 1103, Makati Commercial Centre, Makati, Metro Manila. *Pres.* Jose C. Benedicto.
Philippine Educational Publishers Assn., 927 Quezon Ave., Quezon City 3008, Metro Manila. *Pres.* Jesus Ernesto R. Sibal.

Poland

Polskie Towarzystwo Wydawców Książek (Polish Publishers Assn.), ul. Mazowiecka 2/4, 00-048 Warsaw.
Stowarzyszenie Ksiegarzy Polskich (Assn. of Polish Booksellers), ul. Mokotowska 4/6, 00-641 Warsaw. *Pres.* Tadeusz Hussak.

Portugal

Associação Portuguesa de Editores e Livreiros (Portuguese Assn. of Publishers and Booksellers), Largo de Andaluz 16, 1, Esq., 1000 Lisbon. *Pres.* Fernando Guedes; *Gen. Secy.* Jorge Sá Borges; *Service Mgr.* José Narciso Vieira.

Romania (Socialist Republic of)

Centrala editorială (Romanian Publishing Center), Piata Scînteii 1, R-79715 Bucharest. *Gen. Dir.* Gheorghe Trandafir.

Singapore

Singapore Book Publishers Assn., Box 846, Colombo Court Post Office, Singapore 0617. *Secy.* Peh Chin Hua.

South Africa (Republic of)

Associated Booksellers of Southern Africa, Box 326, Howard Place 7450. *Secy.* M. Landman.

Book Trade Assn. of South Africa, Box 326, Howard Place 7450. *Dir.* M. Landman.

South African Publishers Assn., Box 326, Howard Place 7450. *Secy.* M. Landman.

Spain

Federacion de Gremios de Editores de España (Spanish Federation of Publishers Assn.), Paseó de la Castellana, 82-7°, 28046 Madrid. *Pres.* Francisco Pérez González; *Secy.-Gen.* Jaime Brull.

Gremi de Llibreters de Barcelona i Catalunya (Assn. of Barcelona and Catalunya Booksellers), c. Mallorca, 272-274, 08037 Barcelona.

Gremi d'Editors de Catalunya (Assn. of Catalonian Publishers), Valencia, 279, la Planta, Barcelona 08009. *Pres.* Andreu Teixidor de Ventós.

Instituto Nacional del Libro Español (Spanish Publishers and Booksellers Institute), Santiago Rusiñol 8-10, 28040 Madrid. *Dir.* Rafael Martinez Alés.

Sri Lanka

Booksellers Assn. of Sri Lanka, Box 244, Colombo 2. *Secy.* W. L. Mendis.

Sri Lanka Publishers Assn., 61 Sangaraja Mawatha, Colombo 10, *Secy.-Gen.* Eamon Kariyakarawana.

Sweden

Svenska Antikvariatföreningen, Box 22549, S-104 22 Stockholm.

Svenska Bokförläggareföreningen (Swedish Publishers Assn.), Sveavägen 52, S-111 34 Stockholm. *Managing Dir.* Urban Skeppstedt.

Svenska Bokhandlareföreningen (Swedish Booksellers Assn.), Skeppargatan 27, S-114 52 Stockholm. *Secy.* Per Nordenson.

Svenska Tryckeriföreningen (Swedish Printing Industries Federation), Blasieholmsgatan 4A, Box 16383, S-10327 Stockholm. *Managing Dir.* Per Galmark.

Switzerland

Schweizerischer Buchhändler-und Verleger-Verband (Swiss German-Language Booksellers and Publishers Assn.), Bellerivestr. 3, CH-8034 Zurich. *Managing Dir.* Peter Oprecht.

Società Editori della Svizzera Italiana (Publishers Assn. for the Italian-Speaking Part of Switzerland), Box 2600, Viale Portone 4, CH-6501 Bellinzona.

Société des Libraires et Editeurs de la Suisse Romande (Assn. of Swiss French-Language Booksellers and Publishers), 2 av. Agassiz, CH-1001 Lausanne. *Secy.* Robert Junod.

Vereinigung der Buchantiquare und Kupferstichhändler der Schweiz (Assn. of Swiss Antiquarians and Print Dealers), c/o Walter Alicke, Pres., Schloss-Str. 6, FL 9490 Vaduz.

Thailand

Publishers and Booksellers Assn. of Thailand, 25 Sukhumvit Soi 56, Bangkok. *Secy.* W. Tantinirandr.

Tunisia

Syndicat des Libraires de Tunisie (Tunisian Booksellers Assn.), 10 av. de France, Tunis.

Turkey

Türk Editòrler Derneği (Turkish Publishers Assn.), Ankara Caddesi 60, Istanbul.

United Kingdom

Assn. of Learned and Professional Society Publishers, Sentosa, Hill Rd., Fairlight, East Sussex TN35 4AE. *Secy.* A. I. P. Henton.

Book Trust, Book House, 45 E. Hill, London SW18 2QZ. *Chief Exec.* Martyn Goff, O.B.E.

Booksellers Assn. of Great Britain and Ireland, 154 Buckingham Palace Rd., London SW1W 9TZ. *Dir.* T. E. Godfray.

Educational Publishers Council, 19 Bedford Sq., London WC1B 3HJ. *Dir.* John R. M. Davies.

National Federation of Retail Newsagents, Yeoman House, Sekforde St., Clerkenwell Green, London EC1R OHD.

Publishers Assn., 19 Bedford Sq., London WC1B 3HJ. *Secy./Chief Exec.* Clive Bradley.

Uruguay

Cámara Uruguaya del Libro (Uruguayan Publishing Council), Carlos Roxlo 1446, piso 1, Apdo. 2, Montevideo. *Pres.* Arnaldo Medone; *Secy.* Walter Peluffo; *Mgr.* Ana Cristina Rodríguez.

Yugoslavia

Assn. of Yugoslav Publishers and Booksellers, Kneza Milosa str. 25, Box 883, Belgrade. *Pres.* Vidak Perić.

Zambia

Booksellers and Publishers Assn. of Zambia, Box 35961, Lusaka.

Zimbabwe

Booksellers Assn. of Zimbabwe, Box 3916, 69 Stanley Ave., Harare. *Chpn.* C. K. Katsande.

Calendar, 1987–1988

The list below contains information (as of January 1987) regarding place and date of association meetings or promotional events that are, for the most part, national or international in scope. State and regional library association meetings also are included. For those who wish to contact the association directly, addresses of library and book trade associations are listed in Part 6 of this *Bowker Annual*. For information on additional book trade and promotional events, see the *Exhibits Directory*, published annually by the Association of American Publishers; *Chase's Calendar of Annual Events*, published by the Apple Tree Press, Box 1012, Flint, MI 48501; *Literary Market Place* and *International Literary Market Place*, published by R. R. Bowker; and the "Calendar" section in each issue of *Publishers Weekly* and *Library Journal*.

1987

May

4/28–5/5	Quebec International Book Fair	Quebec, Canada
4/29–5/2	New Jersey Library Association/ Educational Media Association of New Jersey/New Jersey Library Trustees Association	Cherry Hill, N.J.
1–3	British Columbia Library Association	Vancouver, B.C., Canada
2	American Society of Indexers	New York, N.Y.
2	Council of National Library and Information Associations	New York, N.Y.
2	Philadelphia Book Show	Philadelphia, Pa.
2–5	Library Binding Institute	Charleston, S.C.
3–5	Massachusetts Library Association	Framingham, Mass.
3–7	International Reading Association	Anaheim, Calif.
4–8	Association of Research Libraries	Pittsburgh, Pa.
5–9	Florida Library Association	Clearwater, Fla.
7–8	Maryland Library Association	Rockville, Md.
7–9	Advertising Typographers Association of America, Inc.	Boston, Mass.
9–10	Texas Publishers Association	Austin, Tex.
11–13	New Hampshire Library Association	Waterville Valley, N.H.
15–21	Medical Library Association	Portland, Oreg.
17–19	Maine Library Association/Maine Educational Media Association	Orono, Maine

May (*cont.*)

17–20	American Society for Information Science	Cincinnati, Ohio
18–20	Associated Information Managers	Washington, D.C.
18–20	Information Industry Association	Washington, D.C.
21–22	Women's National Book Association	Washington, D.C.
21–23	Saskatchewan Library Association	Regina, Sask., Canada
21–26	Warsaw International Book Fair	Warsaw, Poland
23–26	American Booksellers Association	Washington, D.C.
26–29	Society for Scholarly Publishing	New Orleans, La.
27–28	Vermont Library Association	Burlington, Vt.
28–29	Atlantic Provinces Library Association	Saint John, N.B., Canada
*	Guild of Book Workers	New York, N.Y.

June

2–3	New York Rights and Permissions Group	Ottawa, Ont., Canada
6–11	Special Libraries Association	Anaheim, Calif.
11	Association of Book Travelers	Bedford, Hills, N.Y.
11–17	Canadian Library Association	Vancouver, B.C., Canada
13–18	British Columbia Library Association	Vancouver, B.C., Canada
14–17	Association of American University Presses	Tucson, Ariz.
14–19	American Theological Library Association	San Rafael, Calif.
18–23	Educational Film Library Association	New York, N.Y.
21–24	Association of Jewish Libraries	Livingston, N.J.
25–29	Canadian Booksellers Association	Toronto, Ont., Canada
27–7/2	American Library Association	San Francisco, Calif.
27–7/2	Asian/Pacific American Librarians Association	San Francisco, Calif.
28	Chief Officers of State Library Agencies	San Francisco, Calif.
28–30	Church and Synagogue Library Association	Philadelphia, Pa.
29	Theatre Library Association	San Francisco, Calif.
30	Chinese-American Librarians Association	San Francisco, Calif.
*	Book Industry Study Group	New York, N.Y.
*	PEN International Congress	Republic of Korea

*To be announced.

July

5–8	American Association of Law Libraries	Chicago, Ill.
11	Evangelical Christian Publishers Association	Anaheim, Calif.
11–16	Christian Booksellers Association	Anaheim, Calif.
12–15	Pi Beta Alpha	Hershey, Pa.
22–25	National Association of Government Archives and Records Administrators	Atlanta, Ga.
26–29	International Association of Printing House Craftsmen, Inc.	Toronto, Ont., Canada

August

4	Arkansas Association of School Librarians	Little Rock, Ark.
12–14	Pacific Northwest Library Association	Tacoma, Wash.
16–22	International Federation of Library Associations and Institutions (IFLA)	Brighton, Sussex, U.K.
19–20	International Association of Law Libraries	Brighton, Sussex, U.K.
28–29	Kentucky School Media Association	Frankfort, Ky.

September

2–6	Society of American Archivists	New York, N.Y.
3–5	American Institute of Graphic Arts	San Francisco, Calif.
8–14	Moscow International Book Fair	Moscow, U.S.S.R.
16–18	Missouri Library Association	St. Louis, Mo.
23–26	Mountain Plains Library Association/ North Dakota Library Association/ South Dakota Library Association	Bismarck, N.D.
26	American Printing History Association	New York, N.Y.
27–29	New England Library Association/New England Educational Media Association	Boxborough, Mass.
30–10/2	Kentucky Library Association	Fort Mitchell, Ky.
30–10/3	Educational Media Division, Idaho Library Association	Sun Valley, Idaho
*	International Archival Round Table	Venice, Italy
*	Pacific Northwest Booksellers Association	*Oregon

October

1–2	Idaho Library Association	Sun Valley, Idaho
4–5	Mid-Atlantic Booksellers Association	Atlantic, City, N.J.
4–7	Pennsylvania Library Association	Erie, Pa.

*To be announced.

October (*cont.*)

4–8	American Society for Information Science	Boston, Mass.
6–9	Michigan Library Association	Lansing, Mich.
7–9	Minnesota Library Association	Brainerd, Minn.
7–10	Nevada Library Association	Winnemucca, Nev.
7–10	Wyoming Library Association	Gillette, Wyo.
7–12	Frankfurt Book Fair	Frankfurt, West Germany
8–10	Oregon Educational Media Association	Salem, Oreg.
8–10	Washington Library Media Association	Seattle, Wash.
8–10	West Virginia Library Association	Beckley, W. Va.
8–11	American Translators Association	Albuquerque, N. Mex.
10–13	Colorado Library Association	Fort Collins, Colo.
11–18	Advertising Typographers Association of America, Inc.	Carefree, Ariz.
14–16	Iowa Library Association	Waterloo, Iowa
14–17	South Carolina Library Association	Greenville, S.C.
16	Delaware Library Association	*
18–20	Chief Officers of State Library Agencies	Columbus, Ohio
19–22	ARMA (Association of Records Managers and Administrators) International	Anaheim, Calif.
19–23	Association of Research Libraries	Washington, D.C.
21–23	Mississippi Library Association	Biloxi, Miss.
21–25	Georgia Library Association	Columbus, Ga.
21–25	New York Library Association	Lake Placid, N.Y.
22–25	Florida Association for Media in Education	Orlando, Fla.
24–31	Belgrade International Book Fair	Belgrade, Yugoslavia
25–28	Evangelical Christian Publishers Association	Nashville, Tenn.
26–28	Online, Inc.	San Francisco, Calif.
27–29	Chief Officers of State Library Agencies	Seattle, Wash.
27–30	North Carolina Library Association/ North Carolina Association of School Librarians	Winston-Salem, S.C.
28–30	Nebraska Educational Media Association	Kearney, Nebr.
28–30	Nebraska Library Association	Columbus, Nebr.
28–30	Wisconsin Library Association	Eau Claire, Wis.
28–31	Ohio Educational Library Media Association	Dayton, Ohio
*	Oklahoma Association of School Library Media Specialists	Tulsa, Okla.
*	Vermont Educational Media Association	Burlington, Vt.

*To be announced.

November

1–2	Massachusetts Association for Educational Media	Chicopee, Mass.
1–4	Book Manufacturers Institute	Naples, Fla.
4–7	Arizona Library Association/Arizona School Library Association/Arizona Educational Media Association	Phoenix, Ariz.
4–7	Midwest Federation of Library Associations	Indianapolis, Ind.
5–7	Virginia Library Association/District of Columbia Library Association	Arlington, Va.
7–12	Association of American Medical Colleges	Washington, D.C.
14–18	California Library Association	Santa Clara, Calif.
15	Hawaii Association of School Librarians	Honolulu, Hawaii
15–18	Information Industry Association	Chicago, Ill.
18–22	California Media and Library Education Association	San Diego, Calif.
19–24	Salon du Livre de Montreal/Montreal International Book Fair	Montreal, P.Q., Canada
24–12/9	Cairo International Children's Book Fair	Cairo, Egypt
*	Council of National Library and Information Associations	New York, N.Y.

December

2	Bookbuilders West	San Francisco, Calif.
3–4	Research and Engineering Council of the Graphic Arts Industry	Chicago, Ill.
4	Association of Book Travelers	New York, N.Y.
27–30	Modern Language Association	San Francisco, Calif.
*	Society of Authors' Representatives	New York, N.Y.

1988

January

6–8	Association for Library and Information Science Education	San Antonio, Tex.
9–14	American Library Association	San Antonio, Tex.
10	Chief Officers of State Library Agencies	San Antonio, Tex.
27–30	Special Libraries Association	Williamsburg, Va.

*To be announced.

February

4-11	Art Libraries Society of North America	Dallas, Tex.
9-13	Music Library Association	Minneapolis, Minn.
18-20	Colorado Educational Media Association	Colorado Springs, Colo.
28-3/2	Technical Association of the Pulp and Paper Industry (TAPPI)	Atlanta, Ga.
*	Chicago Book Clinic	Chicago, Ill.

March

16-18	Louisiana Library Association	Lake Charles, La.
*	Alaska Library Association	Fairbanks, Alaska.
*	Association of American Publishers	Key Biscayne, Fla.

April

4-7	Catholic Library Association	New York, N.Y.
11-15	National Association of College Stores	Cincinnati, Ohio
14-16	Oklahoma Library Association	Afton, Okla.
14-16	Pennsylvania School Librarians Association	Hershey, Pa.
18-19	Chief Officers of State Library Agencies	Washington, D.C.
19-23	Texas Library Association	Corpus Christi, Tex.
19-24	Quebec International Book Fair	Quebec, Canada
21-23	Iowa Educational Media Association	Cedar Rapids, Iowa
27-29	Washington Library Association	Wenatchee, Wash.
27-30	Public Library Association	Pittsburgh, Pa.
29-5/3	Council of Planning Librarians	San Antonio, Tex.
*	Maryland Library Association	Baltimore, Md.
*	Puerto Rico Library Association	San Juan, P.R.

May

1-5	International Reading Association	Toronto, Ont., Canada
3-6	Association of Research Libraries	Berkeley, Calif.
4-7	Florida Library Association	Miami, Fla.
5-7	Advertising Typographers Association of America, Inc.	Toronto, Ont., Canada
11-13	Illinois Library Association	Chicago, Ill.
11-14	New Jersey Library Association	Atlantic City, N.J.
18-23	Warsaw International Book Fair	Warsaw, Poland
20-26	Medical Library Association	New Orleans, La.
28-31	American Booksellers Association	Anaheim, Calif.
*	Council of National Library and Information Associations	New York, N.Y.

*To be announced.

June

11–16	Special Libraries Association	Denver, Colo.
11–17	Canadian Library Association	Halifax, N.S., Canada
14–17	Association of Christian Librarians	Elgin, Ill.
19–21	Church and Synagogue Library Association	Oberlin, Ohio
26–29	American Association of Law Libraries	Atlanta, Ga.

July

9–14	American Library Association	New Orleans, La.
11	Theatre Library Association	New Orleans, La.

August

10–12	Pacific Northwest Library Association	Juneau, Alaska
*	International Association of Printing House Craftsmen, Inc.	Cincinnati, Ohio
*	International Federation of Library Associations and Institutions (IFLA)	Sydney, Australia

September

19–22	Association of Research Libraries	York, England
28–10/2	Society of American Archivists	Atlanta, Ga.

October

3–6	ARMA (Association of Record Managers and Administrators) International	Baltimore, Md.
5–7	Minnesota Library Association	Rochester, Minn.
5–10	Frankfurt Book Fair	Frankfurt, West Germany
6–8	West Virginia Library Association	Huntington, W. Va.
6–9	Michigan Library Association	Lansing, Mich.
8–11	Colorado Library Association	Breckenridge, Colo.
9–12	Pennsylvania Library Association	Philadelphia, Pa.
9–16	Advertising Typographers Association of America, Inc.	Naples, Fla.
12–15	Florida Association for Media in Education	Orlando, Fla.
12–16	New York Library Association	Buffalo, N.Y.
13–15	Oregon Educational Media Association/Washington Library Media Association	Portland, Oreg.
19–21	Iowa Library Association	Ames, Iowa

*To be announced.

October (*cont.*)

19–23	Nebraska Library Association/ Mountain Plains Library Association	Omaha, Nebr.
23–25	New England Library Association/New England Educational Media Association	Sturbridge, Mass.
25–28	Virginia Library Association/ Southeastern Library Association	Norfolk, Va.
26–28	Wisconsin Library Association	Lake Geneva, Wis.
26–29	Arizona School Library Association/ Arizona Educational Media Association	Phoenix, Ariz.
27–29	Ohio Library Association/Ohio Educational Library Media Association	Columbus, Ohio
30–11/3	Book Manufacturers Institute	Laguna Niguel, Calif.
*	American Translators Association	Seattle, Wash.
*	Nevada Library Association	Reno, Nev.

November

2–11	Arabic Book Exhibition	Kuwait
12–16	California Library Association	Fresno, Calif.
12–17	Association of American Medical Colleges	Chicago, Ill.
16–19	California Media and Library Educators Association	Fresno, Calif.
*	Council of National Library and Information Associations	New York, N.Y.

December

27–30	Modern Language Association	*

*To be announced.

Index

A

AALL, *see* American Association of Law Libraries

AAP, *see* Association of American Publishers

AASL, *see* American Association of School Librarians

ABA, *see* American Booksellers Association

ABN, *see* Australian Bibliographical Network

ACL, *see* Association of Christian Libraries

ACRL, *see* Association of College and Research Libraries

AECT, *see* Association for Educational Communications and Technology

AFFIRM, *see* Association for Federal Information Resources Management

AIM, *see* Associated Information Managers

AJL, *see* Association of Jewish Libraries

ALA, *see* American Library Association

ALISE, *see* Association for Library and Information Science Education

ALSC *see* Association for Library Service to Children

ALTA, *see* American Library Trustee Association

ANSI, *see* American National Standards Institute

APALA, *see* Asian/Pacific American Librarians Association

ARL, *see* Association of Research Libraries

ARLIS/NA, *see* Art Libraries Society of North America

ARMA International, 601–603

ASCLA, *see* Association of Specialized and Cooperative Library Agencies

ASIS, *see* American Society for Information Science

Abstracting, bibliography of, 462

Academic books, North American, price indexes, 1983/84–1985/86 (*table*), 438–439

   See also Association of American Publishers, Professional and Scholarly Publishing Division

Academic libraries, *see* College and research libraries

Acquisitions

   bibliography, 471

   expenditures, 355–359

   school and academic libraries price indexes, 360–362

   See also Collection development; and specific types of libraries, e.g., Public libraries

Adults

   literacy programs, *see* Literacy programs

   services, *see* American Library Association, Reference and Adult Services Division; Senior citizens, library services for

Agencies, library, *see* Library associations and agencies

Agresto, John, 169–170

Agricultural libraries, *see* Inter-American Association of Agricultural Librarians and Documentalists; International Association of Agricultural Librarians and Documentalists; National Agricultural Library

Allen, Kenneth B., 235

American Association of Law Libraries (AALL), 563–566

American Association of School Librarians (AASL), 38, 167, 347–348, 570–573